The Discoverers

The Discoverers

An Encyclopedia of Explorers and Exploration

Edited by

Helen Delpar

McGraw-Hill Book Company

New York   St. Louis   San Francisco   Auckland
Bogotá   Düsseldorf   Johannesburg   London
Madrid   Mexico   Montreal   New Delhi
Panama   São Paulo   Singapore
Sydney   Tokyo   Toronto

Library of Congress Cataloging in Publication Data

Main entry under title:

The Discoverers.
   Includes bibliographies and index.
   1. Explorers—Biography—Dictionaries. I. Delpar,
Helen.
G200.D53   910'.92'2   79-9259
ISBN 0-07-016264-6

234567890 HDHD 89876543210

*The editors for this book were Robert A. Rosenbaum and Tobia L. Worth,
the designer was Naomi Auerbach, and the production supervisor
was Thomas G. Kowalczyk. It was set in Trump Medieval
by University Graphics, Inc.*

Printed and bound by Halliday Lithograph Corporation

In his poem "The Explorer" (1898), Rudyard Kipling describes the adventures of an explorer driven by a whisper which commands him: "Something hidden. . . . Something lost behind the Ranges. Lost and waiting for you. Go!" Eventually, overcoming hardship and discouragement, the explorer reaches his goal. The explorers whose travels are recounted in this book were often less fortunate than Kipling's protagonist, succumbing to disease, a hostile natural environment, or human foes as they pursued their quest. But they too were driven—whether by curiosity, ambition, or greed—to see what lay over the mountain, to investigate the unknown shore or the uncharted island.

Kipling's poem also makes it clear that the hidden land the explorer has unveiled—"White Man's country past disputing"—is "God's present to our nation" and that settlers will soon arrive to exploit its agricultural and mineral resources. In the history of exploration too, the trader, the colonizer, and the imperial administrator usually followed close upon the heels of the discoverer. Indeed, they were often one and the same.

Although exploration has been inseparable from the colonization and exploitation of new found lands, this volume concentrates on geographical discovery and on those who were the first to examine and describe the various unmapped regions of the globe. Articles discussing the geographical knowledge and concepts of the ancient and medieval worlds have been included, but emphasis has been placed on the age of discovery that began in fifteenth-century Europe and continued virtually unabated until the twentieth century. Explorers of Western European origin are stressed, but the contributions of Chinese, Muslims, and Russians have not been slighted.

Articles in this volume are of two types. The biographical articles relate the careers of preeminent explorers. The other articles deal with the principal geographical regions and with a variety of related topics, such as cartography and oceanography. The geographical articles trace the course of exploration in a single continent or region, developing such themes as obstacles to discovery and reviewing the achievements of the major explorers as well as those of less celebrated figures. Among the continents Africa, Antarctica, Australia, and South America have been treated as units, while North America and Asia have been divided into subregions because of the complexities of the exploratory process in the latter. The editor hopes that the articles in the volume will not only provide readers with clear and concise factual data but will also convey something of the courage, tenacity, and endurance displayed by the great explorers throughout the ages. To extract the maximum amount of information available in the volume, readers should make use of the cross-references and consult the Index.

The production of *The Discoverers* has been a collaborative enterprise, and the editor is grateful to the contributors, whose efforts have made it possible. Special thanks are due to James A. Casada, who, in addition to his articles, gave much valuable help. The editor also wishes to acknowledge the assistance of the staff of McGraw-Hill's Professional and Reference Book Division, especially Robert A. Rosenbaum and Tobia L. Worth.

Helen Delpar

Contributors

Peter J. Anderson
Assistant Director
Institute of Polar Studies
Ohio State University
Columbus, Ohio

J. M. R. Cameron
Lecturer in Geography and Education
University of New England
Armidale, New South Wales

James A. Casada
Associate Professor of History
Winthrop College
Rock Hill, South Carolina

Jiu-fong L. Chang
Seattle, Washington

Kuei-sheng Chang
Associate Professor of Geography
University of Washington
Seattle, Washington

Lawrence A. Clayton
Associate Professor of History
University of Alabama
Tuscaloosa, Alabama

Tom D. Crouch
Assistant Curator, Astronautics
National Air and Space Museum
Smithsonian Institution
Washington, D.C.

Max Fajn
The Harvard School
Chicago, Illinois

Barry M. Gough
Associate Professor of History
Wilfrid Laurier University
Waterloo, Ontario

André Gschaedler
Professor of History
Salem College
Salem, West Virginia

Clive A. Holland
Assistant Librarian and Curator
Scott Polar Research Institute
Cambridge, England

Howard Jones
Associate Professor of History
University of Alabama
Tuscaloosa, Alabama

Matti Enn Kaups
Professor of Geography
University of Minnesota, Duluth
Duluth, Minnesota

H. G. R. King
Librarian
Scott Polar Research Institute
Cambridge, England

George Kish
Professor of Geography
University of Michigan
Ann Arbor, Michigan

Dorothy Middleton
London, England

Robert W. Olson
Associate Professor of History
University of Kentucky
Lexington, Kentucky

Milton Osborne
Senior Research Fellow
Department of International
Relations
Australian National University
Canberra, Australian Capital
Territory

Richard A. Pierce
Professor of History
Queen's University
Kingston, Ontario

D. H. Simpson
Librarian
Royal Commonwealth Society
London, England

Bruce B. Solnick
Associate Professor of History
State University of New York at
Albany
Albany, New York

Irene M. Spry
Professor Emeritus of Economic
Science
University of Ottawa
Ottawa, Ontario

Phillip Drennon Thomas
Professor of History
Wichita State University
Wichita, Kansas

Norman J. W. Thrower
Professor of Geography
University of California, Los Angeles
Los Angeles, California

Martin Torodash
Professor of History
Fairleigh Dickinson University
Rutherford, New Jersey

William Tucker
Assistant Professor of History
University of Arkansas
Fayetteville, Arkansas

B. H. Warmington
Reader in Ancient History
University of Bristol
Bristol, England

Bernerd C. Weber
Professor of History
University of Alabama
Tuscaloosa, Alabama

A

Aerial Exploration

The invention of the airplane provided a revolutionary new tool for those who sought to explore unknown portions of the globe. For the first time, geographic barriers that had frustrated the progress of explorers for centuries could be crossed quickly and in relative comfort by air.

The role that the flying machine would play in exploration was apparent from the dawn of the air age. As early as 1784, only 6 months after the first manned balloon ascent, Thomas Jefferson remarked that the new invention would prove most useful in "traversing deserts . . . pathless and inaccessible mountains" and would lead to "the discovery of the Pole, which is but one day's journey in a balloon from where ice has hitherto stopped adventurers."

Balloon voyages Aerial voyages over unknown lands were a popular theme in nineteenth-century literature. The French novelist Jules Verne provided one of the best-known stories of this type in his *Cinq semaines en ballon (Five Weeks in a Balloon)*, which chronicled a fictional aerial voyage across Africa. Flying-machine expeditions to far corners of the world were also a staple of pulp fiction during this period. The reality of balloon flight fell short of the dreams of the novelists, however. In spite of numerous attempts to develop a navigable aerostat, the free balloon remained a captive of the winds. Few explorers were willing to gamble their lives on a journey over unexplored territory in a craft whose course they could not direct.

One of these few was Salomon August Andrée (1854–1897), chief engineer of the Swedish Patent Office. Andrée first announced his intention to cross the North Pole in a balloon in 1894. The scheme appealed to Swedish national pride and attracted financial support from Alfred Nobel and King Oscar II. Andrée's balloon, the *Ornen (Eagle)*, stood almost 100 feet (30 meters) high and measured 65 feet (20 meters) in diameter. The enclosed gondola housed three men and supplies and survival equipment including sledges and a collapsible boat. The giant balloon featured sails and a special dragline designed to allow some control over the direction of travel.

Danskøya (Dane Island), near Spitsbergen (Svalbard), Norway, was chosen as the point of departure for the polar journey. All preparations were complete by July 1896, but constant southerly winds prevented a departure that summer. Andrée returned to Danskøya with his two traveling companions, Knut Fraenkel and Nils Strindberg, the following year. On the morning of July 11, 1897, the *Ornen* rose into strong winds blowing toward the pole. As the three acronauts flew toward the northeast, their precious dragline became disconnected and fell from the gondola. Five days later one of the pigeons carried aboard the *Ornen* was shot by the captain of a Norwegian

Salomon August Andrée (left) and two companions making preparations for their polar flight. [Smithsonian Institution]

ship. A message dated July 13 attached to the bird reported that all was well. This was the last contact with the Andrée Expedition for 33 years, during which time the fate of the party became one of the great mysteries of the Arctic.

The riddle was solved on August 5, 1930, when a shore party from the sealer *Bratvaag* discovered a tattered camp and the remains of Andrée, Fraenkel, and Strindberg on Kvitøya (White Island) in the Arctic Ocean. A logbook and rolls of exposed film told the tragic story of the last months of the Andrée expedition.

The *Ornen* had traveled 250 miles (402 kilometers) on course for the pole during the first day of the flight. A dense fogbank had been encountered soon thereafter, and a sheet of ice forming on the gasbag had forced the craft onto the ice cap, where it was abandoned on July 14. From July 17 to October 6 the three men traveled south toward Spitsbergen, subsisting on the supplies salvaged from the balloon and on polar-bear meat. Early in October they made camp on an ice floe that drifted to Kvitøya before breaking up. The men established a permanent winter camp on the island, confident that they could survive by hunting local seals and bears. Diary entries indicate that the three men sickened and died during the winter of 1897, however. Carbon monoxide poisoning from a stove used in the closed shelter has been suggested as the cause of death.

The fate of the Andrée party failed to discourage others who sought to reach the pole by air. Walter Wellman, an American newspaper publisher, was the first to attempt a polar crossing in a dirigible balloon. Wellman's airship measured 228 feet (69 meters) in length and was borne aloft by 350,000 cubic feet (10,000 cubic meters) of hydrogen. Powered by twin 90-horsepower engines, the craft carried a crew of four and supplies to sustain the party if forced down on the ice. Like Andrée, Wellman chose Spitsbergen as the starting point for his polar flight. The *America* arrived at Vigo Bay in June 1906, but unfavorable winds

and poor flying conditions prevented a start for more than a year. On September 2, 1907, Wellman, his engineer Melvin Vaniman, and two crew members were at last able to begin their voyage. After only 3 hours in the air, head winds and engine trouble forced a return to Spitsbergen. Exhausted and discouraged, Wellman abandoned the venture.

Arctic flights of the 1920s By the 1920s, improvements in airplane and engine design presented explorers with a reliable vehicle capable of carrying them over untraversed lands in relative safety. The Norwegian explorer Roald AMUNDSEN, leader of the first party to reach the South Pole, was one of the first to realize the potential of the airplane. He remarked: "I had ... become obsessed with the vision of a new method of attacking the Arctic problem ... which, I felt sure, would revolutionize the whole practice of ... exploration ... aircraft for use in the Arctic."

Amundsen first contemplated a flight over the Arctic Ocean from Point Barrow, Alaska, to Spitsbergen. He purchased a Junkers JL-6, a low-wing metal monoplane that had recently established a world endurance record. A Curtiss Oriole was also acquired for reconnaissance flights that would precede the crossing of the polar sea in the Junkers. Having completed the first two flights over the Arctic Ocean, the Oriole was destroyed in a crash. Flights continued with the Junkers in the spring of 1923, but Amundsen lost faith in the airplane when it damaged a ski on landing. He became convinced that emergency landings on the rough ice of the polar cap would damage an airplane on skis so seriously that a takeoff would be impossible. An amphibious aircraft capable of landing and taking off on the open water of the polar leads would be much safer, he believed.

With the financial assistance of Lincoln ELLSWORTH, a wealthy American, Amundsen purchased two Dornier-Wal seaplanes in which he could fly from Spitsbergen to Alaska. The Dornier-Wal was an all-metal high-wing monoplane with tandem engines mounted over the wing. While the two flying boats were being prepared for the flight, Amundsen and Ellsworth learned that the Italian semirigid airship *N-1* could be purchased. Ellsworth agreed to provide additional funds so that the Dorniers could be used for immediate reconnaissance, while the airship would be held in reserve for a full-scale attempt on the pole during the spring of 1926.

Amundsen and Ellsworth left Kongsfjorden (Kings Bay) in the two flying boats on May 21, 1925. Amundsen flew in airplane *N-25* with a pilot and a mechanic, while Ellsworth, also accompanied by two crewmen, commanded the second Dornier, *N-24*. *N-25* developed engine trouble 7 hours after takeoff and was forced to land in the water of a lead only 135 miles (217 kilometers) from the pole. The engine and hull of the second airplane were seriously damaged when Ellsworth ordered a landing to render assistance. By the time that the faulty engine of *N-25* had been repaired, the lead was frozen. The airplane was dragged ½ mile over the ice to an area of packed snow that could be used as a runway. All nonessential equipment was jettisoned on June 15, 1925, 24 days after the start of the flight, as the six men climbed aboard *N-25* for a successful flight back to Kongsfjorden. In spite of their harrowing experience, Amundsen and Ellsworth were determined to continue with their plans for the polar crossing in an airship.

The spring of 1925 found a second American aerial expedition in Arctic waters. Commanded by Capt. Donald B. MacMillan, with Lieut. Comdr. Richard Evelyn BYRD in charge of the three Loening amphibians on loan from the U.S. Navy, the party established a base camp near Etah, Greenland. The three aircraft surveyed more than 30,000 square miles (77,700 square kilometers) of unexplored territory, including a foray by Byrd and his copilot, Floyd Bennett, over the Greenland ice cap. Like Amundsen, Byrd was quick to recognize the utility of the airplane in Arctic exploration: "I was stirred with the conclusion that aviation could conquer the Arctic.... I came back with secret confidence that I was perhaps very close to the biggest thing in my life." After his return, the young naval officer persuaded automobile heir Edsel Ford to donate a Fokker trimotor, to be named *Josephine Ford.* Byrd and Bennett intended to return north with their airplane in 1926 for an attempt to fly to the pole.

Amundsen and Ellsworth were able to conclude arrangements for the purchase of the Italian dirigible *N-1,* which was to be renamed the *Norge (Norway).* They were also able to secure the services of the airship's designer, Umberto Nobile, who was to serve as pilot for the polar voyage. The two leaders of the expedition returned to Kongsfjorden in the spring of 1926 to prepare for the arrival of the *Norge.* The ship *Chantier,* carrying Byrd, Bennett, and the *Josephine Ford,* dropped anchor on April 29. Nobile was on hand with the *Norge* a week later. In spite of protestations by both parties, newspapermen began to speak of an aerial race for the pole.

Byrd immediately experienced a series of problems with the skis fitted to the big Fokker. These difficulties were finally overcome with the advice and assistance of Bernt Balchen, a young Norwegian pilot employed by Ellsworth and Amundsen.

The *Josephine Ford* was pulled to the top of the snow ramp from which it would begin its takeoff run during the early hours of May 9, 1926. Floyd Bennett lifted the heavy trimotor into the air as Byrd charted a course to the pole. In spite of an oil leak in the starboard engine, Byrd announced their arrival at the pole shortly after 9 A.M. The return to Spitsbergen was uneventful, with a safe landing and a hearty welcome by the Amundsen-Ellsworth party at about 4:30 P.M. Accounts by Balchen and other students of exploration have questioned the validity of Byrd's claim to have reached the pole, but to date no definitive evidence refuting the long-accepted version of the flight has been presented.

Amundsen, Ellsworth, and Nobile planned a much more ambitious flight than Byrd's. The *Norge,* a semirigid airship, featured a keel on the underside of a 348-foot (106-meter) gasbag. The craft carried a sixteen-man crew and was powered by three Maybach engines. The airship left Kongsfjorden on May 11 and passed over the North Pole at about 1:30 A.M. the following day. The moment was especially significant for Amundsen and helmsman Oscar Wisting, for they now became the first men to have visited both poles. The *Norge* continued over the top of the world, battling fog and ice to complete the journey of 3180 miles (5118 kilometers) to Teller, Alaska, in 70 hours and 40 minutes. The flight was marred by ill feeling between Nobile and his Italians and the rest of the crew as to who deserved credit for the success of the expedition.

Captain George Hubert WILKINS and Carl Ben Eielson led the third memorable polar assault of 1926. Wilkins, an Australian, had persuaded a group of Detroit backers to finance an aerial expedition to search for unexplored land north of Alaska. Wilkins purchased two airplanes, a Fokker trimotor and a single-engine Fokker, for the proposed flights. His backers insisted on an extended flight over the polar cap from Point Barrow, Alaska, to Spitsbergen. Eielson, one of the best-known bush pilots in Alaska, was hired to pilot the Fokkers. A series of tragic accidents, ranging from the decapitation of a crew member who walked into a propeller, to crashes that seriously damaged

Andrée and his companions depart from Danskøya, near Spitsbergen, in the balloon Örnen. *Their fate was to remain a mystery for 33 years. [National Archives]*

Aerial Exploration

George Hubert Wilkins and Carl Ben Eielson in Paris after they crossed the Arctic Ocean in one of the first Lockheed Vegas. [National Archives]

both airplanes, prevented the proposed distance flight, although Wilkins and Eielson were able to fly farther into the unexplored territory north of Point Barrow than anyone had before.

The Detroit backers provided two new Stinson airplanes for a new attempt to reach Spitsbergen in 1927. Wilkins and Eielson left Point Barrow in one of these aircraft on the morning of March 29, 1927. At 11:15 the pair landed on the ice roughly 550 miles (885

The disastrous voyage of Umberto Nobile's Italia proved to be the last long-distance flight intended solely to explore unknown Arctic territory. [National Archives]

kilometers) from Point Barrow to adjust the engine and take depth soundings. The necessity for further engine repairs combined with strong head winds made it impossible to complete the return flight. A final landing was made in the face of a blizzard shortly after 9 P.M. that evening. The pair were trapped in the cabin of the Stinson by snow and high winds for 5 days. When the weather improved, Wilkins was able to estimate their position as 80 miles (129 kilometers) northeast of Point Barrow. The two aviators then walked to safety, dragging sledges built of aircraft parts.

Disappointed by Wilkins's failure to produce a newsworthy flight after 2 years of effort, the Detroit backers withdrew from the venture. Determined to make a final effort, Wilkins sold the Fokker trimotor (rebuilt as the *Southern Cross,* this airplane would become the first to fly from the United States to Australia) and the remaining Stinson. With the cash thus obtained he was able to purchase one of the first Lockheed Vegas produced. A high-wing, closed-cabin monoplane powered by a Wright J5 Whirlwind, the Vega had a top speed of 136 miles (219 kilometers) per hour. With extra fuel tanks in the plywood wing and fuselage, the Vega was to become one of the most popular and successful airplanes for long-distance flying.

On April 15, 1928, Wilkins and Eielson took off on a 20-hour flight that carried them across the Arctic Ocean, laying to rest the rumors that a landmass existed in the polar sea. Nearing Spitsbergen, they encountered a blizzard and were forced to land on an island. When the storm passed 5 days later, they took off once again and made a final landing at Green Harbor, Spitsbergen.

Umberto Nobile returned to the Arctic in 1928 with a new airship, the *Italia,* that had been especially designed for polar flying. His goal was to conduct extensive aerial mapping operations and scientific studies of the ice cap. After a series of short flights, the *Italia* weighed off for a major voyage on May 23, 1928. The dirigible passed over the pole shortly after midnight and turned back toward Spitsbergen in the face of strong head winds. On the morning of May 25 the combination of a heavy ice load and the loss of gas forced the dirigible onto the polar ice. The control car was ripped from the gasbag, spilling nine men, including Nobile, onto the ice and killing a mechanic in one of the engine gondolas instantly. Free of this weight, the gasbag rose into the air once again carrying six crew members. No trace of this portion of the airship or its occupants was ever seen again. The nine survivors found themselves less than 40 miles (64 kilometers) from Spitsbergen, but the ice was so rugged that it seemed impossible to walk to safety. The party was able to salvage enough food to last 25 days, one sleeping bag, a radio, a pistol, a tent, and an assortment of metal scraps.

An international air search for the *Italia* survivors was launched at the request of the Italian government and Oslo newspapers. Roald Amundsen, ignoring the ill feeling that marked his own relationship with Nobile, was one of the first to volunteer. Wilkins, Eielson, Ellsworth, and other Arctic veterans announced their own willingness to assist in the search.

Nobile, incapacitated with a broken leg, ordered the transmission of continuous SOS signals, but to no avail. On May 30, he finally gave permission for three of his crew members to attempt to walk over the treacherous ice to safety. On June 3, an amateur radio operator in Archangel (Arkhangelsk), U.S.S.R., picked up the SOS from the *Italia,* but the crew proved very difficult to locate from the air. Planes frequently passed near the camp without spotting the party. Moreover, it quickly became apparent that the would-be rescuers were in very real danger themselves. Amundsen, his pilot, and four passengers were lost while on a search flight.

The Nobile party was finally spotted from the air on June 20. While supplies could now be airlifted to the survivors, poor ice conditions made it impossible to land anything but light aircraft. Nobile was the first to be airlifted to safety on June 24. The other survivors had convinced the general that he should be the first to return to Spitsbergen in order to supervise the rescue of the others, but the action would brand Nobile as a coward in the eyes of many for the rest of his life. Deteriorating weather conditions prevented continued attempts to airlift the crew. Not until July 11 did the Russian ship *Krasin* take the main body of the *Italia* party on board. The following day the *Krasin* located and rescued the three crewmen who had attempted to walk to Nordaustlandet (Northeast Land).

Soviet flights The *Italia* disaster brought one phase of the aerial exploration of the Arctic to a conclusion. Long-distance flights intended solely to explore unknown territory were now replaced by those designed to open air routes connecting Europe and the Americas. Soviet airmen made impressive long-distance flights from Moscow to Kamchatka in a single-engine ANT-25 and from Los Angeles to Moscow with stops in Alaska and Siberia. In June 1937, three Soviet airmen flew the trans-Siberian ANT-25 from Moscow to Vancouver, a distance of 5288 miles (8510 kilometers). The following month, a second ANT-25 flew from Moscow to San Jacinto, California, setting a world's distance record of 6296 miles (10,132 kilometers). In August 1937 the six-man crew of a large four-engine aircraft were lost during an attempt to duplicate the ANT-25 flights. These Soviet flights presaged the day when polar skies would serve as a highway traveled by scheduled commercial airliners.

Antarctic flights The introduction of the airplane had a greater impact on the exploration of Antarctica than on that of any other continent. George Hubert Wilkins was the first to make use of the airplane to map large areas of the southernmost landmass. With the financial assistance of William Randolph Hearst, the Australian went south in 1928 with two Lockheed Vegas and pilots Carl Ben Eielson and Joe Ben Cross.

Herbert Hollick-Kenyon (left) and Lincoln Ellsworth beside the Polar Star, which carried them across Antarctica in 1935. [National Archives]

On December 28, Wilkins and Eielson began a flight from Deception Island that would carry them over completely unknown territory. They demonstrated, for example, that Graham Land, which had been considered a peninsula, was, in fact, a series of islands. The following year Wilkins continued flights over Antarctica with pilots Parker Cramer and Al Cheeseman.

Richard Byrd had begun to make plans to fly over the South Pole soon after completing a transatlantic flight in 1927. With the financial assistance of Henry and Edsel Ford, the young naval officer obtained a Ford trimotor and two single-engine aircraft, a Fokker Super Universal and a Fairchild FC2W2. Bernt Balchen, Harold June, Dean Smith, and Alton Parker served as Byrd's key subordinates. The eighty-man party moved south on four ships, establishing the base camp that was to become world-famous as Little America in January 1929. Early forays into the interior resulted in a number of significant discoveries, notably the Rockefeller Mountains. For Byrd, however, the flight to the pole on November 28, 1929, was the climax of the expedition. Balchen served as pilot on this flight, with Byrd himself navigating, June serving as copilot, and Ashley McKinley as photographer. To rise through the Queen Maud Range, the party was forced to jettison food and survival equipment. The remainder of the flight was uneventful, however, with a return to Little America 19 hours after takeoff.

While Byrd was making his reconnaissance and polar flights from Little America, a Norwegian party outfitted with two seaplanes probed the Princess Martha Coast on the opposite side of the continent. At the same time, Sir Douglas Mawson and Flight Lieut. S. Campbell surveyed MacRobertson Land from the air.

The way was now open for a more complete mapping of the Antarctic continent. The three Wilkins-Ellsworth expeditions of the mid-1930s climaxed in the epochal flight of Lincoln Ellsworth and the Canadian pilot Herbert Hollick-Kenyon across the continent in the Northrop Gamma *Polar Star* in November and December 1935. The 1934–1935 Byrd expedition boasted a two-engine Curtiss Condor which mapped 200,000 square miles (518,000 square kilometers) of new territory.

Surveys of other areas The continuing scientific and geographic exploration of the Antarctic has remained dependent on aircraft for aerial mapping, the establishment of forward camps, and the mass movement of men and supplies. While the airplane made its greatest contribution to exploration in the icy skies of the poles, other little-known areas of the world were also opened by aircraft. The rain forests of South America, for example, remained almost totally unknown until the air age.

As early as 1925 Dr. A. Hamilton Rice included a Curtiss Seagull as part of his expedition to the upper reaches of the Amazon. Lieut. Walter Hinton, who had piloted the Navy *NC-4* on the first transatlantic flight, was in charge of aerial operations for the expedition. Capt. Albert W. Stevens, on leave from the U.S. Army Air Service, served as photographer. Hinton and Stevens proved invaluable in maintaining communications between the base camp and exploration parties in the field. In addition, the aircraft was used to scout routes for forward parties, providing film of the hazards to be faced upstream and offering suggestions as to the easiest route to travel. During 9 months of operation the Rice Expedition's Seagull logged more than 12,000 miles (19,312 kilometers) of flying over some of the most difficult and least accessible terrain in the world.

Perhaps the clearest example of the importance of the airplane in opening the rain forests of South America can be seen in the fact that Angel Falls, the world's highest waterfall, remained undiscovered until 1935, when first seen by the legendary bush pilot Jimmy Angel from the cockpit of his Travel Air monoplane. After service with the Royal Canadian Air Force during World War I, Angel had been employed as a barnstormer, a movie stunt pilot, and an organizer of the Chinese Air Force prior to finding his way to Latin America. Flying aircraft ranging from an aging Bristol fighter to modern closed-cabin monoplanes, Angel traversed Central and South America, carrying freight and passengers in and out of almost inaccessible jungle and mountain flying fields. At the time of his death of a cerebral hemorrhage in 1956, Angel was still an active pilot, the embodiment of all the solitary men whose gift of wings enabled them to open new territory for the benefit of mankind.

In addition to its role in the exploration of totally unknown lands, the airplane, coupled with specially developed aerial cameras, completed large-scale photographic surveys that made possible the production of much more accurate maps than could be prepared by using older techniques. The aerial survey conducted between Ketchikan and Anchorage, Alaska, by three U.S. Navy amphibians between May and August 1926 is an outstanding illustration of the way in which the airplane was placed in the service of geographers. Operating at the request of the Department of the Interior, these Loening aircraft provided detailed photographic coverage of more than 10,000 square miles (25,900 square kilometers) of wilderness.

The Houston Mount Everest Expedition, organized by L. V. S. Blacker in 1933, was yet another outstanding example of the use of aircraft to prepare photographic maps of otherwise-inaccessible regions. The Blacker party made the first flights over Mount Everest in two specially prepared Westland P.V. 3 airplanes powered by supercharged Pegasus engines. The planes were equipped with oxygen for the pilot and crewmen and heating gear for men and cameras. A total of eight cameras provided motion-picture footage, as well as oblique and vertical strip photographs. During the course of two survey flights over the Himalayas, members of the expedition braved head winds of up to 110 miles (177 kilometers) per hour to return a photographic record of the roof of the world.

By 1940 airplanes and the intrepid men who flew them had filled the blank spots that dotted the maps of 1900. Men and machines had overcome the final geographic barriers.

See also ANTARCTICA; ARCTIC OCEAN.

BIBLIOGRAPHY: Roald Amundsen, *My Polar Flight*, London, 1925; Roald Amundsen and Lincoln Ellsworth, *The First Flight across the Polar Sea*, New York, 1927; Bernt Balchen, *Come North with Me*, New York, 1958; Latham Valentine Stewart Blacker et al., *First over Everest*, New York, 1934; Richard Evelyn Byrd, *Skyward*, New York, 1928; Lincoln Ellsworth, *Air Pioneering in the Arctic*, New York, 1926; id., *Beyond Horizons*, New York, 1938; C. V. Glines, *Polar Aviation*, New York, 1964; Charles Gibbs-Smith, *Aviation: An Historical Survey from Its Origins to the End of World War II*, London, 1970; John Grierson, *Challenge to the Poles*, Hamden, Conn., 1964; id., *Sir Hubert Wilkins: Enigma of Exploration*, London, 1960; Umberto Nobile, *With the Italia to the North Pole*, New York, 1931; C. R. Roseberry, *The Challenging Skies*, New York, 1966; Per Olaf Sundman, *The Flight of the Eagle*, New York, 1970; George H. Wilkins, *Flying the Arctic*, New York, 1928.

Tom D. Crouch

Africa

Africa was the last of the world's great populated regions to be thoroughly explored, and any analysis of the process of geographical discovery on the continent logically begins with a discussion of the special conditions that caused what might appear, at first glance, to be an inexplicable delay in unraveling its secrets. After all, the exploration of Africa was not completed until the final years of the nineteenth century; yet its northern reaches lie only a few miles across the Strait of Gibraltar from Europe and the origin of most exploring expeditions to the continent. The reasons that the completion of African exploration came long after the contours of North and South America, Australia, the islands of the Pacific, and other regions remote from Europe had been clearly delineated are many. They may, however, be conveniently summarized in four general categories. Africa resisted outside penetration because of its physical features, size, climate, and indigenous population.

Obstacles to Exploration From the earliest stages of revealing the continent's geographical secrets to the Western world (it is in these terms that African exploration is herein defined, although admittedly there is a bit of inherent artificiality in speaking of the discovery of a continent which was the home of millions of human beings) the variegated natural and climatic characteristics of Africa formed major obstacles impeding the efforts of would-be geographical pioneers. So significant were these conditions that they form a central thread which is tightly interwoven throughout the fabric of the history and development of African reconnaissance. Indeed, to a considerable degree these factors dictated the nature and direction of the exploration of the continent.

Physical features Africa is an enormous inverted triangular island encompassed by the Atlantic Ocean on the west, the Indian Ocean and the Red Sea on the east, and the Mediterranean Sea to the north. Yet ironically the continent's proximity to the sea historically proved a barrier rather than an open highway beckoning to adventurers. Virtually all of Africa's eastern and western coastline is devoid of sheltered natural harbors, and only on its Mediterranean-washed northern shores is there an appreciable number of safe ports and landing sites. Furthermore, early seagoing pioneers soon found that the scarcity of suitable anchorages was only the first of a multitude of related problems they had to face. Most of the initial steps in African exploration and virtually all that focused on coastal regions were completed in the days of sail. This meant that the difficulties of finding safe harbors were exacerbated by many other impediments to discovery. In the equatorial waters of the Atlantic Ocean sailors faced the dreaded prospect of days or even weeks of motionlessness in the doldrums while they waited for a breath of wind to fill their sails. If they successfully survived this hazard as they progressed southward, they then faced the terrible storms which raged around the Cape of Good Hope with frightening regularity. Finally, there were the seasonal monsoons to be braved along the continent's Indian Ocean coast. As if such perils were not trying enough, Africa's rivers, for all their size, were equally uninviting.

Every river that seemingly might have opened a smooth and easily traversed route into the interior actually presented, in an almost perverse fashion, major navigational problems. The mightiest of them all, the Nile, successfully withstood every attempt at approaching its source by travel upstream. Indeed, when John Hanning SPEKE eventually solved the ancient mystery of the Nile's origin in the middle of the nineteenth century, his discovery came as the culmination of an expedition that had traveled overland from the East African coast. The cataracts of the Nile, together with the collections of sudd (massed floating vegetation) which periodically clogged the stream's upper reaches from Gondokoro southward, meant that what might have been a highway into the interior instead presented a virtually insurmountable barrier. Similarly, the Zambezi River, which Dr. David LIVINGSTONE styled "God's highway" before being confronted with the bitter truth concerning its navigability, was marked by rapids and waterfalls. In the case of the Zambezi, even entrance to the stream was hazardous, because its mouth contained shifting sandbars constantly pounded by dangerous and unpredictable surf. The Congo (Zaire) River was navigable for some distance upstream, but as disasters taught Henry Morton STANLEY, it was full of treacherous whirlpools even in its lower reaches, and waterfalls dotted its upper levels. The Niger River was in some ways the most perplexing of all. At its mouth it spreads out into a morass of impenetrable mangrove swamps so dense that there scarcely is a perceptible current or outlet to mark any stream at all, much less give an indication of the river's true size. Only after numerous expeditions, marked by tragedy and deaths, were explorers finally able to determine the exact nature of its course and the manner of its exit to the sea.

Land routes to the interior proved even more of an impediment to travelers than did Africa's rivers. To the north the vast expanse of the Sahara Desert loomed as a major barrier interposed between Europe and Africa. To be sure, Arab merchants and Muslims anxious to spread the teachings of Prophet Muhammad managed to resolve many of the mysteries of the trackless, scorching desert long before Europeans penetrated its immense reaches, but for the Western world the Sahara remained both a geographical riddle and an effective obstacle to a direct overland approach to the continent's heart well into the nineteenth century. At the opposite end of Africa, back of the Cape of Good Hope, there were no obstacles comparable to those posed by the Sahara. Still, rough terrain and the Kalahari Desert were less than inviting to explorers. Sandwiched between these two extremes was the meat of the continent, the tropical and subtropical regions of Africa. Here vistas ranging from the harsh, thorny *bundu* of the East African hinterland to dense vegetation produced by rainfalls of up to 400 inches (10,160 millimeters) annually stood ready to thwart expeditions to the interior.

Size Closely related to these natural features inimical to the process of geographical exploration was the obvious immensity of Africa. The continent comprises about one-fifth of the world's landmass and is thus twice the size of Europe. Moreover, Africa is so shaped (its compactness may be contrasted with the endless irregularities that form the outline of Europe) that much of its interior lies at an immense distance from the sea. Large areas in the heart of Africa are more than 500 miles (805 kilometers) from any coast, and there are points more than 800 miles (1,287 kilometers) removed from ocean highways.

Climate Yet neither size nor rugged physical features ranging from perpetually snow-clad mountains on the equator to deserts with a temperature variance of 80°F (44°C) in a 12-hour period proved the greatest deterrent to exploration of the continent. What weighed more heavily than any other consideration in preserving Africa as *terra incognita* insofar as the outside world was concerned was its climate, which produced an environment extremely hostile to European health.

Early in the process of African reconnaissance the continent's tropical regions earned well-deserved opprobrium as the "white man's grave." Only in the latter half of the nineteenth century did Europeans make significant progress in the understanding, prevention, and cure of the myriad maladies which had troubled them from their initial contacts with tropical Africa. The stifling heat, oppressive humidity, and dense vegetation of much of the African interior provided fertile breeding grounds for the insects which carried a multitude of virulent diseases such as encephalitis, blackwater fever, yellow fever, and malaria, the deadliest and most widespread of all Africa's ailments. Even if explorers somehow survived the inevitable array of fevers that struck them, decimation of pack animals by tsetse-fly attacks left them totally dependent on human transport for the progress of their expeditions.

Only with the advent of quinine as a preventative medicine and the corollary use of mosquito netting did travel become even moderately safe as regards disease. Until that time, which came at a late stage in the history of African exploration, the most common result of geographical missions was abrupt conclusion through the death of many or all of the European members. Thus there was, in an African context, more than a modicum of truth in Louis Simpson's caustic remark that "grave by grave we civilized the ground." Or, in the appropriately if unintentionally fatalistic wording of the ditty sung by generations of English sailors in West African waters:

> Beware and take care in the Bight of Benin,
> For one that comes out there are forty that goes in.

Population The climatic perils of Africa were buttressed by the continent's fauna. Deadly vipers and savage beasts were more than largely imaginary dangers written large for the benefit of a European readership which thrived on the often-sensational accounts published by African explorers; in many regions they were a factor to be reckoned with. One only need recall Livingstone's famous adventure with a lion, when he had his arm mangled and narrowly escaped

death, to be reminded of this fact. But it was the human, not the animal, population of Africa that constituted a major barrier. The vast cultural chasm that separated the peoples of Africa from those of Europe proved a deterrent to mutual understanding which has not been entirely superseded even today. For countless centuries Africans had for the most part lived and developed in isolation, and this was particularly true of the Negroid peoples indigenous to all save the northernmost portions of the continent. Many of the same obstacles that prevented outside access to Africa had an equal but opposite effect in that they imposed a special sort of continental insularity on Africans. Seldom did Africans travel, of their own volition, beyond the continent's encircling walls of water. It is true that much of the precolonial history of Africa is contained in the theme of transcontinental migration and movement of peoples, but these travels were strictly of an internal nature. When Africans were exposed to the world beyond their continent in a major way, the exposure took the form of a tragedy perhaps unsurpassed in the annals of man's inhumanity to man: the vast and terrible migration that was the transoceanic slave trade.

Given their naturally xenophobic propensities and desire for isolation, Africans might well have been expected to offer ceaseless resistance to outside intrusion. Such was not always the case; in fact, one marvels at the benevolence of the continent's peoples in the face of the woes visited upon them first by the Arabs and then by Europeans. Nonetheless, both consciously and as a result of the technological and sociological differences that separated them from pioneering travelers, Africans thwarted attempts by outsiders to advance into the interior. Their resistance derived from a variety of reasons, ranging from shrewd economic assessments to sheer superstition. These considerations were reinforced by the horrors the continent's initial penetrators brought in such forms as smallpox, venereal disease, and the slave trade. The people of Africa were the final major barrier to exploration, and their activities, when viewed in combination with the other obstacles already mentioned, meant that the continent presented its discoverers with a formidable task. Yet these very difficulties lent an aura of romance and mystery to the quest for Africa and helped ensure that there was no lack of adventurers anxious to remove the geographical mantle veiling the continent.

Development of European Knowledge The process of lifting this mantle took place in four or possibly five distinct phases of European endeavor. Arabs also contributed significantly to the solution of Africa's geographical secrets, but the exploits of Arab travelers were little known outside the Muslim world and accordingly exerted relatively little influence on European thinking on and exploring activity in Africa. For these reasons Arab efforts figure only marginally in the account that follows. The initial European contacts with Africa were those established by the classical world, and these surprisingly extensive links mark the first major phase of exploration. There then followed a lengthy hiatus corresponding with the Middle Ages and the breakdown of European culture and large-scale political organization. The second phase of the continent's exploration, dominated by Portugal, was an outgrowth of Renaissance Europe's renewed curiosity about the uncharted portions of the world. The capable Portuguese seamen, sponsored and schooled by their remarkable leader, Prince HENRY the Navigator, learned much about Africa. Yet, as we shall see, they jealously guarded their discoveries by revealing relatively little of the great amount of knowledge they amassed. It was only in the third and incomparably the greatest phase of African discovery that European interest in and knowledge of the continent underwent an immense expansion.

This third phase was a product of the Age of Reason, and given the Enlightenment's adulation of the "noble savage," its humanitarian impulses, and imperialist ideas stimulated by mercantilism, Africa was a logical focal point of interest. The era opened with the travels of James BRUCE and the publication of his *Travels to Discover the Source of the Nile* (1790) and concluded slightly over a century later with the onset of what is known as the Scramble for Africa. In the intervening years the major geographical problems were solved and, beginning with the creation of the AFRICAN ASSOCIATION in 1788, public attention turned to the continent in unprecedented fashion. The third phase completed the exploration process insofar as great discoveries were concerned, and in so doing yielded to a fourth, completion of African cartography in detail and a concomitant discovery of the political and economic possibilities the continent offered. A possible final phase would be that of scientific exploration and the belated discovery of the distinctiveness of Africa's peoples and their past. Inasmuch as this is not a geographical discovery, it deserves only passing mention here, but it should be noted that the departure from the traditional Eurocentric view of Africa is truly the latest "discovery" associated with the continent.

Knowledge of the Greeks and Romans The beginnings of European knowledge of Africa came through trading contacts with ancient Egypt, and later the Greeks and Romans amassed a considerable corpus of data concerning the continent's geography. From the dawn of recorded history the Nile River, in particular, had been an object of wonder and fascination. Geographers looked on the mighty stream which traced a verdant strip through hundreds of miles of arid desert to make Egypt its gift and pondered its origins. HERODOTUS OF HALICARNASSUS collected extensive information about the Nile during the course of his travels in Libya and Egypt in the middle years of the fifth century B.C. Thanks to his own researches and secondhand knowledge of expeditions such as the one

undertaken by Pharaoh Necho II (r. ca. 610–594 B.C.), Herodotus had an accurate grasp of Nile geography as far south as Gondokoro and the region of the sudd. He also learned much of the desert (recently the accuracy of his descriptions of areas he visited personally has been fully verified) and heard, from the people of Cyrene, of "a swift and violent river, flowing from the West to the East." He wrongly concluded that this was a part of the Nile; in reality it is likely that the stream being described was either the Komadugu Yobe at the point of its entrance into Lake Chad or the upper reaches of the Niger before it makes its great bend toward the Atlantic Ocean. The *History* of Herodotus also contained other intriguing if not always accurate tidbits (for example, references to Pygmies and "Aethiopian troglodytes") and the account remained the standard description of Africa for the next four centuries.

At that point Roman expansion into North Africa gave rise to works by PLINY the Elder, PTOLEMY, and others which added to existing knowledge of Africa. Unfortunately for posterity, the Romans were surprisingly taciturn regarding their geographical exploits in Africa. Richard Jobson, a British trader on the Gambia River who read Roman accounts in an effort to expand his intellectual horizons on the continent, succinctly expressed the bewilderment and disappointment which greets anyone undertaking to delve deeply into the subject: "The Romans, careful relaters of their

The European exploration of Africa.

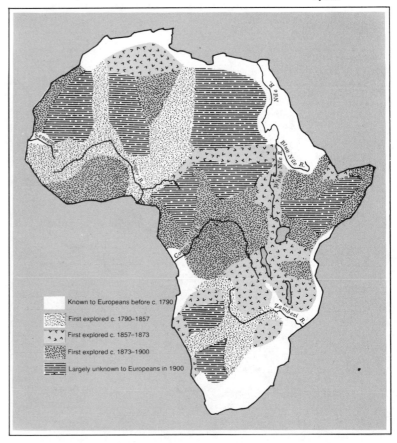

Known to Europeans before c. 1790

First explored c. 1790–1857

First explored c. 1857–1873

First explored c. 1873–1900

Largely unknown to Europeans in 1900

great victories, do speak little of the interior parts of Africa." Nonetheless, Pliny's massive *Natural History* does contain tantalizing data on the findings of Roman military expeditions. These include a list of towns visited by Lucius Cornelius Balbus in an expedition late in the first century B.C. which may have taken him to the banks of the Niger and information taken from the Berber king Juba II on the source of the Nile. Pliny also incorporated other references to the Sahara and Sudan in his writings, but his accounts are exasperating both because of their brevity and because of their inconsistency in accuracy, which makes it difficult to separate geographical fact from myth.

Ptolemy, the renowned second-century geographer who resided in the intellectual center Alexandria, was generally more reliable than Pliny. Yet, insofar as Africa is concerned, Ptolemy's justly famous *Geography* suffers from the same defect as Pliny's *Natural History*. It is so severely compressed that frequently it tantalizes readers rather than providing them with meaningful insights. However, Ptolemy rightly distinguished between the Nile and Niger Rivers; he first suggested that the source of the former stream was to be found in the legendary "Mountains of the Moon" located somewhere in the region of the equator, and his map of Africa was little improved upon until the era of Portuguese exploration. His *Geography* was a convenient compendium of existing knowledge of Africa, and as such it is a commentary on the still-rudimentary nature of clssical geography as it related to the continent.

Portuguese explorers in small ships along the African coast. [The Pierpont Morgan Library]

In essence, the ancients accumulated fairly substantial knowledge of the whole of North Africa including the Sudan, they knew something of the continent's northeastern coastline, and on its western shores Europeans probably penetrated as far south as Sierra Leone (or at least conversed with those who had). But for ancient Europe, Africa remained a land that "inspired always emotions of wonder and curiosity, mingled with terror." It was a continent of mystery and romance, and it harbored wonderfully strange beasts such as one with "a cloven foot like a boeufe; the backe, maine and hire of an horse; and he hath his neighing also. His muzzle or snout turneth up: his taile twineth like the bores, and his teeth like wise are crooked and bending downwards as the bores tusks but not so hurtfull; the skin or hide of his back [is] unpenetrable." This description of a hippopotamus is excellent, but if such beasts existed in reality, can one wonder at exotic creations of the ancients such as ants "as big as a mastiff" or men with their mouths and eyes in their chests? The problem was that, save for portions of the writings of Herodotus, virtually all geographical information gathered by the ancients was of a secondhand nature and reflected in full measure the problems inherent in such data. Thus the misconceptions that bedeviled Europeans throughout the history of African reconnaissance (they exist even today in Hollywood stereotypes such as Tarzan and wild, half-naked natives) were an integral part of the opening chapter of the continent's exploration. Even these misconceptions, together with the important truths garnered by the Greeks and Romans, disappeared in the fourth and fifth centuries A.D. The initial phase of European contact with Africa ended abruptly with the advent of the Dark Ages. Not until centuries later, when the adventurous Portuguese mariners inspired by Prince Henry the Navigator began to sail southward in their caravels, would the contact be renewed.

Era of Portuguese Exploration A precise date can be affixed to the onset of Portugal's exploration of Africa, yet ironically it is not that of a great discovery or of a notable geographical breakthrough. In 1415 Portuguese forces, in an affray growing out of a protracted struggle between the Christian nation and Muslims which had begun in the thirteenth century, successfully invaded and seized the Moroccan port of Ceuta. This was in itself a momentous occasion, for it marked Portugal's first foray into enemy territory and heralded a whole series of conquests on southern Mediterranean shores. However, the greatest significance of the seizure of Ceuta lay in the participation of Portugal's youthful Prince Henry in the siege. Spurred by the conquest and motivated by a host of interrelated ambitions, he returned home determined to open Africa's heretofore tightly secured doors to Portuguese enterprise.

Prince Henry the Navigator The astute young prince readily recognized the implications of his nation's contact with and proximity to Africa, and he envisioned Portugal as a funnel through which the gold of West Africa could flow into Europe. For several centuries the region that eventually came to be known as the Gold Coast had been Europe's principal supplier of the precious metal, but it had traveled to the continent via overland routes through the western Sudan and across the Sahara. This meant that Muslim rulers of territories through which caravans carrying the gold traveled were the middlemen of the transferral process. They accordingly reaped the bulk of the immense profits derived from the gold trade. Prince Henry was determined to circumvent these Muslim entrepreneurs, and to this end he initiated a series of maritime expeditions that reached ever farther south along Africa's uncharted Atlantic coast. In the process he earned an appropriate appendage to his name: he has become known to posterity as Prince Henry the Navigator. Each passing year saw an expansion in Portugal's knowledge of Africa, but there were factors beyond mere hopes of monopolizing the gold trade which accounted for this small country's adventurousness.

As was true of gold, Europe traditionally had received its spices through indirect and expensive channels. This involved a complex trade in which spices, carried by both sea and land, ultimately traveled from the spice-producing islands of the Indian Ocean to the Mediterranean. The Portuguese hoped to discover a new sea route which would take them directly to the East Indies and enable them to avoid any contact with profit-reducing middlemen or the notorious pirates who plagued traders sailing in Mediterranean waters. Should they be successful, their small nation could establish an economic stranglehold on a trade that potentially was even more lucrative than that in gold.

The motives of Portuguese endeavor were not solely economic in nature, however. As the Portuguese chronicler in Prince Henry's service, Gomes Eannes de Zurara, aptly wrote, men were attracted to discovery not merely "to engage in great and noble conquests, but above all to attempt the discovery of things which were hidden from other men." Certainly the lure of the unknown always has been in the forefront of geographical enterprise, and religious impulses have likewise played a major role in stimulating exploration. In the latter context, the PRESTER JOHN saga formed an important chapter in Portugal's contacts with Africa. The legend of the mythical monarch was a well-established one long before Portuguese caravels began their first tentative Atlantic voyages. Purportedly the Christian sovereign ruled a fabulously wealthy kingdom through which there flowed a mighty river whose banks were sprinkled with gems and precious stones of every hue and description. Gold was everywhere plentiful, and the King daily entertained thousands of guests at a table of solid emerald. Most marvelous of all, Prester John supposedly possessed perpetual youth, which he periodically renewed at a fountain of life. Such tales

Woodcut of Prester John, mythical monarch of fabulous wealth with whom Henry the Navigator hoped to join forces to defeat the Muslims. [Library of Congress]

would in themselves have been sufficient to stimulate Portuguese interest or even avarice, but overriding these stories of incalculable riches was the fact that Prester John's great ambition was to stamp out Islam. Thus those two motivations that were so frequently linked in the process of European expansion, God and gold, meshed to form an integral part of Portugal's approach to Africa. Prince Henry, ever alert for opportunities to enrich his nation and simultaneously cripple the Muslims, aspired to a link with Prester John. Jointly their forces could enfold the Muslims and, like a gigantic pincer, gradually crush them. In reality the Prester John legend had little enough foundation (only the Coptic Christianity of Ethiopia cloaked it with the vestiges of truth), but it remained a major magnet attracting Portuguese attention to Africa. Yet this alluring legend and the motivations previously mentioned constitute only one factor in explaining the striking success that the small European nation enjoyed in exploring Africa. The second factor upon which this success was predicated lies in the skills, technological advances, and accumulated maritime information that emerged from Prince Henry's tireless efforts to school his seamen.

At Sagres, suitably situated on a narrow finger of land almost surrounded by the forbidding Atlantic Ocean, Prince Henry brought together an unusual group of individuals who ranged from scholars to sailmakers and from cartographers to caravel captains. Inspired by the sweeping vision of Henry and determined to make Portugal a true mistress of the sea, they approached their collective task with bold inquisitiveness.

The men of Sagres did not lack a foundation upon which to build. The technology of shipbuilding had made great strides by the fifteenth century, and as a result the Portuguese ventured forth in long, narrow vessels ideally designed to withstand the swells of the open sea. Moreover, new and sophisticated instruments such as the astrolabe removed much of the guesswork from navigation.

One major breakthrough in marine technology for which the Portuguese were primarily responsible was the introduction of the lateen sail. This sail, triangular in shape, when used in combination with several masts, allowed a ship to sail much closer to the wind than had been the case with the awkward, single-masted square-riggers. A ship with three graduated masts, fitted with a properly rigged lateen sail and a sternpost rudder located along its median, could reduce its tacking angle by many degrees. This not only meant shorter, quicker voyages; it meant that Portugal's three-masted vessels, called caravels, could sail in almost any type of wind conditions. Therein lay the carefully guarded secret to its success in exploring Africa's Atlantic coast. Portuguese ships could sail along the coast on their outbound southward journey, then follow a westerly course on the homeward voyage until they caught the prevailing trade winds to the north and east. It was a vital discovery, and the necessity of keeping this type of knowledge hidden from potential rivals goes far in explaining the fact

that even today many aspects of Portuguese expansion are little understood by scholars.

As caravels inched their way southward along the African coast, Portugal's mariners carefully recorded their observations and mapped their positions. Vagaries in tides, winds, and currents were duly noted, depths in coastal waters carefully checked, and exact astronomical fixes obtained. The latter were of special importance, because the map makers at Sagres could translate such calculations onto charts for consultation by those involved in future voyages. Cartographers were a central, indeed a vital, feature of Prince Henry's training procedures for his seamen, and later, under King John II, the master of charts became an important royal official. Generations of map makers, drawing on a wealth of data that grew as each successive expedition returned from Africa, contributed immeasurably to Portugal's exploration of the continent.

Coastal exploration Initially Portugal's African overtures were tentative and slow-paced, but by 1434 Gil Eannes (Eanes), Henry the Navigator's principal mariner, had rounded Cabo Bojador. Passing this dangerous, reef-encrusted promontory was heralded as a major breakthrough, and it served to speed up the process of Portuguese exploration. Eannes' accomplishment placed his nation at a point on the African coast which had not been reached by ship since the time of the Phoenicians, and it disproved many prevalent speculations about the waters beyond Cabo Boja-

The lionlike hills of Sierra Leone, so named by Pedro de Sintra, probably the first European to see them. [Library of Congress]

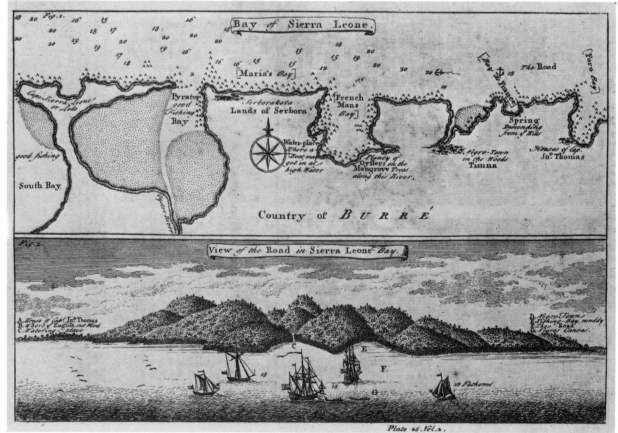

dor. Instead of encountering dragons, boiling seas, and currents so strong as to make return to European waters impossible, Eannes had conquered a bit of the unknown. In so doing he gave validity to Prince Henry's maxim: "You cannot find a peril so great that the hope of reward will not be greater." Henceforth this thought would become almost a watchword with Portuguese sailors. The pattern of discovery had been established, and from Eannes onward new discoveries became almost routine.

By 1445 the Portuguese had sailed as far as the Senegal River and the island of Gorée. A decade and a half later Pedro de Sintra reached Sierra Leone, so named because of the stormy, lionlike appearance of the mountains in back of the coast when he first witnessed them. The same year of Sintra's discovery, 1460, Henry the Navigator died, but the Portuguese commitment to African exploration he had initiated continued unabated. The Cape Verde Islands were settled in 1469, the Pope acknowledged the scope of Portugal's achievement by promising to recognize its sovereignty over newly discovered lands, and merchants working under the auspices of the government began to trade in African waters. The most notable of these early traders was Fernão Gomes, who was granted a monopoly on commercial enterprise beyond Cape Verde in return for an agreement to extend Portugal's knowledge of the African coast by some 400 miles (644 kilometers) annually. Gomes proved as good as his word, and by 1475 Portugal was active in the prosperous Bight of Benin, and the first ships had sailed beyond the equator. Diogo Cão discovered the mouth of the Congo River in 1483, and 4 years later, in January 1488, Bartolomeu Dias completed the steady Portuguese advance to the south when he rounded the Cape of Good Hope.

The initial conquest of Africa's western coast was now complete, and between 1497 and 1499 Vasco da Gama would realize Prince Henry's cherished dream of finding a water route to the east. Sailing past the Cape of Good Hope and turning northward, da Gama, with stops at Mozambique (Moçambique), Mombasa, and elsewhere, eventually reached Calicut on the Malabar coast of India. This remarkable journey, undertaken by the most renowned of all Portugal's mariners, meant that the coastal contours of virtually the whole of Africa were now in outline form.

Exploration of the interior   The logical sequel to the completion of exploration of Africa by sea was an approach to the interior. Yet for a variety of reasons Portugal's land discoveries never assumed anything approaching the dimensions of its pioneering activities at sea. As a small nation with limited resources and population, Portugal chose to concentrate its energies on the maintenance of coastal fortresses from which trade links to the interior could be established. Events also soon proved that excursions to the interior were hazardous and frequently unprofitable. Moreover, the real forte of the Portuguese was sea travel, and with good sense born of materialism they

reasoned that there was little use in searching for wealth inland when Africans would readily bring it to them. Considerations such as these mitigated against major discoveries in the African hinterland, but this is not to say that Portuguese adventurousness stopped at the continent's beaches.

The major contribution the Portuguese made to geographical knowledge of the interior came from Jesuit missionaries. The earnest fathers made significant advances in Angola and elsewhere, and the missionary Gonçalo de Silveira reached the dominions of the legendary Monomotapa (Mwenemutapa) in present-day Rhodesia (Zimbabwe). Silveira even succeeded in converting this powerful ruler, but his success with the monarch responsible for the remarkable stone structures of Zimbabwe was short-lived. In 1561 intrigues by Arab traders led to the murder of the Jesuit priest. Still, travel by Portuguese missionaries continued, and another notable focal point of their Christian endeavor was Ethiopia. Here the Prester John legend was a tempting attraction. Early in the sixteenth century Francisco Alvarez published an account of the country growing out of his experiences as a member of an embassy to Ethiopia. A few years later Portugal undertook a military excursion into the region for the purpose of freeing the land from invading Islamic forces. The leader of this enterprise was Cristoval da Gama, son of the famous navigator, and eventually his forces defeated the Muslims. Da Gama was decapitated in the process, but his work resulted in the creation of close ties between Ethiopia and Portugal which would endure for more than a century.

One outgrowth of this relationship was expanded geographical knowledge of Ethiopia, but here as elsewhere the unfortunate Portuguese practice of concealing discoveries from other European countries meant that the information they collected did not get the wide circulation it deserved. For example, Pedro Páez, a Jesuit priest, anticipated any number of the discoveries normally credited to James Bruce, and recently it has been established that the Portuguese actually were the first to travel in many of the areas supposedly discovered by Dr. David Livingstone. Yet so obscure is this knowledge that even today it is known only to specialists. Thus the story of Portuguese exploration on African soil remains in many ways something of an enigma. The Portuguese never publicized their land travels to an appreciable degree, nor did they, for that matter, evince any great interest in mapping the continent's vast interior. Yet in other ways the Portuguese experience in Africa left indelible impressions which extended far beyond the imposing forts guarding their coastal stations.

It was the Portuguese who revived the contact between Europe and Africa which had been nonexistent since the decline of the Roman Empire, and they initiated the first large-scale interaction with black Africa. Economic considerations were the primary basis for Portuguese interest in the continent, although their expeditions and subsequent endeavors had obvious political and cultural ramifications as well. However, the commencement of the transatlantic slave trade was unquestionably the area where the Portuguese had the greatest impact on Africans (and for that matter, on European interest in Africa). They began, initially on a small scale, the pernicious traffic in human beings which would grow to affect millions and to become the central feature of African history in the colonial era. As other European nations explored the New World and established colonies in the West Indies and on the mainlands of North and South America, the demand for slaves grew, and the "ebony trade" expanded rapidly. Even more lucrative than the trade in gold, the slave trade soon drew French, British, and Dutch competitors to West Africa. Yet these nations, if possible, showed even less interest in the continent's interior than did the Portuguese. The latter at least made some attempts at settlement and at saving African souls. But all the European countries were more interested in what they could take from Africa—precious metal and black men—than what they could learn of it. The result was a centuries-long process of economic extraction and exploitation which destroyed the fabric of existing African polities and cultures and permanently tinctured relations between the two continents. Yet the slave trade, for all its historical importance, added little to knowledge of the African hinterland, and in retrospect the Portuguese contribution to the continent's exploration must be reckoned an essentially maritime one.

Great Age of African Discovery Because of the participation of African middlemen in the slave trade and the climatic and health factors already mentioned, little was added to the sum of knowledge of African geography between the fifteenth century, when Portugal completed the bulk of its reconnaissance of the African coast, and the late eighteenth century. Thus in the latter century Jonathan Swift could write in *Poetry, a Rhapsody*, with his characteristic acerbity and in this instance also with considerable accuracy, of an interior that was unmapped and unknown:

> So geographers, in Afric-maps,
> With savage-pictures fill their gaps;
> And o'er unhabitable downs
> Place elephants for want of towns.

But soon the Age of Reason, with its belief in progress, faith in the virtues of science, and glorification of the idea of the noble savage, would provide the intellectual framework necessary to fill Africa's cartographical gaps. Beginning with the journey of James Bruce, the first of many Scots who would play a prominent role in this phase of African exploration, into Ethiopia in the late 1760s, attention was directed to the Afri-

European soldiers and Africans in fierce battle at Elmina, on the Gold Coast, in the late seventeenth century. [Library of Congress]

can interior and remained focused there until the last of the continent's geographical mysteries had been resolved.

This renewal of interest in Africa resulted from a combination of interrelated circumstances. The questing spirit produced by an age which gloried in all types of scientific inquiry was complemented by growing humanitarian sentiments. The 1st Earl of Mansfield's famous judgment (1772) in the Somerset case, in which he freed a West Indian black who had resided in Great Britain, stirred the zeal of British abolitionists and gave added impetus to their cause. In fact, the whole of the burgeoning antislavery movement directed attention to Africa, and growing evangelical fervor had a similar effect. Then, too, Bruce's multivolume *Travels to Discover the Source of the Nile* stimulated great interest. Bruce did not seek wealth, nor was he moved by deeply rooted feelings of patriotism. He simply was interested in ascertaining the truth and was drawn by Africa's magnetism. The forces which attracted Bruce to Africa continued to exert a pervasive influence on explorers over the course of the next century and form a significant ingredient in any consideration of African exploration in the late eighteenth and the nineteenth centuries.

By the 1860s and 1870s, when African reconnaissance was at its apex, Victorians had developed a shrewd appreciation of the aura of romanticism which surrounded the discoverers involved in unraveling Africa's tangled geographical secrets. Laurence Oliphant, a well-known commentator on such subjects, reviewed several decades of travel and summarized its appeal to the individuals involved by stating: "The object which has impelled these gentlemen to place themselves in these various attitudes of discomfort and danger, has, in the majority of cases been simply 'the fun of the thing'—a love of adventure." Another writer described Africa's attraction through use of a striking analogy: "The European upon whom has once shone the tropical sun of Africa, like the moth that flies to the candle, ever feels drawn again to the land of the palms." The writings of the explorers themselves bear eloquent testimony to the accuracy of such statements. Richard BURTON, one of the most renowned of the nineteenth-century African travelers, beautifully summarized the continent's appeal for him and his fellow adventurers: "The theme [African discovery] has remoteness and obscurity of place, difference of custom, marvellousness of hearsay; events passing strange yet credible, sometimes barbaric splendour, generally luxuriance of nature, savage life, personal danger and suffering always borne with patience, dignity, and even enthusiasm." In short, much of the appeal of Africa in the great era of exploration lay in a peculiar disease which defied ordinary diagnosis, a malady that might best be called Afromania.

Work of the African Association An early and characteristic outbreak of Afromania demonstrated the strength of its hold on those it infected and showed that its effects were by no means limited to explorers.

This came with the founding of the African Association in 1788. If the travels of James Bruce marked the dawn of new departures in African exploration, it was the support that the association lent to such endeavors which placed the age of reconnaissance in the hinterland on solid footing. Always small in terms of membership, the association offset from its inception any liabilities that might have resulted from its size through the enthusiasm and influence of its leaders, among whom was Sir Joseph Banks, himself a noted explorer and president of the Royal Society. Banks and other individuals active in the association's affairs enjoyed extensive contacts with high-placed persons in society and government and were thus able to obtain official support and to propagandize on behalf of expanded British knowledge of Africa.

The principal focus of the association, particularly in its early years, was on western Africa. The problem of the Niger River's course and outlet, combined with interest in the fabled city of Timbuktu and overtones of humanitarian concern, led to sponsorship of a series of expeditions in the region. From the outset death dogged the tracks of the association's explorers, but men such as Daniel Houghton, Friedrich Hornemann, and Mungo PARK made substantial progress in geographical discovery along the Niger.

This was particularly true of Park, a Scottish seventh son and with Bruce among the first of a remarkable group of men from that portion of Britain who were to be active in African exploration. Park departed for the region of the Niger in 1795 and in the course of the next 18 months conclusively established the direction of the river's flow as well as traveling extensively on the Gambia. Park then returned to England to write a best-selling account of his experiences under the title *Travels in the Interior Districts of Africa*. After an interlude of a decade that included marriage, Park, like so many of his successors, once more succumbed to the enticement of unknown Africa. This expedition, which left England early in 1805, was the first to travel not only with official approbation but also with government support. Park's plans called for "the extension of British commerce and the enlargement of our Geographical knowledge," and the economic portion of this statement offers one explanation of why financial aid was forthcoming from the government. However, Park personally was primarily interested in discovery, and, convinced that the Niger and the Congo were connected, he proposed to locate their juncture and then follow the latter stream downriver to the Atlantic. In tones reminiscent of those soon to be associated with Nile discovery, he proclaimed that accomplishment of this feat "was certainly the greatest discovery that remains to be made in the world."

Park's lofty aims ultimately were dashed in the absolute finality of death that so often short-circuited African expeditions. Henceforth the African Association, after almost two decades of remarkable vibrancy and continuity of effort, would gradually decline.

Shorn of the leadership and organizational genius of Joseph Banks in 1804, when recurrent attacks of gout forced retirement from his long-time post as treasurer, and faced with the stark realities of a series of Niger expeditions that had ended in tragedy, the body's membership and vitality dwindled. Still, the explorers mentioned above had, together with other less renowned representatives of the association, done much to clarify geographical outlines of North Africa and the western Sudan. They had also set in motion a chain of Niger exploration that continued unabated until the entire course of the river was known. In 1831, when the association finally closed its books with only fourteen members remaining on the roll, it passed on a firmly established legacy of supporting African exploration to the newly founded ROYAL GEOGRAPHICAL SOCIETY.

Further Niger exploration With the dogged perseverance that is a national characteristic commonly ascribed to the British, the government continued to subsidize Niger exploration. Once committed to Park, it seemed that officials were determined to see the matter through to a successful conclusion. In so doing the government took up the slack left by the African Association's post-1805 decline. In 1815, when the conclusion of the Napoleonic Wars once more permitted such activities, both the Colonial Office and the Admiralty sponsored separate expeditions to the Niger. These undertakings had the now-predictable outcome of death for their leaders, John Peddie and James K. Tuckey, as well as for thirty-five of the fifty-four individuals comprising the latter's entourage. Nonetheless, John BARROW, second secretary of the Admiralty and the man primarily responsible for the dispatch of these expeditions, remained as determined as ever to solve the problem of the Niger.

Shortly after the failure of the undertakings led by Peddie and Tuckey, the possibilities of an approach to the Niger originating in Tripoli came to Barrow's attention. He became increasingly captivated by the idea, and the upshot of his interest was a series of new expeditions beginning in Tripoli. Several of these missions made appreciable geographical progress, and the one led by Walter Oudney, Hugh CLAPPERTON, and Dixon Denham achieved truly remarkable results. These men became the first Europeans to penetrate the kingdom of Bornu and to look out over the waters of Lake Chad. Meanwhile, a rival expedition under Alexander Gordon LAING had reached Timbuktu in 1826, only to have its leader killed in the Niger bend under circumstances that even today remain unclear. Two years later, a Frenchman, René CAILLIÉ, reached the legendary Saharan entrepôt and survived to recount his experiences. His story, as told in *Travels through Central Africa to Timbuctoo* (1830), was an exciting one, but many Frenchmen doubted his veracity. Indeed, Caillié died impoverished and a hero without honor in his own country less than a decade after first sighting Timbuktu. The same year that Caillié described his adventures in print, Richard

Medina, in what is now Mali, pictured as it was early in the nineteenth century.

Lemon LANDER and his brother John were writing what was in essence the final chapter in Niger exploration proving conclusively that the river emptied into the Gulf of Guinea. *See also* NIGER RIVER.

Southern regions and the work of Livingstone In recognition of his achievement Richard Lander became the Royal Geographical Society's first gold medalist, and two decades later that organization would expand to the point at which it had the influence and financial wherewithal to be well to the forefront in the search for the Nile's sources. In the interim, however, great progress was to be made in the ongoing process of geographical discovery elsewhere in Africa. This was especially true of the southern regions of the continent, where European settlers had established a foothold some two centuries earlier. For most of this period though, the Boers, as the Dutch Calvinists who had settled there came to be popularly known, had remained fairly close to the coast. But their simple agrarian existence altered dramatically in the mid-1830s with the onset of the wholesale migration that was the Great Trek. Impelled by a search for *Lebensraum* and freedom from what they deemed unwarranted interference in their life-styles on the part of British officials, the hardy pioneers simply packed bag and baggage and trekked into the interior. In so doing they opened up new lands and added to the sum of European knowledge of South Africa. More important for the annals of discovery (the Boers had little save a practical interest in geography), they helped create the situation which gave one of the greatest men in African exploration, Dr. David Livingstone, his first introduction to the continent and its peoples.

Of all the great Scottish explorers, Livingstone was perhaps most affected by wanderlust. From 1840, when he first departed for Africa as a representative of the London Missionary Society, until his death in 1873, Livingstone was almost completely absorbed in work on the continent. He did return to England for short periods between 1856 and 1858 and in 1864, but even these occasions were devoted largely to writing and speaking on Africa. The frequently quoted couplet concerning the Scottish love of travel and distant places certainly rang true for Livingstone:

> Had Cain been Scot, God would have changed his doom.
> Not made him wander, but continued him home.

In truth, once he had savored the full taste of African exploration, Livingstone virtually abandoned traditional missionary travel for geographical pursuits. This metamorphosis involved some mental gymnastics whereby Livingstone convinced himself that he was performing God's chosen duty. Undeniably he was a deeply religious man, but even the extraordinary lengths he went to in order to justify his travels cannot hide the fact that he was totally enamored of African exploration.

In the first segment of his African career, which spanned 16 years and concluded with his return to

Victoria Falls, so named by David Livingstone, drop 360 feet in the Zambezi River. [Library of Congress]

England in 1856, Livingstone did much to lift the veil from the South African interior. The full title of his timeless travelogue describing his geographical and other exploits during this period, *Missionary Travels and Researches in South Africa; Including a Sketch of Sixteen Years' Residence in the Interior of Africa, and a Journey from the Cape of Good Hope to Loanda, on the West Coast; Thence across the Continent, down the River Zambesi, to the Eastern Ocean* (1857), offers a convenient summation of his exploratory endeavors. Judith Listowel, in her recent work *The Other Livingstone* (1975), conclusively demonstrates that the credit for these striking South African travels and discoveries was not Livingstone's alone. Indeed, largely forgotten individuals such as William Cotton Oswell, László Magyar, and Candido Cardoso performed much of the geographical work generally credited to Livingstone. Yet the fact of his preeminence remains, and by the time he broke his long period of South African vagabondage to return to England, he was an acclaimed Victorian lion. It was now the late 1850s, and the stage was set for a concerted onslaught on the vast unexplored regions of tropical Africa.

Livingstone was an integral and important part of this onslaught, which centered on the search for the sources of the Nile and exploration of Africa's other great rivers (*see* NILE RIVER: SEARCH FOR ITS SOURCE). Livingstone left Quelimane, Mozambique, on the first stage of a government-sponsored expedition on the

Simonstown, near Cape Town. On the right is Admiralty House, where Grant and Speke stopped during their expedition to verify Speke's conclusions about the source of the Nile. [James A. Casada]

Zambezi. Over the next several years this undertaking would make major contributions to African discovery. Livingstone and his subordinates mapped much of the Shire and Zambezi Rivers as well as exploring on the Ruvuma (Rovuma). They also discovered Lake Nyasa (Lake Malawi) and traveled along extensive portions of its western shores, and Livingstone made other notable geographical reconnaissances. Still, the Zambezi Expedition was by no means an unqualified success. For one thing, Livingstone's expectations that the river would prove to be God's highway to the interior were dashed in the rocky, unnavigable Quebrabasa Falls. Likewise, the Universities Mission to Central Africa that had been founded on the basis of his poignant 1857 appeal encountered disease and death. Finally, Livingstone demonstrated his inability to work in harmony with other Europeans, and his deficiencies as a leader doubtless were a factor in his decision to travel alone (that is, with no other Europeans) from this juncture onward. At any rate, the final decade of Livingstone's life is marked by a desire for solitude and freedom from the impediments to exploration posed by weaker, less determined mortals.

Source of the Nile In 1863 the Zambezi Expedition was recalled in shambles. By this time, new forces and

John Augustus Grant's drawing of a Cape bullock cart and a horse wagon with ten Cape mounted riflemen who accompanied him and Speke on their Nile expedition. [James A. Casada]

personalities were at work in the unfolding drama of African exploration, and the next two decades were to prove the most exciting in the entire history of the quest for Africa. A few years earlier, two of Livingstone's fellow Britons, Richard Burton and John Speke, had taken the first major steps in unraveling the perplexing geography of the Nile's headwaters. Acting on the basis of information supplied by two German missionaries in the service of the Church Missionary Society, Johann Ludwig Krapf and Johann Rebmann, Burton and Speke took a novel approach to the Nile's "coy fountains" by advancing inland from a starting point on the East African coast opposite Zanzibar. Jointly they discovered Lake Tanganyika, and on their return journey homeward Speke, acting on reports garnered from Arab traders, made an unimpeded flying march northward from Tabora, in what is now Tanzania. At the end of his remarkably easy side trip he sighted a vast body of water which he intuitively concluded was the source of the Nile and which he impulsively named Lake Victoria in honor of his sovereign. Upon Speke's rejoining Burton, the latter belittled his grandiose claims for the importance of this discovery, and the remainder of their journey back to Zanzibar was marked by steadily deteriorating relations.

These differences degenerated into outright hostility after Speke, who sailed on to England while Burton stayed in Aden to rest and recuperate, broke a promise by advancing his claims to be the discoverer of the elusive source of the Nile. Speke's certitude apparently carried conviction, because the Royal Geographical Society, at the instigation of Sir Roderick Murchison, forthwith made arrangements for him to head a second African journey. On this expedition, accompanied by an ideal subordinate, James Augustus GRANT, Speke discovered Lake Victoria's outlet and named it the Ripon Falls. He and Grant also traveled in other previously unexplored regions, but once they had what Speke deemed sufficient confirmation of his theories they set out northward to follow the Nile downstream. However, tribal differences in the region forced them to leave the river at several points, and while Speke himself evinced no doubts concerning his methods of verifying his discovery, upon his return to England in 1863 critics made capital of his failure to stick to the stream until he reached known regions of the Nile. Accordingly, Speke's claims and the whole question of the Nile became matters of keen interest and debate. Then in 1864, when Speke killed himself in a hunting accident the day before a scheduled debate with Burton on the Nile controversy, interest in the matter was further intensified. Indicative of this was the fact that Livingstone, who was to have been in the audience for this confrontation that never came off, spent his long and ultimately tragic last journey obsessed with the watersheds of the Nile and the Congo.

Meanwhile, Samuel White BAKER was traveling in the intralacustrine regions of Central Africa. He too had been captivated by the Nile's allurement and wrote that "nothing but death shall prevent me from discovering the *sources* of the Nile." In company with his second wife, Baker had met Speke and Grant at Gondokoro in the course of their downriver journey. Utilizing information they provided, he continued his march, still hoping to pluck a remaining leaf of Nile laurel, and after overcoming assorted obstacles discovered Lake Albert.

Livingstone and Stanley While Baker was still in Africa, Livingstone was making preparations for what would prove to be his final journey. In 1866, armed with little save authority from his British government "to deal with native chiefs in all the area between the frontier of Portuguese East Africa and those of Abyssinia and Egypt," Livingstone once more entered Africa. His resolve encompassed a determination to unravel the remaining mysteries of Central African geography, and such was his energy and singleness of purpose that he came close to accomplishing this objective. He discovered Lakes Mweru and Bangweulu, explored portions of Lake Tanganyika in search of its still hidden outlet, and traveled along the Lualaba River (which eventually proved to be the headwater of the Congo). By late 1871, however, exhausted by his prodigious labors and short of much-needed medicines, Livingstone had returned to the Arab trading town of Ujiji. It was here that the enterprising Anglo-American reporter Henry Stanley "found" him. His famous if somewhat-ludicrous initial greeting, "Dr. Livingstone, I presume," heralded the completion of a search for Livingstone and an unprecedented scoop for Stanley's sponsor, the *New York Herald.* The renowned missionary long had been incommunicado and was feared dead, but Stanley replenished his supplies and nursed him back to health. In turn, Livingstone imbued him with the inspiration and a sense of almost filial piety that would be the catalysts in his transformation into the greatest of all African explorers.

Indeed, in a very real sense, Stanley became Livingstone's heir apparent in Africa. Their sojourn together was a brief one of some 2 months, after which Stanley reluctantly left the old man to return to civilization and share his momentous news. Livingstone, his Nile fixation undiminished, continued his travels. On May 1, 1873, literally lost for the only time in his career, he died in the swampy regions south of Lake Bangweulu. The news of Livingstone's end had a profound effect on Stanley, who expressed the hope that he might "be selected to succeed him in opening up Africa."

In the course of three separate undertakings spread over the next decade and a half, Stanley fulfilled his dreams by throwing open the portals of tropical Africa to the outside world. Between 1874 and 1877 he made a transcontinental journey which originated in Zanzibar and concluded in Boma, where the Congo emptied into the Atlantic. The expedition lasted for 999 days and entailed travel under the most arduous conditions. In the course of his travels Stanley clarified many of the remaining ambiguities concerning the Nile's fountains by circumnavigating Lake Victoria,

"Doctor Livingstone, I presume!" [Library of Congress]

Henry Morton Stanley, who was instrumental in opening tropical Africa to the European world, crosses the Makata Swamp.

discovering Lake Edward, and traversing the country between the lakes. Later he sailed on Lake Tanganyika, although like previous travelers he failed to locate its outlet. Stanley then moved onward to the Lualaba, doggedly sailed down this stream until it became the Congo, and then traveled the mighty river to its mouth. This incredible journey, perhaps without parallel in any age of African travel, brought Stanley to the attention of King Leopold II of the Belgians and led to his employment as an administrator in the Congo (now Zaire). While primarily occupied with duties of a nongeographical nature during his Congo years (1880–1885), Stanley nevertheless found time for further travel on the river and discovered Lakes Tumba and Leopold II (now Mai-Ndombe). Then, in 1888, his nomination as the leader of an expedition to rescue Emin Pasha in Equatoria once more took him to the watershed of the Nile. In this expedition geographical concerns were distinctly of secondary importance (the onrushing political scramble for colonial possessions had signaled the end of the great age of Victorian reconnaissance), but it did result in a final resolution of the perplexing Nile question. Stanley explored the Semliki River and determined that it linked his Lake Edward with Baker's Albert, discovered the Ruwenzori Mountains and rightly equated them with the legendary Mountains of the Moon, and, most important, provided full and final confirmation of Speke's preeminence as a Nile explorer.

Late-nineteenth-century exploration At the time Stanley learned of Livingstone's death another intrepid adventurer, the Englishman Verney Lovett CAMERON, was in the heart of the continent. Cameron's expedition had originated as a Royal Geographical Society–sponsored mission to relieve Livingstone, but when he learned of the missionary's death Cameron determined to direct his energies to recovering Livingstone's journals and to exploring on his own. As a result he became the first man to cross tropical Africa from east to west, and in the course of this epic journey he mapped much of Lake Tanganyika, discovered its Lukuga River outlet, and further delineated Livingstone's Lualaba. During the same period, a number of other explorers were active in the region, and an international conference on African geography assembled by King Leopold II in Brussels in 1876 symbolized the extensive interest all Europe had in African travel.

Indeed, explorers sponsored by the International African Association, which grew out of the Brussels meeting, and by its English counterpart, the African Exploration Fund, made substantial contributions to geographical discovery in tropical Africa. This was particularly true of the British explorer, Joseph THOMSON, who combined courage and chicanery in his African *modus operandi*. He became the first European to penetrate the land of the dreaded Masai people of eastern Africa. He also confirmed Cameron's supposition that the Lukuga River was Lake Tanganyika's outlet, and he discovered Lakes Rukwa and Baringo as well as Mount Elgon. In the same decade, the 1880s, the Hungarian travelers Samuel Teleki and Ludwig von Höhnel discovered Lakes Rudolf (Turkana) and Stefanie, and in the 1890s female explorers made their presence felt in a major fashion. The American adventuress May French Sheldon won fame as Bébé Bwana (Lady Boss) and for her discovery of Lake Chala, in what is now Tanzania, which she circumnavigated in a copper pontoon that had belonged to Count Teleki. In West Africa Mary Henrietta Kingsley, an Englishwoman, won lasting fame (admirers created the African Society in her honor) for her travels, always without European companions, in the interior behind Old Calabar (now Calabar, Nigeria).

Elsewhere in these eventful final decades of exploration for exploration's sake on the continent, the remaining major geographical mysteries were fast disappearing. Georg August SCHWEINFURTH, a German explorer with impressive scientific credentials, clarified a number of details regarding the watersheds of the Nile and Congo. John Petherick, who, in company with his wife, had been sent up the Nile to succor Speke and Grant, likewise contributed to the sum of knowledge of Nile geography. The same was true of Emin Pasha, the object of Stanley's final African journey, and of Charles CHAILLÉ-LONG, an American lieutenant of Gen. Charles Gordon. Another American, Paul Belloni DU CHAILLU, explored extensively along the lower reaches of the Gabon and Ogowe (Ogooué) Rivers, and many others who were active in tropical Africa from the 1860s to the 1890s are perhaps equally deserving of mention. This was the last great era of African discovery, and unquestionably it is the most crowded from the standpoint of participants. The career of one of these individuals, Harry Hamilton JOHNSTON, marks a convenient point for a chronological break. Johnston, popularly known as the "prancing proconsul," effectively brought to an end what might be termed primary discovery in east central Africa. His travels in the region of Mount Kilimanjaro were as much political as they were geographical in nature, and his transformation from explorer to the administrator responsible for the founding of the Uganda Protectorate symbolized the transition from exploration to colonial exploitation in the 1890s.

Sahara Desert By the final decade of the nineteenth century, the conquest of the Sahara was also well on the way to completion. Geographically, culturally, and for the most part racially distinct from the remainder of Africa, the Sahara-dominated north of the continent presented special obstacles to would-be explorers. Incredibly arid, characterized by vast distances, and generally inhospitable to an inordinate degree, the Sahara offered, in its own scorching fashion, challenges as demanding as those posed by the heart of Africa. The nomadic peoples of the desert had

known and traveled its desolate expanses for untold centuries, and the ancient Greeks and Romans had gained some knowledge of the region from these inhabitants and their own peripheral journeys. However, the fourteenth-century North African traveler IBN-BATTŪTA perhaps deserves recognition as the first great Saharan explorer. One phase of his remarkable career in travel (he also journeyed extensively in Arabia, along the East African coast, and in Asia) included a crossing of the Sahara to the kingdoms of West Africa. He visited Mali and the legendary entrepôt of Timbuktu before returning to the North African coast by an alternate route that carried him to Takedda, an important caravan and copper mining center in the heart of the desert whose precise location is not known.

Ibn-Battuta's exploits, which deserve wider recognition, presaged later ventures of a similar nature. Indeed, until late in the nineteenth century most Saharan travel was a by-product of attempts to reach the great West African kingdoms and the upper Niger River. These endeavors have already been described, and in one sense even the travels of the greatest Saharan explorer, Heinrich BARTH, form a concluding chapter to the search for the Niger. However, in the decade from 1845 to 1855, Barth did much more than simply reach, as numerous others had done before him, the upper reaches of the Niger and the fabled city of Timbuktu. He explored the entire northern coastline of Africa and then, in company with Adolf Overweg, turned his attention to the Sahara. They started at Tripoli, traversed the desert, and explored Lake Chad and its environs. Overweg died before the expedition's completion, but year after year Barth doggedly pushed on, and before he eventually returned to the coast of the Mediterranean, he had made great strides toward filling in the map of the Sahara.

An African village as Henry Stanley might have seen it during his voyage down the Lualaba River. [Library of Congress]

He had also, through his incomparable achievements, laid the groundwork for the full-scale conquest of the desert.

Among the first to follow in Barth's Saharan footsteps was Henri DUVEYRIER, a French adventurer. His ethnological discoveries among the Tuareg tribes proved of greater lasting significance than his geographical researches, but he did expand European knowledge of the northern portions of the Sahara considerably. Then, in the 1860s and 1870s, two German explorers, Gerhard ROHLFS and Gustav NACHTIGAL, made further inroads in previously trackless reaches of the desert. Rohlfs, in four separate expeditions that spanned two decades, accounted for numerous scientific and geographical discoveries of the first magnitude. Among the latter, the most important was becoming the first European to cross Africa from the Mediterranean to the Gulf of Guinea. For his part Nachtigal, between 1869 and 1874, complemented his countryman's efforts by his travels in the Sahara-Sudan region, where he explored the Tibesti Massif and established, for the first time, the linkage between the region around Lake Chad and the Nile.

The 1870s, a decade that proved as crucial to Saharan exploration as it was to that in Central Africa, encompassed the early work of yet another German, Oskar Lenz. In effect, Lenz reversed René Caillié's path by traversing the Sahara from the Atlas Mountains to Timbuktu. Later he became one of a select handful of explorers (Joseph Thomson was another) whose exploits included important travel in both Saharan and sub-Saharan regions. In the mid-1880s Lenz journeyed up the Congo and thence onward to Lake Tanganyika. Meanwhile, the Fench government, spurred in part by fears of German encroachment in the North African sphere they traditionally had viewed as their preserve, undertook sponsorship of a major trans-Saharan expedition. This venture was as much an exercise in empire building as a geographical enterprise, but before a projected railway could be built across the desert it was necessary to explore the route thoroughly. Accordingly, two military expeditions under Paul-Xavier Flatters conducted preliminary survey work. They succeeded in traveling as far south as the Ahaggar Mountains, but the second undertaking ended in tragedy when Tuareg tribesmen killed Flatters and most of his party. Eventually, however, French persistence would result in the subjugation and pacification of the nomadic desert peoples.

The most notable of these efforts began in 1898, when France dispatched three separate military exploring parties in a concerted attempt to conquer both the desert and its recalcitrant inhabitants. These were the Sahara Mission, led by the experienced desert traveler Fernand Foureau, the Congo-Chad Mission, and the Central African Mission headed by two young officers, Captains Paul-Gustave-Lucien Voulet and Charles-Paul-Jules Chanoine.

The latter undertaking was disastrous as a result of inept leadership which culminated in seeming madness on the part of both commanders. Ultimately they were murdered by their subordinates (who may have had little choice). The remaining men then continued onward toward Lake Chad, the final destination of all three missions. The other two groups fared considerably better, although they did encounter widespread local resistance (Maj. L.-J.-A. Lamy, who headed Foureau's military escort, died in a battle with an army from Bornu), and early in 1900 remnants of all three expeditions joined forces. The united missions now defeated the powerful Mahdist chieftain Rabah and thereby effectively ended large-scale resistance to outside incursions in the region. France had secured political hegemony in the area around Lake Chad, Foureau's findings had substantially furthered knowledge of the central Sahara, and it was now possible to

Timbuktu, from the terrace of Heinrich Barth's house.

pursue such geographical puzzles as the desert still retained in relative safety and security. Thus by the turn of the twentieth century, in desert and jungle alike, the major tasks of African exploration had been completed.

Non-European contribution This is not, however, to suggest that the story of discovery in the continent was at an end. Nor does the foregoing coverage constitute anything like a total picture of the vast panorama that was the African reconnaissance. At best it is an overview that touches the grand moments and delineates the major achievements of exploration on the continent up to the filling in of the map of Africa. In conclusion, therefore, it seems appropriate to mention briefly several factors which deserve consideration in any overall appraisal of a complex and endlessly fascinating subject. One obvious but frequently ignored point is the substantial role that Africans themselves played in making their home known to the outside world. Without the assistance and local knowledge of porters, guides, interpreters, and others, the penetration of Africa would have been both long delayed and infinitely more difficult. *See* AFRICA: CONTRIBUTION OF NON-EUROPEANS.

Impact on Indigenous Societies Similarly, the ongoing process of exploration eventually had a profound impact on indigenous societies. The contacts between Africa's explorers and the peoples they encountered received relatively little attention, at least from the standpoint of appreciable internal changes, until the last two decades. Belatedly, however, scholars began to recognize that any complete appreciation of exploration necessitates going beyond traditional Eurocentric approaches. This awareness is largely predicated on the recent revolution in African studies, and for this reason there has been considerable overreaction in some quarters, even to the extent of belittling or ignoring the place of exploration in the history of Africa. Given the long-standing imbalance in the opposite direction, this is understandable if unacceptable in a scholarly sense. However, the time is now at hand for a reasoned evaluation of the interaction between the pioneering representatives of the outside world and the peoples with whom they came in contact.

At present we have nothing approaching a synthesis on the subject, but research is sufficiently far advanced to permit some initial conclusions. Basically, when viewed in a strictly African context, the immediate impact of the explorers seems minimal. Ordinarily, their passage through a given region had little effect on native life and institutions. They may have been objects of curiosity and awe, and at times their scientific instruments, weapons, medicines, strange clothing, and alien mannerisms caused considerable sensation. Yet this was but a passing phenomenon which, like the sudden influx of wealth in the form of beads or other trade goods that frequently resulted from an expedition's visit, soon gave way to a return

Lake Chad, which Gustav Nachtigal explored in the late nineteenth century.

to normal conditions. By the same token, the explorers normally avoided local quarrels or any intercession in political disputes, although there were instances (Stanley is an example) when they intervened if they thought it would serve their own ends or loftier goals such as the introduction of Christianity or the abolition of some culturally abhorrent practice. For the most part, though, the explorers minded their own business. Often their lives or at the least their chances of success depended on native goodwill and assistance, and they astutely cultivated cordial relations while consciously avoiding any action that might give offense. Moreover, it seems fair to conclude that neither the explorers nor the peoples they encountered were fully aware of the processes of change the former were setting in motion.

It is only when one examines the entire scope of the explorers' activities from a broad, long-range perspective that their profound impact becomes readily recognizable. As has been mentioned previously, the lasting trauma of the slave trade followed close on the heels of the early Portuguese explorers, and by the same token the great exploring explosion of the Victorian era paved the way for the onset of full-scale imperialism. The latter period was the culminating phase of the quest for Africa, and during this era the influence of explorers had ramifications that far transcended the realm of geography. The writings of the Victorian lions, often both sensational and propagandistic in nature, titillated large reading audiences and directed the attention of the public as well as entrepreneurs, officialdom, and humanitarians to Africa. Indeed, there are many strands, some tenuous, others well defined and strong, that connected explorers with the burgeoning of European interest in the continent. Particularly in the nineteenth century, explorers embraced the idea of hegemony in Africa with some of the singleness of purpose and devotion which marked their journeys of discovery, and in the final analysis their achievements as prophets must be recognized as standing in juxtaposition to their work as geographers. Collectively they opened Africa to the outside world and released the floodgates through which flowed new technology and culture as well as the unfolding historical processes of colonialism, nationalist reaction, and independence.

Another area which has suffered the same type of neglect as the impact exploration had on Africans is what might be called, for want of a better term, "secondary exploration." Throughout the entire process of discovery, individuals whose primary responsibility lay in some area other than geographical undertakings added substantially to the ever-growing corpus of knowledge of Africa. From ancient times well into the twentieth century, soldiers, merchants, missionaries, sportsmen, treaty makers, colonial administrators, and a host of others in a variety of capacities all did their part in opening up Africa geographically. Yet as a general rule their geographical work was distinctly secondary to other pursuits, and more often than not they were devoid of the wanderlust which characterized the true explorers and branded them as a breed apart.

In fact, it is in the impulses which drew men to Africa and in the type of men who responded to the continent's undoubted qualities of allurement that one discerns the most important threads of continuity in the lengthy history of African discovery. Throughout the quest for Africa fundamental motivations such as restlessness, egocentric romanticism, and an innate love of adventure led men to the continent. Often dreamers or vagabonds cast aside by a world which whirled those vested with idiosyncrasies into its eddies, they found in Africa a natural outlet for their inner turmoil and insatiable curiosity. Even today, with the veil lifted from the continent's long-held and carefully guarded secrets, Africa still retains a certain special attraction for those who heed adventure's call. Within the past few years Geoffrey Moorhouse has taken a desert journey in search of himself (and in an attempt to cross the Sahara on east-west lines) that he poignantly describes in *The Fearful Void* (1975), and in 1974–1975 John Blashford-Snell led the Zaire River Expedition that traced Stanley's path a century after he had become the first man to travel the course of the foreboding Congo. So the magnetism remains, and certainly the same holds true for the great legion of armchair geographers. For those of us in this category the story of African exploration is a timeless one of endless pleasures.

BIBLIOGRAPHY: Norman R. Bennet, *Africa and Europe: From Roman Times to the Present*, New York, 1975; Robert Brown, *The Story of Africa and Its Explorers*, 4 vols., London, 1911; Hubert J. Deschamps, *L'Europe découvre l'Afrique: Afrique occidentale, 1794–1900*, Paris, 1967; Sanche de Gramont, *The Strong Brown God: The Story of the Niger River*, Boston, 1976; Richard Hall, *Discovery of Africa*, London, 1970; Robin Hallett, *The Penetration of Africa: European Exploration in North and West Africa to 1815*, New York, 1965; Harry H. Johnston, *The Nile Quest*, London, 1903; Egon Klemp (ed.), *Africa on Maps Dating from the Twelfth to the Eighteenth Century*, New York, 1972; Alan Moorehead, *The Blue Nile*, London, 1962; id., *The White Nile*, London, 1960; Margery Perham and Jack Simmons (eds.), *African Discovery: An Anthology of Exploration*, London, 1942; Gail Roberts, *An Atlas of Discovery*, with an introduction by Sir Francis Chichester, London, 1973; Robert I. Rotberg (ed.), *Africa and Its Explorers: Motives, Methods, and Impact*, Cambridge, Mass., 1970; Heinrich Schiffers, *The Quest for Africa*, tr. by Diana Pyke, New York, 1957; Timothy Severin, *The African Adventure: Four Hundred Years of Exploration in the "Dangerous Continent,"* New York, 1973.

James A. Casada

Africa: Contribution of Non-Europeans

Every European traveler in Africa in the era of exploration was dependent to some extent on local cooperation and participation. Some expeditions traveled with escorts provided by coastal rulers, such as the Pasha of Tripoli or the Sultan of Zanzibar; other explorers attached themselves to trading parties following the pre-European routes in the interior; carriers, canoeists, interpreters, and guides might be recruited at the coast or engaged on a temporary basis for local knowledge; and, above all, Africans of initiative and enterprise employed as caravan leaders, as personal servants, or for special skills could make a major contribution, particularly in the caravans which were essential in the exploration of East Africa. An experienced and trusted man could also bring an element of companionship to the solitary life of an explorer. Many are mere names in the record, but enough information is given in the published and unpublished writings of some explorers to provide a vivid picture of the characters and achievements of the more noteworthy men; there are also a few glimpses of the subject from the viewpoint of the Africans themselves.

West Africa Explorers of West Africa needed interpreters and sought them at coastal settlements where they might find men of experience, such as ex-slaves from Africa and the West Indies, whose background would give them a smattering of various tongues and a degree of resourcefulness which would add to their value as traveling companions. Such a man was Johnson, engaged as a Mande interpreter by Mungo PARK at Pisania (now Karantaba, Gambia) in 1795; he had been taken to Jamaica as a slave and had also spent some years in England. Ten years later Park employed another Mande interpreter, Isaaco, whose linguistic knowledge had probably been acquired while working with slaves. Isaaco was a courageous and reliable man; Park sent him back from Sansanding with his journal and traveled on with a guide, Amadi Fatuma. In 1810 Isaaco was sent by the Governor of Senegal to discover Park's fate, and with information from Amadi Fatuma he produced a substantial and, it appears, broadly accurate account of the circumstances of the explorer's death.

For some years Tripoli was an important base for expeditions to explore West Africa. Several journeys were undertaken with the cooperation of the Pasha, who in return for substantial payments provided escorts which, however, mainly served his own interests. Joseph Ritchie and George Lyon, Dixon Denham, Hugh CLAPPERTON, and Walter Oudney, and Alexander Gordon LAING all received this dubious protection, which landed them in greater difficulties. The man whom a generation of explorers from the north found most useful was Hatita ag-Khuden, of the Ajjer Tuareg near Ghāt, in what is now southwestern Libya. He first became known to British travelers in 1820, when he helped Lyon, who sent him a sword as a gift. Denham, who brought it to him, called him "a man with whom I would trust myself anywhere," and he was specially commended by the 3d Earl of Bathurst for his services to the Bornu Mission. He also assisted Laing, who, though considering that Hatita's influence had been exaggerated, nevertheless "never met a better man in any country." It was perhaps Hatita's friendliness in a hostile land, rather than specific aid, which earned him the title "the old friend of the English," in the words of Heinrich BARTH, who met him in the 1850s.

Among personal servants engaged by explorers was "honest Jack Le Bore," as Laing called him. Born in Saint-Domingue, he had been a trumpeter in the French Army and was present at the Battle of Austerlitz. After the Napoleonic Wars he enlisted in the Royal African Corps and became a bugle major. He accompanied Maj. John Peddie on his disastrous expedition, went to Ségou with Dr. Dochard, and entered Laing's service in 1822. He accompanied Laing on his last expedition and died of illness in June 1826. Laing said: "I could have ill spared him at any time; but never less so than at the present."

Another widely traveled servant was Adolphus Sympkins from St. Vincent. From his journeys as a seaman he acquired the nickname Columbus; he later served the Pasha for several years. He spoke Arabic and three European languages, and Dixon engaged him for the Bornu Mission, to which he was "of the greatest service"; he returned with Dixon to England. In 1825 he sailed with Hugh Clapperton but died shortly after landing on the west coast of Africa. Richard Lemon LANDER, who also went as one of Clapperton's servants, did not share this high opinion and thought Sympkins "malicious and vengeful."

A third servant of this expedition was perhaps the best-known African in the exploration of the area, William Pascoe (Pasko). He was born in Gobir, in Hausa country, and named abu-Bakr, but had been kidnapped as a slave. The Royal Navy released him from a Portuguese slaver, and he joined the service. He was in the crew of HMS *Owen Glendower* in October 1823 when the eccentric archaeologist and traveler Giovanni Belzoni arrived at Cape Coast on a journey in search of the Niger. He engaged Pascoe, who said he wished to return to his own people, as guide and interpreter, but Belzoni died on December 3. Lander has much to say of Pascoe. He was an

elderly man, about 5 feet (1.5 meters) in height, with one leg shorter than the other. His face bore the traditional Hausa scars, and he had a broad grin, "but there was an undefinable expression of low cunning in his dark, wandering eye, and an habitual restlessness in his manner which induced one to suspect that there was more of evil in him than he was willing should be detected." During the expedition he was involved in a series of amorous adventures and also deserted several times with money and goods, though always recaptured, and at Sokoto in December 1825 Clapperton dismissed him. He was reengaged when Clapperton's fatal illness threw a new strain on Lander, and he also looked after Lander in his sickness following Clapperton's death. He eventually accompanied Lander throughout the rest of the expedition and went with him to England.

Pascoe later returned to Cape Coast, and, despite his shortcomings, when Richard and John Lander arrived there in February 1830, they "were fortunate enough to engage old Pascoe whose merits as an interpreter are unquestionable." With his two wives, he endured the hazards of the expedition, "a most valuable servant to us, and the only staunch fellow among all our people." Inevitably, he was reengaged by Lander on Macgregor Laird's expedition of 1832, for he was a capable cook, messenger, and interpreter, but early in 1833 he died of poison administered on the orders of the ruler of Idah because he had advocated that the expedition trade higher upstream.

Another trusted servant of Lander was Jowdie, a slave freed after the 1825–1827 expedition and reengaged in 1830, when he was "the strongest and most athletic." By 1832 he had become a reliable interpreter and envoy, an interesting example of the developing capacities of one man on successive expeditions.

The Laird and Oldfield expedition of 1832 was the first of a series of boat expeditions which relied largely on Kru men. (The tragic expedition of Capt. James K. Tuckey to the Congo in 1816 had been undertaken with a European crew, though Africans were engaged for overland porterage.) The Kru people, living on the grain coast of West Africa, acquired a good reputation as seamen in merchant vessels and those of the Royal Navy, and twenty were engaged on this occasion. About 100 Africans, mostly Kru, were employed in the Niger Expedition of 1841, 33 accompanied Dr. William Balfour Baikie in 1854, and an unrecorded number went with him on his 1857 expedition. Praise for their work on these journeys is almost universal. They had their own organization under headmen, and disciplinary problems were rare. Whether working on steam vessels, cutting wood for fuel, canoeing, or swimming, they were particularly useful for river work. On land they acted as carriers. Their "lying and pilfering" were far outweighed by their loyalty and courage. In 1841, for example, Thomas Osmond, a Kru, and Thomas Guy, a Gambian, saved a man from drowning and were awarded

Royal Humane Society medals. Above all they kept healthy. Some were poisoned for making too free with local women by the ruler who had Pascoe murdered, and at least two were killed when Lander was fatally wounded in 1833, but none died of disease on this expedition, nor did any of the much larger number engaged in 1841. The Kru suffered from scurvy owing to bad provisioning in 1854, but all recovered.

Of more individual importance in these expeditions were the interpreters. In 1841 the missionary J. F. Schön engaged fourteen men, who spoke nine African languages between them, for his expedition. Though not formally engaged as an interpreter, the outstanding African was Samuel Adjai Crowther. Adjai, born about 1806, was a Yoruba who had been seized as a slave in 1821, freed by a British ship in 1822, and landed in Sierra Leone, where in 1825 he was baptized. He was a schoolmaster in Sierra Leone and the first scholar of Fourah Bay College. He went with Schön on the 1841 expedition to assess missionary prospects and afterward went to England, where he was ordained in 1843. He accompanied both of Baikie's expeditions and, though nominally a guest, gave valuable aid as an interpreter and from his knowledge and experience. In 1857 he was joined by another African, the Rev. W. E. Taylor, and founded the mission at Lokoja, in what is now Nigeria. Crowther wrote books on all three journeys; he was consecrated bishop of the Niger in 1864 and died in 1891.

Also on these three expeditions was Simon Jonas, an Ibo ex-slave from Sierra Leone, who stayed with the Obi of Abo, in the Niger Delta, at his own request in 1841, had a similar assignment in 1854, and later joined Crowther at Lagos for linguistic work. In July

Abeba (left) and Dorugu, who accompanied Heinrich Barth when he returned to England from Timbuktu in 1855.

1857 he accompanied Taylor in establishing a mission at Onitsha; he taught, interpreted, and accompanied Taylor in journeys in the area. Jonas was taken ill and died on Fernando Po on November 15, 1858, a "zealous servant of God."

Aliheli, a Hausa who accompanied Lander in 1832, was engaged again in 1854; "our valiant little interpreter" was "most faithful and most valuable," but he proved less satisfactory in 1857. Thomas Cook, a Nupe interpreter, had been a freed slave landed at Sierra Leone in 1811 and became a sergeant in the West India Regiment. After his discharge he was a butcher in Freetown, and he was elderly when he volunteered to accompany Baikie in 1857; he died aged 70 just after the founding of Lokoja. Jacob Meheux (Mieux) was an interpreter who served as chief of Lokoja from 1870 to 1896.

Heinrich Barth's book has much to say of his following, notably Mohammed el-Gatroni, "the most useful attendant I ever had," who remained with him, apart from a break of some months, from June 1850 to July 1855. He was widely traveled, resourceful, and reliable in undertaking separate responsibilities. Subsequently he was with Henri DUVEYRIER, Eduard Vogel, and Moritz von Beurmann in the Sudan, and he accompanied Gerhard ROHLFS to Kukawa in 1866 and Gustav NACHTIGAL to Lake Chad 2 years later. His son Ali was with Rohlfs on the Kufra Expedition of 1879.

Barth's expedition is also interesting for the two Africans, formerly servants of his colleague Adolf Overweg, whom he brought to England in 1855. Dorugu, born about 1840 in Hausa country, had been bought out of slavery by Overweg; Abeba (abu-Bakr) from Margi, in the Bornu Kingdom, was about 4 years older. Abeba returned to Africa after 2 years, worked with Crowther and Baikie, occupied official posts under the French and British, and succeeded Meheux as chief of Lokoja from 1896 to 1904. Dorugu dictated his memoirs to J. F. Schön while in England, and these give an African viewpoint on Barth's travels as well as reactions to European ways of life. After his return to Africa in 1864 Dorugu became an interpreter, was later a teacher, and died in 1912.

Livingstone in southern Africa No explorer had a wider experience of different types of African followers than did David LIVINGSTONE. He paid tribute to the Christians of Kuruman and Kolobeng, but though men such as Mebalwe Molehane (David) traveled with him in his early journeys, his only companions during the major expeditions of 1853–1856 were the Makololo. The true Makololo were a people of Sotho stock who had migrated north into Barotseland some 20 years before, but the name is also extended to apply to their varied Tswana subject peoples. Sebetwane, their ruler, welcomed Livingstone in 1851, and his successor, Sekeletu, provided an escort of twenty-seven, under two Makololo, Pitsane and Mohorisi, when Livingstone traveled north in 1853. They escorted him by canoe and on land to Luanda, Angola, and in spite of some internal quarrels he thought them "decidedly the best I ever travelled with." Livingstone refused the offer of a ship home from Luanda in order to lead them back to their capital, Linyanti, which they reached in September 1855. Within 2 months he again set off, this time with an escort of 114, on the journey east which included his naming of Victoria Falls and which ended at Tete, Mozambique, where Livingstone left the majority of the Makololo, undertaking to return and take them back to Linyanti. A few accompanied him to the coast, and he attempted to take the leading man, Sekwebu, "a person of great prudence and sound judgement," to England, but the strange surroundings unsettled the Makololo, who jumped overboard at Mauritius.

Livingstone returned to Africa in 1858 both to investigate the potentialities of the Zambezi and to take the Makololo to their home. The Zambezi Expedition was planned on the same lines as those on the Niger: transport by a Macgregor Laird vessel, the *Ma-Robert,* a team of British specialists, and Kru. In contrast to their good record in West Africa, the Kru were a comparative failure on the Zambezi. Their health suffered in the unfamiliar climatic conditions, and they had no experience of local customs and languages. The hazards of navigating the Zambezi and the shortcomings of the *Ma-Robert,* necessitating a greater number of land journeys, lessened the value of their seamanship, and the public quarrels between Livingstone and Comdr. Norman Bedingfeld, nominally in charge of them, undermined discipline. They were sent home in 1859, but 4 years later, after employing various other Africans, Livingstone wrote to the Admiralty that he would welcome another group. The expedition ended before that request was implemented.

The main African support after the Kru came from the Makololo, initially from those who had remained at Tete and, later, after Livingstone had repatriated them, from a group of sixteen brought back from Linyanti. They worked on the river steamer *Pioneer* and were particularly useful on overland journeys. Their value varied; they tended to be independent and aggressive and set up their own rule, taking wives and property from the local villages. Livingstone, though reprimanding them, never lost his affection for them, and indeed they were always ready to come to his aid or that of the English missionaries of the Universities Mission, which was established during his sojourn on the Zambezi.

Third, there were local pilots, boatmen, woodcutters, and porters, engaged on a short-term basis and proving an amenable and helpful people; and, fourth, Johanna men, engaged on Johanna (Anjouan) Island in the Comoros. The first contingent was enlisted in 1861 to replace European crew members of the *Pioneer* who had fallen sick, but their reliability and freedom from illness led Livingstone to engage two more groups in succession; these, however, proved much less satisfactory.

When Livingstone was recalled in 1863, he sailed to India in his steam launch, the *Lady Nyassa,* taking a crew of three Europeans, seven Zambezians, including Susi and Amoda, and two youths freed from slavery by the Universities Mission, Chuma and Wekotani. These last four were to play a significant part in his last expedition.

Though Livingstone never again saw the Makololo, they never forgot him, and when in 1867 Gunner E. D. Young led an expedition to discover the truth of a report of Livingstone's death, the Makololo supported and helped him. Eight years later they again assisted Young, who was on his way to Lake Nyasa (Lake Malawi) to found the Livingstonia Mission.

East Africa Zanzibar, a cosmopolitan commercial center, was the gateway to the East African mainland, over which its rulers claimed a vague but far-reaching suzerainty. There was a substantial pre-European trade, in which human porterage was essential, for the climate hampered the use of animals, and navigable rivers were virtually nonexistent. A regular Arab-dominated route led to the straggling settlement of Unyanyembe and thence to Ujiji on Lake Tanganyika. Many of the Africans had well-established trading contacts, notably the Swahili in the Mombasa area and the Kamba farther north. The Nyamwezi people of the area south of Lake Victoria were great travelers, both in their own caravans and as employees of others. European explorers therefore used Zanzibar as a base for supplies and manpower, and this built up a pattern of caravan organization and a continuity of personnel in successive expeditions.

The first European explorers, the missionaries Johann Ludwig Krapf and Johannes Rebmann, had no resources for elaborate expeditions and traveled with small bands of Nyika and Swahili; this policy involved them at times in setbacks and dangers arising out of African disputes. When John Hanning SPEKE and Richard Francis BURTON arrived at Zanzibar in 1856 to seek the source of the Nile, the need for an escort was emphasized by the fate of M. Maizan, murdered while traveling with inadequate protection, and by their own experiences in Somaliland, culminating in an attack on their camp in which both were wounded. They therefore welcomed the Sultan's assignment of a half-caste Arab, Said bin-Salim, to represent his authority and act as caravan leader, and also had a contingent of eight Baluchi drawn from the Sultan's mercenary force. Said, however, was an ineffectual leader, unable to control the Baluchi, the "Sons of Ramji" engaged through an Indian merchant and using the expedition to trade on their master's account, and the porters and donkeymen.

The most valuable man was an African, formerly in the Sultan's troops, who was engaged by Speke as a servant. Bombay, a Yao ex-slave whose original name had been lost and who was called after the home of his former master, was hardworking, honest, and resourceful, and his knowledge of Hindustani was particularly appreciated by Speke, who could not speak Arabic or any African tongues. He brought with him another ex-slave named Mabruki (subsequently known as Mabruki Speke), who, though morose and clumsy, had a dogged loyalty that was to prove of value to many explorers. Burton, generally critical of Africans, found praiseworthy qualities in these two and eventually promoted Bombay to take charge of the stores in place of Said. Bombay was with Burton and Speke when they reached Lake Tanganyika and accompanied Speke on his journey north to Lake Victoria.

Bombay and Mabruki were therefore reengaged when Speke returned to Africa in 1860 accompanied by James Augustus GRANT. They in turn found twenty-seven more men from among the Wanguana (freemen) of Zanzibar: ex-slaves, long separated from their traditional backgrounds, adaptable, good-humored, and erratic, the first of many who were to form an essential element in expeditions for the next 30 years. Sultan Majid supplied thirty-six slaves from his gardens, porters were recruited on the mainland, and an escort was provided by ten Cape Mounted Riflemen, soldiers of mixed stock who had volunteered while Speke and Grant were in South Africa on the outward journey. Said bin-Salim was again engaged as caravan leader, but he proved as ineffective as before as the expedition traveled inland. The health and morale of the Cape Mounted men deteriorated rapidly, many porters deserted, but Bombay's recruits "do all the work . . . and do it as an enlightened & disciplined people." Even here, however, all was not well, for Bombay was at odds with Baraka, a colleague of superior abilities who resented the status that Bombay derived from his earlier service.

At Unyanyembe, after delays due to the fighting between the Arabs and the Nyamwezi, Speke engaged more men, sent back the Cape Mounted Riflemen, and also left Said bin-Salim. The latter remained at Unyanyembe as governor, welcomed Henry M. STANLEY, Livingstone, and Verney Lovett CAMERON, and was deposed in 1878. Bombay was given charge of the caravan. His dispute with Baraka continued until the

latter was sent off to try to make contact with John Petherick, who was supposed to bring supplies for Speke, while Speke went with Bombay and a dwindling following to the source of the Nile. Soon after, about half of the remainder, believed to be those who favored Baraka, deserted; Speke and Grant traveled on and eventually reached Khartoum with eighteen men and four women. Bombay had been "the life and success of the expedition," a valuable interpreter and envoy, and a man capable of undertaking independent journeys to obtain recruits and of acting independently when Grant was incapacitated by illness. His own loyalty to Speke had kept the remnant of the Africans together, and his occasional drunkenness was a minor blemish on his sterling qualities. Speke showed his gratitude to his "faithfuls" by purchasing them small plantations in Zanzibar where they could settle, and he continued to take an interest in their welfare after his return to England and until his untimely death in 1864.

When, 7 years later, Henry Stanley arrived in Zanzibar to organize his search for Livingstone, his first thought was to seek Speke's faithfuls. Bombay was found in Pemba; Mabruki Speke, still in Zanzibar, had accompanied Baron Karl Klaus von der Decken on his expedition to Somaliland, had survived the attack in which the baron and some of his followers were killed, but later had lost the use of one hand in a dispute with a neighbor. Both joined Stanley, as did four other faithfuls and another Speke veteran, Manua Sera, who had gone with Baraka to find Petherick. Other Zanzibari were also recruited. During the journey to the interior Stanley decided that Bombay's value had been overrated and that he was often dilatory and ineffective; Mabruki Speke proved "true and staunch" and was mainly responsible for frustrating an incipient mutiny on the Gombe River. On November 10, 1871, Stanley reached Ujiji, to be greeted by Susi and taken to meet Livingstone.

Livingstone's journey of 1866–1871 had been frustrated almost from the beginning by the shortcomings of his manpower. He brought to Zanzibar from India Chuma, Wekotani, Susi, and Amoda; thirteen sepoys to act as an escort and to look after the various animals intended for transport in place of porters; and nine former slaves from the Church Missionary Society school at Nasik, India. He also engaged ten Johanna men. Within 5 months of his landing at Mikindani, in what is now Tanzania, in April 1868, this company had disintegrated. The sepoys had been dismissed after neglecting and ill-treating the animals, all of which had died; they had also had a bad effect on the impressionable Nasik "boys." Wekotani had returned to his own people, three Nasik boys had gone, and the Johanna men deserted in September.

With his stocks depleted by the need to pay local carriers in place of the animals, with only nine followers, and hampered by ill health, Livingstone journeyed erratically in the next 5 years. He traveled for a time with Arab traders, who showed him hospitality

John Hanning Speke's eighteen "faithfuls," photographed at the conclusion of his expedition in East Africa.

despite his dislike of their activities, but they had a corrupting influence on his followers. Chuma, who was potentially a lively-minded and able youth, temporarily succumbed to the leisurely Arab way of life and was one of those who remained behind when Livingstone went with only four followers to Lake Bangweulu in July 1868. At other times different men failed him; by 1871 he had five left: Chuma, Susi, Amoda, and two Nasik men, Edward Gardner and Mabruki. With them were Susi's wife Mochosi and Amoda's wife Halima, the cook.

When Stanley arrived, Livingstone declined to return to the coast and asked that his inadequate following be augmented so that he could continue his explorations. On reaching Zanzibar, therefore, Stanley organized a caravan of fifty-seven men: an Arab, Mohammed ben-Galfin, who was named leader; 50 Zanzibar Africans, some of whom had just returned with him, including Manua Sera and Mabruki Speke; and six Nasik boys who had come from India to join the abortive Livingstone Relief Expedition under Lieut. L. S. Dawson. Bombay was not included, for Livingstone had accepted Stanley's unfavorable assessment of him.

When the column arrived at Unyanyembe, Livingstone dismissed the Arab and appointed three African "heads of departments": Susi, Manua Sera, and another of Stanley's men, Chowpereh. With this party and some additional porters recruited locally, he set off south on his last journey. Through months of his deteriorating health (he had to be carried in the final stages) the party held together, and Susi and Chuma gave good service in exploring unknown country. Just before dawn on May 1, 1873, Livingstone was found dead in his hut at Chitambo's by his Ganda servant Majwara. His followers decided to take the body with his papers to the coast; first they roughly embalmed it and buried the internal organs near a tree on which Jacob Wainwright, a Nasik boy, carved an inscription with the name of the heads of departments.

The hazardous journey of 1600 miles (2575 kilometers) took 9 months, but eventually the body was brought to Zanzibar, whence it was shipped to England; Jacob Wainwright accompanied it and was a pallbearer at the funeral in Westminster Abbey. Chuma and Susi also spent some months in England, where they assisted Horace Waller to edit Livingstone's journals by dictating their firsthand account of events, which he recorded in his notebook (now in Rhodes House). Two other Africans, Matthew Wellington and Carus Farrar, also dictated their reminiscences, but it was many years before these were published.

Livingstone's last journey aroused widespread interest in the role of the Africans. Chuma, Susi, and Jacob were given ROYAL GEOGRAPHICAL SOCIETY medals, and later a special medal was struck by the society for all the sixty men who had accompanied the body to the coast. When these medals reached Zanzibar in 1876, the majority of the recipients had

Kalulu, pictured with Henry Stanley, whom he served as personal attendant during the expedition to find Livingstone.

left the island, many of them on Stanley's transcontinental expedition of 1874–1877, which was intended to finish Livingstone's work.

In recruiting his personnel, Stanley drew on his earlier experience; in his total of more than 350 men and women, he had 21 experienced "chiefs," most of whom had traveled with him and many with Livingstone also. Manua Sera was chief captain; Chuma and Susi were not available, having entered the service of the Universities Mission. Stanley also had a body of 32 stalwart carriers for the sections of the boat, the *Lady Alice,* with which he explored the great lakes; these men, like the chiefs, had the privilege of bringing their wives.

At one time Stanley traveled with a Ganda escort; for 2 months he was accompanied by the caravan of the famous Arab trader Hamed bin-Muhammad (Tippu Tib), who had also met Livingstone and Cameron, but for the most part he was dependent on his own leading men, and their responsibilities were increased by his own absences from the main body when visiting King Mutesa of Buganda and on several occasions when the expedition was split up on land and water. Frank Pocock, the Kentish boatman, whose two British colleagues died early in the journey, developed valuable qualities but relied on the experienced Africans.

Manua Sera, a resourceful if unscrupulous man with a strangely reckless streak in his nature, took effective command of the camp when Stanley was away. Uledi, a skilled boatman and swimmer, came to the fore in the river portion of the journey and saved thirteen men from drowning, though unable to help

Frank Pocock when he was swept to his death at the Massassa Falls. Wadi Safeni, who had traveled with Livingstone on his last journey, was the most reliable of the chiefs, but toward the end of the journey he became insane and wandered off. His wife, Muscati, accompanied the expedition and gave Pocock problems when he was in charge of the camp in Stanley's absence by refusing to obey his orders. She died just as the expedition returned to Zanzibar. Indeed the death toll, in battle, by accident, and from disease, reached the heavy total of 114. Among those who died were Mabruki Speke, Amoda, Gardner, and several more who had followed Speke or Livingstone. Stanley showed his gratitude to the survivors by sending them rings to wear as signs that they had accompanied him, and he also urged Sir John Kirk, British vice consul in Zanzibar, to accept a pay claim on behalf of the Livingstone veterans. On investigation it emerged that this claim was based largely on evidence manufactured by Manua Sera, and it was rejected, though an *ex gratia* payment was made to the dwindling band of Livingstone's men.

Bombay was still alive, having accompanied Cameron across Africa between 1873 and 1876. He had become less effective with age, and Cameron, perhaps because of his naval background, was exasperated by Bombay's casual discipline, but in spite of such criticisms, it is clear that he still commanded personal loyalty from Africans, for nearly all the fifty-four men who reached the West African coast were those he had recruited. After a brief spell in missionary service, he retired on a Royal Geographical Society pension and died in Zanzibar in 1885.

Of other noted Africans, Chuma had an outstanding, though short, career. He worked with Bishop Edward Steere of the Universities Mission and other missionaries on journeys to found and sustain stations in the interior during the 1870s. In 1879 he was chosen as headman for the Royal Geographical Society Expedition led by Alexander Keith Johnston and Joseph THOMSON and was one of those who recommended men for the carefully selected caravan. When Johnston died, it was the experience of Chuma which enabled young Thomson to bring the expedition to a successful conclusion with the loss of only one man, and he took efficient charge of the camp when Thomson went on his disappointing journey to the Lukugu. Chuma, declared Thomson, was not always truthful and liked to act the "big man," sometimes by the lavish distribution of the expedition's goods to local women, but his humor and oratory, his popularity combined with forceful authority, made him unequaled as a caravan leader. He was presented with a sword by the Royal Geographical Society and accompanied Thomson again on his expedition to the Ruvuma (Rovuma) River in 1881. At the close of 1882, however, he died at the age of about 30.

Susi was dismissed from missionary service for drinking and was thought unsuitable for employment by Johnston in 1879, but Stanley, returning to Zanzibar to recruit men for service in the new Congo Free State later that year, enlisted him as "head chief of the foreign native employes," most of whom were Zanzibari who had formerly been with Stanley or knew him by reputation. Susi played an important part in the establishment of the stations which Stanley founded along the Congo (Zaire) River and was a resourceful and trusted leader during the 3 years of his contract. After his return to Zanzibar he was reengaged by the University Mission, led its caravans for some years, was baptized as David in 1886, accompanied Bishop Charles Alan Smythies to the mainland during the rising of Chief Bushiri in 1888, and died in 1891, an honored member of the mission and "a good friend from the first" to the bishop.

Stanley returned to Africa in 1887 to recruit men for the Emin Pasha Relief Expedition and was warmly welcomed by many of his old followers. The Zanzibari gave good service in the confused and tragic trans-African journey. Uledi, the coxswain, who had also been on the Congo with Stanley, was the outstanding man for his courage and experience, especially with boats. Stanley entered into an uneasy alliance with Tippu Tib for the supply of porters, and the failure of this plan was one of the causes of the tragedy that befell the rear column.

On the more northerly route into the interior of East Africa, through the dreaded Masai country, several European explorers relied on traders with experience of the area, but it is possible that such men exaggerated the perils of the journey to preserve their trading advantages. Among them were Sadi ben-Ahedi, who went with Von der Decken in 1862, Charles New in 1871, and Thomson in 1883–1884; Muhinna, also with Thomson; and Jumbe Kimameta, who accompanied Thomson and later went with Count Samuel Teleki and Ludwig von Höhnel in 1887–1888.

Manua Sera's long career ended on this route. He was Thomson's headman in 1883–1884 but was past his best and had become "lazy and unprofitable." He served with Frederick Jackson in 1885–1886, enlisted as a guide with Teleki and Höhnel in 1887, provoked a fracas by carrying off a woman from a village, gave some courageous and able help in crises, and died of tuberculosis on the shores of Lake Baringo early in 1888. On the same expedition there were two other notable men. Dualla Idris was a 24-year-old Somali, handsome, arrogant, and courageous, who had been with Stanley on the Congo as a youth and accompanied F. L. James into the interior of Somaliland in 1884–1885. As headman for Teleki and Höhnel, he was a skilled negotiator and an able leader. He was later to be a trusted interpreter and friend to Frederick Lugard when the latter was administrator for the Imperial British East Africa Company in Uganda from 1890 to 1892. Shortly after, he was drowned off Somaliland. The other was probably the longest-serving veteran of all, Mhogo Chungo (Ferrajji). His career began in 1860 with Speke. He went as a cook with Stanley to find Livingstone, accompanied Cameron across Africa, and carried the flag in the escort which received Livingstone's body at Unyanyembe. He was with Harry Hamilton JOHNSTON at Kilimanjaro in 1884, traveled with Teleki in 1887–1888, and enlisted with Lugard in 1890. However, Lugard found him unsatisfactory, though "a droll character," and he was sent back to the coast, perhaps to a well-earned retirement.

In the years spanned by Ferrajji's career, the outstanding Africans—Bombay with Speke, Susi with Livingstone, Manua Sera with Stanley, and Chuma with Thomson, for example—were not merely valuable members of expeditions but essential contributors to their success.

BIBLIOGRAPHY: E. W. Bovill (ed.), *Missions to the Niger*, 4 vols., Cambridge, England, 1964–1966; T. W. W. Crawford, "Account of the Life of Matthew Wellington in His Own Words, and of the Death of David Livingstone and the Journey to the Coast," *Northern Rhodesia Journal*, vol. VI, 1965, pp. 99–102; S. A. Crowther, *Journal of an Expedition up the Niger and Tshadda Rivers*, London, 1855; S. A. Crowther and J. C. Taylor, *The Gospel on the Banks of the Niger*, London, 1859; Edinburgh University Centre of African Studies, *The Exploration of Africa in the Eighteenth and Nineteenth Centuries*, Edinburgh, 1971 (includes A. H. M. Kirk-Greene, "West African Exploration: Africans, Auxiliaries, and Also-Rans," and D. H. Simpson, "The Part Taken by Africans in the European Exploration of East and Central Africa"); J. M. Gray, "The Correspondence of Dallington Maftaa," *Uganda Journal*, vol. XXX, 1966, pp. 13–24; id., "Livingstone's Muganda servant," *Uganda Journal*, vol. XIII, 1949, pp. 119–129; vol. XXVIII, 1964, pp. 99–100; A. H. M. Kirk-Greene and P. Newman, *West African Travels and Adventures*, London, 1971 (includes Dorugu's memoirs); Mungo Park, *Journal*, London, 1815 ("Isaaco's Journal," pp. 289–335); F. Pridmore and D. H. Simpson, "Faithful to the End," *The Numismatic Circular*, vol. LXXVII, 1970, pp. 192–196; Robert I. Rotberg (ed.), *Africa and Its Explorers*, Cambridge, Mass., 1970; J. F. Schön, and S. A. Crowther, *Journals . . . 1841*, London, 1842; D. H. Simpson, *Dark Companions: The African Contribution to the European Exploration of East Africa*, London, 1976; H. B. Thomas, "The Death of Dr Livingstone: Carus Farrar's Narrative," *Uganda Journal*, vol. XIV, 1950, pp. 115–128; id., "Jacob Wainwright in Uganda," *Uganda Journal*, vol. XV, 1951, pp. 204–205.

D. H. Simpson

African Association

The Association for Promoting the Discovery of the Interior Parts of Africa was founded on June 9, 1788, by the twelve members of a London dining club. Not only was the African interior virtually unknown to Europeans in the late eighteenth century, but political, commercial, and humanitarian considerations combined with scientific curiosity to stimulate interest in unveiling the mysteries of the continent at this time. Among the founders of the association were Sir Joseph Banks, president of the Royal Society, who served as treasurer (1788–1804) and as secretary (1795–1797, 1799), and Henry Beaufoy, a Whig member of Parliament, who was secretary from 1788 until his death in 1795. The association's activities were financed by the members' annual subscriptions of 5 guineas each; during the 43-year history of the association, 212 persons became subscribing members.

Initially focusing its activities on northern and western Africa, the association engaged the services of several explorers, including Daniel Houghton (1740?–1791), who visited the kingdom of Bambuk, famous for its gold, and indicated that the Niger River flows from west to east, contrary to the accepted belief of the day; Mungo PARK; Friedrich Hornemann (1772–1801), a young German who succeeded in reaching Bornu and the Hausa city of Katsina before dying of dysentery in the town of Bokani in Nupe; and Johann Ludwig BURCKHARDT. After 1820, as government-sponsored expeditions succeeded in revealing the geography of West Africa, the association turned to eastern Africa and the problem of the sources of the Nile. The most important explorer whom it engaged in this period was Louis-Maurice-Adolphe Linant de Bellefonds (1799–1883), a French naval officer who reached a point on the White Nile 150 miles (241 kilometers) beyond the confluence of the two Niles. The difficulties of exploration in East Africa, the dwindling membership of the association, and the organization of the ROYAL GEOGRAPHICAL SOCIETY in 1830 led to the association's merger with the latter in 1831.

BIBLIOGRAPHY: Robin Hallett (ed.), *Records of the African Association, 1788–1831*, London, 1964.

Alexander the Great (Alexander III; 356–323 B.C.) King of Macedon. Son of King Philip II, he showed while still very young dynamic qualities of military leadership and boundless ambition. In 336 B.C. he succeeded his father as king. Philip had previously built up the most thoroughly professional army yet known and had made Macedonia the most powerful state in the Greek world. He planned to lead a united force of Macedonians with Greek allies in an attack on the Persian empire, whose military weakness had recently became clear. The plan was put into effect by Alexander in 334. His meteoric success, which went far beyond anything dreamed of by Philip, brought about a major political and cultural revolution in the East. The Persian empire was destroyed, Asia as far as the Indus came under Macedonian control, and Greek civilization was planted in the Near East, which it was to dominate for many centuries. The conquest was naturally of great importance in the history of geography since it opened the way for detailed examination of areas hitherto known to the Greek world only indirectly, by way of small numbers of traders and envoys to the Persian court.

From 334 to 331 Alexander's campaigns took him through Anatolia, Syria, and Egypt. In 331 he crossed the Euphrates and Tigris Rivers and inflicted a further defeat on the Persian king Darius III at Gaugamela (near Mosul); from this time on he was campaigning in lands known only by name to the Greeks. After taking Babylon and Susa, he entered the area of modern Iran, the heart of the Persian empire, capturing the royal cities of Persepolis and Pasargadae, then traveled northwest to Ecbatana (Hamadan). Passing through the Sirdar Pass (named by the Greeks the Caspian Gates and often confused with other more prominent passes), he traveled along the south of the Caspian Sea eastward in pursuit of Bessus, who had removed Darius and proclaimed himself king. By way of the Gurgan (Gorgan) River and Meshed (Mashhad) he turned south, founding Alexandria in Ariis (Herat) and, in 329, Alexandria Arachosia (Kandahar). He then proceeded northeast, crossing the mountains to the Kabul Valley. A city called Alexandria ad Caucasum was founded at the foot of the Hindu Kush; the name indicates that it was thought the mountains were part of the real Caucasus range. The following year Alexander crossed the Hindu Kush, probably by the Khawak Pass, and went northward through the open country of Bactria by way of Bactra (Balkh), across the Oxus (Amu Darya) to Maracanda (Samarkand) and on to the Jaxartes (Syr Darya), founding his most distant city, Alexandria Eschate (Khodzhent;

Leninabad). It appears to have been believed that the Jaxartes was in fact a reach of the Tanais (Don) and that the Oxus flowed into the Caspian. It is clear that at this limit of his march Alexander could rely only on hearsay, no doubt often garbled and tendentious, about what lay beyond his ken. The Aral Sea was unknown to him and indeed to the rest of antiquity, nor was there any conception of the vastness of the landmass of Asia extending eastward.

In 327 Alexander recrossed the Hindu Kush and made for the Indus; his route is not certain until his arrival in Swat, but apparently he did not use the Khyber Pass. In 326 he crossed the river and went on, via Taxila, across the Hydaspes (Jhelum) and reached the Hyphasis (Beas). Here his army refused to go on. How much farther he wished to go is uncertain. Although informed about the Ganges, it is probable that he thought he was not far from the "Ocean Stream," which he like all Greeks believed surrounded the known landmass. Returning, he had a fleet built on the Jhelum and sailed down it and the Indus to the delta, his intention probably now being to make the river the eastern boundary of his empire, as it had been of the Persian. He returned to Mesopotamia with part of his army through the harsh Gedrosian Desert (Baluchistan), sending NEARCHUS with the fleet to explore the coast as far as the head of the Persian Gulf. Alexander died from fever and exhaustion in 323. Apart from the political aims of his conquests he had genuine ambitions to explore; when he died, projects to send one fleet to circumnavigate the Caspian and another to sail round Arabia were suspended. He had with him a staff of "bematists," literally, "pacers," surveyors who surveyed the routes and produced esti-

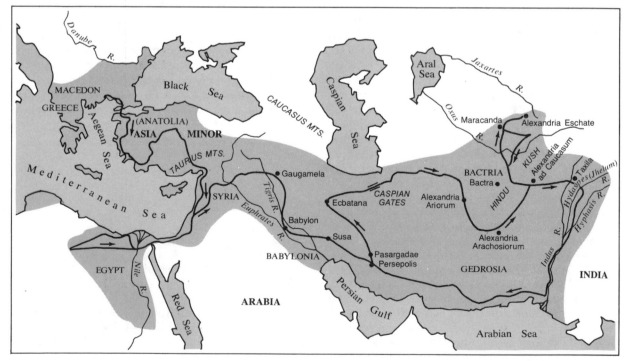

Alexander the Great's empire. Arrows indicate his route to the east.

mates of distances, some references to which survive. He also had with him Greek experts in various sciences and perhaps owed this interest, if little else, to Aristotle, who had been his tutor. Accounts of his campaigns, of which several were produced within a generation of his death, were major sources of information about Asia to subsequent generations.

BIBLIOGRAPHY: W. W. Tarn, *Alexander the Great*, 2 vols., Cambridge, England, 1948; Ulrich Wilcken, *Alexander the Great*, tr. by G. C. Richards, London, 1932.

B. H. Warmington

Almagro, Diego de (ca. 1478–1538) Spanish conqueror and explorer. A native of a village called Almagro in Extremadura, Almagro was of illegitimate birth. In 1514 he traveled to Panama with Gov. Pedro Arias de ÁVILA and there became acquainted with Francisco PIZARRO, whom he joined in efforts to explore and conquer the rich lands rumored to lie in South America. He shared in Pizarro's two probes along the western coast of South America from 1524 to 1528, and in 1525 he lost an eye and several fingers in a skirmish with the Indians. Later he devoted himself to financing and organizing a third expedition, which left Panama under Pizarro's leadership in 1531. Almagro himself arrived in Cajamarca with about 200 men in April 1533, several months after the capture of the Inca emperor, Atahuallpa. Although Almagro and his followers were denied a share of Atahuallpa's ransom, they took part in the subsequent phases of the conquest, and in December 1534 Almagro was named governor of Cuzco by Pizarro. Shortly afterward, however, news came from Spain that King Charles I had appointed Almagro governor of the province of New Toledo, which was to extend for 200 leagues from the southern boundary of Pizarro's province of New Castile.

Conflict soon arose over whether Cuzco lay within the borders of New Toledo or New Castile, but open warfare was averted when Almagro decided to lead an expedition to Chile, part of which lay within his jurisdiction and which the Indians said was rich in gold. Almagro left for Chile in mid-July 1535. The Spanish contingent of the expedition eventually totaled 750; in addition, thousands of Indians accompanied the Spaniards. To reach Chile, Almagro followed a route used by the Incas which crossed parts of modern Bolivia and Argentina. After an arduous trek across the Andes through the San Francisco Pass, Almagro traveled west to the Copiapó Valley and then south to the Aconcagua Valley. From here several exploratory parties set out in different directions; one of them, led by Gómez de Alvarado, reached the Itata River. These expeditions confirmed what had already become evident to the Spaniards: Chile was not rich in metals or the center of a high Indian civilization like that of Peru. The party now decided to return to Peru, following a route across the Atacama Desert that brought them to Arequipa early in 1537.

Almagro returned to Cuzco to find it besieged by the Inca leader, Manco. After lifting the siege, Almagro captured the city, which he claimed as his own. In the ensuing civil war the Almagrists were defeated at Las Salinas, near Cuzco, on April 26, 1538. Almagro was captured after the battle and was garrotted several weeks later.

BIBLIOGRAPHY. John Hemming, *The Conquest of the Incas*, New York, 1970; Rolando Mellafe and Sergio Villalobos, *Diego de Almagro*, Santiago de Chile, 1954; H. R. S. Pocock, *The Conquest of Chile*, New York, 1967.

Alvarado, Pedro de (1485–1541) Spanish conqueror and explorer. A native of Badajoz in the province of Extremadura, Alvarado traveled to the New World in 1510 and settled in Santo Domingo. Having taken part in the expedition of Juan de Grijalva to Yucatán and Mexico in 1518, Alvarado joined the expedition of Hernán CORTÉS the following year and played a leading role in the conquest of Mexico. On the Sorrowful Night (June 30–July 1, 1520), during which the Spaniards fled from the Aztec capital of Tenochtitlán, he is said to have made a remarkable leap across a wide gap in the causeway over which the Spaniards were escaping.

Late in 1523, on the instructions of Cortés, Alvarado embarked upon the exploration and conquest of Central America, overcoming fierce Indian resistance and establishing Spanish authority in what are now the republics of Guatemala and El Salvador. In 1526 he left Guatemala for Spain, where he was named captain general and governor of that province. With the conquest of Guatemala complete, however, Alvarado sought new fields of action, and the news of fabulous discoveries by Francisco PIZARRO in Peru led him to organize an expedition to the adjacent province of Quito. He left Guatemala in 1533 with 500 Spaniards, only to find that Pizarro had already staked a claim to Quito. After agreeing to a payment of 100,000 gold pesos in exchange for his army and equipment, Alvarado returned to Guatemala. In 1540 Alvarado's last exploratory project took him and a fleet of thirteen vessels to the west coast of Mexico, whence he intended to sail for the Spice Islands. The viceroy of Mexico, Antonio de Mendoza, persuaded him to postpone his Pacific voyage in order to take part in the search then under way for the Seven Cities of Cíbola. Alvarado interrupted his plans to join Spanish officials in quelling the Indian revolt known as the Mixtón War and was killed when a rearing horse fell upon him.

BIBLIOGRAPHY: John Eoghan Kelly, *Pedro de Alvarado, Conquistador*, Princeton, N.J., 1941.

Amundsen, Roald Engelbregt Gravning (1872–1928) Norwegian polar explorer. Amundsen was born in Borge, near Oslo, on July 16, 1872, the son of Jens Amundsen, a shipowner. He studied medicine for 2 years, then went to sea. In 1897 he joined the Belgian

Diego de Almagro, Spanish explorer of Peru and Chile, whose early partnership in conquest with Francisco Pizarro soon gave way to rivalry. He died in a civil war near Cuzco. [Library of Congress]

Pedro de Alvarado, Spanish explorer who took part in the conquest of the Aztec empire and went on to crush Indian resistance to Spanish authority in Central America. [Library of Congress]

Antarctic Expedition as first mate of the ship *Belgica.* This vessel was the first to winter in the Antarctic, and Amundsen, aided by the American physician-explorer Frederick A. COOK, was largely responsible for the crew's successful combating of scurvy. *See also* ANTARCTICA.

From 1903 to 1906, on an expedition to the Canadian Arctic in the 47-ton sloop *Gjøa,* he completed the NORTHWEST PASSAGE from east to west, becoming the first man to navigate the legendary waterway in either direction. His track took him via Lancaster Sound, Peel Sound, Franklin Strait, King William Sound (where his ship was iced in), and then along the north coast of the mainland to Bering Strait. He had sailed secretly from Norway in 1903 to escape his creditors, who had demanded payment within 24 hours. During this voyage he determined the precise position of the North Magnetic Pole (70°30′N, 95°30′W). As the first man through the Northwest Passage, he received world attention; subsequently he began to focus on the spectacular in exploration and to join in the enthusiasm that then existed for polar voyaging.

His next plan was to drift across the North Pole in the *Fram,* the old ship of Fridtjof NANSEN. But as he was preparing for sea, news reached him that the American Robert E. PEARY had attained that objective. Still making his preparations, he concealed his new intention of trying to reach the South Pole instead. When he left Norway in June 1910, only his brother knew that he was bound for the South rather than the North Pole. He sailed via the Madeira Islands directly to the Bay of Whales, Ross Sea, at the edge of Ross Barrier, in Antarctica. Here he set up a base 60 miles (97 kilometers) nearer the South Pole than that of the English explorer Robert F. SCOTT, who was also seeking to be the first to the pole. Amundsen wintered in his post, then marched due south with a dog sledge and four companions. He reached the pole on December 14, 1911, a month before Scott, after an amazing journey. His journey covered new ground, added much to knowledge of the continent's interior,

Roald Engelbregt Gravning Amundsen, Norwegian explorer who, after an impressive career of "firsts," died searching for his rival, the explorer Umberto Nobile, in the Arctic ice. [Norwegian Information Service]

and clearly showed that the pole was situated on a landmass.

With funds earned from his books and lectures, Amundsen took up the shipping business and built a new ship, the *Maud,* with which he intended to prosecute his original plan of drifting over the North Pole. He left Norway in July 1918, escaped German submarines, and sailed through the NORTHEAST PASSAGE to Bering Strait. Later, however, he abandoned his plan of a northern drift in favor of an attempt to fly over the North Pole by airplane (*see* AERIAL EXPLORATION). In 1925 he flew with the American explorer Lincoln ELLSWORTH on a venturesome journey that took them within 135 miles (217 kilometers) of the pole. He and Ellsworth tried once more, in 1926, in the dirigible *Norge,* and succeeded, flying from Spitsbergen (Svalbard) to Teller, Alaska. Their partner was Gen. Umberto Nobile of Italy, and disputes over whether Amundsen or Nobile deserved credit for the voyage lasted for years.

Amundsen died in the Arctic in June 1928 when the airplane he was flying failed. At the time he was searching for Nobile's downed dirigible *Italia,* with which Nobile had again flown over the North Pole. Amundsen wrote several books on polar exploration and an autobiography.

BIBLIOGRAPHY: Roald Amundsen, *Roald Amundsen: My Life as an Explorer,* New York, 1927; Lincoln Ellsworth, *Beyond Horizons,* New York, 1938; Bellamy Partridge, *Amundsen,* London, 1953.

Barry M. Gough

Anabara, Semyon *(fl. early eighteenth century)* Yakutsk cossack who discovered, with Ivan Bykov, the Shantar Islands (Shantarskiye Ostrova) in the Sea of Okhotsk. In 1713 he went with a detachment from Yakutsk along the rivers of the Lena Basin to Ude on the Sea of Okhotsk and crossed from the mainland to the Shantar Islands, until then known to the Russians only by hearsay. He visited three of the islands and returned with furs to Yakutsk in 1714.

Richard A. Pierce

Ancient Exploration and Travel

By the term "ancient world" is meant primarily the world of the ancient Greeks and Romans, who transmitted to the Byzantine, European, and Islamic Middle Ages, and hence to the Renaissance, the knowledge and concepts of the known world which they had acquired over many centuries. Indeed the whole concept of geography, like the word itself, is of Greek origin. Earlier civilizations such as those of Mesopotamia and Pharaonic Egypt certainly knew something of the areas immediately surrounding them but apparently had no economic or intellectual incentive to explore further. Likewise, there undoubtedly existed

trade routes of great antiquity linking parts of Neolithic Europe in the fourth and third millennia B.C., using the major river valleys and even the western Atlantic seaboard. Although these trade routes were further developed in the Bronze Age (second millennium B.C.), modern archaeology considers that the volume of trade was extremely small and that knowledge of the routes in any part of the Mediterranean world was negligible. Hence, when Greek knowledge of the world outside the eastern Mediterranean (an aspect of the development and expansion of classical Greek civilization itself) increased from about 800

B.C. on, its basis was the traditional and largely local lore of sailors handed down from generation to generation.

Ships and navigation A precondition of expansion was of course adequate knowledge of ships and their handling. Modern research has dispelled earlier views about the inefficiency of ancient navigation. The cradle of ancient nautical development was not in the river-oriented civilizations of Mesopotamia and Egypt but in the open waters of the eastern Mediterranean, especially Crete, the islands of the Aegean, and coastal communities in mainland Greece. Basic forms of oared galleys with low, slender hulls emerged in the third millennium B.C., and steering oars and a square sail are attested not much later. Cretan merchant vessels had a more rounded hull but were likewise oared and carried a single square sail and were perhaps 50 to 75 feet (15 to 23 meters) in length. At the time of the Homeric epics, which seem to give us a picture of the Aegean world at the beginning of Greek expansion (800–750 B.C.), the regular warship, no doubt doubling as a trading and pirate vessel, was the penteconter, a fifty-oared low, narrow ship, again with sail and steering oars. Merchant ships as such became more specialized, though less is known about their early forms. Their shape was distinctly rounded (the Phoenician type was called *gaulos*, a "tub") and relied more heavily on sail. Nevertheless, because of the frequent calm weather in the Mediterranean summer, the oared merchant ship remained a basic form. From the fifth century B.C. through the fourth century A.D. the standard warship was the trireme, with the rowers in three banks. The capacity of merchant ships is now better known than it used to be. The smallest considered suitable for seagoing in classical times was 70 to 80 tons burden, 100 to 150 tons being common, and in Roman times ships of more than 1000 tons were used in the grain trade between Egypt and Rome.

It does not appear that new types evolved when the Greeks and Romans ventured into the Atlantic and Indian Oceans. The substantial tides in these waters were a surprise when first encountered but presumably were soon mastered. In Mediterranean waters, winter sailing was avoided whenever possible, not so much because of storms as because of the obscuration of sun and stars, on which correct navigation depended. The old view that all ancient shipping preferred to coast rather than sail in the open sea is not now held (in any case, in conditions of good visibility it is impossible to be out of sight of land in Mediterranean waters for long). Although ancient sailing was primarily with the wind astern, experiment has shown that the square-rigged ships could sail as close to the wind as 7 points. From information given in various sources, we know that with favorable winds a speed of 4 to 6 knots overall (that is, night and day sailing) could be achieved, with a speed of 2 to 2½ knots in unfavorable conditions.

Phoenicians and Carthaginians The classical Greeks attributed a major part in the opening up of the Medi-
terranean to the Phoenicians, inhabitants of a thin strip of territory including the cities of Tyre, Sidon, and Berytus (Beirut) along the coast of Lebanon. Their seafaring activities are also referred to in the Old Testament. Much of the information in our sources is unreliable, and the speculations of the eighteenth and nineteenth centuries about the extent of Phoenician voyaging and trade are now discarded. Hard archaeological evidence of the Phoenicians' presence in the western Mediterranean does not date before the ninth century B.C. at the earliest. The traditional dates of their foundations of cities at Gadir (Cádiz; 1110 B.C.) and Utica (1101) are too early, and they are more likely to be around the more reliable date for the founding of Carthage (814 B.C.). The eighth and seventh centuries B.C. appear to have been the most vigorous period of Phoenician voyages. These involved the discovery and opening up of two routes from Phoenicia to Spain, one following the coast of North Africa and the other going by way of Sicily, Sardinia, and the Balearic Islands. A number of anchorages and watering places along both routes, became the sites of small permanent settlements, among them Sousse, Tangier, Motya (San Pantaleo), Palermo, and Cagliari. There can be little doubt that the objective of the Phoenicians, the most vigorous traders in antiquity, was primarily the acquisition of silver and tin from the Iberian Peninsula. The prime market was at Gadir, the first, and for long the only, establishment of a Mediterranean people on the Atlantic coast of Europe. Some small settlements were also established on the Atlantic coast of Morocco.

Greek exploration before Alexander The voyages of the Phoenicians in the west and their earliest colonies preceded only briefly the much more significant and better-known colonial movement of the Greeks. A number of cities, particularly Corinth, Megara, Eretria, Phocaea, and Miletus, were concerned in this movement. The normal practice was that the emigrants founded new cities which in most cases soon became autonomous, though reproducing the political and cultural life of the cities of Greece and thus extending the effective area of Greek civilization. In the western Mediterranean the most important areas of colonization were Sicily (colonies included Syracuse, Naxos, and Agrigentum) and Italy as far north as the Bay of Naples (for example, Cumae, Sybaris, and Tarentum).

Farther west still, the most enterprising colonists were the Phocaeans, whose chief foundation was Massilia (Marseille) and who also founded other cities on the coasts of southern France and northeastern Spain. It was probably Phocaeans who provided most of the scanty information about the Atlantic which got through the Phoenician blockade, including the earliest knowledge of the Armorican Peninsula (Brittany) and the British Isles. A quite separate area with important results for geographical knowledge was the coast of the Black Sea, in which the chief colonizing power was Miletus. In addition to colonies on the southern coast at Trapezus and Sinope, sites in the Crimea also were settled. The discovery of suitable sites in all areas no doubt generally resulted from knowledge acquired from trading voyages as the Greeks followed the Phoenicians in searching for sources of primary products of various sorts, particularly metals. Some of the earliest colonies in Italy (late eighth century B.C.) are connected with the sea route to the Etruscan cities of central Italy. No names of the actual discoverers of sites are known, but there is evidence that the religious center at Delphi was a place where information about areas of potential settlement circulated. So intensive was the activity of Phoenician and Greek settlers in the eighth and seventh centuries B.C. that almost the entire coasts of the Mediterranean and Black Seas were fully known and settled when the political or military weakness of the indigenous inhabitants made settlement possible. Even where settlement was not possible, as in Syria, Egypt, Etruria, and the Dalmatian coast, more intensive patterns of trade made for better knowledge.

During the sixth century B.C. the Greek cities of Ionia saw the beginnings of the great intellectual advances of Greek civilization in philosophy and science. Among other things this development produced the first-known attempts, however speculative, to give rational explanations of natural phenomena and also to systematize and record the accumulating knowledge of the *oikoumenē* (the inhabited world). This was traditionally viewed as a disk surrounded by a flowing river (*not* a sea) named Oceanus. The sun and most stars rose from and set in this Ocean Stream. This notion was the Homeric concept and long continued to have adherents. Even when the notion of the earth as a globe became accepted and knowledge of the inhabited world grew to include the landmass of Europe and Asia, the idea of the Ocean Stream continued, though existing seas could be regarded as inlets from it. Anaximander of Miletus (ca. 610–540 B.C.) was later believed to have been the first man to draw a map of the earth's surface as he understood it; he is also credited with the invention (more

A Greek merchantman from the period (ca. 500 B.C.) when the Greeks saw the world as a disk surrounded by a flowing river called Oceanus.

probably introduced to the Greeks from Babylonia) of the gnomon, or primitive sundial, of importance afterward to the Greeks in determining latitudes. The notion of the earth as a sphere became current in the late fifth century B.C. The first systematic description of the world appears to have been made by Hecataeus of Miletus between 520 and 500 B.C. It has not survived, but from later writers we have some knowledge of its contents. It was based on a description of the coasts of the Mediterranean and adjoining seas and hence had the form of a PERIPLUS. Naturally most of the information is of Greek colonies, but Hecataeus included information about their neighbors and also notices of economic character, on mineral resources, for example. He appears to have had no knowledge of the west beyond the Strait of Gibraltar. In the east he included notices of the Caucasus and the Caspian Sea and, more significantly, of India and the Indus; these names first appeared in a European language in his work. Their inclusion reflects the political change which occurred in his lifetime: the incorporation of the Ionian cities into the Persian empire, which at the same time under Darius I had extended its control to the Indus Valley (which was all that India meant to Hecataeus and his successors for some two centuries). Darius appears to have recognized that his new Greek subjects, though few in number, were energetic and enterprising, and he employed one, Scylax of Caryanda, to sail down the Indus and round to the Red Sea. It is possible that some knowledge of this voyage was available to Hecataeus, who himself visited Egypt and ascended the Nile as far as Thebes, where he talked with the priests. Hecataeus was the first of countless travelers in antiquity to be fascinated by Egypt and the problem of the source of the Nile, which he believed derived from the waters of the Ocean Stream.

A much clearer concept of the world as it appeared to an educated Greek of the next century can be derived from the *History* of HERODOTUS OF HALICARNASSUS, published before about 420 B.C. Herodotus included many digressions of a geographical character; he was especially interested in ethnography, an interest common to many Greek writers. He frequently criticized Hecataeus but made use of his work, and he also had a lot of new material based on travel in southern Italy, Babylonia, Egypt, and the Black Sea area. He no longer held to the view that the landmass was circular and believed that its east-west dimension was much larger than its north-south. In practice he included Africa as an extension of Asia. The division between Europe and Asia lay along the Phasis (Rioni) River. To the north of this line Europe extended indefinitely, and Herodotus could not say whether it ended in a sea or not. As for Asia as we understand it, this was known as far as the Indus but was uninhabited and unknown beyond it. From the point of view of subsequent thinking, a most interesting belief in Herodotus is that Africa could be and in fact had been circumnavigated. His story is that Pharaoh Necho II (r. ca. 610–594 B.C.) sent Phoenician mariners to sail down the Red Sea, circumnavigate Africa, and return by the Strait of Gibraltar. They took more than 2 years on the journey, having halted twice to sow and reap a crop of wheat. Herodotus believed the story in spite of a circumstance which he found incredible, that while sailing round Africa the sailors had the sun on their right hand. He adds that the Carthaginians also believed that Africa could be circumnavigated. His story was variously viewed in antiquity, as it has been in modern times. It can be said to be not impossible but highly improbable; even the report about the sun, which obviously looks like proof that the voyage did occur, could have been invented on the basis of contemporary astronomical knowledge and observations.

Herodotus also included a report of another, certainly unsuccessful attempt in the opposite direction. Between 485 and 465 B.C. a Persian prince was ordered to sail through the Strait of Gibraltar and round Africa. After a voyage of many months with no end in view, he returned. According to his report, at the point where he turned back, the inhabitants were of small stature, peaceful, dwelling in towns and possessing cattle, which on the whole must indicate some area of equatorial West Africa. These attempts did not have successors known to us. If Necho's Phoenicians achieved their objective, the vast distance and lack of useful commerce would have inhibited others from following them. It must not be forgotten that the economic demands which encouraged the search for a route to India in the Renaissance did not exist for classical antiquity, since contact between the Mediterranean world and India steadily became easier, not more difficult. From the geographical point of view, those who rejected Herodotus's story came to believe that along the east coast of Africa the land turned east to join some distant part of Asia.

Herodotus also tells of a gold trade on the west coast of Africa south of the Sahara, conducted between the Carthaginians and the indigenous inhabitants by dumb barter, a method of trade found in the same area in the Muslim period (thirteenth century A.D.). This trade is often associated with the voyage down the west coast of Africa by the Carthaginian HANNO in the fifth century B.C. What purports to be a Greek version of his report survived but has been subject to serious criticism and presents many problems of interpretation. It makes no mention of trade as an objective but indicates the foundation of new colonies and the strengthening of existing ones on the Moroccan coast. It seems that the voyage certainly passed Cape Verde by some distance. The report contained some stories of the ferocity of the indigenous inhabitants, and some of its features were perhaps designed to intimidate possible Greek ventures into an area which the Carthaginians wished to keep for themselves. It was this monopoly which prevented Herodotus from improving much on the ignorance of

Hecataeus about Western Europe. On the other hand, the Greek colonies of the Black Sea were no doubt the source of much-improved knowledge of some of the features of southern Russia including the major rivers Dniester, Bug, Dnieper, and Don; Herodotus grossly exaggerated the size of the Sea of Azov but knew that the Caspian was a vast lake. He had considerable information on the way of life of many of the tribes, above all the Scythians. Farther east still, there are hints of sources of gold presumably in the Ural or Altai Mountains, but though there are travelers' tales about the tribes, the geography is vague in the extreme.

In the century separating Herodotus from ALEXANDER THE GREAT, reference may be made to a lost work on India by Ctesias, a Greek physician at the Persian court, written after 398 B.C. From many later references, both critical and credulous, it can be seen that India already had the reputation of a land of marvels, since Ctesias's book was a farrago of such fables set down with unblushing confidence. Quite different is the surviving report (the *Anabasis*) of Xenophon, leader of an army of Greek mercenaries in the pay of Cyrus, a claimant to the throne of Persia. Xenophon successfully extricated the army after Cyrus's defeat and death at Cunaxa (on the Euphrates north of Babylon) and marched it through unknown and hostile territory up the Tigris River and across Armenia to Trapezus on the Black Sea. His report includes details of distances from point to point and provides the most detailed account of such a march surviving from antiquity. From later in the fourth century we have an extant guide to the coasts and harbors of the Mediterranean and Black Seas.

Alexander and his successors The conquest of the Persian empire between 336 and 323 B.C. by Alexander the Great introduced a new epoch in both political and cultural history throughout the East lasting for many centuries. The whole area from Mesopotamia to the Indus Valley was now open for detailed examination, whereas previously it had been little more than names. Alexander himself, for whom military and political considerations were paramount, nevertheless had elements of an explorer's interests and on occasion allowed these priority. On his march he traveled along the southern coast of the Caspian, crossed the Hindu Kush in each direction, proceeded by way of Bactra (Balkh) and Maracanda (Samarkand) to the Jaxartes (Syr Darya), and founded a city at Khodzhent (Leninabad). In 327 he entered India by an uncertain route (but not the Khyber Pass), crossed the Indus, and reached the Hyphasis (Beas) River, where his troops mutinied and refused to go on. Although informed about the Ganges, he probably thought it was relatively close. Returning, he sailed down the Indus, which he intended to be the boundary of his empire. He returned to Mesopotamia through Gedrosia (Baluchistan), while ordering his fleet under NEARCHUS to explore the coast from the Indus Delta to the head of the Persian Gulf. After his death in 323, a plan to have a fleet circumnavigate the Caspian and another sail round Arabia was abandoned. A number of accounts of his conquest written within a generation of his death are lost, but they formed the basis for much future work on the geography of the East.

Although Alexander's empire soon split into several kingdoms, Greco-Macedonian contacts with India survived and for a time increased. On several occasions between 302 and 290 B.C. a Greek named Megasthenes went as ambassador from Seleucus I to the Indian king Chandragupta, founder of the powerful Mauryan dynasty in north India, at his capital, Palibothra (Pataliputra; now Patna), on the Ganges. Megasthenes's account of India, which included information on its geography, political and religious institutions, caste system, fauna, and flora, is lost but was much used by later writers. While not excluding fables entirely and prone to exaggerations, it was clearly of good quality and largely instrumental in determining the favorable view of India held by most of antiquity. Megasthenes describes the route from the Indus to the Ganges across the Sutlej and Jumna Rivers, but his distances appear to have been garbled in transmission. Probably the first Greek ever to reach the Ganges, he heard of its source in the "Indian Caucasus" (Himalayas) but knew nothing of its lower reaches. He provided the new information that India was larger from north to south than from west to east,

though the figures he gave (about 2300 miles by 1800; 3701 kilometers by 2897) are in excess of reality. He was the first to obtain any information about the island of Taprobane (Ceylon) but believed it was 7 days' sail from the mainland. His account of the natural products of India (for example, rice and cotton) was generally accurate, but it should be stressed that there was no question as yet of commercial interest of any size. In the generations following Megasthenes, Greco-Macedonian control of areas east of Mesopotamia gradually weakened so that further good information on India had to wait until the establishment of the Roman Empire and the development of more active commerce between the Mediterranean world and India via Egypt.

One fragment of Alexander's empire was Egypt, where a dynasty was founded by one of his generals, Ptolemy. Under Ptolemy İI Philadelphus (r. 285–246 B.C.), one of the few known state enterprises in exploration in antiquity took place. This involved the exploration of the western coast of the Red Sea as far as Ras Asir (Cape Guardafui) and the establishment of a number of anchorages and watering places. The most important were Berenice and Arsinoe, from which merchandise was carried overland to Coptos and then down the Nile to Alexandria. The original purpose of the enterprise was to organize the capture of elephants in the interior of Ethiopia, these animals being

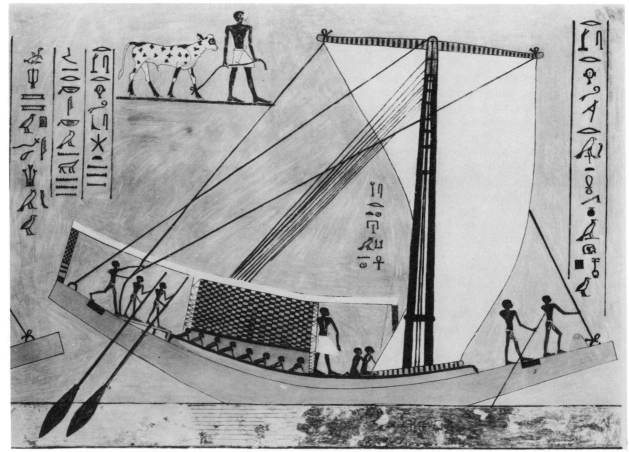

An Egyptian ship. Although the Egyptians themselves did little exploring, their country was a source of curiosity to outsiders long before the third century B.C., when it was the scene of a rare state-sponsored expedition of discovery. [Library of Congress]

considered essential for significant armies after experience of them in India. From the Bab el Mandeb on, the Somali coast was of great interest as producing myrrh and frankincense and so much cinnamon that the whole stretch was called the Cinnamon Land. The opposite shore (Yemen) was also a source of spices and incense. It appears that the inhabitants, known as Sabaeans, were the middlemen in trade between India and the Ptolemaic kingdom until the latter became part of the Roman Empire. Some further knowledge about the Nile naturally accrued, particularly when the native kingdom of Meroe became virtually a dependent. The Alexandrians became well acquainted with the great bend of the river, the Second Cataract (referred to as the Great Cataract), and the junction of the Blue and White Niles, but they had nothing further on its sources. Among those who made Alexandria a center of learning in many spheres was the geographer Eratosthenes (ca. 275–194 B.C.). Chiefly known for his mathematical approach, he calculated the circumference of the earth to 25,000 miles (40,233 kilometers) and was apparently the first to attempt to give a list (now lost) of distances and directions covering the known world. Those who believed in the possibility of circumnavigating Africa made much of the attempt of a certain Eudoxus, a Greek from Cyzicus. About 117 B.C. he made two voyages direct from Egypt to India, clearly still a rarity at this time. The first was at royal command and had a shipwrecked Indian as guide. On returning from the second, Eudoxus was forced to put in on the East African coast, where he came upon the prow of a wreck, of a type which he was told at Alexandria was in use at Cádiz. He took this as evidence that Africa could be circumnavigated and made two attempts from Cádiz. The first took him only a short distance down the Moroccan coast, and on the second he and his ship disappeared. Clearly the evidence on which he based his attempt was worthless, but it is interesting that another reason for it was his resentment at control over trade exercised by the Ptolemaic government of Egypt. This is the only such reference we have from antiquity, and most Indian trade with the Mediterranean continued to come through Egypt without opposition.

General ignorance about Western Europe obtained until the establishment of the Roman Empire with one exception, provided by PYTHEAS. His voyage between 330 and 300 B.C. through the Strait of Gibraltar, along the Atlantic coast of Europe to the English Channel, circumnavigating Britain and sailing along the coast of the North Sea as far as the Elbe, was one of the most daring known to us from antiquity and also the longest in distance covered. Pytheas's report has not survived, but there are references in later writers, often unjustly critical, sufficient to show that his general reliability and observations were within the margins of error common in antiquity. He included ethnographic material on the tribes he met and a well-known reference to tin mining in Cornwall.

The most controversial item was a reference to an "island of Thule," said to be some 6 days' sail from the most northerly point of Britain but only 1 day's sail from a "frozen sea." The land apparently had inhabitants with a lowly standard of life who grew crops of millet and used honey to make mead. It is impossible to be certain what Pytheas said in detail about Thule (and he did not visit it himself); some authors rejected the story because of the belief that life in the latitudes in which Pytheas obviously placed it was impossible. Most modern scholars favor a hearsay report about southern Norway. The name of Thule, in spite of doubts, became established in the concepts of antiquity as the most distant point of the inhabited world in the northwest.

Pytheas had no immediate successors, since Carthage still controlled the Gibraltar passage, and in any case a satisfactory trade route with the area of the English Channel is specifically stated by him to have run across Gaul. The situation changed with the destruction of Carthage by Rome (146 B.C.). The Greek historian Polybius, a friend of Scipio Africanus the Roman general, was present at its fall and was afterward entrusted with a fleet to explore the Atlantic coast of Africa. He also traveled widely in Spain and Gaul expressly to investigate their geography as a preparation for his historical work. The geographical portion of this work has not survived, but references show that he did not know much about northern Europe, partly because he disbelieved Pytheas. He had a fair knowledge of the Alps, and followed Hannibal's route across them, but not of areas farther north and east. In the following century a leading Greek philosopher named Posidonius, a man of extremely wide interests including geography and natural science, profited from his friendship with leading Roman statesmen to travel widely in the western Mediterranean. He spent some time at Cádiz, where from his own observations and information from the inhabitants he worked out, apparently the first to do so, the nature of the tides and their association with phases of the moon.

Roman exploration Julius Caesar's conquest of Gaul (59–50 B.C.) brought Roman control to the North Sea and the west bank of the Rhine, while under Augustus (emperor, 31 B.C.–A.D. 14) the empire was pushed to the Danube throughout its length, and Roman control extended to the Euphrates and over Egypt and North Africa. With the addition of Britain (whose conquest began in A.D. 43) and Dacia (part of modern Romania, conquered in A.D. 106) the empire remained roughly the same size for some four centuries. It is remarkable that knowledge of areas beyond the limit of Roman political control showed only a negligible increase throughout this period. In northern Europe we hear of a Roman who traveled from the Danube at Carnuntum (Petronell, near Vienna) to the Baltic in the time of the emperor Nero in search of amber, but no fresh geographical information reached our sources. Archaeological evidence shows that trading contacts existed with all parts of Germany and Eastern Europe at various times throughout the first four centuries A.D., but again this left hardly a trace in geographical literature. In North Africa, punitive or semiexploratory military expeditions brought the Romans to Garama (Jarmah; Germa) and Cydamus (Ghudāmis, Ghadames), and before the mid-second century a certain Julius Maternus certainly crossed the Sahara from Garama. His journey took 4 months and ended in a district called Agisymba, where there were rhinoceroses; this is generally believed to be Chad. This exploit also had no visible economic or scientific result. Exceptionally, the emperor Nero (r. A.D. 54–68) sent a small exploratory expedition from Egypt specifically to try to find the source of the Nile. The expedition certainly reached the sudd, the great marshes on the White Nile, a point not reached again by Europeans until the nineteenth century.

To the east of the Euphrates the empire of the Parthians constituted an obstacle to knowledge of the Far East, but over the centuries a certain amount of information was gathered about a people known as the Seres. These were the inhabitants of northern China from which silk (Latin, *serica*) was obtained, a luxury whose manufacture was a source of mystery but which was eagerly sought from the time of Augustus on. One trade route was across Central Asia, but it was known or deduced that the land of the Seres also lay beyond India, since another route went through modern Afghanistan and ran down the Indus Valley, and a third crossed the Himalayas to Pataliputra and went across India and also to ports visited by Greco-Roman traders. Perhaps in the early second century a certain Maes, a Macedonian also known as Titianus, compiled an itinerary from the Euphrates to a city of the Seres called Sera, on information from his agents in the silk trade. This followed the relatively well-known route as far as Mary (Merv) and Balkh, then on to a market at Stone Tower (Tashkurghan), and finally into Honan. The route through Parthia is held to have been less used than those through India, and Chinese annals record that the Parthians prevented direct contact between China and the Roman Empire.

The most notable area where trading interests led to further voyaging and additional knowledge was the lower part of the Red Sea, the east coast of Africa, and the Indian Ocean. During Augustus's reign, Aelius Gallus led an expedition down the east coast of the Red Sea as far as the boundary of Yemen, but the aim, to extend Roman domination over the Sabaeans, who had amassed great wealth as intermediaries in trade between Egypt and India, failed. However, within the next half century a detailed knowledge of the coast of Africa from Ras Asir as far as the region of Zanzibar, or some 1200 miles (1931 kilometers) had been obtained. The voyagers who opened up the area are anonymous, but the information was recorded by the author of the so-called *Periplus of the Erythrean Sea*, who no doubt had firsthand knowledge himself. He also recorded, as did PLINY, the discovery, probably about 50 years earlier, by a pilot named Hippalus, of the operation of the monsoons in the Indian Ocean. This knowledge transformed the trade routes from Egypt to the East. Traders no longer had to rely on the Sabaeans as middlemen or to follow the hostile Arabian and Persian coastline but could sail direct from the mouth of the Red Sea to the Indus Delta, Broach, or ports in south India. In recent times archaeological evidence from Arikamedu, near Pondicherry, has spectacularly demonstrated the extent of trade between the Roman Empire and India in the first century A.D. The *Periplus* also has some information about Ceylon, but like that in all ancient authors it is extremely inaccurate. This is true even of information derived from the only known voyage to the island by an inhabitant of the Roman Empire. Between A.D. 41 and 54 a Roman collector of taxes in the Red Sea was driven by the north wind from the Arabian coast to Ceylon. He returned with an embassy to Rome, but Pliny's information derived from this episode is highly romanticized. Beyond the region of Pondicherry the *Periplus* evidently relies more on hearsay, though it has some indication of the Malaysian Peninsula, thought of as an island.

The geographical authors of the Roman period tended to follow in the steps of their predecessors and to ignore information provided by Roman conquests even in areas included within the empire; this applies even to leading figures like STRABO and Pliny. The most important of them from the historical point of view was PTOLEMY. His *Geography*, written between about A.D. 127 and 147, included almost all the knowledge which had accumulated up to that time and, still more important, provided his estimates of the latitude and longitude of towns and natural features from which a coherent map of the known world could be drawn. The translation of this work into Latin in A.D. 1410 was of profound significance in forming the geographical conceptions of the early Renaissance at the beginning of the era of modern exploration.

Purposes and achievements Most ancient exploration took place in connection with the search for new sources of raw materials, particularly metals for the Greek, and later but to a lesser extent, the Roman world. This led first to the western Mediterranean; but when this area was incorporated into the Roman Empire, the resources now available within it appear to have been adequate, and no economic imperative for further searches existed. Although exports of goods from the Mediterranean world into central, northern, and eastern Europe tended to grow throughout ancient times, it does not seem that the converse was true. The Romans had no interest in areas beyond their northern frontiers except in a military sense. Similarly, no commercial needs led to extensive exploration in the interior of Africa. In the East the situation was somewhat different. Starting from the political circumstance that part of the Greek world was for a time within the orbit of the Persian empire, which extended as far as the Indus, exotic products, particularly spices, pepper, and later silk, gradually came to be demanded in the Mediterranean world. Trade between the Mediterranean and India was at its height in the first two centuries A.D. Nevertheless, such trade was largely in luxuries rather than necessities, and the Roman government had no concern in promoting it; rather, important circles in Rome tended to frown on it. In view of these facts, it is not surprising that the Phoenicians are the only major exception to the rule that ancient states were not concerned to promote major exploratory voyages.

Traders in most of antiquity were not of high social status. This circumstance affected not only their influence on governments but the distribution of knowledge of their discoveries. The greater part of ancient geographical literature comes from the hands of men from literary and philosophical circles who were of higher social standing. Though interested in the geographical results of trading voyages, they were rarely involved themselves. Those with philosophical interests were also somewhat prone to geographical theorizing on the basis of scanty observation. On the other hand, most had a lively interest in describing the way of life of distant peoples. The concept of exploration for its own sake did exist in the case of search for, or at least inquiry about, the sources of the Nile, but it never became general. Furthermore, because the age did not know the printing press, the circulation of new knowledge was slow and haphazard. Within these limitations the achievement of antiquity in discovering and recording the knowledge of

such a substantial portion of the northern temperate zone was a considerable one and of great importance when the geographical authors began to be studied again at the end of the Middle Ages.

BIBLIOGRAPHY: E. H. Bunbury, *A History of Ancient Geography*, London, 1883; M. Cary and E. H. Warmington, *The Ancient Explorers*, London, 1929; Lionel Casson, *Ships and Seamanship in the Ancient World*, Princeton, N.J., 1971; W. W. Tarn, *Alexander the Great*, 2 vols., Cambridge, England, 1948; J. O. Thomson, *History of Ancient Geography*, Cambridge, England, 1948; B. H. Warmington, *Carthage*, New York, 1960; R. E. M. Wheeler, *Rome beyond the Imperial Frontiers*, London, 1954.

B. H. Warmington

Andreyev, Stepan *(fl. mid-eighteenth century)* Russian army officer, explorer of the East Siberian Sea, and discoverer of the Novosibirskiye Ostrova (New Siberian Islands). Sent out by F. Kh. Plenisner, commandant of the Anadyr fort, he explored the Medvezhi Ostrova (Bear Islands) in March-April 1763. From one of the islands he saw a blue-black patch to the north. Plenisner decided that Andreyev had seen a large new landmass and sent him there again in 1764. Andreyev and his companion sighted the island but saw sledge tracks of a large party of "unknown persons" and decided to return. "Andreyev Land" was later sought north and northeast of the Medvezhi Ostrova, where there is no land, instead of northwest. In 1951 the Soviet polar geographers Konstantin Sergeyevich BADIGIN and N. N. Zubov, using archival sources, showed that the land seen by Andreyev in 1764 was actually Ostrov Novaya Sibir, part of the Novosibirskiye group, rediscovered in 1806.

Richard A. Pierce

Antarctica

The southernmost continent surrounding the South Pole, Antarctica was the last of the continents to be discovered and explored. It is some 5,000,000 square miles (12,950,000 square kilometers) in size, mostly covered by ice.

As late as 1800 Antarctica was undiscovered. Its existence had been suggested, however, by the ancient Greeks, who postulated that a frozen landmass must lie beyond the tropic zone to their south to balance the frozen zone of the Arctic.

Discovery and early exploration Discovery came in the early 1800s by sealers from England and the Connecticut sealing ports. During the eighteenth century men had sailed close to Antarctica but had not seen the continent. In 1738–1739 J.-B.-C. Bouvet de Lozier led a French expedition which sailed 1000 miles (1609 kilometers) along the great Antarctic ice pack without breaking through. He reported huge tabular icebergs which could only have been produced by continental ice fields beyond the pack ice. Thirty years later another Frenchman, Yves-Joseph de Kerguélen-

Trémarec, sailed south and in 1772 discovered land. A year later he returned to realize that his discovery was a cluster of islands covered by scrub vegetation. Also in 1772 England's Capt. James COOK sailed along the pack ice and circumnavigated the continent. When he compared his chart with those of Bouvet and Kerguélen, he realized that if an Antarctic continent existed, it was south of the pack ice, which he could not penetrate.

Conflicting claims of discovery exist, usually involving Americans, British, and Russians. American claims rest with Nathaniel Palmer of Capt. Benjamin Pendleton's sealing fleet out of Stonington, Connecticut, who sailed along the Antarctic Peninsula in November 1820. The British claim rests on the voyage of Edward Bransfield, who sailed along the Antarctic Peninsula in January 1820, repeating the voyage of a cargo ship which had been blown off course.

In 1819 the Russians sent Fabian von BELLINGSHAUSEN to the Antarctic to seek a southern continent. Between January 1820 and January 1821 he repeated

Cook's circumnavigation but within the pack ice. He probably sighted land on several occasions; his log reported frozen-in icebergs which probably were ice-covered mountains. Bellingshausen was a careful, cautious explorer who probably realized that he had discovered a continent.

During the 1821–1822 season about 100 British and American sealers swarmed to the waters bordering the Antarctic Peninsula to slaughter seals. Voyages of the next several years sought new breeding grounds to continue to kill. James Weddell, a Scot, sailed east of the Antarctic Peninsula and reached 74°15'S before turning back. He never reached the pack ice and turned back only because of the lateness of the season.

The sealers did not always return successfully. A London whaling and sealing firm, Enderby Brothers, sent many ships to the Antarctic in the early nineteenth century. They lost several crews to scurvy and had several ships destroyed by heavy ice and severe storms. These disasters contributed to the realization that the return in furs was not worth the losses of men and ships, and the number of sealing voyages declined.

The coming of modern science was the next impetus to Antarctic exploration, an impetus which would continue into the present. The German Alexander von Humboldt was successful in establishing magnetic observatories on a continuous line from Sitka, Alaska, across China and Russia into Europe. His scientific discoveries enabled Karl Friedrich Gauss to devise a formula relating the three elements of earth magnetic force to any point on earth. This led to the realization that a South Magnetic Pole must exist opposite the North Magnetic Pole. To prove this theory and locate the South Magnetic Pole, Britain, France, and the United States ordered expeditions to Antarctic waters in the mid-1800s.

Antarctica, with its penguins, mountains, and ice, has changed little since the continent's first visitors viewed it around 1820. [U.S. Navy]

The French were the first to arrive. Jules DUMONT D'URVILLE reached land nearest the South Magnetic Pole on January 20, 1840, and landed a party to collect rock specimens at Pointe Géologie. The pole lay inland, and Dumont d'Urville was frustrated in his attempt to sail over it. A week later his ships met up with the *Porpoise,* a brig of Lieut. Charles Wilkes's squadron of American ships.

The United States government had an interest in the southern oceans dating from the first sealers' reports. The furs were an important part of American commerce in the early 1800s. There was much pressure in the 1820s to improve the charting of Antarctic waters after uncharted reefs had taken their share of American lives. Congress finally authorized an official expedition in 1836, but it was not until 1838 that Charles Wilkes was able to lead the U.S. Exploring Expedition southward. The Antarctic was reached in January 1840, and for weeks Wilkes sailed along the coast in a charting voyage complicated by severe weather and icebergs. One of his four ships was lost with all hands. *See also* WILKES EXPEDITION.

The British expedition under Capt. James Clark Ross sailed in 1839 in two ice-reinforced ships designed for penetrating the pack ice directly. Ross plunged into the ice at the International Date Line, breaking through into open water 4 days later. An iceless voyage 500 miles (805 kilometers) farther south brought Ross to an immense mountain range which developed into a coastline. He named this Victoria Land and sent boats ashore to claim the land for Great Britain. Continuing to sail southward, Ross was amazed to discover an active volcano surrounded by huge snow and ice fields blocking his path. He named the volcano and its dormant sister Erebus and Terror and called a nearby embayment McMurdo Bay (now McMurdo Sound). His route farther south was blocked by a barrier of ice and snow now named the Ross Ice Shelf. The party sailed along its front for hundreds of miles to the east without interruption. Pack ice and the lateness of the season caused Ross to discontinue his explorations and winter in Tasmania. He returned for a second season for further discovery but was not followed by other explorers until the end of the century.

Late nineteenth and early twentieth centuries The impetus for the resumption of Antarctic exploration in the twentieth century was the Sixth International Geophysical Congress, held in London in 1895. The conferees concluded that the exploration of Antarctica was the greatest piece of exploration still to be undertaken. They urged the world's scientific societies to promote expeditions. During the next 8 years Belgium, Great Britain, Sweden, Germany, and France sent expeditions southward. In 1897 the Belgian expedition under Adrien de Gerlache sailed in a converted sealer named *Belgica* to explore the west coast of the Antarctic Peninsula. The ship became trapped in the ice, and the entire crew of eighteen was forced to drift

*Wilkes's flagship,
the USS Vincennes,
in Disappointment
Bay. [U.S. Navy]*

with the pack. Scurvy set in, and only the insistence of the surgeon, Dr. Frederick A. COOK, that they eat seal meat saved the captain and the crew. When summer arrived, there was no assurance that they would escape the ice. Through ice 7 feet (2 meters) thick they cut a canal more than 2000 feet (610 meters) long and were within 100 feet (30 meters) of the ship when changing winds closed the ice tight. The winds later shifted, and *Belgica* was able to escape.

While the Belgians were returning home in 1899, expeditions were being prepared in Britain, Sweden, and Germany. The German expedition under Professor Dr. Erich von Drygalski explored along 90°E. Its members also became caught in the ice and were forced to winter. They escaped by laying a trail of ashes on the ice which attracted sufficient radiation to melt a trench and cause the ice to separate. The Swedish expedition, led by Nils Otto Gustaf Nordenskjöld, included a staff of nine scientists. Nordenskjöld and his companions were landed on Snow Hill Island off the east coast of the Antarctic Peninsula with plans to spend one winter exploring and taking scientific observations in that area. When their ship, the *Antarctic*, failed to return the following summer, they concluded that ice conditions had prevented its arrival; they prepared for a second winter by killing large numbers of seals and penguins for food and fuel. During the second summer Nordenskjöld and one companion sledged to the peninsula. From a high

point they saw three skin-covered creatures walking toward them. Soon they discovered that the skin-covered men were also members of the Swedish expedition, landed at Hope Bay at the tip of the peninsula the previous summer when the *Antarctic* tried to reach Nordenskjöld's camp. It never returned, and the unprepared men had to winter as best they could. They built a shelter of rocks, roofing it with their tent. They made clothing, shoes, and fishing lines from the hundreds of seals and penguins they killed and caught fish for food. They were able to collect large numbers of fossils despite their privation.

The *Antarctic*, meanwhile, had been caught in the ice early in 1903 and, despite heroic efforts to save it, was crushed by the pressure and sank. The twenty men on board managed to save the ship's boats and eleven boatloads of provisions. For 16 days they lived on the ice floes until favorable winds let them reach Paulet Island. To survive the winter they killed between 3000 and 4000 penguins. As soon as summer arrived, Capt. C. A. Larsen set out in an open boat to recover the men at Hope Bay. On his arrival he found the fossils and a note explaining that the three men had set out for Snow Hill Island. Larsen continued overland to Snow Hill Island and arrived simultaneously with an Argentine ship which had been sent to search for the Nordenskjöld expedition.

A British expedition in 1899 had landed at Cape Adare, south of New Zealand, and wintered on the coast at a site first visited by the Norwegians under Henrik Bull in 1895. The next British expedition sent to the Antarctic was a national expedition, sponsored by the ROYAL GEOGRAPHICAL SOCIETY and the Royal Society, and financed by the government. Robert Falcon SCOTT was the leader of this expedition, which sailed in the specially built ship *Discovery*. Scott arrived off the Ross Ice Shelf in late 1901 and continued Ross's attempt to sail along the barrier to its end. Rather than finding a route farther south, Scott discovered a high ice-covered land which he named Edward VII Land (now Edward VII Peninsula). Turning to the west, they moored at an inlet so that Scott could go aloft in a captive balloon to see what lay to the south. The ice shelf stretched on as far as the eye could see.

Scott selected Ross Island as his winter base and built his huts in the shadow of Mount Erebus. In the spring Scott, Ernest Henry SHACKLETON, and Dr. Edward A. Wilson used dog sledges to travel to the south on the ice shelf parallel to the mountains for 7 weeks. They reached Shackleton Inlet before they turned back, but the ice shelf and the high mountains continued as far as they could see. On the return trip all three men suffered from scurvy and from lack of food, and Shackleton almost died. When the last of their dogs died, they were reduced to using their tent as a sail to take advantage of winds from the south. During the southward journey a second expedition party under Lieut. Albert Armitage penetrated the mountains to the west by climbing a glacier to the interior, now named the Ferrar Glacier. As they climbed, the ice grew to cover the mountains. On January 3, 1903, they reached the great interior plateau of Antarctica. They eventually reached an elevation of 9000 feet (2743 meters) before they turned back. The next season Scott led a party up the same glacier. At the summit he sent the supporting party back and with two husky seamen, Edgar Evans and William Lashly, continued on into the interior for 200 miles (322 kilometers). The ice-covered scenery never changed. On their return they left the Ferrar Glacier briefly to examine a parallel valley. They were amazed to discover that the glacier abruptly ended and the ice-free valley continued onward. They explored it and found evidence of previous glaciation, running water coming out of the warm sands of the valley floor, a carcass of a seal, but absolutely no life. They had discovered the dry valleys of Antarctica.

Attainment of the South Pole When Scott returned to England, the attempts to reach the North Pole were under way. This turned men's minds to reaching the less accessible South Pole. In 1907 Shackleton, recovered from the 1901–1904 expedition, returned to Antarctica in an attempt to reach both the geographical South Pole and the South Magnetic Pole, believed to lie a few hundred miles inland from the Victoria Land coast. The journey of 1700 miles (2736 kilometers) to the geographic pole and back to base would be supported by fourteen Manchurian ponies, known to be a reliable means of transportation in Siberia. When Shackleton and three men began the South Pole trek, only four ponies were left, the other ten having died. They followed the mountains south until they gradually curved to the east. A gap was discovered in the mountains filled by the great Beardmore Glacier, which averaged 15 miles (24 kilometers) wide and 100 miles (161 kilometers) long. In the 2 weeks that it took them to climb the Beardmore, they discovered fossil plants in the boulders and petrified wood and coal seams laid down in sandstone. At the top of the glacier they set a direct course south across the Polar Plateau for the pole, some 325 miles (523 kilometers) farther. On January 9, 1909, they reached a point only 97 miles (156 kilometers) from the pole and decided to turn back. Shackleton realized that they did not have the energy or the food to continue and halted the march. The next 7 weeks were a race against starvation as they walked north from cache to cache. Finally, they reached a well-stocked depot near McMurdo Sound and were safe. In the meantime T. W. Edgeworth David, Douglas Mawson, and Dr. Alistair Forbes Mackay, three other members of Shackleton's expedition, were attempting to reach the South Magnetic Pole. In October 1908 they started out with a ski-wheel automobile. The car lasted only 2 miles (3 kilometers) before it stuck in the snow; they continued on foot on the sea ice attached to the south Victoria Land coast for 200 miles (322 kilometers), then climbed the Larsen Glacier to the inland plateau. For 3 weeks they crossed the plateau until on January 16, 1909, the dip needle of their magnetic compass indicated that they had reached their goal. Returning to the coast, they were picked up by the expedition relief ship, *Nimrod*, and on March 4, 1909, left for England.

Within 6 months of Shackleton's news reaching England, Scott announced that he was returning to Antarctica to attempt the journey to the South Pole. He planned a scientific expedition, setting one base in McMurdo Sound and a second on the east end of the Ross Ice Shelf. Scott called at Melbourne en route to the south and received a message that Roald AMUNDSEN, the Norwegian explorer, was also planning to attempt the South Pole. After establishing the main expedition base at Ross Island, *Terra Nova* was sent east to establish the second base. The party discovered that Amundsen had built a base at the Bay of Whales, the place where Scott had used his balloon in 1902. Amundsen was 60 miles (97 kilometers) nearer the pole than Scott was. A third expedition, led by Lieut. Naoshi Shirase of the Imperial Japanese Navy, planned to join the race to the South Pole, but his ships were unable to pass through the pack ice.

Amundsen, a professional explorer, was able to build his base Framheim and establish several large depots of food and fuel to the south before the winter arrived. During the winter darkness men, equipment, and dogs were prepared for the pole trip. When spring appeared, Amundsen and his men started for the pole, but their early September departure was too early. They encountered temperatures of more than 70°F below zero (−57°C) and were forced back. On October 19 they set out again: five men, four sledges, and fifty-two dogs. For 4 weeks they sledged south until they reached the mountains. They found several glaciers coming down from the mountains but selected the Axel Heiberg, a narrow and steep glacier, to climb to the Polar Plateau. At 10000 feet (3048 meters) they thought they had reached the top and killed twenty-four of the weakest dogs. On December 7 they passed Shackleton's farthest south point and on December 14, 1911, reached the South Pole. The Norwegians spent 3 days at the pole before returning to Framheim.

Scott's party of five got a later start than the Norwegians did. Once they reached the Beardmore Glacier, the planned route to the pole, they man-hauled their sledges. After a journey during which the men probably began suffering from scurvy or another dietary deficiency, Scott neared the pole. Their enthusiasm was dampened by the sight of a black speck on the horizon. It was a black flag, a Norwegian trail marker. When they arrived at the pole on January 18, 1912, they found a Norwegian tent with letters to Scott and King Haakon VII, a precaution in case Amundsen failed to survive the return trip. When the Englishmen began the return journey, all were in serious trouble with severe frostbite and injuries. Despite these troubles and a dwindling food supply, they took time to collect geologic samples. On March 19, 1912, they camped only 11 miles (18 kilometers) from a large depot of food and fuel. A blizzard hit them, and they died in their tent. They were found the following spring and buried in place. Their diaries, especially Scott's, are records of heroic exploration. The other members of Scott's expedition were active during the pole trek. They explored Victoria Land from the Pacific as far south as McMurdo Sound and were able to discover and explore several more dry valleys.

Once the pole was reached, men developed other reasons to go to Antarctica. The German Dr. Wilhelm Filchner explored in the area of the Weddell Sea to determine if the Ross and Weddell Seas were connected, thus splitting Antarctica into two adjacent continents.

Shackleton returned south with the Transantarctic Expedition. He planned to march from Vahsel Bay (Duke Ernst Bay), on the Atlantic side, across the continent to McMurdo Sound on the Pacific side. He established support bases at both points but was frustrated when his ship *Endurance* was caught in the Weddell Sea pack ice in January 1915. After drifting with the ice for 11 months, the *Endurance* was crushed by the pressure of the ice, and the crew took to ice floes with ship's boats and provisions. By mid-April they reached Elephant Island, where Shackleton left twenty-two men; he and five other men took one boat and crossed the violent seas to South Georgia, the site of permanent whaling stations. Once safe, Shackleton organized five successive relief expeditions before reaching Elephant Island in August with the Chilean steamer *Yelcho* to rescue the rest of his party.

Expeditions of the 1920s and 1930s World War I demanded the attention of explorers, and it was not until 1928 that they returned to Antarctica. The war-developed technology of transportation was applied to exploration with the introduction of airplanes, aerial cameras, and modern communications.

Two expeditions vied to be the first to fly an airplane in Antarctica. George Hubert WILKINS made the first flight with Carl Ben Eielson as pilot, taking off from the warm lava sands of Deception Island to survey the Antarctic Peninsula. On the Ross Ice Shelf, the American Richard E. BYRD was building a base, Little America, at Scott's Balloon Inlet, known to Byrd as the Bay of Whales. Byrd had raised $800,000 to field an expedition of forty-two men and took three airplanes for long-range exploration. The airplanes were used to explore the region east of the Ross Ice Shelf, where several major mountain ranges were discovered, and to fly to the South Pole on November 28–29, 1929. A geologic party headed by Dr. Laurence Gould sledged south to investigate the Transantarctic Mountains for 11 weeks.

Upon Byrd's return to the United States, he began planning for a second expedition. This also was based at Little America, from 1933 to 1935. Airplanes again were used for long-range exploration, but new equipment included an early snowmobile and several other oversnow motor vehicles. Byrd himself spent the 1934–1935 winter in a one-man meteorological station 125 miles (201 kilometers) south of Little America, where he almost died from carbon monoxide poisoning. He was rescued in August, when three men came out from Little America for aurora investigations. Additional geologic investigations were conducted in Marie Byrd Land and in the Transantarctic Mountains, several long-range flights of discovery were made to the east, and biological research was undertaken.

Also active in Antarctica was another American, Lincoln ELLSWORTH. He developed a plan to fly across the continent, landing when visibility became difficult, in an effort to determine if the continent was divided by an ice-covered strait. His plane was damaged in January 1934 when the bay ice gave way and a second attempt was frustrated in late 1934–early 1935, when he had only 12 hours of acceptable flying weather in 3 months. Finally, in November 1935, he and his pilot, Herbert Hollick-Kenyon, were able to fly from Dundee Island off the northeast tip of the Antarctic Peninsula to Little America, landing four times to check their position or to wait out bad weather. They ran out of fuel 20 miles (32 kilometers) from Little America and had to trek in to the now-

empty base. A month later they were picked up by their ship. Ellsworth returned to Antarctica in 1938 with a plan to fly across the full width of the continent. Sailing from Cape Town, he was delayed by heavy ice and did not arrive off the continent in the Indian Ocean sector until late in the season. He explored 250 miles (402 kilometers) inland of the coast, but it was too late to attempt a transcontinental flight. Ellsworth's primary contribution to Antarctic exploration was to prove that airplanes could land deep in the unknown interior for observations and successfully take off again.

Other nations were active in the Antarctic in the 1920s and the 1930s. Two Norwegians, Lars Christensen and Hjalmar Riiser-Larsen, explored the region between Enderby Land and the Weddell Sea between 1926 and 1930. The Australian Douglas Mawson met the Norwegians off the coast of Enderby Land, and both agreed that the 45° meridian would mark the division of Norwegian and Australian regions of exploration and their territorial claims.

In 1933 Riiser-Larsen returned to Antarctica to sledge along the entire coastline of Queen Maud Land to Hope Bay at the tip of the Antarctic Peninsula. Three men would travel with a minimum of supplies and depend on seal hunting for their food. During one of their first days in the field, the ice broke up and scattered them and their equipment in the sea. They were eventually rescued by a whaling ship.

During the 1938–1939 summer Germany sent a government expedition to Antarctica to stake a claim for future whaling operations. Two seaplanes were launched from a catapult ship off Queen Maud Land to explore 300 miles (483 kilometers) deep along 1500 miles (2,414 kilometers) of coastline. Extensive use was made of stereophotography, but the negatives were destroyed during World War II. The Germans named the area they explored Neu-Schwabenland.

In response to the German explorations, the United States sent a government expedition to Antarctica in 1939. The U.S. Antarctic Service established bases at Little America and at Stonington Island off the Antarctic Peninsula. Exploratory flights were made from both bases, and scientific and sledge parties sent out. The expedition was withdrawn to the United States in 1941 as the threat of war caused government officials to concentrate on other problems.

Post-World War II exploration During World War II no exploration occurred in Antarctica, but German commerce raiders frequented the peninsula region. The Norwegian whaling fleet was captured early in the war, and many transports were sunk as a result of the raiding operations. To counter the Germans the British sent a military expedition to Deception Island and Hope Bay in the Antarctic Peninsula. During their operations the British removed an Argentine claim marker at Deception Island and replaced it with a British marker. The Chileans also had claimed Antarctic territory, including the Antarctic Peninsula. When the war ended, responsibility for the British Antarctic bases was transferred from the jurisdiction of the Admiralty to the Colonial Office and designated as the Falkland Islands Dependencies Survey. The base at Hope Bay burned in 1948 and was not rebuilt until 1952. When the construction team arrived, they found the site occupied by an Argentine party which used machine-gun fire to discourage the British from reoccupying their base. Diplomatic protests were followed by an Argentine declaration that the resistance had been in error.

The United States returned to Antarctica after World War II, in 1946–1947, for a major fleet exercise, Operation Highjump. Three fleet groups were to explore the continent. The Central Group established a base and an airfield at Little America, where ski-fitted military transports were used to photograph and explore the interior. The Eastern Group was to stay outside the pack ice and use its seaplanes to explore some 600 miles (966 kilometers) of the coast of Antarctica inland from the Amundsen and Bellingshausen Seas. The Western Group sailed along the Indian Ocean coast and photographed Wilkes Land, Queen Mary Coast, Enderby Land, Princess Ragnhild Coast, and the regions in between. The three groups discovered some 350,000 square miles (906,500 square kilometers) of Antarctica and took more than 70,000 aerial-mapping photographs, one of the expedition's major accomplishments.

During 1947–1948 the U.S. Navy sent two icebreakers with helicopters to Antarctica to land survey teams on prominent landmarks to take ground-control surveys to ensure more accurate mapping from the Highjump photography. During these helicopter flights the Bunger Oasis, a second area of dry valleys, was discovered.

In 1947 a privately financed American expedition, the last of its kind since governments were becoming more deeply involved, arrived at Stonington Island. Finn Ronne, the leader, shared the island with a British expedition, and the two leaders developed joint scientific and exploration projects. Several long-range flights were conducted by Ronne, exploring the peninsula and Filchner Ice Shelf, which terminates in the Weddell Sea. Sledge journeys were sent out to explore the coast of the peninsula. On his return to the United States Ronne received high praise for his work, especially the practice of landing in new territory to take sun sights so that accurate maps could be drawn.

Chile, Argentina, and Great Britain all established bases on the peninsula to protect their territorial claims. By mid-1955 there were eleven bases occupied by some 150 men. Taking note of the emotional situation, the United States had sent notes in 1948 to seven nations with published Antarctic claims—Argentina, Australia, Chile, France, New Zealand, Norway, and Britain—suggesting some sort of internationalization of Antarctica to prevent an outbreak of fighting. Only Britain and New Zealand responded favorably, while the Soviet Union insisted that its interests be considered because of Bellingshausen's discoveries and modern Soviet whaling. In 1955 Britain applied to the International Court of Justice to arbitrate the question of sovereignty. Chile and Argentina refused to be bound by any decision, maintaining that a papal bull of 1493 had granted the lands to them as Spain's successors in the Western Hemisphere.

In the post-World War II period, France also was active in Antarctica. Paul-Émile Victor organized expeditions to both Greenland and Antarctica, the latter doing detailed coastal mapping of the Adélie Coast, the area south of Australia. French scientists also conducted extensive research on emperor penguins until the expedition was withdrawn in early 1953.

Between 1949 and 1952 the Norwegian-British-Swedish Antarctic Expedition established a scientific station in Queen Maud Land, where the Weddell Sea meets the Atlantic Ocean. This first international expedition conducted extensive scientific observations.

International Geophysical Year and Later Exploration

In 1952 the International Council of Scientific Unions established a committee to plan the International Geophysical Year (IGY), a period of coordinated scientific observations throughout the world with special attention being devoted to Antarctica. Between 1952 and 1957, the opening of the IGY, Australia, Argentina, Chile, Britain, South Africa, and the United States sent expeditions to Antarctica to survey for bases or continued to maintain existing stations by increasing scientific observations. The United States planned an ambitious research program with bases at the geographic South Pole, in the heart of Marie Byrd Land, and on the coast at Little America. When advance elements of the expedition arrived at Little America, they discovered that the Bay of Whales was gone. The ice front had broken off and gone out to sea.

During the IGY twelve nations established about fifty bases in Antarctica. The United States expanded its program to six bases; Britain planned a scientific base and a transcontinental surface traverse led by Vivian Fuchs which would cross Antarctica from the Weddell Sea to the Ross Sea by way of the South Pole; New Zealand planned a base on Ross Island to support a traverse led by Edmund Hillary toward the South Pole to meet Fuchs; the Soviet Union planned a coastal base in Queen Maud Land and year-round inland bases at the Geomagnetic Pole and the Pole of Inaccessibility, the farthest point from the sea; Australia built a base at the site of Mawson's earlier base; and France planned a base at the Magnetic Pole. Chile and Argentina continued their bases in the Antarctic Peninsula. Japan, Belgium, South Africa, and Norway established bases along the Queen Maud Land coast.

After the conclusion of the IGY in 1958, most of the

U.S. Navy icebreakers. After World War II exploring Antarctica became an international enterprise, culminating in the International Geophysical Year in 1957–1958. [U.S. Navy]

McMurdo station, a United States base in Antarctica. Although basic research continues, a major aim of Antarctic exploration in the late twentieth century is the search for valuable minerals. [U.S. Navy]

participating nations continued their scientific explorations in Antarctica. An Antarctic Treaty setting aside the continent for peaceful purposes, demilitarizing the area, and putting all national claims aside for the life of the treaty became effective in 1961. Scientific research has continued at a high level, most of IGY nations still being involved. Basic research will continue to be the primary motivation for Antarctic exploration in the late twentieth century, but in-

creased attention will be devoted to finding and examining potential deposits of exploitable minerals.

See also AERIAL EXPLORATION.

BIBLIOGRAPHY: Roald Amundsen, *The South Pole,* London, 1912; Richard E. Byrd, *Discovery,* New York, 1935; id., *Little America,* New York, 1930; Vivian Fuchs and Edmund Hillary, *The Crossing of Antarctica,* London, 1959; H. R. Hill, *The Siege of the South Pole,* London, 1905; Finn Ronne, *Antarctic Conquest,* New York, 1949; Walter Sullivan, *Quest for a Continent,* New York, 1957.

Peter J. Anderson

Arabia

Arabia is the area represented by the landmass between the Red, Mediterranean, and Arabian Seas and the Persian Gulf. It is bounded on the north by approximately 30° or 32°N, a line stretching north of 'Aqaba and Basra. The ancients divided Arabia into three parts: Arabia Petraea, the northwestern region; Arabia Deserta, the northern section between Syria and Mesopotamia; and Arabia Felix, the rest of the peninsula. Later, the last of these names came to be applied only to Yemen.

Western interest in Arabia has always been occasioned by metals, materials, or spices: copper, pearls, incense, coffee, or petroleum. Access to such products, rather than the adventure of successfully penetrating the Ka'bah, the holy Muslim sanctuary at Mecca, was the goal of Europeans. Only greed for profit could overcome the hostile geography of Arabia, thus described by the celebrated English traveler Charles Montagu DOUGHTY: "The desert day dawns not little and little, but it is noontide in an hour. The sun, entering as a tyrant upon the waste landscape, darts upon us as a torment of fiery beams, not to be remitted till the far off evening."

Sixteenth and seventeenth centuries In the early sixteenth century it was the aroma of coffee that at-

tracted Europeans to Arabia. While the journey of the Bolognese Lodovico di VARTHEMA in 1503–1504 does not seem to have been directly connected to the trade in coffee, it corresponds to the increased European, especially Portuguese, interest in Arabia. The coffee craze of the sixteenth century was started, it seems, by a *muftī,* a Muslim religious official, in Aden when he learned that coffee had the virtue of delaying sleep among his religious adepts and enabled them to pass their nights more easily in prayer. The citizens of Aden were not tardy in appreciating, in a manner less mysterious, not to say less spiritual, the virtues of the beverage. From Aden the use of coffee passed to Mecca (Makkah) about 1500 and then to Cairo. By 1554 it had reached Istanbul and resulted in the creation of the famous coffeehouses of that city in which checkers and trictrac were played for hours. At the beginning of the seventeenth century coffee appeared in Venice, and a little later in London.

The desire of the Portuguese to protect their hegemony in the Far East brought Afonso de Albuquerque to Arabian waters early in the sixteenth century. Hormuz fell to the Portuguese as did other strategic sites in the Persian Gulf, and while an effort by Albuquerque to capture Aden (1513) proved unsuccessful, the

Portuguese were able to harry competitors in the Gulf and the Red Sea. The old desire for control of the spice route and for coffee resulted in a struggle between the Ottoman Empire and European powers (notably the British and the Dutch, who soon displaced Portugal in the East) which continued throughout the seventeenth century. Clashes among European rivals became more frequent as each competing group had the backing of newly created East India companies, such as the English Levant Company, established in 1583. With its headquarters in Istanbul and several consulates in Syria, it provided points of departure for European travelers. The security offered by the consulates encouraged a new type of traveler to visit the Middle East and Arabia. These epigones were curious to know more of the Eastern world and enjoyed the adventure of this pursuit. The seventeenth-century European travelers knew more about the classical world than about the Middle East or Arabia in which they wanted to travel and explore.

Eighteenth century   The wars between French, British, and Dutch did not end in the eighteenth century, but they became less intense and permitted scientific investigations which included the use of surveying equipment and the methodical cataloging of all information. Carsten NIEBUHR, a Dane in the service of King Frederick V, is the first chronicler, by virtue of being the only survivor of such an expedition. While Niebuhr's expedition is usually referred to as a new (that is, scientific) kind of exploration, it differed little from former forays in its objectives. Niebuhr's main charge was to observe and record the products of Yemen and to judge the possibilities of trade with Denmark. The goal, as before, was profit with the desire to limit the competition of rivals. While the objectives were similar to those of former explorations, the results were patently different, largely because of the accuracy, detachment, and eighteenth-century rationalism of Niebuhr. He was also the first European to mention the Wahhābī revolution which was occurring in Arabia.

This upheaval was inspired by Muhammad ibn 'Abd-al-Wahhāb, who was born in the southern Najd (Nejd) in 1703. While a young man, he made the pilgrimage to Mecca, where he imbibed the ideas of early Islamic reformers and became convinced that Islam must be reformed and reduced to its original simplicity and purity. Niebuhr wrote that 'Abd-al-Wahhāb "has gone further, perhaps, than some other reformers; but an Arab can hardly be expected to act in such matters with a delicate hand. Experience will show whether a religion, so stripped of everything that might serve to strike the senses, can maintain its ground among so rude and ignorant a people as the Arabs." Wahhabism suffered vicissitudes in the next two centuries but was to be the main lever by which the Saudi family consolidated its control of central Arabia. Niebuhr's view agrees with that of D. G. Hogarth, the twentieth-century historian of Arabian travel, who stated: "There is more hope of stability, religious and political, for an Arabian society in Wahhabism than in traditional Arab liberalism as expressed in the Bedouin society of Jabal Shammar."

Nineteenth century   Napoleon's invasion of Egypt and Syria between 1798 and 1801 created a new interest in the entire Middle East, opening the gates to savants as well as travelers. New fields of study such as hieroglyphics and Egyptology were created. The rise to power of Mehemet Ali (Muhammad 'Alī) in Egypt (r.1805–1848) and his clash with the Wahhābī also increased the penetration of Arabia by Europeans.

Ulrich Jaspar Seetzen, a German botanist and Arabist, was one of the first Europeans to take advantage of the new opportunities for travel. In 1809 he visited Mecca and traveled in Yemen, reaching the capital, San'ā; unfortunately, on his return to the coast he was murdered at Ta'izz. Seetzen represented a new kind of traveler in Arabia, one who was willing to spend years in preparation to acquire the necessary language and scientific skills.

The first detailed account of Mecca available to Europeans was the *Travels* of Ali Bey al-Abbasi, published in Paris in 1813 and in London in 1816. Ali Bey was in reality Domingo Badía y Leblich, a wealthy Spaniard who visited Mecca in 1807 while the Hejaz (Hijāz) was under Wahhabite domination. He was able to give a rather pitiful description of Mecca after the Wahhābī sacking of 1803.

Better descriptions of Mecca were soon written. In the same year, 1809, in which Seetzen was murdered, another learned and well-prepared Arabist, Johann Ludwig BURCKHARDT, arrived in Aleppo (Halab). An agent of the AFRICAN ASSOCIATION, he had as his main objective the exploration of the Niger River, but to appear as a bona fide Muslim he first wanted to make the pilgrimage to Mecca. His descriptions of Mecca, Medina (Al Madīnah), and their environs were so detailed that Richard BURTON, who followed Burckhardt, grudgingly conceded that there was little he could do but expand on the nuances of Burckhardt's account. Destined for Africa, by happenstance Burckhardt became one of the chief European interpreters of the social life, characteristics, and religion of the Arabs to Europeans. His *Notes on the Bedouins and Wahábys*, published posthumously in 1830, was the first detailed account of the origins and history of the Wahhābī movement.

A traveler who was to become more famous than Burckhardt, largely because of his explorations in Africa and his translation of erotic Eastern literature into English, was Richard Burton. He, like Burckhardt, realized the danger of being caught in the Islamic holy precincts of Mecca, which left one with a choice "between death or circumcision." Burton preferred the latter, not for sensation, as is sometimes alleged, but to earn the title *hajjī* (pilgrim), which would facilitate his passage to the Rub'al Khālī, the great expanse of desert in southeast Arabia. This was an objective he failed to achieve and a feat which was delayed for nearly 80 years, being accomplished only in 1931 by Bertram Thomas. Burton was also the last non-Muslim to visit Medina, excepting only the Englishman John F. Keane, until 1908. Burton's account of the lands of Midian, between the Gulf of 'Aqaba and Al Wajh (Wejh) on the east coast of the Red Sea, published in 1878, was the first detailed geographical description of this famous ancient land. It was not to be surpassed until *The Land of Midian* of Harry St. John PHILBY in 1957.

A worthy successor of Ali Bey, Burckhardt, and Burton was the distinguished Dutch Arabist J. Snouck Hurgronje, who spent 5 months in Mecca in 1885. But Hurgronje also marked the advent of a different type of traveler, the academic scholar-traveler. While other travelers were learned, with the exception of George Augustus Wallin none of them were university professors. Hurgronje typified the professor in residence whose goal was to absorb as much as possible and to turn the acquired material into lectures and learned articles.

In 1818, after a decade of war, Ibrahim Pasha, the son of Mehemet Ali, succeeded in defeating the Wahhābī on their home ground. The following year Capt. George Forster Sadlier was sent to Arabia by the British administration in India to meet with Ibrahim Pasha to elicit his support in completely crushing Wahhābī power. Unaware that Ibrahim Pasha was in the process of evacuating the Najd, Sadlier relentlessly pursued him and in so doing established his fame by becoming the first European to cross the peninsula, an amazing feat accomplished in 70 days. Sadlier was also the first European to visit Dar 'iyah, the stronghold and capital of the Wahhābī, and he saw it almost immediately after it had been destroyed by the Egyptians. Razed to the ground, it was devoid of a single soul.

The six decades between 1837 and 1897 witnessed a decline in Wahhābī-Saudi power in central Arabia and the rise of the Shammar tribal confederation in the northern Najd. Under the brilliant leadership of 'Abd-Allah ibn-Rashīd and centered at Ha'il, which was situated on the main trade routes across Arabia, it established virtual independence. Ibn-Rashīd avoided quarrels with the Saudi, and he kept in touch with the Turks and Egyptians. This changed alignment of power in central Arabia is the background for the next series of explorations in central Arabia.

George Augustus Wallin, a Finno-Swede and subsequently professor of Arabic at Helsingfors (Helsinki) University, ostensibly wanted to go to Yemen to study Himyaritic inscriptions. However, D. G. Hogarth, in his book on Arabian travel, states that Wallin's purpose was to investigate the possibilities of an alliance between his patron, Mehemet Ali, and 'Abd-Allāh ibn-Rashīd against the Wahhābī. Wallin's biographers vehemently deny the charge. Nevertheless,

Muslim pilgrims at the Great Mosque in Mecca. A number of European explorers made this pilgrimage in Muslim disguise. [Library of Congress]

the direction of Wallin's journey in 1845 lends credibility to Hogarth's statement. As a result of his journeys Wallin left the first lucid account of the Shammar confederation, a description of its conquests and its administration. He noted that Shammar leadership was sustained by traditional Bedouin virtues rather than by religious ideology, as was the Wahhābī. He observed, correctly, but to the amazement of many Europeans who by now were used to being regaled by stories of Wahhābī and Bedouin fanaticism, that the Bedouin were largely ignorant of religion. In fact, it was not until the twentieth century, after the demise of the Rashīdī and the conquests of the Saudi king 'ibn-Saud (ibn-Su'ūd) that many Bedouin became Islamized. With the exception of William Gifford PALGRAVE, Wallin was the last nineteenth-century explorer to enter virgin territory in Arabia.

Wallin's singular effort to explore virgin ground was exceeded only by that of Palgrave, who in 1862–1863, with a Syrian Greek companion, became the second European to cross the peninsula and the first to do so from west to east. (The east-west crossing had been made by Sadlier in 1819.) Palgrave's journey took 13 months and covered more than 1500 miles (2414 kilometers). An adventurous, charismatic man, Palgrave undertook his journey as an agent of Napoleon III to investigate the possibilities of French expansion into Syria, Egypt, and Arabia. His *Narrative of a Year's Journey through Central and Eastern Arabia* (1865) because of its informative and lively style was widely read in Europe. Palgrave was accused by his successors, especially Harry St. John Philby, of exaggeration and outright prevarication.

The Blunts—Lady Anne Blunt, granddaughter of Lord Bryon, and Wilfrid Scawen Blunt, diplomat and poet—visited the Shammar tribes in 1878–1879. Their journey was distinguished from previous ones in that they traveled openly as Christians. An account of their journey was brilliantly provided by Lady Anne's lucid *A Pilgrimage to Nejd* (1881), which gives a succinct history of the Rashīdī. Lady Anne Blunt was the first European woman to travel in the interior of Arabia, paving the way for such later intrepid travelers as Gertrude Bell, a political assistant to Sir Percy Cox in Iraq after World War I, and Freya Stark, both of whose travels were undertaken without the comforts enjoyed by Lady Anne. *See also* WOMEN IN TRAVEL AND EXPLORATION.

The southern fringe of the Arabian Peninsula—Yemen, the Hadramawt, Dhufar (Zufār), and Oman—was largely unknown until the nineteenth century, when the politics of profit dictated that the East Indian authorities send an expedition, headed by James Wellsted, to Oman to determine the effective power of the Sultan of Muscat (Masqat) in the interior. Working from the ship *Palinurus*, captained by S. B. Haines, Wellsted made a detailed reconnaissance of the Hadramawt and of the east Yemen border during the years 1834–1836. His investigations were cut short in 1836, when he shot himself in a fit of delirium. The *Palinurus* continued its survey of the Hadramawt coast to Dhufar, giving the first and best information of an obscure area until Bertram Thomas published *Across Arabia Felix* in 1932.

In 1843 Alfred von Wrede, a Bavarian in the service of King Otto of Greece, penetrated the interior of the Hadramawt, becoming the first European to see the southern edge of the Rub'al Khālī. Unfortunately his complete journal was not published until 1870, long after he had emigrated to Texas, where he killed himself. One of the most fascinating studies (1885) of the Hadramawt is that of the Dutch Arabic scholar L. W. C. van den Berg, which he based on interviews with Hadramawt immigrants in Java.

In 1893 Leo Hirsch, a German archaeologist and Himyaritic scholar, taking advantage of the Pax Britannica in the Indian Ocean, was the first European to see the Wādī Hadramawt, the main drainage system for the entire area. Before Hirsch could complete his studies, fanatical *sayyids,* alleged descendants of the prophet Muhammad, forced him back to the coast. The same year, the Englishman James Theodore Bent and his wife, who was one of the few European women to travel in the interior of Arabia, followed Hirsch's tracks. Because of their deficiency in Arabic, the Bents, like the Blunts, traveled as Europeans. Bent, who was much interested in the ancient lore of south Arabia, observed that the decline of trade in frankincense and myrrh had done much to ruin the country and had contributed to the silting up of the *wādī.* The studies of Hirsch, Von Wrede, Bent, the Dutch Orientalist Van der Meulen, and the German Hermann von Wissmann contributed greatly to European knowledge of south Arabia.

The greatest traveler of Arabia in the nineteenth century was Charles Montagu Doughty. *Arabia Deserta* (1888), his account of his 15-month stay among the Arabs of the western Najd, is a singular work. Filled with descriptions of Bedouin life and mixed with pictures of men, animals, birds, and reptiles, it is, as T. E. Lawrence put it, "a bible of its kind." Doughty traveled openly as a Christian and bore the brunt of much abuse, but his suffering inspired him to greater feats of observation. He discovered the Aramaic inscription at Taymā', mentioned in the Book of Job, which the Alsatian Charles Huber obtained for the Louvre in 1883. Doughty's perception and deep knowledge of Arab tribal affiliations served as a bridge between the nineteenth-century travelers, who usually traveled alone with two or three Arab tribesmen, and the twentieth-century travelers, who had the resources of governments and, indeed, armies behind them. British intelligence units made much use of *Arabia Deserta* when planning the Arab revolt of 1916.

Twentieth century World War I ushered in new modes of travel in Arabia. Cars, trucks, and all the machines that could be mustered by modern military states were now at the disposal of geographers and geologists. The lone traveler was intimidated further by the advent of countless oil exploration drilling teams in the 1930s. Oil rigs were to become as familiar as Bedouin tents in the sands of Arabia.

By the 1930s the last unexplored region of Arabia, one which amounted to a quarter of its entire area, was the 250,000-square-mile (647,500-square-kilometer) expanse of the Rub'al Khālī, "the Abode of Emptiness." Only three Europeans had glimpsed it: James Wellsted in 1836 from the Jabal al Akhḍar in Oman; Alfred von Wrede, the Bavarian, in 1843 from north of the Wādī Hadramawt; and a Frenchman, Joseph Halévy, in 1870.

In 1929 T. E. Lawrence suggested that the Royal Air Force fly over it in an airship: "Nothing but an airship can do it, and I want it to be one of ours which gets the plum." The plum fell to the British, but to a man on a camel. Bertram Thomas, longtime British political officer in the Persian Gulf, was the first European to cross the Rub'al Khālī. He accomplished this unprecedented feat in the winter of 1930–1931, crossing the "sands of my desire" from Salālah in Dhufar to Doha (Ad Dawḥah) in Qatar.

Thomas's feat enraged St. John Philby, who had long planned the crossing of the Rub'al Khālī but had not been granted permission by King ibn-Saud of Saudi Arabia, permission which Thomas had not bothered to obtain. Philby, the second European to cross the sands, did so a year after Thomas's passage. Philby followed a more arduous route than Thomas had, but the fame of the first crossing was what captured the imagination of Europe. Philby represented the great transition in Arabian travel from the camel to mechanized vehicles. He was a close confidant and adviser to King ibn-Saud and hence had the resources of a government at his disposal. Philby's prodigious collections of flora and fauna of Saudi Arabia introduced Arabia to millions of twentieth-century Europeans.

Wilfred Patrick THESIGER, an Englishman, was the last European to cross the Rub'al Khālī in the traditional mode—on camel, barefoot, and with just two or three Arab guides—in 1946–1947 and again in 1947–1948. Thesiger abhorred mechanized travel. He represented a new European traveler, one who was alienated from the industrialized West. Thesiger found his soul in the abundance of sand and spirituality of its nothingness. Nothing illustrates the difference between Philby and Thesiger better than an incident from their travels. Near Laylah, on the route to Dubai (Dubayy), Thesiger, much to his disgust, heard the desert night disrupted by the sounds of a car stuck in the sands and the smell of gasoline from the racing engine. He wondered what kind of barbaric European or American was destroying the virginity of the desert quiet. The next day, to his amazement, he learned that it was, of all people, Harry St. John Philby.

BIBLIOGRAPHY: Mohamad Ali Hachicho, "English Travel Books about the Arab Near East in the 18th Century," *Die Welt des Islams*, new ser., vol. IX, nos. 1–4, pp. 1–216; D. G. Hogarth, *The Penetration of Arabia*, London, 1904; R. H. Kiernan, *The Unveiling of Arabia: The Story of Arabian Travel and Discovery*, London, 1937; Jacqueline Pirenne, *À la découverte de l'Arabie: Cinq siècles de science et d'aventure*, Paris, 1958.

Robert W. Olson

Arctic Ocean

There have been three distinct themes in the 400-year history of the exploration of the Arctic Ocean. Initially, before explorers recognized the extent and impenetrability of the ocean's permanent ice cover, there were numerous attempts to sail across it, mainly from the region of Spitsbergen (Svalbard) to Bering Strait. The impossibility of that achievement gradually became apparent during the nineteenth century, and explorers then turned their attention from the practical to the symbolic act of conquest: the attainment of the North Pole. Finally, there is the period of scientific exploration, which has lasted from the end of the nineteenth century to the present day.

Search for a sea route When Arctic exploration commenced during the sixteenth century, explorers were concerned with the Arctic less for its own sake than as a potential short trade route from Europe to the Pacific. Thus, the Arctic Ocean first aroused interest as a possible alternative to the elusive Northwest and Northeast Passage routes to the Orient (*see* NORTHEAST PASSAGE; NORTHWEST PASSAGE). The first recorded suggestion that explorers should attempt the Arctic Ocean route was made by the merchant Robert Thorne in a letter to Henry VIII in 1527. Thorne's letter brought no immediate response, but it contained the germ of a theory that was developed at the beginning of the seventeenth century and persisted until quite late in the nineteenth, namely, that once the initial belt of Arctic ice was passed, the climate grew warmer toward the pole and the ocean became ice-free.

This theory was first tested in 1596 during the third attempt on the Northeast Passage by the Dutch explorer Willem BARENTS. On his first two voyages, in 1594 and 1595, Barents had kept close to the European Arctic mainland but had made little progress beyond the Barents Sea. On his third voyage the commander of one of his two ships, Jan Corneliszoon Rijp, persuaded him to keep a more northerly course. In consequence, Barents discovered Spitsbergen, reaching about 80°10′N off its northwest coast before ice stopped him. He then reverted to his planned course eastward toward Novaya Zemlya, near which he subsequently perished.

In 1607 Henry HUDSON followed Barents in testing the theory of the polar passage. Hudson traced part of the east coast of Greenland and later, like Barents, followed the west coast of Spitsbergen northward and reached a new record of 80°23′N, where he, too, was defeated by ice.

After Hudson's failure, explorers lost interest in the Arctic Ocean and concentrated their efforts on the Northwest Passage, the search for which continued intensively for a further 25 years. Then, for the remainder of the seventeenth century and for much of the eighteenth, commercial exploitation of the explored areas of the Arctic, in the form of whaling, sealing, and the fur trade, supplanted exploratory ventures. The only really active Arctic explorers during this period were the Russians, who throughout their steady eastward expansion systematically explored the north coast of Siberia. The discovery in the 1730s of the eastern limit of their empire, Bering Strait, incited them to search for a short sea route to the east, and it was they who, frustrated in their efforts to take ships through the Northeast Passage, revived the idea of an Arctic Ocean route. Vasily Yakovlevich Chichagov was sent to attempt this route twice, in 1765 and 1766, but he achieved little more than Barents and Hudson had, reaching only 80°28′N off northwest Spitsbergen.

In England, meanwhile, geographical theorists began again to assert that the Arctic Ocean was navigable. Most active among them was Daines Barrington, who drew up a list of whalers who claimed to have reached improbably high latitudes north of Spitsbergen and used it to persuade the Admiralty to attempt a crossing of the Arctic Ocean. Capt. Constantine John Phipps was given command of the expedition of two ships, *Racehorse* and *Carcass,* which sailed in June 1773. Phipps established a new record of 80°37′N off Spitsbergen before being stopped by an impenetrable barrier of ice.

Despite this, belief in the navigable Arctic Ocean persisted. Even John BARROW, the distinguished promoter of British naval Arctic exploration in the early nineteenth century, was at first inclined to think that Phipps had merely encountered an unfavorable ice season. He reasoned that there was a narrow wall of ice which commonly reaches between Greenland and Spitsbergen at about 80°N but which, in good seasons, breaks up to allow access to the open polar sea. Thus, when the Royal Navy launched its new program of Arctic exploration in 1818, it began with a fresh attempt to cross the Arctic Ocean from Spitsbergen. This expedition, led by Capt. David Buchan with HMS *Dorothea* and *Trent,* achieved no more than Phipps had done. Buchan's attempts to enter the ice between Greenland and Spitsbergen resulted only in the near wreck of the *Dorothea.* He returned home having reached no more than 80°34′N.

After that experience the Royal Navy, at least, had no further illusions about sailing across the Arctic Ocean. Instead, some naval officers set their minds on the more limited objective of attaining the North Pole by crossing the ice on foot. In 1827 the Admiralty accepted a plan put forward by William Edward PARRY, a veteran of four Northwest Passage expeditions, to travel to the pole with sledge boats, boats mounted on sledge runners which could be used either for sailing through open water or for hauling across ice. Parry set out that same year with HMS *Hecla* and launched his sledge boats to the north of Spitsbergen. He found travel over the ice extremely arduous, but, worse still, he discovered that the drift of the ice carried him south almost as rapidly as he

HMS Trent *was one of many ships that braved the hazardous waters of the Arctic. Here walruses attack the ship's boat during the 1818 voyage.* [Library of Congress]

progressed north. He struggled to a record 82°45′N but then, realizing the hopelessness of his task, turned back.

After that, British explorers were naturally discouraged from further attempts on the pole, and 50 years passed before the Royal Navy again tackled the issue. But outside Britain theories about the accessibility of the pole and the navigability of the Arctic Ocean remained unshaken. Furthermore, a fine opportunity to propound and test such theories arose when the Northwest Passage expedition of 1845 of Sir John FRANKLIN disappeared in the Canadian Arctic. The German geographer August Petermann reasoned that Franklin could have passed northward through the Canadian Arctic archipelago into the Arctic Basin and suggested in 1852 that he might be found somewhere between Bering Strait and the pole. He accompanied his suggestion with an early version of his "open polar sea" theory, which he was to promote vigorously for a further 20 years. The theory was complex, but his main argument was that ships could enter the supposedly ice-free Arctic Ocean by the hitherto-untried passage between Spitsbergen and Novaya Zemlya and thence sail across it toward Bering Strait. *See also* FRANKLIN EXPEDITION AND SEARCH.

Nothing came of Petermann's proposed Franklin search expedition, but at the same time a search expedition was being prepared in the United States on the basis of the same theory that Franklin had passed northward into the open polar sea. This expedition, Elisha Kent Kane's Second U.S. Grinnell Expedition in search of Franklin, adopted a new line of approach

to the Arctic Ocean, by the strait between Greenland and Ellesmere Island, Canada, which was then known only at its southern extremity, Smith Sound. Kane set out in *Advance* in 1853, hoping to find either an ice-free strait leading to an open polar sea or the landmass of Greenland extending north to within proximity of the pole. In the event, ice conditions prevented Kane from sailing far beyond Smith Sound, but his sledge parties did succeed in exploring the shores of Kane Basin and Kennedy Channel north to 81°22′N. Moreover, their discovery of open water in Kennedy Channel provided the incentive for other expeditions to attempt to reach the open polar sea and the pole by this route.

The first explorer to follow Kane was Isaac Hayes, who had been with Kane on the *Advance* and was quite convinced of the existence of the open polar sea. He set out on board *United States* in 1860 but, like Kane, was unable to penetrate far beyond Smith Sound. His sledge parties added little to Kane's discoveries. In 1871 another American ship, *Polaris*, commanded by the veteran Arctic explorer Charles Francis Hall, set out to attain the pole by the same route. Hall made a most encouraging start by taking his ship to 82°11′N, almost at the extreme northern end of the channel between Greenland and Ellesmere Island, but at the beginning of the first winter he died. His officers' enthusiasm for the venture collapsed after his death, and they chose to return home in 1872 with little further accomplished.

In Europe, meanwhile, the persistent campaigning of August Petermann was beginning to bear fruit in

Elisha Kent Kane's expedition to locate Sir John Franklin, lost trying to find the Northwest Passage through Arctic waters. [*Library of Congress*]

the form of two German and two Austro-Hungarian expeditions to the seas between Greenland and Novaya Zemlya. The German expeditions, led by Karl Christian Koldewey in 1868 and 1869–1870, were confined to the region between Greenland and Spitsbergen and made no greater progress toward the Arctic Ocean than had their many predecessors. More important were the Austro-Hungarian expeditions led by Karl Weyprecht and Julius von Payer in 1871 and between 1872 and 1874. The preliminary expedition of 1871 on the *Isbjorn* confirmed Novaya Zemlya as their intended point of departure for the north, but on the second voyage Weyprecht and Payer failed to reach their landing site. Their ship, *Tegetthoff*, was beset in the ice off the west coast of Novaya Zemlya and began to drift north. The drift continued throughout the winter and the following spring until, in August 1873, they discovered a new archipelago, Zemlya Frantsa Iosifa (Franz Josef Land). They remained beset close to land for a further winter. Payer surveyed the southernmost islands of the archipelago in the spring of 1874; then, fearing yet another winter locked in the ice, they abandoned ship and returned south to be rescued by a Russian vessel off Novaya Zemlya.

Attainment of the pole   The remarkable drift of Weyprecht and Payer was, in a sense, a turning point in the exploration of the Arctic Basin. It put paid to all remaining speculation about an open polar sea, but it enhanced curiosity about the nature of that seemingly unapproachable region and marked the beginning of an intensive international effort to penetrate toward the North Pole. The Royal Navy reentered the scene with its British Arctic Expedition of 1875–1876, an attempt to attain the pole by way of Smith Sound. Remarkably, the leader of that expedition, George Strong Nares, managed to take one of his ships, *Alert*, right through the channel between Greenland and Ellesmere Island and wintered at Alert, on the very shores of the Arctic Ocean. The leader of his main sledge journey toward the pole in the spring of 1876, Albert Hastings Markham, reached only 83°20′26″N, but he surpassed Parry's northernmost record of 50 years' standing and put beyond doubt the existence of a permanent ice cover on the Arctic Ocean.

Three years later, the American George W. De Long set out on an attempt to reach the pole by the only remaining untried route, Bering Strait. He was attracted by a new theory put forward by the irrepressible Dr. Petermann, who, having jettisoned his open-polar-sea theory, now reasoned that the landmass of Greenland stretched across the pole to reappear as Ostrov Vrangelya (Wrangel Island), of which explorers had thus far sighted only the southern coast. De Long sailed for Bering Strait on board *Jeannette* in 1879 but in September of that year, to the east of Ostrov Vrangelya, was permanently beset in the ice. The ship drifted to the north of the island for more than a year, then, early in 1881, set into the steady westward drift which carried her to the north of the Novosibirskiye Ostrova (New Siberian Islands), where she was

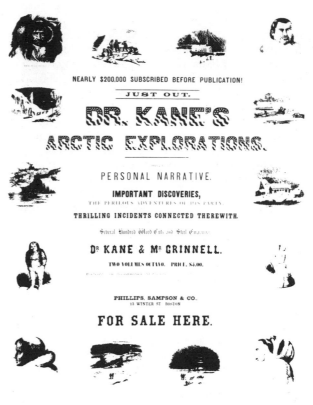

Explorers' journals and memoirs were popular in the nineteenth century; witness this placard advertising Elisha Kane's work. [Library of Congress]

crushed and sank. The crew set off over the ice to the Siberian mainland and, after much hardship, reached the Lena Delta. There many men, including De Long, either drowned or starved to death; only thirteen of the original thirty-two survived.

De Long's expedition made several important discoveries regarding the nature of the Arctic Ocean. It established the insularity of Ostrov Vrangelya, discovered some of the northernmost islands in the Novosibirskiye group, and showed the existence of a westerly drift of the pack across the Siberian side of the ocean. There was a remarkable postscript to this last point, for in 1884 relics belonging to the *Jeannette* were discovered in the ice off southwest Greenland. It was this chance discovery which prompted the organization of the first truly scientific expedition to the Arctic Ocean. Some years later, the Norwegian explorer Fridtjof NANSEN proposed that if those relics could drift right across the ocean, then a properly constructed ship could do likewise. Nansen supervised the construction of the *Fram*, a small, light vessel designed to ride upward under pressure from the ice, then in the summer of 1893 took her to the north of the Novosibirskiye Ostrova, near where *Jeannette* had sunk, and deliberately beset her in the pack. As the ship settled into her predicted drift, westward and slightly northward toward the pole, Nansen commenced the scientific work which alone would have justified the venture, notably the observations demonstrating that the central Arctic was a deep ocean and not the shallow island-studded sea that many had expected him to find. In March 1895, when the *Fram* was at 84°N, Nansen and one com-

George W. De Long, who died attempting to reach the North Pole through Bering Strait. The luckless voyage produced posthumous evidence that led to better-prepared assaults on the pole. [U.S. Navy]

panion left the ship and set out over the ice for the pole, but they reached only 86°14′N before finding themselves caught in the same southward drift that had frustrated Parry in 1827. They had no chance of rejoining the *Fram*, whose position they could no longer predict, so they set off over the ice to Zemlya Frantsa Iosifa, where they spent the winter of 1895–1896. In the following spring they met there the English explorer Frederick George Jackson, who had been engaged in charting the archipelago since 1894 and whose ship, *Windward*, carried them home to Norway. There they learned that the *Fram*, continuing her drift, had broken out of the ice to the west of Spitsbergen in the summer of 1896. She had returned to Norway just a day before them.

The 10 years after Nansen's drift saw a flood of further attempts on the pole. In July 1897, the Swede Salomon August Andrée and two companions made the first attempt by balloon, launched from Spitsbergen. Nothing more was heard of them until 1930, when their remains and journals were found on a small island off Nordaustlandet. They had come down on the ice at 82°56′N, 3 days after taking off, and had perished 3 months later while attempting to walk back to the mainland. In 1899 the Italian Luigi Amedeo di Savoia, Duke of the Abruzzi, sailed for the Arctic on *Stella Polare* to make a more conventional attempt on the pole, by sledge; but unlike his predecessors he chose Zemlya Frantsa Iosifa as his starting

point. The leader of his pole party, Umberto Cagni, reached 86°34′N in April 1900, just beating Nansen's record. The American promoter William Ziegler also chose Zemlya Frantsa Iosifa for his polar expedition, led by Anthony Fiala, between 1903 and 1905, but Fiala's two attempts on the pole ended in complete failure. During the same period, other explorers operating on land were pushing back the boundaries of the Arctic Ocean. Frederick Jackson, the rescuer of Nansen, continued his surveys of Zemlya Frantsa Iosifa until 1897. Otto Neumann SVERDRUP, Nansen's captain on the *Fram* drift, took the little ship back to the Arctic and spent the years from 1898 to 1902 in the extreme north of the Canadian Arctic archipelago, discovering and mapping the Sverdrup Islands (Axel Heiberg, Amund Ringnes, and Ellef Ringnes Islands) and the west coast of Ellesmere Island.

In the midst of all this endeavor, the man whose name is most closely associated with the North Pole, Robert Edwin PEARY, was slowly preparing himself for his final assault. He had begun his Arctic training as early as 1886, on an expedition to the Greenland ice cap, and he had continued to explore north Greenland on a series of expeditions between 1891 and 1897. Thereafter, he had set his heart on the pole.

All Peary's attempts on the pole were made by the Smith Sound route. Between 1898 and 1902, he located the nothernmost point of Greenland, Cape Morris Jesup, but found ice travel northward from there impracticable and reached only 83°50′N. On his second North Pole expedition, in 1905–1906, he chose to set out from the north coast of Ellesmere Island and attained a new record, 87°6′N. On both of these expeditions, he carefully developed the kinds of equipment and techniques best suited to his singular purpose: his dog sledges were specially designed for travel over rough sea ice, he organized depot-laying and support parties to help prolong his journeys, and he enlisted large numbers of Eskimo hunters to maintain his fresh-food supply. With so much preparation and experience behind him, he felt certain of success of his third expedition, in 1908–1909, and indeed he attained the pole from Cape Sheridan, Ellesmere Island, on April 6, 1909. But Peary's triumph, the culmination of more than 20 years' endeavor, was soon to turn to bitterness. He returned home in September 1909 to receive the shattering news that another explorer, Frederick Albert COOK, was claiming to have reached the pole a year before him, on April 21, 1908. Cook maintained that he had made the journey from the northernmost point of Axel Heiberg Island, in the company of two Eskimos. A furious argument ensued, with Peary's supporters dismissing Cook as a fraud and Cook's supporters simply pointing to the apparently flawless record of his journey in his published journals. Peary's claim to priority has won more general acceptance, but even now the dispute continues; there is still a regular flow of new books and articles supporting or debunking one or other of the two rival claims.

Robert E. Peary's ship in Arctic ice. Admiral Peary made reaching the North Pole his life's work and evolved what amounted to a polar-expedition technology. [U.S. Navy]

The airship Norge, flown over the North Pole by Ellsworth, Amundsen, and Nobile. Their success was marred by quarrels over who deserved the most credit for the achievement. [Library of Congress]

The conquest of the pole did not entirely put an end to the heroic age of exploration in the Arctic Basin, and many years were to pass before regular scientific exploration took precedence over adventure. The 1920s saw a series of attempts to reach the pole by new means. On May 9, 1926, Comdr. Richard E. BYRD, USN, reached the pole by air from Spitsbergen on the three-engine Fokker aircraft *Josephine Ford.* In the same year, the wealthy American engineer Lincoln ELLSWORTH, the Norwegian explorer Roald AMUNDSEN, and the Italian airship designer Umberto Nobile combined their resources to make the first flight over the pole by powered airship. Their craft *Norge* landed safely in Alaska on May 13, 1926, after a 70-hour flight from Spitsbergen. This success encouraged Nobile to set out in 1928 on a more ambitious project, a systematic survey of the whole Arctic Ocean from the airship *Italia.* He made two flights, covering the region between Spitsbergen and Novaya Zemlya, then between Spitsbergen, Greenland, and the pole, but crashed to the north of Spitsbergen while returning from the pole. Some of his men were lost when *Italia* drifted away after the crash; the rest camped on the ice to await relief. They were rescued by the Soviet icebreaker *Krasin* after an extensive search, by air and by sea, lasting 48 days. *See also* AERIAL EXPLORATION.

Scientific exploration There were other, less noteworthy expeditions to the Arctic Basin during that period, but the modern age of systematic scientific exploration did not really begin until 1937. It was then that Soviet explorers acted out an idea that had been debated for some years: to set up a scientific station on a drifting ice floe. The station (retrospectively named *North Pole-1*) was established from the air at the North Pole on May 21, 1937, and drifted steadily southward toward the Greenland Sea while the staff, headed by Ivan Papanin, carried out a wide range of scientific observations. They were relieved by ship off the east coast of Greenland on February 19, 1938.

The program was interrupted by World War II but was resumed in 1950 when *North Pole-2* was established at 76°N, 166°W, north of the Chukchi Sea. The scale of the operation was stepped up in 1954, when three North Pole drifting stations, *NP-3*, *NP-4*, and *NP-5*, were established at different points on the ocean's surface. Since then the Soviet program has been continuous: at no time in the past 25 years have there been fewer than two drifting stations in operation. In addition, the support expeditions, which put new stations in the field and relieve old ones, codenamed North and numbered in sequence like the drift stations, have independently gathered data to provide a vast range of scientific information about the ocean. Very little of this information, however, has been published or released outside the Soviet Union.

Other nations, though slower off the mark than the Soviets, have also engaged in systematic scientific exploration of the Arctic Ocean since the war. The Americans occupied their first drifting station, *Ice Island T-3 (Fletcher's Ice Island)* in 1952–1953 and have since established many more. American, British, and Soviet nuclear submarines have also been used in recent years to probe the underside of the Arctic ice. After centuries of probing around the fringes of the

Arctic Ocean and another 100 years of aimlessly tramping across the top of it, explorers are now, at last, engaged in intensive scientific investigation of its mysterious nature.

BIBLIOGRAPHY: George Bryce, *The Siege and Conquest of the North Pole*, London, 1910; W. J. Gordon, *Round about the North Pole*, London, 1907; Farley Mowat, *The Polar Passion*, Toronto, 1967; L. H. Neatby, *Discovery in Russian and Siberian Waters*, Athens, Ohio, 1973.

Clive A. Holland

Ashley, William Henry (1778–1838) American mountain man. Born in Virginia, Ashley moved in the early 1800s to Missouri, where he served as a militia officer and as a local and state politician and eventually joined a friend from Pennsylvania, Andrew Henry, in manufacturing gunpowder. But the fur trade captured Ashley's imagination, and the two men established the Rocky Mountain Fur Company. Henry, veteran of the defunct Missouri Fur Company, controlled field operations, while Ashley at first remained in St. Louis to handle organization and finances. Their work opened the central Rockies' beaver trade and pointed the way overland to the great Pacific Northwest.

Though the company's first attempts to trap in the northern Rockies failed because of Indian opposition, its misfortunes turned out to be good fortune in disguise. The fall of 1823 found Ashley $100,000 in debt and desperate, and he sent a party including Jedediah SMITH and Thomas Fitzpatrick to find a passage through the mountains. They traveled along the Sweetwater River and across the continental divide by using South Pass during the dangerous month of February and found a region rich in beaver along the upper Green River. Fitzpatrick's triumphant return to

St. Louis in the spring of 1824 with packhorses loaded with pelts signaled a new era in Ashley's career: the opening of the central Rocky Mountain fur trade.

Early in November 1824 Ashley himself, guided by Fitzpatrick, led twenty-five men out of Fort Atkinson and up the Platte River, bound for the Rockies. Despite the Pawnees' warnings against winter travel, the excitement of the hunt prevailed. Ashley decided against Fitzpatrick's direct route to South Pass and gave orders to follow the South Platte River because of its better-wooded areas. At long last the men reached the Rockies, and after 3 days of difficult travel they crossed the Front Range. Westward across the Laramie and Medicine Bow Mountains of southern Wyoming the men trudged, closely following the route later used by the Union Pacific Railroad. After a short period of trapping they crossed the second mountainous obstacle between Elk Mountain and Medicine Bow, rimmed the Red Desert in south central Wyoming, and followed the North Platte River until they turned west just below South Pass. From there they took Morrow Creek, Pacific Creek, and Sandy and Little Sandy Creeks and in mid-April, frostbitten and almost starved, reached the Green River.

Ashley immediately went to work. Assigning his men to construct a bullboat, he prepared to lead an exploration of the southern Green to determine whether it was the Colorado River or the fabled Buenaventura, which allegedly emptied into the Pacific. Three other parties were to trap the waters out of the Uinta Mountains, the northern sources of the "Shetskedee" (i.e., the Green), and the western mountains in the direction of the Bear River. When Ashley asked

The American trader-explorer William Ashley was the first to establish the summer rendezvous on a large scale as a method of conducting the fur trade. [Library of Congress]

them to reassemble with their furs on Henry's Fork of the Green River in July, he inaugurated the annual American rendezvous, a meeting place for the MOUNTAIN MEN to trade their year's catch for supplies from the East. In the meantime Ashley and six men set out on the perilous rapids of the Green (later found to be the Colorado River).

On May 16, near the mouth of what some have called Ashley's Fork, they encountered two Frenchmen from Taos whose leader informed Ashley that the Green River was the Colorado and agreed to guide the men across the Wasatch Range. Two months later, the party reached the mouth of Minnie Maud Creek in eastern Utah (north of Desolation Canyon), turned upriver to the Uinta (Duchesne) River, followed it and its upper tributary, the Strawberry River, toward the Wasatch River in the west, marched overland north, west, and east around the Uinta Mountains, and at last kept Ashley's July appointment at the rendezvous. About 120 men gathered on the Green River, where Ashley sold supplies from the East and purchased more than 9000 pounds (4080 kilograms) of beaver, which later brought him $50,000 in St. Louis.

The rendezvous over, Ashley moved north through South Pass, along the Sweetwater and Popo Agie Rivers, down the Bighorn, then down the Yellowstone River to the Missouri. There, on August 19, after several Blackfoot and Crow attacks, he met a military expedition out of Fort Atkinson, whose leader agreed to escort Ashley to the fort. The following year, 1826, was Ashley's last as a mountain man. After transporting a supply of Eastern goods to the rendezvous in Cache Valley, he sold his share of the Rocky Mountain Fur Company to Jedediah Smith, David Jackson, and William Sublette and agreed to serve only as middleman in supplying trade goods and selling beaver in the East. From 1823 to 1827 he made a profit of nearly $60,000 a year. He eventually became a Missouri congressman.

Ashley's contributions to the westward movement of the United States were immense. In 4 years he transformed the fur trade into a highly lucrative business, encouraged Eastern investment in the West, fascinated thousands with the frontier's potential, and furnished a general guide west for emigrants. His men had discovered the Great Salt Lake, advertised Yellowstone Park's wonders, crossed the Great Basin, explored the Green River, opened the central Rocky Mountain fur trade, brought romance and success to the Mountain Men by initiating the rendezvous, completed the outline of the Oregon Trail, and proved the feasibility of using wagon trains west. Ashley also urged the federal government to encourage Western settlement by reducing tariffs, furnishing military protection for settlers, and supplying other aids in erasing the barrier.

BIBLIOGRAPHY: Harrison C. Dale, *The Ashley-Smith Exlorations and the Discovery of a Central Route to the Pacific, 1822–1829*, Cleveland, 1918; rev. ed., Glendale, Calif., 1941; William H. Goetzmann, *Exploration and Empire: The Explorer and the Scientist in the Winning of the American West*, New York, 1966; Dale L. Morgan, *The West of William H. Ashley*, Denver, 1964; Dale Van Every, *The Final Challenge: The American Frontier, 1804–1845*, New York, 1964.

Howard Jones

Asia

The exploration of Asia lasted for centuries and was affected by many different factors, such as geographic and climatic conditions in the various Asian regions, their propinquity to Europe, and the policies of both European and Asian states. In addition, while discussions of exploration in Asia usually emphasize the activities of Europeans, it should be kept in mind that the first explorers of Asia were the Asians themselves.

Much of Western Asia—Asia Minor and Syria, for example—was part of the Mediterranean-centered civilization of the ancient world and was therefore relatively well known to the geographers and travelers of Greece and Rome. This can be seen in the *History* of HERODOTUS OF HALICARNASSUS, who was a native of Asia Minor and traveled in Babylonia and the Black Sea area. His geographical knowledge of Western Asia was limited, however; this is true even for PERSIA despite its central role in his *History*.

In the era of classical antiquity the least familiar section of Western Asia was the Arabian peninsula, which was never conquered by Persia or by Rome. Herodotus knew that ARABIA was large and that it extended far to the south, and he associated it with spices. At the same time he described Arabia as a land of marvels whose denizens included winged serpents that guarded the frankincense trees and great birds that used cinnamon sticks to make their nests. The Sabaeans, who inhabited southwestern Arabia, subsequently became known for the wealth they acquired through the production and sale of spices and incense. A Roman expedition into Arabia led by Gaius Aelius Gallus during the reign of Augustus failed to conquer the Sabaeans and apparently contributed little to knowledge of the peninsula. PTOLEMY provided accurate data on the coastal areas, and his conception of Arabia's shape was approximately correct, yet he filled the interior with tribes and towns of dubious authenticity.

The birth of Islam in Arabia in the seventh century A.D. and its rapid spread into North Africa, Southern Europe, and much of Asia were to contribute in many ways to the advancement of exploration and geographical thought (*see* MUSLIM TRAVEL AND EXPLORATION IN THE MIDDLE AGES). For centuries, however,

European exploration of the peninsula itself was deterred by the harsh climate and terrain and by the hostility of the inhabitants.

The ancient world had but a faint notion of the old and complex civilizations of INDIA and CHINA. "India" meant only the region of the Indus Valley to Herodotus, but over the centuries new information about the subcontinent was accumulated, especially about the western coast and Ceylon. By the first century A.D. there was considerable trade between India and the Roman Empire, and there are reports that envoys were sent from India to Augustus and later Roman emperors. Even so, European ignorance about the eastern coast and the interior of India remained virtually complete until the Portuguese, Dutch, and English incursions of the sixteenth and seventeenth centuries.

If Herodotus at least knew the name of India, he was unaware of the existence of China, for he believed that to the east of India lay an uninhabited wilderness. Gradually, as Rome began to import Chinese silks after the second century B.C., bits of information, usually ambiguous, started to appear in geographical literature. It was not until the Mongol conquest of China and much of Asia in the thirteenth century that Europeans were able to obtain more reliable, if incomplete, data from travelers like Marco POLO.

Meanwhile, the Chinese themselves had traveled extensively to the south and west for a variety of motives, political, commercial, and religious, before the fifteenth century, when the government adopted a policy of retrenchment and isolation from the rest of the world. *See* CHINESE EXPLORATION.

The earliest travelers to SOUTHEAST ASIA were Indians, who visited the area before the Christian era. The first European to visit and describe Southeast Asia, Marco Polo, did not appear on the scene until the thirteenth century.

Penetration of CENTRAL ASIA by the Chinese began in the second century B.C. with the expeditions of CHANG CH'IEN. Much of the silk sold in the Roman Empire passed through this region, and place names and geographical details associated with the silk route began to appear in the writings of Ptolemy and others. From about 1250 to 1350 Central Asia received an influx of European missionaries and merchants, who were welcomed by the Mongol khans, not yet converted to Islam.

Isolated travelers continued to venture into the Asian heartland afterward, notably Jesuits who sought to reach inaccessible Tibet. In the nineteenth century the exploration of Central Asia was furthered by the rivalry of Great Britain and Russia, each of which wanted to extend its influence into the area.

The vast reaches of Northern Asia were explored by the Russian people as they began to expand to the east during the Middle Ages. The first-known expedition to SIBERIA took place in 1483. The following centuries saw the gradual subjugation of the Siberian tribes and the annexation of the region to the Russian empire.

See also ANCIENT EXPLORATION AND TRAVEL; MEDIEVAL EXPLORATION.

Atkinson, Thomas Wittlam *(1799–1861)* English traveler, painter, and architect. In 1842, in St. Petersburg, Atkinson gave up architecture to be a traveler and artist. On the advice of Alexander von Humboldt he turned his attention to Asiatic Russia and, encouraged by the Russian government, set out in February 1848 with his newly married wife, Lucy. His travels extended over 39,500 miles (63,567 kilometers), across the Urals to the Altai (Altay), across the Kazakh steppe to the foothills of the Alatau, and through Kobdo (Jargalant) and Uliassutai (Javhlant) to the heart of Mongolia. At the end of 1853 he returned with hundreds of watercolors. His book on the Amur (1860) was highly praised but later was shown to be mainly a plagiarism of Richard Karlovich Maack's work on the same subject, published in St. Petersburg in 1859, and doubts were raised as to whether Atkinson had himself traveled to the Amur. His wife wrote *Recollections of the Tartar Steppes and Their Inhabitants* (1863).

BIBLIOGRAPHY: Thomas Wittlam Atkinson, *Oriental and Western Siberia*, London, 1858; id., *Travels in the Region of the Upper and Lower Amoor*, London, 1860.

Richard A. Pierce

Atlasov, Vladimir Vasilyevich *(d. 1711)* Conqueror of Kamchatka. An Ustyug peasant, he settled in Siberia, became a Yakutsk cossack, and in 1695 was made *prikashchik* (manager) of the Anadyr *ostrog* (fort). Learning about Kamchatka from a reconnaissance by the cossack Luka Morozko, Atlasov himself led an expedition there in the spring of 1697. During the next 3 years he captured many Koryak and Kamchadal settlements and established an *ostrog*, Verkhnekamchatsk, on the Kamchatka River. In 1700 he was ordered to Moscow to report. In 1706 he was sent back to Kamchatka as *prikashchik*. Goaded by his cruelty, his men mutinied, and in 1711 he was slain.

Richard A. Pierce

Australia

Little was known about Australia when Capt. Arthur Phillip landed at Botany Bay in January 1788 to begin the convict colony of New South Wales. Admittedly, the eastern coast of the continent had been examined by Capt. James COOK 18 years before (indeed, this colony was one of the many results of Cook's voyage), and the other coasts had received sporadic attention from the Dutch in the 100 years after 1606, when the *Duyfken* sailed along the western fringe of Cape York Peninsula. But no European had been more than a few miles inland. The vast interior, an area of nearly 3,000,000 square miles (7,770,000 square kilometers), was totally unknown.

This is not to say, however, that there was no speculation about the nature of the interior, for this was Terra Australis, the legendary Great Southland, which had so captured the imagination of the ancient Greeks. They had viewed it as the perfect mirror of the most fertile lands bordering the Mediterranean Sea, the then-known world. Exploration changed this, for the Dutch had everywhere encountered a forbidding and barren coastline. Nevertheless, favorable speculations continued.

As North America was the nearest-known analogy for Australia, it is not surprising that the idea of an inland sea, similar perhaps to the Great Lakes, and a great river like the Mississippi claimed the greatest attention. Like earlier Dutch visions of an antipodean paradise, these were completely illusory and were dashed by the harsh realities of the Australian environment. This did not happen, however, before the illusions had influenced the nature and direction of inland exploration for the first 60 years of the continent's European occupation. Moreover, they were replaced by an equally illusory belief in a gigantic horseshoe-shaped lake which seemed to be an impenetrable barrier to all movement north of Adelaide.

Australia is really very different from early explorers' pictures of it, and this too was a major influence on exploration. It is an old, low land where a thin, fertile rim encloses an arid, infertile, and inhospitable core, the central third of which is desert. The desert is surrounded by a further third which receives less than 20 inches (508 millimeters) of rainfall annually. The best-watered parts are also the most rugged and difficult to traverse. The highlands bordering the eastern coast form the major barrier. Only the Kilmore Gap north of Melbourne and the valley of the Hunter River west of Newcastle allow ready access to the inland plains. Neither has been as significant as the Cumberland Gap or the Hudson-Mohawk Gap, their North American counterparts. Elsewhere on the eastern coast, small and discontinuous lowlands are flanked on their inland margins by steeply eroded highlands into which the headwaters of the short, coastward-flowing rivers have cut deep, steep gorges.

Once through the highlands, physical barriers decline in significance, but it is here that explorers were forcibly introduced to Australia's harsher qualities. As rivers flow toward the progressively drier and flatter interior, they lose much of their water to seepage or evaporation. In flat country they spread over the surface in small channels or anabranches, and many degenerate into a string of water holes which are joined only in very wet seasons.

Conditions on the barren shield of the western three-fifths of the continent are even worse. Rivers here are seasonal and restricted to a narrow coastal fringe, and while there are many large surface depressions containing moisture, nearly all are alkaline or salt. It was here that the explorers' skills and endurance were put to the greatest test.

Giving force to the difficulties which the land surface imposed were sudden and frequent climatic fluctuations in which flood could quickly follow drought. The flora and fauna, while extremely varied and unfamiliar, provided little nourishment, and all provisions had to be carried. Explorers therefore clung to the precarious lifelines offered by the rivers. Only after accumulating much experience did they venture across the waterless interfluves and through the desert. Not all succeeded.

Australia was clearly a hard continent to come to terms with, yet its exploration was accomplished with striking speed. Settlers took 25 years and several attempts to cross the eastern highlands, and then only because they followed the ridges instead of the valleys, but within 10 years they had explored a semicircular area 150 miles (241 kilometers) from Sydney. Thereafter, the pace of exploration quickened, and the broad configurations of the continent were virtually determined in the 50 years following the epic boat trip

Capt. James Cook lands in New South Wales in 1770. Anchoring in a sheltered harbor which he named Botany Bay because of the many rare plants found on its shores, Cook and his party landed their boats not far from an aboriginal camp. [National Library of Australia]

each colony fostered its own exploration, exploratory parties spread out fanlike and almost simultaneously from all colonial capitals, often being spurred on, as in the case of the north-south crossings in the 1860s and the east-west crossing in the 1870s, by considerable intercolonial rivalry.

Added to this was the fact that exploratory activity was always closely linked to the spread of settlement. The nature of the Australian environment and a rapidly expanding market in Europe encouraged pastoral activities on an extensive scale, and the rapid expansion of flocks and herbs generated a continued land shortage. It is significant that major breakthroughs like the 1813 crossing of the Blue Mountains and Sturt's 1828–1829 discovery of the Darling River occurred during periods of acute drought, while the rapid expansion of flocks in Western Australia in the 1840s and in northern Australia in the 1860s initiated major exploratory activity.

Hastening the pace were the explorers themselves. While motivated by a spirit of adventure, most were employed or sponsored by government agencies and were attracted by the tangible rewards successful exploration bestowed. For military officers in particular, exploration was a major avenue for self-advancement, although rewards tended to be in proportion to the value of lands discovered rather than the difficulties which were overcome. Rivalry, therefore, was sometimes intense. Very few explorers, even in later periods, were Australian-born, but most were competent, courageous, and resourceful. A few, notably Friedrich Wilhelm Ludwig LEICHHARDT and Robert BURKE and William John Wills, became victims of

of Charles STURT down the Murray River in 1830. Later explorers had the task of filling in the details.

The speed of discovery is in marked contrast to the pace in other parts of the globe but can be readily accounted for. Aboriginal inhabitants, although uncommunicative about their territories, offered little resistance, so that there were few barriers to impede progress once the highlands had been successfully penetrated. There was little to see or report on, and large segments of country had an overwhelming sameness and could be quickly examined and passed through. In any event, exploration was tied largely to the rivers, and these were very few in number. As

their own mismanagement, and even they, through their needless deaths, sponsored further exploration.

If we look at Australia's exploration overall, it falls into five distinct phases, each with a particular focus and a distinctive set of characteristics. The first, which spanned the first 27 years, was the longest and perhaps the least eventful.

First contacts, 1788–1815 Speculations worried early explorers very little. Survival was the immediate priority, and this required their getting to know and understand their immediate surroundings. The importance and urgency of this task and the extent of their ignorance were underlined with their first confrontation with Australia's bewildering environment. Botany Bay had been chosen as the site of the first settlement because it was one of the few stretches of coastline examined in detail and described favorably by Joseph Banks and James Cook in 1770. Arriving at the height of summer 18 years later, Phillip realized that their assessment had been grossly optimistic, for Botany Bay's sandiness and swampiness made it totally unsuitable. He was forced to sail north, enter Port Jackson, which had been bypassed by Cook, and establish his tiny penal outpost on the more fertile shores of Sydney Cove, where a small freshwater stream trickled into the sea. The site was severely hemmed in on the west by the sandstone barrier of the Blue Mountains, but this Phillip did not know, for they were not sighted until 3 months later.

Exploration in this early period was characterized by progressively bolder probings outward from Sydney. Phillip actively fostered discovery, taking part in several expeditions and commissioning others, and at the end of his governorship in December 1792 the area from Broken Bay in the north to Botany Bay in the south and the Nepean River in the west, approximately 40 miles (64 kilometers) square, was well known. On more fertile soils within this area, notably near Parramatta and at Richmond, a beginning had been made in agriculture. These became centers for the future spread of settlement and so fostered further exploration.

With their increasing confidence, explorers spread even farther afield and particularly to the north and south. They were spurred on by continuing escapes among the predominantly Irish convict population, who believed that China was no great distance to the north. This led to major discoveries, for Lieut. John Shortland, in search of escapees, examined the Hunter Valley and the future site of Newcastle in September 1797.

Even more significant was the convicts' belief that a colony of white people lay less than 400 miles (644 kilometers) to the southwest. Here they would "receive all the comforts of life without the necessity of labour," a very heady vision after life on the chain gang. In January 1798, in an attempt to stop the resultant flow of escapees, Gov. John Hunter sent four

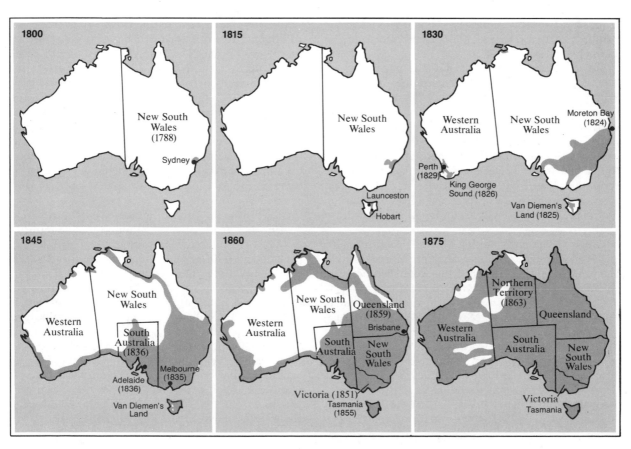

Opening up the continent of Australia. Shaded areas indicate explored territory.

convicts, four soldiers, and two civilians under the guidance of the ex-convict John Wilson in the general direction of the supposed utopia. The convicts returned within 10 days complaining that the land of leisure required too much effort to get there, leaving Wilson and the civilians to continue to the junction of the Wingecarribee and Wollondilly Rivers. Within a month of their return, Wilson followed this expedition with a second journey which took him as far south as Mount Towrang near the present site of Goulburn. Little is known about this journey, but the distance traveled marks it out as one of the most significant achievements of the period.

While the bounds of knowledge had thus been extended northward more than 70 miles (113 kilometers) and southward more than 100 miles (161 kilometers) by 1800, knowledge of what lay west of the Nepean was still hidden by the rugged, tortuous terrain of the Blue Mountains. At least eight attempted crossings of these were made between 1789 and 1804, but while each seemed more successful and penetrated deeper than its predecessors, all were repulsed. William Dawes (1789), Watkin Tench (1790), William Paterson (1793), Henry Hacking (1794), George Bass (1796), Francis Luis Barrallier (1802), and George Caley (1804, 1806) all returned to the settled areas utterly exhausted to declare that the gorges were invincible. It was widely agreed "that this formidable barrier is impassable for man." Perhaps because of these difficulties on land, attention turned to the sea. During this period most of Australia's coastline was mapped, notably by George Bass (1795–1799), Nicolas Baudin (1801–1803), and Matthew FLINDERS (1796, 1798–1799, 1801–1803).

But the lack of progress did not go unnoticed. Banks, a major advocate of Australian exploration, expressed his concern as early as 1798. He held great hopes for the inland, believing that its vastness contained "vast rivers capable of being navigated into the heart of the continent" and that it would reveal "some native raw material of importance." He therefore urged its examination. But the crossing of the mountains came not from the desire to find great rivers but from the need for grass, a need brought on by the prolonged drought beginning in the summer of 1810.

Gregory Blaxland, looking for fresh pastures along the Warragamba River, had determined by then that the range could be crossed if the watershed between the Warragamba and the Grose was followed, but he did not act until pastures had further deteriorated. Leaving South Creek on May 11, 1813, and accompanied by William Lawson, a surveyor, the pastoralist William Charles Wentworth, and four convicts, he climbed the first spur and proceeded west across the plateau. Traveling as little as 2 miles (3 kilometers) a day, but always keeping to the ridges, the party forced its way through heavy brush until it reached Mount Blaxland on May 28. It then turned for home, a few

miles short of the watershed. The mountains had been severely breached but were still unconquered.

Perceiving the significance of this journey, a privately sponsored one, Gov. Lachlan Macquarie sent surveyor George William Evans out in November 1813 to confirm and extend Blaxland's discoveries. From Mount Blaxland, Evans plunged across the Great Dividing Range to the Fish River. This he followed northwest to its junction with the Campbell before tracing the main stream, which he named the Macquarie, northward for 20 miles (32 kilometers) through rich grassy plains. Evans, having conquered the mountains, returned to Sydney, where his news so excited Macquarie that William Cox was ordered to construct a road over the 101 miles (163 kilometers) of the Blaxland-Evans track. This was finished in 6 months, and in April 1815 Macquarie used it to cross the mountains and fix the site of the new town of Bathurst. Evans, sent to examine the country to the southwest, returned to Bathurst to state that he had traversed much good land before encountering the Lachlan River flowing strongly to the west. With this good news, the stage was set for the exploration and occupation of the inland.

Into the inland, 1816–1827   Convinced that the rivers Evans discovered would join farther west into a mighty stream which would then flow either to the Indian Ocean or into Spencer Gulf, Macquarie ordered Surveyor General John OXLEY in April 1817 to trace the course of the Lachlan. Starting where Evans finished in 1815, Oxley proceeded downstream until stopped by extensive marshes. Unable to bypass these and hoping to intersect further rivers, Oxley struck southwest but after crossing thick, desolate scrub swung north 25 miles (40 kilometers) short of the Murrumbidgee to follow the Lachlan downstream. Again he was thwarted by impenetrable swamps. Concluding that the Lachlan could not possibly enter the sea, that it did not join the Macquarie, and that the interior was a marsh and uninhabitable, he retraced his steps to the point where the river emerged from the first marshes. Heading off across country, he came on the Macquarie from the west and traced its course back to Bathurst.

Oxley was so deeply impressed with the Macquarie's size and fertile surroundings that he returned in May 1818 intending to examine its entire length. Both he and the Governor were hopeful that this was the mighty river they sought. Its strong flow, bolstered by recent heavy rains, was most reassuring, and Oxley sailed from Bathurst northward for more than 220 miles (354 kilometers) through attractive open grassy plains. But then the Macquarie, like the Lachlan, branched into many small channels and vanished into swamps. Being unable to penetrate these, Oxley concluded that he was on the edge of an apparently worthless sea. Disheartened, he set off to the east, passing through the fertile Liverpool Plains and across the southern edge of the New England Plateau (New

England Range) before following the Hastings River down to the sea. On his return to Sydney so effectively did his report puncture Macquarie's vision that all major exploration ceased.

Minor sorties continued, however, as settlers pushed out from the growing number of small settlements. It was south of Sydney that progress was most impressive. In near-annual assaults, Hamilton HUME, Charles Throsby, and James Meehan, sometimes alone but more often together, peeled back the frontier, reaching the Bargo Brush and Berrima in 1814, Bong Bong in 1816, Sutton Forest in 1817, and Jervis Bay and Lake Bathurst in 1818. By 1821 Throsby had seen the Murrumbidgee. Two years earlier he had linked Bathurst with these newly discovered areas and the coast. Almost simultaneously, John Howe blazed a trail from Windsor on the Hawkesbury to Newcastle, where a small convict post had been established from the sea 15 years earlier.

These short journeys proved a sound training for Hamilton Hume when he resumed the examination of the inland. Acting on Gov. Sir Thomas Brisbane's desire to know what lay south of the Lachlan, he and William Hovell, a former sailor, decided to make for Westernport on the south coast. Leaving Hume's station near Lake George on October 17, 1824, they plunged southwesterly into a tangle of hills, crossing river after river and rich intervening grassland until they emerged on the shores of Corio Bay on December 16. Through a navigational error, they assumed this was Westernport and returned to Sydney praising its fertility. Although they had effectively disproved Oxley's view that the country to the south of the Lachlan was uninhabitable, the disappointment their error generated among those colonists who arrived to exploit Westernport's supposedly abundant grass helped to direct the main stream of settlement to the north of Sydney. This led to the expedition of Allan CUNNINGHAM in 1827.

Cunningham, a botanist, had been with Oxley in 1817 and had in 1823 explored an extensive area to the north of Bathurst and found, after several attempts, a pass into Oxley's Liverpool Plains. Now, starting from the upper Hunter River, he passed through the Liverpool Plains north to the Namoi River and then through broken country on the west of the New England Plateau to cross the Gwydir and Macintyre Rivers flowing west. Swinging slightly east, he struggled through unattractive country to burst on a broad black-soil plain covered with succulent grass. This, a major find, he named the Darling Downs after the new governor, Sir Ralph Darling. His homeward path, farther to the east, crossed the very fine pastures of the New England Plateau. These were soon occupied.

With Hume and Hovell, Cunningham had opened up a broad belt of country from near Moreton Bay (Brisbane) in the north to Port Philip (Melbourne) in the south. This was of major significance and, for a time, satisfied the need for grass. Only the extremely rugged southeast remained unseen, and this was soon to be traversed by Angus Macmillan (1839) and Paul Edmund de Strzelecki (1840). But their journeys had another significance. They had crossed many large rivers, and Cunningham had heard aborigines speak of large waters to the west where men used canoes and caught gigantic fish. The journeys therefore revived speculations about mighty rivers and inland seas.

Riddle of the rivers, 1828–1836 It was to these that attention now turned. Determined to resolve the riddle of the rivers, Governor Darling selected Charles Sturt, a young army officer who had been in the colony less than 18 months, to find out what happened to the Macquarie beyond Mount Harris, Oxley's end point of 1818. Darling's choice was a wise one, for Sturt not only unraveled the mystery but did it in a way that inspired later explorers to emulate his unparalleled example of courage, endurance, and leadership. To offset Sturt's inexperience, Darling appointed Hamilton Hume as his assistant. With their party, they left Wellington on December 7, 1828, hopeful that the prolonged dry conditions would ease their passage through Oxley's swamps.

Their hopes were not realized. The marshes were still impenetrable. So, after brief sallies east and west, they headed west, then north across the Bogan River and through the drought-stricken country of Oxley's tableland to come on the "banks of a noble river . . . seventy to eighty yards broad." Their joy at finding at least one mighty river, appropriately named the Darling, was cut short by the saltiness of its contents, but, now believing they were on a branch of the inland sea, they headed downstream. On finding brine springs flowing strongly into the river, they retraced their steps to Mount Harris before heading east to follow the dry bed of the Castlereagh north to the Darling. In returning to Mount Harris, they again crossed the Macquarie, now clear of the swamps and flowing strongly north.

On his return to Sydney, Sturt expressed the view that the Darling would continue southwesterly until it joined the Murrumbidgee and would then swing in a great loop toward the northwest, probably to enter an inland sea. It was therefore decided that he should now examine the Murrumbidgee to determine if it ended in marshes like the Lachlan, if it united with the Darling River as Governor Darling thought, or if it emptied into the sea on the southern or some other coast. Thus began a voyage characterized by great achievement and great hardship. The homeward journey was so rigorous that Sturt went blind temporarily and never regained perfect health.

Leaving Sydney on November 3, 1829, Sturt cut across to follow the Murrumbidgee to near its junction with the Lachlan. Deciding to sail from here, he assembled the whaleboat brought from Sydney and with seven companions, three of them convicts, entered the Murrumbidgee on January 7, 1830. Twenty-

Allan Cunningham, who discovered fine grasslands in the Darling Downs and the New England Plateau. [National Library of Australia]

six days later he emerged on the shores of Lake Alexandrina, having sailed more than 900 miles (1448 kilometers), most of them on the "broad and noble river" which he encountered shortly after his departure and which he named the Murray, and after having passed a "new and beautiful stream" from the north which he correctly guessed to be the Darling. Lake Alexandrina was disappointing. Its narrow entrance was hazardous for shipping, and after examining it for 3 days, the party turned for home. It took them another 3½ hard months to reach Sydney, but in this one voyage they had explained the drainage of the continent's major river system and had opened up much good land for settlement. Subsequently, in 1838 Sturt followed this up by tracing the Murray from its source to its junction with the Murrumbidgee.

Thomas Livingstone MITCHELL, appointed surveyor general on Oxley's death in 1828 and jealous of Sturt's success, now requested permission to go exploring. He firmly believed that a great river lay north of the Darling and had visions of this becoming a major trade route to India. His first expedition, precipitated by aboriginal tales of a great river called the Kindur, was disappointing. As each major river he encountered—the Namoi, Gwydir, Macintyre, and Barwon—eventually turned west, it became obvious that they were tributaries of the Darling. The killing of two of his party by aborigines gave him an excuse for turning home. Over the next few years, he became convinced that it was the Darling which flowed northwest, and in 1835 he sallied forth to satisfy his curiosity. After following the Darling southwest for more than 300 miles (483 kilometers) from the depot he established at Fort Bourke, he accepted defeat of his theory and turned back.

But the Darling's course had not been confirmed,

and Mitchell was sent back in 1836 to travel from the Murray junction to the point he had reached the previous year. He first followed the Lachlan in the hope that this was the river Sturt had seen entering the Murray, but being able to penetrate the marshes, he found it joined the Murrumbidgee. Marching to the Murray (Mitchell's expeditions had a distinct military flavor), he satisfied himself that Sturt's unnamed stream was the Darling and then, instead of returning to the settled areas as instructed, swept southward into an area of such fine grass that he named it Australia Felix. On his homeward journey he made two detours, one to Portland Bay, where James and Thomas Henty, pioneer pastoralists, had established themselves 2 years previously, and the other to Mount Macedon, from which he saw the first signs of the pastoral occupation of the Port Philip district by squatters from Van Diemen's Land. These illegal pastoral incursions heralded a new age, for the pace of exploration now snowballed.

Around the edge and into the middle, 1837–1859

With the southeast corner becoming well known, explorers now began to grope their way around the rim and make occasional tentative jabs at the center. The southwest corner was known in outline when Sturt sailed down the Murray, for the small settlement at the Swan River, established in June 1829, was already linked with the convict depot at King George Sound. Later expeditions to the inland pastures of the Avon Valley and its extensions consolidated this knowledge, which was dramatically augmented with George Grey's desperate race south from Gantheaume Bay in 1839. Van Diemen's Land, renamed Tasmania in 1855, was also well known. Hobart and Launceston, established in 1803 to forestall supposed French territorial ambitions, were linked by 1807, and this

A branch of the Darling River. Charles Sturt's discovery of the Darling in 1829 led him to solve the problem of the drainage of Australia's major river system, which had baffled explorers for decades. [Library of Congress]

link provided a starting point for a number of sorties east and west. The activities of the Van Diemen's Land Agricultural Company, formed in 1825, opened up much of the northwest, so that by 1830 the only extensive unexamined areas lay in the mountainous south and west.

But it was from Adelaide, established in 1836, that progress was most effective. Overlanders, driving sheep and cattle to the buoyant Adelaide market, had almost immediately linked it with Sydney and Melbourne. Curiosity now turned to the north with Edward John EYRE, an overlander and a friend of Sturt, in the vanguard. In 1840, on his third trip north and again thwarted by the salt Lake Torrens, which he thought to be part of a great east-west horseshoe lake, he decided to leave most of his party behind and strike west until a way through could be found. Some 1300 miles (2092 kilometers) and more than 4 months later, unable to swing north and being forced to keep close to the coast by the waterless surface of the Nullarbor Plain, he arrived at Albany (previously King George Sound) with his aboriginal servant Wylie. John Baxter, his white companion, had been murdered en route by the other two aborigines, who then fled. The nine horses and six sheep had also perished.

Eyre had, by this epic journey, strengthened the conviction that South Australia was a fertile island surrounded by desert and a semicircular salt-lake barrier and had seemingly destroyed any prospect of finding an inland sea. But his discovery of Lake Torrens had so revived Sturt's hopes that Sturt, now employed by the South Australian Survey Department, offered to make a north-south and east-west crossing of the continent within 2 years. This was considered too ambitious, but Sturt was nevertheless given the task of finding the divide supposed to lie west of the Darling. So strong was his belief in an inland sea and so confident was he of finding it, that Sturt took a boat with him when he left Adelaide in August 1844.

The voyage began well, but Sturt walked into the most ferocious drought yet experienced and became marooned for 6 months at the Depot Glen water hole, where the heat was so intense that the men's hair stopped growing. When the drought broke, and after a brief trip west which seemed to confirm the existence of the horseshoe lake, Sturt and a small party pushed northwest for 450 miles (724 kilometers) until the harshness of the Stony Desert forced their retreat just 150 miles (241 kilometers) short of the center. On reaching the depot, Sturt and his draftsman, John McDouall STUART, went north until the drought and the desert again forced them to withdraw. Now almost totally incapacitated by scurvy and without seeing Lake Eyre, the inland sea he sought, Sturt agreed to return to Adelaide. His health was so undermined in the 18 months this journey took that he explored no more.

In New South Wales, meanwhile, Mitchell and others discussed the desirability of a trail northwest from the Darling Downs which would tap the wealth of India. All were forestalled before they could act on this by Ludwig Leichhardt, an impoverished and inexperienced German who, beginning in August 1844, walked overland with seven companions from Moreton Bay (now Brisbane) 2000 miles (3219 kilometers) to Port Essington (Darwin). The trip took 15 months and was completed in appalling conditions, for Leichhardt's faith in his abilities was not matched by his actions. But it had thrown northern Australia open to pastoral occupation, and Leichhardt was lionized on his return to Sydney. Here he evolved the idea of crossing the continent to Perth. His first attempt (1846) was a fiasco, and further support was difficult to attract. Eventually, in April 1848, with Adolf Classen, a relative, and five others he headed west across the Darling Downs and vanished.

Edward John Eyre, whose 1840 expedition overland from Adelaide west to Albany convinced explorers that the fertile southern part of South Australia was surrounded by desert and a salt lake, dashing their hopes for finding a great inland sea. [Australian Information Service]

Mitchell, anxious for further fame, finally took to the field in December 1845 while the fate of Leichhardt's northern crossing remained unknown. He, too, with his huge party of twenty-eight men, 17 horses, 112 bullocks, and 250 sheep, intended making for Port Essington, but when a courier caught up with him and described Leichhardt's triumphant return to Sydney he continued due northward to the Belyando River. In so doing, he traversed the rich pastures of the Maranoa district and came across a major river flowing northwest. This, "the realization of my long cherished hopes," he named the Victoria after his gracious Queen, seeing it as "a reward from Heaven" for his perseverance and personal sacrifice. His desire for fame and fortune satisfied, he returned to Sydney.

A year later (1847), Mitchell's assistant Edmund Kennedy was sent out to confirm and extend these discoveries. Following the course of the Victoria, he demonstrated that it was actually the Barcoo and that it eventually flowed southwest. He followed this up in the next year with an overland expedition from Rockingham Bay to Cape York. This was a tragic failure. Only three of his party of thirteen survived, and Kennedy was killed by aborigines before reaching the cape. It was not until 1864–1865, when Frank and Alexander Jardine blazed a trail north, that the details of the Cape York Peninsula became known.

Leichhardt's disappearance prompted further discovery, particularly by Augustus Charles GREGORY. With his brothers Francis and Henry, all products of J. S. Roe's Western Australian Survey Department, Gregory had already made a major contribution, having opened the Champion Bay area to pastoralists in 1846 and the Murchison Basin in 1848. This Francis followed up with the Gascoyne district in 1858 and the North West in 1861. Together with Roe's 1848 expedition and Robert Austin's expedition of 1854, these laid the basis of Western Australia's pastoral expansion.

Augustus was commissioned in 1855 to traverse northern Australia in an eastward direction, keeping a lookout for traces of Leichhardt. Landing at the mouth of the Victoria River, he followed its course to the south before tracing Sturt Creek to the edge of the

Great Sandy Desert. Finding some good pastoral country, he retraced his steps and headed east on a route parallel to Leichhardt's. The crossing, which took only 4 months against Leichhardt's 15, revealed much rich grassland, which was quickly occupied.

Sent out again 2 years later, Gregory found traces of Leichhardt's expedition after crossing the Warrego and Barcoo Rivers but was forced by drought to give up his search. Returning to the Barcoo, he followed it downstream to determine whether it was the Cooper's Creek Sturt examined in 1845. Convinced that it was, he diverged southward along Strzelecki Creek and between Lakes Frome and Torrens before making for Adelaide. He had by this solved the mystery of Australia's second major river system, had destroyed the belief that central Australia was totally worthless, and had challenged the theory that there was a horseshoe lake and that it posed an impassable barrier. Benjamin Herschel Babbage, Stuart, and Peter Egerton Warburton completed the challenge and within 2 years located and mapped all the major lakes north of Adelaide.

Continental crossings, 1860–1879

By 1860 only the center and northwest remained unseen. These areas were crossed and recrossed in the next 20 years by skilled professional explorers who had no delusions about how harsh and unforgiving the land could be and who took few risks. No sea or great river was expected now. The discovery of adequate grazing land was considered sufficient reward. It is therefore surprising that the period should open with a tragedy unparalleled in Australian exploration for mismanagement and misplaced enthusiasm.

The Burke and Wills Expedition was marked for tragedy from the outset. It was to be exploration by a committee of the Philosophical Institute of Victoria, no member of which had any practical experience but all of whom were attracted by visions of the fame which would accrue to themselves and to Victoria, newly rich with gold, for making the first crossing of the continent. They selected Robert O'Hara Burke, a contagious enthusiast but no bushman or leader, to lead the expedition and instructed him to go north between Sturt's and Gregory's tracks and link Cooper's Creek with Leichhardt's northern traverse. Speed was urged, for Stuart, sponsored by the South Australian government, was known to be in the field.

The expedition, the most expensive ever undertaken, left Melbourne on August 20, 1860. Quarrels broke out almost immediately, and the party was in complete disarray when it reached Menindee on the Darling. From here Burke made for Cooper's Creek with a small advance party, leaving instructions that the rest were to follow with provisions. Impatient at their nonarrival (they never got there), Burke with William Wills, his surveyor assistant, John King, and his foreman Charles Gray dashed north on foot on December 16. They reached the Gulf of Carpentaria on February 9, 1861, but were stopped from seeing it by mangrove swamps. Now very short of food, they returned, arriving at Cooper's Creek on April 21 "in time to find it deserted." William Brahe, left in charge but with no clear instructions and his men suffering severely from scurvy, had departed that morning. Making the fatal decision to head southwest instead of following Brahe's tracks, Burke and Wills perished. Gray was already dead. An emaciated King, kept alive by friendly aborigines, was rescued by a relief party led by Alfred William Howitt in September.

As for the journey itself, it was hardly exploration. Burke kept no journal, and the speed of the crossing allowed no time for scientific observations. It is ironic that only by their deaths did Burke and Wills foster major discovery. The four expeditions sent out to find them—led by Howitt, William Landsborough, Frederick Walker, and John McKinlay—opened up much good pastoral country in eastern and northern Australia.

It was equally ironic that Stuart should return to Adelaide from his successful crossing only 9 days after Howitt arrived there with the bodies of Burke and Wills. Stuart's achievements were of epic proportions and rank among the greatest in modern exploration. In three successive raids, he plunged progressively farther north, reaching beyond Lake Eyre in November 1859, Attack Creek in June 1860, and Newcastle Waters in July 1861. On each occasion the harshness of the land beat him back, but his fourth assault was successful, and he reached the mouth of the Adelaide River on July 24, 1862. By now his health was completely undermined (he had spent 38 of the last 55 months in the field, usually suffering from scurvy), and for much of the return journey he lay in a litter, paralyzed and blind. He was rewarded with £2000 for his efforts, but, his health broken, he returned to England to die.

Within 10 years the overland telegraph line snaked north along Stuart's trail, finally conquering the center and linking Australia with the outside world. The chain of repeater stations along its length now provided convenient jumping-off points for incursions into the deserts of the Western Plateau. But the first assault came from the west, not the east, and again Leichhardt was the inspiration.

In 1869 a report reached Perth of an attack on white men many years before and the discovery of their skeletons. The colonial government, thinking these were Leichhardt's remains, sent John FORREST, a Western Australian–born pupil of both Roe and the Gregorys, to investigate. The bones turned out to be those of horses lost by Austin in 1854, but Forrest took the opportunity of continuing into the desert as far as Mount Weld. He followed this up the next year by blazing a trail from Perth across the Nullarbor Plain to Adelaide. This paralleled Eyre's route of 29 years before and is near the site of the present highway. Then, in 1874, having fulfilled instructions to examine the headwaters of the Murchison and Gascoyne Rivers, Forrest crossed the Gibson Desert and passed between the Macdonnell and Musgrave ranges to connect with the overland telegraph line at Alberga.

Meanwhile, interest in a crossing from South Australia had heightened. First to make the attempt was Ernest GILES, who started from Charlotte Waters in August 1872. But, privately sponsored and poorly equipped, he got no farther than Lake Amadeus before being beaten back by the shortage of water and grass. William Christie Gosse and Peter Egerton Warburton joined him in the following year. Both left Alice Springs in mid-April, but Gosse, after discovering the giant monolith of Ayer's Rock, returned, "having pushed on as far as is safe." Warburton, the first to make exclusive use of camels, continued on. Although he hoped to reach Perth, the lack of water repeatedly diverted him northward so that he reached the west coast 1000 miles (1609 kilometers) from his destination and after nearly 10 months of extreme hardship. He afterward wrote that "no exploring party ever endured such protracted suffering . . . nor did anyone ever cross so vast an extent of continuous bad country."

Giles, beaten back again in August 1873, later concluded that camels held the key to a successful crossing. After collecting twenty-four animals from Thomas Elder's stud at Beltana Station in May 1875, Giles traversed the 2500 miles (4023 kilometers) from Port Augusta to Perth in little more than 5 months. The camels were invaluable, having at one point crossed a waterless, desolate stretch of 325 miles (523 kilometers) in a region "utterly unknown to man and as utterly forsaken by God." Further proving their worth and his mastery of the desert, Giles returned to Adelaide by a more difficult northern route after little more than 2 months' rest. Thereafter, camels became the accepted mode of transport in the interior.

With Alexander Forrest's careful examination of the Kimberleys in 1879, the broad outlines of the entire continent were sketched in. Areas suitable for stock were already occupied, and only the most hostile and inaccessible pockets remained unseen. Over the next few years, spurred on by the discovery of gold in Western Australia's arid interior, a number of notable explorers including Ernest Favenc (1879), David Lindsay (1891), David Wynford Carnegie (1894), Frank H. Hann (1896–1898) and Alfred Wernam Canning (1901) completed their examination. The honor of making the last discovery fell to C. T. Madigan, who in 1939 with nine men and nineteen camels explored and mapped that part of the Simpson Desert which had so convincingly defeated Sturt in 1845.

A concluding comment When we look back at the story of Australian exploration, three key features stand out. The first is the underlying logic to the spread of discovery. Explorers served their apprenticeships in the humid, milder landscapes of the southeast before pushing irresistibly outward to the harsher west and north. The second is the small number of men who were actually involved and the very close ties that existed between them. A. C. Gregory spoke of an apostolic succession among explorers, and there was some truth in this, for he had been trained by Roe and in turn trained his brothers and both Forrests. And Roe had earlier surveyed the coastline with Philip Parker King, whose father had arrived with the first fleet. Evans introduced Oxley to the inland, Hume introduced Sturt, and Sturt introduced Stuart.

But the most striking feature perhaps was the nature of the exploration itself. This Ernest Favenc, himself a noted explorer, so neatly captured: "It is the spectacle of one man pitted against the whole force of nature . . . where even the physical laws do not assimilate with those of other continents." That men were the victors in this conflict testifies to their single-minded courage and determination.

BIBLIOGRAPHY: J. H. L. Cumpston, *The Inland Sea and the Great River: The Story of Australian Exploration*, Sydney, 1964; Ernest Favenc, *The Explorers of Australia and Their Life Work*, Christchurch, 1908; id., *The History of Australian Exploration from 1788 to 1888*, Sydney, 1888; E. H. J. Feeken and Gerda E. E. Feeken, *The Discovery and Exploration of Australia*, Melbourne, 1970; Kathleen Fitzpatrick (ed.), *Australian Explorers: A Selection from Their Writings, with an Introduction*, London, 1958; Garry Hogg, *The Overlanders*, London, 1961; Egon Kunz, *A Continent Takes Shape*, Sydney, 1971.

J. M. R. Cameron

Ávila, Pedro Arias de; Pedrarias; Pedrarias Dávila (1442–1531)

Spanish soldier and colonial administrator. Born in Arias, Segovia, of Jewish origin, he served as an officer in Africa in campaigns against the Moors in 1510. He was married to Doña Isabel de Bobadilla y de Peñalosa, a strong-willed woman who bore him eight children and insisted on accompanying him to the New World, a singular act at that time. On July 27, 1513, he received a commission to assume the governorship of Darién as a result of complaints by Martín Fernández de Enciso against Vasco Núñez de BALBOA, news of whose discovery of the Pacific Ocean had not yet reached Spain. He sailed in a large fleet from Sanlúcar de Barrameda on April 12, 1514, and arrived on June 29 with 1500 men.

As a governor Pedrarias has been universally characterized as hard, cruel, and rapacious—the worst governor the Indies had ever known. In his youth he had been called El Galán (the Gallant One) and El Justador (the Jouster), tributes to his gallantry and prowess; in his later years, however, he was deservedly referred to as Furor Domini (Wrath of God). Pedrarias instituted an official review of Balboa's conduct but was unsuccessful in convicting him of any misdeeds. He then arranged a proxy marriage of one of his daughters to Balboa and bided his time, waiting until Balboa relaxed his guard, when he accused him of treason and, after a trial, ordered him beheaded in January 1519. That same year, he founded Panama City, the oldest existing European settlement on the American mainland.

Pedrarias encouraged, and may even have backed, Francisco PIZARRO and Diego de ALMAGRO in their search for Peru. A promoter of exploration in Central America, he seized control of Nicaragua, where he died, on March 6, 1531, in León. He had been made governor in 1527 after having been superseded at Panama by Pedro de los Ríos.

See also WEST INDIES, CENTRAL AMERICA, AND MEXICO.

BIBLIOGRAPHY: Pascual de Andagoya, *Narrative of the Proceedings of Pedrarias Dávila*, tr. by C. R. Markham, London, 1865.

Martin Torodash

B

Badigin, Konstantin Sergeyevich (1910–) Soviet naval captain and Arctic specialist. In 1935–1936 Badigin first sailed in the Arctic Ocean as third mate on the icebreaker *Krasin.* In 1937 he was second mate on the icebreaker *Sadko,* which on October 23, 1937, with the icebreakers *G. Sedov* and *Malygin,* was trapped by drifting ice in the Laptev Sea at 75°21′N, 132°15′E. In April 1938, when at 79–80°N planes took most of the personnel off the vessels, he was transferred from the *Sadko* to the *G. Sedov* as captain. At the end of August, after the icebreaker *Yermak* had pulled the *Sadko* and *Malygin* out of the ice, he and a crew of fourteen continued drifting on the *G. Sedov,* which had a damaged rudder. On August 29, 1939, the *G. Sedov* was at 86°39′30″N, 47°55′E, the highest latitude reached by a vessel drifting with the ice. The drift, lasting 812 days and extending 3750 miles (6035 kilometers), ended at the Greenland Sea, northwest of Spitsbergen (Svalbard), 80°30′N, 1°50′E, on January 13, 1940, when the *G. Sedov* was freed by the icebreaker *I. Stalin.* During the drift the crew made scientific observations and repaired the vessel so that it could go to Murmansk under its own power. Badigin received the title Hero of the Soviet Union, as did the rest of the fourteen Sedovtsy.

Richard A. Pierce

Baffin, William (1584?–1622) British Arctic explorer. The earliest record of Baffin dates from 1612, when he was chief pilot of the *Patience* on James Hall's fourth Arctic expedition. This expedition explored the west coast of Greenland to about 68°30′N. On his return,

Baffin entered service with the Muscovy Company, which in 1613 sent north a fleet of seven ships to establish a claim to exclusive rights over the Spitsbergen (Svalbard) whale fishery. Baffin was chief pilot of the fleet, sailing on the *Tiger.* He joined the company's fleet again in 1614, on board *Thomasine,* and this time explored a large stretch of the coast of Spitsbergen.

Baffin then joined the Northwest Company and, in 1615 and 1616, made his two famous voyages in search of a NORTHWEST PASSAGE as the pilot of Robert BYLOT on board *Discovery.* Their discovery and meticulous examination of Baffin Bay during the second of these voyages was one of the most remarkable single advances in the history of Arctic exploration. Later explorers, however, ignored the area; lack of confirmation led to considerable skepticism about the authenticity of their discoveries, and Baffin Bay was eventually eliminated from maps. It was not until 1818 that their discoveries were confirmed by John Ross.

Baffin spent the rest of his life in the service of the East India Company. He died during a warlike engagement with the Portuguese in the Persian Gulf.

BIBLIOGRAPHY: C. R. Markham (ed.), *The Voyages of William Baffin 1612–1622,* London, 1881.

Clive A. Holland

Baker, Samuel White (1821–1893) English explorer. A member of a wealthy family with colonial property and commercial interests, Baker was educated in private schools and completed his studies in Germany.

On his way to find the source of the Nile, Samuel Baker met James Grant and John Speke as they were returning from their successful journey to the same goal. Nothing daunted, he went on to discover Lake Albert and the Murchison Falls. [Library of Congress]

After marrying the daughter of an English clergyman in 1842, Baker traveled to Mauritius, where his father owned sugar estates, and then to Ceylon, where he established an English agricultural colony and indulged his passion for sport. Following the death of his wife in 1855 soon after their return to England, Baker spent several years in aimless wandering through Asia Minor and the Balkans.

In 1861 Baker and his second wife, Florence von Sass, a Hungarian woman 15 years his junior, went to Egypt, where Baker planned to embark upon a quest for the sources of the Nile. He also hoped to meet John Hanning SPEKE and James Augustus GRANT, who had begun a similar search the previous year. After spending 14 months in Sudan learning Arabic and exploring the tributaries flowing into the Nile from Ethiopia, Baker went to Khartoum, whence the expedition set sail for Gondokoro, which was reached on February 2, 1863. On February 15, the sound of musketry heralded the arrival of Speke and Grant, who brought the news that they had solved the riddle of the Nile sources. Baker's disappointment was assuaged somewhat when Speke told him of a large undiscovered lake called the Luta N'zige, which reputedly was connected with the Nile system. Baker started for the southeast in March 1863, being forced to accept the company of a slave trader's caravan. It was not until January 1864 that the party reached the kingdom of Bunyoro, whose ruler, Kamurasi, was suspicious of Baker's intentions and deputed his younger brother to impersonate him. On March 14, 1864, Baker sighted the Luta N'zige, which he named Lake Albert. Obtaining some canoes, he paddled to the point where the Nile enters the lake and then traveled eastward for a short distance until he reached the waterfall which he named the Murchison Falls in honor of the president of the ROYAL GEOGRAPHICAL SOCIETY.

Baker was awarded the gold medal of the Royal Geographical Society even before his return to England, and in 1866 he was knighted. In 1869 the Bakers accompanied the Prince of Wales to Egypt to attend the ceremonies held in honor of the opening of the Suez Canal. On that occasion the modernizing viceroy of Egypt, Ismail, invited Baker to lead an expedition to the upper Nile to extend Egyptian rule in that region and to suppress the slave trade. Baker accepted Ismail's offer but met with much opposition not only from the Arab slavers but also from Africans, notably Kamurasi's son and successor, Kabarega, who resented Baker's efforts to establish Egyptian hegemony in Bunyoro. Baker's principal achievement was the construction of a fort at Fatiko, which became the southernmost outpost of the expedition. Baker returned to England in 1873 at the expiration of his 4-year appointment, being regarded until his death as a leading expert on African matters. His books include *The Albert N'yanza, Great Basin of the Nile, and Explorations of the Nile Sources* (1866) and *Exploration of the Nile Tributaries of Abyssinia* (1868).

Vasco Núñez de Balboa, Spanish explorer who climbed a hill in Darién and discovered the Pacific Ocean. Although he also amassed a treasure in gold and pearls for the Spanish crown, the envy of Governor Ávila led to Balboa's execution on trumped-up charges of treason.

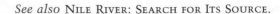

See also NILE RIVER: SEARCH FOR ITS SOURCE.

BIBLIOGRAPHY: Anne Baker, *Morning Star*, London, 1972; Robert Collins, "Samuel White Baker: Prospero in Purgatory," in Robert I. Rotberg (ed.), *Africa and Its Explorers*, Cambridge, Mass., 1970; Dorothy Middleton, *Baker of the Nile*, London, 1949; T. Douglas Murray and A. Silva White, *Sir Samuel Baker: A Memoir*, London, 1895.

Bakhov, Ivan **(d. 1762)** Russian seafarer and explorer of the Bering and East Siberian Seas. In 1748, en route from the Anadyr River to Kamchatka, he was wrecked on Ostrov Bering (Bering Island). He wintered there and in the summer of 1749, in a sloop built of wreckage, reached Kamchatka. In 1755 a Senate *ukaz* (decree) allowed him and Nikita Shalaurov to sail "along the north sea coast from the mouth of the Lena River to Kolyma and Chukotka nos [cape]." He and Shalaurov began this voyage in the summer of 1760 and wintered at the mouth of the Yana River. In 1761 they wintered at the mouth of the Kolyma River, where early in 1762 Bakhov died of scurvy.

Richard A. Pierce

Balboa, Vasco Núñez de **(1475–1519)** Spanish explorer. Balboa was born in Jerez de los Caballeros in the province of Badajoz. In his youth he served as a page to Don Pedro Puertocarrero, lord of Moguer. Balboa sailed from Spain in 1501 with Rodrigo de Bastidas, a wealthy notary, to trade for pearls along the northern coast of South America, where Christopher COLUMBUS had learned they were to be found. The party sailed beyond Cabo de la Vela to the mouth of the Magdalena River. Farther west, they found a fine harbor which they named Cartagena. They followed the shoreline when it bent southward and came to the Gulf of Urabá. There the ships began to leak, and they turned around and sailed to Hispaniola.

Balboa settled in Santo Domingo as a planter but fell into debt. To escape his creditors he stowed away with his dog Leoncico on a ship owned by Martín Fernández de Enciso which was carrying relief provisions to a party that had sailed for Darién under the command of Alonso de OJEDA. Meeting the survivors of that expedition, who were under the command of Franciso PIZARRO, Enciso forced them to return to San Sebastián, a town founded by Ojeda on the eastern side of the Gulf of Urabá. Upon their return they found that the settlement had been destroyed by the natives. At this juncture Balboa made his bid for leadership. He recalled from his voyage with Bastidas that a town existed on the western shore of the gulf, and the party sailed across to the Darién River, where they founded the town of Santa María de la Antigua del Darién. Here the Indians may not have been friendly, but they did not use poisoned arrows, and food and even some gold were available.

Balboa then turned his attention to the neighboring region of Coiba. He made an alliance with the local chief, Careta, who sealed it by offering his daughter in marriage to Balboa, and arranged an alliance with another powerful *cacique*, Comogre. This led to a fortuitous occurrence. The eldest of Comogre's sons, disgusted by the greed of the Spaniards, declared that if they were so insatiable for gold, he would lead them to a sea on the other side of the mountains where the streams were rich in gold if they would help shatter the power of Tubanamá, the richest king of all and the enemy of his father. Arming 190 men and accompanied by 800 natives, Balboa left Darién on September 1, 1513. The party plunged into the jungle and climbed mountains in what is still some of the least penetrable terrain in the world. After engaging in a fierce battle with the natives in the Sierra de Quareca and following this by the putting to death by dogs of a number of chiefs who engaged in "the abominable sin" (homosexuality), the party looted the village and rested briefly.

On the morning of September 27, accompanied only by his dog, Balboa climbed the "peak in Darién" and became the first European to look upon the Pacific from its eastern shore. Sixty-seven Spaniards, among them Francisco Pizarro, erected a pile of stones and a cross, knelt, and sang a Te Deum. Balboa and his men spent some days marching to the sea so as to take formal possession. When they reached the ocean, Balboa strode into the sea and raised a standard bearing the Virgin and the arms of Castile and Aragon. Twenty-six of the men accompanied him in this act on September 29, St. Michael's Day, and Balboa called the place the Golfo de San Miguel. He spent a month amassing gold and pearls before he began the return journey to Darién. Choosing another route than that by which he had crossed the isthmus, Balboa conquered other local chiefs and gathered still more gold. Finally, on January 19, 1514, he returned to Darién. He could announce not only the triumph of the discovery of the South Sea but also the accomplishment of the venture without the loss of a single Spanish life.

The triumph was short-lived. King Ferdinand, heeding the complaints of Enciso and others, appointed Pedro Arias de ÁVILA as governor. The latter, filled with hatred and envy, bided his time (he even arranged the marriage by proxy of one of his daughters to Balboa) and then tricked Balboa into relaxing his guard. Arrested by Francisco Pizarro, Balboa was tried for treason and publicly beheaded in Acla between January 13 and 21, 1519.

BIBLIOGRAPHY: Ángel de Altoguirre y Duvale, *Vasco Núñez de Balboa,* Madrid, 1914; Pascual de Andagoya, *Narrative of the Proceedings of Pedrarias Dávila,* tr. by C. R. Markham, London, 1865; Charles L. G. Anderson, *Life and Letters of Vasco Núñez de Balboa,* New York, 1941, reprinted Westport, Conn., 1970; Bartolomé de las Casas, *Historia de las Indias,* ed. by Agustín Millares Carlo, Mexico City, 1951; Peter Martyr, *De Orbe Novo: The Eight Decades of Peter Martyr D'Anghiera,* tr. by Francis A. MacNutt, New York, 1912, reprinted New York, 1970; José Toribio Medina, *El descubrimiento del Océano Pacífico: Vasco Núñez de Balboa,* Santiago de Chile, 1913–1914; Gonzalo Fernández de Oviedo y Valdés, *Historia general y natural de las Indias,* Asunción, 1944–1945, Madrid, 1959; Kathleen Romoli, *Balboa of Darién: Discoverer of the Pacific,* Garden City, N.Y., 1953; Martin Torodash, "Balboa Historiography," *Terrae Incognitae,* vol. VI, 1974, pp. 7–17.

Martin Torodash

Baranov, Aleksandr Andreyevich (1746–1819) Chief manager of the Russian settlements in North America from 1790 to 1818. Born in Kargopol, northern Russia, he became a trader in eastern Siberia. Invited by G. I. SHELEKHOV to manage his American interests, he sailed from Okhotsk on the company galliot *Tri Svyatitelya (Three Saints)* to Unalaska, where the vessel was wrecked. During the winter he built *baidaras* (large skin boats) and in 1791 went to Kodiak, then the company center. From 1791 to 1793 he rounded Kodiak, explored Cook Inlet and Prince William Sound, and organized new settlements. In 1795 he examined the north and east shores of the Gulf of Alaska as far as Sitka (now Baranof) Island. En route he raised the Russian flag at Yakutat Bay. In 1799 he went from Kodiak to Sitka, where he founded the fort of New Archangel. In 1804 he sent the first fur-hunting party of Aleuts under Russian supervision from Kodiak to California on the Boston ship *O'Cain* on a share arrangement.

After Indians destroyed New Archangel in 1802, Baranov went from Kodiak to Sitka with several vessels in 1804. With the help of Yury LISIANSKY and the round-the-world ship *Neva,* he retook the site, built a new fort, and transferred the center of Russian settlements in North America there. From New Archangel he sent trading and exploring expeditions along the west coast to California. In 1812 his assistant I. A. Kuskov founded Fort Ross 50 miles (80 kilometers) north of the Spanish port of San Francisco. Baranov dreamed of trade with Latin America, China, and the Philippines and of securing the coast for Russia, but he was dogged by misfortune and inadequate means. A trade agreement with John Jacob Astor's Pacific Fur Company fell through because of the War of 1812. The attempt by a subordinate, Dr. G. A. Schäffer, to acquire the Sandwich (Hawaiian) Islands for Russia in 1815–1817 was a costly failure. Baranov was replaced in 1818 and left America in the fall of that year on the ship *Kutuzov.* He died on the homeward voyage, at Batavia (now Jakarta), on April 16, 1819.

BIBLIOGRAPHY: Hubert Howe Bancroft, *History of Alaska, 1730–1885,* San Francisco, 1886; Hector Chevigny, *Lord of Alaska: Baranov and the Russian Venture,* New York, 1942; K. T. Khlebnikov, *Baranov,* tr. by Colin Bearne, Kingston, Ontario, 1973.

Richard A. Pierce

Aleksandr Andreyevich Baranov, Russian trader who explored the Pacific Coast of America and dreamed of developing a Russian trading empire from his Alaskan base. [Library of Congress]

Barents (Barentz), Willem (William; d. 1597) Dutch navigator and explorer. In the years 1594, 1595, and 1596 he made three separate voyages to the Arctic regions searching for a NORTHEAST PASSAGE in order to establish trade relations with China. On the first voyage Barents reached the bleak land of Novaya Zemlya, consisting of two major islands separated by a narrow strait, sailed up the west coast, and by the end of July discovered the Orange Islands, so named in honor of the house of Orange-Nassau. Here many walruses (or sea horses, as they were called) were found. By mid-September, after a voyage of somewhat over 3 months, Barents had returned to Amsterdam. On the second voyage the Dutch reached Vaygach Island, located between Novaya Zemlya and the Russian mainland. The Kara Sea was entered for a short distance, but the ice posed many navigational difficulties. This expedition returned to the Netherlands having accomplished very little. During the third expedition Bjørnøya (Bear Island), north of the Norwegian coast, was discovered, and still farther north the archipelago of Spitsbergen (Svalbard) was reached, although at the time the Dutch thought they had touched the coast of Greenland. Then proceeding southward across the wide northern sea named after him, Barents finally made land on the northern coast of Novaya Zemlya.

Harassed by the extreme cold, floating ice, and heavy winds, Barents and his crew members were finally obliged to stay at Ice Haven, a bay on the northeast coast of Novaya Zemlya. Fortunately for them a lucky find of large amounts of driftwood enabled them to build a house as their shelter. Here they remained as prisoners for the long winter months. They managed to survive on the flesh of bears and of foxes, caught in traps. By June they were able to begin their homeward journey. Barents, who had been seriously ill, died at sea. On August 4 the Dutch crew members saw the mainland of Russia. By November 1 they finally arrived in Amsterdam.

Succeeding Dutch navigators collected much additional information about Spitsbergen, Novaya Zemlya, the Kara Sea, and the northern coasts of Russia. Such information proved to be particularly valuable for various Dutch companies interested in the whaling trade. In September 1871 the simple structure built by Barents and his men was discovered by Capt. Elling Carlsen, a Norwegian seal hunter who visited Ice Haven. The Norwegians also recovered a large number of relics pertaining to Barents's third and last

On a search for a Northeast Passage, Willem Barents's vessel is locked in the ice. The Dutch explorer's unsuccessful attempts to find a passage to China provided invaluable information about the northern coasts of Russia and the Arctic islands.

expedition. Eventually these relics were obtained by the Dutch government and placed in a museum.

BIBLIOGRAPHY: Gerrit de Veer, *The Three Voyages of William Barents to the Arctic Regions (1594, 1595, and 1596)*, 2d ed., Hakluyt Society, 1st ser., no. 54, London, 1876.

Bernerd C. Weber

Barrow, John *(1764–1848)* English promoter of exploration. Barrow was born of humble origins in Dragley Beck, north Lancashire. Educated at the local grammar school in Ulverston, he acquired as a youth an interest in mathematics, geography, and astronomy. His parents wished him to enter the church, but instead he became a timekeeper for a Liverpool iron foundry. In Liverpool he met a Captain Potts, who took him on a voyage in a Greenland whaler, an expedition which gave him an appreciation of the hazards of ice and the necessity for him to complete his navigational training. Subsequently he was engaged by a Dr. James of Greenwich as a mathematical assistant.

Barrow's horizons now began to broaden. He was appointed comptroller of the household for the 1st Earl Macartney's embassy to China, and from his travels he acquired an important knowledge of China which was used by the government. His observations appeared in *Travels in China* (1804), a life of Lord Macartney (1807), and articles in *The Quarterly Review*. Next he went to Cape Colony, southern Africa, with Macartney, traveled extensively there, and decided to settle there as a country gentleman. However, England restored Cape Colony to the Netherlands in 1802, and Barrow returned to England. He entered the Admiralty Office in 1804, when his patron, the 1st Viscount Melville (who had also been in southern Africa), became first lord. Barrow was made second secretary, a position he occupied almost uninterruptedly for 40 years. In 1817 he reported the movement of icebergs into the Atlantic, an auspicious development which led to several Admiralty Arctic expeditions. During the 1820s and 1830s he was also responsible for the reorganization of the Admiralty Office and for a new plan of dockyard management. He resigned in 1845, the friend of countless distinguished explorers, John FRANKLIN and Frederick William BEECHEY among them.

Barrow was active in a number of societies and clubs, including the ROYAL GEOGRAPHICAL SOCIETY, of which he was the founder in 1830. In 1821 the University of Edinburgh awarded him an honorary LL.D. In 1835 he became a baronet. He was a prolific author, and in addition to the published works already cited he wrote, among other titles, *An Account of Travels into the Interior of Southern Africa* (1801–1804), *A Voyage to Cochin China* (1806), *A Chronological History of Voyages into the Arctic Regions* (1818), *The Life of Richard Earl Howe, K.G.* (1838), *Voyages of Discovery and Research within the Arctic*

Regions (1846), and *An Autobiographical Memoir* (1847).

See also NIGER RIVER.

BIBLIOGRAPHY: Christopher Lloyd, *Mr. Barrow of the Admiralty*, London, 1970.

Barry M. Gough

Barth, Heinrich *(Henry; 1821–1865)* German explorer and scholar. The son of a prosperous businessman, Barth was born in Hamburg and was educated at the University of Berlin (1838–1844). After traveling extensively in the Mediterranean region and becoming fluent in Arabic, he was named *Privatdozent* in the department of archaeology at the University of Berlin in 1848. The following year he accepted an invitation to join an expedition to Central Africa which was to be sponsored by the British government and led by James Richardson (1806–1851), an agent of the British and Foreign Anti-Slavery Society who had previously traveled as far as Ghāt, 600 miles (966 kilometers) south of Tripoli. Barth had been nominated for the expedition by the Prussian Ambassador to Great Britain, the Egyptologist Christian von Bunsen, to whom he had been recommended by the geographer Karl Ritter of the University of Berlin. The third member of the expedition was the German geologist Adolf Overweg (1822–1852). Although the principal objects of the mission were to seek the suppression of the slave traffic and to encourage legitimate trade, Barth was interested primarily in the scientific possibilities of the expedition.

Arriving in Tripoli on January 18, 1850, Barth was to remain in Africa for more than 5 years and to travel a total distance of over 10,000 miles (16,090 kilometers), usually without any European companions and with little cash. After he reached the Bornu capital, Kukawa, on April 2, 1850, he used that city as a base while he made four exploratory journeys around Lake Chad. During a trip south to Yola, he became the first European to see and explore the upper waters of the Benue River, which he showed had no direct connection with Lake Chad. Leaving Kukawa on November 25, 1852, he arrived in Timbuktu the following September and remained there until mid-May 1854. As he began his homeward journey, he returned to Kukawa, where he met Eduard Vogel, who had been dispatched to reinforce the expedition, of which Barth was now the only surviving member. Vogel himself would be killed in Wadai in 1856.

Barth arrived in England in September 1855 and spent the next 3 years writing a five-volume account of the expedition, *Travels and Discoveries in North and Central Africa* (1857–1858), which appeared in German as well as in English. Although Barth was awarded the Patron's Gold Medal of the ROYAL GEOGRAPHICAL SOCIETY in 1856 and was appointed professor of geography at the University of Berlin in 1863, his work attracted relatively little attention from con-

Heinrich Barth's travels in Africa, 1850–1855.

temporaries. Today, however, he is generally considered one of the great scholarly explorers of Africa because of the comprehensiveness and accuracy of his geographic, historical, and linguistic observations.

BIBLIOGRAPHY: Brian Gardner, *The Quest for Timbuktoo*, New York, 1968; Anthony H. M. Kirk-Green (ed.), *Barth's Travels in Nigeria*, London, 1962; id., "Heinrich Barth: An Exercise in Empathy," in Robert I. Rotberg (ed.), *Africa and Its Explorers*, Cambridge, Mass., 1970; R. M. Prothero, "Heinrich Barth and the Western Sudan," *The Geographical Journal*, vol. CXXIV, no. 3, September 1958, pp. 326–339.

Basargin, Grigory Gavrilovich *(d. 1853)* Russian vice admiral and explorer of the Caspian Sea. Between 1819 and 1821, commanding the corvette *Kazan* and the transport *Kura*, he took part in the military exploring expedition of N. N. Muravyev-Karsky, examining the southeast coast of the Caspian Sea. From 1823 to 1826 he headed a hydrographic expedition on the northwest coast of the Caspian. He compiled a map of the Caspian coast from Lenkoran to the mouth of the Kura River and an atlas of the mouths of the Volga and parts of the west coast of the Caspian Sea (1831).

Richard A. Pierce

Although Heinrich Barth attracted little attention from his contemporaries, he is recognized today as one of the most conscientious observers of the African scene. [Library of Congress]

Bashmakov, Pyotr *(fl. mid-eighteenth century)* Russian maritime fur hunter and explorer of the Aleutian Islands. In 1753, with A. Serebrennikov on the *Yeremiya*, he went from Nizhnekamchatsk to Bering Island (Ostrov Bering) and then eastward, where he sighted five islands. When the vessel was wrecked on a sixth island, Bashmakov and his men were saved, but the fur cargo was lost. During the next 2 years they built from the wreckage a small vessel in which they returned to Nizhnekamchatsk in 1755. In 1756, with A. Vsevidov on the *Pyotr i Pavel*, he went from Kamchatka to Bering Island and wintered there. In 1757 he sailed farther, sighted eight islands, but could reach only two. On the last of these, Tanaga Island, he spent the winter and in 1758 returned to Nizhnekamchatsk.   *Richard A. Pierce*

Batakov, Anton *(fl. late eighteenth century)* Russian seafarer and explorer of the North Pacific and Chukotka (Chukotsky Poluostrov). In 1785 he was appointed senior navigator in the Northeastern Secret Geographical and Astronomical Expedition led by Joseph BILLINGS. He crossed Siberia to Okhotsk and in 1786 and then went to Verkhnekolymsk. In 1787, on the vessel *Pallas* built there, he went down the Kolyma River and sailed in the East Siberian Sea beyond Mys Bolshoy Baranov. Returning overland to Okhotsk, he spent two winters there. In the fall of 1789 he sailed to Petropavlovsk on the *Slava Rossy* under Billings. In the summer of 1790 he sailed to Kayak Island in the Gulf of Alaska and in summer of 1791 to Unalaska Island, then to the islands of St. Matthew and St. Lawrence and to the American and Asian coasts of Bering Strait. In the fall of 1791 he and Billings left the ship at Zaliv Lavrentiya (St. Lawrence Bay) and on reindeer went across Chukotka to the Kolyma River. In 1794 he crossed Siberia and returned to St. Petersburg.   *Richard A. Pierce*

Beechey, Frederick William *(1796–1856)* British naval officer and geographer. In 1818–1819 he sailed with Lieut. (afterward Sir) John FRANKLIN and Lieut. William Edward PARRY on polar expeditions. With his own ship, *Blossom*, he embarked on a 3-year voyage of exploration in 1825. Passing through Bering Strait, he discovered a fine harbor near Cape Prince of Wales, Alaska, and continued east along the northern Alaskan coast. Before turning back, he was only 146 miles (235 kilometers) from Return Reef, Alaska, the westernmost point attained by the concurrent expedition of Franklin, who was prevented by bad weather from proceeding farther. Thus the planned rendezvous of the two expeditions did not take place. Beechey went south to the Pacific Ocean, where he discovered a number of islands. Subsequently he was employed in surveying the coasts of South America (1835–1837) and Ireland (1837–1847). He was raised to the rank of rear admiral in 1854 and became president of the ROYAL GEOGRAPHICAL SOCIETY in 1855.

BIBLIOGRAPHY: Frederick William Beechey, *Narrative of a Voyage to the Pacific and Bering's Strait . . . in the Years 1825, 26, 27, 28*, London, 1831; Barry M. Gough (ed.), *To the Pacific and Arctic with Beechey: The Journal of Lieutenant George Peard of H.M.S. 'Blossom' 1825–28*, Hakluyt Society, 2d ser., no. 143, Cambridge, England, 1973.

Richard A. Pierce

Begichev, Nikifor Alekseyevich *(1874–1927)* Russian Arctic explorer. Between 1900 and 1902 he served as boatswain on the ship *Zarya*, belonging to a polar

Frederick William Beechey's depiction of the brig Trent, during his polar expedition with John Franklin in 1818. [Library of Congress]

expedition led by the Russian explorer Baron Eduard von Toll, which through two winters rounded Cape Chelyuskin and reached Ostrov Bennett (Bennett Island), north of Ostrov Novaya Sibir. In 1903 Begichev took part in an expedition sent to look for Toll, who had disappeared after setting out on a journey with three companions. In the spring, with dogs pulling a whaleboat on sledges, the party went from the mouth of the Yana River to Ostrov Kotelny in the Novosibirskiye Ostrova (New Siberian Islands). The following summer they traveled on a whaleboat to Bennett Island, where they found Toll's hut and a letter indicating that he and companions had perished.

After taking part in the defense of Port Arthur in 1904, Begichev lived in the north of Siberia, working in the fur trade from the summer of 1906 on. In 1908, while going around the peninsula at the exit of the Khatangsky Zaliv (Khatanga Gulf) he discovered that it was an island, which was named Bolshoy Begichev. West of it he discovered another island, Maly Begichev. Between 1910 and 1913 he visited "his" islands three times. In 1915 he carried the sick from the icebreakers *Taymyr* and *Vaygach*, which were stuck in the ice off the northwest coast of the Taymyr Peninsula, on reindeer.

In 1921 he took part in a Soviet-Norwegian expedition organized to search for two men of the party of Roald AMUNDSEN who had disappeared in 1919 on the vessel *Maud*, and on the northwest shore of the Taymyr Peninsula he found the remains of one of them. In 1922, taking part in the Soviet Taymyr Geological Expedition, he traveled to the mouth of the Pyasina River, went to sea, and on the south shore of the Pyasinsky Zaliv (Gulf of Pyasina) found objects belonging to Amundsen's other man, and on Ostrov Dikson his skeleton. In the summer of 1926 he organized a fur-hunting cooperative, went on reindeer to the Pyasina, descended it a second time, remained at its mouth for the winter, and died of scurvy in May 1927.   *Richard A. Pierce*

Beketov, Pyotr (fl. mid-seventeenth century)   Explorer of Siberia. In 1628 he led thirty cossacks from Yeniseysk into the land of the Buryats. At the mouth of the Uda River he built the small post of Rybnoy, pacified some rebellious Tungus, and continued up the Upper Tunguska River (Verknyaya Tunguska) to the mouth of the Oka River, where he collected the first fur tribute from the Buryats. In 1631 he portaged from Yeniseysk to Ilimsk and from there to the Lena with thirty men. He left ten men at Ust-Kut and led the rest up the Lena as far as the mouth of the Kulenga, where he turned west into the Buryat steppe. Besieged by the Buryats, he and his men stole the besiegers' horses and reached safety on the Lena at the mouth of the Tutura River among friendly Tungus. There Beketov built a fort, Tutursk. In the spring of 1632 he took his force down the Lena, where he conquered most of the Yakuts and built a fort which became the future

Yakutsk. In the territory of the Lena Tungus he built the small post of Zhigansk. In 1633 he had similar success along the Aldan River, an eastern tributary of the Lena.

In 1648, while serving as commandant at Bratsk, he tried to introduce agriculture. In 1652 he was sent with 100 men to secure the route from Barguzin to the Shilka River. He went around the southern end of Lake Baykal and built the fort of Ust-Prorva at the mouth of the Selenga River. He ascended the Selenga and the Khilok to Lake Irgen, where he built the fort of Irgensk. He then went to the Ingoda River and descended it on rafts until halted by winter ice. He sent a small group under one Urasov to build a fort on the Shilka opposite the mouth of the Nercha, the future Nerchinsk. In the spring of 1654 Beketov descended the Amur and wintered at the fort of Kumarsk, where in the spring of 1655 he helped repulse a Manchu attack. He remained on the Amur until 1660, when he returned to Yeniseysk by way of Yakutsk and Ilimsk with a rich cargo of furs.

BIBLIOGRAPHY: George V. Lantzeff and Richard A. Pierce, *Eastward to Empire: Exploration and Conquest on the Russian Open Frontier, to 1750*, Montreal and London, 1973.

Richard A. Pierce

Bekovich-Cherkassky, Aleksandr (d. 1717)   Kabardinian prince in Russian service and explorer of the Caspian coast. Taken from his native Kabardia to Russia in childhood, he was sent abroad in 1707 by Peter I to study navigation. In 1715 Peter sent him to find the lower course of the Amu Darya, thought to fall into the Caspian Sea, which could provide the Russians with a waterway into the heart of Asia, where Peter hoped that gold deposits existed. He returned with a report, based on hearsay, that the Khivans had diverted the Amu Darya from its supposed old outlet in the Caspian into the Aral Sea and with a proposal that it could be restored to its natural course. In 1716, at the head of more than 3000 men, he went by sea from the mouth of the Volga to the mouth of the Ural River and then by land across the Ust-Urt Plateau to Khiva. After failing to stop the Russians by force, the Khivan Khan lured Bekovich and his men to Khiva as if for negotiations, persuaded him to divide his force into small groups "for easier quartering," and then slaughtered them piecemeal, enslaving the survivors.   *Richard A. Pierce*

Belalcázar, Sebastián de   *See* BENALCÁZAR, SEBASTIÁN DE.

Belcher, Edward (1799–1877)   British naval officer and hydrographer. After serving as a surveyor on the expedition of Frederick William BEECHEY to Bering Strait and the Pacific Ocean in 1825, he conducted surveys of his own on the coast of Africa, around Great Britain, and, on the *Sulphur*, on the west coast

Immersion in the Sarawak River of Edward Belcher's exploratory ship Samarang. From this vessel Belcher surveyed the coasts of the East Indies and the Philippines. [Library of Congress]

of South America, where he continued Beechey's task. He served in the war with China in 1840–1841 and was knighted in 1843. During the next 4 years he surveyed the coasts of the East Indies and the Philippines aboard the *Samarang*. In 1852 he succeeded Capt. Horatio Austin in command of the Admiralty's last expedition to search for Sir John FRANKLIN but drew criticism for abandoning in the ice a ship which later floated free, was recovered by an American vessel, was refitted by the United States government, and was presented to Great Britain as a gift. *See also* FRANKLIN EXPEDITION AND SEARCH.

BIBLIOGRAPHY: Edward Belcher, *The Last of the Arctic Voyages*, 2 vols., London, 1855; id., *Narrative of the Voyage of H.M.S. "Samarang" during 1843–1846*, 2 vols., London, 1843; id., *Narrative of a Voyage Round the World Performed in H.M.S. "Sulphur,"* 2 vols., London, 1843.

Richard A. Pierce

Bellingshausen, Fabian Gottlieb Benjamin von (Russian: *Faddey Faddeyevich Bellingsgausen;* 1778–1852)

Admiral, seafarer, and discoverer, with Mikhail Petrovich LAZAREV, of Antarctica. Born on Ösel (Saaremaa) of old Baltic German landed gentry, he served as a midshipman in the round-the-world voyage (1803–1806) of the sloop *Nadezhda* under Adam Johann von KRUSENSHTERN. During the voyage he was made lieutenant, and on his return to Russia captain lieutenant. From 1819 to 1821 he commanded the sloop *Vostok* and with the *Mirny* (Lazarev commanding) made a round-the-world voyage during which Antarctica was discovered and the first scientific exploration of the region was carried out. He discovered Annenkov Island, near South Georgia, and the Traversay Islands. In southern Polynesia the expedition discovered in July–August 1820 several islands in the Tuamotu Archipelago and several islands southeast of the Fiji Islands. Bellingshausen later served in the Mediterranean and Baltic Seas and in 1843 was made an admiral.

BIBLIOGRAPHY: Frank Debenham (ed.), *The Voyage of Captain Bellingshausen to the Antarctic Seas, 1819–1821*, 2 vols., Hakluyt Society, 2d ser., nos. 91 and 92, London, 1945.

Richard A. Pierce

Benalcázar (Belalcázar), Sebastián de (ca. 1490–1551)

Spanish conqueror and explorer. Very little is known about Benalcázar's early life. Born in a village called Belalcázar in the province of Córdoba, he was of plebeian background and was illiterate. His original surname was probably Moyano. Benalcázar went to the Indies at an early age and by 1522 was well established in Panama. After taking part in the conquest of Nicaragua, he joined Francisco PIZARRO after the latter had begun his third expedition to Peru in 1531 and shared in the division of Atahuallpa's ransom at Cajamarca. In 1534 he struck northward from San Miguel (modern Paita) to undertake the conquest of Quito. Although the Incas put up a stiff resistance, the Spaniards formed an alliance with the Cañari Indians, who resented Inca domination. Benalcázar found that Quito had been burned and evacuated by the Indians, but the Spaniards were able to repel their assaults and remained in possession of the city.

In 1536 Benalcázar, hoping to carve out a domain where he would be independent of Pizarro's authority, set out for the north, traveling through extremely rugged terrain into what is now Colombia, and founded the cities of Popayán (1536) and Cali (1537). After returning to Quito, he set out again in 1538 and moved east across Colombia's Cordillera Central in search of a kingdom rich in gold and emeralds about which he had heard from a Colombian Indian captured in 1535. Benalcázar has been credited with coining the term EL DORADO to refer to this fabulous land. He eventually reached the valley of the upper Magdalena River, only to find that Gonzalo JIMÉNEZ DE QUESADA had already established himself in the nearby states of the Chibcha Indians. Leaving behind some of his men and 300 pregnant sows, Benalcázar, accompanied by Jiménez de Quesada and Nicolás Féderman (Nikolaus Federmann), who had recently arrived from Venezuela, now traveled to Spain to present his claims to King Charles I. He was denied the powers he sought in Quito, but in 1540 he was named governor and captain general of the province of Popayán.

Having returned to Popayán and fought on behalf of the royal authorities during the rebellion of Gonzalo PIZARRO, Benalcázar was later arrested for his execution in 1541 of Jorge Robledo, who had been encroaching upon his territory. He was condemned to death but was allowed to appeal the sentence. He died at Cartagena while en route to Spain for that purpose.

BIBLIOGRAPHY: J. Jijón y Caamaño, *Sebastián de Benalcázar,* 2 vols., Quito, 1936–1938; James Lockhart, *The Men of Cajamarca,* Austin, Tex., 1972.

Bering, Vitus Jonassen *(1681–1741)* Danish explorer in Russian service and pioneer of Russian Arctic exploration. In his youth Bering sailed to the East Indies on a Dutch ship. On his return in 1703 he became a sublieutenant in Peter the Great's fleet. In 1724 Peter promoted him to captain of first rank and chose him to lead the First Kamchatka Expedition, the main task of which was to learn whether Asia was connected with North America. In 1728 Bering sailed with a crew of forty-four from the mouth of the Kamchatka River to the Anadyrsky Zaliv (Gulf of Anadyr), and as far north as 67°18′N; en route he discovered St. Lawrence Island and "Diomede Island" (actually two islands), but he did not sight the American coast. After an unsuccessful attempt in 1729 to reach islands east of Kamchatka, he returned in 1730 to St. Petersburg, where he was made a captain commander. The results of his voyage were held to be inconclusive, and Bering appealed to Empress Anna for a second expedition. Instead, in 1733 he was made commander of a grandiose Great Northern Expedition of about 600 men, charged with exploring the unknown Arctic coast of Siberia and the Kuril Islands, as well as a Second

Kamchatka Expedition. Not until 1740 did Bering get the American part of the expedition under way.

Bering, commanding the ship *Sv. Pyotr* (*St. Peter*), and Aleksey Ilyich CHIRIKOV, commanding the ship *Sv. Pavel* (*St. Paul*), left Okhotsk for Bolsheretsk, rounded Kamchatka, and arrived in Avachinskaya Guba (Avacha Bay) on the east coast of the peninsula, where they founded Petropavlovsk. On June 5, 1741, both vessels left this harbor. After wasting time in search of a mythical "Gama Land," the vessels lost contact with each other. On July 17, Bering saw the American coast at 58°14′N and sailed along it for 4 days, discovering and landing briefly on Kayak Island. Chirikov made another brief landing farther south. On their return voyages both commanders sighted the Kenai Peninsula and several of the Aleutian Islands. Chirikov returned to Kamchatka, but on November 6 Bering discovered and was wrecked on the island later named after him. During the winter nineteen men died of scurvy, including Bering, on December 8. The survivors built a small boat from the wreckage of the *Sv. Pyotr* and on August 27, 1742, reached Kamchatka.

See also STELLER, Georg Wilhelm.

BIBLIOGRAPHY: Frank A. Golder (tr. and ed.), *Bering's Voyages,* 2 vols., New York, 1922.

Richard A. Pierce

Billings, Joseph *(d. 1806)* British seafarer in Russian service and explorer of northeastern Siberia and northwestern North America. Between 1776 and 1780, Billings took part in the third expedition of Cap. James COOK as assistant astronomer. In 1783 he was taken in the Russian Navy and in 1785, as captain lieutenant, was given command of the Northeastern Secret Geographical and Astronomical Expedition with the aim of sailing from the Kolyma River through Bering Strait to the northwest coast of North America and of exploring the northeast coast of Siberia. The expedition arrived in Okhotsk in 1786, and while part of his command built ships, Billings tried

Sitka, Alaska, one of the scenes of Joseph Billings's halfhearted attempts, while in Russian service, to explore northwestern North America. [Library of Congress]

in 1787 unsuccessfully to pass Mys Shelagsky and Chukotka (Chukotskiy Poluostrov). Returning to Yakutsk for the winter, Billings occupied himself in trading and had to be ordered by the Admiralty to resume exploration. In 1789 he tried unsuccessfully to go through Bering Strait toward the northwest. In 1790–1791 with his assistant, Gavriil Andreyevich SARYCHEV, and the ship *Slava Rossy* he sailed to Russian America, exploring the Aleutian Islands and following the coast as far east as Cape St. Elias. In 1791–1792 he explored Chukotka by land. He returned to Irkutsk in 1793 and to St. Petersburg in the following year.

The expedition mapped the coasts of Chukotka, the Sea of Okhotsk, the Aleutian Islands, and the coast of Prince William Sound and described the ways of the native peoples, but in general it did not justify the considerable expenditures that were made. Billings was of mediocre ability, and the achievements of the expedition were due in large measure to the more talented Sarychev.

BIBLIOGRAPHY: G. A. Sarychev, *Account of a Voyage of Discovery to the North-East of Siberia, the Frozen Ocean, and the North-East Sea,* London, 1806; Martin Sauer, *An Account of a Geographical and Astronomical Expedition to the Northern Parts of Russia, Performed in the Year 1785, to 1794, Narrated from the Original Papers,* London, 1802.

Richard A. Pierce

Bocharov, Dmitry Ivanovich *(fl. late eighteenth century)* Russian seafarer. In May 1771 Bocharov was taken from Bolsheretsk, Kamchatka, by Count Beniowsky and other mutinous exiles to the Kuril Islands, Japan, and Canton. From there he went to France on a French vessel and with the aid of the Russian Ambassador returned to Russia. Court-martialed, he was imprisoned, later was exonerated, and returned to the Far East. In 1782 he sailed on the ship *Natalya* of G. I. SHELEKHOV. In 1786, In Shelekhov's service, he sailed as navigator's apprentice on *baidaras* (large open boats made of skins stretched over wooden frames), under Y. I. Delarov, from Kodiak Island to the Aleutians. In 1788, as assistant navigator on the galliot *Tri Svyatitelya* (*Three Saints*), with G. A. IZMAILOV he explored the north coast of the Gulf of Alaska from the Kenai Peninsula to Lituya Bay, including Yakutat (Bering) Bay. In 1790, commanding the *Tri Svyatitelya* (*Three Saints*) with A. A. BARANOV on board, he sailed from Okhotsk for Kodiak, but the vessel was wrecked on Unalaska on October 6. The party wintered on Unalaska; Bocharov took two *baidaras* to Bristol Bay, completing the discovery of the north coast of the Alaska Peninsula begun by the expedition of Pyotr KRENITSYN and Mikhail D. Levashev. In 1791 he crossed the Alaska Peninsula at its base, discovering the shortest water and land route between Bristol Bay and Shelikof Strait by way of Egegik River and Becharof Lake.

Richard A. Pierce

Boone, Daniel *(1734–1820)* American frontiersman, Indian fighter, and explorer. Of Pennsylvania stock, Boone moved at 15 to the primitive Yadkin Valley of North Carolina before fighting briefly in the Seven Years' War and serving as wagoner in British Gen. Edward Braddock's ill-fated expedition of 1755. There he met John Finley, who later joined him in exploring Kentucky. Boone's goals in Kentucky were mixed: furs, land, perhaps spying on Indian and foreign influence. But the probability is that he simply loved the freedom of the back country. His most notable achievement was opening the famous Wilderness Road.

Boone's first attempt to reach Kentucky's bluegrass region in the winter of 1767–1768 was a failure, but he set out again in May 1769 from the Yadkin Valley with a small party, including his brother-in-law John Stuart, his brother and Baptist preacher Squire Boone, and John Finley, who served as guide. Provisioned by Judge Richard Henderson of North Carolina, a land speculator and an acquaintance of Daniel, the men reached the Cumberland Gap and took Warriors' Path across Kentucky to Station Camp Creek, where they divided into two groups. Boone's party followed the South Fork of the Kentucky River north to an area near the present town of Irvine before moving down the Kentucky and Red Rivers to the Eskippikithiki area (Indian Old Fields). Amusing themselves in the evening by reading *Gulliver's Travels,* the men by day carefully explored the tableland between mountain and bluegrass which comprises much of central Kentucky. In December, Shawnee Indians captured Boone and Stuart and stole most of the party's supplies and ammunition. Boone and Stuart escaped into a giant canebrake, but the rest of the men thought they were dead.

For a time only Daniel and his brother-in-law remained in the wilderness. But before moving camp to the Red River's mouth, they were delighted to see Squire and a companion return with supplies. The winter of 1769–1770 nonetheless was disheartening. Stuart did not return from a hunting trip he took alone, and Squire's friend returned east. In spring Daniel explored the area by himself, while his brother returned to North Carolina for ammunition. The next few months Boone wandered alone through the Kentucky and Licking River Valleys and explored the Ohio River down to the falls near present Louisville. By late July 1770, he rejoined his brother at Red River camp. After a summer of hunting along the Kentucky River, they wintered in the Green and Cumberland Valleys. In March 1771 Boone and Squire loaded a rich supply of furs onto packhorses and prepared for the homeward trip. But near Cumberland Gap the brothers met a band of Cherokee Indians, who took their horses, supplies, and furs and sent them to North Carolina with nothing to show for 2 years of hunting.

Boone's third and most memorable journey over the mountains, the one which culminated in the Wilderness Road, began in March 1775. Two years earlier he and his family had accompanied seven other families in a disastrous attempt to pierce the Cumberland Gap. There they were ambushed in October 1773 by Indians, who killed Boone's sixteen-year-old son James and five others. The entire party, against Daniel's advice, turned back. But by the mid-1770s interest in Kentucky and Tennessee was widespread, and Judge Henderson organized the Transylvania Company (without charter) and bought land, illegally, from the Cherokees through the Watauga Treaty. He planned to sell it to settlers.

After consummating the treaty with the Indians, Henderson dispatched Boone and twenty-eight companions to mark a trail across Cherokee territory to Cumberland Gap and into Kentucky as far as the south bank of the Kentucky River. Thus the Wilderness Road started at the Watauga settlements at the Long Island of the Holston River, moved through Powell Valley and the gap to the Rockcastle River, and terminated at the Kentucky River. At a spot north of the present town of Richmond in Madison County, Kentucky, Boone and his axmen fought off hostile Indians and built cabins which in 1775 became the heart of Boonesborough. Unfortunately for Boone and Henderson, the colony fell victim to the independent spirit of the frontier, and in June of the following year George Rogers Clark usurped authority in Virginia's name.

The rest of Boone's life is epilogue. One of his sons founded a settlement called Femme Osage in 1796 in the St. Charles district north of the Missouri River and near St. Louis. Here, 3 years later, Daniel joined him, serving as a magistrate under the Spanish flag until 1804. Boone died in his eighties after several strenuous seasons of hunting and trapping which, some say, led him as far west as the Rocky Mountains. It is difficult to discern Boone's real contributions from the tales spun so ingeniously by television, contem-

porary stories, and his *Autobiography* (1784), which supposedly relates his adventures as told to John Filson. But he left an impenetrable legend as well as a rich store of information about the trans-Appalachian West.

BIBLIOGRAPHY: John Bakeless, *Daniel Boone, Master of the Wilderness*, New York, 1939; Lawrence Elliot, *The Long Hunter: A New Life of Daniel Boone*, New York, 1976; Reuben G. Thwaites, *Daniel Boone*, New York, 1902.

Howard Jones

Bougainville, Louis-Antoine de (1729–1811)

French officer, scientist, and circumnavigator. Bougainville was born in Paris on November 12, 1729. His father, Pierre-Yves de Bougainville, a lawyer, was ennobled in 1741. Bougainville had a successful career in the world of science and the military before embarking upon his circumnavigation. Following studies with the famous mathematicians Alexis Clairaut and Jean d'Alembert, he published in 1752 the first part and in 1755 the second part of his *Traité du calcul intégral*, for which he was elected to the Royal Society of Great Britain in January 1756. Meanwhile, the well-connected Bougainville had begun his military career in 1750 in the fashionable Black Musketeers, stationed in Versailles. During the Seven Years' War he participated in the Battle of Quebec in September 1759 and in the defense of Lake Champlain. He was taken prisoner on September 7, 1760, at the Île aux Noix near Saint-Jean, Quebec, but returned to France on his own recognizance.

Bougainville's circumnavigation of the world had its origin in his interest in the strategic location of the Malouines (Malvinas, or Falklands), islands off the coast of Argentina, which were considered the key to passage into the South Seas, the only area of the world where Great Britain did not have a naval base. In December 1761 Bougainville submitted to the French government a plan for the creation in these islands of a naval station and a settlement of displaced Acadians. His plan was approved in 1763, but Bougainville and two of his relatives financed its execution. He was appointed *capitaine de vaisseau* on June 15, and he left Saint-Malo on September 6. The next 2 years saw Bougainville make several trips to the Malouines, where the French colony grew steadily. However, at the end of 1765, when Great Britain created its own settlement there and Spain protested the inroads made into its territories, France decided to give up the islands to Spain rather than share them with Great Britain. To compensate Bougainville for his expenses, the French government offered him the governorship of the islands of France and Bourbon (today Mauritius and Réunion), but instead he requested and obtained authorization to lead a voyage of exploration into the Pacific. After some negotiations, Spain agreed to reimburse Bougainville the cost of the Malouines settlement.

Far left: Although Daniel Boone opened up the Wilderness Road through the Appalachians and founded the settlement Boonesborough, his mythical adventures have probably had a greater impact on American life than have his actual achievements. [Library of Congress]

Bougainville, who had never had any naval training, was given command of two ships, the frigate *La Boudeuse* and the storeship *L'Étoile*. Fortunately, the second officer on *La Boudeuse*, his friend Pierre Duclos-Guyot, was a seasoned naval officer familiar with the Pacific. Bougainville's instructions were to verify the size of the Patagonian natives, allegedly giants; to locate the southern continent believed to exist in the Pacific; to lay claim to all lands discovered; to seek out likely sites for ports of call; to bring back drawings and samples of everything; and to obtain spice plants to strengthen the economy of the Île-de-France.

After a false start at Nantes and delays at Brest, *La Boudeuse* left on December 5, 1766, and reached Montevideo on January 31, 1767, a day before *L'Étoile* began its voyage. Bougainville visited Argentina and Paraguay and turned over the Malouines to Spain on June 2 before sailing for Rio de Janeiro to meet *L'Étoile*. The two ships left Rio in November and spent 52 days in the Strait of Magellan, charting the location of harbors, anchorages, and the direction of tides, collecting plants, and ascertaining that the Patagonians were not giants.

On January 26, 1768, the expedition headed into the Pacific. It was unable to find Easter Island, and it did not reach a large island until April 4, when it arrived at Tahiti (Nouvelle-Cythère), whose friendly people and ideal climate made a deep impression on the explorers. On April 15 the expedition left Tahiti and began its search for the southern continent and particularly the so-called Land of the Holy Spirit. Bad weather and low morale forced Bougainville to give up a search he concluded was futile and to turn once again toward charted oceanic islands. The expedition coasted Samoa, the New Hebrides, the Solomons, Bismarck, New Holland, and New Guinea, looking for a passage from the Pacific to the Molucca Sea and gathering a wealth of geographical knowledge. Two passages, one in the New Hebrides and another in the Solomons, commemorate Bougainville's voyage in this area. Foul weather, unapproachable islands, and hostile natives increased the hardships of the crews. When the ships reached Buru Island, in the Moluccas, on September 1, 1768, all the leather equipment on board the ships had been eaten. The expedition reached the Île-de-France on November 8, by way of the Louisiades, Choiseul in the Solomons, New Britain, and Batavia (now Jakarta). On December 12, after a month of rest and repairs, *La Boudeuse* alone left for France, arriving at Nantes on March 6, 1769, *L'Étoile* reaching Rochefort on April 24, 1769.

Bougainville's expedition was a colonial and economic failure. It had cost 1,544,000 livres, some of which was advanced by Bougainville, and nine lives (seven from *La Boudeuse*), but it had not resulted in the acquisition of new territories, and it had failed to secure the spice plants the Île-de-France so much needed. However, its scientific accomplishments were numerous. It was the first expedition to make systematic longitude readings; forty boxes of samples had been collected by Philibert de Commerson; many islands had been charted, by the constellation method; the Louisiades and part of the Solomons had been discovered; and the myths of the giant Patagonians and the southern continent had been exploded. The expedition made a great impact on popular imagination and the movement of ideas. Bougainville's account of life and society in Tahiti, the *Relation de la découverte*, which was published in October 1769, and Aoutourou, the Tahitian prince whom the expedition brought back to France, influenced the then-fashionable discussion of man's natural state and the noble savage and particularly Denis Diderot's *Supplément au voyage de Bougainville*.

Bougainville was elected to the Academy of the Navy in 1772 and appointed *secrétaire du roi*. He failed to obtain authorization for an expedition to the North Pole, but his career in the Army and the Navy progressed rapidly, and he was promoted to major general of the army in March 1780. During the first years of the French Revolution, he avoided the limelight as much as possible and in September 1791 refused the post of secretary of the navy. He was jailed briefly in 1794, but after the Terror scientific appointments and high honors were heaped upon him by succeeding governments.

Bougainville had married the 20-year old daughter of a naval officer on January 27, 1781. Hyacinthe, their first son, became a rear admiral and the leader of an expedition in the Pacific in 1824–1826. Family tragedies darkened the last years of Bougainville's life. On August 2, 1801, his second son drowned in front of his mother, who died despondent 4 years later. Bougainville died at his Paris home on August 31, 1811.

BIBLIOGRAPHY: Louis-Antoine de Bougainville, *Voyage autour du monde, par la frégate du roi La Boudeuse et la flûte L'Étoile en 1766, 1767, 1768 & 1769*, Paris, 1771; John Dunmore, *French Explorers in the Pacific*, vol. I, *The Eighteenth Century*, Oxford, 1965; Jean-Étienne Martin-Allanic, *Bougainville navigateur et les découvertes de son temps*, 2 vols., Paris, 1964; Maurice Thiery, *Bougainville: Soldier and Sailor*, London, 1932.

Max Fajn

Brendan (Brandan), St. (ca. 484–ca. 577) Irish monk, abbot, and traveler noted for a legendary Atlantic voyage. The historical Brendan was born in or near Tralee in County Kerry. Ordained in 512, he founded monasteries at Ardfert, north of Tralee, and at Clonfert in Galway. Although the historical Brendan apparently visited the Hebrides, Wales, and Brittany, he was subsequently depicted as a more far-ranging traveler in several medieval works, notably the *Navigatio Sancti Brendani*. This Latin narrative in prose, probably written by an Irishman early in the tenth century, relates the adventures of Brendan and other Irish monks after they had set out in a curragh (coracle) for the Saints' Promised Land. During their voyage they visited, among other places, an island filled with huge white sheep and another island where they found talking birds. After 40 days of continuous sailing, they

reached their destination, which turned out to be a place of continental proportions. The story of Brendan's voyage gained rapid currency throughout medieval Europe, and maps frequently depicted St. Brendan's Isle, usually to the south of Europe (sometimes in the vicinity of the Canaries, Madeira, or the Azores).

Because of the verisimilitude of many of the nautical details in the *Navigatio,* efforts have been made to identify Brendan's landfalls with real places. The islands of the sheep and of the talking birds, for example, have been identified with two of the Faeroe Islands. A crystalline column seen by Brendan and topped by a silvery canopy is said to have represented an iceberg covered by fog. Finally, the voyage has been cited as evidence in favor of a pre-Columbian discovery of America by Brendan himself or by Europeans prior to the composition of the *Navigatio.*

BIBLIOGRAPHY: Geoffrey Ashe, *Land to the West: St. Brendan's Voyage to America,* London, 1962.

Broughton, William Robert (1762–1821)

British naval officer. Little is known of Broughton's early life before 1791, when he took command of the brig *Chatham* and sailed with George VANCOUVER on his voyage of discovery. After surveying the Columbia River and adjacent coasts, Broughton sailed with Vancouver to Monterey, California, where he was ordered to return to England with dispatches relating to the Nootka Sound question. He made the journey by way of Mexico, arriving in England in 1793. Broughton returned to the northwest coast of North America in 1796 with the *Providence* but found Vancouver gone. He then turned to a survey of the North Pacific coast of Asia, which supplemented the work done by Jean-François de Galaup, Comte de LAPÉROUSE in the previous decade. On May 16, 1797, the *Providence* was wrecked on a coral reef near the coast of Formosa (Taiwan), but the men were saved. Broughton continued the survey in the ship's tender, a schooner, until May 1798, when he was ordered back to England.

BIBLIOGRAPHY: William R. Broughton, *A Voyage of Discovery to the North Pacific Ocean,* London, 1804.

Richard A. Pierce

Bruce, James (1730–1794)

Scottish explorer. Born on the family estate of Kinnaird, Stirlingshire, Bruce was educated at Harrow and at Edinburgh University, where he began to study law in 1847. His poor health soon put an end to his formal education, and after a period of recuperation he went to London, married the daughter of a wine merchant, and joined her family's firm. The death of his wife in November 1754, less than a year after their marriage, drove him to seek distraction in travel and study.

On March 15, 1763, Bruce arrived in Algiers, having been named consul general there. He had also been instructed to examine and make drawings of classical ruins in North Africa; according to Bruce, by this time he had determined to discover the source of the Nile

James Bruce's account of his journeys throughout Ethiopia and along the Nile were greeted as travelers' tales until the importance of his discoveries was established long after his death. [Library of Congress]

as well. His consulship ended ingloriously in 1765, but he continued his studies of ancient remains with the assistance of Luigi Balugani (1737–1771), an Italian draftsman whom he engaged the same year. In 1768, accompanied by Balugani, he began a journey up the Nile to investigate its source, which he believed lay in Ethiopia. The hazards of travel in Sudan led him to proceed eastward from Aswan across the desert to Quseir and thence to Jidda in Arabia; recrossing the Red Sea, he landed at Massawa, Eritrea, on September 19, 1769. He reached Gondar, then the capital of Ethiopia, on February 14, 1770. Bruce, who was proficient in both Arabic and Amharic and had also acquired considerable knowledge of medicine, was well received by the young emperor, Takla Haymanot, and by the vizier, Ras Michael, who was the real ruler of the country. Accompanying the royal army in a campaign against a rebellious chief, Bruce saw the Tissisat Falls, the great cataract formed by the Blue Nile near Lake Tana, which had been described by the Portuguese Jesuit Jerônimo Lobo (1595–1678). In November 1770 he reached the reputed source of the Blue Nile at Gish, although here again he had almost certainly been preceded by another Jesuit, Pedro Páez (d. 1622). After spending another year in war-ravaged Ethiopia, Bruce began his journey home on December 26, 1771, traveling by way of Sudan. Near modern Khartoum he saw the juncture of the Blue and White Niles, but he remained convinced that the river he had explored was the principal stream, although he acknowledged that the latter was the larger of the two. After an excruciating 20-day desert trek from Berber to Aswan, he sailed down the Nile to Cairo, where he arrived on January 10, 1773.

Bruce now traveled to France, where he won the admiration of Georges-Louis Leclerc de Buffon, and to Italy, where he was chagrined to learn that a woman to whom he had become engaged before leaving Europe had married someone else. After he reached London on June 21, 1774, he had an interview with George III, but fashionable society doubted the veracity of Bruce's stories about Ethiopia, especially about the eating of raw meat carved from living animals, and some wondered whether he had even been to Ethiopia. Among the skeptics was Samuel Johnson, who had published (1735) a translation of Father Lobo's *Voyage to Abyssinia* and had written *Rasselas* (1759), a tale prominently featuring an Edenic Ethiopian valley. Although he was elected a fellow of the Royal Society, Bruce retired in disgust to Scotland. It was not until after the death of his second wife in 1785 that he could be persuaded to write an account of his travels. Five illustrated volumes, *Travels to Discover the Source of the Nile,* appeared in 1790, only to be greeted with the same derision Bruce had already experienced. He was also criticized for slighting the contribution of Balugani, who had died in Gondar. Although the volumes may be inaccurate in some respects, as in the account of conversations that took place many years earlier, Bruce's work contains much valuable scientific and geographic information about Ethiopia which was confirmed by later travelers. Bruce died on April 27, 1794, after a fall from the great staircase at Kinnaird.

See also NILE RIVER: SEARCH FOR ITS SOURCE.

BIBLIOGRAPHY: F. B. Head, *The Life of Bruce, the African Traveller,* 3d ed., London, 1838; Alan Moorehead, *The Blue Nile,* New York, 1962; J. M. Reid, *Traveller Extraordinary: The Life of James Bruce of Kinnaird,* New York, 1968.

Bukhgolts, Ivan Dmitryevich *(fl. early eighteenth century)* Russian officer, sent by Peter the Great in 1715 from Tobolsk with a detachment of 2000 men to seek gold deposits on the Amu Darya and Yarkand Rivers by way of the Irtysh River. The expedition ascended the Irtysh by boat as far as Lake Yamyshev, where they were attacked and besieged for 3 months by more than 10,000 Kalmyks. Without food or reinforcements, Bukhgolts retreated with his remaining 700 men and went down the Irtysh to the Omi River, where he established a fort, from which grew the city of Omsk.

Richard A. Pierce

Burckhardt, Johann Ludwig *(Jean-Louis or John Lewis; 1784–1817)* Swiss explorer. Born in Lausanne, Burckhardt was the son of a wealthy businessman who went into exile in Germany after the French overran Switzerland in the 1790s. After studying at the Universities of Leipzig and Göttingen, the younger Burckhardt went to England in 1806 in the hope of finding employment. In 1808 he offered his services to the AFRICAN ASSOCIATION, proposing to travel from North Africa to Timbuktu and other cities on the Niger River in the guise of a Moorish merchant. Having been engaged by the association, he left England on March 2, 1809, and went to Syria, where he remained for nearly 3 years, perfecting his knowledge of Arabic, which he had begun to study earlier.

In 1812, en route to Cairo, Burckhardt visited Petra, which he was the first modern traveler to describe. While he awaited the appearance of a caravan for the interior, he traveled up the Nile from Cairo and discovered the Temple of Ramses II at Abu Simbel, which had not been seen by Europeans since antiquity. He also visited Mecca disguised as a pilgrim. Back in Cairo, he was preparing to join a caravan when he died of dysentery.

Burckhardt made no remarkable geographical discoveries during his years in Africa and Syria, but the careful observations of his journals, which were published posthumously by the African Association, resulted in his being considered one of the great scholarly travelers, in the mold of Heinrich BARTH and Richard BURTON. He bequeathed his library and 300 volumes of Arabic manuscripts to Cambridge Univer-

Far left:
The Syk, a mile-long gorge cutting through towering cliffs, is the only entrance to the Nabataean city of Petra, described to Europeans for the first time by Johann Burckhardt. [Jordan Information Office]

sity. The African Association published five volumes describing his travels: *Travels in Nubia* (1819), *Travels in Syria and the Holy Land* (1822), *Travels in Arabia* (1829), *Arabic Proverbs* (1830), and *Notes on the Bedouins and Waháhys* (1830).

BIBLIOGRAPHY: Katherine Sim, *Desert Traveller: The Life of Jean Louis Burckhardt*, London, 1969.

Burke, Robert O'Hara *(1821–1861)* Australian explorer. Born St. Clerans, County Galway, Ireland, Burke was the great tragic figure of Australian exploration. He served in the Austrian Army and the Irish Mounted Constabulary before migrating in 1853 to Australia, where he joined the Victorian police force. In 1860 he was selected to lead Victoria's Great Northern Exploration Expedition and cross the continent from south to north. The choice was surprising, for Burke was no bushman or leader and displayed none of the caution which characterized Australia's best explorers. His chief qualifications seemed to be his desire for glory and his reckless bravery.

The expedition, consisting of eighteen men, twenty-six camels, twenty-eight horses, and 21 tons of provisions (including 4 gallons of brandy for the men and 60 gallons of rum for the camels), left Melbourne on August 20, 1860, amid much fanfare and celebration. But trouble struck within weeks. Burke's leadership was challenged, the camels fought with the horses and with one another, and the baggage frequently became bogged. Menindee was reached on September 23, and here the trouble flared. George Landells, the camel master and second-in-command, resigned. His place was given to William Wills. William Wright, a local man, was hired as guide and appointed third-in-command.

Impatient at the delays, Burke now left the bulk of the baggage here and dashed with a small party to Cooper's Creek, where he made preparations for the major northward assault. Wright was to have followed immediately with the provisions and remaining men, but he dallied in Menindee for 3 months and then got lost.

While they waited at Cooper's Creek, Burke and Wills made several short sorties to the north, but Burke's patience finally gave out, and on December 16 he resolved to "dash into the interior and cross the continent at all hazards." Wills, John King, and Charles Gray were selected as companions, and William Brahe, now put in charge of the Cooper's Creek depot, was told to wait 3 months for their return.

Walking 12 hours a day, they reached the Gulf of Carpentaria on February 9, but as provisions were already running low, they turned for home without seeing the sea and after only a day's rest. Conditions steadily worsened as the food ran out. Gray died, and the others were in dire straits when they stumbled back to Cooper's Creek on April 21, only to discover that Brahe had left 7 hours earlier.

Instead of following Brahe, as Wills suggested, Burke insisted on making for the outpost at Mount Hopeless, 150 miles (241 kilometers) away. He dug up the provisions Brahe had left, replaced them with a letter and, after carefully camouflaging the hole so that its contents would not be discovered by aborigines, headed downstream. The setting for the tragedy was now complete, for Brahe meanwhile had met Wright and with him returned to Cooper's Creek. Seeing no sign of Burke's return, they swung back to

Robert O'Hara Burke (left) and William Wills starved to death in the Australian wilderness after crossing the continent from south to north. [Australian Information Service]

Menindee, leaving Burke and Wills to perish from starvation. King, who unlike Burke was willing to accept aid from aborigines, survived to be rescued by the relief party led by Alfred William Howitt on September 15.

In the subsequent royal commission "to enquire into the sufferings," Burke was censured for having more zeal than prudence, but his death, pointless and unnecessary as it was, had captured the imagination of the Victorian people, and he and Wills are commemorated by a monument outside Parliament House, Melbourne.

BIBLIOGRAPHY: M. Colwell, *The Journey of Burke and Wills,* Sydney, 1971; A. Moorehead, *Cooper's Creek,* London, 1963.

J. M. R. Cameron

Burnes, Alexander (1805–1841)   British explorer and political envoy. In service with the Bengal Army from 1821 on, Burnes was placed on political duty in Kutch, where he first became interested in the geography of Afghanistan and Central Asia. In 1831 he was sent up the Indus on a mission to Maharaja Ranjit Singh of Lahore and the following year traveled in disguise by way of Peshawar and Kabul to Bukhara, Meshed (Mashhad), and the Caspian through Teheran to Bushire (Bushehr) on the Persian Gulf. In 1836 he was sent on a political mission to Emir Dost Mohammed at Kabul. Contrary to Burnes's advice, the Earl of Auckland, the governor-general, decided to support the claim of the unpopular emir Shah Shujah to the Afghan throne, and in 1839 Burnes was sent back under Sir William Macnaghten to Kabul to reinstate him. He became India's political agent at Kabul and was assassinated there on November 2, 1841.

BIBLIOGRAPHY: Alexander Burnes, *Travels into Bokhara . . . in the years 1831, 1832, and 1833,* 3 vols., London, 1834.

Richard A. Pierce

Burton, Richard Francis (1821–1890)   English Orientalist, ethnographer, and explorer. Born in Torquay, the son of an Anglo-Irish army officer, Burton was educated haphazardly on the Continent and briefly attended Oxford University, where he began to teach himself Arabic. In 1842 he joined the Indian Army and remained in India for 7 years, traveling extensively and studying languages. In 1849 he was forced to leave India, evidently because of unfavorable reaction to a report by him on homosexual brothels in Karachi. He was allowed to remain in the army, however, and in 1853, having received a year's leave of absence to study Arabic, he traveled to the Muslim shrines of Medina and Mecca in the guise of an Afghan doctor. The following year he joined three other Indian Army officers—John Hanning SPEKE, G. E. Herne, and William Stroyan—for the purpose of exploring Somaliland. Before the main expedition got under way, Burton, again in disguise, traveled to the

Although Richard Burton was the discoverer of Lake Tanganyika, he was better known during his lifetime for his unexpurgated translation of the Arabian Nights. [Library of Congress]

Muslim city of Harar, Ethiopia, which no European was known to have penetrated before. The expedition came to an end after a Somali attack on its members at Berbera, during which Stroyan was killed and Burton and Speke were wounded. After recuperating from his wounds and serving in the Crimea during the Crimean War, Burton proposed to return to Africa to investigate reports of a great inland sea variously called the Sea of Ujiji or Sea of Tanganyika. His primary objective, however, was undoubtedly discovery of the sources of the Nile. For the expedition Burton obtained the sponsorship of the ROYAL GEOGRAPHICAL SOCIETY and £1,000 from the Foreign Office. Accompanying him as his second-in-command was Speke. *See* NILE RIVER: SEARCH FOR ITS SOURCE.

After following the route of Arab slave traders from Bagamoyo, in what is now Tanzania, to Kazeh (moden Tabora), Burton sighted Lake Tanganyika on February 13, 1858, near Ujiji. Both he and Speke had been seriously ill during the trek to the lake, and on this occasion Speke was virtually blind. After partially surveying the lake, they returned to Kazeh, whereupon Speke departed to look for an even larger lake reported by the Arabs to lie to the north. On August 25, 1858, Speke returned to Kazeh. Not only had he seen the lake, which he named Lake Victoria, but he had concluded that it was the source of the Nile. Burton was unconvinced by Speke's arguments, and relations between the two men now began to deteriorate. Burton, who reached England 2 weeks after Speke, claimed that the latter had violated a promise not to make any statements about the expedition until his own arrival. He was also indignant over Speke's publication in *Blackwood's Magazine* (September, October 1859) of two articles describing their expedition and advancing the thesis that Lake Victoria was the source of the Nile. He retaliated with disparaging references to Speke in his own two-volume *The Lake Regions of Central Africa* (1860).

After a trip to North America and marriage to the adoring Isabel Arundell in defiance of her parents' wishes, Burton returned to Africa in 1861 in the relatively insignificant position of consul to the bights of Benin and Biafra. In August 1864, Burton went to England, where he found Speke and James Augustus GRANT, who had recently returned from their successful expedition to Lake Victoria. Burton again questioned Speke's assertions regarding the size and importance of the lake, maintaining that Lake Tanganyika was the major source of the Nile, but a public debate between the two men was forestalled by Speke's sudden death on September 15, 1864.

During the remainder of his turbulent and controversial career, Burton also held consular appointments in Brazil, Damascus, and Trieste, where he died. In 1877–1878 he led a fruitless expedition for gold in Arabia, and in 1881–1882 he joined the explorer Verney Lovett CAMERON in a similarly unsuccessful quest on the Gold Coast of Africa. A prolific writer and gifted linguist who mastered more than forty languages and dialects, Burton published fifty full-length works, including a translation (1880) of Luis Vaz de Camões's *Os Lusíadas* and the scholarly but unsuccessful *The Book of the Sword* (1884). The most notorious of his publications was a sixteen-volume translation (1885–1888) of the unexpurgated *Arabian Nights* with notes and commentary on subjects, such as homosexuality, considered shocking by Victorian standards. He was also secretly involved in the publication of several translations of Oriental erotica. Although Burton was a pioneer of African exploration, his reputation rests primarily on his achievements as an Orientalist. His African writings are remarkable for their wealth of ethnographic detail as well as for their author's contempt of Africans.

BIBLIOGRAPHY: Fawn M. Brodie, *The Devil Drives: A Life of Sir Richard Burton*, New York, 1967; Richard Francis Burton, *The Nile Basin*, with an introduction by Robert Collins, New York, 1967; Caroline Oliver, "Richard Burton: The African Years," in Robert I. Rotberg (ed.), *Africa and Its Explorers*, Cambridge, Mass., 1970; Norman M. Penzer, *An Annotated Bibliography of Sir Richard Francis Burton, K.C.M.G.*, London, 1923, reprinted, New York, 1970.

***Bylot, Robert** (fl. 1610–1616)* British Arctic explorer. Nothing is known of Bylot's life except his contribution to four major NORTHWEST PASSAGE expeditions. He was mate on board the *Discovery* during the discovery and partial exploration by Henry HUDSON of Hudson Bay in 1610–1611, and it was he who managed, against great odds, to bring the ship and seven survivors home after the mutiny of June 1611. In 1612–1613, he returned to Hudson Bay on Sir Thomas Button's Northwest Passage expedition.

Bylot's renowned partnership with William BAFFIN began in 1615, when he was appointed commander of *Discovery* for a voyage to northern Hudson Bay. They coasted along the north shore of Southampton Island but turned back at Frozen Strait, having concluded, correctly, that there was no hope of a Northwest Passage in that direction. The two men set out again with the *Discovery* in 1616 to attempt a passage through Davis Strait. They charted in detail the unknown coasts of Baffin Bay and discovered Lancaster Sound, the only feasible entrance to the Northwest Passage, although neither recognized it as such. On their return, they dismissed the prospect of a passage by way of Davis Strait, and so their great discovery, Baffin Bay, was ignored by subsequent explorers for two centuries and even began to disappear from the maps.

Baffin, who as mate and pilot on the two voyages made most of the scientific observations, has generally received greater credit for their discoveries. But as Baffin himself acknowledged, Bylot was a fine ice navigator, and their success could hardly have been possible without his skills.

BIBLIOGRAPHY: C. R. Markham (ed.), *The Voyages of William Baffin 1612–1622*, London, 1881.

Clive A. Holland

***Byrd, Richard Evelyn** (1888–1957)* American polar explorer. Byrd was born in Winchester, Virginia, on October 25, 1888. A scion of one of the first families of Virginia, he was educated at the Virginia Military Institute and the U.S. Naval Academy, graduating as an ensign in June 1912. An ankle injury incurred during a gymnastic exhibition at Annapolis made him ineligible for promotion and led to his retirement in 1916. He was recalled only 2 months later, however, to serve as a training officer. Anxious for a more active assignment, he entered Pensacola as a flying cadet in the fall of 1917, graduating as Naval Aviator No. 608.

Byrd immediately became interested in a proposal to fly the Atlantic in a large flying boat. As part of the preparations for the flight, he developed the first drift indicator, an instrument designed to measure an airplane's deviation from course due to shifting winds. He also perfected a sextant featuring an artificial horizon for use by aircraft navigators. Now a lieutenant, he was charged with establishing a fueling station in Nova Scotia that could be used as a jumping-off point for the transatlantic flying boats. In spite of his technical contributions to the success of the expedition, Byrd was not permitted to serve as a member of the flight crews of the large Navy Curtiss airplanes that undertook the first aerial crossing of the Atlantic in May 1919.

The first man to make an aerial crossing of the North Pole, Richard Evelyn Byrd was the great pioneer in modern technological exploration. [U.S. Navy]

With the completion of the ocean flight, Byrd was assigned to draft a bill creating the Navy Bureau of Aeronautics, and he continued to serve as the new bureau's congressional liaison. In this capacity he played a particularly important role in preserving the independence of the Navy air arm in the face of Gen. William Mitchell's attempt to create a unified American air force.

In 1921 Byrd was named one of the navigation officers assigned to the *ZR-2 (R-38),* a British airship purchased by the Navy. He traveled to England in August to join the *ZR-2,* then undergoing final acceptance trials at Howden, but had not yet flown on the craft when it exploded and burned over the Humber River on August 24.

Following several years spent in directing Naval Reserve activities, Byrd took command of three Loening amphibians and a six-man contingent of Navy pilots and mechanics attached to Donald B. Mac-Millan's 1925 expedition to Greenland. During the course of this expedition the three airplanes logged a total of 6000 miles (9656 kilometers) in the air, observing more than 30,000 square miles (77,700 square kilometers) of new territory. For the first time Byrd had seen how the airplane could be used in the exploration of the Arctic.

Immediately after his return to the United States, Byrd and Floyd Bennett, one of the MacMillan Expedition pilots, began planning a flight over the North Pole. They obtained the sponsorship of the National Geographic Society and the financial support of industrialists, including John D. Rockefeller, Jr., and Edsel Ford. A Fokker trimotor, renamed the *Josephine Ford,* was purchased for the flight.

Byrd's ship, the *Chantier,* arrived at Kongsfjorden (Kings Bay), Spitsbergen (Svalbard), on April 29, 1926. The Byrd Expedition was not the only party that hoped to make a polar flight from Spitsbergen that spring. Roald AMUNDSEN, the Norwegian who had led the first party to reach the South Pole, and the American explorer Lincoln ELLSWORTH were awaiting the arrival of the *Norge,* an Italian-built airship in which they hoped to fly over the top of the world to Alaska.

The overloaded *Josephine Ford,* fitted with skis, finally took off for the pole at 1:58 A.M. on May 9, 1926, with Bennett at the controls and Byrd navigating. Shortly after 8 A.M. Byrd noted a spray of oil trailing from the starboard engine. Realizing that they could not return to safety on only two engines, Bennett suggested a landing to attempt repairs. Byrd, however, feared that they would damage the Fokker in landing and ordered the flight to continue. The leak proved to be from a loose rivet and ceased as soon as the oil fell below the level of the hole. The remainder of the flight was uneventful, with a polar crossing at 9:02 A.M. and a safe landing at Spitsbergen at about 4:30 P.M. In the years after this epic flight some authorities questioned Byrd's account, claiming that he turned back short of the goal when the oil leak appeared. To date, however, no substantial evidence has

been presented to buttress this contention. Byrd's first aerial crossing of the pole remains one of the great moments in the history of exploration.

In June 1927, Byrd and a three-man crew flew the Atlantic in the Fokker trimotor *America.* While the flight can be seen as an anticlimax following the successful Lindbergh and Chamberlain crossings, it nevertheless added to Byrd's reputation as a distance flyer.

It was in the Antarctic, however, that Richard Byrd was to make his most important contribution to geographic knowledge. The first Byrd Antarctic Expedition sailed for the southernmost continent on August 25, 1928. Its aircraft included a Ford trimotor in which to attempt the first flight over the South Pole, as well as a single engine Fokker monoplane and a Fairchild for use in shorter exploratory flights.

By January 1, 1929, Byrd had planted the base camp that was to become world-famous as Little America. Flights in the Fokker began in late January and resulted in major geographic discoveries. For Byrd, however, the polar flight was the primary goal of the expedition. The *Floyd Bennett,* as the Ford had been dubbed, was hauled from its shelter in preparation for the polar flight on November 28, 1929. Bernt Balchen and Harold June were to serve as pilots, while Ashley McKinley was to provide a photographic record of the trip. Once again, Byrd would navigate. The big Ford lifted off the runway at 3:29 P.M. and began its climb toward the towering Queen Maud Range. Unable to clear the 10,000-foot (3048-meter) passes onto the Polar Plateau, Byrd ordered his crew to dump 250 pounds (113 kilograms) of food and survival gear that might prove essential if the party were forced down. The remainder of the flight proved uneventful, however, with a passage over the pole at 1:14 A.M. on November 29, a return stop at a fuel cache, and a final landing at Little America at 10:08. The first Byrd expedition to the Antarctic sailed for New York on February 19, 1930.

Richard Byrd returned to the United States the best-known explorer of his generation. Planning a new expedition in the depths of the Depression proved more difficult than even Byrd had imagined, but by 1933 preparations for a return to Little America were complete. This time he was equipped with four airplanes: a large two-engine Curtiss Condor, a Fokker, a Pilgrim monoplane, and a Kellett autogiro. The expedition members were ensconced in Little America by January 1934. The emphasis of the second Antarctic expedition was on science. With the polar flight accomplished, all effort was now to be placed on the acquisition of new knowledge in such fields as physics, biology, geology, meteorology, and, of course, geography.

The establishment of a three-man advance base to be occupied by scientists who could make a detailed record of conditions during the long Antarctic winter was a primary objective. When it became apparent that it would be impossible to provision a multiman base, Byrd decided to occupy the station himself. The advance base was finally located near a supply depot roughly 125 miles (201 kilometers) down the trail from Little America. Byrd arrived at the site on March 22, 1934, and his small portable shelter was soon erected. The construction party began the return journey to Little America on March 28, leaving Byrd totally isolated. While he could maintain radio contact with Little America, there was no hope of rescue or assistance until spring. All went well from March through May. On May 31, however, he was overcome by fumes from a portable generator while sending a message to the main party. For the remainder of his stay Byrd was to battle the effects of carbon monoxide poisoning and the terrible cold. When relief finally arrived on August 10, Byrd was so weak that he required 2 months of nursing before he could be flown to Little America. When the expedition members abandoned Little America for the second time on February 7, 1935, they returned with a wealth of scientific data.

The experience at the advance base had not destroyed Byrd's enthusiasm for Antarctic exploration. By 1939 he was planning a third journey to the frozen continent. Unlike the earlier expeditions, the U.S. Antarctic Service, as the third Byrd expedition was to be known, was heavily supported by the United States government. Its primary purpose was to solidify American claims in Antarctica. As always, Byrd was to be in command, but this expedition was to differ from its predecessors in other ways. Little America, which was located in an area now claimed by New Zealand, was to be replaced by two separate bases, each commanded by a veteran of earlier trips. The complexity of the equipment and of the scientific tasks to be performed was also an important factor in guaranteeing that Admiral Byrd would exercise less personal supervision than on earlier trips. By late 1940 both camps were established, and Byrd had returned to the United States, allowing his men to winter alone. The third expedition came to an end that summer, as preparations for war took precedence over science and exploration.

During World War II Admiral Byrd led several tours through the Pacific islands, locating suitable bases from which American airmen could launch strikes against Japan. His report on conditions in the Pacific and on the potential of postwar air routes through the islands proved valuable to American planners.

Interest in Antarctica reappeared with the close of the war. A new expedition, Operation Highjump, was authorized in August 1946. Byrd was named commander, with Rear Adm. Richard Cruzen commanding the accompanying Task Force 68. Highjump, by far the most ambitious American effort to date, included thirteen ships, 4100 men, nineteen airplanes, and four helicopters. The expedition's airplanes flew over thousands of miles of unexplored territory. The high point was a two-plane flight over the unknown land beyond the pole in which Byrd participated. By mid-March 1947 Task Force 68 had weighed anchor for home.

As plans for the International Geophysical Year (July 1, 1957–December 31, 1958) matured, American scientists planned a return to Antarctica. Byrd, whose name was synonomous with the southernmost continent, was a key figure in lobbying for funds and was appointed officer in charge of United States Antarctic programs. Rear Adm. George J. Dufek commanded Operation Deepfreeze, as the naval support unit was termed. During the course of the Deepfreeze Program Admiral Byrd made his final trip south. On January 8, 1956, he completed a third flight over the South Pole. Following his return to the United States, Byrd continued planning for Deepfreeze II and working toward a treaty that would guarantee international cooperation in opening Antarctica. He died in his sleep on March 11, 1957.

The career of Richard Evelyn Byrd bridged the gap between an older tradition in which small groups of men relied on personal heroism to push back the unknown and the age of sophisticated equipment and precise planning. His name symbolizes an era in the history of polar exploration.

See also ANTARCTICA.

BIBLIOGRAPHY: Bernt Balchen, *Come North with Me*, New York, 1958; Richard Evelyn Byrd, *Alone*, New York, 1938; id., *Discovery: The Story of the Second Byrd Antarctic Expedition*, New York, 1935; id., *Exploring with Byrd: Episodes from an Adventurous Life*, New York, 1937; id., *Little America*, New York, 1930; id., *Skyward*, New York, 1928; Alden Hatch, *The Byrds of Virginia*, New York, 1969; Edwin P. Hoyt, *The Last Explorer: The Adventures of Admiral Byrd*, New York, 1968.

Tom D. Crouch

Cabeza de Vaca, Álvar Núñez (ca. 1490–?1556)
Spanish explorer. Cabeza de Vaca was born of an
illustrious family in Jerez de la Frontera. Very little is
known about his early life, save that he fought in Italy
and Navarre and entered the service of the Duke of
Medina Sidonia about 1513. In June 1527 Cabeza de
Vaca set sail from Spain as royal treasurer of an expedition to the New World led by Pánfilo de Narváez,
who had been authorized by the crown to explore and
conquer the area lying between the Río de las Palmas
in northeastern Mexico and Florida. The expedition,
consisting of approximately 600 men and five ships,
made stops in Santo Domingo and Cuba and landed at
the head of Tampa Bay in April 1528. Soon afterward
Narváez decided to march inland while the ships
sailed northward in search of a port which the pilots
said they knew. According to Cabeza de Vaca, he
opposed leaving the ships but was overruled. The
ships were not seen again, and it was later learned
that they had eventually sailed for Mexico.

With a force of approximately 250 to 300 Spaniards,
Narváez set out for Apalachen, where they were told
they would find gold. They arrived at Apalachen (at or
near present-day Tallahassee) and found large quantities of maize but no gold. About a month later, with
Indian archers harassing them as they marched, they
moved to another Indian town called Aute. Having
lost hope of making contact with the ships, they
decided to try to reach the Spanish settlement of
Pánuco in northeastern Mexico by water. To this end

they built five barges and sailed from a bay (variously
identified with Apalachicola, Apalachee, and St. Andrew Bays) which they called the Bay of the Horses
because they killed and ate their last-remaining
horses here. The Spaniards sailed west in their over-
crowded craft, staying close to the shore and sorely
afflicted by the lack of fresh water. After they had
passed the mouth of a river which flowed into the sea
like a torrent (the Mississippi) and had been carried
seaward by the river's current and the wind, the
barges became separated. Cabeza de Vaca's barge
eventually reached Galveston Island in Texas, as did a
barge commanded by Alonso del Castillo and Andrés
Dorantes. During the winter the weather was so severe and food was in such short supply that most of
the Spaniards and many of the local Indians died.

In the spring of 1529 nearly all the Spaniards left
Galveston Island for the mainland while Cabeza de
Vaca stayed behind because of illness. For several
years he lived among the Indians of eastern Texas as a
trader, traveling inland and along the coast. At the
beginning of the winter of 1533 he met Castillo and
Dorantes, as well as the latter's Moorish slave Esteban (Estebanico), along the Colorado River of Texas,
where the Indians gathered yearly to eat pecans. They
reported that they were the only survivors of those
who had separated from Cabeza de Vaca in 1529 and
that they had spent the intervening years as slaves of
various Indian tribes. The four men agreed to meet
the following summer in a district to which the Indi-

ans traveled to feed upon tunas (prickly pears). They would then attempt to reach Mexico together. The rendezvous was effected at tuna thickets near modern San Antonio, whereupon the party of four traveled north and spent the winter with a tribe they called the Avavares. They resumed their westward journey in the summer of 1535, being conducted by Indian guides all the way. They in turn ensured a respectful reception as they traveled by healing the sick by praying and making the sign of the cross over them. After crossing the Rio Grande at Rincon, in what is now New Mexico, they moved south through the modern Mexican state of Sonora. Near Culiacán they made their first contacts with Spaniards and, after resting for several weeks, continued their trek. Their arrival in Mexico City in the summer of 1536 caused much excitement, and they were warmly received by Viceroy Antonio de Mendoza. Their account of their travels stimulated the Viceroy's interest in northern exploration, which in turn led to the expedition of Francisco Vásquez de CORONADO.

Cabeza de Vaca left for Spain in 1537, making a stop in Santo Domingo, where he submitted to the *audiencia* (royal tribunal) a report by him, Castillo, and Dorantes describing their recent adventures. This so-called *Joint Report* is one of the two principal sources of information about their odyssey, the other being a narrative by Cabeza de Vaca published in Spain as *Los naufragios* in 1542. While in Spain, Cabeza de Vaca turned down an invitation to return to Florida in the expedition being organized by Hernando de SOTO, but in 1540 he accepted appointment as governor of the province of Río de la Plata in South America. After landing on the island of Santa Catarina, Brazil, he traveled overland to the Spanish settlement at Asunción, arriving in March 1542 after a journey of more than 4 months during which he probably became the first white man to see Iguaçu Falls, located near the confluence of the Iguaçu and Paraná Rivers. Cabeza de Vaca resumed his explorations in September 1542 in an effort to reach a kingdom rich in precious metals

American bison as described by the Spanish explorer Álvar Núñez Cabeza de Vaca in the sixteenth century. [Library of Congress]

believed to exist in the interior of South America. At the head of an expedition of about 400 Spaniards and 800 Guaraní Indians, he sailed up the Paraguay River to a place called Puerto de los Reyes. Leaving part of his force behind, he then turned westward but was soon compelled to return to Puerto de los Reyes by his followers, who feared the thick forests that lay ahead.

Two weeks after his return to Asunción in April 1544, Cabeza de Vaca was deposed as governor by a group of Spanish conspirators who resented what they considered his high-handed interference in the affairs of the colony. In 1545 he was sent to Spain for trial on a variety of charges, including the accusation that he had attempted to usurp royal authority in Asunción, and was found guilty after years of litigation. Despite appeals, he was unable to obtain revocation of the verdict, though his sentence was made less severe. His last years were evidently spent in poverty, for in 1556 he requested and received financial aid from the Royal Treasury.

BIBLIOGRAPHY: Morris Bishop, *The Odyssey of Cabeza de Vaca*, New York, 1933; Enrique de Gandia, *Historia de la conquista del Río de la Plata y del Paraguay*, Buenos Aires, 1932; Cleve Hallenbeck, *Álvar Núñez Cabeza de Vaca: The Journey and Route of the First European to Cross the Continent of North America*, Glendale, Calif., 1940; Carl O. Sauer, *Sixteenth Century North America*, Berkeley, Calif., 1971.

***Cabot, John** (d. ?1498)* Italian-born explorer whose voyage to North America in 1497 gave England its claim to the continent. Cabot's life is sparsely documented, and neither the place nor the year of his birth is known with certainty. He was probably born in Genoa and became a citizen of Venice in the early 1470s after meeting a residence requirement of 15 years in the latter city. In Venice he was a merchant or a merchant's factor. He later told a contemporary that he had traveled as far as Mecca while engaged in the spice trade and that, after learning that spices originated in the Far East, he had conceived a plan to reach Asia by sailing westward across the North Atlantic. Documents in the archives of Valencia reveal the presence there and in Barcelona of a Venetian called Johan Caboto Montecalunya in 1492–1493. If this was indeed John Cabot, he was undoubtedly aware of the first voyage and triumphal return to Spain of Christopher COLUMBUS.

By the end of 1495 Cabot was in England, where his efforts to secure royal sponsorship for his projected voyage were successful. On March 5, 1496, Henry VII granted letters patent for the voyage to John Cabot and his three sons, one of whom was Sebastian CABOT. They were authorized "to sayle to all partes, countreys, and seas, of the East, of the West, and of the North" and to seek out and discover lands unknown to Christians. According to a letter from an English merchant named John Day to an admiral presumed to be Columbus which was first published in the *Hispanic American Historical Review* in 1956,

Cabot made an attempt to carry out his design in 1496 but was forced to turn back. There is, however, no other evidence of an unsuccessful first voyage by Cabot.

Cabot set sail from Bristol about May 20, 1497, with eighteen or twenty men, perhaps including Sebastian, in a single small vessel, *Mathew.* He proceeded to Dursey Head, Ireland, then sailed westward, and landed on North American soil on June 24. There is much controversy over the site of Cabot's landfall; among the places most frequently mentioned are Cape Breton Island, Newfoundland (Cape Bonavista or Cape Dégrat, on the northeastern tip of the island), Labrador, and Maine. Upon landing, he took possession in the name of Henry VII but soon returned to the ship. The Europeans found signs of human occupation but saw no one. After a coastal voyage, the direction and extent of which are also in dispute, Cabot sailed back to Europe, landing first in Brittany. He was in Bristol by early August and had an interview with King Henry in London on August 10. In the belief that Cabot had reached Asia, preparations began for a second voyage. He left Bristol with a fleet of five ships in May 1498. One of the ships soon put into Ireland in distress, but the fate of Cabot and the other four ships remains a mystery.

BIBLIOGRAPHY: Henry Harrisse, *John Cabot: The Discoverer of North-America and Sebastian His Son,* New York, 1968, reprint of 1896 ed.; Samuel Eliot Morison, *The European Discovery of America: The Northern Voyages, A.D. 500–1600,* New York, 1971; James A. Williamson, *The Cabot Voyages and Bristol Discovery under Henry VII,* Hakluyt Society, 2d ser., no. 120, Cambridge, England, 1962.

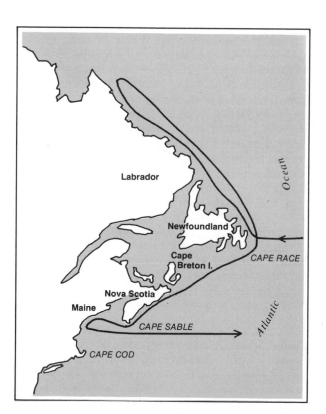

Far left: A reconstruction of the route John Cabot may have followed in 1497.

Cabot, Sebastian *(ca. 1484–1557)* Italian-born navigator and explorer. Cabot is a controversial figure, regarded by some scholars as a charlatan with a gift for prevarication. As a result, there is much disagreement about the number and extent of his voyages, only one of which, an expedition to South America between 1526 and 1530, is thoroughly documented. The son of John CABOT, Sebastian was probably born in Venice while his parents were living in that city. He claimed to have accompanied John Cabot to North America in 1497 and may have done so. In a mappemonde dated 1544 which he designed, the younger Cabot calls himself joint discoverer with his father and gives the date and hour of the first landfall. Sebastian has also been credited by some historians with a voyage in search of the NORTHWEST PASSAGE, which may have taken place in 1508.

In 1512 Cabot entered Spanish service and in 1518 was appointed *piloto mayor* (chief pilot) of Spain, a position previously held by Amerigo VESPUCCI and Juan Díaz de Solís. On April 3, 1526, he left Seville as captain general of a Spanish expedition of four ships and approximately 200 men which was intended to be a successor to that of Ferdinand MAGELLAN. Its destination was the Far East and the biblical lands of Tarshish and OPHIR. Near the Cape Verde Islands Cabot ordered a course that brought the fleet to the Brazilian port of Recife. After leaving Recife on September 29, 1526, Cabot sailed down the coast of Brazil until he reached the vicinity of Santa Catarina Island, which he named in honor of his wife. From several Spaniards whom he encountered in Brazil (survivors of earlier voyages) Cabot learned of a "white king," rich in silver, who dwelled in the Río de la Plata region, and after the loss of his flagship he decided to explore this part of South America instead of sailing to Asia. Several of his officers objected to the change in plans, but Cabot dealt with the dissenters by marooning them. *See also* EL DORADO.

Cabot reached the entrance to the estuary of the Río de la Plata on February 21, 1527. He would spend nearly 3 years exploring the great waterways of this area, thereby opening up a major highway for Spanish penetration of South America. He sailed up the Paraná River to a point about 50 miles (80 kilometers) above its confluence with the Paraguay; the latter river was also explored, probably to a point near Asunción. The Spaniards failed to find the white king, though they did obtain some gold and silver objects of Peruvian origin. Lack of food and the hostility of the Indians led to a decision in October 1529 to leave South America. After Cabot arrived in Spain in July 1530, he was accused and convicted of misconduct on his South American voyage but was soon restored to royal favor and to his position as *piloto mayor.*

Cabot returned to England in 1548. In the 1550s he was named governor of the Company of Merchant Adventurers (Muscovy Company), which attempted to find a NORTHEAST PASSAGE to Asia and engaged in trade with Russia. The precise date of Cabot's death is not known, but the payment of his pension was stopped in 1557.

BIBLIOGRAPHY: Henry Harrisse, *John Cabot: The Discoverer of North-America and Sebastian His Son*, New York, 1968, reprint of 1896 ed.; Samuel Eliot Morison, *The European Discovery of America: The Southern Voyages, 1492–1616*, New York, 1974; James A. Williamson, *The Cabot Voyages and Bristol Discovery under Henry VII*, Hakluyt Society, 2d ser., no. 120, Cambridge, England, 1962.

Pedro Álvares Cabral, Portuguese explorer who made an accidental (or perhaps not accidental) stop at Brazil on his way to India and helped substantiate Portugal's claim to the territory. [Library of Congress]

Cabral, Pedro Álvares **(ca. 1467–1520s)** Portuguese navigator. Cabral departed for India on March 9, 1500, in command of a fleet of thirteen caravels, one squadron of which was commanded by Bartolomeu DIAS, the first Portuguese to double the Cape of Good Hope, in order to capitalize on the discovery by Vasco da GAMA of the sea route to India. On March 18 the Canary Islands were sighted. Four days later, on March 22, the party passed the Cape Verde Islands, by which time they had lost one ship. Instead of following the West African coast as Dias had done, Cabral, following Vasco da Gama's instructions, sailed south after leaving the Cape Verdes until he crossed the doldrums, then southwest in order to take advantage of the trade winds until the latitude of the Cape of Good Hope, and then east to approach the cape.

On April 22, during Easter week, the fleet sighted Monte Pascoal on the eastern coast of South America, 200 miles (322 kilometers) south of Bahia (Salvador). Cabral named the land Terra (or Ilha) da Vera Cruz and immediately dispatched a ship back to Lisbon with the news. The fleet sailed northward to Porto Seguro (present-day Baía Cabrália), where a landing was made. On May 2 the fleet resumed the voyage to the Cape of Good Hope.

The appearance of a comet in the sky on May 12 boded ill, and disaster was not long in striking. Two weeks later a storm struck, sending four ships to the bottom of the sea. Cabral's much-reduced fleet of seven ships was blown around the Cape of Good Hope and regrouped at Mozambique. He sailed to Kilwa and Malindi on July 20 and reached Calicut on the Malabar coast of India on September 13. Muslim opposition here made his stay both dangerous and not too profitable. He bombarded the city, left for Cochin and Cannanore, where he was more successful, and returned to Portugal in July 1501. Passed over in favor of Vasco da Gama for the command of the third voyage to India, Cabral retired to Santarém, where he died in the 1520s. His voyage firmly established the sea route to India, and his discovery secured Brazil for Portugal.

Although most authorities believe Cabral's discovery of Brazil was fortuitous, he may have been carrying secret instructions which caused him to sail farther west than necessary for a doubling of the Cape of Good Hope in order to determine what, if anything, lay at the extreme western part of the area assigned to Portugal under the Treaty of Tordesillas. Credit for the discovery of Brazil properly belongs to Vicente Yáñez PINZÓN, who reached the easternmost point of South America on January 20 or 26, 1500.

BIBLIOGRAPHY: William B. Greenlee, *The Voyage of Pedro Álvares Cabral to Brazil and India*, London, 1938; Samuel Eliot Morison, *Portuguese Voyages to America*, Cambridge, Mass., 1940, reprinted New York, 1965.

Martin Torodash

Cabrillo, Juan Rodríguez **(Portuguese: João Rodrigues Cabrilho; d. 1543)** Portuguese-born explorer of the California coast. Cabrillo is known to have gone to Mexico in 1520 as a soldier in the party led by Pánfilo de Narváez and to have taken part in the conquest of the Aztec empire. Later he went to Guatemala, probably with Pedro de ALVARADO, and prospered there. On June 27, 1542, he left the Mexican port of Navidad with two ships to explore the coast of California. The southern part (Baja California) had been explored by earlier expeditions, notably several sponsored by Hernán CORTÉS, and by 1542 the region was already known as California. This was the name of the island home of Calafia, queen of the Amazons, in *Las sergas de Esplandián*, a popular tale of chivalry written by Garci-Rodríguez de Montalvo and published about 1510. Since the fictional island was located "on the right hand of the Indies" and the existence of Amazons in the vicinity of Mexico had long been rumored, the application of this name to what was first thought to be an island is not surprising.

According to a contemporary account of Cabrillo's voyage, California was sighted on July 2. The ships sailed up the coast, passing the present international boundary, and on September 2 put in at a harbor Cabrillo called San Miguel (present San Diego). In October they sailed through the Santa Barbara Channel, visited Santa Catalina and other islands, and found the Indians there and on the mainland friendly and helpful. After being buffeted by severe storms, Cabrillo decided to winter on San Miguel, another of the Santa Barbara Channel Islands. He died there on January 3, 1543, from the effects of a fall. Bartolomé Ferrer (Ferrelo), whom Cabrillo had appointed as his successor, attempted to sail northward on January 19, but bad weather kept the ships in the Santa Barbara Channel for another month. By the end of February they had reached their most northerly point, about 41°. After overcoming more bad weather during which the two ships became separated for a time, they returned to Navidad on April 14, 1543. The voyage had little immediate impact, and it was not until the seventeenth century that it was followed up by Spain.

BIBLIOGRAPHY: Henry R. Wagner, *Spanish Voyages to the Northwest Coast of America in the Sixteenth Century*, San Francisco, 1929.

Caillié (Caillé), René **(1799–1838)** French explorer. Born at Mauzé in the department of Deux-Sèvres, the son of a baker, Caillié was orphaned at an early age and had little schooling. Having developed a strong desire to become an African explorer, he traveled to Senegal in 1816 as a servant in a French colonizing expedition. He later returned to France but remained drawn to Africa and to his dream of exploration. In 1824 he went back to Senegal in the hope of being able to travel to Timbuktu, the mysterious city on the Niger River virtually unknown to Europeans, and to this end began to acquaint himself with Arabic and Moorish culture. Caillié learned that the Geographical Society of Paris was offering a prize of 10,000 francs to the first man to reach Timbuktu and return with a detailed account of his observations, but since he lacked a sponsor to finance his expedition, he had to wait until he had saved enough money to meet his necessary expenses en route.

Caillié began his quest for Timbuktu in March 1827 at the mouth of the Rio Nunez, in what is now Guinea, and reached the Niger at Kouroussa in June. To disarm suspicion along the way, he claimed to be an Egyptian of Arab parentage who had been taken to France as a youngster and was now returning to the land of his birth. From August 3, 1827, until January 9, 1828, he was forced to remain at Tiéme, being felled first by foot trouble and then by a bout with scurvy. He reached Timbuktu on April 20, 1828, and stayed there until May 4, thereby becoming the second European (after Alexander Gordon LAING) to visit the city of his own volition and the first to survive the journey.

Having returned to France by way of Morocco, Caillié was awarded the Geographical Society prize and was made a chevalier of the Legion of Honor. His account of his travels was published in three volumes in 1830 as *Journal d'un voyage à Temboctou et à Jenné dans l'Afrique centrale,* and was translated into English the same year. Some critics, especially in England, charged that he was a fraud and had never been to Timbuktu at all, but the accuracy of his description was confirmed by Heinrich BARTH, who visited Timbuktu in the 1850s.

BIBLIOGRAPHY: Galbraith Welch, *The Unveiling of Timbuctoo: The Astounding Adventures of Caillié,* London, 1938.

Cam, Diogo See CÃO, DIOGO.

Cameron, Verney Lovett **(1844–1894)** English explorer. Born in the village of Radipole near Weymouth, Dorset, the son of a clergyman, Cameron entered the Royal Navy at the age of 13. He subsequently saw service in various places, including the Indian Ocean, where his experiences on antislavery patrols left him with an abiding hatred of slavery. In 1870 he was assigned to the Steam Reserve at Sheer-

ness. Shortly afterward Cameron volunteered to lead a ROYAL GEOGRAPHICAL SOCIETY expedition to Africa to search for David LIVINGSTONE. His offer was refused, but when the society proposed another such expedition after the meeting of Henry STANLEY with Livingstone in 1871, Cameron was put in charge.

Cameron's instructions as head of the Livingstone East Coast Expedition were to locate and offer assistance to the celebrated explorer, but Cameron was evidently planning to undertake independent exploration on his own as well. Besides Cameron, the expedition consisted of a one-time messmate of his, Assistant Surgeon W. E. Dillon, Lieut. Cecil Murphy of the Royal Artillery, and Robert Moffat, a nephew of Livingstone. By the end of March 1873 they had left Bagamoyo on the East African coast, and they reached Tabora the following August. On October 20, 1873, while still in Tabora, Cameron was informed by letter of Livingstone's death, and the party bearing the latter's body arrived a few days later. By this time Moffat had died, and Dillon and Murphy now decided to leave Africa. Cameron, however, set out for Ujiji to recover Livingstone's books and personal effects, which eventually did reach England. Meanwhile, Cameron explored Lake Tanganyika and plotted ninety-six rivers flowing into the lake but only one flowing out of it, the Lukuga. Interested in exploring the sources of the Congo (Zaire) River, Cameron traveled to Nyangwe, on the Lualaba River, on which he hoped to travel to determine its relationship to the Congo. At Nyangwe he was unable to procure canoes for his trip down the river and, following the advice of the Arab slave trader Hamed bin-Muhammad (later known as Tippu Tib), decided to seek the Atlantic Coast by a more southerly route. After many hardships he reached the West African coast at Catumbela, a village north of Benguela, Angola, on November 7, 1875, thus becoming the first European to cross tropical Africa from east to west.

Cameron was lionized upon his return to England on April 2, 1876, and was awarded the Founder's Medal of the Royal Geographical Society for 1876. The same year he was a British delegate at the conference on Africa convened in Brussels by King Leopold II and warmly supported the King's projects. Regarded as an expert on Africa, he frequently spoke out against the slave trade and urged development of the continent's commercial potentialities. He returned briefly to Africa in 1882 with Richard Francis BURTON to investigate mining concessions on the Gold Coast.

BIBLIOGRAPHY: James A. Casada, "Verney Lovett Cameron: A Centenary Appreciation," *The Geographical Journal,* vol. 141, part 2, July 1975, pp. 203–215; id., "Verney Lovett Cameron: A Centenary Bibliography," *Library Notes of the Royal Commonwealth Society,* new ser., no. 214, September 1975, pp. 1–5; new ser., no. 215, October 1975, pp. 1–5; James R. Hooker, "Verney Lovett Cameron: A Sailor in Central Africa," in Robert I. Rotberg (ed.), *Africa and Its Explorers,* Cambridge, Mass., 1970, pp. 255–294.

The French explorer René Caillié's fascination with the Arab world led him to become the second European to reach Timbuktu and the first to live through the experience.

Canada

Surrounded on three sides by great oceans—the Atlantic, Pacific, and Arctic—and bordering the United States on the south and in Alaska, Canada is a North American nation in northerly latitudes. The story of Canada's exploration involves an understanding of Canada's links with the rest of North America by land and sea and its links with Europe and Asia by sea. The history of human exploration in Canada is an integral record of the attempt to delineate and map North America, to exploit its resources of field, forest, shore, and mountain, to discover routes of travel and commerce, and to find suitable sites for occupation and settlement.

At the time that Europeans began to explore Canada in about A.D. 1000 native Indians and Eskimos already knew much about the landmass of Canada. In their respective localities they knew the rivers, lakes, and seas, and they had developed technological aids to assist in their travel. The birchbark canoe and the kayak are two important and well-known legacies, but to these could be added techniques for survival in the wilderness, such as tent making, berry collecting, and dehydrating food. European explorers adopted many of these important aids, and from the natives they gained a greater degree of knowledge about the land they were exploring than they were prepared to give credit for in their writings. On the other hand, with their sailing ships the Europeans had a deepwater capability. They also had the skills and astronomical aids to make accurate maps and charts. They compiled literary and visual records of their travels and explorations by land and sea. The process of compiling an accurate map of Canada began with the earliest European explorers, but it is only in recent times, with the aid of aerial photography, satellite photography, and infrared detectors and other computer-based technologies for determining soil values and usages, that a full knowledge of Canada's landform has been acquired.

From the earliest times of human occupation in Canada, the occupants knew that they were dealing with a northern land. From the western cordillera to the Appalachians in the east, from the 49th parallel to the Labrador mountains and outer Arctic islands in the north, the environment is northern. Much of the climate is Arctic or sub-Arctic, but in some southerly latitudes more moderate climates occur. Precipitation is heavy on the Pacific Coast, while on the Atlantic shore a lesser rainfall occurs. In between, much of Canada experiences continental climates of warm summers and cold winters. This continental climate corresponds to the principal geographical feature of Canada that affected the exploration of the area, the Precambrian (Canadian) Shield surrounding Hudson Bay on three sides. This vast structure of granite and gneiss provides the anchor for North America. At the time of European-Amerind contact it was the home-

land of numerous tribes that shared their woodland skills and knowledge with the Europeans. Along the shield's forested southern margin Indians and fur traders traveled the natural (though somewhat intricate) east-west water route. This so-called Voyagers' Highway linked together, from east to west, Lakes Superior, Winnipeg, and Athabasca. These lakes are the hubs of three low-elevation drainage saucers which lead respectively to the Gulf of St. Lawrence, Hudson Strait, and via the Mackenzie River to the Arctic. On the west portages could be made to the rivers that drained into the Pacific. This made a transcontinental water highway that fur traders developed and used successfully in the eighteenth and nineteenth centuries. The early exploration of the Canadian landmass, tied as it was so closely with the fur trade, is at bottom the discovery of this east-west route and its links to the north and south. And by the same token the emergence of modern Canada is tied to this same great chapter of exploration. The North West Company, dating from about 1776, the first commercial concern to trade from the Atlantic and Pacific, was, as the great social scientist Harold Innis rightly said, the forerunner of the Canadian Confederation.

Canada also is a maritime state. It is surrounded by great seas, the Atlantic, Arctic, and Pacific. The ice-free quality of the Pacific made it the easiest to explore, though its intricacies demanded careful hydrographic surveying that was not completed fully until the twentieth century. Its distance from Europe meant that it was discovered and explored later than the Atlantic or eastern Arctic shores. The Arctic's ice conditions posed a very special problem for Canadian exploration by sea, and the search for the NORTHWEST PASSAGE, begun by the French in the early sixteenth century, was not successful until the mid-nineteenth. The Atlantic was the most accessible of the three seas to Europe; consequently it provided the entry to the hinterland through two important gateways, the St. Lawrence River on the south and Davis and Hudson Straits on the north. These seas were the links of the European explorers with the wider world, and their role in the discovery of Canada is often mistakenly taken for granted, for the discovery of Canada occurred by sea and by land. On each of these seacoasts aboriginal peoples already exploited the local resources at the time of the arrival of white explorers, and their helping hand to the scientific delineation of the Canadian landmass was significant; like the woodlands Indians, they often welcomed and aided the discoverers.

Aboriginal exploration before A.D. 1000 In terminal Pleistocene–early Holocene (Recent) times, persons of basically Mesolithic culture crossed Beringia from Siberia and penetrated the Pacific cordillera. Later, ancestral Aleuts and Eskimos came to northern North

America. Subsequently Indians populated the western coast, central plains, and eastern woodlands. They build up a considerable knowledge of the land which they retained in their oral tradition, and many place names currently used (Canada, Quebec, Ontario, and Saskatchewan among them) date from early Indian appellations.

European exploration, A.D. 1000–1871 The second phase of Canadian exploration dates from about 1000, when Norsemen coasted along Newfoundland's shores and reconnoitered the continental coast (*see* NORSE MARITIME DISCOVERIES). The Norse made no lasting settlements, and the task of further discovery devolved to other Europeans. Only 5 years after the first voyage of Christopher COLUMBUS, the Italian-born navigator John CABOT sailed from Bristol to find a route from England to the Cathay made legendary by the travels of Marco POLO. This began a major trend in Canadian exploration: to find a navigable route to the East which would shorten trade distances and costs and strengthen the commercial power and, accordingly, the military strength of Great Britain.

A similar aim was pursued by France. In 1524 France sent Giovanni da VERRAZZANO to find the Northwest Passage, which the court hoped would counteract Spain's newly discovered southwestern passage, by Magellan Strait, to the "blessed shores of Cathay." Instead of finding a passage between Spanish Florida and Newfoundland that would have put France directly in touch with the Far East, Verrazzano found the North American shore unyielding.

Verrazzano's navigations, however, had uncovered a large landmass which merited closer inspection. Perhaps some water route to the West lay hidden in the secret recesses of the continent. Thus it was the duty of Jacques CARTIER in three voyages beginning in 1534 to determine the lay of the land south and west of Newfoundland. In 1534 he explored the Gulf of St. Lawrence and claimed its shores for France. In 1535 he ascended the river itself and visited Indians at Stadacona (Quebec) and Hochelaga (Montreal). So favorable were his reports that the French court decided to challenge rival Spanish claims by setting up a fortified settlement. In 1542 Jean-François de la Rocque, Sieur de Roberval, founded France-Roy, near Stadacona. Cartier meanwhile discovered mineral resources. But the samples he sent home proved worthless. Nonetheless, this initiated an important feature of Canadian exploration: the search for precious metals. Meanwhile, the French, like Cabot, were discovering other resources: the great cod fishery of the Grand Banks and the apparently endless fur trade of the continental shore and interior. Ultimately the search for resources proved more rewarding than the search for a navigable waterway to Asia.

Canada's continental interior and shore were more accurately defined by Samuel de CHAMPLAIN, later known as "the father of New France." A geographer and cartographer of repute, Champlain examined the Bay of Fundy in 1604. The next year he explored the

The Cabot Trail, a loop road 185 miles long on Cape Breton Island in Nova Scotia, was named after John Cabot, who sighted the island in 1497. [Canadian Government Travel Bureau]

New England coastline and determined that French settlement there would conflict with that of the English. Thus his superior, Pierre du Gua, Sieur de Monts, decided to erect a defensible settlement at Port Royal, on Annapolis Basin in what is now Nova Scotia. In 1608 Champlain founded Quebec at the St. Lawrence River narrows, and from this base the exploration of the river basin went ahead as rapidly as French resources and Indian friendship would allow. The Iroquois Confederacy south of the St. Lawrence tended to deflect French exploration toward the north and west before the 1660s. In 1611 Champlain selected Montreal as a site for a summer post. After 1609 he explored the country lying upriver of Montreal, including the Ottawa River, Georgian Bay, Lake Ontario, and the Richelieu River. He made great contributions to European knowledge about North America by delineating the principal rivers and lakes of the St. Lawrence River empire.

Much subsequent Canadian exploration emanated from the local Canadian centers of Trois-Rivières (Three Rivers), Montreal, and Quebec. The Jesuits established a number of missions on the frontiers of southwestern Ontario, then called Huronia by the French, and recorded their life experiences in the *Jesuit Relations*. At the same time *coureurs de bois*, the fur traders and voyagers in the upper country (*pays d'en haut*), expanded knowledge of the hinterland for commercial reasons. They did so sometimes without the consent of the chartered company which had the monopoly of trade or without the approval of the Governor of New France, as the colony of Canada was called. Pierre Esprit Radisson and Médard Chouart, Sieur des Groseilliers, were two *coureurs de bois* who explored new rivers and lakes and pushed the fur trade back into the hinterland between Lake Superior and James Bay in the 1640s and 1650s. Official expedi-

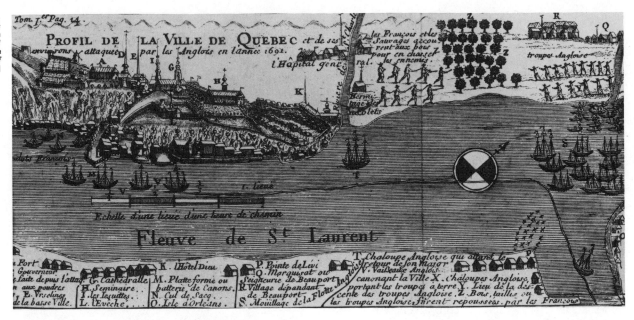

tions by Louis JOLLIET down the Mississippi to the Arkansas in 1673, by the Sieur de LA SALLE to the Mississippi Delta in 1682, and by the Sieur de LA VÉRENDRYE across the continental plains in the 1740s added considerable knowledge about the continental interior.

Meanwhile, European rivals were making inroads in territory claimed by France in the New World. This resulted in new explorations in new areas. In 1613 the Scot Sir William Alexander settled Nova Scotia (New Scotland). In 1668 the Hudson's Bay Company syndicate, aided by Radisson and Groseilliers, began exploration of the southern and western shores of Hudson Bay. Subsequently the company built a number of posts there, though rivalry with France made its situ-

ation precarious for much of the late seventeenth and eighteenth centuries. At the same time the English had been seeking the Northwest Passage. In about 1508-1509 Sebastian CABOT may have entered Hudson Bay, in 1576 Martin FROBISHER penetrated to Baffin Island, in 1586 John DAVIS explored Davis Strait into Baffin Bay, and in 1610 Henry HUDSON passed through Hudson Strait before entering Hudson Bay and James Bay. There were other English voyages as well (by Thomas Button, Robert BYLOT, William BAFFIN, Luke Fox, Thomas James, and others), and by the early seventeenth century these explorations provided a rough outline of the entries and shoreline of the eastern Arctic. Invariably and despite hardships of climate and disease, the English clung passionately to their dream of a passage in northern latitudes. "The North-west passage is a matter nothing doubtful," Davis wrote in 1585 with the perennial optimism that characterized his countrymen's feelings, "but at any time about to be passed, the sea navigable, devoid of ice, the air tolerable, and the waters very deep." But the next stage of exploration in this region did not begin until Hudson's Bay Company servants undertook the exploration of the mainland and the shores of the bay.

In 1670 the Hudson's Bay Company received its charter and the sole rights of English trade in Rupert's Land, that vast area drained by the numerous rivers flowing into Hudson Bay. The charter required the company to find "a new passage into the South Sea" and to prosecute the trade in furs, minerals, and other valuable commodities. By 1682 trading posts had been set up at Rupert River, Albany River, Hayes Island, Port Nelson, and Fort Severn. By the Treaty of Utrecht (1713) France gave Britain undisputed possession of Hudson Bay.

From these posts the exploration of the interior was

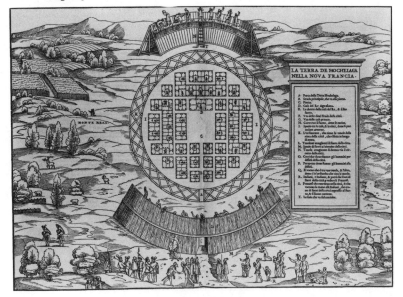

undertaken by employees of the Hudson's Bay Company. In 1691–1692 Henry Kelsey pushed through to the plains, where he visited various Indian tribes and hunted buffalo. In 1754–1755 Anthony Henday (Hendry) explored the country between the north and south branches of the Saskatchewan and opened interior trade to his company. Samuel HEARNE began his great exploration of the interior in 1769. In 1770 he reached the Coppermine River and followed it to the sea, thereby becoming the first white man to see the tundra area (the barrens) and the Arctic Ocean. On the way back he discovered Great Slave Lake. His journey added important data to the geographical knowledge of the interior and its Indian and Eskimo inhabitants. It served also to counter critics of the company such as Arthur Dobbs and Joseph Robson, who had taken pains to condemn the Hudson's Bay Company as being averse to discoveries.

Now the exploration of Canada was spurred by fur-trade rivalry. In 1774 Hearne built Cumberland House to check the growth of the rival North West Company from Montreal, which came via the Great Lakes, Grand Portage, Rainy Lake, and Lake Winnipeg. The Nor'westers were on the Sasketchewan in 1767. In 1772 Joseph Frobisher built a post, also called Cumberland House, and soon thereafter the Nor'westers were pushing their trade into the Saskatchewan and Athabasca systems, at Île-à-la Crosse, Slave River, and Great Slave Lake. Peter Pond went northwest even farther and discovered the Methye Portage, which linked the Churchill River system with the Athabasca-Mackenzie system. In 1788 two men under Pond built Fort Chipewyan on Lake Athabasca, subsequently to become the real starting point for the journey of Alexander MACKENZIE in 1789.

In the meantime, the western coasts of modern Canada had been explored by sea. Spanish and Portuguese voyagers may have made uncertain probes toward the Strait of Juan de Fuca in the sixteenth century, but in 1579 Sir Francis DRAKE made a certain voyage along the coasts of Oregon and California, perhaps as far as 48°N. In 1741 Vitus BERING and Aleksey CHIRIKOV made Russian explorations along the North Pacific coast of North America. In 1774 the Spaniard Juan José Pérez explored Dixon Entrance and Nootka Sound, and in 1778 Capt. James COOK of the Royal Navy made explorations at Nootka, the Gulf of Alaska, and Bering Sea. France and the United States were also interested in the future of the northwest coast of North America. Jean François de LA PÉROUSE laid claim to Lituya Bay, Alaska, in 1786, and Yankee maritime fur traders such as John Kendrick and Robert Gray coasted north from the mouth of the Columbia River (first discovered by the Spaniard Bruno de Hezeta in 1775), extending United States claims by priority of discovery. By the time of the Nootka crisis between Spain and Britain for rights of trade and settlement at Nootka Sound, Vancouver Island, and adjacent coasts in 1790, Russia, Britain, Spain, France,

and the United States had made explorations of the northwest coast (all of them important in themselves, given the geographical obstacles). However, it was not until 1792–1794, when Capt. George VANCOUVER made his surveys of the coast with scrupulous exactness, that Canada's western ocean gate was recorded on the charts with any completeness.

These approaches of the British by sea were frequently related to the probes of their countrymen by land. Cook's voyage attempted to find the western entrance to the Northwest Passage in high latitudes suggested by the discoveries of Peter Pond and Samuel Hearne. Similarly, Vancouver's voyage corresponded to the westward probes of the Nor'westers, particularly Mackenzie.

By the late 1780s the remaining unknown land of Canada was that vast quadrilateral of the Far West and North bounded on the south by the 49th parallel, on the north by the Arctic, on the east by the headwaters of the Saskatchewan, and on the west by the Pacific. Much of this was mountainous or foothills territory, the last-known preserve of fur-bearing animals and a land of great unmapped rivers: the Saskatchewan, the Mackenzie, the Yukon, the Skeena and the Nass, the Fraser and the Thompson, and the Columbia. Most of these rivers were explored by North West Company employees who now were pushing their trade into the Far West.

Among the most spectacular of these penetrations were two by Alexander Mackenzie. This Scot was seeking a commercial route for furs from the Athabasca to the Pacific that would be linked with the growing oceanic trade with China as first developed by the maritime fur traders on the northwest coast. In 1789 he made an exploratory expedition which led him north rather than west. Almost by accident, then, he discovered what he called the River of Disappointment, the great Mackenzie River flowing north to the Arctic and flanking the Rocky Mountains on the east. In 1793 he achieved his original goal. By the Peace, Parsnip, Blackwater (now West Road), and other rivers he reached Pacific tidewater at Dean Channel, British Columbia. His transcontinental journey preceded that of Meriwether LEWIS and William CLARK by more than a decade; it was the first transcontinental journey by a white man north of the Rio Grande. Accounts of Mackenzie's explorations were published in London, Paris, and New York and stimulated interest in Canada and in exploration. Fur traders and cartographers incorporated his newly acquired knowledge in their own realms. Mackenzie was the lineal heir to the sixteenth- and seventeenth-century mariners who had sought the Pacific from the north and east and the followers of Champlain who had paddled west in their canoes. The Northwest Passage had been found, but it was a passage by land rather than by sea.

As significant as Mackenzie's explorations were, they had not determined all. Among the other great explorations was that of David THOMPSON, a professional and scientific surveyor, who not only delineated the features of the Saskatchewan system but traced the headwaters of the Red River of the North, Missouri, and Mississippi systems. In 1807 he crossed the Rockies and determined the headwaters and watershed of the Columbia system. He built posts and opened trade in much of Montana, Idaho, Washington, Oregon, and southern British Columbia, tracing the Columbia to its mouth in 1811. Previously, Simon FRASER, whose work corresponds to Thompson's but in higher latitudes, had crossed the Rockies in 1805, set up posts at Stuart Lake, Fraser Lake, and elsewhere, and, in 1808, followed the great but tortuous river which now bears his name to its mouth on the Strait of Georgia.

During the latter phase of European exploration of Canada the search for the Northwest Passage had been intensified by the British Admiralty. The outline of most of Canada's northern continental shore was provided by the land and sea voyages of John Ross to Lancaster Sound (1818); of John FRANKLIN to the Arctic shore east of the Coppermine River (1819–1822); and of Franklin and Frederick William BEECHEY to delineate the Arctic shore west of the Coppermine to Icy Cape, Alaska (1826). The Hudson's Bay Company's Peter Warren Dease and Thomas Simpson completed the details of the western Arctic in 1837. Meanwhile, in the 1820s two other traders, Samuel Black and Peter Skene Ogden, explored respectively the waterways parallel to and west of the Mackenzie River and the Snake River country in Idaho and Oregon. These explorations were designed to keep Russian and American traders at a distance from Hudson's Bay Company domains, which after 1821 incorporated North West Company fur posts. In the late 1830s and 1840s Robert Campbell pushed Hudson's Bay Company interests into the Yukon and Stikine territories and determined the headwaters of the great Yukon system which flows through Alaska

into Bering Sea. He did so long before Lieut. Frederick Schwatka of the U.S. Navy made his presumptuous claim to priority of discovery in 1883. Farther east Sir John Franklin made a last, fatal attempt to find the Northwest Passage by sea in 1845. The search for Franklin's lost party resulted in the discovery and exploration of many islands north of the continental shore and in much-increased knowledge about the Arctic, its lands, and its peoples (*see* FRANKLIN EXPEDITION AND SEARCH).

Canadian exploration after 1871 At the time the Confederation of Canada was formed in 1867, the main outlines of Canada's topography were known. But much remained to be done: accounts, maps, and charts were still needed; geological appraisals had to be made; and ethnological reports were just beginning to be made with any degree of authority. The final phase of Canada's exploration belongs to Canadians themselves. In 1871 the Dominion Lands Branch, an agency of the federal government, was formed to facilitate land surveys that would permit settlement of the West to develop apace. In more remote areas another federal agency, the Geological Survey, which had been organized in 1842, moved to expand its traverses. Soon its reconaissance parties were seen on distant rivers and islands, especially in British Columbia, the Yukon, and the Northwest Territories. Under the direction of George Mercer Dawson, geologist and ethnologist, the Geological Survey piled up an impressive mound of data, published in its *Reports*. By the end of the century Canada had acquired a full knowledge of its land resources.

In 1880 Britain transferred the sovereignty of its Arctic islands to Canada, and subsequent exploration in that area by Canadians, Americans, Norwegians, and others expanded knowledge of the archipelago. Between 1903 and 1906 Roald AMUNDSEN traversed the Northwest Passage from east to west in the *Gjøa* and determined the precise position of the North Magnetic Pole. The *Karluk* expedition (1913–1918) of Canadian-born Vilhjalmur STEFANSSON under Canadian government auspices extended contemporary knowledge by finding land north of Prince Patrick and Axel Heiberg Islands. During World War II the Royal Canadian Mounted Police vessel *St. Roch*, Henry A. Larsen commanding, completed the passage both ways. But not until the oil tanker *Manhattan*'s voyage in 1969 (aided by the Canadian icebreaker *Sir John A. Macdonald*) did the northern sea-lane offer a commercial route across the top of Canada.

To the end geographical obstacles had hindered Canadian exploration. Few persons accepted Stefansson's claim that the Arctic was "friendly." But the air age and satellites finally conquered distance and terrain and completed the long drama of the exploration of Canada.

Interior of an igloo, photographed by the Canadian Geological Survey, whose reconaissance parties brought back invaluable reports from the interior during the late nineteenth century. [Library of Congress]

BIBLIOGRAPHY: John Bartlett Brebner, *The Explorers of North America, 1492–1806*, London, 1933; L. P. Kirwan, *A History of Polar*

Exploration, New York, 1960; T. J. Oleson, *Early Voyages and Northern Approaches, 1000–1632*, Toronto, 1963; Glyndwr Williams, *The British Search for the Northwest Passage in the Eighteenth Century*, London, 1962.

Barry M. Gough

Cão, Diogo (Cam) (ca. 1450–1486) Portuguese navigator. Although Cão was one of the most important precursors of Bartolomeu DIAS and Vasco da GAMA, little is known of his early life except that he sailed on voyages to Guinea, where he captured three Spanish ships in 1480 and where he may have struck up an acquaintance with Christopher COLUMBUS. In June 1482, Cão captained a continuation of the Henrician voyages of exploration down the African coast. He was the first to carry limestone pillars *(padrões)* surmounted by a cross and bearing inscriptions proclaiming Portuguese suzerainty which were to be erected as signposts of discovery. Passing Cabo Santa Catarina (Pointe Sainte-Catherine in present-day Gabon), the farthest point previously reached, he set up the first pillar on the north bank of the great river known today as the Congo (also called Zaire). After sending an exploring expedition upstream, Cão continued southward until he reached Cabo de Santa Maria (Cape St. Mary), Angola, where a second *padrão* was erected on August 28, 1483. This *padrão* is now in the museum of the Sociedade de Geografia in Lisbon. On his return voyage Cão stopped at the Congo to pick up the members of the exploring expedition. Not finding them, he kidnapped four local potentates to be used as hostages and sailed back to Lisbon, returning on April 8, 1484, when he was knighted by King John II.

Cão left Portugal in 1485 on a second voyage on which two more pillars were erected, the first at Cabo Negro, in present-day Angola, and the second at Cape Cross, in present-day Namibia, at 21°51′ S; the latter *padrão* is now housed in the Museum für Deutsche Geschichte in Berlin. Once again he stopped at the mouth of the Congo and this time collected the missing members of the first voyage's exploring expedition. He also ascended the Congo for a distance of 100 miles (161 kilometers), a feat of great seamanship. The evidence of his achievement is immortalized in one of the most famous and enduring specimens of graffiti, consisting of carved inscriptions and signatures of the Portuguese on the side of a cliff at Yellala Falls.

Cão's expedition returned to Portugal in 1486 supposedly with an African prince called by Portuguese chroniclers Caçuto (but whose real name was probably Nsaku), baptized João da Silva early in 1489. The prince, powerfully impressed by Europe and particularly by Portugal, was returned to the Congo in 1490 or 1491 and proved instrumental in establishing Portuguese hegemony in the region. The Caçuto episode, however, may have occurred during Bartolomeu Dias's return voyage since Cão probably died at a place identified as Serra Parda ("dark range") on the Namibian coast south of Cape Cross in 1486.

BIBLIOGRAPHY: Eric Axelson, *Congo to Cape: Early Portuguese Explorers*, New York, 1973; Damião Peres, *Diogo Cão*, tr. by M. Freire de Andrade, Lisbon, 1957; E. G. Ravenstein, "The Voyages of Diogo Cão and Bartholomeu Dias, 1482–88," *The Geographical Journal*, vol. XVI, no. 6, December 1900, pp. 625–655.

Martin Torodash

Carpini, John of Plano (Giovanni de Piano Carpini; fl. mid-thirteenth century) Italian Franciscan friar and traveler to the Far East. Brother John of the Order of Friars Minor played an important role in the development of the Franciscan Order in Western Europe, having served both in Spain and in Saxony as provincial of the order. In 1245 he was sent by Pope Innocent IV (r. 1243–1254) as an envoy to the Great Khan of the Mongols. Friar John proceeded from the French city of Lyon to Poland, where he was joined by Friar Benedict of the same order, who served as both companion and interpreter on the long journey eastward. They traveled to Kiev and then across the Dnieper and Don Rivers until they reached the camp of Batu, khan of the Golden Horde, on the banks of the Volga. He granted them permission to continue eastward to the court of the Great Khan in Mongolia. Traveling through Central Asia north of the Caspian Sea and the Aral Sea, they finally reached the camp of Kuyuk, near Karakorum in Mongolia, in July 1246. A timely arrival enabled them to be witnesses at the great assembly *(kuraltai)* at which Kuyuk was installed as the Great Khan of all the Mongols. Not until November were the friars dismissed from the Mongol court. On their return journey they carried with them a letter from the Great Khan to the Pope. This long journey they accomplished successfully despite incredible difficulties and hardships.

Friar John wrote a book on these travels after he had returned to the West. His account became one of the most widely known of all the early reports concerning the Mongols, revealing to Christian Europe firsthand information about these nomadic peoples. The French Dominican scholar Vincent of Beauvais incorporated much of this new material in his famous encyclopedia, the *Speculum majus*, an outstanding reference work of the later Middle Ages, but the full text of Friar John's work was not published until 1839.

After Friar John's return to Western Europe, the Pope sent him on a mission to King Louis IX of France. In 1248 the friar was elevated to the rank of archbishop of Antivari (Bar) in Dalmatia. He became involved in a dispute with the Archbishop of Ragusa (Dubrovnik) on questions of ecclesiastical jurisdiction and died while these controversial matters were still under consideration by the Roman Curia.

BIBLIOGRAPHY: Christopher Dawson (ed.), *The Mongol Mission: Narratives and Letters of the Franciscan Missionaries in Mongolia and China in the Thirteenth and Fourteenth Centuries*, tr. by a nun of Stanbrook Abbey, New York, 1955.

Bernerd C. Weber

Carteret, Philip (1733–1796) English naval officer and explorer. Born at Trinity Manor on the island of Jersey, Carteret followed the tradition of his distinguished family by joining the British Navy at an early age. During the Seven Years' War he served in the English Channel and in the Mediterranean, receiving the rank of second lieutenant in August 1758. In 1764 John Byron, under whom he had previously served, invited Carteret to join his round-the-world expedition. During the circumnavigation of 1764–1766 Carteret served as first lieutenant of the *Tamar* and later of the *Dolphin.*

When the 2d Earl of Egmont, first lord of the Admiralty, planned an expedition to search for a southern continent in the Pacific Ocean, Carteret was given command of the sloop *Swallow,* consort of the *Dolphin.* The latter was to be commanded by Samuel WALLIS, the leader of the expedition. Despite his unhappiness over the poor condition of the 20-year-old *Swallow,* Carteret sailed from Plymouth on August 21, 1766, with Wallis and the *Dolphin.* Disagreements between the two men ensued, culminating in the separation of the *Dolphin* and the *Swallow* near the western entrance of the Strait of Magellan in April 1767.

After the separation Carteret was able to embark on an independent course of exploration, though his freedom of movement was limited by the defects of the *Swallow* and his need for antiscorbutics and other supplies. During his voyage across the Pacific he discovered Pitcairn Island and several islands in the Tuamotu Archipelago. He became the first European to rediscover Santa Cruz and the Solomons, though he failed to recognize them as the islands first seen by Álvaro de Mendaña and Pedro Fernández de Quirós in the sixteenth century. In addition, he discovered St. George's Channel separating New Britain from New Ireland and was the first to realize that the latter and New Hanover, both of which he named, were separate islands divided by a strait which he named after Byron.

In mid-December 1767 Carteret anchored near the Dutch port of Makassar in Celebes but received an unfriendly reception from local officials. After stops in Batavia (now Jakarta) and Cape Town, he sailed for England in January 1769. His discoveries overshadowed by those of Wallis and James COOK, Carteret received little recognition for his circumnavigation from the Admiralty. From 1779 to 1782 he commanded the *Endymion* but after that was never again called to active service.

BIBLIOGRAPHY: Helen Wallis (ed.), *Carteret's Voyage round the World, 1766–1769,* 2 vols., Hakluyt Society, 2d ser., nos. 124 and 125, Cambridge, England, 1965.

Cartier, Jacques (1491–1557) French explorer and navigator in North America and the discoverer of the St. Lawrence River. Cartier was a substantial citizen of Saint-Malo, the ancient and famous seaport in Brittany. Although relatively few details are known of his early life, it is a matter of record that in the spring of 1520 he married Catherine des Granches, the daughter of Chevalier Jacques des Granches, constable of the city of Saint-Malo. At the time of his marriage Cartier had attained the rank of master pilot and apparently had already made voyages across the Atlantic to Brazil and to Newfoundland.

In April 1534, while in the service of King Francis I, Jacques Cartier set forth from Saint-Malo with two ships and a small company. Presumably he sought a NORTHWEST PASSAGE to China, for the narrative of his first voyage expressed his disappointment in failing to find a passage to Asia. Cartier arrived at the eastern coast of Newfoundland and made landfall at Cape Bonavista after an Atlantic passage of only 20 days. He then proceeded along the coast in a northerly course until he reached the narrow and ice-cluttered Strait of Belle Isle between the island of Newfoundland and the coast of Labrador. Passing through this strait he eventually reached the Gulf of St. Lawrence. Numerous bays, islets, and islands were explored, but Cartier later described the bleak northern shore of the gulf in very uncomplimentary terms. In June he turned southward and skirted the western side of Newfoundland and the Magdalen Islands (Îles de la Madeleine), a chain of islets. He discovered Prince Edward Island without realizing, however, that it was an island, explored beautiful Chaleur Bay, and then proceeded northward to Gaspé Bay. Natives in great numbers were seen there. Before leaving this area, Cartier raised a great wooden cross at the entrance to the harbor and took possession of the land in the name of the King of France. He continued to Anticosti Island in late July, but contrary winds made further exploration too difficult. By early August the homeward journey had begun.

Francis I, well pleased with the results of the first voyage, ordered a second one to be organized. Three vessels departed from Saint-Malo in May 1535. Included among the passengers were two young Indians who had been brought back from Gaspé during the previous expedition. After a 50-day crossing Cartier reached Funk Island off the coast of Newfoundland. On August 10, 1535, the feast day of St. Lawrence, Cartier anchored in a small bay on the coast of the present province of Quebec. The two Indian boys told Cartier of a mysterious kingdom named Saguenay located in the interior, a kingdom reputed to be rich in gold and precious stones. Searching for this kingdom, Cartier continued up the St. Lawrence River, which he always referred to as "la Grande Rivière." He reached the Indian village of Stadacona, where modern Quebec is located, and was well received by the natives. Leaving some of his men behind to prepare winter quarters, Cartier and the other members of his group continued farther up the river, and on October 2 they reached the palisaded village of Hochelaga, located on the site of the present city of Montreal. Cartier climbed the nearby mountain (Mont Réal, or

Mount Royal), from which he could survey the fertile valley and see ahead the rapids which blocked further progress westward. Cartier and his men therefore returned to the area of the St. Charles River, where a fort had been built and where they all spent the winter. Unfortunately for them the winter of 1535–1536 was a severe one, and the hardships suffered by the French were made even more difficult by an outbreak of scurvy which took a number of lives. A friendly Indian provided some relief for the situation by telling the Frenchmen about a useful remedy, a concoction prepared from the bark of the common arborvitae.

In May Cartier began his homeward journey, carrying with him several Indians, including a local chief named Donnacona. The port of Saint-Malo was finally reached on July 15. Much valuable information concerning the natural and human resources of Canada had been obtained by the French, and furthermore they had found a great waterway which would enable them to penetrate the interior of North America.

Cartier once again set sail for the New World in May 1541, his expedition on this occasion consisting of five ships and a crew of more than 1000 men. In charge of this expedition was a Protestant gentleman named Jean-François de la Rocque de Roberval, who had been designated as the King's lieutenant general.

The Sieur de Roberval planned to follow Cartier at a somewhat later date. On this third voyage Cartier established a settlement at Cap Rouge, situated above Quebec, visited once more the Indian village of Hochelaga, and sought to clear the way past the rapids. The winter was again spent in Canada with the local Indians becoming increasingly unfriendly. In June 1542, Cartier struck camp to return to France. At St. John's port, Newfoundland, he encountered the Sieur de Roberval's ships, which had finally arrived in the New World. Disregarding Roberval's orders to turn back, Cartier continued on his way to France.

The remainder of his life was spent in Saint-Malo or at his country estate of Limoilou. The *Bref récit*, an account of his second voyage, appeared in 1545. He died in Saint-Malo on September 1, 1557. Cartier was the first known European to survey the coasts of the Gulf of St. Lawrence and to explore the St. Lawrence River, which in time became the axis of the French colonial empire in North America.

One of the numerous seekers of the elusive Northwest Passage to China, Jacques Cartier found the St. Lawrence River instead and claimed Canada for France. [Library of Congress]

BIBLIOGRAPHY: Gustave Lanctot, *Jacques Cartier devant l'histoire*, Montreal, 1947; Stephen Leacock, *The Mariner of St. Malo: A Chronicle of the Voyages of Jacques Cartier*, Toronto, 1914; Samuel Eliot Morison, *The European Discovery of America: The Northern Voyages, A.D. 500–1600*, New York, 1971.

Bernerd C. Weber

Cartography

The special importance of cartography to geographical discovery is due to the fact that a place has not really been discovered until it has been recorded with sufficient accuracy so that it can be visited again. Although, of course, there are other means of expressing locational information, such as lists and tables, spatial relationships are best shown on maps. Furthermore, while it is true that specific, individual points on the surface of the earth can be satisfactorily indicated by latitude and longitude notations, appreciation of even simple linear and certainly more complex areal phenomena requires a graphical means of delineation.

Before the development of aerial photography in the middle of the nineteenth century (using at first the balloon as a platform and later heavier-than-air craft), maps and diagrams were the only adequate means of displaying earth features in the orthographic, or plan, view which is essential to an understanding of their true form. Thus the map was and, even in the space age, to a large extent remains the most desirable tool for expressing physical elements such as coastlines, rivers, and mountains or cultural ones, including canals, roads, and settlements. Therefore it is not without good reason that geographical discovery has been regarded as unrolling the world map. Naturally many maps made in the past were crude and even contained quite erroneous information. However, whether more or less accurate, various cartographic products served purposes other than the important one of recording geographical location. Maps were often the basis of speculation on the nature of the earth by philosophers or spurred further discoveries by explorers.

When we speak of geographical discovery, we generally have in mind the European explorations and subsequent settlement initiated by Prince HENRY of Portugal in the early fifteenth century. Much geographical discovery, including that by the Portuguese, depended on maps, often those made by cartographers of other nations, sometimes in earlier times. Obviously the earlier maps were in manuscript form and, especially those by so-called primitive peoples, frequently employed unusual materials. While manuscript maps were of value to discoverers along with the expertise of local navigators, it was only after the invention of printing that the achievements of explorers became well known through published maps. Printed compiled maps became a feature of tracts, essays, and books by or about travelers.

Non-European cartography It was a fortunate circumstance for Europeans that the geographical discoveries of the Renaissance coincided with the invention of printing in Europe, through which these explorations were publicized in both written and graphic form. By contrast, the epic journeys in the Pacific of those "Vikings of the Sunrise," the Polynesians, have no comparable documentation. We must rely in such cases largely on ethnographic, linguistic, and archaeological evidence rather than upon the written or graphic record. Accordingly, while it is certainly desirable to give greater emphasis to non-European geographical exploration than has been usual in the past, the lack of an adequate cartographic record makes this impossible in this article on the relationship of the map to discovery. We know that the Marshall Islanders created ingenious stick charts before the European contact, but these are less records of exploration than practical navigational aids. Similarly the Eskimos made maps of localities familiar to them on pieces of carved wood pasted on sealskin, but again these are of limited value in recording specific contributions to discovery since they are a composite of much geographical lore.

In addition to maps made by peoples of less advanced civilization, we also have early examples of the cartography of Babylon, Egypt, and China. In fact, the earliest printed maps from China anticipate those of Europeans by at least three centuries. However, the Sinocentric attitude of the Chinese makes these maps of only marginal concern in the history of discoveries, even though they are of great interest in the general study of cartography. Although the maps of the Arabs at first reflect the cartography of the Greeks and later of Western Europeans, they also incorporate data from the extensive journeys of certain Islamic travelers.

The European cartographers benefited from this body of information and especially from the astronomical and mathematical attainments of the Arabs. But, as indicated before, this article focuses upon the European contributions to discovery and map making while not, it is hoped, minimizing the contributions to these fields of the peoples who were "discovered."

Ancient and medieval contributions A good point to begin this discussion of the relationship of the map and geographical discovery would seem to be the contributions of PTOLEMY, a Greek mathematician and astronomer who flourished in Alexandria in the second century A.D. Ptolemy's cartographical work, which was embodied in a book now known as the *Geography*, depended both on his own researches and, whether acknowledged or not, on those of his predecessors. These include Eratosthenes, who provided an accurate measure of the circumference of the earth; Crates of Mellos (Mallus), who formalized a global concept; Hipparchus, who developed an earth grid; Marinus of Tyre, who compiled a simple world plane chart; and Posidonius, who "corrected" the figure of the earth's circumference, determined some four centuries earlier by Eratosthenes. Unfortunately Ptolemy accepted the smaller measure of the circumference of the earth of Posidonius rather than the larger and more accurate figure of Eratosthenes. Nevertheless, the contributions to cartography of Ptolemy were of fundamental significance and remained

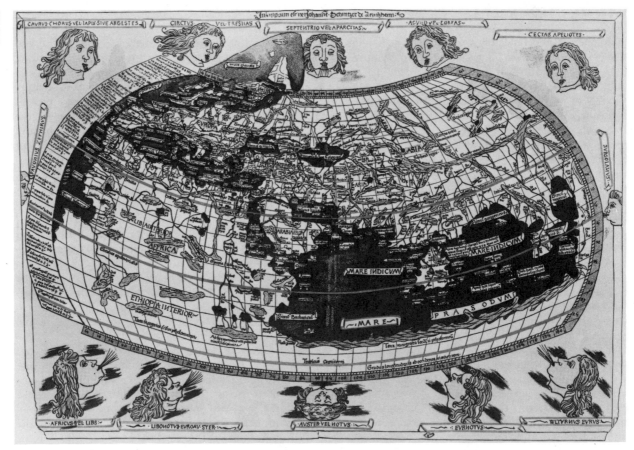

Ptolemaic map of the world published at Ulm in 1482. [Library of Congress]

essentially unchallenged for fourteen centuries following his time. These contributions include instructions for making map projections and a list of some 8000 coordinates of places on the earth. After the destruction of the Library of Alexandria, Ptolemy's *Geography* most fortunately was preserved by the Arabs, who at first accepted and soon improved upon it. Centuries later, when the Turks expanded westward, Greek texts of the Ptolemaic corpus were taken for safety to Florence, where in the early fifteenth century they were translated into Latin. From these instructions, maps of the world known to Ptolemy were constructed and became the model against which the progress of Renaissance exploration could be measured.

The world of Ptolemy was a largely terrestrial rather than water-covered earth consisting of the three continents of Europe, Asia, and Libya (North Africa). This last continent extended eastward to Asia, enclosing the Indian Ocean. The whole of the Mediterranean and Black Seas was well depicted, but only the extreme northeastern fringes of the Atlantic (the Sea of Darkness) were shown. It must not be imagined that there were no European contributions to cartography between those of the later Greeks of antiquity and the Renaissance rediscovery of Ptolemy. However, much of the work of the Europeans in the Middle Ages was religious and symbolic in nature and added little to the knowledge of the earth or, indeed, to cartographic methodology. However, a considerable advance in the latter category came in the fourteenth century with the development of portolan charts, which are extremely accurate and beautiful haven-finding aids for the Mediterranean and Black Seas particularly. They are thought to be based on records of traverses made possible by the then recently invented magnetic compass. The compass was developed in the Italian coastal cities of Amalfi, Pisa, and Genoa and spread thence to the Balearic Islands. Although at first restricted in its geographical delineations, the portolan chart, especially as the Europeans ventured into the Atlantic, was later extended to cover the coasts of Africa and also northern Europe.

Fifteenth and sixteenth centuries

At the same time that this mapping advance was in progress Prince Henry established his navigational "school" at Sagres near Cabo de São Vicente, Portugal, the southwesterly point of Europe. Cartographers, including portolan chart makers, were employed by the prince in his efforts to find ways of outflanking the Moors. Prince Henry's older brother, Pedro, brought back to Portugal from Italy a *mappa mundi* (mappemonde; believed to be by Pietro Vesconte, accompanying Marino Sanudo's *Liber secretorum* . . .) and a copy of *The Book of Messer Marco Polo.* The thirteenth-century journeys by Marco POLO and his father and uncle in eastern Asia had given Western Europeans a glimpse of a world beyond Islam, but much of this information was discredited and, in fact, added little solid map data. However, using information from several sources including maps, ships sent out by Prince Henry rediscovered Madeira (1419) and the Azores (1427–1432).

While these Atlantic islands were being explored, expeditions under Prince Henry's sponsorship were penetrating farther and farther southward along the coast of Africa. By the time of his death in 1460, Gambia (latitude 13°N) had been reached and Islam at last outflanked. Gradually information on these discoveries was added to the cartographic record, but the great contribution of Prince Henry was his initiation of a continuous tradition of European maritime discovery. Other Atlantic states—Spain, France, England, and the Netherlands—joined in this activity, so that in the following 400 years most of the coasts of the world were discovered and mapped by explorers of various European nations. Our purpose now is to present cartographic highlights of this remarkable development by which Europe, from being a rather poor peninsula of Eurasia in the later Middle Ages, became the center of world trade in the seventeenth, eighteenth, and nineteenth centuries.

Although the Iberians were the first Europeans to sponsor geographical discoveries in the Renaissance, they were assisted in their explorations and mapping by workers of several nations. Thus, an early portolan-style map of the Henrician discoveries along the coast of Africa from the Canary Islands to Cape Verde was drawn by the Venetian Andrea Bianco in 1448. A much-better-known summary map which shows the southern terminus of Africa, arising from the discovery of the Cape of Good Hope by Bartolomeu DIAS, is that of Henricus Martellus Germanus (ca. 1490). Obviously such a work pointed up the inadequacy of the Ptolemaic map.

Between the return of Dias to Portugal in 1488 and the completion of the discovery of the sea route from Europe around southern Africa by Vasco da GAMA, who reached India in May 1498, great events were in progress toward the west which were to alter radically the world map. The knowledge of land and water relations immediately before the discovery of the Americas is well shown on the globe *(Erdapfel)* made by Martin Behaim of Nürnberg in the early 1490s. Behaim's globe indicates the earlier discoveries of the Polos and, like the Martellus map, the terminus of southern Africa, suggesting a sea route to "the gorgeous East." The globe also owed much to Ptolemy, including a truncated India and an earth circumference which was too short by one-sixth of the total, and, of course, included no new continents.

Discoverers who preceded Christopher COLUMBUS had learned the value of maps, used them, and employed cartographers. However, Columbus was himself a chart maker and on his voyage to Hispaniola (1492–1493) made a sketch map of the northern part of that island. The objective of Columbus was to reach the coast of eastern Asia, which he believed he had found by sailing westward. His subsequent voy-

Columbus's sketch of the northern coast of Hispaniola, which he thought was part of Asia. [Library of Congress]

ages up to the year 1504 only confirmed this view in his mind, and it was left to the Florentine Amerigo VESPUCCI to propose that a new world *(mundus novus)* had been found. Vespucci embarked on an Iberian ship in 1501 headed for Brazil, which had been discovered the previous year by the Portuguese Pedro Álvares CABRAL on his way to India. On his return from South America, Vespucci claimed to have found a new continent, and this information was embodied in a woodcut map of the world made by Martin Waldseemüller in the Rhineland in 1507. On this most important map Waldseemüller drew the new continent, with discoveries up to that time including those of John CABOT in the north (1497–1498), as a separate entity and engraved the word *America* on the larger, southern part. This new continent was of limited longitudinal extent, being forced into a Ptolemaic framework. It was only

The Waldseemüller map of the world (1507) was one of the first printed maps. [Library of Congress]

after the navigation by Ferdinand MAGELLAN of the strait which now bears his name on the first circumnavigation of the earth (1519–1522) that there could be any real appreciation of the width of the Americas and of the Pacific Ocean. As this largest of oceans was traversed in the next three centuries, its delineation was gradually improved, but not always without retrogression, as in the case of California, which was represented at first as attached to the mainland but later as an island.

The momentous geographical discoveries of the Renaissance were matched by other events which had a great effect on the course of cartography. We have referred to the invention of printing in Europe and indicated that it was soon employed for maps. The first European printed map (1472) was a simple woodcut of a medieval symbolic diagram, but it was not long after this that Ptolemaic printed maps accompanied the recently translated and published *Geography.* The Waldseemüller map of 1507 is another example of an influential printed map.

However, there were other developments besides printing which led to considerable progress in the art and science of map making. Perhaps the most important of these was the application of a new scientific method to cartographic problems. Renaissance mathematicians experimented with various map projections to accommodate the new geographical data, and

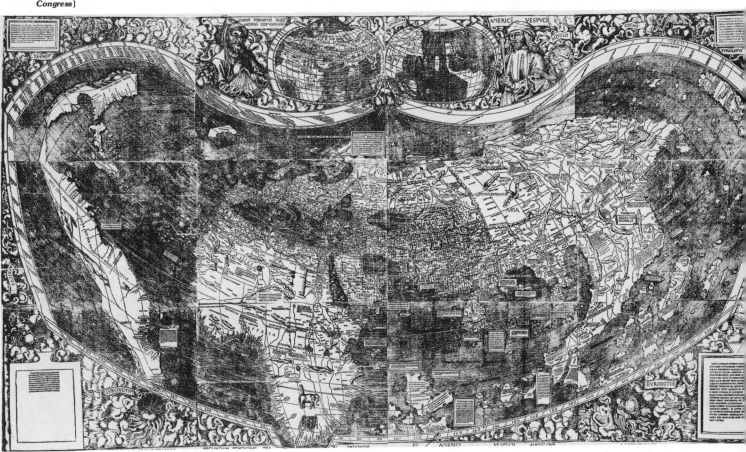

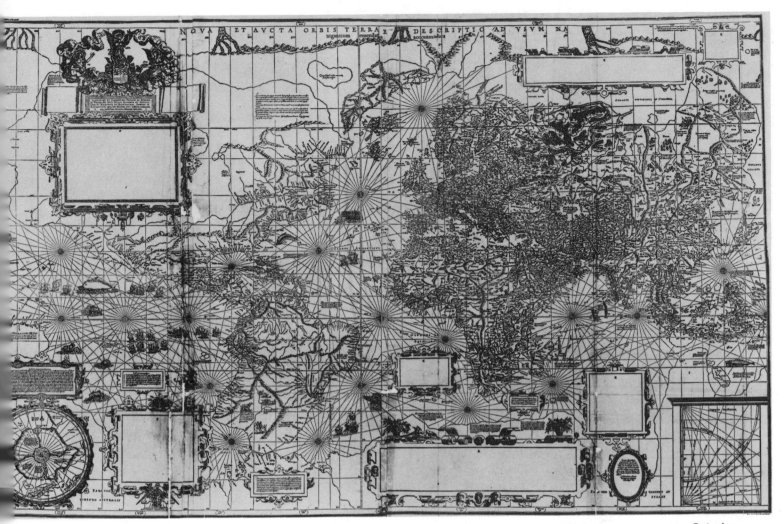

one solution was the cordiform, or heart-shaped, rendering of the earth grid. The Waldseemüller map may be thought of as a special truncated case of this type of projection, which was formalized by Johannes Werner. Several variations of heart-shaped projections were developed, including a double cordiform by Gerhardus Mercator in 1538. Mercator's greatest contribution to cartography was the famous projection of 1569 which has since borne his name. This is a conformal projection; that is, the correct shape of features is maintained around a point. But it has another quality which was of transcendent value to the navigator, namely, that all straight lines on the projection are lines of constant compass direction (loxodromes, or rhumb lines). Although many sailors were slow to adopt this new device, the projection was used by some of the most influential explorers, and the idea was embraced by scientists and publicists. Thus, the Cambridge mathematician Edward Wright provided an analysis of the properties of the Mercator projection in 1599. It was also used for a world map of the same date by Wright (formerly called the Wright Molyneaux map) that was bound with *The Principall Navigations, Voiages and Discoveries of the English Nation* of Richard HAKLUYT, which indicates the results of the travels of Sir Francis DRAKE, the second circumnavigator.

With the development of improved instruments and better ships the cartographic representation of the world's coastlines began to take on an appearance which more closely resembles the modern map. Between the publication of the Waldseemüller map and that of Wright, a period spanning almost the whole of the sixteenth century, the shape of Africa and of Asia was notably improved. An especially striking difference was the delineation of all of South America and much of North America except the Pacific Northwest and the Arctic coast. The work of many explorers besides those mentioned earlier had made this possible: Giovanni da VERRAZZANO, who explored the east coast of North America on behalf of the King of France (1524); Jacques CARTIER, in the St. Lawrence (1534–1542); Juan Rodríguez CABRILLO, on the Pacific Coast from Mexico to central California (1542–1543); and Sir Walter Raleigh, from Cape Hatteras to the Guianas (1584–1595), among many others. Nor were land journeys neglected, as in the cases of Hernán CORTÉS in Mexico (1519–1520), Francisco PIZARRO in

Measuring device, 1581. [Library of Congress]

Peru (1531–1533), and other conquistadores, but these were not usually as productive in a cartographic context as coastal voyaging was. In fact, accurate mapping of the continental interiors had to await the development of more refined methods of surveying in the eighteenth century, a result of the scientific revolution of the preceding century.

Seventeenth and eighteenth centuries Although much refinement in the delineation of these coasts would be undertaken in the seventeenth century, the broad outlines of Europe, Africa, South America, and large parts of Asia and North America appeared in such a world map as that of Wright (1599). *Terrae incognitae* included much of the Arctic coasts of Asia and North America and the northeast and northwest portions of these continents respectively. There was a hint of the existence of Terra Australis on the maps of the period, but explorations of the Spanish along the coast of this area were not part of the general cartographic record. Antarctica and many islands, particularly in the Pacific, awaited discovery. As the Portuguese and Spanish had been most prominent in exploration in the fifteenth and sixteenth centuries, so the Dutch and English became leaders in these activities in the seventeenth and eighteenth centuries. Not only did these powers dominate, in turn, in the discovery of new lands, but they also dominated in the charting of many areas. The Dutch ascendancy dates from the time when the United Provinces threw off the yoke of Spain at the beginning of the seventeenth century.

The focus of Dutch interest overseas was the East Indies and, by extension, an area from Japan to New Zealand. Following Mercator and his friend and rival Ortelius (Abraham Oertel), who compiled the first true atlas (first published in 1570), the Low Countries had no peer in the map and chart trade. Much of the cartographic work emanating from this area at the

time has never been surpassed from an artistic point of view, and as new discoveries were charted, they were added to compiled maps. These included various landfalls by the Dutch on the north, west, and southwest coasts of Australia (New Holland), which culminated in the discovery of New Zealand by Abel TASMAN in 1642. Detailed charts of all of these areas were made by the Dutch, who by the 1660s had mapped eastern New Guinea and much of Australia (except for the important southeast and east coasts) and the west coast of New Zealand. Cartographers of the Dutch East India Company Hydrographic Office— Petrus Plancius, Hessel Gerritsz, and Willem Janszoon Blaeu and his son Cornelius—successively supervised the work of adding this information to general charts.

In the person of William Dampier (1652–1715) particularly, the English presence was felt in the area of Dutch overseas control in the latter part of this period. Dampier's most important discovery was of the strait between New Guinea and New Britain which soon appeared on maps as Dampier's Passage (now Dampier Strait). It was shown thus on the world isogonic chart of Edmond Halley, which followed his Atlantic chart on the same subject. These charts, the first published isoline maps, resulted from Halley's great journey in the Atlantic from 1698 to 1701. This voyage, which has been described as the first sea journey undertaken for a purely scientific purpose, and those of Dampier were the forerunners of a series of English expeditions in the eighteenth century which unraveled many of the remaining secrets of the world map. John Byron, Samuel WALLIS, Philip CARTERET, and others were involved in these ventures, but they were all overshadowed by James COOK, who began his surveying career by mapping the approaches to the St. Lawrence in the mid-1700s. In 1768 Cook was chosen as the leader of an expedition to Tahiti to observe the transit of Venus, which had been predicted by Halley 90 years before. Cook's secret instructions called for him to proceed southward to attempt to find Terra Australis after the astronomical observations had been completed. This he did, exploring and charting all the New Zealand coast and the important east coast of Australia, which he called New South Wales. Soon after his return to England in 1771, Cook embarked on a second voyage (1772–1775) to test the hypothesis advanced by Alexander Dalrymple, hydrographer of the East India Company (and many others before him since antiquity), that there was a great southern continent comparable to Eurasia. By circumnavigating the globe in the mid-latitudes of the Southern Hemisphere, Cook demolished the concept of symmetrical continents in both hemispheres and postulated the existence of Antarctica. On his third and final voyage (1776–1779), Cook attempted to find a NORTHWEST PASSAGE (from the Pacific) and, in doing so, discovered the Sandwich Islands (Hawaii) and charted large areas of the Pacific Northwest of North America. Cook was killed on his return to Hawaii, but his work in charting the Pacific Coast of North America was continued later by George VANCOUVER, who had served under Cook. By the work of Cook and Vancouver, the relationship of discovery and exploration on the one hand and surveying and mapping on the other is exemplified in the best manner possible. These explorers employed entirely scientific methods, including the use of the newly perfected marine chronometer, which solved the age-old problem of determining longitude at sea.

Polar areas With this reconnaissance mapping accomplished, it required only the charting of the polar areas to complete the delineation of the world's coasts, at least at this level. Although many earlier attempts had been made to find a NORTHEAST PASSAGE around Asia and a Northwest Passage around North America, these areas were conquered and adequately charted only in the nineteenth century. Almost from the time that the Portuguese and Spanish had reached the Indies and tried to prevent others from using sea-lanes which they considered their own, northern Europeans had attempted to reach the Orient by the Northeast or Northwest Passages. This attempt gave rise to many expeditions, some of which were productive cartographically and others unsuccessful in every particular. Among those who sailed the Northeast Passage in the sixteenth, seventeenth, and eighteenth centuries were the Englishmen Hugh Willoughby, Richard CHANCELLOR, and Stephen and William Borough (who was a skilled chart maker); Willem BARENTS, a Dutchman; Semyon DEZHNEV, a cossack; and Vitus BERING, a Dane in the employ of Empress Anna of Russia. A passage was finally forced through in 1878-1879 by the Swede Nils Adolf Erik NORDENSKIÖLD, who was interested in both contemporary and historical cartography. A number of these men left their names on the world map, as did those who attempted the equally difficult Northwest Passage, through lack of an easier water route through North America in the mid-latitudes. Those whose names are associated with a Northwest Passage include John DAVIS, who like other early polar explorers navigated by globe and helped construct these devices (1585–1587); Henry HUDSON, whose discoveries (1607–1608) were shown on a chart (1612) by Hessel Gerritsz; and Luke Fox and Thomas James, who mapped Hudson Bay (1631) and assumed that the magnetic and astronomical poles were not at the same point. Apart from Cook's attempt to discover the Northwest Passage from the Pacific, there was less interest in this problem in the eighteenth century. However, the search was renewed with vigor when John FRANKLIN sailed in 1845. The loss of Franklin in 1847 and attempts to find him led to a flurry of Arctic exploration and charting (*see* FRANKLIN EXPEDITION AND SEARCH). Less than a decade later the Northwest Passage was conquered by Robert MCCLURE by a combination of ship and sled travel.

It remained now to chart the coasts of Antarctica, which Cook on his second voyage had inferred was an ice-covered continent. Like much exploration, this developed into a thoroughly international endeavor, with the Russian commander Fabian von BELLINGSHAUSEN, in 1820, being the first to sight land beyond the Antarctic Circle. Whaling and sealing captains such as James Weddell, in 1822, added information, including running surveys, until the governments of France, Great Britain, and the United States sent out scientific expeditions. Among the most successful of these were those led by James Clark Ross in 1839–1843, Charles Wilkes in 1838–1842 (*see* WILKES EXPEDITION), and Jules DUMONT D'URVILLE in 1837–1840. Although particular segments of the coasts were mapped by these exploring parties, large areas of Antarctica, including the interior, were less well known until the twentieth century than one face of the moon.

Scientific development From the earliest coastal surveys to those of the nineteenth century, the instruments used improved considerably. However, there has perhaps been greater development in instruments in the past century than in all previous time. But in treating the relationship of cartography to exploration, especially in the early modern period, we shall not be particularly concerned with these latest technological developments. From quite remote times latitude could be determined with considerable accuracy, even on the unstable deck of a ship, by a succession of instruments: the astrolabe and its later refinements, the quadrant, octant, and sextant. It was quite otherwise with longitude determination at sea, a problem which was not solved until the second half of the eighteenth century by the invention of the marine chronometer. Obviously mapping became more accurate as more and more captains used these instruments in the nineteenth century. The sponsorship of the charting of coasts by trading companies and by governments has also been noted. Thus the Casa de Contratación de las Indias in Seville had responsibility for the training of pilots and mapping for sixteenth-century Spain. Among its duties were the updating of world discoveries on a master map, the *Padrón General*. The Casa da Guiné (later Casa da India), founded in Portugal in the fifteenth century, performed similar functions in that country. These traditions were continued by the hydrographic offices of the English and Dutch East India Companies. In modern times the French were the first to establish an official government hydrographic office, in 1720, with the British following in 1795. It is therefore ironic that France was to be denied primacy in discovery in so many areas, especially in the Pacific, but its contributions to marine surveying were considerable. Detailed charting of the coasts of the world, incorporating explorations which had gone on for several hundred years, was accomplished in large measure in the nineteenth century by the hydrographic offices of France, Britain, and the United States. The signal contributions to the scientific exploration and charting of the seas by Matthew Fontaine Maury of the

U.S. Navy in the mid-nineteenth century deserve special mention.

Land mapping So far we have concentrated our attention on the discovery and charting of coastlines, which is certainly a very large part of the story of exploration. However, land journeys which were productive of mapping should not be neglected, even though they are not treated in as much detail. It was the largely overland travels of the Polos that, as we have seen, sparked the interest of Europeans in geographical discovery in the Renaissance. We have also mentioned the land journeys of Cortés and Pizarro and should recall that it was as a result of a short land journey that Vasco Núñez de BALBOA first saw the Pacific in 1513. However, all these men were also concerned with ships, as was John SMITH, who explored Chesapeake Bay in 1608 and noted on his map, by crosses, land areas he had not visited but about which he had gained information "by relation." This is an early example of "reliability" and points up the fact that much information, especially away from coasts, rivers, and the like, was gained, at best, secondhand. The lack of land exploration on the part of the English colonists on the Atlantic seaboard illustrates a reluctance to penetrate far inland. It was only after nearly a century and a half of settlement that the English, intrepid enough on the seas, effectively crossed the Appalachians and two centuries before the continent was traversed from sea to sea by Meriwether LEWIS and William CLARK. The maps arising from such endeavors were, at best, of reconnaissance quality, as were those of the Russians arising from similar journeys into Siberia. The continents of Africa, South America, and Australia likewise resisted exploration and mapping until the nineteenth century, when such travelers as Alexander von Humboldt, David LIVINGSTONE, and Friedrich Wilhelm Ludwig LEICHHARDT made epic journeys into the interiors.

It does nothing to deprecate the work of these and scores of other scientific travelers to say that such areas are not thoroughly explored until they are mapped topographically. The French had shown how this might be accomplished in their own country, but it took almost the whole of the eighteenth century to complete the survey. Naturally such detailed mapping methods could not be applied at once to whole continents. Nevertheless, the British produced topographic maps for India which rivaled or even surpassed those of a number of European countries in the nineteenth century. Large areas of the world still lack topographic maps suitable for engineering purposes and are in this sense unexplored, if not undiscovered. Along the same line it has been said, with truth, that the greater part of the world has been discovered in the past 25 years. This statement refers to the fact that the morphology of the ocean beds has only recently been appreciated and charted through sonic soundings. Since the 1950s the space programs of the United States and the U.S.S.R. have yielded information about the face of the earth which is not at all evident to travelers on the surface of the planet. Remote sensing of the environment is exploration of a kind which continues, elaborates, and enhances in our own age the charting which has gone on since time immemorial among peoples both primitive and civilized.

BIBLIOGRAPHY: Leo Bagrow, *History of Cartography*, rev. and enl. by R. A. Skelton, Cambridge, Mass., 1974; id., "The Origin of Ptolemy's 'Geographia,'" *Geografiska Annaler*, vol. XXVII, 1945, pp. 318–387; Lloyd A. Brown, *The Story of Maps*, Boston, 1949; Fredi Chiappelli (ed.), *First Images of America: The Impact of the New World on the Old*, Berkeley and Los Angeles, 1976; Armando Cortesão and Avelino Teixeira da Mota, *Portugaliae monumenta cartographica*, Lisbon, 1960; Gerald R. Crone, *Maps and Their Makers: An Introduction to the History of Cartography*, London, 1966; Sir George H. Fordman, *Some Notable Surveyors and Map-Makers of the Sixteenth, Seventeenth and Eighteenth Centuries and Their Work*, Cambridge, England, 1929; Herman Friis (ed.), *The Pacific Basin*, New York, 1967; Derek Howse and Michael Sanderson, *The Sea Chart*, Newton Abbot, England, 1973; H. Arnold Karo, *World Mapping 1954–55*, Washington, 1955; George Kish, "The Cosmographic Heart: Cordiform Maps of the 16th Century," *Imago Mundi*, vol. XIX, pp. 13–21; Clara E. Le Gear, "Map Making by Primitive Peoples," *Special Libraries Association Bulletin*, vol. XXXV, March 1944, pp. 79–83; Charles L. Lewis, *Matthew Fontaine Maury: The Pathfinder of the Seas*, Annapolis, Md., 1927; Sir Henry Lyons, "Sailing Charts of the Marshall Islanders," *Geographical Journal*, vol. LXXII, no. 4, October 1928, pp. 325–328; Joseph Needham and Wang Ling, *Science and Civilisation in China*, vol. 3, Cambridge, England, 1959; John Parker (ed.), *Merchants and Scholars*, Minneapolis, 1965; David B. Quinn (ed.), *The Hakluyt Handbook*, vol. 1, London, 1974; Carl Schoy, "The Geography of the Moslems of the Middle Ages," *Geographical Review*, vol. XIV, 1924, pp. 257–269; Raleigh A. Skelton, "Captain Cook as a Hydrographer," *The Mariner's Mirror*, vol. XXXX, no. 2, 1954, pp. 109–113; id., *Explorers' Maps: Chapters in the Record of Geographical Discovery*, London, 1958; Eva G. R. Taylor, *The Haven-finding Art*, London, 1956; Norman J. W. Thrower, "The Discovery of the Longitude," *Navigation*, vol. V, no. 8, 1957–1958, pp. 174–181; id., "Edmond Halley as a Thematic Geo-cartographer," *Annals of the Association of American Geographers*, vol. LIX, no. 4, 1969, pp. 652–676; id., *Maps and Man: An Examination of Cartography in Relation to Culture and Civilization*, Englewood Cliffs, N.J., 1972.

Norman J. W. Thrower

Central America *See* WEST INDIES, CENTRAL AMERICA, AND MEXICO.

Central Asia

The principal objective of exploration in Asia during the nineteenth century and the first half of the twentieth century was Central Asia. There were other parts of the continent that attracted the attention of explorers: the desert of Arabia, the complex world where China and India meet, the little-known wilderness of northeastern Siberia. But the heart of Asia—that huge area lying north of the Himalayas, south of Siberia, west of the eighteen provinces comprising China proper, and east of the Aral-Caspian depression—saw literally scores of travelers, geographers, geologists, surveyors, and archaeologists, military men and civilians, trudging across its mountains and plateaus, crossing high passes, and struggling with obstacles posed by nature and by humans, to describe and map this, the interior of the largest continent.

For purposes of definition, the plateaus and high peaks of what is called the Pamir knot, locally known as the "Roof of the World," may be conveniently selected as the center of this area. To the north and northwest of the Pamir lie those territories called Russian Turkestan before World War I and for a short while thereafter; they are now known as Soviet Central Asia. To the east of the Pamir lies the area known, again prior to the 1930s, as Chinese Turkestan, the Chinese administrative unit called Sinkiang. Southeast of the Pamir is Tibet, while farther east lies Mongolia, its northern part now an independent state, its southern portion part of China. The term "Turkestan," a term created by Europeans, refers to land inhabited mainly by people speaking languages of the Turki group, now represented in Soviet and Chinese territory. Mongolians inhabit the easternmost and northeasternmost portions of Central Asia, Tibetans its southern parts.

Early exploration Prior to the nineteenth century the exploration of Central Asia proceeded slowly and by several stages. Several missionaries, members of the Society of Jesus, left behind detailed reports on their travels: Bento de Goes (1562–1607), Antonio de Andrade (1580–1634), João Cabral (b. 1599), Francisco de Azevedo (1578–1660), Johann Grueber (1623–1680), and Albert d'Orville (1621–1662), in the seventeenth century; and Ippolito DESIDERI and Manuel Freyre (b. 1679), in the eighteenth century. Grueber and Desideri reached Lhasa and spent some time in Tibet. Several Englishmen penetrated Tibet from the south, from India; their knowledge, however, was limited to the area between the Himalayan borders of India and Lhasa.

Russian-British rivalry Although the attention of Great Britain and Russia, the two great colonizing powers in Asia, was attracted by the relatively unknown expanse of what is now Chinese territory, available information was confined almost entirely to description of the people, customs, and settlements of the area. Until scientific reconnaissance and mapping began in earnest in the late 1860s and 1870s, the best available maps of Central Asia contained little exact information.

Virtually all the territory referred to in these pages by the term "Central Asia" was either under Chinese sovereignty or loosely connected with China prior to 1800. But the westernmost parts of Central Asia, at that time and well into the nineteenth century, were ruled by a number of local princes who even then owed the survival of their sovereignties to their position midway between the expanding European powers, Russia and Great Britain. The history of Central Asia during the nineteenth century was, in fact, the

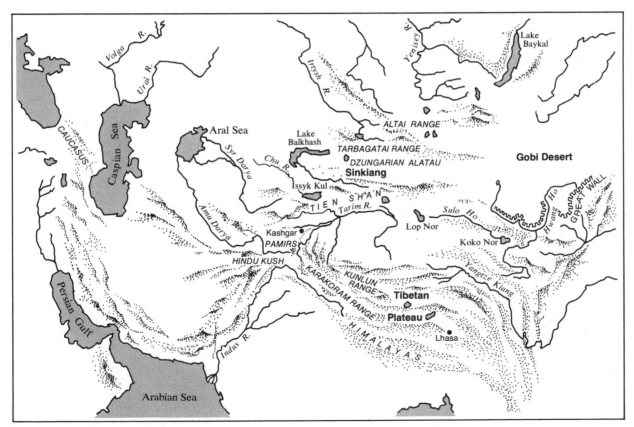

Central Asia.

history of conflict between Russia, gradually expanding its territories into Central Asia from the north, pushing southward and southeastward, and Britain, vitally interested in extending its influence, if not its direct rule, from its base in India northward across the Himalayas.

The motives of exploration in Central Asia were, as a result of this great-power rivalry of overriding importance, mixed, to say the least. Russia and Britain were both directly interested in acquiring as much information as possible about what might well be called the Central Asian marchland, looking forward to possible conquest and direct rule. There was, to be sure, a strong geographical interest in unraveling the complex physical structure, orography, and hydrography of the area. As accurate trigonometrical surveys, based on Russian-controlled and British-controlled land, were gradually expanding, there was a desire to connect these surveys, for purely scientific reasons, to achieve greater geodetic accuracy. There was, and continues to be, great interest in further knowledge of the Turki, Tibetan, and Mongolian cultural complexes. Archaeologists and historians desired to acquire greater knowledge in this Asian heartland, where commerce once passed between the civilizations of Europe and Eastern Asia. It is small wonder that, with so many interests at stake, an attempt to draw a map showing the routes of even the more important explorers is likely to produce an almost illegible set of overlapping tracks, as individuals and organized expeditions set out, with greater and greater frequency, to open up Central Asia.

Just as the overriding fact about the exploration of Central Asia after 1800 was the Russian-British rivalry, so it was that the largest number of explorers working in this area came from those two nations. But there were others as well: Frenchmen, Germans, Swedes, Italians, and Hungarians. The reports of their exploits did, in fact, dominate the geographical literature of the nineteenth century, forcing even the opening up of the least-known continent of the time, Africa, into second place.

Nineteenth-century explorers The exploration of Central Asia was based, as could be expected from the foregoing considerations, in Russia, India, and China. The first forays, as they might well be called, represented thrusts into a little-known world, undertaken for a variety of reasons that were typical of the time.

From the south, from India, came Thomas Manning, a servant of the East India Company, who actually reached the forbidden city of Lhasa, capital of Tibet, in 1811, the first European to do so since Desideri's sojourn there early in the eighteenth century. Also from India, supported reluctantly by the East India Company, came the Hungarian linguist Sándor Csoma de Körös, steeped in the mistaken belief that there remained, somewhere north of the Himalayas, lost groups of Hungarians, left behind in the Hungarian trek to Europe. Csoma did not find any Hungarians, but before he died in Darjeeling in 1842, he spent

many years in Tibetan lamaseries, wrote the first Tibetan grammar, and compiled the first Anglo-Tibetan dictionary. From China came two Vincentian missionaries, Fathers Évariste-Régis Huc and Joseph Gabet, who traversed Mongolia and reached Lhasa in 1846.

Less romantic in his purpose, but possibly more so in his appearance (he disguised himself as a Turkish dervish) was Armin Vámbéry, another Hungarian linguist. Eager to expand his already imposing command of Turki tongues, he journeyed in the early 1860s to what were then the forbidden cities of Central Asia, Bukhara and Samarkand, and returned with a wealth of observations on those areas, soon to be conquered by the Russian empire.

Other travelers were stricter in setting their goals. In 1812 William Moorcroft and Hyder Jung Hearsey traveled into the as yet little-known mountainous regions on the Indian-Afghan border in connection with the beginnings of the great Survey of India, undertaken by British engineers. John Wood traveled, between 1835 and 1838, first to Afghanistan, then north into the Pamir highlands, for the same purpose. From the east, from China, came the first explorer of the borders of Central Asia who was interested in geography only, Baron Ferdinand von Richthofen; he crisscrossed the interior of China between 1860 and 1872 and wrote the first modern geography of the Middle Kingdom.

The first concerted attempt to explore and eventually to conquer parts of Central Asia came from Russia. After initial journeys east of the Caspian that took them as far as the Aral Sea, the Russians, having secured a base of military operations on the west shore of the Caspian, in the Caucasus, and being already in control of southern Siberia, mounted a carefully planned campaign that, by 1881, secured for them complete control of Central Asia as far south as the borders of Persia and Afghanistan, as far east as the Pamir and the ranges extending northeastward from the Pamir, principally the Alai (Alay) and the Altai (Altay).

But even while the military conquest of what became known as Russian Turkestan was going on apace, Russian geographers, both civilians and military men, were far ahead of the armed forces, exploring what were to become Russia's borders with China. Pyotr Petrovich Semyonov-Tianshansky, trained as a geographer first in Russia and later in Berlin, where he was a student of Karl Ritter and became acquainted with Alexander von Humboldt (who himself had traveled along the northern fringes of Central Asia in the 1820s), spent several field seasons in the Tien Shan and, in 1857, climbed one of the high peaks, Khan Tengri. In the 1860s his work was continued by other Russians: N. A. Severtsov, T. von der Osten-Sacken, Aleksandr Vasilyevich von Kaulbars.

In 1871 Aleksey Pavlovich Fedchenko (1844–1873) established the height of what he believed to be the highest peak of the Pamir and named it Mount Kaufmann (now Pik Lenina), in honor of Konstantin Petrovich Kaufmann, commander of Russian forces in the Central Asian campaign of conquest. Fedchenko's name, in turn, is commemorated there; it was given to one of the largest glaciers in the Pamirs. But the outstanding figure among the Russian explorers of Central Asia was Nikolay Mikhailovich PRZHEVALSKY, who in four expeditions between 1871 and 1884 did more than any of his countrymen to contribute to our knowledge of the area.

Przhevalsky Przhevalsky was a career officer in the Russian Army. His interest in geography and ethnography became evident when he was first posted in Siberia. His writings on these subjects attracted the attention of his superiors, and in 1870 he was given leave to carry out explorations in the interior of China. Accompanied only by three men, he entered China from Siberia, traveled through western Kansu as far as the great Tsaidam depression, and returned to Siberia via Mongolia. In 1876 he worked in Sinkiang, exploring and describing the Tien Shan and the Tarim Basin and locating accurately the little-known lake Lop Nor. Lop Nor, a shallow lake east of the Tarim Basin, was of particular interest to geographers because of its unexplained changes in location: available Chinese records indicated that the lake had occupied different positions in the course of the past 2000 years. Von Richthofen called attention to this phenomenon at about the same time as Przhevalsky, and both advanced theories as to its cause.

In 1879, on his third expedition, Przhevalsky crossed Sinkiang and entered Tibet from the north, hoping to reach Lhasa. That city, Tibet's capital, had been a great magnet, attracting explorers for centuries, because of its remoteness and the manner in which the rulers of Tibet had, at all times, maintained their isolation from the outside world. Throughout the nineteenth century and, in fact, until 1950, Tibet was ruled by a theocracy, personified by the Dalai Lama, incarnation of earlier priestly rulers, and was administered by a complex ecclesiastical hierarchy. Nominally subject to China, Tibet managed to maintain near-independent status and continue its secluded existence, protected by the natural barriers of mountains, deserts, and a harsh climate. Nikolay Przhevalsky was within 125 miles (202 kilometers) of Lhasa when Tibetan military forces stopped him and made him turn back.

Between 1883 and 1885 Przhevalsky undertook his last major expedition, concentrating this time on the Tarim Basin and the Kunlun range. His writings, describing eloquently the lands and peoples of Central Asia, made him a world figure and brought him honors from all over Europe. He returned once more to his beloved mountains and died in 1888, at the age of 49, on the shores of Issyk Kul, a mountain lake near the Russian-Chinese border. Przhevalsky's achievements, shedding light on the nature of the mountain systems of Central Asia and describing the region's flora,

The Chinese lake Lop Nor, whose exact location had puzzled geographers for centuries, was located accurately by Nikolay Mikhailovich Przhevalsky in 1876. [Library of Congress]

fauna, and ethnographic features, place him high among explorers.

British and Russian surveys Russia was in a favored position when it came to the exploration of Central Asia. Even before the Russian conquest of the lands between the Caspian and the Pamirs was completed, Russian explorers encountered little if any resistance from Chinese officials when entering the area from Siberia, and the environment of Sinkiang was never as hostile as that of Tibet. Britain, on the other hand, not only had to contend with the immense barrier of the Himalayas, separating the Indo-Gangetic lowland from Tibet, but ran head on into the uncompromising determination of Tibetan authorities to keep all foreigners out of their mountainous realm. Thus, while a handful of men did attempt to enter the land beyond the Himalayan crests, did in fact penetrate Ladakh, Tibet's northwestern neighbor, and went even beyond the Kunlun range to the rim of the Tarim Basin, the main burden of exploring and mapping Tibet was undertaken by British authorities in India through native Indian surveyors. These men, referred to as pundits, were carefully trained as surveyors but had to rely on the simplest instruments, since they entered Tibet disguised as Buddhist pilgrims.

The Indian surveyors used prayer beads as counting devices for the number of steps they had taken, having learned to estimate the length of their stride: this enabled them to measure, with a surprising degree of accuracy, distances covered each day. They relied very heavily on memory to retain information, and committed field notes, pertaining to astronomical positions and to the elevation of mountain peaks, to tiny parchment rolls, concealed within the circular prayer wheels that every pilgrim carried. Over a period of 30 years, these surveyors managed to traverse all Tibet, from its Chinese frontier in the east to Ladakh in the west. The two most prominent pundits, Nain Singh, who worked in Tibet between 1865 and 1875, and Kishen Singh, who followed him, brought back large numbers of accurate observations that enabled the

Survey of India to prepare the first modern maps of the land beyond the Himalayas.

By the mid-1880s British and Russian relations with China were close enough for the two powers to insist that they be given the right to maintain diplomatic posts in the interior provinces of China. The most important concession made by China was the establishment of foreign consulates in Kashgar (K'oshih), the principal town of the Tarim Basin, accessible with relative ease from Russian Central Asia but with greater difficulty from northwestern India. Kashgar thus became the base of operations for a number of individual explorers. Chief among the British explorers working in the general area of Sinkiang were Arthur Douglas Carey and A. Dalgeish, in 1885–1886, and Francis Younghusband, between 1886 and 1895.

The fact that territories under the sovereignty of the two world powers contending for mastery of the heart of Asia, Britain and Russia, were only partially known in precisely those frontier zones where open conflict could bring the two powers close to war led to the establishment of the Pamir Boundary Commission in the 1890s. The work accomplished by this British-Russian group not only included the accurate delimitation and partial demarcation of the boundaries between Russian and British territory, the two being separated by a strip of land, called the Wakhan Corridor, under the sovereignty of Afghanistan, extending to the western boundary of China, but contributed substantially to the knowledge of the Pamir. By 1914, relations between Britain and Russia having been stabilized by accords relating not only to the Pamir but to Persia (Iran) as well, the Indian and Russian triangulation networks across the Pamirs had been connected, a step that marked truly important progress in the accurate mapping of Asia.

While an understanding between Britain and Russia contributed substantially to the knowledge of the Pamir, Tibet remained a closed land. British insistence on establishing trade relations between Tibet and India received no response, and in 1904 a mission was sent to Tibet, charged with opening the country. The mission, containing a sizable contingent from the Indian armed forces and directed by Younghusband (1863–1942), a man with extensive firsthand knowledge of Central Asia, penetrated Tibet against Tibetan armed resistance, overcame the poorly equipped Tibetan forces, and entered the forbidden city of Lhasa on August 2, 1904. But the difficulties in maintaining year-round contact with interior Tibet as well as possible tensions in British-Russian relations led, after the withdrawal of Younghusband's "expedition," to a British-Russian agreement, concluded in 1907, that recognized Tibet's status as a territory under Chinese sovereignty. In reality, the 1907 agreement did nothing more than to recognize the value of Tibet as a buffer separating the two world powers in the heart of Asia.

Hedin and Stein These events, while more of a political-military than of a scientific nature, did contribute to the exploration of Central Asia in a few small areas. But the very remoteness of Central Asia and the continuing attraction to explorers of replacing the areas shown on the map as blanks, with the word *unexplored* in overprint, brought another group on the scene. Two among them stand out, a Swede and an Anglo-Hungarian, one mainly a geographer and the other an archaeologist, both concerned with shedding light on hitherto unknown or little-known lands.

Sven Anders HEDIN, a native of Sweden, first entered Central Asia in 1890, on a reconnaissance survey of eastern Persia, the Pamir, and part of the Tarim Basin. His first major expedition, between 1894 and 1897, concentrated on the Tarim Basin, resulting, among other observations, in the discovery of ruins of ancient cities, once on the Silk Road that connected China with the West, and in accurate maps of the western part of the Tarim Basin.

Between 1899 and 1902 Hedin returned to Sinkiang, undertook a detailed survey of the course of the Tarim River and of the present and past location of the lake Lop Nor, and discovered yet another important city of the past, Lou Lan, in the Lop Nor area. He continued southward into Tibet but, like Przhevalsky some years earlier, was turned back by Tibetan authorities before he could reach Lhasa. The results of the journey were important because they included accurate surveys of the heart of the Tibetan plateau.

Between 1906 and 1908, Hedin entered Tibet from the west, having traversed and mapped the salt desert of eastern Persia on the way, and devoted his efforts to surveying and mapping the ranges north of the Himalayas, which he named the Transhimalaya. The results of this expedition were incorporated in a nine-volume work, directed and written in part by Hedin, *Southern Tibet,* one of the key sources to the historical geography of Central Asia.

Following World War I, Hedin, this time initially under the sponsorship of Lufthansa, the German aviation concern, came back to Central Asia to survey a possible air route between Europe and Peking across Chinese territory. The work continued, under joint Chinese and Swedish sponsorship, until 1935, with Hedin directing a group of Swedish, German, and Chinese scientists who collected a vast number of observations in all fields of the earth sciences, as well as in archaeology. The publication of the more than fifty volumes of the scientific results of the 1926–1935 expedition, expected to be concluded in the late 1970s, combined with Hedin's own voluminous writings, presents an indispensable corpus of information, both scientific and popular, on Central Asia.

Hedin was first and foremost a geographer, a man of many talents, a loner originally, in the grand tradition of nineteenth-century exploration, a superb organizer and leader in his last, great Sino-Swedish expedition. His great contemporary Sir Aurel Stein (1862–1943), who with Hedin dominated the history of Central Asian exploration during the half century between the Afghan Wars and World War II, was first and foremost a historian cum archaeologist. Born in Hungary, educated there and in Germany and England, Stein went to India as a teacher and college administrator but soon turned, as a staff member of the Archaeological Survey of India, to his favorite subject. His main concern was the study of trans-Asian relations and connections, the contacts between civilizations of South and East Asia on one hand and Western Asia and the Mediterranean on the other. He spent a good part of the years between 1897 and 1943 in the field, excavating sites in northwesternmost India, in the Tarim Basin, and in western China, interpreting and correlating his finds, and establishing their place in the overall chronology of Asian history. At the same time, he contributed detailed and accurate observations on the environment of the sites where he worked, providing valuable geographical information as well.

Stein's most important work was done in northwest India and adjacent areas, firmly establishing the nature of the Gandhāra civilization, that blend of Indian and Greco-Hellenistic features that not only dominated northwest India at one time but extended its influence clear across Asia to the Far East as well. In Central Asia, his work at Lou Lan, the site discovered by Hedin, contributed greatly to our knowledge of the historical geography of the area; among other things Stein located the westernmost extension of the Great Wall of China. His other contribution was the excavation, presentation, and partial interpretation of written documents and works of art he found at Tunhuang in western China.

Continuing Russian and Chinese work Comparing the map of Central Asia, as presented by Sven Hedin and his collaborators in an atlas published after World War II, with the best available maps of the late 1800s provides an accurate means of gauging the contributions of explorers to our knowledge of the area. But explorations in Central Asia, though temporarily slowed by World War I, did not stop. In what was once called Russian Turkestan, a vast amount of detailed scientific work in all the biological and earth sciences went on, only partially interrupted by World War II. Thus, to mention one of two examples, N. L. Korzhenevsky led a series of expeditions to the mountainous areas of Soviet Central Asia between 1921 and 1932. Among the more spectacular results of this series of endeavors was the first accurate measurement of the highest mountain on Soviet territory, now called Pik Kommunizma (Mount Communism), with an elevation of 24,590 feet (7495 meters). In 1943 another expedition, led by P. N. Rapasov, measured the elevation of the second highest Soviet peak, Pik Pobeda (Mount Victory), 24,406 feet (7439 meters).

Soviet exploration of Central Asia also took place in the great deserts of the Aral-Caspian depression,

Outdoor kitchen in front of the palace of the Dalai Lama in Lhasa, Tibet, around 1935. [Library of Congress]

where soil, climate, geological, and geographical studies have continued since 1920. In 1935 the lowest point on Soviet territory, 433 feet (132 meters) below sea level, was measured by an expedition equipped and supported like all others by the Soviet Academy of Sciences.

The lack of detailed information from the People's Republic of China prevents a detailed review of accomplishments of Chinese exploration in Central Asia. But the fact that by far the greater part of Central Asia is under Chinese sovereignty and that, for the first time in centuries, central Chinese authority prevails over all parts of the territory of that state, leads one to believe that explorations, conducted by the Chinese state and by Chinese scientific bodies, are going on. The progress achieved in Central Asia, building railroads and all-weather highways and exploring and exploiting fuels, metals, and minerals, presupposes exploration carried out by extensive cadres, carefully planned and fully supported by the Chinese state.

BIBLIOGRAPHY: J. N. L. Baker, *A History of Geographical Discovery and Exploration*, new ed., rev., London, 1948; L. S. Berg, *Geschichte der russischen geographischen Entdeckungen*, Leipzig, 1954; N. A. Gvozdetsky, *Soviet Geographical Explorations and Discoveries*, Moscow, 1974; Sir Percy Sykes, *A History of Exploration from the Earliest Times to the Present Day*, 3d ed., London, 1950; C. Wessels, S. J., *Early Jesuit Travellers in Central Asia*, The Hague, 1924.

George Kish

Chaillé-Long, Charles (1842–1917) American soldier, diplomat, and explorer. Chaillé-Long's education at Washington Academy was terminated by the outbreak of the Civil War, in which he rose through the

The American explorer Charles Chaillé-Long used his time in military service in the Sudan to acquaint himself with the lake regions of Africa and the upper reaches of the White Nile. [Library of Congress]

ranks to a captaincy in the Union Army. This experience in turn led to an appointment as a lieutenant colonel in the Egyptian Army in 1869. Some 5 years later he became chief of staff to Gen. Charles Gordon and in this capacity conducted treaty-making negotiations with King Mutesa of Buganda. In the course of his travels in the lake regions of Africa he carried out geographical researches which resulted in the discovery of Lake Ibrahim (now Lake Kioga) and added to the incomplete reconnaissance by John Hanning SPEKE of the upper reaches of the White Nile. His work in Uganda is described in *Naked Truths of Naked People* (1876), but this book, like his autobiography, is not always reliable. In particular, Chaillé-Long vaingloriously attached too much importance to his own role as a Nile discoverer. In the year following his discovery of Lake Ibrahim, he made another journey in the region dividing the watersheds of the Nile and

Congo (Zaire) Rivers which added to the geographical information earlier obtained by Georg August SCHWEINFURTH.

After his African travels Chaillé-Long took a law degree at Columbia University which launched him on a new career in international law. In later years he held various official posts for the United States government. These included consulships in Cairo and Korea. He continued to write prolifically, mainly on African subjects, and his publications included many articles as well as a number of books in French and English. He was a gold medalist of the American Geographical Society.

BIBLIOGRAPHY: Edward A. Alpers, "Charles Chaillé-Long's Mission to Mutesa of Buganda," *Uganda Journal*, vol. XXIX, 1965, pp. 1–11; Charles Chaillé-Long, *My Life in Four Continents*, 2 vols., London, 1912.

James A. Casada

Challenger Expedition

The role of Great Britain in maritime exploration in the eighteenth and nineteenth centuries is well known, but less familiar is its support of and participation in the first great voyage of oceanographical exploration, the Challenger Expedition of 1872–1876. During a 41-month circumnavigation of the globe, the 2300-ton steam corvette HMS *Challenger* visited all the oceans of the world, with the exception of the Arctic, in a program of oceanographical research.

Inspiration for the expedition came from the naturalists William B. Carpenter, an early supporter of Charles Darwin, and Charles Wyville Thomson (1830–1882), a student of deep-sea fauna. Their success in deep-sea dredging in the North Atlantic in 1868 and 1869 had convinced them of the wealth of

HMS Challenger *under sail on the world's first oceanographical voyage.*

scientific information that could be obtained from a sustained, systematic investigation of the sea. At the request of the Royal Society, the British Admiralty provided a vessel and crew for a voyage of marine exploration. Naval command was given to Capt. (later Sir) George Strong Nares, while the civilian leadership of the scientific contingent was delegated to Thomson.

The Admiralty's instructions stated that the purpose of the expedition was "to investigate the physical condition of the deep sea throughout the three great ocean basins, that is, to ascertain their depth, temperature, circulation, &c., to determine the distribution of organic life throughout the areas traversed, at the surface, at intermediate depths, and especially at the deep ocean bottom." At sea the *Challenger* assumed a station for sounding, dredging, and recording serial temperatures approximately every 200 miles (322 kilometers). In the course of the expedition, she performed these arduous and time-consuming tasks at 362 stations. Dredging at depths down to 3000 fathoms (5486 meters) was difficult, and the trawl frequently failed to return to the surface with any specimens of deepwater fauna.

While in the Pacific, the *Challenger* verified the fundamental differences between this ocean and the Atlantic. The Pacific Ocean was not only larger but also consistently deeper, and its abyssal floor was characterized by a clay bottom which contained substantial amounts of manganese, quartz, pumice, and mica. While sounding in depths beyond 4000 fathoms (7315 meters), it was discovered that the floor was covered with radiolarian ooze.

In a voyage which covered almost 69,000 miles (111,041 kilometers) and which crossed the equator six times while examining the nature of life in the ocean's depths, the scientific accomplishments were numerous. More than 700 genera and 4000 new species were added to zoology. In addition to the discovery of new fauna, the expedition provided conclusive evidence that life could exist in the depths of the abyssal sea and that 300 fathoms (549 meters) was not the limit to life within the sea, indicated the presence of manganese nodules on the floor of the Atlantic and Pacific Oceans, revealed the nature of the sea bottom, obtained seawater from various depths for chemical analysis, and collected data for the further study of oceanic circulation. It was an epoch-making voyage of inquiry into the life and phenomena in the depths of the sea.

See also OCEANOGRAPHICAL EXPLORATION.

BIBLIOGRAPHY: H. L. Burstyn, "Science and Government in the XIXth Century: The Challenger Expedition and Its Report," *Bulletin de l'Institut Océanographique*, Monaco, numéro spécial 2, vol. II, 1968, pp. 603–611; Margaret Deacon, *Scientists and the Sea, 1650–1900,* New York, 1971; William Abbott Herdman, *Founders of Oceanography and Their Work,* London, 1923; Eric Linklater, *The Voyage of the Challenger,* Garden City, N.Y., 1972; Phillip Drennon Thomas, "Explorers of the Ocean Depths: The Challenger Expedition of 1872–1876," *Oceans,* vol. VI, December 1973, pp. 41–45, 77; Charles Wyville Thomson, *The Voyage of the Challenger: The Atlantic,* 2 vols., London, 1877.

Phillip Drennon Thomas

Champlain, Samuel de (ca. 1570–1635) French explorer, navigator, and geographer in North America and the founder of Quebec. He was born at Brouage on the Bay of Biscay, in the province of Saintonge, but the exact day, month, and year of his birth are unknown. His father was an experienced sea captain. As a young man Champlain fought during the 1590s in Brittany under Henry IV, when that Bourbon monarch was engaged in driving out the Spanish invaders of France. When the conflict was over, Champlain went to Spain, where his uncle Guillaume was in Spanish maritime service. From the Spanish port of Sanlúcar Champlain sailed to the New World, visiting Cuba, Puerto Rico, Mexico, and Central America. During the period 1599–1601 he made three voyages to the New World. Returning to France, he entered the service of Aymar de Chastes, vice admiral of France and governor of Dieppe, who had been granted a trade monopoly in New France by Henry IV. Under the auspices of this patron and in an expedition led by François Gravé du Pont, Champlain made his first voyage to Canada in the spring of 1603. The expedition made its way up the great St. Lawrence waterway to Tadoussac, which was then the center of the Laurentian fur trade. Proceeding farther up the St. Lawrence in a pinnace, Champlain reached the formidable Lachine Rapids, which he named Sault Saint-Louis. In mid-August the expedition headed back to France. The fur pelts and dried fish which were brought back proved to be very profitable to those who had invested in this enterprise. Upon his return from the voyage Champlain described his experiences in a book entitled *Des sauvages* (1603).

De Chastes had died during the summer of 1603,

and his company was reorganized. A new royal patent was conferred in 1604 upon Pierre de Gua, Sieur de Monts, a Protestant gentleman of Saintonge, who was given a fur-trading and colonizing monopoly between the latitudes 40 and 46°N.

The company formed by the Sieur de Monts founded three settlements in North America, Sainte-Croix, Port Royal, and Quebec. Of these establishments the first two were unsuccessful, but Quebec became the first permanent French colony in North America. Quebec, with its splendid natural fortifications on the banks of the St. Lawrence, was founded by Champlain on July 3, 1608, and in the course of time became the focal point from which a number of continental explorations were carried out. These explorations eventually brought the French to the Gulf of Mexico and to the great prairies of the West. During the period 1604–1607 Champlain also carried out three explorations along the New England coast, ultimately continuing as far south as Martha's Vineyard. The precise maps which he made during these voyages attest to his excellent cartographic skill.

In the summer of 1609 Champlain accompanied a group of Huron and Algonquin warriors who were traveling southward to fight the Iroquois (the Five Nations) in the area which is now central New York. On the way Champlain discovered the beautiful lake which bears his name. An armed clash between the rival Indian groups occurred near Crown Point in July 1609, and the firearms of the French put the more numerous Iroquois to flight. Quite naturally this defeat caused the Iroquois to hate the French most bitterly.

During the years 1613–1616 Champlain carried out further explorations, hoping that he might discover a route to the western sea. In the summer of 1613 he traveled up the Ottawa River, crossed country from one lake to another, and after many difficulties reached Allumette Island. Two years later in the company of Huron Indians he traveled to the shores of Georgian Bay of Lake Huron. The impetus which Champlain gave to Western expansion continued after his death when the intrepid *coureurs de bois* (French Canadian woodsmen) served as spearheads for French penetration of the heart of the North American continent. Champlain had been named lieutenant of the king's viceroy in Canada (1612) and much later became lieutenant and representative of Cardinal Richelieu when that famous minister of the French crown took New France under his direct supervision. The Company of One Hundred Associates (Cents Associés), of which Champlain was an important member, was established to correct abuses and to advance French interests in the New World.

In 1627 Acadia was seized by the English during an Anglo-French war, and in 1629 Quebec also fell to the English. Champlain returned to Europe, where he spent the next several years negotiating for the return of Quebec. By the Treaty of Saint-Germain-en-Laye (March 1632) French sovereignty was restored over

Known as the father of New France, Samuel de Champlain opened up the St. Lawrence region to the fur trade, made far-sighted treaties with the Indians in the area, and through his writings brought France improved knowledge of the New World. [Library of Congress]

Champlain attacks an Indian fort in western New York, 1615. [Library of Congress]

both Acadia and Canada. Champlain returned to Quebec in May 1633 and never again left this colony. He suffered a paralytic stroke in Quebec in October 1635 and died on Christmas Day of that year. He left a wife, Hélène, but no children. Hélène, who was living in Paris at the time of his death, entered an Ursuline convent after she heard of her husband's demise and spent the rest of her life as a nun.

Champlain was essentially a man of action, a robust soldier and an energetic sailor, a colonizer of the first rank. Despite frequent indifference in official circles he persisted in the maintenance and development of French authority in the area of the St. Lawrence, and he succeeded in building up in this region an effective fur-trading organization. His farsighted policies also provided the foundation for French domination over the Montagnais, Algonquin, and Huron tribes. His extensive writings and his excellent maps contributed to a much better understanding of the geography of the North American continent. Because of his many achievements he truly deserves his posthumous title of "the founder of Canada."

BIBLIOGRAPHY: Morris Bishop, *Champlain: The Life of Fortitude*, New York, 1948; N. E. Dionne, *Champlain*, Toronto, 1963; Samuel Eliot Morison, *Samuel de Champlain: Father of New France*, Boston, 1972.

Bernerd C. Weber

Chancellor, Richard *(d. 1556)*

English navigator. In 1553 Richard Chancellor was the pilot general of an expedition fitted out by London merchants and under the command of Sir Hugh Willoughby to discover and explore a NORTHEAST PASSAGE to the Far East. The expedition, which consisted of three ships, sailed from Gravesend in May 1553. A severe storm off the coast of Norway separated the vessels. Chancellor, who commanded the *Edward Bonaventure*, eventually found the entrance to the White Sea and, sailing southward, reached the Russian shore after dropping anchor near the mouth of the Northern Dvina River (Severnaya Dvina). Willoughby's two vessels, after some aimless wandering, finally found refuge in a bay on the coast of Lapland and there stayed the winter. The long and terrible Russian winter took the lives of all. In the spring of 1554 Russian fishermen found the two vessels and the frozen men aboard.

Meanwhile, Chancellor made the long and difficult overland journey to Moscow, where he was cordially received by the Russian tsar, Ivan IV (Ivan the Terrible). In the summer of 1554 Chancellor returned to the White Sea and sailed to England. The news of his discoveries led to the establishment in London of a new association commonly known as the Muscovy Company. In 1555 Chancellor made his second voyage to Russia and obtained from the Tsar a formal grant to develop trading operations. On this occasion Chancellor also learned of Willoughby's fate and recovered his papers. In the summer of 1556 the homeward journey was begun, but in November a shipwreck occurred in Pitsligo Bay in Aberdeenshire. Some of the crew were saved, but Chancellor lost his life. Among contemporaries he was sometimes known as "the incomparable Richard Chancellor," a fitting characterization for this skilled and intrepid navigator who had made possible the development of Anglo-Russian trade relations in the sixteenth century.

BIBLIOGRAPHY: Lloyd E. Berry and Robert O. Crummey (eds.), *Rude & Barbarous Kingdom: Russia in the Accounts of Sixteenth-Century English Voyagers*, Madison, Wis. 1968.

Bernerd C. Weber

Chang Ch'ien *(Chang K'ien; d. 107 B.C.)*

Early Han Chinese envoy and explorer. When Emperor Wu-ti (r. 140–87 B.C.) of the Han dynasty ascended the throne, he initiated a dynamic policy to deal with the menacing posture of the Hsiung-nu nomads on China's northwestern frontier. In order to seek a military alliance with the Yueh-chih, who had just been crushed by the Hsiung-nu and forced to migrate westward, Chang Ch'ien, a young officer from Hanchung, was chosen as the head of a diplomatic mission. Venturing through the Kansu corridor in 138 B.C., the party was captured by the Hsiung-nu and brought to their headquarters in the Altai Shan (Altay Mountains). After being detained 10 years, Chang Ch'ien made his escape and resumed his journey southwestward, passing through such countries as Wusun in the Ili Valley, Tawan (Ferghana), and K'angchu (Sogdiana) before arriving in Tahsia (Bactria), which had by then been conquered by the Yueh-chih. Resettled in the fertile Oxus (Amu Darya) Valley, the Yueh-chih showed no interest in allying themselves with China in a joint struggle against their common enemy.

In spite of the failure of the mission, the information gathered by Chang Ch'ien on numerous countries beyond Han China and the impact of his report upon China's view of the world and its external relations certainly place him among the greatest explorers in the ancient world. In addition to the countries he visited, Chang Ch'ien reported on Shentu (India), Ants'ai (the Caucasus), Anhsi (Persia), T'iaochih (Mesopotamia), and Lihsuan (the Roman Orient). His return journey followed a southern route, skirting the Kunlun Mountains toward Lop Nor and crossing the Tsaidam, where he again failed to avoid capture by the Hsiung-nu. He escaped a year later and made his way back in 126 B.C.

Having seen certain Szechwan products in Bactria that had come by way of India, Chang Ch'ien proposed to Wu-ti that a new route to the West be opened from Szechwan through India. Four missions were dispatched to explore the Tibet-Yünnan borderlands, but none survived the hostilities of the warlike tribes along the way.

In 115 B.C., Chang Ch'ien headed another mission to Wusun, also seeking an alliance to outflank the Hsiung-nu. Like the previous mission to the Yueh-chih, this attempt did not succeed. From Wusun, however, Chang Ch'ien sent assistant envoys to a number of other countries, bringing silk products as gifts to their rulers. A long era of silk trade was thus begun, and the Silk Road later became the main artery in East-West communications. The great contribution of Chang Ch'ien in overcoming the formidable barriers which separated China from other civilizations lay in the widening of China's geographical horizons and the establishing of contact and exchange with countries to the far west.

BIBLIOGRAPHY: Friedrich Hirth, *China and the Roman Orient*, Shanghai, 1885; id., "The Story of Chang K'ien, China's Pioneer in Western Asia," *Journal of the Amerian Oriental Society*, no. 37, 1917, pp. 89–116.

Kuei-sheng Chang

Cheadle, Walter Butler (1835–1919), and Milton, Viscount (William Fitzwilliam; 1839–1877) English explorers. Many young gentlemen of rank and wealth in the nineteenth century visited Rupert's Land and the Indian territories of British North America "in search of adventure and heavy game." Among these travelers Viscount Milton, who had accompanied the Red River fall buffalo hunt in 1860, and Dr. Walter Cheadle were more than merely tourists: they intended to discover a direct way through British territory to the Cariboo gold diggings in British Columbia and a "North West Passage by land" to the Pacific that would be more practicable than the long-sought Arctic route.

They reached Quebec on July 2, 1862, proceeding by rail and boat via Toronto, Detroit, and Chicago to St. Paul, by stagecoach to Georgetown on the Red River, and by canoe to Fort Garry (modern Winnipeg). There they procured supplies, horses, and guides, leaving on August 23 for Carlton House on the North Saskatchewan River. They wintered in a log cabin they built on "La Belle (Jolie) Prairie," 80 miles (129 kilometers) to the northwest, near White Fish (Witchekan?) Lake, hunting and trapping with local Indians and *métis*. They set off again on April 9, 1863, via Fort Pitt and Edmonton, for the mountains. At Jasper House they secured an Iroquois guide to take them through the Yellowhead (Leather) Pass. Little was known of this pass or the country beyond, though some of the Overlanders, gold seekers headed for the Cariboo diggings, had gone that way, and one of the few mountain guides, André Cardinal, had, at Edmonton, discussed the route with them.

The little party crossed the continental divide to the Fraser River without being aware of it. Here the Iroquois turned back; now without a guide, unskilled in mountain travel, and inadequately equipped, Milton and Cheadle, their *voyageur*, Louis Battenotte ("the Assiniboine"), with his wife and small son, and a hitchhiker, the egregious Mr. O'B, a classical pedant who was both helpless and demanding, could not find a trail and gave up the attempt to make the supposed 6-day journey straight across country to the Cariboo. Instead, they turned down the North Thompson River and for more than a month toiled through a "primeval forest where trees of gigantic size had grown and fallen undisturbed for ages." They struggled with muskegs, precipices, and flooded rivers. Starving and exhausted, forced to eat one of their horses, they finally emerged into the open country near Kamloops, to be succored by Shuswap Indians and Hudson's Bay Company personnel from the fort. They went on to New Westminster and Victoria and thence north to the Cariboo—a very roundabout route.

Home again, they published a book and many articles about their journey, as well as giving numerous lectures. Impressed by the agricultural potential of the Saskatchewan country and British Columbia's wealth in minerals, forests, and fish, they advocated a "connection" through the mountains. Despite the difficulties they had experienced, they thought this quite feasible. Lord Milton lived only a decade more, but Cheadle returned to his profession, making important medical discoveries in his long and distinguished career as a children's doctor.

BIBLIOGRAPHY: Viscount Milton and W. B. Cheadle, *The North-West Passage by Land, Being the Narrative of an Expedition from the Atlantic to the Pacific, Undertaken with the View of Exploring a Route across the Continent to British Columbia through British Territory, by One of the Northern Passes in the Rocky Mountains*, London, 1865, and many subsequent editions; W. B. Cheadle, *Cheadle's Journal of a Trip across Canada, 1862–63*, with introduction and notes by A. G. Doughty and Gustave Lanctot, Ottawa, 1931.

Irene M. Spry

Cheng Ho (1371–?1434) Early Ming Chinese voyager. Cheng Ho was born into a Muslim family at Kunyang in Yünnan at the beginning of the Ming dynasty. In 1381, when the region was pacified, he was one of the children selected to be castrated for imperial eunuch service. Later he was assigned to the retinue of Chu Ti, who was to become the celebrated Emperor Yung-lo. In his early twenties, Cheng Ho accompanied Chu Ti on a series of campaigns against the Mongols and took up a career in the military. During the rebellion by means of which Chu Ti usurped the throne, Cheng Ho played a significant role and hence became one of the new Emperor's most trusted aides. The dethroned ruler, Chu Yun-wen, reportedly fled from Nanking, the capital, amid a conflagration and was later rumored to be wandering abroad. For this and other unspecified reasons, Chu Ti sent expeditions overseas under the command of Cheng Ho which resulted in the most extensive maritime enterprise in Chinese history. On seven occasions between 1405 and 1433, Cheng Ho directed the fleets which visited no fewer than thirty-seven countries from the Vietnam coast in the east to the Persian Gulf, the Red Sea, and East Africa in the west.

The first voyage began from the Yangtze Estuary with a 27,800-man crew and 62 large and 255 small vessels. Sailing southward across the South China Sea, the fleet first anchored at Qui Nhon, Indochina, and later encountered the fleet of the pirate Chen Tsu-i, then in control of Palembang, Sumatra. The latter was defeated in a large-scale sea battle and brought to Nanking for execution.

The second voyage took off in 1407. Its objective was to reach Calicut, which then commanded a focal position in maritime trade in the Indian Ocean. On its way back, the expedition also visited Siam (Thailand) and Java before returning home in 1409. During the third voyage (1409–1411), which reached the same destination as the second, excursions were made to Siam, Malacca, Sumatra, and Ceylon.

The fourth voyage (1413–1415) took the fleet farther afield, and stops were made at the Maldives, Hormuz (Hormoz), the Hadramawt coast of Arabia, and Aden. The fifth (1417–1419) and sixth (1421–?1425) expeditions visited the shores of East Africa, at such places as Mogadishu, Brava, Juba, Malindi, Mombasa, Zanzibar, Kilwa, and others near the Mozambique Strait. Before the return of the sixth voyage, a serious blow to the maritime cause occurred with the death of its patron, Emperor Yung-lo. Soon the idea of another such undertaking came under attack from those who regarded the enterprise as unnecessary and wasteful, but the seventh voyage was given the go-ahead by another new emperor, Chu Chan-chi, in 1431. Between 1433 and 1435 this final expedition revisited a score of states as far as eastern Africa, and as before gifts and tributes were brought by foreign ambassadors who traveled to China with the fleet. Cheng Ho died at Calicut between 1433 and 1435 and was later buried near Nanking.

Details of Cheng Ho's voyages were carefully recorded by his aides, among them Ma Huan, Fei Hsin and Kung Chen, all participants in the various voyages. Nautical charts of one of the voyages have been preserved in the *Wu pei chih* compiled by Mao Yuan-i in 1621.

BIBLIOGRAPHY: Kuei-sheng Chang, 'The Ming Maritime Enterprise and China's Knowledge of Africa Prior to the Age of Great Discoveries," *Terrae Incognitae*, vol. III, 1971, pp. 33–44; J. J. L. Duyvendak, *China's Discovery of Africa*, London, 1949.

Kuei-sheng Chang

China

During classical antiquity Western contact with China was limited and indirect and stemmed primarily from the silk trade. Chinese sources relate that Emperor Wu-ti sent CHANG CH'IEN to locate and conclude an alliance with a people called the Yueh-chih who had been forced to flee by the Hsiung-nu nomads. After many difficulties Chang Ch'ien reached Tawan (Ferghana) and found the Yueh-chih north of the Oxus River (Amu Darya) near Bukhara (128 B.C.) soon after they had conquered Tahsia (Bactria). Although Chang Ch'ien failed to negotiate an alliance with the Yueh-chih, his journey resulted in the expansion of diplomatic and commercial relations between China and the peoples of Western Asia and in the eventual introduction of silk to Europe.

By the Augustan age silk had become a familiar if costly commodity in Italy. China received glass, textiles, and other products from Rome, but the balance of trade was unfavorable to Rome, and in the first century A.D. PLINY complained that China, India, and Arabia together drained 100 million sesterces from the Roman Empire each year. The transparent silken garments favored by Roman women also provoked the censure of moralists like Seneca, who considered them immodest. At this time the Romans did not know how silk was produced, believing it to be a fleece found growing on leaves.

The people whom the Romans associated with silk (Latin, *serica*) became known to them as the Seres. The earliest reference in European literature to the name from which China is derived occurs in the *Periplus of the Erythrean Sea* (first century A.D.; *see* PERIPLUS). The anonymous author speaks of a great city called Thinae from which an overland trade in silk was conducted. The origin of this name has been much debated, but it is generally believed to have come from the Ch'in dynasty of the third century B.C. The silk trade continued during the period of Rome's decline, although it eventually became a Persian monopoly. During the reign (527–565) of Justinian silkworms were smuggled into Byzantium, thus assuring the West a supply of silk independent of China and the many intermediaries in the trade.

The Western fund of knowledge about China greatly increased during the thirteenth and fourteenth centuries while China and much of Asia were under Mongol domination. Initially Europeans reacted to the Mongol conquests with fear and horror, but the Mongols' uncertain religious orientation and their attacks on Muslim states later led Europeans to regard them as potential converts to Christianity and allies against Islam. The result was the dispatch of numerous missionaries to Central Asia and Cathay, as China came to be known in Europe during the Middle Ages. European merchants were also able to travel to the Far East because the most important trade routes were in Mongol hands and were relatively safe.

The earliest European emissaries to the Mongols did not visit China but brought back much information about that country. However, when Khubilai (Kublai) Khan established his capital at Cambaluc (Peking) in 1264, China became more accessible to the West. The first-known visitors were the Polo brothers, Nicolò and Maffeo, who made a celebrated second journey in the company of Nicolò's son Marco POLO. The Polos were merchants, but the next prominent European traveler to China was the Franciscan missionary John of Monte Corvino, who arrived in Cambaluc about 1292 bearing a letter to Khubilai Khan from Pope Nicholas IV. John remained in China until his death in 1328 and succeeded in developing a Christian community numbering several thousand in Cambaluc and Zayton (Ch'üanchou). When the Pope learned of his success, he created the see of Cambaluc in 1307 and appointed John archbishop. Other clerics followed, among them Odoric of PORDENONE and John de' Marignolli. The latter was an Italian Franciscan sent to China in 1338 in response to a request from the Great Khan for a papal benediction and a gift of European horses. Marignolli spent 4 years in China and returned to Avignon in 1353 with a letter from the Khan asking the Pope for more missionaries. The overthrow of the Mongol (Yüan) dynasty in China in 1368 put an end to the work of Christian missionaries there. Between that time and the arrival of the Portuguese in the early sixteenth century, there are only a few references to China in the writings of travelers. Among these is the narrative of Nicolò di Conti, dictated to Poggio Bracciolini in the mid-fifteenth century, but it is unlikely that Conti even visited China.

Portuguese expansion in the Far East began after the voyage of Vasco da GAMA from 1497 to 1499. At Malacca, which they captured in 1511, the Portuguese came into contact with Chinese ships and captains. Portuguese traders from Malacca arrived in Canton in 1514; although they were not permitted to land, they sold their cargo at a profit. A Portuguese effort 3 years later to establish diplomatic relations with the Chinese government proved unsuccessful, but trade grew, and in 1557 the Portuguese were permitted to settle in Macao. In the following decade the Spanish under Miguel López de Legazpi entered the Far East with their conquest of the Philippines.

In the seventeenth century Iberian preeminence in the Far East was successfully challenged by the Dutch and the English. Although European commerce with China continued to flourish, the only Europeans who were able to penetrate the interior were Roman Catholic missionaries, starting with the Italian Jesuit Matteo Ricci, who was allowed to reside in Chaoch'ing (Kaoyao) in 1583 and to move to Peking in 1601. The missionary endeavors of Ricci and his successors resulted not only in the conversion of some Chinese to Christianity but also in the introduction to China of recent advances in Western science, especially in astronomy, mathematics, and cartography. Ricci himself made for the Chinese a map of the world, based on that of Ortelius (Abraham Oertel) of 1570, which gave them for the first time an accurate idea of the continents and oceans as they were known in that day. The work of the missionaries also provided Europe with much new information about China. Uncertainty over whether China and Cathay were the same place was removed by the investigations of Ricci and by the expedition (1602–1607) of Bento de Goes, who made the first overland journey to China since the fourteenth century. A Jesuit lay brother, Goes set out from Agra, traveled to Kabul, and crossed the Pamirs to reach Yarkand (Soch'e) more than a year after his departure. Goes eventually reached the western border of China proper but was not permitted to travel farther. He entered into communication with Ricci but died at Suchow on April 11, 1607, shortly after the arrival of a messenger from Ricci. The Jesuits were also responsible for the preparation of many outstanding maps of China. From 1708 to 1717 a team of nine Jesuits with their Chinese assistants conducted a survey of the entire empire. The resulting maps were engraved in Paris under the direction of Jean-Baptiste Bourguignon d'Anville and were published as a supplement to Father Jean-Baptiste Du Halde's *Description . . . de la Chine* (1735).

The opening of China to large numbers of Europeans in the mid-nineteenth century was followed by extensive exploration of the interior. Perhaps the most distinguished achievement during this period was that of the German geographer and geologist Baron Ferdinand von Richthofen, who made seven expeditions from Shanghai between 1868 and 1872. The results of his investigations were published in his monumental *China: Ergebnisse eigener Reisen und darauf gegründeter Studien* (1877–1912).

BIBLIOGRAPHY: G. F. Hudson, *Europe and China: A Survey of Their Relations from the Earliest Times to 1800*, London, 1931; Joseph Needham, *Science and Civilisation in China*, vol. 1, Cambridge, England, 1961; Henry Yule (ed. and tr.), *Cathay and the Way Thither*, rev. by Henry Cordier, Hakluyt Society, 2d ser., nos. 33, 37, 38, 41, London, 1913–1915.

Chinese Exploration

The saga of human exploration invariably begins with the immediate environment. So in ancient China, where agricultural societies first began in the middle Yellow River Basin, the earliest geographical treatise, the *Shan hai ching*, compiled during the Chou dynasty (1030–221 B.C.), testifies to a strong interest in the mountain chains and river systems which directly affected the life of the inhabitants.

Chou and Han dynasties As the horizons of the Chinese gradually widened, the next stage was the probing of routes and passages through which the natural barriers to the west and the northwest might be surmounted. This frontier sector, characterized by forbidding mountains and vast desert expanses, had since time immemorial held a special fascination for the ancient Chinese. The story of Emperor Mu's western expedition in the tenth century B.C., as preserved in several classical historical works, contained considerable information on the routes, mountains, deserts, and products beyond Chou China's northwestern frontiers. Although an element of romance is intermingled in the chronicle and doubts exist as to the date of its composition, it is nonetheless indicative of what was known during the late Chou dynasty. The intermittent streams, the shifting sands, the open steppes, and the lofty mountain peaks are physical features frequently mentioned in the narrative. The accounts of jade deposits in the Kunlun Mountains and the hospitality of a land ruled by the "Western

Camel train coming from Mongolia through the Great Wall via the Nank'ou Pass. [Library of Congress]

Royal Mother" held allure for the Chinese during many centuries that followed. In contrast, interest in lands on other frontiers seems to have been more sporadic, and maritime orientation was a much later phenomenon.

When the Chou dynasty weakened during the fifth century B.C. and the various feudal states began to struggle among themselves for supremacy, there was an increase in exploration and expansion into lesser-known regions. The northern state of Yen extended its control over parts of southern Manchuria and northern Korea, the state of Ch'u in the central Yangtze Valley opened routes deep into Hunan, Kueichou (Kweichow), and Yünnan, while the northwestern state of Ch'in managed to conquer the rich basin of Szechwan. During this period of political turmoil and intellectual ferment, a theory of the "greater nine continents" was developed by Tsou Yen, one of a class of traveling occultists who achieved considerable popularity through predicting the future and peddling fantastic tales about lands beyond the "Eastern Sea" where people could find peace and immortality. This theory, which could have revolutionized the course of Chinese exploration, was vehemently opposed by Confucianists, as it threatened to undermine the traditional concept of the single "celestial continent" surrounded by the "four seas." During the short-lived Ch'in dynasty (221–207 B.C.) however, one of the best-known traveling occultists, Hsu Fu, did use the promise of seeking the elixir of life in obtaining the support of the emperor Shih-huang-ti in his scheme to found a colony in Japan. The Emperor's campaigns to consolidate control took him to many parts of his empire. In the north the Great Wall was completed by joining existing sections built by a number of states in defense against the Hsiung-nu; to the south a series of river routes were established to link the central Yangtze lake country with the Hsi (Si) River Basin. By the Early Han dynasty (202 B.C.–A.D. 9), the southern frontier had reached the Gulf of Tonkin, and Hainan Island was used as a penal settlement.

From the early part of the second century B.C. on, the greatest concern of the Han emperors was the incessant harassment by the powerful Hsiung-nu nomads from the north and the northwest. Since neither force nor appeasement was successful in securing peace on the frontiers, Emperor Wu-ti initiated a new strategy immediately after ascending the throne in 140 B.C. A mission was dispatched to seek out and conclude an alliance with the Yueh-chih, a nomadic people who had just migrated westward from western Kansu after having been defeated by the Hsiung-nu. As the Emperor's chosen envoy, CHANG CH'IEN made two historic journeys to a number of states in Central Asia between 138 and 109 B.C. and became the most renowned pioneer explorer in China's early history.

On his first journey, Chang Ch'ien and his party promptly fell into the hands of the Hsiung-nu and remained prisoners for 10 years. After making an escape, he resumed the mission of diplomacy and visited several important states, including Wusun, Ferghana, Sogdiana, and Bactria. Although Chang Ch'ien failed to work out an alliance with the Yueh-chih, who by then had subdued Bactria and resettled in a fertile valley with a warmer climate, the vital link he forged between Eastern and Western Asia was to have a profound influence upon both sides for many centuries to come. His report to the Emperor contained not only detailed information on the countries he visited but also knowledge gathered secondhand concerning areas beyond Bactria. From his account, China learned for the first time of the existence of such cultured lands as India, Persia, Mesopotamia, and the Roman Empire (under the respective names Shentu, Anhsi, T'iaochih and Lihsuan). His second journey was also a diplomatic mission, seeking a military alliance with Wusun in the Ili Valley. Notwithstanding a second failure, contact with a number of neighboring and distant countries was established by his assistant envoys.

The importance of Chang Ch'ien's pioneer activities was threefold. First, through the publication of his report in the *Shih chi* by the grand historian Ssuma Ch'ien, China became aware of the existence of faraway civilizations, and its traditional geographical thinking was irreversibly altered. Second, through Chang Ch'ien's personal efforts as well as other missions dispatched by him or at his suggestion the routes in the northwest became established, and attempts were also made to reach India directly through the southwestern borderlands adjoining Yünnan: Tibet and Burma. Third, the breakthrough in physical barriers led to a flourishing trade in silk, iron, and other products along the Silk Road during the centuries that followed. The introduction of alfalfa, grapes, and other crops to China is directly attributable to Chang Ch'ien's explorations.

The overland route so vital to the linking of China with Western Asia was, however, periodically disrupted by warfare with the Hsiung-nu during much of the Han dynasty. To safeguard the Silk Road, one of the ablest generals, Pan Ch'ao, sent a special envoy, Kan Ying, from the Turan Basin to initiate direct communications with the Roman Empire, then known to the Chinese as Ta Ch'in. Seeking passage across the Persian Gulf, Kan Ying was discouraged from making the voyage by Persian seamen, who told horrifying tales of danger and sickness on the high seas. With the information brought back by this mission, China's interest in the Roman world continued unabated, while the increased volume in the silk trade made the Seres (people of silk land) famous around the Mediterranean.

Judging from a few clues which have come down from that period, attempts were undoubtedly made to bypass the route monopolized by the Persians and other middlemen. In the annals of the Late Han dynasty (A.D. 25–220), one finds the arrival of an envoy from Macedonia at Loyang, then the capital city, shortly after Kan Ying's return. There is one report on a Roman juggler who came by way of Burma and reached the capital in A.D. 109, and another tells of an envoy from Emperor Marcus Aurelius Antoninus to the court of China in A.D. 166 via Tonkin. The Roman historian Lucius Annaeus Florus made mention of the arrival of a Chinese envoy in Rome as early as the reign of Augustus (27 B.C.–A.D. 14). Through the enterprise and courage of nameless explorers and adventurers both Chinese and foreign, the alternate sea route was eventually established, and more accurate information concerning the Near East and Southern Europe made its appearance in Chinese geographical literature after this time.

Warring states and T'ang dynasty After the collapse of the Han, when the country was divided into three warring states, contact with the outside world was more frequently motivated by the need for diplomatic representation and territorial consolidation. Thus the northern kingdom of Wei (A.D. 386–534) took control of part of Korea and sent a mission to the court of the Yamato Queen in Japan. A remarkable account of the conditions on the islands of Tsushima, northern Kyushu, and western Honshu is to be found in the *Wei shu*, shedding much light on the geography, customs, and social conditions of Japan before the Taika reforms of 646.

The Wu kingdom (A.D. 222–280) was in control of the eastern and southern coast from the Yangtze Delta to Annam. Interest in the sea route to India and the West led to the sending of two ambassadors, K'ang T'ai and Chu Ying, to Funan in present Cambodia and the Mekong Delta. Through their encounters with envoys and merchants from India and other lands, the Chinese learned much about India, Ceylon, and other countries in Southern Asia, thus paving the way for future contact with the homeland of the Buddhist religion.

The landlocked kingdom of Shu (A.D. 221–264) was situated in the Szechwan Basin. In an attempt to rid itself of harassment from hostile tribes on its southwest, it launched a series of campaigns into Yünnan and northern Burma. As a result, this hitherto dangerous and inaccessible area became better known to the Chinese. In sum, the knowledge obtained during this period of diplomatic and military activity contributed to the completion of an important study of the river systems, the *Shui ching,* as well as to a major compilation of existing maps of the world then known to China by P'ei Hsiu in the middle of the third century.

Up to this time, political, military, and, to a lesser extent, economic motives had been the major underlying factors in the exploits of the Chinese in exploration. When political instability continued into the third and fourth centuries A.D., religions of both domestic and foreign origin made rapid inroads among the Chinese, and priests and monks became an active and influential sector of society. Religion thus took over as the primary motivating force in the exploration of unknown and far-off places. Taoist priests traveled widely in search of sacred mountains in the land, and many left records of their journeys on difficult mountain trails. In a map of T'ai Shan, a mountain beloved of the Taoists, one finds the earliest use of contour lines in depicting relief and other topographic features.

More prominent were the Buddhist travelers, who may be divided into two groups: those intent on saving souls in distant lands and others bent on visiting the holy places in India and learning more about the doctrine through firsthand inquiry. Large numbers of both groups left China by land and by sea; some never returned alive, while others left no record of their experiences. A number of important documents, however, have survived, telling of far-flung lands, daring adventures, and unprecedented journeys beyond the Chinese sphere of knowledge.

Among the records of geographical interest, Hui-shen's narrative as recorded in the *Liang shu* is by far the most perplexing and controversial. It tells of the monk's journey during the latter part of the fifth century to a land called Fusang, whose direction and distance from China and other physical and cultural characteristics have given rise to speculation that it was probably southern Mexico on the North American continent. It is perhaps not impossible to envisage such a voyage along the great-circle route, given the prevailing winds and currents and the navigational know-how and religious zeal of the time. In the *Ssu-hai tsung-t'u*, one of the extant maps of a later period, Fusang appears directly east of China and far beyond the Japanese islands. Further archaeological evidence is, of course, needed before the controversy can be laid to rest.

Among the pilgrims who vowed to visit the homeland of Buddhism and its numerous holy sites, FA-HSIEN was the first to travel to India by land and return by sea. In A.D. 399 he took the rarely traveled route westward through the Tsaidam and Tarim Basins and entered India from the upper Indus River and through the Swat Valley and the Khyber Pass. His descriptions of the desolate landscape beyond Lop Nor and his hair-raising experiences in crossing the canyons of the upper Indus are immortal passages in the travel literature of all time. For the next 6 years he collected Buddhist scriptures and visited the major holy places in the lower Ganges Valley, besides making a trip by sea to Ceylon, the important center of Hīnayāna Buddhism. His return journey took him first to western Java, then northward to the coast of Shantung after encountering dangerous storms in the South and East China Seas. Having traveled through more than thirty countries during 15 years, Fa-hsien wrote a book on his experiences and observations which revealed a large part of the Buddhist world to the Chinese and showed that both the overland and the sea routes were open to pilgrims and traders to and from India.

The T'ang dynasty (618–906) was undoubtedly one of the most favorable periods for Buddhism in China. Hardly had Emperor T'ai-tsung brought the country unity, order, and economic recovery and subdued the Turk khanate in Central Asia than pilgrimages were begun in earnest. The spearhead was HSÜAN-CHUANG, the most learned monk and observant explorer ever produced by China, and his travels constituted the most celebrated journey in the history of Chinese exploration and literature. His records compiled by a disciple, Pien-chi, and his itinerary edited by another student, Hui-li, together with a novel of adventure based on his journey written several centuries later, combine to immortalize Hsüan-chuang as one of the greatest explorers of all ages.

During a span of 16 years and traveling mostly by land, Hsüan-chuang visited a large portion of Central Asia and the Indian subcontinent, observing, inquiring, and systematically recording all that he saw and heard. As a scholar and a linguist, he was uniquely qualified to study the religious doctrines and cultural life of India; as an explorer and geographer, he gathered an enormous amount of information which helped to fill many gaps in the political and social history of the subcontinent. As a result of this historic journey, Buddhism in China became further enriched, and the two cultural centers were brought closer together.

Among the many Buddhist pilgrims who followed the examples of Fa-hsien and Hsüan-chuang, I-CHING was certainly the best known. This Buddhist pilgrim undertook his travels almost entirely by sea, as the overland route had by this time been disrupted by the Tibetans and the Arabs. He went southward from Canton, voyaging on a Persian vessel to Palembang, and then headed northwestward through the Strait of Malacca before boarding a Sumatran ship which took him across the Bay of Bengal to the mouth of the Hooghly River. His sojourn in India was confined to the holy places in the lower Ganges Valley, where he remained for 10 years, learning the law and collecting sacred books. On his return, he again stopped in Palembang, the center of Buddhism in Southeast Asia, and spent several years there in the work of translation. A keen observer and an inquirer of details, I-ching was the first traveler to provide a comprehensive account of the major islands and states in the East Indies and of the states on the coast of the Malay Peninsula.

During the heyday of the T'ang dynasty, China's power came into direct conflict with that of the Arabs, who had extended their control over the Turan Basin. In a decisive battle near Talas in A.D. 751, Chinese troops under the command of Kao Hsien-chih were badly defeated, and Chinese and Buddhist influence in Central Asia was soon permanently replaced by that of the Arabs and Islam. An accidental result of the encounter was the capture of an educated young Chinese named Tu Huan, who was taken by his Arab captors to Mesopotamia. After 10 years he was set free, returned to China via the Persian Gulf and around southern India and Southeast Asia, and wrote an account telling his experiences. The information he brought home has been preserved in a well-known historical work written by his uncle Tu Yu, through which a number of states in the Near East and North Africa became known to the Chinese. Although this inadvertent explorer was probably not the first Chinese to reach the areas he described, he was certainly the first to give a substantial report of the rising Islamic empire and of its western territories in North Africa in particular.

Sung and Mongol dynasties The fall of the T'ang and, after a break, the succession of the Sung dynasty (960–1279) witnessed a gradual southeastward shift of the center of political power and economic activities in China, and the number of foreign traders and settlers showed a steady increase in the major coastal cities. Without the emergence of any explorer of significance, China's geographical horizons were nonetheless vastly expanded through contact with seamen and merchants from foreign lands, especially the Arabs and the Persians. One result was the appearance of a number of geographical treatises and encyclopedic compilations on foreign countries such as Lo Shih's *T'ai-p'ing huan-yu chi,* Chu Yu's *P'ing-chou k'o-t'an,* Chou Ch'u-fei's *Ling-wai tai-ta,* and Chao Ju-kuo's *Chu-fan chih.* These works were written by scholars or officials in responsible positions in charge of maritime trade or with access to such information. The coverage by the thirteenth century had extended the geographical horizons to most of the major countries around the Mediterranean, the east coast of Africa, the East Indies and the lands of the Tungus and Yakuts in the Siberian taiga.

The Mongol conquest of China and the accession of the Yüan dynasty (1260–1368) ushered in a new era in China's relation to the rest of the world. With north China firmly under their control, the Mongol rulers continued their wars of conquest across the heartland of the Eurasian continent, thus enabling numerous Chinese to reach faraway lands in a variety of capacities. The best-known account is that of a journey of the eminent Taoist Ch'ang-ch'un Chen-jen in the early thirteenth century. He was invited by Genghis Khan, a conqueror who was also deeply curious about all religious teachings, to visit him at his western campaign headquarters at Samarkand. Together with a young disciple, the aged recluse traveled from Peking to Central Asia via a northerly route beyond the Gobi Desert and then westward across the Mongolian plateau. After crossing the Dzungarian Basin and passing the Ili Valley, the two followed the old caravan route through the Turan Basin, and the first meeting between the Taoist and the Khan took place near Kabul, where the Khan was conducting military oper-

ations against India. Following further discussions in Samarkand, the Taoist returned by way of the central Mongolian desert, thus twice traversing northern frontiers rarely visited by Chinese before this time.

Other records tell of officials, diplomats, and generals who traveled across the extended territories of the Mongol empire at the Khan's bidding. Some, like the general Kuo K'an, under Hulagu Khan, and Ch'ang Teh, an emissary of Mangu Khan, reached as far as Baghdad, Mecca, and northern Egypt. A merchant, Wang Ta-yüan, who responded to the prospect of widening maritime trade, traveled as far as Somalia and left an account of his experiences and observations. Khubilai (Kublai) Khan himself was responsible for several noteworthy efforts in exploration in connection with an attempt to colonize northern Borneo, reopening the road to Burma, and the search for the true source of the Yellow River. With the establishment of Hsingsu Hai, a lake deep in the Tibetan highlands, as the origin of the great river, erroneous beliefs long shrouded in mythology were finally laid to rest.

Two other outstanding achievements in geography during the Mongol dynasty were also attributable to the cultural crosscurrents of this era. One was a large map prepared by Chu Ssu-pen in the early fourteenth century, which survived in the form of an atlas. This work on China and the surrounding countries is distinguished by an outline of Africa with place names, suggesting that Chinese knowledge had encompassed the source of the Nile, the correct orientation of the Guinea coast, the location of the Congo, and the islands in the southern Indian Ocean. The other was a wooden model of the globe constructed by a central Asian for the Khan in 1273 and described in the official history of the Yüan dynasty. From the descriptions, the ratio of water to land on the globe was approximately 7 to 3. Furthermore, the use of square grids to indicate distances and locations of a number of Chinese cities was a surprisingly advanced technique.

Ming expeditions After Mongol rule was replaced by that of the house of Ming (1368–1644), China experienced a period of respite and consolidation under the founding emperor, T'ai-tsu (Hung-wu). When his second son, Chu Ti, who was later to become Emperor Yung-lo, usurped the throne from the designated heir, Chu Yun-wen, the latter reportedly fled overseas during the upheaval. The stage was thus set for the largest maritime undertaking in Chinese history, the announced purpose of which was to search for the deposed monarch. Considerations of international prestige and the gathering of strange animals and exotic products from abroad may also have contributed to the number and scope of the maritime expeditions. From 1405 to 1433 the eunuch commander CHENG HO conducted seven expeditions to the South China Sea, the Indian Ocean, the Persian Gulf, and the Red Sea, establishing diplomatic contact and tributary relations with scores of countries along the way. The total number of ships involved in the long voyages reached well over 1000, while the large crew on each voyage (averaging 27,500 men) included scholars, linguists, medics, astronomers, and technicians with a variety of skills.

Very detailed records were kept, and scholarly reports were written by several of Cheng Ho's aides who accompanied him on the expeditions. A unique nautical chart, preserved in a seventeenth-century work, provides further illustration of the routes, itinerary, and navigational techniques of the voyages. From the Yangtze Estuary, the first voyage went southward as far as the Strait of Malacca, where a local Chinese pirate was captured in a sea battle and brought back to Nanking for execution. During the second and third voyages, the fleet ventured into the Indian Ocean as far west as the Malabar coast of southern India, making visits along the way to many coastal states and insular countries in South and Southeast Asia. The fourth expedition went farther afield into the Persian Gulf and along the Hadramawt coast, while the fifth and sixth voyages explored the east coast of Africa from Mogadishu to Zanzibar and Kilwa and possibly beyond the Mozambique Channel. The seventh expedition, which called at most of the previously visited states, was delayed for several years by the death of its patron, Emperor Yung-lo, and Cheng Ho himself died during a stop at Calicut.

Summary   In viewing the record of Chinese exploration as a whole, several important stages are clearly recognizable. The first period, from the early Chou to the Late Han, is one of pioneer activities in several directions. The western expedition of Emperor Mu, the opening up of Szechwan and Yünnan, the search for the fabled islands in the "Eastern Sea," Chang Ch'ien's opening of the route to Western Asia, and the mission of Kan Ying to the Near East were all efforts to break out of physical isolation and establish contact with other lands and cultures.

The second era is characterized by the extensive travels of Buddhist pilgrims as a result of the spread of Buddhism in China. Seeking the true law of the religion and inspired by the heroic examples of such great pioneers as Fa-hsien and Hsüan-chuang, the pilgrims reached all parts of Central Asia, the Indian subcontinent, and many islands of Southeast Asia from the fourth to the seventh century.

The third period, from the end of the T'ang to the end of Mongol rule in China, is distinguished by an upsurge in maritime activities and an intensification of international contacts. An impressive accumulation of geographical knowledge resulted from the exchange with the Arabs and Persians, highlighted by the map of Chu Ssu-pen, which covered the world then known to China, including the African continent.

The fourth is a short period at the beginning of the Ming dynasty, marking the pinnacle of Chinese maritime activities. Utilizing the best navigational tech-

niques and the most up-to-date geographical information available, the expeditions under Cheng Ho covered nearly all the coastal regions in the Indian Ocean as well as the insular countries of Southeast Asia. This glorious but short-lived era was followed by the arrival of the Jesuit missionaries from Europe and the ensuing predominance of Western influence in China's knowledge of the world.

Judging from the level of technological capabilities displayed by the Ming expeditions as well as from the data on winds, currents, and coastal outlines at their disposal, it would not have been difficult for the fleet to have extended its journeys to the northern coast of Australia or around the Cape of Good Hope into the Atlantic. Such large-scale government-sponsored enterprises, however, came to an abrupt end in 1435, when a new policy of retrenchment and withdrawal was put into effect. The self-imposed isolation prevented the Chinese from communicating directly with the outside world, and soon the coastal waters were made hazardous by Japanese and other pirates. During this long period of inactivity in exploration, one man distinguished himself as a tireless visitor to mountains, rivers, and scenic spots in southwest China. Author of a famous travel journal and noted also for his literary attainment, Hsu Hung-tsu was not on any official assignment or religious quest but traveled purely for the sake of satisfying his curiosity. As a result, he became the first person to ascertain the true sources of the Yangtze and the Mekong in the Tibetan highlands.

With the arrival of the Jesuits at the end of the sixteenth century, China became the recipient of the latest European scientific knowledge on astronomy, mathematics, cartography, and the geography of the newly discovered continents. From Matteo Ricci's map of the world of 1584 to the work of Ferdinand Verbiest completed in 1764, the Chinese were able to obtain a clear picture of the earth's surface, including the spherical shape, the delineation of continents, and the locations of important countries and places in both the Old World and the New World. When distance was rapidly being conquered as a result of the industrial revolution in the West, China's inward-looking isolationism continued while the vitality of the empire waned. The nation was sadly unprepared to meet the challenge when the emergent Western powers appeared on its doorstep in the nineteenth century. For more than 100 years, unabating external pressures and incessant internal strife combined to drain away China's will and energy, and its once-active and colorful role in exploration has not been regained.

BIBLIOGRAPHY: Samuel Beal (tr.), *Si-Yu-Ki: Buddhist Records of the Western World*, London, 1884; Emil Bretschneider, *Medieval Researches from Eastern Asiatic Sources*, London, 1888; Chang Hsing-lang, *The Materials for a History of Sino-Foreign Relations* (in Chinese), 6 vols., Taipei, 1962; Kuei-sheng Chang, "Africa and the Indian Ocean in Chinese Maps of the Fourteenth and Fifteenth Centuries," *Imago Mundi*, vol. XXIV, 1970, pp. 21–30; id., "The Maritime Scene in China at the Dawn of Great European Discoveries," *Journal of the American Oriental Society*, vol. 94, no. 3, July–September 1974, pp. 347–359; Te-k'un Cheng, "The Travels of Emperor Mu," *North China Branch Journal*, Royal Asiatic Society, vol. LXIV, 1933, pp. 124–142, vol. LXV, 1934, pp. 128–149; Hui-chaio, *Kao-seng chuan* (in Chinese; biographies of eminent Buddhist monks), Nanking, 1889; Charles G. Leland, *Fusang, or The Discovery of America*, London, 1875; Ma Huan, *Ying-yai Sheng-lan: The Overall Survey of the Ocean's Shores*, tr. and ed. by J. V. G. Mills, Cambridge, England, 1970; Jeannette Mirsky (ed.), *The Great Chinese Travelers*, Chicago, 1974; Joseph Needham, *Science and Civilisation in China*, vol. 4, part 3, London, 1971; Paul Pelliot, "Li-Kien, autre nom du Ta-tsin," *Toung Pao*, vol. XVI, 1915, pp. 690–700; Ryusaku Tsunoda (tr.) and L. Carrington Goodrich (ed.), *Japan in the Chinese Dynastic Histories*, South Pasadena, Calif., 1951; Arthur Waley (tr.), *The Travels of an Alchemist*, London, 1931; id., *The Real Tripitaka*, London, 1952.

Kuei-sheng Chang and Jiu-fong L. Chang

Chirikov, Aleksey Ilyich *(1703–1748)* Russian seafarer. In 1715 he entered the Moscow School of Navigation, and in 1716 the St. Petersburg Naval Academy, where he was later assigned as a teacher of navigation. Between 1725 and 1730, as a lieutenant, he assisted Comdr. Vitus BERING on the First Kamchatka Expedition, organized by Peter I to establish whether Asia was connected with America. In 1728 on the ship *Sv. Gavriil (St. Gabriel)*, under Bering's command, he sailed to the Anadyrsky Zaliv (Gulf of Anadyr), discovering Zaliv Kresta (Krest Sound) and Guba Preobrazheniya (Preobrazheniya Bay) on its north shore. From there the vessel sailed as far as 67°18′N; he discovered St. Lawrence Island and "Diomede Island" (actually two islands) en route but did not sight the North American coast.

Between 1733 and 1741 Chirikov assisted Bering in organizing the complex Great Northern Expedition and within it the Second Kamchatka Expedition, which had the task of reaching the coast of North America. In 1740 Chirikov, commanding the ship *Sv. Pavel (St. Paul)*, left Okhotsk for Bolsheretsk on the west coast of Kamchatka, then rounded Kamchatka and arrived at Avachinskaya Guba (Avacha Bay) on the east coast, where he wintered. On June 5, 1741, the *Sv. Pavel* and Bering's *Sv. Pyotr (St. Peter)* left this harbor. After a vain hunt for the nonexistent "Gama Land," the two vessels lost each other. Chirikov sighted the American coast on July 15–16 at 55°36′N, mistaking the Alexander Archipelago for the mainland. At 57°58′N, fifteen men and both of the ship's boats were lost, and Chirikov was forced to turn back. On the return voyage he sighted the Kenai Peninsula and the islands of Afognak and Kodiak, Umnak, Adak (where they first met with Aleuts), Agattu, and Attu. On October 10, 1741, the *Sv. Pavel* arrived at Avachinskaya Guba. Chirikov's report is the first description of the northwest coast of North America and of the Aleuts. He repeated his voyage eastward but reached only Attu Island. On the way back he again discovered (after Bering) the Komandorskiye Ostrova (Commander Islands). On August 16, 1742, he went to Okhotsk and Yakutsk.

Ordered in 1743 "to undertake no more sea voyages," he was made captain commander in 1747 as a reward for his services. He spent the last years of his life in Moscow.

BIBLIOGRAPHY: F. A. Golder, *Bering's Voyages*, 2 vols., New York, 1922.

Richard A. Pierce

Clapperton, Hugh *(1788–1827)* Scottish explorer. The son of a Dumfriesshire surgeon, Clapperton went to sea at an early age as a cabin boy and later entered the British Navy. In 1820, having served on the East India Station and on the Great Lakes in Canada, he was asked to join Dr. Walter Oudney (1790–1824), who had been named by the British government to undertake a journey to the Bornu kingdom for the purpose of exploring the interior of Africa and tracing the course of the Niger River, which was believed to flow through Bornu. Oudney and Clapperton arrived in Tripoli in October 1821 and were soon joined by Dixon Denham (1786–1828), an army officer who claimed that he, not Oudney, was to be leader of the expedition, and by William Hillman, a shipwright. The following April they reached Marzūq (Murzuk) in Fezzan, where they were detained by the Bey, whose military assistance they initially felt was necessary for their progress southward. The expedition eventually left Marzūq under the care of a wealthy merchant, Abū-Bakr bu-Khullum, and reached the border of the Bornu kingdom in December 1822. On February 4, 1823, they became the first Europeans to see Lake Chad, and two weeks later they arrived at the Bornu capital, Kuka (modern Kukawa, Nigeria). On February 13, they saw the Komadugu Yobe River, and Oudney and Clapperton discovered the Chari (Shari) River in April.

Hugh Clapperton, Scottish explorer who traveled extensively in West Africa but failed to receive the recognition enjoyed by other explorers. [Library of Congress]

On December 14, 1823, Oudney, who believed that the answer to the Niger question could be found in Nupe, which lay southwest of Bornu, left Kuka with Clapperton while Denham stayed behind. When Oudney died on January 12, 1824, Clapperton continued alone into the Hausa country. After spending a month at Kano, he reached Sokoto, where the sultan, Muhammad Bello, gave him a cordial reception but informed him that it would be too dangerous to proceed to Nupe. Clapperton was therefore forced to give up his plan; he believed, however, that the real reason for the obstacles placed before him was that the local Arab merchants feared the consequences to themselves if he should succeed in reaching the sea and thereby open a path to British commerce. Bearing a letter from Bello to George IV, Clapperton returned to Kuka and, with Denham and Hillman, made his way back to Tripoli and London, which they reached in June 1825.

Despite the fact that his health had been shattered by his African journey, Clapperton immediately began to make plans to return, this time by way of the

Bight of Benin. According to his instructions, his primary objective would be "to establish a friendly intercourse" between Great Britain and Sokoto, but he was also to work for abolition of the slave trade, trace the course of the Niger, and visit Timbuktu. Clapperton set sail for Africa in August 1825, accompanied by a naval captain, two doctors, and four "domestics," including Richard Lemon LANDER.

After landing at Badagri, Nigeria, on November 30, 1825, the expedition set out for Katunga (Old Oyo), the Yoruba capital, which was reached on January 23, 1826. By this time Clapperton and Lander were the only surviving European members of the expedition. On March 31, Clapperton had his first glimpse of the Niger at Bussa, the site of the death of Mungo PARK. He and Lander crossed the river at the Komie ferry on April 10. They then proceeded to Kano and Sokoto, where Clapperton died on April 13, 1827. According to E. W. Bovill, Clapperton ranks among the most important African explorers but failed to get the recognition he deserved for three reasons: his own modesty and reserve; the enmity of Dixon Denham, who claimed for himself the principal achievements of the Bornu Mission in his *Narrative of Travels and Discoveries in Northern and Central Africa* (1826); and the fact that Clapperton's accurate belief that the Niger flowed into the Gulf of Guinea contradicted the cherished convictions of the influential John BARROW, Second Secretary of the Admiralty. Clapperton's account of his 1825–1827 journey was published as *Journal of a Second Expedition into the Interior of Africa* (1829).

BIBLIOGRAPHY: E. W. Bovill, *The Niger Explored*, London, 1968; Christopher Lloyd, *The Search for the Niger*, London, 1973; *Missions to the Niger: II, III, IV. The Bornu Mission, 1822–1825*, ed. by E. W. Bovill, Cambridge, England, 1966.

Clark, William *See* LEWIS, MERIWETHER, AND CLARK, WILLIAM.

Cocking (Cochin), Matthew (1743–1799) English fur trader and explorer. Cocking came to Rupert's Land, the domain of the Hudson's Bay Company, in 1765 in the service of the company as a "writer" at York Fort (York Factory) on Hudson Bay. Increasing competition from rival traders from Canada led the company to send servants inland to encourage the Indians to continue to bring furs down to the bay. Their accounts of the interior were "unintelligible and incoherent"; so when Cocking volunteered to go inland, his chief, Andrew Graham, gladly sent him off in 1772 in the hope that he would bring back a "rational account" of the little-known inland country. This hope was amply fulfilled. Cocking's log and journal, still to be seen in the archives of the Hudson's Bay Company in Winnipeg, Manitoba, describe the country and its people, the difference between the prairies (Cocking's "Barren Ground") and the "Woody Country," the fauna, vegetation, and weather.

Cocking, who did not even know how to steer the canoe he traveled in, made the arduous journey with a party of Indians returning home from York. Much troubled by illness, they went up the Hayes, Fox, and Minago Rivers, portaging to the Saskatchewan. Near the site of the old French Fort à la Corne the Indians "threw away" their canoes, traveling on, overland, to cross the South Saskatchewan, southwest of modern Battleford, to the Eagle Hills. They spent the winter wandering on the prairies and in the parklands, impounding buffalo and hunting. They encountered friendly Assiniboines, Blackfoot, and Cree but dreaded the Snakes, who then lived nearby. In April they returned to the river to build canoes for the journey down to York, where they arrived on June 18, 1773.

Sent in 1774 to help Samuel HEARNE establish the company's first inland post, Cocking went by Lake Winnipeg to test the feasibility of the route for large canoes. Delayed when he found two company servants left stranded by their Indians, Cocking was eventually taken on by other Indians, not to Basquia (The Pas) to meet Hearne but to their own country. He seized the opportunity to study the new region, the valley of the Red Deer west of Lake Winnipegosis.

Back at York in 1775, he was sent inland again despite "an ugly rupture," traveling by the Nelson River, to take over Cumberland House from Hearne. After yet another journey inland he was allowed to take up an appointment as master at Severn House. In 1781 he went to York as acting master. In failing health, Cocking returned in 1782 to the city of York, where he died, leaving an annuity to each of his three mixed-stock daughters in Rupert's Land.

The observations and records he had made on his inland journeys gave his employers "great satisfaction." Today, they are an invaluable source of information about western Canada in the early days of the fur trade.

BIBLIOGRAPHY: L. J. Burpee (ed.), "An Adventurer from Hudson Bay: Journal of Matthew Cocking, from York Factory to the Blackfoot Country, 1772–73," Royal Society of Canada, *Transactions*, 3d ser., vol. 2, sec. 2, 1908, pp. 91–121; A. S. Morton, *A History of the Canadian West, to 1870–71*, London, 1935.

Irene M. Spry

Collinson, Richard (1811–1883) British naval officer and Arctic explorer. Born in Gateshead, England, Collinson joined the Royal Navy as a midshipman in 1823. During the early part of his career, he established a good reputation as a surveying officer, first under Capt. Henry Foster on an expedition to South Atlantic and Antarctic waters between 1828 and 1831; then, during the 1830s, on the west coast of Africa and in the Pacific Ocean under Capt. Edward BELCHER. These activities brought him to the attention of the hydrographer, Francis Beaufort, who had him appointed surveying officer to the fleet during Britain's first Chinese war (1839–1842). He remained in China, surveying its coasts and rivers, until 1846, and his activities there won him promotion to captain and nomination as commander of the Bath.

His record as a nautical surveyor made him a natural choice as commander of one of the expeditions sent to search the uncharted waters of the Canadian Arctic for the missing 1845 expedition of Sir John FRANKLIN (*see* FRANKLIN EXPEDITION AND SEARCH). He was appointed to command HMS *Enterprise* and *Investigator,* which set out to search by way of Bering Strait in January 1850. The two ships were separated in the Pacific, and *Investigator,* under Comdr. Robert MCCLURE, passed through Bering Strait first. Collinson arrived there too late in 1850 and entered the Arctic only in July 1851. By then McClure had already explored Prince of Wales Strait and the south and west coasts of Banks Island, and Collinson unwittingly duplicated these discoveries. In 1852 he took his ship through Coronation Gulf and Dease Strait, a dangerous, rocky channel previously navigated only by small boats, and found a winter harbor in Cambridge Bay, Victoria Island. In the following spring, he took a sledge party to examine part of the east coast of Victoria Island. Finally, after a third Arctic winter on the north coast of Alaska, he set off homeward through Bering Strait and reached England in May 1855.

Through no fault of his own, Collinson's long Arctic expedition produced few tangible results; his extensive explorations merely repeated discoveries made a year or two earlier by McClure and others. Moreover, disciplinary problems throughout the voyage and the Admiralty's unwillingness to punish the offenders afterward left him disillusioned with the Navy; he never again accepted an appointment. Instead, he spent the rest of his life in the service of Trinity House. In 1875 he became deputy master, the effective head of that establishment, and in the same year received his knighthood in belated recognition of his services to the Royal Navy.

BIBLIOGRAPHY: Richard Collinson, *Journal of H.M.S. Enterprise, on the Expedition in Search of Sir John Franklin's Ships by Behring Strait, 1850–55,* London, 1889.

Clive A. Holland

Columbus, Christopher (Italian: **Cristoforo Colombo;** Spanish: **Cristóbal Colón; 1451–1506**)   Italian navigator in the service of Spain and discoverer of America. There is no reason to doubt that Columbus was born in Genoa, the son and grandson of weavers, though some writers have claimed him for other nationalities. He became a seaman at an early age and in 1476 sailed with a convoy of merchant ships bound for Lisbon and England. When a French war fleet attacked and scattered the convoy off the southern coast of Portugal, Columbus took refuge in the town of Lagos. He then traveled to Lisbon, where there was a large colony of Genoese—captains and seamen, businessmen, scientists, and artisans—among whom was Columbus's younger brother Bartholomew, who had left Genoa before Columbus and had learned the map maker's trade in Lisbon.

In Portugal, at that time the leading nation in exploration, the poorly educated Columbus had an opportunity to expand his navigational skills and his knowledge of geography and cosmography. In 1479 he married Filipa Perestrelo e Moniz, daughter of one of the first colonizers of Madeira, who bore him a son, Diego, about 1480 and died a few years later. Meanwhile, Columbus had made several voyages, including at least one to the Gold Coast of Africa. There is also a possibility that he may have sailed to Iceland in 1477.

Although Columbus had prospered in his adopted country, by 1484 he was prepared to abandon everything, for he had become possessed by an idea which dominated him completely: to reach the Orient, not by struggling overland or by sailing around Africa (if that were ever proved possible), but by striking boldly across the Atlantic, the "Ocean Sea" that was then imagined to circle the inhabited world.

Columbus was not the first person to think of sailing west to Asia. Nor did anyone seriously challenge the theoretical possibility of such a voyage; every educated person knew that the world was round. The problem was a practical one. According to the ancient Greek geographer PTOLEMY, whose teachings were still accepted by most of Columbus's contemporaries, the ocean distance from the westernmost point of Europe to the easternmost point of Asia was more than 10,000 miles (16,090 kilometers). No ship of that time could accomplish so great an ocean voyage. Even if the ship held together, no crew could hope to survive the inevitable hazards and diseases of many months at sea.

Although Ptolemy, as it turned out, underestimated the size of the earth by a full quarter, Columbus, after studying other Greek and Arab authorities, concluded that the earth was smaller still. Furthermore, he believed that the Eurasian landmass stretched farther around the globe than Ptolemy said. And finally, from reading the famous account of Marco POLO of his sojourn in China, Columbus believed in the existence, some 1500 miles (2414 kilometers) off the eastern coast of Asia, of the fabulously wealthy island kingdom of Cipangu, or Japan. Thus, according to Columbus's calculations, the distance from the Canary Islands (the westernmost jumping-off place for an Atlantic crossing) to Japan was only 2400 miles (3862 kilometers), a distance well within the range of contemporary sailing ships.

In 1484 Columbus presented his project, which he called the "Enterprise of the Indies," to King John II of Portugal. John turned it over to a committee of maritime experts, who rejected it. Angry and disappointed, Columbus determined to take the Enterprise of the Indies elsewhere: to Spain, Portugal's traditional enemy.

Columbus in Spain   Soon after landing at Palos, Columbus called at the nearby Franciscan monastery of

Christopher Columbus, Italian navigator sailing for the Spanish crown, who discovered America by mistake and died believing that he had found the fabulous Indies. [Library of Congress]

La Rábida. The hospitable monks agreed to provide shelter and schooling for Diego while Columbus went about his business in Spain. Moreover, they gave him introductions to learned and influential people. Within a few months Columbus was invited to present himself at the royal court, then in Córdoba. At the beginning of May 1486, in the Alcázar at Córdoba, Columbus was received by King Ferdinand and Queen Isabella. As in Portugal, the Enterprise of the Indies was turned over to a specially appointed commission of scientists, scholars, and mariners for examination.

It was not until 1490 that the commission made its report, rejecting Columbus's proposal. A second appeal in 1491 apparently brought a favorable report from another committee, but the project almost foundered because of Columbus's demands in the event he succeeded: a patent of nobility; the title Admiral of the Ocean Sea and all the privileges of a Castilian admiral to be hereditary in his family; the offices of governor and viceroy of all the lands he should discover, these also to be hereditary in his family; a tenth of all profits to be derived from his discoveries. The Royal Council rejected the enterprise and Columbus was dismissed, but the Queen changed her mind after Luis de Santangel, keeper of King Ferdinand's privy purse, pointed out to her that the risks of such a voyage and even Columbus's price were not too large compared with the advantages Spain would derive if he succeeded.

The first voyage Back in Palos, Columbus obtained three ships, the *Niña, Pinta,* and *Santa María.* The first two were caravels, small and fast. The *Santa María* was a *nau,* a somewhat larger, rounder, and slower ship. All together, Columbus recruited about ninety men and boys for the voyage. Among them were three members of a prominent seafaring family of Palos; Martín Alonso Pinzón, who became captain of the *Pinta;* his younger brother, Vicente Yáñez Pinzón, who took command of the *Niña;* and a third brother, Francisco, who was first mate of the *Pinta.* Columbus himself was captain of the *Santa María* and captain general of the fleet.

After leaving Palos on August 3, the little fleet put in at Las Palmas on Gran Canaria (Grand Canary Island), where a damaged rudder on the *Pinta* was rebuilt and the *Niña* was equipped with a square rig like those of its consorts. The remainder of the voyage was fast and uneventful. However, as each day carried the Spanish mariners farther into an ocean that, according to the most respected authorities, was for all practical purposes shoreless, the men became increasingly alarmed, and by October 10 the crew of the flagship was near mutiny. The next day there were undeniable signs of land, and on October 12 land appeared 2 hours after midnight.

Columbus's first landfall, Guanahaní, is now officially San Salvador or Watling Island and is one of the Bahama Islands. Columbus soon realized that this was not Cipangu. Only the little gold ornaments that the friendly, marveling natives (naturally he called them Indians) wore in their noses suggested that he was anywhere near Japan, perhaps somewhere in the Japanese archipelago. The Indians assured him that the gold came from islands west and southwest of Guanahaní. Columbus did not tarry, and on October 14 the ships put out to sea. Cuba, which he reached on October 28, was no different: the same green forest, the same palm-thatched huts. Cuba, however, was

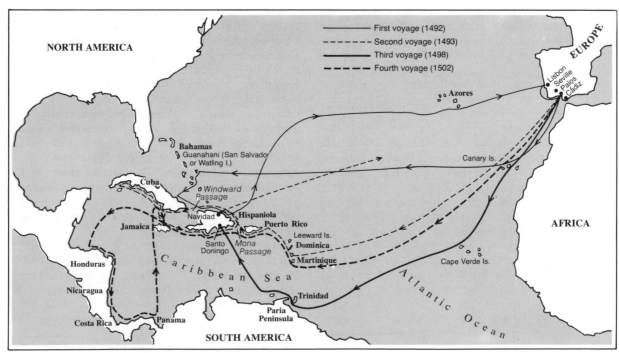

Christopher Columbus's voyages, 1492-1504.

large. "It is certain," wrote Columbus on November 1, "that this is the mainland, and that I am before [the Chinese cities] Zayto and Quisay, a hundred leagues, a little more or less, distant from one and the other."

From mid-November to December 5, the *Santa María, Niña,* and *Pinta* worked their way eastward along the northern coast of Cuba. Disappointment, perplexity, exasperation mounted. On November 22 Martín Alonso Pinzón, hearing that there was gold on Great Inagua Island, deserted the others. Helplessly Columbus watched the *Pinta* disappear to the east. The *Santa María* and *Niña* continued alone along the Cuban shore.

On December 5 they crossed the Windward Passage to Hispaniola. Now at last Columbus began to see gold in quantity. The gold, the Indians told him, came from mines in the interior of the island, a region they called Cibao. To Columbus, Cibao sounded enough like Cipangu to convince him that the object of his expedition was close at hand, but on Christmas Eve the *Santa María* grounded on a coral reef; its seams opened, and it filled with water.

With only the *Niña* remaining of his three vessels, Columbus decided to return to Spain as soon as possible. Leaving thirty-nine men at a fort that he named La Navidad for the day of its founding, Christmas, he sailed in the *Niña* for Spain on January 4, 1493. Two days later, while beating eastward along Hispaniola's northern coast, the *Niña* encountered the errant *Pinta.* After a difficult return voyage, both vessels arrived safely at Palos. In Barcelona Columbus was well received by Ferdinand and Isabella, but instead of basking in his triumph he began to prepare for a second voyage.

The second voyage Columbus embarked from Cádiz on September 25, 1493. This time he commanded a fleet of seventeen vessels carrying some 1500 men, not only seamen but soldiers, artisans, priests, and royal officials. Besides provisions for the voyage the fleet carried seeds, plants, domestic animals, and tools of every kind, for the primary object of this voyage was to establish a permanent colony in the Indies. Columbus also took his youngest brother, Diego, to serve him as confidant and trusted lieutenant.

On November 3, 21 days after leaving the Canaries, he sighted the island of Dominica. For 3 more weeks the fleet worked its way north and west through the Leeward Islands to Puerto Rico, then across to Hispaniola. On November 28 Columbus anchored before the charred, deserted ruins of La Navidad, which had been leveled by the Indians. Abandoning the site as unhealthy, he established a new capital farther east, which he called Isabela.

The admiral himself was eager to resume his explorations. In February he sent twelve of his seventeen ships back to Spain with an urgent appeal that three or four caravels be sent immediately with provisions of every kind. In April, leaving his brother Diego in charge of the colony, Columbus with three caravels sailed off to the west. From Hispaniola he crossed over to Cuba's southern coast. For 6 weeks he picked his way laboriously among many small islands and through treacherous shoal waters. Fifty miles (80 kil-

Columbus and his fleet set sail for the Indies with the blessings of Ferdinand and Isabella. [Library of Congress]

ometers) from the southwesternmost point of Cuba the coast bends southward. Here, on June 13, Columbus turned back. Although sorely troubled to have found no evidence that he was in China, he was nevertheless satisfied that Cuba, just as he had suspected, was a peninsula of the Asian mainland. During July and August the little fleet beat its way eastward, in torrid heat, against head winds and currents. From Cabo Cruz, Cuba, it turned south to Jamaica, then crossed the Windward Passage to the southern coast of Hispaniola.

Sick with arthritis and malaria, Columbus returned to Isabela in September to find the colony in a state of anarchy. Diego had proved an ineffectual governor. There was, however, one cause for rejoicing: the arrival of Christopher's other brother, Bartholomew. To reestablish his control over the mutinous Spaniards, Columbus, reluctant to exercise his great authority as viceroy, turned them upon the inoffensive Indians. Many were rounded up and shipped off to Spain as slaves, the only product of the island that was readily exportable.

The third voyage Despite the complaints of returned colonists, Columbus found his sovereigns' confidence in him still unshaken. He immediately proposed a third voyage of discovery, this one to seek a mainland that he had heard of lying south of the islands already discovered. Ferdinand and Isabella agreed, but they were preoccupied with European politics, and it was 2 years before Columbus was able to assemble eight ships. Two he sent ahead, in January 1498, with much-needed supplies for Hispaniola. Six others departed from Seville in May.

At the Canaries Columbus dispatched three ships directly to Hispaniola. With the other three he continued south to the Cape Verde Islands before turning west. On July 31 he raised the island of Trinidad. Passing along the southern shore of Trinidad, he turned north through the Gulf of Paria toward Venezuela's mountainous Paria Peninsula. From the great quantities of fresh water being emptied into the gulf by rivers, he correctly deduced that he was skirting a continent. If Marco Polo was correct, this southern continent was separated from Asia to the north by a strait that led to the Spice Islands and India. Despite his eagerness to explore farther, he left the coast of Venezuela on August 15 and hurried north to Hispaniola. On August 31 he reached Santo Domingo, the new and permanent capital of the island, whose location, on Hispaniola's southern coast, he had fixed before leaving for Spain in 1496.

Here Columbus found a Spanish rebellion in progress against Bartholomew. Although Columbus came to terms with the rebels, complaints about his conduct reached Ferdinand and Isabella, who sent Francisco de Bobadilla to Hispaniola with full powers not only to investigate the Viceroy's conduct but to replace him if necessary. After arriving in Santo Domingo on August 24, 1500, Bobadilla ordered the Columbus brothers arrested and sent home for trial.

The fourth voyage In Spain Ferdinand and Isabella ordered Columbus released but said nothing about his returning to Hispaniola to resume the governorship. Instead he was kept idly in attendance at court.

Meanwhile other mariners, both Spanish and Portuguese, were busy extending Columbus's discoveries. Gradually Europeans begin to suspect that this was not Asia at all but a "new world," stretching perhaps from the Arctic to deep within the Southern Hemisphere. Columbus, however, still believed that he had been to the Indies and was eager to return and prove it. In March 1502, Ferdinand and Isabella authorized a fourth voyage by Columbus. The admiral's plan was to push beyond Cuba into the western Caribbean, there to search for the imagined strait between the northern and southern continents that opened into the Indian Ocean. He sailed from Cádiz on May 11, 1502, with four ships and 140 men and boys. With him on the flagship was his 14-year-old illegitimate son, Ferdinand. Bartholomew commanded one of the other ships.

This time Columbus retraced the route of his second voyage: first to the Canaries, then west by south across the Atlantic. On June 15 he sighted Martinique, then turned north through the Leeward Islands to Puerto Rico and across the Mona Passage to Hispaniola. At Santo Domingo on June 29 the new governor, Nicolás de Ovando, refused Columbus's request for permission to enter the harbor.

On July 14, Columbus left Hispaniola behind, passed between Jamaica and Cuba, and continued into the western Caribbean, reaching the coast of Honduras at the beginning of August. Against head winds and in foul weather, he followed the coast eastward for a month, then southward past Nicaragua and Costa Rica to Panama in search of a strait. From the Indians he learned that he was coasting an isthmus between two seas. This, he was sure, was the Malay Peninsula; China lay to the north, and India was only a few days' sail across the sea on the other side.

In Panama gold was plentiful, and Columbus's zeal to find the strait diminished. In February 1503, he established a settlement at Santa María de Belén near the gold. The Spaniards, however, soon provoked the Indians to hostilities. Belén had to be abandoned with the loss of ten men and a ship. The remaining three ships followed the coast of Panama to the east. In April another ship was lost. At the beginning of May the two surviving ships left the coast and turned north toward Hispaniola. The ships were in such poor condition, however, that Columbus was forced to put in at St. Ann's Bay, Jamaica. The ships could go no farther, and Columbus ordered them beached. He was marooned.

Early in July Columbus dispatched his most trusted captain, Diego Méndez, with two large dugout canoes manned by a dozen Spaniards and twenty Indians to carry the news of his situation to Santo Domingo. Méndez delivered Columbus's message to Ovando, but the Governor was in no hurry to rescue the troublesome admiral. Not until June 1504 did a small, barely seaworthy caravel sent by Méndez arrive to remove about 100 survivors.

Exhausted and ill upon his return to Spain in November 1504, Columbus settled in Seville. Although he was now a wealthy man, he had many grievances against the crown, and he devoted his last years to a fruitless effort to secure confirmation of the titles, offices, and pecuniary privileges promised him in 1492. He died in Valladolid on May 20, 1506, still believing that he had four times sailed to Asia. He was buried in Valladolid, but his remains were later transferred to Seville. Finally, in 1541 they were carried across the Atlantic and interred in the cathedral at Santo Domingo.

BIBLIOGRAPHY: Fernando Colón, *The Life of the Admiral Christopher Columbus by His Son Ferdinand*, tr. by Benjamin Keen, New Brunswick, N.J., 1959; Samuel Eliot Morison, *Admiral of the Ocean Sea: A Life of Christopher Columbus*, 2 vols., Boston, 1942; id., *The European Discovery of America: The Southern Voyages, A.D. 1492–1616*, New York, 1974; Charles E. Nowell, "The Columbus Question: A Survey of Recent Literature and Present Opinion," *American Historical Review*, vol. XLIV, 1939, pp. 802–822; Martin Torodash, "Columbus Historiography since 1939," *Hispanic American Historical Review*, vol. XLVI, November 1966, pp. 409–428.

Cook, Frederick Albert (1865–1940) American explorer who claimed to have been the first man to reach the North Pole. Cook was born in Callicoon Depot on the Delaware River in New York, the son of a German immigrant who had changed his name from Koch to Cook. After the elder Cook died in 1870, the family moved to Brooklyn. Like his father, Frederick was trained as a doctor, studying first at the College of Physicians and Surgeons of Columbia University and later at the Medical College of New York University.

Cook's Arctic career began in 1891, when he was engaged as surgeon and ethnologist on an expedition to Greenland led by Robert E. PEARY. After two subsequent voyages to Greenland in 1893 and 1894, Cook in 1897 joined the Belgian Antarctic Expedition led by the oceanographer Adrien de Gerlache and described his experiences in *Through the Antarctic Night* (1900). Cook next turned his attention to Mount McKinley, the highest peak in North America, and announced in September 1906 that he had become the first man to climb the mountain to its summit. This effort led to his second book, *To the Top of the Continent* (1908).

Cook left Gloucester, Massachusetts, on the first leg of his North Pole expedition on July 3, 1907, aboard the schooner *John R. Bradley*. From Annoatok, Greenland, he traveled across Ellesmere Island and reached Svartevoeg (now Cape Stallworthy) on the northern tip of Axel Heiberg Island on March 17, 1908. The next day he left Svartevoeg for his final dash to the pole, accompanied by four Eskimos, two of whom were sent back at the end of the third day. According to Cook, he reached the pole on April 21, 1908. He followed a different route on his return from the pole but arrived at Annoatok in the spring of 1909.

The American explorer Frederick Albert Cook, who claimed to be the first man to reach the North Pole. Although he would maintain the truth of his claim until his death, a later conviction for fraud did nothing to convince his audience, and majority opinion has awarded the polar laurel to his rival, Robert E. Peary. [Library of Congress]

Finding sportsman Harry Payne Whitney there, Cook said, he decided to leave his field notes and instruments with him for safekeeping while he traveled south. At Egedesminde, Greenland, he took ship for Copenhagen. During the voyage he announced his conquest of the pole and was hailed as a hero in Denmark and in New York, where he received a tumultuous reception on September 21, 1909.

Meanwhile, however, Cook's claim had been publicly challenged by Peary, who had himself reached the pole on April 6, 1909. Cook steadily lost credibility in the bitter controversy that followed, especially after a committee of experts appointed by the University of Copenhagen concluded on December 21, 1909, that the material submitted by Cook was insufficient for them to accept his claim. Peary and other critics of Cook attacked him on several grounds. They pointed to his lack of verifiable observations and questioned his assertion that he had left any field notes with Whitney. They said that the two Eskimos who had supposedly accompanied him to the pole denied being there. Not only were many other questions raised about Cook's North Pole expedition, but it was also charged that he had perpetrated earlier frauds: that he had never ascended Mount McKinley to its summit and that he had tried to pass off as his own a dictionary of a South American Indian language he had acquired during the Belgian Antarctic Expedition. For his part, in *My Attainment of the Pole* (1911) and in public lectures, Cook steadfastly maintained that his account of reaching the pole was truthful. He retained a following of believers who argued that the charges leveled against him were untrue and that they were orchestrated by an influential lobby of Peary supporters.

The controversy died down during World War I, but Cook again gained notoriety in 1923 when he was sentenced to 14 years in prison for using the mails to defraud oil-company investors. After serving 5 years in the federal penitentiary at Leavenworth, Kansas, he was paroled in 1930 and pardoned in 1940 shortly before his death.

BIBLIOGRAPHY: Andrew A. Freeman, *The Case for Doctor Cook*, New York, 1961; John Edward Weems, *Race for the Pole*, New York, 1960; Theon Wright, *The Big Nail: The Story of the Cook-Peary Feud*, New York, 1970.

Capt. James Cook, known as a great dispeller of myths, brought his crews twice across the world without one death from scurvy. [Library of Congress]

Cook, James (1728–1779) English naval officer, surveyor, and explorer. Cook was born on October 27, 1728, in Marton-in-Cleveland, Yorkshire, the son of James Cook, a Scottish agricultural laborer, and Grace Pace, a local woman. Cook's childhood was spent mostly at Great Ayton, Yorkshire, near his birthplace. He was a scholar between the ages of 8 and 12 and an apprentice to a grocer and dry-goods merchant at the age of 16. In 1746 he became a sailor in the Whitby coal trade under agreement with a shipowner named John Walker. As a mate to a shipmaster sailing collier cats to and from the port of London, young Cook found the spirit of ships and the sea compelling. The tricky and dangerous navigation of the North Sea was for him his seaman's nursery. Perhaps the sight of great three-decker armed ships at Chatham dockyard on the banks of the Thames or news of the wider world caught his imagination, but in any case at the age of 27 Cook volunteered as an able seaman in the Royal Navy.

Volunteers of Cook's type were rare; within weeks he was master's mate of HMS *Eagle,* on which he was to become acquainted with his future patron, Capt. Hugh Palliser. In June 1757 he passed his master's examinations. Master, RN, was a prestigious though uncommissioned service rank which pointed Cook out as a career professional in the handling of ships and in the surveying of waters. A varied service of patrols, conquests, and surveys took him to Ireland, Halifax, Louisbourg (Louisburg), Quebec, and Newfoundland during and immediately after the Seven Years' War. In those years he distinguished himself by charting the St. Lawrence as far as Quebec, a service which allowed the amphibious expedition under Maj. Gen. James Wolfe and Vice Adm. Sir Charles Saunders to dislodge the French from dominant power in Canada. Then, for 5 years, he patiently made charts of Newfoundland which facilitated the continued safety of that other important nursery of seamen, the cod fishery of the Grand Banks, and, moreover, the security of traffic coming in and going out of the St. Lawrence, whether through the Strait of Belle Isle on the north or Cabot Strait on the south. Surveying was the harbinger of commerce and settlement, and on Canada's eastern coasts Cook's surveys were in themselves an important imperial service. His *New Chart of the River St. Lawrence,* published in 1760, and his soundings, coastal profiles, and sailing notes which were published in the famous *North American Pilot* (1775) provided a firm basis of hydrographic knowledge about the great river and the great island that was to be useful for a century. His work marked a new standard in British hydrographic surveying, combining land-based trigonometrical surveys with small-boat work on the seaward side.

In the spring of 1764 Cook was given his first command, the 68-ton schooner *Grenville.* He converted her to a brig in order to make her more effective, an index of his intent on perfection. In July 1766 he carried out observations of the sun's eclipse; his figures were printed in the Royal Society's *Philosophical Transactions* for 1768. When Cook returned to England for the winter of 1767–1768, his Newfoundland work was completed in its main outline. By this time he had mastered surveying, and his skills and industry had bought him to the attention of the Lords of the Admiralty at a critical time of British overseas expansion.

In April 1768 he was given command of a Whitby collier cat renamed HMS *Endeavour* to make a British observation of the transit of the planet Venus and to determine the existence of lands in the Southern Pacific Ocean. On May 25, he was appointed first lieutenant, and in August he left in her for the South Seas. At Tahiti on June 3, 1769, Cook fulfilled the principal objective of the expedition by observing the transit of Venus across the disk of the sun. Thereafter he charted and claimed the Society Islands, so named because they were contiguous to one another. Then he began his search for the Unknown Southern Land (Terra Australis Incognita) widely believed to exist in the Pacific. On October 8, 1769, he reached the northern tip of New Zealand, and 6 months later he proved the insularity of New Zealand's two main islands by circumnavigating them. In mid-1770 he mapped 2000 miles (3200 kilometers) of Australia's eastern coast, claimed it for Great Britain, and named it New South Wales. He nearly lost the *Endeavour* on the Great Barrier Reef but reached home on July 12, 1771, without a single death from scurvy, a historic feat. These discoveries won him prominence, promotion to captain, and the opportunity to sail again.

A year later, on July 13, 1772, Cook sailed again for the Pacific, this time in HMS *Resolution* and *Adventure.* His object was to press the search for the Unknown Southern Continent. From Cape Town the party sailed south, becoming the first men in history to cross the Antarctic Circle. When progress was blocked by ice, Cook moved north. He spent 1773 in Polynesian discoveries. In January 1774, Cook headed south again and reached his southernmost point at 71°10′S. On his long voyage Cook charted and named the New Hebrides, New Caledonia, and South Georgia. He arrived in England on July 30, 1775, having completed a sea journey of 70,000 miles (113,000 kilometers) during which none of his crew had died from scurvy. He had also destroyed speculation of a great and fertile southern continent. Now he was, as the 4th Earl of Sandwich, the first lord of the Admiralty, rightly said, "the first navigator in Europe." In 1776 the Royal Society awarded him the Copley Medal for his report on scurvy.

In August 1775, Cook was appointed to a post of retirement as captain at Greenwich Hospital. He rejected this in favor of yet a third voyage to the Pacific, one that would take him to new places and doubtless win him new honors. In April 1776 he accepted the challenge to find the NORTHWEST PASSAGE, a quest that had defeated Europe's best seamen for several centuries. The overland discoveries of Samuel HEARNE in 1771 indicated a seaway in northern latitudes across the North American continent. Russian maps published in 1774 indicated that Alaska was an island, separated from the North American continent by a strait which ran to the north. For these reasons Cook was instructed to search for the western entrance to the Northwest Passage in about 65°N on the northwest coast of North America and to penetrate to the north and east via Bering Strait. Meanwhile the Admiralty sent two expeditions, commanded by Richard Pickersgill and Walter Young, to search for the Atlantic entrance near Baffin Bay.

On July 12, 1776, the *Resolution* sailed again for the Pacific, this time accompanied by her new consort, the *Discovery.* In December 1777, after numerous stops at South Pacific islands, they entered the North Pacific, where Cook discovered Christmas Island. On January 18 they saw and visited the Sandwich (Hawaiian) Islands, perhaps not the first Europeans to call there but influential enough in the history of the islands to be mentioned. From March 7 to August 18, 1778, Cook's ships charted the coast of North America from Oregon to Bering Strait. Cook spent little time on the southern section of the coast, for his instructions specified that he was to spend his time in searching for the Northwest Passage in higher latitudes. He missed the entrance to the Strait of Juan de Fuca and was of the opinion that there was little probability that such a strait existed. He spent most of April at Nootka Sound, Vancouver Island, where he and his men compiled authoritative accounts of Indian life on the northwest coast. After refitting the ships, Cook sailed northward to Unalaska and through Bering Strait. He reached his farthest north in 70°44'N, where ice prevented further advance. The ships returned to Hawaii to winter. There, on February 14, 1779, an encounter with natives cost Cook and four marines their lives. Clashes with natives had occurred elsewhere (though not everywhere) during his three Pacific voyages, but in this case Cook showed perhaps less than his usual judgment. Their commander gone, the ships sailed north again, but the Northwest Passage eluded them. On October 4, 1780, the *Resolution* and *Discovery* returned to England from one of the longest voyages of discovery in history.

Cook died in his fifty-first year, leaving a wife, Elizabeth, and three living children in London. His memorials are many: his discoveries and surveys contributed to the rise of British power in Canada, the development of the cod fishery, the colonization of Australia and New Zealand, the sending of missionaries to the South Pacific, the beginnings of the maritime fur trade between the northwest coast of North America and China, and the origins of British political

James Cook's three voyages, 1768–1780.

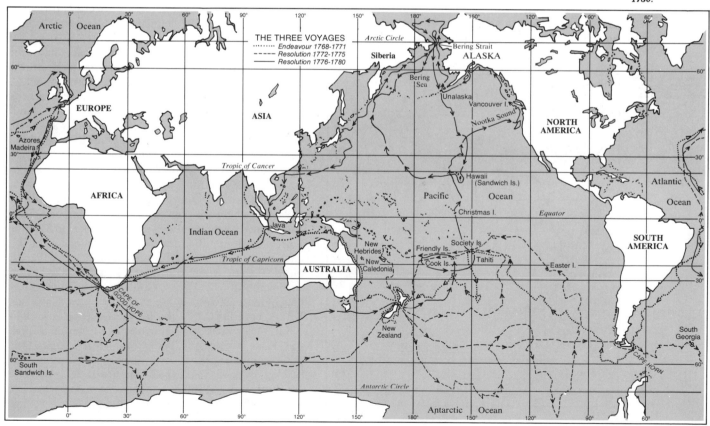

involvement in British Columbia. By his work also, myths of great unknown lands and northwest passages were disproved. And, not least, he proved that long-distance voyaging by sail was practical and could be healthy.

See also NATURAL-HISTORY EXPLORATION.

BIBLIOGRAPHY: J. C. Beaglehole (ed.), *The Journals of Captain James Cook*, 3 vols. in 4, Cambridge, England, 1955–1967; id., *The Life of Captain James Cook*, Stanford, Calif., 1974; Alan Villiers, *Captain James Cook*, New York, 1967.

Barry M. Gough

Coronado, Francisco Vásquez (Vázquez) de *(ca. 1510 – 1554)* Spanish explorer. Born in Salamanca of a noble family, Coronado arrived in the New World in 1535 in the party of Antonio de Mendoza, first viceroy of New Spain (Mexico). He married Beatriz de Estrada, wealthy heiress of a royal official, and in 1538 was named governor of New Galicia, a province on the west coast of Mexico. In this capacity he provided supplies and other assistance to Fray Marcos de Niza, a Franciscan who had been selected to investigate the country north of the Mexican frontier and to verify the reports of Álvar Núñez CABEZA DE VACA. Accompanied by the slave Esteban, who had been a member of Cabeza de Vaca's party, Fray Marcos left the Mexican town of Culiacán on March 7, 1539, and returned to Mexico about 5½ months later with news of a rich and populous city called Cíbola, which he said he had seen at a distance, and of cities even more impressive than Cíbola farther off. There has been considerable disagreement among scholars over the extent of the friar's travels and the truth of his assertion that he had actually seen Cíbola. Mendoza, who had been interested in northern exploration for several years, was convinced by the friar's tales, however, and named Coronado to head an expedition to Cíbola.

Mendoza reviewed the expeditionary force of approximately 335 Spaniards and hundreds of Mexican Indians at Compostela, the capital of New Galicia, on February 22, 1540. The army spent several days at Culiacán, from which Coronado set out on April 22 with about 100 Spaniards and some Indians while the main force stayed behind. After traveling up the Sonora Valley, crossing the Gila River, and entering the Colorado Plateau, they reached the Zuñi pueblo of Hawikuh in what is now western New Mexico on July 7, 1540. This was the city of Cíbola, which Fray Marcos had depicted in such glowing terms, but the Spaniards found none of the riches described by the imaginative friar, who had accompanied the expedition and was now sent back to Mexico in disgrace. With him went Melchior Díaz, who was instructed to make contact with the main army, which he found in the Sonora Valley near modern Ures and started for Cíbola in mid-September. Díaz then set out for the Gulf of California in the hope of finding a supporting fleet commanded by Hernán de Alarcón, which carried supplies needed by the Spaniards at Cíbola. Díaz and his party arrived at the Colorado River near its confluence with the Gila River, where they found a message from Alarcón, who had concluded that he would not be able to locate Coronado and had returned to Mexico. Díaz then led his party across the Colorado, but their explorations were cut short when Díaz was accidentally wounded by a lance in December and died 3 weeks later.

Meanwhile, on July 15, 1540, Coronado had sent Pedro de Tovar and Fray Juan de Padilla to the northwest from Cíbola to a province called Tusayan, where they found seven Hopi settlements and heard of a great river to the west. García López de Cárdenas and a small group of Spaniards set out on August 25, 1540, to find this river, which they saw from the rim of the Grand Canyon. The Spaniards spent 3 days trying to descend to the river, the Colorado, but were able to get only a third of the way down. On August 29, 1540, Coronado sent out another party led by Hernando de Alvarado which traveled east to the pueblo of Acoma and thence northeast to Tiguex in the Rio Grande Valley north of Albuquerque. After exploring the Tiguex area, the Spaniards moved east to Cicuye (Pecos, New Mexico), where they met a Plains Indian whom they dubbed "the Turk." Guided by the Turk, they continued eastward along the Pecos and Canadian Rivers, entering the Plains and getting their first sight of buffalo, which they said were as numerous as fish in the sea. Meanwhile, both Coronado's force and the main army had set out for Tiguex, which became the headquarters of the expedition for 2 years despite conflicts with the Indians during the severe winter of 1540–1541.

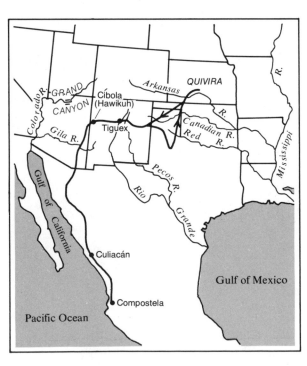

Francisco Vásquez de Coronado's route, 1540–1542.

Coronado and the army left Tiguex on April 23, 1541, to search for a land called Quivira, which the Turk had described as being rich in gold and silver. Heading east, the Spaniards traveled to Cicuye, crossed the Pecos River, and moved into the seemingly endless high plains of the Texas Panhandle known as the Staked Plains (Llano Estacado). When they came to a great *barranca* (canyon; identified with Tule Canyon by Herbert E. Bolton), the change in the terrain, coupled with the statements of the local Teyas (Texas) Indians, convinced Coronado that he had been deceived by the Turk, who now confessed that he had indeed led the Spaniards astray. As their supplies were growing low, it was decided that Coronado should continue the quest for Quivira with thirty horsemen while the rest of the army returned to Tiguex. Traveling to the northeast, Coronado reached the Arkansas River, which was forded near what is now Dodge City, Kansas, and followed it downstream to Great Bend, where he met some Quivira (Wichita) Indians. He left the river and continued in a northeasterly direction until he came to the end of Quivira in the vicinity of modern Lindsborg, Kansas. Once again he was disappointed to find only villages of straw-thatched houses without any evidence of precious metals. The Turk was executed, and the Spaniards returned to Tiguex, where they spent the winter of 1541–1542. In December Coronado was seriously hurt when he fell from his mount and was struck in the head by a companion's horse. He began the return trek to Mexico the following April. At least two Franciscan friars, Juan de Padilla and Luis de Escalona, and possibly a third, Juan de la Cruz, elected to stay behind to proselytize the Indians.

Viceroy Mendoza was disappointed by the outcome of Coronado's expedition, but relations between the two men remained harmonious, and Coronado continued to serve as governor of New Galicia until 1544. He then retired to Mexico City, where he was a member of the municipal council, but his health deteriorated rapidly, for he never recovered fully from the injuries suffered at Tiguex. During an official inquiry (1544–1545) into his leadership of the Cíbola expedition Coronado was accused of misconduct for several reasons, including the execution of the Turk and his withdrawal from the lands he had explored, but he was exonerated by the *audiencia* (royal tribunal) of Mexico City. Although Coronado's search for riches in the north had proved futile, his expedition was a significant milestone in the exploration of North America and, with the contemporaneous venture of Hernando de Soto, helped to provide a realistic conception of the width of the continent.

BIBLIOGRAPHY: Herbert E. Bolton, *Coronado on the Turquoise Trail: Knight of Pueblos and Plains*, Albuquerque, 1949; A. Grove Day, *Coronado's Quest*, Berkeley, Calif., 1940; George P. Hammond, *Coronado's Seven Cities*, Albuquerque, 1940; Carl O. Sauer, *Sixteenth Century North America: The Land and the People as Seen by the Europeans*, Berkeley, Calif., 1971; George Parker Winship (ed.), *The Journey of Coronado*, New York, 1904.

Corte-Real, Gaspar (d. 1501) and Miguel (d. 1502)

Portuguese navigators and explorers in North America. These men were two of the three sons of João Vaz Corte-Real, a military official who served the crown as the captain of the island of Terceira in the Azores. The Corte-Real were a branch of the famous Portuguese family of da Costa.

In May 1500, King Manuel I authorized Gaspar, the youngest son and a gentleman of the court, to undertake a voyage of exploration and gave him extensive powers over any lands he might discover. During this voyage he visited a land which one chronicler says he named Terra Verde. The land in question was probably Newfoundland, though some have argued that he rediscovered Greenland on this voyage. Gaspar returned to Lisbon in the autumn of 1500. The following year he set out once more for the New World. Two of the three vessels in this expedition returned to Portugal in October 1501, bringing for the King a present of more than fifty kidnapped Indians. The third vessel, on which Gaspar himself sailed, was lost at sea.

In May 1502, Miguel Corte-Real by royal authorization led an expedition of two vessels from Lisbon to North America. One vessel ultimately returned to Portugal, but the flagship carrying Miguel Corte-Real was lost.

The results of these voyages were vague and unsubstantial. The Portuguese government did not press land claims in northern North America, but Portuguese fishermen continued to visit Newfoundland waters to catch *bacalhau* (codfish), an important item in the national diet.

BIBLIOGRAPHY: Henry P. Biggar (ed.), *The Precursors of Jacques Cartier, 1497–1534*, Ottawa, 1911; Samuel Eliot Morison, *The European Discovery of America: The Northern Voyages, A.D. 500–1600*, New York, 1971; id., *Portuguese Voyages to America in the Fifteenth Century*, Cambridge, Mass., 1940; Fridtjof Nansen, *In Northern Mists*, vol. II, London, 1911.

Bernerd C. Weber

Cortés, Hernán (Hernando; 1485–1547)

Spanish conqueror and explorer. Cortés was born to a family of the petty nobility in Medellín in the province of Extremadura. At the age of 14 he was sent to the University of Salamanca to study law, but for reasons that are not known he went back home 2 years later to the apparent annoyance of his parents. In 1504 he sailed to Santo Domingo, where he was appointed public notary in the town of Azua. Seven years later he took part in the conquest of Cuba under Diego Velásquez and became a resident of the island, prospering as a miner and stock raiser and serving as a treasury official and as *alcalde* (magistrate) of Santiago. Although Cortés had had his disagreements with Velásquez, the latter named him commander of a large expedition which was to investigate reports of rich lands to be found in Yucatán and adjoining areas. Velásquez's

Although Hernán Cortés's sanguinary conquests appear less than admirable from today's vantage point, he showed considerable statesmanship in his administration of New Spain. [Library of Congress]

Cortés, conqueror of Mexico, greets Montezuma, ruler of the Aztecs. [Library of Congress]

instructions called upon Cortés to learn all he could about the land and its people and to verify rumors that among them were Amazons and individuals with the faces of dogs. Velásquez later decided to rescind Cortés's appointment, but before he could act Cortés slipped away from Santiago on November 18, 1518.

The events of the conquest of Mexico—the arrival in Yucatán in February 1519; the meeting with Mal-

Hernán Cortés's route to Tenochtitlán.

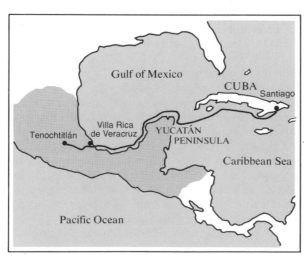

inche (also known as Doña Marina), who became Cortés's mistress and interpreter; the battles and alliances with the Indians encountered en route to the Aztec capital at Tenochtitlán; the capture and death of Montezuma (Moctezuma) II, the Aztec emperor; the rebellion of the Indians which forced the Spaniards to flee from Tenochtitlán on the Sorrowful Night; and the subsequent siege and recapture of the city (mid-1521)—constitute one of the most stirring if sanguinary tales in the history of New World discovery (see WEST INDIES, CENTRAL AMERICA, AND MEXICO). On October 15, 1522, Cortés's exploits were rewarded by King Charles I, who named him governor and captain general of New Spain, as the newly conquered region was called. Despite his statesmanlike concern for the administration and development of his domain, Cortés remained committed to exploration and, in particular, to the search for an interoceanic strait, a subject in which the King also displayed a lively interest, and several expeditions were sent to explore both coasts of New Spain. In 1524 Cortés himself set out on an arduous trek to Las Hibueras (Honduras) in pursuit of a rebellious lieutenant, Cristóbal de Olid.

Cortés's later years were embittered by his unavailing efforts to retain his authority in New Spain, which was increasingly undermined by royal officials. While in Spain in 1528 he was made Marqués del Valle de Oaxaca, with extensive rights over a large section of central Mexico, but real power came to be exercised by the *audiencia* (royal tribunal) and by New Spain's first viceroy, Antonio de Mendoza, who arrived in 1535.

After returning from Spain in 1530, Cortés continued his exploration of the Pacific Coast of New Spain, for which he had received royal authorization in 1529. An expedition (1532) commanded by his cousin Diego Hurtado de Mendoza discovered the Tres Marías Islands, while the survivors of a second expedition returned with reports of a pearl-rich "island" (probably La Paz Bay, Baja California). Deciding to investigate personally, Cortés sailed from Mexico with three ships and about 170 men on April 18, 1535. On May 3 he landed in La Paz Bay at a place he called Santa Cruz. He made an attempt to start a colony on the site (the first in California), but food was scarce and treasure was lacking, and Cortés himself decided to return to Mexico City the following year, partly because of the arrival of Mendoza in the capital. In 1539–1540, in defiance of an edict by Mendoza, Cortés sponsored a voyage by Francisco de Ulloa, who explored the Gulf of California, rounded Cabo San Lucas, sailed northward to Cedros Island and thence to an unknown point beyond, thereby proving that California was not an island but a peninsula. Meanwhile, Cortés went to Spain in 1540, fought in a campaign in Algeria (1541), but had no success in winning the honor and recognition he sought. He died on December 2, 1547, near Seville.

BIBLIOGRAPHY: Hernando Cortés, *Five Letters, 1519–1526*, tr. and ed. by J. Bayard Morris, New York, 1962; Salvador de Madariaga, *Hernán Cortés, Conqueror of Mexico*, New York, 1941; Robert Ryal Miller, "Cortés and the First Attempt to Colonize California," *California Historical Quarterly*, vol. LIII, 1974, pp. 5–16.

Cunningham, Allan *(1791–1839)*   Australian botanist and explorer. Born in Wimbledon, Surrey, England, on July 13, 1791, Cunningham was educated privately at Putney before joining the staff of Kew Gardens, London, in 1808. On Sir Joseph Banks's recommendation, he spent 2 years collecting botanical specimens in Brazil before coming in 1816 to New South Wales, where he joined the 1817 expedition of John OXLEY down the Lachlan River. Following a valuable survey of Australia's coastal vegetation with Phillip Parker King (1817–1822), Cunningham resumed land exploration in 1823 with his discovery of a practical stock route from the Hunter Valley north through Pandora's Pass to the Liverpool Plains, discovered by Oxley in 1818. After a brief collecting trip to New Zealand, Cunningham went north again in 1827 to discover the fertile Darling Downs and a possible pass to the sea. This pass, later called Cunningham's Gap, he explored from the coast in 1828. The headwaters of the Brisbane River he examined in 1829. After a brief visit to Norfolk Island, Cunningham returned to England in 1831. Appointed colonial botanist, he came back to New South Wales in 1837 but died of tuberculosis on June 27, 1839, following his second visit to New Zealand. Primarily a botanist who found he could "blend discovery with botanical research," Cunningham is buried appropriately in the Sydney Botanical Gardens.

BIBLIOGRAPHY: W. G. McMinn, *Allan Cunningham, Botanist and Explorer*, Melbourne, 1970.

J. M. R. Cameron

Daurkin, Nikolay (fl. ca. 1760–1792) Explorer of Siberia. A Chukchi (native of northeastern Siberia), Daurkin was a cossack of the Anadyr garrison. In 1760 F. K. Plenisner, commandant of the Anadyr fort, sent him to Chukotka (Chukotsky Poluostrov), where he collected from the natives information about their country and about the lands to the east, the "Great Land" (North America). In October 1763 he himself went on reindeer to Ratmanova Island in Bering Strait. The information he collected was used in a "Map of the Seacoast from the Mouths of the Anadyr River to the Mouth of the River Kolyma and of the Coasts Opposite." In 1774 he again visited Chukotka, and from 1787 to 1792 he took part in the expedition of Joseph BILLINGS as an interpreter.

Richard A. Pierce

Davis (Davys), John (1550?–1605) British Arctic explorer. Davis was born in Sandridge, Devon. Little is known of his early life, but it seems evident that he had a good education before going to sea, and by 1579 he was already well known as a navigator. In the early 1580s, Davis held a series of consultations with John Dee, the mathematician, and Sir Francis Walsingham, Queen Elizabeth's secretary of state, on the possibility of discovering a NORTHWEST PASSAGE. In consequence, Davis secured financial backing for his three expeditions of 1585, 1586, and 1587. On the first expedition, he discovered Davis Strait and explored part of the west coast of Greenland. He also discovered Cumberland Sound, Baffin Island, where he felt confident that a Northwest Passage would be found. He returned to Davis Strait and Cumberland Sound on his two subsequent voyages, charting long stretches of the Greenland, Baffin Island, and Labrador coasts, but by the end was less hopeful of a passage through Cumberland Sound.

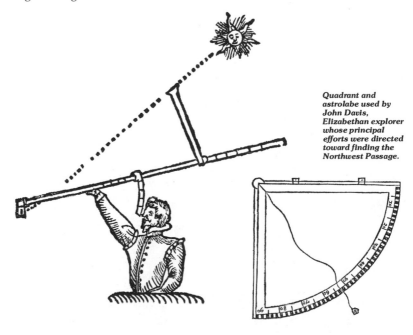

Quadrant and astrolabe used by John Davis, Elizabethan explorer whose principal efforts were directed toward finding the Northwest Passage.

Between 1591 and 1593 Davis took part in Thomas Cavendish's second attempted circumnavigation, hoping that, on reaching the Pacific, he might seek the western entrance of the Northwest Passage. The expedition, however, failed to penetrate the Strait of Magellan, where Davis's ship, *Desire*, was separated from the rest of the fleet. Returning home, he discovered the Falkland Islands. From 1598 on, Davis served as pilot on three voyages to the East Indies, including the successful first voyage of the East India Company. On his third voyage, Davis was killed by Japanese pirates off the coast of Malaya.

BIBLIOGRAPHY: A. H. Markham (ed.), *The Voyages and Works of John Davis the Navigator*, London, 1880; C. R. Markham, *A Life of John Davis, the Navigator, 1550–1605, Discoverer of Davis Straits*, London, 1889.

Clive A. Holland

Davydov, Gavriil Ivanovich (1784–1809) Russian naval lieutenant and explorer of Russian America and the Kuril Islands. Educated in the Naval Cadet Corps, he entered the service of the Russian-American Company in 1802 at the age of 18. In the company of his close friend Nikolay Aleksandrovich Khvostov (1776–1809), he crossed Siberia, sailed from Okhotsk to Russian America and back, recrossed Siberia, and at the end of January 1804 was again in St. Petersburg. In 1805 Davydov and Khvostov crossed Siberia again, traveled to Kamchatka, and from there went to Sitka on the brig *Maria* with the imperial plenipotentiary N. P. Rezanev and Dr. Georg Heinrich von LANGSDORFF. In 1806 Davydov returned to Okhotsk. In 1807, commanding the tender *Avos*, with Khvostov and the *Juno*, he visited southern Sakhalin, the southern Kurils, and "Matsmai" (Hokkaido), where on ambiguous orders from Rezanov they destroyed Japanese trading installations. In Okhotsk Davydov and Khvostov were arrested for this depredation by the local commandant but escaped; in St. Petersburg both were exonerated.

After taking part in the Swedish war in 1808, Davydov settled in St. Petersburg, where Adm. A. S. Shishkov urged him to write an account of his travels. He had finished the account of his first voyage when, in September 1809 after a late reunion with friends, he and Khvostov drowned together in the Neva River while on their way home. Shishkov put the rest of the account together from Davydov's notes and letters and published it as *Dvukratnoye puteshestviye v Ameriku morshikh ofitserov Khvostova i Davydova* (1810–1812).

BIBLIOGRAPHY: G. I. Davydov, *Reise der russisch-kaiserlichen Flott-Officiere Chwostow und Dawydow von St. Petersburg durch Siberien nach Amerika und zurück in den Jahren 1802, 1803 und 1804*, Berlin, 1816.

Richard A. Pierce

Desideri, Ippolito (Hippolyte; 1684–1733) Italian Jesuit missionary and explorer in Asia. Born in Pistoia in December 1684, Desideri entered the Society of Jesus in April 1700 and was ordained in August 1712. In April 1713, in the company of two other priests, he took ship from Lisbon for India, disembarking finally in Goa. He spent several months in India studying the Persian language. In September 1714 he proceeded from the old city of Delhi northward to Lahore and thence slowly to Tibet. On this expedition Manuel Freyre, a Portuguese, was his superior and traveling companion. This northern journey was a long, dangerous, and difficult one. Not until March 18, 1716, did the two priests set foot within the holy city of Lhasa. Father Freyre, whose health was impaired, soon returned to India by way of Nepal. Desideri, however, received permission to dwell in Lhasa, where he diligently studied the Tibetan language. He was permitted also to preach. Desideri was an eyewitness of the Tatar invasion and temporary Tatar domination of Tibet (1720) and the subsequent annexation of the country by the Chinese.

Early in 1721 Desideri received a letter from Rome ordering him to abandon the Tibetan mission at the earliest opportunity. His journey southward was arduous. In India he fell gravely ill, but he recovered eventually in Delhi. He spent some additional years in India, and in the first part of the year 1727 he took the long sea journey around the Cape of Good Hope to Europe. In August 1727 he landed at Port-Louis, a small Breton port, and then traveled by way of Paris, Marseille, and Genoa to Rome. He reached Rome in January 1728. He wrote a lengthy and interesting account of his mission, for his long stay in Tibet had furnished him with detailed information about that relatively unknown land and the manners and customs of its inhabitants. Desideri died suddenly in Rome on April 14, 1733.

BIBLIOGRAPHY: C. Wessels, S. J., *Early Jesuit Travellers in Central Asia, 1603–1721*, The Hague, 1924.

Bernerd C. Weber

Dezhnev, Semyon Ivanovich (ca. 1605–?1673) Yakutsk cossack leader and polar seafarer. Dezhnev served as cossack in Tobolsk, Yeniseysk, and finally (from 1638) Yakutsk. In 1640–1641 he was on the Yana River; in 1642 he crossed to the upper Indigirka River. He descended the Indigirka to its mouth in 1643 and went by sea to the mouth of the Alazeya River. About 1644 he went overland to the lower Kolyma River, recently discovered from the sea by Mikhail Stadukhin. He took part in 1647 in the unsuccessful attempt of Fyodot Alekseyev Popov to cross by sea from the mouth of the Kolyma to the mouth of the Anadyr River, where it was rumored there was a large rookery of walrus, with deposits of ivory. In 1648 he and Popov set out again, but of ninety men and six boats only Dezhnev's boat with twenty-five men survived to reach the mouth of the Anadyr. Some of the men tried to go up the Anadyr during the winter and perished. The twelve survivors,

*Mountains of Tibet,
visited by Ippolito
Desideri, Italian
Jesuit missionary
and explorer who
preached the Gospel
in Lhasa for 5 years.
[Library of
Congress]*

headed by Dezhnev, went up the river in the summer and established the post of Anadyrsk. In 1652 Dezhnev went around the Gulf of Anadyr (Anadyrsky Zaliv) by boat and discovered a large rookery of walrus on its north shore. He stayed on the Anadyr until 1662, when he returned overland to Yakutsk. About 1664 he arrived in Moscow with rich proceeds for the crown. In 1665 he was made a cossack *ataman* (leader) and assigned to Yakutsk, where he remained until 1671. He died in Moscow in 1672 or 1673.

BIBLIOGRAPHY: Frank A. Golder, *Russian Expansion on the Pacific, 1641–1850,* Cleveland, 1914.

Richard A. Pierce

Dias [*de Novaes*], Bartolomeu (Bartholomew Diaz; ca. 1450–1500) Portuguese navigator. Dias's early life is shrouded in mystery, one reason being that his name was a common one among Portuguese navigators of the period. In 1481 he commanded a ship which was part of an expedition to the Gold Coast. He was a gentleman at the court of John II when the King chose him for the exploring expedition which was to find Ptolemy's Prassum Promontorium (the southernmost extremity of Africa) and unlock the sea route to India. Commanding a fleet of three ships, Dias left Lisbon in August 1487 and proceeded to sail beyond the last pillar of Diogo CÃO at Cape Cross, Namibia. On December 8 he reached Walvis Bay, and on December 26, Elizabeth Bay; on December 31, 1487, he probably passed the mouth of the Orange River, the present boundary between Namibia and the republic of South Africa. Beyond 32°S the caravels stood out to sea and were blown around the southern tip of Africa. Dias landed at Mossel Bay on February 3, 1488, and made contact with Hottentot warriors, one of whom was killed in a fracas. The ships continued to the Great Fish River, or more probably farther east to the Keiskama River, when Dias was compelled by his crew on March 12 to return to Portugal, where he arrived in December 1488. Credit should go to Dias for naming the famous promontory the Cape of Good Hope (which he saw for the first time on his *return* voyage). The story that he called it Cabo Tormentoso (Cape of Storms) and that King John changed it to the more felicitous appellation is probably apocryphal. (And while the Cape of Good Hope is the renowned cape, the southernmost point of Africa is Cape Agulhas, 100 miles, or 161 kilometers, east-southeast.) Inexplicably, no exploring expedition of record was sent out to exploit Dias's discovery until 10 years later, when Vasco da GAMA achieved his great success.

Dias was named to the staff of Guinea House in 1494. He supervised the construction and outfitting of the ships that were to be employed by da Gama and accompanied that fleet as far as the Cape Verde Islands. He sailed to the Guinea coast, where he engaged in profitable trading and was later named by King Manuel to establish a trading post at Sofala on the East African coast. In March 1500 he commanded

a squadron in the fleet led by Pedro Álvares CABRAL which discovered Brazil. This voyage was commissioned by Manuel to capitalize on da Gama's discovery of the sea route to India. After leaving Brazil, a savage storm struck on May 24, and four ships were lost, including that commanded by Dias.

BIBLIOGRAPHY: Eric Axelson, *Congo to Cape: Early Portuguese Explorers*, New York, 1973; Edgar Prestage, *The Portuguese Pioneers*, London, 1933, reprinted 1966; E. G. Ravenstein, "The Voyages of Diogo Cão and Bartholomeu Dias, 1482–88," *The Geographical Journal*, vol. XVI, no. 6, December 1900, pp. 625–655; Avelino Teixeira da Mota, *Bartolomeu Dias, Discoverer of the Cape of Good Hope*, Lisbon, 1955.

Martin Torodash

Doudart de Lagrée, Ernest-Marc-Louis de Gonzague (1823–1868)

French explorer. Doudart de Lagrée joined the French Navy after receiving his education at the École Polytechnique in Paris. He served with distinction in the Crimean War but subsequently had to abandon service at sea because of a chronic throat infection. He then sought an appointment in France's new colonial possessions in Indochina and was named French representative at the court of King Norodom of Cambodia in 1863.

Once in Cambodia, Doudart de Lagrée demonstrated a lively interest in the history and geography of that then little-known land. He traveled widely, visited the great temple ruins at Angkor, and saw the first major obstacle to navigation on the Mekong River, the Sambor Rapids, as early as July 1863. Given his knowledge of these rapids, it was ironic that he should have been chosen to lead the Mekong Expedition that left Saigon in June 1866 to investigate the commercial possibilities of a riverine route to China.

As leader of the expedition, Doudart de Lagrée was responsible for five other French explorers, three interpreters, and an escort consisting of four Frenchmen, two Filipinos, and seven Vietnamese. The size of the party and the masses of stores it was expected to carry with it were a cause for immediate concern to Doudart de Lagrée and an undoubted reason for the mission's slow progress even at the beginning, when illness and disease had not yet taken their toll.

Under his direction the Mekong Expedition made the first scientific survey of the Angkor ruins before starting its investigations of the river itself. After the expedition traversed the Sambor Rapids and then encountered the Khone Falls on the border of Cambodia and Laos, it was clear that hopes for using the Mekong for commerce were unrealistic. Doudart de Lagrée and his companions therefore pressed on with scientific aims as their principal concern.

As an expedition devoted to extending human knowledge, the French Mekong exploration was a notable success. But success was bought at a heavy cost in terms of original hopes and human suffering. Doudart de Lagrée himself suffered a severe bout of fever in the course of exploring the Bolovens Plateau region east of the Mekong in southern Laos. Then after leaving Luang Prabang, he grew progressively weaker as the result of amoebic dysentery. His illness did not prevent his making a grueling detour from the Mekong to the Shan state of Keng Tung in August 1867. Once the party entered China, however, his health rapidly declined, and he died in Huitse (formerly Tungchwan) in March 1868.

See also GARNIER, Francis.

BIBLIOGRAPHY: Milton Osborne, *River Road to China: The Mekong River Expedition, 1866–73*, New York and London, 1975; A. B. Villemereuil, *Explorations et missions de Doudart de Lagrée*, Paris, 1883.

Milton Osborne

Doughty, Charles Montagu (1843–1926) English explorer and poet. Doughty is best known for *Arabia Deserta* (1888), his account of his travels in western and central Arabia from November 1876 to August 1878. A singular work, it gives not only geographical descriptions of seldom-seen towns like Ha'il but the most detailed descriptions of Bedouin life. T. E. Lawrence called it "a bible of its kind." Many early explorers of Arabia were gifted linguistically, but Doughty was the lone poet and he was recognized subsequently for his works of poetry, such as *The Dawn in Britain* (1906) and *Mansoul* (1920).

Doughty was born of good English stock. In early childhood he suffered from a speech impediment and ill health, but they did not prevent him from matriculating at Cambridge, where he studied geology. It was the desire to study geology that thrust Doughty into extensive travel. His interest in glaciers took him to Norway in 1865. The next decade found him studying in Oxford, Leiden, Copenhagen, and Louvain. He wandered alone in Southern Europe, Egypt, North Africa, Palestine, and Sinai. He traveled to satisfy his insatiable curiosity and to acquire a background in the languages of the peoples who had played a role in early English history. In this effort Doughty hoped to restore English, at least to his mind, to its greater sixteenth-century qualities.

The clash between Doughty's poetic soul, rational mind, and patriotic heart is evident in his reflections and observations on Arabs. He was the first European to travel for an extended period as a Christian among Arab Bedouin. He was slightly contemptuous of travelers such as Johann Ludwig BURCKHARDT and Richard BURTON who adopted Muslim attire. He was not a zealous Christian, though he found Islam distasteful. Doughty had a total cultural and racial reaction in Arabia. He chose in a deliberate and masochistic manner the word *Nasrany,* a pejorative Arabic term for Christian, to describe himself. The abuse heaped upon the Nasrany, the hunger, weariness, and tribulations he endured, sharpened his poetic images. Doughty is the only European to have captured the spirit of the desert as depicted by the pre-Islamic poets, and he was the only explorer to write his account in "poetry."

Doughty discovered the Aramaic inscription at Taymā', mentioned in the Book of Job, which the Alsatian Charles Huber obtained for the Louvre in 1883. In 1876 he entered Ha'il, the only European to have done so since William Gifford PALGRAVE in 1862, and by so doing he was able to update the history of the Rashīdī dynasty, rulers of the Shammar tribal confederation. He was the first European to take "squeezes," impressionable facsimiles, of the Nabataean inscriptions at Madā'in Ṣāliḥ, which enabled a comparison to be made with those of Petra and provided philologists and epigraphers with a basis that resulted in a breakthrough in the study of Nabataean civilization. Doughty was also the first European to discuss correctly the drainage system and origins of the Wādī al Ḥamḍ between Al Wajh (Wejh) and Yanbu on the Red Sea and to define the great *harras* (lava beds) on the western edges of the Nafūd and Najd (Nejd) Deserts.

BIBLIOGRAPHY: Charles M. Doughty, *Arabia Deserta*, 2 vols., 3d ed., New York, 1921; Barker Fairley, *Charles M. Doughty: A Critical Study*, London, 1927; D. G. Hogarth, *The Life of Charles M. Doughty*, New York, 1929; R. H. Kiernan, *The Unveiling of Arabia*, London, 1937.

Robert W. Olson

Charles Montagu Doughty, English explorer and poet whose Arabia Deserta T. E. Lawrence called "a bible of its kind." [Library of Congress]

Drake, Francis **(ca. 1543–1596)** English navigator, pirate, privateer, and admiral. Drake was born near Tavistock, Devonshire, of obscure parentage. He was one of twelve sons, most of whom became seamen. Drake himself went to sea as a boy, being apprenticed to an old master of a small bark. He engaged in the coasting trade and in piloting for a while but in 1566 was employed in voyages to Guinea and the Spanish Main and learned that Spain, England's adversary, would resist encroachments on its commercial monopoly. In 1567 he sailed with his kinsman John Hawkins to Africa for slaves and thence to the Caribbean, escaping capture by the Spanish during a skirmish at San Juan de Ulúa (Veracruz) in Mexico. Back in England in 1569, he informed Sir William Cecil of the disaster and was thus brought to the notice of the great minister. He made several subsequent voyages to the Caribbean as pirate or privateer. In 1572 he sacked several towns on the Spanish Main and climbed the mountains in Panama to have a look at the Pacific. Returning to England in 1573 with a large store of bullion, he was now a comparatively rich man.

Between 1577 and 1580 Drake sailed around the world; his was the second circumnavigation and the first by an Englishman. In the *Golden Hind* he sailed to Brazil, the Río de la Plata estuary, and south to Patagonia. After passing through the Strait of Magellan, he was driven south, perhaps as far as 57°, by a gale and was therefore able to disprove the existence of a southern continent (Terra Australis) in that region. Drake then sailed up the west coast of the Americas as far north, some claim, as Vancouver Island. In 1579 he anchored near Coos Bay, Oregon, and repaired his ship in Drake's Estero (of Drake's Bay), California, before sailing for the Philippines and the Spice Islands, across the Indian Ocean, and around the Cape of Good Hope to London. In 1581 he was knighted by Queen Elizabeth I for his spirited and highly successful venture.

In 1585 Drake sailed with a fleet to attack the Spanish in the West Indies. Of mixed success, the expedition took him to Santo Domingo, Cartagena, Florida, and Fort Raleigh, North Carolina. In 1587 he led another privateering expedition into the Atlantic and greatly increased England's treasure. Back home again, he assumed direction of England's naval forces (in the administration of which he had had a hand since his return from the Pacific) and in 1588 defeated

Long before sailing out into the English Channel against the Spanish Armada, Sir Francis Drake had circumnavigated the globe in the Golden Hind. [Library of Congress]

Indians welcome Sir
Francis Drake to
American shores.
[Library of
Congress]

cal and other calculations. Armed with this new knowledge, he again approached the West African interior in 1867. During the course of this expedition, which is described in *A Journey to Ashango-Land* (1867), he further clarified Ogowe geography and this time backed his work with solid observations of his positions. Du Chaillu later traveled in Scandinavia and wrote a number of popular works on Africa for boys. By the time of his death in Russia in 1903, his once-dubious claims had been fully vindicated.

BIBLIOGRAPHY: K. David Patterson, "Paul B. Du Chaillu and the Exploration of Gabon, 1855–1865," *The International Journal of African Historical Studies,* vol. VII, 1974, pp. 647–667; E. G. Ravenstein, "Paul Belloni Du Chaillu," *The Geographical Journal,* vol. XXI, 1903, pp. 680–681; Michel Vaucaire, *Paul Du Chaillu: Gorilla Hunter,* New York, 1930.

James A. Casada

the Spanish Armada. In 1589 he attacked the coasts of Spain and Portugal. After a few peaceful years on shore, he again commanded an expedition to the West Indies, in 1595. He died on board his ship off the coast of Panama on January 28, 1596, of dysentery.

BIBLIOGRAPHY: Kenneth R. Andrew, *Drake's Voyages,* London, 1967; Henry Raup Wagner, *Sir Francis Drake's Voyage around the World,* San Francisco, 1926.

Barry M. Gough

Du Chaillu, Paul Belloni (1831–1903)

Franco-American explorer, natural historian, and sportsman. The circumstances of his birth are clouded, but it is clear that Du Chaillu, who later became an American citizen, was born in France. From early childhood he had firsthand experience of Africa thanks to the fact that his father was a trader in the region of the Gabon River. What little formal education he had came at the hands of missionaries, but his practical training and experiences stood him in good stead as an explorer. After a trip to the United States, where his own newspaper articles drew attention to his prowess as a hunter, Du Chaillu undertook a mission to West Africa for the Academy of Natural Sciences of Philadelphia. For almost 4 years, from 1855 to 1859, Du Chaillu traveled extensively on the Gabon River and delineated the geography of the lower reaches of the Gabon and the Ogowe (Ogooué). He also became the first Westerner to kill a gorilla. His somewhat sensationalized account of his travels, *Explorations and Adventures in Equatorial Africa* (1861), stirred great controversy because many doubted the existence of the gorilla and questioned Du Chaillu's geography. While his account ultimately proved to be essentially accurate, Du Chaillu was sufficiently sensitive of the criticism directed at him to study in order to improve his abilities as an observer and in making astronomi-

Dumont d'Urville, Jules-Sébastien-César (1790–1842)

French navigator. Dumont d'Urville was born at Condé-sur-Noireau, Calvados. Following his father's death in 1797, he was brought up by his mother and her brother, the Abbé de Croisilles, whose influences may be responsible for Dumont d'Urville's austere, proud, and somewhat pompous character.

He began his career in the French Navy in November 1807 as a *novice* at the blockaded naval base of Toulon, where he started to study botany, entomology, and various languages. Assigned in 1817 to a ship sent to the Aegean Sea, he was instrumental in the identification and the purchase by France of the *Venus de Milo,* today at the Louvre in Paris. Dumont d'Urville was rewarded for his role in this enterprise with membership in the Legion of Honor and promotion to the rank of *lieutenant de vaisseau* in August 1821.

In 1822 Dumont d'Urville was assigned to the Louis-Isidore Duperrey Expedition into the Pacific. This expedition, which resulted in the serious reconnoitering of the Gilbert and Caroline Islands, allowed Dumont d'Urville to demonstrate his scientific ability and set the course for his subsequent career. He brought back 3000 plant specimens (of which 400 were totally unknown) and 1200 species of insects (of which 450 had never been described). His botanical findings were published in the *Annales des sciences naturelles,* and his *Flore des Îles Malouines* by the Linnaean Society. However, contrary to his expectations, he was neither promoted nor invited to join the prestigious Institut de France: a Cross of St. Louis was his only reward.

A day after the return of the Duperrey Expedition, on May 23, 1825, Dumont d'Urville submitted to the Minister of the Navy a proposal for a new Pacific expedition. Provisional approval was forthcoming on November 10, his promotion to the rank of *capitaine de frégate* on November 11, and final approval on December 25, 1825. He was given command of Duperrey's *La Coquille,* which he renamed *L'Astrolabe,* and instructed to make maps of the hydrography of the Pacific islands, to collect materials on native languages, flora, and minerals, and to search for the remains of the expedition of Jean-François de Galaup, Comte de LA PÉROUSE, which had disappeared in 1788.

Dumont d'Urville's expedition lasted 3 years, from April 25, 1826, to March 25, 1829, and was highly successful. The islands of Totoya and Matuku in the Fijis, Cannac Island near the Laughlan Islands, and the great Astrolabe Reef off Vatulele were discovered; the Loyalty Islands were thoroughly charted; the New Zealand coast and especially Cook Strait were carefully surveyed; knowledge of the hydrography of the South Pacific was so greatly increased that the islands in the area were henceforth divided into the three distinct groups of Polynesia, Micronesia, and Melanesia; a large collection of specimens (1600 plants, 900 rocks, and 500 insects) and many drawings (3350 drawings of 1263 animals) were brought back; and the remains of La Pérouse's ships were located off Vanikoro Island.

However, Dumont d'Urville's expectations of rewards and praise were once again dashed. He was not promoted to the rank of *capitaine de vaisseau* until August 1829, and in 1830 he failed in his bid for a seat at the Institut de France. His management of the expedition came under heavy criticism, because only fifty out of a crew of seventy-nine completed the trip, and his scientific observations were criticized as well, particularly by François Arago, who ridiculed Dumont d'Urville's claim that on August 15, 1826, *L'Astrolabe* had been hit by waves 90 feet (27 meters) high south of Africa. Dumont d'Urville was once again posted to Toulon, where he spent 8 years at a desk job, except for the strictly political mission of conveying into exile ex-King Charles X and his family after the Revolution of 1830.

Dumont d'Urville's naval and scientific reputation recovered after the publication of the monumental *Voyage des découvertes autour du monde* (1832–1834) and the more popular *Voyage pittoresque autour du monde* (1834–1835). In 1837 he was able to obtain command of another Pacific expedition. He was given two ships, *L'Astrolabe* and *La Zélée*, and instructed to make a scientific and hydrographic survey of the South Pacific islands, to explore the Weddell Sea beyond 74°S, and to seek suitable locations for French whalers.

The expedition left Toulon on September 7, 1837, and sailed toward the Pacific by way of the Strait of Magellan. The first attempt to explore Antarctica was not very successful. The ships were unable to go beyond 63°S, and for 5 days (February 4–9, 1838) they were caught in the ice. Nevertheless, the expedition collected numerous geological specimens on Weddell Island in the Falklands; the South Orkney Islands were charted; temperature tests and depth soundings were made in the South Shetlands; experiments in

magnetism and meteorology were carried out; and Louis-Philippe and Joinville Lands (the northern tip of Graham Land and Joinville Island) were discovered in Antarctica.

After rest at Valparaiso, Chile, in April and May 1838, the expedition crisscrossed the South Pacific, visiting Tahiti, the Tonga Islands, the Fijis (where the village responsible for the earlier murder of a French officer was burned down), the New Hebrides, Vanikoro Island, the Solomons, the Carolines, the Netherlands East Indies, and New Guinea, where valuable charts were gathered. However, by the time that the ships stopped at Hobart, Tasmania, on December 12, 1839, scurvy and dysentery had severely depleted the size of the crews. Dumont d'Urville launched his second assault against Antarctica without the sick, who were left behind with *La Zélée*. This time the expedition crossed the Antarctic Circle, reached 73° S, and discovered Adélie Land, named after Dumont d'Urville's wife. On its way back, the Loyalty Islands and the Louisiade Archipelago, off New Guinea, were explored and charted.

The expedition returned to Toulon on November 6, 1840, after a very successful journey. In Antarctica, it had traveled farther south than had any other French expedition and discovered Adélie Land and Louis-Philippe and Joinville Lands; and the mass of accurate and reliable hydrographic charts it compiled was the most important single contribution to the map of the Pacific. Once again, Dumont d'Urville's leadership was questioned, because twenty-five crew members had died during the voyage, but this time recognition and rewards came more quickly than before. On December 31, 1840, he was promoted to the rank of rear admiral; the Société de Géographie awarded him its gold medal; and the government ordered the immediate publication of the account of the expedition, *Voyage au Pôle Sud et dans l'Océanie* (1841–1854). Dumont d'Urville was unable to complete this last assignment: together with his wife and their only surviving son, he died on May 8, 1842, in a train accident at Versailles.

The French explorer Dumont d'Urville's two voyages to the Pacific resulted in the exploration of Antarctica and the gathering of much scientific information. [Library of Congress]

BIBLIOGRAPHY: G. Day, *Dumont d'Urville*, Paris, 1947; Jules-Sébastien-César Dumont d'Urville, *Voyage au Pôle Sud et dans l'Océanie sur les corvettes L'Astrolabe et La Zélée exécuté . . . pendant les années 1837–1838–1839–1840*, 23 vols., Paris, 1841–1854; id., *Voyage des découvertes autour du monde . . . sur la corvette L'Astrolabe pendant les années 1826–1829*, 5 vols., Paris, 1832–1834; John Dunmore, *French Explorers in the Pacific*, vol. II, *The Nineteenth Century*, Oxford, 1969; C. Vergniol, *Dumont d'Urville*, Paris, 1930; Olive Wright (tr.), *New Zealand, 1826–1827, from the French of Dumont d'Urville*, Wellington, New Zealand, 1950; id., *The Voyage of the Astrolabe, 1840*, Wellington, New Zealand, 1955.

Max Fajn

Dupuis, Jean (1829–1912) French explorer. Dupuis traveled to China as a young man, eventually, in 1861, establishing himself in Hankow, where he built up a prosperous business selling military equipment. From his base in Hankow he was in touch with Chinese officials and soldiers in a number of provinces, including Yünnan. According to Dupuis, as early as 1864 he had started searching for a riverine link that would permit commerce to pass directly from the sea into southwestern China. It is more likely that his later discovery of such a route was inspired by members of the Mekong Expedition when they passed through Hankow in 1868. Although the expedition had explored only a brief section of the Red River, there is firm evidence that its leader, Ernest DOUDART DE LAGRÉE, and its second-in-command, Francis GARNIER, had already begun thinking in terms of the Red River as a route for commerce.

Whatever the inspiration, Dupuis successfully descended the Red River from Yünnan into Vietnam in 1871. He was probably not the first European to do this, but he was the first to provide a detailed account of his achievement. Subsequently, in 1873, Dupuis forced a passage up the Red River in opposition to the Vietnamese authorities. His actions at this time led to the temporary seizure of sections of northern Vietnam by Francis Garnier in late 1873, an episode that led to Garnier's death and French withdrawal.

Although Dupuis could rightly claim to have been the most important explorer of the Red River and subsequently to have played a part in bringing the French advance into northern Vietnam in the 1880s, he died in obscurity and near poverty.

BIBLIOGRAPHY: Jean Dupuis, *Les origines de la question du Tong-kin*, Paris, 1896.

Milton Osborne

Duveyrier, Henri **(1840–1892)** French explorer and ethnologist. Born in Paris, Duveyrier met the noted traveler Heinrich BARTH as a youth. He was intrigued by Barth's account of his journeys in the western Sudan, and this apparently provided the impetus that launched his own career as an African explorer. At the age of 19 he explored the northern Sahara to such good effect that he was awarded a gold medal by the Paris Geographical Society. Duveyrier subsequently described this expedition in *Exploration du Sahara: Les Touareg du nord* (1864). Following imprisonment by German forces in the Franco-Prussian War, he resumed his Saharan travels. In the course of a number of journeys he contributed significantly to the expansion of European knowledge of the regions lying south of the Atlas Mountains. He also made a special study of the culture of the Tuareg and became the recognized authority on their speech and customs. Much of his intimate knowledge of the Tuareg derived from the fact that he lived with them for long periods of time. His publications on his later Saharan researches included *La Tunisie* (1881) and *La confrérie musselmane de Sidi Mohammed Ben Alî Es-Senôusi et son domaine géographique* (1884). By the time that Duveyrier died, at Sèvres in 1892, his endeavors had placed him in the first ranks of the explorers of the Sahara.

BIBLIOGRAPHY: René Pottier, *Un prince saharien méconnu: Henri Duveyrier*, Paris, 1938.

James A. Casada

Eiríksson, Leifr *(Leif Erikson, Eriksson, Ericson, or Ericsson; Leif the Lucky; ca. late 970s–ca. 1020)* Iceland-born Norse explorer of the eastern seaboard of North America. For years erroneously credited with the discovery of America, he voyaged to and named Helluland, Markland, and VINLAND in about the years 1001–1002. He was the son of Eirík the Red and Thjodhild. Except for his early years, most of his life was spent in Greenland. When Eirík the Red was exiled from Iceland for murder in 982, the family spent the 3-year sentence exploring Greenland. In 985 or 986, they emigrated to Greenland, settling permanently in the southwest of the country at Brattahlid on Eiríksfjord.

Leifr's reputation and fame rest on his supposed discovery of Vinland, or America, and on his alleged role in proselytization of the Norse in Greenland at the behest of King Olaf Tryggvason of Norway. These achievements of Leifr's, however, are no longer tenable. They had their origin in the long-held opinion that the source describing the events, *Eirík the Red's Saga (Eiríks saga rauda),* narrates trustworthy history. According to the saga, Leifr sailed from Greenland to Norway in the year 999, reaching the court of King Olaf after first being driven off course to the Hebrides, where he and Thorgunna sired a child, Thorgils. The Christian king Olaf is said to have "bestowed great honor" on Leifr and directed him to Greenland with the royal mission of preaching Christianity to the Norsemen. On his return voyage, Leifr's ship experienced navigational difficulties and for a

long time was "tossed about upon the ocean, and came upon lands of which he previously had no knowledge." It was a land with "wild wheat" (wild rice, *Zizania aquatica*?), vines, and *mausur* (maples?). Significantly, Leifr did not name the littoral he had discovered. Its location remains a mystery. The name Vinland is not mentioned until years later, in connection with the planning of Thorfinn Karlsefni's voyage to settle the land Leifr had found. For his role in rescuing shipwrecked seamen and "bringing Chris-

Greenland, home of Leifr Eiríksson, who although he explored the eastern seaboard of North America, is no longer credited as the continent's discoverer. [Danish Tourist Board]

tianity" to Greenland, Leifr earned the cognomen Leif the Lucky. Recent critical textual studies of the two versions of *Eirík the Red's Saga, the Hauksbók* and the *Skálholtsbók,* dating from the early fourteenth and late fifteenth centuries respectively, have confirmed conclusively that the saga is in large measure a deliberate revision of the older and far more reliable *Saga of the Greenlanders (Graenlendinga saga),* committed to writing in Iceland about 1200. It is now evident that Leifr did not bring Christianity to Greenland. The legend of Leifr's journey to King Olaf's court, the proselytization of the Norse in Greenland by Leifr, and his discovery of a land with wild wheat, vines, and *mausur,* was the invention of the monk Gunnlaug Leifsson in Iceland in the late twelfth century.

The more trustworthy *Saga of the Greenlanders* does not contain the legend the monk originated. It recognizes Bjarni Herjólfsson as the discoverer of lands unknown to the Norse located to the west and southwest of Greenland in the year 985 or 986. Leifr Eiríksson is associated with the role of exploring the general region which Bjarni had sighted. In about the years 1001–1002, Leifr with a crew of thirty-five visited and named Helluland, Markland, an unnamed island, and Vinland. The expedition wintered in Vinland, where several dwellings were erected. Leifr was thus instrumental in reconnoitering the eastern seaboard of North America, along which Thorfinn Karlsefni attempted a permanent settlement in about the years 1010–1013.

Although little is known about the person of Leifr Eiríksson, the *Saga of the Greenlanders* describes him in splendid terms as "tall and strong and very impressive in appearance. He was a shrewd man and always moderate in behavior." After the death of Eirík the Red, Leifr came into possession of the family estate at Brattahlid, which in turn was inherited by Thorkell, the second of Leifr's progeny, after Leifr's death at Brattahlid in about 1020.

Even though Leifr is no longer credited with the discovery of America, the myth lives on. Its iconography includes numerous statues of Leifr in urban America. A congressional resolution authorizing the President of the United States to proclaim October 9 in each year as Leif Erickson Day and its approval by President Lyndon B. Johnson in 1964 provide a veneer of official credibility to the tenacious Leifr–Discoverer of America cult. Little did the monk Gunnlaug Leifsson suspect that his historical revisions would someday make Leifr Eiríksson a folk hero, symbolizing the medieval Norse geographical discoveries in the westernmost North Atlantic. *See also* NORSE MARITIME DISCOVERIES.

BIBLIOGRAPHY: Finn Gad, *Grønlands Historie,* vol. I, Copenhagen, 1967; *Grønlands historiske Mindesmaerker,* 3 vols., Copenhagen, 1838–1845; Jón Jóhannesson, "The Date of the Composition of the Saga of the Greenlanders," tr. by Tryggvi J. Oleson, *Saga-Book of the Viking Society for Northern Research,* vol. XVI, part 1, 1962, pp. 54–66; Matti Enn Kaups, "Shifting Vinland: Tradition and Myth; A Rejoinder," *Terrae Incognitae,* vol. III, 1971, pp. 97–105; Magnus Magnusson and Hermann Pálsson, *The Vinland Sagas,* Harmondsworth, England, 1965.

Matti Enn Kaups

El Dorado (Spanish, "The Gilded One") One of several names applied to legendary native kingdoms of great wealth believed to exist in South America in the sixteenth and seventeenth centuries. Belief in the existence of such kingdoms was encouraged by widespread acceptance of medieval tales about terrestrial paradises and by the very real treasure found by Spanish conquerors in such places as Mexico and Peru. Moreover, even Indians who lived far from Cuzco and other centers of high civilization had often heard of their wonders or possessed objects originating there. They readily passed on their information to the Spaniards, who were always eager to hear such news.

The term "El Dorado" may have been coined by Sebastián de BENALCÁZAR, who in the mid-1530s was told of an Indian ruler who was periodically covered with gold dust and floated onto a sacred lake into which emeralds and gold objects were thrown. It is generally believed that the tale heard by Benalcázar had its origin in a similar ceremony held annually by the Chibcha Indians at Lake Guatavita in what is now the republic of Colombia.

Even before Benalcázar had heard of this fabulous kingdom, the existence of such a place (called Xerira) was reported to Ambrosio Alfinger, the German governor of Venezuela, during an expedition that took him to the Magdalena River Valley of Colombia. Alfinger's death in 1533 prevented him from pursuing the search for Xerira, but it was continued by other Germans based in Venezuela who explored an area stretching from the Magdalena Valley to the *llanos* (plains) of Colombia and Venezuela: Nicolás Féderman (Nikolaus Federmann; 1505/10–1542); Georg Hohermuth von Speyer (d. 1540), known in Spanish as Jorge de Espira; and Felipe de Hutten (Philipp von Hutten; 1511–1545). In 1539 Féderman reached the Chibcha states of highland Colombia, where he found Benalcázar and Gonzalo JIMÉNEZ DE QUESADA, who had recently conquered the region. Ironically, neither Féderman nor the Spaniards recognized the area as the source of the El Dorado myth. In fact, in 1541 Hernán Pérez de Quesada (d. 1544), brother of Gonzalo Jiménez de Quesada, led an unsuccessful search for El Dorado in the *llanos* of the Orinoco Basin, and from 1569 to 1572 Jiménez himself was similarly engaged.

Meanwhile, other Spaniards had sought El Dorado farther south. In 1541 an expedition led by Gonzalo PIZARRO traveled eastward from Quito in the hope of finding a land of cinnamon and a golden kingdom that lay beyond. The major result of this unhappy venture was the navigation by Francisco ORELLANA of the Amazon River to its mouth, during which he heard of the rich kingdom of the Omaguas lying to the north of the river. A tale by a Brazilian Indian of an El Dorado in this region prompted an expedition headed by Pedro de Ursúa which got under way in 1560 on the banks of the Huallaga River in Peru. However, El Dorado was forgotten as conspirators led by Lope de Aguirre murdered Ursúa in 1561 and made plans to return to Peru to organize a rebellion there.

Even farther to the south Aleixo Garcia, a Portuguese member of the Juan Díaz de SOLÍS Expedition of 1515–1516 who was shipwrecked off Santa Catarina Island, was told of a white king in the interior whose realm contained a mountain of silver. This story clearly derived its origin from the as-yet-undiscovered Inca empire. Starting from a point on the Paraguay River north of present-day Asunción, Garcia led an Indian army that reached modern Bolivia before being repelled by the Incas. Garcia was able to acquire some plunder during this expedition, and although he was killed by Indians in 1525, Europeans on the coast received part of his booty, along with letters describing his adventures. The story of the white king was relayed to Sebastian CABOT in 1526 and led him to alter the original objective of his expedition and to devote himself to a search for the silver-rich monarch. Cabot's exploration of the Paraná and Paraguay Rivers yielded some gold and silver objects but not the personage in question. The legend of the white king survived the Spanish conquest of the Incas and inspired several other expeditions, including that of Álvar Núñez CABEZA DE VACA to the upper Paraguay in 1543–1544.

In the late sixteenth and early seventeenth centuries seekers of El Dorado again turned their attention to the northern part of the continent and especially to Guiana. As early as 1532 Diego de ORDAZ, who explored the Orinoco River to a point near its confluence with the Meta, was told of the riches to be found in Guiana. Antonio de Berrío (ca. 1520–1597), who married a niece of Jiménez de Quesada and became the latter's heir, explored the region in the 1580s and 1590s in the belief that in Guiana he would find a golden city or cities called Manoa. In 1595 Berrío was captured and interrogated in Trinidad by Sir Walter Raleigh, who was interested in destroying Spanish power in South America and possibly in locating an El Dorado there. Raleigh was able to get no farther than the juncture of the Orinoco with the Caroní River during his 1595 expedition. He returned to Guiana in 1617, but his second effort was a disastrous failure and led directly to his execution by King James I in 1618.

BIBLIOGRAPHY: Constantino Bayle, *El Dorado fantasma*, Madrid, 1943; Walker Chapman, *The Golden Dream: The Seekers of El Dorado*, Indianapolis, 1967; Juan Friede, *Los Welser en la conquista de Venezuela*, Caracas and Madrid, 1961; V. T. Harlow, *Ralegh's Last Voyage*, London, 1932; Charles E. Nowell, "Aleixo Garcia and the White King," *Hispanic American Historical Review*, vol. XXVI, 1946, pp. 450–466; Walter Raleigh, *The Discoverie of the Large and Beautiful Empire of Guiana*, ed. by V. T. Harlow, London, 1928.

Ellsworth, Lincoln (1880–1951)   American pioneer in Arctic and Antarctic exploration by air and the first man to fly across both polar regions. Born in Chicago to wealthy parents, Ellsworth dedicated himself to physical fitness following a sickly childhood. He was not a successful student and left college to work on the first Canadian transcontinental railroad survey. During World War I he was trained as an aviator, but illness cut short his service.

In 1924 Wilkins led a geological transect of the Peruvian Andes from the Pacific to the headwaters of the Amazon. The following year he partially financed a joint expedition with Roald AMUNDSEN to fly from Spitsbergen (Svalbard) to the North Pole. Their two planes were forced to land at 87°44′N, and only after 24 days of arduous work were the six men able to crowd into one airplane and fly back to Spitsbergen. Amundsen later credited Ellsworth with saving the entire expedition.

In 1926, with Amundsen and Umberto Nobile, Ellsworth flew from Spitsbergen to Alaska via the North Pole in the dirigible *Norge*. He represented the American Geographical Society on the Arctic flight of *Graf Zeppelin* and for a time supported the early attempts of George Hubert WILKINS at Arctic submarine exploration. The two men joined forces in four expeditions to Antarctica, and in 1935 Ellsworth and pilot Herbert Hollick-Kenyon flew across the continent, landing four times to wait out bad weather. During Ellsworth's Antarctic expeditions he claimed almost 400,000 square miles (1,036,000 square kilometers) of territory for the United States. *See also* AERIAL EXPLORATION.

Of all the polar explorers of the 1920s and 1930s, Ellsworth alone could personally finance his expeditions. His inherited fortune freed him from seeking

The American polar explorer Lincoln Ellsworth on board a ship carrying his supplies to Antarctica. [National Archives]

financial backers and advertising their projects. His courage, leadership, stamina, and accomplishments resulted in many tributes from governments and, more important, from his colleagues.

BIBLIOGRAPHY: Roald Amundsen, Lincoln Ellsworth, and others, *Our Polar Flight*, New York, 1925; Lincoln Ellsworth, "Arctic Flying Experiences by Airplane and Airship," in *Problems of Polar Research*, New York, 1928; id., *Beyond Horizons*, Garden City, N.Y., 1938; id., *Search*, New York, 1932; id., and E. H. Smith, "Report of the Preliminary Results of the Aero-Arctic Expedition with 'Graf Zeppelin,' 1931," *The Geographical Review*, January 1932, pp. 61–82.

Peter J. Anderson

Erikson *(Eriksson; Ericson; Ericsson),* **Leif** *See* EIRÍKSSON, LEIFR.

Ermak Timofeyevich *See* YERMAK TIMOFEYEVICH.

Etholén, Arvid Adolf *(Russian: Adolf Karlovich Etolin; 1799–1876)* Rear admiral and explorer of Russian America. Etholén was born in Finland of a Swedish-speaking family. In 1817–1818 he sailed to North America on the sloop *Kamchatka*, there taking service with the Russian-American Company as a commander of company ships. In 1821 he and V. S. Khromchenko took the brig *Golovnin* and the cutter *Baranov* to study the northern parts of the colonies. They investigated Hagemeister Island and Strait, described Goodnews Bay, entered the Nushagak River, studied part of the Kuskokwim River, and observed the natives. Between 1840 and 1845 he served as chief manager of the Russian-American Company colonies. During that time he explored the mouth of the Anadyr River and Ayan Bay. Returning to Russia, he was released from service as a rear admiral and served from 1847 to 1859 in the Russian-American Company administration in St. Petersburg.

Richard A. Pierce

Evliya Çelebi *(full name: Evliya ibn-Dervis Mehmed Zilli; 1611–1684)* Ottoman traveler. Evliya Çelebi was born into a powerful and wealthy family on the auspicious day of Muḥarram 10 (March 21), 1611. This date commemorates the martyred death of Ḥusayn, the son of 'Alī and nephew of the prophet Muhammad, at the hands of an Umayyad general. Ḥusayn's death marks the growth of Shī'ism as a political party in Islam, and its anniversary is the occasion of a great festival. Although Evliya Çelebi was a Sunnī, the coincidence of his birth played a role in nearly 40 years (1640–1680) of travel that took him to Eastern Europe, the Balkans, and the Near East. On his twenty-ninth birthday he had a dream in which he saw the prophet Muhammad and interpreted it to mean that he, Evliya, would embark on a great journey. This dream of legend and myth, which Evliya would recall several times, is indicative of the exaggeration he employed in his travel book.

Evliya Çelebi was unusual in that, unlike most Muslims of the sixteenth and seventeenth centuries, he had an insatiable curiosity about the world in which he lived. He seems to have had no desire to travel outside Ottoman lands, and in this he conformed to the constraints of other Muslim travelers. It should be mentioned, however, that in the seventeenth century the Ottoman Empire stretched from Hungary to Sudan and possessed as diverse peoples as any area on earth. Evliya began his journey around 1640 as a private person, although at times he served in an official capacity as well. His parents' connections at the Porte supplied him with credentials which made him welcome wherever he went. His private means assured that he could travel in comfort with many companions and servants. His entourage seemed at times to resemble a small caravan.

Evliya Çelevi had other attributes which assured his success as a traveler. He was a witty, intelligent, and charming man and a great raconteur. He had been a favorite of Sultan Murad IV, who at times of great sorrow would cry, "Ah help! Bring Evliya." He had little formal education but learned quickly, and he became a good calligrapher, musician, and painter. The display of his talents endeared him to his hosts. While Evliya liked to think of himself as a great poet, Cavid Baysun, his Turkish biographer, does not agree. Nor was he a great stylist in the Ottoman language, a fact which ironically assured his success. Choosing to write in a language which reflected the spoken Turkish of his day, Evliya availed himself of a wide audience and endeared himself to those who spoke Turk-

Evliya Çelebi's map of a section of Constantinople. While this Ottoman explorer's records of his travels tend to entertain rather than to instruct, they nevertheless contain much valuable information on the Turkish empire of his time. [Library of Congress]

ish but were increasingly being induced to speak the Persian and Arabic of the court. His *Seyahatname (Travel Book;* 1896–1938) is a piece of light literature which satisfied the need of Turkish intellectuals of his time for entertainment and instruction about the world which the Turks ruled. His narrative style, with an admixture of Arabic and Persian sayings taken from court jargon, made the work readily comprehensible.

Evliya's obvious intent of entertainment explains his lack of concern for historical fact, his exaggeration, and, in some instances, his prevarication. He describes journeys which he obviously did not make. As a result, his account may be used as a historical source only when controlled by additional sources. Despite these reservations, the *Seyahatname* offers a wealth of information on cultural history, folklore, geography, folk medicine, music, and architecture.

In the *Seyahatname* Evliya used Latin, Greek, and Hungarian sources, which he supplemented with the records of provincial officials with whom he stayed. In this alone he ranks with Francesco Guicciardini and offers relief from court historians with their tiresome litany of court events. While Evliya presented an aristocratic view, at least it was interspersed with gleanings from the provinces. The seventeenth century saw a swift deterioration of the Ottoman state, which Evliya witnessed on many occasions, which he did not comprehend, but which he recorded in his ten-volume work.

Some authorities contend the *Seyahatname* was written at the end of Evliya's career, possibly during his year's stay in Egypt. However, Cavid Baysun, the best authority on Evliya, thinks the work was written during the years of travel.

BIBLIOGRAPHY: Evliya Celebi, *Seyahatname*, 10 vols., Istanbul, 1896–1938; Joseph von Hammer-Purgstall, *Narrative of Travels in Europe, Asia by Ewliya Efendi*, London, 1834–50.

Robert W. Olson

Eyre, Edward John (1815–1901) Australian explorer and colonial administrator. Born on August 5, 1815, at Whipsnade, Bedfordshire, England, the third son of a clergyman, Eyre migrated to Australia in 1833 and ran sheep properties in the Hunter Valley and near modern Canberra before making a series of successful trips overlanding stock from established areas for sale in new settlements. He settled in 1838 in Adelaide, from which he made several important exploratory journeys in search of new grazing lands.

In May 1839, Eyre traced the Flinders Ranges north as far as Mount Arden, from which he sighted the "dry and glazed bed" of Lake Torrens, and in August, after crossing Eyre Peninsula, he followed the coast west as far as Streaky Bay. Mount Deception and Mount Hopeless, which he named, reflect his assessment of the harsh, dry country he traversed. Nevertheless, after successfully overlanding sheep from Albany to the Swan River settlement early in 1840, he offered to lead and partly finance an expedition to find a land route from Adelaide to Perth.

Eyre first went north, but beaten back by Lake Eyre and Lake Torrens, made for Fowlers Bay, where he decided to dash over the 850 miles (1368 kilometers) to Albany with only his assistant, John Baxter, and three aboriginal servants. They left Fowlers Bay on February 25, 1841, and almost immediately encountered a difficult, arid terrain. By mid-April they suffered acutely from the desert cold. When Baxter was murdered by two of the aborigines on April 29, Eyre and the remaining aborigine, Wylie, continue westward, always short of food and water, until rescued on June 2 by the French whaler *Mississippi,* After a 12-day rest, Eyre insisted on completing his journey, and he and Wylie reached Albany on July 7. They discovered nothing of value, their route was impracticable, but Eyre was later honored by the ROYAL GEOGRAPHICAL SOCIETY for his courage and perseverance.

After a period as protector of aborigines in South Australia, Eyre become lieutenant governor of New Zealand in 1846 and served in the West Indies before becoming governor of Jamaica in 1864. Severely condemned for his handling of rebellion in Jamaica, although subsequently exonerated, Eyre retired to Walreddon Manor near Tavistock, England, where he died on November 30, 1901.

BIBLIOGRAPHY: G. P. H. Dutton, *The Hero as Murderer: The Life of Edward John Eyre, Australian Explorer and Governor of Jamaica, 1815–1901*, Sydney, 1967; M. J. L. Uren and R. Stephens, *Waterless Horizons*, Melbourne, 1945.

J. M. R. Cameron

~~~~~~~~~~~~~~~~~~~~~~~~~~~~~~

F

Fa-hsien *(Fa-hien; fl. early fifth century)* Buddhist pilgrim and explorer. When the spread of Buddhism took on momentum in the late fourth century A.D., existing translations of Sanskrit scriptures proved to be grossly inadequate. Fa-hsien, a north Chinese monk, was moved by the desire to go to India in order to obtain sūtras (Buddhist texts) still unknown to China. In 399 he took a rarely traveled route from Ch'angan (Sian) to Changyeh, then to Hsining, and through the south side of the Nan Shan to Tunhuang. Beyond Lop Nor, he followed the Tarim and Khotan Rivers before making a major stop in the prosperous Buddhist state of Khotan. A journey of 25 days took Fa-hsien to Yarkand (Soch'e), and another month's travel to Kashgar (K'oshih). After a difficult passage across the Pamir, he headed southwestward toward the upper Indus River.

Descending into the Swat Valley and then following the Kabul River, Fa-hsien approached the historic route through Gandhara and Peshawar and across northern Punjab. East of the Jumna River, his travel covered a number of major cities and holy sites. In the capital (near present Patna) of Magadha, then the richest and most powerful state in India, he spent 3 full years collecting and copying Buddhist texts. He also spent 2 years at Tamralipti, a great seaport at the mouth of the Hooghly River. Afterward, he sailed for Ceylon and spent another 2 years in this important center of Hīnayāna Buddhism.

On his homeward journey, Fa-hsien began by sailing eastward from Ceylon. The vessel soon encountered a tempest and became grounded on a small island off the southern coast of Sumatra. Another 90 days' sailing took Fa-hsien to Java, where he remained for 5 months before boarding another vessel bound for Canton. A severe storm blew the ship off course, and for more than 70 days it drifted without sighting any landfall. Finally, when the crew turned the course to a northwesterly direction, it soon arrived on the southern coast of Shantung. All the sūtras which Fa-hsien carried back from abroad were later turned over to the Buddhist monastery in Nanking.

As the first Chinese to have traveled across the Takla Makan Desert, the Pamir Plateau, the upper Indus, and the Indo-Gangetic Plain and to have visited Ceylon and returned to China by sea through Southeast Asia, Fa-hsien left an account entitled *Fo-kuo chi*, which not only contains detailed descriptions of the routes and countries he visited but also throws much light on the size and equipment of seagoing vessels, navigational skills, and the viciousness of piracy during that period.

BIBLIOGRAPHY: Samuel Beal (tr.), *Travels of Fah Hian and Sung Yun*, London, 1869; Herbert A. Giles (tr.), *The Travels of Fah-hsien*, Cambridge, England, 1923.

Kuei-sheng Chang

Fawcett, Percy Harrison *(1867–?1925)* English soldier and explorer. A native of Torquay, Fawcett attended the Royal Military Academy at Woolwich and was commissioned in the Royal Artillery in 1886. After assignments in Ceylon, Malta, and Ireland, he became engaged in 1906 in boundary delimitation for the Bolivian government and in this capacity traveled widely in relatively unknown parts of South America. He retired from the Army in 1910, though he returned to service during World War I.

After the armistice, he returned to South America to undertake a search for the ruins of ancient civilizations which he was convinced lay undiscovered in the heart of the continent. In particular, he sought a city in the interior of Brazil which had been found in 1753 by Portuguese pathfinders who had later disappeared. After an unsuccessful attempt in 1920, Fawcett renewed his quest in 1925 in the company of his son Jack and a friend, Raleigh Rimell. The trio left Cuiabá, the capital of the Brazilian state of Mato Grosso, on April 20, 1925, and traveled north. By May 29 they had reached a place called Dead Horse Camp (11°43′S, 54°35′W) but were never heard from again. The mysterious disappearance of Fawcett and his companions prompted several search expeditions, starting with that of George Dyott in 1928, but the fate of the party has never been ascertained.

BIBLIOGRAPHY: P. H. Fawcett, *Exploration Fawcett*, ed. by Brian Fawcett, London, 1968.

Flinders, Matthew (1774–1814) English navigator and explorer. The son and grandson of surgeons, Flinders was born at Donington, Lincolnshire, and was educated at the Donington Free School and Horbling Grammar School. By his own account, the reading of *Robinson Crusoe* turned his thoughts to a career at sea, and he was enrolled in the Royal Navy in 1789. From 1791 to 1793 he served as a midshipman in HMS *Providence* under Capt. William Bligh, who was making his second, successful attempt to transplant the breadfruit tree from Tahiti to the West Indies. After taking part in the Battle of Brest (June 1, 1794) in HMS *Bellerophon*, Flinders sailed to Australia in 1795 in HMS *Reliance*, in which George Bass (1771–1803) was serving as surgeon. While the *Reliance* was stationed in Sydney, Flinders and Bass, both singly and together, made several voyages in small boats during which they explored the eastern and southern coasts of Australia. During a 3-month expedition in 1798–1799 in the sloop *Norfolk* they circumnavigated Van Diemen's Land (Tasmania), thereby proving its insularity; the strait separating it from the mainland was later called Bass Strait. When Flinders returned to England in 1800, he was, despite his youth, an experienced navigator and hydrographer. Therefore, when he proposed to Joseph Banks, president of the Royal Society, that he head a hydrographic and scientific expedition to explore the coasts of Australia, Banks approved and secured official sponsorship.

Flinders, now with the rank of commander, sailed

Matthew Flinders, English navigator who, together with George Bass, began explorations of the Australian coast in 1795. [Australian Information Service]

from Spithead on July 18, 1801, in the *Investigator*. He began his survey of the south Australian coast, much of which was unknown, at Cape Leeuwin, which was sighted on December 7, 1801. He discovered and explored Spencer and St. Vincent Gulfs, and on April 8, 1802, at a place he called Encounter Bay he met the French navigator Nicolas Baudin in *Le Géographe*. Although the two men were rivals, the meeting was not unfriendly.

After a stay at Port Jackson, Flinders sailed up Australia's eastern coast, passed through Torres Strait, and surveyed the Gulf of Carpentaria. Because scurvy had broken out among the exhausted crew, he reluctantly decided to end the survey. After a visit to Timor and with his men now suffering from dysentery, he returned to Port Jackson by rounding the western and southern coasts of Australia. He arrived on June 9, 1803, having circumnavigated Australia and, in the words of K. A. Austin, having "literally marked the true outline of Australia on the map of the world."

Flinders hoped to resume the unfinished survey, but since the *Investigator* was unseaworthy, he was compelled to go to England to obtain another ship. On August 10, 1803, he set sail as a passenger in HMS *Porpoise*, which was wrecked on a reef soon after leaving Port Jackson. Nearly all the passengers and crew found refuge on a coral sandbank, while Flinders sailed to Port Jackson for help in the ship's cutter. In a remarkable feat of navigation he arrived at Port Jackson on September 8, having sailed 700 miles (1127 kilometers) in 14 days. After making arrangements for the rescue of the shipwreck victims, Flinders sailed for England in the schooner *Cumberland*. Because the ship was in poor condition and rations were low, he decided to seek help at the island of Mauritius, then held by France, which was at war with Great Britain. For reasons that are still unclear, the governor, Comte Charles Decaen, detained Flinders and kept him in captivity on Mauritius for more than 6 years. He was not released until June 13, 1810.

After his return to England, Flinders devoted his last years to preparing an illustrated account of his expedition, *A Voyage to Terra Australis*, which was published on July 18, 1814, the day before he died. Flinders had married Annette Chappelle shortly before his departure for Australia in 1801 and had been disappointed when he could not take her with him. In 1812 she gave birth to a daughter who subsequently became the mother of the celebrated Egyptologist Sir William Matthew Flinders Petrie.

BIBLIOGRAPHY: K. A. Austin, *The Voyage of the "Investigator," 1801–1803*, Adelaide, 1964.

Forrest, John (1st Baron Forrest of Bunbury; 1847–1918) Australian explorer and statesman. The most distinguished of Western Australia's native-born explorers, Forrest was born in Bunbury on August 22, 1847, and educated at the Bishop's School, Perth. He entered the colony's survey department in 1866, aged 18, and 3 years later led an expedition to the edge of the Great Victoria Desert near Mount Weld in search of the party of Friedrich Wilhelm Ludwig LEICHHART or its remains. His search was unsuccessful, but Forrest traversed more than 2000 miles (3219 kilometers), most of it over good pastoral country. In 1870 he crossed from Perth to Adelaide on a parallel route to the epic 1841 journey of Edward John EYRE and again discovered country suitable for grazing. His 1874 west-east crossing was the longest, most demanding, and dangerous of his three major expeditions. Leaving Perth on March 18 with five other men and eighteen packhorses, Forrest first explored the headwaters of the Murchison River before striking east through Weld Springs and Fort Mueller to the overland telegraph line, which he followed south to reach Adelaide on November 3. Conditions in the Gibson Desert were so severe that the party nearly perished. Only four horses survived. Rewarded with a land grant of 5000 acres (2023 hectares) for his discoveries, Forrest subsequently became deputy surveyor general (1876), surveyor general (1883), and premier (1890) of Western Australia and in these capacities did much to develop its rich agricultural, pastoral, and mineral resources. He entered the federal Parliament on its establishment in 1901 and represented Western Australia until his death at sea on September 3, 1918, while returning from London, where a peerage, the first granted to an Australian, had been conferred on him.

BIBLIOGRAPHY: F. K. Crowley, *Forrest 1847–1918*, vol. 1, *1847–91: Apprenticeship to Premiership*, St. Lucia, Queensland, 1971.

J. M. R. Cameron

Franklin, John (1786–1847) British naval officer and Arctic explorer. Born in Spilsby, Lincolnshire, Franklin joined the Royal Navy on October 23, 1800, as a first-class volunteer on board HMS *Polyphemus*. Britain was then engaged in the Napoleonic Wars, and Franklin was soon involved in the action: on April 2, 1801, *Polyphemus* took part in the Battle of Copenhagen. Soon after the battle, he joined HMS *Investigator* under Capt. Matthew FLINDERS for an expedition to the uncharted coasts of western Australia. Flinder's task was to make a thorough survey of the Australian coastline, of which only the eastern part was known in any detail. This task was only half complete, however, when *Investigator* showed signs of breaking up. Flinders abandoned the survey and returned to Sydney, where ships were found to take his crew home. After numerous difficulties, including a shipwreck in Torres Strait and an attack by French warships in the Strait of Malacca, Franklin finally reached home in August 1804.

Immediately after his arrival, Franklin returned to war duty. He was first appointed to HMS *Bellerophon*, on which he took part in the Battle of Trafalgar. In October 1807, he joined HMS *Bedford*, which was

stationed in South America until 1810, when she returned to the North Sea. Franklin was promoted lieutenant on February 11, 1808. In September 1814, *Bedford* sailed for North America to take part in the attack on New Orleans. Franklin returned home in May 1815, just as the war in Europe was ending, to begin a period of inactivity on half pay.

Franklin returned to sea in 1818 when the Admiralty embarked on a program of Arctic exploration as a means of employing some of its surplus manpower. He was appointed second-in-command to Capt. David Buchan on an expedition to attempt the passage across the Arctic Ocean from Spitsbergen (Svalbard) to Bering Strait on the *Dorothea* and *Trent*. The expedition was, of course, doomed to failure. The party spent about a month in Magdalenefjorden, northwest Spitsbergen, waiting for favorable ice conditions, then were imprisoned in the ice north of Spitsbergen for 3 weeks before Buchan ordered their return home.

John Franklin, British explorer who was generally acknowledged to be a good man in the wrong profession, was lost in the Arctic while searching for the Northwest Passage. [Library of Congress]

The Admiralty then chose to concentrate its efforts on the search for a NORTHWEST PASSAGE. Its first objective was to locate an entrance to the passage from Baffin Bay, a task assigned to William Edward PARRY. At the same time, realizing that explorers attempting the passage would be aided by some knowledge of the whereabouts of the north coast of North America, they appointed Franklin to command an overland expedition with the object of tracing that coast from the Coppermine River to Hudson Bay.

Accompanied by two midshipmen, Robert Hood and George Back, a naturalist, Dr. John Richardson, and two seamen, Franklin sailed for York Factory on a Hudson's Bay Company supply ship on May 23, 1819. From the outset, he was heavily dependent on the fur-trade companies. He intended to follow their supply lines northwest to Great Slave Lake, and he also relied on them for transport, manpower, accommodation, and provisions. This dependence proved to be a major handicap, for the two main companies were then engaged in bitter trade warfare in the north, and their ability to help the expedition fell far short of Franklin's expectations. After many early difficulties, Franklin entered the unknown territory north of Great Slave Lake in the summer of 1820, and built his base camp, Fort Enterprise, on Winter Lake near the Coppermine River. On July 14, 1821, his party, now swelled by some twenty canoemen recruited from the trading companies, finally set out for the north coast. It was then that the fur traders' inadequate support proved critical; with only poor equipment and provisions and a mediocre crew, Franklin faced innumerable problems. He made only slow progress along the coast and had explored eastward only to Turnagain Point, on Kent Peninsula, before the approach of winter, shortage of food, and mounting unrest among the crew forced him to stop. Moreover, because his canoes were now badly damaged, he was forced to return overland to Fort Enterprise. On that journey, half of the canoemen died of starvation, and another canoeman killed the officer Robert Hood and was executed under suspicion of cannibalism. The rest of the party arrived half-starved at Fort Enterprise to find it bare of the expected provisions and were saved only after Back managed to make contact with Indians.

After one more winter in the north, Franklin returned home to a hero's welcome in the autumn of 1822. He was made a post captain on November 20 and was elected a fellow of the Royal Society. On August 19, 1823, he married Eleanor Anne Porden, a poet, who died only 2 years later.

Within a year of his return, Franklin began to plan a second expedition to the north coast, this time with the intention of exploring east and west from the Mackenzie Delta. This time, he chose to take British seamen to replace the Canadian canoemen, to supply his own boats, and to send out equipment and provisions well in advance, in other words, to relieve himself as much as possible from dependence on the fur traders. He set off on February 16, 1825, again accompanied by Back and Richardson and with E. N. Kendall as surveyor. The party made good progress northward to Great Bear Lake, where they built their base, Fort Franklin. They set off on the main journey on June 22, 1826. In the Mackenzie Delta, the party separated: Richardson and Kendall turned east to explore the area to the Coppermine River, and Franklin and Back turned west to explore the coast to Bering Strait, where they hoped to meet HMS *Blossom*, under Frederick W. BEECHEY. Richardson and Kendall accomplished their task with little difficulty, but Franklin, hampered by bad weather, was obliged to turn back at Return Reef, Alaska, only halfway to his planned rendezvous at Icy Cape. Nevertheless, by contrast with the first journey, this expedition was a great success; Franklin accomplished most of his objectives with few problems and with minimal loss of life.

After his return home in September 1827, the Admiralty decided to discontinue its program of Arctic exploration. Franklin's services were rewarded with a knighthood in April 1828. On November 5, 1828, he married his second wife, Jane Griffin.

Franklin commanded the frigate *Rainbow* in the Mediterranean from November 1830 to January 1834. After that, however, he failed to secure another naval appointment, and in 1836 he accepted the post of lieutenant governor of Van Diemen's Land (Tasmania). His arrival there in January 1837 marked the beginning of the unhappiest period of his life. His wish to diminish the island's role as a penal settlement and to institute social reforms was opposed both by the Colonial Office and by a vociferous minority of settlers. In the face of this opposition, Franklin maintained his administration for 6 years before resigning and returning to England, his spirit broken.

Not long after his return in 1844, the Admiralty invited him to submit plans for the renewal of the search for a Northwest Passage. For Franklin, the invitation came as a much-needed tonic: from the start, he was determined to lead the venture himself. Moreover, despite his age (he was then 58), most of his Arctic contemporaries supported him. He was appointed to command the new expedition in February 1845 and set sail, with the ships *Erebus* and *Terror*, in May of that year. Two years later, in Victoria Strait in the Canadian Arctic, Franklin died. *See* FRANKLIN EXPEDITION AND SEARCH.

Two of Franklin's three expeditions were manifest failures, and it is generally acknowledged that he was no great explorer. In many ways, he was unsuited for exploration: his portly physique made him a poor overland traveler, and his limited talent for original thought led him into difficulties which better explorers would have avoided. But the courage with which he faced those difficulties, allied with a good-natured, gentle personality, won for him the enduring respect and affection of both his naval colleagues and the public.

BIBLIOGRAPHY: H. D. Traill, *The Life of Sir John Franklin, R.N.*, London, 1896.

Clive A. Holland

Franklin Expedition and Search

The 1845 expedition of Sir John FRANKLIN was intended as the culmination of a sustained effort by the Royal Navy to discover a NORTHWEST PASSAGE, the short sea route through American Arctic waters to the Pacific that had eluded explorers for more than three centuries. The Navy had already made great advances in the search. When its campaign began in 1818, a great swath of unexplored territory, some 2000 miles (3219 kilometers) wide, still separated Baffin Bay from Bering Strait. Within 20 years, naval ships had penetrated almost half of that distance, discovering Lancaster Sound, Barrow Strait, and Viscount Melville Sound; and successive overland expeditions had explored nearly the entire Arctic coastline of North America. Thus, the main task facing Franklin in 1845 was to discover a navigable communication between Barrow Strait and the north coast, an achievement which was generally believed to present few difficulties. He was instructed to commence his search in the unexplored region to the south and west of Russell Island in Barrow Strait. His alternative, if that should fail, was to search for an open sea in the equally unknown region north of Barrow Strait.

The expedition sailed from the Thames on May 19, 1845. It consisted of 129 men and two ships, HMS *Erebus* (commanded by Franklin himself) and HMS

Terror (Capt. F. R. M. Crozier), and was provisioned for 3 years. The expedition was last seen at the end of July by whalers in northern Baffin Bay; after that, it was never heard from again.

Two years passed before any general concern was expressed at home, and it was not until 1848 that the Admiralty felt any need to send out relief expeditions. But during the next few years anxiety increased considerably, and the search gathered momentum to become perhaps the biggest, and certainly the best-known, rescue attempt ever mounted in the polar regions. Even so, more than 10 years elapsed before the fate of Franklin and his men was fully revealed. His instructions, so precise in their appearance, proved so vague in fact that he could have come to grief almost anywhere in the Canadian Arctic archipelago, and indeed the search expeditions were obliged to explore almost the whole archipelago before the site of the Franklin tragedy was uncovered on King William Island.

The search began in 1848, when the Admiralty responded to mounting pressure from the public by sending out three separate relief expeditions: one following Franklin's prescribed route through Lancaster Sound, another sailing to Bering Strait in the hope that he might be found within reach of his goal, and one setting off overland through Canada to the Mackenzie River Delta.

The main expedition was commanded by Sir James Clark Ross on HMS *Enterprise* and *Investigator*. It left London on May 12, 1848, passed through Lancas-

ter Sound, and wintered at Port Leopold, northeast Somerset Island. In the spring of 1849, sledge parties searched the shores of Prince Regent Inlet but found nothing. Ross himself led a sledge party along the north coast of Somerset Island and into Peel Sound but found no indication that he was actually on the track of the missing ships.

In the meantime, Sir John Richardson's overland expedition had reached the Mackenzie Delta in August 1848 and had searched the coast eastward to the Coppermine River before wintering at Fort Confidence on Great Bear Lake. Richardson returned to England in 1848, leaving the Hudson's Bay Company's Dr. John Rae to continue the search in that region.

The third expedition to set out in 1848 was commanded by T. E. L. Moore on HMS *Plover*. He was directed to Bering Strait but arrived there too late to make any contribution to the search that year. A boat expedition left *Plover* in 1849 to examine the coast between Point Barrow, Alaska, and the Mackenzie River, but otherwise the ship's main role was to wait for Franklin's appearance in Bering Strait. She remained there, with occasional relief from HMS *Herald*, until 1854.

The unsuccessful return of both Ross and Richardson in the autumn of 1849 caused considerable disappointment and greatly increased anxiety at home. Yet in the public mind hope remained strong that Franklin and his men might still be alive (it was frequently recalled that John Ross had survived four Arctic win-

Lady Franklin, who refused to give up hope that her husband would return. She herself organized public sponsorship for the McClintock search in 1857, which finally found on King William Island concrete evidence of the fate of the expedition. [National Portrait Gallery, London]

ters, from 1829 to 1833), and in recognition of this hope the Admiralty laid plans for a massive new effort in 1850.

In all, the Admiralty sent out eight ships and more than 360 men in 1850, and privately sponsored expeditions added four more vessels to that total. Two ships, HMS *Enterprise* and *Investigator*, set out in January for Bering Strait; all the others sailed in spring on the more familiar voyage to Lancaster Sound. Capt. Horatio Austin commanded the largest fleet, consisting of HMS *Resolute* and *Assistance* and the steamers *Pioneer* and *Intrepid*, while an experienced Arctic whaling master, William Penny, took out HMS *Lady Franklin* and *Sophia*. At the same time, Lady Franklin launched her own campaign. She sent out *Prince Albert* under Charles Forsyth and also prompted the United States to join in with two ships, *Advance* and *Rescue*, sponsored mainly by the New York merchant Henry Grinnell. Finally, the veteran Sir John Ross, now more than 70 years old, took his schooner *Felix* to join the fleet heading for Lancaster Sound.

Capt. Erasmus Ommanney, commanding *Intrepid*, was the first into Lancaster Sound and, in mid-August, found the first traces of the Franklin Expedition at Cape Riley, Devon Island, and on Beechey Island. Penny's ships arrived soon after, and his men scoured Beechey Island, finding positive evidence that Franklin had wintered there in 1845–1846 but no written records or any indication of Franklin's future intentions.

Soon after, the Lancaster Sound fleet put into winter quarters, Penny and Ross in Assistance Harbour, Cornwallis Island, and Austin's ships not far away in Barrow Strait. Forsyth's *Prince Albert* returned home before winter to report the finds on Beechey Island, and the two American ships also withdrew prematurely from the search, albeit unintentionally. They drifted with the ice from Barrow Strait into Baffin Bay and, when finally released in Davis Strait in June 1851, had no choice but to return to New York.

In the spring of 1851, Austin and Penny divided between themselves the task of searching the unexplored coasts of the Arctic islands by sledge. It was in this task that Lieut. Francis Leopold MCCLINTOCK rose to prominence. After his experiences on James Ross's expedition of 1848–1849 he had perfected the technique of man-hauling sledges to such an extent that, under his management, Austin's sledge parties were each able to explore hundreds of miles of new coast without mishap. They charted much of the coastline of Prince of Wales, Bathurst, Byam Martin, and Melville Islands, while Penny undertook the exploration of Wellington Channel. In most circumstances, their efforts would have been acclaimed a triumph. But, for all that, they failed to find a single indisputable trace of the Franklin Expedition, and they returned home in 1851 to face widespread public disappointment.

While Austin and Penny were exploring in the Bar-row Strait region, *Enterprise* and *Investigator* were making significant discoveries farther west. *Investigator*, under Comdr. Robert MCCLURE, passed through Bering Strait in 1850 and discovered Prince of Wales Strait, between Banks and Victoria Islands, where she wintered. In 1851 McClure sent out sledge parties to explore the north coasts of those islands. Heavy ice prevented him from taking his ship through into Viscount Melville Sound; so he retreated from Prince of Wales Strait and took his ship around the west coast of Banks Island into McClure Strait, where he found a safe harbor in Mercy Bay. McClure was never able to extricate his ship from Mercy Bay: he remained beset there until rescue arrived in 1853.

In the meantime, Capt. Richard COLLINSON on board *Enterprise* arrived too late in Bering Strait to enter the ice in 1850; and when he reached the Arctic in 1851, he unwittingly duplicated many of McClure's discoveries in Prince of Wales Strait and on the west coast of Banks Island. Unlike McClure, though, he was unable to reach McClure Strait and eventually returned to winter on the west coast of Victoria Island. He went on to examine the south coast of Victoria Island (which, unknown to him, had already been discovered by John Rae in 1851) and came nearer than any before him to discovering the site of the Franklin tragedy when he examined the western shore of Victoria Strait in 1853. It was not until 1854 that Collinson finally set off for home through Bering Strait.

The long absence of both Collinson and McClure was partly the reason for the Admiralty's decision to continue the Franklin search after all but the most persistent optimists had abandoned hope. Fearing as much for the safety of the crews of *Enterprise* and *Investigator* as for those of *Erebus* and *Terror*, they elected to send out Austin's four ships, plus HMS *North Star*, on one final search expedition in 1852. Sir Edward BELCHER replaced Austin in command of the fleet, but many of Austin's officers, including McClintock, remained on board.

After passing through Lancaster Sound, Belcher's squadron divided into three parts to cover as wide a range as possible. Belcher himself took two ships into Wellington Channel; Henry Kellett and McClintock took two ships to Melville Island to search for Collinson and McClure as well as for Franklin, and *North Star* remained at Beechey Island. In the spring of 1853, McClintock again organized the exploration of an extensive area by sledge. One of the parties managed to locate *Investigator* in Mercy Bay and arranged the evacuation of the crew, while others added to the map the coastlines of Prince Patrick, Eglinton, and Emerald Islands and completed the charting of Melville Island.

In 1854 both Belcher and Kellett experienced difficulty in extricating their ships from the ice, and Belcher made a sudden (and, many believed, premature) decision to abandon them. The crews of Belcher's entire fleet and of *Investigator* returned home on *North Star* and on two supply ships that had arrived at Beechey Island.

Belcher's return home signaled the end of the official Franklin search. Despite pleas from Lady Franklin and her supporters, the Admiralty concluded that no member of the expedition could have survived nearly 10 years in the Arctic and that the addition of further expense to an already considerable total was not worthwhile.

In view of the great expense and the large numbers of ships and men that the Admiralty had committed to the search over a period of 7 years, it is ironic to reflect that, while all this effort failed to reveal a single clue as to the fate of Franklin, the truth was uncovered, just as the search was being called off, by a lone explorer who was not even looking for the Franklin Expedition. In the spring of 1854, as Belcher was planning his return home, the Hudson's Bay Company's Dr. John Rae set out for Boothia Peninsula to chart the last remaining unexplored section of the north coast of America, between Castor and Pollux River and Bellot Strait. When passing Pelly Bay, he met Eskimos who had seen a party of emaciated Europeans traveling down the west shore of King William Island several years earlier. Later, they had found the graves and corpses of this same party on the mainland, near the mouth of the Back River. Rae purchased from the Eskimos some relics, such as silver spoons and forks, which provided conclusive evidence that those Europeans had belonged to the Franklin Expedition.

Even after Rae's findings were reported, the Admiralty could not be tempted to reopen its investigation, and Lady Franklin was forced to seek public sponsorship for an expedition of her own. She won enough support to purchase and fit out the yacht *Fox*, which sailed under the command of McClintock in 1857. Following early difficulties, McClintock was unable to begin his search of King William Island until 1859. But when his sledge parties finally did reach the island, they found enough relics to permit a summary reconstruction of Franklin's voyage and to confirm its tragic conclusion. Most significantly, Lieut. W. R. Hobson discovered two brief notes, the only written records of the expedition ever to have been found, outlining Franklin's wintering at Beechey Island in 1845–1846, his circumnavigation of Cornwallis Island, and his second wintering (after almost certainly passing through Peel Sound and Franklin Strait) to the northwest of King William Island. An addendum to one of the notes records Franklin's death on June 11, 1847, the ships' besetment off King William Island throughout 1847–1848, and their abandonment, followed by an attempt to walk to Back River, in the spring of 1848. This story was completed by a trail of relics, graves, and skeletons along the western and southern shores of King William Island. It appears that no member of the expedition survived beyond 1848; starvation and scurvy rapidly overtook them all.

The Franklin search did not end with McClintock's return. During the next two decades the American explorers Charles Francis Hall and Frederick Schwatka both visited King William Island and its vicinity in the hope of discovering a more extensive written account of the expedition. And, despite evidence that any surviving records were almost certainly destroyed by Eskimos, the search has continued sporadically up to the present day. Most recently, as the survival of a written record appears increasingly improbable, searchers have concentrated on seeking the whereabouts of Franklin's ships. So far, however, nothing has been found to add substantially to the story revealed by McClintock. The reason for the Franklin tragedy will probably never be fully known.

BIBLIOGRAPHY: Richard J. Cyriax, *Sir John Franklin's Last Expedition: A Chapter in the History of the Royal Navy*, London, 1939; Leslie H. Neatby, *The Search for Franklin*, London, 1970; H. D. Traill, *The Life of Sir John Franklin, R.N.*, London, 1896; Noel Wright, *Quest for Franklin*, London, 1959.

Clive A. Holland

Fraser, Simon (1776–1862) Canadian fur trader and explorer of the Far West. Fraser was born in Bennington, in what is now Vermont. His father, a Scot fighting for the Loyalists, died during the American Revolution. In 1784 his mother took the family to Canada, and they settled in Cornwall, Ontario, where Simon grew up. In 1793, the year that Alexander MACKENZIE reached the Pacific overland, the 17-year-old Fraser was working as a clerk for the North West Company.

Rising in the company's service, he was elected a partner in 1801. In 1805 he was sent to establish the first trading posts west of the Rockies and to find new sources of furs. Aided by Indians, in 1805 he established Rocky Mountain Portage House (now Hudson Hope, British Columbia), followed Mackenzie's route by the Peace and Parsnip Rivers, then explored the Pack River to McLeod Lake, where he established Fort McLeod, the first white settlement west of the Rockies. In 1806 he explored various rivers to Stuart Lake and build Fort St. James on that lake and Fort Fraser on Fraser Lake. This great mountainous interior which he opened as the link between the plains and the Pacific in those latitudes reminded him of his mother's description of Scotland; consequently, he named it New Caledonia.

In 1808 Fraser explored to its mouth the river that now bears his name. It did not offer the company a navigable river, nor was it the Columbia, for which the company had been searching. In 1811 Fraser took charge of the company's Red River Department; he was one of the Nor'westers arrested by the 5th Earl of Selkirk of the Hudson's Bay Company as a participant in the "battle" (June 1816) at Seven Oaks, Red River of the North, stemming from a conflict between the North West Company and settlers supported by Selkirk and the Hudson's Bay Company. Retiring before 1820, Fraser settled in St. Andrews, Upper Canada

(Ontario). He died on April 19, 1862. Simon Fraser University in Burnaby, British Columbia, is named for him.

BIBLIOGRAPHY: W. Kaye Lamb, *The Letters and Journals of Simon Fraser, 1806–1808*, Toronto, 1960.

Barry M. Gough

John Charles Frémont's supposedly scientific expeditions to explore the American West eventually to the conquest of California. [Library of Congress]

Frémont, John Charles (1813–1890) American soldier, explorer, and politician. Three westward expeditions led by John C. Frémont from 1842 to 1845 constitute the first significant use of exploration as a diplomatic and scientific implement in acquiring territory for the United States. Born in Savannah, Georgia, and educated at Charleston College in South Carolina from 1829 to 1831, Frémont became an assistant engineer in the Topographical Corps in 1835 and was commissioned a second lieutenant 3 years later.

Preparations for Frémont's first major expedition in 1842 (June through October) began years before. In 1838 he accompanied the French scientist Joseph Nicollet westward from Fort Snelling on the Mississippi River in Minnesota to the Red Pipestone Quarry along the Minnesota River. The next year he joined Nicollet up the Missouri River to Fort Pierre, northeast over the plateau called the Coteau de Missouri, down to Joseph Renville's post near Lac Qui Parle, and along the Minnesota River back to the Mississippi. Frémont's experience and the expansionist interests of his influential father-in-law, Sen. Thomas Hart Benton of Missouri, came together in 1842, when they sought to establish American claims in Oregon. From St. Louis in the spring, the spirited explorer set out with a German cartographer and partner in many future ventures, Charles Preuss. A few miles upriver Frémont met Kit Carson (soon to be his lifelong friend), who agreed to serve as guide. Though making few discoveries, the group crossed the plains and mountains along the Oregon Trail and through South Pass. In a futile effort to establish his country's sovereignty, Frémont planted an American flag on the highest peak (named Frémont Peak) in present-day Wyoming.

Frémont's second expedition began in May 1843. It was ostensibly scientific, but its military features raise questions about its real objectives. In fact, his venture constituted an invasion of Mexican territory by an official armed party of the United States. Benton suggested that Frémont "connect the reconnaissance of 1842 with the surveys of [Naval] Commander [Charles] Wilkes on the coast of the Pacific Ocean, so as to give a connected survey of the interior of our continent." Frémont was to map the Oregon Trail, collect information pertaining to the possible construction of a line of forts, and locate the Buenaventura River, a mythical waterway that allegedly led to the sea. Late in May Frémont and around forty others, including Kit Carson and Thomas Fitzpatrick, pulled out of Kansas City.

After taking his men south along the Kansas River and through the mountains at the Cache la Poudre River in northern Colorado, Frémont moved across the desolate Laramie Plain to rejoin the well-known emigrant road at the Sweetwater River. Turning south at Soda Springs, his band reached the Great Salt Lake in early September. Bursting with excitement, the party's leader wrote: "I am doubtful if the followers of Balboa felt more enthusiasm when from the heights of the Andes, they saw the great Western Ocean." For some unexplained reason Frémont believed that the lake was unexplored. After several days of exploration the men pushed northward to the area below Fort Hall and along the Snake River toward Oregon. They completed this stage of the journey by following the Oregon Trail to the American mission run by Marcus Whitman at Fort Walla Walla and then moving to The Dalles in November. Setting camp, they visited Dr. John McLoughlin's Hudson's Bay Company's headquarters at Fort Vancouver.

Several days of rest passed before the Frémont party embarked for California and an eventual return across the Rockies. Late in November the men turned south toward Nevada, where they discovered Pyramid Lake. In January 1844 they began a westward crossing of the Sierra Nevada despite Indian warnings that it was dangerous at that season. Thirty days elapsed before the survivors made it through the treacherous passes, high drifting snow, and zero temperatures and stumbled through Carson Pass and onto John Sutter's ranch on the American River. Eventually the men made their way down the Sacramento and San Joaquin Valleys, through Tehachapi Pass (which they erroneously thought was Walker Pass), into the Mojave Desert, and eventually back to Independence in July 1844.

The trip had substantial results. After naming the western half of the desert the Great Basin, Frémont submitted a report (10,000 copies published as a government document) which advertised the West's agricultural capabilities, eventually guided emigrants west via the Platte River and South Pass, no doubt affected the Mormon decision to settle near the Great Salt Lake, and spread the explorer's fame throughout the nation.

It was Frémont's expedition beginning in July 1845 which aroused the great controversy still surrounding him. His instructions were to survey the Arkansas and Red Rivers and determine the points at which the 100° longitudinal boundary line of the United States touched these rivers. More than sixty men, including Carson and Fitzpatrick again, set out across the hot and dusty plains in summer. Going up the Arkansas River through Bent's Fort, they skirted the Royal Gorge, moved through the Tennessee Pass and along the White River, crossed the Grand and Green Rivers, went down the Duchesne and Timpanogos Rivers, and touched the Great Salt Lake. They then cut west across the Great Basin, naming Pilot Peak and the Humboldt River, both in present-day Nevada. Frémont's expedition had opened a new transcontinental route southwest from Great Salt Lake to northern California. By September he and his men again were at

Sutter's Fort. Frémont soon left for Monterey to engage in a long private talk with the American consul in California, Thomas O. Larkin.

Frémont's secret meeting has raised speculation about his motives in California. Though the explorer informed the Mexican commandant, José Castro, that his was a mission of peace, the presence of American troops aroused suspicions. Frémont received permission to winter in California, but in March 1846 Castro ordered him to leave. Confronted by a superior Mexican force, Frémont moved northward, near Upper Klamath Lake, where he received a government agent, Marine Lieut. Archibald Gillespie. He had a packet of letters from Senator Benton as well as an order from Secretary of State James Buchanan: Frémont was "to watch over the interests of the United States, . . . conciliate the feelings of the people of California, and encourage friendship towards the United States."

Frémont was not present when the Californians declared themselves the Bear Flag Republic and took Sonoma in June 1846, but his location nearby doubtless encouraged the move because it implied protection from the United States government. In any case he freely advised the rebels and offered to guard their prisoners. Almost 2 weeks after the skirmish at Sonoma, Frémont marched into the settlement, took command of the army, and led 134 MOUNTAIN MEN and Bear Flaggers southward to challenge General Castro. On the way they killed three Mexicans to avenge the deaths of two Americans. When they reached Monterey in late July, Mexican forces already had fled to the border. Frémont's men joined those of Commo. Robert Stockton in taking Los Angeles in August, and the conquest of California was complete.

The aftermath of Frémont's activities in California was also colorful. Near the end of the Mexican War, an intense argument developed between Frémont and Gen. Stephen Kearny over who was supreme commander in California. Though orders from Washington assigned the responsibility to Kearny, Frémont refused to obey and was court-martialed and found guilty in January 1848 of mutiny, disobedience, and conduct unbecoming an officer. President James K. Polk approved the sentence but remitted the penalties. Frémont, however, resigned his commission and left the Army.

His exploratory career was not over. During the summer of 1848, Senator Benton persuaded a friend and two St. Louis businessmen to support an exploration of a central route to San Francisco which would lead to construction of a railroad. Not surprisingly, he asked Frémont to lead the expedition. Gathering thirty-five men, Frémont in October again headed for the Rockies. He was to trace the 38th parallel through the Cochetopa Pass leading over the San Juan range, thereby establishing a new passageway connecting the San Luis Valley of Colorado with the Green River Valley. After following the Kansas River to the Arkansas River and Big Timbers Creek, the party took the south bank upstream past Bent's Fort to the Pueblo settle-

Frémont Peak, Wyoming: a romantic view appropriate to the public image John Charles Frémont strove to establish throughout his career. [Library of Congress]

ment. Though warned of a severe winter ahead, Frémont foolishly continued past Lancaster Lupton's Hardscrabble Post, over the Sangre de Cristo range at Robidoux Pass, and to the upper Rio Grande in San Luis Valley. Mid-December brought temperatures of −20°F (−29°C) and snow 10 feet (3 meters) deep as they attempted to cross the San Juan Mountains by Wagon Wheel Pass. Eventually the starving men had no alternative but to return to the upper Rio Grande and seek relief at Taos.

Despite the loss of more than ten men, Benton and Frémont called the expedition a success and prepared for a new venture. Frémont talked confidently of the coming southern railroad and planned to make his way west again, this time along the 32d parallel into California. In February 1853 Benton urged his Senate colleagues to consider a Pacific railway based on Frémont's "discoveries." But the plan did not materialize. In September he sent Frémont west on a private survey that brought him to the Green River and across Utah to Parowan by early 1854.

Frémont's major contributions were symbolic and inspirational. If anyone in the nineteenth century depicted the romance and heroism of the American pioneer blazing trails west, it was Frémont, whose persistent effort to become the spokesman for America's "manifest destiny" combined with widespread exaggerated publicity to portray him as the "great pathfinder." Although his "explorations" largely were over well-worn trails, his maps furnished the most accurate work on the Far West until the 1870s, and at least one historian has insisted that Frémont took the first major step toward destroying the widely held view that much of the trans-Mississippi West was the Great American Desert.

Because of the successes and failures of Frémont's Western ventures, it is understandable and perhaps fitting that he became one of California's first two United States senators in 1850 and the Republican party's first candidate for the presidency in 1856; yet he also was an unsuccessful Union commander in the Civil War (eventually removed by President Lincoln) and a failure in postwar railroad enterprises. He completed his public career by serving as territorial governor of Arizona from 1878 to 1883 and was restored to the rank of major general with retirement pay just before he died in 1890.

BIBLIOGRAPHY: Ferol Egan, *Frémont: Explorer for a Restless Nation,* Garden City, New York, 1977; John C. Frémont, *Memoirs of My Life,* 2 vols., Chicago, 1887; William H. Goetzmann, *Exploration and Empire: The Explorer and the Scientist in the Winning of the American West,* New York, 1966; Allan Nevins, *Frémont: Pathmarker of the West,* New York, 1939; id., *Frémont: The West's Greatest Adventurer,* 2 vols., New York, 1928; Mary Lee Spence and Donald Jackson, *The Expeditions of John Charles Frémont,* 2 vols., Urbana, Ill., 1973.

Howard Jones

Frobisher, Martin (ca. 1535–1594) English navigator, explorer, and adventurer. He was born in Yorkshire and was one of three children in a family of country gentry. After the death of his father young Frobisher was sent to London to be brought up by his uncle, Sir John York. Through his uncle's influence Frobisher obtained a place in the West African expedition of Thomas Wyndham in 1553 which partly explored the little-known area of lower Guinea. The commander and more than two-thirds of his men died from fever, but Frobisher managed to survive. In 1554–1555 he took part in another expedition to West Africa, was kidnapped by Negroes, and turned over to the Portuguese. After a period of imprisonment the Portuguese authorities released him and shipped him back to England. During the next few years Frobisher became involved in a number of maritime enterprises, accepting commissions from various parties and taking part in some activities of doubtful legality. On one occasion he spent some time in an English jail for having seized a cargo of wines belonging to a London merchant.

Frobisher's real claim to fame, however, rests on his three voyages to North America in search of the NORTHWEST PASSAGE. The first expedition, which got under way in June 1576, consisted of two ships, the *Gabriel* and the *Michael,* and an unnamed pinnace. Michael Lok, the London merchant, was the principal financial backer of this expedition, which unfortunately experienced unexpected difficulties. The pinnace was lost in a storm off the Shetland Islands. Both the ships reached the eastern coast of Greenland early in July, but shortly after their arrival the master and crew of the *Michael* deserted and returned to England. Frobisher and his men, meanwhile, pressed on in these northern waters and eventually discovered what is now Resolution Island off the southeastern cape of Baffin Island. In proceeding northward, Frobisher discovered a large bay, later named after him, which he thought was the passage to Cathay. This bay was explored for a distance of approximately 150 miles (241 kilometers). Some trading with the Eskimos was carried on, but Frobisher lost five of his men when they were carried off by the natives. This unexpected loss persuaded Frobisher to return to England, for his one ship was seriously undermanned. Before making the return journey, however, he took possession of the land in the name of Queen Elizabeth, seized one male Eskimo to bring to England, and stowed aboard a piece of coal-black stone which a crew member had picked up on shore. By its weight this stone seemed to be some kind of metal. Frobisher reached London on October 9. Rumors circulated that the black stone he had brought back contained gold, and there was a rush of excitement over the proposed second expedition.

Michael Lok formed the Cathay Company, a joint-stock corporation which received a charter from the crown. Lok was named governor for life, while Frobisher received the title of high admiral. The second expedition took its departure toward the end of May 1577 with three ships, the *Gabriel* and the *Michael* of the first expedition and the *Aid,* a fine vessel of some 200 tons provided by the Queen. Elizabeth also subscribed to this enterprise. Early in July this expedition reached Greenland. A determined search for the ore supposedly containing gold was undertaken by the crew members on the southwest shore of Frobisher Bay, for mining operations now superseded any interest in geographical exploration. In all some 200 tons of ore were stored in the three ships before they returned to England in September. In addition, three Eskimos—a man, woman, and child—were brought back, but they did not live long after coming to England.

Frobisher's third expedition consisted of fifteen ships including again the *Gabriel,* the *Michael,* and the *Aid,* which served as the flagship. The fleet left Harwich in May 1578 and bearing westward reached southern Greenland in the latter part of June. This area Frobisher named West England, and he took possession of the land in the name of the Queen. Sailing farther west through fog and mist, the fleet became separated. Frobisher missed the entrance to his bay because of the turbulent weather and entered what he called the Mistaken Straits, the waterway now known as Hudson Strait, which lies between Baffin Island and the northern coast of Labrador and Quebec. Not until the end of July did the fleet finally reassemble in Frobisher Bay. One vessel earlier had the misfortune of ramming an iceberg and was lost although the crew was saved. The summer was well advanced before suitable sites for the ore digging were finally found and the necessary work started. Under very difficult conditions somewhat more than 1300 tons of ore were loaded on the ships. So long had Frobisher remained in these northern waters that several ships just managed to clear the ice. All of them finally reached England in one port or another during the month of October. On the homeward journey a number of crew members died.

The ore brought back proved worthless insofar as precious metals were concerned, and the Cathay Company finally went bankrupt. Michael Lok, who had held such high hopes for success and who had expended so much of his own fortune in this venture, went to a debtors' prison. Many individuals sustained heavy financial losses in this unfortunate enterprise.

Frobisher himself now turned his attention to Ireland and received from the Queen the command of the *Foresight.* He devoted his attention to carrying on blockading duties off the Munster coast. During the rest of his life he continued in the Queen's service. In 1585 he held the rank of vice admiral in Sir Francis DRAKE's voyage to the West Indies. Three years later he received the honor of knighthood for his courageous activities in the Armada campaign. His later command involved an attack against a Spanish fort in Brittany, and in these military operations he received a bullet wound in his leg. Gangrene developed, and he died in Plymouth on November 22, 1594.

Martin Frobisher sailed to the Americas to find the Northwest Passage but instead brought back a lump of ore that started a sixteenth-century gold rush. [Library of Congress]

BIBLIOGRAPHY: William McFee, *Sir Martin Frobisher,* London, 1928; Samuel Eliot Morison, *The European Discovery of America: The Northern Voyages, A.D. 500–1600,* New York, 1971; Vilhjalmur Stefansson, *The Three Voyages of Martin Frobisher,* 2 vols., London, 1938.

Bernerd C. Weber

G

Gama, Vasco da *(ca. 1460–1524)* Portuguese navigator. Vasco da Gama was born at Sines in southern Portugal to a family of the lesser nobility and probably served as a soldier before taking to the sea, where he engaged in expeditions (and probably piracy) against the French in 1492. Da Gama was chosen by King Manuel to command the expedition to exploit the discovery by Bartolomeu DIAS of the Cape of Good Hope, the key to the sea route to India, because of his rank (he sailed as *capitão mor*, or captain major) and capabilities as a leader. His fleet consisted of four ships, *São Gabriel, São Rafael,* the *Berrio,* and a storeship. He left Lisbon with approximately 150 men on what was to be one of the epochal voyages in the history of the Western world on July 8, 1497. The fleet passed the Canaries on July 15 and on July 26 reached the Cape Verde Islands, where it remained at São Tiago until August 3.

Instead of following the West African coast, as the Henrician explorers had and as Bartolomeu Dias had on his pioneering voyage in 1487–1488, da Gama swung out into the Atlantic on a great looping course to escape the doldrums. The correctness of this procedure was verified on November 7, when he made his landfall at St. Helena Bay (32°40′S), about 125 miles (201 kilometers) north of the cape, where he remained for refitting until November 16. The Cape of Good Hope was easily doubled on November 22, and the ships entered Mossel Bay, where the storeship was broken up and a *padrão* (pillar) was erected, on No-

vember 25. The ships sailed on December 8 and reached Natal on Christmas Day. On January 11, 1498, an anchorage was made near the mouth of the Rio de Cobre. The fleet arrived at the Rio dos Bons Sinaes (Quelimane River) on January 25 and erected another *padrão*. Mozambique (Moçambique), the frontier of Muslim East Africa, was reached on March 2, and Mombasa on April 7. Here the Muslims attempted to capture and destroy the Portuguese fleet.

One week later, on April 14, da Gama reached Malindi, in what is now Kenya, where the single most fortuitous event of the voyage occurred. Da Gama met Ahmad ibn-Mājid, the celebrated pilot of the Indian Ocean, who agreed to show the Portuguese the ocean route to India. The ships left Africa on April 24 and after an uneventful voyage of 23 days sighted the Malabar coast of the Indian subcontinent, where they erected a *padrão* at Calicut on May 20.

The reception accorded to da Gama by the Hindu ruler, the Zamorin, was not very warm, and the Muslim traders were positively hostile to the intruding Portuguese. Inexplicably, da Gama had nothing of value to trade, and he departed from Calicut at the end of August on the homeward voyage. A stop was made at Angediva Island in the Indian Ocean before the ships made port on January 7, 1499, at Malindi after an arduous voyage of almost 3 months. A *padrão* was erected here and another one (the last) at Mozambique, which they reached on February 1. The Cape of Good Hope was rounded on March 20, and the *Berrio*,

Vasco da Gama shown above the city of Calicut, his first landfall in India, where he helped to establish the Portuguese sovereignty that became so important in East-West trade.

under Nicolau Coelho, reached the Tagus River on July 10. The flagship, *São Gabriel,* under da Gama sailed for Terceira in the Azores in a vain attempt to secure medical aid and a salubrious climate for Vasco's ailing brother Paulo. Vasco da Gama reached Lisbon on September 9 and entered the city in triumph on September 18. He was made Almirante do Mar das Indias, and sometime between 1499 and 1502 he married Catarina d'Atayde.

In February 1502, da Gama sailed in a fleet of twenty ships on a second voyage to India, where he established Portuguese suzerainty. He also demonstrated his legendary cruelty by bombarding Calicut before sailing for Cannanore and Cochin, where he established trading posts and made the local ruler a Portuguese vassal. He returned to Portugal in September 1503 and settled down to profit from the special privileges granted to him by the crown as a reward for his services. The King created him Count of Vidigueira in 1519 after some protracted negotiations. Da Gama returned to India as viceroy in 1524 and died there at Cochin on December 24. His remains were returned to Portugal in 1538 and interred at Vidigueira, but in 1880 they were supposed to have been exhumed and reburied in the Church of Santa Maria de Belém in Lisbon. However, there is reason to be-

Vasco da Gama's route to India, 1497–1499.

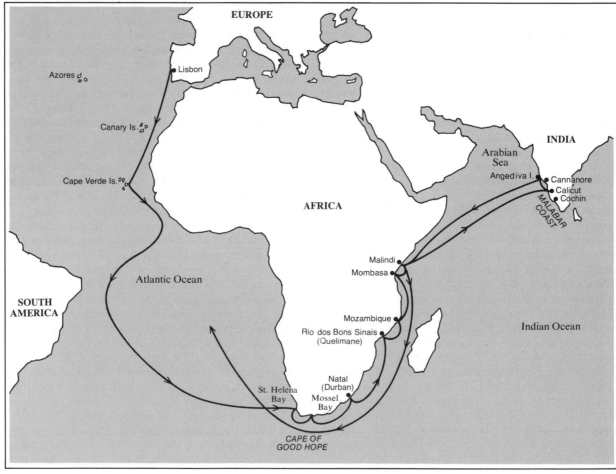

lieve that the wrong tomb was opened and that da Gama's body is still buried on his estate.

Da Gama is the hero of Luiz Vaz de Camões' epic poem, *Os Lusíadas (The Lusiads),* published in 1572. Indeed, it may be said that the discoverer owes his fame to the poet, who took a near-contemporary event as his theme to exalt the history of his native land and the magnificent accomplishments of its sons.

BIBLIOGRAPHY: Luiz de Camões, *The Lusiads,* tr. by Leonard Bacon, New York, 1950; id., *The Lusiads,* prose tr. by William C. Atkinson, Harmondsworth, England, 1952, reprinted 1973; Henry H. Hart, *Sea Road to the Indies,* New York, 1950; K. G. Jayne, *Vasco da Gama and His Successors,* London, 1919; Charles E. Nowell, "Vasco da Gama, First Count of Vidigueira," *Hispanic American Historical Review,* vol. XX, no. 3, August 1940, pp. 342–358; Ernest George Ravenstein (ed. and tr.), *A Journal of the First Voyage of Vasco da Gama, 1497–1499,* London, 1898; Henry E. J. Stanley, *The Three Voyages of Vasco da Gama,* London, 1869.

Martin Torodash

Garnier, Francis *(Full French name: Marie-Joseph-François Garnier; 1839–1873)* French explorer. Francis Garnier is deservedly the best-known of the French explorers active in mainland Southeast Asia during the nineteenth century. His name is linked most particularly with the Mekong Expedition of 1866–1868. Garnier was the son of an army officer. Contrary to his parents' wishes, he trained as a naval officer and was a member of the French forces that defeated the Vietnamese near Saigon in 1861. Attracted by the potential interest of colonial life, he joined the French administration in southern Vietnam in 1863. While serving as a colonial official between 1863 and 1866, he conceived a plan to explore the Mekong River, arguing that the river could be used as a commercial route into southwestern China.

In making his suggestion that the great river be explored for commercial purposes, Garnier was relying upon hope rather than on any available evidence that the Mekong could serve as a navigable trade route. Indeed, the scant information that was available to Garnier and his colleagues suggested that any ascent of the Mekong would be difficult if not impossible. None of this mattered, however, as Garnier played the major role in promoting the idea of exploration and was rewarded by gaining the post of second-in-command of the expedition, which was placed under the leadership of Comdr. Ernest DOUDART DE LAGRÉE.

The Mekong Expedition left Saigon in June 1866, apparently well equipped except for the absence of sufficient scientific instruments. In fact, as soon became clear, the expedition was excessively large and greatly hampered by the mass of stores that its members were expected to take with them in circumstances that often made travel difficult even for the most lightly equipped traveler. As second-in-command of the expedition, Garnier had to leave all the major decisions to Doudart de Lagrée until his leader's health grew so bad that collective decisions became the order of the day. Nonetheless, Garnier

was able to claim the right to undertake some secondary exploration with only the most limited assistance in terms of the numbers accompanying him. With only a single French companion he descended the worst section of the rapids dominating the Mekong in northeastern Cambodia. Next he undertook a mammoth journey on foot from southern Laos to Angkor and return, a distance of approximately 1000 miles (1609 kilometers), with only one Vietnamese orderly for company on the return leg of the journey. And once the expedition reached China, in late 1867, he traveled away from the main party to explore the navigational possibilities of the Red River, again accompanied only by his Vietnamese orderly.

Vasco da Gama as an old man, presumably enjoying the many profitable honors that came his way after his two voyages to India. [Casa de Portugal]

After the explorers had been forced to abandon their efforts to follow the course of the Mekong and Doudart de Lagrée had fallen dangerously ill, Garnier made one final effort, accompanied by three others of the French party and five Vietnamese of the escort, to chart the course of the Mekong closer to its source. They failed to achieve this goal and reached no farther than the city of Tali in western Yünnan Province. In reaching this far, however, they overcame great physical and political obstacles, and in the course of their travel through southwestern China they were the first men from Europe since Marco POLO to chart the course of the Yangtze River so far from the sea.

With Doudart de Lagrée's death in March 1868, Garnier automatically became leader of the expedition, and under his command the party returned to Saigon in June 1868. Garnier's major role in the achievements of the expedition, most particularly in terms of determination to continue in the face of grave difficulties and in relation to the collection of information, is undeniable. Equally important was the part he played as a cartographer. He personally mapped no less than 3100 miles (4989 kilometers) of previously uncharted territory. But as he quickly found once he returned to Paris, these achievements were resented by an important segment of French opinion that felt he had tried to place his own efforts in a more prominent light than those of his dead leader. The matter is open to argument, and there can be no doubt that Garnier was on occasion indiscreet and sometimes immodest. Nevertheless, his role was recognized and praised by those outside France who were in a position to make impartial judgments. In this regard it is striking to record the award conferred upon him and Dr. David LIVINGSTONE, the famed explorer of Africa, at the International Geographical Congress in 1871 and the medal he received from the ROYAL GEOGRAPHICAL SOCIETY of London.

After service in the Franco-Prussian War, Garnier returned to the East, first to solitary travel in China with the hope of finding the source of the tea and silk Chinese merchants sold to the West, then to the command of an unauthorized attempt to seize part of northern Vietnam for France. This latter effort was an outgrowth of the Mekong Expedition, since Garnier was sent to assist Jean DUPUIS, a French arms trader

The French explorer Francis Garnier charted thousands of miles of unexplored territory in Vietnam and became the first European since Marco Polo to penetrate southwestern China.

who had successfully used the Red River as a commercial route to Yünnan after having been alerted to the river's possibilities when Garnier and his companions passed through Hankow in 1868.

Garnier died in a minor engagement outside the Hanoi citadel in December 1873, at a time when his efforts were being disavowed by his superiors. His rash death matched the rashness of much of his life. Yet however rash and ready to act against the weight of evidence he was, his courage ensured that he pursued and achieved his goals as an explorer even under the worst conditions. Although his achievements were little known to the English-speaking world, his contemporaries were correct in judging them to be the equal of the achievements of the better-known explorers of Africa such as John Hanning SPEKE, Richard Francis BURTON, and Livingstone.

BIBLIOGRAPHY: Francis Garnier, *Voyage d'exploration en Indo-Chine*, Paris, 1885; Milton Osborne, *River Road to China: The Mekong River Expedition, 1866–73*, New York and London, 1975; Georges Taboulet, "Le voyage d'exploration du Mekong (1866–68): Doudart de Lagrée et Francis Garnier," *Revue Française d'Histoire d'Outre-Mer*, 1970.

Milton Osborne

Gilbert, Humphrey *(Humfry; ca. 1539–1583)* English explorer, soldier, and adventurer. He was born in Devonshire, the son of Otho Gilbert and of Katherine, daughter of Sir Philip Champernowne of Modbury. When Humphrey was 8 years old, his father died, and his mother became the third wife of the elder Walter Raleigh, also of Devon. Their firstborn child was the future Sir Walter Raleigh, who was born in 1552. Thus Humphrey and his brothers John and Adrian became the half brothers of Walter and Carew Raleigh.

Young Humphrey was educated at Eton and at Oxford. During the reign of Mary Tudor he entered the service of Princess Elizabeth, and he remained a member of her household after her accession to the throne in November 1558. In the early 1560s Humphrey Gilbert fought in the English Army in northern France, assisting the Huguenots in their struggle against the French crown. Later in that decade he served in Sir Henry Sidney's army in Ireland and was knighted in 1570 for his military achievements. In 1571, upon returning to England, Gilbert represented Plymouth in the House of Commons, where he supported the policies of Elizabeth I. The following year at the secret command of the Queen he led more than 1000 men to the Netherlands to aid the Dutch in their war against Spain.

Gilbert published in 1576 *A Discourse of a Discoverie for a New Passage to Cataia* (that is, Cathay), a work which had already circulated in manuscript form for 10 years. This account set forth in clear and vigorous terms Gilbert's ideas about the search for a NORTHWEST PASSAGE to the Far East and effectively developed public interest in the cause of overseas expansion. In June 1578 Gilbert received letters patent from the crown authorizing him to discover and explore such lands and territories not possessed of any Christian prince or people. He was also authorized to establish a colony with English subjects and to exercise viceregal powers of government. The first expedition of 1578–1579, in which Gilbert and Raleigh both participated, failed completely. Gilbert's second and last expedition sailed from Plymouth in June 1583 with five ships. Two days after this departure one of the ships deserted and returned to England. The other ships finally reached St. John's Bay, Newfoundland, where Gilbert found a number of fishing vessels manned by crewmen of various nationalities. On August 5 Gilbert formally took possession of the land in the name of the English Queen and set up the royal arms engraved in lead on a wooden post. Approximately a fortnight was spent in exploring the country and in prospecting for mineral wealth. During this time one ship was sent back to England with the sick and ailing, thus leaving only three vessels out of the original five. Gilbert's largest ship, the *Delight*, was wrecked on a reef, probably off what is now Sable Island, and many crew members were drowned. This loss was a serious one, for the *Delight* had been the supply vessel for the fleet.

By the end of August the homeward journey had begun with Gilbert commanding the *Squirrel* (10 tons) and Edward Hayes commanding the *Golden Hind*. North of the Azores the ships ran into a severe storm, and during the night of September 9 the *Squirrel* disappeared with all hands aboard. Only the *Golden Hind* remained to bring back to England the news of this disaster. In the broad story of English overseas expansion during the Elizabethan age Gilbert was more important for his unwearied advocacy of continued maritime endeavors than for any practical achievements of his own.

BIBLIOGRAPHY: William G. Gosling, *The Life of Sir Humphrey Gilbert, England's First Empire Builder*, London, 1911; Samuel Eliot Morison, *The European Discovery of America: The Northern Voyages, A.D. 500–1600*, New York, 1971; David B. Quinn (ed.), *The Voyages and Colonising Enterprises of Sir Humphrey Gilbert*, 2 vols., Hakluyt Society, 2d ser., nos. 83 and 84, London, 1940.

Bernerd C. Weber

Giles, Ernest *(1835–1897)* Australian explorer. Born on July 20, 1835, in Bristol, England, and educated at Christ's Hospital, London, Giles emigrated in 1850 to join his parents in Adelaide. He worked in the Victorian goldfields and as a clerk in Melbourne before spending the years from 1861 to 1865 assessing the pastoral potential of the country inland from the Darling River. Subsequently sponsored by Baron Ferdinand von Mueller, a noted botanist, and several wealthy Victorians, Giles investigated country to the west of the overland telegraph line between Adelaide and Darwin in 1872 and again in 1873 but on both occasions was beaten back by the aridity of the Gibson Desert, which he named in memory of an assistant who perished in its wastes. His 1875 journey, when he took little more than 5 months to cross the 2500 miles (4023 kilometers) from Port Augusta to Perth with camels, is one of the outstanding feats of Australian exploration, to be matched only by his return trip over the even more forbidding country just south of the Tropic of Capricorn. Although honored by several European learned societies for this double crossing over some of the most difficult country in the world, Giles received little recognition in Australia because he found no good pastoral land. He was again working as a clerk and in obscurity, this time at Coolgardie in the Western Australian goldfields, when he died of pneumonia on November 13, 1897.

BIBLIOGRAPHY: G. P. H. Dutton, *Australia's Last Explorer: Ernest Giles*, London, 1970; L. Green, *Ernest Giles*, Melbourne, 1963.

J. M. R. Cameron

Glazunov, Andrey *(fl. mid-nineteenth century)* Explorer of Alaska. A native-born employee of the Russian-American Company, he was sent by the chief manager, Ferdinand Petrovich von Wrangel, to explore the Kwikpak (Yukon) Delta by kayak in 1834. In 1835–1836 he described the lower Yukon from the mouth of the Anvik River and the region between the Yukon and the Kuskokwim, thus completing the exploration of the coastal area from Norton Sound to Kuskokwim Bay. He established the Russian settlement at Ikogmiut in 1842. *Richard A. Pierce*

Golovnin, Vasily Mikhailovich *(1776–1831)* Russian vice admiral, explorer of the Pacific Ocean and Kuril Islands, scholar, and writer. Between 1795 and 1800, as a midshipman and a lieutenant, Golovnin sailed with Russian naval vessels in the North Sea. Between 1802 and 1806, as a volunteer, he sailed on British warships in the Mediterranean, the Atlantic Ocean, and the Caribbean. In 1807 he set out from Kronshtadt for Kamchatka as commander of the sloop *Diana*. Unable to round Cape Horn because of contrary winds, he tried to go by way of the Cape of Good Hope but was detained at Simonstown because of the Anglo-Russian war. Held for a year, he finally evaded a large British squadron by night and escaped, arriving at Petropavlovsk in the fall of 1809. In 1810 he sailed from Kamchatka to Russian America, and in 1811 he surveyed the central and southern Kuril Islands. Landing at Kunashir Island for water, he, two officers, and four seamen were taken prisoner by the Japanese. He was kept for 2 years and 3 months on the island of Hokkaido until, in 1813, he was freed by the crew of the *Diana* under the senior officer, P. I. Rikord. Returning to Petropavlovsk, Golovnin then returned overland to St. Petersburg. Between 1817 and 1819, commanding the sloop *Kamchatka*, he made a round-the-world voyage to Kamchatka and Russian America. In 1830 he was made a vice admiral, and in the following year he died in St. Petersburg of cholera. His

The Australian explorer Ernest Giles leads a party through rough country. [Australian Information Service]

accounts, in Russian, of his imprisonment in Japan (1816), of his first voyage (1819), and of his second voyage (1821) and a history of famous shipwrecks display keen observation and literary ability.

Richard A. Pierce

Grant, James Augustus *(1827–1892)* British explorer and Africanist. Born in Scotland, Grant joined the Indian Army at an early age. While in India he met John Hanning SPEKE, and they joined together for traveling and hunting expeditions in the Himalayas. They become close friends, and later, after Grant had returned to England as a result of wounds suffered in the siege of Lucknow, Speke invited Grant to join him in his second journey to Africa's lake regions to ascertain the nature of the Nile's sources. Grant, a calm, unassuming man, proved an ideal counterpoise to the mercurial Speke. Their expedition provided further (although not absolute) confirmation that Lake Victoria was the source of the Nile. They also traveled in previously unexplored regions of Uganda and made significant contributions in various fields. Grant was especially useful as a collector and natural historian, as is evidenced by his description of the expedition, *A Walk across Africa* (1864).

Speke's accidental death shortly after the two returned to England led to Grant's emergence as the principal spokesman for his companion's controversial geographical theories. It also signaled the beginning of Grant's long career as an Africanist. He returned to Africa only briefly, as an intelligence officer in the Abyssinian campaign of Sir Robert Napier (later Baron Napier of Magdala), but he devoted the remainder of his life to various activities associated with the continent. His efforts included an extensive, lavishly illustrated description of the botanical collections made by the Speke-Grant expedition which com-

After the death of his friend and leader John Speke, James Grant carried on their work and became one of the foremost authorities on Africa in the nineteenth century. [James A. Casada]

Grant's drawing of a Zulu of the Delagoa Bay area. [James A. Casada]

prised the entire twenty-ninth volume of the *Transactions of the Linnean Society* (1872) and a slender volume entitled *Khartoom as I Saw It in 1863* (1885). He was a member of the Emin Pasha Relief Expedition Committee and saw long service on the Council of the ROYAL GEOGRAPHICAL SOCIETY and various committees of that body. He died in his native Nairn-

shire, widely loved and generally recognized as one of the great Victorian specialists on Africa.

BIBLIOGRAPHY: James A. Casada, "James A. Grant: A Bibliographical Survey," 2 parts, *Library Notes of the Royal Commonwealth Society*, new ser., nos. 184 and 185, September and October 1972, pp. 1–4, 1–4; id., "James A. Grant and the Royal Geographical Society," *The Geographical Journal*, vol. CXL, July 1974, pp. 245–253.

James A. Casada

Greenland

Greenland, the largest island in the world (840,000 square miles, or 2,175,600 square kilometers), is a Danish province situated mostly north of the Arctic Circle. It is buried by a thick ice sheet, and only 15 percent of its mass is unglaciated. This ice-free zone along the coasts is where Greenland's population (48,-581 in 1972) lives.

Eskimos were the first inhabitants of Greenland. Arriving from northern Canada, they lived on the north coast in a warmer time with some groups migrating southward along the east and west coasts, where they found hunting and fishing abundant. Archaeological sites which date to about 600 B.C. have been found.

The first white settlers in Greenland were Vikings from Iceland and Scandinavia. They settled in the mildest region, the southwest coast near Godthåb and Julianehåb. Ruins of their farms, churchyards, and burial grounds exist to this time. Walrus and narwhals were hunted to the north for commercial purposes. The printed record indicates that Vikings ventured onto the great ice cap but that settlement was impossible. *See also* NORSE MARITIME DISCOVERIES.

The first permanent white settlement after the Vikings was made in 1721 by Hans Egede, a Norwegian missionary. Other European missionaries followed and, failing to find the hoped-for Vikings, stayed to

work among the Eskimos. Scientific explorers did not investigate Greenland until the early nineteenth century. In 1806 the Danish government sent Karl Ludwig Giesecke, an itinerant actor and amateur mineralogist, to Greenland to prepare a survey of the geology of the island. In the 1850s Henrik Rink was assigned to Greenland, where he served for 20 years, primarily as governor. Trained in medicine, Rink studied and published material on the geology, glaciology, linguistics, and ethnology of Greenland. During the second half of the nineteenth century the Danish Commission for the Conduct of Geological and Geographical Research in Greenland was formed, and from 1876 to the present it has published more than 200 volumes of research.

The west coast of Greenland was delineated during the search for a NORTHWEST PASSAGE to Asia. The east coast was long unknown because of the heavy ice which congregates along the coast as it drifts down from the Arctic Ocean. The east coast became better known in the early twentieth century, when the ice drifting south decreased in volume. Northwest Greenland was explored by British and American expeditions which delineated the northern regions and used Greenland for explorations farther north toward the North Pole. Exploration of the coastal region was completed in 1907 when a Danish expedition rounded the northeast coast of Greenland and reached Cape Bridgman, which had been reached earlier from the west by the American Robert E. PEARY.

The great interior ice cap drew explorers' curiosity and scientific interest only after 1850, when it was realized that at one time great ice sheets had covered much of North America and Europe. After several unsuccessful attempts, the first serious expedition to explore the interior was made in 1883 by Nils Adolf Erik NORDENSKIÖLD, who penetrated for 84 miles (135 kilometers). Five years later Fridtjof NANSEN, Otto SVERDRUP, and four companions made the first crossing of the inland ice in the southern region from the uninhabited east coast near Kjoge (Køge) Bay to Godthåb on the west coast, a distance of 260 miles (418 kilometers). Nansen used skis and devised special sledges and cooking stoves for his expedition. He determined conclusively that the inland ice was unbroken and reached an elevation of some 9000 feet (2743 meters).

Greenland today is still habitable only along the coast, as 85 percent of the enormous island is covered by ice. [Danish Tourist Board]

In 1892 and 1895 Robert Peary crossed the north of Greenland twice; Knud Rasmussen, a Dane, repeated these journeys in 1912. These crossings served mainly as access routes to the northeast corner of Greenland and did not produce major scientific results. The first crossings, accompanied by important scientific discoveries, occurred in 1912 and 1913. The Swiss Alfred de Quervain used dogs and sledges to travel from the middle west coast to Angmagssalik. Johan Peter Koch, accompanied by the German meteorologist and geophysicist Alfred Lothar Wegener, made a crossing from Upernavik on the west coast some 700 miles (1127 kilometers) to the east coast at about 77°N. Koch reached elevations of nearly 10,000 feet (3048 meters) and suffered temperatures as low as −30°F (−34°C). Both expeditions made important studies of the climate and the snow and ice conditions of the ice cap.

These crossings, where scientific research had to be stolen from the time available for travel, proved unsatisfactory for the scientific explorers. In 1930 the systematic exploration of the inland ice began as it continues today, with inland year-round stations. Wegener established research stations at Weststation near the west coast and Eismitte near the geographical center of the ice sheet. Meteorological observations were made for the full year, and seismic measurements which determined the thickness of the ice were taken. Other studies determined that the 2 billion tons of ice on Greenland depressed the rock base some 1800 feet (549 meters) into the earth's surface. Also in the early 1930s, a British expedition led by H. G. Watkins maintained a research station in the south of Greenland for 6 months and photographed much of the coast.

During World War II the Germans used submarines to establish meteorological stations along the east coast. These were destroyed by the U.S. Coast Guard. Large transport air bases were built on the west coast by the U.S. Army Air Force and were used heavily in the movement of airplanes and men to England.

Since the end of World War II scientific exploration has been characterized by permanent bases along the

Modern-day Greenland continues to fascinate scientists, who explore the interior from permanent research stations, often using dog sledges not unlike those of the earlier explorers. [Danish Tourist Board]

coast and on the inland ice, helicopter and ski-fitted airplanes to transport explorers, and tracked vehicles for traverses. Glaciologists have drilled ice cores through the ice sheet to determine past climate from records stored in the ice and have developed airborne sounders to measure electronically the thickness of the ice and to plot the terrain under the ice.

In 1977 the Danish and United States governments joined in a multiyear research program, the Greenland Ice Sheet Program (GISP), to study the inland ice. Greenland will continue to be explored in the future, but the men and women who search there will be scientific investigators, not geographical explorers.

BIBLIOGRAPHY: Finn Gad, *The History of Greenland*, 2 vols., Montreal, 1971–1973; L. P. Kirwan, *A History of Polar Exploration*, New York, 1960; Fritz Loewe, *The Scientific Exploration of Greenland from the Norsemen to the Present*, Institute of Polar Studies Report No. 35, Columbus, Ohio, 1970; P. E. Victor, *Man and the Conquest of the Poles*, London, 1963.

Peter J. Anderson

Gregory, Augustus Charles (1819–1905) Australian explorer and surveyor. The second son of a retired army officer who helped colonize Western Australia, Gregory was born in Farnsfield, Nottingham, England, on August 1, 1819. He joined the Western Australian Survey Department in 1841. Five years later, with his brothers Francis and Henry, he explored an extensive area to the north of Perth and discovered coal in the Irwin River. In 1848, while examining the pastoral potential of country inland from Shark Bay, he discovered lead in the Murchison River. His major northern Australian expedition of 1855–1856, financed by the British government, reversed the 1844 route of Ludwig LEICHHARDT with

considerable success and opened up much new land for pastoral occupation. His 1858 expedition from Brisbane to Adelaide was also successful, for in addition to finding further good land, he demonstrated that many rivers drained into Lake Eyre and thus solved the puzzle of Australia's inland drainage. Gregory became surveyor general of the newly established state of Queensland in 1859 and served in several official positions until his death in Brisbane on June 25, 1905. He was knighted in 1903 for his contribution to Australian exploration.

BIBLIOGRAPHY: J. H. L. Cumpston, *Augustus Gregory and the Inland Sea*, Canberra, 1972.

J. M. R. Cameron

Augustus Charles Gregory's 1858 expedition across Australia finally solved the riddle of the continent's inland drainage system. [Australian Information Service]

H

Hakluyt, Richard *(ca. 1552–1616)* English geographer, translator, and historian of explorations. He was born in or near London, probably in 1552. His family, of Welsh extraction, had been settled in Herefordshire at least since the thirteenth century. After the early death of his parents Richard was brought up under the guardianship of a cousin, also named Richard Hakluyt, a lawyer of the Middle Temple. The elder Hakluyt had a keen interest in geography and awakened the interest of his youthful charge in geographical matters. Young Richard was a queen's scholar at Westminster School, and in 1570 he entered Christ Church, Oxford, where he received his B.A. degree in 1574 and his M.A. degree in 1577. After completing his formal training he was ordained in the Church of England.

Hakluyt made definite contributions to the fields of geography and historiography as well as holding a number of important ecclesiastical positions. He was the first scholar to lecture on modern geography at Oxford, and in his own day he became known as a vigorous and effective advocate of English maritime enterprise in the New World. Between 1583 and 1588 he served as chaplain to the English Ambassador in Paris, Sir Edward Stafford. This Continental sojourn afforded Hakluyt a valuable opportunity to learn much about the maritime activities and interests of other countries.

In 1584, at the request of Walter Raleigh, he wrote an important state paper which is conventionally ab-breviated as *A Discourse of Western Planting.* This work circulated in manuscript form for nearly three centuries, not being published until the reign of Queen Victoria. In this discourse Hakluyt cogently presented the arguments for English overseas expansion, pointing out that a colony in North America would provide an important base for the discovery of a NORTHWEST PASSAGE to the Far East.

Hakluyt was tireless in his efforts to collect travel accounts. He wished to publish these records in order to stimulate his countrymen to further efforts in maritime exploration and discovery as a counterpoise to the great power of Spain. His most important publication was the second edition of *The Principall Navigations, Voiages and Discoveries of the English Nation,* which appeared in three large volumes in 1598–1600. This monumental work constitutes an important source book of geographical knowledge and provides a remarkable insight into the nature of the Elizabethan age. Hakluyt not only collected and edited material on English voyages but also sought out and translated himself the travel literature of other countries.

Hakluyt died in London in November 1616 and was buried in the south transept of Westminster Abbey. The grave was not marked, and no portrait of him is known to exist. His writings are his true memorial and establish his just claim to fame.

BIBLIOGRAPHY: George B. Parks, *Richard Hakluyt and the English Voyages,* 2d ed., New York, 1961.

Bernerd C. Weber

Hanno *(fl. probably fifth century B.C.)* Carthaginian navigator. Hanno was perhaps a leading statesman of the Phoenician colony of Carthage at a time when the Carthaginians had suffered setbacks in wars with the Greeks of Sicily and were concerned to consolidate monopolistic control over the western Mediterranean and the Atlantic coasts beyond. Carthage had already established small settlements or watering points along the Moroccan coast at least as far south as Mogador, and it was in this direction that Hanno sailed. A Greek version of what was said to be a report of his voyage has survived; it is mentioned by several ancient writers. Unfortunately the report raises so many problems of interpretation that certainty about the motives and scope of the voyage cannot be obtained. It is improbable that the notoriously secretive Carthaginians would have published a report unless it was as likely to deter or mislead as to encourage competitors.

The first European to reach the Arctic overland from Hudson Bay, Samuel Hearne made his journey across Canada by one-man sled and canoe. [Library of Congress]

The report says that the expedition was ordered to found colonies, no mention being made of trade. However, most scholars associate it with a report in HERODOTUS OF HALICARNASSUS of about the same date of a gold trade between indigenous tribes and Carthaginians on the West African coast. The size of the fleet (sixty fifty-oared galleys) looks feasible, but 30,000 passengers is a gross exaggeration. It is, however, reasonable to suppose that some new colonies were established, though only two of those mentioned in the report were heard of again. A major error, perhaps deliberate, put the Lixus River (Oued Loukkos) south of Cape Soloeis (Cabo Cantim) instead of north of it; perhaps the Darat (Oued Dra) was meant. The most southerly colony was Cerne (named by a later Greek writer apparently independently as a Carthaginian trading post), which is generally identified with Hern Island at the mouth of the Río de Oro. Beyond Cerne, the effective limit of navigation along this coast according to the Greek writer, Hanno undertook two missions, perhaps for purposes of exploration. A river named Chretes was probably the Senegal River (known to the Romans as Bambotum). If Cerne was really Hern Island, 12 days' sailing apparently brought Hanno to Cape Verde. On an island off "West Horn" (perhaps Bissagos, or Bijagós, Bay) the explorers came across hairy savages called by the natives "gorillas," the source of the modern term. At almost the final point of the voyage they came to a "region from which came streams of fire," named by them Chariot of the Gods. This has been taken to be a volcano, perhaps Mount Cameroun, but may refer to bush fires and be no farther than Mount Kakoulima, in Guinea.

The extent of Hanno's voyage has sometimes been minimized in view of the many difficulties experienced by the Portuguese along this coast, though it may have had antecedents of which we are ignorant. However, the trading possibilities in the area appear to have been limited; none of the Carthaginian colonies attained much importance, and when after the destruction of Carthage in 146 B.C. the Romans dominated the western Mediterranean, they showed no interest whatever in the West African coast, even after they founded the province of Mauretania, extending as far south as the area of Rabat.

BIBLIOGRAPHY: B. H. Warmington, *Carthage*, New York, 1960.

B. H. Warmington

Hasan ibn-Muhammad al-Wazzan al-Zayyati, al- *See* LEO AFRICANUS.

Hearne, Samuel *(1745–1792)* English explorer of the Canadian north. Hearne was born in London. At the age of 11 he entered the Royal Navy, but at about 20 he joined the Hudson's Bay Company and was sent to Fort Prince of Wales (now Churchill) at the mouth of the Churchill River. In 1769 he examined the west coast of Hudson Bay. He then traveled inland from the fort to the south of Chesterfield Inlet and to Dubawnt Lake. In 1770 he again set out, this time via Clinton Lake to the mouth of the Coppermine River on the Arctic Ocean, returning home via Great Slave Lake. Hearne thus became the first white man to reach the Arctic overland from Hudson Bay. He traveled with Indians only, dragging a one-man sled overland in winter and traveling by canoe in summer. Hearne was the first explorer to give a clear account of the barren lands and of Eskimo life in these latitudes. In his journals he recorded his observations of Indian-Eskimo violence (this was the first such report).

In 1774 Hearne built Cumberland House, the Hudson's Bay Company's first post in the interior, as a counter to North West Company expansion. In 1775 he became governor of Fort Prince of Wales and was captured by the French naval officer Jean-François de Galaup, Comte de LA PÉROUSE in 1782. He was taken to France, where he was released on condition that his account of his Arctic travels be published (it appeared in 1795 with the title *Journey from Prince of Wales's Fort in Hudson's Bay to the Northern Ocean*). In 1783 the company sent him out to reestablish a post at Churchill. He remained there until 1787, when ill health forced him to return to England, where he died.

BIBLIOGRAPHY: Richard Glover (ed.), *A Journey to the Northern Ocean*, Toronto, 1958; J. B. Tyrrell (ed.), *Journals of Samuel Hearne and Philip Turnor*, Toronto, 1934.

Barry M. Gough

Hedin, Sven Anders *(1865–1952)* Swedish explorer. Hedin's lifelong interest in Asia began when, upon graduating from high school in Stockholm in 1885, he was offered a post as tutor to a Swedish youngster whose father was an engineer in the Baku oil fields, on the Caspian shore of the Caucasus. At the close of his work there, Hedin traveled first to Teheran, then continued on horseback across Persia (Iran) to the Persian Gulf, thence to Baghdad, and returned across western Persia to Teheran. Although his journey was an adventure rather than a scientific undertaking, it opened to him the vista of a life as an explorer.

After graduating from Uppsala University, Hedin went to Berlin to study geography under the direction of Ferdinand von Richthofen, the leading authority on Asia. His studies were interrupted, however, by his appointment as interpreter to a Swedish diplomatic mission traveling to Persia, Hedin having acquired the reputation of being an unusually skilled interpreter. He left the Swedish mission in Teheran, traveled across northern Persia to Russia's newly acquired domain in Central Asia, and went as far east as Kashgar (K'oshih) in Chinese Central Asia.

Returning to Europe, Hedin completed his studies in Germany and in 1899 embarked on the first of his scientific expeditions to Central Asia. Having crossed the highlands known as the Pamir, he attempted to climb Mount Muztagh Ata, continued on to Kashgar in the Tarim Basin, and undertook the crossing of the Takla Makan desert, which occupies the central portion of that basin. That journey almost ended in tragedy, for Hedin underestimated the time needed to cross the desert, supplies of water ran out, and several members of the expedition died. It was only Hedin's will to live and his finding a watercourse at the last moment that saved his life and that of his guide. His next goal was the terminal lake of the Tarim Basin, called Lop Nor. This shallow lake had long been the object of speculation among geographers because of its changing position, attested by ancient Chinese records and by a survey by Nikolay PRZHEVALSKY. Hedin pinpointed the location of Lop Nor and, in the course of his journey, discovered in its vicinity the ruins of cities covered by desert sands. He made a first, short excursion into northern Tibet and completed his expedition by crossing Chinese Central Asia to Peking.

In 1899 Hedin embarked on his second expedition. He traveled by boat down the Tarim River, mapping accurately its meandering course, and made further studies in the area of Lop Nor. Thence he turned southward to Tibet but was stopped by Tibetan authorities short of his goal, the "forbidden city" of Lhasa, Tibet's capital. Turning westward, he then mapped part of the great mountain system that forms the northern boundary of the Tibetan plateau, named by Hedin Transhimalaya.

Hedin's third expedition began in 1905, under serious political difficulties. Both Britain and Russia forbade him to enter Tibet, the goal of the expedition, from their respective territories, for they did not want to disturb the status quo of the land they considered a buffer zone. During the first part of his journey, Hedin crossed the desert of eastern Persia and completed the first geodetic route survey of that area. He then en-

tered Tibet from Ladakh, from the northwest, explored and mapped Transhimalaya in great detail, and determined the sources of the Indus, the Sutlej, and the Brahmaputra.

With great skill Hedin made continuous and carefully controlled traverses of much of central and western Tibet, and his exceptionally accurate sketches and panoramas served as the basis of the first reliable maps of that part of Central Asia. His collections of geological specimens were equally valuable to scholars studying the geology and geomorphology of the area.

Hedin traveled alone on these expeditions, accompanied only by native servants, and relied entirely on his own observations, maps, panoramas, drawings, and journals while preparing the first of his reports on these journeys, addressed largely to the general public. Later he obtained the collaboration of specialists and published detailed scientific reports. *Scientific Results of a Journey in Central Asia* (1904–1907) and *Transhimalaya* (1909–1913), among others, remain milestones in the scientific description of Tibet and of its northern borderlands.

Following World War I, Hedin returned once more to Central Asia, this time concentrating entirely on western China rather than on Tibet. The germ of this fourth expedition, begun in 1926, was the desire of Lufthansa, the German airline, to survey an air route from Berlin to Peking, passing through western China. This time Hedin was accompanied by a small group of meteorologists charged with establishing ground weather stations preparatory to the opening of the air route. Difficulties in Germany prevented the completion of the work, but Hedin managed to obtain funds to continue the expedition, concentrating on scientific rather than on practical matters.

The Sino-Swedish Scientific Expedition to the Northwestern Provinces of China spent nearly 8 years in the field, from 1928 to 1935. Hedin recruited a distinguished group of specialists, both Swedish and Chinese, representing geology, geomorphology, paleontology, geodesy and astronomy, botany, meteorology, archaeology, and ethnography. Their reports, now exceeding fifty volumes, are still being pub-

Sven Anders Hedin, left, and F. A. Larsson look their camels over before setting out across the desert. [Swedish Information Service]

Prince Henry the Navigator combined organizational and leadership talents to catalyze the great era of Portuguese exploration and discovery. [Portuguese National Tourist Office]

lished; together with an atlas of Central Asia, they represent the last major contribution by an international team of scholars to the knowledge of Central Asia past and present. The last phase of this, Hedin's last expedition, was a survey, headed by Hedin, of a possible motor road from China proper to the province of Sinkiang.

Through the earlier years of his career Sven Hedin was a loner who considered himself a pioneer, surveying territories as yet unexplored, gathering a mass of observations, and skillfully presenting them both to the general public and to the scientific community in books, articles, and public lectures. On his last expedition, between 1926 and 1935, he accepted the role of leader and coordinator of a group of highly specialized scholars, exploring in depth and with the greatest accuracy possible the problems presented by Chinese Central Asia. The results of the nearly 40 years he spent in the heart of Asia stand as a monument to his energy and skill as an observer.

BIBLIOGRAPHY: Sven Hedin, *My Life as an Explorer*, tr. by Alfhild Huebsch, Garden City, N.Y., 1925; Karl F. Kohlenberg, *Sven Hedin: Vorstoss nach Innerasien*, Balve, Sauerland, Germany, 1976; Sten Selander, *Sven Hedin, En äventyrsberättelse*, Stockholm, 1957.

George Kish

The coast of West Africa explored by Portuguese mariners under the direction of Prince Henry the Navigator.

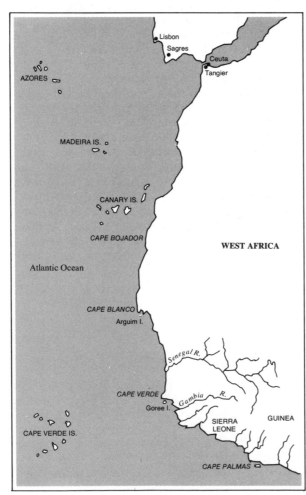

Henry *(Henrique, known as the Navigator; 1394–1460)* Portuguese nobleman and promoter of navigation. Born in Porto (Oporto) on March 4, 1394, Infante Dom Henrique was the third surviving son of five born to John I, founder of the House of Aviz, and Philippa of Lancaster, daughter of John of Gaunt. His surname, the Navigator, was not employed by the Portuguese during his lifetime (indeed, Henry never went to sea) but was conferred by his English biographer, Richard Henry Major, in 1868. Henry, although not a scholar, was well grounded in science, mathematics, and astronomy.

His participation in the assault and conquest of Ceuta, the Muslim stronghold in northern Morocco, on August 21, 1415, marked his emergence as a figure in history. He was knighted, and his father rewarded him for his services with the titles of Duke of Viseu and Lord of Covilhã and with the governorship of Algarve, the southernmost province of Portugal, where he established headquarters at Sagres and surrounded himself with scientists and cosmographers, most of whom were Jews. Great advances were made in map making and shipbuilding, the crowning achievement of the latter program being the development of the caravel. At Sagres he evolved a definite program of geographical exploration, as opposed to casual commercial voyaging, and provided the organization, encouragement, knowledge, and money for discoveries, revenues being derived from Henry's position as governor and administrator of the Order of Christ. Two distinct directions were taken: westward exploration into the Atlantic and exploration along the west coast of Africa. Henry's purposes were to find the African sources of gold which had been reaching Morocco via the caravan routes, to locate the lengendary Christian kingdom of PRESTER JOHN, and possibly to reach the Indies. In 1419 the Madeira group of islands was rediscovered by João Gonçalves Zarco and Tristão Vaz Teixeira, and colonization was begun in 1425. Between 1427 and 1432 expeditions to and discovery of the Azores by Gonçalo Velho were achieved.

The African voyages did not achieve anything of note until 1434, when Cabo Bojador, the known southern limit of the Atlantic Ocean and the West African coast, was rounded by Gil Eannes (Eanes), an achievement not merely over a geographical barrier, but over a more formidable psychological unknown. This first real step on the sea road to India, made on the fifteenth attempt, was Henry's most important achievement in the field of discovery and exploration. During the next 2 years his ships advanced more than 250 miles (402 kilometers) down the coast, an advance interrupted only by Henry's failure to conquer the Canary Islands, title to which was reaffirmed to Castile by a papal bull in 1436. The next year, 1437, Henry led a disastrous military expedition to Tangier, where his brother Ferdinand was surrendered as a hostage to the Moors and subsequently died in captivity. Henry returned to Algarve and built the Vila do Infante at Sagres.

In 1441 Cape Blanco (Cap Blanc) was discovered by Nuño Tristão. The same year, Antão Gonçalves reached the Rio do Ouro (Río de Oro), where he captured some natives and took them to Portugal. This marked the beginning of the slave trade, which subsequently was headquartered on the island of Arguim (Arguin), which Tristão reached in 1443 and fortified in 1448. During 1444 and 1445 Dinis Dias discovered the Senegal River and Cape Verde (Cap Vert) and reached the island of Gorée, beyond which the African coast trends eastward. In 1445 Álvaro Fernandes reached the Cape of Masts on the Guinea coast. By this time the search for gold and slaves seems to have supplanted any scientific or religious aims.

The Cape Verde Islands were discovered in 1456 by Alvise da Cadamosto and Antoniotto Usodimare; Cadamosto had reached the Gambia River the previous year. On the last of the Henrician voyages in 1460, Pedro de Sintra reached Sierra Leone, about 1500 miles (2414 kilometers) down the West African coast. This is commonly considered to be the farthest point reached, although Henry's statement in a document of 1458 that he had knowledge of "300 leagues of the land of Guinea" indicates that Cape Palmas may have

been reached. He died on November 13, 1460, at Sagres. Although he left no corpus of writings and eschewed the limelight, he can truthfully be said to have been the instigator of the great age of discovery and exploration and, even if only inadvertently, the precursor of Christopher COLUMBUS, Bartolomeu DIAS, and Vasco da GAMA.

BIBLIOGRAPHY: C. Raymond Beazley, *Prince Henry the Navigator*, London, 1895; Richard Henry Major, *The Life of Prince Henry of Portugal*, London, 1868; Edgar Prestage, *The Portuguese Pioneers*, London, 1933, reprinted 1966.

Martin Torodash

Herodotus of Halicarnassus (ca. 490–420 B.C.)

Greek historian. Conventionally described as the Father of History, he wrote about the war between the Persian Empire and the Greeks that ended in a Greek victory in 478 B.C. This great work, which has survived, was based to a considerable degree on personal researches involving widespread traveling in the Aegean, southern Italy, Babylonia, Egypt, and the Black Sea. Herodotus had a great interest in the ethnographical aspect of geography and included digressions on many of the peoples he encountered, especially where relevant to his theme. From these digressions and other indications we can construct a model of the known world as

The world according to Herodotus, Greek historian of the fifth century B.C. [H. F. Tozer, A History of Ancient Geography, Cambridge, England, 1897]

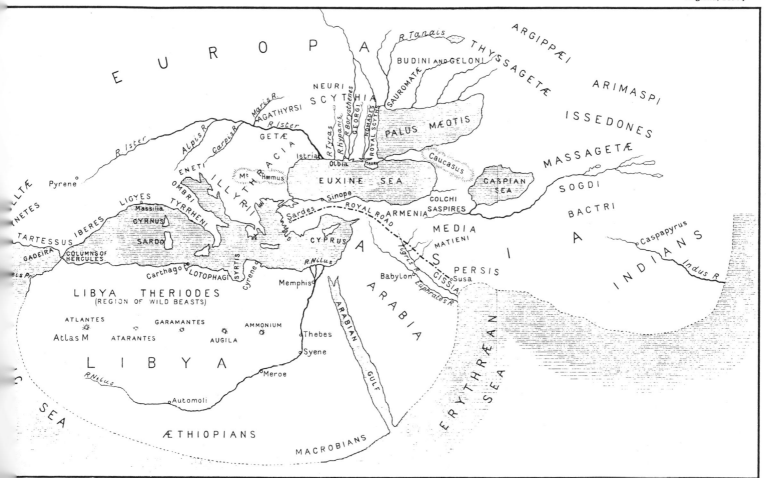

it appeared to educated Greeks of his time. He also drew material from the lost work of Hecataeus of Miletus (fl. ca. 520–500 B.C.), who wrote the first-known quasi-geographical work, on the cities and tribes surrounding the Mediterranean.

Herodotus rejected the view of the known inhabited world as being circular and surrounded by the Ocean Stream, and considered its east-west dimension to be much greater than its north-south. Although he accepted an already-established division into three continents, Europe, Asia, and Africa, he also regarded Africa as an extension of Asia. Europe was separated from Asia not by a north-south line but by an east-west one, along the Phasis (Rioni) River with a projection eastward. To the north and east of this line Europe extended indefinitely, while to the south and east land extended to beyond the Indus; whether both continents ended on the sea he did not know. On the other hand, he believed that Africa had been circumnavigated but had no concept of its true size, putting its southern coast at about the same latitude as Aden.

His knowledge of the far west and northwest was limited to the Phoenician colony of Gadir (Cádiz); Phoenician control undoubtedly prevented Greek knowledge of this area. He knew of the great length of the Danube. From Greek colonies in the Black Sea he obtained some information of relatively distant parts of south Russia and Siberia and as far as possible rejected the more fabulous stories. Misconceptions included a gross exaggeration of the east-west dimension of the Black Sea and the general size of the Sea of Azov. The Dniester, Bug, Dnieper, and Don were correctly enumerated. Herodotus did not know of the Volga but, unlike most later writers, correctly viewed the Caspian as a vast lake.

In Asia he could enumerate, presumably from Persian sources, the administrative divisions of the Persian Empire as far as the Indus Valley but had little information beyond this. He informs us that Darius I had employed a Greek sailor, Scylax of Caryanda, to sail down the Indus Valley and along the inhospitable Persian and Arabian coast to the Red Sea.

His information about Egypt south of Meroe (Merowe) was vague, and he believed that the Nile flowed from west to east here. Like countless others after him, he inquired about its source but got no good information. He believed the oases in North Africa stretched at regular intervals from Egypt to the Atlantic and knew of the Sahara but nothing south of it. He also had a story (often disputed) that Africa had been circumnavigated by the Phoenicians. Herodotus is a prime example of a combination of interest in both physical geography and the cultural traits of non-Greek peoples which dominated much of the Greek approach to geography.

BIBLIOGRAPHY: *Herodotus*, Loeb Classical Library ed., 4 vols., London and New York, 1920–1924; J. O. Thomson, *History of Ancient Geography*, Cambridge, England, 1948.

B. H. Warmington

Hind, Henry Youle (1823–1908) Canadian geologist, chemist, teacher, and explorer. Hind came from Nottingham, England, to Canada in 1846 after studying in Germany, Cambridge, and France. He taught chemistry and mathematics at the provincial normal school in Toronto, from 1848 to 1853. Then, on obtaining his master's degree from Trinity College, Toronto, he became a professor of chemistry there.

In 1857 the Canadian government organized an expedition under the command of George Gladman, a former officer of the Hudson's Bay Company, to explore the country and canoe route between Lake Superior and Red River Settlement (modern Winnipeg) with Hind as geologist. The following year Hind was put in charge of one section of the Canadian Expedition, while his colleague Simon James Dawson took charge of the other. Hind and his team, traveling partly in canoes they carried with them and partly by horse and cart, examined the Assiniboine and Qu'Appelle Rivers and the connection between the Qu'Appelle and South Saskatchewan at the Elbow. Hind suggested that the waters of the South Saskatchewan be diverted down the Qu'Appelle to give a more direct water communication. The Gardiner Dam today does indeed back water up into the connecting valley, but for purposes of irrigation and hydroelectric-energy generation, not for transportation.

Hind and his team followed the South Saskatchewan down to its fork with the North Saskatchewan and on to Lake Winnipeg, with side trips to Lake Winnipegosis to examine salt springs and to the Souris River to investigate rumored coal measures. They cut across country from Fort à la Corne to Fort Ellice and visited Fort Pelly. They skirted Duck and Riding Mountains and followed the Minnedosa and Whitemud Rivers back to Portage la Prairie and Red River.

These journeys led Hind to emphasize the difference between parklands and semiarid plains and to stress the potential of the "Fertile Belt." His findings largely agreed with those of the expedition led by John PALLISER, but he was more optimistic about the possibility of communication with Canada north of the international boundary.

Eager to go west again, to complete the examination of the South Saskatchewan and to traverse one or more passes through the Rockies, Hind submitted specific plans for further exploration to the British government in 1859 and to the Canadian government in 1867 but failed to secure financial support. Instead, in 1861, with his brother, William George Richardson Hind, as artist, he explored Labrador and its river systems.

In 1864 Hind resigned from Trinity College and undertook a geological survey in New Brunswick, going on in 1869–1871 to examine goldfields in Nova Scotia. Exploring for minerals in northeastern Labrador (now part of Newfoundland), he discovered extensive new cod fisheries but was drawn away from

further study of these fisheries when in 1877 his services were required in connection with the Fisheries Commission set up in Halifax in accordance with Clauses XVIII to XXV of the Washington Treaty of 1871. In 1890 he became president of a new church school in Edgehill, Nova Scotia.

A prolific writer, Hind also edited three periodicals in the 1850s and 1860s. He became involved in the 1880s in acrimonious controversy, attacking a variety of alleged "frauds" and hotly defending contentions based on his own explorations.

BIBLIOGRAPHY: Henry Youle Hind, *Explorations in the Interior of the Labrador Peninsula, the Country of the Montagnais and Nasquapee Indians*, 2 vols., London, 1863; id., *Narrative of the Canadian Red River Exploring Expedition of 1857 and of the Assiniboine and Saskatchewan Exploring Expedition of 1858*, 2 vols., London, 1860; id., *A Sketch of an Overland Route to British Columbia*, Toronto, 1862.

Irene M. Spry

Hsüan-chuang *(Hsüan-tsang; Hiuen-tsiang; b. 603)* Buddhist pilgrim and explorer. During the early part of the seventh century, Buddhism in China was plagued by doctrinal differences. Anxious to resolve the textual discrepancies, Hsüan-chuang, a young Buddhist monk from Loyang, set out for India even though a ban on Western travel was in effect. In 629 he slipped out of Ch'angan (Sian) and journeyed through the Kansu corridor to Turfan (T'ulufan). After passing through Kucha (K'uch'e), Aqsu (Ak'osu), and the Bedal Pass, he skirted the southern shore of the Issyk Kul toward the capital of the Turkic empire on the Chu River. He then proceeded along the historic route via Talas, Tashkent, Samarkand, and Keshm (Kishm) to Tukhara, once known as Bactria. Having crossed the Hindu Kush, Hsüan-chuang rested in Kapisa (Bagram), near Kabul, during the summer of 630 before traveling along the Kabul River through Peshawar to Taxila. On an excursion to Srinagar, he met the famed Mahāyāna philospher Sanghayases, under whom he studied until early 633.

Proceeding southward to Sialkot and crossing the Jumna, the pilgrim reached the Ganges at Hardwar. A major stop was made at Kannauj before sailing down the sacred river, where he narrowly escaped death at the hands of Durga pirates. Visits were made to Allahabad and Benares (Varanasi), and homage was paid at Sravasti (Set Mahet), where Buddha worked the great miracle, and at Kasia, where Buddha entered Nirvana.

It was at Nalanda in Magadha, in present southern Bihar, that Hsüan-chuang found the highest authority on the idealist school of Buddhism. After studying there for 5 years, he achieved a certain measure of fame as the learned master from China. Resuming his journey down the Ganges, the pilgrim stopped at Tamralipti, whence he took the coastal land route southward. Before reaching the Godavari River, he turned inland to Anhara in interior Deccan and then headed for the coast and arrived at Conjiveram (Kanchipuram), the capital of Dravida.

Unable to visit Ceylon, which was then in turmoil, Hsüan-chuang went across the lower Indian peninsula and reached the west coast at the mouth of the Narbada River. An extended excursion inland brought him to the eastern end of the Satpura Range, whence he backtracked and then headed northwestward across the Thar Desert and upstream along the Indus.

On his return journey, he chose the route via Kashgar (K'oshih), Yarkand (Soch'e), Khotan, Tunhuang, and Yümen and arrived back at the capital, where he received a royal welcome.

During a span of 16 years, Hsüan-chuang traveled about 40,000 miles (64,370 kilometers), ranking him as the greatest land traveler of the premodern age. The records and itinerary of his travels, edited by two faithful disciples, contain the most comprehensive and accurate details on the Buddhist world in the Middle Ages.

Henry Hudson makes a trading stop on his return journey down the Hudson River. [Library of Congress]

BIBLIOGRAPHY: Samuel Beal, *The Life of Hiuen-tsiang,* London, 1911; René Grousset, *In the Footsteps of the Buddha,* London, 1932.

Kuei-sheng Chang

Huc, Évariste-Régis (1813–1860) French Catholic missionary and explorer in Asia. Born in Caylus in the department of Tarn-et-Garonne, Huc entered the Vincentian order in the fall of 1836. After his ordination in 1839 he left for China as a missionary. Much of his time in the Far East was spent in Mongolia, where he carried on his religious duties and where also he took advantage of the opportunity to study the dialects, manners, and customs of the Tatars. He traveled extensively through the area. In October 1845, in the company of Father Joseph Gabet, also a Vincentian, Huc joined the caravan of a Tibetan embassy just returning from a mission to Peking. After many hardships the two missionaries reached Lhasa, the capital of Tibet, in January 1846. Their stay in Lhasa, however, was brief. Although Tibetan officials were friendly, the Chinese *amban* (official) was hostile to the two Westerners and forced their expulsion from the country.

After a few months of travel the two priests arrived in Macao in the early part of October 1846. Father Huc remained in China for nearly 3 years, but Gabet sailed for Europe and subsequently went to Brazil, where he died in 1853. Huc, meanwhile, returned to France in 1852, his health seriously impaired. He left the Vincentian order in 1853. In addition to writing a detailed and famous account of his travels in the Far East, Huc is remembered also for his two-volume work *L'empire chinois* (1851).

BIBLIOGRAPHY: Évariste-Régis Huc, *Travels in Tartary, Thibet and China, 1844–1846,* tr. by William Hazlitt and ed. by Paul Pelliot, 2 vols., London, 1928.

Bernerd C. Weber

Hudson, Henry (d. 1611) English navigator and explorer. The place and date of his birth are unknown, as are the facts of his early life. However, he enjoyed the reputation of being a skilled navigator when he was chosen in the spring of 1607 to lead an expedition in search of a NORTHEAST PASSAGE to China. This expedition was undertaken on behalf of the English Muscovy Company. In late April 1607 Hudson sailed from Gravesend in his ship *Hopewell* along with a few crew members and his young son John. He reached Greenland in June but failed to find any sea passage that would take him to the Far East. Tracing the boundary of sea ice eastward, he eventually reached a hitherto-unexplored section of the coast of Spitsbergen (Svalbard). Thereafter Hudson headed homeward and reached the Thames by mid-September. This voyage was significant because it opened up for the English the very profitable whale fisheries in the area of Spitsbergen.

In April 1608, Hudson undertook a second voyage in search of a Northeast Passage, and on this voyage part of Novaya Zemlya was explored. The ultimate purpose of this expedition, however, was not realized, and the Muscovy Company lost interest in making further efforts to find a shorter trade route to the Far East. In 1609 the Amsterdam Chamber of the Dutch East India Company gave Hudson a contract to search again for a Northeast Passage. On this occasion he received command of the *Half Moon,* a vessel with a mixed crew of Dutch and English seamen, and Amsterdam was the assembly point for this expedition. When Hudson and his crew approached Novaya Zemlya, a mutiny among the seamen brought about a change in the original plans, and the *Half Moon* sailed toward the North American coast at 40°N. This idea had been suggested to Hudson by some maps and letters which some time before he had received from his friend Capt. John SMITH of Virginia. Newfoundland was reached early in July. Some exploration of the coast southward was undertaken, and then the *Half Moon,* turning northward, finally anchored off what is now Sandy Hook, New Jersey, for several days. The *Half Moon* then proceeded up the river now named after this English explorer. On the return journey Hudson landed at Dartmouth, England, fully intending to return to the Netherlands. He was refused permission, however, by the English government to continue in Dutch service. The very next year the Dutch East India Company began its trading operations in what is now the Hudson River Valley.

In April 1610 Hudson began his fourth and last voyage. On this occasion he sailed in the interests of a group of London merchants and enterprisers. In June Greenland was reached, and in July Hudson passed through the strait that now bears his name and explored the great inland body of water now known as Hudson Bay by proceeding generally along its eastern side. In November Hudson's ship, the *Discovery,* went into winter quarters in the southwest corner of what is now called James Bay. The crew endured many hardships during the long cold winter, and mutinous attitudes developed. In June 1611, just 3 days after the *Discovery* finally broke free from the ice, rebellious crew members seized Hudson, his son John, and seven others and set them adrift in a small boat without any provisions. By September the *Discovery* reached England with only a handful of men who had survived the terrible ordeal. Nothing was ever heard again of Henry Hudson and his companions.

BIBLIOGRAPHY: George M. Asher (ed.), *Henry Hudson the Navigator: The Original Documents in Which His Career Is Recorded, Collected, Partly Translated, and Annotated, with an Introduction,* Hakluyt Society, 1st ser., no. 27, London, 1860.

Bernerd C. Weber

Australian-born Hamilton Hume began exploring his country at seventeen, subsequently making major discoveries in the Yass Plains, Clyde River, Sydney, and Port Phillip Bay areas. [Australian Information Service]

Hume, Hamilton (1797–1873) Australian explorer. The eldest son of a disreputable convict superintendent, Hume was born at Parramatta, New South Wales, on June 19, 1797, and began exploring 17 years later from Appin, where his family finally settled in 1812. He examined the Berrima and Bong Bong districts briefly in 1814 and followed this, 3 years later, with a more thorough examination of Sutton Forest. For the next few years he acted as a government guide, going 95 miles (153 kilometers) southwest of Sydney with James Meehan in 1817, to Goulburn and Lake Bathurst with Meehan and Charles Throsby in 1818, and to Jervis Bay with John OXLEY, Meehan, and Throsby in 1819. In 1821 he explored the Yass Plains and followed this in 1822 with an examination of land bordering the Clyde River. His major exploration of the area between Sydney and Port Phillip Bay, made with William Hovell, took place 2 years later. On being awarded a government grant of 1200 acres (486 hectares) for his discoveries, Hume withdrew to his pastoral property near Yass, briefly coming out of retirement to blaze a new road over the Blue Mountains in 1828 and to act as assistant to Charles STURT in 1828–1829. Hume died at Yass on April 19, 1873, his later years being marked by bitter arguments with Hovell over mistakes in their joint expedition of 50 years before.

BIBLIOGRAPHY: F. O'Grady, "Hamilton Hume," *Journal of the Royal Australian Historical Society*, vol. 49, 1963, pp. 337–359.

J. M. R. Cameron

I

I-ching *(I-tsing; b. 634)* Buddhist pilgrim and explorer. Following the return of the great pilgrim traveler HSÜAN-CHUANG to China in 645, a large number of Buddhists were inspired to make the journey to India by land and by sea. Among them, I-ching was the most renowned for the geographical information he gathered on the Southeast Asian islands during his pilgrimage.

In the winter of 671, I-ching boarded a Persian ship at Canton bound for Palembang, Sumatra, then the capital of Sribhoja. After a 6-month sojourn, he skirted the coast of Sumatra and reached the northern end of the island. Traveling on a Sumatran vessel to India, he made a stop on the Nicobar Islands before disembarking at the great seaport of Tamralipti at the mouth of the Hooghly. He remained there for a year to learn the Sanskrit language.

The route taken by I-ching to reach Magadha with its numerous holy sites and the cultural center of Nalanda was apparently different from those used by FA-HSIEN and Hsüan-chuang. Passing through a region of mountains, woods, and swamps, he was plagued by illness and bandits before arriving at Nalanda. He spent 10 years there, studying Buddhist doctrines and collecting sacred books. By the time of his departure, he had acquired more than 500,000 *slokas* (Sanskrit stanzas), which by his own estimation would fill 1000 volumes in Chinese translation.

Taking the same route homeward, I-ching once again stopped at Palembang, where he hoped to complete his work of translation in 10 years. He soon realized that the task was beyond the power of a single man, and in 689 he went to Canton to recruit help. He and his staff remained in Palembang until 695, translating the sūtras and editing his personal notes, which were published and have survived to this day.

The geographical knowledge accumulated by I-ching during his 24 years abroad covers both India and the insular countries in the "Southern Sea." It is in the latter category that his contribution is the most original and valuable. In the centuries that followed, his records were regarded as an indispensable reference for the study of the early history, culture, and religions of the peoples of the East Indies.

BIBLIOGRAPHY: Édouard Chavannes (tr.), *Mémoire. . .sur les religieux éminents*, Paris, 1894; Junjiro Takakusu (tr.), *A Record of the Buddhist Religion*, Oxford, 1896.

Kuei-sheng Chang

Ibn-Baṭṭūṭa, Abū ʿAbd-Allāh Muḥammad *(1304–1377)* Arab traveler. Ibn-Baṭṭūṭa, one of the most famous travelers of the medieval Near East, was born in Tangier, Morocco, and died in Morocco at the age of 73. His various journeys occupied a period of more than 20 years. Between 1325–1326 and 1332 his itinerary included North Africa, Egypt, Syria, Arabia, Iraq, various parts of Persia, Yemen, Aden, East Africa, Oman, and the Persian Gulf. In the next period of travel, he visited Egypt, Syria, Asia Minor, the lands of the Golden Horde Mongols, Constantinople, Persia, Afghanistan, and India. Afterward, he spent some time in the Maldive Islands, Ceylon, Indochina, the Indonesian archipelago, and China. Further voyages touched a number of the same places but also new areas such as Sardinia, Spain, and parts of black Africa.

The range of experience and observations gained during this peripatetic life were recorded in the most famous travel book in Islamic history, the *Rihla (Journey)*. Ibn-Baṭṭūṭa did not actually write this work himself; rather he dictated it to a scholar named ibn-Juzayy, who completed it toward the end of 1357. Although modern specialists have pointed out certain exaggerations or discrepancies in it, the *Rihla* remains a formidable and exceptionally valuable source of historical and geographical details.

Ibn-Baṭṭūṭa's descriptions of Asia Minor, India, and parts of Africa are usually said to have been of particular significance. Even a brief glance at the *Rihla*, however, will yield some idea of the great variety of subjects touched by the author. One can find in it, for example, important facts about the religious beliefs and practices of various peoples, including Shī'ite extremists in Syrian territory. It is also very informative about the customs and ideas of the Turkish Futuwwa brotherhoods in Asia Minor in the fourteenth century. Similarly, the author provides useful and interesting details about Christian monastic establishments in Constantinople.

Ibn-Baṭṭūṭa was a keen observer of commercial activity and economic life. He mentions some of the goods to be seen in the markets of various cities, also noting the sorts of commodities grown in rural districts. One may learn, furthermore, of the myriad occupations encountered in the various countries in the course of the journeys.

Those interested in diet, dress, and forms of entertainment can also benefit considerably from the pages of the *Rihla*. One reads, for instance, of the styles of dress and types of musical instruments which ibn-Baṭṭūṭa saw in the region of the Niger River. In addition to these subjects, the work of ibn-Baṭṭūṭa provides useful, if brief, information about the effects of the great bubonic plague pandemic of 1348–1349 in the Near East.

BIBLIOGRAPHY: Ibn-Baṭṭūṭa, *The Travels of ibn-Baṭṭūṭa*, tr. by H. A. R. Gibb, 3 vols., Hakluyt Society, 2d ser. nos. 110, 117, 141, Cambridge, England, 1958–1971.

William Tucker

Ibn-Faḍlān, Aḥmad (*fl. first half of 10th century*) Muslim traveler and author. Ibn-Faḍlān was a non-Arab Muslim who lived in the eastern part of the Islamic world, probably in Baghdad, during the first part of the tenth century. The details of his life are virtually unknown except for the period of a journey which he undertook in 921–922. He went on this trip as part of a mission which the 'Abbāsid ruler al-Muqtadir sent to the court of the Volga Bulgars in Russia. His role in this embassy was to convey a message to the Bulgar Prince, to distribute presents from the Caliph in Baghdad, and to examine the activities and progress of legal experts sent by the Islamic government to the Bulgar court.

The journey began in 921 in Baghdad, the participants in it moving from there into Persia, Central Asia, the Caspian regions, and Russia. The mission arrived at the Bulgar capital in the spring of 922. Upon the return of the embassy to Baghdad, at an undetermined date, ibn-Faḍlān penned an account of his experiences and observations in a work entitled simply *Kitāb (Book)*, frequently incorrectly known by the title *Al-Risāla (The Epistle)*. This book is of capital

The town of Ghat, Libya, visited by the great Arab traveler ibn-Baṭṭūṭa.

importance for anyone concerned with the ethnography and geography of Russia and Central Asia. Various Turkic groups, such as the Oghuz (Ghuz) and the Pechenegs (Petchenegs), are examined in some detail. As would be expected, the author speaks at length about the Bulgar state. He also provides fascinating details about the Khazars, a Turkic people of Jewish faith who ruled a state on the lower reaches of the Volga River from about the late seventh century to some time in the latter part of the tenth century. This state was of considerable importance commercially and militarily because of its location and because of Khazar military prowess. In addition, we find in ibn-Fadlān's book interesting details concerning the customs and practices of the Rus (Russ), the pagan Scandinavian settlers in early medieval Russia.

BIBLIOGRAPHY: D. M. Dunlop, *The History of the Jewish Khazars*, New York, 1967.

William Tucker

Ibn-Ḥawqal, Abū al-Qāsim ibn-ʿAlī al-Naṣībī (d. after 973)

Arab traveler and geographer. Ibn-Ḥawqal was a native of Naṣībīn in Mesopotamia (Iraq). He appears to have been a merchant or a religious teacher, or both, as well as an author. Although the dates of his life are not available, his journeys can be dated from information given in his book *Kitāb Ṣūrat al-Arḍ (Book of the Image of the Earth)*. His travels began in 943 and continued at intervals until about 973 or 974. Among the countries he visited were Spain, Armenia, Iraq, various provinces of Iran, Sicily, the Maghreb (North Africa), Egypt, and other parts of Africa.

His observations and experiences were set down in his book, which was based to a certain extent on a previous work by al-Iṣṭakhrī that appeared in several versions or editions. The book is essentially a descriptive geography of the Islamic lands, although it also includes interesting and valuable data about peoples and countries bordering on the Islamic world. There is a good deal of information about the economic life of the places visited or discussed. One finds details, for example, of products, prices, and other features of the economy of a given country or region. Ibn-Ḥawaal's text demonstrates implicitly that his information was based very much on firsthand observation rather than upon a simple copying of Iṣṭakhrī's work. His additions can be seen particularly in the sections devoted to Egypt, the Maghreb, Spain, and Sicily.

Apparently, as the title of the book would suggest, ibn-Ḥawqal originally intended to prepare a collection of maps of the Muslim world with commentary. The finished product, however, turned out to be much more than explanatory notes for maps. The topics treated in the work include towns, rivers, and other physical features of the areas as well as the nature and activities of the people living there. Ibn-Ḥawqal's written information and his maps were important contributions to medieval Islamic geographical literature, since they considerably extended Muslim knowledge of certain peoples and regions, especially parts of Africa.

BIBLIOGRAPHY: Ibn-Ḥawqal, *Configuration de la terre*, tr. by Gaston Wiet, Paris and Beirut, 1964.

William Tucker

Ibn-Jubayr, Abū al-Ḥasan Muḥammad (1145–1217)

Muslim traveler and author. Ibn-Jubayr was born in Valencia, Spain, into a Muslim family which traced its presence in that country to the eighth century. His father belonged to the bureaucratic or secretarial class, and ibn-Jubayr was educated in conformity with the training and values of that group. He studied Arabic grammar, literature, and various subjects associated with the Islamic faith, such as Qurʾānic (Koranic) exegesis. He also became a member of the bureaucratic group, receiving an appointment as secretary to the Governor of Granada. He was to become famous in the annals of Islamic literature for the travels which he undertook beginning in 1182.

Leaving Spain that year, he began a voyage to Mecca for the purpose of accomplishing the Muslim rite of pilgrimage. During the course of this trip, he stopped at a number of intermediate points in the Mediterranean, including the islands of Sardinia and Crete. He landed at Alexandria and traveled to the Islamic holy cities in Arabia by way of Cairo. Ibn-Jubayr stayed in Arabia for nearly a year and then traveled to Iraq and Spain. He returned to Spain via Sicily, arriving home in 1185.

Between 1189 and 1191 he traveled once more to the Near East. Finally, he embarked on another Eastern journey in 1217, and it was in the course of this trip that he died (autumn of 1217). These two latter voyages were not as important as the first one, which is the subject of ibn-Jubayr's work the *Riḥla (Journey)*.

The *Riḥla* is one of the most exciting and informative Muslim travel accounts of the medieval period. It contains many interesting details about the rituals and practices associated with the pilgrimage in Mecca. The book gives numerous insights into the state of Near Eastern society at the time of the Crusades. One can also gain from it an idea of the methods and hazards of navigation in the Mediterranean, and the latter part depicts an extremely severe and terrifying storm at sea which ibn-Jubayr and his fellow passengers endured on the return voyage from the Near East to Europe.

BIBLIOGRAPHY: Ibn-Jubayr, *The Travels of Ibn Jubayr*, tr. by R. J. C. Broadhurst, London, 1957.

William Tucker

Idrīsī, ʾAbū ʿAbd-Allāh Muḥammad al-Sharīf al- (1100?–1165 or 1166)

Arab traveler and geographer. Al-Idrīsī was one of the most famous geographers and cartographers in the medieval world. There is a good deal of uncertainty about the details of his life. It is said that he was born in Spain, scion of the Idrisid

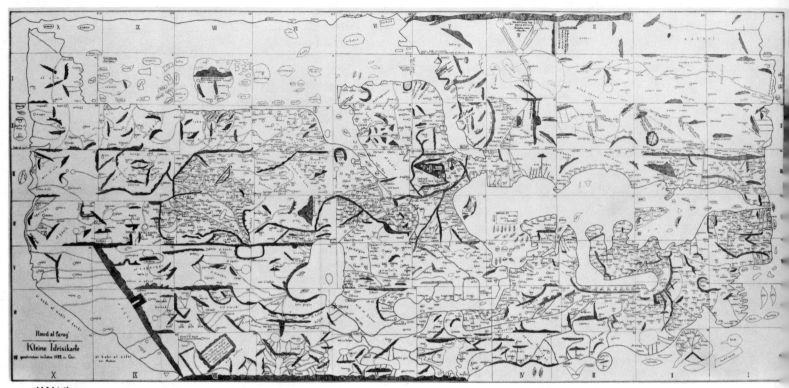

family which had ruled the region of Fez, Morocco, from the end of the eighth until the first part of the tenth century. He appears to have traveled throughout the portions of the Middle East between North Africa and Asia Minor. Finally he was invited to come to the court of the Christian king Roger II of Sicily. There he constructed a large planisphere and wrote a book entitled *Nuzhat al-Mushtāq fi Ikhtirāq al-Āfāq (The Stroll of One Wishing to Traverse the Horizons of the Globe)*, which was intended to be a key to understanding the device. Since the work was commissioned by King Roger, it is frequently known simply as *Kitāb al-Rujār* or *Kitāb al-Rujayr (The Book of Roger)*.

Six complete manuscripts of the book have survived, and we learn from information included in them that it was finished about 1154. The treatise was based upon both personal travel experiences and those of other voyagers. Al-Idrīsī discussed in a lucid fashion all known countries of Asia, Africa, and Europe, providing particularly significant details of the ethnography and cultures of these areas. Economic life and commerce were given a prominent place in the discussion, and the book remains to the present a valuable source for the economic situation in the twelfth century.

The Book of Roger, as it has survived, contains some seventy maps in addition to the text. The maps are arranged according to the medieval Islamic grouping of the seven climatic zones. They are generally judged by specialists to be among the most accurate maps to have been produced in the medieval world, whether in Europe or in the Near East.

BIBLIOGRAPHY: D. M. Dunlop, *Arab Civilization to AD 1500*, New York, 1971.

William Tucker

India

The earliest European writer to mention India was Hecataeus of Miletus (ca. 500 B.C.), who wrote only a short time after the annexation of an Indian province to the Persian empire by Darius the Great. To Hecataeus, as well as to HERODOTUS OF HALICARNASSUS, "India" meant the valley of the Indus River. To the east of India, Herodotus believed, Asia was devoid of inhabitants. Like other ancient writers, he described India as a land of marvels where all birds and four-legged animals (except the horse) grew larger than anywhere else and where gold was dug by huge ants. One of the few other Indian products mentioned by Herodotus came from a wool tree (that is, cotton). Herodotus also reported the voyage of Scylax, an admiral of Darius, who descended the Indus and reached Egypt after a voyage of 30 months.

The fabulous qualities of India were even more prominent in a treatise, preserved only in an abstract, by Ctesias of Cnidus, a physician who spent 17 years at the Persian court and returned to Greece in 398 B.C. Although there are a few kernels of fact in his work—for example, the general direction of the Oxus River (Amu Darya) was given correctly for the first time—he populated India with monstrous creatures of the sort that would frequently reappear in classical and medieval literature: unicorns, dog-headed men, and men with a single foot so large that it could serve as an umbrella.

More reliable firsthand information about India was acquired as a result of the campaigns of ALEXANDER THE GREAT, who crossed the Indus River in 326 B.C. and had reached the Beas River when his men refused to go any further. Alexander then sailed down the Indus to the delta and turned west to begin his march home. Meanwhile, he sent NEARCHUS to explore the ocean which he believed flowed around India.

The most important ancient description of India was written by Megasthenes, who was sent as an envoy to the court of Chandragupta in northern India by King Seleucus I about 300 B.C. Megasthenes remained in India for several years and may have been the first Greek to see the Ganges River. Although his account contained some erroneous and fabulous material (he repeated the story of the gold-digging ants, for example), he provided much accurate ethnographical and geographical information, as when he observed that India is larger from north to south than from east to west. He was also the first to obtain data on Ceylon (Sri Lanka).

There is evidence of considerable commerce between India and the Roman Empire by the first century A.D. Initially, the traffic in Indian wares was indirect and involved numerous intermediaries. There is a tale recounted by STRABO of two direct voyages from Egypt about 120–115 B.C. by Eudoxus of Cyzicus, who agreed to accompany an Indian sailor, found adrift in the Red Sea, to his homeland. Eudoxus returned from the journey with a cargo of spices and gems, only to have them seized by the King. Undaunted, he made a second journey and again returned safely to Egypt. On his way home, however, he was blown far down the East African coast, an experience that later led him to undertake a circumnavigation of Africa. Regardless of the truth of this story, by the time of PLINY and the anonymous author of the *Periplus of the Erythrean Sea* (*see* PERIPLUS) seamen of the empire were regularly sailing from the Red Sea across the open ocean to India instead of relying on middlemen or hugging the Arabian and Persian coasts. A Greek mariner called Hippalus is said to have pioneered this route after he had observed the regularity of the monsoons.

Although the *Periplus* gives many details about the ports and products of India's western coast, the author's knowledge of the eastern coast was extremely imprecise. PTOLEMY had many more place names for the eastern coast, but he erred with respect to the location and shape of the subcontinent, virtually suppressing its peninsular conformation. Ptolemy also grossly inflated the size of Ceylon.

After the second century A.D. little new information about India appeared in Western writing. Direct trade between Rome and India was curtailed, though Indian products continued to be imported. There were communities of Christians on the Malabar and Coromandel coasts at an early date, but the origins of Christianity in India are obscure. According to the apocryphal Acts of Thomas, the apostle Thomas preached, performed miracles, and was martyred in India, where his supposed tomb was venerated at Mailapur (Mylapore), near Madras.

The most valuable description of India during the early Middle Ages appears in the *Topographia Christiana,* a sixth-century treatise written to refute the pagan notion that the world is round. Its author, Cosmas, was a monk, probably from Alexandria, who had previously been a merchant in Eastern waters. He discusses the commerce of western India and Ceylon, as well as the Christian churches there, though some scholars have doubted that his statements were based on personal observation.

It was not until the late Middle Ages that the Western fund of knowledge about India was significantly expanded as a result of the flowering of religious, commercial, and diplomatic contacts between Europe and Asia that started in the thirteenth century after the establishment of Mongol rule over much of the latter continent. Among the better-known travelers to India during this period are Marco POLO and the Franciscan missionary John of Monte Corvino, who spent a year (about 1291) on the Malabar and Coromandel coasts before going to China. However, the best medieval discussion of India is contained in the

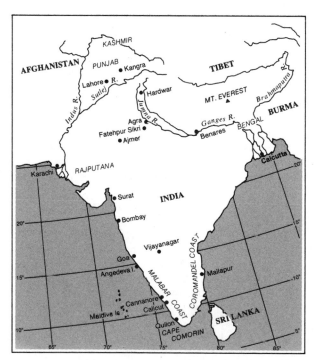

India.

Mirabilia (Book of Marvels) by Jordanus of Sévérac, a French Dominican. Jordanus first appeared in India in 1321 with three Italian Minorites and a Franciscan lay brother, all of whom were murdered on Salsette Island by fanatical Muslims during Jordanus's absence. He remained in India for many years, being named bishop of Columbum (Quilon) in 1330. His *Mirabilia,* probably written between 1329 and 1338, is noteworthy for its details on the ethnography and the flora and fauna of the coastal regions of India. Jordanus was also the first writer to make a clear association of PRESTER JOHN with Africa.

Another excellent account of India, as well as of Southern Asia in general, was dictated to Giovanni Francesco Poggio Bracciolini, secretary to Pope Eugenius IV, by Nicolò di Conti in 1444. Conti, a Venetian merchant, began his Eastern travels about 1419. After a sojourn in the Middle East, he sailed to the Gulf of Cambay on the northwestern coast of India. He traveled extensively in India, seeing the inland city of Vijayanagar, the shrine of Thomas at Mailapur and the Ganges, as well as in Burma and Southeast Asia. Along the way he acquired an Indian wife and fathered four children, but she and two of the children died of the plague in Egypt while en route to Europe.

If European travelers to India were rare at the beginning of the fifteenth century, the last years of the century would mark the beginning of the large-scale European penetration that culminated in British domination of the subcontinent by 1800. The earliest arrivals were the Portuguese, who had sought for years to reach India by sailing around the southern tip of Africa. The first Portuguese to visit India, however, did not arrive by that route, but rather sailed from Aden and landed at Cannanore on the Malabar coast. This was Pero da Covilhã, who was sent to India in 1487 by King John II to complement the simultaneous voyage of Bartolomeu DIAS. Covilhã also visited Calicut and Goa before embarking on an odyssey that took him to Sofala in East Africa, to Arabia (and perhaps to Mecca as a pilgrim), and finally to Abyssinia (Ethiopia), where he remained for 30 years. Cavilhã sent back to Portugal a report on his travels that was probably used in the planning of the epochal voyage of Vasco da GAMA to India (1497–1499). The subsequent establishment of Portuguese hegemony over much of Asia was followed by the arrival of large numbers of administrators, clerics, traders, and soldiers, many of whom wrote about their experiences. Among these may be cited Duarte Barbosa, who lived in India from 1500 to 1516 or 1517 and later joined the round-the-world expedition of his brother-in-law, Ferdinand MAGELLAN. Of non-Portuguese travelers to India in the early sixteenth century the most celebrated is Lodovico di VARTHEMA, whose account (1510) of his extensive Eastern wanderings became an immediate best seller.

Portuguese predominance in the East was soon challenged by other Europeans, notably the Dutch and the English. The weaknesses of the Portuguese empire and the profits to be made in Eastern trade were pointed out to the Dutch by a compatriot, Jan Huyghen van Linschoten, who spent more than 5 years (1583–1589) in Goa in the service of the Archbishop of that Portuguese enclave. Upon his return to Holland, he composed his famous *Itinerario* (1596), which described his experiences in India in addition to providing detailed navigational information for seamen interested in venturing into the unfamiliar waters off Asia and the Americas.

The first Englishman known to have settled in India was Thomas Stevens, a Jesuit, who lived there from 1579 until his death in 1619. Father Stevens was not only a missionary but a scholar and poet as well. His major work was a long religious poem, *The Christian Purana* (1616), written in the Marathi language for the spiritual guidance of recent converts.

Father Stevens is also remembered for his assistance to the first group of Englishmen who traveled to India for commercial purposes. Led by John Newbery, the party of six left England in 1583 carrying letters of introduction from Queen Elizabeth to Akbar, the great Mogul (Mughul) emperor of India, and to the King of China, whose name and title she did not know. Having been arrested in Hormuz (Hormoz) by the Portuguese authorities, three of the group—Newbery, Ralph Fitch, a merchant, and William Leeds, a jeweler—reached Goa late in 1583 and were released shortly afterward. They eventually made their way to Fatehpur Sikri, Akbar's new capital near Agra, but they were unable to conclude a commercial agreement. While Leeds stayed behind at Akbar's court and Newbery left for Lahore on the first leg of his return trip to England (he was never heard from again), Fitch began a lengthy journey that he hoped would bring him to China. He was unable to reach his destination, but he did travel throughout India and also visited Burma, Siam, Malacca, and Ceylon. After his return to London in 1591, he was frequently consulted by merchants interested in Eastern commerce, including the founders of the East India Company, which was established in 1600.

Determined Dutch competition prevented the English company from gaining a foothold in Southeast Asia. As a result, the East India Company turned its attention increasingly to the Indian mainland, starting with the voyage of the *Hector,* which landed at Surat on the Gulf of Cambay on August 24, 1608. Aboard the *Hector* was William Hawkins, who proceeded to Agra, capital of Akbar's successor, Jahangir. Hawkins was well received but was unable to negotiate a commercial treaty. In 1612, however, Thomas Best succeeded in winning some concessions for his countrymen; he also promised that an English representative would be sent to reside at the Mogul court. This ambassador was Sir Thomas Roe—"well spoken, learned, industrious, and of a comelie personage"—

who arrived in India in 1615. Roe remained there until 1618 and was able to improve the company's position considerably.

Early English travelers to India often wrote narratives of their journeys, among the best of which are those by Fitch and Roe. Edward Terry, an Anglican cleric who served as chaplain to Roe from 1616 until they left India together in 1618, wrote *A Voyage to East-India* (1655), which not only describes his own journey but also gives an authoritative and comprehensive picture of the society of northern India at the time of his visit. In the future many other Englishmen would publish similar volumes. Among these may be mentioned *A New Account of East India and Persia* (1698) by John Fryer, a surgeon for the East India Company who spent 7 years in India and 2 in Persia between 1673 and 1682.

French interest in entering the lucrative Indian trade is evidenced by an ill-fated expedition of two ships which sailed from Saint-Malo in 1601. Aboard one of the vessels, which was wrecked on a reef in the Maldive Islands, was François Pyrard of Laval, who survived the mishap. He spent five years in the Maldives, lived among Malabar pirates for a time, served with the Portuguese forces in Asia, and was wrecked off the coast of Brazil before returning in 1611 to France, where he promptly penned a narrative of his adventures.

Not all the early travelers to India had commercial, religious, or diplomatic motives for their journeys. Thomas Coryate, an eccentric Englishman already famous for his *Crudities* (1611), an account of a walking tour in Western Europe, set out for the East in 1612 merely for the sake of travel. From Aleppo (Halab) he walked to the Holy Land and to Persia, where he hoped in vain for an audience with the Shah. In India he visited Lahore, Agra, and Ajmer, as well as Hardwar, a famous Hindu shrine on the upper Ganges. According to Edward Terry, Coryate also traveled to Kangra in the northeastern Punjab, probably becoming thereby the first Englishman to penetrate the Himalayas. Since Coryate died in India in 1617, he was unable to write a full relation of his wanderings; what is known about his journey comes mainly from five letters he wrote while in Ajmer and Agra.

While much of India, especially the coastal regions, became known to Europeans through the writings of sixteenth- and seventeenth-century travelers, it was not until the eighteenth century that scientific geographical data began to be gathered, largely through the labors of surveyors employed by the East India Company and the British government in India. A pioneer in this work was James Rennell, a former midshipman in the Navy who was appointed surveyor general of the East India Company's territory in Bengal in 1764. Two years after his departure from India in 1777, Rennell published the *Bengal Atlas*, which Clements Robert Markham called "a work of the first importance both for strategic and administrative purposes" and "a lasting monument to the ability and perseverance of Rennell." Rennell also constructed the first approximately accurate map of India, the first edition of which appeared in 1783, along with an explanation of the plan by which it was prepared.

In 1802 Col. William Lambton launched the enterprise that was later designated the Great Trigonometrical Survey with the help of an enormous theodolite especially imported from England. He started the triangulation with a base line measured at Madras and, after running the triangles across the peninsula from east to west, he carried the survey south to Cape Comorin and then worked northward along the 78th meridian of longitude. Lambton's work was continued by his successor as superintendent of the Great Trigonometrical Survey, George Everest, who adopted the gridiron system of triangulation. The survey was eventually extended to cover all of India as well as Burma and other neighboring regions. The completion of the great meridional arc in 1841 made it possible to determine the altitude of the Himalayan peaks, one of which, known at first as Peak XV, was named after Everest. Meanwhile, topographical surveys were also conducted, covering virtually all of India by 1900.

BIBLIOGRAPHY: C. Raymond Beazley, *The Dawn of Modern Geography*, vol. III, Oxford, 1906; E. H. Bunbury, *A History of Ancient Geography*, with a new introduction by W. H. Stahl, 2 vols., New York, 1959; G. F. Heaney, "Rennell and the Surveyors of India," *Geographical Journal*, vol. 134, part 3, September 1968, pp. 318–325; Clements R. Markham, *Major James Rennell and the Rise of Modern English Geography*, New York, 1895; Boies Penrose, *Travel and Discovery in the Renaissance*, Cambridge, Mass., 1963; R. C. Prasad, *Early English Travellers in India*, Delhi, 1965; J. Oliver Thomson, *History of Ancient Geography*, New York, 1965; Cecil Tragen, *Elizabethan Venture*, London, 1953.

Iran *See* PERSIA.

Izmailov, Gerasim Alekseyevich *(fl. late eighteenth century)* Russian seafarer. In May 1771, with D. I. BOCHAROV, he was taken from Bolsheretsk, Kamchatka, by the mutineer Count Beniowsky but was put ashore in the Kuril Islands. In 1775 he explored the west and northeast shores of Kamchatka. Between 1783 and 1786, as assistant navigator, he took part in the expedition of G. I. SHELEKHOV to Kodiak. In 1788, on the galliot *Tri Svyatitelya (Three Saints)*, he explored the north coast of the Gulf of Alaska with Bocharov, burying several plates to indicate the region as Russian territory. In 1789 he explored the southeast shore of the Kenai Peninsula, and he made many other voyages until at least 1797. Izmailov was one of the ablest navigators in Russian America at that time.

Richard A. Pierce

Jiménez de Quesada, Gonzalo (1509-1579) Spanish explorer and conqueror. Born either in Córdoba or in Granada, Jiménez studied at the University of Salamanca and was practicing law in Granada by 1533. The circumstances of his departure for America are not known, but he arrived in Santa Marta on the Caribbean coast of South America in 1536 in a large expedition led by Pedro Fernández de Lugo, the new governor of the province. Shortly afterward the difficulties of colonization in Santa Marta, coupled with the prevailing ignorance of South American geography, led the Governor to organize an expedition that would attempt to reach Peru by way of the Magdalena River. Having been named commander of the expedition, Jiménez left Santa Marta on April 5, 1536, at the head of approximately 600 men. In addition, four ships carrying supplies were to sail up the Magdalena and join the land party at the confluence of the Magdalena and César Rivers.

To avoid a region known to be inhospitable and occupied by hostile Indians, Jiménez initially traveled eastward toward the present-day Venezuelan border, skirting the Sierra Nevada de Santa Marta. After a stop at Chiriguaná in the César River Valley, he proceeded to Tamalameque, the spot where the land party was to meet the ships. When it became evident that the ships were not going to appear, Jiménez and his men continued their march inland along the Magdalena, suffering severely from lack of food and the rigors of travel in the tropical terrain. They eventually learned that the ships had been unable to sail up the Magdalena as planned, but 80 leagues from Tamalameque they met another fleet dispatched by Fernández de Lugo. In October 1536 the expedition reached La Tora (modern Barrancabermeja), where a decision was made to abandon the Magdalena and penetrate the mountains that lay to the east and were reportedly inhabited by Indians of an advanced culture. On March 9, 1537, the party reached the territory of he Chibcha Indians. In the next 2 years the Spaniards conquered the Chibchas, amassed a large quantity of gold and emeralds, and founded the city of Santa Fe (modern Bogotá).

Early in 1539 two other Europeans arrived on the scene: the Spaniard Sebastián de Benalcázar and the German Nicolás Féderman (Nikolaus Federmann), who had traveled south from the Venezuelan town of Coro in search of a rich land called Xerira. Féderman maintained that the newly conquered region, which had been named New Granada, came under the jurisdiction of the German governors of Venezuela, and a violent conflict over the matter might have taken place, but he and Jiménez agreed on March 17, 1539, to submit their respective claims to the Council of the Indies in Spain. Shortly afterward Jiménez and Féderman left together for Spain, accompanied by Benalcázar. Other claimants for control of New Granada soon appeared, and it was eventually awarded to Alonso Luis de Lugo, son of Pedro Fernández de Lugo, who had inherited the governorship of Santa Marta upon the death of his father. Meanwhile, Jiménez, who had probably expected to be named governor of New Granada himself, left Spain in 1541 and traveled in France and Portugal. He returned to Spain in 1545 to find that he had risen in the estimation of the court, and he was given several honors, including the title of marshal of New Granada.

By 1551 Jiménez was back in New Granada, where he remained for the rest of his life. In 1569, having been authorized to search for an EL DORADO believed to be located east of the Andes, he led a large expedition across the mountains to the *llanos* (plains) of modern Colombia. Jiménez returned to Santa Fe with the remnants of his expedition 3 years later after suffering terrible privations but without having found El Dorado. Well educated in comparison with other sixteenth-century Spanish explorers, Jiménez wrote several works, including an accurate and objective account of the conquest of New Granada.

BIBLIOGRAPHY: Germán Arciniegas, *El caballero de El Dorado*, Madrid, 1969; Juan Friede, *Gonzalo Jiménez de Quesada a través de documentos históricos*, Bogotá, 1960; id., *Invasión del país de los Chibchas*, Bogotá, 1966.

Linguist, explorer, artist, and administrator, Harry Johnston played an important role in the development of colonial rule in Africa.

Johnston, Harry Hamilton (1858–1927) British explorer, linguist, artist, and administrator. Johnston was born in Kennington and, given his scholarly accomplishments, had surprisingly little formal education. He did study at King's College, London, and the Royal Academy but took no degree. Johnston early evinced marked abilities in such diverse fields as art, languages, and science, all of which subsequently were to be central to his career. In 1879, while scarcely beyond adolescence, Johnston followed up a Continental tour with an 8 months' visit to Tunis. Here he sketched, wrote articles for newspapers, and, most important, found himself greatly enamored of Africa. The direction of his life's work was thereby established, and in 1882 he joined an expedition under the 7th Earl of Mayo which was to hunt and collect in Angola. After a time with the expedition he received permission to set out on his own, and Johnston explored the Congo and visited Henry Morton STANLEY.

During these travels he developed his remarkable abilities as an observer and scientific reporter, and at least partly on the basis of these achievements he was chosen to head the Kilimanjaro Expedition. This expedition, jointly sponsored by the British Association and the Royal Society, ostensibly was purely scientific in nature. Yet Johnston combined treaty-making activities with his scientific pursuits and thereby signaled a new departure in his career. Henceforth he would be an individual linking the final stages of African exploration with the onset of formal colonial rule. Although he would fill, usually in outstanding fashion, a number of consular and administrative positions in Africa, he always combined exploration and scientific inquiry with the more mundane requirements of office, and throughout the course of his African years he recorded every scrap of information

Far right: Exploration of the Mississippi River by Louis Jolliet and Jacques Marquette, 1673.

he could obtain on the Bantu and semi-Bantu languages. Between 1899 and 1901 he was instrumental in founding the Uganda Protectorate. Afterward, recurrent attacks of blackwater fever and differences with Colonial Office officials, notably Clement Hill, led to a premature retirement.

Johnston's extraordinary energy now found new outlets, and his literary output, already immense by most standards, quickened. He was instrumental in founding the African Society and was one of its first presidents, and he played a major role in the establishment of the School of Oriental and African Studies. By the time of his death in 1927, his multifaceted African activities justly merited the claim of his most recent biographer that he was "the completest Africanist."

BIBLIOGRAPHY: James A. Casada, *Sir Harry Johnston: A Bio-Bibliographical Study*, Basel, Switzerland, 1977; Alex Johnston, *The Life and Letters of Sir Harry Johnston*, London, 1929; Harry H. Johnston,

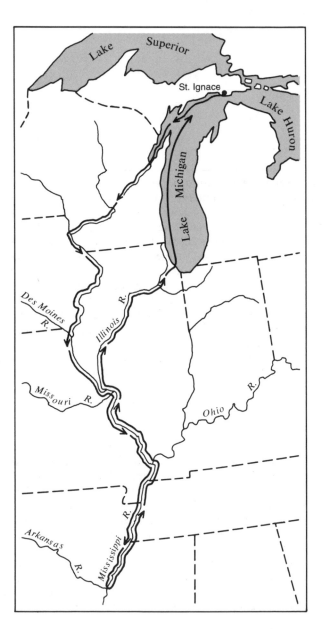

The Story of My Life, London, 1923; Roland Oliver, *Sir Harry Johnston and the Scramble for Africa,* London, 1957.

James A. Casada

Jolliet (Joliet), Louis *(ca. 1645–1700)* French explorer in North America, cartographer, organist, royal hydrographer, businessman, and seigneur. He was born in Quebec Province, the son of Jean Jollyet, a humble wheelwright, and of Marie d'Abancourt. Educated at the college of the Jesuits in Quebec, he originally planned to enter the priesthood, and he did take minor orders in August 1662. The study of music also greatly interested him, and he learned to play the harpsichord, the flute, the trumpet, and the organ. His plans for the priesthood changed, however, and in October 1667 he traveled to France. The purpose of this journey is unknown, but in the fall of 1668 he returned to New France and soon became actively engaged in fur-trading activities.

Late in 1672 he joined with Father Jacques Marquette (1637–1675) and several others to make preparations for a journey in search of the great river toward the west which the Indians had reported as wide, deep, and beautiful and worthy of comparison with the St. Lawrence. Various French missionaries had gained some ideas about such a river from their contacts with the Indians of the Great Lakes. Jolliet's expedition finally got under way in May 1673 and eventually reached the great waterway now known as the Mississippi River by way of Lake Michigan and the Fox-Wisconsin route. Following the Mississippi to its junction with the Arkansas, the exploring party was able to ascertain that the Mississippi emptied into the Gulf of Mexico and was not a passage to the East China Sea. The explorers then returned to Lake Michigan by way of the Illinois River. Jolliet's brief narrative of this exploration was written from memory, his personal papers and other important records having been lost as the result of an accident in the rapids near Montreal. Jolliet subsequently explored in the Hudson Bay area and in Labrador, and he prepared an extensive description of the Labrador coasts and their inhabitants as well as a number of cartographic sketches. In 1697 he received the appointment as royal hydrographer and obtained a seigneury on the Etchemin River. Details of his last years are obscure. He died in the summer of 1700, and the place of his burial is unknown.

BIBLIOGRAPHY: Jean Delanglez, *Life and Voyages of Louis Jolliet (1645–1700),* Institute of Jesuit History Publications, Chicago, 1948; Virginia S. Eifert, *Louis Jolliet: Explorer of Rivers,* New York, 1965.

Bernerd C. Weber

K

Kashevarov, Aleksandr Filippovich (1808–1866)
Explorer of Russian America and cartographer. Born
on Kodiak Island of a Russian father and an Aleut
mother, he was sent by the Russian-American Company to the navigation school in St. Petersburg. Between 1828 and 1830, as navigator on the company
ship *Elena* (V. S. Kromchenko commanding) he made
a round-the-world voyage to Russian America. In
1831–1832 he was sent to Russian America on the
military transport *Amerika* (V. S. Kromchenko commanding) and sailed on company vessels until 1843.
In 1838 he was commander of a hydrographic expedition studying the northern coasts of Russian America.
From the redoubt St. Michael on Norton Sound he
took the company vessel *Polifem* through Bering
Strait to Cape Lisburne. Then on *baidaras* (large open
boats made of skins stretched over wooden frames) he
studied the shore from Cape Lisburne to a point 30
miles (48 kilometers) beyond Point Barrow. Returning
by way of Siberia to St. Petersburg, he was assigned in
1845 to the Hydrographic Department of the Naval
Ministry to compile maps for the *Atlas Vostochnogo
okeana s Okhotskim i Beringovym moriam (Atlas of
the Eastern Ocean Including the Okhotsk and Bering
Seas)*, published in St. Petersburg in 1850. Between
1850 and 1856, as a captain lieutenant, he was commandant of the port of Ayan on the Sea of Okhotsk.
From 1857 to 1862 he again worked in the Hydrographic Department.   *Richard A. Pierce*

**Khabarov, Yerofey Pavlovich (*fl. mid-seventeenth cen-
tury*)** Russian explorer. Born in Ustyug, he moved
about 1636 to Siberia, where he achieved success in
agriculture and the fur trade. In 1649 he organized at
his own expense at Yakutsk an expedition to explore
the as yet virtually unknown Amur Valley. With a
force of 150 men he ascended the Olekma and the
Tungir Rivers, crossed the Yablonovy Range in January 1650, then descended the Urka or the Amazar to
the Amur. Finding that conflict with the native Dau-
rians could mean a war with China, which claimed
suzerainty over the region, he returned in Yakutsk in
1650. His recommendations, forwarded to Moscow,
led to plans to send an army to conquer and hold the
Amur, but this idea was later abandoned.

In 1650 Khabarov returned to the Amur on a second
expedition and settled in the fortified native village of
Albazin. In the spring of 1651 he started down the
Amur fighting the natives. He built the *ostrog* (fort) of
Achansk, where he and his men spent the winter of
1651–1652, repulsing native attacks and, in March
1652, an attack by the Manchus. Going back up the
river, he built the *ostrog* of Kumarsk at the mouth of
the Kumara River, then was recalled to Moscow on
charges of excessive cruelty to his men. Exonerated,
he was made commandant of the *ostrog* of Ilimsk.

BIBLIOGRAPHY: Frank A. Golder, *Russian Expansion on the Pacific,
1641–1850*, Cleveland, 1914.

Richard A. Pierce

197

Inhabitants of Kotzebue Sound, discovered by the Russian explorer Otto von Kotzebue. [Library of Congress]

Kotzebue, Otto von *(1787–1846)* Russian seafarer. Born in Reval (Tallinn), the second son of the well-known German dramatist August von Kotzebue, he accompanied Adam Johann von KRUSENSHTERN on his round-the-world voyage in the *Nadezhda* between 1803 and 1806. In 1815 Kotzebue commanded a similar expedition in the brig *Rurik*. Entering the Pacific by way of Cape Horn, he visited Easter Island and the Tuamotu Archipelago, where a number of islands were discovered, charted a large part of the northwest coast of Alaska, and discovered the sound that now

A native of the Russian peninsula of Kamchatka, which Stepan Petrovich Krasheninnikov studied extensively in the mid-eighteenth century. [Library of Congress]

Habitant du Kamtchatka

bears his name. Finding that he could not return to the Atlantic through the Arctic, he turned south, visiting the Marshall Islands on his way back to Europe. Between 1823 and 1826 he made another voyage around the world in the sloop *Predpriyatiye,* carrying out valuable oceanographic researches and discovering additional islands in the Society and Marshall groups. In 1830 he retired because of ill health.

BIBLIOGRAPHY: Otto von Kotzebue, *A New Voyage round the World,* 2 vols., London, 1830; id., *A Voyage of Discovery,* 3 vols., London, 1821.

Richard A. Pierce

Krasheninnikov, Stepan Petrovich *(1711–1755)* Russian scholar and explorer of Kamchatka. Born in Moscow, Krasheninnikov studied in the Moscow Slavonic-Greek-Latin Academy (1724–1732) and the Academic University in St. Petersburg (1732–1733). From 1733 on he served in the Great Northern Expedition, and until 1736 he traveled about Siberia with Johann Georg Gmelin. In 1737 he was assigned to study Kamchatka, and during the next several years he traveled over many parts of the peninsula, compiling a massive account of its history, ethnography, geology, botany, and zoology. In 1741 he left Kamchatka and continued his work in the Academy of Sciences in St. Petersburg, completing his monumental *Opisaniye zemli Kamchatki* in 1751, published in modern translation in 1972.

BIBLIOGRAPHY: E. A. P. Crownhart-Vaughan (tr.), *Explorations of Kamchatka, North Pacific Scimitar,* Portland, Oreg., 1972.

Richard A. Pierce

Krenitsyn, Pyotr Kuzmich *(d. 1770)* Russian naval officer and explorer of the North Pacific. In 1764 Krenitsyn was given command of an expedition which sailed from the mouth of the Kamchatka River in 1768. With his assistant, Mikhail D. Levashev, he explored the islands of Umnak, Unalaska, and Unimak and the western part of the coast of the Alaska Peninsula. In 1770 they returned to Kamchatka, where Krenitsyn drowned in the Kamchatka River. In 1771 Levashev took the materials of the expedition to St. Petersburg; a map of the Aleutian Islands based on them was compiled in 1777. Krenitsyn's name remains on the strait between Onekotan and Kharimkotan Islands in the Kuril chain, a volcano and a cape on Onekotan Island, and the Krenitzin Islands in the Fox group of the Aleutians.

Richard A. Pierce

Krusenshtern, Adam Johann von *(Russian: Ivan Fyodorovich Krusenshtern; 1770–1846)* Russian admiral and circumnavigator. Member of a Baltic German family, Krusenshtern took part in the war with Sweden in 1787–1790 and served in the British Fleet in Africa, Asia, and North America from 1793 to 1798. In 1799, after a year in Canton, he returned on a British ship by

Iliulink (now Unalaska), principal settlement on the island of Unalaska, explored by Pyotr Kuzmich Krenitsyn in 1768. [Library of Congress]

way of England. That year he presented a proposal for a round-the-world voyage to promote trade communication between Russian ports in the Baltic Sea and Russian America, and in 1802 he was appointed commander of such an expedition. This first Russian circumnavigation was accomplished between 1803 and 1806 with the ships *Nadezhda* and *Neva,* which was commanded by Yury Fyodorovich LISIANSKY. While the *Neva* visited Russian America, Krusenshtern took the imperial plenipotentiary N. P. Rezanov to Japan and sailed along the west coast of Hokkaido, along the east coast of Kamchatka, and to Sakhalin and the Kurils. Krusenshtern Strait (also known as Tsushima Strait), between Japan and Korea, is named after him. From 1827 to 1842 he was director of the Naval Cadet Corps.

BIBLIOGRAPHY: A. J. von Krusenshtern, *Voyage round the World, in the Years 1803, 1804, 1805, and 1806,* tr. by A. B. Hoppner, 2 vols., London, 1813.

Richard A. Pierce

L

Laing, Alexander Gordon *(1794–1826)* Scottish explorer. Born in Edinburgh, Laing attended Edinburgh University before obtaining a commission in a West India infantry regiment. When his regiment was stationed in Sierra Leone, Laing expressed a desire to explore the interior of Africa, especially to determine the course of the Niger River. His request was denied, but in 1822 he was placed in command of a patrol that traveled near the source of the Niger. The low elevation of the area convinced Laing that the Niger did not join the Nile and that efforts to explore the former should originate in West Africa instead of North Africa. Having been chosen to report personally to the 3d Earl Bathurst, secretary of state for war and colonies, on the progress of a campaign against the Ashanti of the Gold Coast, Laing arrived in London in August 1824. He resumed his efforts to secure support for his plans of exploration, and Lord Bathurst proved receptive. The latter argued, however, that Laing's expedition should commence in North Africa on the ground that travel across the Sahara was known to be feasible. Laing acquiesced and was named head of a mission that would travel from Tripoli to Timbuktu, from which it would follow the Niger to its termination.

Accompanied by his West Indian servant and two West African boatbuilders, Laing arrived in Tripoli in May 1825 but was not able to start on the southward journey until July 18. In the meantime he fell in love with Emma Warrington, daughter of Hanmer War-rington, British consul in Tripoli, and prevailed upon the latter to marry them. From his letters to Warrington and others, it is known that Laing and his companions traveled to Ghudāmis (Ghadames) and Aïn Salah, in what is now Algeria. All the while he expressed concern about "my dear Emma" and about the possibility that Hugh CLAPPERTON, who had begun his second African expedition in August 1825, might solve the Niger problem before him. Laing left Aïn Salah on January 9, 1826, venturing into territory so violent that seasoned desert merchants were fearful of traversing it. Early the following month he was attacked by Tuareg at the Wadi Ahenet and was nearly killed, but despite his severe wounds he proceeded southward. On August 13, Laing, by now the only surviving member of his original party of four, arrived in Timbuktu, becoming the first European to have visited that fabled city of his own volition in modern times. In contrast to René CAILLIÉ, who was disappointed by the city, Laing wrote that it met his expectations in every respect. Laing remained in Timbuktu for 5 weeks, his departure being urged by the local sheikh, who feared for his safety. By now Laing had abandoned his intention of sailing down the Niger to its end and planned to return by way of West Africa. On September 24, 1826, 2 days after leaving Timbuktu, he was murdered by his guide, who had been suborned by fanatical Muslims. A passerby buried him nearby; in 1910 his remains were exhumed by the French and reburied in Timbuktu. Despite the fact that Laing traveled over much territory unknown to Europeans, he provided little information for scholars; his journal was apparently lost, and his letters after he passed Ghudāmis were uncommunicative, perhaps because he was saving his news for the account he hoped to write after his return. *See also* NIGER RIVER.

BIBLIOGRAPHY: E. W. Bovill, *The Niger Explored*, London, 1968; Brian Gardner, *The Quest for Timbuktoo*, New York, 1968; *Missions to the Niger: I. Friedrich Hornemann and Gordon Laing*, ed. by E. W. Bovill, Cambridge, England, 1964.

Richard Lemon Lander, who was to discover the termination of the Niger River, began his African adventures as a "domestic" to Hugh Clapperton. [Library of Congress]

Lander, Richard Lemon *(1804–1834)* English explorer. The son of a Cornish public-house keeper, Lander had traveled to the West Indies and South Africa, as well as to Europe, as a servant to several masters when he was engaged as a "domestic" by Hugh CLAPPERTON in 1825. Lander nursed Clapperton devotedly during the latter's last illness, although he was often ill with recurrent fever himself. With the help of William Pascoe, a Hausa servant who had been engaged in England, Lander was able to travel safely from Sokoto to Badagri on the Bight of Benin, and he arrived in Portsmouth on April 30, 1828. His account of this journey was published as *Records of Captain Clapperton's Last Expedition to Africa* (1830).

Despite the illness and other dangers he had experienced in Africa, Lander volunteered to return when the government proposed another Niger expedition. His instructions were to reach the river and "to follow its course, if possible to its termination, wherever that might be." Accompanied by his younger brother, John Lander (1806–1839), he left Portsmouth on January 9, 1830, and, after recruiting some servants, including Pascoe, at Cape Coast Castle, landed at Badagri. The Landers then traveled northward to Bussa, where they began their voyage down the Niger by canoe. Their plans nearly went awry when they were taken captive at the Ibo market town of Kiri and kept prisoners by a king (obi) of the Ibo until Englishmen at nearby Bonny or Brass should ransom them. They were released, however, when a Brass trader called King Boy offered to redeem them provided that he be compensated at the coast. While John stayed at Brass as a hostage, Richard and King Boy reached the Nun River, the principal mouth of the Niger, on November 18, 1830. Although the captain of an English brig in the vicinity refused to give King Boy what was owed to him, the latter agreed to relinquish the two brothers, who were now able to begin their homeward voyage.

Having solved the mystery of the Niger's termination, which had baffled so many earlier explorers, Lander was awarded the first annual premium of 50 guineas of the recently founded ROYAL GEOGRAPHICAL SOCIETY. The brothers' narrative of their epochal journey appeared in three volumes as *Journal of an Expedition to Explore the Course and Termination of the Niger* (1832).

In 1832 Richard went back to West Africa as a member of a private trading expedition organized by the Liverpool merchant Macgregor Laird. Joining Lander at Cape Coast Castle was Pascoe, who was later poisoned on the orders of an African chief. Lander himself was injured in a skirmish with some Africans at Angiama, about 100 miles (161 kilometers) up the Niger, and died of his wounds on February 2, 1834, on the island of Fernando Po. *See also* NIGER RIVER.

BIBLIOGRAPHY: E. W. Bovill, *The Niger Explored*, London, 1968; Robin Hallett (ed.), *The Niger Journal of Richard and John Lander*, London, 1965.

Langsdorff, Georg Heinrich von *(Russian: Grigory Ivanovich Langsdorff; 1774–1852)* German physician and naturalist in Russian service. Between 1803 and 1805 Langsdorff sailed on the sloop *Nadezhda*, commanded by Adam Johann von KRUSENSHTERN, on the first Russian circumnavigation, going from Copenhagen around Cape Horn to Petropavlovsk and Japan and back to Petropavlovsk. He sailed to Russian America with the imperial plenipotentiary N. P. Rezanov in the summer of 1805 and visited Spanish California the following spring in Rezanov's company. In 1807 Langsdorff returned to European Russia by way of Kamchatka, Okhotsk, and Siberia. In 1812 he published an account of the expedition and was appointed Russian consul general in Rio de Janeiro. Between 1821 and 1828 he studied different regions of Brazil, sending valuable collections on zoology, botany, and ethnography to the Russian Academy of Sciences, but in 1829 he came down with an incurable mental illness and was taken back to Europe.

BIBLIOGRAPHY: G. H. von Langsdorff, *Voyages and Travels in Various Parts of the World, during the Years 1803, 1804, 1805, 1806, and 1807*, London, 1813.

Richard A. Pierce

La Pérouse, Jean-François de Galaup, Comte de *(1741–?1788)* French sailor and navigator who explored the Pacific. La Pérouse was born on August 22, 1741, near Albi in southern France, the eldest son of a middle-class family. He entered the French Navy as a *garde de la marine* at the age of 15. He fought off the east coast of America during the Seven Years' War and in the 1760s served in the Indian Ocean. During the War of American Independence La Pérouse, now a captain, led a French naval attack on British trading posts on the shores of Hudson Bay. He surprised and captured Fort Prince of Wales and York Factory, two key posts on the bay. One of his prisoners was Samuel HEARNE, the explorer of the Coppermine River, then in charge of Fort Prince of Wales. Hearne and his manuscript journals of his famous 1770–1772 journey to the Arctic Ocean were taken to France, where La Pérouse, a geographer himself, arranged for his captive's release on condition that the journals be published (as they were in 1795).

On August 1, 1785, La Pérouse sailed from Brest with two French government ships, *L'Astrolabe* under Paul-Antoine de Langle and *La Boussole* under his personal command, to complete the geographic discoveries of James COOK in the Pacific. His lengthy instructions also called upon him to inquire into the prospects of the maritime fur trade of the northwest coast of North America north of the Spanish possessions, to lay claim to a site for French traders, and to investigate the possibility of a NORTHWEST PASSAGE from Bering Strait. In addition, he was to explore the Asian coast and sections of the South Pacific and to return to France in 1789.

On June 23, 1786, he reached Yakutat Bay, near Mount St. Elias, Alaska, via Cape Horn, Easter Island, and the Hawaiian Islands. While the expedition was in Alaska, the party discovered and took possession of Lituya Bay, found that the Bering's Bay of Captain Cook did not exist, did much to refute the idea of a Northwest Passage, and collected valuable scientific material. Leaving Lituya Bay on July 30, the ships coasted southward to Monterey, California, crossed the Pacific, and reached Macao on January 2, 1787. La Pérouse then sailed north to Kamchatka via the Sea of Okhotsk, having failed to round Sakhalin and to prove it to be an island, separated from the Manchurian mainland. At Petropavlovsk, Kamchatka, where he arrived in September, he sent Baron Jean de Lesseps to France by way of Siberia with dispatches and the expedition's journals. The two vessels then sailed southward to the Samoan group, where, at Manua, de Langle and eleven members of the expedition were murdered by natives.

From Samoa La Pérouse sailed via Tonga and Norfolk Island to Port Jackson, New South Wales. He left Botany Bay in February 1788 to continue his explorations but was never seen again. In 1791 an expedition commanded by Antoine-Raymond-Joseph de Bruni, Chevalier d'Entrecasteaux, was sent to search for La Pérouse but found no traces. Only in 1826 did Peter Dillon, a British merchant captain, hear of La Pérouse at Tikopia in the Santa Cruz group. His investigations and those of Jules DUMONT D'URVILLE in 1828 indicated that the ships had been wrecked near Vanikoro Island in the Santa Cruz group. The natives had killed some of the survivors; the others built from the wreckage of one of the vessels a sloop on which they went to their final unknown fate. Fortunately, La Pérouse's journals of the voyage from Kamchatka to Botany Bay had been sent to Paris before his departure from Australia and were published in 1797.

BIBLIOGRAPHY: Peter Dillon, *Narrative . . . of a Voyage . . . to Ascertain the Actual Fate of La Pérouse's Expedition*, London, 1829; John Dunmore, *French Explorers in the Pacific*, vol. I, *The Eighteenth Century*, Oxford, 1965; N. L. A. Milet-Mureau, *Voyage de la Pérouse*, 3 vols., Paris, 1797.

Barry M. Gough and Richard A. Pierce

La Salle, René-Robert Cavelier, Sieur de (1643–1687) French explorer in North America and the discoverer of the mouth of the Mississippi. He was born in Rouen, Normandy, the second son of Jean Cavelier and of Catherine Geest. His family was well to do and belonged to the *haute bourgeoisie* of provincial France. La Salle studied at the Jesuit college in Rouen and in 1658 entered a Jesuit novitiate in Paris, but he subsequently he left the religious life. In 1666 he went to Canada, where his elder brother, Jean Cavelier, was a member of the Order of Saint-Sulpice.

La Salle obtained from the Sulpicians a grant of land in the western end of the island of Montreal, and there he carried on for a while his activities as a pioneer farmer. Contacts with the Indians, however, aroused his interest in exploration projects. After selling back his estate to the Sulpicians, La Salle took part in an expedition in the summer of 1669 which explored the southern shore of Lake Ontario and the land south of the lake. Relatively little is known of La Salle's activities during the next few years, but in 1674–1675 during a trip to France he obtained the grant of Fort Cataracoui (which he renamed Frontenac) and patents of nobility for himself and his descendants. A second visit to France in 1677 resulted in further privileges which allowed him to participate in the exploration and the exploitation of the West.

Upon his return to New France in 1678, La Salle was accompanied by Chevalier Henri de Tonty, who had served as a cadet in the French Army and who became La Salle's trusted lieutenant and confidential agent in later enterprises. La Salle cooperated with the Comte de Frontenac, governor-general of New France, in making plans for further explorations and the development in the West of an empire for the glory of Louis XIV. These plans involved the construction of a shipyard near the present site of Buffalo on the Niagara River. In the summer of 1679 *Le griffon*, named in honor of Frontenac's coat of arms, was launched. This vessel was the first sailing ship to ply the Great Lakes west of Ontario. An exploration of Green Bay (Baie des Puants), an arm of Lake Michigan, was carried out, and *Le griffon* was loaded with a great store of furs which had been assembled by La Salle's traders. These pelts were intended for Fort Frontenac to appease La Salle's creditors, but the valuable cargo never reached its destination because *Le griffon* was lost, possibly in a storm.

Meanwhile, La Salle himself with a party of men established Fort Miami on the site of present-day St. Joseph, Michigan, and then proceeded to Lake Peoria, where Fort Crèvecoeur was built. La Salle decided to go himself to Fort Frontenac for additional supplies after having sent Father Louis Hennepin and two other men on an exploring expedition to the upper reaches of the Mississippi River. The difficult journey to Fort Frontenac, undertaken during early spring when snow and ice were melting, required just over 2 months to accomplish. When La Salle eventually returned from his eastern journey, he found that the Illinois post had been abandoned. Tonty and his men had been forced to flee before an invasion of hostile Iroquois. A reunion with Tonty was effected at Michilimackinac by the end of May 1681.

A man of great vision, La Salle explored the Mississippi and claimed the Louisiana territory that was to become the southern base of the French North American empire. [Library of Congress]

One of La Salle's ships unloads at anchorage. The great French explorer was the first to launch a sailing ship on the Great Lakes west of Ontario. [Library of Congress]

Early in the year 1682 La Salle, Tonty, and a small party proceeded down the Mississippi River. They marveled at the luxuriant nature of the country which they saw. Early in April they finally came within sight of the Gulf of Mexico, and on April 9, 1682, in the delta of the Mississippi River La Salle formally took possession of the entire region, naming it Louisiana in honor of the Bourbon king, Louis XIV. This

The explorations of René-Robert Cavelier, Sieur de La Salle.

event marked the climax of La Salle's distinguished career.

The return journey began almost at once. Tonty reached the Illinois River and began the construction of another fort. He was later joined by La Salle, and Fort Saint-Louis, located on a bluff below the present city of Ottawa, Illinois, was completed (1682–1683). This fort became the hub of Tonty's fur trade for a decade. In 1683 La Salle was deprived of his authority by the recently appointed governor of New France, the Sieur de la Barre. La Salle journeyed to Quebec and took passage for France, arriving there shortly before Christmas, 1683. Tonty, meanwhile, was left in charge of the fur-trading activities in the West.

In France La Salle reported his discoveries to government officials and eventually received from the King the authority to colonize and to govern the region between Lake Michigan and the Gulf of Mexico. He set out from La Rochelle in July 1684, intending to go to the mouth of the Mississippi, but he never succeeded in reaching it. Instead, La Salle and his men landed on the eastern coast of Texas and there established a settlement. Between 1685 and 1687 three major efforts were made to reach the Mississippi by land, but all these attempts proved fruitless. On the third effort the men became mutinous, and La Salle was shot to death near the Brazos River in March 1687 by one of his disaffected companions. La Salle's outstanding achievement was the discovery of the last 700 miles (1127 kilometers) of the lower course of the Mississippi and of claiming for France the vast territory of Louisiana. He was an explorer of tenacity, vision, and courage, and his efforts made possible the realization of a great French empire in North America.

BIBLIOGRAPHY: Isaac J. Cox (ed.), *The Journeys of René Robert Cavelier, Sieur de La Salle as Related by His Faithful Lieutenant, Henri de Tonty*, 2 vols., New York, 1905; Leo Vincent Jacks, *La Salle*, New York, 1931; Francis Parkman, *La Salle and the Discovery of the Great West*, Boston, 1878; John Upton Terrell, *La Salle: The Life and Times of an Explorer*, New York, 1968.

Bernerd C. Weber

La Vérendrye, Pierre Gaultier de Varennes, Sieur de

(1685–1749) French Canadian fur trader and explorer in western Canada and in the United States. Born in Trois-Rivières (Three Rivers) on the St. Lawrence, he was the son of René Gaultier de Varennes and of Marie Boucher. His father was a French military officer who served for a time as governor of Trois-Rivières, and his mother belonged to one of the most illustrious families of Canada. Entering the French colonial army as a youth, Pierre saw military service in New England, in Newfoundland, and later in Europe, where he participated in the War of the Spanish Succession (known in North America as Queen Anne's War). In the bloody Battle of Malplaquet in Flanders (September 1709) he was severely wounded and taken prisoner by the enemy. Returning to Canada after the war, he married Marie-Anne Dandonneau du Sablé, daughter of a well-to-do family. Six children, four sons and two daughters, were born of this marriage.

La Vérendrye took an active part in the development of the French fur trade and in the extension of the western frontiers of New France. In these ventures he received no financial aid from the government. Instead, he obtained his supplies on credit, with prospective profits from the fur trade serving as the basis for repayment. Assisted by members of his family, he established forts, explored in detail the Winnipeg Basin, discovered and mapped the upper Missouri, and attempted to search for the western sea. In the summer of 1736 his eldest son, Jean Baptiste La Vérendrye, and several companions were murdered by Sioux Indians on Massacre Island in Lake of the Woods. Despite many discouragements La Vérendrye showed remarkable persistence and fortitude in his exploration efforts. During the winter of 1742–1743 two of his sons made a circuitous journey on foot and on horseback which took them far to the west to mountains which some scholars have identified as the Black Hills of South Dakota. In the last year of his life La Vérendrye was awarded the Cross of St. Louis in recognition of his extensive explorations. He was making preparations for still another journey to the West when he died in Montreal on December 5, 1749.

BIBLIOGRAPHY: Antoine Champagne, *Les La Vérendrye et le poste de l'ouest*, Quebec, 1968; N. M. Crouse, *La Vérendrye: Fur Trader and Explorer*, Ithaca, N.Y., 1956.

Bernerd C. Weber

Lazarev, Mikhail Petrovich (1788–1851) Russian naval officer and circumnavigator. In 1803 he was sent with thirty-one other volunteers to England for sea training. During the next 5 years he served in various ships of the British Fleet in the Atlantic Ocean and the West Indies. Between 1813 and 1816 he took the Russian-American Company vessel *Suvorov* to Sitka and back to Kronshtadt. Between 1819 and 1821 he commanded the sloop *Mirny* under Fabian Gottlieb Benjamin von BELLINGSHAUSEN on a voyage to the Antarctic, and from 1822 to 1825 he commanded the frigate *Kreiser* on his third round-the-world expedition. Subsequently he distinguished himself in the Battle of Navarino (1827) and other battles with the Turks, became the organizer and commander of the Black Sea Fleet, and in 1843 was made a full admiral.

Richard A. Pierce

Ledyard, John (1751–1789) American traveler. Born in Connecticut, Ledyard studied briefly (1772) at Dartmouth College, then went to sea. In 1776 he sailed with James COOK on the *Resolution*. His *Journal of Captain Cook's Last Voyage* (1783) was the first step in a project to urge the exploitation by American merchants of the tremendous commercial possibilities of the fur trade on the northwest coast of

North America. He tried in vain to find sponsors to provide him with a ship to reach the coast, where he wanted to set up a post. Others got the credit for pioneering the trade; Astoria was ultimately built at the mouth of the Columbia River between 1811 and 1813. Ledyard next tried to cross North America, an idea that was to preoccupy him for the rest of his life. Unable to acquire backing for this, he hit upon the idea of doing it from west to east, first crossing Siberia. Starting in Sweden, he walked around the Gulf of Bothnia to St. Petersburg and from there to Tomsk, Krasnoyarsk, Irkutsk, and Yakutsk. Turning back to Irkutsk, he was arrested there on January 16, 1788, for unknown reasons and expelled from the country. In May 1788, back in London, he engaged to explore the African interior but died in Cairo on January 10, 1789.

BIBLIOGRAPHY: John Ledyard, *A Journal of Captain Cook's Last Voyage to the Pacific Ocean*, 2d ed., Chicago, 1963; Stephen D. Watrous (ed.), *John Ledyard's Journey through Russia and Siberia, 1787–1788*, Madison, Milwaukee, and London, 1966.

Richard A. Pierce

Leichhardt, Friedrich Wilhelm Ludwig (1813–?1848) Australian explorer and naturalist. Born in Trebatsch, Prussia, on October 23, 1813, and educated at the Universities of Berlin (1831, 1834–1836) and Göttingen (1833), Ludwig Leichhardt arrived in Sydney on February 14, 1842, not trained for any particular profession and having evaded compulsory military service.

Determined to achieve fame by exploring central Australia, "that kernel of the dark continent," he offered his services to Sir Thomas MITCHELL, the surveyor general of New South Wales. Spurned, he spent the next 2 years lecturing on botany and geology and making minor botanizing trips, including an epic overland walk in January 1843 from Newcastle 480 miles (772 kilometers) to Moreton Bay. Early in 1844, after a proposed official expedition to northern Australia was refused as being too expensive, Leichhardt successfully sought private support for his own expedition of volunteers.

This assembled in Sydney in August 1844 and sailed north to Brisbane, where it was joined by John Gilbert, an ornithologist and the only competent bushman among its eight members. Leaving Jimbour on October 1, the expedition meandered slowly north, occasionally losing Leichhardt in the bush, until early February, when Leichhardt calculated that only one-quarter of the journey had been completed but three-quarters of the provisions had been consumed. The pace was now quickened, and after crossing the Great Dividing Range in mid-May, the party swung toward the Gulf of Carpentaria. Before this was reached, Gilbert was killed by aborigines, and two others received bad spear wounds. Now very short of provisions and hampered by two wounded men, Leichhardt skirted the gulf and made for Port Essington (Darwin), which was reached on December 17, 1845. The last part of

Although he made some valuable discoveries in the form of excellent grazing land, the Australian explorer F. W. L. Leichhardt is remembered chiefly for his incompetence and for his mysterious end. [*Australian Information Service*]

the journey was chaotic. Everybody suffered severely from scurvy. Most of the botanical specimens were lost or destroyed. Nevertheless, excellent pastoral country had been discovered, and Leichhardt received a hero's welcome and a reward of £1500 (the first money he ever earned) when he reached Sydney on March 25, 1846.

After preparing his journal for publication, Leichhardt began organizing his second major journey, which was to be a continental crossing linking the Darling Downs with the Swan River settlement. This was even more badly managed and equipped. Within 6 months of its departure in December 1846, the party of eight returned, suffering from malnutrition and malaria and having covered only 500 miles (805 kilometers).

Undaunted, Leichhardt began preparations for his final journey, but sponsors and competent companions were now difficult to find, and the expedition was not ready until March 1848. It was last seen on April 3, heading west along the Condamine River. The seven men and seventy-seven animals it contained vanished without trace.

Honored by his contemporaries for his learning and his discoveries, Leichhardt is now remembered chiefly for his incompetence and self-centeredness and for the mystery which still surrounds his fate.

BIBLIOGRAPHY: M. Aurousseau, *Letters of F. W. Ludwig Leichhardt*, Cambridge, England, 1968; A. H. Chisholm, *Strange Journey: The Adventures of Ludwig Leichhardt and John Gilbert*, 2d ed. rev., Adelaide, 1973.

J. M. R. Cameron

Leif the Lucky   *See* EIRÍKSSON, LEIFR.

Leo Africanus *(Arabic: al-Hasan ibn-Muhammad al-Wazzan al-Zayyati; ca. 1485–ca. 1554)* Spanish-born traveler and geographer. Leo was born in Granada, but after the expulsion of Muslims from Spain in 1492, he emigrated with his parents to Morocco, where he was educated. Starting in 1507, he traveled widely in North and Central Africa and the Middle East, often in a diplomatic capacity. He visited Timbuktu twice, and on the second occasion (1512–1514) he traveled from there to Egypt by way of Lake Chad. He was returning from an assignment in Constantinople in 1518 when he was captured by the Sicilian pirate Pietro Bovadiglia and taken to Rome, where he was presented as a slave to Pope Leo X. Upon discovering that his slave was a man of learning, the Pope freed him, installed him in Castel Sant' Angelo, and ordered three bishops to instruct him in Christianity. Pope Leo himself baptized him in 1520 and bestowed his own names, Giovanni Leone, upon him. Leo eventually returned to North Africa.

Leo is best known for his *Descrittione dell' Africa et delle cose notabili che quivi sono,* which provided much valuable information about Africa at a time when Europeans knew very little about the continent. Completed in Italian in 1526, the manuscript came into the hands of Giambattista Ramusio, who published it in his collection of *Navigationi et viaggi* (1550). It was translated into English by John Pory as *A Geographical Historie of Africa* (1600).

BIBLIOGRAPHY: Jean-Léon L'Africain, *Description de L'Afrique*, tr. by A. Épaulard, 2 vols., Paris, 1956.

Lewis, Meriwether *(1774–1809),* **and Clark, William** *(1770–1838)* American explorers. Perhaps no other series of events in United States history stirs more thoughts of romance and adventure than the great westward expedition which Lewis and Clark led to the Pacific Ocean and back between 1804 and 1806. Even before the transfer of the vast, largely unknown Louisiana Territory to the United States in March 1804 (under an agreement of May 1803), President Thomas Jefferson was inquisitive about its geographical features. In a secret message to Congress on January 18, 1803, he announced plans to explore the trans-Mississippi West. Jefferson's association with the American Philosophical Society no doubt encouraged his scientific curiosity about the fabled NORTHWEST PASSAGE supposedly linking Europe and Asia. No less important were his economic and military goals. Both the sea otter of the northwest coast and the riches of the Far Eastern market seemed limitless. In addition, exploration might yield important findings about British, French, and Spanish influence in the West. Congress responded with $2500 (the total cost eventually exceeded $50,000) "for the purpose of extending the external commerce of the United States." Jefferson also intended to strengthen the United States claim to the Columbia River and gather information about the Indians.

To head the expedition Jefferson turned to his friend and personal secretary, Meriwether Lewis, who called for assistance from his longtime friend and military associate William Clark, brother of George Rogers Clark. This was not Lewis's first flirtation with such a project; he had tried unsuccessfully in 1792 to lead a group up the Missouri River.

Departure from St. Louis came about 4:00 P.M. on May 14, 1804. The expedition consisted of forty-five men, twenty-nine of whom were the "permanent detachment" and would travel to the Pacific and back, while the others would journey as far as Mandan country and return to St. Louis with specimens of rocks, plants, and animals from the area explored. The first 1600 miles (2575 kilometers) did not promise new adventures. Frenchmen in the early 1700s already had explored as far as the 43d parallel, the southern boundary of South Dakota. During these 166 days, the men roughed it against the Big Muddy's strong currents, countless sandbars, and numerous snags. Lewis and Clark continually complained of "ticks, musquiters and knats," as well as boils, stomach disorders, lost oars, and other mishaps. Yet there were remarkably few casualties, and only one man died.

The party's contacts with Indians had mixed results. After a few brief, uneventful meetings with Oto, Missouri, and Yankton Sioux, the expedition, in late September, experienced trouble with the pro-English Teton Sioux near present-day Pierre, South Dakota. But a show of force backed them down. Lewis and Clark optimistically noted that they had broken the Sioux blockade and opened the Missouri River to Americans. Passing into friendly Arikara Indian territory, they acquired provisions and persuaded a chief to guide them to Mandan country.

In October the expedition entered the five Mandan Indian villages (near Bismarck, North Dakota) and began a winter of preparation for the great westward trek the following spring. About 3 miles (5 kilometers) below the villages, they constructed log houses and a stockade, which they named Fort Mandan. Here they met the captive wife of a French trader, a Shoshoni Indian girl named Sacajawea, who, with her husband, Toussaint Charbonneau, as companion, served as interpreter and guide for the push to the Pacific. Evidence indicates that, contrary to tradition, Sacajawea's work as guide was *not* indispensable to the expedition's success. Yet she deserves recognition: Sacajawea interpreted the white men's wishes to the Shoshoni and assured her people's trust in them.

On April 7, 1805, the most important segment of the expedition began when thirty-one white men, Sacajawea, her husband, and their newborn baby set out west. The difficulties were enormous. Besides frequent encounters with bears, a problem arose when

Left: Portrait of William Clark, who with his friend Meriwether Lewis helped to dispel the myth that a Northwest Passage existed in the latitudes they explored in 1805. [Independence National Historical Park Collection]

Right: Portrait of Meriwether Lewis. Probably the most important contribution of the Lewis and Clark Expedition to the Pacific was to reemphasize the importance of the Oregon territory to American development. [Independence National Historical Park Collection]

the party reached a fork in the Missouri River. The decision to take the southwestern branch instead of the northwestern branch, the Marias River, as Lewis called it in honor of his cousin, was correct; in just 10 days the men came upon the Great Falls of the Missouri. A month passed before they could build carts and complete the portage around the falls and treacherous cascades beyond.

In July the party was desperately low on supplies. The men had passed through rugged mountainous terrain, only to confront the Three Forks of the Missouri, which they named the Jefferson, Madison, and Gallatin. Following Sacajawea's advice, they chose the westernmost stream, the Jefferson. Lewis and his men passed Shoshone Cove, crossed the continental divide at Lemhi Pass, and captured two terrified Shoshoni squaws who agreed to direct them to the tribe's

Interior of the hut of a Mandan chief. When Lewis and Clark visited the Mandans and established Fort Mandan, they also encountered Sacajawea, the Shoshoni Indian who served as interpreter and guide on their push to the Pacific. [Library of Congress]

chief. Though the Indians at first seemed hostile, they backed off when they saw Sacajawea, who was the chief's sister. A council followed, during which the Indians agreed to furnish horses, guides, and supplies for the excursion across the Rocky Mountains.

It took 50 days to move 300 miles (483 kilometers) over the dangerous mountain trails. After entering the Bitterroot Valley, they turned west and for 10 days pushed through snow and rain. Finally, in late September, the men came upon the sprawling valley of the Clearwater River, where friendly Nez Perce Indians supplied food and helped the white men build canoes. The expedition floated down the Clearwater, Snake, and Columbia Rivers and on November 15, 1805, finally gazed upon the Pacific Ocean.

There was little time for celebration, however, for winter was upon the men. Carefully avoiding the mountain passes, Lewis and Clark established quarters in a crudely constructed, flea-ridden stockade they called Fort Clatsop. Located near present-day Astoria, Oregon, it was burdened with endless coastal rains and bitter, cold weather. Only 6 days of sunshine lifted the men's spirits between January and late March.

The long-awaited spring signaled time to journey back to St. Louis. After a brief discussion, Lewis and Clark rejected President Jefferson's recommendation to return by sea and prepared to go overland again. On March 23, 1806, the men broke camp. After crossing the Rockies, the expedition split in June when Lewis and some of the men decided to explore the Marias River, while Clark and the others (including Sacajawea, her husband, and child) retraced their steps through present-day Yellowstone Park. Lewis eventually returned to the Great Falls of the Missouri. After a mild skirmish with Blackfoot and Gros Ventre Indians in the Marias River Valley, he went on to hunt elk in the Marias bottomlands, but was disabled for a month after being shot in the leg by his companion, a nearsighted French hunter who thought he was a bear. In the meantime Clark took the old route to Three Forks and moved eastward to the Yellowstone River, a considerable distance north of Yellowstone Park. He then followed the stream to the Missouri River. He also had Indian troubles; a small band of warriors stole his horses.

At last, in early fall, the two explorers reassembled for the final leg of the journey. Pausing at the Mandan villages to persuade Chief Big White to go with them to visit the eastern United States, the expedition quickly proceeded down the swift current of the Missouri. On September 23, 1806, more than 2 years after their original departure up the Missouri River, the men entered St. Louis, surprising numerous onlookers who had given them up for dead.

The Lewis and Clark Expedition made several notable contributions. It destroyed the myth of a Northwest Passage in the latitudes visited, collected information about thousands of miles of previously unknown territory, established good relations with many Indian tribes, marked several passageways through the mountains (some not practical), stimulated interest in the fur trade, and, perhaps most important, aroused American concern over Oregon by

Lewis and Clark's route, 1804–1806.

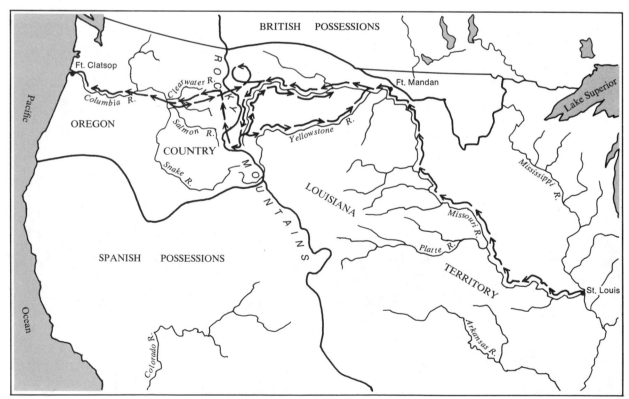

reinforcing claims to the area between the Mississippi's headwaters and the Pacific Ocean. Unfortunately, only four of the men's journals have been found. Though their official map of the West was not always accurate and did not appear until publication of the expedition's report in 1814, it was indispensable to many explorers for years. On it was the first use of the term "Great Plains" in describing the vast treeless lands west of the Missouri River.

There is an aftermath. Lewis became governor of Louisiana Territory in 1806, a position he held until he was mysteriously shot to death 3 years later in a lonely cabin in Tennessee. Clark became a partner in the Missouri Fur Company, governor of Missouri until it reached statehood, and superintendent of Indian affairs for Louisiana and then for Missouri Territory until his death in 1838. Animal skins, Indian relics, and other specimens and souvenirs gathered during the trip were placed on display at Monticello and in the American Museum in Philadelphia. Lewis and Clark College, a Presbyterian institution in Portland, Oregon, bears the explorers' names, and in 1905 Congress appropriated $1 million to coin Lewis and Clark commemorative gold dollars, a move which helped promote the Lewis and Clark Centennial Exposition in Portland.

BIBLIOGRAPHY: John Bakeless, *Lewis and Clark: Partners in Discovery*, New York, 1947; Elliott Coues, *History of the Expedition under the Command of Lewis and Clark*, 4 vols., New York, 1893; Paul R. Cutright, *Lewis and Clark: Pioneering Naturalists*, Champaign-Urbana, Ill., 1969; Richard Dillon, *Meriwether Lewis: A Biography*, New York, 1965; C. S. Kingston, "Sacajawea as Guide: The Evaluation of a Legend," *Pacific Northwest Quarterly*, vol. 35, January 1944, pp. 3–18; Reuben G. Thwaites (ed.), *Original Journals of the Lewis and Clark Expedition, 1804–1806*, 8 vols., New York, 1959; U. S. Department of the Interior, National Park Service, *Lewis and Clark*, Washington, 1975.

Howard Jones

Lisiansky, Yury Fyodorovich (1773–1839) Russian naval officer and circumnavigator. After education in the Naval Cadet Corps and service in 1788 during the war with Sweden, Lisiansky was made a lieutenant in 1793 and by order of the empress Catherine II was among sixteen Russian naval officers sent to England to serve as volunteers in the British Fleet. During the next 5 years he took part in several sea campaigns against the French, moving to Canada, the Lesser Antilles, and India. Returning to Russia in 1798, he was made a captain lieutenant and in 1801 given command of a frigate. In 1802 he was placed in charge of the *Neva*, which was to make a round-the-world voyage under Adam Johann von KRUSENSHTERN, with the *Nadezhda*. The two ships left Kronshtadt on August 7, 1803 (New Style). Separating in the following year in the Pacific Ocean, the *Neva* proceeded to Russian America, while the *Nadezhda* sailed to Kamchatka and Japan. At Sitka, Lisiansky helped A. A. BARANOV retake the area from the local natives, who in 1802 had destroyed the Russian port of New Archangel. In 1805, laden with a cargo of furs, the *Neva* crossed the Pacific, discovering on the way the uninhabited Lisianski Island and Neva and Krusenshtern reefs. The ship met the *Nadezhda* in Macao, and the two vessels turned homeward, arriving at Kronshtadt on August 3, 1806. After 3 more years in active service, Lisiansky retired in 1809 with the rank of captain of the first rank. His large collection of native costumes, weapons, and tools, acquired on the voyage, was willed to the Rumiantsev Museum.

BIBLIOGRAPHY: Yury Lisiansky, *A Voyage round the World in the Years 1803, 4, 5 & 6 . . .*, London, 1814.

Richard A. Pierce

Literature and Exploration

Throughout the history of the written word the activities of travelers and explorers have had a major impact on literary endeavor. The travelogues and other accounts that form a logical emanation of exploits and discoveries in strange and distant lands have invariably appealed to a wide readership in a manner that the student of the history of exploration early comes to recognize. Whether one refers to the splendid series of volumes published by the Hakluyt Society or to a single-volume account written by the explorer himself or one of his contemporaries, the literature *of* exploration is a readily recognized genre. It also has long been a well-tilled field of scholarly study, and considerable energy and erudition have been devoted to tracing and describing the development of geographical literature. However, there is another literary aspect of discovery which transcends straightforward narratives devoted to a realistic recounting of achievements in some distant land. This is what might be styled exploration *in* literature, and as a general theme it deserves broader recognition alongside the better-known factual accounts. To date such has not generally been the case, although there are encouraging signs of a turnabout in the appearance of several recent books and in the creation of an ongoing Modern Language Association seminar on "Travel and Exploration." The seminar has begun annual publication of a journal entitled *Exploration*, and in time it may become a widely recognized medium for the study of this theme in literature.

Ancient literature　There are any number of logical beginning points for such a study, but perhaps a chronological approach is best. Even such early peoples as the ancient Egyptians and Mesopotamians produced literature related to travel and exploration. For example, a surviving papyrus from the period of the Middle Kingdom describes the wanderings of a mythical hero who was shipwrecked, endured much suffering and hardship, and then miraculously obtained another ship upon which to return home. Similarly, Gilgamesh, the hero of the well-known Mesopotamian epic, was a wayfarer who crossed seas and trackless deserts. These tales and other ancient works are in many ways prototypes of the saga of Odysseus. The timeless chronicle of his travels, based on a collection of oral traditions commonly ascribed to the blind poet Homer, epitomizes the travel romance. *The Odyssey* contains elements which recur throughout the development of such literature.

The Greeks probably originally borrowed the basis for the legend of Odysseus from the Egyptians or the Mesopotamians. Moreover, given the fact that the Greeks were a seafaring people, it is not surprising that *The Odyssey* is characterized by a real feeling for the Mediterranean and its crosscurrents, changeable weather, and other conditions of importance to navigation. Nor is the Greek contribution by any means limited to this masterpiece. Mythical figures such as the Argonauts and various deities, including Heracles and Dionysus, were, among other things, explorers. The theme also occurs in Greek humor, in which the example of Aristophanes's Cloud-Cuckoo-Land in his comedy *The Birds* embodies a rather special approach to mythical regions. Likewise, Greek literature incorporates varied concepts of utopian regions such as the persistent legend of Atlantis as well as wondrous inhabitants and creatures in the then barely known locales of Africa and India.

Other ancient literature also abounds in allusions to travel and exploration. The words of Alfred Tennyson's Ulysses, in describing the motivating forces at work within him, go far in capturing the essential attractions that subjects of this nature have exercised on an endless succession of writers from the earliest literate times to the present:

The lights begin to twinkle from the rocks;
The long day wanes; the slow moon climbs; the deep
Moans round with many voices. Come, my friends.
'Tis not too late to seek a newer world.

Push off, and sitting well in order smite
The sounding furrows; for my purpose holds
To sail beyond the sunset, and the baths
Of all the western stars, until I die.

This search for "a newer world," a beckoning land "beyond the sunset," has perhaps been the single most readily distinguishable feature of exploration in literature. The West early came to symbolize man's last journey, the underworld, or the earth's farthest reaches, and there was a continuing preoccupation with exploring the strange new worlds that lay beyond the sun's final gleaming. Most of these concepts found full play in Greek literature, and the Romans, as was true in so many areas, simply built on the foundations their cultural predecessors had so conveniently laid. However, thanks to their vast empire and practical interest in geographical knowledge, the Romans collected much new information which their writers could utilize. Both on land and at sea they expanded far beyond the bounds of the Mediterranean, and one result of this was a wealth of new material and imagery to be incorporated into literature. Nowhere is this better exemplified than in the writings of PTOLEMY. He was arguably the greatest geographer of the ancient world, but his works are a wonderful blend of fact, half-truth, and fantasy. In the latter categories, his influence was pronounced in many ways. For example, his conception of Africa's great rivers flowing from juxtaposed fountains in the heart of the continent appears repeatedly in subsequent literature. His works offer an index to the abundant usage of travel and exploration as literary themes in classical times, and they also attest to the continuing appeal of such imagery to later writers. A much higher proportion of fantasy appears in the work of the fabulist Gaius Julius Solinus, who wrote in the third or fourth century A.D. His *Collectanea rerum memorabilium* relies heavily on the *Natural History* of PLINY and the work of other classical authors, but Solinus concentrates on the marvelous, purveying tales of dog-headed apes, werewolves, and a race of men who cannot die from snakebites. Solinus was frequently cited by later writers, including St. Augustine.

Medieval literature Somewhat surprisingly, the medieval period, traditionally regarded as rather barren ground in literature as well as in other areas of humanistic achievement (more a time of partial preservation than of progress), is also rich in a wide variety of works which fall within the scope of this article. Many medieval legends, deriving mostly from events of classical antiquity, contain geographical elements. The exploits of ALEXANDER THE GREAT were magnified to the point of becoming associated with travel throughout Asia and eventually were even intermeshed with the stories and prophecies of Gog and Magog. Geoffrey of Monmouth, in his *Historia regum Britanniae,* incorporated mythical discoveries, and the travels of St. BRENDAN among unknown isles of the Atlantic (the Western Ocean) form a central fea-

The ship of Odysseus, from Homer's Odyssey. *Here Odysseus is tied to the mast to keep him from following the music of the Sirens to his death on the treacherous rocks they guard.*

ture of Irish folklore. Likewise, outside Western Europe, where intellectual decline was less noticeable, various works in Greek and Arabic, such as those by Zemarchus and the *Meadows of Gold* of Al-MASŪDĪ, recounted real and imaginary travels in distant lands. The Bible was, of course, already an enduring example of literature, originating in oral form, in which geographical conceptions loomed large. In medieval times, there was particular emphasis on paradisiacal concepts such as the Garden of Eden and the four sacred rivers of eternity. The supposed locales of paradise itself varied widely, but as an idea, in either allegorical or real form, it was generally accepted. Here we have a noteworthy extension, albeit in somewhat modified form, of classical utopian ideas. It is not in these works, however, but in those of the late medieval period, that we find the best examples of the use of travel and exploration themes in literature.

Perhaps the best-known work of this type is the *Travels of Sir John Mandeville*, which was written in Norman French in the third quarter of the fourteenth century and purports to relate the author's experiences in the Near and Far East. Among the subjects discussed are the palace of the Great Khan of China, a fruit containing a little beast like a lamb, and the Fountain of Youth, which Mandeville locates in Malabar. The identity of the author is unknown, though he claimed to be an English knight from St. Albans who embarked on his travels in 1322. Whether the author actually visited any of the places mentioned is also unknown since most of the book is based on the writings of earlier medieval travelers, especially Odoric of PORDENONE. However, because of the skill with which Mandeville selected, embellished, and presented his material, the *Travels* quickly acquired great popularity, and more than 250 manuscripts in ten languages have survived. The *Travels* influenced Christopher COLUMBUS and other explorers and, in the words of Josephine Bennett, "was read by Ariosto and Tasso, Cervantes, Rabelais, and Montaigne, as well as by every great English writer from the *Pearl* poet to William Morris."

The religious pilgrimage, the most common type of sustained travel during the Middle Ages, is the setting of Geoffrey Chaucer's incomparable *Canterbury Tales*. The entire series of tales revolves around the pilgrims' progress to Canterbury, and journeys to holy shrines are a feature of many other works. Yet it should be recognized that Chaucer's characters and their fellow travelers normally moved through relatively well-known populated regions. Not so others, however. The medieval period also encompassed the daring Atlantic voyages of the rugged, courageous Vikings and other Scandinavian peoples, and the sagas, eddas, and epic poems associated with them teem with examples of exploratory endeavor in literature. Even to the present these delightful tales of reconnaissance remain at the heart of the Scandinavian and Icelandic cultural heritage. *See* NORSE MARITIME DISCOVERIES.

For the more southern regions of Western Europe, the Crusades constitute the closest comparable literary inspiration to the Atlantic voyages of Leifr EIRÍKSSON, Eirík the Red, and others. Out of these religiously inspired but in many ways supremely secular undertakings came numerous chronicles and related writings. The beginning of the renewed expansion of European horizons is also associated with the impact of the Crusades, and from the period would emerge such diverse matters as the monumental travels of Marco POLO and a growing interest in crushing the Muslims through linkage with the Christian kingdom of the mythical PRESTER JOHN. Marco Polo's account of his adventures, *The Book of Messer Marco Polo*, created a sensation in Europe and is at least as notable for its revelations of other cultures as for its contributions to geographical knowledge. Moreover, it serves as a needed reminder that Oriental cultures had thrived while the West was in decline, and certainly the literature of these cultures included much of relevance to this study. *See also* MEDIEVAL EXPLORATION.

Both India and China long had been the home of highly advanced civilizations, and their traditions included many tales of noble discoveries. Substantial amounts of material of this nature still have not been translated into English, but reference to the career of one individual provides some indication of the rich-

The Squire, from Chaucer's Canterbury Tales. The religious pilgrimage was the most common form of sustained travel in medieval times.

Frontispiece from an early edition (Nürnburg, 1477) of Marco Polo's account of his travels.

Das ist der edel Ritter · Marcho polo von

ness of such literature. Indeed, it is somehow fitting that an Orientalist who himself was a renowned explorer, Sir Richard BURTON, was responsible for translating a considerable corpus of such literature into English. Burton's first love may have been the sexual lore and customs of various cultures, but he was also responsible for making available several Indian works which include tales of travel. He also prepared editions of *A Thousand and One Nights* and of *Os Lusiadas* of Luis Vaz de Camões which still are widely used. The latter work of course belongs to the Renaissance, but the adventures of Sinbad the Sailor deserve to rank well to the forefront of any list of outstanding examples of exploration in literature. Sinbad's seven voyages are fictional, but they are undoubtedly based on the experiences of Muslim merchants in the Indian Ocean, and many of the creatures and places mentioned have been identified with genuine counterparts. For example, the Old Man of the Sea, whom Sinbad meets during the fifth voyage, has generally been identified with the huge apes of Borneo and Sumatra. Some of Sinbad's other experiences, however, are similar to episodes in Western literary works dealing with travel and exploration. Thus the island in the first voyage which turns out to be a whale's back is very much like one visited by St. Brendan's companions.

Renaissance   The Renaissance era, which comprehended the single most important period of discovery in human annals, witnessed a tremendous growth in both the literature of exploration and exploration in literature. Spain and Portugal, which provided most of

the early impetus in Renaissance exploration, also pioneered in the literary field.

From early in the fifteenth to well into the seventeenth century, the Portuguese historicogeographical narrative was a dominant form. Prose chronicles of this kind, while essentially factual in origin, deserve mention in the context of exploration in literature because of their unusual derivation. It was Portuguese policy to maintain secrecy about new discoveries, and accordingly the information gained by the nation's intrepid navigators first became available through the literary efforts of João de Barros, Gaspar Correa, Fernão Lopes de Castanheda, Afonso de (Braz) Albuquerque, and others. Their accounts, while not fictional, frequently were romanticized and embellished. From a rather different perspective, these chronicles are totally eclipsed by *Os Lusíadas (The Lusiads)* of Camões, which is based on the voyage of Vasco da GAMA to India (1497–1499). In the words of one noted authority, "The *Lusiads* is indeed the national poem par excellence and the supreme epic of Portugal's conquests in the East." Certainly the work stands alone as a testament to the country's rather fleeting moment of grandeur, and it is unsurpassed by similar writings in the literature of any language.

Spain had its parallel to Camões's work in *La Araucana* of Alonso de Ercilla y Zúñiga, although his effort was by no means of the same quality as *Os Lusiadas*. Nonetheless, it is a noted epic poem which describes the conquest of Chile in graphic terms, and there were other contemporary Spanish writings of a similar nature. Different in style, but certainly belonging to the same literary classification, were Lope de Vega's poem on the misdeeds of Sir Francis DRAKE, *La Dragontea* (1598), and Juan de Castellanos's narrative poem *Elegías de varones ilustres de las Indias*. The literature of the period for the rest of continental Europe is not of the same quality as that of Portugal and Spain, but given the lead of these two countries in actual geographical endeavor it is to be expected that inspiration for literary endeavor was highest in the Iberian Peninsula. Still, the work of at least one other individual certainly deserves special mention. LEO AFRICANUS defies national classification, but inasmuch as his actual writing took place under the patronage of Pope Leo X, it is logical to speak of him in a European context. Leo X freed him from slavery upon discovering the man's immense erudition and literary ability, and the result was the famous *Descrittione dell' Africa*. Although this work is intended as a factual account and remains an important reference source, it is also full of flights of poetic fancy.

It was in England, where the Renaissance spirit bloomed late but with an exceptional autumnal beauty, that exploration as a theme in literature saw particularly widespread usage. In Elizabethan times in particular, flushed by the overseas achievements of daring sea dogs such as Sir Francis Drake, Sir Humphrey GILBERT, Sir John Hawkins, and myriad lesser

An illustration from Os Lusíadas, epic poem by Luis Vaz de Camões based on Vasco da Gama's voyage to India. Here a Portuguese (probably da Gama) is welcomed to Indian shores. [Library of Congress]

figures, writers glorified new found worlds and their conquerors in an ecstasy of patriotic fervor. What A. L. Rowse, in *The England of Elizabeth*, has styled "The Elizabethan Discovery of England" is well known, and it was but a single logical step from glorification of the beauties of parish and shire to directing attention to the broader and more wondrous spectrum of new worlds.

As in all things Elizabethan, Shakespeare can be relied on to provide insight. He readily realized, with his uncanny ability to capture the essence of his countrymen's spirit, that new forces were at work. It was an era, as he wrote in *The Two Gentlemen of Verona*, when

> . . . men, of slender reputation,
> Put forth their sons to seek preferment out:
> Some to the wars, to try their fortune there;
> Some to discover islands far away.

Allusions of a similar nature which focus on the adventurous enterprise of the age abound in his works, and Shakespeare was very much aware of and readily used the newly acquired geographical lore which Richard HAKLUYT and others were making widely known and available. One of the witches in *Macbeth*, in an anachronistic but typical statement, refers to the journey (1583–1591) of Ralph Fitch to India by way of Mesopotamia: "Her husband's to Aleppo gone, master of the *Tiger*." And in *Othello* one glimpses the legends of the supernatural or bizarre which the period found so attractive and which so permeated rapidly accumulating geographical data. There were those regions

> Wherein of antres vast and desarts idle,
> Rough of quarries, rocks and hills whose heads touch heaven,
> . . . .
> And of the Cannibals that each other eat,
> The Anthropophagi and men whose heads
> Do grow beneath their shoulders.

The most obvious reference to the impact exploration had on Shakespeare, however, is found in *The Tempest*. The play was suggested by the wreck of the *Sea Venture*, flagship of a fleet bound for Virginia under the command of Sir George Somers, which ran aground on Bermuda in 1609.

Shakespeare stands apart from the crowd, yet many of his contemporaries or near contemporaries made significant contributions to literature of this genre. Emphasis on that which is new and novel in exploration and discovery greets one in Christopher Marlowe, Edmund Spenser, Ben Jonson, and others, nor should the contribution of Sir Walter Raleigh, who knew firsthand that of which he wrote, be forgotten. Moreover, in the Elizabethan Renaissance there was exciting variety in modes of expression. Distant lands and noble travelers figure in mediums ranging from sonnets to plays and including collections and propagandistic literature. In the last two categories Richard Hakluyt is in a class by himself. While *The Principall Navigations, Voiages and Discoveries of the English Nation* is firmly rooted in fact, it also conveys a stridently patriotic promotional message as well as offering fertile fields of imagery to eager writers who were anxious to traverse the bounds between real and imagined.

On either side of the Elizabethan era, writings in English involving exploration or travel were less extensive, but they still existed in abundance. Sir Thomas More's *Utopia* embodies something of the idealistic concepts previously mentioned, although the work itself is basically political in orientation. Just over a century later, John Milton combined political concerns with the concept of a perfect earthly kingdom gone awry in *Paradise Lost*. This was a new aspect of the now long-standing interest in such idyllic worlds, and to it Milton brought abundant reliance on geography. As he wrote, he found "the study of Geography is both profitable and delightfull," and so extensive was his reliance on it that Robert R. Cawley has made a book-length study of *Milton. and the Literature of Travel*.

Seventeenth and eighteenth centuries Definition of the earth's final frontiers was by no means completed in the Renaissance, and the ongoing pattern of new discoveries continued to provide inspiration for writers on many subjects. Both the scientific revolution and the Enlightenment spawned their own brands of concern with distant places and alien peoples. Much of this curiosity derived from scientific or intellectual bases, but leading writers of the seventeenth and eighteenth centuries exhibited a ready propensity to utilize exploration and travel information in shaping their works. To a considerable degree efforts at geographical reconnaissance in the first half of the seventeenth century focused on commercial expansion. Naturally such mundane economic pursuits had less literary attraction than journeys motivated by a simple desire to probe the unknown. The latter half of the century, however, witnessed a considerable change in this pattern.

The Royal Society, created in England early in the reign of Charles II, had a marked impact on scientific travel, and both the society and its French counterpart (created a few years later) included many literary figures in their membership. Guidebooks for travelers also became increasingly common in the latter part of the seventeenth century, and these, together with the popular grand tour, provided ready fuel for literary fires. However, it was voyages to and journeys in strange and distant lands that continued to attract the most attention and provided the greatest impetus to those who used such imagery in their writings. Alexandre Olivier Exquemelin's *De americaenische zeeroovers* (1678), which was translated into English as *Bucaniers of America* in 1684, is a fine example of the attractiveness of seemingly exotic subjects such as the activities of pirates in distant seas. William Dampier's *A Voyage to New Holland,* John Churchill's *Collection of Voyages and Travels,* and other less enduring works had a profound impact on imaginations of the time, and eventually they bore fictional fruit in the writings of individuals such as Daniel Defoe and Jonathan Swift. Dampier's account undoubtedly influenced Swift, as is evidenced by his use of the Great Australian Bight as the setting for Lemuel Gulliver's experiences in *Gulliver's Travels.* This book as a whole is a splendid example of a fictional work centering on travel, and one encounters similar methods in other pieces by Swift. His lines in *Poetry, a Rhapsody* are frequently quoted, and they are suggestive of the manner in which writers adopted the techniques he attributes to geographers:

> So geographers, in Afric-maps,
> With savage-pictures fill their gaps;
> And o'er unhabitable downs
> Place elephants for want of towns.

In a similar fashion recourse to exploration themes could fill literary gaps by bringing pen to paper in a rewarding manner.

Swift's contemporary Daniel Defoe illustrates the fascination of the time not only with distant and unknown places but with their inhabitants as well. His *Robinson Crusoe,* which this writer considers the finest sustained narrative of the type under discussion, was probably based on the experiences of Alexander Selkirk, a Scottish navigator who was marooned from 1704 to 1709 on Isla Más a Tierra (now Isla Robinson Crusoe) in the Juan Fernández group off the coast of Chile, which was a favorite haven for English corsairs and privateers in the seventeenth and eighteenth centuries. Selkirk's story was told by his rescuer, Capt. Woodes Rogers, in *A Cruising Voyage round the World* (1712), and an interview with Selkirk by Richard Steele appeared in *The Englishman* in 1713. *Robinson Crusoe* was published in 1719.

Defoe's moving tale demonstrates the period's con-

Robinsoe Crusoe and his pets. [Library of Congress]

victions regarding the innate ingenuity of man and his ability, if circumstances pressed him sufficiently, to master all things. Friday is the prototype of what Jean-Jacques Rousseau termed the "noble savage," and in Crusoe himself are embodied all the virtues of the true explorer. The prominence Defoe gives to Friday is very much in keeping with the spirit of the age as well, because the inhabitants of strange lands, always exciting, exercised extraordinary fascination on figures of both the scientific revolution and the Enlightenment. John Locke, Richard Bentley, and other serious writers used information on the beliefs and habits of native peoples to support a wide range of political and philosophical arguments. The deists cited the concepts of natural religion among primitive peoples as validation for their own beliefs and as an indication of the manner in which clerical organization and established churches had corrupted true religion in highly civilized states.

Before we leave Defoe, the wider ramifications of one other aspect of *Robinson Crusoe* deserve mention. This is what might be called the shipwreck setting as a literary device. Mention of it has been made in several different settings, and in truth one encounters it with astonishing regularity throughout the development of exploration in literature. An indication of its enduring qualities is *The Swiss Family Robinson* (1813) by Johann Wyss. This work has enjoyed almost as much popularity and longevity as *Robinson Crusoe,* and if a momentary transfer to another medium is permissible, the adaptability of the shipwreck theme is emphasized in an American television series based on Wyss's book.

As well known as the writings of Swift, Defoe, and Wyss are, they are certainly rivaled if not actually surpassed by the philosophes in resort to subject matter employing travel settings. Mention has been made of Rousseau's noble savage, and this idealized aboriginal type appealed immensely to those who were at the heart of the French Enlightenment. Indeed, offshoots of travel and exploration, in their many varieties, permeated the very core of philosophic thought during the period. The philosophes saw endless possibilities in discovery, and they rightly reckoned that the impact of European expansion would bring about profound and lasting changes in worlds old and new. This can be seen in Voltaire's *Candide* (1759), whose title character travels to South America, visiting the Jesuit missions in Paraguay and EL DORADO. The latter is a hospitable land where children play quoits with precious stones and pieces of gold and there are no monks, law courts, or prisons. Before writing *Candide,* Voltaire read *Voyages de François Coréal aux Indes Occidentales,* a work by a seventeenth-century Spanish traveler which he also consulted for his *Essai sur les moeurs.*

Strangely enough, the period, for all its richness in the field of exploration in literature, was not a particularly productive one in actual discovery. This situation changed dramatically in the final decades of the eighteenth century and henceforth, save for the hiatus occasioned by the Napoleonic Wars, exploration by land and sea continued apace until earthly frontiers were no more. The voyages of Capt. James COOK in the Pacific, the travels of James BRUCE in Ethiopia, the ongoing search for the NORTHWEST PASSAGE and the NORTHEAST PASSAGE, and the creation of the AFRICAN ASSOCIATION in 1788 all heralded a new age in discovery. They also marked the dawn of a new era in literature, when the romantic writers reacted sharply to what they considered the emotional barrenness and sterility of the Age of Reason. Given their preoccupation with nature and the mysterious, supernatural, and unknown, the romantic poets, from a different perspective, found as much to appeal to them in travel and exploration as did the philosophes. That two schools of literary thought which were poles apart could find abundant inspirational material on common ground attests the flexibility and versatility of the theme.

Nineteenth century   Examples drawn from the work of two of the best-known romantic writers, Samuel Taylor Coleridge and Lord Byron, will suffice to give a general if necessarily limited indication of how travel and exploration figure in the literature of the period. Coleridge's *The Rime of the Ancient Mariner* as a whole is a recounting of a bizarre and terrible journey, and the author derived his use of the albatross from reading George Shelvocke's little-known *A Voyage round the World* (1726). His *Kubla Khan,* which often has been reckoned as the finest piece of romantic craftsmanship, fragmentary though it is, also carries its readers to "a stately pleasure-dome" in Xanadu

> Where Alph, the sacred river, ran
> Through caverns measureless to man
> Down to a sunless sea.

By Coleridge's own account, the poem came to him in a dream after he had fallen asleep while reading a passage about Khubilai (Kublai) Khan's palace in *Purchas His Pilgrimes* (1613), a survey of religion and customs around the world by Samuel Purchas.

Like Coleridge, Byron frequently utilized factual material on travel to good advantage. His grandfather, the circumnavigator John Byron, had written a well-known description of the wreck of Lord Anson's ship the *Wager,* and he in turn used this as the basis for the storm and shipwreck in *Don Juan.* Furthermore, the whole of *Childe Harold* is a literal and literary pilgrimage, and appropriately enough two of the most frequently quoted lines in the work are

> Adieu, adieu! my native shore
> Fades o'er the waters blue.

Poetry, as these and other romantic writers demonstrated, could embody either passing references to travel or sustained imagery which carried the entire poem.

By the mid-nineteenth century romanticism had declined, and new areas of discovery were being opened to the world and its writers. Foremost among these in the period between 1850 and 1900 was tropical Africa; and the advent of the new imperialism, the "scramble" for colonial possessions on the continent, and the popularization (and sometimes bastardization) of the ideas of Charles Darwin opened up a whole range of new vistas in literature. However, although Africa was the primary focal point of both actual geographical discovery and literature relating to the subject during this period, many notable developments in this literature fell outside the so-called dark continent. Countless novels touched on varying corners of the globe. Among the most prominent were Charles Kingsley's *Westward Ho!* and Robert Louis Stevenson's *Treasure Island.* Another new feature of this period was the great demand for juvenile literature. Writers like G. A. Henty filled reams of paper in boys' books in which faraway places and daring discoveries were a predominant theme. Similarly, travel tales dotted the pages of the dozens of popular youth magazines. In adult reading, much the same tastes prevailed, and serialized novels on travel found comfortable companion berthing with the latest true tale of African adventure in the quarterlies which figured so prominently as reading matter during this period.

In English literature of the time, distant isles and places with unpronounceable names were omnipresent. And why not, given the proud dominion of a small nation over an empire on which the sun never set? This was grist to the mills of Alfred, Lord Tennyson, H. Rider Haggard, and that prolific portrayer of imperial scenes, Rudyard Kipling. The latter two writers again brought Africa into the spotlight, although Kipling wrote about Mandalay, up-country India, or the Fuzzy-Wuzzies of the Sudan with equal facility. Haggard's range was more limited, but he demonstrated an unerring knack for capturing the allurement of Africa. The mysteries of the continent's great rivers, and in particular the Nile, had a fascination that excited the public in a manner comparable to today's interest in space missions. Accordingly, Haggard and many others read the explorers' travelogues carefully and avidly searched for the tidbits that would give their readers a fictional taste of Africa's rapturous delights. In truth, there was something of a mania for all things African, and the whole of Western Europe discovered, at least in a literary sense, the validity of the Arab proverb: "He who has drunk of the waters of Africa must needs return after many days to quench his thirst thereat." For the actual explorers, this thirst was virtually unquenchable, and the broad segment of the literate public that followed their exploits eagerly awaited each new revelation from Africa.

Heretofore, for the most part, explorers had confined their literary endeavors to full and careful reports on their geographical, scientific, and related findings. With Africa, though, there is a discernible difference, which in part was occasioned by the drug-like attraction the continent had for its explorers.

Beginning with James Bruce's massive five-volume *Travels to Discover the Source of the Nile* (1790), there was a pronounced tendency among the most noted explorers of Africa to dress up their travelogues with that which was sensational or outré or which served to call to notice the inferiority of the peoples among whom they traveled. This is not to suggest that all these explorers intentionally distorted; rather, they tended to write what their audiences, which thanks to the advent of cheap printing and mass education were much larger than in earlier times, wanted to read. They also exhibited a marked propensity to view everything African through a cultural prism with pronounced refractory qualities.

Thus the classic works of the period—*Missionary Travels and Researches in South Africa* of David LIVINGSTONE, Richard Burton's *The Lake Regions of Central Africa, Journal of the Discovery of the Source of the Nile* of John H. SPEKE, *The Albert N'yanza* of Samuel White BAKER, *Through the Dark Continent* and *In Darkest Africa* of Henry M. STANLEY, and *The Kilima-Njaro Expedition* of Harry H. JOHNSTON—to some extent bridge the gap between the literature of exploration and exploration in literature. They also provide a pointed reminder of the too-little-appreciated reality that the distinction between the two genres is often a blurred one. Works of fiction frequently provide just as much of a feeling for a geographical region, just as keen a sense of the complex motivational forces that have impelled discovery in all ages, as do actual accounts written by explorers. Perhaps this is why the lions of Victorian discovery found the transition from fact to fiction such an alluring one.

Stanley, Johnston, Baker, Verney CAMERON, Joseph THOMSON, and others tried their hand at fiction with varying degress of success. Johnston, who wrote several novels based in large measure on his African experiences, was the best of the lot, but all enjoyed the advantages of prior renown and an abundance of firsthand experiences which they could tap. And who was to gainsay a bit of poetic license, be it in a travelogue or in a work of fiction, if it produced the desired result? There was scarcely an iota of truth in Johnston's poem "Ode to a Cannibal's Aunt," yet it strikes the reader straight on and typifies the type of material which led half-believing readers to envision Africa as a dark continent (this legacy of the era of imperialism still lurks in the shadows of many Western minds):

> Search through the crowded market
> Visit each cannibal feast.
> Where will you meet
> With a corpse so sweet
> As that of the dear deceased?
>
> Juicy she was, and tender,
> And little did we discern,
> The good we should reap
> From the cost of her keep.
> She has made us a noble return.

> Beauty we scarce remember,
> Virtues we soon forget.
> But the taste of our Aunt Eliza
> Clings, clings to my palate yet.

Twentieth century The major feats of African discovery had been completed by the turn of the twentieth century, and there was a rapid decline soon thereafter in fictional works based on its grand geographical mysteries (C. S. Forester's *The African Queen* is a particularly notable exception). The last unexplored areas of earth now lay in the polar regions, and just as Kipling assured his readers that condemned mortals would find his character Gunga Din "squattin' on the coals givin' drink to poor damned souls," these frozen frontiers provided their own icy imagery. The polar regions have perhaps engendered less writing than has travel in warmer though not necessarily more hospitable climes, but then it is a comparatively new field. Yet one example must be mentioned. The poems of Robert Service, with their singsong style and catchy internal rhyme, earned him the sobriquet "poet of the Yukon," and certainly he glorified travel in the vast frozen expanses of the Arctic. Seldom have explorers as a breed been more accurately depicted than in his "The Men That Don't Fit In":

> There's a race of men that don't fit in,
> A breed that can't stand still;
> So they break the hearts of kith and kin,
> And they roam the world at will.
>
> They range the field and they rove the flood,
> And they climb the mountain's crest;
> Theirs is the curse of the gypsy blood,
> And they don't know how to rest.

With the conquest, or at any rate the complete charting, of the Arctic and Antarctic, space remained as the final frontier. Space also provides a fitting point of conclusion to this coverage, because in this century a continuing fixation with the universe that we are just now beginning to probe has led to a distinct and immensely popular type of literature, science fiction. With pioneering works such as *The War of the Worlds* by H. G. Wells paving the way, in the course of only a few decades an amazing amount of material of this sort has appeared. It ranges in quality from sheer trash to excellent works by writers like Ray Bradbury, but in its totality science fiction comprises a class of literature based almost entirely on travels in time of space and the imaginary events that might derive therefrom. Thus there remain, in the words of television's "Star Trek" (which has spawned a veritable cult of devotees), opportunities to "seek out brave new worlds" and to go "where no man has dared to go before." In a literary sense, at least, this will always be the case, and doubtless future editions of John Bartlett's *Familiar Quotations* will see a continuing expansion of the hundreds of index entries under travel, its derivatives, and related words.

BIBLIOGRAPHY: J. R. Anderson, *The Ulysses Factor,* New York, 1961; Josephine Waters Bennett, *The Rediscovery of Sir John Mandeville,* New York, 1954; Marc Cary and Eric H. Warmington, *The Ancient Explorers,* London, 1929; Robert R. Cawley *Milton and the Literature of Travel,* Princeton, N.J., 1951, id., *Unpathed Waters: Studies in the Influence of the Voyagers on Elizabethan Literature,* New York, 1967; Edward G. Cox, *A Reference Guide to the Literature of Travel,* 3 vols., Seattle, 1935–49; R. W. Frantz, *The English Traveller and the Movement of Ideas, 1660–1732,* New York, 1968; Preston E. James, *All Possible Worlds: A History of Geographical Ideas,* New York, 1972; J. H. Parry, *The Age of Reconnaissance,* London, 1967; J. H. Parry (ed.), *The European Reconnaissance: Selected Documents,* New York, 1968; Boies Penrose, *Travel and Discovery in the Renaissance, 1420–1620,* Cambridge, Mass., 1952; John K. Wright, *Geographical Lore of the Time of the Crusades,* New York, 1925.

James A. Casada

Litke (Lütke), Fyodor Petrovich (1797–1882) Russian admiral, circumnavigator, and Arctic explorer. Between 1817 and 1819, as a midshipman, Litke made a round-the-world voyage on the sloop *Kamchatka* (Vasily Mikhailovich GOLOVNIN, commander) to Kamchatka and Russian America; en route he was promoted to lieutenant. Between 1821 and 1824, commanding the brig *Novaya Zemlya,* he mapped the Murmansk coast of the Barents Sea and the west and south coasts of Novaya Zemlya. Between 1826 and 1829, holding the rank of captain lieutenant and commanding the sloop *Senyavin,* he made his second round-the-world voyage to Russian America and to Kamchatka. During this voyage he mapped St. Matthew Island in the Bering Sea. In the winter of 1827–1828 he explored the Caroline Islands in Micronesia; in the eastern part of the archipelago he discovered the inhabited Senyavin Islands, among them Ponape, the largest of the Caroline Islands, and two atolls, Pakin and Ant.

In the summer of 1828 Litke determined astronomically the most important points of the east coast of Kamchatka north of Petropavlovsk and studied Ostrov Karaginsky (Karaginsk Island) in detail, the strait separating it from the mainland (Litke Strait), and Ostrov Verkhoturye. In the northern part of the Bering Sea he mapped the coast of the Chukotsky Peninsula and discovered and mapped Senyavin Strait, which lies between the mainland and the islands of Arakamchechen and Ittygran. During the winter of 1828–1829 he explored the central part of the Caroline chain, discovering additional atolls.

In 1845 Litke was one of the founders of the Russian Geographic Society, and in 1864 he was chosen president of the Academy of Sciences. He was made an admiral in 1855.

BIBLIOGRAPHY: Fyodor Petrovich Litke, *Voyage autour du monde . . . sur la corvette Le Seniavine,* 3 vols. and atlas, Paris, 1835–1836.

Richard A. Pierce

Livingstone, David (1813–1873) Scottish missionary and explorer. No British explorer of the nineteenth century so captured the imagination and esteem of his compatriots as this tenacious Scot, born in Blantyre, near Glasgow, the son of a traveling tea vendor who distributed religious tracts along with his tea. Although David was employed full time in a cotton mill from the age of 10, he managed to acquire an education by studying in his spare moments. In 1836, having been moved by an appeal for medical missionaries to serve in China, he decided to prepare himself for such a career; by the end of 1840 he had received a diploma from the Faculty of Physicians and Surgeons in Glasgow, had been accepted by the nondenominational London Missionary Society, and had been ordained as a nonconformist minister. The outbreak of the Opium War, however, led him to select South Africa as a mission field instead of China.

Livingstone reached Cape Town on March 14, 1841, and traveled 530 miles (853 kilometers) north to Kuruman, Bechuanaland, an isolated mission station founded by Robert Moffat, whose daughter Mary would become Livingstone's wife on January 2, 1845. From 1841 to 1849 Livingstone devoted himself primarily to missionary labors, founding three new mission stations to the north of Kuruman: at Mabotsa in Bechuanaland (1843); at Chonuane, 40 miles (64 kilometers) north of Mabotsa and the residence of the Bakwena (Kwena) chief Sechele, where Livingstone moved after quarreling with fellow missionary Roger Edwards (1845); and at Kolobeng, 40 miles northwest of Chonuane, where he and Sechele were driven by worsening drought (1847).

In 1849 Livingstone, who was becoming convinced of the desirability of working as an itinerant missionary to the tribes north of Kolobeng in the belief that the presence of missionaries there would help prevent annexation of the region by the Boers, made the first of three journeys which would alter the course of his life. On the first (1849) he and two companions became the first Europeans to see Lake Ngami, which they reached by skirting the Kalahari Desert and following the course of the Zouga River. Following a second trip to Lake Ngami (1850), he embarked on a journey that brought him to the upper reaches of the Zambezi River at Sesheke on August 4, 1851. It was during this expedition that Livingstone was exposed to the slave trade for the first time.

After sending his family to Great Britain in 1852, Livingstone moved to the Kololo settlement of Linyanti on the Chobe River to begin an unsuccessful search for a suitable mission site on the upper Zambezi. Since access to this region from the south was difficult, especially because of the presence of the Boers, Livingstone now sought a route to West Africa via the Zambezi that might be used by traders and missionaries. This quest led him to undertake one of his most significant journeys of exploration. Leaving Linyanti on November 11, 1853, he traveled to the

The self-educated missionary-explorer David Livingstone became his era's symbol of endurance and determination. Even after Henry Stanley "found" him, ill and impoverished, at Lake Tanganyika, he insisted on remaining in Africa to continue his explorations. [Library of Congress]

West African coast at Luanda, Angola, where he arrived on May 31, 1854. After returning to Linyanti, he turned eastward and, again following the course of the Zambezi, arrived at the port of Quelimane, Mozambique, on the Indian Ocean, on May 20, 1856. During this stage of his journey he saw the falls which he named Victoria in honor of the Queen. He then returned to England for the first time since his departure in 1840 to find himself acclaimed as a national hero.

Although Livingstone was probably the first European to make a coast-to-coast crossing of south central Africa, the territory he traversed had previously been penetrated by the Portuguese, and the continent had been crossed before by two native traders (1802–1811) and by a party of Arab slavers (1851–1854). However, accounts of these journeys were little known to the British public, while Livingstone provided large quantities of sound geographic details which showed that, contrary to accepted belief, southern Africa did not consist solely of desert but contained fertile and well-watered sections inhabited by people skilled as farmers, craftsmen, and traders. To Livingstone's contemporaries, the region thus seemed a promising field for English commerce as well as missionary enterprise.

Although Livingstone severed his connection with the London Missionary Society in 1858, he remained interested in the conversion of Africans to Christianity and encouraged the dispatch of missionaries to the Kololo and the Matabele (Nolebele). Having received a consular appointment, he himself headed an expedition aimed at making the lower Zambezi a "path for commerce into the Interior"; the development of British commerce in the area, he felt, would contribute to the demise of the slave trade. The Zambezi Expedition, which consisted of six Europeans besides Livingstone, including his younger brother Charles, forms one of the most controversial aspects of his career. A serious blow was the discovery that the Quebrabasa Falls of the Zambezi, which Livingstone had heard about but had not seen on his previous journey, prevented navigation of the river. Undaunted, Livingstone sailed up the Shire River to determine its suitability as a highway to the interior but found the way barred 200 miles (322 kilometers) upstream by the rapids he called the Murchison Cataract. On later treks through adjacent country he discovered Lakes Chilwa and Nyasa (Malawi). In 1861 a group of Anglican missionaries led by Bishop Charles Frederick Mackenzie joined Livingstone in East Africa. They established a station at Magomero near Lake Chilwa and became involved in combating the slave trade, but death and disease weakened the party, and Magomero was soon abandoned. Meanwhile, two efforts by Livingstone to test the navigability of the Ruvuma (Rovuma) River had also proved unsuccessful.

Recalled by the British government in 1863, he returned to England by way of India, arriving in London on July 23, 1864. By early 1866 he was back in Africa, with the purpose of exploring the Central African watershed while endeavoring in his contacts with the people to enlighten them as to the virtues of Christianity and the evils of the slave trade. Starting from Mikindani, on the East African coast north of the Ruvuma River, Livingstone marched along the river, skirted the southern end of Lake Nyasa, then moved north toward the upper reaches of the Congo and discovered Lakes Mweru and Bangweulu. After suffering extreme hardships caused by refractory and disloyal servants, lack of food, and sickness (aggravated by the loss of his medicines), he reached Nyangwe in the Congo, on the eastern bank of the Lualaba River, on March 29, 1871, but was prevented by the hostility of the slave traders and the reluctance of his own followers from venturing on the river to determine whether it was the Nile or the Congo. On July 15, 1871, he was a horrified witness to an unexpected massacre of hundreds of Africans in Nyangwe by the slavers.

The following November found him weak and destitute at Ujiji on Lake Tanganyika, where he met Henry M. STANLEY, who had been commissioned to search for him by the American newspaper magnate James Gordon Bennett, Jr. Livingstone and Stanley explored northern Lake Tanganyika, determining that the Ruzizi River flowed into and not out of the lake and therefore that the lake was not an extension of Lake Albert and part of the Nile system. Livingstone accepted supplies offered by Stanley, but refused to leave Africa with him. The two men separated at Unyanyembe, near modern Tabora, Tanzania, and Livingstone pressed forward with his explorations while his health seriously deteriorated. He died in a small village on Lake Bangweulu in the early morning hours of May 1, 1873. His embalmed, eviscerated body was carried by a procession of Africans to the coast, and from there his remains were taken to England and interred in Westminster Abbey on April 18, 1874.

Livingstone was a complex man whose motives and achievements have often provoked controversy. He believed that he had been divinely appointed to spread the truths of Christianity among Africans whose souls he felt were otherwise destined to perish, yet he made but a single convert and one who turned out to be a backslider at that. Nevertheless, armed with his strong sense of purpose, he exhibited extraordinary powers of endurance against hunger, illness, and discomforts and dangers of all kinds that felled lesser beings. The inability of others, both Europeans and Africans, to match his strength and dogged perseverance often led to strained relations, especially with the former. Livingstone has been accused of callous treatment of his wife, Mary, whom he took on his arduous journeys of 1850 and 1851 despite the fact that she was pregnant on both occasions. She traveled to Africa to join him in 1862, only to succumb to fever shortly afterward. Similarly, his children were left virtually fatherless during his long years in Africa.

Livingstone was remarkable for his curiosity about African nature, but the ethnographic content of his writings is relatively poor. He was often critical of African customs and institutions, such as nudity, but he frequently remarked on the virtues of Africans and believed that the flaws he perceived could be corrected by contact with Christianity and European civilization. Although he did not consider himself a pacifist, he eschewed the use of violence in his dealings with Africans and, in contrast to many other nineteenth-century Europeans in Africa, detested the wanton slaughter of wildlife. Despite his strictures against the slave trade, he could find much to praise in individual Portuguese and Arabs, such as the slave traders who aided him during his last travels. Perhaps his greatest importance lies in his impact on his contemporaries in Great Britain, for his writings and public appearances stimulated an interest in Africa that was soon translated into the economic and political exploitation of the continent. His books include *Missionary Travels and Researches in South Africa* (1857) and *Narrative of an Expedition to the Zambesi and Its Tributaries* (1865).

BIBLIOGRAPHY: Norman Robert Bennett, "David Livingstone: Exploration for Christianity," in Robert I. Rotberg (ed.), *Africa and Its Explorers*, Cambridge, Mass., 1970; James A. Casada, *Dr. David Livingstone and Sir Henry Morton Stanley: An Annotated Bibliography*, New York, 1976; Tim Jeal, *Livingstone*, New York, 1973; I. Schapera (ed.), *Livingstone's African Journal, 1853–1856*, 2 vols., Berkeley, Calif., 1963; George Seaver, *David Livingstone: His Life and Letters*, New York, 1957; Jack Simmons, *Livingstone and Africa*, London, 1955.

Long, Stephen Harriman *(1784–1864)* American explorer. In four explorations of the trans-Mississippi West (1817, 1819, 1820, 1823), Maj. Stephen H. Long of the U.S. Topographical Corps placed an imprint on the present-day Great Plains which took nearly 30 years of explorations and settlement to remove. Dubbing the barren lands between the 98th meridian and the eastern slope of the Rockies the "Great American Desert," he reinforced one of the greatest frontier myths and, by so doing, delayed settlement of the American interior. Long's expeditions led to the establishment of strategic military posts and to the gathering of scientific information, but their overall effect on the westward expansion of the United States was negative.

Long's first expedition was military and scientific in nature. A Phi Beta Kappa from Dartmouth College and a former instructor of mathematics at West Point, he was well equipped to survey the country's frontier defenses from Arkansas to Minnesota. His small party moved up the Mississippi River to the Falls of St. Anthony (present Minneapolis) to select sites for military posts as part of a government effort to protect the United States fur trade from the British and to ward off unfriendly Indians. Within 2 years, Congress authorized construction of Fort Smith on the Arkansas River and Fort Snelling at the confluence of the Mississippi and Minnesota Rivers. A third post had to

await another westward expedition, also involving Long, in 1820.

Long's second venture, the Yellowstone Expedition in 1819, was an elaborate military and scientific failure. This project marked the first use of steamers on the Missouri River as well as the first time that an official group of explorers into the West was accompanied by scientists, including zoologist Thomas Say, botanist William Baldwin, and Titian Rembrandt Peale, assistant naturalist. The scientific party left St. Louis on June 21 with the steamboat *Western Engineer* and set up winter quarters in September near Council Bluffs, Iowa, where the troops of the expedition had halted. Long went to Washington, where he found Congress unwilling to appropriate additional funds for the expedition. He was now ordered to ascend the Platte River to its source and to return to the Mississippi by way of the Arkansas and Red Rivers.

Thus Long's third expedition was an extension of the previous year's venture. On June 6, 1820, he led nineteen men out of Council Bluffs. Among them was Dr. Edwin James, a replacement for Baldwin, who had died. The trip to the Rockies passed without incident. Following the north bank of the Platte River, the men pushed through huge herds of buffalo and at the Loup River in central Nebraska visited the Pawnee villages. Securing the services of two French guides in the vicinity, Long's men continued along the Platte River to its forks and then crossed to the south bank of the South Fork. Moving about 25 miles (40 kilometers) a day, the men saw the mountains (Longs Peak) on June 30. Almost a week later they reached the site of present Denver and the next day gazed upon Platte Canyon. The party then followed Plum Creek south and crossed the continental divide to Fountain Creek. From a spot near present Colorado Springs, Dr. James became the first man to climb Pikes Peak. The group eventually turned south toward the Arkansas River after the botanist, by now the chronicler of the expedition, had recorded his discovery of numerous species of mountain plants and animals.

After Long and his companions reached the Arkansas near Pueblo, Colorado, James and several others ascended the river as far as the Royal Gorge. Near La Junta, Colorado, the party was divided into two groups. While one group continued down the Arkansas, Long began a search for the sources of the Red River. He touched upon a large waterway near Raton Pass in New Mexico and followed it eastward, only to find that it returned him to the Arkansas River. What Long had been charting was the Canadian River across the Texas Panhandle and into Oklahoma. And when the two groups of explorers were reunited on September 13 near Fort Smith in present Arkansas, Long discovered that three deserters from the other party had taken rifles, packs, horses, and nearly all the journals and scientific notes.

Long's expedition of 1820, despite its obvious failures, deserves notice because it spread the myth of the Great American Desert. The barren picture of the

By naming all the territory between the 98th meridian and the Rockies the "Great American Desert," Stephen Long succeeded in delaying American settlement of the Great Plains for more than 30 years. [Independence National Historical Park Collection]

Plains portrayed in James's two-volume account (1823) of the expedition discouraged settlement west of the Mississippi River and affected the writing of schoolbooks and the marking of maps for years.

Congress authorized Long's fourth and last expedition in 1823; it was to explore the area between the Mississippi and Missouri Rivers. With a party including a geologist, a landscape painter, a mineralogist, and a zoologist, he left Philadelphia in late April and traveled west through Fort Wayne, Fort Dearborn, Prairie du Chien, and Fort Snelling. Down the Mississippi River and then up the Minnesota, the expedition explored the headwaters of the Minnesota and the Red River of the North and then marked the international boundary along the 49th parallel just north of Pembina in North Dakota. Long's return took him along the Red River to Lake Winnipeg in Canada, across Lake Superior, and by the other Great Lakes to New York State. His arrival in Philadelphia on October 26, 1823, marked his only triumphant return after a venture west.

BIBLIOGRAPHY: William H. Goetzmann, *Exploration and Empire: The Explorer and the Scientist in the Winning of the American West*, New York, 1966; W. Eugene Hollon, *The Great American Desert: Then and Now*, New York, 1966; Edwin James, *Account of an Expedition from Pittsburgh to the Rocky Mountains*, 4 vols., in Reuben G. Thwaites (ed.), *Early Western Travels, 1748–1846*, 32 vols., Cleveland, 1904–1907; Richard G. Wood, *Stephen Harriman Long, 1784–1864* Glendale, Calif., 1966.

Howard Jones

Lütke, Fyodor Petrovich *See* LITKE, FYODOR PETROVICH.

McClintock, Francis Leopold (1819–1907) British naval officer and Arctic explorer, renowned for his development of the man-hauling technique of sledging and for his discovery of the fate of Sir John FRANKLIN. Born in Dundalk, Ireland, McClintock joined the Royal Navy as a first-class volunteer in June 1831. He served on board HMS *Samarang* on the South American Station until January 1835, then was on duty in England for 2 years before joining HMS *Crocodile* on the North American Station. McClintock returned to England in 1841 to pass his lieutenant's examinations and was appointed to HMS *Gorgon,* on the Brazilian Station, in January 1843. He was transferred to HMS *Frolic* for a 2-year cruise in the Pacific when his promotion to lieutenant came through on July 29, 1845.

McClintock was studying at Portsmouth in 1848 when the Admiralty launched its search for the missing NORTHWEST PASSAGE expedition of Sir John FRANKLIN, and he was appointed to the search expedition of Sir James ROSS on board HMS *Enterprise* and *Investigator* (see FRANKLIN EXPEDITION AND SEARCH). The expedition wintered at Port Leopold, Somerset Island, and the search was conducted by sledge from there in the spring of 1849. It was McClintock's experience of sledge travel on this voyage which brought his particular talent to the fore. Naval sledging techniques were then at a primitive stage of development, and he saw many ways of improving them. On his return home in the autumn of 1849, he experimented with different types of equipment, prepared a system

of depot laying to prolong journeys, then joined Capt. Horatio Austin's search expedition of 1850–1851 to test his new methods. His researches were thoroughly vindicated by the success of Austin's traveling parties. From their winter quarters in Barrow Strait, the six main sledge teams and their numerous support parties dragged their sledges over more than 5000 miles (8047 kilometers), discovering many hundreds of miles of new coast, with relative ease. McClintock himself covered an unprecedented 770 miles (1239 kilometers) in 80 days in exploring parts of Bathurst, Byam Martin, and Melville Islands.

McClintock again took charge of sledging on the Admiralty's next search expedition, led by Sir Edward BELCHER between 1852 and 1854, on which he had command of HMS *Intrepid.* His sledge teams again ranged over a wide area from their winter quarters at Melville Island, and McClintock made an even longer journey than before, covering 1210 miles (1947 kilometers) and discovering much of Prince Patrick and Eglinton Islands. After his return home, in October 1854, he was promoted post captain.

The Franklin search was officially called off in 1854, but many officers continued to appeal for a last effort to determine Franklin's fate. Lady Franklin herself raised the funds for an expedition, purchased the yacht *Fox,* and asked McClintock to take command. He sailed in July 1857 and 2 years later, on the shores of King William Island, found conclusive proof of Franklin's death.

McClintock was knighted for his Arctic services in

Francis Leopold McClintock is remembered for his innovations in Arctic exploratory techniques and for finding proof of the fate of the expedition of Sir John Franklin. [National Portrait Gallery, London]

1860. In the same year, he returned briefly to the Arctic on HMS *Bulldog* when sounding a route for the North Atlantic telegraph. He remained in active naval service until 1882, with appointments in the North Sea, as admiral superintendent of Portsmouth Dockyard, and on the North American and West Indies Station. He reached the full rank of admiral on July 7, 1884, and in that year was elected to Trinity House, of which he remained an active member until his death.

He continued to advise on the preparation of polar expeditions during his later life, and man hauling remained the navy's standard mode of polar travel throughout that period. McClintock is sometimes accused of having delayed the introduction of dog sledging to naval exploration by placing such emphasis on man hauling; on the contrary, he actually favored dog transport but simply never had dogs of sufficient quality at his disposal. Instead, like any truly great explorer, he made the finest possible use of the limited resources available to him.

BIBLIOGRAPHY: Clements Markham, *Life of Admiral Sir Leopold McClintock*, London, 1909.

Clive A. Holland

McClure, Robert John Le Mesurier (1807–1873)

British naval officer and Arctic explorer. Born in Wexford, Ireland, McClure was educated at Eton and Sandhurst and entered the Royal Navy in 1824. He saw service in various parts of the world during his early career and first visited the Arctic in 1836–1837 as mate on board HMS *Terror* during Capt. George Back's expedition to Hudson Bay. McClure was promoted lieutenant on his return in September 1837. He served subsequently on the Great Lakes and in the West Indies and was attached to the Coast Guard in 1848, when he was selected to take part in the Arctic expedition of Sir James Clark Ross in search of Sir John FRANKLIN. On the unsuccessful return of that expedition in the autumn of 1849, Ross's ships, *Enterprise* and *Investigator*, were fitted out to renew the search by way of Bering Strait. McClure was appointed to command *Investigator* under the general command of Capt. Richard COLLINSON, on board *Enterprise*. They sailed together on January 10, 1850, but were separated on the outward voyage.

McClure reached Bering Strait first and decided to proceed alone. He charted the south coast of Banks Island and discovered Prince of Wales Strait, in which he spent the winter of 1850–1851. During the winter, he traveled north through the strait to the shores of Viscount Melville Sound and thus, by reaching from the west a sea which William Edward PARRY had discovered from the east in 1819, became the discoverer of a NORTHWEST PASSAGE. Ice stopped him from taking his ship through into Viscount Melville Sound in 1851, so he sailed back around Banks Island, hoping to approach the sound from the north. He was again stopped by ice in McClure Strait and found refuge in Mercy Bay, on the north coast of Banks Island, where

Investigator became inextricably beset. By the spring of 1853, McClure was planning to abandon ship and to march to the mainland, but members of the Franklin search expedition of Sir Edward BELCHER arrived to rescue him just in time. His crew was distributed among Belcher's ships and finally sailed home through Baffin Bay in 1854.

After the voyage, McClure was promoted captain and knighted, and he received a substantial parliamentary award for the discovery of a Northwest Passage. He served in the Pacific from 1856 to 1861 but then had no further service. He was promoted rear admiral on March 20, 1857, and vice admiral on May 29, 1873.

McClure's Arctic journals were edited for publication by Sherard Osborn, a fellow Arctic officer. Osborn's popular narrative helped to perpetuate McClure's name as the first discoverer of a Northwest Passage. More recently, however, historians have preferred to restore that honor to Franklin, who, unknown to the world, had discovered another passage 4 years before McClure.

See also FRANKLIN EXPEDITION AND SEARCH.

BIBLIOGRAPHY: Sherard Osborn (ed.), *The Discovery of the North-West Passage by H.M.S. "Investigator," Capt. R. M'Clure, 1850, 1851, 1852, 1853, 1854*, London, 1856.

Clive A. Holland

Mackenzie, Alexander (1764–1820)

Fur trader and explorer in areas now part of Canada. Mackenzie was born near Stornoway, Isle of Lewis, Scotland. His mother died when he was a child; in 1774 he emigrated with his father and two aunts to New York, where an uncle was in business. On the outbreak of the American Revolution, his father obtained a commission in Sir John Johnson's Royal Greens, and young Alexander was sent north to school in Montreal.

Mackenzie entered the service of the fur-trading company Finlay, Gregory & Co. as a clerk. When this company was absorbed into the North West Company, he went west in 1785 as a wintering partner of the firm, trading all year round in the wilderness, and in 1787 became a partner. In 1789 he made an exploratory expedition from Fort Chipewyan to the mouth of the Mackenzie River via the Slave River and Great Slave Lake. He called the stream now named after him River of Disappointment, for it led to the Arctic rather than the Pacific Ocean. On May 9, 1793, aided by Indians, he began his famous overland voyage to the Pacific from Lake Athabasca. His route was by the Peace, Parsnip, Blackwater (now West Road), and Bella Coola Rivers. He reached tidewater at Dean Channel, British Columbia, on July 22. He made a remarkably rapid return journey and was back at the fork of the Peace and Smoky Rivers on August 24.

Mackenzie's expedition to the Pacific showed the intricacies and difficulties of travel in that latitude. No great river of the west was found there, nor was there an appropriate watercourse for the shipment of

Chiangmai in January 1837 and then began the major part of his exploration as he headed north through the Shan States with the aim of entering the southwestern Chinese province of Yünnan. The route he followed to the town of Keng Tung from Chiangmai had never been traveled before. From Keng Tung to Keng Hua farther north McLeod traveled over territory that was equally unknown to Europeans of the time. For most of this journey he traveled on elephant back.

By the time he reached Keng Hung in March 1837, McLeod had penetrated farther toward China's southern border than any other explorer of his time. But he was not permitted to enter Yünnan and so did not, contrary to some accounts, become the first European to travel into Yünnan by a southern route. (That distinction fell to the French Mekong Expedition members in 1867.) Although preserving a tenuous independent identity, the region of which Keng Hung was the capital, the Sip Song Panna, was a vassal of China, and the authorities were unprepared to allow McLeod to proceed into China without the proper passports. (Keng Hung has subsequently been absorbed into China as Yünchinghung.)

McLeod's journey to Keng Hung was important in itself, but it should also be seen as characteristic of a wide range of similar expeditions made by men attached to the developing British administration in Burma in the 1830s and 1840s. Although these expeditions, McLeod's included, had no immediate political or commercial result, they formed the basis for later efforts to establish a reliable transport link between Burma and China.

BIBLIOGRAPHY: W. C. McLeod, *Journal of a Mission from Moulmein to the Frontiers of China*, London, 1849.

Milton Osborne

furs out of the Athabaska region, where the Nor'westers were rapidly expanding their Indian trade. Mackenzie's transcontinental journey was the first crossing of North America by a white man north of Mexico, and it preceded the explorations of Meriwether LEWIS and William CLARK by more than 10 years.

In 1799 Mackenzie went to England, where his journals were edited and published as *Voyages from Montreal . . . to the Frozen and Pacific Oceans* (1801). He was knighted in 1802 and returned to Canada, where he became involved with the XY Company, rivals to the Nor'westers. Mackenzie lived in Montreal and sat as a member of the Lower Canada Assembly (1804–1808). He later retired to Scotland and lived until his death on March 12, 1820, at Avoch, Black Isle, Ross-shire.

BIBLIOGRAPHY: W. K. Lamb (ed.), *The Journals and Letters of Sir Alexander Mackenzie*, London, 1970; Walter Sheppe (ed.), *First Man West: Alexander Mackenzie's Journal of His Voyage to the Pacific Coast of Canada in 1793*, Berkeley and Los Angeles, 1962; M. S. Wade, *Mackenzie of Canada*, Edinburgh and London, 1927.

Barry M. Gough

McLeod, William C. *(d. 1880)* British explorer. As a captain in the Indian Army, McLeod undertook an important exploration of the eastern and northeastern regions of Burma. Leaving Moulmein in December 1836, he traveled up the Salween River before striking overland to the northern Thai city of Chiangmai, then part of a quasi-independent principality. He reached

Madoc Legendary Welsh prince, son of King Owen Gwynedd of North Wales, who supposedly discovered America and founded a colony there in 1170. Starting in the sixteenth century, the story of Madoc's colony became linked to persistent reports of a tribe of fair-skinned, Welsh-speaking Indians in the New World.

The first printed work to assert the discovery of America by Madoc was a pamphlet (1583) by Sir George Peckham which sought to establish a British claim to the New World. The following year Dr. David Powel published *The Historie of Cambria*, which was based on a work by the geographer Humphrey Llwyd left unfinished at the time of the latter's death in 1568. Here Madoc is said to have reached Mexico or Florida and to have established a colony there, thus anticipating Spanish discoveries.

Powel believed that the Welsh colonists had been absorbed by local Indians, who still exhibited signs of their Welsh origin. He was but one of many who discerned Welsh influences among American Indians. One such account, for example, was that of Morgan Jones, a New York minister, who affirmed in 1686 that he had been saved from death at the hands of the

Tuscarora Indians when he uttered some words in Welsh that were understood by an Indian of the Doeg tribe who was present. In *The Course of Empire*, Bernard De Voto counted thirteen real tribes that had been identified as the Welsh Indians as well as several imaginary tribes.

Jones's account was first published in 1740 during the War of Jenkins's Ear between Spain and Great Britain. In the following decades interest in the Madoc legend and the Welsh Indians mounted as a result of an upsurge of Welsh cultural nationalism and missionary zeal. Accordingly, in 1792 a group of Welshmen sponsored an expedition to the United States by John Evans for the purpose of finding the Welsh Indians, who were now believed to be located near the upper Missouri River. After many vicisstudes Evans reached the Mandans of modern North Dakota in 1796. He lived with them for more than 6 months and concluded on the basis of his experiences with them and other tribes that there were no Welsh Indians.

Despite Evans's negative report, the legend flourished. Robert Southey celebrated the exploits of the Welsh prince in a long poem, *Madoc* (1805). The American artist George Catlin, who spent several years among the Mandans in the 1830s, found some Welsh traces in their language and culture and conjectured that the name Mandan might be a corruption or abbreviation of Madawgwys, or followers of Madoc. In 1858 the Llangollen Eisteddfod offered a prize for the best essay on the theme "The Discovery of America in the Twelfth Century by Prince Madoc ab Owain Gwynedd." An essay by Thomas Stephens was considered the best submitted, but since he argued that Madoc had *not* discovered America, no prize was awarded. The publication of Stephens's essay in 1893 was a severe blow to the Madoc legend, but it continued to win adherents, especially in the United States, In 1953 the Daughters of the American Revolution erected a tablet at Mobile Bay, Alabama, to commemorate an alleged landing by Madoc on that site.

BIBLIOGRAPHY: Richard Deacon, *Madoc and the Discovery of America*, New York, 1966; Bernard De Voto, *The Course of Empire*, Boston, 1952; David Williams, "John Evans' Strange Journey," *American Historical Review*, vol. LIV, 1948–1949, pp. 277–295, 508–529.

Magellan, Ferdinand (Portuguese: *Fernão de Magalhães*; Spanish: *Fernando de Magallanes*; ca. *1480–1521*) Portuguese-born explorer. Born in northern Portugal, either in the province of Entre Douro e Minho or in that of Trás os Montes, Magellan was appointed a page to Queen Leonor at the age of 12. In 1505 he sailed to India with the fleet of Viceroy Francisco de Almeida; Francisco Serrão, with whom he would be closely associated in the future, also embarked with Almeida. In 1509, after having fought at the Battle of Diu, Magellan, together with Serrão, joined an expedition to Malacca led by Diogo Lopes de Sequeira which ended

in a Portuguese defeat at the hands of the local ruler. Magellan and Serrão returned to Malacca in 1511 in an armada of nineteen ships that succeeded in bringing the city under Portuguese rule. To follow up this victory, the Portuguese dispatched three caravels to the clove-rich Moluccas, which apparently had never been visited by any European. Serrão was in command of one of the ships, and some believe that Magellan may have taken part as well; in any event, although the commander of the expedition, Antônio de Abreu, failed to achieve his goal, Serrão did reach Ternate after many adventures. There he soon became a confidant of the ruler and wrote to Magellan extolling the riches of the Moluccas, which he described as being much farther from Malacca than they actually are.

Magellan, meanwhile, returned to Portugal in 1513 but soon left once more to participate in a successful campaign in Morocco. Accused of improperly selling some cattle, he went back to Portugal without leave. Although Magellan was later cleared of the charges against him, he had evidently lost the favor of King Manuel, for the sovereign denied him a trifling increase in his monthly allowance and refused to permit him to undertake a voyage to the Moluccas.

Having decided to seek employment in Spain, Magellan arrived in Seville on October 20, 1517, and was soon joined by Ruy Faleiro, a Portuguese astronomer with whom he had become acquainted earlier. The two succeeded in persuading King Charles I that the Moluccas lay within the area assigned to Spain by the Treaty of Tordesillas and that the islands could be reached by way of a strait leading from the Atlantic to the Pacific; in this way the route around the Cape of Good Hope, monopolized by the Portuguese, could be avoided. To help convince the King, they may have used a map or globe based on the globe of Martin Behaim (1459–1506), which depicted South America as a long peninsula extending southward from southern Asia; also shown was a strait lying between the peninsula and an inaccurately located Ceylon.

The King quickly agreed to sponsor Magellan's voyage, and on September 20, 1519, a fleet of five ships— *Trinidad* (Magellan's flagship), *San Antonio*, *Concepción*, *Victoria*, and *Santiago*—bearing approximately 240 men left San Lúcar de Barrameda on the first leg of the journey. After taking on supplies in the Canaries, the fleet sailed along the African coast as far as Sierra Leone, then south-southwest until it reached the coast of Brazil. The fleet spent 2 weeks at what is now known as Rio de Janeiro, on the Bay of Guanabara, and then sailed down the coast of South America as Magellan searched in vain for the entrance to the strait he expected to find at about 35°S. At San Julián (49°12'S), a port where the fleet spent 5 months, Magellan quelled a mutiny led by Spaniards who had personal grievances against him and resented his Portuguese origin. On October 21, 1520, the fleet came upon the strait which now bears the name of Magellan and on November 27 or 28, 1520, it entered the

South Sea, which Magellan called the Pacific. By now Magellan's fleet had been reduced to three vessels: *Santiago* had been wrecked before reaching the strait, and *San Antonio* had deserted while the newly discovered waterway was being explored.

Upon entering the Pacific, Magellan sailed northward, later turning to the west. Experts disagree over the precise route followed by Magellan in crossing the Pacific, though it is known that only two islands, both of them uninhabited, were sighted. Meanwhile, the men suffered extreme hardships from lack of fresh food and water, and a number succumbed to scurvy.On March 6, 1521, the fleet reached the Marianas, whose light-fingered inhabitants led the Europeans to call the islands the Ladrones (islands of thieves). Ten days later Magellan sighted the island of Samar in the archipelago that would later be called the Philippines. The fleet visited other islands in the group, notably Cebu, trading with the inhabitants and attempting to convert them to Christianity. On April 27, 1521, in a fruitless effort to subdue a hostile chief of the island of Mactan, Magellan was killed.

With the death of Magellan, leadership of the expedition first devolved upon Duarte Barbosa and Juan Rodríguez Serrano, but both were killed a few days later. On May 1, 1521, the surviving members of the expedition, who now numbered 108, selected the pilot João Lopes Carvalho as their leader and decided to abandon and burn *Concepción*. For the next few months Carvalho sailed aimlessly in the East Indies, apparently unable to find the Moluccas, plundering any vessel he came upon and maintaining a harem of captured women. In September he was supplanted by Juan Sebastián de Elcano (1487?–1526), an exerienced Basque navigator, and by Gonzalo Gómez de Espinosa, who reached Tidore in the Moluccas on November 8. There they learned that Francisco Serrão had been poisoned and that a Portuguese expedition was expected momentarily. The two ships were quickly loaded with spices and provisions and on December 21, 1521, Elcano sailed for Spain on *Victoria* by way of the Cape of Good Hope. *Trinidad,* delayed by the need for repairs, left Tidore on April 6, 1522, under the command of Espinosa, who planned to recross the Pacific in order to reach Panama. After many misadventures Espinosa was forced to return to the Moluccas, where he surrendered to the Portuguese, who kept him a prisoner until 1526. Meanwhile, after an arduous voyage, Elcano and seventeen other survivors reached Seville on September 8, 1522, having completed the first circumnavigation of the world.

The significance of this achievement was clearly understood at the time, and several accounts of the voyage soon appeared. The most important of these was by Antonio Pigafetta (1491?–after1523), a native of Vicenza, Italy, who had sailed with Magellan as a *sobresaliente* (supernumerary). Pigafetta was a warm admirer of Magellan, but some other writers, particularly those of Portuguese nationality, have been less enthusiastic about his qualities as a navigator and leader of men. There has also been disagreement as to the achievement of Elcano in completing Magellan's voyage. Elcano left once more for the Moluccas on May 24, 1525, in an expedition led by Francisco García Jofre de Loaysa, only to die, probably of scurvy, in the Pacific north of the equator.

BIBLIOGRAPHY: Samuel Eliot Morison, *The European Discovery of America: The Southern Voyages, A.D. 1492–1616,* New York, 1974; Charles E. Nowell (ed.), *Magellan's Voyage around the World: Three Contemporary Accounts,* Evanston, Ill., 1962; Charles McKew Parr, *Ferdinand Magellan, Circumnavigator,* New York, 1964; Martin Torodash, "Magellan Historiography," *Hispanic American Historical Review,* vol. LI, no. 2, May 1971, pp. 313–335.

The Portuguese-born Ferdinand Magellan mounted the first expedition to circumnavigate the world for King Charles I of Spain. Although the voyage was successful, Magellan did not live to complete it. [Library of Congress]

Maritime Exploration

The great age of maritime exploration is generally perceived as encompassing primarily the fifteenth and sixteenth centuries, beginning with the first hesitant probes by the navigators of Portuguese Prince HENRY on the waters around the African continent. They were followed rapidly by the magnificent accomplishment of the visionary Christopher COLUMBUS, the expedition of Ferdinand MAGELLAN that circumnavigated the earth, and other epic voyages by English, Dutch, Italian, and French explorers that helped to flesh out the true dimensions and geography of the world. Yet maritime exploration was neither bound by the confines of these centuries nor linked inexorably to European genius. Ancient Phoenicians, enterprising Polynesians, and far-ranging Chinese certainly shared some of the qualities of curiosity and courage shown by the great eighteenth-century English sea captain and scientist James COOK. For a proper beginning one must thus turn briefly to the explorers of the ancient and medieval and non-Western worlds.

Ancient exploration Possibly the earliest-known craft that ventured abroad from well-known waters were reed boats and barges built along the Nile River by Egyptians several millennia ago. How far they ranged is subject to conjecture, but they most probably remained well within the confines of the Mediterranean, and the eastern Mediterranean at that. Thor Heyerdahl, a Norwegian anthropologist, has speculated that ancient Egyptians might have made voyages across the Atlantic and thus contributed to the peopling and culture of the Americas. He built two reed craft, *Ra I* and *Ra II,* and succeeded in crossing the Atlantic in 1970.

More intrepid were the Phocnicians, a commercial

and sailing people who originated in Lebanon and became the ubiquitous carriers of the ancient world. From the coastal city of Byblos, perhaps one of the oldest in biblical times, they explored and ranged over the entire Mediterranean on fine ships fashioned from the famed cedars of Lebanon. Egyptian imperial curiosity and Phoenician skills were combined about 600 B.C. to make a most remarkable exploratory voyage. According to the Greek historian HERODOTUS OF HALICARNASSUS, Phoenicians in the service of Pharaoh Necho II circumnavigated Africa from east to west in a 2-year voyage that reentered the Mediterranean through the Strait of Gibraltar. Carthage, a prosperous Phoenician colony later conquered by the rising Roman Empire, also sent voyages of exploration in the fifth century B.C. that reached as far north as Britain, probably in search of commodities such as tin.

While practical mariners explored the reaches of the Mediterranean and its neighboring seas, Greek and Roman thinkers plumbed and conjectured on the mysteries that lay beyond. These academicians of antiquity argued that the earth was round and made estimates of its circumference that were remarkably accurate. Of the many learned treatises that were produced during the flowering of ancient Western civilization perhaps none subsequently produced such an impact as the *Geography* of PTOLEMY, a second-century Hellenized Egyptian.

Ptolemy's great work *Geography* concerned itself principally with the making of maps and charts, navigational instruments quite as important to later maritime explorers as the quadrant and the compass. He divided the earth into 360 degrees of latitude and longitude, made an estimate of the circumference of the earth, and provided instructions for such processes as the measuring of longitude in different latitudes. Nonetheless, in spite of Ptolemy's substantial achievements, the legacy that he left for his Renaissance rediscoverers included numerous errors. While his arrangement of lands and islands in the Mediterranean was remarkably accurate, his guesses as to what lay beyond were as remarkably inaccurate. Great landmasses were placed where none existed, open oceans were depicted as landlocked seas, and Asia projected inordinately far to the east. Indeed, the world beyond the Mediterranean represented a vast unknown to the ancients. They nevertheless conceived some valid astronomical theories, made reasonably accurate estimates of basic global dimensions, and laid down the preliminary groundwork for chart making and celestial navigation. These classical

A 15th-century version of Ptolemy's map of the world. [Library of Congress]

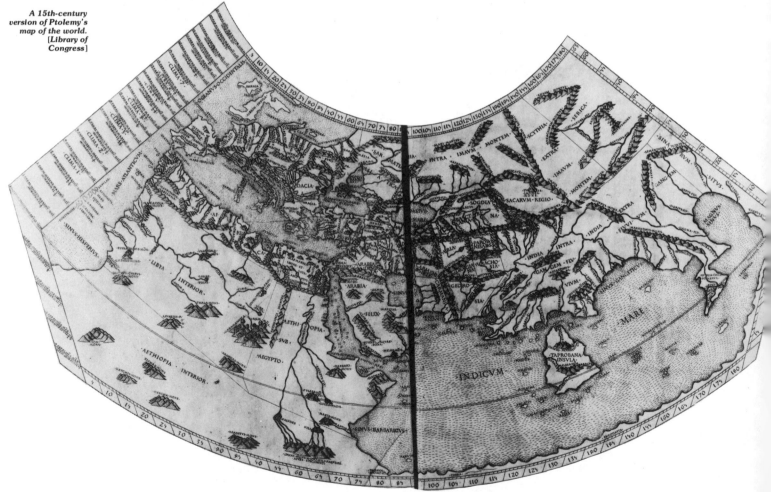

scholars provided the thinkers and explorers of the later Renaissance with some knowledge and certainly not a little inspiration to try and prove or disprove empirically the validity of their perceptions of the earth and its universe. The long eclipse in maritime knowledge and exploration between Ptolemy and Columbus reflected the fall of the Roman Empire and the subsequent seclusion and parochialism of the European world during the Middle Ages.

The Polynesians While the great Western age of exploration was being gestated, other peoples in the vast and remote area of the Pacific were themselves embarking on a maritime adventure. Between about 1000 B.C. and A.D. 1000, Polynesia was explored and settled by peoples who had originated in the far western archipelagoes and lands of Taiwan, the Philippines, and Indonesia. The settlement of Polynesia, an immense space roughly bounded by Hawaii in the north, Easter Island in the southeast, and New Zealand in the southwest, was accomplished by a mastery of navigation and a skill in watercraft building that was unmatched by other cultures of that epoch. From the islands of Tonga and Samoa, probably inhabited as early as 3000 to 4000 years ago, the exploration of Polynesia radiated outward. Navigation was a blend of the observation of the stars with a feeling for the swells, the currents, and the winds that provided the experienced sailor with an uncanny sense of position and direction. Stars were observed not only to provide courses but also to determine latitude. The size and frequency of swells were interpreted for signs of land. Perhaps even more remarkable was the navigational technique of *te lapa*. Underwater streaks or flashes called *te lapa* were observed and interpreted by Polynesian navigators in such a fashion as to provide them with clues to the directions of the islands.

The great voyaging canoes supplied the physical means and combined the necessary qualities of seaworthiness, ample size, and durability. The canoes were up to 55 or 60 feet (17 or 18 meters) in size and were constructed of wide planks lashed to the ribs of the frames by a type of cordage called sennit made from coconut fibers. These double-ended constructions were then lashed together by broad planking in outrigger or catamaran fashion to offer greater stability and more room and comfort than single-hulled canoes could do. Sails were fashioned of woven leaves. With a fair wind these great voyaging canoes could make long sea voyages, and great expeditions, either of exploration or of settlement, could last for weeks and cover thousands of miles. The exploration, discovery, and settlement of the farthest reaches of Polynesia, Easter Island and Hawaii, for example, attest to an exemplary maritime expertise that went unchallenged in the Pacific until Magellan crossed that greatest of oceans in the early sixteenth century.

Chinese exploration The mainland of East Asia also produced a maritime culture of significance, based largely on commerce but encompassing the art of exploration as well. Chinese invention had culminated in the evolution of the junk, a rather flat-bottomed, shallow-draft vessel that carried a balanced, sometimes retractable rudder and battened sails. Chinese navigators learned the use of the compass more than 1000 years ago and were also competent at measuring latitude from star altitudes, reckoning time by burning given amounts of incense, and making other computations relating to longitude and speed. It is not surprising that in the 2d century B.C. voyages of exploration had been sent from the mainland to Japan. Fables even imply that a Chinese junk, lost and storm-driven, reached the North American coast a millennium ago.

Perhaps the most spectacular voyages undertaken by the Chinese occurred when a series of seven expeditions, political, commercial, and exploratory in nature, was dispatched from China to the Indian Ocean between 1405 and 1433. Commanded by a court eunuch named CHENG HO in the service of the Ming dynasty, the first three expeditions reached India, the next three stretched as far west as Aden and Hormuz (Hormoz) on the Persian Gulf, and the seventh sent traders far down the east coast of Africa. The junk had arrived in seas furrowed in times past only by the Arab dhow, and it was even recorded that seven Chinese reached Mecca.

The size of the expeditions alone, some carrying more than 25,000 men in sixty vessels or more, merits our admiration and awe, especially when compared with the very small Portuguese fleets that sailed into these waters a little less than a century later. The junks themselves were most impressive. Some exceeded 400 feet (122 meters) in length, carried up to four decks, and were built with watertight compartments, another Chinese invention. *See also* CHINESE EXPLORATION.

Arab exploration The Indian Ocean penetrated by the Chinese junks produced more than 1000 years ago another extraordinary maritime culture, which explored the limits of that ocean and subsequently dominated its trade and commerce. The Arab dhow, a rather rakish and weatherly lateen-rigged vessel, enabled Arab seafarers in the eighth and ninth centuries to extend their influence from Africa to the East Indies. Encouraged by the teachings of the prophet Muhammad to spread the faith, Arab sailors and merchants explored and prosyletized widely. They became carriers of cloves, cinnamon, pepper, silks, tea, sandalwood, and other exotic items that would later draw the European explorers irresistibly to this area in the fifteenth and sixteenth centuries. Navigators utilized the alidade and the astrolabe, while master mariners such as Aḥmad ibn-Mājid, whose services Vasco da GAMA fortuitously employed in 1498, were not only accomplished astronomers and mathematicians but chart makers and practical seafarers as well. *See also* MUSLIM TRAVEL AND EXPLORATION IN THE MIDDLE AGES.

Norse discoveries Contemporaries of the flourishing Arabian seafarers, the Norsemen of Scandinavia forged a maritime legend in the North Atlantic that also survives in convincing testimony to the abilities of pre-Renaissance explorers. Between about A.D. 860 and 1000, Scandinavian adventurers and explorers discovered and colonized Iceland and Greenland and placed a tiny settlement on the coast of North America. The movement of the Norsemen into the North Atlantic mirrored the Scandinavian expansion, spearheaded by the famed Vikings, into other parts of Europe such as England, Spain, and even Sicily in the far Mediterranean.

Norsemen sailed the North Atlantic in a beamy, clinker-style–built ship called a *knarr* that was propelled by a big square sail which could be supplemented by manning long sweeps or oars. Although lacking a compass, these mariners could calculate latitude by utilizing Polaris (the North Star, or polestar) or the sun. While their instruments were crude

and their errors sometimes immense, they nonetheless established fairly regular, if not entirely reliable, connections with their colonies in Greenland and Iceland that endured until the late thirteenth or early fourteenth century. *See also* NORSE MARITIME DISCOVERIES.

Opening of the European age of exploration As can be readily ascertained from the above, the great oceans of the world did not lack intrepid and knowledgeable explorers throughout the ages. What distinguished the Europeans of the fifteenth and sixteenth centuries from their predecessors was an apparently fathomless drive to experiment and explore that recognized no bounds. This led to a recognition of the immensity of the world and the unity of the seas and, ultimately, to the Europeanization of much of the world about those seas.

The Europeans of the great age of exploration be-

Spice plants of the East Indies, highly coveted by trader-explorers since the Middle Ages. [Library of Congress]

longed intellectually, emotionally, and mystically to two different ages, that of the Renaissance and that of the modern world, which were intertwined and contradictory at the same moment. Being part of a transitional age meant embracing values and goals that sometimes were conflicting and sometimes complemented each other. Perhaps this set of circumstances explains some of the great successes of the age, for it was not unusual to find combined in one man the inquisitive scientist, the zealous crusader, and the perceptive and dynamic merchant. It is within the successful attempts to realize these roles that one can best perceive the motivations and the means that launched the age.

One of the major concerns of medieval Europe was the availability of certain imports from India and the East. Europeans had long depended upon the Orient for the spices that flavored and preserved foods; cinnamon came from Ceylon, pepper from Java and Sumatra, nutmeg from Borneo and Celebes, and cloves from the Moluccas and the Banda Islands. Although sericulture had been widely developed in Italy by the fifteenth century, silk from Persia and China also fetched high prices on the European market.

Communications and commerce with the East had worked relatively well in the centuries preceding the fourteenth and fifteenth. Italian city-states such as Venice and Genoa maintained contacts with their suppliers through a lengthy conduit that included Mediterranean shipping, camel caravans, Indian Ocean dhows, and a host of middlemen. Under the Mings, however, China turned inward and exclusive while coincidentally the Muslim faith, largely through the efforts of the rising Ottoman Empire based in Turkey, assumed an escalating hostility to Christian commerce and Christianity in general. Trading through the Levant to the sources in the Indian Ocean became an increasingly costly, dangerous, and finally impossible enterprise by the fifteenth century. The idea of circumventing this obstacle by finding an alternative route represented an important strand in the web of motives that underlay maritime exploration in this age.

The force of religion acted as a powerful agent as well. In the Iberian Peninsula both Spanish and Portuguese warriors had long been engaged in the expulsion of Moors, who had occupied much of the peninsula in the eighth century. The reconquest culminated in 1492 with the capture of the last of the Moorish kingdoms, Granada, by King Ferdinand of Aragon and Queen Isabella of Castile. The Portuguese had meanwhile carried the war to Africa and captured the city of Ceuta as early as 1415. Why not carry the righteous crusade further? Rumors compounded of facts and fables told of the existence of long-isolated pockets of Christianity in India and the East. Why not try to reach these brethren, such as the legendary kingdom of PRESTER JOHN or the Christian community that had allegedly been founded by St. Thomas in India, and

Different types of vessels used by the Portuguese in the Indian Ocean.

strengthen Christianity in the face of the Ottoman threat?

Early Portuguese exploration A practical man whose vision was influenced by some of these dreams and ambitions emerged in the first half of the fifteenth century. Prince Henry of Portugal inspired and supported Portuguese mariners who made the first significant voyages by Western explorers into the Atlantic and down the African coast. From his home at Sagres on Cabo de São Vicente he encouraged his captains to explore west past the Canaries and south toward Cabo Bojador on the coast of West Africa. To foster the mingling of the practical with the theoretical, Henry attracted learned men, such as astronomers and cartographers, and craftsmen, such as shipwrights and instrument makers, to Sagres. By 1434 Bojador, a fearful obstruction to superstitious mariners bred by ignorance of what lay beyond, was rounded by Gil Eannes, while by 1443 a caravel had brought back the first commercial fruits of these early explorations: gold dust and black slaves. Henry's explorers had also ranged far enough west to have discovered a group of islands collectively named the Azores (Isles of the Hawks). Additionally, the Madeira Islands, long known to Portuguese mariners, were now colonized and developed to produce sugar and wine, two profitable products reaching the markets of Europe by the mid-fifteenth century.

When Prince Henry died in 1460, the great Western age of exploration had been launched. By then it was realized that Africa trended east and south beyond the equator. Perhaps that great continent might be rounded by sea, and hence a clear route to India discovered. Profits were also being realized, and as early as 1448 an armed trading post, called a factory, had been constructed at Arguim (Arguin) on the coast of Mauritania. Converts were also being harvested, and the blessings of the church were freely bestowed on Henry's sailors and explorers. The successes of the Portuguese were nonetheless due as much to their techniques and vessels as to their vision and ambition.

The basic vessel which served Henry's mariners was called a caravel. It was a small ship, almost always less than 100 tons and in most cases less than 50 or 60 tons, propelled by triangular-shaped lateen sails adopted from the Arab maritime culture of the Indian Ocean. Caravels outfitted with lateen sails possessed the distinct advantage over traditional European square sail designs of being able to sail close to the wind. Square sails simply could not be arranged to utilize contrary winds in the manner of lateens,

which could spread a long, taut edge into the wind. Square-rigged ships *(naus)*, on the other hand, could carry a great deal more sail with safety and ease because of their configuration. This enabled ships equipped with square sails to be larger and sometimes faster than caravels, but nonetheless clumsy and totally inadequate when winds were encountered forward of the beam. Small lateen-rigged caravels provided Henry's explorers with the maneuverability so vital when faced with uncharted coasts, lee shores, and other menacing unknowns.

A major breakthrough occurred sometime during Henry's lifetime when imaginative and no doubt experienced mariners combined the advantages of lateen and square sails in one vessel known as the *caravela redonda.* The idea, which certainly seems brilliant in retrospect, probably was put into practice by chance rather than by design. Whatever the origin, the result represented a major innovation. Lateen-rigged vessels could be enlarged only slightly because of the limits imposed by the lateen sail. It was difficult to tack (the sail and spar had to be hauled laboriously *over* the mast) and thus was unworkable past a certain size. Square sails could be more easily shifted to change tack and could be easily enlarged, especially by dividing them into different parts; therefore, larger ships could be built, fitted, and propelled well by the square sails. During the longer voyages of exploration that followed Henry's time it was necessary to enlarge the capacity and staying power of ships at sea. A *caravela redonda,* or *navío,* as it later was called in the Spanish service, could be enlarged to carry an expedition far, could be sailed with a certain margin of safety and security close to strange coastlines, could be tacked and steered with relative ease depending on the combination of sails employed, was well suited for running before the steady trade winds, and generally served the explorer well. The description supplied of Christopher Columbus's flagship, *Santa María,* by Samuel Eliot Morison in *Christopher Columbus, Mariner* (1955) is well worth quoting:

> Her rig was the conventional one of the period, when ships were just emerging from the one-big-mast type of the Middle Ages: a mainmast higher than she was long, a main yard as long as the keel, carrying an immense square sail—the main course—which was counted on to do most of the driving. Above the main course was spread a small main top sail. The foremast, little more than half the height of the mainmast, carried only a square fore course or foresail. The mizzenmast, stepped on the high poop, carried a small lateen-rigged sail, and under the bowsprit, which pointed up from the bows at a sharp angle, was spread a small square sail called the spritsail, which performed rather inefficiently the function of the modern jib.

The climax to Portuguese exploratory efforts in this long initial period occurred in the last 13 years of the century. The Treaty of Alcaçovas, signed with Castile in 1479, awarded to Portugal all island groups in the Atlantic except the Canaries and a clear sphere of influence over exploration and settlement of the African

Portuguese caravels from a manuscript on navigation. [The Pierpont Morgan Library]

coast. Furthermore, by the 1480s Portuguese explorers, who had already reached as far south as the mouth of the Congo River and Cape Cross, in what is now Namibia, were under constant encouragement to venture further by King John II. In 1487 a captain in John's service, Bartolomeu DIAS, was caught in a storm for 13 days and, while out of sight of land, was blown around the Cape of Good Hope and into the Indian Ocean. Equipped only with small caravels and discouraged from ranging farther by low supplies and a mutinous crew, he returned to Portugal with the news. Within a decade of Dias's voyage the Portuguese crown launched a major expedition of four vessels—three mixed-rigged ships and one caravel—led by Vasco da Gama to explore and trade where Dias had left off. The great Portuguese century of exploration begun by Prince Henry reached a climax in 1498, when da Gama landed on the Malabar coast of India, having sailed directly from Portugal.

Da Gama's voyage represented the typical combination of luck, skill, and determination that afforded success to most explorers of this era. Sailing south into the Atlantic, he stood well out to sea to search for the best winds. Not only did he accomplish the longest voyage then made out of sight of land by a European, but he picked up favorable winds and thus shortened the passage around Africa. After rounding the Cape of Good Hope and sailing up the East African coast, da Gama chanced upon ibn-Mājid, an extremely capable navigator of the Indian Ocean who helped in the voyage to Calicut on the Indian coast.

The Portuguese followed up da Gama's voyage with determined and warlike expeditions that by 1515 culminated in the establishment of Portuguese bases at key points of the Indian Ocean all the way from the Persian Gulf to the Strait of Malacca. Not only had strategic ports been secured, but Muslim competition on the sea had been substantially suppressed. How did a small nation that sent tiny fleets manned by small complements into a sea filled with thousands of sailors, hundreds of dhows, and implacably hostile rulers manage to triumph? The answer lay in the technical superiority of Western vessels and, more important, in the cannon they carried.

Guns, as much as sails, ships, and skilled navigators, were responsible for the success of European explorers. While both the Chinese and the Muslim worlds possessed the knowledge of guns and gunpowder and certainly the practical expertise to have developed some effective weapons, it was nonetheless the Europeans who conceived of guns and ship as one and then forged this formidable combination into an irresistible weapon. Basically, while non-Western people retained a dependence upon embarked warriors, Europeans employed shipborne cannon as the primary instruments of combat at sea. In 1509 a numerically inferior Portuguese fleet defeated an Egyptian-Arab fleet carrying more than 15,000 men off the Indian coast near Diu. The lethal power of the cannonball, shot at a distance from a strong, maneuverable, and defensible platform, overwhelmed the crafts and sailors of the Indian Ocean. Indeed, when the Portuguese arrived off the port of Canton in 1517, the fame of their ships and guns had preceded them to China.

Columbus's voyages The exploits of Christopher Columbus mirror well the duality of Renaissance explorers, who were usually conquerors and traders as well. After the Portuguese succeeded in forestalling Spanish expansion down the African coast, the Genoese navigator persuaded the Spanish sovereigns Isabella and Ferdinand to try another route to India and the East. He argued simply that if one sailed far enough directly west one would eventually arrive in the East.

Columbus's enterprise contained elements of inspiration, practical knowledge, and some significant miscalculations concerning the true dimensions of the earth. From classical sources and contemporary scholars, such as the famed Florentine astronomer and map maker Paolo Toscanelli, Columbus fashioned two major geographical estimates, both flawed. First, he underestimated the circumference of the globe by about one-sixth of its actual size. Second, he grossly overestimated the length of Asia's coastal projection toward the east. In consequence, he deduced that if one sailed about 3000 miles (4828 kilometers) west from Portugal or Spain, one would eventually reach the Orient, probably touching at Cipangu (Japan) in the first instance. Columbus first proposed his project to the Portuguese but was rejected upon the recommendation of a committee of learned advisers to the crown. They quite rightly concluded that Columbus's estimates contained serious errors and that the adventure as conceived could never succeed. Overtures to the French and English courts were also rejected before Isabella sanctioned the Columbian adventure in 1492.

The three vessels selected for the voyage, the *Santa María*, *Niña*, and *Pinta*, were characteristically small, ranging from about 60 to 100 tons, and were rigged with varying combinations of square and lateen sails. The fleet was prepared at the small port of Palos on the southwestern Atlantic coast of the province of Andalusia, and the crews were recruited largely from the local inhabitants, many with long attachments to the sea. The fleet sailed on August 3, 1492.

Columbus's plan involved dropping south to the latitude of the Canary Islands, 28°N, and then turning to catch the northeast trade winds that blew steadily toward the west and Cipangu. The voyage itself was remarkably rapid, marred only in its later stages by a frightened crew whose faith in the mission was not as deep as Columbus's. On October 12, 1492, land was sighted, and God was thanked. Columbus bestowed the name San Salvador (Holy Savior) on that small island in the Caribbean which today bears the English name Watling.

To Columbus, San Salvador represented the outer fringes of the fabled Orient. He sailed through some of the islands of the Bahamas, and then, while exploring the Cuban coast, a party was landed with the mission of discovering the whereabouts of the Grand Khan. Simple homes and primitive natives who understood none of the Castilian, Latin, or Arabic spoken to them did not deter the admiral. The fleet moved on to another large island, given the name of La Isla Española (Hispaniola). Here again little evidence of Cipangu, China, or India was readily apparent. Nonetheless, there was gold, and the many native inhabitants were potential converts and workers. Columbus returned to Spain in early 1493 with grandiose plans. He had left a small complement of sailors on the north coast of Española at a tiny settlement called La Navidad near where the *Santa María* had foundered on a reef on Christmas Eve, 1492. This was the first, albeit short-lived, settlement made by Europeans in America.

Columbus subsequently returned to his discoveries three more times, between 1493 and 1496, 1498 and 1500, and 1500 and 1504. On each succeeding voyage he ranged farther into the waters of the New World. On the third voyage he discovered the South American mainland and recognized it for what it was: a continent of vast although unknown proportions. Characteristically, Columbus had arrived at this conclusion as a practical and experienced explorer of the Renaissance. The heavy discharge of fresh water into the sea from the mighty Orinoco River in northern South America provided unchallenged evidence of a vast hinterland. Columbus, ever the pilgrim to the East, conjectured that this continent must surely represent the outer edge of China, Cipangu, or another area tantalizingly near his goal.

Columbus the explorer had also been Columbus the master navigator. By modern standards, the tools of his trade would seem wildly inaccurate and hope-

Columbus lands on Hispaniola in 1492. [Library of Congress]

lessly inadequate. The boldness and genius of Renaissance explorers such as Columbus are magnified when one considers the rudimentary instruments and methods that were relied upon to cross unknown oceans, explore unknown coasts, and then return the equally vast distances home.

Compasses had been employed in European waters at least 200 years before Columbus's time and were depended upon commonly by European explorers. A compass provided the sailor with a good approximation of north by relying on the magnetic quality that lodestone imparts to a needle. A needle that could freely pivot and seek north was fastened to a card which was divided into 32 points, each representing 11 ¼ degrees. The navigator, of course, steered in the direction indicated by the needle. Variation, or the tendency of the compass to err from true north because of differences in the earth's magnetic field, was known to exist. Compensation could be made by trial and error, and a good navigator such as Columbus certainly was always aware of the possibility of mistakes, especially in new waters.

Closely allied to the compass in importance were charts. They were employed by mariners to portray the outlines of coasts and islands, to describe the prevailing winds and currents, and to plot courses. The construction of portolans, charts drawn for short-range piloting in European waters, had begun as early as the thirteenth century, and by the fifteenth had evolved into a fine craft. Drawn on these charts were prominent headlands, rivers, harbors, and other important or distinguishing features to aid the navigator. Rhumb lines which indicated compass courses between different points were also shown. A major drawback of portolans was not overcome until the sixteenth century, when a Flemish geographer, Gerhardus Mercator, published a true projection of latitude and longitude. Portolans did not compensate for the narrowing of longitudinal distances as they extended away from the equator and approached the poles. Distortions thus occurred if portolans were attempted on a large scale. Nonetheless, for short-range coastal piloting and as records for observations of new and strange coasts, they were indispensable. They not only permitted the accumulation of practical knowledge but, in many cases, proved to be excellent vehicles for the explorer and geographer as artist.

The compass, charts, and other assorted devices and methods available to Renaissance explorers were employed to estimate one's position and progress at sea. This practice, called dead reckoning, never found a more adept master than Christopher Columbus. He supplemented his instruments' information with an uncanny instinct that helped him solve the problem of distance traveled, direction followed, and time elapsed. The half-hour glass measured time and was reasonably accurate for local conditions. Not until the eighteenth century would an accurate and dependable sea clock, the chronometer, be invented and perfected. Time thus remained uncertain, and the lack of a chronometer forestalled a celestial solution to the problem of longitude.

A vessel's speed was estimated by the pilot largely through his senses. Experience at sea, knowledge of a ship's sailing qualities, and careful attention to flotsam or weeds as they drifted by were all invoked in the formula to arrive at speed. A chip log, or log line, was a device to measure speed. Knots marked regular intervals on a line that was paid out into the water and observed for the frequency in which the knots passed out. This method, however, was not generally used until the late sixteenth century. Thus da Gama, Columbus, and others of their generation relied on the more empirical approach. Estimates of the speed or distance traveled were made at half-hour intervals and recorded in the ship's logbook. Compensation for tacking, leeway, or drifting sideways with the wind and currents, if known, all complicated the problem.

When in shallow water, the lead line could be employed to find depth. A bottle-shaped lead plummet was attached to a long line. Heaved outboard, it provided the leadsman with a rough estimate of depth when he felt the lead strike bottom. Soundings were used not only to navigate safely but to make charts more accurate. Heaving the lead is indeed such a reliable piloting technique that modern ships, equipped as they might be with all the latest fathometers, sonar, and other highly sophisticated gear, still post a leadsman under certain conditions.

The practice of finding one's latitude at sea by celestial observation also formed part of the explorers' navigational baggage. The fixture of the star Polaris above the North Pole and the predictability of the sun's orbit were the two constants that enabled navigators to determine latitude. Instruments such as the cross-staff, the astrolabe, and the quadrant measured the angle between Polaris or the sun and the horizon. Latitude could be determined simply by shooting Polaris. If the star were 39° above the horizon, the observer's latitude was 39°N; if 20° above, 20°N, and so forth. The first-recorded latitudinal fixes by Polaris were made in the 1460s, but this technique was probably employed by Prince Henry's explorers earlier. The disappearance of Polaris from view in the Southern Hemisphere presented a considerable problem that was solved by Portuguese mathematicians, astronomers and navigators in the second half of the fifteenth century by turning to the sun for a determination of latitude. An observation of the sun's altitude, or angle between the horizon and the sun, was made at midday. Tables of the sun's declination, or the sun's altitude north and south of the equator at noon on any given day of the year, had been compiled and made available to Portuguese navigators by the middle 1480s. These were consulted, and the sun's declination was added or subtracted to the observed altitude of the sun according to the hemisphere and the season. The result was the observer's distance from the equator, or his latitude.

The crudeness of the instruments, the movement of

Artist's conception of sixteenth-century mariners observing the North Star. [Library of Congress]

the ships, and the very elementary knowledge possessed by even the most capable navigators made celestial navigation a chancy supplement to the more reliable means of dead reckoning. Even Columbus only infrequently made use of his quadrant, preferring to rely more generally on practical than on celestial observations. The determination or knowledge of latitude nonetheless helped to trace and fix new routes to

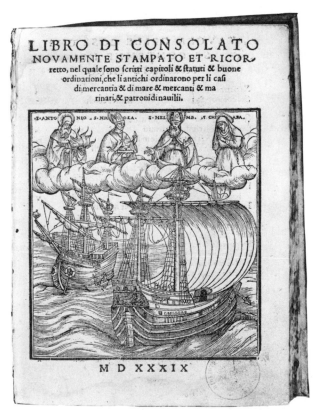

A book of 1539 on maritime law. This title page shows the mariners' guardian saints Antonio, Nicola, Elmo, and Chiara in the clouds. [Library of Congress]

newly discovered lands and islands. It also provided explorers with the confidence necessary to undertake some of the extremely long transits made through unknown waters in this era.

Coasts of North and South America   Columbus's voyages triggered scores of emulative expeditions that sailed from the ports of Western Europe and the British Isles. They were in search of various things: a route to the East, a better knowledge of the Columbian discoveries, and gold, precious stones, or other forms of wealth. Competition between the emerging nation states of Spain, Portugal, France, and England also stimulated explorations.

In the late 1490s, England, then emerging from a long series of internal wars under the sovereignty of the parsimonious Henry VII, gingerly initiated its role in the age of exploration through the services of John CABOT, who approached Henry about 1495. Cabot persuaded the King to sponsor a Columbian-style voyage to seek a more direct route to the East by sailing along the higher latitudes of the North Atlantic. He sailed from Bristol in late May 1497 in one tiny ship, *Mathew*, of about 50 tons.

Cabot followed the high latitudes aound 50°N on the solid premise that the shortest distance to China lay across the northern third of the globe. However, he did not land on the exotic coast of some Oriental empire but fetched what was probably the stark, rugged outline of Newfoundland on June 24. He explored a goodly portion of the Newfoundland coast, discovered great stands of trees, found much codfish in the surrounding seas, and then returned to England. Cabot felt that he had discovered part of the Asian continent, although some evidence suggests that he recognized those coasts as a "new land" not previously accounted for by the ancients or his contemporaries. In any case, Cabot's confidence and the King's curiosity produced a second expedition that sailed for America in 1498. Of this voyage we know nothing. Cabot and all but one ship of his small fleet disappeared in stark testimony to the hazards of the trade.

Far to the south another contemporary of Columbus, Pedro Álvares CABRAL of Portugal, made a discovery that later aided his countrymen in claiming colonial rights in America. Cabral had been dispatched to India in 1500 to capitalize on the successful da Gama voyage. Proceeding into the Atlantic, Cabral ranged far west in the search for the best trade winds and bumped into the eastern bulge of Brazil at about 17°S. He naturally claimed it for Portugal. According to the Treaty of Tordesillas signed between Spain and Portugal in 1494, this new land, whether island or continent, fell within that part of the world reserved for the Portuguese.

As the uniqueness and dimensions of America became slowly apparent to explorers and monarchical patrons as well, an increased effort was launched to find a way through or around this new world to the still much-desired spice and silk ports of the East. The broad Río de la Plata Estuary offered the possibility of being a passageway, and it was explored by Juan Díaz de SOLÍS on behalf of the Spanish crown in 1515–1516. Meanwhile, Spanish explorers in the Caribbean were gradually establishing the fact that no easy way to the Orient lay in that direction. The Central American and northern South American coasts, known as Tierra Firme, appeared unbroken. When Vasco Nuñez de BALBOA crossed the Isthmus of Panama late in 1513 and sighted the Pacific, which he named the South Sea, he correctly identified that body of water, briny and possessing sizable tides, as a newly discovered ocean. How far away did China lie from here? The answer was supplied by the epic voyage of Ferdinand Magellan, a Portuguese explorer in the service of Spain.

Magellan's voyage   Magellan, who had had a long and distinguished record of service in the East, made a fairly simple proposition to the Spanish. He offered to sail to South America, find the strait or southernmost tip, pass through or around it, and complete the transit to Asia. This route would represent a new, all-Spanish track to those islands and lands in the East which lay within the Spanish concessions delimited by the line of the Treaty of Tordesillas that presumably girdled the globe. Magellan's argument was persuasive, and in 1518 King Charles I (Emperor Charles V) approved it. Five ships were outfitted for the expedition and departed from the port of Seville on Monday, August 10, 1519.

The expedition sailed to Brazil first and, after making landfall at Cabo de São Roque on the northeastern tip, moved south in search of the passage. It was not until October 1520 that Magellan discovered the entrance to the strait that now bears his name. He then began the careful probing that culminated 38 days later in the successful transit to the Pacific. The way to the Indies was now clear.

The voyage was marked by near-indescribable hardships, for the quick passage to the East that Magellan had anticipated dragged on for more than 3 tortuous months out of sight of land. Water turned putrid, what little food remained spoiled horribly amid the maggots, while scurvy with all its horrors of bleeding gums, sores, falling teeth, and terribly aching joints took a heavy toll. Rats fetched a high price until this source of food was exhausted. Even the chafing gear, soaked for days in brine to soften it and then grilled, was eaten. The Philippines were reached in March 1521, but tragedy ensued amid the joy of finding food and water and a friendly reception, for Magellan was killed shortly afterward.

Command of the expedition eventually devolved upon Juan Sebastián de Elcano. In a voyage no less remarkable for its endurance than the crossing of the Pacific, he returned to Spain and anchored at Seville on September 8, 1522, with a cargo of cloves and seventeen other survivors. The profits from these spices not only paid for the entire voyage but left a sizable profit for all who had invested in the trip. Magellan's voyage certainly demonstrated the commercial rewards that could be reaped by the bold and the hardy.

Of equal importance, Magellan's circumnavigation of the world (for he indeed had circumnavigated it if one considers that his voyage west had reached the approximate area where he had sailed previously in the service of the Portuguese) had proved the unity of the world's oceans. The old Ptolemaic dimensions of the world (too small) and the errors (a landlocked Indian Ocean, for example) were dismissed in favor of the knowledge provided by Magellan's trip. The East could, in truth, be reached by sailing west, but a difficult strait had to be weathered, and an awe-inspiring ocean had to be crossed. While navigators in the service of Spain and Portugal plowed new seas in the Southern Hemisphere, the English and French joined the probing Iberians in the north.

Search for a northern passage Numerous voyages, some to explore and some to fish for cod off the Grand Banks of Newfoundland, had been made to the far northern coast of North America following and perhaps even before John Cabot's voyage of 1497. The Portuguese brothers Gaspar and Miguel CORTE-REAL, Cabot's own son Sebastian CABOT, and unknown fishermen touched North American shores at various times but left little precise knowledge of their discoveries. Another Italian, this time in the French service, made the first significant exploration in the sixteenth century of that continent's waters and coast.

Giovanni da VERRAZZANO wished to discover the northern sea route to Cathay. If not successful in that endeavor, he at least hoped to find a strait or passageway leading to the Orient. Verrazzano sailed to the New World in early 1524, arrived somewhere near Cape Fear, North Carolina, and made an initial exploration southward before turning north and coasting as far north as Maine or Newfoundland. In the course of this voyage he eventually arrived at the conclusion that North America certainly was not part of Asia but indeed a new world. He did make a rather serious error by assuming that the waters on the other side of the Carolina Outer Banks (Pamlico Sound) represented the Pacific and that that strip of low-lying land was but an isthmus between the two great oceans. But conjecture still formed a very important ingredient in the making of explorers' reports, and the strength of Verrazzano's clear realization of North America as a new world certainly outweighed the flawed conception of how close the Pacific lay to the Atlantic.

French interests in discovering a strait through the North American continent were carried forward by Jacques CARTIER of Saint-Malo, who made three voyages to North America between 1534 and 1542 and thoroughly explored the Gulf of St. Lawrence. Cartier found no straits but helped fashion French claims to that part of the world. By the second half of the sixteenth century emboldened Englishmen had taken up the challenge of finding the elusive northern sea route to Cathay, if not through a NORTHWEST PASSAGE then through a NORTHEAST PASSAGE.

English exploration of the Arctic regions from Baffin Bay in the west to the Kara Sea off northern Siberia transcended the Elizabethan era and represented one of the most determined and ultimately fruitless efforts launched by any one nation in the great age of exploration. The first expedition was led by Sir Hugh Willoughby, who in 1553 took three small vessels into the North Sea, around Norway's North Cape, and then east. Caught by the harsh and frozen winter, Willoughby, with two ships and their entire crews, perished. A third vessel, *Edward Bonaventure,* under Richard CHANCELLOR, reached Archangel (Arkhangelsk) in the White Sea. In 1556 a small vessel, *Searchthrift,* commanded by Stephen Borough, again attempted the Northeast Passage but reached no farther than the Novaya Zemlya archipelago. The Kara Sea was ice-blocked, and after wintering near Archangel Borough returned to England. An attempt in 1580 by Arthur Pet and Charles Jackson met with equal frustration in the ice-choked Kara Sea.

Before the sixteenth century ended, one last effort was made to forge the Northeast Passage by a small nation that developed into one of England's greatest maritime and naval rivals. Sailing for the Netherlands, William BARENTS launched three unsuccessful expeditions to reach beyond the Kara Sea. On the last of these, in 1596, he discovered Spitsbergen (Svalbard), but this great explorer died in the spring while trying to go home in two open boats from Novaya Zemlya. The expedition's ship had become stuck fast in the ice, another of the perils of Arctic exploration. (The first ship to make the passage across northern Asia was a Swedish vessel, *Vega,* in 1878–1879.)

While the Northwest Passage was equally impenetrable, it nonetheless irresistibly attracted Elizabethans with the tempting possibility that its mysteries could easily be solved. Sir Humphrey GILBERT was the greatest champion of the virtues of the Northwest Passage. He argued forcibly in *A Discourse of a Discoverie for a New Passage to Cataia* that the route over or through North America was the easiest and shortest to China. The theories were first put to the test by Martin FROBISHER in three voyages between 1576 and 1578. He probed about the entrance to Hudson's Bay, brought home Eskimos and samples of black stone that were thought to contain gold, but certainly did not find the passage, nor did he produce a profit in any other way. Another triad of voyages was undertaken between 1585 and 1587 by John DAVIS. His third voyage took him into the high latitudes of Baffin Bay, which separates Greenland from Baffin Island (part of North America), but the ice turned him back. In 1610 Henry HUDSON, a navigator in the service of the English, explored the immense bay named after him. However, Hudson Bay did not lead to the Pacific, and Hudson passed a terrible winter ashore in the southern part of the great bay. He perished tragically after mutineers set him, his young son, and seven crew members adrift in a small boat. While maritime explorers in the Arctic discovered the narrow frozen limits imposed by the permanent Arctic ice pack, others turned to reach that vast and open ocean that had been first traversed by Magellan.

Pacific exploration Pacific explorers were motivated to find land, in contrast to Arctic explorers, who sought water passages. However, not unlike their Arctic brethren, Magellan's successors speculated optimistically on the existence of land where none lay, and the search for land, especially for the great southern continent Terra Australis Incognita, lasted for several centuries. Terra Australis Incognita had been manufactured by ancient geographers and cartographers who felt a need for the existence of a great landmass in the Southern Hemisphere to balance the land in the north. Furthermore, land was thought to cover a great percentage of the globe's surface. When the dimensions of the Pacific slowly began to emerge after Magellan's voyage, the theory of the southern continent was reinforced.

Spanish mariners crossed the Pacific in both directions innumerable times in the sixteenth century not only in search of Terra Australis Incognita but for imperial and religious reasons as well. Wishing to exploit claims laid by Magellan to Spanish sovereignty in eastern islands, several voyages were launched into the Pacific from the mother country and the colony of New Spain (Mexico) between 1527 and 1565. Álvaro de Saavedra, for example, sailed from Mexico in 1527 to try to discover a route to and from the Spice Islands. He reached the western Pacific, but storms and contrary winds foiled his return.

Spanish reverses, on account of the elements and Portuguese resistance, prompted Charles V to sell his claims in the East, except for the Philippines, to the Portuguese in 1529 for a cash sum. Thereafter the Spanish concentrated on discovering a viable route to and from the Philippines from the west coast of New Spain. This was accomplished in 1565, when an expedition under the command of Miguel López de Legazpi founded the colony of Manila. On the same voyage the great navigator Fray Andrés de URDANETA pioneered the route back to New Spain. He sailed far north to about latitude 40°N and discovered the prevailing westerlies that brought him back to the North American continent. Urdaneta's voyage alone exemplified the marked contributions to the knowledge of the Pacific made by the Spanish in this era.

While the interests of the empire were being advanced in the Philippines, Spanish explorers from the colony of Peru in South America set out to discover and colonize Terra Australis Incognita, Álvaro de Mendaña made two voyages from Peru into the South Pacific, in 1567–1569 and 1595–1596. On the first trip he discovered the Solomon Islands, so called because they were thought to be the land of OPHIR where the biblical King Solomon's mines were located. The second voyage constituted a full-fledged colonial expedition, replete with women, children, livestock, and all the tools for settlement. The Marquesas and Santa Cruz Islands were discovered, but the colony, attempted in the latter group, proved a failure.

The clipper ship **Red Jacket** *in the ice off Cape Horn. The cape was rounded for the first time in 1615–1616 by Dutch sailors in search of a new route to the East.* [Library of Congress]

In 1579 and 1587 two other great navigators, the Englishmen Francis DRAKE and Thomas Cavendish, also crossed the Pacific. Both entered through the Strait of Magellan, raided Spanish possessions along the west coast of the Americas, and returned to England by circumnavigating the globe. Drake is claimed to have explored as far north as Vancouver Bay in Canada in search of the western terminus of the elusive Northwest Passage. He discovered only that the coast appeared unbroken and trended westward. Drake then returned south to about the latitude of San Francisco and made sail for the Moluccas.

In the very early seventeenth century Pedro Fernándes de Quirós (Pedro Fernandez de Queirós) set out to find Terra Australis Incognita, which he confidently felt was located not very far south of the Solomon Islands. New discoveries were indeed made, among them the New Hebrides Islands. Quirós calculated these to be the northern tip of his great southern continent. During this expedition two vessels under the command of Luis Vaez de Torres got separated from the main fleet and made another important discovery. On their way to Manila they passed through the strait (subsequently named after Torres) that divides Australia from New Guinea and raised the issue of Australia's existence. Did Torres see Australia? Was it Terra Australis Incognita? The riddles of the Pacific nonetheless remained unsolved by the Spanish in this era. As the empire went into a long eclipse, emphasis was placed on consolidating and defending gains rather than on exploration and expansion. Dutch seamen picked up the thread where the Spanish left off. Curious, ambitious, and extremely competent, the Dutch not only were beguiled by the possibility of finding and settling the great southern continent but were attracted by the lucrative trade between the East and Europe which Portugal had monopolized for more than a century.

Dutch exploration in the Pacific commenced in the late sixteenth and early seventeenth centuries when the great East India Company and its predecessors began to challenge Portugal for control of the major spice islands and entrepôts of the East. Australia was probably discovered by Dutch seamen as early as 1606. Its west coast became familiar after 1611, when Dutch mariners discovered the quickest route to the East. From the Cape of Good Hope they would sail 4000 miles (6437 kilometers) directly east and once having reached the longitude of western Australia sail north to their colonies of Java and Batavia (now Jakarta). Much of the Australian coast was subsequently explored by experienced navigators such as Abel Janszoon TASMAN.

In the southeastern Pacific, in 1615–1616, two Dutch mariners discovered Cape Horn in addition to the southernmost strait off Tierra del Fuego. Jacob Le Maire (whose name was given to the strait) and Willem Schouten were in search of a new route to the East when they discovered Le Maire Strait. They then rounded Cape Horn (named after their hometown of

A view of Kealakekua Bay, Hawaii, where Captain Cook died. [Library of Congress]

Hoorn) for the first time and pioneered this new route into the Pacific.

Cook's voyages Other additions to the basic knowledge of the Pacific were made in the seventeenth and eighteenth centuries by such disparate individuals as the enterprising and observant English buccaneer William Dampier and the eminent French scientist-navigator Louis-Antoine de BOUGAINVILLE. Nevertheless, it remained for the great English explorer and scientist Capt. James Cook to cap the exploration of the limits of the Pacific in a distinguished set of voyages between 1768 and 1779.

During the course of these expeditions Cook's scientific and navigational observations excelled to a degree unapproached by any of his predecessors. In his first voyage he sailed more than 2000 miles (3219 kilometers) along the east coast of Australia, sometimes inside the Great Barrier Reef, and left charts and sailing instructions that have only been supplemented and never truly superseded. In his second voyage he plunged below the Antarctic Circle for the first time in search of the great southern continent. He did not discover Antarctica, but his voyage finally disabused contemporaries of the notion that a rich, inhabitable continent lay somewhere yet to be found. In his third and last voyage he put in at the Hawaiian Islands and then proceeded to the northwest coast of North America, up through the Aleutian Islands, and through Bering Strait, which divides Alaska from Siberia. (The strait had been discovered in 1728 by Vitus BERING, a Dane in the Russian service.) Again, as in the waters of the Antarctic, the ice and intolerable weather caused Cook to realize decisively that the Northwest Passage either did not exist or was virtually impassable.

Cook's contribution to maritime exploration had not been merely geographical. He tested successfully the first accurate chronometer for use at sea, made by John Harrison, and thus helped to solve the problem of determining longitude, which had long plagued navigators. The good captain also experimented, quite successfully, with various means of coping with another problem that had invariably caused great hardships, scurvy. By carefully constructing and enforcing a diet of onions, citrus fruits, and other foods, he overcame this age-old enemy.

By the end of the eighteenth century almost all the inhabitable lands that could be reached on the navigable oceans and seas of the world had been explored. In the wake of the explorers followed fellow Europeans to colonize, exploit, and spread their culture and power to the newly discovered world. The maritime navigators of the great age of exploration both shrank the world and expanded the limits of men's lives, and their legacy helped create the modern world as we know it.

See also ARCTIC OCEAN; MODERN EXPLORATION: FIFTEENTH TO SEVENTEENTH CENTURY; MODERN EXPLORATION: EIGHTEENTH TO TWENTIETH CENTURY; PACIFIC OCEAN.

BIBLIOGRAPHY: J. C. Beaglehole, *The Exploration of the Pacific,* 3d ed., Stanford, Calif., 1966; Charles R. Boxer, *The Dutch Seaborne Empire, 1600–1900,* New York, 1965; Carlo M. Cipolla, *Guns, Sails and Empires: Technological Innovation and the Early Phases of European Expansion, 1400–1700,* New York, 1965; Ernest S. Dodge, *Northwest by Sea,* New York, 1961; Kenneth P. Emory, "The Coming of the Polynesians," *The National Geographic,* vol. 146, no. 6, December 1974, pp. 732–746; John R. Hale and the editors of Time-Life Books, *Age of Exploration,* New York, 1966; Henry H. Hart, *Sea Road to the Indies,* New York, 1950; David Lewis, "Wind, Wave, Star, and Bird," *The National Geographic,* vol. 146, no. 6, December 1974, pp. 747–755; Samuel Eliot Morison, *Admiral of the Ocean Sea,* 2 vols., New York, 1942; id., *The European Discovery of America: The Northern Voyages, A.D. 500–1600,* New York, 1971; id., *The European Discovery of America: The Southern Voyages, A.D. 1492–1616,* New York, 1974; J. H. Parry, *The Establishment of the European Hegemony, 1415–1715,* New York, 1966; id., *The European Reconnaissance,* New York, 1968; Boies Penrose, *Travel and Discovery in the Renaissance, 1420–1620,* Cambridge, Mass., 1952; Frederick J. Pohl, *Amerigo Vespucci, Pilot Major,* New York, 1944; Edouard Roditi, *Magellan of the Pacific,* New York, 1972; Alan Villiers, *Men, Ships, and the Sea,* Washington, 1973.

Lawrence A. Clayton

Mas'ūdī, Abū al-Ḥasan 'Alī ibn al-Ḥusayn al- *(d. 956)* Arab historian and traveler. Al-Mas'ūdī, one of the most important writers on history and geography in the medieval world, was born in Baghdad on an undetermined date. He claimed to have been a descendant of Masūd, one of the companions of Prophet Muhammad. An avid student and investigator all his life, he traveled through much of the Islamic world and beyond, making some interesting and long ocean voyages. He wandered through Persia (Iran) and the southern shores of the Caspian Sea and undertook a trip from the South China Sea to the Red Sea. In the course of the long sea voyage, he stopped and spent some time in Ceylon and Madagascar. After visiting the regions of Palestine and Syria, he settled in Egypt, where he died in the month of Jumādā II, 956.

His journeys helped him add to his fund of knowledge of geography, ethnography, and history. Not only did he learn from his own experiences and observations, but he also met and learned from many scholars of various creeds and ethnic backgrounds. He set down his insights in a thirty-volume work entitled *Akhbār al-Zamān (Reports of the Age),* which was begun in 943. Only a portion of this chronicle has survived, under the title *Murūj al-Dhahab wa*

Ma'ādin al-Jawāhir (Meadows of Gold and Mines of Precious Stones). This book, published originally in a nine-volume edition between 1861 and 1877, is a history of the ancient peoples and the Islamic world up to 947. It contains much valuable historical and occasional geographical information. As Mas'ūdī himself liked to point out, one may find in it materials pertaining to prophets, kings, continents, and the seas.

Of perhaps greater interest to the geographer is the book which he called *Kitāb al-Tanbīh wa al-Ishrāf (The Book of Warning and Supervision).* This book includes a short summary of history but begins with a short geographical section. From the latter we can gain some idea of what Masūdī saw and learned in the course of his wide travels. In breadth of knowledge and the universal nature of his ideas, al-Masūdī ranks as one of the great scholars of the medieval Muslim East.

BIBLIOGRAPHY: Tarif Khalidi, *Islamic Historiography: The Histories of Masudi,* Albany, N.Y., 1975; al-Masūdī, *Maçoudi: Le livre de l'avertissement et de la revision,* tr. by Baron Bernard Carra de Vaux, Paris, 1897.

William Tucker

Medieval Exploration

With the political decline and collapse of the Roman Empire in the West during the fifth century there was a noticeable decline in both geographical exploration and geographical knowledge. The great migrations of various barbarian tribes along with the political disintegration and economic instability of the times virtually closed large areas of Europe to any travelers.

Early Middle Ages In the early Middle Ages the state of geographical knowledge was illustrated perhaps best by the encyclopedic accounts of St. Isidore of Seville (d. 636). Despite the curious blend of fact and fable in his writings, Isidore of Seville did preserve much of the geographical lore of the ancient Romans. His work entitled *Etymologies* contains twenty books, of which the thirteenth and fourteenth deal with geographical topics. Christian medieval scholars frequently did not consider geography a distinct science but treated it incidentally along with the study of other subjects. Medieval Arab scholars made some significant advances in the study of geography. Particularly important in this respect was the traveller al-Idrīsī, who lived for a time at the Norman court of Roger II in Sicily. At the King's command al-Idrīsī made a celestial sphere out of silver and painstakingly compiled a description of the inhabited earth as it was then known. Geography was a practical matter to the Arabs because of their extensive commercial interests and activities. *See also* Muslim Travel and Exploration in the Middle Ages.

Probably the most important contribution to geographical exploration in the early Middle Ages came from the seafaring activities of the Norsemen, Northmen, or Vikings, as they are variously designated. Roughly from the middle of the eighth century to the middle of the eleventh century a tremendous migration from the Scandinavian north brought about the creation of new states and the discovery of new lands (*See* Norse Maritime Discoveries). Scandinavian rule was established in Ireland, on the Isle of Man, in the Hebrides, Orkney, Shetland, and Faeroe Islands, and in northern and central England. Of the kingdoms of the old Anglo-Saxon heptarchy, only Wessex in southern England managed to survive politically despite repeated raids of the Norsemen, or Danes, as they are called in English history. Viking voyages westward brought about the discovery of Iceland, Greenland, and the northern coast of North America, which was named Vinland. The duchy of Normandy, established in northern France in the early part of the tenth century, began as a Scandinavian settlement. Finland and Lapland were explored and colonized. Trade was carried on in the White Sea and eastward to the Ural Mountains. The Swedes not only controlled the Baltic coast of Russia but founded the Russian state itself in the ninth century. Some Scandinavian adventurers traveled as far south as Constantinople and entered the military service of the Byzantine Empire. Around 1000 many of these northern adventurers became personal military attendants of the Byzantine Emperor, achieving fame as the Varangian Guard.

From the duchy of Normandy itself a remarkable expansion occurred during the eleventh century and thereafter. In 1066 Duke William conquered England and successfully established a dynasty of Norman kings. Other Norman military leaders extended their political control over southern Italy and Sicily and became involved in the political affairs of the Byzantine state. Normans played a part in the First Crusade and were successful at the end of the eleventh century in establishing in northern Syria the Norman principality of Antioch. These widely scattered exploits of one group of people constitute a significant chapter in the history of medieval expansion and the further extension of geographical knowledge.

In general, the crusading movement made significant contributions to the development of medieval travel and exploration. Western Europeans became aware of the nature and diversity of the Muslim

A Viking ship. The Vikings' far-ranging voyages, which reached, some say, as far as North America, made the Norsemen the principal explorers of the early Middle Ages. [Library of Congress]

world; the commercial interests of Italian city-states vastly increased, and land travel and maritime enterprise both prospered. Trade stimulated the spirit of inquiry and also provided opportunities for the acquisition and transmission of geographical information. In the Mediterranean area Italy's central geographical position linked its seaports with the Levant and Asia in the East and with ports on the Atlantic seaboard in the West. Land routes in the north of Europe connected the German states with areas to the east and the southeast of Europe. Geographical knowledge expanded not only through these commercial land routes but also through the sailing voyages of the Hansa towns operating in the North Sea and in the Baltic. Cities of northern Italy, such as Venice, Florence, and Milan, provided an important link between the Mediterranean and Baltic Seas.

In regard to land journeys the activities of Benjamin of Tudela, who flourished during the second half of the twelfth century, seem especially significant, for he was probably the greatest Jewish traveler of the Middle Ages. His wanderings carried him from the western Mediterranean to the shores of the Levant and from there to Mesopotamia and into Persia. His *Book of Travels* has been translated into almost every European language and has served as an invaluable source of information for the Mediterranean world in the twelfth century. A contemporary of Benjamin of Tudela was Pethahiah of Regensburg in Bavaria. He made his way from Prague through Poland and Russia, then to the Crimea, Armenia, Babylonia, Syria,

and Palestine. His travel account was not written by himself but by others who heard a report of his extended journeys. He was particularly interested in the condition of various Jewish communities which he visited, in the collection of Jewish legends and miracle stories, and in the holy places of Palestine and the traditions associated with them.

Thirteenth century The expanding commercial activities of the Italians, Catalans, French, and Portuguese brought about a noticeable improvement of the portolans, the medieval sailing maps. Among Western peoples nautical science reached maturity in the Mediterranean Basin, and from this area some groups extended their trading activities to the Black Sea, while others bore their share of North African commerce. The Vivaldi brothers from Genoa set out in 1291 with the apparent intention of trying to establish an all-sea route to India. Although these two explorers were lost somewhere off the coast of Morocco, other European navigators continued their interest in islands in the Atlantic Ocean and in the shoreline of West Africa. Eventually the southward push of Portuguese explorers would culminate in the triumphant opening of an all-sea route to India by Vasco da GAMA in 1497–1498.

The thirteenth century was a golden age for the expansion of geographical knowledge. One of the significant phases of this expansion centers in the establishment of new contacts between Western Europe and the Far East. Travelers of this period contributed much to the accumulation of geographical data relating to distant and frequently unknown areas, and their travel accounts stimulated further interest in geographical exploration. The contacts which were made between East and West were facilitated in the early thirteenth century by the establishment of Mongol authority over a vast territory which stretched from the coasts of China to the eastern borders of Europe. From the religious point of view the Mongols were relatively tolerant, and the possibility that they might be converted to Christianity encouraged some Western leaders to take definite actions which might bring about closer relationships. Moreover, the possibility of an alliance with the Mongols suggested an opportunity to challenge the forces of Islam.

In 1245 John of Plano CARPINI, an Italian Franciscan friar, received a commission from Pope Innocent IV to visit the court of the Great Khan in Mongolia. On the long and arduous journey to the East Friar John was accompanied by another Franciscan named Benedict. Not until July 1246 did the friars finally arrive at the *ordu* (camp) of Kuyuk in Mongolia, and here the Western travelers had the unusual opportunity of witnessing the formal installation of Kuyuk as the Great Khan of all the Mongols. The two friars remained for several months in Mongolia, and finally in November 1246 they began their return journey westward, arriving in Italy in the summer of 1247. Carpini was a careful and competent observer, and the report which he prepared on his travels gave Europeans one of the most important of the early European accounts concerning the Mongols.

Another early description of these nomadic peoples was provided by William of RUBRUCK, a Franciscan friar from French Flanders, who was sent by King Louis IX of France to the court of the Great Khan. Making the long and difficult land journey across Asia and following the same general route as Carpini, William of Rubruck came to the *ordu* of the Great Khan in Mongolia on December 27, 1253, and there he remained for several months. By the first week of May 1255, he had arrived on the coast of Cilicia. Although differing in details, the reports of John of Plano Carpini and William of Rubruck provide a wealth of new information on the geography of Russia and Central Asia. Furthermore, the two narratives describe in considerable detail the life, customs, and beliefs of the Mongols in the days of two of their great political leaders, Kuyuk (d. 1248) and Mangu (d. 1259).

One of the most important contributions to European knowledge concerning the Far East was made by a Venetian family, the Polos. The elder Polos, brothers Nicolò and Maffeo, traveled to far-off Cathay (the medieval name for China) and were kindly received at the imperial court by Khubilai (Kublai) Khan. In 1269 they returned to Italy as ambassadors of the Khan, bearing with them a letter to the Pope as well as a golden tablet which the Khan had given to them as a guarantee of safe-conduct through his extensive do-

Venice. Italy's many seaports, linking the peninsula to the Levant, made the Italian city-states central to Mediterranean trade during the Middle Ages. It was from Venice that the Polos made their remarkable journeys. [Library of Congress]

minions. Two years later the Polo brothers began their return journey to Cathay, taking with them this time young Marco POLO, the son of Nicolò. Their long land journey to Cathay, which began after they had arrived in the Levant, led them from Syria eastward through Mesopotamia and Persia, through Turkestan, and across the great Gobi Desert until at last they reached Shangtu, the summer residence of Khubilai Khan. His court was truly the political center of the Eastern world, for Khubilai Khan ruled over an empire greater in territorial extent and inhabited by more people than any other ruler of his time.

After many years of living in China, the Polos eventually were able to return to their native city, taking this time the long sea route. They had been authorized by the Great Khan to be a part of the escort of a Mongolian princess to the court of the Khan of Persia, a commission which they successfully fulfilled before they returned to Venice. Marco Polo in a later period of his life, when he was a war captive of the republic of Genoa, dictated while in prison a lengthy description of his travel experiences, a work which became very popular and one which remains as one of the best-known travel accounts of the medieval period. Marco Polo described with clarity, detail, and accuracy the high civilization of Cathay, and opened to Europeans a vision of its great wealth and power. The numerous manuscripts of Marco Polo's travels which still survive attest to the popularity of his account. In the fifteenth century an early printed edition of this work came into the possession of Christopher CoLUMBUS and is now preserved in the Bibliotheca Columbina in Seville.

Still another outstanding visitor to Cathay who arrived there toward the end of the thirteenth century was John of Monte Corvino, a native of southern Italy

Khubilai Khan, ruler of the greatest empire in the Middle Ages, directs a battle from his headquarters on the backs of four elephants. Marco Polo remained in Cathay, as the Great Khan's trusted adviser and administrator, for many years before returning to Venice. [Library of Congress]

and a Franciscan friar. He had taken part in the Franciscan mission to Armenia and Persia and had finally returned to Italy bearing a letter from the King of Armenia to the Pope. John was again sent from Italy by Pope Nicholas IV with letters to the patriarchs and princes of the East, including a letter to the Great Khan in Peking. In 1291 Friar John left Tabriz, the capital of the Il-khans, and proceeded to Hormuz (Hormoz), where he boarded a ship for India. He also visited the Moluccas before continuing on to China, finally arriving in Peking in 1294. There he was courteously received by government officials. John of Monte Corvino carried on vigorously his missionary endeavors in China, finally being elevated in 1307 by Clement V to the rank of archbishop. He also received Christian helpers from the West to assist him in carrying on missionary activities. John of Monte Corvino, who died in China in 1328 at an advanced age, was deeply loved in the country of his adoption.

During the late thirteenth century a famous Nestorian monk, traveler, and diplomat made a journey from the East to the West. Rabban Bar-Sauma, born near Peking, was the envoy of Arghun Khan, the sovereign of the Mongol Persian realm. This Nestorian monk was sent to the West for the primary purpose of seeking an alliance of Western powers with the Mongols against a common enemy, the Muslims. This embassy started in 1287. Rabban Bar-Sauma was received in audience in Constantinople by the emperor Andronicus II Palaeologus, in Paris by Philip IV, and in Gascony by Edward I, the Plantagenet king of England. He also visited Rome and received the Eucharist from Nicholas IV on Palm Sunday, 1288. Although from a political point of view no concrete results were achieved from this embassy, Rabban Bar-Sauma's account of his Western embassy is particularly valuable as a general and perceptive view of medieval Europe at the close of the period of the Crusades.

Fourteenth century The fourteenth century was a period of continued Christian interest in Far Eastern countries. Among the famous Christian missionaries who went to the Far East during this period were Andrew of Perugia, Jordanus of Sévérac, Odoric of PORDENONE, and John de' Marignolli. Of these missionaries, Jordanus of Sévérac and Odoric of Pordenone were probably the most important. Jordanus of Sévérac achieved distinction as a French Dominican missionary and explorer in India and was elevated to the rank of bishop in 1330. In addition to his missionary activities he is remembered for a geographical treatise entitled *Mirabilia*. This work contains a wealth of information on various regions of India, including their principal products, the manners and customs of the people, and the flora and fauna of the country. Probably this account is the best description of India during the Middle Ages written by a Westerner. Friar Odoric visited India, Ceylon, and some of the islands in the East Indies and spent at least 3 years in Peking. His return journey to the West was made by the long and difficult land route. Odoric's account of his travel experiences attracted much attention from contemporaries and enjoyed a favorable reputation similar to that of Marco Polo's description in the previous century.

Besides missionaries various commercial travelers also made valuable contributions to geographical knowledge. Around 1313 Marino Sanudo, who had spent many years in the Near East, prepared an important descriptive treatise on Palestine and embellished his narrative with a number of maps. A Genoese named Pietro Vesconte, who later moved to Venice, collaborated with Sanudo in this important work. The Florentine traveler Francesco Balducci Pegolotti, who also lived for many years in the Near East, wrote his *Practica della mercatura,* which was especially valuable for its discussion of fourteenth-century trade routes and its information about the imports and exports of various regions. The Venetian merchant Nicolò di Conti is probably the most famous of Western commercial travelers to the East during the later Middle Ages. He began his extensive travels from the Syrian city of Damascus, where he had stayed for some time to learn Arabic. His eastward journeys included the Arabian Desert, Mesopotamia, Persia, India, Ceylon, Burma, Sumatra, Java, and the Malay Peninsula. On his return journey he visited Calicut, Socotra, Aden, Jidda (Juddah), and Cairo, finally arriving in Venice in 1444 after an absence of 25 years. At the insistence of Pope Eugenius IV he dictated the report of his incredible travels to the famous humanist Poggio Bracciolini, a secretary at the papal court. This detailed account of southern Asia is one of the best ever written by a European during the Middle Ages.

Eastern Europe in the thirteenth and fourteenth centuries Geographical exploration and colonization efforts in Eastern Europe during the thirteenth and fourteenth centuries were mainly the work of the Order of Teutonic Knights (Deutscher Ritterorden). Originally established in the Holy Land during the Third Crusade as a military religious order for members of the German nobility, this militant organization later transferred its activities to Prussia and the shores of the eastern Baltic, undertaking with great zeal the conquest of land then occupied by various Slavic tribes. Emperor Frederick II granted members of the order extensive privileges in the Golden Bull of Rimini (1226), and in this document the grand master also received the same rights as a prince of the empire. In 1237 the Teutonic Knights merged with another group known as the Livonian Knights, a famous order which had been founded about 1202 by Albert, bishop of Riga.

The members of the combined orders made important geographical advances in Eastern Europe. Prussia was eventually conquered, rural and urban colonization successfully carried out, and centralized authority with an elaborate officialdom effectively established. In the course of this military expansion new

towns were founded, among them Thorn (Toruń), Memel (Klaipėda), Marienburg (Malbork), and Königsberg ("the King's city"; now Kaliningrad), named in honor of the warrior monarch Ottokar II (d. 1278), king of Bohemia. Marienburg, on the Nogat River southest of Danzig (Gdańsk), became the seat of the grand master *(Hochmeister)* in 1309. The important city of Reval (Tallinn) was purchased from Denmark in 1346. A steady flow of German immigrants, particularly of merchants and peasants, came into those districts where the native population had been killed or driven even farther east. Pacification of this area facilitated the rapid expansion of trade in the eastern Baltic on the part of the Hansa, and the settlement of the eastern marches (*Ostmarken*) laid the foundations for the growth of the modern state of Brandenburg-Prussia. The *Drang nach Osten* of the Teutonic Knights reached the zenith of its success during the fourteenth century and marked a significant chapter in the history of geographical expansion and Eastern colonization. This thrust into the northeast may be considered one of the last major phases of exploration and conquest on the European continent during the later Middle Ages. As a consequence of this expansion the area of habitable German territory increased enormously.

Role of fables and legends Remarkable in the history of late medieval expansion is the role played by the fabulous in influencing and directing the course of geographical exploration. Tradition peopled the earth with strange animals and weird and monstrous races of men. Legends induced some explorers to seek the elusive land of OPHIR, allegedly the source of much of the gold and jewels of the court of King Solomon. Others were lured by the reports of the kingdom of PRESTER JOHN, a Christian state said to be of enormous size and incredible opulence, variously located in Mongolia, China, India, and finally East Africa. In this kingdom there were reputedly rivers of gold and of silver, amazons and centaurs, a curious race of shrinking giants, and a wonderful fountain of life which imparted youthful vigor to those who bathed in its soothing waters.

Many of the fables which generally circulated in the later Middle Ages seemed to be localized in the area called India, long considered a land of mystery and one abundantly filled with astonishing wonders and strange marvels. There, it was said, could be found pygmies and giants, horned wild men who grunted like pigs, men who had dog's heads and barked and snarled, and men who had no heads at all but who did have eyes in their stomachs. The word *India* in the Middle Ages had no precise geographical meaning to most Europeans but rather served as a convenient way to refer to that part of the East beyond the Muslim world of the eastern Mediterranean.

One of the most important compilations of travelers' tales, fables, and anecdotes of the Near, Middle, and Far East in this period was the pseudonymous work of "Sir John Mandeville." This compilation presented much fanciful material and bizarre descriptions of exotic places. Written in an entertaining style, it was widely read in manuscript in the fifteenth century and in printed form in the sixteenth. Although prepared originally in French, the work was soon translated into English and other Western European languages, and the stories which it contained greatly stimulated interest in geographical exploration.

One of the persistent and curious legends of this period concerned an island in the Atlantic Ocean where seven cities allegedly were located. Common belief held that to this place seven bishops, together with many Christian followers, had fled from Moorish Spain, trying to find a secure place of refuge. According to the legend, the descendants of these early migrants lived peacefully in the seven cities, practicing faithfully Christian virtues and enjoying economic prosperity. To find this island with its happy inhabitants and its reputed wealth was the hope and dream of many Iberian navigators during the fourteenth and fifteenth centuries. Sailors' yarns always insisted on the reality of these mysterious cities, which some seamen even claimed they had sighted on the far-distant horizon of the Atlantic Ocean. Other accounts reported that in the mid-sixth century the Irishman St. BRENDAN in traveling westward had discovered somewhere in the Atlantic a beautiful and fertile island where strange marvels could be seen. For centuries this island, although never found, continued to be located on scientific maps. Medieval writers also commented on the existence of the terrestrial paradise, which supposedly was situated so far in the East that it was also to be found at the extreme end of the West.

The influence of such a large body of myth, legend, and fiction cannot be discounted in considering the motivation for geographical exploration during the Middle Ages and the Renaissance. In the pursuit of the fabulous, the remote, and the unknown, men were willing to endure incredible hardships and suffering and themselves encounter strange and unusual experiences which perhaps were almost as remarkable as the objectives that first had inspired them to take such calculated risks.

BIBLIOGRAPHY: Leo Bagrow, *History of Cartography*, rev. and enl. by R. A. Skelton, Cambridge, Mass., 1964; John N. L. Baker, *A History of Geographical Discovery and Exploration*, new ed., rev., New York, 1937; William K. Ferguson, *Europe in Transition: 1300 to 1520*, Boston, 1962; George H. T. Kimble, *Geography in the Middle Ages*, London, 1938; Arthur P. Newton, *Travel and Travellers of the Middle Ages*, New York, 1930; Wilcomb E. Washburn, "The Meaning of 'Discovery' in the Fifteenth and Sixteenth Centuries," *American Historical Review*, vol. LXVIII, October 1962, pp. 1–21.

Bernerd C. Weber

Messerschmidt, Daniel Gottlieb (1685–1735) German scientist in Russian service, traveler, and explorer in Siberia. Messerschmidt completed the course in medicine at the University of Halle, acquiring great knowledge for that time of natural history, geography, archaeology, and other sciences. In 1716 he was called by Peter the Great to St. Petersburg, where he contracted to go to Siberia to study "the geography of the country, natural history, medicine, medicinal plants, and epidemic diseases, and to describe the Siberian peoples, philology, monuments, antiquities and all other unusual things." He worked first alone, and then had the Swedish prisoner of war Tabbert (Strahlenberg) assigned to him. He collected plants, mounted birds and made drawings of them, determined at each prominent place the height of the polestar, and made maps. He requested the Siberian authorities to turn over to him all antiquities including pagan idols, mammoth bones, and old Kalmyk and Tatar manuscripts, collected words from the languages of the Siberian natives, and was the first to understand the historic importance of their relationships. The results of his 7 years of travel are in ten volumes of manuscript, in Latin, which have never been published. They remain, together with his collections, in the Academy of Sciences. He married in St. Petersburg and lived in poverty during his last years.

Richard A. Pierce

Good luck rather than good leadership guided Thomas Mitchell's expeditions to valuable discoveries of fertile pastureland in Australia. [Australian Information Service]

Mexico See WEST INDIES, CENTRAL AMERICA, AND MEXICO.

Milton, Viscount (William Fitzwilliam) See CHEADLE, WALTER BUTLER, AND MILTON, VISCOUNT.

Mitchell, Thomas Livingstone (1792–1855) Australian explorer and surveyor. Born at Craigend, Stirlingshire, Scotland, on June 15, 1792, Mitchell worked with his colliery-owning uncle before joining the British Army and serving under Wellington in the Peninsular War, chiefly as a surveyor and draftsman. Appointed deputy surveyor general of New South Wales in 1827, he took control of the survey department on the death of John OXLEY in May 1828 and immediately initiated an extensive program of road and bridge building. But this failed to satisfy his overwhelming ambition or to overcome his jealousy of the achievements of Charles STURT, and he made preparations to go exploring.

He led four expeditions, all of them conducted with military precision and all of them influenced by his belief that northern Australia contained a mighty river which would link the settled southeast with the riches of Asia. The first two expeditions (1831 and 1835) were connected with Charles Sturt's 1828–1829 discovery of the Darling, which Mitchell thought was the "mighty river" he sought. They added little to existing knowledge. The third (1836) was also a follow-up to Sturt's discoveries, for Mitchell was instructed to determine whether the Darling flowed into the Murray, as Sturt thought. Largely disregarding his instructions, a practice he perfected throughout his official life, Mitchell swept farther southward to discover the fertile Western District of Victoria. His final expedition (1845–1846) was intended to be the first crossing of the continent from Sydney to Port Essington (Darwin) but beaten by Friedrich Wilhelm Ludwig LEICHHARDT, Mitchell continued north into the fertile plains of central Queensland. On his return journey, he was greatly relieved to come across a broad stream flowing northwest. Convinced that this was the headwaters of the river that flowed into the Joseph Bonaparte Gulf 1250 miles (2011 kilometers)

away, he named it the Victoria. It was actually the Barcoo, as his assistant Edmund Kennedy discovered a year later, and ends in the desert wastes surrounding Lake Eyre.

Mitchell's explorations were not particularly significant or difficult, but he had the good fortune to discover excellent agricultural and pastoral land, for which he was richly rewarded. He made several trips to Britain to publish his exploration journals and to seek the knighthood he received in 1838. He died of pneumonia in Sydney on October 5, 1855, while a royal commission was inquiring into major shortcomings in the survey department he had ruled for the previous 27 years.

BIBLIOGRAPHY: J. H. L. Cumpston, *Thomas Mitchell: Surveyor General and Explorer*, London, 1954.

J. M. R. Cameron

Modern Exploration: Fifteenth to Seventeenth Century

The impulse for European discovery and exploration in the early modern period may be said to have emanated from several sources; chief among them were the eternal goals and goads of mankind. In addition, from time to time there has been proposed a theory stressing what might be termed the inexorable westward movement of mankind and, more particularly, the ideas and ideals of Western, that is, European civilization. It should always be borne in mind that discovery and exploration were European, specifically Western European, movements; Europe was not an attraction for China, India, or Japan.

Motivation The reasons why men set forth in ships to explore the unknown and the conjectural might well be joined to the question of why the era of early modern exploration occurred *when* it did. Certainly, one of the most important and felicitous concatenations in the history of civilization was the development of printing by Johann Gutenberg and the consequent spread of knowledge, especially geographical knowledge, which occurred coincidentally with the European desire to expand horizons. Academic treatises on geography, cosmography, cartography, and navigation, Arabic works, and travelers' tales may not have ben "popular" literature, but their dissemination was widespread and their availability made possible the systematic organization of voyages of discovery. Christopher COLUMBUS, for example, is known to have read the *Imago mundi* of Pierre Cardinal D'Ailly, a compendium of astronomical knowledge published in 1480–1483, in which the conclusion that China was little more than 3000 miles (4828 kilometers) west of the Canary Islands was reached. He also owned Aeneas Sylvius's *Historia rerum ubique gestarum*, a description of Asia published at Venice in 1477 which was largely a digest of PTOLEMY

but which differed on one important point: a belief in the circumnavigability of Africa. *The Book of Messer Marco Polo* was the most popular and influential book of its genre. This account of the East was widely read and certainly stimulated interest in travel and exploration.

As one historian of the age of discovery, John Parry, insists, the fifteenth-century explorers were practical men who sought not new lands but new routes to old lands. Thus, the motivations for the great discoveries and explorations of this period have been euphoniously, if simplistically, listed as God, glory, and gold. This trinitarian motivation, however, overlooks a primal force: thirst for knowledge. Simple curiosity, knowledge for its own sake, which has blessedly afflicted humans ever since the creation, is the basis of modern scientific exploration. Another historian, J. H. Plumb, has written of an "inner dynamic of exploration which has a long, long Atlantic history stretching back to the Vikings."

Messianic Christianity, the desire to spread the Gospels and convert the heathen, was a factor which affected some men more than others. Certainly, Prince HENRY of Portugal was imbued with religious zeal, and Columbus seems to have had powerful Christian inspiration for his project. It should be noted that the allurement of bringing Christ to the unbelieving indigenous populations also embraced an unhealthy dose of fierce anti-Islamism, tinctured with hatred and violence. Christopher Columbus sought the gold of the Indies not merely for reasons of greed but also as the means of financing a last crusade which would liberate Jerusalem and the Holy Sepulcher. Arnold Toynbee, when he ascribed the westward expansion of Iberia to the consequences of "Syraic pressure" exerted on the peninsula by the Moors, held this view. Spaniards considered the Indies a combination of consolation prize and trophy from God for their centuries of struggle against the Moorish infidels and compensation for their losses and the losses of the church.

In his *Quest for Eastern Christians* (1962), Francis M. Rogers emphasized another aspect of the religious allure: the desire for union with distant Christians in the East (India and Ethiopia), knowledge of whom existed from the earliest days of Christianity. Vasco da GAMA, when queried as to why he had come to India, is supposed to have replied "Christians and spices." The legend of PRESTER JOHN, a rich and powerful potentate reigning in Central Africa, was persistent and strong. The domains of this paragon of Christianity, according to legend, constituted a paradise where rivers flowed with gold, jewels abounded, and a fountain of youth poured forth the elixir sought by humanity since the beginning of time. He was supposed to have controlled not only vast wealth but also thousands of warriors who would be available for the reconquest of Jerusalem. It does not matter that the reality of this legend turned out to be a minor native ruler, the Negus of Ethiopia. The desire to find and reunite with members of the faith was a powerful stimulus. And according to Samuel Eliot Morison, another quest which was never attained was for "some 'land of pure delight where saints immortal reign'; where (in the words of Isaac Watts's hymn) 'everlasting spring abides, and never fading flowers.'" The search of Juan PONCE DE LEÓN for a fountain of youth may well have been motivated by this impulse.

Glory, as an impetus for discovery and exploration, takes two forms, the national, which spurred those who wanted to claim new lands for the glory of their country, and the personal. As the great Spanish philosopher Miguel de Unamuno posited, the most basic human desire is for immortality. In its most sublime form, this quest can bring forth the most unselfish qualities, resulting in boons for humanity; in its worst form, the most self-serving forms of self-glorification: the naming of a continent, a river, or a cape or the acquisition of a title. "Ego tripping" may be a term coined in the 1970s; it is singularly appopriate when applied to some mariners of the sixteenth and seventeenth centuries.

Above all, the reasons for discovery and exploration were economic in nature. The Turkish capture of Constantinople in 1453 jeopardized overland trade routes to the East. The search in Africa for the mythical Prester John conveniently included a search for the sources of the gold which had been transported across the Sahara to North African centers. By the time da Gama sailed, spices were an important reason for finding a sea route to the Indies. Food was incredibly dull in Western Europe, and means of preservation other than salting and pickling did not exist. Spices such as pepper enhanced the flavor of food made dull by desiccation and smoking, while cloves were useful for preserving. The Venetians held a mo-

nopoly on the overland spice trade and exacted high prices. Therefore, it should not be considered strange that Europeans developed colonies, enclaves, entrepôts, and suzerainties for their economic value. Trade followed the flag. Extractive industries such as mining, timber cutting, and fishing were the common pursuits. And the importance of land itself cannot be overestimated. Land was desired for the cultivation of valuable commodities, for occupation and settlement, for prestige, and for security. In addition, the royal houses of Europe always coveted land for dynastic purposes.

Breadth of vision, coupled with greed, then becomes the keynote of the age of discovery. The cosmic human restlessness, the intense curiosity about the world, and the need to implement the incentives provided by a freely soaring spirit drove the discoverers abroad not only to seek answers to metaphysical questions but to fulfill economic and political needs as well.

The Portuguese Early modern discovery, that is, systematic and not merely accidental discovery, may be said to have begun with the voyages commissioned by the Portuguese Prince Henry the Navigator. The establishment of his school at Sagres on Cabo de São Vicente resulted in the coordination of knowledge in the fields of cartography, ship design and construction, astronomy, navigational instruments, and weaponry. Henry himself probably never went to sea, and the school at Sagres was not an academy in the sense that men enrolled as students for courses or formal training. It was, rather, a postgraduate seminar where experts were gathered by Henry for intensive study and discussion and where mariners became acquainted with the latest developments in the navigational arts. Here maps and charts were updated with the return of the captains sent out by Henry to advance the frontiers of geographical knowledge. A definite connection thus exists between European technological developments and overseas exploration and expansion.

Map making was, to say the least, an inexact science in the Middle Ages. Without the knowledge necessary for drawing an accurate representation, cartographers let imagination fill the gaps. The so-called *mappa mundi* centered on Jerusalem and were Christian in purpose. Ptolemaic maps, accurate in their depiction of Europe and the North African coastline, portrayed the Indian Ocean as an inland sea and contained vast masses of *terrae incognitae*. Practical seamen attempted to remedy this state of affairs by drawing portolan charts. Essentially accurate coastal depictions with loxodromes, or rhumb lines, drawn from port to port, these were sufficient for use in the Mediterranean

When Prince Henry sent his ships down the West African coast, the concept of latitude was developed. A line was drawn on the meridian of Cabo de São Vicente, and this served as a reference point against which explorers could mark and measure their ac-

Prince Henry the Navigator. Though he probably never went to sea, his school for the navigational arts trained the Portuguese captains who colonized the Cape Verde Islands and reached Sierra Leone.

complishments. However, the determination of latitude by celestial observation was very difficult. The instrument available for this purpose was the astrolabe, consisting of a sighting device, a plumb line, and a degree scale. The angle which the North Star makes with the horizon is the latitude. Not only was this difficult to determine from the deck of a ship, but it became impossible south of the equator when the North Star disappears. This problem was overcome by Portuguese Jewish astronomers, especially Abraham Zacuto, who developed a method of calculating latitude by measuring the height of the sun at noon. In 1478 an almanac which calculated the sun's declination, the distance of its zenith from the equator on each day, was compiled. By the end of the fifteenth century, the quadrant, a simpler instrument than the astrolabe, had been developed, and navigators, having agreed on a fairly accurate length of a degree of latitude (actually 69 statute miles, or 111 kilometers), could plot their positions and observations. A solution to the problem of the determination of longitude, dependent upon the development of a very accurate timepiece, was not made until the latter part of the eighteenth century, too late to play a role in the early period of the age of discovery.

The design of ships improved tremendously during the fifteenth century, a development which augured well for oceanic exploration. When trade was confined to inland seas such as the Black Sea and the Mediterranean, oared galleys were preferred for the obvious reason that they were not dependent upon the vagaries of the wind. Sailing ships were square-rigged, a fact which for the most part limited their usefulness to periods when the wind was astern. The Portuguese adapted the lateen sail from the Arabs. This triangular sail enabled a ship to cope better with head winds and follow the contours of coastlines. Constant refinements and improvements were made until the best features of both riggings, square and lateen, were combined in one vessel, the *caravela redonda*, which dominated the period of discovery and exploration until the Spanish *nau*, a much larger ship, was developed. The search for the ideal ship was a continuing one. This ship had to be a vessel that could go anywhere, and at the same time it had to be large enough to carry the crew necessary for the operation of the ship, supplies and provisions to sustain them, and, of course, sufficient cargo space to hold the cargoes to be traded and those to be bought and brought home.

The development of new forms of weaponry must also be considered, for discovery and exploration, more often than not, involved the conquest and subjugation of native peoples. It was the superiority of their guns and firepower which enabled the numerically inferior Europeas to overcome the resistance of indigenous people to their incursions. Innovations in naval weaponry, such as the cutting of portholes for cannon, not only increased capacity but also aided stability. A human element which is always part of warfare is morale. The fanaticism with which the Portuguese, especially, were imbued should not be underrated as a factor. Spanish soldiers charging into battle crying "Santiago" were fearsome enough. When astride horses, an unknown and strange combination in the Americas, they were fearsome beyond belief.

Portuguese sea captains, under Prince Henry's tutelage, began their quest for the sea route to the Indies after the conquest of Ceuta on the Moroccan Mediterranean coast in 1415. The discovery (or rediscovery) and colonization of Madeira and the Azores was achieved during the last years of the first quarter of the fifteenth century. However, the first major accomplishment of the Portuguese was the doubling of Cabo Bojador in 1434. Until this comparatively insignificant geographical, but formidable psychological, barrier on the West African coast had been overcome, men had believed it to mark the extreme southern limit of the navigable Atlantic. During Henry's lifetime the Cape Verde Islands were reached and colonized, and in the year of his death, 1460, Sierra Leone was reached. Thus, the Portuguese explored approximately 1500 miles (2,414 kilometers) of the West African coastline.

With John II (r. 1481–1495), the Portuguese found their second great royal patron of discovery. The voyages of Diogo Cão (1482–1484 and 1485–1486) continued the exploration of the African coast south of the Congo River. In 1487 the King sent Pero da Covilhã (Covilham) on an overland journey to India and Ethiopia. Covilhã obtained information of the most precious sort, namely, that an ocean route around Africa did indeed exist. The same year witnessed the departure by sea of Bartolomeu Dias. In the first

Shipwrecked Europeans building a new vessel. Though the seaworthiness of ships improved tremendously during the fifteenth century, the sea remained a formidable adversary. [Library of Congress]

weeks of 1488 he rounded the Cape of Good Hope, and to him belongs the credit for finding the key to the ocean route to the Indies. A querulous crew forced Dias to turn back soon after he had entered the Indian Ocean. However, it was now known that the coastline stretched unmistakably northward, and the route remained for the next explorer to exploit.

The Portuguese did not capitalize upon Dias's accomplishment for a decade. Finally, in July 1497, under the patronage of Manuel I the Fortunate, Vasco da Gama left Lisbon on what was to be one of the most important sea voyages in history. Although he did not follow Dias's pathfinding route, da Gama doubled the Cape of Good Hope in November 1497. In April 1498 he reached Malindi on the East African coast, where he secured the services of an experienced pilot, and reached Calicut on the Malabar (western) coast of India almost a month later. The Portuguese, under Pedro Álvares CABRAL, reached the Brazilian coast on the way to India in 1500. Their overseas expansion, from South America to the East Indies, was severely limited by considerations of manpower; the total population of the home country was probably less than 2 million. Nevertheless, the opening years of the sixteenth century saw the beginnings of modern empire building in the East at Goa, Muscat, and Malacca under Afonso de Albuquerque. Macao, an entrepôt on the Chinese coast, was founded in 1557, and even Japan was penetrated before 1550. As the great epic poet of the Portuguese, Luis Vaz de Camões, wrote in *Os Lusiadas*, "If there had been more of the world they would have discovered it" (Canto VII, 14).

A major turning point in the history of the world had been reached. Discovery was no longer to be the province of individuals. Western European governments were now actively engaged, often in partnership with private banking houses and merchant companies, in the planning and financing of voyages to find new routes to the sources of spices, gold, slaves, and other riches. Furthermore, exploration during the sixteenth century was to be almost exclusively oceanic. The sea, not overland routes, was to be the highway of the Western world.

The Spanish The Portuguese exploitation of their discovery of the Cape of Good Hope water route to the Indies was followed by the Dutch, English, and French in the erection of colonial empires in the East and almost simultaneously by the Spanish in the Western Hemisphere.

Christopher Columbus, an Italian navigator, believed that Asia could be reached by sailing west. His reading of such works as Pierre d'Ailly's *Imago mundi* convinced him that China was approximately 3000 miles (4828 kilometers) due west of the Canaries. He attempted to secure aid from the Portuguese crown. Failing to get the necessary financial backing from John II, he departed for Spain, where he arrived at a propitious moment, for the country was approaching unity after years of turmoil. A dynastic marriage had taken place, and Ferdinand of Aragon and Isabella of Castile were remodeling the internal machinery of the country, modernizing the army, and expelling the last of the Moors from the Iberian Peninsula. Columbus's proposals were carefully, although dilatorily, considered. What seems to have been decisive in securing royal approval was the willingness of Genoese merchants, resident in Seville, to supply financial backing; Isabella's willingness to pawn her jewels is one of the better-known fictions of history and little more. The Spanish crown thus had nothing to lose and, literally, a world to gain.

The first Columbian voyage was a comparatively uneventful cruise which "discovered" the major islands of the West Indies, Cuba and Hispaniola. The significance of this voyage was even more profound than da Gama's subsequent discovery of the sea route to the East Indies. This was soon evident when the Spanish monarchs attempted to secure a monopoly for Spanish exploration in the western Atlantic from Pope Alexander VI. His response was in 1493 to issue four papal bulls, the essence of which was to confirm Castile's rights of discovery in the West as long as they did not infringe upon the rights of another Christian ruler. A north-south line of demarcation along a meridian 100 leagues west of the Azores and Cape Verde Islands was drawn. Spain was awarded all lands west and south of the line; Portugal was given all lands east and south.

The Portuguese, alarmed and angry (the Pope was a Spaniard, Rodrigo Borgia), opened direct negotiations with the Spaniards which led to the signing of the Treaty of Tordesillas in 1494. Under the terms of this document, the line of demarcation was set 370 leagues west of the Cape Verdes, thus granting to Portugal all of Africa, India, and, as a result of Cabral's discovery in 1500, Brazil.

King Ferdinand II of Aragon points across the Atlantic, while Columbus and his three ships prepare to land in the New World. [Library of Congress]

Columbus made three additional voyages to the Western Hemisphere, during which he explored the West Indies and the coastlines of Central and northern South America. Although he must have known that he had not reached the spice islands of *the* Indies, he never publicly acknowledged his failure to reach Asia and died an embittered man.

Columbus was followed to the New World by a succession of navigators, discoverers, explorers, and conquistadores. The age of discovery was in full bloom. In rapid succession Newfoundland, Labrador, and the North American coast were reached by English ships in 1497 and 1498. The Spaniards Alonso de OJEDA and Vicente Yáñez PINZÓN explored the South American coast in 1499 and 1500. Rodrigo de Bastidas attempted to colonize in Central America in 1501, and from 1499 to 1501 Amerigo VESPUCCI made his controversial voyages of discovery during which he may have explored as far south as the Río de la Plata. What may be termed the second great landmark in American discovery took place in 1513, when Vasco Núñez de BALBOA became the first European to set eyes on the Pacific Ocean from its eastern shore. The geographical significance of his discovery is that North and South America were now recognized as separate continents, separated from the "old world" by two oceans. In the same year, Juan Ponce de León made his first expedition to Florida in search of the legendary fountain of youth.

In 1519 two events of momentous consequence began. One, the voyage of Ferdinand MAGELLAN, a Portuguese sailing under the Spanish flag, ended 3 years later in the first circumnavigation of the world. Magellan, like Columbus, offered his services to the Spaniards after having been turned down by the Portuguese, his idea being a western route to the spice islands which would enable Spain to challenge Portuguese hegemony in that area. His voyage proved that, in John H. Parry's words, "all the seas of the world are one," but his route was not commercially useful. The second event of this portentous year took place on land: the invasion by Hernán CORTÉS of Mexico, where he discovered and conquered an empire which had attained an advanced degree of civilization and possessed enormous wealth.

The consequences of the discovery of Mexico and the resultant influx of wealth into Spain transformed the nature of the era and necessitated the establishment of a political and economic infrastructure for an American empire, a process which was to be extended and enlarged when Francisco PIZARRO conquered the fabulously rich Inca empire, centered in Peru, in the 1530s. Viceroys were sent to rule over the new territories in the name of the crown. *Corregidores* and *alcaldes mayores,* governors of municipal districts, were more directly involved in colonial administration. An *audiencia,* or high court of review, checked on their performance and exercised considerable power in other ways. *Encomiendas* and *repartimientos* for the assignment and distribution of Indian labor

Columbus and his men among the Indians at Isla de Margarita in the Caribbean. In the foreground Indians dive for oysters. [Library of Congress]

to individuals were established. A host of other bureaucratic institutions and individuals were necessary for the efficient administration of this vast new land and its agricultural and mineral wealth. The church also expanded its activities, being ever concerned with the souls of both the conquerors and the conquered.

The Dutch, French, and English   While the Spaniards were making their discoveries at sea and exploring the interiors of the North and South American continents and the Portuguese continued to consolidate their positions in the East, the latter part of the sixteenth century and the beginning of the seventeenth century saw the English and Dutch becoming the principal participants in exploration activity. The capture of Malacca by the Dutch in 1641 ended the period of Portuguese suzerainty in the East. The successful siege was the culmination of years of activity which effectively began with the voyage of Jan Huyghen van Linschoten to Portuguese India in 1583. His remarkable *Itinerario* (1596) inspired his countrymen to exert themselves to enter the spice trade. Led by Jan Pieterszoon Coen, governor-general of the East Indies, the Dutch achieved feats of greatness mainly because of supremacy developed on the high seas. The Netherlanders deserve credit for the discovery of Cape Horn, thus finding a new western passage to the East Indies. The Dutch had but one motive for their voyages of exploration: profit. In 1602, to facilitate their quest, they founded the East India Company, a private monopoly with close governmental ties. Their single-mindedness is evidenced not only by the large numbers of traders who went to the Indies but also by the almost complete absence of clergymen. The Dutch were singularly successful in their commercial activity in the East Indies, spurning opportunities to take possession of either Australia or New Zealand, which offered no commercial possibilities. They colonized and controlled their island empire until World War II.

The Netherlands also expanded its commercial empire to the Western Hemisphere, where the Dutch put down, if not roots, at least footholds. They established themselves in the present-day states of New York and New Jersey as well as in Brazil and the West Indies. The Dutch West India Company, though, was never as successful as its counterpart in the East Indies for many reasons, not the least of which was the infinitely superior wealth of the latter area. Furthermore, the rise of Great Britain and France eventually forced the withdrawal from the North American continent and a general colonial contraction.

The French had made sporadic attempts at discovery in the sixteenth century, culminating in the arrival of Jacques CARTIER in Canada on three voyages during 1534–1542. The area was not conducive to European colonization, and new attempts were made in Brazil in 1555 and in Florida in 1564. However, it was not until 1603, when Samuel de CHAMPLAIN sailed up the St. Lawrence River, that French efforts began to bear fruit. Missionary activity was an important part of the French pioneering experience in Canada, although, because of the indifference of the Indians, it cannot be said that the results were gratifying.

The exploratory ventures of the French in the North American heartland constitute their greatest accomplishments during the latter half of the seventeenth century. The missionaries expanded geographical horizons better than theological ones in the Great Lakes area. Father Jacques Marquette, accompanied by a fur trader, Louis JOLLIET, descended the Mississippi River, a feat also accomplished by Robert de LA SALLE, who reached the Gulf of Mexico and named a large portion of the continent Louisiana.

The seventeenth and eighteenth centuries saw the French gain footholds in Senegal in West Africa and the large Indian Ocean island of Madagascar. On the Indian subcontinent they established enclaves, such as Pondichéry on the Coromandel coast, some of which were held until the twentieth-century independence movement. However, enmity with Britain was to prove to be the undoing of the French. The commercial superiority of the British and their vaunted power on the waves eventually drove the French effectively from the Indian subcontinent and the North American continent. French hearts never seemed to be in empire building; their efforts were either too little or too late.

England embarked on overseas discovery and exploration in earnest more than a century after the Spanish and Portuguese began to find new lands and new routes to old lands, although a Genoese, John CABOT, left Bristol in 1497 on a voyage which took him and probably his son Sebastian CABOT to North America. Other voyages were made by Englishmen in an attempt to find a NORTHWEST PASSAGE or a NORTHEAST PASSAGE during the sixteenth century, but without success in either direction. Ice effectively blocked all such attempts for centuries. After the accession of Elizabeth to the throne in 1558, Martin FROBISHER, John DAVIS, Henry HUDSON, and William BAFFIN continued the search for a navigable Northwest Passage, a search which was not to be rewarded, and even then not profitably, until the twentieth century.

Francis DRAKE, sailing on what was essentially a grand expedition of piracy, circumnavigated the globe between 1577 and 1580. This was the first time Magellan's voyage had been replicated. Although Drake's voyage was a magnificent feat of seamanship and derring-do, it did not open any new geographical frontiers. Nor did it establish England as an overseas power.

Humphrey GILBERT and Walter Raleigh attempted to found colonies in North America during the last decades of the sixteenth century, but both failed. It was not until 1607 that the first permanent English colony was established at Jamestown, Virginia, and it

John Cabot and his son Sebastian discovering Newfoundland in 1497. Like Columbus a Genoese, Cabot also sailed under a foreign flag—the English. [Library of Congress]

was not a rousing success. Thirteen years later, in 1620, the *Mayflower* arrived with a party of religious dissenters who founded a colony at Plymouth, Massachusetts. Probably the most famous of all American settlements, it was soon annexed by the more prosperous and powerful Massachusetts Bay colony.

Additional settlements were made on the North American coast by various groups of Englishmen. Far more valuable were the West Indian ventures of the English trading companies. Engaged in monocultural farming, with the burden of the work being done by slaves imported from Africa, these plantations continued to supply the mother country with profits until well into the twentieth century.

In India the English East India Company began its operations during the first years of the seventeenth century. Although the English could not obtain a foothold in the spice islands, after the Seven Years' War (1756–1763) they drove out the French and established an all-powerful hegemony on the subcontinent which endured until after World War II.

The great age of oceanic discovery may be said to have run its course by the middle of the eighteenth century. Few coasts remained to be explored and most of them were visited by the greatest navigator who ever lived, the Englishman James COOK, who made three remarkable voyages during the years 1768–1779 and filled in most of the blanks on the map. The contribution of the Frenchman Louis-Antoine de BOUGAINVILLE during the years 1766–1769 also helped to answer some of the Europeans' geographical questions.

Effect Europeans left their homelands and took risks and faced dangers beyond present-day comprehension for profit, glory, escape, and even altruistic reasons. Some areas of the world were settled; some were plundered. The European empires brought progress and uplifted the indigenous inhabitants in many instances. However, the price was often enslavement or extinction and, almost always, loss of native culture. The early modern period of discovery was a triumph of oceanic and navigational and scientific expertise which enabled the white Christian peoples of Western Europe to exert their dominance over the colored races of the rest of the world for three centuries. Even after European political control ended, the cultural and religious legacies remained. *See also* CARTOGRAPHY; MARITIME EXPLORATION.

BIBILIOGRAPHY: J. N. L. Baker, *A History of Geographical Discovery and Exploration*, 2d ed., London, 1937; reprinted New York, 1967; C. R. Boxer, *The Dutch Seaborne Empire: 1600–1800*, New York, 1965; id., *The Portuguese Seaborne Empire: 1415–1825*, New York, 1969; Frank Debenham, *Discovery and Exploration: An Atlas-History of Man's Journeys into the Unknown*, Garden City, N.Y., 1960; Samuel Eliot Morison, *Admiral of the Ocean Sea: A Life of Christopher Columbus*, Boston, 1942; id., *The European Discovery of America: The Northern Voyages, A.D. 500–1600*, New York, 1971; id., *The European Discovery of America: The Southern Voyages, A.D. 1492–1616*, New York, 1974; J. H. Parry, *The Age of Reconnaissance*, Cleveland, 1963; id., *The Discovery of the Sea*, New York, 1974.

Martin Torodash

Modern Exploration : Eighteenth to Twentieth Century

The history of exploration and discovery from the eighteenth to the twentieth century is a complex, ever-changing mosaic of the personal courage and daring of individual explorers set against a background of national ambitions, international rivalries, and competing economic interests. The nature, pattern, technology, and problems of geographical exploration changed dramatically during these years. The quickening pace of exploration dispelled myths that had entranced geographers for centuries and resolved problems that heretofore had defied solution. The nature of the NORTHWEST PASSAGE and the NORTHEAST PASSAGE was determined. The question of the existence of Terra Australis Incognita was answered. The sources of the Nile and Niger Rivers were found. Both poles were reached. With the exception of Antarctica, the interiors of the continents were probed and mapped. By the last quarter of the twentieth century, the fundamental features of the great oceans had been recorded, and the first tentative steps into space had been taken.

Scientific and technological advances The modern era of exploration begins with the eighteenth century, an age of reason in human thought and an age of war in human conduct. It is a creative epoch in European history with fundamental advances occurring in the sciences. Exploration profited from these scientific and technological advances. In the eighteenth century the vast stretches of the world's largest ocean, the Pacific, began to be systematically explored as a result of the evolution of marine technology and the adoption of new shipboard practices. Voyages of discovery had been restricted previously by the manifold problems of shipboard hygiene. With the publication in 1753 of James Lind's *A Treatise of the Scurvy* and its advocacy of the use of citrus fruits to prevent this common and debilitating disease, seamen began to acquire the medical knowledge necessary for the maintenance of shipboard health. The dimensions of the devastation that could be wrought by scurvy on a long voyage can be noted in the tragedy which beset George Anson (later Baron Anson) on his circumnavigation of 1740–1744. Almost two-thirds of his 961 men died of scurvy and other nautical hazards during this cruise. Fortunately for Anson's career, the wealth of plundered treasure he brought home redeemed this voyage in the eyes of the nation. Lind's work demonstrated that improper shipboard hygiene took a far greater toll of seamen's lives than did war, shipwrecks, capture, famine, or fire. In addition to a proper diet, other practices such as frequent baths for the crew, weekly washing of clothing and bedding, and periodic fumigations of the ship reduced the chances of disease and illness on long cruises. Capt. James COOK paid careful attention to the health of his men, and his missions of exploration were not handicapped as those of Vitus BERING had been with men who were dying of scurvy.

The vessels of exploration themselves changed during the 1700s. In earlier centuries awkward, bulky cargo-carrying vessels had served as ships of discovery. In the seventeenth century Dutch East Indiamen with their broad, deep hulls that could transport trade goods from Europe to Asia had carried mariners into virgin waters, but in the eighteenth century these ships were neither well enough armed or maneuverable enough to escape the attacks of men-of-war or to explore the shallow waters of a coral island. Consequently, these vessels began to be replaced by ships which were better suited to the particular needs of exploration. In the first half of the eighteenth century, when a nation's strategic goals were tied inextricably to its maritime ventures and when the possibilities of armed conflict at sea were common, warships were usually chosen as the ships of exploration. With the development of voyages of scientific exploration and of international respect for these voyages in the latter half of the century, new ships began to be utilized. Cook selected as the vessels for his voyages small, ruggedly built shallow-draft colliers (coal carriers) which, as the *Endeavour*'s grounding on the Great Barrier Reef demonstrated, possessed the strength and maneuverability to withstand the dangers of exploring uncharted coastal waters. In the nineteenth century vessels such as the *Fram* of Fridtjof NANSEN would be specially designed to meet the rigors of polar exploration. In the twentieth century the whole genius of man's technology was placed at the disposal of explorers.

The Harrison chronometer provided a simple mechanical solution to the problem of determining longitude at sea. [National Maritime Museum, Greenwich, England]

Before marine explorers could satisfy the growing requests of cartographers for precise information about the location of newly discovered islands and lands, the vexing problem of establishing a definite position at sea had to be worked out. For without the establishment of the specific location of islands, continents, or reefs it was difficult to refind them. In the Pacific, which covers approximately one-third of the earth's surface, it was almost impossible to find islands, reefs, or ice formations which reputable mariners claimed to have visited or seen. On land rivers, mountains, and deserts gave explorers coordinates, but at sea the horizon-stretching sameness of the ocean's waves failed to produce such clues to one's position. Seamen had been able roughly to calculate their latitude, their position north or south of the equator, for centuries. In 1731 the English instrument maker John Hadley brought greater accuracy to this procedure. He developed the reflecting quadrant, which allowed one to obtain accurate latitude readings down to 1 minute of an arc. Hadley's instrument

evolved into the marine sextant. While knowing latitude at sea was an important aid to mariners and explorers, they still needed to know not only their north-south position but also their east-west position.

The establishment of a system for determining longitudes was a more difficult task than that of developing a method of fixing accurate latitudes. To encourage scientists to turn their attention to this subject, the British Parliament created a prize of £20,000 for the development of an accurate and reliable method of determining longitude at sea. The principles for fixing this coordinate had been known since the fifteenth century, but instruments which would allow the consistent application of these principles were lacking.

Essentially the question of longitude is the determination of one's eastern or western position at a given moment. As the earth completes its diurnal rotation, the position of the sun changes in respect to particular locations on the earth's surface. When the sun is directly overhead, it is noon along the arc of that particular meridian; east of this location it is past noon, and west of this location it is before noon. Since the earth makes one rotation in 24 hours and since it revolves through 360 degrees, it is clear that the earth passes through 15 degrees in an hour. With an accurate timepiece and an arc of longitude which serves as the base for one's calculations, it is then possible to calculate one's longitude. Longitude can also be established by astronomical observations and calculations, but the time and complexity of this method prevented the average mariner from adopting it. The natural relationship between distance and time in the progression from one meridian of longitude to another suggested that a mechanical solution to this problem would be simpler.

An accurate chronometer for this purpose was developed and tested by John Harrison in 1762, and with the support of George III chronometers began to be used on ships of the Royal Navy. The marine chronometer was the most significant navigational instrument developed since the advent of the compass. Cook utilized chronometers during his voyages, and he became the first marine explorer who had at most times a reliable indication of his position. Initially, nations used their capitals as the basis for establishing the standard, or prime, meridian from which to calculate longitude for the ships of their countries. In 1884 the Washington Meridian Conference established the meridian of Greenwich, England, as the prime meridian for determining longitude. These developments in navigational technology were complemented by the beginning of the systematic publication of nautical almanacs which included data on coastlines, ports, reefs, and tides.

Russian expeditions to the east The growing complexity of international politics and the subsequent increasingly political and strategic demands that were attendant upon voyages of discovery brought the planning for these missions under the closer scrutiny of a nation's sovereign. In Russia, Peter the Great looked eastward, seeking to learn more about the lands that were claimed by his nation. Venturesome cossacks had wandered through much of Asiatic Russia and Siberia in the seventeenth century, and by 1696 the Kamchatka Peninsula had been reached and partially explored. A Russian attempt in 1719 to explore the connection between northeastern Asia and North America had been unsuccessful. Six months before his death in 1725, Peter the Great named Vitus Bering to the command of an expedition to determine if Asia and North America were connected and to establish a Russian priority in the area. In the course of this expedition Bering charted the Kamchatka Peninsula, encountered islands that had previously been unknown, but did not prove conclusively that a strait separates Asia from North America.

Russia's interest in its eastern provinces continued to grow. Bering returned to Okhotsk in 1734 at the head of the most ambitious Arctic expedition yet undertaken by any nation with instructions systematically to map the Arctic coast from the Obskaya Guba (Gulf of Ob) to the Anadyr River, to seek land across Bering Strait, and to investigate the Kuril Islands and the waters of Japan. The latter objectives were delegated to Bering's second-in-command, Martin Spanberg. The German naturalist Georg Wilhelm STELLER and the French astronomer Louis Delisle de la Croyère joined Bering's force. Sailing eastward, they sighted the Alaskan coast in July 1741. Steller was allowed to go ashore on Kayak Island to collect specimens of northern flora and fauna. The party discovered the Aleutian Islands, but further exploration was restricted by an outbreak of scurvy and the approach of winter.

Bering's landings upon the American coast would enable the Russians to establish a foothold in North America, and his hesistant exploration in Arctic waters began to dispel many of the erroneous ideas about the geography of the north. Steller's work was the initial chronicling of the unique flora and fauna of these high polar latitudes. During the reign of Catherine the Great, Russian interest in northwestern America increased, with settlement following the path of exploration.

French and British in the Pacific In the same decades that the Russians were learning more about the waters and coastlines of the North Pacific, the French were seeking to obtain more information about the Pacific Ocean in its southern latitudes. Near the end of the seventeenth century, France established the Compagnie Royale de la Mer Pacifique to coordinate and to encourage activities in this ocean. Frequent eighteenth-century speculation about the potential wealth of a southern continent inspired both France and Great Britain to search diligently for this land.

The existence of Terra Australis Incognita, the unknown Southern Land, had been posited by geographers since the first century A.D. Classical and Renaissance geographers assumed that a large southern landmass was needed to counterbalance the weight of Europe, Asia, and Africa in the northern half of the globe. In the context of their knowledge of the earth, it was a reasonable assumption. Renaissance cartographers included this southern continent on their maps; and since the vast dimensions of the Pacific and the inadequacies of sixteenth- and seventeenth-century navigational skills frustrated systematic exploration of that ocean, there was no proof that a wealthy, hospitable southern continent did not exist.

In France the dreams of this land were nourished by the naturalist Georges de Buffon and by Charles de Brosses. The Treaty of Paris in 1763, which brought both diplomatic humiliation and the loss of most of France's American possessions, further accentuated that nation's desire to find a prosperous southern continent which could renew its declining fortunes through trade, resources, and possibilities for settlement.

In 1766 Louis-Antoine de BOUGAINVILLE, an adherent of De Brosses's ideas on Terra Australis, set sail aboard the frigate *La Boudeuse* for a voyage of southern exploration. After discovering new islands in the Pacific archipelago of Tuamotu, he arrived at Tahiti in April 1768. He named that delightful island La Nouvelle-Cythère but then learned to his dismay that the English seaman Capt. Samuel WALLIS had been there 10 months earlier. Accompanied by the naturalist Philibert de Commerson and the astronomer Pierre-Antoine Véron, Bougainville contributed to the growing scientific awareness of the uniqueness of the Pacific Basin. Commerson discovered the presence of marsupial mammals in the East Indies, and Véron, by obtaining the longitude of the Philippine Islands, enabled geographers to begin to perceive the enormous width of the Pacific Ocean. Bougainville had not discovered the southern continent, but he had obtained important data about the Pacific, discovered new islands, and completed an arduous voyage with the loss of only seven men. The details and accomplishments of his circumnavigation were presented to the French public in his very popular *Voyage autour du monde,* which was published in 1771.

In the eighteenth century, published accounts of voyages and travels became very popular and appeared in a variety of inexpensive editions. This tradition began in England with the appearance of William Dampier's *A New Voyage round the World* in 1697. Rivaling works of theology in public popularity, these often-personal narratives of the tribulations and accomplishments of travel and discovery maintained their attraction throughout the nineteenth century and created enthusiasm for geographical exploration.

Britain's growing confidence in its abilities at sea encouraged assumption of the task of ascertaining the existence of the continent which maps testified to but which no seaman had seen. It was a Yorkshire seaman, Capt. James Cook, who shattered the illusion of the fertile, densely populated southern continent. In 1768 the 40-year-old Cook sailed the 368-ton collier

Endeavour toward the island of Tahiti to observe the transit of Venus. The Royal Society had petitioned George III for the support of a scientific expedition to observe the passage of Venus between the earth and the sun. Since this observation had to be performed in a cloudless area, Tahiti was selected. Observations of the transit collected from a variety of locations would present scientists with the data necessary for determining the distance of the sun from the earth. This information could later be used to calculate the parameters of Newton's universe.

With the successful completion of this phase of his instructions, Cook opened his sealed instructions from the Admiralty. They began with a preamble which could serve as an embodiment of British motives for global exploration: "The making of Discoverys of Countries hitherto unknown, and the attaining a knowledge of Distant Parts which though formerly discover'd have yet been but imperfectly explored, will redound greatly to the Honour of this Nation as a Maritime Power, as well as to the Dignity of the Crown of Great Britain, and may tend greatly to the advancement of the Trade and Navigation thereof." More specifically, Cook's instructions directed him to sail southward from Tahiti seeking the southern continent. If he had not discovered it by the time he reached 40°S, he was to sail westward until he reached New Zealand. In the course of a cruise which lasted from 1768 to 1771, Cook charted and sailed around New Zealand proving its insularity, discovered and charted the east coast of Australia, confirmed the existence of Torres Strait, and passed by New Guinea and Java while completing a global cir-

cumnavigation. While he had failed to find the southern continent, the successes of this first voyage were notable. The accomplishments of Cook and the naturalists Joseph Banks and Daniel Carl Solander, who had accompanied him, in geography, hydrography, ethnography, zoology, and botany were manifold.

With the question of the southern continent's existence still remaining a tantalizing mystery and with highly imaginative Englishmen such as Dr. Alexander Dalrymple maintaining that there lay in high southern latitudes a land which surpassed "the whole civilized part of Asia, from Turkey to the eastern extremity of China," attention continued to be focused on the earth's southern extremity. Dalrymple's enthusiasms were not restrained by Cook's recent experiences, and to whet the appetites of British imperial interests he observed that "the scraps from this table [the southern continent] would be sufficient to maintain the power, dominion, and sovereignty of Britain."

In France, Yves-Joseph de Kerguélen-Trémarec returned from a southern voyage to the Indian Ocean in which he had discovered the Kerguélen Islands in 1772. Naming his discovery La France Australe, he extravagantly claimed that this land would revitalize France by giving it a secure route to India, treble its maritime trade, and provide it with wood, minerals, and diamonds. Kerguélen's view of the inhabitants of this land reveals how fanciful speculations could still be in the Age of Reason. "If men of a different species are not discovered, at least there will be people in a state of nature living in their primitive manner, ignorant alike of offence and remorse, knowing nothing of the artifices of civilized society. In short, France Australe will furnish marvellous physical and moral spectacles." The edenic qualities of this land quickly disappeared when on a return visit Kerguélen had a better opportunity to examine his discovery. He then termed his cold, windswept discovery the Land of Desolation; so vanished La France Australe.

Against this background, Cook proposed a new voyage of exploration into southern waters to resolve finally the question that was so much on the public mind. Sailing in 1772 with two converted colliers, the *Resolution* and the *Adventure,* Cook again circumnavigated the globe, but this time at much higher southern latitudes. He ultimately reached 71°10′S, a latitude which was not surpassed in the eighteenth century, and he and his crew became the first men to cross the Antarctic Circle. With his return to England in 1775 after a voyage of 70,000 miles (113,000 kilometers), the myth of Terra Australis Incognita was at last laid to rest. With the use of chronometers on this voyage, Cook had been able to locate more precisely many of the island and island groups of the Pacific, including Easter Island, Tonga, New Caledonia, the Marquesas, and the New Hebrides. Charts had been prepared for portions of Tierra del Fuego, South Georgia, and the South Sandwich Islands.

Cook's third and final voyage was designed to re-

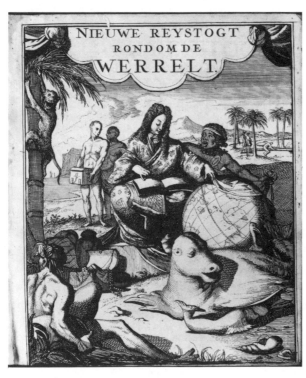

Title page of a Dutch translation of William Dampier's A New Voyage around the World, the first of many popular accounts of world travel to be published in England during the years of discovery. [Library of Congress]

NIEUWE REYSTOGT RONDOM DE WERRELT.

solve another persistent geographical mystery, the existence of the Northwest Passage, the search for which had begun in the sixteenth century. To encourage the search for the Northwest Passage, the British Parliament had offered a prize of £20,000 for the discovery of such a navigable artery from Hudson Bay. In 1776 Parliament renewed its offer, but with the stipulation that the route be beyond 52°N. Cook's plan was to sail along the Pacific coast of northwestern North America until he found an opening or passage eastward that would lead to Hudson Bay or Baffin Bay.

Sailing northward in the Pacific toward North America, Cook discovered uninhabited Christmas Island and the populous Hawaiian Islands. By March 1778, he had reached the North American coast; and by August of that year, he had passed through Bering Strait, crossed the Arctic Circle, and entered the Chukchi Sea. He reached 70°44′N before ice fields forced him to turn back. Returning to Hawaii to take up winter quarters, Cook was slain by natives on February 14, 1779. Thus died the pathfinder of the Pacific, a mariner whose agile intellect and able seamanship had led his ships on the greatest voyages of exploration since the age of discovery.

Changing motives By the beginning of the nineteenth century, the great voyages of Pacific exploration were over. The major island and island groups of this ocean had been discovered and charted. The important features of the Pacific were now known. Men had penetrated the Antarctic. While scientific discovery had been an important element in many of the expeditions of the eighteenth century, the fundamental motive for the majority of them had been the discovery of new lands and people where settlement and trade might be established to the advantage of the discoverer's nation. Patterns, motives, and areas of geographical exploration changed throughout the 1800s; and while economic and commercial advantages were sought as a by-product of discovery, other themes also appeared. Exploration for the attainment of scientific knowledge alone became common. It was the age of natural-history exploration, and naturalists traveled throughout the world seeking that which was unknown to science. At sea, the latter half of this century witnessed the rise of oceanographical exploration, culminating in the British CHALLENGER EXPEDITION of 1872–1876, the first expedition to circumnavigate the globe in order to learn more of the life and character of the ocean's depths. This century was also the era of the great Victorian explorers who left their lives and carved their deeds on the topography of all the continents.

The popularity of travel, exploration, and discovery with the general publics of European nations continued to grow. Explorers became heroes and were lionized by society. Private societies were organized to sponsor and stimulate exploration. In 1788 the AFRICAN ASSOCIATION was founded in England to support discovery in the imperfectly known continent of Africa, and in 1804 the Palestine Association was created to encourage the exploration of Syria and the Holy Land. Geographical societies naturally played a crucial role for developing and focusing public support for exploration. In 1821 the Société de Géographie of Paris was chartered, 7 years later the German Gesellschaft für Erdkunde was established at Berlin, and in 1830 the ROYAL GEOGRAPHICAL SOCIETY of London began its work. In Russia the Imperial Geographical Society of St. Petersburg was founded in 1845.

These societies promoted exploration throughout the world. Explorers wound their way through Central Asia, and the interior of Australia began to be mapped. Journeys were made into the heart of Africa. The nineteenth century was not only a century of well-organized national expeditions involving hundreds of men but also an era of exploration by singular, often ill-prepared individuals sponsored by private associations and missionary organizations.

North and South America North and South America saw more and more details of the mountains, rivers, and deserts of their interiors being added to their maps. In the United States the acquisition of the Louisiana Territory in 1803 stimulated the nation's interest in the Western lands beyond the Mississippi River. The government became a frequent sponsor of Western expeditions in the nineteenth century, and the expeditions of Meriwether LEWIS and William CLARK, Zebulon PIKE, and Stephen H. LONG marked the beginning of a long tradition. With settlers flowing into these lands in the trail of the expeditions, surveyors were required to prepare the charts, maps, and plats which would permit a semblance of orderly settlement. With national boundaries always a subject of sovereign interest, both the Canadian and the Mexican boundaries were surveyed. The desire to link the Atlantic with the Pacific Coast by transcontinental railroad led to the explorations which were attendant to the Pacific Railroad Surveys of the 1850s.

South America has always played an important role in the history of exploration, and in the eighteenth and nineteenth centuries its varied topography attracted many of Europe's most talented naturalists, including Alexander von Humboldt, Alfred Russel Wallace, Henry Bates, and Charles Darwin. It is difficult to find an area that has attracted a greater number of scientific expeditions than South America.

Among the most significant of the early scientific endeavors in South America was the French astronomical expedition of Charles-Marie de La Condamine in 1735, which saw the first descent of a section of the Amazon River by scientists and the introduction of rubber to Europe. From 1789 to 1794 a Spanish expedition under Alejandro Malaspina surveyed a large portion of the lower extremity of South America, preparing charts of the Río de la Plata and the coasts of Argentina, Brazil, Patagonia, the Malvinas

(Falkland) Islands, Tierra del Fuego, Chile, and Peru. From 1799 to 1804 Humboldt and his companion Aimé Bonpland pursued their private explorations in Venezuela, Colombia, Peru, Ecuador, Mexico, and Cuba. The fame which attended their work led Wallace, Bates, and Darwin to South America.

Africa and Asia Africa with its disparate topography and distinctive cultures was indeed the "dark continent" at the turn of the nineteenth century. Although Europeans had sailed along the perimeters of Africa for three centuries, its interior was virtually unknown. The Association for Promoting the Discovery of the Interior Parts of Africa, or more simply the African Association, had encouraged the exploration of that continent's interior since 1788. In particular, the association wished to find the course and mouth of the Niger River and the city of Timbuktu. To find the river the association sent a Scottish surgeon, Mungo PARK, on two expeditions. In July 1796 Park became the first European to see the Niger, but he was unable to follow it to its mouth. Park returned to Africa in 1805 to search once more for the mouth of the Niger, only to die in the attempt. It was not until 1830 that Richard LANDER floated down the Niger and

discovered that it flowed into the Gulf of Guinea, thereby solving the mystery of Africa's third largest river. The French explorer René CAILLIÉ achieved the other goal of the African Association. In 1828 he reached the fabled city of Timbuktu, only to be disappointed to find that it was "nothing but a mass of ill-looking houses, built of earth." With these goals fulfilled, the African Association was absorbed into the Royal Geographical Society. *See also* NIGER RIVER.

The distances involved, the presence of various debilitating diseases, and the hostility of native tribes ensured that the secrets of Central Africa would be obtained with difficulty. In 1841 the Scottish missionary David LIVINGSTONE arrived in Africa. Until his death in 1873, he devoted his energies to gaining an understanding of that continent and its peoples and to pressing for the abolition of the African slave trade. In 1849 Livingstone crossed the Kalahari Desert. A year later he discovered the upper Zambezi River. From 1853 to 1856, while crossing the continent, he encountered Victoria Falls and learned how truly varied the interior geography of Africa was. Lake Nyasa (Lake Malawi) was discovered by Livingstone in 1858. From 1866 to 1871 he discovered Lakes

The French explorer René Caillié reached the fabled city of Timbuktu in 1828, only to find an ordinary village of earthen dwellings. [Library of Congress]

Mweru and Bangweulu south of Lake Tanganyika and had his famous meeting with the *New York Herald* reporter Henry Morton STANLEY.

The sources of the Nile River were another of the fundamental mysteries of African geography. James BRUCE uncovered the headwaters of the Blue Nile in 1770, but it was not until the nineteenth century that the headwaters of the White Nile were finally discovered. The search for the sources of the White Nile involved the most illustrious names in African exploration: Livingstone, Richard BURTON, John Hanning SPEKE, Sir Samuel BAKER, and Henry Morton Stanley. Their collective efforts ultimately demonstrated the origins of Africa's greatest river. *See also* NILE RIVER: SEARCH FOR ITS SOURCE.

Explorers also traveled extensively in ARABIA and SOUTHEAST ASIA during the nineteenth century in an effort to unravel the remaining geographical mysteries of Asia, but the focal point of exploration in that continent was CENTRAL ASIA. The accumulation of geographical information about the still-unknown heartland of Asia was stimulated by the rivalry of Great Britain and Russia for influence in the area, and it was these nations which provided most of the explorers of Central Asia.

Arctic exploration   Even as the nineteenth century was a momentous period in African exploration, it was an equally significant era in polar exploration. Through much of this century, polar exploration would be essentially a British activity. Britain's interests were strategic and scientific. Concerned over the growing Russian interest in the Arctic and North Pacific, Britain wanted to demonstrate its presence in the area. Under John ROSS and Edward PARRY a British naval expedition attempted to find the Northwest Passage in 1818, but it failed to achieved its goal. Its observations of marine life in Arctic waters encouraged whalers to enter those fertile areas. Parry tried again in 1819–1820, 1821–1823, and 1824–1825, but once more success eluded him.

By 1827 the British Admiralty had shifted its attention from the Northwest Passage to seeking the North Pole. In the summer of that year, Parry began a sledge and small-boat journey from the west coast of Spitsbergen (Svalbard) toward the north. While reaching a record latitude of 82°45′N, he was prevented from reaching his goal by the drift of the ices floes. Nevertheless, this latitude was not surpassed for half a century. In 1831 a privately supported English expedition under the command of John Ross enabled Ross's nephew James Clark ROSS to discover the North Magnetic Pole.

Sir John BARROW eloquently pleaded the case for another government expedition to seek the Northwest Passage, and in 1845 the Franklin Expedition was launched. Commanded by the 59-year old Arctic veteran Sir John FRANKLIN, 129 men set forth on the best-equipped polar expedition to have left England's shores. Sailing through Davis Strait in the ships *Erebus* and *Terror*, the Franklin forces entered Lancaster

Sound. Ice prevented them from entering Wellington Channel, and consequently the first winter was spent at Beechey Island. They had supplies for three winters in the ice. During the second winter (1846–1847) they were caught in the ice of Victoria Strait. Franklin died in June 1847. After enduring the ravages of scurvy during their third winter in the ice, they decided in the spring of 1848 to abandon the ships and head for the Back River. These attempts were futile. Not a man of the expedition survived this march.

Apprehension in England about the lack of word from Franklin led to plans to initiate a search for the *Erebus* and *Terror*. From 1848 to 1859 more than forty expeditions searched for Franklin's party. By 1878 the tragic details were known, more than 7000 miles (11,265 kilometers) of Arctic coastline had been explored, and the Northwest Passage had been twice crossed by combined journeys of sledge and boat. The loss of the Franklin Expedition was the greatest disaster that Britain ever experienced in polar exploration. *See also* FRANKLIN EXPEDITION AND SEARCH.

In the latter decades of the century, other nations began to play an important role in Arctic discovery. Baron Nils Adolf Erik NORDENSKIÖLD led a Swedish contingent into polar waters seeking the Northeast Passage. Leaving Tromsø, Norway, in 1878 aboard the steam whaler *Vega*, he made the first shipboard transit through the Northeast Passage, arriving in Bering Strait in 1879.

With the growth of scientific interest in exploring the Arctic, the first International Polar Year was held in 1882. This program of research had the support of Norway, Sweden, Denmark, Russia, the Netherlands, Britain, Germany, Austria, and the United States. One of the most meticulous series of data on polar phenomena was that collected by the Norwegian explorer Fridtjof Nansen during his drift across the polar basin aboard the *Fram* in the years 1892–1896. Another young Norwegian, Roald AMUNDSEN, gained the distinction of making the first naval transit through the Northwest Passage when his *Gjøa* entered Bering Strait in 1906 after having left the waters off King William Island in 1903. The honor of being the first to reach the North Pole was claimed by the American Robert E. PEARY on April 6, 1909.

Meanwhile technology had begun to be called upon to help overcome the hazards of polar exploration. In 1897 a Swedish patent official, Salomon August Andrée, sought to fly over the North Pole in a balloon. Supported by Alfred Nobel and King Oscar II of Sweden, Andrée lifted off from Spitsbergen in a gas-filled balloon made of Chinese silk. Sixty-five hours later, the balloon came down on the ice pack. The crew was lost.

In the era after World War I, the airplane was used as a vehicle of polar exploration. The initial attempts to reach the pole by plane failed, but Comdr. Richard Evelyn BYRD and Floyd Bennett became the first men to fly over the top of the world on May 9, 1926. Between May 11 and May 14, Roald Amundsen, Gen.

Umberto Nobile, and Lincoln ELLSWORTH on board the dirigible *Norge* flew from Kongsfjorden across the North Pole to Alaska and thus successfully completed the first transpolar flight from Europe to North America.

In 1931 Sir Hubert WILKINS attempted a transpolar passage beneath the Arctic ice aboard the United States submarine *Nautilus.* Damage to his diving gear prevented him from attaining his goal. A United States nuclear submarine, appropriately named the *Nautilus,* passed under the pole and completed the Northwest Passage under the ice in August 1958.

Antarctic exploration Sustained scientific exploration of Antarctica developed more slowly than had Arctic exploration. It was not stimulated by the mirage of a bountiful southern continent or spurred by a search for a commercial passage, such as the Northwest Passage. In the years after Cook, American and British sealers were the principal visitors to these waters. In 1820 a Russian expedition under Baron Fabian Gottlieb von BELLINGSHAUSEN entered Antarctic waters. In the following year, it discovered Peter I Island and Alexander Island, the first lands found within the Antarctic Circle. France was represented in these waters during the 1837–1840 expedition of Jules DUMONT D'URVILLE, who discovered Joinville Island, Louis-Philippe Land (the northern tip of Graham Land), and Adélie Land. The most ill-prepared expedition to enter high southern latitudes was the American expedition under the command of Charles Wilkes (1838–1842). In spite of the quality of his ships, Wilkes sailed one of his vessels within sight of the Antarctic continent and proceeded westward along the coastline until blocked by ice. *See also* WILKES EXPEDITION.

British activity in this area was renewed from 1839 to 1843 with an expedition led by Capt. James Clark Ross, the discoverer of the Magnetic North Pole. This well-equipped expedition attempted to reach the Magnetic South Pole but was blocked by a great ice shelf, the Ross Ice Shelf. In 1842 Ross came within 710 miles (1,143 kilometers) of the geographic South Pole, reaching 78°9′S. This latitude would not be surpassed until the efforts of Scott, Edward Wilson, and Shackleton in 1903.

Capt. Robert Falcon SCOTT led a major British expedition into the Antarctic in the years from 1901 to 1904 on the carefully prepared *Discovery.* The accomplishments of this expedition were numerous and significant. Many scientific observations were made. The large Ross Ice Shelf was followed to its eastern extremity. King Edward VII Land (now Edward VII Peninsula)

Roald Amundsen, who later would become the first man to reach the geographic South Pole, arriving in Nome in 1906 after 3 years in the Arctic aboard the Gjøa. [Library of Congress]

was discovered. Surpassing Ross's record, the party reached the high southern latitude of 82°17′. The South Pole itself still lay beyond their reach.

The race for this pole intensified. From 1907 to 1909 a privately financed British expedition led by Ernest SHACKLETON tried for the pole, but a lack of supplies forced the men to turn back when they were within 97 miles (156 kilometers) of it. Three members of Shackleton's expedition reached the South Magnetic Pole on January 16, 1909. The honor and acclaim of having first reached the geographic South Pole fell to Roald Amundsen, who planted the flag of Norway upon the southern polar axis on December 14, 1911. A month later, on January 18, 1912, Robert Scott reached the pole, but he died in a blizzard when trying to return to his base camp.

Surrounded by sea and ice and covered by large ice formations, the 5,000,000 square miles (12,950,000 square kilometers) of Antarctica prevented rapid and easy exploration. Yet its possible resources and its potential for scientific research were so great that nation after nation initiated endeavors in these latitudes. With the sponsorship of the American Geographical Society and William Randolph Hearst, Sir Hubert Wilkins made the first Antarctic flights from 1928 to 1930. American investigations of this land became more protracted with the expeditions of Comdr. Richard Byrd in 1928–1930 and 1933–1935 and the establishment of the camp Little America. In the decades after World War II international cooperation in the Antarctic grew with twelve nations participating in the 1957–1958 activities of the International Geophysical Year. In 1959 these nations signed the Antarctic Treaty, which provided that this region be used only for peaceful and scientific purposes for the next three decades.

Space exploration While the exploration of the polar regions effectively utilized the increasingly complex technology that had been developed during the two world wars of the twentieth century, it was in the exploration of space that this technology began to be most dramatically applied. The dream of exploring the celestial realms had haunted man since the Renaissance, but it was not until 1942 that a rocket was successfully launched into space. Through the development of the Nazi rocket program and the famous V-2s, the Germans gained valuable experience with rocket propulsion systems. With the conclusion of World War II, both the United States and the Soviet Union sought to capitalize upon the German experience. Each nation obtained the services of German engineers.

The intensification of the mutual suspicions of the cold war encouraged both the U.S.S.R. and the United States to develop sophisticated rocket programs. In 1957 the U.S.S.R. successfully launched into orbit the earth's first artificial satellite, *Sputnik I.* Challenged by the evident superiority of Soviet space efforts and comprehending the possible military implications of

The balloon Ornen, manned by Salomon Andrée and his companions, sets off from Danskøya, near Spitsbergen, in an ill-fated attempt to reach the North Pole. [Smithsonian Institution]

this superiority, the United States established the National Aeronautics and Space Administration (NASA) in the spring of 1958. NASA's task was to win the space race. Soviet leadership was both obvious and highly visible. On April 12, 1961, Yury A. Gagarin aboard *Vostok 1* became the first man to enter space.

The Terra Nova icebound in the Antarctic. The leader of the expedition, Capt. Robert Falcon Scott, reached the South Pole on January 18, 1912, but perished in a blizzard on the way back to his camp. [Library of Congress]

The Soviets obtained a scientific and propaganda triumph. Discovery and exploration in space was becoming a race for political and military advantages. President John F. Kennedy clearly indicated United States willingness to participate in this competition when he announced in a special message to Congress of May 25, 1961, that this nation planned to land a man on the moon and return him safely before the end of the decade. For Kennedy and most other Americans, this was to be "a great new American enterprise," but an enterprise with obvious political implications. Kennedy contended that it would help the United States "to win the battle that is going on around the world between freedom and tyranny . . . the battle for men's minds." Eight years later, on July 20, 1969, the American astronaut Neil Armstrong took "one small step for a man, one giant leap for mankind," and became the first man to set foot on the moon.

With the successful conclusion of the program to put a man on the moon, attention could be turned to the more scientific aspects of space exploration. Radio astronomers broadened their attempts to learn more of the characteristics of deep space and began programs of listening for other signs of life in the universe. NASA's Viking Program developed a series of missions which collected data on Mars and the possibilities of life on that planet. The successes of space exploration in the twentieth century have been dramatic, but the discovery of the features of this infinite realm is still in its most primitive stages.

While it is difficult to outline the particular features of future programs of exploration and discovery, it is perhaps reasonable to assume that since people and nations will be involved, the traditional motives of discovery and exploration will remain. Some people will still seek to learn more of the unknown for its own sake. People and nations will strive for the glory of being the first to set foot upon virgin territories. Nations will seek to find new resources and political, military, and economic advantages in the newly discovered domains.

See also AERIAL EXPLORATION; NATURAL-HISTORY EXPLORATION; OCEANOGRAPHICAL EXPLORATION; SPACE EXPLORATION.

BIBLIOGRAPHY: John N. L. Baker, *A History of Geographical Discovery and Exploration*, London, 1931; J. C. Beaglehole, *The Life of Captain James Cook*, Stanford, Calif., 1974; Paul Russell Cutright, *The Great Naturalists Explore South America*, New York, 1940; Margaret Deacon, *Scientists and the Sea, 1650–1900*, London, 1971; Ernest Dodge, *Northwest by Sea*, Oxford, 1961; John Dunmore, *French Explorers in the Pacific*, 2 vols., Oxford, 1965; William H. Goetzmann, *American Exploration in the American West, 1803–1863*, New Haven, Conn., 1959; L. P. Kirwan, *The White Road*, London, 1959; Richard S. Lewis, *From Vinland to Mars*, New York, 1976; Jeanette Mirsky, *To the Arctic*, London, 1949; Alan Moorehead, *The White Nile*, London, 1960; Robert I. Rotberg (ed.), *Africa and Its Explorers: Motives, Methods, and Impact*, Cambridge, Mass., 1970; E. G. R. Taylor, *The Haven-finding Art*, London, 1957.

Phillip Drennon Thomas

Mountain Men (ca. 1825-1840)

American fur traders and explorers. Perhaps no group of American explorers arouses more visions of colorful drama than the small number of free traders referred to as Mountain Men. Usually at the forefront of the nation's westward march to the Pacific, this independent, tough breed of adventurers opened pioneer trails which linked the Mississippi Valley to the Rockies and the southern border of Canada to the Gila River in present Arizona. Their role in the Rocky Mountain fur trade was brief, for they prospered only between the mid-1820s and early 1840s. Their number was small; in no single year were there more than 500 known Mountain Men, and they probably totaled no more than 2000. Yet the names of several are familiar: William ASHLEY, James Beckwourth, Benjamin de Bonneville, Jim Bridger, Kit Carson, James Clyman, Tom Fitzpatrick, Hugh Glass, David Jackson, Jedediah SMITH, Joseph Walker. The mountain man's appearance was exotic and primitive: tanned skin, shoulder-length disheveled hair complete with beard, a cap made of beaver skins, a "possibles sack" of miscellaneous items, a "Hawkins rifle," colorful buckskin pants and hunting shirt decorated with porcupine quills or leather strippings, beaded moccasins, and a wide waist belt holding a pistol, a tomahawk, and a scalping knife. Paradoxically, the trails he opened and the profits he stimulated caused the near extermination of the fur-bearing animal, encouraged the spread of civilization, and thereby hastened the end of his own era in American history.

The mountain man structured most of his life around the fur trade. Meriwether LEWIS and William CLARK first came across two of these people along the Missouri River in 1805; no doubt successors of those pioneers who had opened Kentucky and Tennessee, they were on their way to trap along the Yellowstone River. Since winter was the prime hunting season because of the thickness of the beaver's coat, the mountain man had to have a sturdiness of character and body which enabled him to outlast the travails caused by snow, icy waters, treacherous mountain passes, hostile Indians, and unfriendly grizzlies. A number of these hardy men made it to the spring "rendezvous," a carnival-like, raucous affair instituted in 1825 by William Ashley, which served primarily as the hunters' trading center for Eastern goods. There, at an agreed spot in the central Rockies, they bartered away the year's catch for equipment and supplies brought by fur-company caravans. And there, on sixteen annual occasions, the mountain man celebrated a momentary respite from his rugged life. The rendezvous at Pierres Hole, west of the Tetons, in 1832 was perhaps the most memorable. Among the Mountain Men in attendance were Bridger, Fitzpatrick, Joseph Meek, Zenas Leonard, Alexander Sinclair, William and Milton Sublette, and two nephews of Daniel BOONE. Hundreds of Indians, Flathead, Nez Percé, and Shoshoni, joined the festivities, as did ninety men representing the already-unpopular American Fur Company.

The major reason for the mountain man's demise was the rapid depletion of the beaver. By the 1820s trappers were invading beaver territory from three outposts: Taos, Fort Vancouver, and St. Louis. From Taos in northern New Mexico they moved eastward along the Pecos River, then westward across the Gila River Valley, and eventually into southern California by the close of the decade. In the Far Northwest, from Fort Vancouver, built by Britain's powerful Hudson's Bay Company, they used Dr. John McLoughlin's brigade system to dominate the area's beaver streams. Led by a "partisan," large groups of trappers wound southward into California's Sacramento and San Joaquin Valleys and eastward along the Snake River into the northern Rockies. The third point of departure, St. Louis, constituted the initial step up the Missouri River and into the northern Rockies. By the early 1830s bitter rivalry had developed among three major

concerns: the Rocky Mountain Fur Company, the Hudson's Bay Company, and the American Fur Company. The small catch at the 1834 rendezvous resulted from this conflict. The trade soon suffered from other factors: a change in world fashions from fur to silk hats, excessively cold winters, the onset of smallpox at the American Fur Company's outpost at Fort Union near the mouth of the Yellowstone River. The era of the mountain man closed when fur trappers turned to hunting buffalo and when waves of pioneers pushed back the Western frontier.

What did the Mountain Men do in their twilight years? Some remained permanently marked by the wilderness, while others turned to politics, real estate, mining in Mexico, the transportation and supply business, and employment as government guides. More than 100 settled in California, either to hunt for sea otters or to become farmers, horse and cattle traders, vineyardists, carpenters, blacksmiths, coopers, and, in at least one case, a baker. Some joined John C. FRÉMONT in the shadowy prelude to the Bear Flag Revolution in California, while others served as guides for the U.S. Army during the Mexican War. A few helped Union forces hold off a Confederate advance near Santa Fe during the Civil War.

The Mountain Men's contributions were numerous. Ten wrote personal accounts which were published, while others told their stories to friends or

Portrait of Jim Bridger, one of the small number of hardy and individualistic Mountain Men who pioneered the Rocky Mountain fur trade in the first half of the nineteenth century. [*National Archives*]

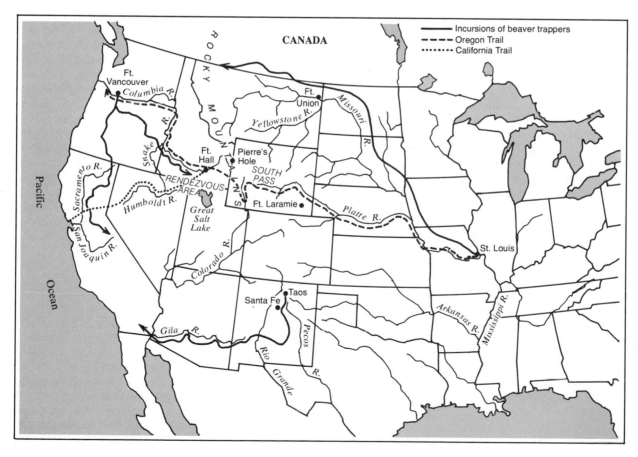

Centers of the fur trade in the Far West and the incursions of the beaver trappers into the Mountain Men's territory.

writers, who in turn had them published. The men helped open the Far West by exploring more than 1,000,000 square miles (2,590,000 square kilometers) of plains, deserts, and mountains and encouraged settlement by advertising new paths, especially the California Trail, which stretched from Fort Hall on the Oregon Trail, in present Idaho, along the Humboldt River across present Nevada and the Sierras, and ultimately into California. They then completed the task by working as guides for pioneers and government explorers. Finally, they left behind a rich legacy of romance; as one writer observed, "The map of the West was drawn on a beaver skin."

BIBLIOGRAPHY: Ray A. Billington, *The Far Western Frontier, 1830–1860*, New York, 1956; Bernard De Voto, *Across the Wide Missouri*, Cambridge, Mass., 1947; William H. Goetzmann, *Exploration and Empire: The Explorer and the Scientist in the Winning of the American West*, New York, 1966; Leroy R. Hafen, *The Mountain Men and the Fur Trade in the West*, 6 vols., Glendale, Calif., 1965; Dale Van Every, *The Final Challenge: The American Frontier, 1804–1845*, New York, 1964.

Howard Jones

Muslim Travel and Exploration in the Middle Ages

In a period of less than a century and a half, the small Islamic state based in western Arabia expanded into one of the great empires in world history, stretching from Spain to the borders of the Chinese empire. The very nature of this large state, the conquests which created it, and the administrative and economic practices meant to maintain it all contributed to a great interest in travel and the study of geography, both descriptive and mathematical. By the eighth century, furthermore, Arab merchants were extending their commercial ventures into the southern seas, and then later deep into Central Asia, with the pacification and conversion to Islam of much of that region. As a result, maritime knowledge and techniques were further developed.

The overwhelming importance of the Islamic pilgrimage to Mecca (the *ḥajj*), one of the five pillars of the faith, also meant that people within the Muslim polity would frequently be on the move. With the growth of Islamic scholarship, there came to be a special interest in the *hadīth*, sayings attributed to Prophet Muhammad and his companions. These sayings became major sources of Muslim norms and mores, and students of *hadīth* began to travel throughout the domain of Islam in search of *hadīth* scholars and new *hadīth*. All this served to generate a good deal of mobility among the people of the Islamic state, a mobility which was not to be found to the same degree in medieval Europe.

Islamic geographical concepts The discoveries and experiences of Muslim travelers constitute a significant part of the large corpus of geographical literature which has come down to us, and it therefore seems appropriate to discuss medieval Muslim travel within the context of Islamic geographical concepts and literature. To understand the nature of Islamic geographical knowledge, it is necessary to examine briefly its non-Islamic antecedents. A reading of the Qur'ān (Koran), the *hadīth* literature, and the pre-Islamic poetry of the Arabs gives some indication of pre-Islamic Arab geographical concepts. In addition to information about wells, tribal camp areas, and places of general interest in Arabia and neighboring areas, one finds evidence of non-Arabic cosmographical ideas derived from ancient Near Eastern peoples such as the Hebrews. This knowledge was expanded a great deal at the time of the Muslim conquests, which began in the early 630s. The conquests brought firsthand knowledge of areas such as Palestine, Iraq, Persia, and, later, the Maghreb (North Africa) and Central Asia. Perhaps of greater significance, the discoveries and observations associated with the conquests stimulated an interest in descriptive and mathematical geography.

After the accession of the 'Abbāsid dynasty to the throne of the Muslim state in 750, Islamic scholarship, including geographical studies, began to flourish in the new capital, Baghdad, under the encouragement of rulers such as al-Ma'mūn (r. 813–833). It was at this time that Indian mathematics and astronomy, Persian geographical and administrative learning, and Greek philosophy and science, including geography, came to play an important role in Islamic intellectual life. In the area of geography, the Muslims borrowed some ideas from India—for example, the belief that the inhabited area of the earth consists of nine parts—as well as from the Persians. From the latter came, for instance, the belief that the world consisted of seven zones of habitation with the *sawād*, or agricultural area, of Iraq at the center. The Greeks also made significant contributions to Muslim geography. The celebrated *Geography* of PTOLEMY was available and was apparently much studied, since we know that it was translated a number of times in the period after 750. A number of Arab geographers indicated that they made use of this and other Greek geographical books, and modern scholars maintain that the Greek influence was paramount and continued to be felt in Arab geography all the way up to the nineteenth century.

Types of geographical literature Medieval Muslim geography was exceptionally varied in the methods utilized and the areas investigated. Since the primary focus of this discussion is travel and discovery, we shall confine ourselves to delineating the major types and representative figures of Islamic geography. One of the important genres of this literature was the treatise devoted to a description of the routes and revenues of the empire, for example, the *Kitāb al-Masālik wa al-Mamālik* of ibn-Khurradādhbih (mid-ninth century). Ibn-Wādih al-Ya'qūbī (d. 897) wrote a similar work entitled *Kitāb al-Buldān*, devoted to a discussion of the routes leading to the frontiers of the empire and a description of territories adjacent to them. Ya'qūbī is of special interest, however, in that he appears to have traveled widely and gathered his information from the people of the areas described. Qudāma ibn-Ja'far (early tenth century) and ibn-Rusta (early tenth century) wrote similar works, although ibn-Rusta also dealt with physical and mathematical geography in his study.

Al-Balkhī (d. 934), al-Istakhrī (first half of the 10th century), Abū al-Qāsim IBN-ḤAWQAL (d. after 973), and al-Muqaddasī (d. 1000) all concentrated upon descriptions of Islamic lands, including experiences of personal travel. Al-Muqaddasī went far beyond mere description, also discussing customs, languages, and characteristics of peoples treated in his book. Abū al-Hasan al-MAS'ŪDĪ (d. 956), who was a historian and geographer, examined the areas of human and physical geography, paying special attention to such considerations as the impact of environment upon human development.

World geographies were another major type of medieval Islamic geographical writing. Writers such as al-Zuhrī of Spain (d. end of twelfth century) and Muhammad al-Sharīf al-IDRĪSĪ (d. 1165 or 1166) compiled information on the physical and descriptive geography of the known world through travel or consultation of other Arabic and of Greek source materials, or both. In the case of al-Idrīsī, at least, important work was carried out in cartography.

Cosmological works also began to appear in the Islamic world in the period following 1100. Here a major figure was the cosmographer al-Qazwinī (d. 1283), whose books included the *'Ajā'ib al-Buldān* and the *Āthār al-Bilād*. The latter work is reported to have been the first systematic book of its sort in the Islamic world. It is of particular interest for its information concerning towns and for numerous biographical sketches. Other cosmographical authors of some note were al-Dimashqī (d. 1327) and ibn al-Wardī (d. 1349).

One of the most important types of geographical literature to appear after the beginning of the thirteenth century was the dictionary. Undoubtedly the major example of this genre and one of the most important titles in medieval Islamic literature was the *Mu'jam al-Buldān* of YĀQŪT AL-RŪMĪ (1179–1229). This multivolume work includes valuable topographical, historical, and economic data. It is organized on the basis of entries given under place names. The introduction includes an excellent summary of Arabic mathematical and physical geographical concepts, many based upon Greek ideas.

One of the most famous medieval Islamic scholars, al-Bīrūnī (d. 1048), wrote a work on the chronology of ancient nations, *al-Āthār al-Bāqīya*, which includes interesting and useful information on the locations of several cities and is especially noteworthy for its mention of their latitudes. In this book he also records a number of observations on the physical characteristics of the earth, among them changes on the surface. In his history of India, *Tārīkh al-Hind*, we have one of the best studies of the physical character, religious life, and social customs of that country to appear before modern times. Al-Bīrūnī's encyclopedic knowledge of the geographical information and methods of his time made his work of singular importance in medieval Islamic intellectual life.

In the later medieval period (1200–1500), what one scholar has termed regional geographies became sig-

Maps of al-Istakhri, a Muslim writer of the tenth century who recounted his travels through Islamic lands.

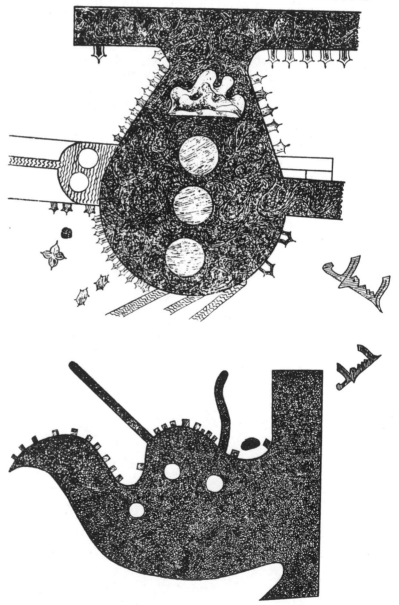

nificant. Writers such as al-Maqrīzī (d. 1442) in Egypt composed works devoted to descriptions of important monuments, quarters, markets, and other features of major cities such as Cairo. These books contain a great deal of information of use to art historians and historical geographers as well as historians. The works centered on the regions of Syria and Egypt. At the same time, authors in Persia and Central Asia were making their contributions to regional geography, some of them written in the new Persian of the Islamic era.

In addition to the types of literature already mentioned, astronomical literature and investigations of considerable sophistication figured prominently in medieval Muslim thought and learning, including geography. Astronomers in observatories in the 'Abbāsid and Tīmūrid (fifteenth century) periods conducted experiments yielding useful information about the geographical coordinates and distances separating locations in the Islamic world.

Maritime travel and exploration As indicated above, commercial, political, and educational motives caused a good deal of movement by people in the Islamic world of the Middle Ages. In many instances this movement involved maritime voyages, and in fact some of the most interesting geographical and travel accounts extant have to do with travel in the southern seas (the Indian Ocean) and the Mediterranean. The Arabs were familiar with ocean travel long before the Islamic conquests, but they had not themselves been involved in it to a great degree. After 750, with the shift of the imperial center to Iraq, Arab navigators were venturing out into the Indian Ocean,

traveling as far as East Africa and China. Arab sailors learned the peculiarities of the monsoon winds, and this knowledge enabled them to sail to India and eventually as far as Indonesia and Malaysia.

The Arab maritime experience was conditioned primarily by the desire for political and economic benefits, *not* by exploratory curiosity per se. As a result, sailors and oceangoing merchants did not explore totally unknown areas. As is evident from a glance at medieval Islamic geographical lore, certain misconceptions or fears kept them from venturing into certain areas; for example, the Atlantic was believed to be a realm of darkness. Even so, the Muslims did expand their reach and thereby their commercial interests. We know that they traded with the tribes of the Nicobar and Andaman Islands. A sizable and flourishing mercantile community established itself in Canton, China, but an antiforeign rising in 878 decimated the community, and trade declined. In fact, the Arabs do not appear to have extended their maritime ventures and Eastern commerce beyond the Malay Peninsula in the wake of the Chinese disaster.

After this time, the Arabs confined their maritime voyages primarily to the Mediterranean, the Red Sea and waters off south Arabia, and the Indian Ocean. In the former areas, trade and especially warfare were the major factors in maritime activity, which continued until the rise of the Ottoman Empire. Muslim navigators were dominant in the Indian Ocean–Persian Gulf area until the coming of the Portuguese in the late fifteenth and early sixteenth centuries.

Muslim navigational techniques and instruments were partially derivative and partially original. Early Muslim techniques did not differ drastically from those of other ancient and medieval seafaring peoples. Muslims passed on from generation to generation a vast amount of lore and knowledge about tides, currents, winds, and other important maritime phenomena. The information was frequently complex, involving such subjects as wave structures, wind directions, and other factors which could alter during the course of the year.

Location at sea was determined in the early period in any of several ways. Coastlines and formations could be sighted by the use of a mast boy or lookout; estimates of speed were made by watching an object thrown astern. Speed combined with the general direction of the ship would yield some idea of one's position. The only other way of finding location in the early days was the use of star sightings. The developments in Islamic astronomy were extremely helpful in this respect.

Astronomical instruments such as the quadrant, astrolabe, sundial, and globe were important also in navigation. The astrolabe, derived from the Greeks, was used to determine the distance of a star from a horizontal plane. It was somewhat difficult to use on board a ship because of the motion of the vessel. On shore, however, it might be used with good effect to determine the latitude of ports. It proved so valuable

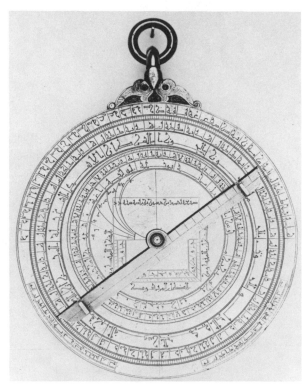

Muslim astrolabe of the fifteenth century. The astrolabe, a Greek invention, was used by the Muslims to determine the latitude of seaports. [NASA]

in this way that it was transported from one port to another, the information thus gained being recorded in sailing manuals.

Having gained the ability to determine latitude, the Muslims produced *rahmānī*, nautical texts in which they recorded the vital statistics of ports and headlands. The *rahmānī*, the earliest mention of which dates from the late tenth century, contained data on general and specific wind directions, reefs, tides, and coasts at all times of the year and in all weather conditions. In addition to general sailing instructions, the *rahmānī* included considerable information about monsoon winds, knowledge of vital importance given the activity of the Muslims in the Indian Ocean.

Muslim navigators had access to rough maps or diagrams. These rudimentary maps were not charts or projections, since they did not allow for the curvature of the earth. In many instances, the Muslim sailor used only a sailing guide or a map in his head. In fact, it appears that the only really good Islamic maps extant are those of al-Idrīsī, which were created for the Norman ruler Roger II of Sicily. The compass was also a part of medieval Muslim maritime equipment. There are reports of its having been used on Arab and Persian sailing vessels at the end of the eleventh century. The device seems to have taken ordinarily the form of an iron fish, magnetized with a lodestone, and floated in a bowl of water.

All these techniques and instruments no doubt left much to be desired. Using the limited techniques and instruments at their disposal, however, Islamic navigators made some impressive long voyages and succeeded, too, in establishing regular trade routes from the Mediterranean to China. Moreover, the lateen rig characteristic of Arab vessels proved of value to the Portuguese and Spanish, who in the fifteenth century adapted it for use in the caravels that sailed to Africa and the New World. *See also* MARITIME EXPLORATION.

Some of the particularly interesting travel observations coming from the pens of Muslim writers were the result of maritime voyages. One of the earliest of these is a travelogue entitled *Akhbār al-Sīn wa al-Hind* composed by a merchant known to us only as Sulaymān, who lived around the middle part of the ninth century. This work, as the title indicates, was a description of the land and people of China and India. It was apparently based upon several voyages to those countries by the author. Al-Mas'ūdī, one of the fine scholars of the medieval Muslim world, also embarked upon a number of maritime voyages on the Mediterranean and Caspian seas. A Persian sea captain named Buzurg ibn-Shahriyār (d. 1009) has left us an interesting work entitled *Kitāb al-'Ajā'ib al-Hind*, which, while containing much legendary or fantastic materials, does seem to provide some accurate information about Muslim navigators in certain parts of the Indian Ocean. Shihāb al-Dīn Ahmad ibn-Mājid, the man who served as the Indian Ocean pilot of Vasco da GAMA in 1498, has left a number of works

dealing with navigation and nautical affairs. His works, together with those of Sulaymān ibn-Ahmad al-Mahrī (first half of the sixteenth century), suggest clearly an improvement in certain methods and navigational knowledge by the late fifteenth century.

Muslim travelers In any chronological examination of Muslim travelers in the Middle Ages, it seems that one must start with al-Ya'qūbī, mentioned above, whose *Kitāb al-Buldān* (composed about 891) was based, according to its author, on travel in many parts of the Islamic empire. The work is similar in some respects to the book of routes of ibn-Khurradādhbih, including topographical data as well as information about routes. Ya'qūbī's travels took him from North Africa to India, and his book is an interesting and useful description of the large cities and, generally, the eastern and western provinces of the Islamic empire.

Ibn-Rusta (early tenth century) wrote an interesting work, *Kitāb al-A'lāq al-Nafīsa*, which includes not only a description of the Islamic lands but also an account of some non-Islamic peoples such as the Slavs and the Hungarians. It is not confined to descriptive geography, for we find in it a good deal of material on mathematical geography. How much of the work was based on that of contemporaries or predecessors and how much on personal observation is difficult to say.

Al-Mas'ūdī, as already noted, was a traveler as well as a sedentary scholar. Much of his geographical information was based upon his personal experiences as well as on knowledge gained from people whom he met on his journeys. Another author of importance, a contemporary of Mas'ūdī, was al-Istakhrī. Not much is known about his life, but it does appear that he traveled a good deal. Observations made during these travels appear in his book *al-Masālik wa al-Mamālik*, a description of routes and regions. Ibn-Hawqal embarked upon a number of voyages in the years between 943 and 973 or 974. He recorded his observations in the book *Kitāb Sūrat al-Ard*, which appeared about 977. He made use of Istakhrī's book in his own work, but it also contains much that was original with ibn-Hawqal. His contributions were not confined to his descriptive accounts, for his work in cartography constituted another useful and significant area of activity.

One of the most systematic and original authors in medieval Islamic geography was Muhammad ibn-Ahmad al-Muqaddasī (d. 1000), a native of Jerusalem, whose travels took him over much of the Muslim world. His work *Ahsan al-Taqāsīm fī Ma'rifat al-Aqālīm* contains, in addition to descriptions of areas, important reports of the languages, religious practices and beliefs, and customs of the people among whom he traveled. The consensus among modern scholars is that he was one of the most reliable and careful geographers of his day.

Diplomatic and commercial missions sent by the Islamic rulers were the occasion for observers to record much interesting and informative data on the lands entered and the peoples encountered. Such reports provided descriptions of customs and institutions not just in Muslim lands but also in non-Muslim areas. Writings of this nature did much to expand Islamic geographical knowledge. One of the authors of such a work was Aḥmad IBN-FAḌLĀN, who was part of a mission sent by the 'Abbāsid ruler al-Muqtadir (r. 908–932) to the court of the Volga Bulgars in central Russia in 921–922. He recorded his experiences in a treatise called *Kitāb (Book)*. In it he included ethnographic information of importance on the peoples of southern and central Russia. We read in his pages of the affairs of the Khazar kingdom in southern Russia and of the manners and customs of the Rus (Russ), the pre-Christian Scandinavian inhabitants of Russia. Another traveler said to have been involved in a mission, this one to the court of an Indian prince, was a man named Abū Dulaf Mis'ar ibn al-Muhalhil (tenth century). He is believed to have traveled through Central Asia, Afghnistan, and India. He has left us an account of his movement and observations in two treatises, one of them somewhat confused.

The great scholar al-Bīrūnī, already mentioned, was also a traveler whose journey to India yielded a mine of information about the people of that country. He traveled in India for several years and thereby studied the land and its people firsthand. Bīrūnī learned Sanskrit and devoted special attention to the religions and philosophies of the country. His work on India remains one of the greatest achievements of medieval Islamic intellectual life.

A contemporary of al-Bīrūnī, the Persian traveler Nāṣir-i Khusraw (d. 1060 or 1061), has left us one of the most interesting travel accounts of the medieval period. Written in Persian and entitled the *Safar-Nāma*, it records the personal experiences of the author in Arabia and Egypt. It is of particular value to the student of the religious and social life of medieval Islam, since it contains one of the best accounts of the religious practices and social structure of the Qarmatians, a Shī'ite group who established a small state in Bahrain at the end of the ninth or the beginning of the tenth century.

Al-Idrīsī, one of the premier Arab geographers, was a man who traveled in a large part of the Islamic world but who, interestingly enough, composed his great work for a Christian monarch, Roger II of Sicily. The book incorporating the fruits of his travels and research is called simply *The Book of Roger (Kitāb al-Rujār)*, finished in 1153–1154. In this book, al-Idrīsī writes of the geography, ethnography, and cultures of Asian, African, and European countries. The book is also important because of the maps included in it.

One of the best travel monographs devoted to one region is the *Kitāb al-Ifāda wa al-I'tibār fī al-Umūr al-Mushāhada wa al-Hawādith al-Mu'āyana bi Ard al-Miṣr* of 'Abd al-Laṭīf al-Baghdādī (d. 1231 or 1232), who recorded in it his observations of life in Egypt in the early thirteenth century. This book contains exceptionally interesting information about plants and crops, as well as detailed descriptions of the effects of famine and earthquake in the period of the author's sojourn in the country.

Muḥammad IBN-JUBAYR was a Muslim from Granada, Spain, who made three journeys to the Near East. One of these took place between 1182 and 1185 or 1186 and took ibn-Jubayr through the countries of Syria, Iraq, and Eqypt to Mecca for the pilgrimage. The return journey was by way of Sicily. The events and observations of this trip are recorded in a book known simply as the *Riḥla (Journey)* of ibn-Jubayr. This work is of special interest because of its description of the pilgrimage ceremonies and the Islamic holy places in Mecca.

Perhaps the most famous of all medieval Muslim travelers was Abū'Abd Allāh Muḥammad IBN BAṬṬŪṬA (1304–1377), a native of Tangier, Morocco. This scholar spent much of his life on voyages to various portions of the world and recorded his observations in a celebrated book, the *Riḥla (Journey)*. He made the pilgrimage to Mecca for the first time at the age of 22 and later was to repeat the journey to Mecca and Medina many times. His travels took him over Asia, Africa, the Far East, and southern Europe. Among the cities which he visited were Bukhara, Constantinople, Calcutta, and Delhi. He also traveled in China, Indonesia, and Ceylon.

Significance All these travel accounts constitute one of the richest sectors of medieval Islamic literature. From them we can gather much useful data about the Islamic world, India, the Far East, and even Eastern and Southern Europe. The information is of very great variety, interesting in itself but also of value to scholars in various fields. Geographers, particularly those concerned with the development of geographical methods and theories, have an obvious interest in works of this nature. A number of these books, for example, provide valuable insight into Greek and other ancient peoples' visions of the form and nature of the universe. From these works historical geographers can glean details of cities, towns, or villages, many of them long disappeared or substantially altered. The historian of art and architecture can find much of value about the nature and location of important monuments or buildings now destroyed or irreparably damaged.

The scholar of comparative religion, Islam, or Muslim sects also can find significant details in many of the travel books. Bīrūnī's work, for instance, is invaluable to the student of Hinduism and medieval Indian religious thought generally. Ibn-Rusta's work includes an interesting section on Islamic heresies.

One of the major beneficiaries of these works, finally, is the historian of medieval Islamic social and economic life. One has only to glance at the notes and bibliographies of most modern books or monographs in these fields to see verification of this statement. The Islamic travelers yield crucial data about taxes, cultivation practices, crops, trade practices and goods, foods consumed, and other features of material life and culture. One may also gain at least some idea of the nature and role of various natural disasters which touched the medieval Islamic world. All in all, the geographical and travel works of the medieval Muslim world are worthy of attention for people interested in a wide range of subjects and disciplines.

BIBLIOGRAPHY: S. M. Aḥmad, ''Djughrāfiyā,'' *Encyclopedia of Islam*, vol. II, 2d ed., Leiden, 1965, pp. 575–587; Sir T. W. Arnold, ''Arab Travellers and Merchants,'' *Travel and Travellers of the Middle Ages*, ed. by A. P. Newton, 1926; reprinted Freeport, N.Y., 1967; R. Blachère and H. Darmaun, *Extraits des principaux géographes arabes*, 2d ed., Paris, 1958; D. M. Dunlop, *Arab Civilization to AD 1500*, New York, 1971; G. F. Hourani, *Arab Seafaring in the Indian Ocean*, Beirut, 1963; D. A. King, *Spherical Astronomy in Medieval Islam: The Ḥākimī Zīj of Ibn Yūnus*, Albany, N.Y., 1977; I. J. Kračkovskij, *Arabskaja geografičeskaja literatura*, Moscow and Leningrad, 1957; J. H. Kramers, ''Djughrāfiyā,'' *Encyclopedia of Islam: Supplement*, Leiden, 1938, pp. 61–73; A. Miquel, *La Géographie humaine du monde musulmane jusqu' au milieu du lle siècle*, 2 vols., Paris and The Hague, 1967–1973; Yāqūt al-Ḥamawī, *The Introductory Chapters of Yāqūt's Mu'jam al-Buldān*, tr. and ed. by Wadie Jwaideh, Leiden, 1959.

William Tucker

Nachtigal, Gustav (1834–1885) German explorer and diplomat. Nachtigal was born in Eichstedt, and his medical studies at several German universities provided him with the opportunity from which his career as an African explorer emanated. He served as a military surgeon in both Algiers and Tunis and while at these stations participated in several expeditions into the Saharan interior. These undertakings brought an invitation from King William I of Prussia to lead a mission to the Sultan of Bornu, who had been influential in assisting several German travelers. Nachtigal successfully completed this task and continued onward into previously unexplored regions of the central Sahara. Ultimately, in 1874, he arrived at Khartoum, having previously visited Wadai and Kordofan. He described this journey in his massive three-volume work, *Sahara und Sudan* (1879–1889), and therein lies his primary claim to renown as an explorer. Nachtigal later served as German consul general at Tunisia, and he figured significantly in the Bismarck-inspired advances in West Africa which added Togoland and the Cameroons to Germany's burgeoning African empire. He died at sea shortly afterward and was buried at Grand-Bassam, Ivory Coast.

BIBLIOGRAPHY: Albert Frankel, *Gustav Nachtigals Reisen in der Sahara und im Sudan*, Leipzig, 1887; Hans Hever, *Gustav Nachtigal*, Berlin, 1937; Josef Wiese, *Gustav Nachtigal: Ein Deutsches Forscherleben im dunklen Erdteil*, Berlin, 1914.

James A. Casada

Far left: Sahara Desert. German-born Gustav Nachtigal served as a military surgeon in Africa and was a member of several expeditions into the Sahara. He told of his experiences in a huge work of three volumes, Sahara und Sudan. [National Archives]

Nansen, Fridtjof (1861–1930) Norwegian explorer, scientist, and statesman. Nansen was born at Store Frøen near Oslo, where he attended school. In 1880 he entered the University of Oslo, eventually specializing in zoology and receiving his doctorate in 1887. In 1882 he was appointed curator of the Zoological Museum at Bergen. Earlier that year he had gained his first experience of Arctic waters when he sailed aboard a Norwegian sealer to the east coast of Greenland, where the vessel was trapped in the ice for 3 weeks.

Nansen launched his career as an explorer in 1888 with an assault on the inland ice of Greenland, which rises from the coast to a height of nearly 9000 feet (2743 meters). He had conceived the expedition in 1883 upon reading of the recent journey of N. A. E. NORDENSKIÖLD, who, like other explorers, had been unsuccessful in his effort to traverse the ice cap. Nansen, an expert skier since childhood, believed that he could achieve this goal with the help of skis. His scheme was generally dismissed as unfeasible, and the Norwegian government refused a request for financial support. Nansen found a benefactor in Augustin Gamél, a Dane, and proceeded to plan the expedition with the meticulous care that was characteristic of all his projects.

Nansen left Norway for Greenland aboard the sealer *Jason* in May 1888 with five companions, among them Otto SVERDRUP. After leaving the *Jason* on two boats, they succeeded, with some difficulty, in landing on the uninhabited east coast of Greenland and began their ascent to the inland ice in mid-August. The going was hard because of bad weather, limited rations, and lack of drinking water, but by September 27 they had reached the west coast at Ameralikfjord. They then headed for Godthåb, where they spent the winter.

The seed of Nansen's next Arctic venture was planted as early as 1884 when he read an article by Professor Henrik Mohn, who reported that relics from the *Jeannette,* an American vessel that had foundered in 1881 north of the Novosibirskiyi Ostrova (New Siberian Islands), had been found on the southwest coast of Greenland. Mohn believed that the relics had drifted on a floe across the Arctic Ocean. From this and similar evidence Nansen concluded that a ship especially designed to withstand the pressure of the ice might be able to drift from the Siberian Arctic across the North Pole to the sea between Greenland and Spitsbergen (Svalbard). Although few Arctic experts believed that the project had any likelihood of success, Nansen received financial assistance from the Norwegian government, King Oscar II, the ROYAL GEOGRAPHICAL SOCIETY of London, and several private individuals, including a Russian, Nikolay Kelch, who paid for east Siberian dogs to be used to haul sledges when necessary. The vessel on which Nansen and his companions would sail was designed by the Scottish naval architect Colin Archer. Called the *Fram (Forward),* she was small, broad, and relatively light, with smooth, sloping sides and especially strong ends. From the many applicants, Nansen selected twelve men to accompany him, one of them being Otto Sverdrup.

The *Fram* left Norway in July 1893, made her way across the Kara Sea and around Cape Chelyuskin, and by September 26 had been frozen in the ice at about 77°44'N. Although Nansen was at first discouraged by the irregularity of their progress, the *Fram* slowly drifted northward in the following months, passing 82°N on October 21, 1894. During the long voyage the men were kept busy at a variety of tasks, including the making of scientific observations. Diversion was provided by a wellstocked library, the publication of a newspaper, the *Framsjaa,* and meals so ample that some of the men began to look like "prize pigs."

Even before the end of the first winter Nansen was mulling over a daring plan to leave the *Fram* with a single companion in an effort to reach the North Pole, and the project matured as it became evident that the ship would not drift so far north as had been originally hoped. Leaving Sverdrup in command of the *Fram,* which had reached 84°N, 101°55'E, Nansen set out on March 14, 1895, with Frederik Hjalmar Johansen. With them they took two kayaks, three sledges, and twenty-four dogs. Nansen at first planned to travel northward for 50 days, but the ice was so rough and leads and pressure ridges so numerous that they turned back on April 8. Even so they had reached 86°14'N, a new record in Arctic exploration. On July 24 they sighted land: Zemlya Frantsa Josifa (Franz Josef Land). They sailed along the coast for several weeks, but finding progress southward blocked by ice, they decided to halt for the winter in late August. For shelter they built a hut of stone and moss, roofed with walrus hides.

On May 19, 1896, they set off again by kayak. On June 17, Nansen was startled to hear what seemed to be the barking of a dog. While Johansen stayed behind at their camp, Nansen went to investigate and, in an encounter as remarkable as the more celebrated meeting of David LIVINGSTONE and Henry M. STANLEY, came across the English explorer Frederick George Jackson, leader of the Jackson-Harmsworth Expedition, which had camped at Cape Flora in Zemlya Frantsa Josifa. The Norwegians were taken to Jackson's camp, where they had their first warm baths in more than a year and awaited the arrival of the relief ship *Windward,* which took them back to Norway. Soon after their arrival, they received a telegram from Sverdrup, who reported that the *Fram* had also returned safely to Norway.

Nansen's achievements were hailed not only in Norway but also in England, where he was awarded honorary degrees from Oxford and Cambridge Universities. The scientific aspects of the expedition received special praise, particularly its demonstration that the polar sea is a deep basin devoid of large land masses. In the years that followed Nansen devoted himself mainly to scientific endeavors, especially in the field of oceanography (see OCEANOGRAPHICAL EXPLORATION). He also became an outspoken defender of Norwegian interests during the events that led to that nation's separation from Sweden in 1905 and was named the first Norwegian Minister to London.

With the outbreak of World War I Nansen became more deeply involved in international affairs. In 1917 he was sent to the United States by the Norwegian government to arrange for the export of American foodstuffs to neutral Norway. Between 1920 and

A man of extraordinary energy and versatile gifts, Fridtjof Nansen achieved distinction first as a zoologist and later as an explorer and statesman. [Norwegian Information Service]

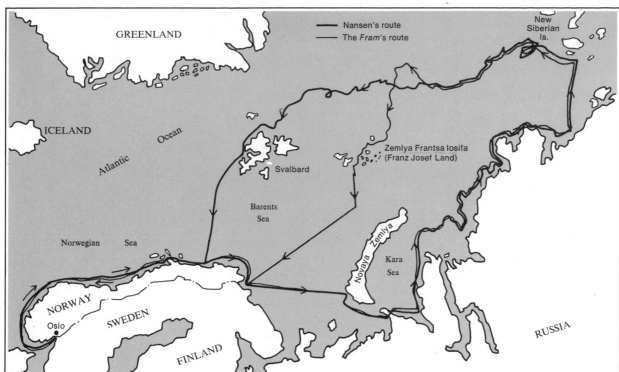

1922, as High Commissioner of the League of Nations, he organized the repatriation of more than 400,-000 prisoners of war; in addition, he directed the resettlement of thousands of Russian, Greek, and Armenian refugees. Meanwhile, when the League proved unwilling to provide aid for the victims of famine in Russia, Nansen collected funds from private sources for this purpose. In 1922 he was awarded the Nobel Peace Prize.

Nansen's dedication to humanitarian causes in his later years did not keep him from producing occasional scientific papers. Nor had he lost his interest in Arctic exploration, the history of which he discussed in a two-volume work, *In Northern Mists* (1911). He was planning to cross the Arctic in the *Graf Zeppelin* when he was taken ill and died on May 13, 1930.

BIBLIOGRAPHY: Fridtjof Nansen, *Farthest North*, 2 vols., London, 1897; id., *The First Crossing of Greenland*, translated by Hubert Majendie Gepp, 2 vols., London, 1890; E. E. Reynolds, *Nansen*, London, 1932.

Natural-History Exploration

Innate within men and women is a curiosity about the world in which they find themselves. This curiosity is of primeval origin and led them early in their history to an examination of their environment. With death, disease, and disaster as constant companions, their explorations of the flora, fauna, and lands which they encountered were naturally cautious. As early religions, myths, and art poignantly testify, they stood in awe before the inexplicable forces of nature. Yet they began to record the manifestations and periods of natural phenomena, and the human experience became enriched by these perceptions of the natural world. The rise of agriculture and the growth of civilization reveal that the first tentative natural-history explorations provided a wealth of knowledge about the geography, plants, animals, minerals, and weather conditions that affected daily life. Much of this early knowledge was of immediate value, for it provided people with food, clothing, and an awareness of the appropriate seasons for performing agricultural tasks.

It is difficult to ascertain when people first consciously went into new lands to explore the varieties of a region's flora, fauna, or geography. In 1495 B.C., Queen Hatshepsut of Egypt sent an expedition to the land of Punt to collect the trees which produced aromatic frankincense—perhaps the earliest example of sponsored plant collecting. Her successor, Thutmose III, collected plants during his military campaign in Syria, and on the walls of his temple at Karnak 275 plants which flourished during his reign have been skillfully carved. If the activities of Queen Hatshepsut and Thutmose III are not actual indications of natural-history exploration, they are at least an early indication of human enthusiasm for plant collecting in foreign lands.

Greek and Roman contributions Serious natural-history investigations were first undertaken by the Greeks. Aristotle's work in biology was unsurpassed in antiquity and the early Middle Ages. He himself collected many specimens in the eastern Mediterranean, and his erstwhile student ALEXANDER THE GREAT included a contingent of naturalists in the army which he assembled for his campaign into hither Asia. From 331 to 323 B.C. these naturalists collected plants, animals, minerals, and observations on the lands through which they marched. The death of Alexander and the subsequent turmoil in Athens prevented Aristotle from analyzing and incorporating these materials in his own writings, but his student and successor as head of the Lyceum, Theophrastus, utilized the data collected by Alexander's forces in his *Enquiry into Plants* and in his teaching.

Roman efforts in scientific investigation were quite restricted, for the Romans never fully assimilated the procedures and methods of scientific inquiry articulated by the Greeks. Intellectually, the Romans stood in awe of the Greek accomplishments, and Roman science is essentially an abridgment of the Greek experience in this realm. Although the Romans were able to expand the frontiers of their empire almost at will, their efforts at the exploration of unknown regions were limited. It was not in the Roman character to explore an area in order to learn more of its natural history.

The tradition in Roman science, and hence in natural-history investigations, became the practice of gathering and restating the knowledge previously recorded by Greek authors. The search for authors, and therefore authorities, was substituted for empirical investigation. Encyclopedic works were preferred to analytical works, and the appearance of learning was substituted for the actual attainment of knowledge. Scholarship and scientific investigation became confused with the citation of antique authors, a tradition which maintained itself in Latin Christendom from the first to the thirteenth century.

In his *Quaestiones naturales*, Seneca attempted to present an explanation of natural phenomena, but the work quickly deteriorated into a potpourri of unrelated information on astronomy, meteorology, physics, and physical geography. In this highly didactic work, nature and natural events are presented as providing man with moral instructions. Seneca's first-century contemporary, PLINY the Elder, produced one of the more voluminous and arcanely intriguing treatises on natural history written in antiquity. Edward Gibbon termed the thirty-seven books of Pliny's *Natural History* an "immense register where Pliny has deposited the discoveries, the arts, and the errors of mankind." This protracted and highly anthropocentric encyclopedic study with its wealth of fascinating information about strange and exotic plants, animals, and minerals nourished the meager interest people had in natural history in the early Middle Ages.

Medieval outlook Ultimately, the medieval pursuit of truth became no less diligent than that of the Greeks, but the basic premises were different. Medieval scholars' sense of evidence lay beyond this world in the realm of metaphysics. The transience of this world and the things of this world did not appear to be a fruitful field of study for Christians. Nevertheless, in spite of the admonitions of the fathers of the church, people were curious about the world in which they were only passing shadows. As even a cursory examination of medieval bestiaries, herbals, or tapestries will reveal, the medieval world was resplendent with fabulous animals and miraculous plants. People's disdain for empirical evidence and their acceptance of the supernatural led them to accept the existence of exotic flora and fauna with strange and marvelous properties that inhabited the fringes of the known world. While the skepticism of the late Middle Ages began to question the nature of these creations, it was not until the Renaissance was mature that nature began to be explored in such a fashion that the unicorn, basilisk, harpy, kraken, and satyr were relegated to the land of myth and folk memory.

Renaissance explorers The Renaissance voyages of discovery encountered not only new worlds but also new plants, animals, and peoples which challenged the interpretive skills of historians, cartographers, and naturalists. Classification of these new forms became of crucial importance, for they rendered obsolete the previous compilations of naturalists. The selection of an appropriate nomenclature for these discoveries was a problem that scholars such as Konrad von Gesner and Ulisse Aldrovandi sought to resolve. Taxonomy became a major and persistent dilemma for naturalists until the appearance of Carolus Linneaus's binomial system of classification in the eighteenth century.

Thousands upon thousands of new species now awaited their investigators, and naturalists, or at least people who had an interest in natural history, became part of the expeditions which set sail from the ports of Europe for the yet-unexplored regions of the globe. Even as naturalists were setting forth on these voyages, greater interest began to be demonstrated in the flora and fauna of Europe itself. The Renaissance delight in the life of this world brought local plants, birds, and animals under more careful scrutiny. The sense of beauty and love of accuracy nourished by Renaissance humanists encouraged artists, illustrators, and engravers to portray with greater accuracy the plant and animal specimens collected by those early visitors to the shores of the New World. Natural-history illustrations became more precise, and scientific drawings began to be an important aid in study and classification.

Spanish participation in sixteenth-century natural-history exploration began auspiciously with the activities of Gonzalo Fernández de Oviedo (1478–1557) and José de Acosta (1540–1600). An Asturian aristocrat, Oviedo has the honor of having produced the first treatise on the natural history of the New World. Sailing to Panama in 1514, he held several royal offices in the West Indies and also chronicled early Spanish activities in this realm. Although his *Historia general y natural de las Indias,* which he began in 1535 but which was not published in full until 1851, is uneven in quality, the work does provide Europe with the first descriptions of the tapir, manatee, iguana, armadillo, anteater, sloth, pelican, hummingbird, and ivory-billed woodpecker.

More widely respected as an accurate natural historian is the Spanish chronicler José de Acosta. A Jesuit, Acosta forsook appointment to a chair in theology at Rome to pursue the career of a missionary among the Indians of the New World. During the 15 years he spent in the Western Hemisphere, 14 in Peru and 1 in Mexico, Acosta studied the native languages and customs as well as carefully observing the natural history of the lands in which he labored. His *Historia natural y moral de las Indias* (1590) is clearly the most important of the early Spanish treatises on the natural history of the New World, although its methodology is at times restricted by Acosta's adherence to the scholastic conventions of medieval thinkers. Acosta informed his readers that he wished "to touch upon the naturall historie of the heavens, ayre, water, and earth at the West Indies, also of their beasts, fishes, fowles, plants, and other remarkable varieties of nature."

This work was quite sophisticated for the sixteenth century, for in it Acosta not only chronicled the characteristics and habitats of many new animal species but also described the presence of fossil bones (which he presumed were the remains of giant humans), altitude sickness, the domesticated animals of South America, the coca leaf and its uses, and descriptions of Aztec and Inca historical accomplishments. His most perceptive comments on natural history were reserved for his explanation of the distinction between the fauna of Europe and the Americas. In seeking to answer the question "How it should be possible that at the Indies there should be any sorts of beast, whereof the like are nowhere else?" he perhaps deserves recognition as the New World's first zoogeographer, or ecologist.

Sustained English interest in the natural history of the New World was developed by Thomas Harriot (ca. 1560–1621), who in the late summer of 1585 became the first Englishman to embark upon a critical examination of the flora and fauna of North America. An accomplished mathematician and astronomer, Harriot was in service to Sir Walter Raleigh. As a member of Raleigh's ill-fated Roanoke settlement, he had the opportunity to study the natural history of an unknown land. The results of his investigation were published in *A briefe and true report of the new*

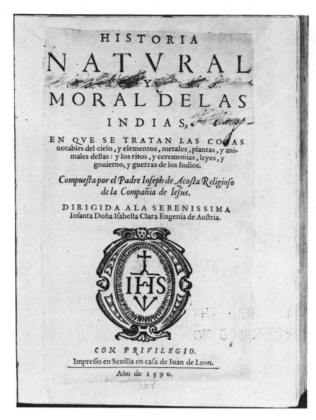

Title page from José de Acosta's account of the natural history of the New World. The New World's first ecologist, Acosta culled the material for his study from his 15 years of experience in Latin America as a Jesuit missionary. [Library of Congress]

found land of Virginia (1588). In this treatise, Harriot noted more than eighty-six species of birds and numerous unknown plants, trees, and shrubs. His descriptions of the American Cervidae would not be equaled for two centuries.

Thomas Harriot's companion in his American odyssey was the talented English artist John White, who produced the earliest extant color illustrations of the plant, animal, and native life of North America. Sixty-three of White's paintings were based upon the flora, fauna, and native life he observed in the New World, and with Harriot's text they provide an important introduction to the natural history of America. These beautiful watercolors, which are in the British Mu-

Diamondback terrapin, painted by John White. A member of the ill-fated Roanoke settlement, White produced the first color illustrations of the flora, fauna, and native life of North America. [Library of Congress]

seum, became the basis for the engravings which accompanied Harriot's 1588 treatise.

Catesby English interest in the natural-history exploration of North America was maintained by Mark Catesby (1683–1749). Influenced by the eminent English naturalist John Ray, Catesby was the most talented naturalist to explore the lands in which English colonists were seeking to establish a new life for themselves. Catesby made two trips to America. From 1712 to 1719 he collected plants and seeds along the Atlantic coast, traveling as far west as the Blue Ridge Mountains and as far south as Bermuda and Jamaica. While in America, he won the esteem of natural historians in England by sending them numerous rare plant specimens. In 1722 Catesby returned to America as a plant collector.

This 3-year endeavor culminated in Catesby's highly literate and handsomely illustrated two-volume *The Natural History of Carolina, Florida, and the Bahama Islands* (1731–1743). With its 220 color illustrations, this book remained the most attractive scientific work published on American natural history for the next 100 years. Although some critics have found many of Catesby's illustrations too brightly colored and often lacking in scientific detail, others have praised the ecologically sound settings and marvelously dynamic poses of animals. Catesby popularized the practice, later used effectively by Alexander Wilson and John Audubon, of including on one plate a balanced visual portrayal of zoological, ornithological, and botanical specimens. Catesby's taxonomy was weak, and his contributions to modern

The hooded titmouse and the water tupelo.. An engraving from the drawings of Mark Catesby, the English naturalist who began the practice of combining zoological, ornithological, and botanical specimens on one plate. [Library of Congress]

classification were quite meager. Yet in the field of ornithology he surpassed the descriptive standards of the time. With his attempts to explain the migratory habits of birds, he began the practice of interpretive ornithology in America.

Gmelin and Steller As the pace of exploration increased, so did the number of individuals who participated in the collection of specimens and observations. It is impossible in the brief compass of this article to include more than a representative selection of the more significant accomplishments in natural-history exploration in the eighteenth and nineteenth centuries. Almost every nation in Europe sent expeditions to distant lands, and naturalists and other scientists were almost always a part of an expedition's force.

Russian desire to learn more of the eastern reaches of the Russian empire enabled the German naturalists Johann Georg Gmelin (1709–1755) and Georg Wilhelm STELLER to explore those lands. In 1733 Georg Gmelin joined the Second Kamchatka Expedition, which, with the encouragement of the empress Anna and the support of the Russian Academy of Sciences at St. Petersburg, was going to survey eastern Siberia, the coastline of Arctic Russia, the lands east of those coastlines, and the waters of the North Pacific. The expedition was to consist of two components. The larger force was to march overland across Siberia until it reached the ocean and once there construct vessels for a program of marine exploration under the command of Vitus BERING. The second element consisted of a small contingent of scientists who would proceed overland to Kamchatka, obtaining specimens and records of the flora, fauna, geology, meteorology, and peoples encountered. In addition to Gmelin, this party also included the historian and ethnographer Gerhard Friedrich Müller and the astronomer Louis Delisle de la Croyère. By September 1735, Gmelin's party had reached Yakutsk, having explored the regions along the Irtysh, Ob, and Tom Rivers and having passed through Krasnoyarsk to Yeniseysk and then to Irkutsk near Lake Baykal, steadily marching eastward. For a naturalist, the hazards of travel were often compounded by the frequent disasters which occurred to his specimens, notebooks, and equipment. In November 1736, a fire destroyed most of Gmelin's collections and equipment. By the end of the summer of 1737, Gmelin and his party had explored the lands along the Tunguska and Angara Rivers and had descended the latter river to winter at Yeniseysk.

While in winter quarters they met Steller, who had traveled overland from St. Petersburg. Steller was sent farther eastward to join Bering's party. Gmelin then proceeded up the Yenisey River until he reached 66°N. His party then began the homeward journey, exploring the area between the Yenisey and Ob Rivers, the Baraba, Ishim, and Vagay Steppes, and the region around the Caspian Sea on their return. They reached St. Petersburg in early 1743.

The lands seen, the flora and fauna examined, and

the observations recorded during this expedition of more than 9 years provided Gmelin with a unique insight into the natural history of these heretofore scientifically unexplored regions. Gmelin's *Flora sibirica* (1747–1769) describes more than 1100 species encountered during his travels and provides illustrations of 294 of them. Noting the important distinctions in plants and animals that occur in Siberia once the Yenisey River has been crossed, Gmelin suggested for the first time that this river was a natural frontier between Europe and Asia. In addition to the important general observations that he made in zoology, geology, ethnography, and mineral resources, Gmelin also determined that the Caspian Sea was lower than the Black and Mediterranean Seas. In eastern Siberia he discovered permafrost and made attempts to measure its depth. Gmelin's pioneering efforts in exploring the natural history of Siberia were complemented by the equally momentous accomplishments in the lands and waters farther to the east.

Steller had unusual opportunities to examine a unique natural environment that had not yet been subjected to the scrutiny of science or the exploitation of Europeans. In spite of dangerous and taxing circumstances, he made good use of these opportunities. After joining Bering's forces in Siberia, he sailed with them in June 1741 on board the *St. Peter* (*Sv. Pyotr*) for the exploration of those northern waters that lay between Siberia and North America. Although he was the ship's physician and naturalist, his arrogance and contempt for his companions led to unpleasant and frequently stormy relations with his Russian shipmates. To the detriment of the expedition's health and success, his medical advice was too frequently ignored, and scurvy became a persistent and deadly problem.

On July 16, 1741, the mainland of Alaska was sighted for the first time as Mount St. Elias came into view. A few days later, Steller was allowed to go ashore on Kayak Island in the Gulf of Alaska, becoming the first naturalist to collect in Alaskan waters. Unfortunately, after the time, expense, and hardship expended in reaching this distinctive habitat, Steller was permitted to spend no more than 10 hours ashore gathering examples of the island's life-forms. Bering, fearful of being forced to winter in this ill-known and inhospitable region, sought to return to Kamchatka. While still in those waters, Steller had the opportunity to observe the native Aleuts, and he prepared one of the earliest descriptions of these peoples. By now scurvy had broken out among the crew, and the grim foolishness of ignoring Steller's earlier advice on antiscorbutic herbs became manifest. Bering himself died of scurvy on December 8, 1741. Throughout the winter and in the midst of his ministrations to the ill, Steller conducted an extensive examination of the plant and animal life of the island and surrounding waters. Provided with more time for his investigations than he had previously enjoyed, he performed his famous study of the sea cow (Steller's sea cow, *Hydro-*

damalis gigas), dissecting one of these remarkable marine animals, which weighed almost 8000 pounds (4629 kilograms). His study of the sea cow was one of his principal scientific accomplishments. It provided scientists with the most detailed knowledge available on this large manatee, which could reach a length of 35 feet (11 meters) and a girth of 20 feet (6 meters). Within a century after Steller's study, the sea cow had become extinct at the hands of northern sealers. In his *De bestiis marinis*, which was published posthumously in 1751, Steller presented the results not only of his study of the sea cow but also of his studies of other marine animals including the first detailed account of the sea otter. In ornithology, Steller gained distinction for his descriptions of Steller's jay, Steller's eider, Steller's eagle, and Steller's white raven. Gmelin utilized Steller's botanical notes in his *Flora sibirica*, while scrupulously acknowledging his indebtedness to Steller's work.

Banks and Solander   As the momentum of exploration increased in the latter half of the eighteenth century, more opportunities arose for naturalists to join government-sponsored expeditions. Such an opportunity presented itself to Joseph Banks (1743–1820) when in 1768 he persuaded the British government to allow him to join the naval expedition commanded by James COOK to observe the transit of Venus. The son of a prosperous member of the landed gentry in England, Banks had the leisure and resources which would enable him to participate in a voyage that would be fraught with dangers and last several years. Banks not only paid his personal expenses but also invested £10,000 to acquire equipment for his researches and to pay the expenses of the eight men who accompanied him as part of his scientific party. Prior to his joining Cook on the Transit of Venus Expedition, Banks's experience as an exploring naturalist had been limited to a voyage to Labrador and Newfoundland in 1766.

Banks was accompanied on this expedition by a protégé of Linnaeus, the Swedish naturalist Daniel Carl Solander (1733–1782). One of Linnaeus's most distinguished students, Solander had come to England in 1760 to help implement Linnaeus's binomial system of classification. Although Linnaeus's experiences as a natural-history explorer had been limited to a collecting trip to Lapland in 1732, he became a powerful and enthusiastic advocate of seeking out unexplored areas for the study of natural history. His students wandered into every corner of the earth, seeking to collect, classify, and study unknown flora, fauna, and other natural phenomena. Students of Linnaeus explored, collected, and observed in Egypt, Smyrna, Mongolia, Surinam, the Malabar coast, China, America, Russia, West Africa, the Cape of Good Hope, Java, Ceylon, and Japan.

By August 1768, Banks and Solander had gathered their equipment and awaited Cooks's orders. The English biologist John Ellis commented in a letter to Linnaeus that "no people ever went to sea better fitted out for the purpose of natural history," remarking further that "they have got a fine library of natural history; they have all sorts of machines for catching and preserving insects; all kinds of nets, trawls, drags, and hooks for coral fishing, they even have a curious contrivance of a telescope by which, put into water, you can see the bottom at great depth." This was one of the best-equipped expeditions to set forth from any nation in the eighteenth century, and it was to be further graced by the able command and brillant seamanship of Captain Cook.

The *Endeavour* sailed in August 1768 for the Southern Hemisphere to take up a station at Tahiti where the party could observe the transit of Venus on June 3, 1769. Eighteenth-century scientists were interested in charting the dimensions of Newton's universe, and a careful and meticulous observation of the transit of Venus from various locations would enable them to determine the distance of the sun from the earth. This distance could then be used as a unit of measurement with which to perform the neccesary calculations for establishing the parameters of the universe.

Cook also received secret instructions to search for the great southern continent that was believed to exist before one reached latitude 40°S. If he was unable to find this land, he was to sail westward until he reached New Zealand. In this voyage of global circumnavigation, which lasted from the late summer of 1768 to July 1771, the *Endeavour* sailed down the east coast of South America, rounded Cape Horn, and observed the transit of Venus at Tahiti. Cook then began his search for the southern continent, saw his ship grounded on the coral shoals of the Great Barrier Reef, and surveyed and charted the eastern coastline

of Australia. Rediscovering the Torres Strait, the *Endeavour* passed into the Coral Sea through the East Indies and across the Indian Ocean, rounding the Cape of Good Hope for the return to England.

Banks and Solander enjoyed many unprecedented opportunities for natural-history investigation. On their outward passage, they became the first naturalists systematically to examine the flora and fauna around Tierra del Fuego, albeit at some cost. Two of Banks's servants died of exposure while he collected specimens of alpine flora.

At Tahiti, Banks and Solander broadened the scope of their investigations to include the ethnography of the Polynesians, and Banks gained some knowledge of the Tahitian language. Their collections and specimens grew as they explored the waters off the Great Barrier Reef, the largest coral formation in the world, and the eastern coastline of Australia. The animals encountered there intrigued them, particularly the large marsupial which the natives called the kangaroo. Collecting in New Guinea was restricted by the hostility of the natives, while in Java malaria and dysentery limited activities.

Upon their return in 1771, the preoccupation of both Banks and Solander with other matters postponed the early publication of the results of their investigation. They had encountered hundreds of new species of animals and had collected specimens from more than 100 new plant families with 800 to 1000 new species. The participation of Banks and Solander in Cook's first voyage left an important legacy for natural-history exploration. The two men attracted the attention of the scientific community to the vast Pacific Basin. Their collections and unpublished notes were later used by other scientists. Johann

James Cook arrived in Tahiti in 1769 with a party whose mission was to observe the transit of Venus from various locations in order better to calculate the distance of the earth from the sun. [Library of Congress]

Reinhold Forster used their materials to help work up the collections he made on Cook's second voyage, and their specimens later became part of the natural-history collections of the British Museum. Cook himself profited from his relationship with Banks and Solander, and naturalists played a prominent role on his second voyage. While naturalists did not play a significant role in his tragic third voyage, a precedent was established for naturalists to accompany voyages of exploration sponsored by the British government, although not at government expense. Charles Darwin's fruitful participation in the cruise of the *Beagle* was in the tradition of Banks and Solander.

The Forsters The success of Cook's first voyage and the acclaim that accrued to Cook, Banks, and Solander encouraged the Admiralty to sponsor another voyage. In 1772 Cook was sent forth to resolve the question of the southern continent's existence. With the *Resolution* and *Adventure,* Cook sailed on a voyage which lasted from July 1772 to July 1775. On this expedition, Cook finally demolished the geographers' belief in the great inhabitable Terra Australis Incognita.

The father-and-son team of Johann Reinhold Forster (1729–1798) and Johann Georg Adam Forster (1754–1794) accompanied Cook on the second voyage as naturalists. They were given this opportunity when Banks declined to join the expedition because of a disagreement over the accommodations to be allocated to the naturalists. The Forsters were talented German botanists, and their descriptions of the flora encountered during the cruise of the *Resolution* and *Adventure* in the Pacific became the basis for the systematic botanical knowledge of that immense region. Reinhold Forster described his experiences in his *Observations Made during a Voyage round the World* (1778), an important and methodologically significant delineation of the anthropological, geographical, botanical, zoological, and oceanographical phenomena encountered. His son Georg produced a more general account of the expedition, *A Voyage round the World* (1777), which introduced the popular scientific travel narrative. Six decades later from the deck of the *Beagle,* Darwin would observe, investigate, and speculate upon the origins and importance of some of the same coral reefs and volcanoes that had intrigued the Forsters. The work of both Forsters anticipated and stimulated the work of their countryman Alexander von Humboldt, the elder Forster in terms of methodology and breadth of scientific interest and the younger Forster in the development of a popular travel narrative which described one's scientific travels. Georg Forster also gave personal encouragement to Humboldt to pursue a career of scientific exploration.

Humboldt The tradition of natural-history exploration was ably maintained by the talented and energetic Alexander von Humboldt (1769–1859). Inspired by Georg Forster, the young Humboldt passionately dedicated himself to a life of scientific adventure.

With his companion, the French botanist Aimé Bonpland, Humboldt embarked upon what has been appropriately termed the "scientific discovery of America." Granted permission by King Charles IV of Spain to explore that country's possessions in the New World, from July 1799 to April 1804 they traveled more than 6000 arduous miles (9650 kilometers) through the often-hazardous terrain of present-day Venezuela, Cuba, Colombia, Peru, Ecuador, and Mexico, observing, recording, and mapping the flora, fauna, geology, seismology, geography, history, climate, peoples, and antiquities of those lands. They collected more than 60,000 plant specimens, 6300 of which were unknown to science, and carefully sought to determine their latitude and longitude as they traveled. Notebook after notebook was filled with data and reflections on what they observed, for Humboldt was interested in all subjects, from the treeless expanses of the llanos (plains) to the remarkable shocking powers of the electric eel. Humboldt sought ideas as well as specimens, and he was always attentive to the nuances of nature, appreciating the delicacy with which a hummingbird could balance on a chalice of a flower as well as the majestic forces of the earth which could thrust a mountain range upward.

Humboldt's accomplishments were many. His exploration of the upper Orinoco River and his passage through the feral wilderness of the Casiquiare River or Canal demonstrated the connection between the great South American waterways of the Orinoco and the Río Negro, a tributary of the Amazon, the only natural connection between two great river systems in the world. Humboldt and Bonpland became the first naturalists to explore the luxuriant tropical wilderness between the Amazon and Orinoco Basins, collecting more than 12,000 plant specimens on this journey alone. Having explored these important river systems, Humboldt then turned his attention to the volcanic formations of the high Andes. In June 1802, he ascended to within 1500 feet (457 meters) of the dome-shaped summit of Chimborazo in Ecuador, having climbed to a height more than 19,000 feet (5791 meters), never reached before. This record, which lasted 30 years and was surpassed by one of his own protégés, contributed significantly to Humboldt's popular reputation in Europe. His studies along the cordillera of the Andes were particularly fruitful. They provided him with data on plant distribution, life zones, the formation of rocks, the role of volcanoes in the origin and growth of mountain ranges, and the effect of high altitudes upon humans.

Upon his return to Europe in 1804, Humboldt began the Herculean task of analyzing and publishing the results of his extensive studies. Laboring over this project for more than a quarter of a century, he used up his private fortune in the production of the handsomely illustrated thirty-four volumes of the *Voyage aux régions équinoxiales du nouveau continent . . . par Al. de Humboldt et A. Bonpland . . .* (Paris, 1805–1834). Humboldt was a polymath, and his interests

Alexander von Humboldt, whose interests and accomplishments were encyclopedic, dedicated himself to scientific adventure, making important discoveries in fields as diverse as botany and geomagnetism, [German Information Center]

were universal. His work on geomagnetism enabled him to discover the weakening of the earth's magnetic field as the equator was approached. To compare the climate of various regions, he introduced the use of isothermal lines and developed the methodology for studying tropical storms. When sailing along the coast of Peru, he became the first scientist carefully to measure the temperature and velocity of the cold ocean current that washed those shores. For mapping the oceanographical features of this current, geographers, to his dismay, presented him with the eponymic honor of designating it the Humboldt Current. Humboldt's South American years were his primary experiences as an exploring naturalist, although he made a 6-month trip across Eurasia to Siberia in 1829.

Humboldt was a compassionate humanist who believed in the oneness of the universe. He was interested in describing for the public the nature, methods, discoveries, and beauty of science. At the age of 76, Humboldt published the first volume of a five-volume interpretive synthesis of nature's interrelationships, the *Kosmos* (1845–1862), upon which he labored until his death in 1859. With its citation of more than 9000 sources, the *Kosmos* is a testament to the skill and dedication with which Humboldt sought to intro-

duce society to the wonder and mysteries of nature. The immediate popularity of the work, 80,000 copies of which were sold within 6 years, and its translation into the major European languages speak of the success of his self-ordained task.

Humboldt's ideas and writings nourished a generation of nineteenth-century naturalists. Darwin, Alfred Russel Wallace, Louis Agassiz, and William James considered Humboldt's *Personal Narrative of Travels* to be among their favorite works. Darwin stated that the whole course of his life was due to his having read and reread Humboldt's *Personal Narrative,* and it was Darwin who proclaimed that Humboldt was "the greatest scientific traveler who ever lived."

Darwin The contributions of Charles Darwin (1809–1882) to the development of modern biology are well known and are a direct result of his participation as an unpaid civilian naturalist on HMS *Beagle* during its 57-month cruise from 1831 to 1836. Robert Fitzroy, commander of the surveying ship *Beagle,* suggested to the Admiralty the importance of having a naturalist join the *Beagle* on its mission to survey the coasts of Patagonia, Tierra del Fuego, Chile, and Peru and to obtain a series of meridian distances across the Atlantic, Pacific, and Indian Oceans. With the Admiralty's consent, once more a civilian naturalist set forth upon a ship of the Royal Navy. Fitzroy fulfilled his hydrographical instructions in an efficient and professional fashion, returning with eighty-two detailed and accurate coastal sheets, eighty harbor plans, and forty views of portions of the lands the party visited. He also obtained an accurate sequence of meridian distances with the ship's chronometers and thus satisfied that segment of his orders.

In spite of illness and frequent periods of seasickness, Darwin's years aboard the *Beagle* transformed him from an inexperienced student of nature into a dedicated field naturalist with sophisticated observational and analytical skills. Since the study of natural history was not the primary purpose of the *Beagle*'s voyage, Darwin was able to engage in this pursuit only when it did not interfere with the hydrographical mission of the ship. Whenever possible, Darwin remained ashore to conduct his own investigations while Fitzroy performed his surveying tasks at sea.

At their first port of call at São Tiago in the Cape Verde Islands, Darwin had the opportunity to examine the geological history of an island. With Charles Lyell's *Principles of Geology* as his guide, he began to appreciate the recent geological process by which islands were formed. As his observational skills increased, his awareness of the diverse forces which were involved in geological change developed. On the islands of the Atlantic, Pacific, and Indian Oceans as well as along the coasts of South America, Darwin studied geological phenomena which led him to depart from the catastrophist position in geology. His experiences with earthquakes, his study of volcanoes, and his examinations of fossil beds on the sides of

Darwin's explanation of the role of coral polyps in the creation of atolls was not verified until the twentieth century.

mountains led him to understand the role of elevation and subsidence in the formation of the earth's surface as well as to perceive that many areas were once covered by great seas. Swift-running streams in the Andes led him to comprehend the forces of erosion. Darwin's most salient geological observations centered in the role of coral polyps in the building of atolls, barrier reefs, and fringing reefs. This was a subject which perplexed many Pacific explorers, but it was Charles Darwin who provided the brilliant hypothesis which explained the nature of their origin. In contrast to Lyell's view that atolls were formed by coral polyps on the rims of submarine volcanoes, Darwin correctly argued that coral atolls arose along the edges of volcanic craters that were gradually subsiding. This famous theory testifies both to Darwin's skill as a field naturalist and to his talents as a theoretician. Darwin's explanation was not verified until the twentieth century.

Darwin's thoughts upon the origin and evolution of species matured very slowly and were a consequence of his comparison of the flora and fauna encountered in his explorations of the Cape Verde Islands, South America, and the islands of the Galápagos Archipelago. Having sailed from England with little thought on this question, Darwin tacitly acknowledged the immutability of species. Yet the facts which he began to record in his notebooks led him ultimately to challenge this premise. The data which he could not reconcile with existing theory centered in the extinction of some species and the continuation of similar but not identical species, the existence of similar but not identical species in geographically adjacent areas, the presence of island species which resembled the life-forms on the nearest continent rather than life-forms in similar island habitats, and the variegated forms of similar species that he found in the Galápagos Islands.

The rocky, windswept islands of the Galápagos Archipelago provided Darwin with insight into the diversity of species which perplexed him. On each of these islands located near the equator some 600 miles (966 kilometers) west of South America, there existed such an array of similar but distinct forms of tortoises, lizards, mockingbirds, and finches that Darwin could no longer accept the immutability of species. The paramount question then became one of explaining the mechanism by which species changed, or evolved. Stimulated by Thomas Malthus's *An Essay on the Principle of Population*, Darwin suggested that species evolved into other species as a result of the process of natural selection during the struggle for survival. This insight into the mechanics of evolution coalesced slowly in Darwin's mind from 1837 to 1859, but it was not until he read Wallace's essay on the same subject in 1858 that he began the 13-month process of transforming his copious notes on the transmutation of species into his epoch-making *Origin of Species* (1859). In his *Autobiography*, Darwin acknowledged the importance of natural-history ex-

ploration in his own evolution, noting that "the voyage of the *Beagle* has been by far the most important event in my life and has determined my whole career."

Wallace and Bates Natural-history exploration was equally fruitful in stimulating the evolutionary thought of Alfred Russel Wallace (1823–1913). Wal-

Bird and fish of the Galápagos Archipelago: the many varieties of similar but distinct fauna that Darwin observed here caused him finally to reject the immutability of species.

lace's development of the mechanism of natural selection to explain the origin and evolution of species was also predicated upon observations he had made exploring and collecting in South America and Malaya. Inspired by the works of Humboldt and Darwin and by W. H. Edwards's *A Voyage up the River Amazon* (1847), Wallace and his close companion, the entomologist Henry Walter Bates (1825–1892), sought passage to South America to begin a career as explorers and natural-history collectors. Landing near the mouth of the Amazon at Belém (Pará) in 1848, they began a program of collecting and investigating which lasted for Wallace until 1852 and for Bates until 1859. Until 1850 they explored and collected in the region surrounding Pará, along the Tocantins River, and up the Río Negro; but in that year they separated to collect independently. Wallace continued to work along the Río Negro, while Bates explored the upper Amazon Basin. Carefully recording the locations at which he collected his specimens, Wallace began to be aware of the geographical distribution of plants and animals, a subject that challenged him for the rest of his life. While returning to England in 1852, Wallace was forced to abandon ship when it caught fire. After 15 days in an open boat, Wallace was rescued, but he had lost the specimens and notes he had made during the previous 4 years. The loss of these materials prevented him from publishing the detailed scientific papers that he desired, although he was able to publish a work on the palm trees of the Amazon which contained an analysis of their distribution along the Negro and Amazon Rivers. For the general public, he prepared *A Narrative of Travels on the Amazon and Rio Negro* (1853), but this work never gained the acceptance that Bates's popular account of his travels obtained.

Bates, after his separation from Wallace, devoted the next 7½ years to exploring and collecting in the Tapajós and Solimões River Basins. A dedicated collector and an ardent student of the insect life of the Amazon, Bates obtained more than 14,500 specimens, 8000 of which were unknown to science. These insects, in particular the butterflies, provided Bates with the clue to the understanding of mimicry, the phenomenon by which an unprotected species that is scarce and palatable assumes a resemblance in shape and color to a more abundant and unpalatable species and thus escapes the attention of predators. An early adherent of Darwin's ideas, Bates became an important student of systematic entomology. Upon his return to England, he served for twenty-eight years as assistant secretary of the ROYAL GEOGRAPHICAL SOCIETY. In this position he corresponded with scientists and explorers throughout the world, edited the *Journal* and *Proceedings* of the society, published editions of a number of travel narratives, and performed his own research.

On numerous occasions Wallace and Bates discussed the evolution and geographical distribution of species, but the loss of Wallace's data in 1852 made him reluctant publicly to advocate a mechanism to explain this phenomenon. To gather additional observations for his understanding of the process of evolution and hoping to support himself through the collection and sale of specimens, Wallace sailed in 1854 for the Malay Archipelago. Traveling more than 14,000 miles (22,530 kilometers) before his return to England in 1862, Wallace explored the tropical regions embraced by Celebes in the north, Timor in the south, the Aru Islands in the east, and Malacca and Malaya in the west. During 8 years of wandering, Wallace collected approximately 127,000 specimens and gained evidence to support his belief in the organic evolution of species through natural selection. The descriptions of these travels in his popular *The Malay Archipelago* (1869) won him international acclaim. His accomplishments in natural-history exploration in both South America and Malaya, zoogeography, evolutionary biology, and popular scientific writing ensure that he be considered with Darwin as one of the premier naturalists of the nineteenth century.

Specialization Human curiosity about the world did not abate in the decades after the work of Wallace and Darwin on evolutionary biology, but the growing specialization within science began to restrict the activities of the more general natural historian. The day of the amateur scientist was beginning to disappear, for the masses of data that had been collected by earlier naturalists needed to be integrated into a more sophisticated theoretical framework. Zoologists, botanists, ecologists, anthropologists, ethnologists, geologists, climatologists, vulcanologists, and oceanographers began to assume their specialized researches. These disciplines built upon the explorations and accomplishments of the earlier naturalists who had ventured into the recesses of every continent to gain an understanding of the world of nature.

BIBLIOGRAPHY: Henry Walter Bates, *The Naturalist on the River Amazon*, 2 vols., London, 1863; J. C. Beaglehole, *The Life of Captain James Cook*, Stanford, Calif., 1974; Douglas Botting, *Humboldt and the Cosmos*, New York, 1973; Alice M. Coats, *The Plant Hunters*, New York, 1970; Paul Russell Cutright, *The Great Naturalists Explore South America*, New York, 1940; Charles Darwin, *The Voyage of the Beagle*, ed. by Leonard Engel, New York, 1962; Loren Eiseley, *Darwin's Century*, New York, 1958; Alexander von Humboldt, *Cosmos*, tr. by E. C. Otté, 5 vols., London, 1848–1850; Lotte Kellner, *Alexander von Humboldt*, London, 1963; H. Lewis McKinney, *Wallace and Natural Selection*, New Haven, Conn., 1972; Roy Anthony Rauschenberg, *Daniel Carl Solander: Naturalist on the "Endeavour,"* Philadelphia, 1968; William H. Stahl, *Roman Science*, Madison, Wis., 1962; Leonhard Stejneger, *Georg Wilhelm Steller: The Pioneer of Alaskan Natural History*, Cambridge, Mass., 1936; Phillip D. Thomas, "The Waning Spirit: The Roman Legacy for Early Medieval Science," *Wichita State University Studies*, Wichita, Kans., 1969.

Phillip Drennon Thomas

Nearchus *(Nearchos; ca. 360–312 B.C.)* Officer of ALEXANDER THE GREAT. Born on Crete, he later lived in Amphipolis, Macedonia, and became a boyhood friend of Alexander. He took part in Alexander's campaign against Persia and was made governor of Lycia (southwest Turkey) in 334–333 B.C. In 329 he rejoined Alexander in Bactria with reinforcements. Alexander, prevented by mutiny in his army from advancing in India beyond the Hyphasis (Beas) River, determined to return to Mesopotamia by land along the southern coast of Persia; Nearchus was put in charge of a small fleet built on the Hydaspes (Jhelum) River and given the task of making a coastal voyage from the mouth of the Indus to the Persian Gulf. The object was to pursue a genuinely exploratory voyage, "to investigate the beaches along the coast together with anchorages and islands, to sail round any gulf penetrating inland, to find out what cities were near the sea, what land was capable of bearing crops and what was desert." Nearchus subsequently published an account of the voyage, relatively full extracts of which were used by Arrian in his *Indica*, and there are references in other authors. It appears that neither Alexander nor Nearchus had any direct knowledge of the voyage made along the same coast two centuries earlier by Scylax of Caryanda on the orders of the Persian king Darius I.

Nearchus's fleet, manned by Greeks, Phoenicians, Cypriots, and Egyptians and officered by Macedonians and Greeks, sailed from the mouth of the Indus in September 325 B.C. Apart from a delay caused by adverse winds at Karachi, the voyage was relatively uneventful. Nearchus's narrative gave his estimate of each day's sailing distance (unfortunately not the sailing time from which he estimated the distance) and topographical descriptions in simple factual form. His descriptions of the way of life of the indigenous peoples along the coast (most of an extremely primitive level of life) and of his encounters with them tend to be romanticized and show the influence of literary models, especially of Herodotus. Details in the account show that the fleet took 65 days including stops to get from the Indus mouth to the Anamis (Minab) River and another 40 days to the head of the Persian Gulf. The expedition was clearly well organized and successfully carried out Alexander's orders, even though some credit should go to the chief navigating officer, Onesicratus, honored like Nearchus by Alexander on their return. Nearchus's voyage probably had a negative effect on Greek interest in the area, since the coast seemed totally unattractive and poverty-stricken. When, about three centuries later, the use of the monsoons for sailing in the Indian Ocean was discovered (*see* PERIPLUS), not even the regular trade route between Egypt and Arabia and India followed the coast, which received little further attention until British surveys in the late eighteenth century.

BIBLIOGRAPHY: M. Cary and E. H. Warmington, *The Ancient Explorers*, London, 1929.

B. H. Warmington

Nevelskoy, Gennady Ivanovich (1814–1876) Russian naval officer. In 1848–49, as a captain lieutenant, he commanded the transport *Baykal* during a voyage from Kronshtadt around Cape Horn to Kamchatka. In 1849 he rounded the northern part of Sakhalin to the mouth of the Amur River, showing that the river was accessible to ships. From the Amur he sailed south to the Sea of Japan, proving that Sakhalin was an island. Returning to St. Petersburg by way of Siberia in the winter of 1849–1850, he was promoted and assigned to eastern Siberia. In the summer of 1850 he raised the Russian flag at the mouth of the Amur and founded the Nikolayevsky post. Between 1851 and 1855, as commander of the Amur Expedition, he directed the exploration of the Amur region and Sakhalin, mapped the Tatarsky Proliv (Tatar Strait), and discovered several harbors. In 1853 he raised the Russian flag on both shores of Tatar Strait and southern Sakhalin. He left the Far East in 1855 and returned to St. Petersburg but spent the last 20 years of his life in voluntary exile in Paris.   *Richard A. Pierce*

Nicollet (Nicolet) de Bellesborne, Jean (ca. 1598–1642) French explorer and interpreter in North America and clerk of the Company of One Hundred Associates. A native of Normandy, he came to New France in 1618 in the service of the Company of the Merchants of Rouen and of Saint-Malo. He played an important role as an intermediary between the French and the Indian tribes of the Hudson Bay area. In the summer of 1634 he undertook a long and difficult journey to the West in an effort to find the East China Sea. On this journey he made his way across Lake Huron to the Straits of Mackinac, and then he proceeded along the northern shore of Lake Michigan, which he dis-

covered as far as Green Bay (Baie des Puants). Maps which he made of this area were most useful for fur traders who subsequently came to this region. Upon returning to Trois-Rivières (Three Rivers), he worked as a clerk for the Company of One Hundred Associates and served as an interpreter to the satisfaction of both the French and the Indians. Because he had earlier spent 2 years living among the Algonquin Indians on Allumette Island in the Ottawa River learning their language and an additional 9 years in the country of the Nipissings, he was well qualified to serve as a liaison officer between the French and the natives.

Nicollet de Bellesborne was the first white man to explore the area near the Wisconsin River, a tributary of the Mississippi, and also the area southward toward the Illinois River. Well respected for his linguistic abilities and for his extensive knowledge of Indian lore, languages, and customs, he became a leading citizen of Trois-Rivières. He married Marguerite Couillard in October 1637 and had two children by her. His life was cut short by an accident. While he was traveling by boat between Quebec and Trois-Rivières in October 1642, the boat was overturned by a strong wind and Nicollet de Bellesborne was drowned.

BIBLIOGRAPHY: Auguste H. Gosselin, *Jean Nicolet et le Canada de son temps (1618–1642)*, Quebec, 1905.

Bernerd C. Weber

Niebuhr, Carsten (1733–1815) Danish explorer. A native of Holstein, then under the Danish crown, Niebuhr was one of a party of six commissioned by the King Frederick V to explore Yemen. Besides Niebuhr, who had been trained in mathematics and astronomy, the group included Peter Forskål, Christian Cramer, Frederick von Haven, George William Baurenfeind, and a Swedish servant, Berggren. With the exception of Niebuhr, all died in the course of the journey. With characteristic honesty, Niebuhr incorporated, with acknowledgments, the separate studies of his dead comrades in his own work. Forskål's notes on the flora and fauna of Yemen were edited by Niebuhr and published in 1775.

Like most European travelers to Arabia in the eighteenth century, Niebuhr had a political and economic mission as well as the stated scientific and geographic purposes. He was to ascertain the productivity of the area and the possibilities of increasing trade, which was then largely in the hands of the British and the Dutch, with Denmark. Niebuhr fulfilled his mission extremely well.

His party arrived at Jidda (Juddah) in October 1762. During their stay in Arabia they explored two of three major geographical zones in Yemen. The Tihamah, the coastal belt from Al Luhayyah to Mocha (Al Mukhā), about 60 miles (97 kilometers) at its broadest, was thoroughly documented, leaving little to subsequent scholar-travelers. In the second zone of mountainous highlands which parallel the Tihamah on the east, only the flora of *wādī* (river valleys) were examined by Forskål. The third area investigated included the capital, San'ā', and the great eastern slope which merges into the Al Ahqaf Desert bordering the southwestern corner of the Rub' al Khālī (Empty Quarter). Niebuhr was also the first European traveler to comment on the strict new Muslim creed known as Wahhabism that was then sweeping central Arabia, though he did not realize the vast repercussions of this movement on the future history of Arabia and Islam.

Niebuhr's relation of his travels was the first comprehensive account by an eighteenth-century traveler to Arabia. It was published in German (1772), French (1773), and English (1792). The many editions of his work, the latest in 1968, attest to the accuracy of his descriptions, which gained the respect of contemporaries and the accolades of his successors. His lucid and unemotional observations, especially of the inhabitants of Yemen, led Jacqueline Pirenne, a recent student of Arabian travel, to call him "the perfect reporter."

BIBLIOGRAPHY: D. G. Hogarth, *The Penetration of Arabia*, London, 1904; R. H. Kiernan, *The Unveiling of Arabia*, London, 1937; Carsten Niebuhr, *Travels through Arabia*, 2 vols., Edinburgh, 1792; Jacqueline Pirenne, *À la découverte de l'Arabie*, Paris, 1958.

Robert W. Olson

Niger River

Perhaps no other river in the world baffled the European mind to a greater extent or for a longer period of time than did the Niger River. From the days of HERODOTUS OF HALICARNASSUS until the solution of the Niger mystery in the first third of the nineteenth century, there was uncertainty about all aspects of the river: its source, the direction of its flow, the site of its termination, and indeed its very existence. The difficulty of obtaining accurate information about the river stemmed in part from its length (2600 miles, or 4184 kilometers), the unpredictability of its course through varied terrain inhabited by people of diverse cultures, and the fact that both the Niger and its principal tributary, the Benue River, were known by many different names. In addition, numerous obstacles hindered the access of Europeans to the river. An approach from North Africa required the crossing of the Sahara with all its attendant difficulties, while an approach from the West African coast involved the risk of succumbing to fever or dysentery. Moreover, it was virtually impossible to distinguish the river's mouth because of the swampy, ill-defined nature of its exit into the Gulf of Guinea. Finally, Africans resisted penetration of the interior by Europeans because they feared its commercial implications.

The European quest for the Niger began in earnest with the foundation in 1788 of the AFRICAN ASSOCIATION, which initially devoted itself to the solution of the river's mysteries. In the late eighteenth century knowledge of the Niger had progressed little from the time of Herodotus. After relating a tale of some North Africans who had crossed the Sahara and seen a great river flowing from west to east, the Greek historian conjectured that the river was the Nile, which he believed rose in the interior of Africa at the same distance from its mouth as the Danube from its mouth. Later both PLINY and PTOLEMY spoke of an African river which they called the Nigris or Nigir.

The assertion of Herodotus that the river flowed in an easterly direction was confirmed by IBN-HAWQAL, a tenth-century Arab geographer who visited the Sudan. But al-IDRISI stated in his description of African geography that the Niger flowed from east to west. LEO AFRICANUS, who may have actually navigated the river below Timbuktu in the early sixteenth century, made the same error in his *Descrittione dell' Africa* (*Description of Africa*). According to Leo, the Niger was a branch of the Nile which flowed underground and then emerged from a great lake.

European confusion regarding the Niger was graphically shown in the map of Africa in the 1570 atlas of Ortelius (Abraham Oertel). The map shows the Niger rising near the equator in a Lake Niger, flowing to the north (underground for 60 miles, or 97 kilometers) to Lake Bornu (Lake Chad) and then westward through a Lake Guber, and finally emptying into the Atlantic through a delta of which the Senegal and the Gambia were a part. The mid-eighteenth-century representation of the Niger by Jean-Baptiste Bourguignon d'Anville is little more accurate, although the Senegal is shown to be separate from the Niger.

The first important contribution to knowledge of

The course of the Niger River.

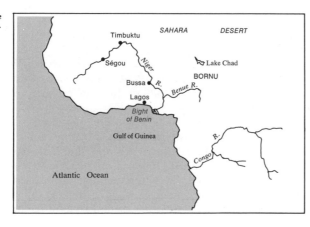

the Niger was made by Mungo PARK, who was sent to Africa by the African Association in 1795. Park saw the Niger near Ségou and confirmed its easterly flow. His narrative of his travels was accompanied by a work by James Rennell, England's foremost geographer, who held that the Niger terminated in a lake in the heart of Africa. Others, notably John BARROW, second secretary of the Admiralty, adhered to the ancient view that the Niger flowed into the Nile, while in 1816 James McQueen, a Scottish geographer, advanced what ultimately proved to be the correct theory: that the Niger emptied into the Gulf of Guinea. Park himself came to the conclusion that the Niger and the Congo were the same river and died in Africa in 1806 while trying to test his hypothesis.

Park's theory was again put to the test in 1815–1816, when the British government sponsored a two-pronged expedition to West Africa. A party led by Maj. John Peddie was to follow the Niger to its mouth, while a scientific expedition organized by the Admiralty and commanded by Capt. James K. Tuckey was directed to explore the Congo River to determine its relationship to the Niger. Neither of these expeditions added to the contemporary fund of information about the Niger.

Meanwhile, a young naval officer, William Henry Smyth, had urged the advisability of making Tripoli the starting point for future expeditions into the interior of West Africa, and his recommendations caught the attention of Barrow, who was disturbed by the unhappy results of previous efforts. In 1818 Joseph Ritchie, a surgeon, and George Lyon (1795–1832), a naval officer, left Tripoli and reached Marzūq (Murzuk) in Fezzan, where Ritchie died; on the basis of inquiries made while in Marzūq, Lyon concluded that the Niger reached Lake Chad and eventually joined the Nile. The Lyon-Ritchie Mission was followed by two other expeditions from Tripoli: the Bornu Mission and the effort of Alexander Gordon LAING, who had earlier traveled near the source of the Niger. Neither of these was able to trace the Niger to its termination, but Laing succeeded in reaching Timbuktu, and the Bornu Mission brought back valuable information about a virtually unknown region of Africa.

In 1825 Hugh CLAPPERTON, who had been a member of the Bornu Mission, returned to Africa to resume the search for the Niger, but he died without accom-

Heinrich Barth crossing the Niger River at Say, in what is now Niger, on an expedition sponsored by the British government and aimed at ending the slave trade.

plishing his goal of following the river to its mouth. In 1830, however, Richard LANDER, who had first traveled to Africa as Clapperton's servant, and his brother John sailed down the Niger from Bussa to the delta through which the river flows into the Gulf of Guinea.

The success of the Landers did not put an end to expeditions to the Niger, but the promotion of commerce and discontinuance of the slave trade now became the principal objectives. In 1832 Macgregor Laird organized a trading expedition which proved unsuccessful and cost the life of Richard Lander and most of the other Europeans who took part in it. In 1850 the British government sponsored an expedition led by James Richardson aimed at extinguishing the slave trade. Although it too failed to achieve its primary purpose, the scholarly work of one of its members, Heinrich BARTH, was of major significance. In 1854 a mission was sent to West Africa to explore the Benue River and, if possible, to make contact with Barth. Barth was not found, but the mission, under the leadership of Dr. William Balfour Baikie (1825–1864), did sail its steamer to a point on the Benue several hundred miles higher than that attained previously. Baikie returned to Africa in 1857 and remained there until 1864. With his death the same year, the great age of Niger exploration came to an end.

BIBLIOGRAPHY: E. W. Bovill (ed.), *Missions to the Niger*, 4 vols., Cambridge, England, 1964–1966; E. W. Bovill, *The Niger Explored*, London, 1968; Robin Hallett (ed.), *Records of the African Association, 1788–1831*, London, 1964; Christopher Lloyd, *The Search for the Niger*, London, 1973.

Nile River: Search for Its Source

For centuries men had marveled at the mighty river which traced a verdant strip through the Egyptian desert and wondered where its life-giving waters originated. Yet in the mid-nineteenth century the primary source of the world's longest stream remained as shrouded in mystery as it had been when the first-century Roman poet Lucan, in *The Civil War*, penned his famous lines on the river's allure:

> Yet still no views have urged my ardour more
> Than Nile's remotest mountains to explore.

Then say what source the famous stream supplies,
And bids it at revolving periods rise;
Show me the head from which, since time begun,
The long succession of his waves have run;
This let me know, and all my toils shall cease
The sword be sheathed, and earth be blessed with peace.

To be sure, many geographers of the carpet-slipper variety were ever ready to propound dogmatically asserted theories relating to the problem. Practically speaking, however, real knowledge of the subject had made little significant progress in 1600 years, since PTOLEMY, with the aid of native reports, had placed the location of the Nile's fountainhead somewhere in the equatorial "Mountains of the Moon," now identified with the Ruwenzori mountain group discovered by Henry M. STANLEY in 1889.

In reality the lower Nile is formed of two rivers, the Blue and White Niles, which have their confluence at Khartoum. The streams, appropriately named because of their coloration, have markedly different characteristics. The vagaries of geography have dictated that the White Nile be known as the principal river despite the fact that for much of each year its sister stream flows with such intensity that it supplies more than 80 percent of the water to the Nile below Khartoum. However, the White Nile is the longer of the two feeders, and solution of its sources proved an infinitely more difficult and intriguing problem than was the case with the Blue Nile.

The Blue Nile The Blue Nile flows out of Lake Tana in the Ethiopian mountains, and on the eve of the great era of Nile reconnaissance its source had been known for three-quarters of a century. The man who had unveiled the Blue Nile's mysteries was James BRUCE, a Scotsman who was a typical product of the Age of Reason. His early years were marked by illness, and his marriage ended in tragedy only 9 months after he and his bride had repeated their vows. Bruce sought solace and release from his grief in what he considered "the noblest of all occupations, that of exploring the distant parts of the globe." His vision fixed on the source of the Nile, which he deemed "a defiance of all travellers, and an opprobrium to geography."

After years of rather aimless wandering about North Africa, in 1769 Bruce's peregrinations carried him to the port of Massawa on the Red Sea in Eritrea, and thence into the unknown Ethiopian hinterland. In just over 3 months he reached the capital city of Gondar on Lake Tana, where he managed to ingratiate himself with local rulers. His connections enabled him to travel with relative freedom, and during 1770 he explored Lake Tana and its immediate environs. Bruce overlooked the Blue Nile's outflow from Lake Tana, but he observed the spectacular Tissisat Falls and most of the other significant features of the river's headwaters. A Portuguese priest, Pedro Páez, had anticipated much of this work by a century and a half, and a similar passage of time would ensue before Col. R. E. Cheesman completed the exploration of the Blue Nile in the 1920s and 1930s. Nonetheless, Bruce's

travels, which culminated with a journey downriver from Ethiopia to the union of the two Niles, take pride of place.

He had persevered against every imaginable obstacle through upward of a decade of exploration, and his copious notes and accurate (if often exaggerated) observations ushered in a new age of African discovery. Bruce waited for many years after his return to Europe before publishing a massive, highly controversial account of his experiences, and owing to rather shoddy treatment at the hands of his contemporaries he died believing that his researches largely had been in vain. In truth the scorn and disbelief he encountered were rather predictable manifestations of the Georgian temperament, and they did little to detract from the singular nature of his achievement. Bruce had initiated the solution of and focused attention anew on the ancient enigma of the Nile. Henceforth, as European imaginations encompassed ever-wider horizons, the question of the Nile's ultimate source would remain well to the forefront in both public curiosity and geographical circles.

Burton and Speke The single greatest breakthrough in Nile discovery came in the mid-1850s, when Richard Francis BURTON and John Hanning SPEKE set out on a journey which had as one of its primary purposes "solution of that great geographical problem, the determination of the sources of the White Nile." This was how their instructions from the ROYAL GEOGRAPHICAL SOCIETY, the sponsoring body, read, and while their goal was ages old, the approach adopted by the two Englishmen was a novel one. Burton, the leader of the expedition, proposed to reach what he termed the Nile's "coy fountains" via an overland route starting on the East African coast opposite Zanzibar. Heretofore every attempt at reaching the Nile's headwaters had proceeded along the stream itself, and in the two decades prior to Burton and Speke's venture, appreciable progress had been made. Indeed, various individuals including members of the Catholic Mission to Central Africa and John Petherick, an English trader who also filled a consular office, had progressed as far upriver as Gondokoro at the navigable head of the Nile. However, the stream's source clearly lay much farther south, and Burton felt a more productive approach might be to travel directly to the great equatorial lakes that reputedly lay in the heart of the continent and thence downstream.

The story of the resultant expedition, which culminated in great discoveries but also in irreconcilable differences between Burton and Speke, is one of the best known in the annals of African exploration. After a lengthy, wearying journey which tried both men mentally and physically, the two companions reached Lake Tanganyika, which Burton believed to be their goal: "the reputed Lake of Nyassa." On the return journey, Speke suggested that they detour to investigate a second lake, "described by the Arabs to be both broader and longer than the Tanganyika . . . which they call Ukerèwe," that he was "burning to see." But

Burton, his patience exhausted by the rigors of African travel and not a little tired of Speke's company, bluntly declared that "he was not going to see any more lakes." Resolutely Speke insisted on the importance of exploring the lake in order to follow the letter of the Royal Geographical Society's instructions. Yet in all likelihood his sanctimoniously expressed sense of duty was tinctured by an intense personal desire to carry out his "long-cherished hopes of discovering the sources of the Nile." Finally Burton, exasperated by Speke's persistence and appreciative of an opportunity to be alone, granted his subordinate permission to explore the inland sea of which the Arabs spoke in such grand terms. Burton, who for the moment preferred solitude and ethnological researches to geographical discovery, was thereby betrayed into a mistake which was to haunt him for the rest of his life.

Speke, spurred by slim bits of evidence concerning a lake that reportedly "extended to the end of the world," made a rapid and relatively trouble-free march to the Ukerèwe. On August 3, 1858, he sighted a vast expanse of water which he intuitively concluded was the source of the Nile: "I no longer felt any doubt that the lake at my feet gave birth to that interesting river, the source of which has been the subject of so much speculation, and the object of so many explorers." Speke's logic was weak (Burton later likened his reasoning to that of a woman), but ultimately, after years of controversy and uncertainty, it would be established that Speke had indeed solved the ancient riddle of the White Nile.

Exultant in his success, Speke hurried back to the town of Kazeh (modern Tabora, Tanzania) to share the good news with Burton. To his surprise he was received rather coolly by Burton, who somehow sensed that the elusive goal he had sought with such ardor had slipped away. For the remainder of the return journey the subject of the lake as the Nile's source was avoided by mutual agreement, but as soon as Speke reached England (Burton had been left behind in Aden to recuperate from the effects of tropical disease), he expressed his firm conviction that his discovery was the source of the Nile. He had named the lake Victoria, after his sovereign, and forthwith he announced plans to return to Africa in order to obtain geographical proof of his claims. Sir Roderick Murchison, the influential president of the Royal Geographical Society, shared much of Speke's enthusiasm and following an interview with the young explorer he announced: "Speke, we must send you there again."

Speke and Grant The stir created in geographical circles by Speke's revelations and subsequent bitter recriminations and denunciations on the part of Burton ensured that there would be no scarcity of volunteers to accompany Speke on his new expedition, and in short order James Augustus GRANT, a former hunting companion in India, was chosen as second-in-command. Speke planned once again to approach the lake with an overland expedition originating in Zanzibar, but there also were arrangements for an auxil-

iary expedition which would travel up the Nile under the leadership of John Petherick. The latter undertaking had as its primary purpose a meeting with Speke and Grant on their journey downriver from Lake Victoria, but Petherick was anxious to have some part in joining Speke in "ripping open Africa together."

On April 27, 1860, Speke and Grant left England and made a leisurely voyage to Zanzibar. After ncessary equipping and preparations on the island, they commenced their journey to Kazeh along the same trade route followed on Speke's previous expedition. After countless interruptions, a standard feature of African travel, they reached Kazeh and marched on to the kingdom of Karagwe, an area near the southwestern shore of Lake Victoria. Here Speke and Grant remained for several weeks as the guests of Rumanika, the sovereign of Karagwe, while awaiting permission to enter the adjacent country of Buganda. Speke discovered a new lake, which he named the Little Windermere, but news of Petherick made him anxious to resume his quest. Ultimately the requisite permission came from Mutesa, the ruler of Buganda, and Speke moved on to his court. At Mutesa's he and Grant found themselves virtual prisoners, and not until July 1862 were they allowed to resume their journey. However, their sojourn had at least one bright spot, because while at Mutesa's Speke had learned that Lake Victoria had a large outlet at its northern end. He surmised that this might well be the outflow of the Nile and accordingly the party moved in this direction. When he and Grant neared the place where the Nile supposedly left the lake, Speke made a decision which later drew bitter attacks from his numerous critics. Instead of allowing Grant the privilege of sharing in the achievement of their long-awaited goal, Speke took a small group of men and made a flying trip in search of the Nile's exit. However, Grant's leg was troubling him, and his diaries make it abundantly clear that he concurred with Speke's decision to go on alone.

Speke made a rapid journey and on July 21, 1862, he sighted his goal: "Here at last I stood on the brink of the Nile. Most beautiful was the scene; nothing could surpass it! It was a magnificent stream from 600 to 700 yards [550 to 640 meters] wide." Speke then marched upstream, and a week later he reached the point where the river left Lake Victoria. He now had, in his personal view, removed all doubts concerning the mystery of the Nile's source. As he gazed on the mighty waterfall that formed the river's exit from Lake Victoria, he concluded: "The expedition had now performed its functions. I saw that old Father Nile without any doubt rises in the Victoria Nyanza [Nyanza was an African word for lake] as I had foretold." So certain was Speke that he lingered at the spot for only 3 days, and after he rejoined Grant, the expedition began a march downriver that maintained only sporadic contact with the river. This was a mistake, because Speke had only to stay in continuous contact with the stream to Gondokoro, and all vestiges of doubt concerning the Nile's source would have been resolved. However, for the sake of expediency and because he personally had no doubts, Speke failed to obtain irrefutable proof to support his discovery. This oversight, together with other factors such as Speke's mysterious death shortly after his return to England and lingering doubts on the part of Burton, Dr. David LIVINGSTONE, and other eminent geographers, served to prolong final resolution of the Nile controversy by more than a decade.

Baker and Stanley   Meanwhile, Speke, heedless of the potential enormity of his failure to follow the Nile, continued downriver on a homeward course. At Gondokoro he and Grant met an old acquaintance of Speke's, Samuel White BAKER, who had undertaken the solution of the Nile's sources from the traditional northern approach. The two parties exchanged notes, and on the strength of information Speke and Grant had obtained regarding a lake to the west of Victoria Nyanza Baker continued southward in hopes that he might yet pluck a remaining leaf of Nile laurel. In March 1864, Baker reached a body of water he named

Murchison Falls, dropping from the Victoria Nile to the level of Lake Albert.

Lake Albert (after the Prince Consort, a fitting choice for the mate of Speke's discovery), and he subsequently verified that the Victoria Nile entered the lake on the northeast and that the White Nile (sometimes referred to as the Albert Nile at this point) left the lake at its northern end, flowing toward Gondokoro. He thus provided general corroboration for Speke's theories, but debate on the exact nature and location of the Nile's sources continued unabated for many years.

Almost a decade later Dr. Livingstone, in the course of his famous last journey, was convinced that he was at the Nile's headwaters. Actually, as journeys by Verney Lovett CAMERON and Henry Stanley soon proved, Livingstone's Lualaba River was the headstream of the Congo. Stanley not only contributed to clarification of Livingstone's geographical endeavors; he also wrote the final chapter in the lengthy story of Nile exploration. In the course of two major expeditions, the Anglo-American one of 1874–1877 and that in relief of Emin Pasha during the years 1887–1890, Stanley resolved most of the questions which still troubled geographers and bolstered Speke's detractors. He circumnavigated both Lake Victoria and Lake Tanganyika during the Anglo-American Expedition, and the same journey saw the watersheds of the Congo and the Nile clearly delineated. Stanley's mission to rescue Emin Pasha in Equatoria clarified the exact nature of Lake Albert as a Nile reservoir (it receives water from Lake Edward via the Semliki River and Lake Victoria via the Victoria Nile—these combine to issue forth from Lake Albert as the White Nile) and for all practical purposes completed the Nile quest.

Speke thus had been premature in his 1863 cable to England saying "The Nile is settled." Indeed, in the interlude between his confidently telegraphed pronouncement and Stanley's last great African journey, a number of individuals in addition to those already mentioned played some part in clarification of the Nile's geography. Notable among these were Georg August SCHWEINFURTH, a German who traveled in the area of the Nile-Congo watershed, Wilhelm Junker, and Charles CHAILLÉ-LONG. Yet in the end Speke's theories were fully vindicated, and he must be given the primary credit for the revelation of what Sir Harry JOHNSTON, himself an eminent Africanist and explorer, termed "the greatest geographical secret after the discovery of America."

BIBLIOGRAPHY: J. N. L. Baker, "Sir Richard Burton and the Nile Sources," *English Historical Review*, vol. LIX, January 1944, pp. 49–61; Samuel W. Baker, *The Albert N'yanza*, 2 vols., new ed. with an introduction by Alan Moorehead, New York, 1962; Fawn M. Brodie, *The Devil Drives: A Life of Sir Richard Burton*, New York, 1967; James Bruce, *Travels to Discover the Source of the Nile*, 2d ed., 5 vols., Edinburgh, 1795; Richard F. Burton, *The Lake Regions of Central Africa*, 2 vols., London, 1860; James A. Casada, "James A. Grant and the Royal Geographical Society," *The Geographical Journal*, vol. CXL, June 1974, pp. 245–253; James A. Grant, *A Walk across Africa*, Edinburgh and London, 1864; Richard Hall, *Stanley: An Adventurer Explored*, London, 1974; Alexander Maitland, *Speke and the Discovery of the Source of the Nile*, Edinburgh and London, 1863; Dorothy Middleton, *Baker of the Nile*, London, 1949; Alan Moorehead, *The Blue Nile*, London, 1962; id., *The White Nile*, London, 1960; J. M. Reid, *Traveller Extraordinary: The Life of James Bruce of Kinnaird*, New York, 1968; Heinrich Schiffers, *The Quest for Africa*, tr. by Diana Pyke, New York, 1957; John H. Speke, *Journal of the Discovery of the Source of the Nile*, Edinburgh and London, 1863; id., *What Led to the Discovery of the Source of the Nile*, Edinburgh and London, 1864; Henry M. Stanley, *Through the Dark Continent*, 2 vols., London, 1878.

James A. Casada

Nordenskiöld, Nils Adolf Erik (1832–1901) Swedish Arctic explorer and scientist. Adolf Nordenskiöld came from a distinguished Swedish family long resident in Finland, one that gave both Sweden and Finland a number of men who served as army and navy officers, civil servants, and scientists. He was graduated from Helsingfors University, having studied chemistry and mineralogy, but came into open conflict with the representatives of the Russian Empire then ruling Finland. In 1858 he chose to leave his native land and, having already become known for his work in mineralogy, was appointed chief of the division of mineralogy of Sweden's National Museum of Natural History, a post he held until his death.

In the same year in which Nordenskiöld left Finland to settle in Stockholm, he had his first opportunity to go to the Arctic, as a member of a small group of scholars exploring the Spitsbergen (Svalbard) archipelago under the leadership of Otto Martin Torell. He returned to Spitsbergen with Torell in 1861, and in 1864 he conducted his own group for the first time, to Spitsbergen once more. Nordenskiöld first attracted world attention in 1868, when, aboard the small Swedish steamer *Sofia*, commanded by F. W. von Otter, a naval officer who later became Sweden's minister of the navy and prime minister, he reached 81°-42′N, an Arctic record. He was feted both in Sweden and in England and honored by the ROYAL GEOGRAPHICAL SOCIETY in London; his career as polar explorer was well under way.

In 1870 Nordenskiöld went to West Greenland to investigate the possible use of dog teams for polar work, and on that occasion he made a brief foray, the first by a scientist, to investigate the nature of Greenland's ice cap, the *inlandsis*. His next polar venture, in 1872–1873, almost ended in disaster. His expedition, intended to take off from northern Spitsbergen to the North Pole, lost its reindeer, which were to be used as pack and draft animals, and he and his men were frozen in by an early ice storm. The expedition weathered the severe winter in good shape, and Nordenskiöld and several companions made a lengthy journey across Spitsbergen's Nordaustlandet to investigate its nature.

On his return to Sweden in 1873, Nordenskiöld decided to abandon the quest for the North Pole and turned his attention to the possibility of navigating across the Arctic Ocean from Europe, past Siberia, to the Pacific: the NORTHEAST PASSAGE. In 1875 and 1876, he sailed on small vessels to the mouth of the Yenisey River, returning on the first of those journeys via the upper reaches of the Yenisey and Siberia to Europe. Encouraged by what he had found out about the navigability of the Kara Sea, and with the financial support of King Oscar II of Sweden, Oscar Dickson, a wealthy Swedish businessman, and Aleksandr Sibiryakov, an equally wealthy Russian mining magnate, Nordenskiöld took off, on a converted whaling vessel, *Vega*, under the command of Louis Palander of the Swedish Navy, with four officers, four scientists, and a crew of twenty, to sail across the Northeast Passage, from Tromsø, Norway, on July 21, 1878. Having rounded Cape Chelyuskin, the northernmost headland of Asia, *Vega* steamed past the Siberian coast and on September 27 anchored in a bay barely 120 miles (193 kilometers) from Bering Strait. But the ship was frozen in the next day, and Nordenskiöld and his crew were icebound there until July 18, 1879.

In retrospect, the forced wintering of *Vega* was a good thing: it allowed the expedition to gather a large and varied amount of scientific information, making it the first polar expedition to do so. When the ice broke up, *Vega* got under way once again, sailed through Bering Strait on July 20, 1879, and returned via Japan, Ceylon, and the Suez Canal to Europe, making its triumphant entry into Stockholm Harbor on April 24, 1880, a day known since then as Vega Day in the Swedish calendar.

Nordenskiöld's report on the voyage was a best seller, translated into many languages, and the five-volume report on the expedition's scientific findings became a milestone in the systematic study of polar regions. Nordenskiöld led one last expedition to the Arctic. Convinced that there was ice-free land in the middle of Greenland, he persuaded his friend Dickson to equip a ship for the journey and in 1883 made a foray into Greenland's interior. The result was equivocal, but it proved that, given the equipment and the time, the Greenland ice cap could be crossed, a feat accomplished by Fridtjof NANSEN in 1888.

On *Vega*'s arrival in Yokohama, Japan, on Septem-

Adolf Nordenskiöld, shown here with his ship Vega. His triumphant return to Stockholm on April 24, 1880, after navigating the Northeast Passage, has been commemorated in the Swedish calendar as Vega Day. [Swedish Information Service]

ber 2, 1879, Nordenskiöld had reported to Oscar II that the ship crossed the Northeast Passage and that "an ocean was opened to navigation without loss of a single man, without illness, and without damage to the ship." In those words Nordenskiöld summed up one important aspect of the expedition, which reflected full preparation, careful management, and attention paid to the well-being of the people on board. The second important aspect of the *Vega* expedition, indeed of his other Arctic voyages as well, was the attention given to the gathering of the greatest possible number of scientific observations. The five volumes of the *Scientific Observations of the Vega Expedition* deal with the zoology, botany, oceanography, geodesy, geophysics, and anthropology of Arctic Siberia, placing the main thrust of the expedition on its scientific achievements, while not neglecting the practical importance of the Great Northern Seaway, as the Northeast Passage became known under the Soviet regime.

Nordenskiöld's expeditions to Spitsbergen stimulated further voyages to that part of the Arctic, by sea and by air, and made the Spitsbergen archipelago among the best known polar areas of the world. Though motivated by the spirit of discovery, Nordenskiöld remained a practical man. As he stated once in an interview, he was concerned in finding the way to the Orient, getting his men and himself over there and back home, rather than in being a hero. Having accomplished that task, he did in fact become the dean of polar explorers and continued to further the cause of discovery in high latitudes. More than anyone else, he was consulted on matters regarding exploration in high latitudes by men who succeeded in their goals, like Nansen, and by others who failed, like Salomon August Andrée, the Swedish engineer who attempted a balloon journey to the North Pole in 1897 and lost his life in the attempt.

Nordenskiöld belongs to that group of explorers who achieved fame in other fields of endeavor as well. While his work in geology and mineralogy is now only of historical interest, his two monumental books on the history of CARTOGRAPHY, *Facsimile-Atlas to the Early History of Cartography* and *Periplus: An Essay on the Early History of Charts and Sailing Directions*, published simultaneously in Swedish and English, in 1889 and 1897, laid the foundations of the field of the history of map making.

BIBLIOGRAPHY: Sven Hedin, *Adolf Erik Nordenskiöld: En levnadsbeskrivning*, Stockholm, 1926; George Kish, *Northeast Passage: Adolf Erik Nordenskiöld, His Life and Times*, Amsterdam, 1973; Adolf Erik Nordenskiöld, *Vega: Expeditionens vetenskapliga iakttagelser*, 5 vols., Stockholm, 1882–1887; id., *The Voyage of the Vega round Asia and Europe*, New York, 1881; Henrik Ramsay, *Nordenskiöld Sjöfararen*, Stockholm, 1950.

George Kish

Norse Maritime Discoveries

The Norse discovery of islands and extensive shorelines along the western periphery of the North Atlantic, of lands nowadays grouped with America, ranks as one of the major contributions to the growth of geographical knowledge in medieval Europe. As a corollary to the discoveries, the Norse voyages established the northwestern limits of what until then was generally regarded as the indefinite Western Sea, established its navigability, and demonstrated the feasibility of European maritime colonization of distant transoceanic lands.

Lasting for more than 300 years, from the eighth through the beginning of the eleventh century, the era of Norse discovery witnessed the geographical expansion of the European world by more than 3000 miles (4828 kilometers) to the west, mainly in the latitudes of 40 to 70°N. Unlike the subsequent efforts of the Portuguese and the Spaniards, the Norse discoveries came about without encouragement and self-serving guidance from religious, political, and commercial interests. Neither was there a Scandinavian Sagres nor a Norse prototype of Prince HENRY the Navigator to promote, motivate, and direct geographical discovery and exploration. All the evidence unearthed so far indicates that the Norse discoveries were folk discoveries, a series of involuntary events which occurred because sail-propelled ships were driven off course by storms or lost their bearings in fog and under clouded skies. The discoveries are substantiated by fragmentary circumstantial evidence that has survived in the form of artifacts and of written sources, most of which are based on oral traditions first committed to writing generations after the events occurred. Given the circumstances, it is understandable why the beginnings of the Norse discoveries are shrouded in obscurity and why the westward expansion in general has generated much speculative thinking. The failure to distinguish between three distinct activities associated with the occupation of newly found lands—the processes of discovery, exploration, and settlement—has also contributed to present-day misconceptions regarding the Norse enterprise.

Scottish islands and Faeroes   It may well be that the Shetlands, the nearest of the islands forming the western rim of the North Sea, located 155 nautical miles (287 kilometers) west of Norway, were the first in the series of discoveries that eventually culminated in landfalls along the final land barrier to maritime discoveries, the North American littoral. The array of artifacts found at the Jarlshof archaeological site in the Shetlands proves conclusively that the Norse occupation of the island group began about A.D. 800. At approximately the same time the Norse commenced settling the Hebrides, the Orkneys, and the Faeroe Islands (Føro). Even earlier, in the eighth century, they must have sailed the North Sea and discovered the islands, for transporting people and goods across the sea to make a settlement assumes, of course, prior discovery and exploration of what was to be settled. The documented Norse raid and destruction of the church and monastery at Lindisfarne (Holy Island) off the North Sea coast of Northumbria in England in 793, subsequent attacks and plundering of monasteries along the coasts of Scotland, Ireland, and England, and the Norse folk etymon for the Picts (Péttar) suggest that the Norse had discovered the western islands years before the beginnings of their permanent settlements there. Once they had reached the Shetlands, the Norse were on the in-sight-of-land sea route to the Orkneys, Scotland, the Hebrides, Ireland, and England.

The medieval Norse literary and historical sources provide no information at all about these discoveries. While the Shetlands and the Hebrides lack written local historical traditions, the *Saga of the Orkney Islanders (Orkneyinga saga)*, first committed to writing in Iceland at the end of the twelfth century, merely notes the Norse colonization of the islands. On the other hand, the discovery of the Faeroe Islands, located 152 nautical miles (282 kilometers) to the northwest of the Shetlands, is noted, though anachronistically, in the *Saga of Harald Harfair* (in Snorri Sturluson's *Heimskringla*, dating from the thirteenth century). The sole reference to the event is embedded in one laconic sentence: "Amid all the unrest, when Harald was seeking to subdue all the land of Norway, the Faeroes and Iceland, lands out beyond the sea, were found and settled." As King Harald's consolidation of power in Norway climaxed in the Battle of Hafrsfjord about 900, the discovery of the Faeroes, according to saga chronology, occurred in the last quarter of the ninth century. In this instance, however, the saga tradition is clearly in error, as the Norse had discovered the island group earlier, probably in the late eighth century.

Iceland In contrast to the virtual dearth of written sources on the Norse discovery of the islands on the western rim of the North Sea and the Faeroes, medieval traditions regarding the discovery of Iceland, Greenland, and lands farther to the west have survived. Except for general references contained in the two rather short Norwegian manuscripts, *Historia de antiquitate regum Norvagiensium*, written sometime between 1170 and 1180 by the Norwegian monk Theodoricus, and the anonymous *Historia Norvegiae*, also written in the late twelfth century, most of the extant information derives from four medieval Icelandic sources. Two are historical works: the *Book of the Icelanders (Íslendingabók)*, written by the Icelandic historian Ari Thorgilsson in the years 1122–1132; and the *Book of the Settlements (Landnámabók)*, probably compiled under the guidance of the same author

early in the twelfth century. The other two are thirteenth-century family sagas of anonymous authorship: the *Saga of the Greenlanders (Graenlendinga saga)* and *Eirík the Red's Saga (Eiríks saga rauda)*. The geographical emphasis in the texts is variously on Iceland, Greenland, and VINLAND. The era of discoveries extends some 125 years from the discovery of Iceland, traditionally thought to have occurred in about 860, to Bjarni Herjólfsson's sighting of the eastern seaboard of what nowadays is a part of the United States or Canada.

The Norse tradition of the discovery of Iceland is narrated in the *Sturlubók* and *Hauksbók* versions of the *Book of the Settlements*. Of the five existing versions of the *Book of the Settlements*, the original of which is not extant, these are the only ones that describe the Norse discovery of Iceland. Although the two versions present dual discoveries (in inverted order), they are in agreement regarding the circumstances of discovery. The *Sturlubók* credits the Norwegian Naddod the Viking with the first voyage. On a journey from Norway to the Faeroes, the ship carrying Naddod and his companions was "storm driven westward [past the Faeroes] into the sea, and there they found a great land," the east coast of Iceland. They probably landed at the mouth of Reydarfjördur, near Reydarfjall, 235 nautical miles (435 kilometers) to the northwest of Myling, the northwestern extremity of the Faeroe Islands. After ascending "a high mountain" in the Reydarfjördur region and observing no evidence of human settlement thereabouts, Naddod's party sailed for the Faeroes. They named the newly discovered land Snaeland (Snowland) for the snow that fell on the mountains at the time of their departure.

The *Hauksbók* version relates that weather conditions similar to those experienced by Naddod were directly responsible for the discovery of Iceland by Gardar Svavarsson the Swede. While sailing through Pentland Firth on his way to the Hebrides, Gardar's ship was "driven west into the sea." He, too, landed on the east coast of Iceland, probably somewhat to the east of Eystrahorn, a conspicuous mountainous headland in the southeast of the island, located 468 nautical miles (867 kilometers) to the northwest of Dunnet Head, the southwestern entrance point to Pentland Firth in Scotland. By circumnavigating the land he had found, Gardar established its insularity. He named it Gardarsholm (Gardar's Island). After spending the winter at Húsavík, on the inhospitable north coast of Iceland, Gardar sailed the following summer for Norway, where he is said to have "praised the [new] land much."

The existence of the two traditions pertaining to the discovery of Iceland points to the probability of additional and earlier but unrecorded Norse contacts with the island and to uncertainty about the events at the time the texts were written. Apparently, several traditions or blends thereof were available to the compilers of the *Landnámabók* and the authors of other volumes as well. Naddod's role in the discovery of the island is a case in point. While the *Hauksbók* relegates Naddod's wind-driven voyage to a secondary position, the monk Theodoricus in his *Historia* ignores him entirely, holding that certain anonymous merchants on their way to the Faeroes experienced inclement weather, whereupon they discovered Iceland in a manner reminiscent of Gardar's and Naddod's adventitious journeys. *Historia Norvegiae* likewise dispenses with Naddod's voyage and recognizes Gardar Svavarsson as the discoverer of Iceland. Yet the tradition of Naddod's voyage, irrespective of the precise nature of his involvement or even lack thereof, is more in keeping with the Norse mode of discovery than is Gardar's journey. Besides the outright statement in *Sturlubók* that Gardar "went to seek Snowland," there are at least three good reasons that support Gardar's role as an explorer of the island and not as its discoverer.

First, wintering without an adequate supply of provisions on the uninhabited north coast of Iceland would be most difficult if not impossible; provisions carried on board for a journey to the Hebrides certainly would not stretch through the winter in Iceland. Apparently, the winter stay of Gardar and his companions on Iceland was planned, and adequate supplies were brought along. Second, besides providing a general name for the land he allegedly discov-

Snaefellsjökull, an ice mountain 65 miles west of Reykjavik. The precise date of the Norse discovery of Iceland is shrouded in tradition, but it is generally supposed to be around A.D. 860. [National Archives]

ered, Gardar, in stark contrast to Naddod, named at least two specific locations, Skjálfandi, and Húsavík, the site at which he wintered. In the surviving Norse traditions, the naming of specific minor geographical features is commonly associated with exploration and settlement rather than with voyages of discovery. Third, Gardar built a dwelling at Húsavík (literally, House, or Cabin, Bay), which probably served as the base for exploring the island.

According to Norse traditions, the next Scandinavian to land on the island was Floki Vilgerdason, a Norwegian who is best remembered for naming the island Iceland and for his abortive attempt at settling it. Permanent Norse settlement of the island began about the year 870, with the arrival of the Norwegian foster brothers Ingolfr Arnarson and Leifr (Hjorleifr) Hrodmarsson and their families and retainers. Thus, while *Landnámabók* and *Íslendingabók* provide approximate dates for the beginnings of settlement, the earlier voyages to Iceland by Naddod, Gardar, and Floki remain dateless. When, then, did the discovery occur? In spite of the oft-repeated assertion that Naddod discovered Iceland sometime between the years 860 and 870, the only evidence regarding the date of his voyage is the reference in *Sturlabók* to the presence of Norse settlers in the Faeroes at the time the discovery occurred. Since the Norse in all likelihood had settled in the islands by the year 800 if not earlier,

the stringent time restriction imposed by present-day interpreters of Naddod's journey to Iceland is quite untenable. There seems to be no good reason or explanation as to why the Norse discovery of Iceland should have been delayed until the year 860 or shortly thereafter. The sufficient and recurring conditions of discovery, inclement weather and the existence of sail-bearing ships capable of being "driven west into the sea," were already present in eighth-century Scandinavia.

Far more important than the identity of the discoverers is the unanimity of the Icelandic sources in identifying the mechanism responsible for the discoveries. The elements associated with the discovery of Iceland—uncertainty as to when the discovery occurred, multiple discoveries, and the textual consensus that wind-driven voyages or the experience of *hafvilla* (literally, "lost at sea") brought about the discoveries—form the very foundation of the Icelandic conception of Norse maritime discoveries in the Atlantic. Although some scholars have seriously questioned it, there is no good reason to reject the proposition outright because the corpus of Icelandic and Norwegian sources lacks alternative traditions on the subject.

The strongest opposition to the Norse model has emanated from those who advocate what for convenience might be dubbed the Irish-guide theory. They surmise that seafaring Celtic anchorites and monks, traveling in search of solitude in seaworthy curraghs (coracles), found Iceland and communicated its existence to the Norse in the western islands. That an undetermined number of Celtic hermits dwelled in Iceland at the time of Norse discovery and settlement is substantiated by toponyms like Papey (Island of the [Irish] Monks) and by texts such as monk Dicuil's *Liber de mensura orbis terrae*, *Íslendingabók*, and *Landnámabók* (both *Sturlubók* and *Hauksbók* versions). The last of these relates that "before Iceland was settled by Northmen there were in it men whom the Northmen call papar [*i.e.*, monks or anchorites]. They were Christian men . . . there were found left by them Irish books, bells and crosiers. . . ." However, these texts lack evidence that might lend support to the conjecture that the Norse learned of Iceland from the Celtic religious in the Hebrides, the Faeroes, or elsewhere or that the monks guided the Norse to the Shetlands, the Faeroes, Iceland, or even Greenland and Vinland. The conflicting life-styles, the language barrier, and the ecological preferences of the two populations were quite incompatible and hardly conducive to the exchange of geographical information. In fact, the Celtic hermits avoided contact with the Norse by withdrawal. After the Norse arrived in Iceland, the *papar*, or Celtic religious, abandoned it because "they would not live alongside heathen" *(Íslendingabók)*. And the recent plundering inroads of the Norse into England, Scotland, and Ireland must have been vivid in the minds of the Celts, thus providing further cause to avoid the Norse rather than guide them westward from island to island.

Greenland According to the singular logic of Icelandic historiography, the settling of Iceland first opened the way for a Norse discovery of Greenland. While *Íslendingabók* merely remarks that Greenland "was found [discovered] and settled from Iceland," both versions of *Landnámabók* and some of the Icelandic sagas as well note that the discovery resulted from a wind-driven voyage. Gunnbjorn Ulfsson is said to have been "driven west of Iceland," presumably to the east coast of Greenland, during a voyage from Norway to Iceland. Following the tradition of Naddod's and Gardar's voyages, the texts do not provide a date for Gunnbjorn's discovery. Circumstantial evidence suggests, however, that the journey took place between 875 and 900, or during the settlement phase of Iceland. The land or islands Gunnbjorn discovered were afterward remembered in Iceland as Gunnbjorn's Skerries. The name Gunnbjorn might have given his discovery is lost. In the circumstances, it is understandable why opinion varies regarding the location of the geographical area Gunnbjorn sighted in Greenland, if indeed it was Greenland that he sighted. Most of the speculation favors the Angmagssalik region, situated 310 nautical miles (574 kilometers) west of Bjargtangar, the nearest point in Iceland.

The next voyage to what seems to have been Greenland occurred in about 970 (or perhaps some years later), when a group of Icelanders under the leadership of two outlaws, Snaebjorn Galti and Rolf of Raudesand, sailed in search of Gunnbjorn's Skerries and established a short-lived settlement somewhere on the inhospitable east coast of the island. It is difficult,

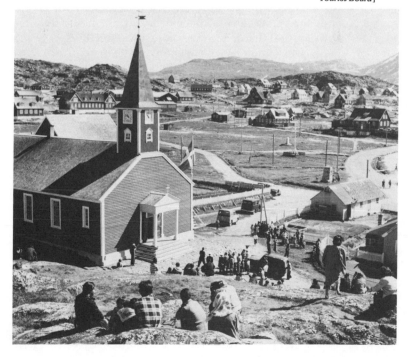

Godthåb, in the southern part of West Greenland, was one of the first Norse settlements, and today it is the largest town and the capital of Greenland. [Danish Tourist Board]

however, to believe that in the 80 or 90 years after Gunnbjorn's voyage there were no wind-driven voyages to Greenland and to lands located farther west, as the hiatus in the Icelandic sources implies. In view of the fact that during the time period numerous ships brought settlers from Norway, the Hebrides, and other western islands to Iceland, the references in Icelandic sources to ships being first wind-driven to the west of Iceland before landing on its shores and the alleged find by Snaebjorn Galti's party of a purse containing coins in a cairn or burial mound on the east coast of Greenland suggest that some ships probably inadvertently reached Greenland but that such events went unrecorded. Somehow the old Icelandic tradition of Gunnbjorn's journey survived, and it is more realistic to think of it as symbolizing repeated experiences (several adventitious discoveries west of Iceland) rather than being the record of a unique event.

The Norse exploration of Greenland is intimately linked with Eirík the Red, father of Leifr EIRÍKSSON. After being exiled from Iceland for homicide in 982, Eirík spent the 3 years of his sentence exploring the coasts of Greenland. Sailing from near Snaefellsjökull, he crossed Denmark Strait and easily found the so-called Gunnbjorn's Skerries, or the east coast of Greenland, as it forms an impenetrable barrier for ships sailing west of Iceland all the way south to Cape Farewell (Kap Farvel) at 59°46'N. Along the west coast of Greenland, Eirík's explorations probably reached as far north as Disko Island at 70°N. Eirík landed at Brattahlid on Eiríksfjord in the southwest of Greenland, named several topographic features, and afterward called the land Greenland because "men would be more ready to go there if it had a good name" *(Íslendingabók)*. In spite of several recent and fanciful interpretations of the appellation, including the suggestion that it is a misnomer, the name Eirík gave the land was, in fact, an appropriate toponym. Considered in the Norse ecological context, the element *green* in Greenland connoted pasturage, promising the land-seeking Icelanders that their predominantly pastoral, mixed-livestock economy could be successfully implemented in the narrow ice-free coastal habitat of southwestern Greenland.

The news of the habitability of the island supposedly reached Iceland first in the year 985 or 986, when Eirík returned from his exile. As all the good land in Iceland had been claimed or settled, Eirík's account of Greenland, coupled with his own desire to settle there, led to Norse colonization of the island. During the summer of 985 or 986, a total of twenty-five ships, each carrying an estimated twenty to twenty-five passengers, livestock, household goods, and tools, left western Iceland for Greenland. Only fourteen of the ships reached Greenland. Of the remaining eleven ships, "some were driven back, and some were lost" *(Landnámabók)*. Although the text in this instance clearly recognizes the vulnerability of Norse maritime ventures to the vagaries of weather, the narrative has, nevertheless, brought about rather remarkable interpretations as to the cause of the mishap. Some authors have speculated that the ill-fated ships were destroyed by a submarine earthquake or volcanic eruption, implying, of course, the presence of tsunamis (earthquake-generated sea waves). But they do not offer evidence as to how a tsunami or a series of tsunamis would bring fourteen of the twenty-five ships to Greenland, force some back to Iceland, and sink yet others. Even more singular would be an alternative hypothesis suggesting there were up to eleven submarine earthquakes, volcanic eruptions, and resultant tsunamis between Iceland and Greenland to cause havoc with navigation in the summer of 985 or 986. The textual phrase "some [ships] were lost" should not be taken to mean or connote sinking vessels or drowning crews and passengers. It is highly probable that the observation rests merely on the visual experience of sailors, meaning that some of the ships were lost to other ships at sea, or on information concerning the failure of a number of the ships to arrive at their objective in Greenland. Some of the "lost ships" may, indeed, have survived the ordeal and been wind-driven to islands and lands located to the west and southwest of Greenland. By odd coincidence, what some claim to be the first recorded Norse sighting of "America" occurred in the summer of 985 or 986.

Vinland   With the settlement of Greenland (Eastern Settlement, located in the southwest near Julianehåb, and Western Settlement, at Godthåb) there began the final and by far the most glamorized epoch of medieval Norse discoveries in the Atlantic. Geographically, the focus shifted to the western periphery of the ocean, to lands located to the west and south of Greenland, which, to the south of Hudson Strait, formed the ultimate and insurmountable barrier to further Norse maritime discoveries westward. According to Icelandic narratives, the Norse discovered several distinct places and regions along the barrier, of which Helluland, Markland, and Vinland are by far the most renowned. It is ironical that the discovery of the ephemeral Vinland, situated on the periphery of a finite ocean, should in time have come to be characterized as a herculean achievement. Viewed more realistically, its discovery was far from being a singular event. In fact, the terminal quality of its location signified the inherent limitations of the Norse mode of maritime discovery and pointed to the impending doom of the era of discoveries as well. Inasmuch as Vinland is said to have been situated somewhere on a littoral extending from Labrador to Florida, a region subject to sighting by crews aboard lost, wind-driven ships, its discovery was predictable.

The paucity of information in the Icelandic historical texts on the discovery of Vinland, while remarkable, is quite in keeping with the treatment accorded discoveries other than that of Iceland and Greenland. To learn more about Vinland and its discovery, it is necessary to consult another, albeit less reliable genre of sources, namely, folklore that has survived in the form of Icelandic family sagas.

Most of the pertinent Norse folk traditions relating to the discovery and location of Vinland are embedded in two so-called Vinland sagas. Of the two, the *Saga of the Greenlanders (Graenlendinga saga)* is the older and is generally considered the more trustworthy. It was first committed to writing about the year 1200. *Eirík the Red's Saga (Eiríks saga rauda)* was written sometime between 1264 and 1284. Its narrative about the discovery of lands to the west and southwest of Greenland by Leifr Eiríksson is a deliberate revision of events as described in the *Saga of the Greenlanders.* The folk traditions about Vinland were seemingly transmitted orally for about 200 years until they were committed to writing by anonymous scribes in Iceland, in surroundings removed hundreds of miles from the environment in which the events occurred. To some degree, the surviving Vinland sagas are, in fact, examples of an elitist, stylized history. The original manuscripts of the sagas no longer exist. The oldest extant text of the *Saga of the Greenlanders* (in *Flateyjarbók*) was written between 1382 and 1395. *Eirík the Red's Saga* survives in two versions, in *Hauksbók*, dating from the early fourteenth century, and in *Skálholtsbók,* compiled in the last quarter of the fifteenth century. It is as yet uncertain how accu-

rately the *Saga of the Greenlanders* narrates the discovery and exploration of lands located to the west and south of Greenland and how closely it resembles the original lost manuscript. Given the circumstances, it is understandable why the two sagas must be approached with caution.

In presenting two contradictory versions of the discovery of lands located to the south and west of Greenland (now known as America), the sagas are in keeping with the Norse model of multiple discoveries of lands in the Atlantic, as described in Icelandic historical texts. According to the *Saga of the Greenlanders,* it was Bjarni Herjólfsson who first sighted new lands beyond Greenland. But in *Eirík the Red's Saga* his voyage is utterly ignored, and Leifr Eiríksson emerges as the discoverer, first of a coastal region and later, after centuries of furtherance, of America. Although both discoveries remain dateless in the sagas, incidental evidence suggests that Bjarni's discovery took place in the year 985 or 986 and Leifr's journey in the year 999.

Although recent textual studies of *Eirík the Red's Saga* have confirmed conclusively that the legend of Leifr's discovery of a land with vines, "wild wheat," and *mausur* was the invention of the Icelandic monk Gunnlaug Leifsson in the late twelfth century, it is worth a review because it forms the foundation for

A Norse ship. According to the Norse sagas, these sturdy craft carried their passengers safely across the Atlantic and back nearly 500 years before Columbus set sail for America.

the long-held erroneous conception of Leifr's discovery of "America." The brief description of Leifr's alleged discovery in *Eirík the Red's Saga* is reminiscent of Naddod's and Gunnbjorn's wind-driven voyages to previously unknown shores. Sailing directly from Norway to southern Greenland, over a latitudinal distance of 1500 nautical miles (2778 kilometers), Leifr's ship was driven off course and for a long time was "tossed about upon the ocean, and came upon lands of which he previously had no knowledge." But, contrary to the opinion of certain Vinland enthusiasts, the voyage was not Leifr's first transatlantic journey, nor was it his first experience of *hafvilla*, or being lost at sea. For in sailing from Greenland to Norway, the *hafvilla*-prone Leifr was first driven off course to the Hebrides. Because the existence of the Hebrides was known to Leifr and the Norse in general, his landfall there did not constitute a geographical discovery.

Although the saga narrative does not reveal the duration of Leifr's ordeal at sea and makes no reference to the discovery of a place called Vinland, it does provide an early botanical glimpse of a segment of the eastern seaboard of North America. Among the plants Leifr found and of which he took samples to Greenland were vines, wild wheat (wild rice, *Zizania aquatica*?), and *mausur* (maples?). More important than the debated identity of the individual species of flora

was the role of vegetation in the Norse environmental perception, a not-unexpected manifestation of their pastoral ways.

Leifr did not name the new land. Only later in Greenland, in connection with the planning of Thorfinn Karlsefni's voyage to settle the new land to the south and west, is the name Vinland first mentioned. The question remains: Was Leifr the first Norseman to visit the shores of the eastern seaboard? Evidently not, for at an unidentified location Leifr found some shipwrecked seamen whom he brought to Greenland. And very likely there had been others before them, anonymous men and women, wind-driven to distant beaches, whose names and exploits never reached the Icelandic clerics who committed some of the surviving folk traditions to writing centuries later in distant Iceland.

In the more reliable *Saga of the Greenlanders*, Bjarni Herjólfsson is said to have been the first to sight lands beyond Greenland. His ship experienced *hafvilla* while sailing from western Iceland to the Eastern Settlement in Greenland in the summer of 985 or 986. After he had lost sight of Iceland, the favorable wind failed, "northerly winds and fog set in, and for many days they did not know where they were drifting." Eventually, either the fog or cloud cover dissipated or the party had sailed out of the region where the conditions had prevailed, so that they ob-

Map showing the routes followed by the four Norse explorers credited with the discovery of Iceland, Greenland, and Vinland.

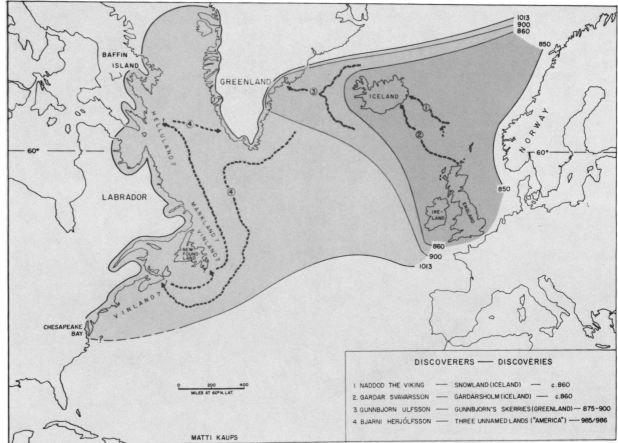

DISCOVERERS —— DISCOVERIES

1. NADDOD THE VIKING —— SNOWLAND (ICELAND) —— c.860
2. GARDAR SVAVARSSON —— GARDARSHOLM (ICELAND) —— c.860
3. GUNNBJORN ULFSSON —— GUNNBJORN'S SKERRIES (GREENLAND) —— 875-900
4. BJARNI HERJÓLFSSON —— THREE UNNAMED LANDS ("AMERICA") —— 985/986

MATTI KAUPS

served the sun again, thus enabling Bjarni to determine their latitudinal position. It is important to note here the reference to a mysterious means of determining latitude and the fact that the technique was rendered entirely ineffective in the presence of fog and cloud cover, resulting in the experience of *hafvilla.* The drift of Bjarni's ship for many days may well mean that it had been moved along to the south and southwest by the East Greenland and Labrador Currents in an area known for its frequent and massive spring and summer fogs. Unwittingly, Bjarni had discovered the currents and the associated fogbanks, leaving for the saga to provide the earliest European account of the phenomena.

Being cognizant of their southerly location, Bjarni sailed northward in search of latitudes more in keeping with what information he might have had about the position of Greenland. Before reaching Greenland, Bjarni and his crew sighted three distinct coastlines, two of which were wooded; the northernmost was "mountainous and topped by a glacier." This is the earliest reference in the Vinland sagas to the Norse sighting of lands beyond Greenland. Surprisingly, Bjarni did not land on, nor did he name, the three lands he had discovered.

If the saga account is credible, and there are several good reasons for doubting it, then there were no voyages, wind-driven or otherwise, beyond Greenland for 16 years, or until 1001 or 1002, when Leifr Eiríksson explored certain of the western lands. Whether he saw any of the places Bjarni had sighted remains unknown. The fact that he obtained Bjarni's ship for the voyage does not, of course, mean that the ship led him to familiar waters of years past, as some authors insist. Unlike Bjarni before him, Leifr did visit and name three of the four lands he reconnoitered, Helluland, Markland, and Vinland, each being an ecological appellation. The outstanding geographical features noted in Helluland (literally, Slabland) were rocks and glaciers. From the Norse pastoral ecological perspective, it was judged "a worthless country" in that there was no "grass to be seen." Leifr's second landfall was in Markland (Forestland), which he named for its "natural resources." It was a forested region with sandy beaches and level topography. Since forests extend as far north as Hamilton Inlet in eastern Labrador, Markland must have been located to the south of it. Helluland probably identified Baffin Island or perhaps northern Labrador. Both toponyms refer to broad ecological regions along the eastern seaboard and not to specific geographical locations. The geographical description of Vinland is somewhat more detailed. Its location and the meaning of its name have been debated at great length for centuries. The linguistic controversy has centered on the orthography of the element *vin* and its concomitant meaning. Vinland means "meadowland" or "fertile land," while Vínland translates literally "wineland." On ecological grounds, the Vínland-Wineland association is bothersome, for the saga clearly states "Leifr named the

country after its natural qualities." Wine, quite obviously, is a processed liquid product and not a "natural quality" of a region. And there is no evidence in the sagas that Leifr and his party established the first winery in America. Far more in keeping with the Norse tradition of place naming and environmental perception is the Vinland-Meadowland interpretation. Yet this interpretation has been challenged on phonological grounds.

Leifr and his companions built dwellings, explored, and wintered in the now-famous Vinland before returning to Greenland the following spring. After Leifr's return to Greenland, the Norse made several efforts to colonize Vinland, the last of which occurred in 1013–1014. These efforts proved unsuccessful, however, partly because of conflict between the Norse and the native Americans, whom they called Skraelings, a contemptuous designation.

There is widespread support in the academic community for the so-called stepping-stone theory of Norse discovery, which holds that the discoveries proceeded from island to island and from east to west in an orderly geographical sequence. For example, the discovery of Iceland had to await the discovery of the Faeroes and the Shetlands; likewise, the discovery of Greenland required an earlier discovery of Iceland; and the discovery of Greenland was in turn a prerequisite for the discovery of Vinland. In reality, however, discovery by *hafvilla* did not require that islands and lands be discovered in geographical sequence, though Norse settlement did generally proceed in this manner. What was required for discovery by *hafvilla* was the development of sail-propelled craft.

The Oseberg ship, excavated in 1904. A stately and richly ornamented calmwater vessel, it contained in its stern an elaborate burial chamber fully equipped with what were considered necessities for the afterlife. [Norwegian Information Service]

There is incontestable evidence that Norse vessels already carried sails in the eighth century, thereby opening the way to geographical discoveries to the west of Norway. Moreover, as with developing systems in general, it is likely that the frequency of Norse ships experiencing *hafvilla* (hence the potential for geographical discovery) was greater at the beginning stage of the Norse contact with the North Sea and the Atlantic than later, when through accumulated experience they were better informed about and accustomed to the vagaries of the western seas. Indeed, the carbon-14 dates from the L'Anse-aux-Meadows archaeological site in northern Newfoundland suggest that the Norse had reached the eastern seaboard by the late seventh or eighth century, or more than a century before the purported Norse discovery of Iceland and Greenland. The house types and other artifacts, coupled with carbon-14 dates, strongly suggest that the site was settled in the ninth century if not earlier. These settlers might well have come directly from the Shetlands or the Faeroes without having to wait for the settling of Iceland and Greenland first. It is highly probably that ongoing archaeological research in Canada will yield evidence of additional early Norse voyages to the eastern seaboard, predating what the Icelandic sources record. Investigations at Pamiok Island in Ungava Bay in northern Quebec and elsewhere clearly demonstrate that the L'Anse-aux-Meadows site is not the only place the Norse inhabited along the eastern littoral.

Other discoveries In addition to the discoveries in the Atlantic, the Norse discovered the small island of Jan Mayen, located some 300 nautical miles (556 kilometers) north-northeast of Iceland, and the island group of Svalbard (including Spitsbergen) in the Arctic Ocean in the late twelfth century. Although the mode of discovery of these islands remains unknown, it is likely that it resulted from *hafvilla,* from ships being wind-driven off course to the north of sailing lanes in more southerly latitudes. The Norwegian trader Ottar (Ohthere) did not discover northern Norway and the White Sea about 880, as some authors maintain, but rather traveled for the purpose of expanding trade to a region whose existence was already known to the Norse. In Greenland, too, the Norse explored the land and sea. Besides ill-fated attempts to explore the glacier-clad interior, the Norse, in search of hunting grounds certainly reached Kingigtorssuaq, near Upernavik, and probably Melville Bay (between 75 and 76°N), and Jones Sound (at about 75°N) in the Canadian Arctic. These were the northern hunting grounds *(Norðresta)*, where the Norse hunted for walrus, ptarmigan, caribou, narwhal, and polar bear and where in time they met the Eskimos.

Knowledge of Norse discoveries There is irrefutable evidence that the Norse geographical discovery of Iceland, Greenland, and Vinland was incorporated into Western European learning shortly after the discoveries occurred. Already in the year 1075, Adam of Bremen in his *Gesta Hammaburgensis* cites the Norse discovery of Wineland, which he identified as an island in the ocean beyond Greenland. Far more important than this singular reference to Vinland in other than the Icelandic and Norwegian texts and sagas was the dissemination of geographical information about Greenland in medieval Europe. The information was available in the form of manuscripts, books, and maps. Of particular importance in advertising the past Norse discoveries was the first map of northern Europe drawn by the Danish cartographer Claudius Clavus, dubbed "the first cartographer of the north," while visiting Italy in 1424. In addition to Scandinavia, his map depicts Iceland and Greenland. Greenland is portrayed as a peninsula joined to Europe, a conception based on and continuing medieval Norse cosmography. As Greenland forms the western extremity of the map, Helluland, Markland and Vinland are not shown. Clavus's map was soon incorporated into European world maps. It appeared first in the *Geography* of PTOLEMY of 1427 made for Cardinal Guillaume Fillastre and thus firmly established the Norse discovery of Greenland in Western European cartographic tradition.

Although direct evidence is wanting as to whether any of the fifteenth-century world maps showing Greenland, such as that of Donnus Nicolaus Germanus of 1474, were available to Christopher COLUMBUS prior to his memorable voyage of 1492, it seems hardly conceivable that in planning his voyage he managed to overlook such obvious information. Whether Columbus was aware of the past Norse voyages to Helluland, Markland, and Vinland is of little significance. What is important is the fact that the fifteenth-century world maps show the existence of lands out in the "western Sea." Though Iceland and Greenland are situated in latitudes far to the north of Columbus's planned journey, they nevertheless conveyed the Norse discoveries, the concept of the navigability of the ocean, and the probability of yet other lands to the west. The ocean was no longer a barrier but rather a manageable avenue of travel. The purported fact-collecting voyage of Columbus to Iceland prior to his first journey to America is indeed questionable. If he did visit the island, then he might have learned of Vinland, thus reinforcing the thought of the existence of lands farther to the west. Since English fishermen had reached the shores of Iceland by the year 1410, it may well be through them that the Venetian navigator John CABOT, considered by some to be the discoverer of the continent of North America, learned of Greenland and of lands beyond.

It was in post-Columbian times that the Icelanders and Scandinavians first became interested in the Vinland voyages. The rediscovery of the Icelandic and Norwegian texts and sagas brought to light geographical and ethnological information which subsequently was used in promoting the campaign of the pre-Columbian Norse discovery of America. The Norse encounters with the Skraelings clearly show that they were not the first to discover America, though they might have been the first Europeans to reach the littoral of the eastern seaboard of North America.

BIBLIOGRAPHY: Leo Bagrow, *History of Cartography*, ed. and rev. by R. A. Skelton, Cambridge, Mass., 1966; A. W. Brøgger, *Den norske bosetningen på Shetland–Orknøyene*, Skrifter utgitt av det Norske Videnskaps, Akademi i Oslo, vol. II, Hist.-Filos. Klasse, 1930, no. 3, Oslo, 1930; Daniel Bruun, *Erik den røde og Nordbokolonierne i Grønland*, 2d ed., rev., Copenhagen, 1931; W. P. Cumming et al., *The Discovery of North America*, New York, 1971; Finn Gad, *Grønlands Historie*, vol. 1, Copenhagen, 1967; *Grønlands historiske Mindesmaerker*, 3 vols., Copenhagen, 1838–1845; J. R. C. Hamilton, *Excavations at Jarlshof, Shetland*, Edinburgh, 1956; Anne Stine Ingstad, "The Norse Settlement at L'Anse aux Meadows, Newfoundland," *Acta Archaeologica*, vol. 41, 1971, pp. 111–154; Helge Ingstad, *Verterveg til Vinland*, Oslo, 1965; *Íslendingabók*, ed. by Finnur Jónsson, Copenhagen, 1930; Jón Jóhannesson, "The Date of the Composition of the Saga of the Greenlanders," tr. by Tryggvi J. Oleson, *Saga-Book of the Viking Society for Northern Research*, vol. XVI, part 1, 1962, pp. 54–66; Gwyn Jones, *A History of the Vikings*, London, 1968; Matti Enn Kaups, "Shifting Vinland: Tradition and Myth," *Terrae Incognitae*, vol. II, 1970, pp. 29–60; id., "Shifting Vinland: Tradition and Myth; A Rejoinder, *Terrae Incognitae*, vol. III, 1971, pp. 97–105; *Landnámabók*, ed. by Finnur Jónsson, Copenhagen, 1900; Thomas E. Lee, *Archaeological Investigations of a Longhouse, Pamiok Island, Ungava, 1970*, Collection Nordicana, Centre d'Études Nordiques, no. 33, Université Laval, Quebec, 1971; T. C. Lethbridge, *Herdsmen and Hermits*, Cambridge, England, 1950; Magnus Magnusson and Hermann Pálsson, *The Vinland Sagas*, Harmondsworth, England, 1965; Samuel Eliot Morison, *The European Discovery of America: The Northern Voyages, A.D. 500–1600*, New York, 1971; Arthur Middleton Reeves, *The Finding of Wineland the Good: The History of the Icelandic Discovery of America*, London, 1895; Carl O. Sauer, *Northern Mists*, Berkeley and Los Angeles, 1968; Erik Wahlgren, "Fact and Fancy in the Vinland Sagas," in Edgar C. Polomé (ed.), *Old Norse Literature and Mythology*, Austin, Tex., and London, 1969.

Matti Enn Kaups

North America

The first Europeans to visit North America were probably the Norse, who discovered the still-mysterious VINLAND and made several attempts to settle there in the eleventh century. Their colonizing efforts proved unsuccessful, however, and had little or no influence on the subsequent development of the continent. The man generally regarded as the first European to reach North America after the Norse is John CABOT, who sailed from Bristol in 1497 in search of the western route to Asia. Where he landed is not known with certainty (Newfoundland is frequently mentioned as the most likely spot), but Cabot himself believed that he had reached China.

There are those, to be sure, who assert the primacy of other individuals and groups in the discovery and settlement of North America. St. BRENDAN, the sixth-century Irish monk who is reported to have sailed to a Promised Land of the Saints, is believed by some to have reached North America. Another popular and persistent myth is based on the travels of MADOC, a Welsh prince who is supposed to have established a colony in North America in the twelfth century.

Others have argued for a discovery of North America before 1497 by either Portuguese or English seamen. The discovery of the Azores by Portugal between 1431 and 1452 was followed by numerous Portuguese voyages in search of other Atlantic islands. It is the contention of Portuguese historians that these voyages resulted in the discovery of North America but that the find was kept secret. Similarly, some English historians believe that Newfoundland was discovered by Bristol seamen before 1497. This hypothesis rests heavily on an undated letter in Spanish, first published in 1956, from John Day, an English merchant, to an admiral believed to be Christopher COLUMBUS. While describing a recent English voyage, clearly that made by Cabot in 1497, Day states that the place where Cabot landed was discovered in other times *(en otros tiempos)* by men from Bristol who had

been seeking the (imaginary) island Hy-Brasil. Since there was a series of western voyages from Bristol starting in 1480, Day's statement has been used to advance the theory that these voyages resulted in the discovery of Newfoundland and the rich fisheries nearby. It has also been suggested that news of these discoveries reached Cabot while he was in Spain or Portugal and influenced the planning of his western expedition.

Whatever the truth of these theories, it was not until the sixteenth century that the exploration and colonization of North America got under way. Exploration of the northern part of the continent was undertaken mainly by individuals who sailed on behalf

Hernando de Soto lands in Florida in 1539 in search of another rich empire for the King Charles I of Spain. He subsequently discovered the Mississippi but found no El Dorado. [Library of Congress]

of France or England, such as Giovanni da VERRAZ-ZANO, Jacques CARTIER, and Martin FROBISHER. Since Spain and Portugal claimed a monopoly of southern routes to Asia, the location of such a passage in northern latitudes remained an important goal of early explorers. It soon became evident, however, that North America was not part of Asia but an obstacle in the path of those who sought the riches of the East. Explorers now began to seek a strait or an all-water passage through the new continent that would permit ships to sail from the Atlantic to the Pacific. The search for this elusive NORTHWEST PASSAGE was to last three centuries.

Meanwhile, the early exploration of the southern portion of the continent was carried out by Spaniards like Juan PONCE DE LEÓN, Hernando de SOTO, and Francisco Vásquez de CORONADO. Sixteenth-century Spanish expeditions to such places as Florida and California were a natural extension of earlier Spanish discoveries and conquests to the south in the islands of the Caribbean and New Spain (Mexico).

Exploration of the northwestern reaches of the continent waited until the eighteenth century. By this time Russian expansion eastward across Siberia had brought rumors of a large region to the east. Questions about the nature of this territory and its relation to Asia were clarified by a series of Russian expeditions in the eighteenth century, notably the one commanded by Vitus BERING in 1741. Further exploration was stimulated by the beginning of the fur trade and the establishment of the first Russian colony in 1784. Maritime exploration of the area in the eighteenth century was also furthered by the commercial and scientific pursuits and international rivalries that brought Spanish, British, and French vessels to the waters of the North Pacific.

See also CANADA; NORSE MARITIME DISCOVERIES; NORTHWESTERN NORTH AMERICA; UNITED STATES.

Northeast Passage

The Northeast Passage is the sea route along the northern coast of the Soviet Union between the Barents Sea in the west and the Chukchi Sea and Bering Strait in the east. The original motivation for efforts to traverse this passage was economic. Navigators following Christopher COLUMBUS to the West soon realized the continental proportions of their discovery, but they were convinced that somewhere there should be a passage through North America to the riches of Cathay. Jacques CARTIER, for example, made three voyages in search of a passage to India and China between 1534 and 1542 and was blocked by his discovery of more than 1800 miles (2897 kilometers) of east-coast America. Because these early voyages were unsuccessful, many eyes turned toward the northeast when Siegmund von Herberstein's *Rerum Muscoviticarum comentarii* appeared in 1549. Von Herberstein reported the observations of a sailor who had rounded Nord Kapp (North Cape) and included a map showing that Asia was just to the east, easily reached by the Siberian coast.

The English This information was well received in England, a nation anxious to break into the Eastern trade but reluctant to challenge the more powerful Spanish and Portuguese traders sailing west or around the Cape of Good Hope. England did, however, hire away Spain's chief navigator, Sebastian CABOT, who organized a three-ship expedition to sail around Nord Kapp to Cathay. Its departure from London in the spring of 1553 was celebrated widely; it was the start of a long history of merchant adventures.

Only one ship survived the voyage. Two ships and the bodies of their crews were later found on the east coast of Lapland, the unprepared victims of an Arctic winter. The third ship, *Edward Bonaventure*, with Richard CHANCELLOR as chief pilot and Steven Borough as master, successfully sailed around Norway and into the White Sea. At Archangel (Arkhangelsk) the party learned that they had reached Russia. Traveling overland to Moscow, they were welcomed by Tsar Ivan IV (Ivan the Terrible), with whom trade agreements were developed. The resulting Muscovy Company was chartered in 1555, and while the expedition did not reach Cathay, important trade developed.

A second expedition was dispatched in 1556 with Borough as chief pilot. Off the Kola Peninsula (Kolsky Poluostrov) he joined Russian fishermen who guided him past the White Sea to the Pechora River. Borough continued eastward and sailed through the strait between Vaygach Island (Ostrov Vaygach) and Novaya Zemlya into the Kara Sea. Ice conditions were so severe in the Kara Sea that Borough returned to England. His reports discouraged any future attempts for 25 years.

England sent only one more expedition in search of the Northeast Passage. Arthur Pet in the *George* and Charles Jackman in the *William* were sent in 1580 to attempt to cross the Kara Sea. Pet sailed through Yugor Strait (Proliv Yugorsky Shar), between Vaygach Island and the mainland, and into the Kara Sea. He was turned back by ice and fog and returned to England. Jackman never returned. With this failure the Muscovy Company halted all attempts at the Northeast Passage and concentrated on developing overland trade with Moscow.

The Dutch The Dutch followed the English in search of the Northeast Passage. They also failed, but they made important discoveries and had one party survive the Arctic winter on the northeast coast of Novaya Zemlya.

In 1565 the Dutch established the White Sea Trading Company in Archangel, a move designed to take advantage of the pioneering efforts of the English 10 years earlier. Oliver Brunel brought success to the White Sea Trading Company before he was imprisoned as a spy. Later paroled, he induced the Stroganov family to develop trading with the Dutch. He also made an overland trip to the Ob River, traveling farther east in Russia than any other European had up to that time. In 1584 Brunel secured financing for an expedition to seek the Northeast Passage and trade with the natives of northern Asia. He sailed from Archangel, and while successful in trading along the coast, he failed to reach the Kara Sea. While returning to Archangel, he ran aground in the Pechora River and lost his cargo.

Some 10 years later Willem BARENTS, an experienced navigator, led three Dutch ships north. Two vessels successfully entered the Kara Sea while Barents attempted to sail north of Novaya Zemlya. Heavy ice forced him back, but the penetration of the Kara Sea was encouraging. Seven Dutch ships attempted the Kara Sea in 1595 but could not even pass Novaya Zemlya because of the ice. In 1596 Barents sailed north from the Netherlands and discovered (or rediscovered) the Svalbard (Spitsbergen) group before sailing east toward Novaya Zemlya. He rounded the northern tip of the island and, with worsening ice conditions, took shelter in a bay, Ice Haven, on the northeast coast. The ship's crew built a house from driftwood and spent the winter. In June 1597 they sailed again around the northern tip of Novaya Zemlya and south in a small ketch. Barents died before the crew completed their heroic voyage by reaching safety on the Kola Peninsula.

Almost 300 years passed before Ice Haven was visited again. In 1871 a Norwegian sealing captain reached Ice Haven and discovered the house, totally sealed with a cover of ice. Inside he discovered equipment, instruments, books, and other sixteenth-century artifacts, as well as Barents's letters, which had been placed in the chimney.

The return of Barents's men to Amsterdam in 1597 coincided with the arrival of the first Dutch fleet to sail around Cape Horn to the East Indies. In 1602 the Dutch East India Company was formed as a trade monopoly. Shipowners not in the company and not privy to the southern routes had to concentrate on finding a northern route to profit from this trade; also, shipowners in the company tried to protect their monopoly by searching for the northern route. The company even hired Henry HUDSON to search for a Northeast Passage. Faced with a mutinous crew, he turned away from Novaya Zemlya and sailed to North America, where he explored the coast from Chesapeake Bay to Newfoundland and discovered the Hudson River.

A drawing of the house built by Willem Barents, a Dutch explorer, and his crew after they were forced to winter at Ice Haven, in Novaya Zemlya.

Several additional Dutch expeditions were sent to northern waters to seek a Northeast Passage, but they were unsuccessful. The northern voyages gradually turned to fishing, and Dutch interest in the sea route subsided.

The Russians The Russians were not inactive in discovering a northern sea route along their north coast. In the early eighteenth century, Peter the Great secretly sent two men to determine whether Asia and America were connected. Sailing from Kamchatka, they probably reached the Kuril Islands, but since they reported verbally only to the Tsar, their achievement is little known. Six months before he

A seventeenth-century vessel icebound off Novaya Zemlya. The seas around the island posed great hazards to early Arctic explorers.

died in 1725, Peter ordered the First Kamchatka Expedition to build boats in Kamchatka or nearby and to sail north along the shore to see if the land connected with North America. Vitus BERING, who was placed in command of the expedition, explored the coast north of Okhotsk and the Kamchatka Peninsula (Poluostrov Kamchatka) to the Gulf of Anadyr (Anadyrsky Zaliv) in 1728 and discovered the Diomede Islands, but fog prevented him from seeing the North American continent.

In 1733 Bering initiated a second expedition, the goals of which included a five-part mapping of the Arctic coast from Archangel in the west to the Gulf of Anadyr on the Pacific Coast. As Bering became more heavily burdened with problems, this work was taken over by the Admiralty College. Men were recruited from the river settlements of northern Siberia to explore the coast in *kochi,* small flat-bottomed boats totally unsuited for oceanic travel. Through 1740 many expeditions worked along the coast, charting the territory as far east as the mouth of the Kolyma River, about 160°E. Finally the Admiralty College called a halt. Vast progress in delineating the coast had been made, but the passage was not completed, and the reports of the explorers convinced most that a Northeast Passage was impracticable.

In the late eighteenth and early nineteenth centuries merchants from Russia pioneered exploration of the Siberian coast in the Arctic. Vast deposits of mammoth ivory were located, and new islands were discovered.

Cook, Billings, and Wrangel

In 1778 JAMES COOK attempted to sail home to England from his third circumnavigation of the world via a Northwest or Northeast Passage. Heavy ice on the American side forced him to turn west. He sailed through Bering Strait and, because the weather was clear, was able to see what Bering had missed, the sea-lane between the North American and Asian continents. Faced again with ice, he turned southward.

Catherine the Great of Russia, in 1788, approved plans to explore the Siberian coast between Great

Bear Cape (Mys Medvezhy), reached by Dmitry Haptev, and North Cape (Mys Shmidta), reached by Cook 10 years earlier. Command was entrusted to Joseph BILLINGS, one of Cook's assistants. This expedition failed because of Billings's lack of leadership and fear of the Arctic.

The coastal survey was finally completed by Baron Ferdinand von Wrangel, who used dogs and sledges to chart the coast by land. After 4 years of work he reached North Cape, and the coastal chart was complete. This was the last attempt of the Tsarist governments to determine the Arctic coast and the relationship between Asia and America.

Nordenskiöld

Nils Adolf Erik NORDENSKIÖLD became interested in the waters of the Siberian coast about 100 years after the Russians had completed their survey. An experienced explorer and geographer, Nordenskiöld saw a commercial route to Siberian ports as but one part of a voyage to China. In 1873 and 1875 he crossed the Kara Sea to the Yenisey River in a reconnaissance voyage. By 1878 he had secured the backing of King Oscar II of Sweden, a financial sponsor, and a Russian merchant. With provisions for 2 years he sailed aboard *Vega,* a steam- and sail-driven ship of 300 tons, from Tromsø, Norway, in July 1878. For the first part of the voyage he was accompanied by three Russian merchant ships. On August 6 they separated at Dickson Harbor, the safe harbor discovered in the 1873 reconnaissance. Two of the Russian ships sailed up the Yenisey River on a commercial voyage while Nordenskiöld's *Vega* and the third Russian ship, the *Lena,* continued eastward. By August 19 they reached Cape Chelyuskin, the northernmost tip of Eurasia. Never before had Cape Chelyuskin been passed by ship; *Vega* and *Lena* reached it in a month. *Vega*'s log indicates it was not an adventurous voyage but almost routine sailing in open water through fog and little ice.

Nordenskiöld briefly turned north to search for new land, but heavy pack ice turned him back toward the coast. On August 28 the two ships reached the Lena River. The last merchant ship ascended the river, and *Vega* continued eastward alone. In early September the party began to encounter snow and drift ice. Heavy fog and shallow water forced them to use a small launch to steam ahead to search for a passage. By September 28 they had passed North Cape, the westernmost penetration by Captain Cook 100 years earlier, but could go no farther as solid ice lay to the east. Only 120 miles (193 kilometers) farther lay the long-sought Pacific Ocean. The *Vega* froze in quickly. By early October the winter routine had been established. Scientific observations begun at sea were continued, and good relations were established with the Chukchi, the natives of the region.

When spring arrived, Nordenskiöld began to prepare for the continuation of his voyage. It was not until July 18, however, that strong winds broke up the ice and freed the *Vega.* In 2 days of sailing *Vega*

Capt. James Cook's men shooting seahorses during Cook's third circumnavigation of the globe. His attempts to complete the journey via a Northwest or a Northeast Passage were unsuccessful and he was forced to turn southward. [Library of Congress]

reached East Cape (Mys Dezhneva) at 11 o'clock in the morning. The men celebrated their achievement by firing their small cannon in a salute and turned southward into the Pacific Ocean.

Twentieth-century developments The Northeast Passage remained quiet for the remainder of the nineteenth century. The Russo-Japanese War, culminating in the destruction of the Russian Fleet during the Battle of Tsushima, provided motivation for the next attempt. To fight the Japanese in the East Tsar Nicholas II sent a naval squadron from home waters in northwestern Russia on a 10-month voyage around the Cape of Good Hope. Many felt that the war would have been concluded on a better note if the fleet had made a more direct journey across the top of Russia and attacked the Japanese much earlier. The Imperial Navy created a study committee under the direction of the experienced Arctic oceanographer and surveyor B. A. Vilkitsky to examine a northern sea route. The study endorsed a northern sea route as possible, but it recognized that detailed mapping and additional surveys were required and that safety would be enhanced by building weather stations, lighthouses, navigational aids, and fuel deposits along the entire coast.

Later the Russian government organized the Arctic Ocean Hydrographic Expedition, for which two steel-hulled icebreakers, the *Taymyr* and the *Vaygach*, were designed and built. Although a west-to-east effort was originally planned, the home port was changed to Vladivostok in the east to counter increasing American influence in Chukotka (Chukotsky Poluostrov). The *Taymyr* and the *Vaygach* were launched in 1909 and arrived in Vladivostok in mid-July 1910. Owing to the lateness of the season, the two ships only rounded East Cape before heavy ice halted their progress; they spent the winter in their home port. During the next three seasons the ships penetrated Siberian waters and worked farther west. Each winter they returned to Vladivostok and resupplied. In the 1914 season they were ordered to complete the survey and break through to Archangel. The onset of World War I delayed their work momentarily while they awaited a change of orders. Finally the Naval Command in St. Petersburg gave *Taymyr* and *Vaygach* instructions to continue the survey. By September they had reached winter quarters south of Cape Chelyuskin. In August 1915 the ships were freed and within a month had reached Archangel. The expedition had discovered Severnaya Zemlya (North Land), a group of islands north of Cape Chelyuskin, and successfully made an east-west traversal of the Northeast Passage.

Many raised doubts as to the practicability of a northern sea route. A two-season voyage with many months spent in enforced wintering did not lend itself to commerce. During the 1920s little use was made of the Arctic route, especially in the east. It was not until 1932 with the creation of the Main Administration of the Northern Sea Route that the Soviet gov-

Vega, the ship which carried Adolf Nordenskiöld on his long voyage through the Russian Arctic to East Cape. [Swedish Information Service]

ernment turned its attention to the sea route. The ship *Sibiryakov*, captained by Otto Y. Schmidt, traversed the passage in one season, sailing into the Bering Sea in 2 months and 4 days after losing her propeller to the ice. The *Chelyuskin* attempted to repeat the voyage in 1934 but was crushed and sunk in the Chukchi Sea. The icebreaker *Lithe* steamed from Vladivostok to Leningrad during the 1934 season, followed the next year by icebreaker-escorted cargo vessels sailing in both directions.

The strategic value of the Northeast Passage was demonstrated in 1940. Following the Soviet-German pact in 1939, the German Navy sought bases in the northern U.S.S.R. These plans failed, but the Soviet response encouraged the Germans to inquire about use of the northern sea route by German ships. To test the route the Germans sent the commerce raider *Schiff-45*, also known as *Komet*, eastward in July 1940. Flying the Soviet flag, *Komet* was assisted by four Soviet icebreakers at various points of the voyage, which encountered little ice. *Komet* emerged in Bering Strait on September 5 and, striking the Soviet flag, embarked on a 15-month cruise during which she sank 64,000 tons of Allied shipping and returned to Germany without losing a man.

Since World War II the Soviet government has devoted great effort to the development of a continuous northern sea route. The world's greatest icebreaker fleet operates along the Soviet Arctic coast throughout the year, escorting cargo ships all along the coast. The commercial dream of the early European merchants has been fulfilled, but instead of spices and tea from China the Northeast Passage ships Siberian timber and other raw materials to industrial centers in western Russia.

BIBLIOGRAPHY: Jeannette Mirsky, *To the Arctic!.* Chicago, 1970; L. H. Neatby, *Discovery in Russian and Siberian Waters*, Athens, Ohio, 1973; N. A. E. Nordenskiöld, *The Voyage of the Vega*, London, 1881.

Peter J. Anderson

Northwest Passage

The Northwest Passage, simply defined, is a shipping route from the Atlantic to the Pacific by way of the Arctic seas of North America. Ideally, it provides a much shorter passage from Europe to the East than the traditional routes by way of the Indian Ocean, Cape Horn, and even, in more recent times, the Panama Canal. This ideal, however, has never been attainable; the severe ice and weather conditions of the North American Arctic have always made the passage impractical, and it remains hazardous even for modern ice-strengthened ships. Moreover, during the period of search for a Northwest Passage, the complex geography of the Canadian Arctic archipelago gave it an added quality of elusiveness: the search spanned just three and one-half centuries and engaged about eighty expeditions before a passage was finally discovered in the 1850s, and a further 50 years elapsed before it was first navigated in full.

Beginnings The search for a Northwest Passage began around the year 1500, when the immediate successors of Christopher COLUMBUS made scattered landfalls off the coast of North America. Initially, it was believed that these landfalls represented sightings of the Asian continent. The first Northwest Passage explorer, John CABOT, thought he had discovered a northeastern extremity of Asia when he landed in the region of Newfoundland in 1497, and the Portuguese Gaspar CORTE-REAL fell victim to a similar illusion when he sighted what was probably Greenland in 1500. Both men believed that they need only coast southwestward from these landfalls to reach the lands of spices, but both were lost without trace when attempting to do that on their respective follow-up expeditions: Cabot's in 1498 and Corte-Real's in 1501.

Within a few years, explorers began to realize that the Orient was not so easily attained and that the discoveries of Cabot and Corte-Real were not themselves the goal but obstructions on the route. John Cabot's son, Sebastian CABOT, may have been the first to understand the new nature of the problem. He claimed to have led an expedition in search of a Northwest Passage in about 1508–1509, to have passed through a strait which corresponds approximately to the latitude of Hudson Strait, and to have entered a sea which he believed to be the Pacific Ocean. He may have discovered Hudson Bay, but whether or not this voyage really took place is still in question.

Other voyagers in this early period of search were attracted by the possibility of a low-latitude Northwest Passage through the new obstacle but succeeded only in proving that the eastern coast of North America continued unbroken for a considerable distance to the north. In 1524 Giovanni da VERRAZZANO searched the coast between Cape Fear, North Carolina, and about 50°N off Newfoundland; Estevão Gomes searched from Florida to Cape Race, Newfoundland, in 1524–1525; and in 1527–1528 John Rut examined part of the coast of Labrador. Finally, Jacques CARTIER explored the one major gap remaining in the coastline, the Gulf of St. Lawrence, in 1534 and 1535–1536.

At this point, the earliest period of search for a Northwest Passage came to an end; the continuity of the North American coastline had been established, and it was known that a Northwest Passage, if it existed, must lie uncomfortably far to the north. Moreover, the Spanish and the Portuguese, who had contributed most to the search so far, had established monopolies over South Atlantic and Indian Ocean shipping and, with their own trade routes around the world secured, had no real need to seek an alternative passage.

Sixteenth-century British exploration It was the monopoly over the Indian Ocean route to the East, maintained first by the Portuguese, then in the seventeenth century by the Dutch, which led to a revival of interest in the Northwest Passage in Britain. British business interests found themselves virtually excluded from the lucrative trade with the East, and the possibility of finding an alternative route, and possibly a much shorter route, became increasingly attractive. The NORTHEAST PASSAGE, around the northern coast of Asia, was first contemplated, and a small number of British expeditions set out to search for it

Jacques Cartier's expedition on the St. Lawrence River, one of three voyages made by the French explorer in search of a passage to China and India. [Library of Congress]

in the 1550s. They, however, made little progress beyond Novaya Zemlya.

Then, beginning in the 1570s, a long series of British expeditions set out to explore toward the northwest. The first in this new line of British Northwest Passage explorers was Martin FROBISHER, an enterprising mariner of proven experience. Frobisher sailed with two ships, *Gabriel* and *Michael*, on June 7, 1576, and by August 11 was lying off a broad channel penetrating the Arctic coast of North America, far to the north of any previous discovery on that coast. He was at once convinced that he had found a northern passage around America, a strait corresponding to Magellan Strait in the south. In fact, it was no more than a large bay, now known as Frobisher Bay, in southern Baffin Island. He examined the bay in some detail (without, however, confirming or disproving the existence of a western outlet) and returned home bearing a few prizes as evidence of his discoveries: a captive Eskimo and his kayak and a rock sample. The Eskimo (who soon died of pneumonia) provided a source of wonderment for the people of London, but it was the rock sample which was of the most enduring interest to Frobisher's sponsors, for it was analyzed and pronounced to be gold-bearing.

The sponsors, now organized as the Cathay Company, thereupon postponed their interest in the passage and instead sent Frobisher on two further expeditions, in 1577 and 1578, to mine the gold on the shores of Frobisher Bay. The second of these expeditions was one of the most ambitious ever sent to the Arctic: fifteen ships carried housing, equipment, and a wintering party of about 100 men to establish a mining "colony." That plan was abandoned following the loss of the ship carrying the prefabricated housing, but the fleet nevertheless arrived back with more than 1000 tons of ore. The sequel to this enterprise was a disaster. Not an ounce of gold was ever extracted from the ore, and the Cathay Company folded up amid much recrimination and with considerable loss of capital. For 2 years Frobisher's sponsors had let themselves be deceived by iron pyrites: "fool's gold."

Ironically, the gold fever robbed Frobisher of a truly important discovery. On his last voyage, he mistakenly entered Hudson Strait and would willingly have explored it in detail had that not been contrary to his instructions. Instead, he turned back and thereby delayed the discovery of Hudson Bay by some 40 years.

Frobisher's successor in the search for a Northwest Passage was John DAVIS, who likewise conducted three expeditions, in 1585, 1586, and 1587. On his first voyage, he examined the west coast of Greenland to Godthåbsfjord, then crossed the strait which bears his name and discovered the entrance to Cumberland Sound, which to him appeared quite as promising as Frobisher Bay had done to his predecessor. He examined the shores of Davis Strait again in 1586, and it was not until the third voyage that he apparently rejected the possibility of Cumberland Sound's leading to the Pacific. On that occasion, he coasted south from Cumberland Sound to the Labrador coast, observing the entrances to both Frobisher Bay and Hudson Strait.

Early-seventeenth-century expeditions After Davis's voyages, some 25 years passed before any further advance was made in the search for a Northwest Passage, but interest in a short northern passage to the East did not lapse entirely. Instead, it was diverted for a time toward the northeast, where Willem BARENTS and Henry HUDSON were making significant discoveries in the service of the Dutch. In the same period two British Northwest Passage expeditions did set out, but they achieved little. George Weymouth coasted between Baffin Island and Labrador in 1602, and in 1606 John Knight visited the Labrador coast, where he lost his life at the hands of Eskimos.

The first major breakthrough came when Henry Hudson, detained in England after his last voyage for the Dutch in 1609, was engaged to exercise his navigational skills on behalf of his own country. On April 17, 1610, Hudson sailed from Gravesend on the little ship *Discovery*, a famous vessel used on several subsequent expeditions. His initial goal was clear from the outset; he knew from several sources, notably from John Davis, of a great tidal strait, now known as Hudson Strait, penetrating the northeastern coast of North America, which then appeared to be the most probable entrance to a Northwest Passage. Hudson discovered the strait with ease (indeed he was swept into it by the tide), and he picked his way through the ice to emerge into Hudson Bay. There can have been little doubt in his mind, as he made his way southward along the eastern shore of the bay, that he was now in the Pacific Ocean. The only cause for doubt was that he was much too far to the east: in more southerly latitudes the Pacific coast of America was known to be thousands of miles farther west. But, before he saw any sign of the coast trending west, winter overtook him in James Bay. Hudson was never to find that westerly trend to the coast. The miseries of winter and an acute shortage of food exposed bitter rivalries on board ship, sparked off largely by Hudson himself in a series of irrational decisions and displays of favoritism. By spring he found himself with a crew sharply divided into two camps, and, almost inevitably, mutiny ensued. Hudson and eight of his supporters were set adrift in a boat, and the mutineers returned home; Hudson was never seen again.

The mutineers' report of Hudson's discoveries so encouraged his sponsors that they decided to embark on an intensive search of Hudson Bay. Now styled the Company of Merchants of London Discoverers of the Northwest Passage (the name implies their confidence in Hudson's achievement), they sent out Thomas Button in *Resolution* and *Discovery* to follow up Hudson's discoveries. Button's voyage of 1612–1613 checked some of the optimism that Hudson's had given rise to. Button sailed southwestward from Hudson Strait across a wide expanse of open sea, but then was stopped by land: the western shore of

Hudson Bay. He wintered at the mouth of the Nelson River, then set about exploring the coastline northward, for it was already clear to him that Hudson had not found the Pacific Ocean but a vast new bay, from which a further outlet into the Pacific had yet to be found. He reached Southampton Island before returning home.

Button's expedition was followed by several others sent out by the same sponsors to find an outlet from Hudson Bay. In 1614 William Gibbons failed to enter Hudson Strait and returned home with nothing accomplished. In the following year Robert BYLOT and William BAFFIN searched among the islands to the north of Hudson Bay, entered Frozen Strait between Southampton Island and the mainland, and concluded that there was no outlet. William Hawkridge examined part of the same area again in 1625. In 1619 the only recorded Danish Northwest Passage expedition, led by Jens Munk, crossed Hudson Bay to Churchill River, where all but three of his sixty-five men died of scurvy in the winter. Munk himself led the survivors home in 1620.

While this thorough examination of Hudson Bay continued, Baffin and Bylot extended the search in a different direction. In 1616 they were sent out in the *Discovery* to search to the north of Davis Strait. On this bold pioneering venture they explored meticulously right to the northern extremity of Baffin Bay, there discovering and naming Smith, Jones, and Lancaster Sounds, but they returned home with a discouraging report on the possibility of a feasible outlet to the west.

Finally, in 1631, two British expeditions set out to complete the examination of Hudson Bay. Luke Fox, on board *Charles*, was sponsored by London merchants, and Thomas James, with *Henrietta Maria*, was supported from Bristol. Fox began where Button had left off, in Roes Welcome Sound between Southampton Island and the mainland, then carefully examined the coastline southward and eastward to the entrance to James Bay, thus joining the discoveries of Hudson in 1610 and Button in 1612–1613. James, too, examined the southern shore of Hudson Bay from west to east, and wintered in James Bay before returning to England.

With the return of James in 1632, this period of intensive British involvement in the search for a Northwest Passage ended abruptly. The apparent absence of a navigable outlet from either Hudson Bay or Baffin Bay, the decline of Britain's sea power under James I and Charles I, and the virtual extinction of the adventurous Elizabethan breed of mariner, plus the establishment by the East India Company of at least a foothold in India, combined to extinguish any remaining interest in the discovery of a Northwest Passage and all remaining hope of a commercially viable passage. Nearly 100 years were to pass before the question of the passage was raised again, and by then the motivating factor was not trade with the East but trade, mineral exploration, and geographical discovery within North America itself.

Hudson's Bay Company   The exploration of Hudson Bay was not entirely fruitless. Its potential as a commercial gateway to the North American interior was spotted eventually, and in 1670 the Hudson's Bay Company was established to exploit that potential. Within 50 years the company had a string of fur-trading posts permanently established on the shores of the bay, and the existence of these posts, notably of one founded at Churchill in 1717, made the unexplored areas of northern Hudson Bay more accessible than ever before. With this in mind James Knight, the company's aging overseas governor, persuaded his employers in London to let him explore those areas with the primary purpose of discovering a passage westward toward rich mineral deposits reported to him by Indians. Knight's expedition in *Albany* and *Discovery*, which set out from London in June 1719, ended in tragedy. After parting with the company's supply vessels in Hudson Bay it was never seen again, and nothing was known of its fate until 1767, when two of the company's ships found relics on Marble Island in northwestern Hudson Bay. Knight and his men had apparently spent two winters on the island, dying one by one of sickness and famine.

Some years after Knight's voyage the Hudson's Bay Company reluctantly resumed the search for a passage at the instigation of one Arthur Dobbs, a theorist who believed almost fanatically in the existence of an outlet from northwestern Hudson Bay. Dobbs goaded the company into further action by means of a sustained attack on its failure to explore its own territories. The outcome was James Napper's halfhearted voyage northward from Churchill in 1737; it accomplished nothing and thoroughly dissatisfied Dobbs, who now drew the Admiralty into the controversy. In 1741 it sent out HMS *Furnace* and *Discovery* with one of the Hudson's Bay Company's ablest captains, Christopher Middleton, in command. Middleton wintered at Churchill and, in 1742, discovered and explored Wager and Repulse Bays and observed the entrance to Frozen Strait before concluding, rightly, that there was no hope of a passage in that direction. Dobbs remained dissatisfied. He publicly accused Middleton of slackness and, convinced that Wager Bay must hold the key to the Northwest Passage, prepared a private expedition to the same area. This expedition, led by William Moor in the *Dobbs* and *California* in 1746–1747, discovered Chesterfield Inlet but otherwise served only to confirm Middleton's observations; on its return, Dobbs finally fell silent.

The conclusion of this acrimonious episode did not entirely put an end to speculation about a passage out of northern Hudson Bay. For many years afterward Hudson's Bay Company ships trading northward from Churchill were expected, in theory at least, to keep a lookout for a possible passage, and they even caused a minor flurry of excitement in the early 1760s with the rediscovery of Chesterfield Inlet. Further, in 1753 and 1754, the American Charles Swaine attempted twice to explore for a passage through Hudson Bay but failed both times to enter Hudson Strait.

Pacific approach This sporadic activity in Hudson Bay was, however, quite isolated from the mainstream of opinion on the Northwest Passage and aroused little interest in Europe, where geographical theorists were developing a completely different approach to the problem. By the last quarter of the eighteenth century, the North Pacific Ocean was firmly established as the new center of attention. Vitus BERING had pointed the way with the discovery of the strait separating Asia and North America on his great overland expeditions of 1725–1741. As the North Pacific became more accessible to European navigators later in the century, the prospect of locating an entrance to the passage in the region of Bering Strait became increasingly attractive.

The Pacific approach to the problem also gave rise to another school of thought that resurrected the question of a low-latitude Northwest Passage. The theory, propounded in Britain by Alexander Dalrymple during the 1770s and 1780s and investigated by Spanish expeditions operating from California in the same period, was based largely on the apocryphal voyages said to have been made by Juan de Fuca in 1592 and Bartholomew de Fonte in 1640, which were then given credence by some geographers. It embodied the novel idea of a series of interconnecting channels and lakes passing through the American continent, commencing on the Pacific coast between 47 and 53°N.

On the other hand, the British Admiralty, initiating its own search for a Pacific entrance, took the more orthodox view of a high-latitude passage and, when dispatching Capt. James COOK to explore the north-

west coast in 1776, directed him to the north of 65°N. Before his death in 1779, Cook established the continuity of the Alaskan coastline as far as Icy Cape in 70°44'N. However, after his expedition's return in 1780, criticism of his instructions mounted, especially when sea-otter hunters, attracted to the northwest coast in the wake of Cook's voyage, began to report deep indentations in the coast far to the south of Cook's survey, namely, in the region of De Fuca's and De Fonte's supposed passages. The Admiralty responded to this criticism in 1791 by sending out George VANCOUVER to survey that area of coast. Vancouver examined the northwest coast south of Cook's discoveries in meticulous detail; in particular, he explored the notorious Strait of Juan de Fuca, where, rather to his surprise, he found a Spanish expedition engaged in the same task. By the time he returned home in October 1795, Vancouver had laid the ghost of the low-latitude Northwest Passage for all time.

Revival of British Arctic exploration By the beginning of the nineteenth century the search for a Northwest Passage had been in progress for 300 years without any significant breakthrough being made. Admittedly, it had brought about the discovery and exploration of Hudson Bay and the coasts of Alaska, Labrador, and Baffin Island; and these achievements had, in turn, benefited the commercial development of northern North America. But as yet not even an entrance to the passage had been found, and 2000 (3219 kilometers) miles of uncharted territory still separated Cook's Icy Cape and the explored areas of Hudson and Baffin Bays. In 1818, however, the British Admiralty, prompted by its energetic second secretary, John BARROW, launched a major assault on this region in a final effort to solve the riddle of the Northwest Passage.

Barrow proposed a revival of Arctic exploration as

The Discovery, grounded on a ledge of submerged rock in Queen Charlotte Sound during George Vancouver's expedition of 1791–1795. [Library of Congress]

an ideal means of providing employment for some of the Royal Navy's surplus manpower at the end of the Napoleonic Wars. His interest in the Northwest Passage was confined to scientific and geographical curiosity (he had no illusions about finding a commercial seaway), but the discovery of a passage was still central to his plans, if only to give his explorers a goal to aim at and to provoke some popular interest. In consequence of his efforts, two Arctic expeditions were planned for 1818. On the one hand, Capt. David Buchan and Lieut. John FRANKLIN were sent with two ships toward Spitsbergen (Svalbard) in an attempt to cross the Arctic Ocean. This expedition, of course, failed hopelessly. At the same time, Comdr. John Ross and Lieut. William PARRY, in HMS *Isabella* and *Alexander,* were directed toward Baffin Bay in search of a Northwest Passage. In planning a course for them, Barrow had recalled from obscurity the voyage of Baffin and Bylot in 1616, which, by the eighteenth century, had been dismissed as fantasy. Barrow saw promise in Baffin's three sounds, Smith, Jones, and Lancaster, in northern Baffin Bay, and encouraged Ross to pay particular attention to them. In the event, Ross's voyage served only to confirm Baffin's discoveries. Ross made only a cursory examination of the entrances to Smith and Jones Sounds, and on entering Lancaster Sound he was deceived by a mirage. Perceiving what appeared to be mountains across the head of the sound, he retreated and sailed home to report the impossibility of a passage by that route. A major disagreement ensued. Parry, who had seen no mountains, submitted an entirely encouraging report of Lancaster Sound, and Barrow chose to prefer his account. In consequence, Parry was appointed to command a second expedition to the sound, while Ross was passed over in disgrace.

At the same time, the Admiralty elected to send out a small expedition under John Franklin to tackle the Northwest Passage overland, a novel approach made possible by the steady encroachment of fur traders into the Canadian sub-Arctic mainland. Their trading posts were still far from the Arctic coast, and the position and trend of that coast were still almost entirely unknown, but the traders had seen it twice: Samuel HEARNE had located it at the mouth of the Coppermine River in 1771, and Alexander MACKENZIE had traced Mackenzie River to its mouth in 1789. By using Hearne's sighting as a target and the trading companies' supply lines as a means of transport into the north, Franklin hoped to trace the line of the coast eastward toward Hudson Bay and thus to chart at least the central portion of the Northwest Passage.

Parry and Franklin set out in May 1819, Franklin on a Hudson's Bay Company ship bound for York Factory on Hudson Bay, and Parry, with HMS *Hecla* and *Griper,* bound for Lancaster Sound. Within 3 months, Parry accomplished the feat which establishes his name among the most famous of polar explorers: he passed through Lancaster Sound to become both the first discoverer of an entrance to the Northwest Passage and the first to enter among the islands of the Canadian Arctic archipelago. Continuing west, he passed through Barrow Strait and Viscount Melville Sound to the southwestern extremity of Melville Island. There, about halfway through the passage, he was finally halted by ice. With no further hope of progress that season, he wintered on the south coast of Melville Island. He returned home the following year after a second unsuccessful attempt to penetrate the ice to the west.

As Parry was arriving home in triumph, Franklin's five-man overland expedition was still only just entering the unexplored territory north of Great Slave Lake where he built his base camp, Fort Enterprise, for the winter of 1820–1821. The main exploratory journey, in 1821, was fraught with difficulties. The party coasted eastward from the mouth of the Coppermine River but made very slow progress and found their canoes too frail and their Canadian boatmen increasingly restless. These handicaps, plus an acute shortage of food, forced them to abandon the voyage at Kent Peninsula, only a quarter of the way to Hudson Bay, and to attempt the journey overland back to Fort Enterprise. Starvation overtook them on this journey; about ten of the boatmen died, an officer, Robert Hood, was murdered, and the rest only just survived.

Franklin reached England again in 1822, by which time Parry was already engaged on his second Northwest Passage Expedition (1821–1823). This time, rather surprisingly, the Admiralty had directed him to the remaining unexplored corner of Hudson Bay, Foxe Basin. During this voyage, he explored the east coast of Melville Peninsula, at the northern end of which he discovered the long-sought western outlet from Hudson Bay: Fury and Hecla Strait. The strait passes via the Gulf of Boothia into Prince Regent Inlet and thus provides a theoretical entrance to the Northwest Passage. But, as Parry learned during two summers' observations, it is permanently choked with ice and unnavigable for sailing ships; only in modern times have icebreakers been able to pass through it.

With the final elimination of Hudson Bay, attention again focused on Lancaster Sound and Parry's route of 1819. This route was known to be icebound at its western end, but Parry had noticed several promising channels leading south from Barrow Strait. From this time on, the main preoccupation of Northwest Passage explorers was twofold: to discover which of these channels provided a navigable link with the north coast of America and to establish that the north coast itself was navigable along its entire length to Icy Cape.

This task commenced in 1824, when Parry set out to examine Prince Regent Inlet, the first major channel leading south from Barrow Strait, while George Lyon sailed for Hudson Bay to explore the north coast by boat from Melville Peninsula to Franklin's farthest on Kent Peninsula. Both expeditions failed completely. Parry returned home after one of his two ships, *Fury,* was wrecked in the ice in August 1825, before the survey of Prince Regent Inlet had properly begun. Lyon met bad weather in Roes Welcome Sound and failed to reach Repulse Bay, where he had planned to commence his boat journey.

In 1825 Franklin began another overland expedition to extend westward his discoveries on the north coast, but from a more accessible starting point, the Mackenzie River Delta, and with better-organized support from the Hudson's Bay Company. This time he accomplished most of his objectives almost without a hitch. On reaching the Mackenzie Delta on July 4, 1826, he divided his expedition into two boat parties; one, led by himself, headed west along the north coast of Alaska, and the other, under Dr. John Richardson, headed east for the Coppermine River. Richardson completed his task without difficulty, but Franklin, hampered by bad weather, turned back only a little over halfway to Icy Cape.

Private ventures At the end of this expedition, with the discovery of a Northwest Passage so nearly in sight, the Admiralty suddenly lost interest in Arctic exploration and began to reject plans for the completion of the task submitted by Franklin and others. For the next two decades, the continuation of the search was left almost exclusively to private enterprise.

The first of the private ventures was organized by John Ross, who was understandably anxious to clear his name after his misfortune in 1818. He secured the sponsorship of Sir Felix Booth, purchased a paddle steamer, *Victory,* and set out in 1829 to search for a passage by way of Prince Regent Inlet. As he sailed southward through the inlet, Ross failed to notice Bellot Strait, the one channel which, in good conditions, might have afforded an outlet to the west. Otherwise, as he learned from Eskimos during the winter, Prince Regent Inlet was an impasse, and his further explorations were confined to overland travel. Ross's nephew, James Clark Ross, undertook most of the overland journeys. Starting from *Victory*'s winter quarters on the east coast of Boothia Peninsula, he crossed the peninsula several times in the summers of 1830 and 1831, explored parts of its western coast, where he also became the first to locate the North Magnetic Pole, and discovered the northern extremity of King William Island.

Ross's expedition remained in Prince Regent Inlet for four winters, much longer than he had intended. He failed repeatedly to extricate *Victory* from the ice, so he finally abandoned her and made his way by boat by Lancaster Sound, where, in August 1833, he was rescued by a whaler. In England, meanwhile, fears for his safety grew, and the public subscribed to an overland search expedition led by George Back, a veteran of Franklin's two expeditions. Back chose to search for Ross by exploring Great Fish (now Back) River, which was known only by Indian report but was believed to enter the sea near Prince Regent Inlet. He made the long journey north through fur-trading territory in 1833 and wintered on Great Slave Lake, where news of Ross's safe return reached him the following spring. He chose nevertheless to explore Great Fish River to the sea before returning home and thus added to the map one of the largest rivers in northern Can-

Capt. John Ross, whose nephew James Ross would discover the North Magnetic Pole, here shown searching for a Northwest Passage in the Canadian Arctic. [Library of Congress]

ada and a short stretch of the northern coastline around its mouth.

Soon after, the Hudson's Bay Company undertook to complete the north-coast survey. In 1837 their servants Peter Warren Dease and Thomas Simpson repeated Franklin's journey west from the Mackenzie and filled in the blank left on Franklin's map by reaching Point Barrow, Alaska. During the next two years, using Fort Confidence on Great Bear Lake as their winter base, they completed the survey east from the Coppermine River to the west coast of Boothia Peninsula and, returning, surveyed the south coasts of King William and Victoria Islands. By the time they had finished, only two stretches of the north coast remained unexplored: the bottom of Prince Regent Inlet and part of the west coast of Boothia Peninsula.

Final achievement The virtual completion of the north-coast survey and Ross's elimination of Prince Regent Inlet made prospects for the discovery of a Northwest Passage so bright that, by 1843, several influential officers and geographers were raising their voices in favor of one last attempt by the Royal Navy. Admiralty and government support were finally granted early in 1845, and the new expedition, with Sir John Franklin commanding, was hastily fitted out.

The Franklin Expedition sailed from London on May 19, 1845, with instructions to search for a passage in the unexplored region southwest of Cape Walker on Barrow Strait. It was last seen heading for Lancaster Sound by whalers in northern Baffin Bay but after that was never heard from again. *See* FRANKLIN EXPEDITION AND SEARCH.

The several expeditions sent to search for Franklin contributed much to the exploration of the Canadian Arctic archipelago; indeed, excepting the Sverdrup Islands far to the north, they put the outline of nearly all the Arctic islands on the map. Moreover, it was the search for Franklin which finally solved the riddle of the Northwest Passage: three different expeditions independently discovered three separate passages be-

Capt. Roald Amundsen and his crew aboard the Gjøa in Nome, 1906. They were the first successfully to navigate the Northwest Passage. [Library of Congress]

tween the years 1848 and 1851. Franklin's own expedition discovered the passage through Peel Sound and Victoria Strait, but none survived to tell the tale. The search expedition of Robert McCLURE on board *Investigator*, which had entered the Arctic through Bering Strait, discovered a second passage through Prince of Wales Strait in 1851; and Richard COLLINSON on board *Enterprise* independently made the same discovery a year later. Heavy ice in Viscount Melville Sound, however, prevented both men from completing the passage. Finally, McClure, having been thwarted in Prince of Wales Strait, took his ship to the north coast of Banks Island to discover a third Northwest Passage through McClure Strait. His ship was beset there for two winters and was finally abandoned when members of the search expedition of Sir Edward BELCHER arrived to rescue him. McClure and his men were taken home by way of Baffin Bay and thus became the first to pass right through the Northwest Passage, but of course they did so partly on their own ship, partly on foot, and partly on Belcher's ships.

Even though the existence of several prospective Northwest Passages was at last proven, nobody had yet demonstrated that any were navigable throughout on a single ship. But the search for Franklin exhausted Britain's passion for polar exploration. When it ended, the Royal Navy turned its back on the Arctic leaving the question of navigability unanswered, and it was not until 1903 that the Norwegian explorer Roald AMUNDSEN set out to settle the matter. He chose a course similar to that followed by Franklin, through Lancaster Sound, Peel Sound, and Franklin Strait but, unlike his predecessor, chose to sail around the east and south of King William Island. From there, he followed the north coast of the continent to Bering Strait, where he arrived in 1906 after three winters in the Arctic.

Twentieth-century developments In many ways, Amundsen's achievement was little more than an academic exercise: he was the first to take a ship through the Northwest Passage, but his 47-ton *Gjøa* was far too tiny to demonstrate its navigability to commercial shipping, and the voyage aroused little interest in the passage as a trading route. Traffic along sections of the passage did increase steadily in the first half of the twentieth century as trading companies and government agencies increased their activities in the Arctic, but it was not until the 1940s that the passage was again navigated in full. Between 1940 and 1942 Henry A. Larsen of the Royal Canadian Mounted Police took the schooner *St. Roch* through the passage from west to east, deviating a little from Amundsen's route by sailing through Bellot Strait instead of Peel Sound. In 1944 he returned from east to west, this time opening up the passage through Prince of Wales Strait.

During the cold war of the 1950s, the Northwest Passage acquired a new but short-lived strategic significance as the United States and Canadian Navies examined its value for supplying the DEW Line stations and for nuclear-submarine maneuvers. Finally, in 1969, the wheel turned full circle, and the prospect of a commercially viable Northwest Passage again rose to prominence after centuries of neglect. The huge tanker SS *Manhattan* was twice used to test the feasibility of transporting oil through the passage from newly discovered reserves on the North Slope of Alaska to the eastern United States. Despite promising results from these voyages, the idea was eventually abandoned in favor of a pipeline through Alaska.

So, after nearly 500 years, the expectations of the earliest Northwest Passage explorers remain unfulfilled. It still appears unlikely that the passage will be developed as a commercial shipping route between

the Atlantic and Pacific Oceans. However, as the economic development of the Canadian Arctic continues, sections of the Northwest Passage will undoubtedly increase in importance as shipping routes between north and south.

BIBLIOGRAPHY: Sir John Barrow, *A Chronological History of Voyages into the Arctic Regions*, London, 1818, reprinted Newton Abbot, 1971; id., *Voyages of Discovery and Research within the Arctic Regions, from the Year 1818 to the Present Time*, London, 1846; Ernest S. Dodge, *Northwest by Sea*, New York, 1961; Leslie H. Neatby, *In Quest of the North West Passage*, London, 1958; George M. Thomson, *The North-West Passage*, London, 1975; Glyndwr Williams, *The British Search for the Northwest Passage in the Eighteenth Century*, London, 1962.

Clive A. Holland

Northwestern North America

The conquest of Siberia brought Russia to the shores of the Pacific. There were rumors of another large region across the sea to the east, but for a long time the question of what the territory was or, if it was North America, whether the two continents were joined, remained unsettled. Semyon DEZHNEV, who unwittingly solved the problem by rounding Chukotka (Chukotsky Poluostrov) in 1648, heard of the Diomede Islands. Vladimir ATLASOV during his exploration in Kamchatka (1697–1699) was told of a "great land" situated opposite Chukotka.

Eighteenth-century exploration Neither Ivan Yevreinov and Fyodor Luzhin in 1719 nor Vitus BERING in 1728 was able to solve the problem conclusively. In 1732 Ivan Fyodorov and Mikhail Gvozdev completed a voyage from the mouth of the Anadyr River to the North American coast, confirming the presence of a strait, but their findings were not known for some years. Therefore, in 1732 the Russian Senate once again ordered Bering, among other objectives, to determine whether Kamchatka and North America were connected and to investigate the American coasts. When the voyage was finally undertaken in 1741, Bering's second-in-command, Aleksey CHIRIKOV, reached the American coast at latitude 57°39′N, but the loss of both of his small boats and their crews, evidently at the hands of natives, prevented further exploration, and he returned to Avacha Bay, Kamchatka, in October. Bering landed only briefly on Kayak Island in the Gulf of Alaska, sighting Mount St. Elias, before he too started back. On the return voyage both parties sighted the Kenai Peninsula and a number of islands in the Aleutian chain. Bering was wrecked on the island in the Komandorskiye group which now bears his name and died there on December 8, 1741.

The survivors of Bering's party reached Kamchatka in a boat built from the wreckage of their vessel. Their reports of an abundance of sea otters in the islands sparked a new fur rush. Siberian merchants began

forming companies that built crude vessels and sent them out to the newly discovered islands. As areas were hunted out, the voyagers sought new islands. Thus, between 1743 and 1746 Yemelyan Basov hunted on the islands of the Komandorskiye group. In 1745 Mikhail Nevodchikov found the most westerly of the Aleutians, the Near Islands. In 1753 a vessel sent out by the merchant Andrey Serebrennikov found the Rat Islands. In 1756 Andreyan Tolstykh reached Amlia and Adak Islands in the group named after him, the Andreanof Islands. In 1758 Stepan Glotov reached Umnak and Unalaska of the Fox group. In 1761 Gavrilo Pushkarev saw the mainland of Alaska: the tip of the Alaska Peninsula.

These Russian activities aroused concern in Madrid, where it was feared that Russia might move south and encroach on lands claimed by Spain. In 1769 Marqués Carlos Francisco de Croix, viceroy of New Spain, on orders from King Charles III tried to block the assumed Russian advance southward. Acting with the visitor general of the Franciscan missions, he sent an expedition to Upper California to establish garrisons and under their protection to start missions to convert and civilize the Indians. Beginning with the establishment of the Mission and Presidio of San Diego, missions were built at intervals in Upper California as far north as San Francisco Bay (1776), thereby establishing Spain's hold on the region.

The Spanish also undertook voyages northward both to make discoveries and to determine the extent of Russian activity. In 1774 an expedition under Juan José Pérez with the ship *Santiago* explored the coast as far as the Queen Charlotte Islands, traded with the Indians, and took possession of the country in the name of the King of Spain. On the west coast of Vancouver Island the party discovered Nootka Sound.

The following year, a second expedition was sent out under Don Bruno Hezeta, with the ships *Sonora* and *Santiago*. At the 49th parallel Hezeta, with the *Santiago*, turned back, but on the way south he discovered the mouth of the Columbia River. Juan Francisco de la Bodega y Quadra and his pilot, Francisco Antonio Mourelle de la Rúa, with the *Sonora,* went north to Sitka (Norfolk) Sound, identified Mount Edgecumbe, and entered and named Bucareli Bay on the west side of Prince of Wales Island.

A third Spanish expedition was planned but had to be delayed several years until another ship was built. Meanwhile, Great Britain, acting from scientific and commercial motives, entered the North Pacific to search for a northern passage from the Pacific Ocean to the Atlantic or westward around Asia. During his third voyage (1776–1779) Capt. James COOK sighted and named Mount Edgecumbe and Prince William Sound, discovered Cook Inlet, ran far enough north in Bering Strait to prove conclusively the separation of the two continents and the impracticality of a northern passage, and charted the coasts on either side of Bering Strait.

In 1779 the Spanish expedition, comprising the vessels *Princesa* and *Favorita,* sailed from San Blas for the north under Lieut. Ignacio Arteaga, assisted by Bodega. Early in May the ships entered Bucareli Sound, carrying out an extensive reconnaissance. Resuming their voyage on July 1, they sighted Mount St. Elias, passed Kayak Island, formally claimed possession of the country for Spain at Nuchek Bay and again at the tip of the Kenai Peninsula, and went as far west as Afognak Island, near Kodiak. Meanwhile, upon arriving at Canton, Cook's sailors had disposed of a stock of sea-otter skins obtained on the northwest coast of North America for such high sums that a rush of British and, later, American skippers began to obtain more. Capt. James Hanna, who sailed from Macao to Nootka in 1785, was followed the next year by Capts. John Meares, Nathaniel Portlock, George Dixon, and others. Soon there were a dozen or more ships a year on the coast. In 1786 two French vessels under Jean-François de Galaup, Comte de LA PÉROUSE came on a voyage of discovery, one of the objectives of which was said to be the acquisition by France of trading posts on the northwest coast.

This activity in the North Pacific and rumors of continued Russian advance southward roused Spain to resume its explorations. In 1788 two vessels were sent northward on a reconnaissance to attempt to ascertain Russian intentions. Don Estevan José Martínez, commander of the *Princesa* and head of the expedition, had accompanied Pérez on his voyage of 1774. Gonzalo López de Haro was second-in-command, in the *San Carlos.* They examined part of Prince William Sound, sailed to Unalaska, and brought back exaggerated reports of Russian interest in the Nootka Sound area. This caused the Viceroy to send the same two commanders and the same two ships out again in 1789 to occupy Nootka Sound, but instead of the Russians they found the English at Nootka, and the celebrated Nootka Sound controversy resulted.

In the Aleutian Islands cutthroat competition, mistreatment of the natives, and exhaustion of the fur resources led the merchant Grigory Ivanovich SHELEKHOV to urge the establishment of permanent colonies, if possible under one company. In 1783 he set out from Okhotsk with an expedition of three ships, one of which soon became separated from the others, and in 1784 founded the first Russian colony in North America on Kodiak at Three Saints Bay. Shelekhov's "discoveries" (he was to be called the Russian Columbus) were minimal, but his colonies provided advance bases which soon made the whole of southern Alaska familiar territory. In 1788 G. A. IZMAILOV and D. I. BOCHAROV in Shelekhov's vessel *Tri Svyatitelya* (*Three Saints*) described the north mainland shore of the Gulf of Alaska from Kenai Peninsula to Yakutat and Lituya Bays. In 1789 Izmailov described the southeast shore of Kenai Peninsula. In 1788–1789 Gavrilo Loginovich Pribylov, a skipper for a rival company, discovered two islands north of Unalaska rich in fur seals, now called the Pribilof Islands.

The empress Catherine II, whenever free of complications in Europe, displayed interest in the explorations in Russian America and in good treatment of the natives by the fur traders. At government expense, expeditions were fitted out to map the newly discovered areas and to oversee the conduct of the private traders. Thus, in 1764 Lieut. Ivan Sindt made an unsuccessful voyage into the Bering Sea. In 1768–1769, Lieuts. Pyotr KRENITSYN and Mikhail Levashev visited the Aleutian Islands and the Alaska Peninsula. In 1786, aware of the interest of foreigners in the northwest coast, Catherine ordered more decisive measures. A flotilla of four ships, under Capt. Grigory Ivanovich Mulovsky, was fitted out to sail around the world to the North Pacific, whereupon two ships would patrol and explore on the Asian coast and two on the American coast. The threat of war with Sweden forced cancellation of the expedition, but plans for another, organized for scientific purposes by the savant Peter Simon Pallas, went forward. Headed by Joseph BILLINGS, an English mariner who had served under Cook, and his more talented second-in-command, Gavriil Andreyevich SARYCHEV, the expedition (1785–1793) explored Chukotka (Chukotsky Poluostrov) and visited Unalaska. Considering the expedition's size and expense, the results were modest.

Russian-American Company Shelekhov's efforts to persuade Catherine to grant his company a monopoly over the fur trade in North America failed, but after his death his son-in-law N. P. Rezanov in 1798 brought the various competing firms together. In 1799 Rezanov obtained from Tsar Paul I a 20-year charter granting a monopoly to the Russian-American Company. From 1790 on the operations of Shelekhov's company and its successor in North America were under the capable Aleksandr BARANOV. Shipwrecked on Unalaska Island on the way to his new post, Baranov spent the winter there and completed his trip to

Three Saints Bay in a 2-month voyage by *baidara* (large skin boat) in 1791. His assistant, D. I. Bocharov, entered Bristol Bay with two *baidaras*, finished the discovery of the north coast of the Alaska Peninsula begun by Krenitsyn and Levashev, then found a short and convenient way across the peninsula to Shelikof Strait via the Egegik River, Becharof Lake, and a short portage to the strait. In 1791–1793 Baranov rounded all of Kodiak in *baidaras*, entered Cook Inlet, rounded Kenai Peninsula, and examined islands in Chugach Bay (Prince William Sound). He organized settlements on Afognak Island, on the shores of Cook Inlet, and at Resurrection Bay (now Seward). At the last-named site he commenced shipbuilding, and elsewhere he investigated coal and iron deposits.

The most pressing problem of the Russian colonies was supply. The transport of goods and foodstuffs by barge and pack train across Siberia and then by ship across the North Pacific was expensive and unsatisfactory. In an effort to achieve a more satisfactory solution, voyages around the world from St. Petersburg were undertaken. The idea had been proposed in the time of Peter the Great and had nearly been realized by the Mulovsky Expedition. Kept alive by Capt. Lieut. Ivan Fyodorovich KRUSENSHTERN and others, the idea was finally put into force in 1803 with the dispatch of the *Nadezhda* under Krusenshtern and the *Neva* under Yury Fyodorovich LISIANSKY. Separating from the *Nadezhda* in the Hawaiian Islands, Lisiansky took the *Neva* to Kodiak and then aided Baranov in the retaking of New Archangel (Sitka), seized by the Tlingit Indians in 1802. He wintered at Kodiak, met the *Nadezhda* in Macao, and returned to St. Petersburg in 1806. Subsequently more than fifty such voyages were accomplished. Many were undertaken for commercial purposes alone, but others

made important contributions to science. Capt. V. M. GOLOVNIN, with the *Diana* in 1807–1809 and the *Kamchatka* in 1817–1819, set a standard for seamanship and provided valuable hydrographic data. Otto von KOTZEBUE, with the *Rurik*, financed by Count N. M. Rumiantsev, made many discoveries in the islands of the South Pacific. On the northwest coast near Bering Strait, Shishmaref Inlet, Sarichef Island, Kotzebue Sound, and Eschscholtz Bay were discovered in 1816. In 1819 M. N. Vasilyev in the *Blagonamerennyi* and G. S. Shishmarev in the *Otkrytiye* with their subordinates Arvid Adolf ETHOLÉN and V. S. Khromchenko in smaller vessels undertook extensive explorations of the American coast of Bering Strait, discovering Nunivak Island in 1821. Between 1826 and 1829 Capt. Lieut. F. P. LITKE with the *Senyavin* and M. N. Stanyukovich with the *Moller* undertook further explorations of the Bering Strait area.

These and other voyages resulted in the accumulation of a valuable fund of navigational information. M. D. Tebenkov, while governor of the colonies, gathered all the facts he could from ship logs and personal recollections of Russian and foreign skippers. He compiled all these data in his *Atlas of the Northwest Coast of America* (St. Petersburg, 1852).

The early explorations of Alaska were almost exclusively of the coastal areas. A notable exception was one Ivanov, with the Lebedev-Lastochkin Company, an early rival of Shelekhov's enterprise, who about 1787 traveled north of Lake Iliamna for more than 27 days. His brief and sketchy account has led some to believe that he reached the lower Yukon.

The Russian-American Company, under orders from the government, began exploration of the interior after the Baranov era. In the winter of 1817–1818 Pyotr Korsakovsky crossed from Kodiak to the south-

Harbor of New Archangel (Sitka), on Norfolk Sound. The Tlingit Indians attempted to capture this Russian base in 1802, but Aleksandr Baranov and Yury Lisiansky retook it. [Library of Congress]

west shore of Cook Inlet, then proceeded north of the Alaska Peninsula to Lake Iliamna and its outlet, the Kvichak River. In 1819 he examined the American shore of the Bering Sea as far north as one of the arms of the delta of the Kwikpak (Yukon) River.

In 1819–1820, Andrey Klimovsky explored the lower reaches of the Copper River. In 1829–1830, Ivan Filippovich Vasilyev studied the rivers entering Bristol Bay, including the Nushagak River. Farther north he discovered the large, navigable Kuskokwim River and followed it to its middle course.

In 1833, on the south shore of Norton Sound and east of the Kwikpak Delta, the company founded the Mikhailovsky redoubt (now St. Michael). Between 1833 and 1835 Andrey GLAZUNOV studied the Kwikpak Delta and the river's lower course up to the mouth of the Anvik River. In 1838 Glazunov and Pyotr Malakhov ascended the Kwikpak to the mouth of the Nulato River. The same year Pyotr Kolmakov traced a great part of the course of the Innoko River, a large lower (left) tributary of the Kwikpak, crossed the Kuskokwim Mountains to the Kuskokwim River, and descended it to the sea.

The most extensive explorations of the interior were performed by Lieut. Lavrenty Alekseyevich ZAGOSKIN. Entering company service in 1838, he was placed in charge in 1842 of an expedition to study the largest rivers of Alaska, the Kwikpak (Yukon) and the Kuskokwim. Starting from the St. Michael redoubt, Zagoskin went to the Nulato redoubt and studied the lower course of the Koyukuk River, the north branch of the Yukon. In the summer of 1843 he reached the mouth of the Tanana River, the main tributary of the Yukon, and in *baidarkas* (kayaks) studied the Yukon from its rapids to its lower bend. In 1844 he traversed the middle and lower reaches of the Kuskokwim and the lower reaches of the Yukon. Zagoskin's account of his explorations is one of the best contemporary works on Russian America.

In 1844 Malakhov explored and made a map of the Susitna River, which collects the waters of many

rivers flowing from the central and western part of the Alaska Range and flows into the northern part of Cook Inlet. During the remainder of the Russian regime, comparatively little land exploration was undertaken. The absence of large fur yields in the northern and interior regions, inadequate means, and in later years uncertainty as to the company's future hindered further effort.

United States contributions　United States contributions to the exploration of Alaska began in 1865 with the Western Union Telegraph Expedition, a private attempt to link Europe with North America by telegraph. The line was abandoned when the Atlantic cable began to operate, but thanks to the planning of Robert Kennecott, the support of the Smithsonian Institution, and the fieldwork of William Dall, major contributions were made in science and exploration. These contributions were expanded by the Coast Survey, in which Dall also took a prominent part, and later by the Army. The Signal Service performed important work in scientific exploration, especially in natural history and meteorology, and the Department of Columbia, under the direction of Gen. Nelson A. Miles, sponsored a series of geographical explorations. In 1883 Lieut. Frederick Schwatka traced the headwaters of the Yukon. In 1884 Lieut. W. R. Abercrombie tried unsuccessfully to explore the Copper River Basin, a task completed brilliantly the next year under Lieut. Henry T. Allen, proving the possibility of a direct route from the coast to the interior.

In the meantime the Navy and the Revenue Marine competed in the exploration of coastal areas, the former in southeastern Alaska and the latter along the western and northern littoral. Expeditions sent to aid the survivors of the Arctic exploration vessels *Jeannette* and *Rodgers* carried on extensive exploration in northeastern Siberia and northwestern Alaska. Coal deposits were found by the revenue cutter *Thetis* in 1888 and by the *Corwin* in 1894. In 1886 the revenue cutters received the report that oil seepage had been observed at Cape Simpson, giving the first inkling of the North Slope deposits.

In 1889 the Coast Survey, newly renamed the Coast and Geodetic Survey, began geodetic work connected with the international-boundary question. The period from 1888 to 1891 also witnessed the vigorous exploration in Yukon Territory directed by George Dawson of the Canadian Geological Survey. The U.S. Geological Survey became active in Alaskan inland exploration in 1895 and 1896 in response to increased mining activity. During the decade that followed a network of surveys connected the principal river systems, and mining areas, sometimes in advance of actual discovery, were mapped and photographed.

In 1899 the Harriman Alaska Expedition toured the Aleutians and the Pribilof Islands. Although dismissed by some as a big game hunt and grandiose outing, the expedition was heavily staffed with leading scientists and produced an impressive body of work in many fields.

John Burroughs (left) and John Muir on St. Matthew Island, Alaska, during the Harriman Alaska Expedition of 1899. Although critics considered the voyage a lightweight undertaking, this tour of the Aleutians and the Pribilof Islands produced much information about the territory. [Library of Congress]

BIBLIOGRAPHY: A. I. Andreyev (ed.), *Russian Discoveries in the Pacific and in North America in the Eighteenth and Nineteenth Centuries: A Collection of Materials*, tr. by Carl Ginsburg, Ann Arbor, Mich., 1952; Hubert H. Bancroft, *History of Alaska, 1730–1885*, San Francisco, 1886; V. N. Berkh, *A Chronological History of the Discovery of the Aleutian Islands*, tr. by Dmitri Krenov, Kingston, Ontario, 1974; Warren L. Cook, *Flood Tide of Empire: Spain and the Pacific Northwest, 1543–1819*, New Haven, Conn., and London, 1973; *Documents on the History of the Russian-American Company*, tr. by Marina Ramsay, Kingston, Ontario, 1976; S. G. Fyodorova, *The Russian Population in Alaska and California: Late 18th Century–1867*, tr. by R. A. Pierce and A. S. Donnelly, Kingston, Ontario, 1973; James R. Gibson, *Imperial Russia in Frontier America: The Changing Geography of Supply in Russian America, 1784–1867*, New York, 1976; Frank A. Golder (tr. and ed.), *Bering's Voyages: An Account of the Efforts of the Russians to Determine the Relation of Asia and America*, 2 vols., New York, 1922; K. T. Khlebnikov, *Baranov, Chief Manager of the Russian Colonies in America*, tr. by Colin Bearne, Kingston, Ontario, 1973; R. V. Makarova, *Russians on the Pacific, 1743–1799*, tr. by R. A. Pierce and A. S. Donnelly, Kingston, Ontario, 1975; Henry N. Michael (ed.), *Lieutenant Zagoskin's Travels in Russian America, 1842–1844: The First Ethnographic and Geographic Investigations in the Yukon and Kuskokwim Valleys of Alaska*, Toronto, 1967; S. B. Okun, *The Russian-American Company*, tr. by Carl Ginsburg, Cambridge, Mass., 1951; Morgan B. Sherwood, *Exploration of Alaska, 1865–1900*, New Haven, Conn., and London, 1965.

Richard A. Pierce

Oceanographical Exploration

Covering seven-tenths of the earth's surface, the oceans of the world have challenged human attempts to fathom their secrets for millennia. The exploration of the frontiers of the sea has required the mastery of not only the techniques of geographical exploration but also the subtle understanding of the principles of chemistry, physics, geology, and biology. Until the nineteenth century, the seas were an unknown realm whose width, breadth, and depth needed to be mapped and whose water-covered rivers, mountains, and valleys still awaited their explorers. It was a world whose dynamic configuration was still unperceived and whose inhabitants awaited taxonomic classification and biological analysis. The dimensions of the problems presented by oceanographical exploration required almost from its inception that there be adequate financial backing for such endeavors. Men, ships, and supplies had to be carefully prepared and supported before a successful program of research and exploration could begin. In their need for funds, early voyages of oceanographical investigation were similar to government-supported polar expeditions in the eighteenth and nineteenth centuries and to space exploration in the twentieth century.

Ancient and medieval contributions The Greeks developed the earliest sustained scientific interest in the sea. Aristotle, the son of the court physician to Philip of Macedon and a student of Plato, was an astute observer of the creatures and phenomena of the Mediterranean Sea. His descriptions of marine animals were unsurpassed in the ancient world and in some cases were not equaled until the end of the Middle Ages. In his *Meteorologica,* Aristotle presented the Greeks of the fourth century B.C. with a cursory survey of tides and an explanation of the sea's origins, its saltiness, and the nature of the evaporation-precipitation cycle.

The Romans had only a limited interest in the sea, and their knowledge of it was essentially an extension of what the Greeks had thought on this subject. PLINY the Elder's thirty-seven-volume *Natural History* included, amid its passages on mythical beasts, magic potions, and marvelous sights, substantial descriptions of the flora, fauna, and physical occurrences of the sea. Indeed, his descriptions of tides were among the more accurate of those presented in the ancient world. Nevertheless, the body of oceanographical knowledge which was passed on to the thinkers of the medieval centuries was meager. With the decline of antiquity there was a perceptible waning of interest in science, and the acquired knowledge of the sea was only imperfectly maintained.

The Venerable Bede made the most important contributions to the understanding of the processes of the oceans during the early Middle Ages. This delightful eighth-century ecclesiastic, teacher, scholar, and historian developed the most comprehensive understanding of tides that had yet appeared. In his calendrical work *De ratione temporum*, which was produced for his monastery in northern England, Bede examined the relationship between the phases of the moon and the corresponding tides and noted the daily retardation which the moon and the tides jointly experienced. His study of this subject led him to understand the principle upon which the "establishment of port" is predicated, thereby affording seamen a method of determining the nature of the tidal flow and the depth of water at the anchorages to which they were sailing. Bede's novel work in this area has often been hailed as one of the few examples of original scientific scholarship to occur between the decline of Rome and the revival of learning in the twelfth century. Throughout the medieval centuries knowledge of the sea was sought for essentially practical purposes. Improvements were made in navigational aids. In the twelfth century Alexander Neckham composed one of the earliest treatises on the use of the mariner's compass. Tide tables were produced, and information on water depths and the character of the bottom for major ports began to be circulated among mariners.

Sixteenth and seventeenth centuries Knowledge of the ocean naturally increased as a result of the voyages of exploration and discovery in the sixteenth and seventeenth centuries. Equally important in increasing knowledge of the sea was the beginning of the abandonment of the traditional classical assumptions about the nature of the sea. Leonardo da Vinci, William Bourne, William Gilbert, Galileo, and Johannes Kepler represent only the most eminent of the thinkers who were beginning to discuss oceanographical questions. In the sixteenth century, the practical experiences of Renaissance explorers began to be woven into the writings of the scientists of the day. European mariners began to record their encounters with the effects of the Gulf Stream, and by the 1540s Spanish seamen had confronted the Equatorial Current of the Pacific Ocean. Attempts at sounding were made, but these were generally failures. The inability of Renaissance ships to establish their longitude prevented them from determining their precise location at sea, and thus they were unable to record accurately where they encountered many of the unusual features of the unexplored waters upon which they were sailing.

As science rapidly developed in the sixteenth and seventeenth centuries, new methods and theoretical premises arose. Experiments began to be conducted to verify the validity of these new hypotheses. While the growth of knowledge in chemistry, biology, and physics provided those who were interested in marine studies with new concepts and experimental techniques, until the conclusion of the nineteenth century it was easier to observe and to record turbulences on the face of the sun than it was to gain a rudimentary knowledge of the life and topography of the world which lay 2 miles (3.2 kilometers) beneath the sea's surface.

Early in its history, the Royal Society of England began to concern itself with examining life and phenomena beneath the sea's surface. In June 1661, the 1st Earl of Sandwich was asked to investigate on his forthcoming voyage to the Mediterranean Sea its depth, its salinity, the tidal flow of the Strait of Gibraltar, and the luminescence of seawater. The society thus began a tradition of requesting such observations from obliging parties. One of the founders of the society, Robert Boyle, was a diligent student of the ocean environment. A powerful champion of the experimental method, Boyle stressed the need for a systematic investigation of the sea. While generally dependent upon the observations of seamen for his empirical knowledge of the sea, Boyle in his four essays on the sea provided a comprehensive assessment of the need for oceanographical exploration.

Eighteenth century The first systematic investigation of the sea in the eighteenth century was undertaken by Count Luigi Ferdinando Marsigli (Marsili; 1658–1730), who in 1724 published his *Histoire physique de la mer*, the first modern treatise on oceanography.

Interested initially in geology, Marsigli came to believe that it was impossible to understand geological formations on land without understanding the features of the sea bottom. Hampered by a lack of adequate equipment, Marsigli sought to investigate select regions of the sea in detail. While still a young man, he had examined the Bosporus and discovered beneath the surface current of the strait a countercurrent with waters of a different density. He later turned his attention to the waters off the southern coast of France. Working from a small port near Marseille, Marsigli ran a series of soundings which enabled him to prepare a profile of the sea floor. This profile was the earliest description of the morphology of a coastline with its continental shelf and slope leading to deeper waters. In his work Marsigli described the flora and fauna encountered in the marine environment; analyzed the temperature, salinity, and color of seawater; and examined the nature of the sea's motion by observing and measuring, when possible, waves, currents, and tides. In opposition to the views of his contemporaries, Marsigli contended that coral was a living organism, although he incorrectly classified it as a plant rather than as an animal. Marsigli's carefully organized examination of a given area within the sea would later become an accepted model for successful oceanographical exploration.

Marine explorers in the eighteenth century occasionally made oceanographical observations regarding temperature, salinity, and tides, but it was not until the voyages of James Cook that the English began to gather such information systematically. While Cook's first voyage of 1768–1771 did not significantly contribute to an understanding of the phenomena of the sea, this expedition has been justly praised for the wealth of geographical, ethnological, and botanical knowledge it produced. The success of this expedition led to Cook's remarkable second voyage of 1772–1775 during which he sailed east from the Cape of Good Hope and circumnavigated the globe. While seeking to fulfill one of the expedition's objectives of proving the existence of a large southern continent, naturalists under Cook's command obtained temperature readings from various depths in the fertile waters of the Antarctic Ocean. They discovered that there were layers of water at 100 and 160 fathoms (183 and 293 meters) that were warmer than the surface layer. Water samples were also obtained for chemical analysis, and tidal ranges were recorded at various sites. Data were beginning to be collected for an understanding of oceanic circulation. Following Admiralty instructions, Cook utilized the chronometer on this voyage and demonstrated its value as a navigational instrument. With the chronometer, it was now possible to fix a ship's longitude and thus, with a knowledge of its latitude, to determine precisely its position at sea.

During the same decade of Cook's explorations, the British Admiralty sent Capt. Constantine John Phipps into Arctic waters seeking a naval route to the North Pole. Better equipped than previous parties entering these frigid waters, the *Racehorse* and the *Carcass* reached farther north than Henry HUDSON had, but ice prevented them from proceeding beyond Spitsbergen (Svalbard). The expedition's scientists, a civilian astronomer and a surgeon-naturalist, utilizing a self-registering thermometer recorded temperatures from 673 and 780 fathoms (1231 and 1426 meters) and carried out other observations.

Even as English naturalists were exploring the secrets of the polar seas from the decks of Royal Navy vessels, other nations also were inquiring into the mysteries of the ocean's depths. French naturalists made observations of the sea's temperature and salinity at different depths during Marc Marion du Fresne's expedition of 1771–1774 and on the cruises of the *Géographe* and the *Naturaliste,* which Napoleon sent on a voyage of circumnavigation under Nicolas Baudin in 1800. The first Russian voyage of circumnavigation under Adam Johann von KRUSENSHTERN in 1803–1806 also made oceanographical observations.

In less hazardous waters, the brilliant and eternally curious Benjamin Franklin was carrying out marine research in the same years that Cook was making his epic voyages. Franklin's interest in the sea was of long duration. From his youth he had been intrigued by the ocean's mysteries, and his eight passages across the Atlantic Ocean provided him with numerous opportunities to study the sea. Franklin's most famous ocean study was of that great river in the Atlantic, the Gulf Stream. With a volume of water which exceeds that of 400 Amazon Rivers, the Gulf Stream is a powerful determinant of the flora, fauna, climate, and current of the Atlantic Ocean itself. By 1775 Franklin had pioneered in the use of a thermometer as an aid to locating and navigating through the Gulf Stream; and even on his last return voyage to America, he was still

experimenting with a special thermometer which enabled him to record Gulf Stream temperatures down to a depth of 100 feet (30 meters). His charting of the Gulf Stream had immediate practical implications, for it reduced the time necessary to make the transatlantic passage from Europe to America.

Early nineteenth century Interest in constructing an explanation for general oceanic circulation grew in the late eighteenth and early nineteenth centuries. Developments in physics began to be applied to an understanding of this subject. The eccentric Benjamin Thompson, Count Rumford, speculated upon the nature of heat in many of his essays, and in his 1798 treatise "Of the Propagation of Heat in Fluids" he anticipated many of the essential features of the modern model of ocean circulation. A little later, the English geographer James Rennell attempted to provide ocean scientists with a comprehensive view of the circulation patterns of the Atlantic Ocean in *An Investigation of the Currents of the Atlantic Ocean,* which appeared posthumously in 1832.

The importance of polar waters in the general circulation patterns of the world's oceans began to be appreciated, and nineteenth-century explorers who ventured into these waters were asked to collect observations which would aid in understanding this problem. In 1820, after years of experience in northern waters, William Scoresby published the first modern study of Arctic geography, an *Account of the Arctic Regions with a History and Description of the Northern Whale-Fishery.* In addition to providing valuable information on Arctic flora, fauna (including plankton), meteorology, magnetism, and water temperatures, Scoresby suggested that the surface layer of Arctic waters was colder than deeper layers of water because of the region's penetration by a finger of the Gulf Stream. More observations were needed before

In 1773 the British Admiralty sent the Racehorse and the Carcass on an expedition to find a naval route to the North Pole.

the validity of this assumption could be tested, but it was a intriguing idea for students of the sea.

In the third and fourth decades of the 1800s, national voyages of exploration continued, and they added to the growing accumulation of diverse data about the sea. France's Vénus Expedition of 1836–1839 and the 1837–1840 expedition of Jules DUMONT D'URVILLE with *L'Astrolabe* and *La Zelée,* while having other primary responsibilities, did provide that nation's scientists with new marine observations. D'Urville conscientiously performed the laborious task of making temperature observations from great depths, even as deep as 1200 fathoms (2195 meters), but he failed to appreciate the effects of pressure at such depths upon his maximum and minimum thermometers, and his readings were thus distorted. These erroneous readings helped to popularize the erroneous idea that beginning at around 600 fathoms (1097 meters) the ocean's universal temperature was approximately 4.4°C (40°F). Fortunately for the scientific honor of France on this subject, the pressure-corrected temperature observations made with protected thermometers during the cruise of the *Vénus* recorded more accurate deep-sea thermal ranges, and from a depth of more than 900 fathoms (1646 meters) a temperature reading of 2.3°C (36°F) was obtained.

Despite some evidence to the contrary and the opposition of Alexander von Humboldt and Matthew Fontaine Maury, the belief in a universal temperature of around 4°C (39°F) at great depths continued. Unfortunately for the quick demise of this theory, the work of the talented physicist and oceanographical explorer Emil Lenz (1804–1865) was either unknown or ignored. Lenz had served as a scientist on board the sloop *Predpriyatiye* of Otto von KOTZEBUE during the Russian scientific circumnavigation of 1823–1826. With equipment invented by G. F. Parrot, Lenz was able to obtain more accurate readings of specific gravities and deep-sea temperatures and secured correct observations from depths down to 2 kilometers (1.2 miles). The demonstration by Lenz and Parrot that

pressure affects an unprotected thermometer's readings was generally neglected by other researchers. Lenz later became a distinguished physicist, producing fundamental work on electromagnetic induction and the thermal action of currents. His contribution to oceanographical exploration was the result of his participation in Kotzebue's expedition and includes, in addition to his accurate measurement of specific gravities and temperatures from great depths, a relatively accurate explanation of several phenomena: the salinity maximums in the Atlantic and Pacific Oceans, the greater salinity of the Atlantic over the Pacific, the decreasing salinity of the Indian Ocean as a ship proceeded eastward, and the fact that at certain latitudes the sea's surface water could be warmer than the air above it.

The plotting of deep-sea temperatures continued to grow as an important phase of oceanographical exploration. Sir James ROSS sought to obtain a record of deep-sea temperatures during his Antarctic expedition of 1839–1843. This expedition into southern polar waters was among the most significant British geographical expeditions of the nineteenth century. Ross's selection for command of this venture was a brilliant choice, for he had gained valuable polar experience while accompanying his uncle, Sir John Ross, and William PARRY during their search for the NORTHWEST PASSAGE. James Ross's name was already etched in the annals of polar exploration, for on June 1, 1831, he had discovered the North Magnetic Pole. On his Antarctic expedition Ross demonstrated the ability to carry out a sophisticated program of oceanographical research while sailing in perilous waters. A testament to the consummate skill with which Ross conducted this expedition is to note that only one man was lost, and he through illness, during the entire expedition.

With the ships HMS *Erebus* and HMS *Terror,* Ross had been instructed to make magnetic observations in far southern latitudes, to seek those sites where land had been previously indicated, to discover and to attain the South Magnetic Pole, and to examine the Antarctic seas in the highest latitudes that could be reached. After the *Erebus* and the *Terror* had been strengthened by the addition of double-coppered hulls and the installation of watertight bulkheads and massive internal bracing, Ross sailed for the south in the early fall of 1839. Learning of the activities of Dumont D'Urville and Charles Wilkes (*see* WILKES EXPEDITION) in these waters, Ross selected a more easterly meridian (170°E) for his penetration of the Antarctic Circle. This easterly penetration of the Antarctic ice led to his discovery on January 10, 1841, of Victoria Land. While in these waters, Ross meticulously, and almost single-handedly, maintained the program of oceanographical investigation outlined by the Royal Society. In spite of his conscientious care for this work, the accuracy of his soundings varies because of his inability to determine precisely when the bottom was reached and because of the difficulty in compen-

Capt. James Ross plants the British flag on the North Magnetic Pole on June 1, 1831.

sating for the effect of undercurrents on the sounding lines. An important accomplishment of this voyage was Ross's successful use of a deep-sea clamm (an oceanographical instrument developed by Ross) and dredge which enabled him to bring back living faunal forms from 400 fathoms (732 meters). In contrast to the opinion of Edward Forbes, who maintained that marine life could not exist beyond 300 fathoms (549 meters), Ross contended that regardless of the sea's depth living creatures could be found on the bottom, that there was no depth which was the limit to life in the sea. Ross's summary of the accomplishments of this expedition was contained in his two-volume account *A Voyage of Discovery and Research in the Southern and Antarctic Regions during the Years 1839 to 1843* (1847).

Even as Ross was searching for the South Pole, the Manx naturalist Edward Forbes (1815–1854) was developing his theory of an azoic zone in the sea. While serving in 1842 as a naturalist on board HMS *Beacon*, Forbes had been unable to find marine life beyond 300 fathoms. As he began his study of the life zones of the sea, he came to believe that life ceased to exist beyond that depth and hence that there was an azoic zone beyond 300 fathoms. His death while still a young man prevented him from continuing his research or from examining evidence collected by the deep-sea dredging expeditions of the latter half of the nineteenth century. It was the evidence collected by these expeditions which finally refuted his azoic theory.

Although the leadership in marine, polar, and oceanographical exploration clearly resided with the

An early leader in American marine sciences, Matthew Fontaine Maury used information gleaned from ships' logs to study the winds and currents of the Atlantic.

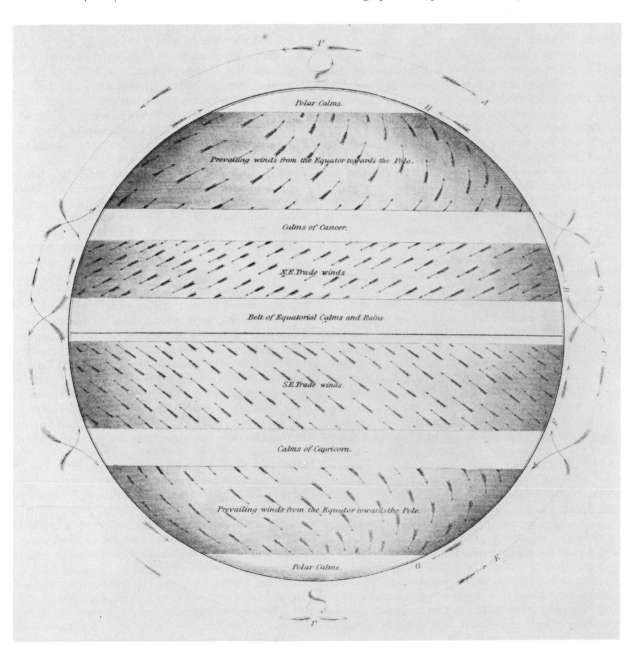

British, the United States was beginning to make tentative efforts in these areas. From 1838 to 1842 the U.S. South Seas Surveying and Exploring Expedition under the command of Charles Wilkes gathered information from the unexplored regions of the world's oceans. While the Wilkes Expedition did not contribute substantively to physical oceanography, it did make important observations and collected many specimens. Asa Gray used materials collected by this expedition for his investigations of plant geography. James Dwight Dana, who accompanied the expedition as a civilian scientist, began a study of zoophytes as a result of his experiences on this expedition. Dana's study of the corals and of the three primary forms of coral islands, atolls, barrier reefs, and fringing reefs, enabled him independently to confirm Charles Darwin's hypothesis on the formation of coral islands.

The work of Matthew Fontaine Maury (1806–1873) also contributed to the growing American study of the sea. Although a strident critic of United States naval policies, Maury was nevertheless appointed in 1842 superintendent of the U.S. Navy Depot of Charts and Instruments. In this position he devoted himself to the practical problems of navigation. Using information collected from ship's logs, Maury began to chart the winds and currents of the Atlantic. Later, he added the Pacific Ocean to the charts he was preparing. In 1847 Maury began to publish these wind and current charts. Maury believed that this oceanographical information was of immediate commercial value since he thought that it would reduce dramatically the sailing time from American ports.

Maury's greatest weakness as an investigator of the ocean's secrets was his inability to digest the vast amounts of material that he collected and to place it in a sound theoretical framework. Always eager to collect more information about the oceans, research vessels sailing under Maury's direction utilized the newly invented Brooke patent sounding lead to gather bottom samples from depths which were previously impossible to collect from. With this new device, sediment from depths of more than 3000 fathoms (5486 meters) was obtained for study and analysis. These samples were utilized in the inaugural studies of marine micropaleontology. With his records of more than 200 deep-sea soundings, Maury began a study of the topography of the North Atlantic. In 1854 he published the first bathymetrical chart which utilized 1000-fathom (1829-meter) contours. This chart of the North Atlantic was also the first attempt to plot the contours of an entire ocean basin. The Atlantic Telegraph Company later utilized this information on the sea floor's contours when it began to lay the first transatlantic telegraph cable.

Maury had a talent for administration, and he played a prominent role in the organization of the first international scientific congress to concern itself with oceanic problems. In 1853 an international conference was held at Brussels to coordinate meteorological observations at sea. Maury summarized his oceanographical investigations in his popular *The Physical Geography of the Sea* (1855). Blessed with a vibrant style, this work quickly went through many editions and was translated into Dutch, German, French, Norwegian, Spanish, and Italian. While the work was attractive to the general public, marine scientists quickly challenged the weak support that Maury marshaled for his theories. With the outbreak of the Civil War in 1861, Maury supported the Confederacy and faded from a position of leadership in American marine sciences.

Late nineteenth century Marine biology grew rapidly in the latter half of the nineteenth century. By this time the flora and fauna of the earth's surface were becoming relatively well known to naturalists, and even the plant and animal life of the shallow coastal waters was becoming more familiar. Yet the life of the deep sea was still mostly unknown, and the floral and faunal mysteries of the depths still awaited systematic exploration. Darwin's publication of his epoch-making *Origin of Species* in 1859 was also a powerful stimulus to further exploration of the sea's deeper reaches. Seeking Darwin's "missing links" became a preoccupation with many naturalists. Darwin had taught that evolution occurred more slowly in the sea since the environment was more stable and changed less frequently than did that on land. The abyssal sea began to be perceived as a place where early faunal forms could be found, and in the 1860s marine animals with apparent similarities to extinct fossil forms were discovered.

The Norwegian naturalist Michael Sars pioneered in the investigation of marine invertebrates obtained from great depths. His collection of the first living stalked crinoids, sea lilies, from the bottom of the Norwegian Sea demonstrated a close relationship between a living animal and an organism which was thought to have been extinct since the Mesozoic era.

Because of the problems involved in such exploration, the resources necessary to support investigations of this kind exceeded those of individuals or small scientific societies. Before a sustained program of deep-sea dredging could begin, it was necessary to obtain access to a large vessel which could carry on the work at sea and then to find funds to maintain the ship and its crew during the program of exploration.

Inspired by the work of Michael Sars, Charles Wyville Thomson and William B. Carpenter in Britain sought support for a program of deep-sea dredging from the Royal Society. The society in turn requested permission from the British Admiralty for civilian scientists to accompany a naval vessel on a cruise in the North Atlantic in order to conduct dredging experiments. Despite inclement weather and the use of a vessel which was demonstrably ill-suited for such purposes, Thomson and Carpenter successfully dredged from the paddle-wheel steamer HMS *Lightning* in the late summer of 1868. From the depths beyond 300 fathoms (549 meters), they obtained species of sponges, rhizopods, echinoderms, crustaceans, mollusks, and foraminifers. Discovering diverse temperatures at similar depths in different regions, they began to question the belief in a constant temperature of 4°C (39°F) in deeper water. The success of this initial cooperation between the Royal Society and the Admiralty led to the British government's placing of the survey ship HMS *Porcupine* at the disposal of the society in the summer of 1869. Again, Thomson and Carpenter were successful in their dredging, collecting animals from depths of more than 2400 fathoms (4389 meters) and also obtaining serial temperatures from various levels. The belief in Forbes's azoic zone and in a submarine constant of 4°C was seriously challenged by the data collected by Thomson and Carpenter in 1868 and 1869.

Having demonstrated the scientific results which could be obtained by civilian scientists sailing on British naval vessels, the Royal Society proposed to the Admiralty to expand the scope of their jointly sponsored oceanographical exploration from the North Atlantic to the oceans of the world. This appealed to Britain's pride as the world's premier maritime power, and for this and other reasons Queen Victoria's government decided to support such an endeavor. Preparations were made for the first great national voyage of oceanographical exploration, the CHALLENGER EXPEDITION.

From 1872 to 1876, the steam-powered corvette HMS *Challenger* made a circumnavigation of the globe to explore the world's oceans for science. Although the British had conducted twelve deep-sea expeditions between Cook's Antarctic voyage and the Challenger Expedition, never before had such a carefully prepared and adequately supported oceanographical expedition set forth. The ship was commanded by Capt. (later Sir) George Strong Nares, who was recalled from the *Challenger* in 1874 and later gained additional fame for his leadership of the British Arctic Expedition of 1875–1876. The civilian scientists on the Challenger expedition were under the direction of Charles Wyville Thomson. During the 3½ years of the expedition, the *Challenger*'s scientific staff sounded at 362 stations; confirmed through dredging that life could be found beyond 300 fathoms; discovered manganese nodules on the floor of both the Atlantic and the Pacific Oceans; revealed that the sea floor at great depths was composed of a clay bottom formed by the chemical decomposition of the calcareous skeletons of foraminifers, mollusks, and other species; discovered in the Pacific that in depths beyond 4000 fathoms (7315 meters) the sea floor was covered with a bottom composed of radiolarian ooze; obtained new data on the diurnal migration of plankton; and became the first steamship to cross the Antarctic Circle.

The Challenger Expedition was an early example of what the twentieth century would term "big science." It was the most expensive voyage of oceanographical exploration in the nineteenth century. By the time the fifty volumes of the *Challenger*'s scientific reports were finally published in 1895, Her Maj-

esty's government had spent more than £200,000 on the project. The large collections of flora, fauna, and bottom samples brought back were analyzed, to the dismay of certain British scientists and newspapers, by an international community of scholars. Specimens collected by the expedition led ultimately to the introduction of 700 new genera and 4000 new species. Although the Challenger Expedition did not make the contributions to physical geography that might have been made for several reasons, among them the inadequacy of the instruments used and the preoccupation of the civilian scientists with the biological and natural sciences, the data it collected did provide ocean scientists with an introduction to the complex dynamics of the ocean's systems.

The Challenger Expedition was the first major deep-sea expedition to have oceanographical exploration as its primary goal. Previously, ocean research had been part of the more general programs of geographical exploration. The expedition demonstrated the value of voyages designed with plans of oceanographical research as their principal objectives.

Seeking to emulate the example of the Challenger Expedition, Germany, Denmark, Italy, Russia, and the United States sent vessels forth to conduct specific programs of ocean research in the last three decades of the nineteenth century. From 1877 to 1910, the independently wealthy Alexander Agassiz (1835–1910) utilized his private fortune to support his oceanographical investigations. His initial work was done on board the U.S. Coast and Geodetic Survey steamer *Blake* on three cruises in the Caribbean and Atlantic. From 1884 to 1890 the *Blake* was utilized by Lieut. John Elliott Pillsbury to survey the current of the Gulf Stream. He developed an ingenious method for anchoring in the Gulf Stream at depths down to 2000 fathoms (3658 meters), and with a current meter

The zoological laboratory of the HMS Challenger, *a British steamship that made the first great national voyage of oceanographic exploration, from 1872 to 1876. [NASA]*

he invented Pillsbury was able to measure the Gulf Stream for a sustained period. By holding to one deep-sea station for as long as 6 days, he could for the first time plot the fluctuations which occurred in the speed, direction, depth, and currents of the Gulf Stream.

In 1882 the first vessel especially constructed for oceanic research in the United States, the 234-foot (71-meter) steamer *Albatross,* was commissioned for service by the U.S. Fish Commission. In 40 years of service, the *Albatross* examined the waters of the Atlantic, the Pacific, and the Bering Sea. With the exception of her last voyage, the cruises of the *Albatross* were concerned more with studying marine flora and fauna than with physical oceanography. Alexander Agassiz sailed with her into the tropical Pacific in 1891 to explore and to collect from waters bypassed

A great bird captured on the deck of the Challenger, one of the many specimens taken on the expedition, which led to the introduction of 700 new genera and 4000 new species.

by the *Challenger.* He was currently studying the marine fauna of the Pacific and Caribbean sides of the Isthmus of Panama to demonstrate his belief in the former connection of the two. In 1899 Agassiz and the *Albatross* examined the South Seas and the waters off Japan. This expedition enabled him to continue his investigation of the formation of coral reefs, a subject which interested him for the rest of his life. On this voyage, the *Albatross,* using equipment designed by Agassiz, dredged from a depth of more than 1200 fathoms (2195 meters).

Disregarding the success and fame which the Challenger Expedition had won for Great Britain and disdaining the growing support for oceanographical exploration by the United States and other nations, the French government was reluctant to support the sys-

tematic investigations of French marine scientists. Talented and wealthy amateur scientists with an interest in the sea sought to obtain their country's aid for programs of marine research. When this failed, they supported the oceanographical research themselves.

In 1885 Prince Albert I of Monaco (1848–1922) began his career as a serious student of the sea. From his yacht *Hirondelle,* he undertook an investigation of the Gulf Stream to determine where it went once it left the waters off New England and Canada. In 1885 and 1886, Prince Albert dropped floats into the eastern perimeters of the Gulf Stream to trace the drift of the current. As the floats were returned, the transatlantic characteristics of the Gulf Stream began to be delineated. Interested in many manifestations of the sea's phenomena, Prince Albert built a series of especially equipped yachts which allowed him to pursue his marine interests. In addition to his study of the drift of the Gulf Stream, he conducted investigations of the meteorological phenomena of the sea; prepared a bathymetric chart of the oceans; studied the venom of the Portuguese man-of-war *(Physalia),* a pelagic coelenterate, and conducted physiological experiments with it on animals; and examined the nature and distribution of plankton from the surface down to 800 fathoms (1463 meters). To popularize the study of the oceans, Prince Albert established the Musée Océanographique de Monaco in 1910 and a famous research center, the Institut Océanographique of Paris, which officially began its work in 1911.

Because of the dimensions of the subject and the resources necessary for marine science to grow, international cooperation appeared to be an effective way of conducting such research. In 1902 Great Britain, Norway, Denmark, Germany, Ireland, Russia, and the Netherlands joined together in the International Council for the Exploration of the Sea. The Council's immediate goal was practical: an exploration of the waters of the North Atlantic in order to develop policies which would allow the wise management of the fisheries in those waters.

Even as oceanographical exploration was becoming more thoroughly institutionalized, there were still singular individuals who developed their own programs of exploration. The strangely driven Norwegian explorer Fridtjof NANSEN contributed significantly to the understanding of the life and features of Arctic waters. Daring and introspective, Nansen had startled veteran polar travelers by his 1888 crossing of the Greenland ice cap by skis and sledges. This success enabled him to win support for another tradition-defying expedition. Contrary to the advice of most established polar authorities, Nansen planned to allow his vessel to be caught in the polar ice west of the Novosibirskiye Ostrova (New Siberian Islands) and remain aboard it as it moved with the ice floes from the east to the west carried by the circulation of the Arctic Current.

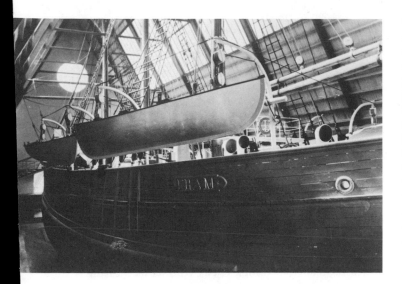

Nansen meticuluuously prepared himself, his men, and his ship, the *Fram*, which was especially constructed for the expedition. By the autumn of 1893, the *Fram* and Nansen and his crew of twelve were locked in the ice. The scientific program began with the taking of meteorological observations every 4 hours. Serial temperatures and salinity readings from various depths were recorded, and a study of ice formations was initiated. Polar currents were of particular interest since the safety of the expedition was based upon their patterns of circulation. The oceanographical work was laborious. Bitter cold amplified the time necessary for sounding and dredging. Some soundings required several days to complete. In opposition to commonly held beliefs, Nansen's 2000-fathom (3658-meter) sounding revealed that the Arctic Sea was not a shallow body of water. The oceanographical and meteorological data collected by Nansen led to a more sophisticated understanding of the complex hydrography of Arctic waters.

Twentieth century The early decades of the twentieth century witnessed the growing theoretical interpretation of the data on oceanic circulation which had been accumulating since the Challenger Expedition. With the outbreak of World War I, oceanographical exploration was restricted to research which would have a practical application. The appearance of submarine fleets led to the development of sonar equipment. The evolution of sonic depth finders brought to an end the many difficulties which had been attendant upon sounding with hemp or wire lines. It now became possible to obtain continuous bottom profiles while a ship was moving. This was an immeasurable aid to physical oceanography, for it permitted the detailed mapping of the sea floor.

In the era following World War I, Germany played a prominent role in oceanographical exploration. With government support, the German Atlantic Expedition began in 1925 a systematic investigation of the dynamics of circulation in the Atlantic Ocean. Under the leadership of Alfred Mertz and Georg Wüst, the steamer *Meteor* was fitted out with sophisticated new equipment including current meters, echo sounders, apparatus for the chemical analysis of seawater, and plankton nets. With a scientific contingent of five physical oceanographers, two meteorologists, a chemist, a geologist, a biologist, and a crew of 120 men, the expedition was prepared for a detailed study of the role of temperature, salinity, and bottom contours in determining circulation patterns. By the conclusion of the voyage in 1927, the *Meteor* had cruised more than 67,000 miles (107,823 kilometers), made fourteen latitudinal cross sections of the Atlantic from 20°N to 65°S, collected more than 9000 temperature and salinity readings, and with the echo sounders obtained more than 33,000 soundings. These soundings enabled her to map out the features of the geophysically important Mid-Atlantic Ridge. The accurate and highly detailed information gathered by the *Meteor* established a new standard for oceanographical exploration and began the more modern phase of the scientific study of the physical phenomena of the sea. The *Meteor*'s scientists compared their empirical data with theoretical projections they made by using the techniques of dynamic modeling. They were pioneers in the methods of dynamic oceanography.

American scientists followed the example of German oceanographers and began to use theoretical techniques in their study of the dynamics of ocean currents. The United States has played a prominent role in oceanographical exploration in the twentieth century through the development of research centers such as the Scripps Institution of Oceanography, the Woods Hole Oceanographical Institution, and the Lamont Geological Observatory. The growth of oceanography was detoured by World War II into once more satisfying practical military needs. War at sea, and in particular the growing sophistication of undersea

*Far left:
The* Fram *on display at the Fram Museum, Oslo. Specially constructed to withstand the strain of being locked in the ice, the* Fram *was used to gather oceanographical data in the icebound Arctic. [Norwegian Information Service]*

A modern oceanographic research vessel, the USNS Hayes, *sets out from Seattle in 1971. The age of discoveries below the surface of the oceans is relatively new, even toward the end of the twentieth century. [U.S. Navy]*

warfare and antisubmarine detection equipment, created an electronic technology that had immediate application as a research tool in the postwar years.

Oceanographical research in the 1960s and 1970s added to its other interests a concern for the fascinating questions posed by geologists on the spreading of the sea floor, continental drift, and plate tectonics. To explore these subjects, the American *Glomar Challenger*, often with the scientists of other nations aboard, conducted an ongoing program of deep-sea drilling and core sampling after 1968.

Oceanographical exploration in the future will combine two of the oldest incentives for exploration, the search for knowledge of the unknown and the search for wealth. And since the oceans of the world still contain much that is unknown and since their wealth is still unchronicled, the final chapter of oceanographical exploration will not be written in the twentieth century.

BIBLIOGRAPHY: Jacqueline Carpine-Lancre, "Les expéditions océanographiques et la publication de leurs resultats (Étude bibliographique)," *Bulletin de l'Institut Océanographique*, Monaco, Numéro spécial 2, vol. II, 1968, pp. 651–664; Margaret Deacon, *Scientists and the Sea, 1650–1900*, New York, 1971; T. F. Gaskell, "The History of the Gulf Stream," *Bulletin de l'Institut Océanographique*, Monaco, Numéro spécial 2, vol. I, 1968, pp. 77–86; William Abbott Herdman, *Founders of Oceanography and Their Work*, London, 1923; Daniel Merriman, "Speculations on Life at the Depths: A XIXth Century Prelude," *Bulletin de l'Institut Océanographique*, Monaco, Numéro

spécial 2, vol. II, 1968, pp. 377–383; G. S. Ritchie, "The Royal Navy's Contribution to Oceanography in the XIXth Century," *Bulletin de l'Institut Océanographique*, Monaco, Numéro spécial 2, vol. I, 1968, pp. 121–131; Susan Schlee, *The Edge of an Unfamiliar World*, New York, 1973; R. B. Seymour-Sewell, "Oceanographic Exploration, 1851–1951," *Science Progress*, vol. 40, July 1952, pp. 403–418; Sir Charles Wyville Thomson, *The Depths of the Sea*, London, 1873; Francis L. Williams, *Matthew Fontaine Maury: Scientist of the Sea*, New Brunswick, N.J., 1963; Georg Wüst, "The Major Deep-Sea Expeditions and Research Vessels, 1873–1960," in M. Sears (ed.), *Progress in Oceanography*, vol. II, New York, 1964, pp. 1–52.

Phillip Drennon Thomas

Odoric of Pordenone   See PORDENONE, ODORIC OF.

Ojeda, Alonso de *(ca. 1468–ca. 1515)*   Spanish explorer and colonial administrator. Born in Cuenca, he served in the household of the Duke of Medina Celi and fought against the Moors. Ojeda commanded a ship under Christopher COLUMBUS on the second voyage to America in 1493 and was quite active on Hispaniola in campaigns against the natives and on exploring expeditions into the interior. Upon his return to Spain he associated himself with Juan de la Cosa and Amerigo VESPUCCI, who sailed under his command on a voyage of exploration of the northeastern coast of South America in 1499, trespassing on Columbus's monopoly. Returning to Spain in 1500 with a cargo of a few pearls, some brazilwood, and enslaved Indians, he was awarded the title of governor of Coquivacoa, the Indian name for the area around the Lake Maracaibo which he explored. (He is supposed to have named the Indian villages built on stilts Little Venice: Venezuela.)

Ojeda made other voyages to this region in 1502 and 1505. In 1508 he was made governor of Nueva Andalucía (present-day Colombia). He recruited a group of Spaniards on Hispaniola and sailed from Santo Domingo in November 1509. Eventually a colony was established on the Gulf of Urabá. However, the colonists soon fell into straitened circumstances, and Ojeda was forced to sail away to seek aid. He tried to reach Santo Domingo but was shipwrecked on Cuba, and when he finally arrived on Hispaniola, he was ruined. His colonists abandoned the settlement and were rescued by Martín Fernández de Enciso.

Ojeda always had troubles with the natives—on Hispaniola, on the Pearl Coast, near Cartagena, and at the Gulf of Urabá—troubles which he often precipitated and brought upon himself by his brutal conduct toward the Indians. His behavior also brought down the wrath of Bartolomé de las Casas on his head. He seems, however, to have had a champion at court in the person of Bishop Juan Rodríguez de Fonseca. Nevertheless, he died at Santo Domingo in dire poverty in about 1515.

BIBLIOGRAPHY: Duquesa de Berwick y de Alba, *Autógrafos de Cristóbal Colón y papeles de América*, Madrid, 1892; Samuel Eliot Morison, *The European Discovery of America: The Southern Voyages, A.D. 1492–1616*, New York, 1974; Boies Penrose, *Travel and Discovery in the Renaissance, 1420–1620*, Cambridge, Mass., 1952.

Martin Torodash

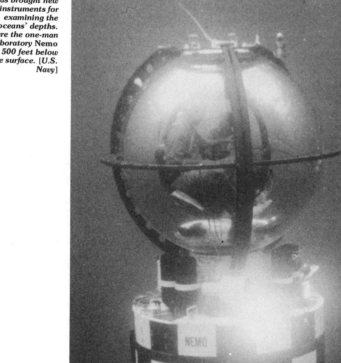

Sophisticated modern technology has brought new instruments for examining the oceans' depths. Here the one-man laboratory Nemo dives 500 feet below the surface. [U.S. Navy]

In the Old Testament, a land to the south or southwest of Palestine from which the navy of King Solomon obtained gold (I Kings 9:28, I Kings 10:11). The biblical Ophir may have been located in Arabia or East Africa, but over the years it was identified with other lands and regions proverbial for their wealth. In the sixteenth century it was placed in the Pacific. In 1526 Sebastian CABOT left Spain for the Pacific to find Ophir and Tarsish, another Old Testament land associated with valuable metals, but failed to complete his mission. Because of the presumed Pacific location of Ophir, the group of islands discovered there by Álvaro de Mendaña in 1568 soon came to be called the Solomon Islands.

The Orinoco River in Venezuela, first explored by the Spanish conquistador Diego de Ordaz in 1531. [Embassy of Venezuela, Washington]

***Ordaz (Ordás), Diego de** (ca. 1480–1532)* Spanish explorer and conqueror. Born in the province of Zamora, Ordaz had traveled to the New World by 1509, when he joined an expedition to the northern coast of Colombia led by Alonso de OJEDA. After participating in the conquest of Cuba in 1511, he played a leading role in the early stages of the conquest of Mexico. In March 1521 he went to Spain to report to King Charles I on developments in Mexico.

In 1530 Ordaz headed an expedition in his own right as he left Spain with three ships and nearly 500 men. He had been authorized by the crown to conquer and settle a vaguely defined territory extending for 200 leagues between the Amazon River and Cabo de la Vela. Unable to land at the mouth of the Amazon, he sailed to the Gulf of Paria, where he was told of a large river, the Huyapari (now the Orinoco), in the vicinity. Ordaz began to explore the rain-swollen river in June 1531 and, after experiencing many hardships, reached a point below its confluence with the Meta, which he also explored for a short distance. During his journey he heard of wealthy Indian lands in the area, including one called Guiana, but no such discoveries

were made. Upon his return to the coast, Ordaz became embroiled in difficulties with Spanish residents of the nearby island of Cubagua, who claimed that he had no rights in northern Venezuela. He was seized and shipped to Santo Domingo, where he was freed, and died while en route to Spain to plead his case.

BIBLIOGRAPHY: Casiano García, *Vida del comendador Diego de Ordaz, descubridor del Orinoco,* Mexico City, 1952; Florentino Pérez Embid, *Diego de Ordás, compañero de Cortés y explorador del Orinoco,* Seville, 1950.

***Orellana, Francisco de** (ca. 1511–1546)* Spanish explorer. A native of Trujillo and a kinsman of Francisco PIZARRO, Orellana went to the Indies as a young man and took part in the conquest of Peru, losing an eye in a skirmish with the Indians. In 1537 he refounded the city of Guayaquil at a different site. When Gonzalo PIZARRO began his expedition to the "land of cinnamon," Orellana was named second-in-command after joining the main body at Zumaque (Zumaco) in March 1541.

The exhaustion of the expedition's provisions and the threat of starvation prompted Orellana and from fifty to sixty others to leave their companions to search for food, and they soon found a well-supplied Indian village below the confluence of the Napo and Aguarico Rivers. However, instead of rejoining Pizarro after leaving the village on February 2, 1542, Orellana's party continued to sail downstream, entered the Amazon River on February 11, and emerged into the Atlantic Ocean on August 26, 1542. Thus Orellana had headed the first expedition successfully to navigate the Amazon, the mouth of which had been discovered in 1500 by Vicente Yáñez PINZÓN, who had called the river the Freshwater Sea. This name was soon supplanted by that of Marañón, but after Orellana's voyage the river came to be called the Amazon. According to Gaspar de Carvajal, a Dominican friar who accompanied Orellana and wrote an account of the journey, the Spaniards passed several

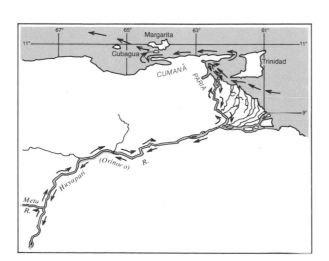

Far left: Diego de Ordaz's exploration of the Orinoco River, 1531.

The Australian explorer John Oxley, whose belief in an inland sea in Australia inspired later explorers and led to many important discoveries. [Australian Information Service]

villages subject to Amazons, and during one battle with the Indians ten or twelve of these women appeared to stimulate the males by their example as warriors. Carvajal described the Amazons as being very tall, robust, and white and armed with bows and arrows.

Despite his impressive exploit, Orellana has been censured by some writers for his apparently callous abandonment of Pizarro. However, the surviving documents give conflicting evidence as to whether Orellana promised to rejoin Pizarro within a specified interval and whether he chose not to do so of his own volition or reluctantly bowed to the arguments of his companions that it would be impossible to sail upstream to Pizarro's camp.

Upon entering the Atlantic, Orellana and his followers sailed northwestward and eventually reached the island of Cubagua. Orellana then traveled to Spain to report his achievement to King Charles I and to seek appointment as governor of the territory he had discovered. This he received in a capitulation of February 13, 1544, in which he was authorized to explore and colonize land south of the Amazon not under the jurisdiction of Portugal. He was also named governor and captain general of this region, which was called Nueva Andalucía. In May 1545 Orellana left Spain for the Amazon with a fleet of four vessels and approximately 300 to 350 men, but the expedition was plagued by problems, and Orellana himself died while exploring one of the mouths of the river.

BIBLIOGRAPHY: Gaspar de Carvajal, *The Discovery of the Amazon,* ed. by H. C. Heaton, New York, 1934; Philip Ainsworth Means, "Gonzalo Pizarro and Francisco de Orellana," *Hispanic American Historical Review,* vol. XIV, no. 3, August 1934, pp. 275–295.

Oxley, John Joseph William Molesworth (1785?-1828) Australian explorer. Born in Westow, Yorkshire, England, Oxley served in the Royal Navy from 1799 until he was appointed surveyor general of New South Wales in 1812. He then became responsible for examining large sections of southeastern Australia. Four of his journeys are significant. In 1817, with his assistant George Williams Evans and the botanist Allan CUNNINGHAM, he traced the course of the Lachlan River. He examined the Macquarie River in 1818. As both rivers vanished in "an ocean of reeds," he concluded that he was "in the immediate vicinity of an inland sea." He thought that the country surrounding the Lachlan was worthless and that the Liverpool Plains, discovered in 1818, while fertile, were too inaccessible to be of value. Jervis Bay and Illawarra District were examined from the sea in 1819, and Oxley, again incorrectly, considered them worthless. His examination of the Moreton Bay area in 1823 and his discovery of the Brisbane River led to the establishment there of a penal station. Oxley's pessimistic assessment of the inland inhibited further exploration for years, but his belief in an inland sea captured the imagination of several later explorers, including Charles STURT and Thomas MITCHELL, and initiated major discoveries. Active in colonial life as a politician, businessman, and pioneer of the Bowral district, Oxley died on May 25, 1828. He is commemorated in many place names. The Oxley Highway follows the route of his 1818 expedition.

BIBLIOGRAPHY: E. W. Dunlop, *John Oxley,* Melbourne, 1960.

J. M. R. Cameron

P

Pacific Ocean

The Pacific Ocean is more than twice as large as the Atlantic Ocean. While the Atlantic has very few islands, the Pacific has thousands of them. The first explorers of the Pacific were the Polynesians and other islanders, but they left no written records. The inhabitants of the Asian continent explored its marginal seas. The history of this exploration and that of the coasts of the Americas does not fall within the scope of this study. It was European explorers who prepared the first accurate charts of the world's largest ocean and its islands.

Penetration of the Pacific by explorers from Europe was an aspect of the age of discovery. After pioneering the sea route to the Spice Islands, the Portuguese reached the outskirts of the vast ocean. Some of their ships ventured among its many islands. The Spaniards came to the shore of the Pacific after exploring the Caribbean area and the Isthmus of Panama. A Spanish fleet under a commander born in Portugal was the first to cross the immense ocean. The Dutch displaced the Spaniards and the Portuguese as Pacific explorers during the seventeenth century. The eighteenth and early nineteenth centuries were essentially an age of English and French exploration. Thanks to new methods of measuring latitude and longitude, the Pacific took on definite contours, and islands which had been discovered and later lost, like the Solomons, were definitely located on charts. Explorations by the Russians early in the nineteenth century revealed little that was not already known, but the Russians as well as navigators of other nationalities made contributions to knowledge.

The Portuguese Portugal was the pioneer country during the age of discovery on account of its location at the extreme southwest of Europe. The Portuguese first sailed around Africa. Under the command of Vasco da GAMA their first fleet reached India in 1498. They arrived in the Moluccas, or Spice Islands, in 1512 under Antônio de Abreu. The letters of Francisco Serrão, a Portuguese who lived in the area for about 10 years, encouraged Ferdinand MAGELLAN to undertake his famous voyage across the Pacific to try to demonstrate that the coveted islands were situated within the Spanish half of the world.

From the Spice Islands the Portuguese undertook several voyages of discovery. It is doubtful that they sighted Australia, but Jorge de Meneses discovered the western part of New Guinea in 1526. It is not believed that Diogo da Rocha sailed any farther than Yap in Micronesia in the voyage that he made from about 1525 to 1527. Another Portuguese, Francisco de Castro, made discoveries in the same area 10 years later. Very momentous, however, were the voyages of explorers from Portugal in the waters bordering Asia. Japan was reached by sea in 1542. Portuguese cartographic work on the western fringes of the Pacific was useful to navigators of other nations. Still more important for the exploration of the Pacific Ocean was the work of Portuguese who served Spain, such as Magellan and Pedro Fernández de Quirós (Pedro Fernandes de Queirós).

The Spaniards It was the voyages of Christopher COLUMBUS which led to the discovery of the Pacific by Europeans coming from the east. In 1513 Vasco Nuñez de BALBOA undertook his famous trip across the Isthmus of Panama and became the first white man to gaze upon the vast expanse of water he called the South Sea. Circumstances prevented Balboa from following up his discovery.

Magellan's voyage is usually remembered as the first voyage around the world, though it was one of his officers, Juan Sebastián de Elcano, who completed it. Like Columbus before him, Magellan experienced a great deal of difficulty in his efforts to obtain the command of a fleet. Columbus asserted that he could reach the Far East by sailing west. Magellan, on the strength of letters received from the Moluccas, claimed that he could reach the Spice Islands by sailing west and that the said islands lay on the Spanish side of the Line of Demarcation determined by the Pope and later modified by mutual agreement between the Spaniards and the Portuguese.

Magellan's fleet of five ships set out from Seville on August 10, 1519. The crossing of the Atlantic and the coasting of South America were nothing new, but Magellan had to travel farther south than any previous navigator to find a strait leading into the Pacific. At the end of November 1520 the fleet, reduced to three ships, emerged from what is now known as the Strait of Magellan into the ocean that the explorer called Pacific.

Three months and 20 days were spent crossing the ocean amid terrible hardships. After a landing on Guam, the southern coast of Samar in the Philippines was reached on March 21, 1521. Magellan's stay in the Philippines ended in tragedy. He was killed in battle, and a number of his men were treacherously murdered. The two remaining ships, the *Trinidad* and the *Victoria*, proceeded to the Moluccas, which were sighted in November 1521, after stops at Mindanao, Palawan, and Brunei.

The Portuguese came to the Moluccas fairly regularly, but they had no fortress there, and no conflict arose at that time. The Spaniards were able to buy spices. It was decided that one ship would return to Spain by sailing west through seas nominally controlled by the Portuguese while the other would attempt to recross the Pacific. The *Victoria* arrived in

Ternate in the Moluccas, Indonesia. Although the Portuguese were the first to land in the Spice Islands in 1512, the Spanish were not far behind. The ensuing controversy over their ownership would not be resolved until the Treaty of Saragossa was signed in 1529. [Library of Congress]

Spain in September 1522, thus being the first vessel to complete the circumnavigation of the globe. The *Trinidad* attempted in vain to recross the ocean and finally fell into the hands of the Portuguese.

After the return of the *Victoria,* Spain fitted out another fleet to claim the Moluccas and establish a governor there. Francisco García Jofre de Loaysa, the future governor, died, and a number of the ships were lost on the way, but the remainder of the fleet reached the islands in January 1527. Sporadic fighting with the Portuguese occurred until news of the Treaty of Saragossa (Zaragoza) was known in the islands. After protracted negotiations Emperor Charles V, who ruled Spain as King Charles I, signed this treaty in 1529 with King John III of Portugal, giving up his claims to the Spice Islands in exchange for a large sum of money. Modern cartography shows that the islands were located within the Portuguese zone.

At the time when Charles V was still planning to uphold his claims to the Moluccas, he ordered Hernán CORTÉS, who had completed his conquest of Mexico, to send an expedition to investigate the fate of the survivors of the two fleets that had left Spain for the Spice Islands. Cortés dispatched Álvaro de Saavedra with three vessels in October 1527. Only the *Florida* succeeded in reaching the Moluccas. Saavedra made two attempts to recross the Pacific. He died in the second one when the party reached about 31°N. It was necessary to sail still farther north to find favorable conditions for the return voyage, and another 37 years were to elapse before the return route to America was found.

The following may be said about the Spanish discoveries up to Saavedra's voyage. Before reaching Guam, Magellan's fleet sighted an undetermined island in the Tuamotu Archipelago and another small one in the Carolines, one of the groups which form Micronesia. After the departure from the Philippines no discovery of importance was made. Very little is known about the course of Loaysa's ships, except that one of the Marshalls, later identified as Taongi, was sighted. Saavedra's voyage was more profitable from the viewpoint of discovery. On his first attempt to recross the Pacific he made discoveries in the Marshalls and on the northern coast of New Guinea. On the second one other islands in Micronesia were discovered. One of them has been identified as Ponape in the Carolines, and the other as Eniwetok in the Marshall group.

Except for an obscure story about a ship under the command of Hernando de Grijalva, there is no record of another Spanish expedition in the Pacific until 1542. The Spaniards believed that there must be some islands in the vast ocean that would not be within the Portuguese sphere and might produce spices or other valuable commodities. The 1542 undertaking started in 1541 as a joint enterprise by Pedro de ALVARADO, governor of Guatemala, and Antonio de Mendoza, viceroy of Mexico. Six vessels under the command of Ruy López de Villalobos left Navidad in Mexico in November 1542, reaching a small island off Mindanao after nearly 4 months at sea. On the way over they came across some of the islands of Micronesia, and landings were made. At one place—probably Fais, a Portuguese discovery—the explorers were welcomed by natives making the sign of the cross. Villalobos's complement of more than 300 men experienced terrible hardships in the Philippines. One of the ships was sent to Mexico to get help, but she was no more successful in recrossing the Pacific than the *Trinidad* and the *Florida* had been. Finally hunger drove Villalobos to the Moluccas in violation of the Treaty of Saragossa, and some fighting took place with the Portuguese. A second attempt was made to sail back to America. It also failed. On the way north the ship discovered or rediscovered some islands near New Guinea. Villalobos died at Amboina (Ambon), attended by St. Francis Xavier, and the survivors of the expedition were repatriated to Spain by way of India.

After Villalobos's failure it was obvious that no Spanish settlement could be made in the western Pacific until a return route to America was found. This was the purpose of Miguel López de Legazpi's voyage in 1564. He took with him Fray Andrés de URDANETA, who had been in the area before and was reputed to be well versed in meteorology. On the way west the smallest vessel of the fleet, the *San Lucas,* disappeared and accomplished one of the greatest voyages in history. After landing at some islands in the Marshalls and Carolines, the *San Lucas* reached the Philippines and succeeded in returning to America by sailing up to 40°N and taking advantage of the Japan Current. Although the veracity of the account of the voyage by the captain, Alonso de Arellano, and the pilot, Lope Martín, was initially doubted, it has so many precise details that there can be no doubt that they succeeded where others had failed. The main islands discovered by the *San Lucas* were Kwajalein in the Marshalls and Truk in the Carolines.

After the disappearance of the *San Lucas,* Legazpi's remaining ships continued their course westward, sailing between 9 and 10°N. A landing was made on an island they called Los Barbudos (The Bearded Men). It has been identified as Mejit, one of the Marshalls. Other islands were sighted, and after a stop at Guam the fleet reached the Philippines in February 1565. On June 1 the *San Pedro* under the command of Felipe de Salcedo, but with Urdaneta in charge of navigation, left to discover the return route to America, unaware that the *San Lucas* was in the process of doing the same thing. The highest latitude reached was 39°-30'N, and the California coast was sighted in 27°N on September 23. The *San Lucas* had arrived in New Spain 2 months earlier. The elusive return route across the Pacific had been found and was used regularly by the Manila Galleon.

After 1565 Spanish exploration shifted to the South Pacific. Three voyages took place with departure from Peru. Traditions among the Indians of Peru that an Inca ruler had undertaken a voyage and brought back some gold appear to have been the main reason for Álvaro de Mendaña's first voyage. The original suggestion for the expedition came from Pedro Sarmiento de Gamboa, Spanish cosmographer and historian, and the plaque commemorating the four-hundredth anniversary of the departure of the fleet credits Mendaña and Sarmiento jointly with the discovery of the Solomons. Departure took place in November 1567. In January an island was sighted; it was probably Nui, one of the Ellice Islands. The next land sighted was either what is now called Ontong Java or the Roncador Reef. The first landing was made at Santa Isabel in February. This was believed to be a part of the mainland until an expedition revealed that it was an island surrounded by others. A brigantine was built and used to explore the middle and southern Solomons. Although this name was given to the archipelago at a later date, the present names of Santa Isabel, Guadalcanal, and San Cristobal go back to Mendaña's first voyage. No gold was found, and no settlement was made. The attitude of the Melanesian natives varied from friendliness to open hostility.

For the return voyage, which began in August 1568, it was decided to sail north in order to reach the zone which had been proved favorable for such a purpose. In October Wake Island was sighted. Then the two ships were separated during a storm at a higher latitude. They were reunited only in January 1569 on the coast of Mexico. Return to Peru was made with much difficulty.

Mendaña was anxious to return to the islands he had discovered but could not leave until 1595. In the meantime the Pacific had ceased to be a "Spanish lake," for Francis DRAKE had entered the vast ocean in 1578, causing great concern to Spain.

On his second voyage Mendaña had with him as chief pilot Pedro Fernández de Quirós, who is better known by his Spanish than by his original Portuguese name. The object of this expedition was to make a settlement in the islands, by that time called the Solomons. Women, including Mendaña's wife, Isabel Barreto, went along. The Marquesas were reached in July 1595 after only 1 month at sea. The party tarried a few days among the Polynesian inhabitants. Mendaña's Santa Cristina has been identified as Tahuata. Mendaña would have liked to leave a small group of people in the Marquesas, but his men were anxious to see the fabled Solomons. As the voyage proceeded and the Solomons failed to appear, discontent increased aboard the ships. Finally in September land was sighted, but the very same day the second ship of the fleet disappeared and was never found again. The party had not arrived in the Solomons but in the Santa Cruz group farther south. Both archipelagoes are populated by dark-skinned Melanesians. The island where the ships cast anchor is now known as Ndeni. Attempts to make a settlement failed on account of internal dissension. Illness also made ravages among the Spaniards, causing the death of Mendaña himself. His widow and heiress decided to sail to the Philip-

pines. The voyage was very difficult, but the *San Jerónimo,* the largest vessel of the fleet, succeeded in reaching Manila thanks to the skill of Quirós, who left an account of the voyage.

After returning to Mexico, Quirós made efforts to gain support for a voyage of his own. He finally succeeded in getting a fleet of three ships and left Callao in Peru in December 1605. The course was first southwest to about 26°S. Had the fleet stayed in this latitude, the eastern coast of Australia might have been discovered, but the course was changed to northwest. Landings were made on some islands. The longest stay occurred on Taumako, one of the Duff Islands, in April 1606. Quirós was very close to Santa Cruz, which he had visited with Mendaña, but on his course south he missed it. On April 27 a great landmass was seen looming over the horizon. Quirós was overjoyed: he thought that he had found the great continent believed to lie undiscovered in the Southern Hemisphere and called the new land La Austrália del Espíritu Santo. In reality he had arrived at the largest of the New Hebrides, still called Espiritu Santo Island. Under the eyes of hostile natives a great religious festival was held, but no settlement was made. As the ships were leaving the bay, the flagship with Quirós aboard became separated from the other two under controversial circumstances. She sailed to Mexico by the North Pacific route of the Manila Galleon.

The two remaining ships waited for some time in the bay, then sailed away. The discoveries which were then made are attributed to Luis Vaez de Torres and Diego de Prado y Tovar. They first sailed south in accordance with sealed instructions which were opened. As no land was sighted in 20°30'S, the course was set to the northwest. Islands in the Louisiade Archipelago were reached. Then, steering through what is now Torres Strait, the ships reached the Moluccas. After his arrival in Manila, Torres wrote a letter to King Philip III about his voyage; Prado y Tovar left a memorial and charts. Quirós sent memorial after memorial to the Spanish crown to arouse interest in the South Seas islands, but it was all in vain. The Spaniards resumed voyages of exploration in the Pacific only much later. In the eighteenth century their most important voyage was that of Alejandro de Malaspina (1790–1793), who made few discoveries, but collected many scientific data. Other nations were busy exploring the ocean.

The Dutch Following their revolt against Spanish rule and the closing of the port of Lisbon to their ships, the Dutch started sailing to the Spice Islands instead of getting their merchandise in Portugal for resale to the people of northern Europe. At first in cooperation with the British, then on their own, the Dutch ousted the Portuguese, who were subjects of the King of Spain from 1580 to 1640, from nearly all their dominions in the East Indies. When Japan closed its doors to foreigners, the Dutch were allowed a limited amount of trade there. The Dutch East India

Company took over the exploitation of the Moluccas and neighboring islands. Exploration was conducted from there.

Dutch navigators made several landfalls on the northern and western coasts of Australia without knowing that they were all on the same continent. In 1606 a Dutch vessel named *Duyfken* under the command of Willem Jansz coasted New Guinea, sailing as far as the strait through which Torres was to sail a few months later. The Dutch did not realize that there was a passage there and returned to their settlements. Ten years later another Dutch ship, the *Eendracht*, under Dirk Hartog made a landfall on the coast of what is now Western Australia. The spot is still called Dirk Hartogs Island. In 1619 another ship touched the area around present-day Perth, and in 1623 yet another vessel discovered Arnhem Land on the northern coast of Australia. Thus the Dutch gradually obtained some knowledge of about one-half of the Australian continent, which was known for a long time as New Holland, but no settlements were made.

All these landfalls had been piecemeal, and Anton van Diemen, governor of the Dutch settlements in the East Indies, decided to take steps to coordinate discoveries. In 1636 he sent out Peter Pietersz, who explored the area of Melville Island. Today Van Diemen Gulf recalls the voyage.

Of much greater consequence were the voyages undertaken by Abel Janszoon TASMAN and Frans Jacobszoon Visscher as a result of instructions from Governor Van Diemen. Their first voyage consisted in sailing from Batavia (now Jakarta) to the island of Mauritius in the Indian Ocean. From there the two Dutch ships set out in a southerly direction. The plan was to navigate to a little more than 50°S, but the weather made them retreat to about 44°. Staying in the same latitude, they sailed east and on November 24, 1642, they sighted the southern coast of what they called Van Diemen's Land to honor the sponsor of the voyage. It is now called Tasmania after the discoverer. The explorers went ashore briefly on the east coast. No individual of the now-extinct Tasmanian people was seen. The Dutch were unable to ascertain that the land was an island; this was determined only at the end of the eighteenth century. Tasman and Visscher continued their voyage in an easterly direction across the Tasman Sea. On December 13 the Alps of New Zealand loomed over the horizon. Tasman landed at a place near the northwestern end of South Island. The first relations between Europeans and Maoris ended in tragedy. Four sailors were killed, and Tasman called the bay Murderers' Bay.

Tasman steered some way in the direction of what is now called Cook Strait but did not discover that it was a passage separating two islands. All of Tasman's exploration was conducted on the western coast of New Zealand. It was left to James COOK to discover the other side of the two islands. The Dutch vessels skirted the coast of North Island. On January 6, 1643, they sighted what is still known as Three Kings Islands, off the northernmost cape of New Zealand. This name is derived from that of one of the provinces of the Netherlands.

On January 19, 1643, the weary Dutch reached the Tonga Islands and stayed for some time among the friendly natives of Tongatapu, which they called Amsterdam. The next archipelago visited was Fiji. No landing was made on account of the reefs, and there was no need for fresh supplies. From Fiji the course was northwest. The Dutch missed the Solomons, as did other navigators before and after them. On the way to Batavia Tasman penetrated what is now the Bismarck Sea. He sighted New Britain but did not notice the channel between New Britain and New Ireland. He coasted New Guinea on his return to Batavia, where he arrived in June 1643. The main discoveries of Tasman and Visscher on this voyage were Tasmania, New Zealand, some of the islands of the Tonga and Fiji groups, and New Britain. This was quite an achievement, but historians have criticized Tasman for his hesitations. For instance, by sailing just a little farther east he could have found Cook Strait in New Zealand. Visscher suspected its existence and left a gap on his chart.

In spite of these discoveries Governor Van Diemen was not satisfied, since no lands which might be profitable for trading had been found. In February 1644 Tasman and Visscher were sent out once again. After rounding the western extremity of Java, they navigated past Amboina to the southern coast of New Guinea. From there the Dutch sailed all the way to Torres Strait but missed its entrances. The remainder of the voyage was along the coast of the Gulf of Carpentaria and Arnhem Land, with a return to Batavia. This voyage made no new discovery except to demonstrate that the various Dutch discoveries from Cape York to Dirk Hartogs Island were part of the same land: New Holland.

The Dutch also came into the Pacific from the east. The first of these expeditions were undertaken for plunder to weaken Spain, as Drake and others had done during the second half of the sixteenth century. Such voyages did little in the field of discovery. However, in 1616 an important voyage took place. The *Eendracht* under Jacob Le Maire (1585–1616) and the *Hoorn* under Willem Schouten (1567?–1625) emerged into the Pacific Ocean not through the Strait of Magellan or around Cape Horn but through what is now known as Le Maire Strait. The party steered north to the Juan Fernández Islands, where some fish were caught and water taken. The vessels changed their course from north to west at the latitude of 15°S. In April they were among the Tuamotus, one of which may have been seen by Magellan. A landing was made on Takapoto, where the Dutch found tattooed natives armed with clubs and slings.

The ships' course next took them into the waters between Tonga, Fiji, and Samoa, and landings were made on smaller islands. In the Hoorn Islands (Îles des Horn), where they stayed a few days, the Dutch witnessed the ceremonial making and drinking of kava. After their departure, to the great relief of the natives, the vessels came across some small islands and in June sighted a land which they thought was New Guinea. It was New Ireland, New Guinea being a little farther to the southwest. As far as can be ascertained, New Ireland had not been seen previously by Europeans. The small fleet reached the Dutch settlements by way of the northern coast of New Guinea. Le Maire and Schouten had made the following main discoveries: some islands in the Tuamotu Archipelago and the Tonga group, the Hoorn Islands, New Ireland and other islands in the Bismarck Archipelago, and some islands in the Admiralty group. They had also found the eastern limits of New Guinea.

William Dampier, English explorer-buccaneer of the seventeenth century. His career is typical of the transition period between the near piracy of earlier British privateering and the great age of scientific exploration. [Library of Congress]

The last important Dutch voyage in the Pacific was undertaken by Jacob Roggeveen, who left the Netherlands in August 1721 and sailed through Le Maire Strait and then beyond 60°S. The presence of icebergs made him think that there must be an Antarctic continent. After that he sailed north to warmer latitudes. He was pleased with Juan Fernández, and on Easter Day, April 5, 1722, he arrived at an island which he appropriately called Easter Island, located at the easternmost angle of the so-called Polynesian triangle, which is also demarcated by New Zealand and Hawaii. Easter Island was a new discovery, and Roggeveen, who was also a scientist, was the first to describe the giant stone statues that have intrigued later navigators. During his stay Roggeveen had an opportunity to write descriptions not only of the land but also of the natives. The expedition next sailed in the direction of the Tuamotus. There was a skirmish on Makatea with deaths on both sides. Three days later Bora-Bora in the Society group was sighted. Roggeveen's men were suffering from scurvy, and he was anxious to reach the Dutch settlements of the East Indies. On the way the party sighted a number of islands which had not been discovered by other navigators, including Tutuila, in the Samoan Islands.

The ships of Le Maire and Schouten and those of Roggeveen, which arrived in the Dutch East Indies after crossing the Pacific from the east, were considered interlopers on the prerogatives of the East India Company. Indeed, Roggeveen's voyage had been sponsored by the Dutch West India Company, a rival. As a result, ships were confiscated, and commanders were arrested and sent back to the Netherlands under guard, a sad sequel to voyages which had contributed a great deal to expand the knowledge of the Pacific Ocean.

Dutch explorers of the Pacific had not been able to prove or disprove the existence of a large southern continent (different from Australia, which is sometimes called the smallest continent), often referred to as Terra Australis Incognita (Unknown Southland). However, the Dutch, who were also experts at cartography, made some useful discoveries which were of great help to the scientific explorers of the second half

of the eighteenth century, most of whom were British or French.

The British The crossing of the Pacific by Francis Drake, which occurred when the Spaniards were the main explorers of the ocean, has been mentioned. Other men from the British Isles followed, mostly bent on privateering. Thomas Cavendish was the first Britisher to capture a Manila galleon, in 1587 near the coast of Mexico. He continued his voyage across the Pacific. Neither Drake nor Cavendish made any discovery worth mentioning. Richard Hawkins, who tried to repeat the exploits of Drake and Cavendish, was captured by the Spaniards. These raids into the Pacific were made from the east. British navigators also came in via the western Portuguese route. For a while they cooperated with the Dutch in displacing the Portuguese. This cooperation ceased after the Amboina massacre in 1623. The Dutch were left masters of the East Indies, and the British concentrated for the time being on their settlements in India.

It has been pointed out that the seventeenth century was essentially a period of Dutch exploration, but the British reentered the scene toward the end of the century. Of special importance was William Dampier (1652–1715), part explorer, part buccaneer. A great observer as well, he resembled in this respect the scientific explorers of the second half of the eighteenth century who left countless volumes. In 1697 he published *A New Voyage Around the World* with observations on winds and currents, a proof of his scientific mind. His first voyage in the Pacific took place in 1683, and he navigated there on other occasions. He explored the northern coast of Australia. Australian history books sometimes quote his disparaging remarks on the Australian aborigines when he first saw them. The names of Dampier Archipelago, off the west coast of Australia, and Dampier Strait, between New Britain and New Guinea, give some idea of Dampier's contributions. He was still busy early in the eighteenth century when his two-volume work *A Voyage to New Holland* (1706–1709) came off the press. Dampier circumnavigated the world three times. His work marks a transition between the British privateering expeditions of the sixteenth century and the scientific explorations of the eighteeth.

However, before the era of British scientific voyages started, the British entered the Pacific Basin on several occasions during wars against Spain. Thus between 1708 and 1710, during the War of the Spanish Succession, Woodes Rogers preyed on Spanish shipping. Between 1741 and 1743, during the War of the Austrian Succession, George Anson roamed the Pacific and brought back to England a large amount of treasure taken from a Manila galleon.

The books written by Dampier and others aroused much interest and a desire to know more about the great ocean. The first voyage with an essentially scientific purpose was that of John Byron (1723–1786), which began in 1764 once peace following the Seven

Years' War made the seas relatively safe again. His instructions called for identifying some reports by other navigators concerning the possible existence of a southern continent.

After emerging from the Strait of Magellan, Byron steered west in about 27°S, where the continent was believed to be located. Had he been able to stay in the same latitude he would have discovered the eastern coast of Australia before Cook. Weather conditions, however, obliged him to change his course to the northwest. Byron is credited, however, with the discovery of two islands of the Tuamotu Archipelago not sighted by earlier navigators, Napuka and Tepoto, which maps call the Îles du Désappointement (Disappointment Islands), as well as Atafu in the Tokelau group and one of the Gilbert Islands. He returned to England via the Cape of Good Hope after a stop at Batavia.

Byron's voyage had not proved that Terra Australis Incognita did not exist, so shortly after his return to England another expedition was prepared. In 1766 two ships left England, the *Dolphin* under Samuel WALLIS and the *Swallow* under Philip CARTERET. As they entered the Pacific, the vessels became separated, and each of them explored different sections of the ocean. Wallis sailed through the Tuamotus and stopped at Tahiti in the Society Islands. He is credited with the discovery of this important island as well as of some of the Tuamotus and the Marshalls. On his side, Carteret discovered Pitcairn Island, later to become famous as the refuge of some of the mutineers of the *Bounty.* Among the other islands sighted was Buka at the extreme northwest of the Solomon Islands. After Mendaña's discovery of this archipelago several explorers had tried in vain to locate it.

Both Wallis and Carteret used a new instrument to determine longitude at sea, the chronometer. They were able to locate definitely on Pacific charts the islands they discovered or rediscovered. However, the mystery of the Unknown Southern Land remained intact, and there were still vast expanses of the ocean where no European vessel had ever sailed. It was left to James Cook to do most of the discovering. His three voyages mark the climax of British exploration, although the French conducted scientific voyages in the Pacific during the same period.

The main object of Cook's first voyage was to observe the transit of the planet Venus across the sun from a site in the South Pacific. This was to happen on June 3, 1769, and would not occur again for another 105 years. He also did some exploring, and this voyage plus the two others rank Cook among the greatest explorers of all times.

In command of the *Endeavour*, Cook entered the Pacific from the east toward the end of January 1769. He sighted several of the Tuamotu chain of islands, some of which had been discovered by other navigators, including the Frenchman Louis-Antoine de BOUGAINVILLE, who was exploring the Pacific at the same

time as the British. Carteret chanced to meet Bougainville, but Cook did not. Cook's purpose was to reach Tahiti, which had been described by Wallis, its discoverer, as a suitable island for a long stay, and to establish an observatory there. The *Endeavour* cast anchor at Tahiti in April 1769. While in Tahiti waiting for the transit of the planet, Cook had ample opportunity to observe the land and the inhabitants. Other islands around Tahiti, some of them new discoveries, also were visited. From Tahiti Cook steered south, then southwest and struck the eastern coast of New Zealand in October 1769. Tasman had skirted the western coast of North Island more than 100 years earlier, but no European explorer had seen the east coast. Cook spent several months in the waters of New Zealand, sailing all around it and demonstrating that there were actually two islands. Cook Strait, which had been suspected by Visscher, Tasman's companion, is a reminder of this discovery. The fact that one could sail all around New Zealand was a definite proof that it was not a part of Terra Australis Incognita. Cook had taken with him a Polynesian boy from Tahiti called Tupaia. The New Zealand Maoris, who were Polynesians too, could understand the boy's speech. In spite of that, their relations with the British visitors had their ups and downs. Years later an old Maori recalled that Captain Cook had patted him on the head when he was a child. However, on several occasions there was bloodshed.

Aboard the *Endeavour* traveled Joseph Banks, a fellow of the Royal Society whose specialty was botany. He collected many plants, some of which were edible and preventives for scurvy, that terrible disease of seamen. Cook and Banks thought that New Zealand would be a good land for a British settlement. Possession of the islands was taken in the name of Great Britain. This action was confirmed only in 1840.

After a lengthy stay in New Zealand waters, the *Endeavour* sailed to the eastern coast of Australia. A harbor was found in Botany Bay, so named because of the many specimens of plants Banks found there. Some aborigines made a show of resistance to a landing but were put to flight by the sound of firearms. Cook took possession in Great Britain's name of the whole east coast of Australia and called it New South Wales.

Cook continued his course in a northerly direction and was the first to sail through Torres Strait since its discovery by the Spanish navigator. There are several islands in the strait, and Cook did not sail in the same channel as Torres had done. On October 10 he was in Batavia and after sailing around the Cape of Good Hope, reached England in July 1771. The whole voyage had lasted a little less than 3 years, of which 2½ years had been spent exploring the Pacific Ocean. Cook's first voyage had begun to destroy the myth of Terra Australis Incognita. By sailing around New Zealand he had shown that it was neither a section of

Terra Australis Incognita nor the eastern coast of New Holland.

Cook left England on his second voyage on July 13, 1772, with two ships, the *Resolution* and the *Adventure,* and sailed to the Cape of Good Hope. After leaving the cape in November 1772, Cook's ships sailed as far south as ice would permit in the Indian Ocean (Terra Australis Incognita was believed to extend there too), and on January 17, 1773, Cook became the first navigator to cross the Antarctic Circle. A latitude of 67°S was the farthest the ships could steer without being trapped by the ice pack, although this was the southern summer. On February 8, 1773, the ships became separated in bad weather and came together again only in New Zealand.

After the separation the *Resolution* under Cook sailed as far as the longitude of Tasmania, then north to New Zealand. South Island was reached in March. A few weeks later the *Adventure* was found at the appointed place where the ships were to meet in case of separation. The *Adventure* had been able to call at small islands north of Tasmania now called the Furneaux Group after the *Adventure*'s commander, but the latter had thought that what is now known as Bass Strait was a large bay, and without investigating any farther he had set out for New Zealand in order not to miss Cook. The latter accepted Furneaux's opinion and until the end of his life believed that New South Wales and Tasmania were linked.

From New Zealand Cook undertook a circular voyage in the South Pacific east of New Zealand, finding only small islands. He was back in New Zealand after 4 months of traveling. Then he undertook a still longer voyage, reaching 71°10'S before returning to New Zealand. No continent was found in that area. Not satisfied, Cook, while en route to England via the Cape Horn route, sailed to about 50°S and searched for Terra Australis Incognita in the South Atlantic as well. He was back in England in July 1775. The second voyage had lasted 3 years. The expedition had made many discoveries, the most important being the southern New Hebrides, New Caledonia, and Norfolk Island. On this voyage Cook had also proved, this time definitely, that there was no great continent in the South Pacific north of ice-covered Antarctica.

Captain Cook was to explore the Pacific once more. His *Resolution* was refitted; the second vessel was the *Discovery.* The plan for the third voyage was to explore the northern Pacific outside the regular route of the Manila Galleon. On July 12, 1776, Cook left England for the last time. He again entered the Pacific from the west. New Zealand was reached in February 1777 after a landing in Tasmania. Cook was anxious to return to the Society Islands a Polynesian called Omai whom he had taken to England. However, the ships had to stop at Tongatapu, where the King was at first entertained, then held as hostage in order to secure the return of some articles that the natives had pilfered. In August Tahiti was sighted, and Omai received a hero's welcome from his people. While in Tahiti, Cook found out that the Spaniards had left missionaries there and had later picked them up.

Death of Capt. James Cook in 1779. The explorer had departed from Hawaii to continue his work in the northern Pacific when a storm forced him to return to the shelter of the islands, where he was killed in a skirmish with the natives. [Library of Congress]

They had not had much success in converting Polynesians to Christianity. Tahiti was at war with Moorea, a nearby island.

After spending about 1 month on Raiatea Island, west of Tahiti, Cook's vessels took a northerly course. The most important part of the voyage was about to start. On Christmas Eve, 1777, a landing was made on a small island appropriately named Christmas Island. Finally, on January 18, 1778, Cook discovered (or rediscovered) the islands of Oahu and Kauai in the Hawaiian group, which Cook called the Sandwich Islands to honor the 4th Earl of Sandwich, first lord of the Admiralty. After exploring the northern Pacific as far as 70°44'N, he decided to winter in the Sandwich Islands. In November Cook sighted Maui, one of the islands which he had not seen during his earlier visit to the archipelago. A few days later he discovered the island of Hawaii. In Kealakekua Bay on the western coast he received a great welcome. According to Hawaiian tradition, a divine chief called Lono was to come back on a big ship bearing gifts.

On February 4, 1779, the expedition left port to continue exploring the northern Pacific. During the night a storm damaged the *Resolution,* and Cook reluctantly decided to return to the bay he had left. After the theft of a boat belonging to the *Discovery,* Cook decided to go ashore and was stabbed from behind. The tragedy which ended a great explorer's life took place on February 14, 1779.

Charles Clerke, Cook's second-in-command, took charge during the remainder of the voyage. The ships sailed north once again, passed through Bering Strait, but could not steer as far as Cook had done previously, and the decision was made to return to England by way of the Asian side of the Pacific. They followed the Kuril Islands and the coasts of the Japanese islands and, after a stop in Macao, sailed back to Great Britain by way of the Cape of Good Hope. The voyage had lasted more than 4 years.

Other British navigators followed Cook. Although the general outline of the Pacific was now known, there was still exploration to do. Near the end of the eighteenth century George Bass discovered the strait which now bears his name. Together with Matthew FLINDERS Bass sailed for the first time all around Tasmania. Early in the nineteenth century Flinders was the first explorer to circumnavigate Australia, the coasts of which had been explored piecemeal over a period of two centuries.

The French Like the British, the French entered the Pacific Basin in the sixteenth century, but there is no French equivalent of Drake's voyage. Only in the second half of the eighteenth century did the French adopt a systematic plan of exploration. The publication in 1756 of Charles de Brosses's *Histoire des navigations aux terres australes* encouraged exploration. De Brosses gave the history of the voyages which had already taken place and wrote about what might yet be discovered, especially Terra Australis Incog-

nita. The work was translated into English and became a source of information for Cook and other explorers.

The first great French voyage of the eighteenth century was that of Louis-Antoine de Bougainville, who entered the Pacific from the east in January 1768. Wallis and Carteret were already in the process of exploring the ocean in different directions. Bougainville's instructions were to take possession of any island which was not claimed by another nation and might be of use for trade. He thus took possession of seven archipelagoes in which earlier navigators had made discoveries. Of the groups of islands which Bougainville claimed for France only two, the Tuamotus and the Society Islands, came under French rule. Bougainville's colorful description of Tahiti, discovered by Wallis, was to have a lasting influence on the French, especially in literature. While some of Bougainville's discoveries were actually rediscoveries, he is credited with discovering some of the Tuamotus and some of the New Hebrides or at least with placing them securely on charts. The largest of the Solomons, which he discovered in June 1768, is named for him. Bougainville had with him two scientists, a naturalist and an astronomer. Many observations of longitudes were made, and after Bougainville's expedition the scientific world had a more accurate notion of the width of the world's largest ocean.

Two other French explorers left for the Pacific after Bougainville's expedition. The first was Jean-François-Marie de Surville (1717–1770), who crossed the Pacific in 1769 by way of New Britain, the Solomons, New Caledonia, and New Zealand. He missed Tahiti. The other was Marc Marion du Fresnes (1724–1772), who left Mauritius in 1771 in order to return to Tahiti a chief whom Bougainville had taken to France. The native died on the way to his home, and the expedition proved of little importance, except for the discovery of the Marion and Crozet groups, named after the explorer and his second-in-command, Julien Crozet.

France's greatest explorer of the Pacific was Jean-François de Galaup, Comte de LA PÉROUSE, who was entrusted by the government of Louis XVI with two ships, *La Boussole* and the *L'Astrolabe.* He was ordered to see whether there were still islands to discover in the Pacific after Cook's three voyages. There were some, but La Pérouse's voyage in the Pacific is far more important from the viewpoint of the distance he covered and the data he collected than for the discoveries that he made.

In April 1786 La Pérouse was at Easter Island, where some very valuable observations were made. Then he steered to the northwest in unknown waters practically devoid of islands. He anchored briefly in Hawaii and sailed on to Alaska. From there he sailed down along the west coast of North America to Monterey Bay, then crossed the Pacific, sailing part of the time in unknown waters. On November 5, 1786, he discovered Necker Island northwest of the main group of the

Jean-François de Galaup, Comte de La Pérouse, eighteenth-century French explorer. He crossed and recrossed the Pacific, touching on Easter Island, Hawaii, Alaska and the Pacific Coast of North America, China, the Philippines, Japan, and Samoa. On his final voyage he set sail from Australia in 1788 and dropped out of sight forever. [Library of Congress]

Hawaiian Islands while on his way to the coast of China. He repaired his vessels in the Philippines before sailing to the Japanese islands. La Pérouse Strait between Hokkaido and Sakhalin is a reminder of his cartographic work in the area.

From the peninsula of Kamchatka La Pérouse sailed south to Samoa, then to Tonga. In January 1788 he cast anchor at Botany Bay in New South Wales to repair his vessels shortly after the arrival there of the British fleet that had come to start a penal settlement in Australia. La Pérouse left the following month but was never seen again.

During the French Revolution the French government sent an expedition led by Antoine-Raymond-Joseph de Bruni, Chevalier d'Entrecasteaux (1737–1793), to try to locate La Pérouse. The expedition found no trace of La Pérouse, but it did gather valuable scientific data and discovered the group of islands named after D'Entrecasteaux at the eastern end of New Guinea and the Trobriand Islands nearby. It was not until the 1820s that evidence was found that La Pérouse's ships had been wrecked near Vanikoro Island in the Santa Cruz group.

Other French explorers, the most important of whom was Jules-Sébastien-César Dumont d'Urville, navigated in the Pacific during the nineteenth century, but there was little left to discover. The French also had a share in the surveying of the western and southern coasts of Australia. Some French names on these coasts are a reminder of the expedition led by Nicolas Baudin from 1800 to 1803. Although the French made relatively few discoveries as compared with the Spaniards, the Dutch, and the British, the data their navigators collected fill a great many volumes which are now a precious source for the study of the Pacific.

The Russians As explained earlier, the exploration of the seas bordering Asia does not fall within the scope of this study. Much of the exploration done by Russians belongs to this category, as does most of what was done by the Japanese and the Chinese. However, in the nineteenth century several Russian expeditions crisscrossed the vast ocean. Two of them were under the command of Otto von Kotzebue, one from 1815 to 1818 and the other from 1823 to 1826. They resulted in the discovery or at least the definite location of some islands in Micronesia which had not been discovered by others such as Thomas Gilbert and John Marshall, two British navigators. One of the Russian discoveries was the island of Bikini, a name which was to pass into the world of fashion in the twentieth century.

It is noteworthy that by the beginning of the nineteenth century the exploration of the Pacific was just about completed when the exploration of the interior of Africa had barely started.

BIBLIOGRAPHY: James C. Beaglehole, *The Exploration of the Pacific*, 3d ed., Stanford, Calif., 1966; Mariano Cuevas, *Monje y marino*, Mexico City, 1943; John Dunmore, *French Explorers in the Pacific*, 2 vols., Oxford, 1965; Otis W. Freeman, *Geography of the Pacific*, New York, 1951; Herman R. Friis (ed.), *The Pacific Basin: A History of Its Geographical Exploration*, New York, 1967; André Gschaedler, "The Discovery of Guadalcanal," *Pacific Discovery*, vol. V, September–October 1952, pp. 24–27; id., "Religious Aspects of the Spanish Voyages in the Pacific during the Sixteenth Century and the Early Part of the Seventeenth," *The Americas*, vol. IV, January 1948, pp. 302–315; Colin Jack-Hinton, *The Search for the Islands of Solomon (1567–1838)*, Oxford, 1969; Edgar Prestage, *The Portuguese Pioneers*, London, 1933; Andrew Sharp, *The Discovery of the Pacific Islands*, Oxford, 1962; Alan Villiers, *Captain James Cook*, New York, 1967; Lawrence Wroth, *The Early Cartography of the Pacific*, New York, 1944.

André Gschaedler

Palgrave, William Gifford (1826–1888) English explorer, missionary, and diplomat. Palgrave was born in Westminster, the son of Sir Francis Palgrave and the grandson of Meyer Cohen, a Jewish member of the London Stock Exchange. Sir Francis became a Christian and adopted Palgrave, the surname of his wife's mother, as the family name upon his marriage in 1823. The elder Palgrave was a distinguished scholar who won renown as the founder of the Public Record Office, the national archives of Great Britain.

Palgrave attended Charterhouse School and Trinity College, Oxford, where he mastered the classical and modern European languages. Before graduating from Oxford, however, he left England in 1846 to join the Indian Army as a cadet in the Bombay Infantry. In 1848, apparently influenced by a desire to proselytize among the Arabs, Palgrave became a Roman Catholic, and the following year he entered the Jesuit college at Negapatam (Negapattinam) as a novice. He remained there until 1853, when he was sent to Rome to continue his studies at the Collegio Romano. Two years later he was posted to Lebanon, near Beirut, where he became involved in missionary and educational work. In 1857 he was ordained a priest.

While in Lebanon and Syria, Palgrave witnessed the great rebellion of 1860 in which the Druze, Muslim sectaries, attacked the Maronites, Christians attached to the Church of Rome. The turmoil and carnage of this conflict temporarily terminated Palgrave's mission, and he was sent to Europe to appeal for funds to aid the victims of the rebellion. Afterward he was instructed to complete his studies in France. There he conceived a plan to bring Christianity to the Arabian Peninsula. Soon afterward he was summoned to the presence of the French emperor, Napoleon III, and agreed to investigate the possibilities of French expansion into Syria, Egypt, and Arabia. Napoleon sought silk and cotton and a market for the commercial goods of France. At the same time he was attempting to reduce British hegemony in the Middle East before the completion of the Suez Canal. Palgrave was to receive 10,000 francs for his efforts.

On June 24, 1861, Palgrave left for Egypt on the first leg of his politicoreligious mission in the Middle East. The following June found him in Arabia at Ma'ān, whence he set out in the guise of a Syrian doctor to cross the peninsula with a Syrian Greek companion, also a priest in disguise. Palgrave crossed the Nafūd

Desert to Ha'il, capital of the Shammar tribe who were fierce opponents of the Wahhābi Saudi, visited Riyadh (Ar Riyād), and, after several near-fatal mishaps, reached Muscat (Masqat). His journey marked only the second time that a European had crossed the peninsula, and the first time from west to east. George Forster Sadlier had accomplished the first crossing (east to west) in 1819.

Palgrave's journey secured his fame, and he was invited to lecture before the ROYAL GEOGRAPHICAL SOCIETY upon his return to England. His account of his exploit, *Narrative of a Year's Journey through Central and Eastern Arabia* (1865), was valuable, for he had been able to explore at a leisurely pace an area unseen by Sadlier. Even so, Harry St. John PHILBY later contended that Palgrave had written of things and places that he had not seen. D. G. Hogarth, the first student of Arabian travelers, however, upheld the authenticity of Palgrave's work, as does his biographer, Mea Allan.

Palgrave renounced the priesthood and Catholicism in 1865 and subsequently entered the British diplomatic corps. For more than 20 years he served as consul and minister in such far-flung posts as Trebizond (Trabzon), St. Thomas in the Virgin Islands, Manila, Sofia, Bangkok, and Montevideo, where he died. In addition to his book on Arabia, Palgrave wrote numerous articles on travel; *Hermann Agha* (1872), a novel set in the Middle East; and *A Vision of Life* (1891), an autobiographical poem.

BIBLIOGRAPHY: Mea Allan, *Palgrave of Arabia: The Life of William Gifford Palgrave, 1826–1888*, London, 1972; David G. Hogarth, *The Penetration of Arabia*, New York, 1904.

Robert W. Olson

Palliser, John (1817–1887) Irish landed gentleman, big-game hunter, traveler, and explorer. Educated largely on the continent of Europe and at Trinity College, Dublin, and a captain in the Waterford Artillery Militia, Palliser was an eager sportsman, as were his friends. In 1847–1848 he emulated his Scottish future brother-in-law, William Fairholme, in making a trip up the Missouri River. He found buffalo hunting a "noble sport" and resolved to return to the prairies. In London, an intimate of a group of friends interested in exploration, he wrote a lively book about his adventures in the American West.

Controversy was raging as to the capabilities of the British West for agriculture and settlement. Palliser, on his election as a fellow on November 24, 1856, submitted to the ROYAL GEOGRAPHICAL SOCIETY a plan for a journey with local hunters and *voyageurs* to examine the plains north of the 49th parallel and passes through the Rocky Mountains beyond. The society applied to the British government for £5000 ($24,250) to finance an expedition enlarged to include a team of scientists. The grant was authorized largely through the influence of Palliser's friend John Ball, undersecretary of state for the colonies. Ball added a third

assignment, an examination of the old North West Company canoe route from Lake Superior to Red River Settlement, where Winnipeg now stands. He enlisted the help of the Royal Society and of outstanding scientists, who selected Dr. (later Sir) James Hector as geologist, naturalist, and medical man, Capt. Thomas W. Blakiston as magnetical observer, Eugène Bourgeau as botanical collector, and John W. Sullivan as secretary and astronomer. Sir George Simpson, governor of the Hudson's Bay Company's territories in North America, contributed advice and essential help in securing canoes and their crews, men, horses, and supplies. The government appointed Palliser leader of the expedition.

On May 28, 1857, Palliser, Hector, Bourgeau, and Sullivan landed in New York, traveling on by Niagara Falls and Detroit to Sault Sainte-Marie, where they picked up two canoes with their *voyageurs*, who paddled them from Isle Royale, Michigan, to Red River Settlement. Then they examined the border country from Pembina, in what is now North Dakota, to the Turtle Mountains, in Manitoba, and the country northwestward to the Elbow of the South Saskatchewan River. Their winter base was Fort Carlton, Saskatchewan, where Blakiston joined them, bringing the magnetical instruments via Hudson Bay. Palliser had gone off to New York via St. Paul, Minnesota, to request the Colonial Office for more time and more money. Hector journeyed to Fort Edmonton, Alberta, to engage men for the coming season.

The second season's work took the expedition west to the mountains, where the party dispersed to test five passes. Palliser and Sullivan made a dash to the international border, then traversed North Kananaskis Pass and North Kootenay Pass before joining the party at Edmonton, the base for the second winter. Hector explored Vermilion and Kicking Horse Passes, and Blakiston both Kootenay Passes.

In the third season the expedition traveled southeast to the fork of the Red Deer and South Saskatchewan Rivers in an attempt to connect with its westernmost point in 1857, and thence south, through Blackfoot country, to the Cypress Hills, from which Hector pushed northwestward to Howse Pass, while Palliser and Sullivan returned across the mountains by North Kootenay Pass to try to find a way onward to the Pacific Coast. By the time that Palliser met an American party running the line for the Boundary Commission of 1857–1862 near modern Midway, British Columbia, he was convinced that although a railroad might be constructed north of 49° to the coast, it would be prohibitively costly. When Hector rejoined Palliser and Sullivan, they made a difficult journey down the Columbia and so to Victoria and New Westminster, British Columbia, before returning to England to write the final report and settle the expedition bills, which, at £13,000, greatly exceeded the authorized expenditure.

Palliser, on January 6, 1862, saw Hector off for New Zealand from Marseille, where they met Blakiston on his way home from exploring the Yangtze Kiang. In 1862–1863 Palliser was in the Caribbean and the Confederate States, and in 1869 he made yet another journey that combined big-game hunting and exploration, to Novaya Zemlaya and the Kara Sea.

Palliser's expedition is best remembered for "Palliser's Triangle" in the semiarid southern prairies of Canada, but it identified a "Fertile Belt" well suited for agriculture, and the Canadian Pacific Railway was built through Hector's Kicking Horse Pass. The expedition's reports and great map were used for many years by geological and boundary surveyors, the Northwest Mounted Police, and other precursors of the change from the buffalo-hunting, fur-trading pattern of prairie life to settlement and agriculture. They are still of basic scientific and historical importance.

BIBLIOGRAPHY: John Palliser, *Solitary Rambles and Adventures of a Hunter in the Prairies*, London, 1853; Irene M. Spry, *The Palliser Expedition*, Toronto, 1963; Irene M. Spry (ed.), *The Papers of the Palliser Expedition*, Toronto, 1968.

Irene M. Spry

Respected for his African explorations by the age of thirty-five, Mungo Park died while tracing the course of the Niger River. [Library of Congress]

Park, Mungo *(1771–1806)* Scottish explorer. Born in Selkirkshire, the son of a farmer, Park studied medicine at Edinburgh University. In London he secured the position of assistant surgeon on the East Indiaman *Worcester* through the influence of his brother-in-law, the botanist James Dickson, who introduced him to Joseph Banks, president of the Royal Society and treasurer of the AFRICAN ASSOCIATION. After a voyage to Sumatra on the *Worcester*, Park offered his services to the association, which engaged him to go to West Africa. His instructions (April 21, 1795) listed several objectives, including investigation of the course of the Niger River and a visit to Timbuktu. Park arrived at Pisania (now Karantaba) on the Gambia River in July 1795 and set out for the interior the following December. On July 20, 1796, he saw the Niger near Ségou, Mali, and traveled along the banks of the river until he reached Silla, thereby determining conclusively the easterly direction of its flow. At this point he decided to turn back because of lack of funds and because the country beyond was controlled by fanatical Muslims. Park returned to England safely in December 1797 and, while he considered and rejected a proposed expedition to Australia, began writing an account of his travels. The resulting work, *Travels in the Interior Districts of Africa* (1799), proved an immediate best seller, and Park earned 1000 guineas from the first edition alone.

By 1804 the British government, determined to establish a British presence on the Niger to forestall possible French encroachment in the area, was making plans to dispatch a military expedition with which Park was to be associated. A change of government put an end to this scheme, but Park, who was now convinced that the Niger and the Congo were the same river, was asked to return to Africa and "to pursue the course of [the Niger] to the utmost possible distance to which it can be traced."

Park left Portsmouth in January 1805, accompanied by his brother-in-law, Alexander Anderson, also a surgeon; George Scott, a draftsman; and four carpenters. His force augmented by two sailors and thirty-five soldiers and an officer recruited from the English garrison on Gorée Island, Park sailed up the Gambia to Kaiaf, where on April 27, 1805, the party began the overland march to the Niger. The onset of the rainy season had a disastrous effect on the health of the members of the expedition, many of whom had succumbed to malaria and dysentery by the time the Niger was sighted on August 19. At the large market town of Sansanding, Park constructed a boat for the journey down the Niger and apparently set sail on November 19 with the four surviving members of the expedition in addition to a guide and three African slaves. Since nothing was ever heard from Park or any of the other Europeans again, the fate of the party was subsequently pieced together from several sources, including an account by the guide, who left Park's service at Yauri. It appears that Park antagonized the chiefs along the river by refusing to pay customary tolls and by firing at all who approached. In March or April 1806, the party was ambushed at Bussa, where rapids made the river impassable. The only member of the group to survive was one of the slaves, who reported that Park had drowned while trying to escape. *See also* NIGER RIVER.

BIBLIOGRAPHY: E. W. Bovill, *The Niger Explored*, London, 1968; Robin Hallett (ed.), *Records of the African Association, 1788–1831*, London, 1964; Christopher Lloyd, *The Search for the Niger*, London, 1973.

Mungo Park's route, 1805–1806.

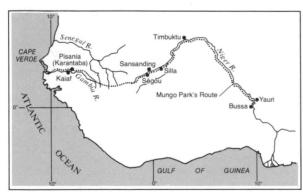

Parry, William Edward *(1790–1855)* British naval officer and Arctic explorer. Born in Bath, Parry joined the Royal Navy on June 30, 1803, as a first-class volunteer on board *Ville de Paris*, stationed in the English Channel. He remained on duty in the channel until May 1808, when he joined HMS *Vanguard* of the Baltic Fleet. He was promoted lieutenant on January 6, 1810, and soon after joined HMS *Alexandria*, also of the Baltic Fleet, which was later engaged in the protection of the Spitsbergen (Svalbard) whalers. In 1813 he crossed the Atlantic to join *La Hogue*, stationed at Halifax. He remained on the North American Station, on a series of different ships, until 1817.

Parry's career as an explorer began in 1818, when the Admiralty's second secretary, John BARROW, impressed by a treatise on nautical astronomy that Parry had published, had him selected for one of two Arctic expeditions which sailed in that year. He was appointed to command HMS *Alexander* on the expedition of Comdr. John Ross to search for a NORTHWEST PASSAGE through Baffin Bay. In the aftermath of that unsuccessful voyage, Ross and Parry disagreed over the prospect of a passage through Lancaster Sound, which they had briefly examined. The Admiralty preferred Parry's more optimistic description of the sound (Ross had maintained that it was a closed bay) and asked him to reexamine it in 1819. It was at this point that Parry embarked on the series of three expeditions which established his fame as an explorer: in 1819–1820, when he sailed through Lancaster Sound to become the first discoverer of an entrance to the Northwest Passage; from 1821 to 1823, when he explored western Foxe Basin; and in 1824–1825, when he led an expedition to Prince Regent Inlet that was cut short after the loss of one of his two ships. In 1827 Parry embarked on his last Arctic expedition, an attempt to reach the North Pole by sledge boat from Spitsbergen, on which he achieved a record northern latitude, 82°45'N, which remained unbeaten for 50 years.

Promotion and honors followed rapidly in the wake of Parry's voyages. He received many awards and medals, was promoted commander on November 4, 1820, and post captain on November 8, 1821, and was appointed acting hydrographer on December 1, 1823. He was knighted on April 29, 1829. In May 1829, he resigned as hydrographer to become commissioner of the Australian Agricultural Company in New South Wales. He returned to England in 1834 and for a short time thereafter was assistant poor-law commissioner in Norfolk. In April 1837, he accepted an Admiralty post as comptroller of steam machinery, which he held for nearly 10 years. Later, he was captain superintendent of Haslar Hospital and, from 1853 until his death in 1855, lieutenant governor of Greenwich Hospital. From 1845 on he also took an active part in the preparation of the Northwest Passage expedition of Sir John FRANKLIN and of the subsequent search expeditions (*See* FRANKLIN EXPEDITION AND SEARCH). He was promoted rear admiral on June 4, 1852.

It was not only the extent of his discoveries which made Parry a famous and highly respected explorer but also the techniques of exploration which he developed. No previous naval expeditions had deliberately wintered in the high Arctic, and Parry inherited no established means of maintaining good health, discipline, and morale throughout the cold, dark Arctic winters. Yet so successfully did he combat these problems that his methods were adopted on subsequent naval expeditions throughout the nineteenth century.

BIBLIOGRAPHY: Ann Parry, *Parry of the Arctic: The Life Story of Admiral Sir Edward Parry, 1790–1855*, London, 1963.

Clive A. Holland

Famous in his time for his discovery of an entrance to the Northwest Passage in 1819–1820 and for the record northern latitudes he reached when exploring the far north, William Parry has since been remembered for his development of polar survival techniques. [National Portrait Gallery, London]

Pavie, Auguste (1847–1925) French explorer. Pavie began his association with the Indochinese region after service with the French Marines. Joining the Telegraph Department of the colonial government in Cochin China (southern Vietnam) in 1868, he took up an appointment in the Cambodian seacoast town of Kampot in 1876. In this isolated setting Pavie demonstrated a keen interest in Cambodian culture, learning to speak the Cambodian language and beginning to explore the surrounding area in an initially limited fashion. In 1879 he sought authorization from the Governor of Cochin China, the chief French official in the Indochinese region, to carry out a major exploration of Cambodia, Laos, and Vietnam. This permission was eventually granted, although in 1880 Pavie's energies were diverted to supervising the construction of the first telegraph line between Phnom Penh and Bangkok.

From 1881 to 1895 Pavie and his associates engaged in a major and sustained survey of the region that was to become known as French Indochina. The series of expeditions has come to be known as the Pavie Mission, and in the course of the mission surveys were made of more than 260,600 square miles (675,000 square kilometers), while the distance covered in the various itineraries exceeded 18,750 miles (30,174 kilometers).

Given the size of the Pavie Mission's achievements, they have received remarkably little attention outside France. Part of the reason for this lack of attention is the fact that the findings were published only in French and have been, as a result, restricted to those with access to material in that language. Perhaps equally important has been the fact that Pavie and his associates did not undertake any single expedition that was the equal of those of their compatriots who explored the Mekong or the major expeditions of such men as Richard BURTON, David LIVINGSTONE, and John Hanning SPEKE in Africa. Such a comparison is, however, essentially unfair. If Pavie and those who worked with him were not absent from their home bases for such protracted periods as others, this did not mean they were encountering territory and peoples that were any better known than those seen by their more famous contemporaries. Moreover, one of the towering achievements of the Pavie Mission was the collection of an enormous amount of scientific, linguistic, and ethnographic information concerning the areas that were explored. The eleven volumes of the mission's findings with their outstanding maps are a notable testimony of this achievement.

In addition to his exploratory work, Pavie was directly concerned with the extension of French power over the Laotian states. During a period of intense imperial rivalry he was able to assert French paramountcy over sections of modern Laos and, finally, to gain both British and Thai acquiescence to the establishment of a French protectorate throughout the Laotian states. While modern commentators might be critical of Pavie's actions, it is nonetheless true that the existence of a modern state of Laos is in part due to his efforts.

BIBLIOGRAPHY: Auguste Pavie, *Mission Pavie*, 11 vols., Paris, 1898–1911.

Milton Osborne

***Peary, Robert Edwin* (1856—1920)** American explorer. Peary was born in Cresson, Pennsylvania, but was taken to his mother's native Maine after the death of his father in 1859. After graduating from Bowdoin College in 1877, he was employed as a draftsman with the Coast and Geodetic Survey in Washington and in 1881 was appointed a civil engineer in the U.S. Navy. In 1884–1885 and in 1886–1887 he traveled to Nicaragua to survey routes for a proposed interoceanic canal. After his return from his first Nicaraguan trip, a childhood interest in Arctic exploration was rekindled by reading *Exploration of Interior Greenland* by N. A. E. NORDENSKIÖLD.

Peary began his career as an explorer in 1886 by traveling to the west coast of Greenland and penetrating the inland ice cap more deeply and at a higher elevation than had ever been done before. He returned to Greenland in the summer of 1891 at the head of a party that included his wife, Josephine Diebitsch Peary, whom he had married in 1888, and his black manservant, Matthew A. Henson, who would accompany him on all his future expeditions. Peary had hoped to be the first man to cross Greenland, but when this feat was accomplished by Fridtjof NANSEN

in 1888, he decided to concentrate on the exploration of northeastern Greenland in order to determine its extension to the north. After recuperating from a broken leg, he set out from Hvalsund (Whale Sound) in the spring of 1892 and struck northeastward across Greenland to a height, Navy Cliff, from which he sighted and named Independence Bay (Independence Fjord). By this time Peary had already adopted the methods that he would employ on his polar expeditions: supplies were kept to a minimum and were carried in sledges pulled by Eskimo dogs.

During his next expedition to Greenland (1893–1895), Peary again crossed the ice cap to Independence Bay and discovered Mount Wistar. He also located the site of an "iron mountain" near Cape York mentioned by earlier explorers. As Peary had suspected, the mountain turned out to be a meteorite. He later found two other meteorites nearby and took all three of them to the United States. Josephine Peary again accompanied her husband during part of the expedition, and on September 12, 1893, she gave birth to a baby girl, named Marie Ahnighito, the first white child to be born that far north.

Peary launched hs first polar expedition in 1898 with the intention of forcing a passage through the strait joining Baffin Bay with the Arctic Ocean and then starting out for the North Pole from the northern tip of Greenland or Ellesmere Island. Soon after the expedition got under way, however, most of Peary's toes had to be amputated because of frostbite. In 1900 he reached the most northerly point of Greenland, discovering Cape Morris Jesup, which he named after the wealthy New Yorker who was president of the American Museum of Natural History and had given important moral and financial support to Peary. Although he had now conclusively proved the insularity of Greenland, his effort to reach the pole, which he began on April 6, 1902, from Cape Hecla on Ellesmere Island, soon ended in failure at 84°16'N. He had, however, traveled farther north in the Western Hemisphere than anyone else up to that time.

In his next attempt to reach the pole, Peary had the use of the *Roosevelt*, a vessel specially designed to withstand the Arctic ice. He sailed from New York on the *Roosevelt*, which was commanded by Capt. Robert A. Bartlett, on July 16, 1905, and arrived at Cape Sheridan, Ellesmere Island, on September 5. Peary began his assault on the pole at Cape Moss on March 6, 1906; though he was soon forced to turn back, he had reached 87°6'N, another farthest north.

Peary launched what he knew would be his last effort to reach the pole on July 6, 1908, when he sailed from New York aboard the *Roosevelt*, again commanded by Bartlett. The other members of the expedition were Henson, Dr. J. W. Goodsell, Ross G. Marvin, a member of the 1905–1906 expedition, George Borup, a recent graduate of Yale University, and Donald B. MacMillan, an instructor at Worcester Academy in Massachusetts. On September 5 the vessel arrived at Cape Sheridan after fighting her way through

Admiral Peary adopted successfully a Spartan approach to polar exploration. Traveling with scant provisions, dog sledges, and few companions, he reached the North Pole in 1909. [U.S. Navy]

nearly impassable ice. The autumn and winter were spent in hunting and making other preparations for the dash to the pole, which was to commence from Cape Columbia. The members of the expedition left the *Roosevelt* for Cape Columbia in February 1909, accompanied by Eskimos, dogs, and sledges. On February 28, Bartlett left Cape Columbia, which was 413 nautical miles (765 kilometers) from the pole, with three Eskimos to open a trail; shortly afterward he was followed by Borup, who was to leave a load of supplies after a march of 3 days, then return for additional loads. The main party, consisting of Peary, Henson, MacMillan, Goodsell, and Marvin, departed on March 1. After being delayed for nearly a week by a wide lead, or channel of open water, Peary passed the 84th parallel on March 11 and a few days later began sending back the supporting parties, starting with Goodsell and MacMillan. During the return journey Marvin, who turned back on March 26, fell through the young ice of a lead and drowned.

By April 2 Peary was alone with Henson, four Eskimos, and thirty-eight dogs 133 nautical miles (246 kilometers) from the pole and ready to begin the final leg of the expedition. He halted at 10 A.M. on April 6 and made camp, calling it Camp Morris K. Jesup, after his recently deceased benefactor. According to observations made at noon, his latitude was 89°57'11",

about 3 nautical miles (5.6 kilometers) from the pole. After making additional observations on April 7 that showed him to be even closer to the pole, Peary started back, arriving at Cape Columbia on April 23. It was not until July 17 that the *Roosevelt* was able to sail southward. From Indian Harbour, Labrador, he sent news of his achievement, but his return to the United States was marred by the claim of Dr. Frederick A. Cook that he had reached the pole on April 21, 1908. Peary's blunt assertion that Cook had handed the public "a gold brick" was soon echoed by knowledgeable persons in the United States and Europe, though Cook himself never abandoned his claim.

In his last years Peary devoted himself to the promotion of aviation and air power, maintaining that "he who commands the air commands all." His books include *Northward over the "Great Ice"* (1898), *Nearest the Pole* (1907), *The North Pole* (1910), and *Secrets of Polar Travel* (1917).

BIBLIOGRAPHY: John Edwards Caswell, *Arctic Frontiers: United States Explorations in the Far North,* Norman, Okla., 1956; Matthew A. Henson, *A Negro Explorer at the North Pole,* New York, 1912; Donald B. MacMillan, *How Peary Reached the Pole,* Boston and New York, 1934; John Edward Weems, *Peary: The Explorer and the Man,* Boston, 1967.

Pedrarias *(Pedrarias Dávila)* See ÁVILA, PEDRO ARIAS DE.

Periplus

Latin transcription of the Greek *periplous,* meaning "circumnavigation," a word used conventionally in two senses with reference to Greco-Roman exploration. The less frequent meaning is a report of a voyage along coasts previously unexplored or at least not generally known. The more common meaning is a sailing manual of simple form describing the coasts of areas known to the Greeks and Romans, giving the names of coastal towns and features such as headlands and rivers in geographical order, with estimates of distance from point to point. Some peripli also gave brief information about the peoples of the hinterland but without any detailed treatment. The second group was specifically designed for traders, whereas some examples of the first group were made at least partly to extend geographical knowledge. In principle, the term applied, as is evident from its meaning, to enclosed areas, primarily the Mediterranean and the Black Sea, but came to be used of navigation along any stretch of coast, not necessarily a round trip. Most peripli are known only from references in later writings, but a few have survived entire. In the first group may be mentioned:

1. An account (not extant), probably written about 520 B.C. by a Greek sailor from Massilia (Marseille), of the Atlantic coast of Spain and France, which also contained references to the British Isles.

2. A Greek version (extant) of what was said to be a report of a voyage down the Atlantic coast of Morocco and West Africa in the fifth century B.C. by the Carthaginian HANNO.

3. An account by NEARCHUS of his voyage from the Indus Delta to the Euphrates, made in 325 to 324 B.C. on the orders of ALEXANDER THE GREAT; substantial portions survive in the *Indica* by the historian Arrian.

4. The account (not extant) by PYTHEAS of his voyage toward the end of the fourth century B.C. along the Atlantic coast of Spain and Gaul and of his circumnavigation of Britain.

In the second group are included the following:

1. An extant periplus of the Mediterranean and Black Sea coasts compiled about 325 B.C. by an anonymous author, generally referred to as Pseudo-Scylax. Although thin on areas of the western Mediterranean under Carthaginian domination, the work is of good quality.

2. A periplus (not extant) of the Red Sea by Agatharchides, about 110 B.C.

3. An account of the Black Sea coasts in the form of a letter to the emperor Hadrian by Arrian (Flavius Arrianus), governor of Cappadocia and Pontus (northern Turkey), about A.D. 132. It is remarkable that the Roman government apparently had no such detailed account of the area in spite of nearly two centuries'

domination of it. Arrian's work is superior to any existing later work until the early nineteenth century.

4. The best-known and most interesting surviving periplus, the so-called *Periplus of the Erythrean Sea*, the sea's name here being used in its wide sense of the Indian Ocean. The date is not certain but is probably about the mid-first century A.D. The work describes the principal routes from Egypt to India and also the east coast of Africa as far as Zanzibar, with a wealth of detail for the ancient trader. The first section lists the harbors on the western coast of the Red Sea and southward down the east coast of Africa. There follows an account of the opposite coast of the Red Sea, the whole coast of Arabia as far as the Strait of Hormuz (Hormoz), and the Persian coast as far as the Indus Delta. Significantly we also learn that at an unspecified date, probably about 50 years earlier, the way to use the monsoons in the Indian Ocean had been discovered or revealed to the Greek sailors of

Egypt, who now dominated the rapidly growing trade between the Roman Empire and India. Ships left Egypt in July and could now sail directly from the exit of the Red Sea to the Indus Delta, to Barygaza (Broach), or to ports in south India. A large number of harbors along the Indian coast as far as Ganges Delta is given. The periplus also has something to say of Ceylon and knows (by hearsay) of the Malaysian Peninsula (thought of as an island) and perhaps of southern China. Substantial lists of imports and exports traded at various points are also provided. Recent archaeological evidence from India confirms the extent of its trade with the Roman Empire.

BIBLIOGRAPHY: Karl (Carolus) Müller (ed.), *Geographici Graeci Minores*, 2 vols., Paris, 1855–1861; W. H. Schoff, *The Periplus of the Erythrean Sea*, New York, 1912; R. E. M. Wheeler, *Rome beyond the Imperial Frontiers*, London, 1954.

B. H. Warmington

Persia

Persia, which was officially renamed Iran in 1935, was better known to Europeans of the ancient world than was most of the rest of Asia. The earliest Greek geographer, Hecataeus of Miletus (ca. 500 B.C.), whose work survives only in fragments, was sufficiently aware of the strength of the Persian empire to warn his fellow Ionians against rebellion, but his advice was ignored. HERODOTUS OF HALICARNASSUS, for whom the Persian Wars constituted the supreme event of human history, provided numerous details

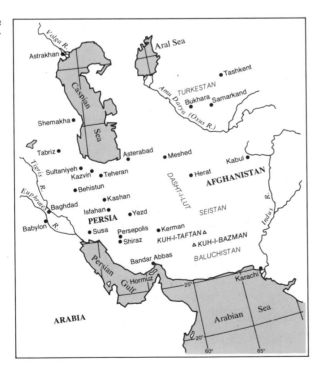

Persia and adjacent lands.

about the empire, such as a list of the twenty satrapies into which it was divided and a somewhat confused description of the royal road from Sardis to Susa, but the geographical content of his work is poor. He appears, for example, to have been ignorant of the existence of the Persian Gulf. Although the conquest of the Persian empire by ALEXANDER THE GREAT greatly increased contemporary knowledge of Persia, that many gaps and errors remained uncorrected for centuries can be seen in the inflated dimensions of the conception of Persia of PTOLEMY. During the centuries of Rome's decline several wars were fought with Persia, and there was some travel by missionaries, but little new geographical information was acquired.

Europe's relations with Persia received a strong if short-lived stimulus with the extension of Mongol rule over the country in the thirteenth century under Hulagu (d. 1265), who took the title Il Khan. Hulagu, whose mother and chief wife were Nestorian Christians, was well disposed toward Christianity. Moreover, he was an enemy of Islam and destroyed the Baghdad caliphate in 1258. Hulagu's successors, Abaga (r. 1265–1282) and Argun (r. 1284–1291), were also sympathetic to Christianity.

The result of the early Il Khans' favorable disposition toward Christianity was an influx of European diplomats, missionaries, and merchants to Tabriz, then the Persian capital. Various popes and monarchs, such as Edward I of England, sent emissaries to the Persian court, while Persian envoys were dispatched to Europe. The Il Khans encouraged trade with Europe, and a community of Italian merchants was soon established in Tabriz. Among the missionaries who preached in Persia and elsewhere in the Middle East during this period was an Italian Dominican, Ricold of Monte Croce (ca. 1242–1320), who described his experience in an *Itinerarium*. For a time Christian prospects in Persia appeared so promising that in 1318 Pope John XXII created the bishopric of Sultaniyeh, to which he appointed the Dominican Francis of Perugia. Other well-known travelers who visited Persia during the Mongol era were Marco POLO and Odoric of PORDENONE.

After the death of Argun, Christian influence in Persia began to wane, and the Il Khan Oljaitu (r. 1304–1316), though baptized a Christian, became a convert to Islam. Missionary efforts continued for a time but declined greatly after the extinction of the Mongol dynasty in 1335. Commercial and diplomatic relations between Persia and Europe also suffered a decline but did not disappear completely. In 1403, for example, a Spanish nobleman, Ruy González de Clavijo, was sent by Henry III of Castile to the court of Tamerlane, who had extended his sway over Persia. Clavijo visited Tabriz, Teheran, and Meshed (Mashhad) before meeting the redoubtable conqueror in Samarkand in 1404. Clavijo's account of his journey was first published in Seville in 1582. In the second half of the fifteenth century concern over Turkish expansionism led Venice to dispatch several merchants as envoys to the court of Uzun Ḥasan, who was also hostile to the Turks. The Venetian envoys—Caterino Zeno, to whom Uzun Ḥasan was related by marriage, Josafa Barbaro, and Ambrogio Contarini—were well received by the Persians, but no permanent alliance against the Turks was achieved.

The subjugation of Hormuz (Hormoz) by the Portuguese between 1507 and 1515 kindled the interest of other European powers in that celebrated entrepôt and the kingdom that lay beyond. The efforts of British traders to penetrate Persia began with the journey of Anthony Jenkinson (d. 1611) in 1562–1563. A member of the Muscovy Company, Jenkinson was instructed to make an attempt to enter into commercial relations with Persia by way of Russia. Having sailed down the Volga to Astrakhan, Jenkinson survived the dangers of navigation on the Caspian Sea and eventually made his way to the capital of Shah Tahmasp I at Kazvin (Qazvīn). He was unable to accomplish his mission at Kazvin, though he did obtain commercial privileges for the English from the friendly ruler of Shirvan. Jenkinson organized a second expedition to Persia in 1564. Its leader, Thomas Alcock, reached Kazvin but was later murdered near Shemakha. Four more expeditions were sent to Persia by the Muscovy Company between 1565 and 1580, but they too failed.

In the latter year John Newbery, a London merchant, left England for Hormuz to survey commercial prospects there. During the course of his journey he became the first Englishman to sail down the Euphrates and to visit Hormuz, Shiraz, and Isfahan (Esfahān); he returned to Europe by traveling from Persia across Asia Minor to Constantinople. Back in England, he agreed to lead a commercial expedition to the East and sailed for Syria in 1583 accompanied by Ralph Fitch and four other Englishmen. Having descended the Euphrates, they reached Hormuz, only to be detained by the Governor, who sent them to Goa, where they were released.

English conflict with Spain, which ruled Portugal from 1580 to 1640, furnished the background of the expedition led by Sir Anthony Sherley in 1598. This murky venture, concocted by Sherley and Venice, apparently aimed at striking a blow at the Portuguese in Hormuz. Once at Isfahan, then the Persian capital, Sherley agreed to serve as a Persian ambassador in Europe. His brother Robert, who had accompanied him to Persia, remained there until 1608, when he too was sent to Europe as an emissary of Shah Abbas I. The expulsion of the Portuguese from Hormuz in 1622 by an Anglo-Persian force was followed by the dispatch of an English embassy under Sir Dodmore Cotton in 1627. He was accompanied by Robert Sherley, who was still in Persian service. Both Sherley and Cotton soon died in Kazvin, but a member of their party, Thomas Herbert, traveled throughout Persia before returning to England and wrote a valuable *Description of the Persian Monarchy* (1634), also known as *A Relation of Some Yeares Travaile*.

Two other seventeenth-century travelers to Persia who wrote important accounts of their journeys were Pietro della Valle (1586–1652) and John Chardin (1643–1712). The former, a native of Rome, began his Eastern travels in 1614. He spent 6 years in Persia, where he visited Isfahan, Shiraz, and other cities as well as the ruins of Persepolis, which he was the first modern European to identify. After a trip to India, he returned to Rome in 1626 and wrote a narrative about his experiences in the form of letters to a friend. Chardin, a Frenchman by birth and a jeweler by profession, lived for several years in Persia in the 1660s and 1670s.

During the nineteenth century Persia was a victim of imperial rivalry between Great Britain and Russia, which vied for hegemony over the kingdom until an agreement assigning a sphere of influence to each power was signed in 1907: Russia was given the northern part of Persia, while Britain received a smaller portion in the southeast. Meanwhile, the exploration of Persia was furthered as a result of the powers' preoccupation with the country.

In the first two decades of the century several of the British officers who accompanied Sir John Malcolm on his diplomatic missions to Persia undertook journeys of exploration. These included John Macdonald Kinneir, later the envoy of the East India Company to Persia, who wrote *A Geographical Memoir of the Persian Empire* (1813) and *Journey through Asia Minor, Armenia, and Koordestan in the Years 1813 and 1814* (1818). Henry Pottinger and Charles Christie explored parts of eastern Persia and western Afghanistan between 1810 and 1812, and the former described his journey in *Travels in Beloochistan and Sinde* (1816).

Starting in 1821, James Baillie Fraser explored the region immediately south of the Caspian Sea. In 1830 Arthur Conolly, whose death in Bukhara in 1842 with Charles Stoddart would be a *cause célèbre*, crossed northern Persia from Tabriz to reach Herat in Afghanistan. Henry Rawlinson, who was a member of a British military mission to Persia in the 1830s, explored Susiana, Luristan, and Persian Kurdistan and was honored by the ROYAL GEOGRAPHICAL SOCIETY in 1840 for his journey in the last of these. It was during his stay in Persia that Rawlinson began the work for which he is chiefly remembered: decipherment of the cuneiform inscriptions hewn into the face of a cliff at Behistun (Bisutun).

The second half of the nineteenth century saw more systematic exploration of Persia by Europeans. In 1858–1859 a Russian scientific expedition headed by Nikolay Khanikov contributed greatly to knowledge of eastern Persia. A similar achievement in southern Persia was accomplished by members of the British boundary commission headed by Maj. Gen. Frederick Goldsmid, which fixed part of the boundary between Persia and Baluchistan and adjudicated Persian and Afghan claims to Seistan (Sistan, 1870–1872).

The single most distinguished European explorer of Persia was Sir Percy Molesworth Sykes (1867–1945). During his first journey (1893) he traveled from Asterabad (now Gorgan, or Gurgan) up the Atrek (Atrak) Valley to Meshed. From there he traversed the great central desert, the Lut, in a southwesterly direction to arrive at Kerman. In 1893–1894 he explored Persian Baluchistan, becoming the first European to climb the volcano of Kuh-i-Taftan and the extinct volcano of Kuh-i-Bazman. Starting in late 1894, he traveled through the interior of Persia from Resht (Rasht) to Teheran, Yezd (Yazd), Kerman, and Baluchistan, to the last two of which he had been named consul. During his fourth journey (1897–1901) Sykes systematically examined the districts of Seistan and Quain (Kain) in eastern Persia. His fifth journey (1902–1906) first took him from Bandar 'Abbas on the Persian Gulf to Kerman and adjacent areas. He then traveled to Meshed, to which he had been appointed as consul general and which became his base for the exploration of Khorasan (Khurasan). Sykes later explored the region between Meshed and Asterabad in northeastern Persia. He resumed his travels in Persia in 1916, when he was ordered to raise a force of Persian troops (South Persia Rifles), with whom he marched for hundreds of miles. Sykes's account of his early explorations, *Ten Thousand Miles in Persia*, was published in 1902; he was awarded a gold medal by the Royal Geographical Society the same year.

BIBLIOGRAPHY: D. W. Davies, *Elizabethans Errant: The Strange Fortunes of Sir Thomas Sherley and His Three Sons*, Ithaca, N.Y., 1967; Ronald Bishop Smith, *The First Age of the Portuguese Embassies, Navigations and Peregrinations in Persia (1507–1524)*, Bethesda, Md., 1970; Sir Percy Sykes, "A Fourth Journey in Persia, 1897–1901," *Geographical Journal*, vol. XIX, 1902, pp. 121–169; id., "A Fifth Journey in Persia," *Geographical Journal*, vol. XXVIII, 1906, pp. 425– 453, 560–587; id., *A History of Persia*, 2 vols., 3d ed., London, 1930; J. Oliver Thomson, *History of Ancient Geography*, Cambridge, England, 1948; Cecil Tragen, *Elizabethan Venture*, London, 1953.

Far right: Denouncing British imperialism and embracing Islam, Philby became the greatest explorer of Arabia. [Royal Geographical Society]

Philby, Harry St. John Bridger (1885–1960) English explorer. The birth in 1885 of Harry St. John Philby in then-exotic Ceylon seems to have played a role in his insatiable curiosity for travel. Philby's family was in straitened circumstances during his childhood, but because of his impressive intellectual gifts he was able to win scholarships to Westminister School and to Trinity College, Cambridge. Philby mastered classical and modern languages at Cambridge. During his stay there, with an energy reminiscent of that of Richard BURTON, he also studied Persian, Hindustani, and Urdu in preparation for his entrance to the Indian Civil Service in 1908. Philby remained in India until November 1915, when he joined the Mesopotamian Expeditionary Force in Iraq as a political officer. There he became aware of policy differences between the Indian government and the British Foreign Office regarding support for the Arab rebellion in 1916. In 1917 he was dispatched to Riyadh (Ar Riyād), capital of the central Arabian kingdom of the puritanical Wahhābī, to encourage ibn-Saud ('Abd-al-'Azīz ibn-'Abd-al-Rahman ibn-Su'ūd), the Wahhābī leader, to attack the pro-Turkish Rashīdī, leaders of the great Shammar tribal confederation in the northern Najd (Nejd) and fierce opponents of the Wahhābī. Philby was also to pacify ibn-Saud's fear of an attack by British-backed Sharīf Husayn of the Hejaz (Hijāz), leader of the Arab revolt.

Harry Philby's 1917 journey—from the Persian Gulf to Riyadh and from there to Jidda (Juddah)—had several important consequences. It established his fame as an explorer and won him the Founder's Medal of the ROYAL GEOGRAPHICAL SOCIETY, for he had become one of the few Europeans to have crossed central Arabia and only the second European to have done so from east to west, the other being George Forster Sadlier in 1819. His sojourn at Riyadh thrust him into the international aspects of the Arab revolt and initiated him into the intricacies of British Arab policy, which he was to oppose for the rest of his life. As a result, he abandoned his staunch conservatism and renounced the imperial British attitude toward the nonwhite peoples of the empire. Like T. E. Lawrence, Philby zestfully took up the cause of the Arabs. Most important, he met ibn-Saud, with whom his life was to be tied intimately for the next 30 years. In ibn-Saud Philby found his life's work. In 1924, after 3 years of service in Iraq and Jordan, Philby proceeded to Saudi Arabia to attach his destiny to the rising fortunes of ibn-Saud. Philby's biographer, Elizabeth Monroe, calls the next 5 years of his life "the lean ones." Not yet a Muslim and not firmly in the confidence of ibn-Saud, Philby undertook a series of commercial ventures, none of which were successful, to remain solvent. This period also demonstrates

Philby's contradictory views. He was at once the champion of Arab independence, an anti-imperialist, a lover of unspoiled Arabia, and an agent for Western capitalists seeking mining, oil, and automobile concessions. Thus Philby sought to introduce to Arabia the very mechanized life of the West with which he felt so uncomfortable.

Philby's luck changed in 1930, when for material reasons and in the hope of obtaining ibn-Saud's permission to cross the Rub 'al Khālī, he became a Muslim. His conversion to Islam proved to be the gateway to the Rub 'al Khālī, which he crossed in 1932. By a coincidence of fortune the journey of Bertram Thomas from Salālah in Dhufar to Doha (Ad Dawhah) in Qatar was to rob him of being acclaimed the first European to cross the great desert. This was in spite of the fact that his journey was through the much more arduous western half of the Rub 'al Khālī and yielded significantly more geographical data than Thomas's traverse did. Philby was to continue his exploration and mapping of Saudi Arabia, in the new mode of Arabian travel, the automobile, for the next 20 years. In the process he provided an array of geographical data which was to be superseded only by the introduction of the airplane and the huge scientific apparatuses of the oil exploration companies. Philby represented a transition between the traditional means of travel, the camel, and the modern, the airplane.

Philby's fame as a traveler would have sufficed to secure his place in history. But his long residence in Riyadh, his intimacy with ibn-Saud and his sons during the crucial period of consolidation of the Saudi dynasty, and his prolific pen earned him the title of the first European historian of twentieth-century Arabia. In addition, he amassed large collections of birds, mammals, moths, snakes, plants, rocks, and fossils which were eventually located in several British and American museums. He introduced, literally single-handedly, Europe to twentieth-century Arabia. Perhaps these efforts explain partially his last words before dying: "I am bored." The inscription on his tombstone reads: "Greatest of Arabian Explorers." After that, what was left?

BIBLIOGRAPHY: Elizabeth Monroe, *Philby of Arabia*, London, 1973; Harry St. John Philby, *Arabian Highlands*, Ithaca, N.Y., 1952; id., *Arabian Jubilee*, New York, 1952; id., *The Empty Quarter*, London, 1933; id., *The Heart of Arabia*, 2 vols., London, 1922.

Robert W. Olson

Pike, Zebulon Montgomery **(1779–1813)** American soldier and explorer. Mystery still shrouds the explorations led by Zebulon Pike of New Jersey in 1805–1806 and 1806–1807. It was his fortune or misfortune to become involved in westward expeditions directed by the notorious Gen. James Wilkinson. Because writers have tied Wilkinson to Aaron Burr and a host of separatist schemes in the trans-Mississippi West, many have associated Pike and Wilkinson as partners in early-nineteenth-century frontier conspiracies. No

one has proved Pike's participation in expeditions allegedly sent to spy on the Spanish in the Southwest, but there remain questions about whether Pike was indeed a "lost" explorer. It seems safe to conclude that he served as an unofficial arm of a government in Washington which wanted to stretch American interests across the Mississippi River. Whether by design or by accident, Pike's adventures joined those of Meriwether LEWIS and William CLARK in stimulating the westward expansion of the United States.

Pike's first expedition west was undertaken in 1805, when as a lieutenant in the U.S. Army he received orders from Wilkinson to find the headwaters of the Mississippi River. From St. Louis he was to explore the upper valley area, conciliate the Indians, and choose sites for fur and military posts. In a sense he was to encourage execution of Jay's Treaty of 1794, which called on the British to evacuate the Old Northwest. Pike's diary records that on August 9 he and twenty companions left St. Louis in a keelboat with 4 months' provisions.

The trip north passed without incident. In less than 2 weeks, the party approached the De Moyen Rapids (near present Keokuk, Iowa), where Pike met a delegation of Sac Indians and assured them of American friendship. A few days later the expedition saw the lead mines at the present site of Dubuque and then passed the village of Prairie du Chien. In late September the party stopped at the mouth of the Minnesota River, where Pike bought two tracts of land from the Sioux, one near present Minneapolis and the other at the mouth of the St. Croix River, as future sites for government posts.

In early December Pike and twelve others pushed northward to locate the Mississippi's headwaters. At first traveling on a pirogue and then forced to sled through the ice and snow-covered regions of Minnesota, they came across two British trading posts about a month later, on Red Cedar Lake and at Sandy Lake (Big Sandy Lake). The second post, belonging to the North West Fur Company, had thrived there for 12 years. Especially disturbing was the fact that the farther north Pike went, the more posts he found flying the Union Jack. Pike's mission seemed complete when he concluded (erroneously) that Leech Lake was the major source of the Mississippi River. The party then began the slow journey home

Hardly had Pike returned to St. Louis when General Wilkinson directed him to head an expedition to the Southwest—the venture which has caused unending controversy about motive. Pike's known orders were to locate the source of the Arkansas River, secure the return of a group of Osage Indian captives, settle problems between the Osage and Kansas tribes, and establish communications and perhaps a treaty with the Comanches. But many writers believe that Pike had secret instructions from Wilkinson to move on to Santa Fe and make a reconnaissance of Spanish strength in the region of New Mexico. In July 1806 Lieutenant Pike and twenty-three men, mostly mili-

Zebulon Montgomery Pike's involvement with the conspirator James Wilkinson has never been satisfactorily explained. Whatever his motives were, his explorations contributed significantly to the expansion of the American West. [Library of Congress]

tary and including Wilkinson's son, also a lieutenant, and Dr. John Robinson, a surgeon-naturalist who claimed he had business in Santa Fe, set out from Fort Belle Fontaine near St. Louis to push westward up the Missouri and Osage Rivers by keelboat and then travel by horseback across the plains of Kansas and Colorado. They were to follow the Arkansas River to its source, turn south to the Red, and continue along it to the Mississippi.

After delivering the Osage refugees to their home near the eastern boundary of present Kansas, the party turned northward and by late September was at the Pawnee villages above the Republican River in southern Nebraska. There Pike learned that a Spanish force of 600 men from New Mexico was intent on ending his penetration of the vaguely defined Spanish hinterland. Pike and his men next rode south until they

reached the great bend of the Arkansas River in Kansas. A small party of six men, led by young Wilkinson, made two canoes and proceeded down the river through Kansas and Oklahoma to its junction with the Mississippi in Arkansas, while Pike and the others moved across the Plains toward the Rockies.

Despite ample warning that it was too late in the year to scale the mountains, Pike decided to trudge on. By mid-November his party of seventeen men caught sight of the Rockies and about a week later reached the present site of Pueblo, Colorado. Pike and three companions then set out toward the peak now named for him. But the seemingly short trek was an illusion. Well into the third day, the cotton-clad, shivering men had reached only a minor summit to the south, the identity of which is not certain.

The party then turned south, ostensibly to explore

Zebulon Pike's expeditions, 1805–1807.

Pike's Peak and Colorado City (now in Colorado Springs), 1866. Pike spent 3 days trying to reach and climb this mountain, but freezing temperatures forced him to content himself with viewing it from afar. [Library of Congress]

the upper reaches of the Arkansas River. The men moved up the Arkansas River to the mouth of the Royal Gorge, then north to the South Platte, and eventually back to the upper Arkansas. At their Royal Gorge campsite (sometimes called the Grand Canyon of the Arkansas River) in January 1807, they built a log shelter on Fountain Creek, tributary of the upper Arkansas, and left two men, the exhausted horses, and part of the baggage. The remaining members of the expedition, led by Pike, crossed the high ranges of the Sangre de Cristo Mountains on foot and moved through the San Luis Valley to construct a stockade near the present southern boundary of Colorado. The 2-week trek through the mountains had taken a heavy toll. Six men lay crippled with gangrene, while two were so frostbitten that they lost their feet.

The rest of the Southwestern trip remains the source of debate. Though Pike later officially declared that he was certain he was on a headwater of the Red River, there are many indications that he knew he actually was on the upper Rio Grande, in Spanish territory. He was soon arrested by Spanish officials, and the next chapter in his life constitutes an odyssey which found him in Santa Fe, Albuquerque, El Paso, Chihuahua, San Antonio, Nacogdoches, and Natchitoches. The American explorer apparently created enough doubt of his guilt that his captors considered prudence the wisest course, and in early July 1807, after several months of questioning, he was released on the American side of the border. Though supposedly stripped of notes and maps during his incarceration, he reconstructed from memory much of what he had heard and seen. Besides, the Spanish had not discovered a private set of papers hidden in the barrels of his guns.

Pike's report had great impact on United States expansion beyond the Mississippi River. Entitled *An Account of Expeditions to the Sources of the Missis-*

sippi and through the Western Parts of Louisiana, it was published in 1810; French, German, and Dutch editions quickly followed. In addition to furnishing maps and information on Spanish influence in the area, Pike's work combined with that of Lewis and Clark and other explorers to attract national attention and prevent special interests from dominating these Western reaches. Yet the real significance of Pike's second journey lies in his dismal description of the Plains which, some historians argue, originated the myth of the Great American Desert.

Pike would not see the results of his labors, for he died in the U.S. Army's attack on York (Toronto) in April 1813 during the War of 1812. The great westward movement began later, gold was discovered near Denver in 1850, and in less than a decade there poured out of Kansas and Missouri wagons which carried these words painted on their covers: "Pike's Peak or Bust!"

BIBLIOGRAPHY: Elliot Coues, *The Expeditions of Zebulon Montgomery Pike*, 3 vols., New York, 1895; William H. Goetzmann, *Exploration and Empire: The Explorer and the Scientist in the Winning of the American West*, New York, 1966; W. Eugene Hollon, *The Lost Pathfinder: Zebulon Montgomery Pike*, Norman, Okla., 1949; Donald Jackson (ed.), *The Journals of Zebulon Montgomery Pike*, 2 vols., Norman, Okla., 1966.

Howard Jones

***Pinzón, Vicente Yáñez** (ca. 1463–1514)* Spanish navigator and explorer. A native of Palos, Vicente Yáñez was the younger brother of Martín Alonso Pinzón, who commanded the *Pinta* on the first voyage of Christopher COLUMBUS. Vicente Yáñez commanded the *Niña* and always remained loyal to Columbus, in contrast to his brother, who deserted Columbus for several weeks. In 1495 Vicente Yáñez was authorized to make another voyage but apparently it did not take place.

Pinzón's next voyage began in November 1499, when he sailed from Palos with four caravels. After taking on supplies in the Cape Verde Islands, he steered south-southwest and on January 20 or 26, 1500, landed in northeastern Brazil at a cape which he called Santa María de la Consolación and which is usually identified with Cabo Santo Agostinho, located near Recife. Pinzón therefore anticipated Pedro Álvares CABRAL in the discovery of Brazil by 3 months, though the Spaniard's claim is disputed by Portuguese and Brazilian historians. From his first landfall in Brazil Pinzón sailed west and northwest toward the Gulf of Paria, making stops at various places along the way. As the Spaniards passed the mouth of the Amazon River, they found fresh water at a distance of 30 leagues from the coast. Pinzón ascended the river, which he called the Freshwater Sea, for 20 or 30 leagues. From the Gulf of Paria Pinzón sailed to Hispaniola and the Bahamas, losing two caravels near Crooked Island. He arrived in Palos on September 9, 1500.

Pinzón returned to South America between 1502 and 1504, sailing first to the Gulf of Paria and then eastward and southward to a point near Cabo de São Roque in Brazil. By July 1504 he was in Hispaniola, where he met Columbus, who had recently been rescued from Jamaica. Two more voyages by Pinzón, both in association with Juan de SOLÍS, are recorded, but very little is known about either of them. The first (1506), as described by Peter Martyr, took them to the section of the Central American coast explored by Columbus on his fourth voyage. The objective of the second, which began in 1508, was the discovery of an interoceanic strait.

BIBLIOGRAPHY: James Roxburgh McClymont, *Vicente Añes Pinçon*, London, 1916; Samuel Eliot Morison, *The European Discovery of America: The Southern Voyages, A.D. 1492–1616*, New York, 1974.

More conqueror than explorer, Francisco Pizarro established Spanish hegemony in Peru (1531–1533) by slaughtering the Incas and appropriating their gold.

Pizarro, Francisco (ca. 1478–1541) Spanish explorer and conqueror. Born in Trujillo in Extremadura, Pizarro was the illegitimate son of a royal captain of infantry and a farmer's daughter. Little can be said with certainty about his early life, though it is known that he remained illiterate and was never able to manage more than an awkward rubric. He went to the Indies in 1502 in the fleet of Nicolás de Ovando, governor of Hispaniola, and took part in the expedition of Alonso de OJEDA to the Gulf of Urabá 7 years later. When Ojeda returned to Hispaniola to obtain supplies, he left Pizarro in charge of the Spanish settlement on the Gulf of Urabá, and Pizarro was among the members of the expedition who eventually moved to the Isthmus of Panama. Pizarro's name came after that of Vasco Núñez de BALBOA on the list of those who saw the South Sea (Pacific Ocean) for the first time in 1513. It was Pizarro who arrested Balboa in 1518.

By 1524 Pizarro was one of the most prominent men in Panama. In that year he received permission from the governor of Panama, Pedro Arias de ÁVILA (Pedrarias), to explore and conquer to the south, where a rich kingdom called Birú was believed to be located. Associated with Pizarro in this venture were Diego de ALMAGRO, a priest, Hernando de Luque, and Pedrarias himself. An expedition in 1524 to the Pacific Coast of modern Colombia brought only a meager return, but Pizarro and Almagro made a second attempt between 1526 and 1528. On this occasion Pizarro and his companions sailed as far south as Santa in modern Peru and from time to time went ashore, where, as at the city of Tumbes, they found increasing evidence of a high native civilization. After returning to Panama with some gold, llamas, and two Indian boys who were to be taught Spanish, Pizarro went to Spain, where he obtained a royal capitulation giving him the right to conquer Peru and the governorship of the province. For Almagro he obtained only the title of commandant of Tumbes. Pizarro returned to Panama in 1530 with approximately 125 new recruits, including four half brothers. Although Almagro was unhappy over the fact that he had been relegated to an inferior position, he was mollified by Pizarro's promises of future honors and consented to continue the partnership. He remained behind in Panama to organize reinforcements while Pizarro left for Peru around early January 1531 with about 180 men and 30 horses.

Landing on the coast of modern Ecuador, the Spaniards marched to a large town called Coaque, where they found gold and silver ornaments, which were sent to Panama. Their strength augmented by new recruits from Panama and Nicaragua, among them Sebastián de BENALCÁZAR, the Spaniards continued down the coast until they reached Puná Island in the Gulf of Guayaquil. Here they were joined by another group of reinforcements led by Hernando de SOTO. In February 1532 Pizarro and his followers crossed to the mainland and, after several weeks in Tumbes, continued southward for about 100 miles (161 kilometers) until they reached a site near the sea considered suitable for a settlement, which they called San Miguel de Piura. Having heard that the Inca emperor, Atahuallpa, was in the highland city of Cajamarca, Pizarro arrived there on November 15, 1532, to find the central square deserted. At the invitation of Pizarro, Atahuallpa, who was encamped nearby with a large army, entered the city the following day and was taken captive. He attempted to win his freedom, or at least preserve his life, by amassing an immense treasure of gold and silver for the Spaniards, but to no avail, for he was executed in July 1533.

With the capture of Cuzco, the Inca capital, in November 1533, the Spanish conquest was complete, though the Spaniards would be faced with a serious Indian uprising in 1536–1537. On January 6, 1535, Pizarro founded a capital for the new colony on the Rímac River; initially called the City of the Kings, it soon became known as Lima through corruption of the word Rímac. Although Pizarro's days as an ex-

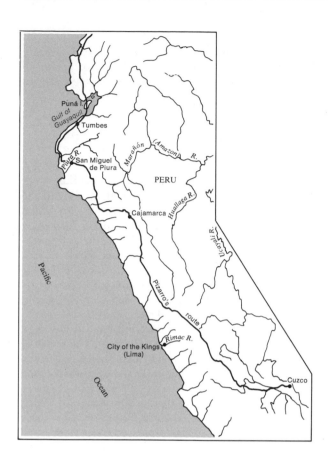

*Far left:
Francisco Pizarro's
route to Cuzco,
1532–1533.*

plorer were over, Peru now became the base for numerous South American expeditions, such as that of Almagro to Chile and those of Benalcázar to the north. The rivalry between Pizarro and Almagro, who had arrived in Cajamarca soon after the seizure of Atahuallpa, led to a civil war in the course of which Almagro was executed. On June 26, 1541, Pizarro was assassinated in Lima by partisans of Almagro's half-Indian son Don Diego, known as the Lad.

BIBLIOGRAPHY: John Hemming, *The Conquest of the Incas*, New York, 1970; James Lockhart, *The Men of Cajamarca*, Austin, Tex., 1972; Rubén Vargas Ugarte, *Historia general del Perú: I: El descubrimiento y la conquista (1524–1550)*, Lima, 1971.

Pizarro, Gonzalo *(ca. 1513–1548)* Spanish explorer and conqueror. The youngest of the four half brothers of Francisco PIZARRO, Gonzalo was of illegitimate birth but was recognized by his father, the royal captain of infantry Gonzalo Pizarro. The younger Gonzalo traveled to the Indies in 1530 with Francisco and took part in the conquest of Peru. Having been named governor of Quito in 1539, Gonzalo at once began to lay plans for an expedition to investigate reports of a "cinnamon tree" in the forests east of the Andes and of a rich kingdom located beyond the forests. At its start the expedition, which got under way in February 1541, comprised approximately 200 Spaniards, 4000 Indians, and thousands of dogs, swine, and llamas. Francisco de ORELLANA, the lieutenant governor of Guayaquil, joined the expedition later and was named second-in-command.

During the first leg of the expedition Pizarro and his followers crossed the Andes, then halted in a valley called Zumaque, or Zumaco, about 60 leagues from Quito. Taking some seventy men, Pizarro embarked on a search for the cinnamon tree in the forest, using torture to extract information from the local Indians. Some cinnamon trees were found, but Pizarro quickly concluded that they were of little value. He still had hopes of finding the golden kingdom and dispatched a party of fifty men led by the campmaster to investigate. The latter returned 2 weeks later to report that he had located a great river. This river was the Coca, which flows into the Napo, a major tributary of the Amazon. The entire expedition thereupon moved to the banks of the Coca and followed its course both along the shore and in canoes. There was much suffering, however, because of the lack of food since the supplies brought from Quito had been exhausted. When the Spaniards heard reports of another important river near which there was ample food, Orellana obtained permission from Pizarro to sail to the river for provisions. Orellana left the main party on December 26, 1541, but was not heard from again. After waiting in vain for Orellana, Pizarro sent out parties by canoe to search for food. One of them, led by Gonzalo Díaz de Pineda, reached the confluence of the Coca and Napo Rivers and, after sailing up the latter, found a large plantation of manioc. Their hunger appeased, Pizarro and his followers began the arduous return journey, entering Quito in August 1542.

Upon his arrival in Quito, Pizarro learned that Francisco Pizarro had been murdered in 1541 and that although the latter had named him his successor in his will, Peru was being governed by a royal appointee. Pizarro's belief that the governorship of Peru rightly belonged to him eventually led him to rebel unsuccessfully against the crown, and he was executed after his defeat.

BIBLIOGRAPHY: Pedro Cieza de León, *The War of Chupas*, tr. and ed. by Clements R. Markham, Hakluyt Society, 2d ser., no. 42, London, 1918; James Lockhart, *The Men of Cajamarca*, Austin, Tex., 1972; Philip Ainsworth Means, "Gonzalo Pizarro and Francisco de Orellana," *Hispanic American Historical Review*, vol. XIV, no. 3, August 1934, pp. 275–295.

Pliny *(full Latin name: Gaius Plinius Secundus; A.D. 23–79)* Roman encyclopedist. The Elder Pliny (so called to distinguish him from his nephew) was a native of Comum (Como) and held a number of posts in the Roman imperial administration in Spain, Gaul, and elsewhere. His leisure was spent in studying and writing. His major surviving work is the *Natural History (Naturalis historia)* in thirty-seven books, completed in A.D. 77. This is a compilation of facts or supposed facts from earlier writers on various sciences as understood in antiquity, including geography. Pliny's enormous energy and curiosity to some extent compensate for his frequently careless use of his sources and his lack of critical standards and of the broader conceptions of Eratosthenes (ca. 275–194 B.C.) and STRABO. Some of his material does not survive elsewhere, however, and he provides some data derived from recent Roman work. He is more interested in the political geography of the Roman Empire than in giving general geographical descriptions even of areas known to him and lacks interest in indigenous peoples. He does not attempt to locate places by latitude and longitude but does include a number of measurements of distance, derived from his sources. Pliny accepted the arguments of Eratosthenes and Hipparchus (ca. 190–126 B.C.) for the correct shape of the globe and has figures for the gradual lengthening of the solstitial day north of the equator.

The geographical books of the *Natural History* are Books 3 to 6, although Book 2, concerning the universe in general with a certain amount of astronomical information, should perhaps be included under this heading. Book 3 covers the Mediterranean world west of the Adriatic. From the point of view of the political geography of the Roman Empire the section on Spain is the most informative and up to date, but here as elsewhere physical geography is negligible; unlike many other writers, Pliny does, however, correctly describe the direction of the Pyrenees. Much of the information on Gaul is no more recent than Julius Caesar's conquest more than a century earlier. Pliny's geographical knowledge of the area between the Alps and the Danube is far in advance of that of Greek sources, but he has little to say of areas north of the Danube. Book 4 contains much uncritical compilation from sources as far back as Homer not only on Greece but also on northern and eastern Europe. It is surprising to find Pliny extremely ignorant about Germany (he had written on Rome's wars with the German tribes), but he has a notion of the configuration of modern Denmark and is the first writer to use the name Scandinavia, which he thinks of as an island. Book 5 on Asia is better and has the fullest account of the Euphrates and Tigris in any ancient author. Pliny still thinks of the Caspian as a gulf of the ocean in spite of recent Roman campaigns in Armenia, but he has an interesting notice of the overland trade route from India to the Caspian and on to the Black Sea. In Book 6 his material on north India is from earlier writers, but he has recent material on south India and the Indian trade including the use of the monsoon (see PERIPLUS). He claims to describe Ceylon on the basis of information from ambassadors to Rome, but the topographical details are very poor, and, like most authors, he vastly exaggerates its size. He has nothing on East Africa to match the almost-contemporary *Periplus of the Erythrean Sea.* On the rest of Africa he owed much to Juba II, the scholar-king of Mauretania, and probably derived from him our first reference to the "Nigris" River, described as being like the Nile and separating Africa (that is, the Mahgreb) from Ethiopia (trans-Saharan Africa). This seems to refer to a large river south of the Sahara and is generally taken to indicate the modern Niger. The reference was important in the history of early modern exploration of West Africa. Pliny perished in the great eruption of Vesuvius in A.D. 79, which he had gone to observe at close hand.

BIBLIOGRAPHY: Pliny, *Natural History,* Loeb Classical Library ed., 10 vols., London and Cambridge, Mass., 1938–1963; J. O. Thomson, *History of Ancient Geography,* Cambridge, England, 1948.

B. H. Warmington

Polo, Marco *(ca. 1254–1324)* Medieval traveler to the Far East. In 1271 young Marco, in the company of his father, Nicolò Polo, and his uncle Maffeo, both merchants, set forth from his native Venice on a remarkable journey to Asia. They first proceeded by ship to the Levantine coast, but the ultimate destination of these three travelers was the far-distant court of the Mongol ruler Khubilai (Kublai) Khan (r. 1260–1294), emperor of China and one of the most famous medieval monarchs in the Far East. Both Nicolò Polo and his brother Maffeo had previously visited the realm of the Great Khan and had been favorably received by the Mongol ruler in his capital city of Cambaluc, the modern Peking.

The three Polos began their land journey to China from the city of Acre ('Akko) in Palestine. They bore with them letters and gifts from the recently elected pontiff, Gregory X (Teobaldo Visconti), and they were accompanied by two learned Dominicans, Nicolas of Vicenza and William of Tripoli. Before they had journeyed far, however, the two friars abandoned their intention of proceeding to China and under the protection of the Knights Templars returned to the seacoast. Meanwhile, the Polos continued their journey. Although the exact route which they took is not known, it is clear that they made use of caravan trails through Mesopotamia, Persia, and Afghanistan, proceeding across the plateau of Central Asia, and traversed the great Gobi Desert. Finally they arrived at Shangtu, the summer residence of Khubilai Khan. The long, difficult, and sometimes dangerous journey had taken approximately 3½ years to complete.

At the Mongolian court the Venetian travelers were honorably and courteously received. Young Marco found favor in the eyes of the Great Khan, who employed this intelligent, discreet, and observant Westerner in various important missions which afforded him the opportunity to travel extensively in the vast Mongol empire. His travels also included parts of India and of Burma. Marco Polo was deeply impressed with the splendor of the imperial court and with the many marvels and curiosities which he encountered in the dominions of Khubilai Khan. The Venetian noted with keen interest the number and the richness of Chinese cities and the extensive nature of the trading operations in which they were engaged. For 17 years Marco Polo faithfully served the Great Khan.

Not until 1292 did the Polos (Marco, Nicolò, and Maffeo) receive a somewhat reluctantly granted permission to begin their return journey to the West. They were chosen as part of an imposing escort for a young Mongolian maiden named Cocachin who had been selected as the bride of Arghun, the khan of Persia and grandnephew of Khubilai Khan. Because the overland route to Persia was imperiled by war, the escort party took the long sea journey which carried them along the shores of southern China, Burma, and India. The fleet also made a long stay at various ports on the island of Sumatra. Because of the difficult and perilous nature of this journey a number of the suite died on the way. This homeward sea journey admirably supplemented the long land journey which the Polos had undertaken years before. When the escort party finally arrived in Persia, Khan Arghun was already dead. Consequently the lady Cocachin later married Ghazan, the son of Arghun. In a leisurely manner the Polos continued their homeward journey northward, tarrying for several months at Tabriz, then proceeding to the port of Trebizond (Trabzon) on the Black Sea. There they took a vessel to Constantinople and journeyed by way of the Mediterranean Sea to Venice, arriving there toward the end of 1295. Not long after returning home Marco Polo became involved in a naval war which had broken out between those two great Italian commercial rivals, Venice and Genoa. During this conflict Marco Polo was taken prisoner, probably in some unrecorded clash between the armed galleys of the two city-states. Marco Polo remained a war prisoner until his release following the conclusion of a peace between Venice and Genoa in May 1299.

As a war prisoner Marco Polo had much time on his hands, which he put to good use by dictating an account of his travels to a fellow prisoner named Rustichello (Rusticiano) of Pisa, a romance writer of some distinction at that time. The unusual partnership which developed between the Venetian merchant adventurer and the professional writer of romances resulted in the appearance of one of the world's most famous travel books. During the Renaissance this book became one of the principal sources of information about the Far East and particularly Cathay, as China was then called. Never before had so much valuable information concerning the flora, fauna, geography, sociology, and politics of Asia been gathered together by one man. Marco Polo's careful observations proved to be of great value to later generations of ethnologists and anthropologists, and in his own time this detailed account of his travels captured the imagination and attention of Europe, especially of Mediterranean Europe. Marco Polo was the first European traveler to reveal China in all its vastness and to provide some definite information about the countries on its borders.

Few details are known of Marco Polo's life in Ven-

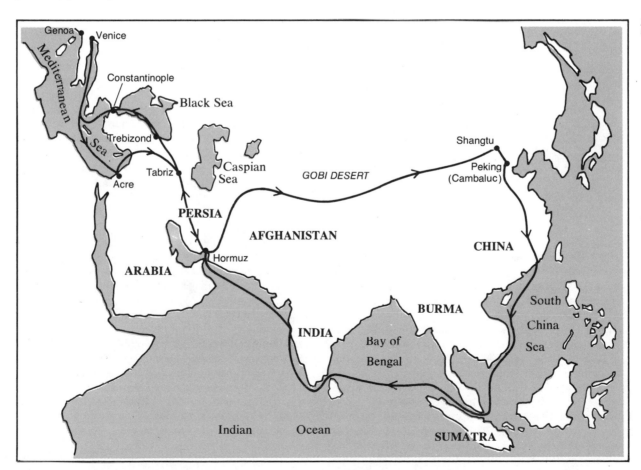

Marco Polo's travels.

Frontispiece of Il
milione, the record
of Marco Polo's
travels as told to a
fellow prisoner in
Genoa around 1299.
Polo is the small
figure in the top left-
hand corner.

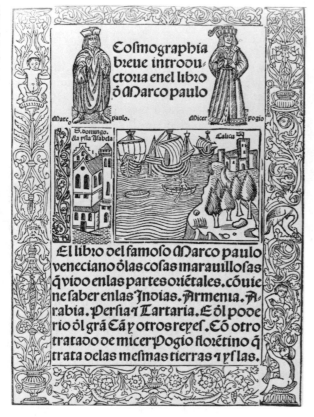

ice after his release from captivity. When he died in January 1324, he left a wife and three daughters. In accordance with the wishes expressed in his will he was buried beside his father in the Church of San Lorenzo.

BIBLIOGRAPHY: Henry H. Hart, *Venetian Adventurer: Being an Account of the Life and Times and of the Book of Messer Marco Polo,* Stanford, Calif., 1941; Arthur C. Moule and Paul Pelliot (eds. and trs.), *The Description of the World,* London, 1938; Leonard Olschki, *Marco Polo's Asia: An Introduction to His "Description of the World" called "Il milione,"* Berkeley, Calif., 1960; Sir Henry Yule (ed. and tr.), *The Book of Ser Marco Polo, the Venetian, Concerning the Kingdoms and Marvels of the East,* 3d ed., rev. by Henri Cordier, 2 vols., London, 1903.

Bernerd C. Weber

Ponce de León, Juan (ca. 1474–1521) Spanish explorer, best known for his discovery of Florida. Ponce de León was born in Santervás del Campo in the province of Valladolid. Virtually nothing is known about his early life except that he came from a distinguished family. He probably sailed to the New World with Christopher COLUMBUS in 1493 and settled in Hispaniola. In 1504 he took part in a campaign against the Indians of the province of Higüey, of which he was appointed governor. In 1508 he began the settlement of the island of San Juan de Borinquen (Puerto Rico), which had been discovered by Columbus on his second voyage, and was named governor by King Ferdinand the following year. However, he was deprived of this position in 1511 when the King recognized the viceregal claims of Diego Columbus, Christopher's son, including the right to make all appointments in the New World. To compensate Ponce de León for his loss, in 1512 the King authorized him to seek out and occupy the island of Bimini. Although a few contemporary writers spoke of an island north of Cuba called Boyuca or Bimini where there was a fountain of youth, there is no real evidence that Ponce de León hoped to find such a fountain except for the assertions of the historians Gonzalo Fernández de Oviedo and Antonio de Herrera. Indeed, very few firsthand documents about any aspect of Ponce de León's two voyages to Florida have been unearthed.

Ponce de León set out from the port of San Germán in Puerto Rico on March 3, 1513, with three ships, *Santa María de la Consolación, Santiago,* and *San Cristóbal.* Sailing to the northwest, the ships passed the Turks and Caicos Islands and on March 14 stopped at the island of Guanahaní (San Salvador), site of Columbus's first landfall in 1492. The voyage was resumed a few days later, and a northwesterly course was maintained until April 2, when the party anchored near what they thought was an island. They called it La Florida because of its many fresh groves and even terrain and because it was the season of Easter (Pascua Florida). The following day Ponce de León took possession of the place. The site of his first Florida landfall was probably in the vicinity of St. Augustine or the inlet near Daytona Beach that now bears his name.

On April 9 the party sailed south but ran into a current stronger than the wind: the Gulf Stream, a discovery as important as that of Florida because it opened the possibility of a new sea route from the West Indies to Spain. When Ponce de León attempted to land, the Indians proved unfriendly, but the Spaniards were able to gather wood and water at a river they called the Santa Cruz (Jupiter Inlet). On May 8 they rounded what they called the Cape of Currents; they then skirted the Florida Keys and turned into the Gulf of Mexico, sailing north to Charlotte Harbor or to the mouth of the Caloosahatchee River. After heading south again, they arrived on June 21 at some islands which they named after the turtles they captured there in large numbers (the Dry Tortugas). Sailing to the southwest, they sighted land on June 26 and went ashore a few days later. Most believed themselves to be in Cuba, but it is possible that they had reached the northern coast of Yucatán.

After returning to Puerto Rico in October, Ponce de León remained deeply involved in the affairs of the island, being named captain general on September 27, 1514. It was not until February 1521 that he was able to sail once more to Florida, where he hoped to establish a colony. However, after landing on Sanibel Island near the mouth of the Caloosahatchee, he was wounded by an Indian arrow. He was taken to Havana to recuperate but died there in July 1521.

BIBLIOGRAPHY: Edward W. Lawson, *The Discovery of Florida and Its Discoverer Juan Ponce de León,* St. Augustine, Fla., 1946; Samuel

Eliot Morison, *The European Discovery of America: The Southern Voyages, A.D. 1492–1616*, New York, 1974; Vicente Murga Sanz, *Juan Ponce de León*, 2d ed. rev., Barcelona, 1971.

Pordenone, Odoric of *(ca. 1265–1331)* Franciscan missionary and explorer in the Far East. His career as a missionary began in 1296 and continued virtually to the end of his life. With other Franciscans he carried on missionary work in south Russia in the Mongol khanate of Kipchak. In 1314 he sailed from Venice for the Near East and did missionary work in Constantinople, Trebizond (Trabzon), and Tabriz. Eight years later this zealous missionary set out with an Irish companion, Friar James, for the Far East to join Archbishop John of Monte Corvino in Cathay. He traveled through Persia and Iraq and sailed from Hormuz (Hormoz) to India.

Friar Odoric visited both the Malabar and the Coromandel coasts of India and the islands of Ceylon, Sumatra, Java, and possibly Borneo. From Ceylon he took a ship to Canton and arrived at this southern Chinese port during the latter part of 1324. Traveling leisurely northward, he visited various cities on the way and finally arrived at Cambaluc (modern Peking) in 1325. Shortly before John of Monte Corvino's death in 1328 he was commissioned to return to Europe to recruit new missionaries for China.

On his return journey to the West, Friar Odoric traveled through Sinkiang Province to Chinese Turkestan, then around the Caspian Sea to Persia, Iraq, Syria, and possibly Palestine. He reached Venice at the close of the year 1329 or early 1330. The journal of his travels was dictated in the Italian city of Udine in 1330. This work was extensively plagiarized in the popular *Travels of Sir John Mandeville*. Among Roman Catholics Friar Odoric is venerated as a patron of Christian missions and of long-distance travelers. His cult was approved by Pope Benedict XIV in July 1755.

BIBLIOGRAPHY: Manuel Komroff (ed.), *Contemporaries of Marco Polo*, New York, 1928.

Bernerd C. Weber

Poyarkov, Vasily Danilovich *(fl. mid-seventeenth century)* Russian explorer and the first European to travel on the Amur River. In 1643 Poyarkov was named to head a military detachment which was ordered to go from Yakutsk to the Shilka River to collect fur tribute, check reports of precious-metal deposits and agricultural prospects, see whether the Shilka offered a route to China, subdue the inhabitants of the Amur region, and secure it for Russia by building forts. He led his party up the Aldan River, its right tributary, the Uchur, and the Gonam. Leaving some of his men in a winter camp on the Gonam, he crossed the mountains with a detachment of ninety men, discovered the Zeya, a tributary of the Amur, and spent the winter on it. In the spring of 1644 the detachment left on the Gonam arrived with supplies, and the party

went down the Zeya to the Amur and along that river. Mistreatment had aroused the hostility of the natives, so that the Russians had to fight wherever they went.

In the summer of 1645, when the mouth of the Amur was free of ice, they sailed into the Sea of Okhotsk, sighting the northwest shore of Sakhalin, and by way of the Gulf of Sakhalin (Sakhalinsky Zaliv) and the western part of the Sea of Okhotsk reached the Ulya River, already known to the Russians after Ivan Moskvitin's 1639 expedition to the Pacific. They wintered on the Ulya and in the early spring of 1646 went up the river on skis, crossed the watershed, and returned to Yakutsk in June 1646 by rivers of the Lena Basin. On his return Poyarkov submitted an elaborate plan for conquest of the Amur region, which led to an effort by Moscow, later abandoned under threat of a war with China, to seize control of the region.

BIBLIOGRAPHY: Frank A. Golder, *Russian Expansion on the Pacific, 1641–1850*, Cleveland, 1914; George V. Lantzeff and Richard A. Pierce, *Eastward to Empire: Exploration and Conquest on the Russian Open Frontier, to 1750*, Montreal and London, 1973.

Richard A. Pierce

Prester John Legendary Christian monarch of the medieval and early modern eras whose kingdom was believed to be located in Asia or Ethiopia. The earliest reference to Prester John appears in the twelfth-century chronicle of Otto of Freising, which mentions an Eastern priest-king called John who was a Nestorian Christian and had won a great victory over an army of Medes and Persians. This encounter has been identified with a battle (1141) near Samarkand in which the Seljuk sultan Sanjar was defeated by the Turkish khan Yeh-lu Ta-shih. The latter, however, may not have been a Christian. About 1165 there appeared in Europe a celebrated letter purportedly addressed by Prester John to Manuel I Comnenus, the Byzantine emperor, and other Christian kings. In this letter Prester John describes his domain, which is located in India, as a place where gold and precious stones abound and where poverty, theft, avarice, and adultery are unknown. Although the letter is based on material from medieval Latin literature and was undoubtedly written by a European, belief in the existence of Prester John became widespread, and such medieval travelers as Marco POLO and Odoric of PORDENONE hoped to find him during their journeys to Asia. Marco Polo thought he had found the prototype of Prester John in the person of a Christian ruler of the Kerait tribe, Ung or Wang Khan, who had been slain in battle by Genghis Khan early in the thirteenth century.

During the fourteenth century, as Europeans established contact with Ethiopia, Prester John came to be identified with the Christian Negus, or Emperor, of that African nation, which was then considered a part of India. When Prince HENRY of Portugal embarked on his program of maritime discovery in the fifteenth century, a contemporary historian, Gomes Eannes de Zurara, listed among his motives the hope of finding a Christian prince who would join him in a holy war against Islam. The Christian prince meant was probably Prester John. In 1487, John II of Portugal, as a complement to the voyage of Bartholomeu DIAS, sent Pero da Covilhã (Covilham) on a quest for Prester John and the lands where spices were found. After visiting Egypt, India, and the Arabian peninsula, Covilhã reached Ethiopia, which he was apparently not permitted to leave. He was thus the first of a series of Portuguese travelers to Ethiopia in the sixteenth and seventeenth centuries, several of whom wrote important works that shed light on Ethiopian history and culture. As Ethiopia became somewhat better known to Europeans, the fabulous qualities attributed to Prester John's realm gradually disappeared.

BIBLIOGRAPHY: Eric Axelson, *Congo to Cape: Early Portuguese Explorers*, New York, 1973; Arthur Percival Newton, *Travel and Travellers of the Middle Ages*, London, 1926, reprinted Freeport, N.Y., 1967; Vsevolod Slessarev, *Prester John: The Letter and the Legend*, Minneapolis, 1959.

Born in Russia in 1839, Nikolay Przhevalsky became the first explorer to contribute a detailed picture of the great spaces of Central Asia. [Library of Congress]

Przhevalsky, Nikolay Mikhailovich (1839–1888)

Russian explorer of Central Asia. Educated at the Smolensk Gymnasium, he entered the Russian Army in 1855 and later taught geography in the military school at Warsaw. In 1867, at his request, he was transferred to Siberia, where in 1867–1868 he explored the Ussuri River region and pursued Chinese bandits on the Manchurian border. The Russian Geographical Society approved his plan for expeditions deep into Asia and provided modest means. Between 1870 and 1873 he made the first of his Central Asian expeditions. Setting out from Kyakhta, he passed through Urga (Ulan Bator), Mongolia, crossed the Gobi Desert to Peking, went southwestward to the approaches to Tibet, and then returned to Kyakhta. In 1876–1877 he went from Kuldja (Ining) southeastward across the Tien Shan and Takla Makan to discover the lake Lop Nor and the Altyn Tagh range and then returned to Kuldja. In 1879–1880 he traveled from Zaysan across Dzungaria and continued southward to within 125 miles (202 kilometers) of Lhasa, where the Tibetan authorities made him turn back. Between 1883 and 1885 he went from Kyakhta south across the Gobi to the lake Koko Nor (Ch'ing Hai) and Tsaidam, to the Altyn Tagh and Kunlun ranges, and then over the Tien Shan to Karakul on Issyk Kul. He intended to lead a fifth expedition but died at Karakul (later renamed Przhevalsk).

Przhevalsky was the first to give the world a clear idea of Central Asia. During his 9 years in the region, he traversed more than 20,500 miles (32,991 kilometers), of which 19,000 miles (30,577 kilometers) were in China and Mongolia. His explorations covered an enormous region from the Pamirs east to the Great Khingan Range (about 2500 miles, or 4023 kilometers) and from the Altai south to central Tibet (about 600 miles, or 966 kilometers). He made valuable collections of plant and animal life, including many new species. His discoveries include the wild camel and the only known wild horse, now known as Przhevalsky's horse. He wrote many scientific monographs and several travel accounts, two of which were translated into English.

BIBLIOGRAPHY: Nikolay Mikhailovich Przhevalsky, *From Kulja, across the Tian Shan to Lob-Nor*, London, 1879; id., *Mongolia, the Tangut Country, and the Solitudes of Northern Tibet*, 2 vols., London, 1876.

Richard A. Pierce

Ptolemy (full Latin name: Claudius Ptolemaeus; fl. ca. A.D. 127–147)

Astronomer, mathematician, geographer, and general polymath at Alexandria, Egypt. His works had greater influence on the science and attitudes of both the European Middle Ages and of Islam than those of any other ancient writer except Aristotle. Among his huge output the most important works were:

1. *Almagest* (Arabic form of the Greek title), a treatise in thirteen books on astronomy. Some of the data are derived from the great Greek astronomer Hipparchus, but Ptolemy added fresh observations of his own about the planetary orbits. As a result of its authoritative presentation and mathematical detail, the *Almagest* was regarded as definitive for more than 1000 years, and only major advances in observations made it possible to disprove its basic feature of a geocentric universe.

2. *Tetrabiblos*, the most influential treatise on astrology throughout the Middle Ages, again because it appeared to give a relatively scientific approach to the subject.

3. *Geography*, a great work that was essentially a vast collection of coordinates of latitude and longitude for making an improved map of the known world. Following the suggestion (not carried out) of Hipparchus that this could be done only by determining the latitude and longitude of the places to be included in the maps, six of the eight books contain tables giving Ptolemy's locations of towns, tribal areas, rivers, and mountains. This wholly admirable scheme was in line with Ptolemy's mathematical and astronomical interests. The essential drawback was the quality of his information; for only a small minority of places was even the latitude based on astronomical observation (primarily by the height of the polestar or of the shadow cast by a measuring rod). For longitudes, no such observations existed or could exist in ancient times (although a method of using simultaneous observations of lunar eclipses at different points was known). In practice, therefore, Ptolemy used transmitted distances based on sailing time or the land equivalent with all the obvious uncertainties. These are seen even in the figures for the Mediterranean world and *a fortiori* for more distant parts. Ptolemy himself realized the limitations of his scheme but nonetheless constructed tables which have an unjustified air of exactitude about them. The

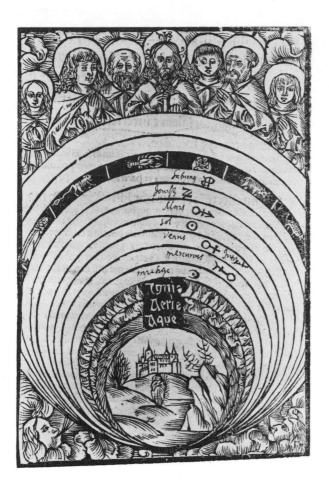

ates the size of Ceylon in spite of a wealth of detail on place names. On the other hand, he is our only authority for ancient knowledge of Asia beyond the Ganges, which certainly included the Malaysian peninsula and the Gulf of Siam. Here are the Sinae (the name from which our China is derived). Ptolemy believed that the coast then bent round southward, ultimately to meet an eastward projection of Africa from somewhere south of Zanzibar. He had heard or read of two large lakes in equatorial Africa as twin sources of the Nile, fed by snows from the "Mountains of the Moon." This information, like a vague reference to a Nigir River in West Africa, was of vital importance to the exploration of Africa until the nineteenth century. Still more important was the fact that Ptolemy placed the eastern part of Asia so far to the east that the distance apparently separating it by sea from Western Europe was diminished. This error was of vital importance to the geographical concepts of the fifteenth century and the idea of voyaging westward to discover the Indies.

BIBLIOGRAPHY: J. O. Thomson, *History of Ancient Geography,* Cambridge, England, 1948.

B. H. Warmington

Pytheas *(fl. ca. 330–300 B.C.)* Greek navigator from Massilia (Marseille). Pytheas's voyage along the Atlantic coast of Europe brought new knowledge of this area to the Greek world. His report (which has not survived) had features which caused some later Greek and Roman writers to disbelieve it, but on the whole it appears to have been trustworthy. The voyage probably dates to a time of weakness at Carthage, which normally prevented ships of other states from passing through the Strait of Gibraltar. Pytheas probably had some hopes of trade (he is said to have been a poor man), but he also had good astronomical knowledge and had calculated the latitude of Massilia to within a few minutes of the correct figure; he made other observations on the voyage. His route is certain from Cádiz to Cape Ortegal, and he seems to have coasted round the Bay of Biscay. He noted correctly (unlike many Greek geographers) that the Armorican Peninsula (Britanny) was an immense westward projection. From it he crossed to Britain, of which he appears to have been the first to provide a description for the Greek world. Significant points included an account of tin mining in Cornwall and remarks on the way of life of the inhabitants. He then circumnavigated Britain, correctly identifying its shape as roughly triangular; his estimates of the length of the three sides are double the real figures, but the proportions are roughly correct. He also gave some details of Ireland but did not visit it.

The most controversial item of his report was a reference to an inhabited "island of Thule," some 6 days' sailing north of the northernmost point in Scotland but only 1 day's sailing from a "frozen sea." It is impossible to be certain what the full account of

bulk of his information derived from a fairly recent predecessor, Marinus of Tyre, and, with some additions made by himself, a map constructed in accordance with Ptolemy's coordinates represents the sum of ancient knowledge or belief about the geography of the world.

Some of the more important features follow. In western Europe, Ptolemy had much good information on Ireland (which had never been brought within the Roman Empire) and located it correctly relative to Great Britain, Scotland's shape is distorted to a west-east direction, and his island of Thule (*see* PYTHEAS) is clearly now Shetland. In contrast to his information on Ireland, there is little new on the tribes of Germany, and his attempts to locate them show the lack clearly. His configuration of Denmark is accurate, but he had little knowledge of the Baltic. In central Europe he was the first to name the Carpathian Mountains. Like other authors, he exaggerates the size of the Sea of Azov and puts it too far north. He is the first to provide much definite information on the Rha River: the Volga. He and Marinus had more new information on the people known as the Seres, that is, of western China, derived from silk traders. He has a number of names for inland cities (which cannot be identified with existing cities) but does not realize that the land is bounded by the sea. He has the shape of the Indian subcontinent quite wrong and exagger-

Pytheas said about it, since most of the references are not only fragmentary but hostile, owing to the general belief that life in latitudes so far north was impossible. Some accepted the account, however, and Thule became a romantic term for the farthest point of the known world. Modern scholarship rejects the Shetlands as the Thule of Pytheas as being too close to Scotland and has come to favor a reference to southern Norway. On his return to the coast of Gaul, Pytheas sailed "beyond" (east of) the Rhine but probably not beyond the Elbe.

Pytheas had no immediate successor, presumably because of continuing or reestablished Carthaginian control, and further knowledge did not accrue until the Roman conquest of Spain and Gaul. In any case, he specifically said that the tin trade with Britain, which was important in antiquity, ran across Gaul to the Mediterranean, the Gallic rivers offering excellent routes. Nevertheless, Pytheas's voyage, in terms of distance covered, is the longest known to us from antiquity and was a remarkable achievement for a Mediterranean Greek unfamiliar with the problems of sailing in the Atlantic.

BIBLIOGRAPHY: M. Cary and E. H. Warmington, *The Ancient Explorers*, London, 1929.

B. H. Warmington

Rohlfs, Gerhard *(1831-1896)* German explorer and Africanist. Born at Vegesack, near Bremen, Rohlfs studied at the Universities of Heidelberg, Würzburg, and Göttingen. In 1855 he enlisted in the Foreign Legion, an experience which gave him some knowledge of Arabic and native customs as well as appealing to his strong spirit of adventure. His travels began in 1862, when he set off from Tangier and journeyed over territory previously visited by only one other European, René CAILLIÉ. Rohlfs described his experiences in *Adventures in Morocco and Journeys through the Oases of Draa and Tafilet* (1874). Scarcely a year later, despite having been wounded in the course of his initial African expedition, he once more set out, this time with the intention of reaching Timbuktu. He was thwarted in this plan but did succeed in reaching Ghudāmis (Ghadames) and thence traveled to Tripoli. A third undertaking was much more successful, for between 1865 and 1867 Rohlfs became the first European to cross Africa from the Mediterranean to the Gulf of Guinea. This journey is described in *Quer durch Afrika* (1874). Rohlfs later traveled from Cyrenaica to Alexandria and then accepted the leadership of an expedition sponsored by Khedive Ismail of Egypt which had as its purpose exploration of the Libyan Desert. The striking scientific results achieved by this undertaking led, in 1878, to the German government's employing Rohlfs on an expedition to Wadai. Attacks by Suaya Arabs aborted this mission, and Rohlfs's last position in Africa was a short and inauspicious term as German consul in Zanzibar. While his scientific geography was not of the highest quality, Rohlfs added substantially to European knowledge of North Africa, and as an outspoken colonial publicist he had a great impact in shaping German views of Africa.

BIBLIOGRAPHY: Konrad Guenther, *Gerhard Rohlfs: Lebensbild eines Afrikaforschers*, Freiburg, 1912; E. G. Ravenstein, "Gerhard Rohlfs," *The Geographical Journal*, vol. VIII, 1896, pp. 184–185; Wolfe W. Schmokel, "Gerhard Rohlfs: The Lonely Explorer," in Robert I. Rotberg (ed.), *Africa and Its Explorers*, Cambridge, Mass., 1970, pp. 175–221.

James A. Casada

Ross, James Clark *(1800-1862)* British polar explorer. James Ross entered the Royal Navy in April 1812 as a first-class volunteer on board HMS *Briseis*, commanded by his uncle, John ROSS. James remained with his uncle on a succession of ships and was still serving as a midshipman under him in 1818, when he commanded HMS *Isabella* and *Alexander* on the first of the Royal Navy's attempts to find a NORTHWEST PASSAGE by way of Baffin Bay. John Ross failed to find an outlet from Baffin Bay and returned home to meet severe criticism. James, however, was spared his uncle's ignominy and was appointed to take part in the Navy's next Northwest Passage expedition, under the command of William Edward PARRY, in 1819. That expedition discovered in Lancaster Sound the main western outlet from Baffin Bay, and spent a winter at Melville

The discoverer of King William Island, locator of the North Magnetic Pole, and first to explore Antarctica, James Ross tired early of his dangerous occupation. He allowed the leadership of the great Northwest Passage venture of 1845 to pass to Sir John Franklin, only to come out of retirement to join in the search for the lost expedition. [National Portrait Gallery, London]

Island, halfway through the passage. James Ross also accompanied Parry's next two Northwest Passage expeditions (1821–1823 and 1824–1825) and was promoted lieutenant on December 26, 1822. He was again with Parry in 1827, when the latter sailed to Spitsbergen (Svalbard) in an attempt on the North Pole, and he took part in Parry's unsuccessful northward march over the ice.

He was rewarded with promotion to commander on November 8, 1827, but thereafter remained without an appointment. He was still on half pay in 1829, when John Ross asked him to take part in his private expedition to attempt the Northwest Passage on the *Victory*. The expedition spent four winters trapped by ice on the east coast of Boothia Peninsula in the Canadian Arctic, and during that period James Ross conducted most of the exploratory work, exploring the coasts of Boothia Peninsula, discovering King William Island, and locating the North Magnetic Pole on June 1, 1831.

James Ross received his promotion to post captain on October 28, 1834. In the next year he embarked on a systematic magnetic survey of the British Isles which occupied him until 1838, but he returned briefly to the Arctic in the early months of 1836 in an attempt to relieve whalers who had been beset throughout the winter in Davis Strait.

In 1839 Ross sailed in command of *Erebus* and *Terror* on the Royal Navy's first major exploring expedition to the Antarctic. He spent three summers in the Antarctic, wintering each year in Van Diemen's Land (Tasmania) and Australia, and discovered Ross Sea, the Ross Ice Shelf, Ross Island, and Victoria Land. On his return to England in 1843, a campaign began to have *Erebus* and *Terror* fitted out for a renewed attempt on the Northwest Passage. Ross, with his unrivaled experience of the polar regions, was almost unanimously considered to be best fitted for the command. However, after having married in 1843, he declined to undertake any further polar voyages; the command went instead to Sir John FRANKLIN, who sailed in 1845. After Franklin's disappearance, Ross was persuaded to lead one more Arctic expedition to search for him (see FRANKLIN EXPEDITION AND SEARCH). He sailed with HMS *Enterprise* and *Investigator* in 1848, wintered at Port Leopold, Somerset Island, and searched the surrounding coasts by sledge, but returned home in autumn without having found any trace of Franklin. He spent the rest of his life in peaceful retirement in Aylesbury.

BIBLIOGRAPHY: Ernest S. Dodge, *The Polar Rosses: John and James Clark Ross and Their Explorations*, London, 1973.

Clive A. Holland

Having failed to discover the Northwest Passage in 1818, John Ross lost favor with the Admiralty until he was able to redeem himself by enduring four winters locked in the ice of the Gulf of Boothia.

Ross, John *(1777–1856)* British naval officer and Arctic explorer. Born in Wigtownshire, Scotland, Ross entered the Royal Navy as a first-class volunteer on board HMS *Pearl* in 1786. After 3 years' service in the Mediterranean, he was transferred to the merchant service, made voyages to the West Indies and the Baltic, then, in 1794, joined the East India Company. He returned to the Royal Navy in 1799 as a midshipman on board *Weasel* in the North Sea. In 1803, when the war in Europe broke out again, he began a 9-year period of service under Adm. Sir James Saumarez, during which he was promoted lieutenant in March 1805. On receiving his promotion to commander in February 1812, he took command of *Briseis* in the Baltic and the North Sea.

After further service on *Actaeon* and *Driver*, Ross was appointed in 1818 to command *Isabella* and *Alexander* on an expedition to Baffin Bay, the first in a long series of British naval expeditions in search of a NORTHWEST PASSAGE. Ross's expedition of 1818 was a failure. He located the three channels leading from northern Baffin Bay (Smith, Jones, and Lancaster Sounds) that William BAFFIN had discovered in 1616 but found no passage through any of them. Most notably, he reported Lancaster Sound to be a closed bay, a matter disputed by his second-in-command, William Edward PARRY. On his return home, Ross became involved in a number of acrimonious disputes with Parry over Lancaster Sound and with others over his scientific results. In consequence, when a new expedition was sent to reexamine Lancaster Sound in 1819, Ross was passed over and Parry received the command.

Ross was never again offered a naval appointment, though he was understandably anxious to undertake another expedition and restore his tarnished reputation after Parry returned in 1820 with the news that Lancaster Sound was indeed an open channel, leading halfway through the Northwest Passage. Having failed to interest the Admiralty in his proposals, Ross finally persuaded a wealthy friend, Sir Felix Booth, to sponsor a private Northwest Passage expedition on the steamship *Victory*. He set out in 1829, passed through Lancaster Sound and Prince Regent Inlet, and spent four winters imprisoned in the ice of the Gulf of Boothia. He explored the region of Boothia Peninsula until he was rescued by a whaler in 1833. This expedition, one of the most arduous ever undertaken by Arctic explorers, did much to restore Ross's reputation. He was knighted and made a companion of the Bath in 1834 and was further honored by geographical societies, but he still received no further naval appointments.

After a spell as British consul in Stockholm, from 1839 to 1846, Ross again approached Admiralty for command of an expedition in 1847, when plans were being made for the relief of the missing Northwest Passage expedition of Sir John FRANKLIN of 1845. On being turned down once more, he organized a private expedition on the small vessel *Felix*. This little expedition spent the winter of 1850–1851 in Barrow Strait, but it was ill equipped and contributed almost nothing to the Franklin search. *See also* FRANKLIN EXPEDITION AND SEARCH.

Ross, who was already 74 at the end of this venture, now finally retired from exploration. But he never abandoned his quarrel with the naval establishment, which he continued, by means of bitterly worded pamphlets, until the end of his life.

BIBLIOGRAPHY: Ernest S. Dodge, *The Polar Rosses: John and James Clark Ross and Their Explorations,* London, 1973.

Clive A. Holland

Rowlands, John *See* STANLEY, HENRY MORTON.

Royal Geographical Society

From its inception, the Royal Geographical Society has been closely identified with support and encouragement of the many forms of geographical exploration. Founded in 1830 as an outgrowth of the Raleigh Club and the AFRICAN ASSOCIATION, the society was to a considerable extent the brainchild of Sir John BARROW, second secretary of the Admiralty. Barrow was an active and vocal proponent of geographical discovery, and, in his capacity first as a vice president and later as president of the society, he saw to it that the organization's medals were awarded to individuals who had made outstanding contributions as explorers. Barrow also began a long-lived tradition of close cooperation and interaction between the society and the British government in exploratory endeavors. Thanks primarily to the fact that it lent financial and other support to Robert Hermann Schomburgk's highly successful expeditions in British Guiana in the 1830s, the society under Barrow's tutelage soon made its mark as a body devoted to furthering discovery. However, several other ventures of the same period had less auspicious outcomes than did Schomburgk's travels. These failures led, during the second decade of the society's existence, to considerable restraint in extending monetary assistance to explorers.

Indeed, by the late 1840s the society was in the doldrums. But the advent of Sir Roderick Murchison as the body's president dramatically altered this situation, and the years of Murchison's supremacy (1851–1870) were to be among the society's greatest. A noted geologist and one of the society's founders, Murchison infused the organization with a new vitality and elevated it to heretofore undreamed-of heights in terms of both membership and prestige. He did this primarily through following Barrow's example in emphasizing exploration, and as H. R. Mill, a chronicler of the society's development, writes: "To relate the doings of the Royal Geographical Society under Murchison's supremacy would be almost to write a history of geographical discovery in the most crowded years of its modern development."

Through his many links with influential figures in government and politics, Murchison brought new prominence to the society, and the succession of geographical "lions" he paraded before the mushrooming membership made interest in exploration quite fashionable. Thanks to the discoveries of those who worked under the society's auspices during this period, notably African explorers such as David LIVING-STONE, Richard BURTON, John H. SPEKE, James A. GRANT, and Samuel W. BAKER, the organization became internationally prominent. Moreover, the impetus and direction provided by Murchison continued little diminished after his death, and the society continued to play a major role in African exploration until most of the continent's geographical mysteries had been resolved. From the onset of the great age of African reconnaissance in the 1850s to its conclusion with the "scramble" for colonial possessions in the 1880s and 1890s, the Royal Geographical Society was a central, if not the predominant, factor in bringing geographical light to the so-called dark continent.

Once Africa had yielded its secrets, the final unexplored land areas of the earth were the polar regions. Here, too, the society assumed the lead in promoting discovery. Several prominent fellows of the society were veterans of the search for Sir John FRANKLIN, and in the two decades following the completion of the exploration of Africa, these individuals, led by Sir Clements Markham, brought considerable renown to the body in the field of polar discovery. Particularly notable in this regard was the work of Robert Falcon SCOTT, but the society was also involved in offering support and advice to a number of other polar explorers.

It was in the area of advice that the society made perhaps its greatest contribution to exploration. In addition to the many expeditions it supported (and continues to assist even today), the Royal Geographical Society acted as a sort of central clearinghouse for the accumulation and exchange of data on travel and exploration. Its book of instructions, *Hints to Travellers* (4th edition, 1878), first compiled by Sir Francis Galton, went through many editions and proved invaluable to generations of explorers, cartographers, and others. Similarly, the society's various serial publications apprised its readership of the latest developments in exploration, its meetings gave both explorers and academic geographers an opportunity to discuss discoveries and exchange ideas, and its library and map room have been, throughout its existence, a storehouse of geographical knowledge of immeasurable value to both explorers and students of exploration.

In the twentieth century, and particularly after World War I, the society relinquished some of its prominence in the field of exploration. However, this derived more from the changed nature of modern

*The Royal
Geographical
Society.*

discovery than from any diminution in the society's efforts in support of exploration. The body continued to recognize outstanding feats in the awarding of its medals, it regularly made grants in support of geographical researches, and it remained a focal point of interest for those involved in the study of exploration. In almost a century and a half of existence, the Royal Geographical Society has fostered modern exploration on many fronts, and it has numbered among its fellows and medalists many of the greatest discoverers of modern times.

BIBLIOGRAPHY: Clements R. Markham, *The Fifty Years' Work of the Royal Geographical Society,* London, 1881; Hugh Robert Mill, *The Record of the Royal Geographical Society, 1830–1930,* London, 1930; publications of the society *(Journal of the Royal Geographical Society, Proceedings of the Royal Geographical Society, The Geographical Journal).*

James A. Casada

Recipients of Royal Medals (Founder's and Patron's), 1839–1978*

1839	Thomas Simpson and Dr. Edward Rüppell
1840	Col. Henry Creswicke Rawlinson and Sir Robert Schomburgk
1841	Lieut. Henry Raper, R.N., and Lieut. John Wood, I.N.
1842	Capt. Sir James Clark Ross, R.N., and Rev. Dr. Edward Robinson
1843	Edward John Eyre and Lieut. J. F. A. Symonds
1844	W. J. Hamilton and Prof. Adolf Erman
1845	Dr. Charles Tilstone Beke and Karl Ritter
1846	Count P. E. de Strzelecki and Prof. Alexander Theodor von Middendorff
1847	Capt. Charles Sturt and Dr. Friedrich Wilhelm Ludwig Leichhardt
1848	Sir James Brooke and Capt. Charles Wilkes, U.S.N.
1849	Austen Henry Layard and Baron Karl von Hügel
1850	Rev. David Livingstone (watch) and Col. John C. Frémont
1851	Dr. George Wallin and Thomas Brunner (premiums)
1852	Dr. John Rae and Capt. Henry Strachey
1853	Francis Galton and Comdr. Edward Augustus Inglefield, R.N.
1854	Rear Adm. William Henry Smyth and Capt. Robert J. L. McClure, R.N.
1855	Karl Johan Andersson (instruments) and Rev. David Livingstone
1856	Elisha Kent Kane and Heinrich Barth
1857	Augustus C. Gregory and Lieut. Col. Andrew Scott Waugh
1858	Capt. Richard Collinson, R.N., and Prof. Alexander Dallas Bache
1859	Capt. Richard Francis Burton and Capt. John Palliser
1860	Lady Franklin and Capt. Sir Francis Leopold McClintock, R.N.
1861	Capt. John Hanning Speke and John McDouall Stuart
1862	Robert O'Hara Burke and Capt. Thomas Blakiston
1863	Frank T. Gregory and John Arrowsmith
1864	Capt. James Augustus Grant and Baron Karl Klaus von der Decken
1865	Capt. T. G. Montgomerie and Samuel White Baker
1866	Dr. Thomas Thomson and W. Chandless
1867	Adm. Alexis Butakov and Dr. Isaac I. Hayes
1868	Dr. August Petermann and Gerhard Rohlfs
1869	Prof. N. A. E. Nordenskiöld and Mrs. Mary Somerville
1870	Lieut. Francis Garnier and George W. Hayward
1871	Sir Roderick Murchison and A. Keith Johnston
1872	Col. Henry Yule and Robert Barkley Shaw
1873	Ney Elias and Henry Morton Stanley
1874	Dr. Georg August Schweinfurth and Col. P. Egerton Warburton
1875	Lieut. Karl Weyprecht and Lieut. Julius von Payer
1876	Lieut. Verney Lovett Cameron, R.N., and John Forrest
1877	Capt. Sir George Nares, R.N., and the Pundit Nain Singh
1878	Baron Ferdinand von Richthofen and Capt. Henry Trotter
1879	Col. Nikolay Przhevalsky and Capt. William John Gill
1880	Lieut. Louis Palander and Ernest Giles
1881	Maj. Alexandre Serpa Pinto and Benjamin Leigh Smith
1882	Dr. Gustav Nachtigal and Sir John Kirk
1883	Sir Joseph Dalton Hooker and E. Colborne Baber
1884	Archibald Ross Colquhoun and Dr. Julius von Haast
1885	Joseph Thomson and H. E. O'Neill
1886	Maj. Adolphus W. Greely and Guido Cora
1887	Lieut. Col. Thomas Hungerford Holdich and Rev. George Grenfell
1888	Clements Robert Markham and Lieut. Hermann von Wissmann
1889	Arthur Douglas Carey and Dr. Gustav Radde
1890	Lieut. Francis Edward Younghusband and Mehmed Emin Pasha
1891	Sir James Hector and Dr. Fridtjof Nansen
1892	Alfred Russel Wallace and Edward Whymper
1893	Frederick Courteney Selous and W. Woodville Rockhill
1894	Capt. Hamilton Bower and Élisée Reclus
1895	Dr. John Murray and the Hon. George Nathaniel Curzon
1896	Sir William Macgregor and St. George Littledale
1897	Pyotr P. Semyonov and Dr. George Mercer Dawson
1898	Dr. Sven Anders Hedin and Lieut. Robert E. Peary, U.S.N.
1899	Capt. Louis-Gustave Binger and Fernand Foureau
1900	Capt. H. H. P. Deasy and James McCarthy
1901	H.R.H. the Duke of the Abruzzi and Dr. A. Donaldson Smith
1902	Gen. Sir Frederick Lugard and Maj. Percy Molesworth Sykes
1903	Douglas William Freshfield and Capt. Otto Neumann Sverdrup
1904	Sir Harry Hamilton Johnston and Comdr. Robert Falcon Scott, R.N.
1905	Sir Martin Conway and Capt. C. H. D. Ryder
1906	Alfred Grandidier and Robert Bell
1907	Dr. Francisco Moreno and Capt. Roald Amundsen
1908	Lieut. Boyd Alexander and H.S.H. the Prince of Monaco

Recipients of Royal Medals (Founder's and Patron's), 1839–1978* (Continued)

1909	Dr. Mark Aurel Stein and Col. the Hon. Milo George Talbot		1942	Miss Freya Stark and Owen Lattimore
1910	Col. H. H. Godwin-Austen and Dr. William Speirs Bruce		1943	No award
1911	Col. Pyotr Kuzmich Kozlov and Dr. Jean-Baptiste Charcot		1944	No award
1912	Charles Montagu Doughty and Douglas Carruthers		1945	Dr. Charles Camsell and Sir Halford Mackinder
1913	Lady Scott (casket) and the late Dr. Edward Adrian Wilson		1946	Brig. Edward A. Glennie and Subinspector Henry A. Larsen, R.C.M.P.

1909 Dr. Mark Aurel Stein and Col. the
 Hon. Milo George Talbot
1910 Col. H. H. Godwin-Austen and Dr. William
 Speirs Bruce
1911 Col. Pyotr Kuzmich Kozlov and
 Dr. Jean-Baptiste Charcot
1912 Charles Montagu Doughty and Douglas Carruthers
1913 Lady Scott (casket) and the late Dr. Edward Adrian
 Wilson
1914 Prof. Albrecht Penck and Dr. Hamilton Rice
1915 Sir Douglas Mawson and Dr. Filippo de Filippi
1916 Lieut. Col. Percy Harrison Fawcett and
 Capt. F. M. Bailey
1917 Comdr. David George Hogarth and Brig.
 Gen. C. G. Rawling
1918 Miss Gertrude Bell and Commandant Jean Tilho
1919 Col. E. M. Jack and Prof. William Morris Davis
1920 H. St. John Philby and Prof. Jovan Cvijić
1921 Vilhjalmur Stefansson and Gen. J.-E.-R. Bourgeois
1922 Lieut. Col. C. K. Howard-Bury and E. de Koven
 Leffingwell
1923 Dr. Knud Rasmussen and the Hon. Miles
 Staniforth Smith
1924 Ahmed Hassanein Bey and Comdr. Frank Wild
1925 Brig. Gen. the Hon. C. G. Bruce and
 A. F. R. Wollaston
1926 Lieut. Col. E. F. Norton and Sir Edgeworth David
1927 Maj. Kenneth Mason and Dr. Lauge Koch
1928 Dr. Tom G. Longstaff and Capt. Sir Hubert Wilkins
1929 Francis Rennell Ross and C. H. Karius
1930 F. Kingdon Ward and Carsten Egeberg Borchgrevink
1931 Bertram Thomas and Rear Adm. Richard
 Evelyn Byrd, U.S.N.
1932 H.R.H. the Duke of Spoleto and
 Henry George Watkins
1933 J. M. Wordie and Prof. Erich von Drygalski
1934 Hugh Ruttledge and Capt. Ejnar Mikkelsen
1935 Maj. R. A. Bagnold and Willy Rickmer Rickmers
1936 G. W. Murray and Maj. R. E. Cheesman
1937 Col. C. G. Lewis and Lincoln Ellsworth
1938 John Rymill and Eric Shipton
1939 A. M. Champion and Prof. Hans Ahlmann
1940 Mr. and Mrs. Harold Ingrams and
 Lieut. Alexander R. Glen, R.N.V.R.
1941 Capt. P. A. Clayton and Dr. Isaiah Bowman

1942 Miss Freya Stark and Owen Lattimore
1943 No award
1944 No award
1945 Dr. Charles Camsell and Sir Halford Mackinder
1946 Brig. Edward A. Glennie and Subinspector
 Henry A. Larsen, R.C.M.P.
1947 Brig. Martin Hotine and Col. Daniel van der Meulen
1948 Wilfred Patrick Thesiger and Thomas H. Manning
1949 Prof. L. Dudley Stamp and Prof. Hans Petterssen
1950 George F. Walpole and Prof. Harald Sverdrup
1951 Dr. Vivian E. Fuchs and Dr. Donald Thomson
1952 H. W. Tilman and Paul-Émile Victor
1953 P. D. Baird and Count Eigil Knuth
1954 Brig. Sir John Hunt and Dr. N. A. Mackintosh
1955 Comdr. C. J. W. Simpson and Dr. John K. Wright
1956 Charles Evans and John Giaever
1957 Sir George Binney and Prof. Ardito Desio
1958 Sir Edmund Hillary and Dr. Paul Siple
1959 Sir Raymond Priestley and Comdr. W. R. Anderson
1960 Phillip Garth Law and Prof. André-Théodore Monod
1961 Dr. John Bartholomew and Dr. M. M. Somov
1962 Tom Harrisson and Capt. E. A. McDonald, U.S.N.
1963 Capitaine de Frégate Jacques-Yves Cousteau and
 Dr. Albert P. Crary
1964 Dr. Louis S. B. Leakey and Dr. Thor Heyerdahl
1965 Prof. Lester C. King and Dr. E. F. Roots
1966 G. Hattersley-Smith and E. J. H. Corner
1967 Claudio and Orlando Vilas Boas and Prof.
 Dr. Eduard Imhof
1968 Walter Brian Harland and Prof. Augusto Gansser
1969 Dr. R. Thorsteinsson and Dr. E. T. Tozer and
 Rear Adm. Rodolfo N. M. Panzarini
1970 Walter William Herbert and Dr. Haroun Tazieff
1971 Sir George Deacon and Dr. Charles Swithinbank
1972 Rear Adm. G. S. Ritchie and Dr. M. D. Gwynne
1973 Norman-Leslie Falcon and Prof. Edgar H. Thompson
1974 C. J. S. Bonington and Dr. Gordon de Quetteville Robin
1975 Sir Lawrence Kirwan and Dr. J. P. Kuettner
1976 Dr. Brian B. Roberts and Rear Adm.
 Sir Edmund Irving
1977 Prof. Michael J. Wise and Prof. Frederick
 Kenneth Hare
1978 Maj. Gen. R. L. Brown and Prof. Mieczysław Klimaszew-
 ski

*The Founder's Medal is awarded annually by the Royal Geographical Society in memory of William IV, who was king when the society was established in 1830 and was its first royal patron. The head of each succeeding royal patron has appeared on the Patron's Medal, also awarded annually. The two medals are of equal value and distinction, and the consent of the sovereign must be obtained before they can be awarded.

Rubruck (Ruysbroeck; Rubrouck), **William of** (ca. 1215–1270) Medieval Franciscan friar and traveler to the Far East. Relatively little may be ascertained about the life of this friar except that which he relates in his travel account. Even the dates of his birth and death are unknown. A native of Flanders, he derived his name from a town near Cassel, now located in French Flanders. The French monarch Louis IX sent him on a religious mission to the Mongolian court. In May 1253 he proceeded by sea from Constantinople to the Crimea, traveled from there to the Don and Volga Rivers, and then crossed the great expanse of Central Asia amid many vexatious difficulties and hardships. He was accompanied by another Franciscan named Bartholomew of Cremona, a clerk, an interpreter, and some assistants. Early in January 1254 he was received by the supreme Mongol ruler, Mangu Khan, near Karakorum, the Mongol capital. William of Rubruck in his report concerning his mission provides an excellent account of the life of the Mongols, describing their food, drink, and clothes, their hunting activities, the status of women in Mongolian society, aspects of Mongolian penal laws, standards of justice, soothsayers, and death and burial customs. At Mangu's court William of Rubruck met representatives of various religious bodies, including Catholics, Nestorians, Armenians, Manichaeans, Buddhists, and Muslims, all attempting to gain the special favor of the Great Khan. However, the Mongol ruler made such use of these groups as might suit his own purposes.

William of Rubruck set forth for Europe in the summer of 1254. He returned to Sarai on the Volga and from there went to Armenia and Cappadocia and finally to Nicosia on the island of Cyprus. From this city he went to Antioch on the Asiatic mainland, which he reached by June 1255. Eventually he traveled westward to Paris, where he met the noted English Franciscan scholar Roger Bacon. Apparently the English friar became much interested in William of Rubruck's travel experiences and referred to his travels at some length in his own encyclopedic book *Opus Majus*. William of Rubruck was an observant and conscientious cleric who wrote one of the most valuable travel accounts of the thirteenth century, an account which presented to Western eyes not only much new geographical material but interesting ethnographical information as well.

BIBLIOGRAPHY: Christopher Dawson (ed.), *The Mongol Mission: Narratives and Letters of the Franciscan Missionaries in Mongolia and China in the Thirteenth and Fourteenth Centuries*, tr. by a nun of Stanbrook Abbey, New York, 1955.

Bernerd C. Weber

S

Sarychev, Gavriil Andreyevich (1763–1831) Russian naval officer, explorer, and hydrographer. From 1785 to 1793 he served as second-in-command in the Northeastern Secret Geographical and Astronomical Expedition led by Joseph BILLINGS, doing hydrographic work in the Aleutian chain and exploring Chukotka (Chukotsky Poluostrov). In 1802, as a captain of the first rank, he checked and corrected maps of the Baltic Sea and the Gulf of Finland. In 1808 he received the title of hydrographer general and was made a vice admiral. He was promoted to admiral in 1830 and died in St. Petersburg of cholera the following year.

BIBLIOGRAPHY: G. A. Sarychev, *Account of a Voyage of Discovery to the North-East of Siberia, the Frozen Ocean, and the North-East Sea,* London, 1806; Martin Sauer, *An Account of a Geographical and Astronomical Expedition to the Northern Parts of Russia, Performed in the Year 1785, to 1794, Narrated from the Original Papers,* London, 1802.

Richard A. Pierce

Schweinfurth, Georg August (1836–1925) German explorer, ethnologist, and natural historian. Born in Riga, Schweinfurth was a student at the Universities of Heidelberg, Munich, and Berlin from 1856 to 1862. In the course of his studies he became interested in Africa through arranging and classifying plant collections brought back from the continent by German travelers. He determined to undertake his own exploration of Africa's geography and natural history, and in 1862–1863 he journeyed up the Nile as far as Khartoum. His activities on this expedition, notably the collection of flora he brought back to Europe, led to a commission from the Humboldt-Stiftung of Berlin for scientific researches in the then little-known regions of the East African interior. Between 1869 and 1871 he discovered the Uele (Welle) River, explored the Bahr el Ghazal, elucidated the hydrography of the latter, and made even more significant finds of an ethnological and biological nature. Schweinfurth described these variegated endeavors in *The Heart of Africa* (2 volumes, 1873). Soon after the work's appearance he again undertook an African expedition, this time in company with Gerhard ROHLFS. Together they journeyed through vast unexplored stretches of the Libyan Desert. Later Schweinfurth was instrumental in the founding of a geographical society in Egypt, and he traveled in the Arabian Desert with Paul Güssfeldt.

Although it is not generally known, in 1885 Schweinfurth was offered the leadership of the Kilimanjaro Expedition (ultimately led by Harry Hamilton JOHNSTON) sponsored by the British Association and the Royal Society. However, he declined the position owing to pressing duties in Egypt and the debilitating effects of his previous African travels. Nonetheless, he undertook one further desert journey and retained an active interest in African developments after his days as an explorer had ended. Evidence of this is provided by his many scientific publications

A German-born explorer and scientist, Georg Schweinfurth traveled extensively along the Nile and the Bahr el Ghazal and through the Libyan Desert between 1862 and 1871. He made an enormous contribution to European knowledge of African geography, flora, and fauna.

and an edited work, *Emin Pasha in Central Africa* (1888). Unlike so many of the great nineteenth-century explorers of Africa, he lived to an advanced age. Schweinfurth's name is seldom mentioned in the first rank of African explorers, yet thanks to the extent and varied locales of his explorations, the catholicity of his interests, and the magnitude of his contributions he deserves better of posterity.

BIBLIOGRAPHY: Anonymous, "Obituary: Dr. Georg Schweinfurth," *The Geographical Journal*, vol. LXVII, 1926, pp. 93–94; L. Keimer, "Bibliographie des ouvrages de Georg Schweinfurth," *Bulletin Société Royale Géographique Égypte*, vol. XIV, 1926, pp. 73–112; Georg Schweinfurth, *Lebenslauf*, Berlin, 1921.

James A. Casada

Although his expedition to the South Pole in 1911–1912 ended in tragedy, Capt. Robert Falcon Scott came to be the British public's ideal of the perfect explorer. [Royal Geographical Society]

Scott, Robert Falcon (1868–1912) English explorer. Scott was born on June 6, 1868, at Devonport, Devonshire, the son of a brewer. Educated at Stubbington House, Fareham, Hampshire, he proceeded to a career in the Royal Navy, receiving his early training on HMS *Britannia*, the equivalent at that time of a maritime university. From here Scott graduated with first-class certificates in mathematics and seamanship and subsequently served on HMS *Boadicea* as a midshipman. Later he decided to specialize as a torpedo officer and in 1887 was appointed to HMS *Rover* in the West Indies Training Squadron. It was during this period that fate took a hand in Scott's future. Along with other young midshipmen he was noted by Sir Clements Markham, a cousin of the squadron commander, as a possible candidate for the leadership of a future Antarctic expedition. Sir Clements, then honorary secretary of ROYAL GEOGRAPHICAL SOCIETY and later to become its president, was determined that the Royal Navy should be in the vanguard of a renewed British presence in the Antarctic, a region neglected by government since the discoveries of Sir James Clark ROSS between 1839 and 1843. It was as a result of a chance meeting with Markham in London in June 1899 that Scott, now a lieutenant, became aware for the first time of the prospective expedition. He promptly wrote applying for the command and in June of the following year was officially appointed.

The 12 months that followed were probably the busiest of Scott's life. "I may as well confess" he admitted, "that I have no predilection for polar exploration." He therefore set to with a will to remedy the deficiencies in his experience, seeking advice from experienced explorers like the Norwegian Fridtjof NANSEN and busying himself with every detail of the equipment, commissariat, and scientific preparation required for a 3-year expedition to a land separated by the world's stormiest ocean from all sources of supply. His task was made the more difficult by the need to obtain decisions from the various committees set up by the Royal Geographical Society and the Royal Society to control scientific and logistic policy. But by sheer perseverance Scott's will prevailed. In March 1901, the expedition's ship, *Discovery*, specially built and strengthened to deal with the Antarctic pack ice,

was launched, and on August 6, 1901, the British National Antarctic Expedition set sail.

The members of the expedition were predominantly Royal Navy men even though its organization was civilian. An exception was Ernest SHACKLETON, an ex-merchant navy officer who was later to gain prominence as an Antarctic explorer in his own right. Among the civilian scientists Dr. Edward Adrian Wilson achieved a reputation as a first-class zoologist and artist and was later to become Scott's close confidant. In January 1902, Scott set up his winter quarters at Hut Point on Ross Island. Instead of returning to New Zealand as planned, *Discovery* remained and was used as a base from which to explore the adjacent ice shelf and the mainland. Exploration took the form of a series of probes, made by sledging parties, one to the southwest and one to the north, skirting the coast of Victoria Land, and lastly the main venture, a southward trek across the Ross Ice Shelf 200 miles (322 kilometers) toward the South Pole. On this occasion Scott, accompanied by Wilson and Shackleton, achieved latitude 82°17′S, a record for that time. The poor performance of the sledge dogs coupled with an outbreak of scurvy compelled Scott and his companions to turn back, and they achieved winter quarters only with the greatest difficulty. In January 1903, the ship *Morning* arrived to relieve *Discovery*, now immovably fast in the ice. Scott was obliged to spend a second winter in Antarctica. During the summer of 1903, with Petty Officer Edgar Evans and Leading Stoker William Lashly, Scott sledged up the Ferrar Glacier to the Polar Plateau at an altitude of 9000 feet (2743 meters), a total distance of 725 miles (1167 kilometers) in 59 days. In February 1904, *Discovery* was freed from the ice and joined the relief ships *Terra Nova* and *Morning* in a triumphant return to New Zealand and home. In addition to extensive topographical and geological discoveries inland, the coast of Victoria Land had been explored and King Edward VII Land (now Edward VII Peninsula), to the west, discovered. "Never," claimed Sir Clements Markham, "has any polar expedition returned with so great a harvest of results."

During the next 5 years Scott, now promoted to captain, held a number of naval appointments both at sea and on shore, his course seemingly set for a successful Navy career. But as early as 1906 he was hankering to return to the south. Soon he was to be challenged by his former subordinate and now rival, Shackleton, who in 1908 achieved a point on the polar plateau of Antarctica within 97 miles (156 kilometers) of the South Pole. In September 1909, Scott publicly announced plans for an "expedition to achieve the South Pole . . . to secure for the British Empire the honour of this achievement." In this ambition he was encouraged by his wife Kathleen (née Bruce), a successful sculptor, whom he had married in 1908.

His immediate task was one that he found personally uncongenial: the raising of funds. For unlike the

Discovery expedition, which had the backing of two learned societies, this was entirely a private venture. A total of £40,000 was required, the Treasury having promised to match half this amount. Added to these worries were the problems of staffing. The estimation in which Scott was held as a leader is evidenced by the number of applications received from prospective explorers: more than 4000. Among these who were eventually chosen were several members of the *Discovery* expedition, including Edward Wilson as chief of the scientific staff. For although achievement of the South Pole was the most publicized aspect of the expedition, for Scott science was to be the rock foundation of all effort in the south.

The expedition ship *Terra Nova* left England in June 1910. In Australia Scott received a tersely

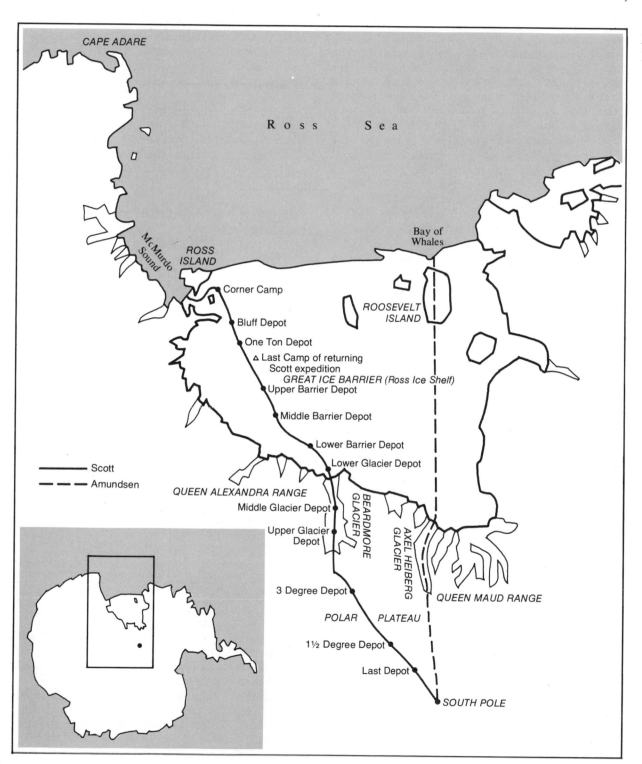

Robert Scott's and Roald Amundsen's routes to the South Pole, 1911–1912.

worded telegram from the Norwegian explorer Roald AMUNDSEN to say that he also was on his way to Antarctica on board the *Fram* with the same goal, the South Pole. The news was a great shock, but Scott determined to carry on with his plans unaltered. After some delays in the pack ice, *Terra Nova* reached Ross Island on January 22, 1911. Winter quarters were established at Cape Evans. Scott lost no time in starting depot-laying parties in preparation for the pole journey the following spring. A party was also dispatched westward on board *Terra Nova* to explore King Edward VII Land, but meeting Amundsen's *Fram* at the Bay of Whales, it changed plans and proceeded north to Cape Adare. At Cape Evans the winter months (May to September) were spent in the hut preparing gear and revising plans for the pole. In June Scott allowed Wilson, Lieut. H. R. Bowers, and Apsley Cherry-Garrard to make a midwinter journey to Cape Crozier to obtain samples of eggs from the rookery of the emperor penguin, a remarkable bird that lays its eggs in the depth of the Antarctic winter. Probably the most extraordinary expedition of its kind ever made, "the worst journey in the world" was accomplished in subzero temperatures and almost complete darkness.

By the end of September all was ready for the march to the pole. Scott planned to achieve the pole with a party of four man-hauling a sledge from the top of the Beardmore Glacier, the route to the plateau discovered by Shackleton in 1908. The pole party was to be accompanied by supporting parties using dogs, ponies, and motor sledges, which, it was hoped, would haul the heavy loads to the foot of the glacier. Toward the end of October 1911 the motor sledges set off, followed by the main party, consisting of ten men, ten ponies, and twenty dogs. The two motors very soon broke down and were abandoned. Weather conditions on the ice shelf rapidly deteriorated, making progress for the ponies especially difficult. At the approaches to the Beardmore Glacier the entire expedition became bogged down in soft snow, and its outcome seemed to be more a question of luck than of planning. Eventually three man-hauling parties ascended the 10,000 foot (3048 meters) Beardmore Glacier, the first turning back on December 21 and the second on January 4. At the last moment, for some reason never satisfactorily explained, Scott selected a fifth man to add to the original pole party of four; this was a representative of the army, Capt. L. E. G. Oates. For the pole party, consisting of Scott, Oates, Wilson, Bowers, and Petty Officer Edgar Evans, the journey across the Polar Plateau was hard going, but morale was high. Then on January 16, 1912, Bowers sighted a black marker flag left by Amundsen. They knew then that the Norwegians had forestalled them (by a month, as it turned out). Scott wrote in his diary: "Great God this is an awful place and terrible enough for us to have laboured to it without the reward of priority."

The return journey of more than 800 miles (1287 kilometers) was a progressive disaster. Petty Officer Evans, physically the toughest member of the party, was the first to show signs of deterioration, finally collapsing and dying near the foot of the Beardmore Glacier on February 17. The others struggled on across the ice shelf, suffering from frostbite and lack of food and warmth. On or about March 16, Captain Oates, unable to walk farther, left the tent during a blizzard and was never seen again. About March 21, another blizzard caught Scott, Bowers, and Wilson only 11 miles (18 kilometers) from fuel and food at One Ton Depot. The tent entombing their bodies was found 8 months later by a search party from Cape Evans together with valuable rock samples and precious diaries and notebooks, one of which contained Scott's immortal Message to the Public, which ended: "Had we lived I should have had a tale to tell of the hardihood, endurance and courage of my companions which would have stirred the heart of every Englishman. These rough notes and our dead bodies must tell the tale. . . . "

Not until the middle of February 1913 did the news of the tragedy burst upon the British public. The effect was one both of grief and admiration. A Memorial Appeal Fund was launched and produced a tremendous response. Adequate provision was made for next of kin, and memorials to Captain Scott went up in various parts of the world. Around Scott himself a legend hardened. Somehow he came to epitomize all the virtues of courage, stoicism, and endurance regarded by the British as being particularly theirs. In consequence the true character of Scott has tended to become concealed beneath the image of a plaster saint. Scott was a highly complex personality, an inward-looking man, fatalistic and highly sensitive. Unlike Amundsen and Shackleton, he was unable to capture completely the loyalty and affection of his men and lacked the self-confidence necessary to the planning and execution of a successful polar expedition. Yet Scott's romantic ideal of polar exploration, symbolized by men hauling sledges and "going forth to meet hardships, dangers and difficulties with their own unaided efforts" still continues to capture the admiration of the public and dwarf the achievements of Shackleton and Amundsen.

BIBLIOGRAPHY: Apsley Cherry-Garrard, *The Worst Journey in the World: Antarctic 1910–1913*, 2 vols., London, 1922; Reginald Pound, *Scott of the Antarctic*, London, 1966; Robert Falcon Scott, *Scott's Last Expedition*, arranged by Leonard Huxley, 2 vols., London, 1913; id., *The Voyage of the "Discovery,"* 2 vols., London, 1905; Edward Adrian Wilson, *Diary of the Discovery Expedition to the Antarctic Regions 1901–1904*, London, 1966; id., *Diary of the Terra Nova Expedition to the Antarctic 1910–1912*, London, 1972.

H. G. R. King

Shackleton, Ernest Henry (1874–1922) English explorer. Born in Ireland on February 17, 1874, the son of a doctor, Shackleton was educated at Dulwich College, London. Determined on a career at sea, he left school at the age of 16 and spent his formative years in the merchant navy. In 1901, by sheer persistence and force of character, he secured the post of third lieutenant on board the ship *Discovery* of Capt. Robert Falcon SCOTT, which was then being fitted out for an expedition to the Antarctic. This was the first scientific expedition to carry out extensive land exploration on the Antarctic continent. Shackleton was chosen to accompany Scott and the zoologist Dr. Edward A. Wilson on a sledge journey across the Ross Ice Shelf to the farthest south then attained, latitude 82°17'S. On the return journey to winter quarters all three men suffered severely from scurvy, Shackleton in particular. As a result he found himself invalided home on the relief ship *Morning* in 1903. This was a blow to Shackleton's pride which kindled in him a determination to return to Antarctica as leader of his own expedition. In 1904 he married and established himself in Edinburgh as secretary of the Scottish Geographical Society, a position which brought him into contact with many influential members of society. In 1907, having achieved the necessary financial backing, he announced ambitious plans for an Antarctic expedition which had as its aims the achievement of both the South Pole and the South Magnetic Pole. It was to be a private venture without any government aid. Always the innovator, Shackleton planned to reach the pole by using dogs, ponies, and a motor car specially designed to haul sledges over the ice. He also took with him the first motion-picture camera to be used in Antarctica.

The expedition sailed from England on board the *Nimrod* in July 1907. Despite promises to Scott to keep clear of the McMurdo Sound region (regarded by his former leader as exclusively his own), Shackleton was obliged by force of circumstances to set up his hut at Cape Royds on Ross Island. The expedition was, in the event, highly successful. The Beardmore Glacier was discovered and ascended by Shackleton and three companions, who in January 1909 crossed the Polar Plateau to within 97 miles (156 kilometers) of the South Pole. Meanwhile, another party under Professor T. W. Edgeworth David succeeded in sledging to the South Magnetic Pole. When Shackleton returned to England in June 1909, he was showered with honors, including a knighthood.

In December 1911 the South Pole was finally achieved by the Norwegian Roald AMUNDSEN and, a month later, by Captain Scott's ill-fated party. Shackleton now turned his restless mind to an even more ambitious plan: the crossing of the Antarctic continent from the Weddell Sea to the Ross Sea. A landing would be effected on the Weddell Sea coast, and the transantarctic party would descend the Beardmore Glacier to the Ross Ice Shelf, picking up supplies depoted by a second party wintering at Cape Evans on Ross Island. The expedition, which left England on August 1, 1914, as World War I was breaking out, was in many ways a disaster. The expedition ship *Endurance* was beset in the ice of the Weddell Sea and had

to be abandoned, the crew escaping in boats to inhospitable ice-covered Elephant Island, in the South Shetland group. From here Shackleton with five companions made an incredible boat journey to South Georgia, crossing its glacier-clad mountains to seek help from the whalers at Grytviken. After further months of unceasing effort Shackleton at last secured the rescue of his Elephant Island party by the Chilean vessel *Yelcho* in August 1916.

During the latter years of the war Shackleton served on an expeditionary force to northern Russia. In 1921, frustrated in his efforts to launch an expedition to the Arctic, Shackleton, accompanied by several of his former Antarctic comrades, set sail on the *Quest* to explore the islands of the sub-Antarctic. It proved to be his last voyage. On January 5, 1922, he died suddenly of a heart attack on board ship off South Georgia. A striking and original explorer, Shackleton harnessed modern inventions to the service of exploration, made full use of publicity and the power of the press, and encouraged scientific research. But it is his powers of leadership for which "the boss," as he was known to his men, is best remembered. In the whole of his career Shackleton never lost a man.

See also ANTARCTICA.

BIBLIOGRAPHY: Margery and James Fisher, *Shackleton*, London, 1957; Ernest Henry Shackleton, *The Heart of the Antarctic: Being the Story of the British Antarctic Expedition 1907–1909*, 2 vols., London, 1909; id., *South: The Story of Shackleton's Last Expedition, 1914–1917*, London, 1919; John R. F. [Frank] Wild, *Shackleton's Last Voyage: The Story of the Quest*, London, 1923.

H. G. R. King

Ernest Henry Shackleton combined modern technological and promotional skills with the leadership qualities common to the greatest explorers of all ages. His polar expeditions were a series of moral victories and practical accomplishments. [Royal Geographical Society]

Shelekhov, Grigory Ivanovich (1747–1795) Russian merchant, fur trader, and founder of Russian America. In 1773 Shelekhov went from his birthplace, Rylsk, Kursk Guberniya, to Irkutsk, where he entered the service of a rich Siberian merchant, I. Golikov. He moved in 1775 to Okhotsk and with Golikov and other merchants organized a large fur company for operations in northeast Asia, the Aleutian Islands, and the northwest coast of North America. In 1783 he went with two galliots he had built, commanded respectively by Gerasim IZMAILOV and Dmitry BOCHAROV, from Okhotsk to Bering Island, where the expedition wintered. In 1784 he sailed to Unalaska and from there to Kodiak, where he founded a permanent settlement. In the next 2 years he founded other settlements on the northwest coast of the Gulf of Alaska and sent parties out to investigate adjoining regions. In the summer of 1786 he left Kodiak to return to Siberia. He died in Irkutsk in July 1795.

Ambitious and unscrupulous, Shelekhov made full use of his men and was harsh in dealing with native resisters. His account of his voyages was published as a book and has gone through many editions but gives an overly laudatory account of his discoveries, his treatment of the natives, and the prospects for his enterprises. Catherine the Great steadfastly refused to grant his company the monopoly of the fur trade which he sought, but after his death his son-in-law N. P. Rezanov was able to persuade the new monarch, Tsar Paul I, to grant permission to form a single company, the Russian-American Company (1798).

BIBLIOGRAPHY: G. I. Shelekhov, *Rossiskago kuptsa Grigorya Shelek-hova stranstvovaniye s 1783 po 1787 god iz Okhotska po Vosto-chnomu Okeanu k Amerikanskim beregam i vozvrashcheniye ego v Rossiyu,* St. Petersburg, 1791; Avrahm Yarmolinsky, "Shelekhov's Voyage to Alaska: A Bibliographical Note," *Bulletin of the New York Public Library,* vol. 36, no. 3, March 1932, pp. 141–148.

Richard A. Pierce

Siberia

The Russian people began to expand eastward soon after forming a state in the ninth century. The principalities of the Kievan state depended to a large extent on trade in forest products, particularly furs, and as fur-bearing animals were hunted out, new regions were explored. Novgorod, in the northeast, developed a virtual fur empire as its hunters and traders pushed farther, following the river systems. Novgorod sent expeditions to what the chronicles term "the country beyond the portage," east of Lakes Onega and Beloye to the Northern Dvina River (Severnaya Dvina), the "Iron Gates" (probably the region of the Pechora River), the "land of Yugra" (the Ural Mountains), and even "the land of midnight," which probably included the lower Ob region.

The decline of Kiev in the eleventh century started a population shift northeastward into the forest area along the Oka and Volga Rivers. There the Russians amalgamated with the Finnish tribes and built the strong principalities of Suzdal and Vladimir, which began to encroach on the Novgorodian lands. The Mongol conquest (1237–1241), which spared Novgorod, gave it a respite from this competition and permitted the continuance of its pioneering. In 1363 Novgorod sent a large expedition to the lower Ob River.

The rise of a new Volga principality, Moscow, brought a push from that quarter. By 1472 Moscow had taken Great Perm, the land of the Komi Permyaks, in the basin of the upper Kama River. There the Russians clashed with another people living farther east, the Voguls. Pursuing them in 1483, the Muscovites made the first-known expedition to the Irtysh region, the Siberian land, or Sibir. Of unknown origin, the term appears in Arab and Persian sources of the first half of the fourteenth century. As a result of the expedition of 1483, Yugorian (of a Finnish tribe occupying the land of Yugra in the Ural Mountains), Vogul, and one of the Siberian (probably Tatar) princes became tributary to Moscow. At the end of the fifteenth century, between 1499 and 1501, Prince Semyon Kurbsky led another Moscow expedition to Siberia. Thus the Russians in the last quarter of the fifteenth century penetrated to the Irtysh River and were already familiar with the lower Ob. Grand Prince Vasily included in his title a claim to sovereignty over "the lands of Obdora and Konda," lands along the lower Ob and along the Konda, a tributary of the Irtysh.

In 1478 Moscow, after a seesaw struggle, annexed Novgorod and its possessions. The conquest in 1552 of the khanate of Kazan by Ivan IV (Ivan the Terrible) brought the central Ural tribes under Moscow rule and opened the way to the east. In 1555 the khanate of Sibir began paying tribute, although this ceased when Kuchum, another Tatar, usurped the throne of the khanate.

The Stroganovs, a leading merchant family, were given extensive lands in the new region. When harassed by Vogul tribesmen from beyond the Urals, the Stroganovs equipped a band of cossacks under YERMAK and about 1581 sent them across the Urals into Sibir. Yermak occupied the site of the old capital of Sibir, Tyumen, and then continued along the Tobol to Isker, the capital of the khanate, and captured it. There followed hard fighting in which the Russians sought to consolidate their hold on the region; in 1584 or 1585 Yermak himself was killed in battle.

After Yermak's death, the Moscow state took over the subjugation of the new territory. Plans for systematic occupation were gradually worked out. The troops sent to Siberia built forts on the Ob River and its tributaries and at the portages. These forts served as centers for the collection of fur tribute *(yasak)* and as bases for the subjugation of the surrounding tribes. The natives, unaccustomed to firearms or to organizing in large numbers, rarely put up effective resistance.

The route first taken to the new territory was from the Chusovaya, a tributary of the Kama, to the Tagil, the Tura, and the Tobol. At the sources of the Tagil the small fort of Verkhnetagilsk was built. This route had to be given up because the mountain rivers were too shallow. A route from the Vishera, another tributary of the Kama, to the Lozva, Tavda, and Tobol Rivers was tried next. In 1590 the fort of Lozvinsk was built on the Lozva, where the river becomes navigable.

The Lozva route was dangerous for a long time because of the warlike and restless Vogul tribe, centered at Pelym, on the eastern slope of the Urals. The Russians subjugated them and built a fort at Pelym in 1593. The destruction of the Pelym principality made the Tavda route safe, but in 1597 Artemy Babinov found a better route by land directly to the Tura River which shortened travel by about 700 miles (1127 kilometers). This remained the principal land route to Siberia until 1763, when the Siberia-Moscow road by way of Kungur and Yekaterinburg (now Sverdlovsk) was established. In 1598 a new town, Verkhoturye, was founded on the Tura, and in about 1600 another fort, Turinsk, was built midway between Verkhoturye and Tyumen. The establishment of these points consolidated the route between the Kama and the Irtysh. This system of transportation and communication firmly attached the newly acquired Siberian khanate to the Moscow state.

From the fourteenth century on the Ostyak tribes on the lower Ob had paid tribute more or less regularly, first to the Novgorodians, then to the Muscovites. The final subjugation of the Ostyaks and the Samoyeds followed the founding (1593) of the fort of Berezovo on the Sosva River about 13 miles (21 kilometers) from its confluence with the Ob and the founding 2 years later of Obdorsk (now Salekhard) near the mouth of the Ob.

The Russians had known of the coast of the Gulf of Ob (Obskaya Guba) for at least a century, and they had visited it to trade with the Samoyeds. On the Taz River the Russian traders had founded their own fort and had gathered abundant furs by barter or by the imposition of *yasak* for their own benefit. About 1600, a party sent from Tobolsk descended the Ob, entered the Gulf of Ob, and continued overland toward the mouth of the Taz. Ascending the Taz, they built the fort of Mangazeya, which became an important fur-trading and administrative center.

Meanwhile, others had gone up the Ob from its confluence with the Irtysh and in 1594 founded the fort of Surgut. Surgut's main significance was military, to keep watch over the Ostyak tribe of the middle Ob. This tribe was subdued in 1598, and a fort, Narym, was built in the center of its territory. The subjugation of the Ostyak tribes was completed in 1602 with the building of another fort, Ketsk, on the Ket River, a tributary of the Ob.

The foundation of Narym and Ketsk brought the Russians to a region inhabited by various Tatar and Kirghiz tribes. In 1604 one of the Tatar princes recognized Russian authority, and the Russians built another advanced southern outpost, Tomsk, on the Tom River, a tributary of the Ob. In 1618 still another step was taken with establishment of Kuznetsk (now Novokuznetsk), farther up the Tom.

Yenisey Basin The conquest of the territories drained by the Ob and its tributaries soon led to another great river system farther east. Following routes discovered previously by private traders, about 1607 government men from Mangazeya went overland from the Taz River to the Turukhan River, a western tributary of the Yenisey River. The small post of Turukhansk founded at the mouth of the Turukhan later supplanted Mangazeya as an administrative center, becoming known as New Mangazeya.

From Turukhansk the advance continued. In 1610 Kondraty Kurochkin and other Dvina merchants in Mangazeya built *kochi* (decked boats) in Turukhansk, sailed down the Yenisey to its mouth, and then proceeded eastward to the Pyasina. In 1614 a fort was built on this river to collect *yasak* from the Samoyeds.

Meanwhile in 1608, men from Ketsk had reached the Yenisey by way of the Ket-Yenisey portage and ascended the Yenisey as far as the Kan River. In 1618 the garrison of Ketsk was augmented, and an expedition composed of men from Ketsk and Tobolsk under Pyotr Albychev and Cherkas Rukin was sent to explore the routes to the Yenisey and Upper Tunguska (Verkhnyaya Tunguska) Rivers. At the head of the Ket they built Makovsk. From this point the territory farther east was explored. In 1619 the founders of Makovsk went farther up the Ket, portaged to the small Kem River, and followed it to the Yenisey, where they built the fort of Yeniseysk. From Yeniseysk cossacks went to the Upper Tunguska and then to the Stony Tunguska (Podkamennaya Tunguska) and Lower Tunguska (Nizhnyaya Tunguska) Rivers.

Lena Basin Men from Mangazeya were also active on the eastern tributaries of the Yenisey. On the Stony Tunguska about 1620 the Tungus told the Mangazeyans of another large river to the east, where there were people who lived in houses, wore clothes like the Russians, and kept horses. These rumors caused a rush to the new region. Men from Mangazeya ascended the Lower Tunguska, portaged to the sources of the Vilyuy River, descended it to the mighty Lena River, and soon encountered the Yakuts, a Turkic people with a more advanced culture than that of most other Siberian tribes.

The first Russians to sail on the Lena were *promyshlenniks* (fur hunters) led by one Penda. Starting from Turukhansk with forty companions, Penda spent 3 years on the Lower Tunguska. Reaching its upper course, he and his party portaged to the Lena at a point opposite the right tributary Kirenga, which they descended to the Lena. Penda went as far as the site of the future Yakutsk, then turned and went back up the river to the mouth of the Kulenga, opposite which, on the right bank of the Lena, was the future site of Verkholensk. From there he crossed the Buryat steppe until he reached the Upper Tunguska, or Angara. This swift-flowing stream brought Penda and his men back to the Yenisey, by which at the end of 1623 they reached Yeniseysk, whence they returned to Turukhansk after a journey of more than 5000 miles (8047 kilometers).

In 1629 the *voyevodas* (commandants) of Tobolsk dispatched an expedition under Samson Navatsky. Like Penda, Navatsky ascended the Lower Tunguska, but portaged to the Chona, descended it to the Vilyuy, and went down the Vilyuy to the Lena, where he built a small fort, Ust-Vilyuyskoye. Other *promyshlenniks* followed, and the Vilyuy soon became a well-known route.

The government men and traders of Yeniseysk were meanwhile approaching the Lena from its upper reaches in the south. In 1628 the petty officer Vasily Bugor left Yeniseysk with ten men, ascended the Upper Tunguska and its small tributary, the Idirma, portaged to the Kuta River, and followed it to the upper Lena. He ascended the Lena as far as the mouth of the Kirenga, collecting *yasak* from Yakuts along the way, then turned and retraced his route, arriving in Yemiseysk in 1630.

The fine quality of furs brought back by Bugor led to the organization of another expedition from Yeniseysk, under the command of Ivan Galkin. He discovered a route from the Ilim, a tributary of the Upper Tunguska, to the Lena that was much better than the Idirma-Kuta portage used by Bugor and secured it by building Lensky Volok, later known as Ilimsk, on the Ilim and Ust-Kut at the mouth of the Kuta.

In 1631 Pyotr BEKETOV of Yeniseysk, with about thirty men, portaged from Ilimsk, ascended the Lena as far as the mouth of the Kulenga, and then turned west into the Buryat steppe. There he and his party clashed with the strong and warlike Buryats, a Mongol tribe. Retreating to the Lena, Beketov built the fort of Tutursk at the mouth of the Tutura River. After wintering at Ust-Kut, Beketov led his force down the Lena in the spring of 1632 and conquered most of the Yakuts. On the right bank of the Lena he built a fort, the future Yakutsk. From there he continued down the Lena, conquering the Tungus, and built the post of Zhigansk. In 1633 he operated with the same success along a large eastern tributary of the Lena, the Aldan.

From Tomsk, in 1636, a detachment under Dmitry Kopylov was sent to the Lena by way of Yeniseysk. Kopylov descended the Lena and then went up the Aldan. Above the mouth of the Maya River, a right-

Approach to a partly dismantled pontoon bridge across the Angara River at Irkutsk. Ivan Pokhabov founded the city as an administrative center in 1652. [Library of Congress]

bank tributary of the Aldan, he established the post of Butalsk and proceeded to collect *yasak* from the Tungus and a related people, the Lamuts. In 1639 Kopylov sent a detachment of twenty men under Ivan Moskvitin to reconnoiter the country to the east. The party went up the Maya and its tributary, the Yudoma, then through a pass in the Dzhugdzhur Range to the Ulya River. Following the Ulya downstream, they reached the Sea of Okhotsk, part of the North Pacific. In less than 60 years, from Yermak's expedition of 1581, the Russians had traversed the entire distance to the Pacific.

Baykal region On the upper Yenisey the Russians heard of the Buryats. As usual, they sent out parties to reconnoiter and build advance posts. In 1627–1628 Maksim Perfilyev of Yeniseysk ascended the Upper Tunguska River as far as the Shaman Rapids, where he built a small post. In 1627 Andrey Dubensky, also from Yeniseysk, reached the juncture of the Kacha and Yenisey Rivers and there built a fort which he named Krasnoyarsk. In 1628 one Ostafyev built the small post of Kansk, on the Kan River. The same year Pyotr Beketov built the post of Rybnoy in the Buryat country, at the mouth of the Uda River, then went up the Upper Tunguska to the mouth of the Oka, and in 1629 returned to Yeniseysk.

These penetrations of their territory had aroused the Buryats, and Maksim Perfilyev was given the task of pacifying them. In 1631 Perfilyev built a fort, Bratsk, on the Angara River. Three years later the Buryats massacred the garrison and burned the fort, but in 1635 it was rebuilt. Bratsk guarded communications between the Yenisey and the Lena and became an important base for *yasak* collection and further exploration.

In 1643 a Yakutsk man, Kurbat Ivanov, made his way from Verkholensk and discovered Lake Baykal. One of his men, named Skorokhodov, went around the north end of the lake as far as the Barguzin River. In 1644 Vasily Kolesnikov of Yeniseysk took a party as far as the Osa River, an eastern tributary of the Angara, and built Verkhne-Angarsk. In 1644 Ivan Pokhabov was sent from Yeniseysk to Bratsk, then up the Angara to Lake Baykal, and across the lake to its main source, the Selenga River, where he obtained information about the Mongols. In 1648 Ivan Galkin founded the fort of Barguzin, and in 1652, taking over command of this post, Pokhabov built a small post on the Angara, Irkutsk, to become the administrative center of eastern Siberia.

In 1653, having been sent out from Yeniseysk, Pyotr Beketov built the fort Ust-Prorva at the mouth of the Selenga, then went up the Selenga to Lake Irgen, where he founded Irgensk. In 1653–1654 one of Beketov's men built Nerchinsk; it had to be abandoned but in 1658 was restored. The same year Telembinsk was built; in 1665 the post of Udinsk (later Verkhne-Udinsk) was founded at the confluence of the Uda and Selenga, and the fort of Selenginsk farther up the Selenga.

Acquisition and loss of the Amur In the late 1630s, rumors of a great river in eastern Siberia began to spread among the Russians on the Yenisey and the Lena. In 1639 Ivan Moskvitin and his men from Tomsk, the first Russians to reach the Pacific, heard of the Amur and Zeya Rivers from the Lamuts. The people who lived along the Amur were said to practice agriculture and to possess rich silver deposits.

The Perfilyev Expedition of 1638–1640 from Yeniseysk, while on the Vitim and its tributary, the Tsipa, heard of the Daurs on the Shilka and the Amur. Expeditions sent out from Yeniseysk to verify these rumors led to the conquest of the trans-Baykal region and the discovery of a direct route into the Amur region from the west, the Barguzin-Nercha route discovered in 1650 by Vasily Kolesnikov. However, it was to be men from Yakutsk, on the Lena, who would first enter this new territory.

The Lena tributaries—the Vitim, the Olekma, and the Aldan—offered three obvious routes to the Amur; so the new center of Yakutsk took the lead in exploring the new region. As soon as the commandants of Yakutsk heard of Perfilyev's expedition, they sent seventy men under Yenaley Bakhteyarov along the Vitim. Bakhteyarov had orders to investigate the sources of the river and to secure accurate information about the Daurs and Daurian silver but failed in this mission.

In June 1643, another Yakutsk official, Vasily Poyarkov, was sent with 120 men to the Amur, this time by way of the Aldan. Poyarkov ascended the Aldan, its right tributary, the Uchur, and the Gonam. Leaving some of his men there, he and 90 men crossed the Stanovoy Range and discovered the Zeya, a tributary of the Amur. Mistreatment of the natives made them hostile, so that the party suffered great hardships during the winter. In the spring of 1644 the party left on the Gonam arrived with supplies, and they went down the Zeya to the Amur and along that river to its mouth, terrorizing the native Daurs, Dyuchers, Olchas, Goldi, and Gilyaks. They wintered at the mouth of the Amur, and in the summer of 1645 sailed into the Sea of Okhotsk, sighting the northwest coast of Sakhalin, and across the western part of the Okhotsk to the Ulya River, already known from Moskvitin's expedition. They wintered a third time at the mouth of the Ulya, and in the early spring of 1646 they ascended that river, crossed the watershed, and by rivers of the Lena Basin returned to Yakutsk in June 1646.

In 1649 Yerofey Pavlovich Khabarov was sent from Yakutsk on a new expedition to the Amur. The Vitim and Aldan Rivers had proved impractical because of many rapids and difficult mountain terrain, so the Olekma River was now chosen. The party ascended the Olekma and the Tungir as far as the mouth of the Nyukzha, where they spent part of the winter. They then crossed the Yablonovy Range and by way of the Urka or the Amazar reached the Amur. Finding the natives hostile and believing that war with them would lead to a conflict with their suzerain, China, he returned to Yakutsk in May 1650 to report. Returning to the Amur the same year, Khabarov conquered the town of the Daur princeling Albaza and fortified it, calling it Albazin. He wintered there, and in the spring of 1651 he and his men built boats and started down the Amur. The natives resisted stubbornly, and at the mouth of the Sungari Khabarov founded the fort of Achansk, where the party spent the winter of 1651–1652. The new Manchu regime in China now sent an army against Achansk. The Russians beat them off, but anticipating another attack, Khabarov in April 1652 abandoned Achansk and moved up the Amur. He built a fort (later Blagoveshchensk) at the mouth of the Zeya, then ascended the Amur to the mouth of the Kumara, where he built the fort of Kumarsk on what is now the Chinese side of the river.

In 1658, a garrison left on the Amur at Albazin was expelled by the Chinese, and for more than a decade the region became a no-man's-land. In 1672 the Moscow government began a cautious attempt to reoccupy the region. Albazin was refortified, but in 1685 it was again lost to the Chinese. Neither side wanted to go to war, however, and in 1689 the Chinese and Russians met at Nerchinsk and concluded a treaty by which the Russians agreed to withdraw from the Amur region.

Chukotka and Kamchatka While exploring and subjugating the Lena, Baykal, and Amur regions, the Russian administration, servicemen, and traders also explored regions farther north and eastward. Using techniques derived from experience in river transport and in the maritime region of northern Russia, they ventured successfully on stormy Arctic seas. In 1633 Ilya Perfiryev and Ivan Rebrov descended the Lena to the Arctic Ocean. From there Rebrov and part of the group followed the coast west to the Olenek River, while Perfiryev sailed east along the coast to the Yana River. In 1638 Rebrov went by sea to the Yana and eastward to the Indigirka River. Between 1635 and 1638 Yelisey Buza explored the Omoloy, the Yana, and Chondon Rivers, subjugating the Yukaghirs inhabiting the region. In 1636 and 1638, Posnik Ivanov found a land route from Yakutsk across the Verkhoyansk Range to the Yana, and in 1640 he reached the Indigirka, subduing the Yukaghirs in that region.

Reports of activities on the Yana and Indigirka and rumors of a Pogicha River somewhere farther east brought other expeditions from Yakutsk. In 1640 Dmitry Zyryan and a small detachment took the overland route to the Indigirka, descended it, subduing the Yukaghirs, and then went by sea to the Alazeya River. Rumors of the Kolyma and other rivers still farther east led to the dispatch in 1644 of an expedition under Mikhail Stadukhin and including the later famous Semyon Dezhnev. Stadukhin and his party sailed down the Indigirka to the sea, thence eastward to the Alazeya, and from there to the Kolyma, establishing Nizhnekolymsk near the river's mouth. In 1648 a party under Fyodot Alekseyev Popov, including Semyon Dezhnev, left Nizhnekolymsk and sailed to the mouth of the Kolyma and eastward along the coast, still in search of the elusive Pogicha River, which now began to be called the Anadyr. On the way all the boats were lost except that of Dezhnev, who made it around Mys Dezhneva (East Cape) to discover the Anadyr River and, by so doing, to solve unwittingly the geographic problem of whether Asia and North America were joined. In 1649 Dezhnev founded the fort of Anadyr, and the following year, having ascended the Bolshoy Anyuy and crossed the mountains, Mikhail Stadukhin also appeared on the Anadyr.

Following the expeditions of Dezhnev and Stadukhin, the fort of Anadyr became the main base for activities in the eastern extremities of Siberia. From Anadyr the cossack hunters and traders imposed *yasak* upon the Koryak reindeer herders to the south as far as the Oklan and Olyutora Rivers. The fort of Aklansk, built in 1669, served as an added guarantee of Koryak submission.

There were rumors at least as early as the 1660s of a land to the south called Kamchatka. In 1696, under orders from Vladimir ATLASOV, in charge at Anadyr, the cossack Luka Morozko led a party down the west coast of Kamchatka as far as the Tigil River. In 1697 Atlasov himself went nearly to the end of the peninsula, conquering the native Kamchadals as he went. Verkhnekamchatsk (1699), Nizhnekamchatsk (1701), and Bolseretsk (1704) became the main Russian strongholds.

In 1711 two cossack mutineers, Danilo Antsyferov and Ivan Kozyrevsky, led a party across the strait from the southern extremity of Kamchatka, Mys Lopatka,

View of the town and harbor of Petropavlovsk in Kamchatka. The Kamchadals were conquered by Vladimir Atlasov in 1697. [Library of Congress]

to become the first Russians to visit the Kuril Islands. The party landed on the island of Shumshu and perhaps on the next island, Paramushir. From the Ainu inhabitants they obtained information about the islands farther south and thus were able to return to Bolsheretsk with a tentative map of the entire Kuril chain. In 1721 two topographers, Ivan Yevreinov and Fyodor Luzhin, sent by Peter the Great to investigate the Kurils, reached the sixth island, Simushir.

Scientific exploration   In the eighteenth century exploration in Russia advanced from the earlier efforts of untrained military men and traders to systematic investigation for scientific purposes by personnel to some degree prepared for their tasks. Much of this change came about through Tsar Peter the Great's own wide-ranging interests and his desire to place Russia in the forefront of modern scientific achievement. Peter, dreaming of an Arctic route to China and India, was particularly interested in the configuration of land at the east end of Asia and in the problem of whether Asia and North America were joined. A Great Kamchatka Command, authorized in 1716 to study the coasts of Kamchatka and Chukotka (Chukotsky Poluostrov) never materialized, but in 1724 Peter ordered what later became known as the First Kamchatka Expedition for similar purposes. Vitus BERING, a Danish seafarer, was appointed to head the expedition, sided by Lieut. Aleksey CHIRIKOV and Martin Spanberg. After surmounting great difficulties of transport and supply, the expedition built the vessel *Sv. Gavriil (St. Gabriel)* at Nizhnekamchatsk, and in July 1728 Bering and his party put to sea. Bering's survey of the strait now bearing his name was inconclusive, and an effort in the following year to reach the coasts of North America was abandoned.

The Russian Senate, dissatisfied with Bering's first expedition, in April 1732 ordered a Second Kamchatka Expedition, part of a grandiose project today known collectively as the Great Northern Expedition, aimed at a wholesale reconnaissance of the Arctic and Pacific coasts of Siberia. The enterprise was to consist of three detachments. One, under Bering, was to try to reach North America; another, under Spanberg, was to explore the islands of Japan; and a third, actually several expeditions, was to explore the Arctic coast. Bering was charged with responsibility for all three.

Despite extreme hardships and a high cost in lives and resources, the groups assigned to explore the northern coasts achieved brilliant success. In 1734–1735, Lieut. Stepan Muravyev and Mikhail Pavlov explored the Kara Sea coast and along the west coast of Poluostrov Yamal, reaching, respectively, latitudes 73°04′N and 73°11′N before being forced back by ice. In 1736–1737 Lieut. Stepan Malygin and Aleksey Skuratov rounded Poluostrov Yamal. Between 1734 and 1737 Lieut. Dmitry Ovtsyn sailed from Obdorsk on the Ob to Turukhansk on the Yenisey, preparing a detailed map of the route. Between 1738 and 1740 pilot Fyodor Minin and Lieut. Dmitry Sterlegov penetrated from the Yenisey eastward to the west coast of Poluostrov Taymyr. Lieut. Vasily Pronchishchev and Lieut. Khariton Laptev explored the east coast of the peninsula in 1735 and in 1739–1740 respectively. Between 1736 and 1743 Lieut. Dmitry Laptev managed, first, to follow the coast eastward from the Lena to the Indigirka and then to continue as far eastward as Mys Bolshoy Baranov, beyond the mouth of the Kolyma, before being stopped by ice.

In the spring of 1738 Spanberg, in the brig *Arkhangel Mikhail*, accompanied by Lieut. William Walton in the double sloop *Nadezhda* and by Lieut. Aleksey Schelting in Bering's old vessel the *Sv. Gavriil*, sailed to investigate the Kuril Islands and the islands of Japan. Spanberg mapped most of the Kurils as far as the island of Urup; Walton reached Hokkaido. In 1739 both Spanberg and Walton independently reached the main Japanese island of Honshu.

Bering undertook his own part of the enterprise in 1741, putting to sea from Petropavlovsk in June. He achieved only minor success before wrecking his vessel on the island that now bears his name and dying there, but the expedition was important for the exploration of the Aleutian Islands. *See also* NORTHWESTERN NORTH AMERICA.

Equally important were studies made by individu-

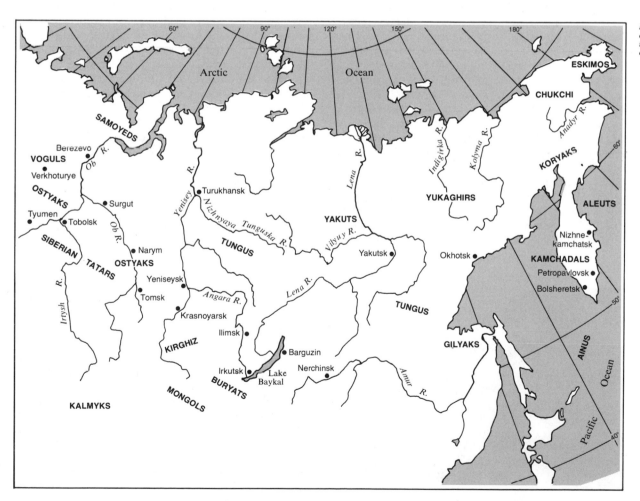

Important towns and native peoples in eighteenth-century Siberia.

als or small groups. Daniel Gottlieb MESSERSCHMIDT, a naturalist and physician of Danzig invited to Russia by Peter the Great in 1716, is credited with beginning the planned study of Siberia. Between 1720 and 1727 he studied the Baraba Steppe, the Kuznetsky Alatau, the Ob, Yenisey, and Lower Tunguska Rivers, the headwaters of the Lena River, Lake Baykal, Dauria (a territory on the upper Amur), and Lake Dalai Nor (Holun Nor) in Inner Mongolia. On the Tom River he found the skeleton of a mammoth; in the trans-Baykal region he found and described extensive mineral resources; and he was the first to discover and describe permafrost. His ten-volume manuscript description of his investigations, written in Latin, has never been translated or published.

Several other savants worked as members of Bering's Great Northern Expedition. The historian Gerhard Friedrich Müller collected a mass of historical materials on Siberia in the years 1733–1743. During the same period Johann Georg Gmelin traveled widely in western Siberia, the trans-Baykal region, and the Yakutsk and Ural regions, obtaining the first scientific information on the flora, fauna, ethnography, and geology of many of the regions he traversed. Georg Wilhelm STELLER, a zoologist and physician who accompanied Bering, made extensive observations on the natural history of Kamchatka, several of the Kuril Islands, and other parts of Siberia. Stepan Petrovich KRASHENINNIKOV accompanied Gmelin between 1733 and 1736 and traveled extensively in Kamchatka between 1737 and 1741, studying its geology, geography, botany, zoology, history, ethnography, and languages. Between 1769 and 1774 Peter Simon Pallas, invited to Russia by Catherine II from his native Berlin, studied the Volga region, the Urals, the northwestern Altay (Altai) Mountains, and the Minusinsk Basin, working out the main characteristics of the relief of the Sayan and Altay systems. In 1722 he went to Irkutsk and studied the trans-Baykal region, the Yablonovy Range, and Lake Baykal. His works are to be found in his *Travels through the Southern Provinces of the Russian Empire* (London, 1802–1803). The doctor of medicine Johann Gottlieb

Goldi along the Amur River, north of Khaberovsk. Although Russia had been excluded from the Amur Valley since 1689, the area remained of great interest in government circles, and in 1850 Lieut. Gennady Ivanovich Nevelskoy claimed the entire region for the Russian crown. [Library of Congress]

Georgi, assigned to Pallas's expedition in 1772, wrote extensively on the peoples and natural history of Russia.

Return to the Amur   Russian exclusion from the Amur Valley, occasioned by the Treaty of Nerchinsk in 1689, was a cause for regret in government circles, but as late as the nineteenth century little was actually known about the region. In 1787 the French navigator Jean-François de Galaup, comte de LA PÉROUSE concluded that Sakhalin was a peninsula, connected with the mainland by a neck of land north of De Kastri Bay. In 1805 the Russian navigator Adam Johann von KRUSENSHTERN, making hasty observations along the same coast, came away convinced that La Pérouse was right and that the mouth of the Amur was unnavigable because of extensive sandbanks. Certain Russian naval officers, on the other hand, referring to old maps and accounts, thought otherwise, and in view of the Amur's potential importance as an eastern waterway, urged the exploration and reoccupation of the Amur Valley. One of these, Lieut. Gennady Ivanovich NEVELSKOY, explored the area in 1849 and found that a strait did exist and that Sakhalin was an island. Gaining imperial approval, Nevelskoy in 1850 was appointed commander of an expedition to establish a post "on the southwest coast of the Okhotsk Sea." Acting on his own initiative, he raised the Russian flag at the mouth of the Amur, claiming as Russian territory all the Amur region and the island of Sakhalin. Several talented assistants (N. K. Boshnyak, D. I. Orlov, A. I. Petrov, and N. V. Rudanovsky) studied the Amur region and Sakhalin, mapped the Tatarsky Proliv (Tatar Strait), discovered harbors, and located ship channels.

The Arctic   The most difficult region of Siberia for exploration remained the Arctic coastline and the landmasses, real or mythical, which lay offshore. In 1710 the Yakutsk cossack Yakov Permyakov, sailing from the Lena to the Kolyma, saw two islands at sea. In March 1712 the Yakutsk cossack Merkury Vagin took a party on sledges from Ust-Yansk across the ice to what became known as Bolshoy Lyakhov Island (Ostrov Bolshoy Lyakhovsky), southernmost of the New Siberian Islands (Novosibirskiye Ostrova). Discovery in 1759–1760 of a huge deposit of mammoth bones on the same island led to the discovery of two other islands in the group, Maly (1770) and Kotelny (1773). In 1800 a hunter named Faddeya discovered another island east of Kotelny, which was named Ostrov Faddeyevsky after him.

Exploring the archipelago further between in 1809 and 1811, Yakov Sannikov sighted a landmass north of the group. Later explorers sought this nonexistent "Sannikov Land" in vain; in 1902 the Russian explorer Baron Eduard von Toll and three companions died in the search, which persisted until 1938 (*see* BEGICHEV, Nikifor Alekseyevich).

The finding of other undiscovered land in the Arctic Ocean was predicted by in 1870 Prince Pyotr Alekseyevich Kropotkin, secretary of the Physical Geography

Section of the Russian Geographical Society, on the basis of the movement of ice. In 1873 the Austro-Hungarian expedition of Julius von Payer found and named Franz Josef Land (Zemlya Frantsa Iosifa), but Kropotkin insisted that still other landmasses must exist. His prediction was borne out in 1913 when a Russian expedition under Boris Andreyevich Vilkitsky discovered northeast of Novaya Zemlya the large archipelago which was named Severnaya Zemlya.

The dream of an Arctic sea route across Europe and Asia existed from the sixteenth century on. In 1764, on the initiative of the Russian scientist Mikhail Vasilyevich Lomonosov, a secret expedition was fitted out to seek a route from Spitsbergen (Svalbard) to Kamchatka by way of the polar basin. Capt. Vasily Yakovlevich Chichagov managed to reach 80°26'N northwest of Spitsbergen, closer to the North Pole than anyone had yet been, before being turned back by ice. In the nineteenth century the dream was revived in 1862, when the industrialist M. K. Sidorov sent two sailing vessels to find the way, but both vessels were crushed by ice off Poluostrov Yamal.

Others were more successful with segments of the journey. The English captain Joseph Wiggins, starting in 1874, made several voyages through the Kara Sea to the mouth of the Ob. In 1875 Nils Adolf Erik NOR-DENSKIÖLD, a Swede, rounded the Poluostrov Yamal and reached the mouth of the Yenisey discovering a good harbor, Dickson. Finally, in 1878–1879 Nordenskiöld made the entire trip in the *Vega*. The development of modern icebreakers made the voyage practicable. In 1914–1915 Boris Vilkitsky made it with the icebreakers *Vaygach* and *Taymyr*. In 1932 the icebreaker *Sibiryakov*, under O. Y. Shmidt, made the voyage in a single season.

See also NORTHEAST PASSAGE.

BIBLIOGRAPHY: V. K. Andriyevich, *Istorichesky ocherk Sibiri po dannym predstavliyaemym Polnym sobraniem zakonov*, 6 vols. in 8, St. Petersburg, 1886–1889; id., *Kratky ocherk istory Zabaikalya ot drevneishikh vremen do 1762 goda*, St. Petersburg, 1887; John F. Baddeley, *Russia, Mongolia and China . . . A.D. 1602–1676*, 2 vols., London, 1919; L. S. Berg, *Ocherki po istory russkikh geograficheskikh otkryty*, 2d ed., Moscow and Leningrad, 1949; id., *Otkrytiye Kamchatki i kamchatskiye ekspeditsy Beringa*, 3d ed., Leningrad and Moscow, 1946; James R. Gibson, *Feeding the Russian Fur Trade: Provisionment of the Okhotsk Seaboard and the Kamchatka Peninsula 1639–1856*, Madison, Wis., Milwaukee, and London, 1969; Frank A. Golder, *Russian Expansion on the Pacific, 1641–1850*, Cleveland, 1914; Robert J. Kerner, *The Urge to the Sea: The Course of Russian History; The Role of Rivers, Portages, Monasteries and Furs*, Berkeley, Calif., 1946; S. P. Krasheninnikov, *Explorations of Kamchatka, North Pacific Scimitar*, tr. by E. A. P. Crownhart-Vaughan, Portland, Oreg., 1972; George V. Lantzeff and Richard A. Pierce, *Eastward to Empire: Exploration and Conquest on the Russian Open Frontier, to 1750*, Montreal and London, 1973; G. F. Müller, *Istoriya Sibiri*, 2 vols., Moscow and Leningrad, 1937–1941; G. A. Sarychev, *Account of a Voyage of Discovery to the North-East of Siberia, the Frozen Ocean, and the North-East Sea*, London, 1806.

Richard A. Pierce

Sinclair, James (1811–1856)

Sinclair, James (1811–1856) Rupert's Land trader, traveler, and Rocky Mountain explorer. Born at Oxford House, the son of a Hudson's Bay Company officer from the Orkneys and a part-Cree mother, Sinclair was educated in Edinburgh, Scotland.

Returning to Rupert's Land in 1826, young Sinclair became the partner of Red River Settlement's leading private merchant, Andrew McDermot. Trading and freighting gave him wide experience of travel with

View of the northern Rockies, which James Sinclair crossed twice, leading Canadian emigrants into what are now Oregon and Washington. [Library of Congress]

boat brigades to Hudson Bay, with Red River cart brigades to St. Peter, Minnesota, and with dog trains in winter. In the struggle against the Hudson's Bay Company's monopoly of trade he became a leader of the mixed-stock *(métis)* population, thereby incurring the hostility of Sir George Simpson, governor in chief of the territories of the Hudson's Bay Company.

As this population expanded, free trading caused the company increasing concern, while anxiety was mounting as to the future of Oregon, then in dispute between Great Britain and the United States. To relieve the pressure of population in Red River and to strengthen the British presence in Oregon, the company decided to promote emigration from Red River to Oregon. A party of emigrants was organized with Sinclair as leader. Twenty-three families (121 men, women, and children with fifty-five carts, horses, and cattle) left Red River on June 5, 1841, and reached Fort Vancouver on the Columbia on October 13. Deserted by their guide at the foot of the mountains, they were rescued by an Indian, Bras Croche, who led them through a pass, probably White Man Pass, that proved shorter and easier than Simpson Pass, traversed by Simpson a few weeks earlier.

Eager to discover the best-possible route across the mountains for travelers by land (the usual Hudson's Bay Company route by Athabasca Pass connected water routes on the two sides of the mountains), Sinclair told John PALLISER in 1848 that he hoped to try another pass of which he had heard. He crossed the mountains again in 1850 by his 1841 pass to spend 2 years in California and Oregon, where he planned to settle. Discouraged by conditions there, he returned via Panama and New York to Red River in 1852. There he was reconciled secretly with Sir George Simpson, accepted an appointment in the service of the company west of the mountains, and organized a second party of emigrants to the Columbia. Twenty-eight men with their families and 250 cattle set off on May 25, 1854. Bras Croche and two Stonies (Assiniboin) were their guides through the mountains, but the new and supposedly better route that they tried turned out to be very bad and difficult for cattle. They traveled up the Kananaskis Valley, but which of the three passes that lead from it over the Rockies was the one they crossed is not clear. They took a month to get through the mountains, but at last emerged in the Kootenay Valley, where Sinclair got his bearings at Canal Flats, which separate the headwaters of the Columbia from the Kootenay River, and eventually reached Walla Walla, Washington, on December 24.

Sinclair planned further journeys with emigrants from Red River to the Columbia but was killed at the Cascades in the Yakima Indian War. The name Sinclair's Pass has fallen into disuse, but Sinclair's Canyon, through which the Banff-Windermere highway runs, still commemorates his pioneering journeys through the Rocky Mountains.

BIBLIOGRAPHY: D. Geneva Lent, *West of the Mountains: James Sinclair and the Hudson's Bay Company*, Seattle, 1963; George Simpson, *Narrative of a Journey round the World during the Years 1841 and 1842*, 2 vols., London, 1847.

Irene M. Spry

Smith, Jedediah Strong (1799–1831) American explorer. Born in New York of a New England family, this "knight in buckskin," as contemporaries called him, was an anomaly because most other traders were from the South or West and because he did not drink much, refrained from smoking and chewing, and took his Bible on the trail. After his family migrated to Pennsylvania, the fur trade drew Jedediah to St. Louis. During his 9-year exploratory career, he traveled more than 16,000 miles (25,750 kilometers) and gathered the first precise information about the Far Southwest.

Smith was only 24 years old, perhaps the youngest man to lead a major expedition westward, when he left Fort Kiowa (Fort Lookout) on the upper Missouri River in late September 1823 to trap in the central Rockies and Columbia River areas. Under contract to William ASHLEY, Smith led eleven men across the Plains via the White River and through the Dakotas' Badlands and Black Hills. There were hardships. Besides nearly dying of thirst, Smith encountered a wounded grizzly along the western slopes of the Black Hills which took his head in its jaws and nearly killed him. While Smith recuperated for 10 days, his men explored the hills; then the entire party moved across the Belle Fourche River, buying horses from the Sioux and Cheyenne, into the Powder River Valley, over the Bighorn Mountains through Granite Pass, and into the basin of the Bighorn River. Foolishly choosing to cross the mountains at Union Pass in early February, Smith had to turn back because of heavy snow. Having learned of another pass from the Indians, he soon set out again for the mountains. This time Smith and his men were a match for the elements. They went through the continental divide to the Sweetwater River and became the first Americans to cross the Rockies westward through South Pass. Their reward came in March when they gazed upon the Green River, an area rich in beaver.

The final stage in this expedition, to the Columbia, held further difficulties. After trapping along the Green to the foot of the Uinta Mountains (the area of Blacks Fork), Smith set out west and northwest with seven men toward Flathead Post, the British-owned Hudson's Bay Company's advance base on the Clark Fork of the Columbia River in eastern Oregon Country (present Eddy, Montana). Along the Snake River, the party met a few Iroquois trappers from the fur company and soon made contact with their leader in the region, Alexander Ross. Smith followed Ross to Flathead Post, where, as unwelcome guests of the company, he and his men spent the winter.

Smith's first expedition west yielded important returns. In addition to furs, his stay with the Hudson's Bay Company disclosed information about British influence in the Columbia River area. He saw the Great Salt Lake, attended the first rendezvous of the MOUN-

TAIN MEN on the Green River in July 1825, and in the fall returned down the Missouri River to St. Louis with Ashley. A short time later, Smith became Ashley's field partner and leader of the Rocky Mountain brigades.

Smith's second great venture began in the spring of 1826, when he joined Ashley's annual Western expedition sponsored by the Rocky Mountain Fur Company. Told by Ute Indians that the Great Salt Lake possibly had a westward link to the Pacific, Smith determined to locate the legendary Buenaventura River. In the spring, he dispatched David Jackson and a few men to explore the area north and west of the lake. Their 24-day excursion in a bullboat uncovered no outlet resembling the fabled Buenaventura.

In July 1826 Ashley, now a rich man, sold his interests in the fur company to the partnership of Smith, Jackson, and [William L.] Sublette. For the next 4 years these men headed brigades which explored and trapped the Rockies and Pacific Coast from Sonora to Canada. In August 1826 Smith led a party of sixteen out of Cache Valley, down the Virgin and Colorado Rivers, and across the Mojave Desert toward the Pacific. His goals were to find the Buenaventura, follow the coast to the Columbia River, trap the country to the Snake River, and meet at the rendezvous in northeastern Utah.

The desert crossing from the Mojave Indian villages at the eastern edge of California to San Diego was arduous. Choosing an old Indian trade route, they followed the twisting and weaving Mojave River, which Smith named the Inconstant, crossed the San Bernardino Mountains, came upon the Mojave's headwaters, and on November 27 reached San Gabriel Mission above San Diego. They were the first Americans to journey overland to California through the Southwest. But their exultation was short-lived; the area they pierced belonged to Mexico, and they soon were embroiled in difficulties with the Mexican Governor in San Diego.

Smith departed from San Diego by ship in January 1827, but when he reached San Pedro Bay and the edge of the desert, he violated the Mexican Governor's instructions and turned northward over the Tehachapi Mountains and into the San Joaquin Valley. His futile search for the Buenaventura ended in May at the American River, about 350 miles (563 kilometers) up the trail. Smith disconsolately moved east toward the Sierras. But snow and freezing temperatures prevented a crossing. Returning down the western slope of the mountains (unaware of the area's gold), the men turned south to the Stanislaus River (or the Merced) and readied themselves for another attempted crossing of the mountains in late May. After traveling up to 40 miles (64 kilometers) a day around the southern rim of Walker Lake in present Nevada, they dragged through the burning Great Basin (partially along present Highway 6 through Nevada), and made their way toward the Bear Lake rendezvous in July 1827 near the Great Salt Lake. They had accomplished what no white men, and probably no Indians, had done: they had crossed North America's highest mountains and its largest desert, the Great Basin.

The next stage in Smith's second westward expedition began after 9 days of rest; on July 13 he was back on the California Trail and moving toward the Columbia River. With eighteen men he traveled south past the Great Salt Lake and toward the Mojave settlements again. Not only did the Indians prove unfriendly on this occasion, but Smith was jailed by Mexican authorities for 2 months. Finally, in late December, he and nineteen companions left California. They reached the Umpqua River in mid-July 1828, and while Smith and two others scouted the trail to the Willamette Valley, a band of Kelawatset Indians attacked and killed all but one of the party. Smith safely arrived at the Hudson's Bay Company's headquarters at Fort Vancouver in August.

In the fall of 1830, Smith and his two partners sold their mountain interests to a group of traders who retained the firm name of Rocky Mountain Fur Company. Claiming to be through with the business, Smith bought a farm and a town house in St. Louis. It would have been better for Smith had he remained in retirement. In 1831 he sought to fulfill a lifelong dream of leading a wagon train to Santa Fe. With Jackson, Sublette, and more than seventy other men, twenty-two wagons, and a 6-pound cannon, they pulled out of St. Louis on April 10. Near Independence they were joined by Thomas Fitzpatrick. On May 27, Smith, who had ridden ahead to look for water, was ambushed and killed by Comanche Indians in the hot and dry stretch beween the Arkansas and Cimarron Rivers. Though the spot of his death is unknown, the Indian stories passed on by Mexican traders attested to Jedediah's violent death. With him went his plans to publish a journal and map of the West. It was not until 1934 that his journal of his Western travels was published for the first time.

Smith's explorations stimulated American interest in the Far West. His work filled in the last great blank spot on the map of North America, and it pointed to the vast agricultural potential of the Far West. Also important, Smith learned much about British operations in the Snake and Columbia River areas. Though he convinced the British Governor that insurmountable difficulties prevented American settlement there, his report to Secretary of War John Eaton in October 1830 contained a remarkably accurate evaluation of British strength in the Far West and a highly optimistic assessment of Oregon's agricultural and commercial possibilities. A major factor in achieving success, he recommended, was federal aid to emigrants. Other explorers soon would sketch in the finer points of Smith's general guide to the West.

BIBLIOGRAPHY: William H. Goetzmann, *Exploration and Empire: The Explorer and the Scientist in the Winning of the American West*, New York, 1966; Dale L. Morgan, *Jedediah Smith and the Opening of the West*, Lincoln, Nebr., 1953; Maurice S. Sullivan, *The Travels of Jedediah Smith: A Documentary Outline*, Santa Ana, Calif., 1934.

Howard Jones

Smith, John (1580–1631) English explorer, colonizer, adventurer, and author. He was born in Willoughby, Lincolnshire, the firstborn son of farmer George Smith and of his wife, Alice. He received a grammar school education and for a time served as an apprentice to a merchant of King's Lynn. At about the age of 16 he became a soldier of fortune on the European continent, fighting in the Low Countries, Hungary, and Transylvania. Wounded in battle and taken prisoner by the Turks, he was sent to Turkey as a slave. Eventually he escaped from a prison camp near the Don River, and after many vicissitudes he finally reached England, probably late in 1604.

Smith participated in the expedition sent across the Atlantic by the Virginia Company in December 1606 and was among those who founded the English colony at Jamestown. He became one of the members of the governing council of this settlement and began the work of exploring the surrounding territory. During his stay in Jamestown Smith explored both the Potomac and the Rappahannock Rivers as well as Chesapeake Bay. Smith's book entitled *A True Relation of . . . Occurrences in Virginia* (1608) is significant as the earliest firsthand account of the Jamestown settlement.

Smith made important contributions to the development of English interest in the New England area. In 1614 he visited this region on behalf of a group of

A composite, taken from the explorer's record of his travels, of Capt. John Smith's adventures in the New World, 1607–1609. [Library of Congress]

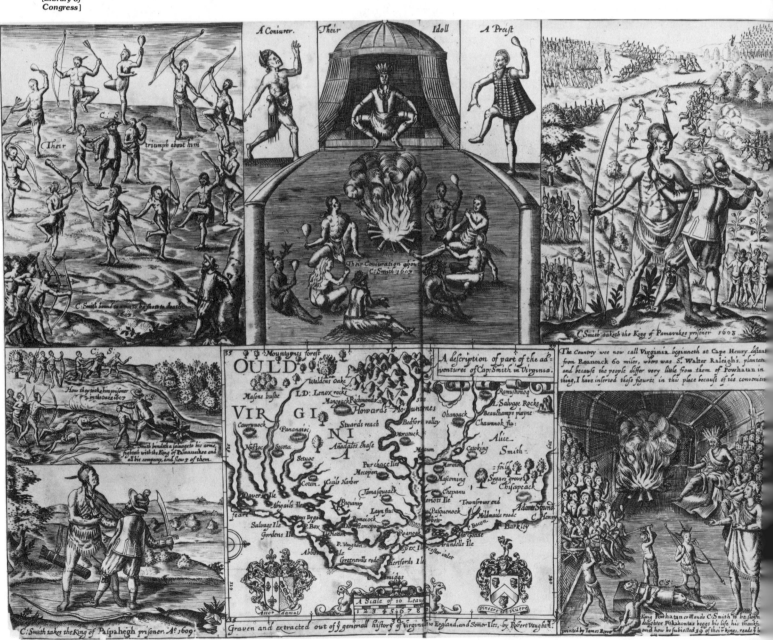

London merchants, made extensive explorations along the coast, and returned to England with a valuable cargo of furs and salted fish. On the occasion of another voyage to the New World in 1615 he was captured by French pirates and shipwrecked off the coast of France. Finally he managed to return to England, where he published in 1616 an important description of New England together with an accurate map of the region.

During his last years Smith devoted his attention to writing and thus became an effective propagandist for English colonial expansion in North America. He also wrote one of the earliest handbooks for seamen in the English language. Smith died in London in June 1631 and was buried in St. Sepulchre's Church in that city.

BIBLIOGRAPHY: Philip L. Barbour, *The Three Worlds of Captain John Smith*, Cambridge, Mass., 1964; Bradford Smith, *Captain John Smith: His Life and Legend*, Philadelphia and New York, 1953.

Bernerd C. Weber

Solís, Juan Díaz de (1470-1516) Spanish navigator. Solís was born in Lebrija. On June 29, 1508, he sailed with Vicente Yáñez PINZÓN in search of a western route to the Spice Islands. The expedition commenced its explorations by circumnavigating Cuba, thus proving conclusively that it was an island. It then continued to the Gulf of Honduras and proceeded carefully to follow the Central and South American coastlines to approximately 41°S, where it discovered the Río Negro. Strangely, the party sailed past and did not discover the Río de la Plata on this voyage. They returned to Spain in 1509.

In 1512, upon the death of Amerigo VESPUCCI, Solís succeeded to the post of pilot major of Spain. On November 12, 1514, King Ferdinand commissioned him to take three ships for a period of 2 years to attempt to find a southwest passage to the Spice Islands. After he entered the Pacific, his instructions were to sail northward as far as the Isthmus of Panama and follow that latitude to his destination. Solís sailed from Sanlúcar de Barrameda on October 8, 1515, and arrived at the Río de la Plata (not named as such until 1527), which he named El Mar Dulce (the Freshwater Sea), in February 1516. The expedition explored what seemed to offer a transoceanic passage as far as the territory of the Charruas. Disaster befell the party when Solís rowed ashore on the Uruguayan coast and was killed and eaten by the natives in August 1516. Thoroughly demoralized, the Spaniards, now under the command of Solís's brother-in-law, Francisco de Torres, returned to Spain, arriving on September 4, 1516.

The discovery of Yucatán during the voyage of 1508–1509 is sometimes attributed to Solís, but there is no reliable evidence attesting to this.

BIBLIOGRAPHY: José Toribio Medina, *Juan Díaz de Solís: Estudio Histórico*, Santiago de Chile, 1897; Samuel Eliot Morison, *The European Discovery of America: The Southern Voyages, A.D. 1492–1616*, New York, 1974.

Martin Torodash

Soto, Hernando de (ca. 1500-1542) Spanish explorer. Born in Jerez de Badajoz in western Extremadura, Soto came from a family of minor hidalgos. He probably arrived in the New World in 1514 as a member of the expedition to Panama led by Pedro Arias de ÁVILA, whose daughter he would marry in 1536. In 1524 he took part in the conquest of Nicaragua under Francisco Hernández de Córdoba and became one of the leading citizens of the new colony. In an effort to obtain an independent sphere of influence for himself, Soto agreed to participate in the third expedition of Francisco PIZARRO to Peru and contributed two ships, about 100 men, and 25 horses, which he brought to Puná Island on December 1, 1531.

Soto went on to play a major role in the conquest of Peru, being the first Spaniard to meet the Inca emperor Atahuallpa, whose execution he is said to have opposed. Despite the fame and wealth which he acquired in Peru, his hopes of an independent governorship were not realized. In 1536 he returned to Spain to pursue this goal, seeking the governorship of Quito or that of Guatemala with a view of launching an expedition of discovery and conquest on his own. In April 1537 the crown granted him the right to conquer and colonize the still vaguely defined Florida and to select 200 leagues along the coast of which he was to be governor and *adelantado* (royal deputy). He was also given the governorship of Cuba, which was to serve as his base of operations.

Soto set sail from Sanlúcar de Barrameda on April 7, 1538, at the head of approximately 650 men and women. After stopping in Cuba to gather supplies and make other preparations, the expedition left Havana on May 18, 1539, and landed on the southeast side of Tampa Bay on May 30. The expedition, whose route was reconstructed by the United States De Soto Commission between 1935 and 1939, then moved inland to the north and northwest, traveling near country traversed by Pánfilo de Narváez in 1528. During an attack on a group of Indians, the Spaniards found a survivor of the Narváez Expedition, Juan Ortiz, who joined Soto as an interpreter.

On October 6 the Spaniards reached the town of Apalachen, at or near modern Tallahassee, where they spent the winter months despite harassment by the unfriendly Apalachee. Having heard from an Indian prisoner of a great and wealthy queen who ruled at a place called Cofitachequi, they set out on March 3, 1540, and crossed most of Georgia before arriving on April 30 at Cofitachequi, which was located on the Savannah River below Augusta. They met the fabled queen but found no treasure save freshwater pearls. Still bent on finding gold, the expedition left on May 13 and turned northward to seek another land, Chiaha, reported to be rich in that metal. After crossing the Appalachian Mountains (they were the first Europeans to do so) and following the Tennessee River, the Spaniards reached Chiaha (on Burns Island, Tennessee) on June 6. While Chiaha provided food in

Soto, Hernando de

Hernando de Soto captures the Indian town of Alibamo, in northern Mississippi, in 1541. Like most explorers of his time, Soto was preoccupied with the search for gold. [Library of Congress]

abundance, it too failed to yield any gold. Now Soto turned to the south, seeking a great chief, Cosa, whom the Spaniards encountered on the Coosa River north of Childersburg, Alabama. On October 10 the Spaniards met another important chief, Tuscaloosa, in a village on the Alabama River. From Mabila (at a point never identified but perhaps near Choctaw Bluff, Alabama), where the Spaniards repelled an Indian attack in a bloody, day-long battle, they marched northward, crossing the Black Warrior and the upper Tombigbee Rivers, and spent the winter near present-day Pontotoc, Mississippi. Here, on March 4, 1541, they suffered a surprise attack by the local Chickasaw Indians which cost the lives of twelve Spaniards and more than 50 horses and 300 pigs while Indian casualties were insignificant.

Leaving their winter quarters on April 26, 1541, the Spaniards traveled to the west and got their first glimpse of the Mississippi River on May 8 in a province called Quizquiz. After four barges had been built, the river was crossed south of Memphis on June 18. Soto then spent several months traveling in what is now Arkansas before stopping at the village of Utiangue (near Calion or Camden, Arkansas), where the expedition wintered. According to "a gentleman from Elvas" who took part in the expedition and wrote a *True Relation* of it, Soto had only 300 fighting men

De Soto's Discovery of the Mississippi, a nineteenth-century painting by William Henry Powell. [State of Alabama, Department of Archives and History]

and forty horses left when Utiangue was abandoned on March 6, 1542. In addition, the interpreter Juan Ortiz soon died, and there was no satisfactory replacement. Soto now moved south along the Ouachita River, seeking the Mississippi and an outlet to the sea, for he had apparently decided to abandon his enterprise, at least temporarily. On May 21, however, he died of fever, and his body, weighted with sand, was lowered into the Mississippi near Natchez.

Led by Luis de Moscoso, whom Soto had designated as his successor, the surviving members of the expedition made an attempt to reach Mexico by land and traveled westward, perhaps reaching the Brazos River before deciding to turn back. During the winter of 1542–1543, which they spent near Natchez, they built seven small boats and embarked upon the Mississippi on July 2, 1543. They entered the Gulf of Mexico on July 18 and reached the Spanish settlements in Mexico the following September.

Although sometimes depicted as a romantic epic, Soto's 3-year trek had little immediate significance.

He has been criticized by some for his abuse of the Indians he encountered and for his emphasis on the search for treasure instead of colonization, but he has also been admired for his courage, endurance, and ability to evoke the respect of his followers. In addition to the account by the gentleman from Elvas, which was first printed in 1557, there are three primary sources for the expedition: a diary kept by Rodrigo Rangel, Soto's secretary, nearly all of which was transcribed by Gonzalo Fernández de Oviedo in his *Historia general y natural de las Indias* (1851); an official report by the factor of the expedition, Hernández de Biedma, presented to the Council of the Indies in 1544; and Garcilaso de la Vega's *La Florida del Inca* (1605), based on the reminiscences of Gonzalo Silvestre, a survivor of the expedition.

BIBLIOGRAPHY: Edward Gaylord Bourne (ed.), *Narratives of the Career of Hernando de Soto*, 2 vols., New York, 1904; James Lockhart, *The Men of Cajamarca*, Austin, Tex., 1972; Carl O. Sauer, *Sixteenth Century North America*, Berkeley, Calif., 1971; United States De Soto Commission, *Final Report of the United States De Soto Commission*, Washington, D.C., 1939.

South America

The exploration of South America began contemporaneously with its discovery by Christopher COLUMBUS in 1498 and was completed in the main within 100 years. After a relatively slack time during the seventeenth century, a second great wave of exploration that began during the Age of Enlightenment washed over the continent and lasted to the near present. Its hallmark was scientific curiosity, and the naturalists, botanists, geographers, and archaeologists who pushed into the pristine interior of the continent completed and complemented the basic explorations done in the sixteenth century.

In the widest-possible interpretation of exploration one can contend that South America was not discovered and explored by Renaissance Europeans alone. Thousands of years ago migrants crossed the Beringian plains that connected North America to Asia, and they then filtered southwest until they reached and settled South America. Much ink has also been spilled over the possibility that many other cultures and civilizations at one time or another spawned expeditions that reached and presumably "explored" South America. Some reputable scholars even today will argue forcibly that Phoenician ships, blown off course while circumnavigating Africa in the pre-Christian era, landed on the east coast of South America and left inscriptions on rocks which recall their adventure. Ancient Polynesian navigators, who certainly were accomplished sailors, have been suggested as possible discoverers and explorers of the west coast. A more convincing theory was tested by the Norwegian anthropologist-adventurer Thor Heyerdahl. He attempted two voyages on papyrus-reed rafts

from Africa to America and succeeded in reaching the Windward Islands on his second try in 1970. Heyerdahl postulated that the great pyramidal structures of native American civilization (those in Middle America especially) were basically the inspiration of outriders of the mighty Egyptian civilization who had purposefully left Egypt to find another world. The list of alleged pre-Columbian explorers of South America can be extended through the implausible to the absurd, with lost and wandering Jewish tribes of the ancient Holy Land representing the former category and extraterrestrial visitors representing the latter. The problem with all these suggestions is that one cannot verifiably reconstruct the past from speculation and fancy. Very little substantial evidence exists to corroborate any of these theories. Whatever merits exist for pre-Columbian incidents of discovery and exploration, there is no doubt that when Columbus happened upon South America in 1498, he initiated the only era of European exploration of South America that endured and eventually transformed the continent into a European colony.

Northern and eastern coasts Columbus was embarked on his third voyage to the Americas when he chanced upon the island of Trinidad and the northern coast of South America near the mouths of the Orinoco River. While at first he merely considered his newest discovery to be another island in a great archipelago off Asia, the vast volume of fresh water that issued from the estuary of the Orinoco into the ocean argued otherwise. Columbus thus recognized the continental properties of the coast. His contemporaries and successors then enlarged upon the knowledge of this mass of land that heretofore had been unknown to contemporary and classical scholars and navigators alike.

In the two decades after Columbus's discovery there occurred numerous voyages to the northern and eastern coasts of South America that helped to establish its unique identity and to outline its geographical configuration. Most of the early voyages were undertaken by Spaniards in search of pearls, gold, assorted treasures, and native kingdoms alleged to exist in great abundance. Among the ambitious conquerors was Alonso de OJEDA, who explored most of the northern coast of South America from the mouths of the Orinoco to the Gulf of Darién in a series of expeditions between 1499 and 1509. The first settlements were attempted on the north coast between Cartagena and the Isthmus of Panama by Ojeda in company with Diego de Nicuesa. An offshoot of these attempts resulted in the first settlement realized by Europeans on the continent. In 1509 or 1510 a small colony was planted on the Gulf of Darién. Subsequently, one of its founders, Vasco Núñez de BALBOA, discovered the Pacific and prepared the way for the exploration of the west coast of South America. While Ojeda, Nicuesa, Rodrigo de Bastidas, and others tilted with the new land and its people, equally adventurous and observant chart makers and pilots such as Juan de la Cosa

and Amerigo VESPUCCI recorded and interpreted their sailing experiences on this new coast.

Juan de la Cosa's famous 1500 map of the world was the first to show the northern South American mainland. Amerigo Vespucci in turn explored much of the eastern and southern coast and inadvertently became associated with the naming of this great continent. Some controversy beclouds Vespucci, who claimed to have sailed and seen a great deal more than he probably did. He indubitably made at least two voyages to South America, once in 1499 in the company of Ojeda and again in 1501 with a Portuguese fleet under Gonçalo Coelho. During this second voyage the expedition coasted southward from about the latitude of Cabo de São Roque on the eastern bulge of Brazil and may have reached Patagonia in southern Argentina. The mainland of Brazil had actually been discovered the previous year by the Spaniard Vicente Yáñez PINZÓN, who made landfall somewhere near modern Recife, and then sailed north. A few months later the Portuguese captain Pedro Álvares CABRAL, who was en route to India, also touched upon the eastern bulge of the continent. Nonetheless, Amerigo's observations, in the form of long letters later published and widely read throughout Europe, helped to implant the perception that this continent slowly being unveiled truly represented a "new" world to the Europeans. Ves-

Cartagena, Colombia. The first Spanish settlements in South America were established between Cartagena and the Isthmus of Panama, 1499– 1509. [Library of Congress]

pucci's observations of the novel flora, fauna, and natives (especially of their odd and sometimes promiscuous sexual habits, which titillated his sixteenth-century readers) served to reinforce the impression that South America constituted a unique and totally different environment from the Oriental mainland that Columbus had searched for in 1492. In 1507 a geographer named Martin Waldseemüller published some of Vespucci's letters in a work that included a map of the world. He placed Vespucci's name, altered to America, on the new continent, and the name popularly became associated with this part of the new world. America was applied to the Northern Hemisphere as well by Gerhardus Mercator, a distinguished sixteenth-century map maker.

During the second decade of the sixteenth century Spanish and Portuguese conquistadores, mariners, woodcutters, pearl seekers, and all manner of men continued drawing in the map of South America as they went about their various pursuits. The discovery of Brazil by Cabral was followed by a marginal Portuguese interest in that part of the continent which lay on its side of the Treaty of Tordesillas. Under the provisions of this treaty, which had been concluded in 1494 between Spain and Portugal, all South America, with the exception of Brazil, fell on the Spanish side of the Line of Demarcation. Portuguese, as well as French and English interlopers slightly later, began extracting brazilwood early in the sixteenth century. Several small Portuguese *feitorias* (trading posts) were established in this period. While little exploration was done immediately into the interior, the coastline of Brazil, named after the wood, became familiar to Portuguese mariners and woodcutters.

Search for a passage to the east From the Caribbean, Balboa struck west in 1513 across the Isthmus of Panama and discovered the Pacific Ocean, or South Sea, as he christened it. Its strong tides and brininess proved it to be an ocean of large proportions. There then arose three questions which helped focus the objectives of explorers in relation to South America. How far across the South Sea did China, Japan, and the Spice Islands lie? Where would the west coast of South America lead to? Could an all-water route be discovered through or around South America to the South Sea? This last question drew the most attention during the second decade of the sixteenth century.

In 1515 Juan Díaz de SOLÍS sailed to South America in charge of an expedition to search for that passage or strait to the East. He discovered the estuary of the Río de la Plata for Spain but was killed in 1516 by native Americans. Despite its disastrous end, the Solís journey prepared the stage for a voyage that not only found the strait but established with near finality the dimensions of South America, the immensity of the Pacific Ocean, and the vast distance of the continent from Asia.

In 1519 a Portuguese in the service of Spain, Ferdinand MAGELLAN, set sail from Seville bound for South America with orders to find the strait (no one doubted it existed), make the transit, and then dart across Balboa's South Sea to China. After a brief and sometimes idyllic interlude at Rio de Janeiro, the fleet coasted southward and explored the Río de la Plata and the Patagonian coast on the far southeastern corner of South America. On October 21, 1520, the fleet rounded Cabo Virgenes, named by Magellan in honor of the Feast of St. Ursula and the Eleven Thousand Virgins. It marked the entrance of the long-sought waterway. The expedition wound its way through the 334 nautical miles (619 kilometers) of the strait and emerged on the Pacific side on November 27 or 28. Then Magellan ran north along the Chilean coast for a few days and neared the latitude of modern Valdivia, where he picked up the westerlies he sought and struck out for the East. The rest of his epic voyage carried him away from South America.

The second Spanish expedition to transit the Strait of Magellan, almost always known by that great explorer's name, was organized in 1525. Commanded by Francisco García Jofre de Loaysa, it carried Juan Sebastián de Elcano as chief pilot and a young page named Andrés de URDANETA, who later distinguished himself in another trans-Pacific voyage. The object of this Second Armada de Molucca was much the same as Magellan's: to reach and exploit the Spice Islands and thus enrich Spain and its subjects. The fleet made landfall at Brazil, sailed south to Patagonia, and struggled through the turbulent strait. The remnants of the expedition that emerged from Cabo Pilar on the Pacific side were scattered by winds and storms. Loaysa and Elcano died in the transit of the Pacific, while the survivors were captured by the Portuguese in the Philippines. One small pinnace, *Santiago,* separated from the others, sailed north for 50 days and landed at Tehuantepec on the Mexican coast in July 1526, thus making the first voyage from Europe to the west coast of the Americas. The Strait of Magellan and the Pacific were proving to be formidable barriers for Spanish mariners interested in that route, but knowledge of the southern cone of the continent was furthered appreciably by the Magellan and Loaysa voyages. Another route around the southern tip of the continent was found in 1616 by Jacob La Maire and Willem Schouten, who passed through Le Maire Strait, discovering Staten Island (Isla de los Estados) and sighting Cape Horn, which was named after the Dutch city of Hoorn, which sponsored the voyage.

Conquest of Peru While the southern part of the continent was explored as a by-product of the search for a viable route to the East, Spaniards began to drop down the west coast of South America from Panama in the 1520s. No straits or passages beckoned here. As early as 1520 Spanish conquerors and settlers in Panama had heard of a powerful civilization rich in gold that lay to the south. In 1522 an expedition under Pascual de Andagoya sailed down the coast of modern Colombia and returned with tales of a rich land and people called Birú or Pirú that lay farther to the south. Two years later Francisco PIZARRO organized the first of three expeditions that would lead ultimately to the discovery and conquest of the great Inca empire.

The first Pizarro expedition, composed of approximately 100 men, explored southward toward the equator, but tropical swamps, hostile natives, and shortages of provisions brought no success on this attempt. A second expedition was launched in 1526. This time one of Pizarro's most capable navigators, Bartolomé Ruiz, ranged far enough south to encounter some real evidence of the fabulous empire sought. Near the equator, which was crossed for the first time on this voyage, Ruiz encountered a balsa raft manned by Indians dressed in fine garments and adorned with gold ornaments. They were from Tumbes, a city located on the north coast of Peru, and they spoke of a great kingdom to the south. After some delays Pizarro and his most faithful followers reached Tumbes, and expectations were fulfilled. Not only did the Spaniards acquire gold, emeralds, and fine fabrics, but they also heard that the heart of a great empire lay in the interior and that civil war currently cleaved it in two. Buoyed by all these possibilities, Pizarro left Tumbes, ranged a little farther south, and returned to Panama. From there he sailed to Spain to recruit his army and to petition for royal sanction for the *entrada,* or armed conquest, of Peru.

In 1531 three ships set sail from Panama with the main body of the future conquistadores of Peru: 180 men and thirty horses. Skirmishes in the Gulf of Guayaquil, a sharp battle with the fierce Indians of Puná Island, the capture of Tumbes, and the founding of San Miguel de Piura nearby all preceded the entrance into the interior in 1532. The in-depth exploration of the Inca empire, which had extended its dominion over wide areas of modern Ecuador, Peru, Bolivia, and Chile, had commenced.

From the coast Pizarro set out east through the Sechura Desert and straight into the high Andes toward the city of Cajamarca. The small army's movement marked the first European approach from the west to this great South American chain of mountains. Pizarro's objectives were clear. After arriving at Cajamarca he seized Atahuallpa, the powerful head of the Inca empire, in a well-laid ambush and obtained from him a ransom of gold and silver that made every Spaniard with Pizarro rich beyond his most inventive fantasies.

The next major step was the capture and subjugation of Cuzco, the Incas' capital, which was located more than 600 miles (966 kilometers) south from Cajamarca. Outriders of the main Spanish army at Cajamarca sent south to reconnoiter were responsible for the first European exploration of this major body of the empire. Pizarro dispatched one of his brothers, Hernando, south to investigate a sacred shrine called Pachacamac located along the coast very near modern Lima. On this march down the coast Hernando Pizarro passed through the innumerable fertile valleys that intersect the coastal desert. They are watered by streams and rivers fed from the steep western slopes of the Andes and were the sites of earlier Peruvian civilizations that eventually were absorbed into the late-rising Inca empire. From Pachacamac he turned inland and proceeded up the river valley to Jauja. Meanwhile another small reconnaissance group had penetrated as far as Cuzco in the southern highlands, and their reports of the capital, along with Hernando Pizarro's news of the coast and Jauja, soon attracted Francisco and the main Spanish army. By November 1533 Pizarro had moved south. He fought several sharp actions with Atahuallpa's generals, who resisted in vain, and captured Cuzco, the heart of the empire. The conquest-exploration radiated north, east, and south from the Cajamarca-Cuzco axis over the next several years. However, contemporaneously and even before Pizarro's *entrada,* Europeans had pushed up the great Río de la Plata Estuary and its feeders from the south and east into the heartland of the continent.

Río de la Plata and the Paraguay and Paraná Rivers The ascension of the Paraguay and Paraná Rivers by Sebastian CABOT between 1527 and 1529 represented the first major exploration of this great river system. Cabot, the pilot major of Spain at the time, was in command of a fleet bound for Magellan Strait and the East Indies when he was sidetracked off the coast of South America by the tales of great riches that lay in the interior.

One of Cabot's sources was Aleixo Garcia, who had been shipwrecked during the ill-fated Solís Expedition of 1516. On the coast Garcia had heard of a great white king bedecked in silver who ruled a magnificent empire in the interior. With other comrades Garcia had marched westward, crossed the Paraná and Paraguay Rivers, and then traversed the Chaco Boreal to arrive at the foot of the Andes within the borders of the Inca empire. Some silver and other treasure were acquired, but Garcia's exhortations to his cronies on the coast to join him failed, and he was assassinated in 1525. When Cabot heard of Garcia's exploits and saw remnants of the plunder, the pilot major was persuaded to explore the Río de la Plata (renamed from the Río de Solís) thoroughly.

Cabot's group began sailing, kedging, and rowing up the Paraná in early 1527. At the confluence of the Paraná and the Paraguay Cabot chose to continue up the Paraguay to near where modern Asunción is located. He then returned to the Paraná and explored northward along this water artery. In early 1528 a Diego García quite unexpectedly appeared downriver with a royal commission to explore the Río de la Plata. After a rather stormy meeting, for Cabot was supposed to be in the Moluccas, the two sponsored some joint probes. The most interesting one was led by a lieutenant of Cabot's named Francisco César. César probably reached the Andes and the outer edges of the Inca empire on his reconnaissance. His reports helped spawn the tale of a "city of the Caesars" that spurred men's imaginations for more than a century and led to later extensive exploration in that area. The remnants of Cabot's expedition returned to Spain in 1529 with enough silver, gold, and Indian slaves to encourage other conquistador-explorers. Furthermore, the first substantial, although not always accurate, reports of the geography and inhabitants of that part of the continent also flowed from Cabot's probes.

In 1534 a substantial, well-equipped expedition under the command of Pedro de Mendoza sailed from Seville to the Río de la Plata. More than a dozen large ships and 2000 men, including not only Spaniards but Germans and Flemings, comprised this impressive force. After founding the city of Santa María del Buen Aire at the mouth of the Riachuelo, the tentative good relations with the Querandí Indians broke down, and the main body of the Spanish army was besieged in Buenos Aires. In spite of these troubles an expedition led by Juan de Ayolas was sent upriver to find the source of silver and gold about which Sebastian Cabot and others had told. Ayolas went up the Paraguay to near 19°S and there traded for silver and other objects that had obviously originated among the Incas of the Andes. He was killed in 1537, but one of his lieutenants, Domingo Martínez de Irala, settled into the newly founded city of Asunción on the Paraguay (named in honor of the Feast of the Assumption of the Virgin) amid the friendly Guaraní. Subsequently, Mendoza withdrew from the Río de la Plata, and Irala then brought the remnants of the Buenos Aires colony to Asunción and assumed command of this first successful settlement in the region. Then, in 1541, one of those peripatetic and amazingly resilient Spanish conquistadores of the era appeared on the local scene.

Álvar Núñez CABEZA DE VACA, that noteworthy traveler who first crossed a great part of the North American continent as an Indian slave and medicine man, had received the King's permission to explore and settle the areas previously granted to Mendoza. After marching overland from the Brazilian coast to Asunción, he set forth with a large expedition up the Paraguay to try to establish contact with Peru. The expedition reached Puerto de los Reyes, a point that Irala had reached earlier on reconnaissance, and continued westward on foot toward the Andes. They were nonetheless forced to turn back before reaching Upper Peru (Bolivia) for want of provisions, hostile Indians, and other hardships. Upon his return to Asunción Cabeza de Vaca was jailed on trumped-up charges and sent back to Spain. In 1548 an expedition sent by Irala toward Upper Peru finally reached the fringes of the growing Spanish empire in the high plains of modern Bolivia. Four men from this expedition subsequently arrived in Lima and thus completed the first links between Spaniards exploring the continent from east to west. Meanwhile, the energy of the Peruvian conquest in the 1530s and 1540s spread far south and north of the captured capital of Cuzco.

Conquest of Chile The early exploration of Chile was born of a feud between Francisco Pizarro and his partner, Diego de ALMAGRO, who thought he deserved a larger share of the booty and territory from the conquest of Peru. Almagro was put off by Pizarro with the dubious assurance that all lands south of Cuzco, dubbed New Toledo, were his to conquer. He set off in mid-1535 for the south with hundreds of Spanish soldiers and thousands of Indians in his train. The crossing of the high Andes and the approach to Chile by way of the mountains took a terrific toll, for Almagro had foolishly launched his *entrada* in the winter. The party descended toward the coast around Copiapó and continued south into the rich and fertile Central Valley. They found little treasure but much resistance as they advanced closer to the home of the fiercely independent Araucanian Indians. Almagro eventually turned back, disgusted with Chile, the bitter cold, the Araucanians, and the lack of treasure. The expedition marched back north along the coastal Atacama Desert, a formidable barrier in itself, crossed the Andes, and reached Cuzco in 1537.

The second major *entrada* that led ultimately to the permanent settlement of Chile occurred in the 1540s under the leadership of Pedro de VALDIVIA. Subsequent Spanish expeditions sent to secure the southern part of the Central Valley reached the Maule River, while most of the coast of Chile was explored in the 1540s and 1550s as well. In the 1550s several expeditions, including one sent by Valdivia in 1553 under the command of Francisco de Ulloa and another ordered by Valdivia's successor, Don García Hurtado de Mendoza, in 1557, explored the archipelagoes and deep mountain-ranged fjords, called *canales* in Chile, in the southern half of the province as far as the Strait of Magellan.

Bogotá and El Dorado Three major *entradas* all aimed toward the area of modern Bogotá in the mid-1530s created perhaps the most interesting incident in the entire and extraordinary history of the conquest and early exploration of South America. One finger of this conquest was projected from the south. This troop was led by Sebastián de BENALCÁZAR, one of Pizarro's lieutenants who had led an army from Piura north and east into Ecuador in 1534–1535, conquered the city of Quito, and begun the pacification of that province. This constituted the first major exploration of the interior of that region. Benalcázar then turned toward the north. In 1536 he struck out for Colombia and founded the cities of Popayán and Cali as he progressed toward the *sabana* (plain) of Bogotá.

From the east there approached a bedraggled troop of Germans and Spaniards who had commenced their penetration of the Colombian highlands several years earlier from the Venezuelan coast. The indebtedness of King Charles I (Emperor Charles V) to Welser banking houses caused this rather anomalous appearance of Germans on the South American continent in the 1530s, for he granted Venezuela to the Welsers for conquest, exploration, and exploitation. Since the early 1530s German expeditions, led by individuals such as Ambrosio Alfinger and Georg Hohermuth, had explored Lake Maracaibo and the Sierra Nevada de Santa Marta and neared the land of the Chibchas, who inhabited the region around Bogotá. A large quantity of gold had been obtained during these expeditions. The legend of an Indian chief who was periodically gilded in gold dust and the rumored existence of a golden idol the size of man helped further to leaven the imaginations of these explorers. The Chibchas of Bogotá, almost inaccessible in highlands that could be approached from the north and east only through long jungle valleys and precipitous cordilleras, were the objects of two unsuccessful expeditions before 1538. In that year Nicolás Féderman (Nikolaus Federmann) launched a third attempt from Venezuela. After a most difficult crossing of the mountains, he began the final approach to Bogotá from the east just as Benalcázar closed in from the south.

The prize, however, belonged neither to the conquerors of Quito nor to the German entrepreneurs. They were both coolly welcomed to the plains of Bogotá by Gonzalo JIMÉNEZ DE QUESADA. This remarkable individual had proceeded up the Magdalena River Valley in 1536–1537. Poisoned arrows, fevers, snakes, and other miseries had decimated his army by the time he reached the Chibchas in 1538. When Féderman and Benalcázar appeared in 1539, their surprise at finding Quesada already there certainly must have been mutual. The tactful Quesada arranged to have the King arbitrate the dispute and distributed ample gifts of gold and emeralds to Féderman and Benalcázar to smooth the negotiations.

The wave of Spanish energy that swept over the high Andean kingdoms and territories of the Incas, Chibchas, and others continued in the decades following the 1530s to disgorge conquerors and explorers into the lower mountains, plateaus, plains, and great river systems of the northeastern part of the continent. The search for other Cuzcos and for the sources of fantastic legends such as that of EL DORADO led to the early exploration of the great Amazon and Orinoco River basins that serve half the continent. On the crest of this wave rode another Pizarro, Gonzalo, half brother to Francisco.

From his governorship of Quito Gonzalo PIZARRO conceived a plan to strike east into the lowlands in search of a land of cinnamon and of a gilded king who ruled a rich province. Pizarro and his retinue dropped down from the Andes in early 1541 but were soon immersed in the trackless jungle. Somewhere on the Coca River Pizarro called a halt and accepted the offer of Francisco de ORELLANA to take a small party ahead to reconnoiter and bring back food. Orellana reached the Napo River, a major tributary of the Amazon, but he did not halt there. Trusting in divine providence, he and his small group paddled downstream toward the Amazon and the odyssey of the first exploration of that great river by Europeans. After issuing from the mouth of the Amazon in August 1542, Orellana returned to Spain to explain his behavior, tell of his adventures, and, inevitably, excite many an imagination. And it was precisely this largely unexplored northeastern quadrant of the continent between the Amazon and the sea which cast the strongest spell over European minds in the second half of the century.

In 1558 there was concocted an expedition in Peru that completed the second crossing of the continent and also set some sort of demonic standard for barbarity and cruelty. Tales of El Dorado, the rich kingdom of the Omaguas, the fabulous city of Manoa, and the warlike but bewitching Amazons circulated widely among a restless population of late-coming conquistadores. An expedition into the interior with the lure of wealth and glory always attracted attention and stalwarts. Consequently, when in 1559 Pedro de Ursúa was named to lead such an *entrada*, a great many undesirables flocked to its standard.

In July 1560 Ursúa's horde, numbering more than 300 Spaniards, began dropping down the Huallaga River, one of the main tributaries of the Amazon. Reaching the Amazon, they then continued downriver, passing its confluence with the Ucayali and arrived near where the Putumayo feeds into the Amazon in December 1560. At this juncture Ursúa was murdered by rebels, whose passage to the sea under the command of Lope de Aguirre was marked by a series of atrocities, including Aguirre's murder of his own daughter. There is some doubt as to whether Aguirre's gang reached the ocean via the Amazon or the Orinoco, but the madman was finally killed in Venezuela, where he was beheaded and quartered and his remains displayed publicly as a reminder to all who would rebel.

Orinoco region The Orinoco region had drawn the attention of many before a nephew by marriage of Jiménez de Quesada, Antonio de Berrío, explored the region persistently in the 1580s and 1590s. In 1531 Diego de ORDAZ had pushed up the river as far as the Atures Rapids. Later, in 1533, one of his lieutenants went high up the Meta River, a major Orinoco tributary, before being dispatched by a poisoned arrow. Several other unsuccessful treasure hunts were launched on the Orinoco area in the next few decades, but Berrío was the individual who capped sixteenth-century Spanish efforts. Between 1584 and the early 1590s Berrío sponsored or himself made at least four incursions into the Orinoco Valley. He never found El Dorado, nor was he able to penetrate the steep and formidable Guianan escarpment to the south of the Orinoco. Yet his expeditions added greatly to the general knowledge of the area and, most specifically, to English knowledge when Berrío was captured and questioned by Sir Walter Raleigh at Trinidad.

Raleigh represented English interests and enterprise in the early history of the exploration of South America. Wishing to harass Spain more effectively, Raleigh focused his energies on South America. According to the best contemporary thinking, South America was the cornucopia which fed the Spanish war machine in Europe. After his initial excursion up the Orinoco and into Guiana Raleigh wrote a marvelously entertaining and propagandistic tract entitled *The Discoverie of the Large and Beautiful Empire of Guiana* (1596). It was one of those inventive sixteenth-century pieces that transformed a jungle or mountain wilderness into arcadia. For 20 years after his initial approach Raleigh attempted to establish some type of English control over the area and to find, of course, El Dorado, or the mines, or the cities. He lost his son in Guiana during this period and ultimately lost his own head as well in 1618. The ax at Westminster fell in part because of his failed expectations in Guiana.

Seventeenth-century missionary and secular exploration By the turn of the seventeenth century when Raleigh had appeared, a watershed of sorts had been passed in the exploration of South America. The main outline of the continent had been drawn with its distinguishing features boldly inscribed: the great Andean chain that dominated the western portion; the mighty Amazon, Río de la Plata, and Orinoco, rivers which collectively drained more than half the continent; and the myriad habitats and climates represented by the steaming jungles of Darién and the barren territory of Patagonia. They had largely been explored and mapped, although with different degrees of accuracy and levels of observation.

Missionaries, whose activity commenced early in the sixteenth century and flourished in the seventeenth, proved to be excellent explorers during this era as well. From Bogotá and Quito Jesuits and Franciscans struck out east. While establishing missions along the major tributaries of the Orinoco and Amazon in the mid-seventeenth century, they explored large stretches of territory previously unseen by Europeans. Father Samuel Fritz, a Jesuit who proselytized among the Omaguas and other tribes along the Amazon at the end of the seventeenth century, compiled one of the first reliable maps of that great river's entire course. Jesuit missionaries in Brazil had as early as the mid-sixteenth century explored the backlands, the *sertão*, of Brazil. To the south other members of the Society of Jesus had traveled extensively from the Uruguay River inland in the course of establishing large missions, or reductions, among the Guaraní Indians.

Secular exploration in this era was born largely of the slow rippling of Portuguese interest from the coast into the Brazilian interior. Pedro Teixeira between 1637 and 1639 led a remarkably successful ascension of the Amazon that reached Quito; he then returned with Spanish companions to Belém (Pará) at the mouth of the river. During the course of this expedition Teixeira helped fix the boundary between Spanish and Portuguese Amazonia, although this frontier continued to cause friction for more than a

Sir Walter Raleigh with the ruler of Guiana in 1595. Seeing the riches of South America as Spain's support in its European wars, Raleigh sought to defeat the enemy at home by harassing them in the New World. [Library of Congress]

century. Much farther to the south, Brazilians, especially from the city of São Paulo, had begun in the sixteenth century *entradas* into the interior that continued with increasing frequency in the seventeenth. These groups of adventurers, known as *bandeirantes*, sought gold, Indian slaves, and other forms of market-

Title page of Willem Piso's Historia naturalis Brasiliae (1648), showing Indians, flora, and fauna. By the seventeenth century the major conquests in South America had been made, and colonizers turned to missionary work and exploitation. [Library of Congress]

able wealth. In the course of more than a century they added to the knowledge of large portions of the interior of Brazil. Between 1648 and 1652, for example, Antônio Rapôso Tavares led an expedition composed of more than 200 Portuguese and 1000 Indians far into the interior. They traversed the upper, swampy reaches of the Paraguay River, marched along the eastern slopes of the Andes, navigated the Madeira River, probably reached the vicinity of Quito farther north, and then floated down the Amazon to Belém. This represented a considerable achievement not only in exploring that vast and largely unfamiliar interior portion of the continent but also in substantiating Portuguese claims to the area.

Eighteenth and nineteenth centuries   In the wake of the conquerors, missionaries, *bandeirantes,* and others who pioneered the exploration of South America in the sixteenth and seventeenth centuries there followed in the eighteenth and nineteenth centuries a brilliant and diverse group nurtured in the Age of Enlightenment. Their enthusiasm flowed from scientific curiosity about the natural and physical world and its rules and aberrations. South America offered the scientists of the Age of Reason the opportunity to explore, describe, and analyze the nature of a pristine land. The reward was personal satisfaction derived from having participated in the discovery of useful knowledge for all humankind. The Frenchman Charles-Marie de La Condamine (1701–1774) was one of the first of this genre of explorer-scientist.

La Condamine came to South America in 1735 with a team of assistants that included a mathematician,

an astronomer, a botanist, several engineers, and a watch and instrument maker. The object of the expedition was to measure precisely the length of a degree of latitude at the equator in order to determine the actual shape of the earth, which was thought by some to be flattened slightly at the poles and by others at the equator. The party's observations were to be compared with the results of similar observations made by another team sent to the Arctic regions. For part of their trip in South America the French party was escorted by two Spanish naval lieutenants, Jorge Juan and Antonio de Ulloa, whose own observations of South America compiled over a number of years added significantly to the knowledge of the continent, its geography, and its inhabitants. La Condamine made his calculations near Quito and then elected to return to France in 1743 via the Amazon River. His trip down the Amazon did not blaze any new pathways, but his notes and subsequent detailed report of the voyage added new perspectives and depth to the European knowledge of South America.

Spanish scientists sponsored by the crown added greatly to the scientific knowledge of South America in the second half of the eighteenth century as well. Men such as José Celestino Mutis, Hipólito Ruiz, and José Pavón explored widely among the flora and fauna of South America. They sent back innumerable samples of plants and medicines and great quantities of information on South America that filtered through Spain and into enlightened Europe. The culmination to this century of scientific exploration occurred at the very end and was brilliantly achieved by the travels and observations of one man, Friedrich Heinrich Alexander von Humboldt (1769–1859).

Baron von Humboldt personified the noblest ideals and ways of the Enlightenment. A Berliner, he had studied geography, chemistry, botany, and physics and made scientific trips around Europe and the Near East before his voyage to America. He was interested in observing, discovering, classifying, and explaining the natural world about him. His travels in Spanish America between 1799 and 1804 produced a galaxy of collections, observations, analyses, and interpretations of the land and its people that has never been duplicated. One of the most intriguing puzzles that Von Humboldt tackled concerned the Casiquiare River or Canal. This stream results from a bifurcation of one of the Orinoco's tributaries. One arm leads into the Orinoco while the other, the Casiquiare, flows into the Río Negro, which feeds into the Amazon. The two great river systems are thus connected by this quirk of geography. Von Humboldt and Aimé Bonpland (1773–1858), a French botanist who traveled with him, went up into this very difficult country, marked by fevers, vipers, insects, and innumerable other dangers, to study the unusual phenomenon. What had been a rather hazy geographical riddle was finally solved by Von Humboldt's precise drawings and explanations that were backed by longitudes, latitudes, and descriptions in detail reflecting his thor-

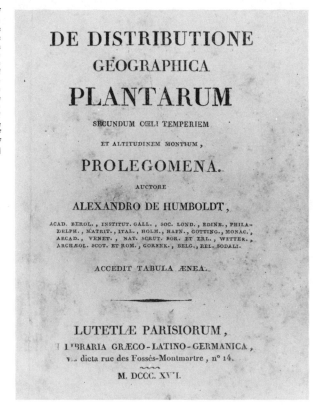

Title page of Alexander von Humboldt's De distributione geographica plantarum. Von Humboldt's New World experiences contributed to his ideas on the relationship between climate and altitude and the distribution of plants. [Library of Congress]

DE DISTRIBUTIONE
GEOGRAPHICA
PLANTARUM
SECUNDUM CŒLI TEMPERIEM
ET ALTITUDINEM MONTIUM,
PROLEGOMENA.
AUCTORE
ALEXANDRO DE HUMBOLDT,
ACAD. BEROL., INSTITUT. GALL., SOC. LOND., EDINB., PHILA-
DELPH., MATRIT., ITAL., HOLM., HAFN., GOTTING., MONAC.,
ARCAD., VENET., NAT. SCRUT. BOR. ET ERL., WETTER.,
ARCHÆOL. SCOT. ET ROM., GORENK., BELG., REL. SODALI.

ACCEDIT TABULA ÆNEA.

LUTETIÆ PARISIORUM,
LIBRARIA GRÆCO-LATINO-GERMANICA,
via dicta rue des Fossés-Montmartre, n° 14.
M. DCCC. XVI.

iosity. In Rio he commented on the nature of clouds and singing frogs, in Patagonia on Indians, and in Tierra del Fuego on the gulf that divided civilized people from the primitive individuals of that stark land. Arriving in southern Chile soon after an earthquake had devastated Concepción, he immediately and characteristically was attracted to this phenomenon and its causes. He crossed the Andes between Santiago and Mendoza, Argentina, and speculated on the origins of those mountains and valleys from the geologic evidence seen on his journey. Not only did Darwin's reports add significantly to knowledge of South America, but his observations during his tour of the continent were of seminal importance in the development of his theories of evolution and natural selection. *See also* NATURAL-HISTORY EXPLORATION.

The exploration of South America by naturalists continued unabated in the nineteenth century. Each expedition or explorer made significant contributions to the knowledge of the area. Some, fascinated by the tropics, added to the books on Amazonia. Others, attracted to the frozen climes, launched out to climb the highest peaks of the Andes. Mount Aconcagua, 22,834 feet (6960 meters) high, was not conquered until 1897, for example. The search for the past civili-

Angel Falls, Venezuela, remained undiscovered until the aviator James Angel flew over it in 1935. [Embassy of Venezuela, Washington]

oughness. His observations on Indian linguistics, poisons, cannibalism, plants, and minerals all formed part of his distinguished contribution. In 1802 he climbed almost to the peak of the volcanic mountain Chimborazo in Ecuador to test some theories on the correlation between elevation and temperature. Later that year he discovered the cold ocean stream that flows north along the west coast of the continent in his search for the answer to the peculiarly dry weather pattern of that area. The current still bears his name. While Von Humboldt's scientific exploration of South America was never equaled in extent or brilliance, he was nonetheless followed in the nineteenth century by individuals whose claims on the limelight of natural history are no less bright.

Of these, perhaps the most famous is Charles Darwin (1809–1882), who visited South America between 1831 and 1833. He traveled as the naturalist aboard the ship *Beagle,* which had been dispatched by England to survey the coasts of Patagonia, Chile, and Peru and to measure different longitudes around the world. In the course of its voyage Darwin made stops or trips through Rio de Janeiro, Buenos Aires, the pampas of Argentina, and Patagonia, Chile, the Atacama Desert, and Callao, Peru. He observed and described the world he saw at great length and with much literary grace and always displayed the scientist's cur-

zations of South America became a passion for explorers in the nineteenth and twentieth centuries. In 1911 an American, Hiram Bingham (1875–1956), discovered the long-abandoned ruins of Machu Picchu that straddled a nearly inaccessible mountain eyrie in the Urubamba Valley of eastern Peru. He thus added another dimension to the exploration of South America through archaelogical endeavor. By and large, however, the exploration of the continent, in almost all respects, had been completed by the nineteenth century, though Angel Falls in Venezuela, the highest waterfall in the world, was unknown until it was discovered in 1935 by an American flier, James (Jimmy) Angel (d. 1956). The scientific and natural exploration during the age of Victoria had crowned brilliantly the bold actions of the continent's early sixteenth- and seventeenth-century discoverers and explorers.

BIBLIOGRAPHY: Paul Russell Cutright, *The Great Naturalists Explore South America,* New York, 1940; Helmut De Terra, *Humboldt: The Life and Times of Alexander von Humboldt, 1769–1859,* New York, 1955; Edward J. Goodman, *The Explorers of South America,* New York, 1972; Robert B. Cunningham Graham, *The Conquest of the River Plate,* London, 1924; Earl Parker Hanson (ed.), *South from the Spanish Main: South America Seen through the Eyes of Its Discoverers,* New York, 1967; Sir Clements R. Markham, *Early Spanish Voyages to the Strait of Magellan,* London, 1917; Samuel Eliot Morison, *The European Discovery of America: The Southern Voyages, A.D. 1492–1616,* New York, 1974; Richard M. Morse (ed.), *The Bandeirantes: The Historical Role of the Brazilian Pathfinders,* New York, 1965; Frederick J. Pohl, *Amerigo Vespucci, Pilot Major,* New York, 1944; William Prescott, *The Conquest of Peru,* New York, 1961; and many other editions; Carl O. Sauer, *The Early Spanish Main,* Berkeley, Calif., 1966; Victor W. Von Hagen, *South America Called Them,* New York, 1945; Louis B. Wright, *Gold, Glory, and the Gospel: The Adventurous Lives and Times of the Renaissance Explorers,* New York, 1970.

Lawrence A. Clayton

Southeast Asia

The exploration of large parts of Southeast Asia by Asian travelers predates the earliest visits by Europeans by at least 1000 years. Before the end of first century of the Christian era travelers from India, traders for the most part, had begun to visit a limited number of Southeast Asian regions, including the southern parts of modern Cambodia and Vietnam. Even earlier than this, perhaps in the second century B.C., Indian traders had traveled to China by a route that took them through northern Burma. Chinese visits to Southeast Asia, to both the mainland and the islands, are clearly documented from the third century A.D. onward. These early contacts by Asian visitors to Southeast Asia underline how late the European world was in gaining any detailed knowledge of a region already familiar to other societies. Although the great geographer PTOLEMY (fl. ca. A.D. 127–147) had some sense of a region beyond India, neither he nor others in the West after him had any detailed information on the character of Southeast Asia until the famous Venetian traveler Marco POLO recorded his visits to Burma, sections of modern Vietnam, and the Indonesian islands of Java and Sumatra in the thirteenth century. Yet during the centuries before Marco Polo became the first European to witness and describe this distant part of the world the states of Southeast Asia were already engaged in extensive political and trade relations with each other and with their great neighbors, India and China. In brief, to write of the exploration of Southeast Asia is to write of the European discovery of a region known by its inhabitants in terms that were meaningful for them even if these were not the later scientific standards of exploration that were such an important European contribution.

Early visitors As the first recorded European visitor to Southeast Asia and as a man of wide-ranging interests, Marco Polo has continued to fascinate scholars with the details of his travels and the sometimes improbable marvels he claimed to have encountered. Yet Polo was like so many of the other Europeans who visited Southeast Asia before the great explorations of the late eighteenth and nineteenth centuries. He recorded visits to a limited number of locations in Burma, Vietnam, and Indonesia but provided little sense of the Southeast Asian world beyond what he saw himself. This observation does not make him any less a mighty traveler, but it emphasizes how much remained unknown.

Similar comments may be made about the other

Marco Polo about to begin his travels. Although Polo visited and commented on isolated parts of the Southeast Asian lands, his records left Europeans with only a scanty knowledge of the region. [Library of Congress]

well-known travelers of this early phase of Western contact with Southeast Asia. There is scholarly fascination in tracing the travels of the Italian friar Odoric of PORDENONE (ca. 1265–1331) through the Strait of Malacca and to the now-vanished state of Champa on the coast of Vietnam. So, too, historians and geographers search for information of importance in the writings of the great Arab traveler IBN-BAṬṬUṬA (1304–1377), whose voyages took him as far as Sumatra. But none of these travelers, whether one as well known and important as Marco Polo or lesser figures such as the Florentine friar John de' Marignolli or another Venetian, Nicolò di Conti, whose visits to Asia took place in the fifteenth century, provide comprehensive information about the Southeast Asian region as a whole or even on a single state within that region. They traveled, often in conditions of great hardship, and their reports still make interesting reading. But the age of true exploration still lay removed from their time.

Iberians in Southeast Asia The sixteenth and seventeenth centuries were marked by a slow accumulation of knowledge concerning the geography of Southeast Asia as Portuguese and Spanish settlements were established on a permanent basis. For the first time the Europeans who traveled in Southeast Asia were linked to settled communities, no matter how threatened with extinction those communities were from time to time.

The Portuguese entry into Southeast Asia was the result of their earlier advances in India, where Goa was captured in 1510. A year later Afonso de Albuquerque captured Malacca, the great port city on the western coast of the Malay Peninsula, and the stage was set for a very considerable advance in European knowledge of Southeast Asia. Portuguese officials traveled to the countries of both mainland and maritime Southeast Asia. Despite the advance in knowledge, however, there were important limitations on the scope of the new information that these Iberian travelers acquired. They journeyed to capital cities, such as Ayutthaya in Siam (Thailand), rather than to provincial centers. And their journeys in the maritime regions were dominated more strongly by the desire to find the source of the spice trade's supplies than by a general interest in questions of geography. For Portuguese missionaries, moreover, despite their feats of travel and endurance, descriptions of their efforts to gain converts usually overshadowed their accounts of the region itself. This was not true of Father Gaspar da Cruz, who reported at length on his visit to Cambodia in 1555, but he like so many others could not penetrate far beyond the then Cambodian capital of Lovek to follow the unknown course of the Mekong River.

As the Portuguese came to the Southeast Asian region from the west, so, not long after, their fellow Iberians, the Spanish, came to the region from the east. Ferdinand MAGELLAN, a Portuguese who had transferred his allegiance to the Spanish crown, dis-

Plants of the Philippines and a boat of the Marianas. Magellan discovered these island groups in the course of his attempted circumnavigation of the globe in 1521. [Library of Congress]

covered the Philippine Islands in 1521 in the course of his attempted circumnavigation of the globe. His discovery was followed almost immediately by his death, but the Spanish state became determined to gain possession of the Philippines. An expedition in 1542 had little practical effect, but Miguel López de Legazpi, whose expedition reached Cebu in 1565, established a settlement there and subsequently, in 1571, another at the site of the modern city of Manila, on the island of Luzon.

The Portuguese and the Spanish achieved some remarkable feats of travel and discovery in the sixteenth century. They were active in Burma, Thailand, and Cambodia no less than in the maritime regions. Among the most interesting of these Iberian adventurers were those, like Blas Ruiz and Diego Veloso, who briefly became important figures in late-sixteenth-century Cambodian politics and others, such as Diogo do Couto, who became the first Europeans to visit the great temples of Angkor. Their accounts of the Angkor region, of the economy on which the center of the Angkorian empire rested, and of their travels as far north as Vientiane in modern Laos were, however, quickly forgotten and have been rediscovered only in the twentieth century. Most of Cambodia, like so many other parts of Southeast Asia, continued to be unknown territory for a further 200 years after Blas Ruiz and Diego Veloso played their briefly dazzling roles. Despite the growing number of port settlements visited and trading posts established, knowledge of Southeast Asia's geography and its cultural patterns remained limited in the extreme. Nor did the situation change greatly when Dutch and then British travelers, traders, and adventurers became a permanent feature of the scene from the beginning of the seventeenth century on.

Slow expansion of knowledge Both the Dutch and the British had penetrated Southeast Asia before the end of the sixteenth century. The circumnavigation of the world by Sir Francis DRAKE had brought him to the eastern Indonesian island of Ternate as early as 1579, while at the other geographical extreme of the region Ralph Fitch visited Burma in 1583. The Dutch came a little later but in ever-greater numbers once their first expedition had reached Bantam, Indonesia, in 1596. In the years that followed both the Dutch and the British ranged widely through both mainland and maritime Southeast Asia as trading posts were established wherever commercial opportunity was attractive and local authority was agreeable.

Many of these early trading ventures were of short duration, but they often served to broaden European knowledge of the region. The Dutch, for instance, were briefly active in Cambodia during the 1630s and 1640s, only to fail in their commercial aims. A Dutch trader, however, Geebaerd van Wuysthoff, who worked in Cambodia at this time, made the difficult journey from near modern Phnom Penh to Vientiane in Laos in 1641 and gave a detailed if sometimes

dubiously accurate account of that city. Van Wuysthoff was typical of many other travelers of his age in his failure to provide an extended account of his journey as opposed to a description of the destination he reached.

European knowledge of Southeast Asia continued to expand slowly in the seventeenth and eighteenth centuries as traders sought commercial opportunity and as others, frequently unrealistically, dreamed of European empires in the East. French hopes in the latter regard led to a clash between the Thai court based at Ayutthaya and a curious collection of traders, missionaries, and adventurers in the late seventeenth century. Before the clash occurred, however, a French missionary, Simon de la Loubère, prepared a detailed account of Thailand and its population. When published in 1691, his book included a surprisingly detailed map of some inland regions. This instance in which knowledge was gained and disseminated must be placed against the many other instances in which no real advance in geographical knowledge took place over a long period. With the failure of the French to establish themselves in Thailand, the only significant European powers remaining in the Southeast Asian region on a permanent basis were the Dutch and the Spanish. In both cases too much emphasis cannot be placed on the extent to which these alien powers were, outside certain essentially limited regions, generally lacking in both administrative and military power and poorly informed about the geographical features of the countries they encountered beyond the trading ports and the environs of these commercial centers.

The situation in the second half of the eighteenth century may be summarized in the following way. Most of the coastal regions of Southeast Asia had been delineated in a general fashion. Some areas, such as the coast of Java, were much better known than others, while other regions, such as the eastern coast of Borneo, were barely known at all. Pioneering voyages such as that undertaken to New Guinea by Thomas Forrest of the English East India Company between 1774 and 1776 sometimes provided many details on particular areas. But these tended to be the exception. Given the mass of islands that make up modern Indonesia, East Malaysia, and the Philippines, it should not be surprising that many coastal regions in maritime Southeast Asia were unexplored in any true sense before the end of the nineteenth century, while the rivers that flowed into these coastal areas were often completely unknown to men from Europe. By the latter part of the eighteenth century the coastline of mainland Southeast Asia was known in some detail, but once again there was lack of knowledge, sometimes approaching total ignorance, about the interior of the states of the mainland.

For both mainland and maritime Southeast Asia the extent to which vital exploration remained to be undertaken is underlined by a brief recital of some of the facts that were unknown at the beginning of the

The temple of Borobodur, near Jogjakarta, Java. The Dutch had controlled Java for 200 years without being aware of its existence and did not find it until the great age of exploration in the nineteenth century. [Library of Congress]

nineteenth century. Although the Dutch had been established in Java for nearly 200 years by 1800, they did not know of the existence of the great Buddhist monument Borobodur, located near the central Javanese city of Jogjakarta (Yogyakarta). The equally splendid monuments of Angkor had been forgotten since they had last been seen by Europeans in the sixteenth century, and no sense of their existence was held in Western circles. The course of the Mekong River was unknown except in the sparsest fashion for certain lower reaches, so that even the best-informed opinion thought that it was likely to rise in a great inland lake that also fed the Chao Phraya (Mae Nam, or Menam, River) of Thailand and the Salween River in Burma. The existence of much of Southeast Asia was, at the beginning of the nineteenth century, guessed at rather than known. But with the advent of the nineteenth century change was on the way, and the great period of Southeast Asian exploration was about to begin.

Age of exploration   The truism that the nineteenth century was a time for accelerated scientific inquiry has particular importance for the Southeast Asian region. In addition, the nineteenth century was a period when the search for imperial and commercial opportunities combined with growing scientific knowledge to give a forceful new impetus to exploration. Increasingly the European powers with interests in Southeast Asia and the men who served those interests sought to open new frontiers of knowledge. In doing so the explorers of the nineteenth century transformed European understanding of the geographical and cultural character of the Southeast Asian region.

Throughout Southeast Asia's long history the possibility of trade with China has been one of the dominant threads running through both indigenous and foreign thought about the area. As Britain slowly extended its control over Burma from the early nineteenth century onward, the prospect that there might be a way into China from Burma fascinated a number of British officials and military men. One of the most significant attempts to prove the viability of a land route between Burma and China was that made by Capt. William C. MᶜLᴇᴏᴅ in 1837. He traveled by elephant, following the course of the Salween and then striking across the Shan States to Keng Hung (now Yünchinghung), still short of the Chinese province of Yünnan. McLeod was only one of a number of British explorers who were active in Burma during the 1830s and who provided detailed and scientifically accurate accounts of regions that had been unknown or barely known before. By the 1860s, with British political dominance over Burma increasingly assured, knowledge of northern and northeastern Burma had increased to the point that discussion began of a possible rail link running through Burma to China. Although this link was never established, the exploratory and survey work associated with it greatly increased the knowledge of northern and northeastern

Burma and led, ultimately, to the successful construction of the Burma Road during World War II.

By the beginning of the nineteenth century European knowledge of Thailand's geography was considerable, but essentially this knowledge was limited to the Chao Phraya Valley region. The remoter areas of the north and northeast still awaited exploration (though the British explorer Dr. David Richardson had reached Chiangmai from Moulmein, Burma, in 1834), and it was not until the 1850s and 1860s that it began. One of the outstanding figures in the exploration of northern Thailand and the Laotian states was the Frenchman Henri Mouhot. A keen student of natural history, Mouhot penetrated as far north as Luang Prabang, Laos, having traveled beside the Mekong from Nong Khai in Thailand.

It was not Mouhot's travels through Thailand and Laos, which ended with his death near Luang Prabang in 1861, that brought him fame. Rather he is remembered as the man who told the world of the forgotten temples at Angkor in Cambodia. Mouhot, who visited the great complex of ruins in 1860, was not the first European to rediscover the temples that had last been seen by Westerners in the sixteenth century. This distinction belonged to Father Charles-Émile Bouillevaux, who reached the ruins in 1850, only to be curiously unimpressed by what he saw. But if Mouhot's description of Angkor and his travels in Thailand and

Pagoda Hill, Moulmein, Burma. It was from Moulmein that Dr. David Richardson traveled into Thailand in 1834. [Library of Congress]

Laos represented a considerable step forward in knowledge of the mainland of Southeast Asia, this advance also served to emphasize how much remained to be done. Most particularly, the route and source of the Mekong River, the longest river in Southeast Asia and the twelfth longest of the world's rivers, remained unknown.

The mystery of the Mekong's source and of the course it followed, combined with a hope that it might offer a route to China, brought a decision by the French colonial authorities in southern Vietnam to explore the river. The resulting expedition accomplished one of the major explorations of the nineteenth century and probably the greatest single feat of exploration for the whole of Southeast Asia. Starting from Saigon in June 1866, the Mekong Expedition traveled slowly and frequently painfully up the river, passing through Cambodia, Thailand, Laos, and Burma before finally abandoning the effort to find the river's source and entering the southwestern Chinese province of Yünnan in October 1867.

In terms of the hopes that the Mekong would provide a commercial link between southern Vietnam and China the expedition was a failure, for there are major barriers to navigation barely 100 miles (161 kilometers) from Phnom Penh, and the Khone Falls on the modern frontier between Cambodia and Laos present an almost insurmountable barrier for vessels of any size. Yet in terms of new areas surveyed and of details of population, flora, fauna, and geology recorded the expedition was an outstanding success. The information compiled by its members, most notably by Francis GARNIER, who became the expedition's leader after the death of Ernest DOUDART DE

The Mekong River. The expedition mounted in 1866–1867 to search for the source of this river was probably the greatest accomplishment of Southeast Asian exploration. [United Nations]

LAGRÉE in China, remains important today. Under conditions of great hardship the expedition mapped some 4000 miles (6437 kilometers) that had never been recorded before. Much of this was along the valley of the Mekong, but it also included the recording of secondary itineraries through northeastern Thailand, southeastern Laos, and parts of the Shan States. In its own time the Mekong Expedition was hailed as a triumph of exploration, and Garnier shared an award with David LIVINGSTONE of African fame. Yet because its records were in French, the expedition has remained almost unknown outside France.

The achievements of the Mekong Expedition led directly to the exploration of the Red River by Jean DUPUIS in 1871. Just as the French had first hoped that the Mekong would provide a commercial route into China, so was the hope held for the Red River. Dupuis was able to show that goods could pass up the Red River into China's Yünnan Province, but this was achieved only with considerable difficulty because of rapids. Political difficulties, moreover, made the Red River an uncertain route even when high water levels minimized the necessity for portage of goods passing up and down the river.

In addition to the achievements of the Mekong explorers and the more limited work of Dupuis, great French exploratory efforts in the nineteenth century included those of Auguste PAVIE. Pavie began his colonial career in Cambodia as a telegraph operator and subsequently supervised the construction of a telegraph line from Phnom Penh to Bangkok. Working in largely unknown regions of the Cambodian interior, he showed an aptitude for exploration and was authorized to carry out a geographical survey of the In-

dochinese region as a whole. The Pavie Mission, as it came to be known, involved a series of expeditions lasting from 1879 to 1895. Pavie and his associates traveled throughout Vietnam, Cambodia, and Laos, and by the time the expeditions were completed, only limited (mostly mountain and upland) regions remained to be explored in Indochina. As a direct result of Pavie's travels through the Laotian states, the French government intervened to establish a colonial presence in that region.

Exploration of maritime Southeast Asia was, in general, more piecemeal than was that of the mainland regions. Individual sea captains mapped sections of coastline according to the importance they attached to trading prospects in different areas. Because of this approach there were still many areas throughout Indonesia and the Philippine Islands that were not known or at least not mapped in any detail at the end of the nineteenth century. The east coast of Borneo, for instance, and in particular the countless river estuaries of that area were known only in an indefinite fashion before the beginning of the twentieth century.

Areas of greater commercial and political importance were, of course, surveyed earlier. During Thomas Stamford Raffles's period as lieutenant governor of Java (1811–1815) the great Buddhist monument Borobodur was rediscovered and surveyed in central Java. Slowly other regions, many of them well known in their coastal outlines, were subjected to serious survey. The northeastern coast of Sumatra (Achin, or Acheh), for instance, had been visited and described before John Anderson's visit in 1823, but his survey was of hitherto-unequalled thoroughness. Emphasis must be given once again to the fact that the extension of knowledge did not mean an immediate expansion of European territorial control. In the case of Achin, most notably, the Dutch were not able to implement administrative control over some regions until the beginning of the twentieth century.

Much of the scientifically important exploration of the Netherlands East Indies (Indonesia) did not take place until the end of the nineteenth century and later. The southern regions of the great island of Borneo were explored in the 1890s by a number of Dutch expeditions, the most important of these being associated with Anton Willem Nieuwenhuis between 1893 and 1898. Other European explorers who contributed significantly to knowledge of Borneo were Carl Sofus Lumholtz and Karl Bock. Exploration of Sulawesi (Celebes) was undertaken in the years 1893–1903 by two Swiss explorers, Paul and Fritz Sarasin. The more distant islands in the Indonesian Archipelago were from the Dutch base in Java, the later, in general, was their exploration, so that in the most distant region of all, Irian Jaya (formerly West New Guinea), some areas were still unexplored even after World War II. Perhaps more surprising is the realization that the island of Bali, a bare few miles from the eastern tip of Java, did not come under full Dutch administration until the first decade of the twentieth century, at

which time it finally became possible to complete a detailed survey of its inland geography.

Exploration of the northern sections of the island of Borneo that fell under British control went on throughout the nineteenth century. In some cases exploration was directly linked with the extension of governmental control. The Brooke family and their administrators in Sarawak, to take the most notable example, played a major part in widening knowledge of the northwestern part of Borneo in direct association with their efforts to impose a governmental apparatus. In other instances, however, knowledge was accumulated as the result of the deliberate pursuit of scientific ends. The work of Alfred Russel Wallace is the outstanding instance here. Wallace's travels (1854–1862) extended beyond Borneo to other parts of the archipelago, leading to his vitally important conclusion concerning the difference that existed between the flora and fauna of the western and eastern islands. His conclusion was summed up in the concept of Wallace's line, which revealed the marked difference in character between fauna, in particular, east and west of a line drawn from Sulawesi and passing north and south between Bali and Lombok. To the west the affinities are with Asia; to the east, with Australia. Spenser St. John was another major traveler with a deep interest in ethnography though not, perhaps surprisingly, in natural history. With Hugh Low he was the first to climb Mount Kinabalu in modern Sabah (previously known as North Borneo), the highest mountain in Southeast Asia, in 1858. And he made a major journey of discovery, also in 1858, up the Limbang River in north central Borneo.

The pattern of exploration in the Philippine Islands, under Spanish control until 1898, was not markedly dissimilar from that of other maritime areas in Southeast Asia. Coastal regions that had been important for trade or were linked with missionary endeavors were relatively well known, while more obscure islands were scantily mapped and barely touched by outside influence. For the whole of the maritime world, indeed, the picture presented by Joseph Conrad in his famous novel *Lord Jim* of parts of the Southeast Asian islands that were still virtually unknown by the Western world in the late nineteenth century was based as much on fact as on Conrad's artistic imagination.

Twentieth century Although the greater part of Southeast Asia was known by the beginning of the twentieth century, many questions of detail remained to be settled, and some areas were almost completely unknown as late as the 1920s and 1930s. The highland regions of central and southern Vietnam, for instance, only came to be known in anything approaching a complete fashion after World War I. Even more strikingly, parts of Irian Jaya remained unexplored until after World War II.

The nineteenth century witnessed the great period of exploration in Southeast Asia, and the twentieth century was a time when much of the work remaining to be done was completed. Despite the details now shown on maps, however, there are still parts of Southeast Asia that can only be described as barely known, even in the last quarter of the twentieth century. The chances of discovering another previously unknown ethnic group, such as happened with Tasaday in the Philippines in 1971, must be rated very low indeed. Yet other mysteries and uncertainties persist, and it is correct to emphasize that the exploration of Southeast Asia is not yet complete.

BIBLIOGRAPHY: E. H. Blair and J. A. Robertson (eds.), *The Philippine Islands, 1493–1898*, 55 vols., Cleveland, 1905; Charles Boxer, *The Dutch Seaborne Empire, 1600–1800*, London, 1965; id., *The Portuguese Seaborne Empire, 1415–1825*, London, 1969; Hugh Clifford, *Further India*, London, 1904; Archibald R. Colquhuon, *Amongst the Shans*, London, 1885; Armando Cortesão (ed.), *The Suma Oriental of Tomé Pires*, 2 vols., London, 1944; Alexander Dalrymple, *Oriental Repertory*, 2 vols., London, 1793; F. C. Danvers, *The Portuguese in India*, 2 vols., London, 1894; Jean Dupuis, *Les origines de la question du Tong-kin*, Paris, 1896; Francis Garnier, *Voyage d'exploration en Indo-Chine*, Paris, 1885; B. P. Groslier, *Angkor et le Cambodge au XVIe siècle d'après les sources portugaises et espagnoles*, Paris, 1958; D. G. E. Hall, *A History of South-East Asia*, 3d ed., London, 1968; George Masselman, *The Cradle of Colonialism*, New Haven, Conn., and London, 1963; M. A. P. Meilink-Roelofsz, *Asian Trade and European Influence in the Indonesian Archipelago between 1500 and about 1630*, The Hague, 1962; Alexandre-Henri Mouhot, *Travels in the Central Parts of Indo-China (Siam), Cambodia and Laos during 1859–60*, 2 vols., London, 1864; Milton Osborne, *River Road to China: The Mekong River Expedition, 1866–73*, New York and London, 1975; Auguste Pavie, *Mission Pavie*, 11 vols., Paris, 1898–1911; Marco Polo, *The Book of Ser Marco Polo, the Venetian, Concerning the Kingdoms and Marvels of the East*, 2 vols., 3d ed., London, 1903; Spenser St. John, *Life in the Forests of the Far East*, 2 vols., London, 1962; B. H. M. Vlekke, *Nusantara*, rev. ed., The Hague and Bandung, 1959; Alfred Russel Wallace, *The Malay Archipelago*, London, 1869; Henry Yule, *A Narrative of the Mission sent by the Governor General of India to the Court of Ava in 1855*, London, 1858.

Milton Osborne

Space Exploration

Humanity's age-old desire to probe the unknown has found ultimate expression in the exploration of space. As the scene of the most awesome natural phenomena in our experience, the heavens have always been a source of mystery and fascination. World myth and legend are filled with tales devised to explain the orderly procession of the sun, moon, stars, and planets across the sky as well as the occasional appearance of spectacular comets and novae.

Rocketry and the dream of space flight The dream of travel into this mysterious realm had to await the development of a sophisticated cosmology. As long as the sky remained a bowl inverted over the earth, space flight was inconceivable. As early as 160 B.C., Lucian of Samos produced a fictional account of a celestial journey, but such tales remained rare until the seventeenth century, by which time the revolution in astronomy sparked by the work of Copernicus, Kepler, Galileo, and Newton produced an accurate portrait of the solar system. By the late nineteenth century stories of travel into space had become a familiar literary theme. Jules Verne's twin novels *De la terre à la lune* (1865) and *Autour de la lune* (1870), Edward Everett Hale's "The Brick Moon" (1869), and H. G. Wells's *The War of the Worlds* (1898) are typical of the genre. Thus the dream of space flight was firmly planted by the early years of the twentieth century. The realization of the dream was to be quite another matter.

The fictional heroes of space-flight adventures had been sent aloft by an incredible variety of devices, ranging from bottles of dew and flights of migrating birds to the giant cannon of Jules Verne. The first generation of scientists and engineers to give serious thought to the possibility of space flight quickly rejected these fanciful and impractical schemes. Not until 1891 did Hermann Ganswindt, a German inventor, point out that the rocket was the only means of propelling a vehicle through the vacuum of space.

The rocket is an engine that carries a supply of fuel to burn and an oxidizer to support combustion. The gaseous products of combustion are exhausted through a nozzle, imparting thrust to the rocket. All rocket motors, from the primitive black-powder devices of the thirteenth century through the giant engines that boosted the Apollo astronauts to the moon, are based upon a physical principle first enunciated by Isaac Newton in 1687: "Reaction is equal but opposite to action; or the actions of two bodies are equal but point in opposite directions."

Rockets appeared almost simultaneously in China and Europe during the thirteenth century. These early weapons consisted of black powder packed into a case that was completely closed on one end and featured a nozzle on the other. A long stick attached to the side of the case stabilized the rocket in flight. The first rockets were inaccurate short-range weapons but could be fired in barrages to frighten enemy troops and horses.

In Europe rocket weapons were eclipsed by improvements in artillery during the sixteenth century but remained in use to produce the spectacular fireworks displays that enlivened coronations, royal weddings, and other ceremonial occasions. Following improvements by the Englishmen William Congreve and William Hale, barrage rockets were reintroduced into European arsenals during the nineteenth century and were effectively used during the Napoleonic Wars, the American Civil War, and various colonial campaigns.

By the late nineteenth century scientists were aware that the space environment was essentially a gasless vacuum in which normal engines that relied on atmospheric oxygen to support combustion would be useless. Only the rocket, which carries its own supply of oxygen, could propel a space vehicle.

Three major figures, working independently at the turn of the twentieth century, laid the foundation for space travel. The first of these, Konstantin Eduardovich Tsiolkovsky, was born in Russia in 1856. A schoolteacher, he published his first account of a journey into space in 1895. His classic study of the problems of space flight, *The Investigation of Space with Reactive Devices*, was published in 1903. The Russian theoretician continued to publish studies of astronautical problems until his death in 1935. Tsiolkovsky, whose work was little noted outside the Soviet Union, supplied the basic mathematical demonstration of the possibility of space travel. In addition, he described a variety of devices ranging from liquid-propellant rockets to earth satellites and manned spaceships capable of interplanetary and interstellar journeys.

Robert Hutchings Goddard was the second of the three great pioneers of space flight. Born in Worcester, Massachusetts, in 1882, Goddard received a Ph.D. degree in physics from Clark University, where he remained as a professor for most of his career. His interest in space flight began when he read a newspaper serialization of *The War of the Worlds* as a boy. By 1914 he had received the first of what would eventually become 214 patents covering virtually every phase of modern rocketry. His classic treatise on space flight, *A Method of Reaching Extreme Altitudes*, was published by the Smithsonian Institution in 1920. Goddard was not content to remain a theoretician, however. During World War I he experimented with rockets under the auspices of the War Department. Convinced that much higher exhaust velocities were available with liquid propellants, he began work in 1920 on a rocket motor burning gasoline and liquid oxygen. This early work was carried on with grants from the Smithsonian. On March 16, 1926, Goddard flew the world's first liquid-propellant rocket from a farm near Auburn, Massachusetts. Additional funds from the Daniel and Florence Guggenheim Foundation for the Promotion of Aeronautics enabled him to establish a permanent rocket construction and test facility at Mescalero Ranch, near Roswell, New Mexico, in 1930. Here he was able to develop and fly a series of increasingly sophisticated rockets prior to World War II. At the time of his death in 1945, Goddard was recognized not only as an astronautical theorist but also as the man who had taken the first practical steps toward developing the liquid-propellant rocket.

Romanian-born Hermann Oberth (1894–   ) was the last of the trio who established modern rocketry. Oberth's classic *Die Rakete zu den Planetenräumen (The Rocket into Interplanetary Space)*, published in Germany in 1923, was a source of inspiration for a generation of German rocket engineers. Banding together to form the German Society for Space Travel (Verein für Raumschiffahrt; VfR) in 1927, these enthusiasts experimented with liquid-propellant rockets near Berlin. Experimenters in other nations were soon following the German example. The American Interplanetary Society (soon to become the American Rocket Society) was founded in 1930. Inspired by the success of the VfR, the American experimenters launched their first rocket in 1933. Under the leadership of Theodore von Kármán rocket experiments were also undertaken at the Guggenheim Aeronautical Laboratory of the California Institute of Technology in 1936. In the Soviet Union, experimental rocket societies were founded in Moscow and Leningrad as early as 1929. As in Germany and the United States, these early Soviet groups produced a generation of well-trained rocket engineers. Sergi Korolyov, perhaps the best-known product of the Russian societies, was later to supervise work on the Sputnik launch vehicle and early Soviet manned spacecraft. While not an experimental group, the British Interplanetary Society, founded in 1933, was also important in providing detailed studies of astronautical problems and in publicizing the potential of space flight.

In addition to the organized effort in Germany, the Soviet Union, the United States, and Great Britain, a number of independent experimenters were also active. Robert Esnault-Pelterie in France; Eugen Sänger, Franz von Hoefft, and Guido von Pirquet in Austria; and Walter Hohmann, Max Valier, Reinhold Tiling, and others in Germany were working to perfect the engines, pumps, propellants, and control systems necessary for large rockets.

The early period of rocket history came to an end with the development of the A-4 (V-2). The work of the VfR had attracted the attention of German military planners as early as 1932. Dr. Wernher von Braun, a veteran of the VfR, had been placed in command of a group of technicians at Peenemünde, an island in the Baltic Sea, by 1936. Their task was to develop an effective long-range ballistic missile for use against cities in England and on the continent. The V-2 stood 45 feet 11 inches (14 meters) tall and weighed 28,299

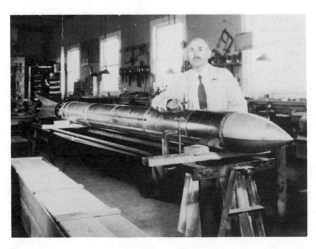

Dr. Robert H. Goddard with his rocket in his workshop at Roswell, New Mexico (1935). Dr. Goddard has been recognized as the "father of American rocketry" and as one of the pioneers in the theoretical exploration of space. [NASA]

pounds (12,836 kilograms) fully fueled and ready for flight. The engine of the V-2, which burned liquid oxygen and alcohol, produced a thrust of 59,500 pounds (26,989 kilograms) at sea level. Under operational conditions the rocket carried 1 metric ton of high explosive to a maximum altitude of 60 miles (97 kilometers) over a range of 190 miles (306 kilometers). The V-2 made its first successful flight on October 3, 1942. By the end of World War II a total of 1027 of the rockets had been fired against Allied targets.

Intended as a weapon of destruction, the V-2 was, nevertheless, a major step toward the development of a genuine space launch vehicle. At the close of World War II captured V-2s were divided among the victorious nations to be used in training rocket technicians and launch crews. The availability of these large rockets also provided an opportunity for scientists to send instrument payloads into the upper atmosphere. Since the nineteenth century experimenters had employed kites, balloons, and aircraft to "sound" the ocean of air. The rocket, capable of reaching much higher altitudes than these earlier vehicles, opened new avenues of approach to the study of atmospheric physics, meteorology, and related sciences. Between March 15, 1946, and June 28, 1951, a total of 52 instrumented V-2 rockets were launched from White Sands, New Mexico, the principal American launch site.

In addition, a number of other sounding rocket types were perfected. The first of these, WAC Corporal, was designed by engineers at the Guggenheim Aeronautical Laboratory of the California Institute of Technology. When used as the upper stage for the much larger V-2, the resulting Bumper-WAC reached a peak altitude of 250 miles (402 kilometers), well beyond the upper fringes of the atmosphere. Yet another American sounding rocket, Viking, was built by the Martin Company for the U.S. Navy. Twelve of these large rockets were launched between May 5, 1949, and February 4, 1955, reaching altitudes of up to 158 miles (254 kilometers). A variety of other sounding rockets have been developed since World War II. In addition to answering the scientists' questions about the mysterious space environment, these vehicles have played a major role in creating the technology that would carry manned and unmanned spacecraft on longer journeys away from their home planet. These precursors of the space age remain important scientific tools, providing a relatively inexpensive means of boosting short-term experimental packages into the upper atmosphere and near-earth space.

Earth satellites The concept of an unmanned, instrumented, earth-orbiting satellite can be traced to 1869, when the American essayist Edward Everett Hale described such a vehicle in his short story "The Brick Moon." Tsiolkovsky, Goddard, Oberth, and other pioneers all discussed the possibility of such a craft. Essentially, the earth satellite was seen as a logical extension of earlier sounding-rocket programs. The new vehicles were designed to carry instruments

similar to those borne aloft by sounding rockets, yet able to provide a continuous flow of information on ever-changing conditions in near-earth space. Satellite feasibility studies were commissioned by the U.S. Navy and Air Force during the years immediately following World War II, but officials remained skeptical, arguing that there was no scientific or military requirement for such a craft. The International Geophysical Year (IGY; July 1, 1957–December 31, 1958) provided the final impetus for the development of the first artificial earth satellite. The IGY offered scientists an opportunity to cooperate with colleagues in other nations in a coordinated investigation of the earth's environment. Both the United States and the Soviet Union announced that satellites would be launched as part of their contribution to the IGY.

In the United States, Project Vanguard, a Naval Research Laboratory proposal, was selected as the official satellite program in 1955. Vanguard called for the construction of a totally new three-stage launch vehicle assigned specifically for the task. Project Orbiter, a rival Army plan, proposed using a modified Redstone ballistic missile to orbit a satellite but was initially rejected in favor of the civilian effort. As the IGY approached, Vanguard officials faced the inevitable difficulties associated with the development of an entirely new launch vehicle, satellite, and tracking network. In spite of these problems, it seemed apparent that the United States would succeed in orbiting the world's first satellite before the end of 1958. Thus the announcement that the Soviet Union had placed a 184-pound (83-kilogram) satellite, *Sputnik I*, into orbit on October 4, 1957, came as a shock to an unprepared world. The fear that the United States had lost a "space race" was compounded by the launch of the 1120-pound (508-kilogram) *Sputnik II* carrying the space dog Laika on November 3, 1957.

The explosion of the rocket that was to carry the first Vanguard satellite into orbit on December 6, 1957, convinced many Americans that their nation had indeed fallen far behind the Soviet Union in science and technology. At this critical juncture, Dr. Wernher von Braun and his team of Army Ballistic Missile Agency engineers were given permission to attempt a satellite launch with their Jupiter-C, a modified Redstone rocket featuring three solid-propellant upper stages. With the successful launches of *Explorer I* on January 31, 1958, and *Vanguard I* on March 17, 1958, the United States finally entered the space age. On July 16, 1958, Congress took a major step toward organizing a space program by voting to establish the National Aeronautics and Space Administration (NASA).

American and Soviet space planners expanded their satellite launch plans over the next decade. Initially, all orbital spacecraft were intended to answer purely scientific questions. Perhaps the most important contribution of the early satellite program was the discovery of the earth's radiation belts and the mapping of the complexities of the magnetosphere by early

Explorer-series vehicles. The satellite has continued to serve as an invaluable research tool, expanding our knowledge in such areas as physics, astronomy, biology, and geology.

By 1960 satellite technology was being applied to improve the quality of life on earth in more direct ways. *Tiros I,* launched on April 1 of that year, became the world's first meteorological satellite, the predecessor of an entire family of spacecraft that have revolutionized weather forecasting. *Transit I-B,* orbited on April 3, was the first satellite designed to assist ships at sea in locating their positions. The first communications satellites, *Echo I* and *Courier I,* followed on August 12 and October 4. The modern global satellite communications network employs a series of vehicles orbiting at synchronous altitude, 22,800 miles (36,692 kilometers) above the surface of the earth. On August 11, 1960, *Discoverer 13* became the first space vehicle to be recovered intact from earth orbit. Since 1960 earth satellites have continued to assist scientists in solving earthbound problems in areas ranging from meteorology and communications to mapping, agriculture, urban planning, and pollution control. Earth satellites have provided the most useful direct benefits of man's entry into space.

Unmanned space probes Since 1957 unmanned spacecraft have pioneered our exploration of the solar system. The first objective was to gain a more thorough understanding of our nearest celestial neighbor, the moon. The Pioneer series of American space probes were designed to return television pictures of the lunar surface. Like so many phases of the American space effort during the years immediately following the launch of *Sputnik I,* the Pioneer program was fraught with difficulties. Nine of these probes were launched between August 17, 1958, and September 26, 1960. *Pioneer 4,* the only one of these craft to reach the vicinity of the moon, did not complete a sufficiently close approach to return photographs.

The Soviet probe *Luna 1,* launched on January 2, 1959, was the first spacecraft to escape the pull of the earth's gravity. *Luna 2* became the first artificial object to impact on the moon, on September 14, 1959. On October 7, 1959, *Luna 3* returned the first photographs of the far side of the moon. A series of Soviet attempts to make a soft landing on the lunar surface failed before *Luna 9* touched down on February 3, 1966, transmitting a series of thirty pictures that gave scientists their first close-up view of the surface of the moon. Three other Soviet probes were placed in lunar orbit during 1966, with a fourth, *Luna 13,* making a second soft landing and returning surface photographs and data on soil cohesion.

As the United States space program moved rapidly toward a manned lunar landing, the Soviets sent a series of ever more sophisticated unmanned vehicles to the moon. *Zond 5,* for example, carried animals on a circumlunar journey in September 1968. *Luna 16,* launched on September 12, 1970, landed on the moon and returned soil samples to earth. *Luna 17* carried a

small automated lunar rover to the moon in November 1970. Known as *Lunakhod 1,* this robot explorer continued to travel over the lunar surface from November 17, 1970, to October 4, 1971. It conducted a series of experiments ranging from soil sampling and testing to x-ray studies. In addition, it returned high-quality television pictures of the lunar surface.

Undaunted by the failure of the Pioneer program, American space planners launched a series of lunar probes, orbiters, and landers early in the 1960s. Unlike the Soviet program, however, the American effort was aimed at the ultimate goal of site selection for an eventual manned lunar landing.

The nine Ranger spacecraft launched between August 23, 1961, and March 21, 1965, were designed to return close-up photographs up to the moment of impact on the moon. The first six Rangers failed as a result either of problems at launch or of internal difficulties with the spacecraft. *Ranger 7,* launched on July 28, 1964, performed flawlessly, transmitting 4316 photographs before crashing into the crater Guericke. The last two spacecraft in this series were similarly successful.

The American Surveyor spacecraft were designed to make soft landings on the lunar surface, returning photographs and information on soil conditions at the landing site. Information derived from the five successful Surveyor flights (May 30, 1966–January 7, 1968) was of critical importance in planning the Apollo manned lunar missions. Five successful Lunar Orbiter spacecraft flown between August 10, 1966, and August 1, 1967, returned thousands of photographs which were used to prepare detailed maps of the moon.

The unmanned space probe has also proved to be an invaluable tool for planetary exploration. *Venera I,*

Surveyor nose fairing for the Centaur launch vehicle undergoes a test in a space environmental chamber at the Lewis Research Center in Cleveland. [NASA]

Mariners 8 and 9. The unmanned space probe has proved invaluable in planetary exploration. [NASA]

A drawing of the Viking mission to Mars in 1976. The Viking program was the first effort to determine the possibility of life on another planet. [NASA]

launched by the Soviet Union on February 12, 1961, was intended to provide the first close glimpse of another world but failed to transmit any information. The first American Venus probe, *Mariner 1*, failed at launch. *Mariner 2*, launched on December 14, 1962, was a complete success, passing within 21,600 (34,-761 kilometers) of the surface of Venus and transmitting information on the surface temperature, radiation levels, and magnetic conditions near the cloudy planet. A large Soviet spacecraft, *Zond 1*, launched

toward Venus on April 2, 1964, and a second Venera probe, launched on November 12, 1965, failed to transmit data. On March 1, 1966, *Venera 3* impacted on Venus but failed to return any information on the planet. *Venera 4* entered the Venusian atmosphere on October 18, 1967. An instrumented capsule was parachuted to the surface but ceased functioning during the descent to the planet. The atmosphere of Venus was found to consist of a high percentage of carbon dioxide with temperatures of up to 536°F (280°C).

The American *Mariner 5* spacecraft, launched on June 14, 1967, also studied the atmosphere of Venus, confirming the data obtained by *Mariner 2* and *Venera 4*. The 1969 probes, *Venera 5* and *6*, which also reached Venus, apparently ceased operation because of excessive temperature and pressure before they reached the surface. *Venera 7* finally became the first artificial object to broadcast from the surface of Venus, on December 15, 1971. The Soviet *Venera 9* spacecraft made another successful descent to the surface, returning yet another series of photographs of another world.

Launched on November 3, 1973, the American *Mariner 10* spacecraft was the first to visit two planets, Venus and Mercury, during the course of a single mission. During an initial approach to Venus in February 1974, *Mariner 10* returned photographs of the cloud cover and additonal data on the planet. Reaching Mercury in mid-March 1974, the spacecraft transmitted pictures showing surface details as small as 300 yards (274 meters) wide. The innermost planet was also found to have a tenuous atmosphere and an unexpected magnetic field. The atmosphere of Venus will be more throughly explored by *Pioneer Venus 1* and *Pioneer Venus 2*, which were launched in 1978.

While Venus was the first target for unmanned space probes, Mars has always been the most fascinating planet in the solar system. Both of the first two spacecraft aimed at the red planet, the Russian *Mars 1* and the American *Mariner 3*, failed. *Mariner 4* passed within 6000 miles (9656 kilometers) of Mars on July 14, 1965, returning twenty-two photographs that gave scientists their first close glimpse of the pocked and cratered Martian surface. *Mariner 6* passed within 2000 miles (3219 kilometers) of Mars on July 31, 1969, investigating the composition and structure of the atmosphere and transmitting another set of surface photographs. *Mariner 7* completed a third pass over Mars on August 5, 1969. *Mariner 8*, launched on May 8, 1971, failed to operate, but *Mariner 9*, which followed on May 30, 1971, was one of the most successful of all planetary probes. The craft was placed in Mars orbit on November 13, 1971, and transmitted a total of 6876 photographs, almost completely mapping the planet's surface before the mission was terminated on October 27, 1972.

Mars 2, launched by the Soviet Union on May 18, 1971, impacted on the Martian surface the following November. *Mars 3*, launched 2 days after *Mars 2*, succeeded in making a soft landing on December 2.

Another chapter in the story of the exploration of Mars was played out by the Viking spacecraft in 1976. Two Viking orbiters circled the planet, gathering data on surface temperatures, atmospheric-water concentration, the appearance of clouds and dust storms, and the topography of the surface. Once in orbit, each of the Viking spacecraft released a landing module designed to make a parachute descent to the Martian surface. Each lander included equipment to identify organic molecules, three different life-detection experiments, meteorological sensors, a seismometer, equipment to analyze the inorganic constituents of the soil, and cameras, magnets, and a boom to retrieve soil samples. The first module landed on Mars on July 20, 1976; the second, on September 3, 1976. The Viking Program represents a genuine milestone, humanity's first attempt to identify life in another part of the universe.

The American *Pioneer 10* and *11* spacecraft have extended the reach of scientific instruments to Jupiter and Saturn. *Pioneer 10*, which carries a specially designed greeting for residents of other worlds, bears the distinction of being the first spacecraft to attain sufficient velocity to leave the solar system. The probe made its closest approach to Jupiter on December 3, 1973. A sister ship, *Pioneer 11*, followed on December 2, 1974. Both spacecraft bolstered the suspicion that the giant planet is composed largely of liquid hydrogen. Jupiter was found to be much hotter at its core (30,000°C) than suspected. The temperature falls rapidly as one approaches the clouds which shroud the surface. *Pioneer 11*, which passed only 29,000 miles (46,670 kilometers) from Jupiter, will continue its journey to Saturn, approaching the ringed planet in 1979 if all goes well.

In 1977 *Pioneer 10* and *Pioneer 11* were joined by *Voyager I* and *Voyager II*, identical 1820-pound (827-kilogram) spacecraft carrying powerful telescopic cameras that were expected to provide more accurate data on Jupiter and Saturn than *Pioneer 10* and *Pioneer 11*. *Voyager I* and *Voyager II* are scheduled to reach Jupiter in 1979 and Saturn in 1980 and 1981. Earth controllers might then decide to send *Voyager II* to Uranus and Neptune.

Manned space flight In spite of the enormous advances in knowledge garnered as a result of unmanned space flights, public attention has focused on the manned space effort. As in the case of the satellite and space-probe programs, the United States and the Soviet Union found themselves in competition in manned space flight. As early as 1961 President John F. Kennedy established the goal of placing an American on the moon by the end of the decade. Thus, the United States Mercury and Gemini Programs were aimed at developing the hardware and gaining the experience that would make possible the realization of this goal. The Apollo program was devoted to manned space flight. In July 1969 *Apollo 11* accomplished the goal President Kennedy had set. While the spacecraft's command module, *Columbia*, orbited

NASA's Pioneer Venus 1 *lifts off from Cape Canaveral in May 1978.* [NASA]

the moon, the lunar module *Eagle* descended to the moon's surface. On July 20, 1969, astronauts Neil A. Armstrong and Edwin E. Aldrin, Jr., walked on the moon.

The full impact of the drive to reach the moon on American society and industry has yet to be fully assessed. The Soviet Vostok, Voskhod, Soyuz, and Salyut spacecraft allowed cosmonauts to gain extensive experience in orbital space flight and opened new opportunities for research to Soviet scientists. The American Skylab Program demonstrated the ability of astronauts to live and work in space for long periods of time, while the Apollo-Soyuz Test Project (ASTP) demonstrated the willingness of both major spacefaring nations to cooperate in joint programs of research and exploration. While Russian cosmonauts will continue to venture into space for the forseeable future, United States astronauts will remain on the ground until the first flight of the *Space Shuttle* opens a new era of space exploration in 1980. Unlike current launch vehicles, which are totally expended during the course of a mission, the *Space Shuttle* is designed

*Astronauts Neil A.
Armstrong (left) and
Edwin E. Aldrin, Jr.,
plant the American
flag on the moon on
July 20, 1969.
[NASA]*

to be flown many times. The *Space Shuttle* will make the exploitation of the unique potential of the space environment possible on a large scale for the first time. The way is open to the exploration of space; unlike the exploration of the earth, it will be a never-ending quest.

The history of the manned space effort through ASTP can best be presented in tabular form.

BIBLIOGRAPHY: Wernher von Braun and Frederick I. Ordway III, *A History of Rocketry and Space Flight*, New York, 1969; id., *The Rocket's Red Glare*, New York, 1976; Arthur C. Clarke (ed.), *The Coming of the Space Age: Famous Accounts of Man's Probing of the Universe*, New York, 1967; William R. Corliss, *Scientific Satellites*, Washington, 1967; F. C. Durant III and George James (eds.), *First Steps toward Space*, Washington, 1974; Eugene Emme, *A History of Space Flight*, New York, 1965; Kenneth Gatland, *Manned Spacecraft*, New York,.1967; id., *Robot Explorers*, London, 1972; Milton Lehman, *This High Man: The Life of Robert H. Goddard*, New York, 1963; Willy Ley, *Rockets, Missiles, and Men in Space*, New York, 1968; William R. Shelton, *Man's Conquest of Space*, New York, 1974; Loyd S. Swenson, James Grimwood, and Charles C. Alexander, *This New Ocean: A History of Project Mercury*, Washington, 1966.

Tom D. Crouch

United States and Soviet Manned Space Flights, 1961–1975

Mission	Crew	Launch date	Time in space (hours and minutes)	Remarks
Vostok 1	Yury A. Gagarin	April 12, 1961	1:48	First man in space.
Mercury Redstone 3	Alan B. Shepard, Jr.	May 5, 1961	0:15	First suborbital flight; first American in space.
Mercury Redstone 4	Virgil I. Grissom	July 21, 1961	0:16	Second United States suborbital flight.
Vostok 2	Gherman S. Titov	August 6, 1961	25:18	First manned flight in excess of 24 hours; 17.5 orbits of earth.
Mercury Atlas 6	John H. Glenn, Jr.	February 20, 1962	4:55	First United States orbital flight.
Mercury Atlas 7	M. Scott Carpenter	May 24, 1962	4:56	Three earth orbits.
Vostok 3	Andrian G. Nikolayev	August 11, 1962	94:22	First tandem flight, with *Vostok 4.*
Vostok 4	Pavel R. Popovich	August 12, 1962	70:57	In visual and radio contact with *Vostok 3.*
Mercury Atlas 8	Walter M. Schirra, Jr.	October 3, 1962	9:13	Landed within 13,000 feet (3,962 meters) of predicted point.
Mercury Atlas 9	L. Gordon Cooper, Jr.	May 15, 1963	34:20	Final Project Mercury flight.
Vostok 5	Valery F. Bykovsky	June 14, 1963	119:06	An 81-orbit flight.
Vostok 6	Valentina V. Tereshkova	June 16, 1963	70:50	First woman in space.
Voskhod 1	Vladimir M. Komarov Konstantin P. Feoktistov Boris B. Yegorov	October 12, 1964	24:17	First multiple-crew launch.
Voskhod 2	Alexey A. Leonov Pavel I. Belyayev	March 18, 1965	26:02	Leonov made first "walk" in space.
Gemini Titan 3	Virgil I. Grissom John W. Young	March 23, 1965	4:53	First manned Gemini mission.
Gemini Titan 4	James A. McDivitt Edward H. White	June 3, 1965	97:56	White completed first American space walk.
Gemini Titan 5	Leroy G. Cooper, Jr. Charles Conrad, Jr.	August 21, 1965	190:55	Longest space flight to date.
Gemini Titan 7	Frank Borman James A. Lovell, Jr.	December 4, 1965	330:35:31	Longest flight of Gemini Program; successful rendezvous with another American spacecraft.
Gemini Titan 6-A	Walter M. Schirra, Jr. Thomas P. Stafford	December 15, 1965	25:51	Rescheduled following failure of Agena target to orbit.
Gemini Titan 8	Neil A. Armstrong David R. Scott	March 16, 1966	10:41	First docking in space led to problems that forced a mission abort.
Gemini Titan 9-A	Thomas P. Stafford Eugene A. Cernan	June 3, 1966	72:21	Cernan completed 2-hour, 7-minute space walk.
Gemini Titan 10	John W. Young Michael Collins	July 18, 1966	70:47	Rendezvous with Agena target vehicle; Collins spent 89 minutes outside spacecraft.
Gemini Titan 11	Charles Conrad, Jr. Richard F. Gordon, Jr.	September 12, 1966	71:17	Docking with Agena; Gordon tethered Agena to Gemini for a 2-orbit flight.

(Continued)

United States and Soviet Manned Space Flights, 1961–1975 (Continued)

Mission	Crew	Launch date	Time in space (hours and minutes)	Remarks
Gemini Titan 12	James A. Lovell, Jr. Edwin E. Aldrin, Jr.	November 11, 1966	94:34	Final Gemini mission; Aldrin completed the Gemini extravehicular activity record of 5 hours 30 minutes spent outside a spacecraft.
Soyuz 1	Vladimir M. Komarov	April 23, 1967	26:40	First flight of Soyuz spacecraft; Komarov died when his main parachute failed during reentry.
Apollo Saturn 7	Walter M. Schirra, Jr. Donn F. Eisele Walter Cunningham	October 11, 1968	260:09	First manned flight of the Apollo command and service module.
Soyuz 3	Georgi T. Beregovoi	October 26, 1968	94:51	The cosmonaut rendezvoused with an unmanned *Soyuz 2* vehicle launched the previous day.
Apollo Saturn 8	Frank Borman James A. Lovell, Jr. William A. Anders	December 21, 1968	147:00	First manned circumlunar flight.
Soyuz 4 *Soyuz 5*	Vladimir A. Shatalov Yevgeny V. Khrunov Aleksey S. Yeliseyev Boris V. Volynov	January 14, 1969 January 15, 1969	71:14 72:46	*Soyuz 4* and 5 rendezvoused in orbit. Khrunov and Yeliseyev transferred and returned to earth in *Soyuz 4*. Volynov returned alone in *Soyuz 5*.
Apollo Saturn 9	James A. McDivitt David R. Scott Russell L. Schweickart	March 3, 1969	241:01	First manned flight of a lunar module (earth orbit).
Apollo Saturn 10	Thomas P. Stafford John W. Young Eugene A. Cernan	May 18, 1969	192:03	First test of a lunar module in lunar orbit.
Apollo Saturn 11	Neil A. Armstrong* Edwin E. Aldrin, Jr.* Michael Collins	July 16, 1969	195:18	Command Pilot Armstrong and Lunar Module Pilot Aldrin became the first human beings to set foot on the moon.
Soyuz 6 *Soyuz 7* *Soyuz 8*	Georgi S. Shonin Valery N. Kubasov Anatoly V. Filipchenko Vladislav N. Volkov Viktor V. Gorbatko Vladimir A. Shatalov Aleksey S. Yeliseyev	October 11, 1969 October 12, 1969 October 13, 1969	118:42 118:41 118:50	These three spacecraft rendezvoused to practice joint maneuvers and performed a series of scientific experiments and observations in concert with one another.
Apollo Saturn 12	Charles Conrad, Jr.* Richard F. Gordon, Jr. Alan L. Bean*	November 14, 1969	244:36	Conrad and Bean spent a combined total of 7 hours 45 minutes on surface of the moon.
Apollo Saturn 13	James A. Lovell, Jr. John L. Swigert, Jr. Fred W. Haise, Jr.	April 11, 1970	142:54	Mission aborted after explosion of an oxygen tank in the service module. The crew returned safely.
Soyuz 9	Andrian G. Nikolayev Vitaly I. Sevastyanov	June 1, 1970	424:59	This flight set a duration record for manned space missions.
Apollo Saturn 14	Alan B. Shepard, Jr.* Stuart Allen Roosa Edgar D. Mitchell*	January 31, 1971	216:02	During their time on the moon Shepard and Mitchell collected 96 pounds (44 kilograms) of lunar sample material.

*Indicates astronaut member of lunar landing party.

United States and Soviet Manned Space Flights, 1961–1975 *(Continued)*

Mission	Crew	Launch date	Time in space (hours and minutes)	Remarks
Soyuz 10	Vladimir A. Shatalov Aleksey S. Yeliseyev Nikolay N. Rukavishnikov	April 22, 1971	47:46	Cosmonauts docked with, but did not enter, a Salyut space station launched on April 19.
Soyuz 11	Georgi T. Dobrovolsky Vladislav N. Volkov Viktor I. Patsayev	June 6, 1971	570:22	This was the first crew to dock with, enter, and work in the Salyut space station. A hatch failure during reentry led to the death of all crew members.
Apollo Saturn 15	David R. Scott* Alfred M. Worden James B. Irwin*	July 26, 1971	295:12	For the first time astronauts traveled over the lunar surface in a battery-powered lunar roving vehicle.
Apollo Saturn 16	James W. Young* Thomas K. Mattingly 2d Charles M. Duke, Jr.*	April 16, 1972	265:51	The crew returned 213 pounds (97 kilograms) of lunar surface material.
Apollo Saturn 17	Eugene A. Cernan* Ronald Evans Harrison H. Schmitt*	December 7, 1972	301:51	Last lunar landing mission of the Apollo program.
Skylab 2	Charles Conrad, Jr. Joseph P. Kerwin Paul J. Weitz	May 25, 1973	672:50	*Skylab 2* astronauts were successful in repairing the Skylab space station, which had been damaged during launch.
Skylab 3	Alan L. Bean Owen K. Garriott Jack R. Lousma	July 28, 1973	1,427:09	The crew completed further repairs to the Skylab and completed a wide range of scientific tests and observations.
Soyuz 12	Vasily G. Lazaryev Oleg G. Makarov	September 27, 1973	47:16	Almost 27 months after the loss of *Soyuz 11*, *Soyuz 12* tested new safety procedures and conducted scientific experiments.
Skylab 4	Gerald P. Carr Edward G. Gibson William R. Pogue	November 16, 1973	2,017:16	The crew of the Skylab conducted an extensive program of experiments and observations, setting a new record for time in space.
Soyuz 13	Pyotr I. Klimuk Valentin V. Lebedev	December 18, 1973	188:55	Astrophysical, earth-resources, and other scientific experiments and observations were undertaken.
Soyuz 14	Pavel R. Popovich Yury Artyukhin	July 3, 1974	377:30	The crew occupied and lived in the space station *Salyut 3*, launched on June 24.
Soyuz 15	Gennady Sarafanov Lev Demin	August 26, 1974	48:12	An unsuccessful attempt to dock with *Salyut 3*.
Soyuz 16	Anatoly V. Filipchenko Nikolay N. Rukavishnikov	December 6, 1974	142:24	A flight to check modifications made to prepare the Soyuz spacecraft for the upcoming ASTP flight.
Soyuz 17	Georgi Grechko Alexey Gubarev	January 19, 1975	709:20	Entered *Salyut 4*, launched on December 26, 1974.
Soyuz 18	Pyotr Klimuk Vitaly Serastyanov	May 24, 1975	1511:20	The crew spent 2 months and 2 days aboard *Salyut 4*.

*Indicates astronaut member of lunar landing party.

United States and Soviet Manned Space Flights, 1961–1975 (Continued)

Mission	Crew	Launch date	Time in space (hours and minutes)	Remarks
Soyuz 19	Alexey A. Leonov Valery N. Kubasov	July 15, 1975	142:31	At 11:15 on the morning of July 17, 1975, these two spacecraft docked, effecting the first international union in space. The craft remained linked while visits were exchanged.
Apollo (ASTP)	Thomas R. Stafford Vanu D. Brand Donald K. Slayton	July 15, 1975	217:28	

John Hanning Speke.

John Hanning Speke's routes in Africa, 1854–1862.

Speke, John Hanning *(1827–1864)* English explorer. Born in Somerset to a landowning family, Speke joined the Indian Army at the age of 17. He fought in the Punjab campaign and in the Second Sikh War and spent his leaves exploring and shooting game. He also developed a desire to undertake exploration in Africa and in 1854, taking advantage of a long leave, embarked for Aden on the first stage of his journey. There he met Richard Francis BURTON and joined his ill-fated expedition to Somaliland; during a Somali attack on Burton and his companions, Speke was badly wounded and briefly made a captive. Returning to Central Africa with Burton in December 1856, he shared in the discovery of Lake Tanganyika although he was temporarily blind at the time and could barely see the lake. While Burton remained at Kazeh (modern Tabora, Tanzania), Speke struck northward to investigate reports of another large lake. He sighted the lake, which he called Lake Victoria, at Mwanza on July 30, 1858, and had his first full view of it on August 3. Although he was unable to explore the lake, he quickly concluded that it was the source of the Nile, a conviction which Burton derided and which was to produce much bitterness between the two men.

Upon returning to England, Speke revealed his theories to the ROYAL GEOGRAPHICAL SOCIETY and soon won financing for a new expedition. Accompanied by James Augustus GRANT, whom he had known in India, Speke arrived in East Africa in 1860 and once again made for Kazeh. The explorers then headed northward, their progress being hindered by illness, by warfare between Arabs and natives, and by the demands of African chiefs for *hongo* (transit fees). Their path became somewhat smoother when they entered the lake area and visited the important intralacustrine Bantu kingdoms of Karagwe and Buganda. While Grant stayed behind in Karagwe because of a troublesome leg, Speke marched eastward toward the Nile, which he reached on July 21, 1862, at a place called Urondogani about 40 miles (64 kilometers) north of Lake Victoria. He followed the river upstream along its left bank until he came to its source at the falls at the north end of Lake Victoria. He named the falls Ripon Falls in honor of the 2d Earl of Ripon, who had been president of the Royal Geographical Society when the expedition was conceived. Speke had planned to begin his homeward journey by sailing down the Nile, but this proved impossible because of the objections of some of the Africans in the area. Having been reunited with Grant on August 19, 1862, Speke was forced to travel to the capital of Bunyoro. The king, Kamurasi, was rather unfriendly and attempted to delay their departure, but they were able to resume their journey on November 9. Continuing northward, at Faloro they fell in with a column of Egyptian and Sudanese soldiers whose commander also engaged in slave and ivory trading. On February

15, 1863, they arrived at Gondokoro, where they expected to meet John Petherick, British vice consul at Khartoum, who had promised to supply them with boats and provisions. Speke's annoyance at Peterick's absence was later made public and cost Petherick his position. On hand at Gondokoro, however, was Samuel White BAKER.

Speke and Grant returned to a tumultuous reception in England. Speke's contention that he had proved his theories concerning the source of the Nile now found many adherents, but some, notably Burton, publicly challenged his claims because he had failed to circumnavigate Lake Victoria or to follow the river downstream continuously from the lake. Speke and Burton agreed to present their arguments before a meeting of the British Association for the Advancement of Science at Bath in September 1864. On the morning of September 16, Burton and an audience of several hundred persons were assembled for the debate when it was revealed that Speke had died the previous afternoon while shooting after his shotgun had gone off as he was climbing a wall. The controversy over the source of the Nile did not end with the passing of Speke, but the subsequent explorations of Baker, David LIVINGSTONE, and Henry M. STANLEY all served to confirm the essential soundness of his views.

See also NILE RIVER: SEARCH FOR ITS SOURCE.

BIBLIOGRAPHY: Roy C. Bridges, "John Hanning Speke: Negotiating a Way to the Nile," in Robert I. Rotberg (ed.), *Africa and Its Explorers,* Cambridge, Mass., 1970; Alexander Maitland, *Speke,* London, 1971; Donald H. Simpson, "J. H. Speke: A Bibligraphical Survey," *Library Notes of the Royal Commonwealth Society,* new ser., nos. 93 and 94, October–November, 1964; John Hanning Speke, *Journal of the Discovery of the Source of the Nile,* Edinburgh, 1863.

Stanley, Henry Morton (born John Rowlands; 1841–1904) Anglo-American journalist and explorer. Stanley was born in the Welsh county town of Denbigh and christened at St. Hilary's Church as the bastard son of John Rowlands and Elizabeth Parry. Thanks largely to Stanley's own efforts at drawing a veil over his origins, both in his highly romanticized, unreliable *Autobiography* (1909) and elsewhere, details of his early years are obscure. Clearly his childhood was a traumatic one, with few vestiges of ordinary home life and paternal affection. From 1847 to 1856 he lived at the St. Asaph Union Workhouse, and it was here that he received his only exposure to formal education. At the age of 15 he left the institution and, after futile attempts to find a secure niche with various relatives, signed on as a cabin boy aboard a ship bound for New Orleans.

When the vessel reached its destination, he jumped ship and soon gained employment as a junior clerk. It was in this bustling American port city that he first found the security he so desperately craved. A cotton broker by the name of Henry Hope Stanley befriended the rootless lad and soon adopted him. It was from the elder Stanley that he got the name under which he became famous, but the relationship remains a mys-

tery compounded by fantasies. What is clear is that the youth continued his wayward propensities. Finally the well-meaning cotton broker, exasperated by the antics of his uncontrollable protégé (Stanley ran away several times), sent him to work on a friend's plantation in Arkansas. The rupture between the two proved a permanent one and, after a brief, restless sojourn in Arkansas, Stanley enlisted as a soldier in the Confederate Army.

Almost immediately he was captured at the Battle of Shiloh and sent to a federal prison in Chicago. He won his release by agreeing to join the U.S. Artillery, only to be stricken by the dysentery which had been rampant in Chicago's Camp Douglas. His condition deteriorated so rapidly that he received his discharge from service and late in the summer of 1862 once more returned to his native Wales. Here Stanley found himself as little loved or wanted as he had been as a child, and after an interlude of rather aimless vagabondizing he returned to New York and enlisted for a 3-year term in the U.S. Navy. However, his restiveness remained strong, and in a few weeks he deserted. Stanley's abandonment of his post with the fleet completed a chain of unending escapism which had begun at the St. Asaph Union Workhouse and culminated in 1865. Clearly he was a deeply troubled young man in search simultaneously of adventure and of a secure place in life, and he soon found an ideal blending of these elements, first in journalism and then as a reporter-explorer.

Stanley's career as a reporter began in 1865, and henceforth journalistic endeavor would be the hub of virtually every phase of his life. Somewhat paradoxically, his early years of uncertainty and soul-searching had produced a tenacity and singleness of purpose rivaled by few, and these factors first evinced themselves when he covered Gen. Winfield Scott Hancock's Indian campaign in the West in 1867. Success here opened new vistas, and Stanley conceived and nurtured the idea which provided him with his initial introduction to Africa. He had read of British preparations for an attack on King Theodore of Ethiopia, and he intuitively sensed that the impending campaign had great news potential. Through a combination of enterprise, ingenuity, and good fortune Stanley brought off a major scoop in Ethiopia in 1868, and it led directly to an assignment by the *New York Herald* to locate Dr. David LIVINGSTONE, who had long been incommunicado in Africa and was feared dead. In a relatively trouble-free fashion, Stanley journeyed to Ujiji in Central Africa and met Livingstone in November 1871. This accomplishment assured him of lasting fame as a journalist, but his brief period of contact with the aged traveler and its immediate aftermath had other important ramifications.

Together the two made a partial circumnavigation of Lake Tanganyika, and from this point onward Stanley would combine exploration with journalism as a single profession. Yet he never abandoned his métier; henceforth he simply expanded and complemented it.

Henry Morton Stanley's turbulent early years molded him into one of the toughest and most successful participants in African exploration.

There is considerable truth in a statement by Sir Francis Galton, who knew many of the explorers intimately, that Stanley was "essentially a journalist aiming at producing sensational articles." Still, in the course of the next two decades, Stanley would accomplish geographical feats in Africa perhaps unrivaled by those of any other explorer of the continent.

His triumphant return to England with news of having found Livingstone enveloped him in a bitter controversy (many segments of the British establishment chose to ignore him or belittled his accomplishment), but he never forgot either the man or the methods that had brought him success and notoriety. Virtually all his subsequent career was molded by his exposure to Livingstone. There are abundant indications that the expedition resulted in Stanley's falling prey to the fascination and magnetism which Africa exerted on virtually all the great Victorian explorers, and this consideration, together with his abiding devotion to Livingstone, led him repeatedly back to Africa. His next venture on the continent was coverage of Sir Garnet Wolseley's Ashanti campaign in 1873, and while in West Africa he learned of Livingstone's death. Deeply moved, Stanley piously but sincerely vowed that "his mission . . . must not be allowed to cease," and he hoped that he might "be selected to succeed [Livingstone] in opening up Africa to the shining light of Christianity." This entry in Stanley's diary, though written in the emotionalism of the moment, was to prove an accurate summary of his future African endeavors.

The desire to honor Livingstone's memory and his own fervid aspirations to resolve Africa's remaining geographical secrets now drew Stanley inexorably to the continent. The journey he envisaged was on the grandest possible scale, and journalism offered the financial resources, in the form of £ 6000 from both the *New York Herald* and the *Daily Telegraph,* that enabled him to undertake his great venture. He planned to cross equatorial Africa from Zanzibar to the mouth of the Congo (Zaire) River and during the journey to clarify the remaining questions regarding the Nile's source, to map all the great lakes of the interior, and to trace the Congo from its origins downriver to the Atlantic Ocean. Furthermore, he aimed to complement these geographical pursuits with efforts to introduce Christianity in Central Africa. Incredibly, between 1874 and 1877 Stanley managed to achieve virtually all these feats. His famous plea for missionaries to King Mutesa of Buganda resulted in the establishment of the Church Missionary Society's Victoria Nyanza Mission; he became the second European, after Verney Lovett CAMERON, to cross the continent from east to west; he charted many of the features of the intralacustrine regions of Africa; and he successfully navigated the turbulent, forbidding Congo downstream. *See also* NILE RIVER: SEARCH FOR ITS SOURCE.

From 1880 to 1885 Stanley was in the employ of King Leopold II of Belgium. Essentially he was an administrator responsible for founding a colony, but his efforts embraced geography as well. He broadened his early researches on the Congo and in 1883 discovered Lakes Tumba and Leopold II (now Mai-Ndombe). Then in 1888, after a period of rest in Europe, Stanley undertook his last great mission, the rescue of Emin Pasha, governor of Equatoria Province in Sudan, who was believed to be in great danger after the fall of Khartoum. The expedition ended in acrimony and controversy, but geographically speaking it should be reckoned the last great exploring venture in Africa. En route to Emin, Stanley explored the Semliki River, established the linkage between Lakes Albert and Edward, and delineated the Ruwenzori Mountains. These discoveries effectively solved the remaining mysteries of the Nile's sources as well as virtually completing the filling in of the map of Africa.

At the conclusion of the expedition Stanley went into semiretirement, and the final decade and a half of his life brought him some of the recognition and love he had always desired. He resumed British citizenship, was knighted, and eventually secured election to the House of Commons. He also, after a lifetime of unsuccessful romantic adventures, found a loving mate and many of the comforts of a settled home life as a result of his marriage to Dorothy Tennant. In the late 1890s, his interest in Africa still undiminished, he made a sentimental journey to South Africa. In 1904, weakened by the privations he had endured in his lengthy periods of African travel, Stanley died. For all the criticism, much of it justifiable, that has been directed at his character and his methods of travel, the fact remains that Stanley was a giant in the annals of exploration.

BIBLIOGRAPHY: James A. Casada, *Dr. David Livingstone and Sir Henry Morton Stanley: An Annotated Bibliography,* New York, 1976; Byron Farwell, *The Man Who Presumed: A Biography of Henry M. Stanley,* New York, 1957; Richard Hall, *Stanley: An Adventurer Explored,* London, 1974; Dorothy Stanley (ed.), *The Autobiography of Sir Henry Morton Stanley,* London, 1909; Henry M. Stanley, *How I Found Livingstone,* London, 1872; id., *In Darkest Africa: Or the Quest, Rescue and Retreat of Emin, Governor of Equatoria,* 2 vols.,

Henry M. Stanley's route in search of Dr. Livingstone, 1871.

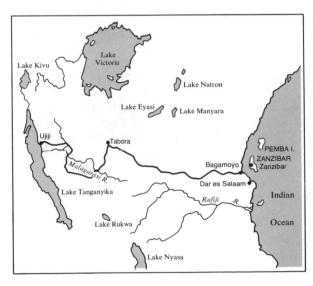

London, 1890; id., *Through the Dark Continent*, 2 vols., London, 1878.

James A. Casada

Stefansson, Vilhjalmur (1879–1962)

Stefansson, Vilhjalmur (1879–1962) Explorer, writer, lecturer, and publicist of the Arctic regions. Stefansson was born in Arnes, near Gimli, Manitoba, on November 3, 1879, the son of Icelandic immigrants who shortly thereafter moved to North Dakota. He studied at the Universities of North Dakota, Iowa (B.A., 1903), and Harvard (M.A., 1923). In 1904 he went to Iceland to study anthropology and archaeology.

Stefansson made three expeditions of note. In 1906–1907 he went to the Mackenzie River Delta of northwestern Arctic Canada with the expedition led by Ernest De Koven Leffingwell and Ejnar Mikklesen and learned to live, speak, eat, and hunt like an Eskimo. Between 1908 and 1912 he conducted an ethnological survey of the central Arctic coast for the American Museum of Natural History and the Geological Survey of Canada. Between 1913 and 1918, under Canadian government auspices, he commanded the Canadian Arctic Expedition, using sleds in his explorations after the loss of his flagship, the *Karluk*, in 1914. During this expedition he extended contemporary knowledge of the Arctic archipelago by finding land north of Prince Patrick Island and Axel Heiberg Island. He also mapped large regions of coastline and gained increased knowledge of Eskimo life. He developed a thesis that the Arctic was a habitable zone—"the friendly Arctic," he called it—where life could be sustained even on ice floes without supplies. By rejecting the idea that Arctic exploration was difficult or venturesome, he invited the censure of other explorers, such as Roald AMUNDSEN. He believed that the north was rich in natural resources and could serve as a shortcut between major centers of commerce and civilization. He also developed a theme of human history, now largely discredited, that great empires in northern climes had supplanted lesser empires in more southerly latitudes.

Realizing that future exploration of the north could best be carried out by airplane, Stefansson retired in 1919 to write and lecture. He lived most of his remaining years in New York City. As an Arctic expert he was much in demand; he advised Pan American World Airways and the United States government on polar routes and compiled manuals on the Arctic for the U.S. Navy. He encouraged, among other ventures, the formation of the unsuccessful Hudson's Bay Reindeer Company.

Stefansson acquired an outstanding library of polar and subpolar literature which found a permanent place in the Baker Library of Dartmouth College in 1951. Among his twenty-four books and numerous articles are the following volumes, which enjoyed a wide reading public: *My Life with the Eskimo* (1913), *The Friendly Arctic* (1921), *The Northward Course of Empire* (1922), *Hunters of the Great North* (1922), *Ultima Thule*, (1940) and his autobiography, *Discovery* (1964). He died in Hanover, New Hampshire, on August 26, 1962.

BIBLIOGRAPHY: D. M. LeBourdais, *Stefansson, Ambassador of the North*, Montreal, 1963; Vilhjalmur Stefansson, *Discovery: The Autobiography of Vilhjalmur Stefansson*, New York, 1964.

Barry M. Gough

Steller, Georg Wilhelm (1709–1746)

Steller, Georg Wilhelm (1709–1746) German scholar and naturalist in Russian service. Steller arrived in St. Petersburg in 1734 and practiced medicine there. In 1737 he was appointed an adjunct of natural history at the Academy of Sciences and at his own request was assigned to the Second Kamchatka Expedition of Vitus BERING. In 1740 he arrived in Okhotsk; from there he went by sea to Bolsheretsk on the west coast of Kamchatka and thence, in March 1741, to Avachinskaya Guba (Avacha Bay) on the east coast of the peninsula. In June 1741 he accompanied Bering on the vessel *Sv. Pyotr (St. Peter)*. On July 20, 1741, he landed in North America, on Kayak Island, where he made valuable observations although he had only a few hours in which to work. On the return voyage the vessel was wrecked on Ostrov Bering (Bering Island).

During the ensuing winter Bering and a number of others died of scurvy and exposure, but Steller wrote one of his most important works, *De bestiis marinis (On Sea Animals)*, made the first full descriptions of Bering Island, and kept a diary, published in 1793. At the end of August 1742, he and the other survivors returned to Kamchatka on a boat built of the wreckage of the *Sv. Pyotr*. Steller then worked on Kamchatka until 1744. His *Opisaniye zemli Kamchatky (Description of Kamchatka)* was published in 1744. He died in Tyumen, western Siberia, while on the way back to St. Petersburg in November 1746.

See also NATURAL-HISTORY EXPLORATION.

BIBLIOGRAPHY: F. A. Golder, *Bering's Voyages*, 2 vols., New York, 1922; G. W. Steller, *Beschreibung von dem Lande Kamtschatka,*

One of the remote areas visited by Georg Wilhelm Steller was Kamchatka, where he worked from 1742 to 1744. Pictured here is a native of that region, traveling in winter. [Library of Congress]

Frankfurt and Leipzig, 1774; id., *Reise von Kamtschatka nach Amerika mit dem Commandeur-Capitän Bering*, St. Petersburg, 1793.

Richard A. Pierce

Strabo *(ca. 54 B.C.–A.D. 21)* Greek historian and geographer. A native of Amasia (Amasya) in the Roman province of Pontus (northern Turkey), he traveled fairly widely in the eastern Mediterranean and in Asia Minor. His historical work is lost, but his *Geography* in seventeen books, completed about A.D. 18, was apparently the first attempt by any writer to bring together all the geographical knowledge available, political and ethnographical as well as physical and topographical. Strabo's limitations are those common to most Greek scientists: love of system and theory relatively unchecked by observation, with approval or criticism of earlier writers on the basis of very slender evidence. His failure to use new topographical (but not ethnographical) material on parts of western and northern Europe recently conquered by the Romans may also be noted, though the Romans themselves seem to have been surprisingly uninterested in such material.

Strabo accepted many figures for distances and directions from the Greek geographer Eratosthenes (though he also criticized him), including his nearly correct estimate of the earth's circumference. He discussed the problem involved in laying out a map on a plane surface instead of on a globe, though he probably did not produce a map himself. From the few coordinates and estimates of distances which he gives his map would have been seriously distorted. He estimated the west-east dimension of the inhabited world from Cabo São Vicente at about 8000 miles (12,874 kilometers) and its north-south dimension at some 3400 miles (5472 kilometers). The latter estimate results partly from his rejection of the reference by PYTHEAS to Thule and partly from his putting Massilia (Marseille), a base point, too far south. He believed

the Pyrenees to run in a north-south direction, parallel to the Rhine; he almost ignored the Armorican Peninsula (Britanny) and clearly considered Ireland to be north of Britain. His knowledge of Central Europe east of the Rhine was vague but not totally distorted; but on areas north of the Black Sea he was inferior to HERODOTUS OF HALICARNASSUS. Books 11 to 16 on Asia are particularly dependent on earlier writers; hence in particular the southward configuration of much of the Indian subcontinent is ignored. However, Strabo presented plenty of good information about India's peoples and trading products, rejecting some, though not all, of the fabulous stories available. By far the larger part of Book 17 on Africa is in fact concerned with Egypt. Strabo followed the accepted view of the shape of Africa as a right-angled triangle. In spite of much interesting ethnographical material, Strabo was little read in antiquity until Byzantine times.

BIBLIOGRAPHY: Strabo, *The Geography of Strabo*, Loeb Classical Library, 8 vols., London and New York, 1917–32.

B. H. Warmington

Stuart, John McDouall *(1815–1866)* Australian explorer. McDouall Stuart was born in Fifeshire, Scotland, on September 7, 1815, the son of an army officer. He arrived in 1838 in South Australia, where he joined the colony's survey department. Between 1844 and 1846 he gained valuable experience as draftsman of the expedition of Charles STURT to central Australia, but he did not begin his own exploration until May 1858. Over the next 5 years, in a nearly continuous series of brilliant assaults, he conquered the center of the continent.

Between May and August 1858, Stuart and a companion explored the "fearful country" between Lake Torrens and Streaky Bay and followed this up the next year with two examinations of good pastoral country west of Lake Eyre. Although he had been "almost blind" on the second of these examinations, he resolved to attempt a south-north crossing of the continent and on March 2, 1860, with two companions left his Chambers Creek depot (30°S) and headed north. The party got as far as Attack Creek (19°S), where an aboriginal attack on June 26 and the shortage of provisions forced their return. Their crossing of the geographical center of the continent on April 22 was celebrated by Stuart's naming a nearby hill Central Mount Sturt in memory of his mentor. It is now called Central Mount Stuart.

Back in Adelaide in October, Stuart was given £ 2500 by the South Australian Parliament to equip a larger expedition. This left on November 29, 1860, reached Attack Creek on April 25, 1861, and Stuart's Plain on May 4, but then the thick scrub, "as great a barrier as an inland sea or wall," slowed it down. The expedition had gone only as far as Newcastle Creek (17°30'S) when the shortage of provisions forced its return on July 12. Stuart reached Adelaide on Septem-

Celebrating his crossing of the center of the Australian continent in April 1860, John Stuart plants the Union Jack on Central Mount Stuart. [Australian Information Service]

ber 23, 1861, quickly reprovisioned, and headed north again on October 26. He was back at Attack Creek on March 28, 1862. After much searching, a path was found through the scrub. Daly Waters (16°S) was reached on May 28, the headwaters of the Roper River on June 26, and on July 24 the party burst on the sea at Chambers Bay, just east of the mouth of the Adelaide River.

On his return to Adelaide on December 18, 1862, Stuart was rewarded with a government land grant and £ 2000 and the gold medal of the ROYAL GEO-GRAPHICAL SOCIETY, but his health was completely undermined. For much of the return journey, he had lain paralyzed on a litter. In April 1864 he went to England. He died in London, in some poverty, on June 5, 1866, almost blind with his memory gone. His achievements are recorded in a number of place names, but undoubtedly Stuart's greatest memorial is the overland telegraph line from Adelaide to Darwin, which follows the trail he blazed.

BIBLIOGRAPHY: I. M. Mudie, *The Heroic Journeys of John McDouall Stuart,* Sydney, 1966; M. S. Webster, *John McDouall Stuart,* Melbourne, 1958.

J. M. R. Cameron

Sturt, Charles *(1795–1869)* Australian explorer and government official. Born in India on April 28, 1795, Sturt was the eldest son of Thomas Sturt, a judge in the service of the British East India Company. He entered the British Army in 1813 and served in Spain, Canada, France, and Ireland before being sent to New South Wales in 1827 in charge of a party of convicts. Here he renewed his acquaintance with Ralph Darling, now governor of the colony, and became his military secretary. He also became friendly with the explorers John OXLEY, Allan CUNNINGHAM, and Hamilton HUME. On November 4, 1828, he received Darling's permission to conduct his own exploration to see what lay beyond the marshes Oxley had encountered on the Macquarie River 10 years before.

The expedition left Sydney on November 10, 1828, and reached Oxley's end point by December 31. From here, Sturt and his twelve companions followed the Bogan, Castlereagh, and Macquarie Rivers north to the Darling. This was a discovery of major significance, for the Darling was still navigable after 3 years of severe inland drought and was apparently fed by tropical rains from the mountainous northeast. Explorers had long dreamed of finding a mighty river like this which would solve the puzzle of just where the continent's inland rivers flowed. Thus, when Sturt returned to Sydney in April, he requested permission to follow the Darling to its assumed outlet in an inland sea. Instead, he was sent to complete Oxley's partial 1817 examination of the Lachlan-Murrumbidgee river system, which it was thought might also flow into the Darling.

The second expedition left Sydney on November 3, 1829, and made for the Murrumbidgee, which Sturt followed downstream to its junction with the Lachlan. As the Murrumbidgee, unlike the Lachlan, was free of marshes, Sturt made the momentous decision to sail from here and so made the voyage which explained the drainage of Australia's greatest river system. On January 7, with seven companions, he set out. Seven days later he sailed into the Murray and 9 days farther on encountered the Darling, which he explored briefly before continuing downstream. Although he was threatened by aborigines on several occasions, the rest of the voyage was uneventful, and on February 9 he reached the barren shores of Lake Alexandrina, the Murray's outlet to the sea. Although Sturt had now solved the riddle of the rivers, this was a disappointing end, for the difficulty of navigating within Lake Alexandrina meant that the Murray would never be a Mississippi. In addition, he and his men had the appalling prospect of rowing 900 miles (1448 kilometers) upstream. They did not reach Sydney until May 25, 1830.

Sturt was now sent to Norfolk Island as commandant of the convict garrison there, but his health, undermined by both expeditions, continued to deteriorate, and in October 1831 he successfully requested permission to return to England on convalescent leave. Here he left the Army, obtained a grant of 5000 acres (2023 hectares) in New South Wales, married Charlotte Greene, and, in September 1834, returned to manage his new pastoral property. But Sturt was no businessman, and after failing as a pastoralist in New South Wales and in overlanding stock to South Australia, he was happy to accept a post in the South Australian Survey Department in 1839. Over the next 4 years, partly because of a conflict with Gov. Sir George Grey, Sturt's fortunes declined. In 1843, as a desperate measure, he prepared a grandiose plan for exploring and surveying the entire unknown interior of the continent within 2 years. This plan was rejected, but approval was given to an attempt to establish the existence of a mountain range west of the Darling near latitude 28°S. Thus began Sturt's final and greatest exploration, even though the country it revealed was almost totally worthless for human settlement. He was then aged 48.

The party of sixteen men left Adelaide on August 10, 1844, and followed the Murray and Darling Rivers before becoming trapped by drought at Depot Glen, near Milparinka, from January 27, 1845, to July 16. Conditions were so hot and dry that thermometers burst, and "we found it difficult to write or draw, so rapidly did the fluid dry in our pens and brushes." Sturt intended sending some men back to Adelaide when the drought broke, but James Poole, his second-in-command, died of scurvy, and he was forced to move the whole party on to Fort Grey. From here, after a short sortie westward to Lake Blanche, Sturt and four others plunged 450 miles (724 kilometers) northwest over the Stony Desert between Cooper's Creek and the Diamantina River until forced back by the sands of the Simpson Desert. He now tried a more

On his great trip down the Murray and Darling Rivers in 1829–1830, Charles Sturt managed to define the major geographical features of Australia and to discover techniques to combat the country's inhospitable climate. [Australian Information Service]

northerly route, but again the desert and the drought beat him. While planning a do-or-die race to the center of the continent, he collapsed from exhaustion and the prolonged effects of scurvy, and the whole party retreated, arriving in Adelaide on January 19, 1846.

Sturt was extremely disappointed with the results, for he had found no good country, no inland sea, and no major mountain range. But he had established the main geographic features of the interior, provided much essential knowledge of its climatic regime and its flora and fauna, and had developed the techniques which later explorers used to conquer its hostile wastes. The expedition itself had been an extraordinary example of courage and endurance. The men had lived in the desert for 18 months and had traveled more than 3000 miles (4828 kilometers) over largely unknown and quite inhospitable country.

Sturt subsequently became colonial secretary of South Australia, but his eyesight, which had been deteriorating since 1829, again failed. He resigned in 1851 and retired to Cheltenham, England. It was here that he died on June 16, 1869, days before the formalities for conferring a knighthood on him were completed.

BIBLIOGRAPHY: J. H. L. Cumpston, *Charles Sturt: His Life and Journeys of Exploration*, Melbourne, 1951; M. Langley, *Sturt of the Murray*, London, 1969.

J. M. R. Cameron

Sverdrup, Otto Neumann *(1855–1930)* Norwegian explorer. Sverdrup was born in Bindalen in Helgeland. He went to sea at the age of seventeen but later settled with his father on a farm near Steinkjer. Through his friendship with a brother of Fridtjof NANSEN, he became a member of the party that crossed the inland ice of Greenland with Nansen in 1888. In 1893 he sailed with Nansen as captain of the *Fram* and was named commander of the expedition when Nansen left the ship to make a dash for the North Pole early in 1895. Sverdrup's instructions were to seek open water and make for home as speedily and as safely as possible. In May 1896 the *Fram*'s engine, which had not been used during the drift, was started, and efforts were begun to free the ship from the ice. The ship had been blasted loose by early June, but it was not until August 13 that she sailed into open water off the coast of Spitsbergen (Svalbard). On August 20 the *Fram* anchored off Skjervøy in Norway, where Sverdrup learned that Nansen was on his way home too.

Almost immediately after his return to Norway, Sverdrup agreed to take the *Fram* through Smith Sound and Kane Basin in an attempt to reach and explore the northern coast of Greenland. According to Sverdrup, there was no intention of trying to reach the pole, though Robert E. PEARY regarded the Norwegians as potential rivals. Sverdrup left Norway on June 24, 1898, with fifteen companions. Because the condition of the ice pack made it impossible to sail up Kane Basin, Sverdrup decided, after spending the winter of 1898–1899 in Rice Strait, to abandon the original goal of the expedition. On August 22, 1899, they headed south for Jones Sound, which had been selected as their new route of exploration. In the next 3 years Sverdrup and the other members of the expedition explored in detail the unknown southern and western coasts of Ellesmere Island and discovered Axel Heiberg Island, Ellef Ringnes Island, and Amund Ringnes Island (named after the sponsors of the expedition and now known collectively as the Sverdrup Islands). In addition, they brought back fifty-three large cases of geological, botanical, and zoological specimens. Sverdrup, who received the Patron's Medal of the ROYAL GEOGRAPHICAL SOCIETY in 1903, described the expedition in a two-volume work translated into English as *New Land* (1904).

In later years Sverdrup sailed several times to the Arctic waters off Siberia, notably in 1921, when he opened a route from England across the Kara Sea to the Ob and Yenisey Rivers. He was also a leader of the campaign to preserve the *Fram*, which was eventually housed in the Fram Museum at Bygdøy, Oslo. He died on November 26, 1930, shortly after receiving the sum of $67,000 from the government of Canada, which had successfully asserted its sovereignty over the Sverdrup Islands.

BIBLIOGRAPHY: T. C. Fairley (ed.), *Sverdrup's Arctic Adventures*, London, 1959; Fridtjof Nansen, *Farthest North*, 2 vols., London, 1897.

T

Tasman, Abel Janszoon (1603-1659) Dutch navigator and explorer. Born in Lutjegast, a village near Groningen, Tasman went to Batavia (now Jakarta) in the Dutch East Indies in 1633 and became a seaman in the employ of the Dutch East India Company. After returning to the Netherlands in 1637, he went back to Southeast Asia, now committed to a long period of service for the company. There followed several voyages, the most important of which took him to the North Pacific with Mathijs Quast in 1639. In 1642 Tasman was named commander of an expedition planned by Anton van Diemen, governor-general at Batavia. Tasman's objectives were to explore the southern and eastern Pacific, including parts of Australia previously visited by Dutch navigators; to search for an unknown Southland; and to seek a passage from the Indian Ocean to the Pacific which might open a short route to Chile.

Accompanied by Frans Jacobszoon Visscher, an experienced pilot and hydrographer, Tasman set sail on August 14, 1642, with two ships, the war yacht *Heemskerk* and the flute *Zeehaan*. After a stop at Mauritius, Tasman sailed south, hoping to reach latitude 52° or 54°, as his instructions directed. However, bad weather forced him to turn east at 44°S. In late November land was sighted, and an anchorage was found on December 1. Tasman called his discovery Van Diemen's Land, a name retained until the nineteenth century, when the island became known as Tasmania. Sailing to the east, Tasman again sighted land (New Zealand) on December 13. He called this discovery Staten Landt, thinking erroneously that it might be connected to a place of the same name visited by Jacob Le Maire in 1616. Tasman anchored near Cape Farewell a few days later, only to lose four men in a skirmish with the Maoris. His course now took him into Cook Strait and along the west coast of North Island. Unable to land at Three Kings Islands to obtain fresh water and provisions, Tasman sailed to the northeast until he came to Tongatapu in the Tonga group; at this island and at Nomuka he found ample supplies of food and water. Confronted with bad weather in the Fiji group, he decided to head north and west. After sighting and naming the large atoll of Ontong Java and sailing along the north coast of New Guinea, Tasman was back in Batavia by mid-June 1643.

Van Diemen and his associates were uncertain as to the potential benefits of Tasman's voyage, but the following year they dispatched him on another expedition, designed to elucidate further the northern coastline of Australia. With two yachts and a galliot and again accompanied by Visscher, Tasman sailed along the south coast of New Guinea (without entering Torres Strait), then explored the waters off the northern and western coasts of Australia from Cape York to North West Cape. Upon his return, his employers expressed disappointment because he had not explored inland.

Although he undertook no more voyages of exploration, Tasman remained in the employ of the East India Company. In 1649, after leading an attack against the Spanish in the Philippines, he was briefly suspended after attempting to hang two young seamen who had disobeyed orders. About 1653 he retired from the company, but he remained in Batavia until his death.

BIBLIOGRAPHY: James C. Beaglehole, *The Exploration of the Pacific*, 3d ed., Stanford, Calif., 1966; Andrew Sharp, *The Voyages of Abel Janszoon Tasman*, Oxford, 1968.

Thesiger, Wilfred Patrick (1910–   ) English explorer and traveler. Thesiger was born in Ethiopia, where his father was British minister, and lived there until he was 9 years old. He spent the next 10 years studying in England, attending Eton and Magdalen College, Oxford. He returned to Ethiopia in 1930 to attend the coronation of Emperor Haile Selassie. In that year and during another visit in 1934 Thesiger embarked on journeys to discover the source of the Awash River and to observe the Danakil tribesmen, who were reputed to collect testicles instead of heads. As was characteristic of Thesiger's explorations, these journeys were undertaken for personal adventure as much as for the advancement of geographical knowledge.

In 1935 Thesiger joined the Sudan Political Service and spent several years in a remote district of the province of Darfur and in the Western Nuer District of Upper Nile Province. His experiences in Ethiopia and Sudan and in the Jabal ad Druz in Syria during World War II proved to be training for his unique explorations in Arabia.

In the autumn of 1945 Thesiger was appointed investigator for the Middle East Antilocust Unit. His responsibility was to locate the breeding places of locusts in southern Arabia. While on the assignment, he explored the Rub' al Khālī (Abode of Emptiness), which he crossed in 1946–1947, traveling from Salālah to the Līwā oasis and back. With this journey Thesiger became the third European to cross the Rub' al Khālī and only the second to do so from the south. Bertram Thomas was the first to do so, in 1930–1931, and Harry St. John PHILBY crossed it from north to south in 1932. Thesiger, however, traveled without the support and resources of the other two men. In 1947–1948 he crossed the western edge of the Rub' al Khālī, becoming the first European to explore this area.

During the next two years (1948–1950), Thesiger attempted to explore the interior of Oman on the western side of the Jabal al Akhdar, a place less known than Tibet. Although it had previously been visited by several Europeans, Thesiger was unable to complete his explorations because of the hostility of the tribes. The tribal leaders felt that all Christians were in the employ of oil companies and wished to seize their lands. The leader of the interior tribes of Oman informed him that to continue his exploration he would need that remarkable innovation of the nationalistic, centralized state, a visa.

Thesiger's explorations in Arabia are memorable and historic as the last conducted with only camel and compass. Even as he completed his travels there, the drone of the airplane, gas fumes of Jeeps, and the massive scientific apparatuses of oil exploration companies signaled the death of this mode of travel.

After leaving Arabia in 1950, Thesiger was able to find another unspoiled region in the Middle East, the marshes of southern Iraq, and spent several months a year there until 1958. He also traveled in Afghanistan, Morocco, Ethiopia, Kenya, and Iran before returning to Arabia in 1966 and joining the royalist forces in the civil war in Yemen.

BIBLIOGRAPHY: Timothy Green, *The Adventurers: Four Profiles of Contemporary Travellers*, London, 1970; Wilfred Thesiger, *Arabian Sands*, New York, 1959; id., *The Marsh Arabs*, London, 1964.

Robert W. Olson

Thompson, David (1770–1857) English fur trader, explorer, surveyor, and geographer, Thompson was born in London on April 30, 1770, of Welsh extraction. His father died when Thompson was 2, leaving the family in poor circumstances. David was educated at the Grey Coat School, a famous Westminster charity school, where he acquired an excellent mathematical knowledge. He was apprenticed to the Hudson's Bay Company in 1784 and sent to Churchill. Thompson spent 13 years at posts on Hudson Bay and in the Saskatchewan country. In 1787–1788 he wintered among Indians in the vicinity of modern Calgary, Alberta. In 1789 he began studying surveying under Philip Turnor, the first surveyor to be employed by the Hudson's Bay Company. His fieldwork took him along the Saskatchewan River to its mouth, then to the Hayes River. In 1792–1793 he worked on the Nelson River and parts of the Churchill River. Between 1793 and 1797 he surveyed territory between Cumberland House and York Factory and in particular, in 1796, explored to Lake Athabasca by the new route of Reindeer and Wollaston Lakes and the Black River.

In 1797 he entered the service of the North West Company, which allowed him to combine fur trading with surveying. He spent the winter of 1797–1798 in an arduous journey of 4000 miles (6437 kilometers) in which he covered a wide area from Lake Superior to Lakes Winnipeg and Winnipegosis. He went on the Assiniboine, Red, and Missouri Rivers to the source of the Mississippi and down river to St. Louis. Subsequent travels in the Northwest took him to Île-à-la Crosse Lake and the Beaver River in 1798, Lesser Slave Lake and the Athabasca River in 1799, and the North and South Saskatchewan Rivers and the Bow River in 1800. He discovered the headwaters of the Saskatchewan. In 1804 he became a partner in the North West Company.

In 1807 Thompson crossed the Rockies with his wife and family by Howse Pass and that summer built Kootenay House, the first fur post on the Columbia River. Subsequently he built many posts on the Columbia and its tributaries, thereby opening to the trade much of Montana, Idaho, Washington, Oregon, and southern British Columbia. His surveying of the Columbia watershed and his securing of the upper reaches of the Columbia and Kootenay Rivers for the North West Company trade delayed his arrival at his ultimate objective, the mouth of the Columbia. Thus, when he reached the Pacific, he found Americans at Fort Astoria. He then returned upriver and completed his survey. He was the first man to travel the full length of the great river of the west and the first to map its course with any accuracy. Thompson River, a tributary of the Fraser, was named for him by his friend Simon FRASER.

In 1812 Thompson left the West forever. He settled near Montreal and prepared for the North West Company a great map of western Canada (now in the Ontario Archives). For 10 years beginning in 1816 he surveyed for the International Boundary Commission the Canadian–United States boundary from Saint-Régis, Quebec, to the northwest corner of Lake of the Woods. Nearly blind and in poverty, he died at Longueuil, near Montreal, on February 10, 1857. In 1799 he had married Charlotte Small, a half-Indian woman, by whom he had sixteen children. He was a pious man who refused to allow the sale of spiritous liquor to Indians.

Thompson was among the great geographer-explorers of the world. His Western travels covered 50,000 miles (80,460 kilometers) by canoe, horse, and foot. He mapped routes through 1,700,000 miles (2,735,800 kilometers) of Canada and the United States. His maps were precise, reflecting his persistent and methodical surveys. Through his labors he unlocked to science and cartography the secrets of two great river systems, the Saskatchewan and the Columbia.

BIBLIOGRAPHY: Richard Glover (ed.), *David Thompson's Narrative, 1784–1812,* Toronto, 1962.

Barry M. Gough

Thomson, Joseph *(1858–1895)* British explorer. Thomson was born near Thornhill, Dumfriesshire, and as a youth he showed considerable aptitude and a great love for natural science. He had the good fortune to study under Sir Archibald Geikie, and through his mentor's influence he obtained the position of geologist in an 1879 expedition to Central Africa. When the expedition's leader, Alexander Keith Johnston, died after only 6 months in Africa, Thomson resolutely took charge and successfully completed the mission. He became the first European to reach Lake Nyasa (Lake Malawi) from the north, and from there he traveled onward to Lake Tanganyika and for some distance along the Lukuga River. He described his experiences in *To the Central African Lakes and Back* (2 volumes, 1880).

The first European to reach Lake Nyasa from the north and the first to travel in Masai country in Kenya, Joseph Thompson had a promising career in Africa until his death at thirty-seven. [Library of Congress]

Thomson had made careful observations of the geology of the regions he traversed, and this consideration influenced the Sultan of Zanzibar to send him in search of coal deposits on the Ruvuma (Rovuma) River and its tributaries. He failed to locate coal, but shortly after returning to England Thomson assumed the leadership of an expedition to Masailand sponsored by the ROYAL GEOGRAPHICAL SOCIETY. Utilizing his persuasive ways and prowess as an explorer to good advantage, Thomson braved the fierce Masai and traveled through previously untrodden territory in present-day Kenya. The results of this expedition, described in *Through Masailand* (1885), were so significant that he was awarded the Founder's Medal of the sponsoring society.

Thomson later was active as a treaty negotiator in both western and southern Africa, and in 1885 he explored the Atlas Mountains. This undertaking, which saw him cross the range twice, was described in *Travels in the Atlas and Southern Morocco* (1889). His devotion to African travel ultimately took its toll on his health, and Thomson died when only 37 years of age.

BIBLIOGRAPHY: E. G. Ravenstein, "Joseph Thomson," *The Geographical Journal,* vol. VI, 1895, pp. 289–291; Robert I. Rotberg, *Joseph Thomson and the Exploration of Africa,* London, 1971; J. B. Thomson, *Joseph Tomson, African Explorer,* London, 1896.

James A. Casada

_U_

United States

The exploration of the territory that now comprises the forty-eight contiguous United States was shaped, especially in its initial phases, by the same forces and motivations—economic, religious, and nationalist— that characterized the exploration of Canada and of the New World in general. From the West Indies and Mexico came sixteenth-century Spaniards who hoped to find in more northerly latitudes densely populated native kingdoms as opulent as those of the Aztecs and the Incas. Meanwhile, the French and the English, faced with the Spanish-Portuguese monopoly of trading routes to the East, looked northward in the hope of finding a waterway, a NORTHWEST PASSAGE (sometimes called the Strait of Anian), that would connect the Old World with the Orient.

The Spanish The first Spanish conquistador in what is now the United States was Juan PONCE DE LEÓN. After helping to bring Puerto Rico under Spanish control, Ponce de León may have heard of an island to the north called Bimini which allegedly contained gold and what the Indians called the Fountain of Youth. Quickly securing a patent to the area, he set forth from Puerto Rico in March 1513 and soon approached a beautifully foliaged stretch of land which he named Florida because it was the Easter season (Pascua Flor-

ida). Other exploratory attempts in the areas of his patent by rivals Alonso Álvarez de Pineda and Lucas Vásquez de Ayllón caused Ponce de León to try again in 1521. After securing a new patent allowing him to settle "the Island of Bimini and the Island of Florida," he and two shiploads of men landed on the west coast of Florida. As before, the Indians proved unfriendly, and Ponce de León was wounded so badly by an arrow that he died shortly after.

In the meantime, Pineda and Ayllón penetrated much of the northern area. Pineda's expedition in 1519, sailing under orders of Francisco de Garay, the governor of Jamaica, mapped the entire northern edge of the Gulf of Mexico from southern Florida to the Pánuco River in Mexico, sighted what some later writers assumed was the Mississippi River but may have been Mobile Bay and River, and showed that Florida was linked to Pánuco and thus with South America. In 1520 Ayllón, a resident of Hispaniola, sent out a ship which later joined forces with another Spanish vessel. The Spaniards reached the mainland at a river they called the Río de San Juan Bautista and seized several Indians, who were taken to Hispaniola as slaves.

Soon afterward Ayllón left for Spain, accompanied by one of the Indian captives known as Francisco Chicora. Before the court of King Charles I, Chicora, a gifted liar, told of the giant kings and queens of his homeland and of people from the sea who had tails so thick and long that they had to dig holes in order to sit. Ayllón won the charter to colonize Chicora. Leaving Hispaniola in 1526 with six vessels carrying 500 colonists and slaves, he landed below present Georgetown, South Carolina, and quickly realized that this area did not hold the wonders described earlier by Chicora. After a series of mishaps destroyed most of the supplies and Chicora himself disappeared into the woods, Ayllón ordered the expedition southward to a large river (the Savannah), where his men constructed a few ragged huts near the site of the present city of Savannah, Georgia. The winter of 1526–1527 took a heavy toll, only 150 surviving to return to Santo Domingo in the spring. Ayllón himself died of fever and was buried at sea. His failures ended Spain's first major attempt to establish a colony in the eastern section of the present United States. In fact, they discouraged interest in Spanish settlements along the mainland of the Atlantic coast for 40 years.

Spain's interest gradually turned to the continental interior, largely because of the conquests of Hernán Cortés in Mexico in 1519–1521 and of Francisco Pizarro in Peru in the 1530s. True conquistadores who associated the sword with the spirit, they looted the rich cities of the Aztecs and the Incas and thus fired dreams of vast wealth in the New World. Optimistic Spaniards believed that the North American interior might even be richer than Central and South America. Thus an intense drive developed for wealth, land, and religious conversions.

Narváez and Cabeza de Vaca One of Spain's most ambitious attempts to colonize the southern part of North America occurred in June 1527, when five vessels with 600 men led by the red-bearded and one-eyed Pánfilo de Narváez set out from Spain. Although Narváez proved an incredibly inept leader and the expedition culminated in death for many of its members, it is noteworthy not only because some of Narváez's men saw the Mississippi River 13 years before its "discovery" by Hernando de Soto, but also because of the remarkable odyssey of the group's trea-

The Spanish battle Indians in Florida, as they extend their empire into what is now the United States during the sixteenth century. [Library of Congress]

surer, Álvar Núñez CABEZA DE VACA. Accompanied by two Spaniards and a Moorish slave named Esteban, Cabeza de Vaca struggled from a shipwreck on a sandbar along the Texas coast (probably Galveston Island) to reach the west coast of Mexico in 1536. His 8-year trek, starting from the initial landing by the Narváez Expedition at Tampa Bay, had covered nearly the breadth of the continent.

Cabeza de Vaca's fascinating accounts of the area's giant cowlike shaggy beasts (the first description of the American buffalo) and its rich cities allegedly containing copper, emeralds, and turquoises caused a renewed burst of exploring activity in 1536. There were valid reasons for this excitement. Florida, it must be remembered, encompassed all unexplored land from Newfoundland to Mexico. In addition, Cortés had taken three ships northward to Baja California in 1535 without seeking permission from the crown. He may have been the first to discover that the Pacific Coast furnished access to the East Indies, but his independent actions had threatened the authority of the first viceroy of New Spain, Antonio de Mendoza. The recently appointed official had heard of another expedition to be led by Hernando de Soto, which ostensibly aimed at Florida but conceivably could spread its interests into the areas above New Spain as well. Other attractions encouraged exploration. There was the Aztec legend of the "Seven Caves" of gold and silver in the north from which their predecessors had fled years before. In addition, Spanish lore told of "Seven Cities" of gold (eventually called the Seven Cities of Cíbola), which could be traced back to the early 700s, when the Moors had overrun the Iberian peninsula and seven bishops had fled by sea to the west and established new episcopates on an island called Antilia located somewhere in the Atlantic. The Spanish felt confident that this rich land lay north of Mexico. And it followed that if the famed Seven Cities were insular, there had to be a sea. If there were a sea, there doubtless would be a strait. Hence the search for the Strait of Anian was again intensified.

Soto The first major attempt to find the Seven Cities came in 1537, when Hernando de Soto, in Spain at the time of Cabeza de Vaca's well-publicized return, immediately secured rights to Narváez's grant, and was named governor and *adelantado* (royal deputy) of the province of Florida. Setting out from Cuba in May 1539 with 600 soldiers, 50 black slaves, 213 horses, a pack of vicious bloodhounds, and a large herd of swine, Soto reached the Florida coast near Tampa Bay later that month. There began 4 years of fruitless wanderings, during which he and his army came across another survivor of the ill-fated Narváez Expedition (Juan Ortiz, who would serve until his death in 1542 as interpreter and guide for Soto) and marched over 350,000 square miles (906,500 square kilometers) of unexplored lands. Evidence suggests that the men went through present Florida, Georgia,

North and South Carolina, Tennessee, Alabama (thus becoming the first Europeans to cross the Appalachian Mountains), Mississippi, Arkansas, Louisiana, and Texas.

Fray Marcos and Coronado While Soto's expedition was en route, Mendoza prepared to ward off further encroachments on the territory of New Spain. Having bought the black slave Esteban who had accompanied Cabeza de Vaca into Mexico City, he sent a Franciscan priest, Fray Marcos de Niza (who had been with Pizarro in Peru), with Esteban and a band of interpreters into the present southwestern United States in March 1539. Their goal was to find the famed Seven Cities.

Fray Marcos's expedition has suffered much criticism, largely because many of his accounts were exaggerated or inaccurate (especially those telling of camels, elephants, and animals similar to unicorns). The major thrust of his travels lay along the northern frontier of New Spain, somewhere in the area of the lower Gila River or the mouth of the Colorado. By now called Sayota ("a man from heaven"), Fray Marcos moved north from Culiacán until he reached Vacapa on the Mayo River. From there he dispatched Esteban on March 23 to investigate the surrounding region, and 4 days later news came back that the black had talked with Indians who had seen seven magnificent cities in a Zuñi Indian province. It was apparently at this point that Fray Marcos first heard the name Cíbola applied to the great country that lay to the north. The vision of another Tenochtitlán quickly drew Fray Marcos's expedition up the Sonora River, through the pass from its headwaters to those of the San Pedro River, and down that valley across a wild range of mountains, woods, and valleys. Finally, on May 21, the men were only 3 days' march from their destination when Fray Marcos learned of Esteban's death at the hands of the Zuñi Indians. Fray Marcos's Indian companions were terrified, but he pushed on, determined at least to see Cíbola. At last, from a point high in the mountains, he looked down on what he called the "handsomest" settlement he had seen (actually the poor Zuñi pueblo of Hawikuh in present western New Mexico) and then turned away "with far more fright than food" to return to Mexico City by late August 1539.

Fray Marcos's report was greeted optimistically— too much so. The year after his return, in 1540, Mendoza hurriedly fitted a major expedition to stake a Spanish claim to this allegedly wealthy area. Nearly 350 volunteers, guided by Fray Marcos and under the command of Francisco Vásquez de CORONADO, set out in February with nearly 1000 Indians, blacks, servants, and Franciscans, hundreds of mules and packhorses, many pieces of light artillery, and several herds of cattle, sheep, goats, and swine. There could be no delay. Francisco de Ulloa, sailing under Cortés's orders in 1539, had discovered that California was a peninsula and could win for his superior an even greater claim to the lands above New Spain.

Coronado's expedition was a bitter and expensive disappointment. Passing through much of the same area earlier crossed by Fray Marcos (including the present locale of Tombstone, Arizona, later found to house tremendous veins of silver), the men reached Cíbola. After a fierce battle with its Zuñi inhabitants, the Spaniards ransacked the city in a futile search for gold. For some unexplained reason, the priest had lied. To protect Fray Marcos from the angry soldiers, Coronado sent him back to Mexico in disgrace. Gloom set in until, somewhere near the site of modern Pecos, New Mexico, a Plains Indian known as "the Turk" (probably because of his headdress) told Coronado about his rich homeland of Quivira far to the north.

Once again the Spanish chieftain's spirits rose, only to be dashed. A year of fruitless wandering finally convinced him that the Indian was a liar; Quivira was only a group of grass or straw huts sheltering the Wichita Indians on the northern plains of present Kansas. There could be little consolation for the Spanish general in the fact that he had spent almost all of 1541 exploring a vast area of land more than 500 miles (805 kilometers) northwest of Soto's journey. Coronado's cheerless entrance into Mexico in 1542 with fewer than 100 men marked the loss of an investment of 1 million pesos, the end of Mendoza's grandiose dreams about finding the Seven Cities, and the beginning of a premature death for the now broken-spirited conquistador.

The survivors of Soto's ill-fated expedition returned in a similar condition the next year. Meanwhile, during Coronado's expedition Melchor Díaz had crossed the Colorado River in 1540, only to learn of the utter desolation of Lower California. In 1542 the Portuguese navigator Juan Rodríguez CABRILLO made it to the outer edge of the peninsula of California, discovered San Diego Bay, and entered the area of Los Angeles. After Cabrillo's death early in 1543, his chief pilot, Bartolomé Ferrer (Ferrelo), resumed the attempt to sail north but succeeded only in reaching about latitude 41° (southern Oregon) before turning back. It became painfully obvious even to the persistent Mendoza that there was no Strait of Anian linking the Atlantic with the Pacific, nor were there rich Indian kingdoms to be found north of Mexico.

Later Spanish exploration Spanish activity thus drew back to the islands of the Caribbean and to the areas surrounding Mexico. After Coronado's ill-fated expedition, Spain's occupation and consolidation of North America never equaled its knowledge of the hinterland. From 1543 to 1769 Spain's exploratory efforts in the present-day United States consisted merely of tracking over old territories or entering scattered unknown lands lying between those already explored. Without sufficient numbers, the Spanish could not overcome the dangers posed by Indians and rugged terrain, the dearth of passable roadways and waterways, and the countless revolts by their own black and Indian laborers. The rest of Spanish expansion remained for farmers, cattlemen, colonizing missionaries, and a few early miners wanting to exploit the northern central plateau in the Sierra Nevada and beyond the Gila and Colorado Rivers in present western Arizona. While Juan de Oñate in the 1590s would found the first white colony west of the Mississippi River, in New Mexico, other Spaniards, such as Sebastián Vizcaíno in 1602–1603, continued to pursue the elusive Strait of Anian (especially when rumor spread that England's Francis DRAKE had found such a waterway during his voyage in the 1570s along the Pacific Coast), and a few competed with other Europeans for the supposed riches of North America. Still, those who again made their way through the southwestern and southeastern portions of the present United States had little hope of reviving the lofty dreams shared by Ponce de León, Soto, Coronado, and others of earlier years. Spanish control in North America proved to be hollow, no match for the French drawing down the Mississippi River Valley and the English working inland from the Atlantic Coast.

The French The initial exploratory efforts by the French in the New World came primarily in the cold lands bordering the North Atlantic Coast. Giovanni da VERRAZZANO explored the area during the 1520s, but France's various internal and external problems prohibited concentrated support by the government. When the Peace of Cambrai of 1529 ended a long series of wars, King Francis I sent Jacques CARTIER in 1534 on the first of three voyages that would lay the foundations of New France along the St. Lawrence River.

South Carolina and Florida When France's wars and domestic quarrels again temporarily subsided in the 1560s, its exploratory efforts revived. The first concentrated attempts seemed designed to test the resolve of the Spanish in Florida. Following the colonial interests of the Protestant admiral of the realm Gaspard de Coligny, 150 Huguenots under Jean Ribaut (Ribault) and René Goulaine de Laudonnière built Charlesfort on the site of Port Royal, South Carolina, in 1562. These early explorers suffered from sickness, desertion, and rapidly depleted supplies. A second expedition under Laudonnière, again engineered by Coligny, in 1564 headed for Florida, landing at Matanzas Inlet south of the present site of St. Augustine. At a settlement on the St. Johns River called Fort Caroline (near present Jacksonville), these Frenchmen tried to establish a base from which to explore the interior in the hope of finding precious metals. Ribaut belatedly arrived with reinforcements on August 28, 1565.

Under King Philip II of Spain, Pedro Menéndez de Avilés, governor and captain general of Florida, prepared to drive out the intruders. He arrived at a site he called San Agustín on August 28, 1565. A futile attempt to capture the French ships followed, after which he ordered construction of St. Augustine, the first permanent white settlement in the present United States. Soon afterward, Menéndez destroyed Fort Caroline, tricked Ribaut into surrendering, and

had him executed. Most of the other Frenchmen in Florida experienced a similar fate. In 1566 and 1567 he established outposts at Santa Elena (then called San Felipe, near Port Royal, South Carolina), San Pedro (on Cumberland Island, Georgia), and San Mateo (on the St. Johns River, where the French had constructed Fort Caroline). To the south of St. Augustine, Menéndez had one fort built on the St. Lucie River, another on the Miami River, and two on the west coast at Tampa Bay and Charlotte Harbor. This elaborate preparation temporarily broke France's southern drive and kept Spanish control of Florida intact.

Champlain and his followers   Though the sixteenth century closed with no major French settlements in North America, the unbounded riches of the St. Lawrence Valley fur trade remained a major attraction. Out of this continuing interest came the work of Samuel de CHAMPLAIN, who explored much of the northeastern sector of the continent from 1603 to 1616. Though making few major revelations, he charted the coast from Cape Breton Island to southern Massachusetts, discovered the Kennebec River and the portage from its headwaters to the Dead River and the Chaudière River, and finally in 1608 established a tiny colony at Quebec, later the capital of New France. Because of Indian problems and divisions among the Frenchmen themselves, Champlain spent the better part of the years 1608–1613 merely trying to consolidate his influence with the Indians and earn

profits for his supporters, who were still seeking a passage to China. His *coureurs de bois* (traders who worked in the forests) and *voyageurs* (those who went into the plains) worked to spread French influence from the St. Lawrence River to the Rocky Mountains and from Hudson Bay to the Gulf of Mexico.

Champlain's explorations had mixed results. He had reached the Sweetwater Sea (what eventually would be called Lake Huron), and he had opened a direct fur traders' route up the Ottawa River to the upper Great Lakes. Yet he did not discover Lake Erie, nor did he ever understand the interrelatedness of the vast water system of Lake Huron, Georgian Bay, and Lake Michigan. Another Frenchman, Étienne Brulé, would fulfill Champlain's dream of finding a shorter water route to the interior than that afforded by the St. Lawrence River. Along the Susquehanna River in 1615, Brulé confirmed Champlain's belief in a waterway connecting the Great Lakes with the Atlantic Ocean. In 1634 Jean NICOLLET DE BELLESBORNE, another of Champlain's followers, took Brulé's route along the North Channel of Lake Huron to Sault Sainte-Marie, moved west to the Straits of Mackinac opening into Lake Michigan, hovered along the northwest shore of that body of water until he got to Green Bay, where he discovered the Fox River, and then turned northward to where the upper arms of the Wisconsin River, a tributary of the Mississippi, were only 3 days away. Unfortunately for the French, domestic

and foreign problems again set in and until 1650 prevented exploitation of these findings.

A brief truce in the Iroquois wars from 1653 to 1658 afforded an opportunity for the French to bolster their New World empire and to initiate further exploration of the continental interior. Two French emigrant brothers-in-law, Pierre Esprit Radisson and Médard Chouart, Sieur des Groseilliers, led the new drive. In 1654 Groseilliers and another Frenchman (once believed to be Radisson) traveled up the old Ottawa River route to Georgian Bay and Lake Huron and probably traversed Lake Saint Clair to reach the site of modern Detroit. Though uncertainty clouds their journeys in the 1650s, it seems that an expedition of 1659–1660 took them to the country south and west of Lake Superior, where they probably became the first Europeans to come in contact with the Sioux.

Jolliet and Marquette After the French curbed the Iroquois in 1666, they turned toward the Mississippi River. Earlier explorers, of course, had touched its waters. Nicollet had marveled at its size; Radisson and Groseilliers may have looked upon it. Though Jesuit priests would dominate exploration of the mighty river, their leader would not be a man of the cloth. A young American-born Frenchman, Louis Jolliet, in 1669 brought more traders to the quarters recently established by Nicolas Perrot. By the spring of 1673, six Jesuit missionaries, including Father Jacques Marquette, had erected stations on Green Bay and on the Fox River in the northeastern sector of the Lake Superior–Michigan triangle. They now were ready to move deeper into Wisconsin territory. Almost inevitably someone suggested a trek to the Mississippi River.

Though responsibility for the river's exploration first went to another Frenchman, Sieur de La Salle, his continued involvement in other areas caused French leaders to turn to Jolliet. Father Marquette, an experienced woodsman who spoke six Indian languages, would accompany him in determining whether the Mississippi was the same waterway as the "Spanish River of the Holy Spirit" and whether it

wound into the Gulf of Mexico, the Gulf of California, or the Pacific Ocean. Though Indians warned of merciless natives, heat so oppressive that it caused death, and "horrible monsters, which devoured men and canoes together," the small party of Frenchmen embarked from Saint-Ignace Mission into the "strange lands" and came upon the Mississippi River on June 17, 1673.

The quest down the great river thus began. Descending the Mississippi past the Missouri and Ohio Rivers, the men eventually turned back when the Indians warned of highly dangerous natives along the southern waters. Though the first expedition did not make it to the Gulf of Mexico, the venture was profitable. The men had reached a spot just above the mouth of the Arkansas River (somewhere around 34°N), which meant that they had paddled their canoes more than 2500 miles (4023 kilometers) in 4 months. More important, they had learned much about the North American heartland and realized that, in the words of the chronicler of the journey, "Beyond a doubt, the Mississippi River discharges into the Florida or Mexican Gulf, and not to the east in Virginia . . . or to the west in California." By mid-September, Marquette was resting at Green Bay, while Jolliet's return to Quebec in 1674 excited the imaginations of both governmental and spiritual leaders of New France, who dreamed of an all-water passageway connecting the Great Lakes and the Gulf of Mexico.

La Salle Two listeners most interested in the prospects raised by Jolliet and Marquette were Louis de Buade, Comte de Frontenac, soon to become governor of New France, and René-Robert Cavelier, Sieur de La Salle, a visionary trader who had had long experience with the Indians of the Ohio Valley and who now shifted his interests to the Mississippi region. Frontenac and La Salle hoped to establish a chain of fur posts linking the Great Lakes with the Mississippi River Valley. Such an action would bring profits and hem in the already-troublesome English colonies along the Atlantic seaboard.

Having support from Paris, La Salle and his companion, a one-armed Italian named Henri de Tonty, prepared to head the grand design. After building Fort Frontenac as a base for penetrating Lake Ontario country, they sailed west in 1678 toward Green Bay, where they acquired a large cache of furs, and then moved by canoe along the southern rim of Lake Michigan. Constructing Fort Miami at the mouth of the St. Joseph River, they took the Kankakee Portage to the Illinois River, where they built Fort Crèvecour. There, La Salle left Father Louis Hennepin to explore the Upper Mississippi River while he returned to Fort Frontenac. At this point another Iroquois war intervened.

In 1681 the frontier calmed enough for La Salle to resume his venture. Moving out of Fort Miami, he and twenty-three Frenchmen again took the Kankakee Portage to the Illinois River and followed it and the Mississippi River to the Gulf of Mexico by early April

Lake Huron in 1703. Étienne Brulé, a companion of the French explorer Samuel de Champlain, may have been the first European to see this lake. [Library of Congress]

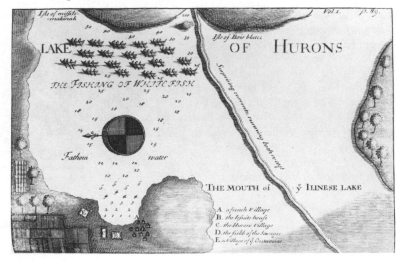

1682. After an elaborate ceremony in which La Salle took formal possession of the Mississippi Delta in the name of King Louis XIV, the men returned home, pausing long enough to construct Fort Saint-Louis on an easily defended spot called Starved Rock which loomed over the Illinois River. His government, La Salle believed, could abandon the St. Lawrence entrance to the Mississippi Valley fur trade in favor of an outpost on the Gulf of Mexico.

Later French exploration Although La Salle's last great effort—to construct such a fort at the mouth of the Mississippi River—led to his death, his explorations had several noteworthy results. His plans to establish a French colony on the Gulf Coast had diverted French fur-trading interests to the more lucrative Lake Superior region. Daniel Greysolon, Sieur Duluth (Dulhut), would explore as far as present Minneapolis and build trading posts on Lake Nipigon and at the western end of Lake Superior in 1684 and 1685, while Nicolas Perrot would construct posts in western Wisconsin and discover the lead mines in present Iowa. Despite La Salle's failures along the Gulf of Mexico, his original objective had been fulfilled: the French would build a string of posts along the St. Lawrence–Great Lakes–Mississippi water passages and temporarily establish themselves on the North American continent.

The irony is that the French were unable to exploit the great interest spreading in New France about the possibilities of an all-water passage from the north to the Gulf of Mexico. By 1672 Louis XIV had set out on a series of costly wars in Europe and the New World which threatened to bring collapse to the entire colonial empire. In Canada the Comte de Frontenac, now governor, could do little with sparse funds and with a home government in France that refused to support any major enterprise on the Mississippi River. No help could come from the Jesuits either, for they entered a period of sharp decline. Though by the middle of the eighteenth century the French had touched the Rocky Mountains and had made notable efforts to reinforce La Salle's claim to the Mississippi Valley, they eventually would lose a disastrous war with the English, the French and Indian War (Seven Years' War), and the terms of the Treaty of Paris of 1763 would drive them from the continent as a major power.

The English For several reasons the English were late in exploring the New World. While the Spanish and

French competed for North America in the early half of the sixteenth century, Tudor England was enmeshed in domestic and foreign troubles which hampered overseas enterprises. Some English sailors had braved the cold waters around Labrador and Hudson Bay in an effort to find the Northwest Passage, while a few fishermen had touched the banks of Newfoundland; but these early ventures served only to whet English curiosity about the North American coastline. When a period of calm set in during the 1570s, the monarchy under Queen Elizabeth prepared to lay claim to the New World.

Elizabethan enterprise The possibility of finding a passage through the continent continued to offer great appeal, thanks largely to Sir Walter Raleigh and his half brother, Sir Humphrey GILBERT, who had popularized the idea in Europe. Gilbert's efforts, combined with the corresponding interest shown by a London merchant prince named Michael Lok, led to three voyages (1576, 1577, and 1578) during which Martin FROBISHER tried unsuccessfully to find such a passage. In the meantime, Gilbert secured a charter from the Queen. Although Gilbert's two attempts (1578, 1583) at colonization of the North American mainland proved abortive, Raleigh's dream of a colony in the New World remained intact.

The early successes of England's Francis Drake in pirating Spanish galleons along the western coast of North America (probably even discovering San Francisco Bay in 1579) and raiding towns in Central and South America further convinced Sir Walter Raleigh that it was time to establish a colony in America. Besides helping to obtain gold, the outpost could slow the growth of New Spain. In addition, Richard HAKLUYT in 1583 had written *A Discourse of Western Planting*, an impressive argument for colonization as a means of halting Spain's northward advance along the Atlantic coast. In 1584, Raleigh, having obtained from the Queen a charter like Gilbert's, sent out two vessels on a reconnoitering mission which reached the North Carolina coast near Roanoke Island. Although an effort in 1585–1586 to colonize this region was unsuccessful, another attempt was made in 1587. However, this Lost Colony vanished before aid could arrive. Yet the English for two decades maintained interest in Virginia, the name they gave to the entire area between Florida and Newfoundland. In the meantime, the crown's efforts culminated in war with Spain and the eventual defeat of the famed Spanish Armada in 1588.

Virginia and the South When peace with Spain came in 1603, England, now under James I of the Stuarts, prepared for colonization again, and in 4 years

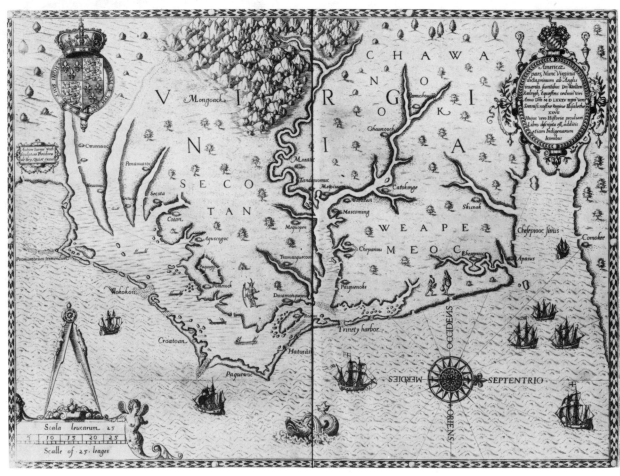

Map of the coast of Virginia, i.e., North Carolina, site of Sir Walter Raleigh's unsuccessful colonizing ventures in the 1580s. [Library of Congress]

the crown-chartered Virginia Company established the first permanent English settlement at Jamestown. Since the English had entered a new era of competition with the French and the Dutch, it was not surprising that these settlers immediately prepared to explore inland and to the north. Henry HUDSON, an Englishman sailing for the Dutch East India Company in search of an opening to the Orient, would probe the North American coast above Chesapeake Bay in late 1609, discovering the river that now bears his name. Shortly thereafter, Dutch sea captains would chart most of the mid-Atlantic coast from Cape Ann to Virginia. Thus the English hardly were in their New World colony when orders came to examine the surrounding area.

Early English explorations out of Virginia were not greatly successful. Christopher Newport and John SMITH led the first ventures in 1608. While Newport made his way up the James River to present Richmond, Smith explored the bays and estuaries near Jamestown. The rivers, they found, led only to a mountain barrier, while Chesapeake Bay halted at the mouth of the Susquehanna River. Yet the Indians insisted that a huge waterway lay deep in the interior of the continent, and Englishmen became certain that it existed somewhere around latitude 40° and slightly beyond the Blue Ridge Mountains. The story became so widespread, in fact, that the Spanish sent spies to Virginia to determine its location, while geographers in England continued for years to locate the Gulf of Mexico, the Great Lakes, and Hudson's Bay in a ring close to Virginia.

During the early 1640s, traders in Virginia became concerned about the rapid decline in furs, and a small contingent petitioned the Assembly for permission to explore farther west. Slowed by an Indian uprising, Gov. Sir William Berkeley in 1645 authorized the establishment of forts along the fall line of the six major rivers. He soon learned that only 5 days away a series of rivers emptied into a great sea, and by 1648 he planned an expedition to move south and west to determine its location. Virginians talked of the elusive "South Sea" (Pacific Ocean) and of great mines which New Spain was too weak to hold. Just when the Iroquois Indians were driving the French from the west in late August 1650, a party of Virginians, under Abraham Wood, pulled out of Fort Henry (located near the mouth of the Appomattox River) and headed toward the present Mississippi Valley.

Success was not to come, however. Accompanied by Edward Bland and a few companions, Wood moved toward the forks of the Roanoke River in the southwest. Entering areas that possibly had been explored before, the men trekked nearly 100 miles (161 kilometers) through the lands between the James and Roanoke Rivers. But once again, problems in England (civil strife followed by foreign troubles) upset conditions in Virginia and prevented further exploration for nearly two decades.

During the late 1660s, the English shifted interest to the southern Piedmont. Berkeley asked the British court in 1668 to authorize an expedition which might reach the Pacific and exploit believed Spanish gold in the surrounding areas. Though King Charles II was deep in his own problems and could not turn to the New World, the Governor took advantage of the timely arrival of a German physician, John Lederer. Berkeley sent three expeditions (1669 and 1670) under Lederer's leadership to find a passageway through the Blue Ridge Mountains. The small group crossed the Rapidan River to the mountains on one foray, moved south to the Indian villages of Sara near present Salisbury, North Carolina, and Ushery near Fort Mill, South Carolina, on another, and wound up along the Rappahannock River on the third.

Lederer's published narrative of his expeditions contained some truth but much fabrication. Londoners in 1672 read, for example, that during his second expedition Lederer had encountered a barren desert and a large brackish lake, but it is difficult to locate these in the region he traversed. Despite such stimuli to the imagination, the essential point remains that he had failed to find a passage from the Piedmont through the Appalachian Mountains.

In 1671 the fortunes of the Virginians changed as an expedition sponsored by Wood accomplished the first recorded English crossing of the Appalachians. In September of that year Thomas Batts and Robert Fallam moved west from Fort Henry, followed the Roanoke River and crossed the mountains to emerge in the beautiful valley of the New River.

Wood now turned his attention to the potential trade of the Carolina back country. In 1673 he sent James Needham and Gabriel Arthur from Fort Henry in a southwesterly direction, past the Occoneechee Indian village near present Clarksville, Virginia, toward the headwaters of the Yadkin River and across the North Carolina Blue Ridge. After they had reached a Cherokee village on an unidentified river (perhaps the French Broad or the Little Tennessee), Needham returned to Fort Henry, only to be murdered by an Occoneechee Indian while on his way back to the Cherokee village. Arthur remained with the Indians for several months, traveling with them from Florida to the Ohio River.

The last significant westward venture by the Southern colonies originated in South Carolina around 1673. Dr. Henry Woodward, attracted by the fur trade as well as by the possibility of casting out Spanish influence in the area, set out to explore the lands between the Santee and Savannah Rivers. From a town inhabited by the warlike Westo Indians, he and other traders followed the Indian trails north to the Catawbas in the region of the Carolina Blue Ridge Mountains, northwest to the Cherokee Indian settlements at the southern tip of the Appalachians, and west toward the Creeks living above the Gulf of Mexico. The rest of his achievements are unknown.

After a brief interlude caused by Bacon's Rebellion of 1676, English fur traders resumed exploring the southern area. By the 1690s some were engaged in the business along the Ohio River, while others concentrated on the Shenandoah Valley. Still other fur traders moved on to the Carolina Piedmont in order to make use of the Tennessee and Savannah River systems. The Great Valley of the Appalachian Mountains attracted the first great waves of settlement. Connecting the northern and southern sections of the Old West, it stretches across Pennsylvania and New York up to Lake Champlain. The rich river bottomlands drew pioneers in the early part of the eighteenth century, and before long they peopled the valleys of the Delaware, Susquehanna, Hudson, Mohawk, upper Connecticut, and Merrimack Rivers and soon poured over the perimeters into the highland and plateau regions beyond. By 1710 Virginia farmers joined the great westward thrust, and when mid-century came, the Great Valley was shaded with numerous wealthy estates.

New England While these Englishmen planted colonies along the southern Tidewater, others set sights on the northeastern sector of the present United States. Their first attempt in 1607, in what is now Maine, failed when the Plymouth Company (Northern Virginia Company) admitted defeat and most of its members returned to England a year later. Not until 1620 did the reorganized members of the company establish the Council for New England and try again. Their royal grant generously gave them the vast area between the 40th and 48th parallels, but they were unable to raise sufficient funds to effect a major success. Yet the few courageous settlers who remained provided the basis for the New England colonies.

The ultimate success in the north came when the Separatists, a religious group advocating a full break with the Anglican Church, reached Plymouth Rock on the Massachusetts coast in 1620 and built a settlement. By the end of the decade, fishermen and traders had moved northward, leaving a string of settlements connecting the New England coast from Casco Bay to Boston Harbor. The most significant of these efforts was by the Massachusetts Bay Company, which in 1628 secured a grant from the Council for New England to settle a belt of land from sea to sea and running from just north of the Merrimack River to a point barely south of the Charles River. By the late 1630s the New Englanders had settled along the coast of Maine, in the outlying regions of Boston Harbor and Plymouth, and as far inland as the Taunton River and Narragansett Bay. The only penetration of the interior was in the Connecticut River Valley (though first accomplished in 1614 by a Dutchman, Adriaen Block) and as far north as Springfield.

With the close of King Philip's War in 1676, New England's expansion spread until by the end of the century settlers had penetrated much of the good coastal areas and tidal valleys. Like their Southern counterparts, they were eager to spread into the Old West. Thus the next phase of Northern exploration would be part of the same westward push which affected the Southern colonies and brought the first major wave of interior settlement.

Boone and the interior The most notable eighteenth-century explorer involved in this early movement west was Daniel BOONE, whose interest centered on the bountiful hunting and farming lands of Kentucky. In 1775 he opened the famous Wilderness Road from Long Island of the Holston River, through the Cumberland Gap, and ending on the Kentucky River, where he constructed a fort called Boonesborough.

Though it appeared that there was much activity among both the Northern and Southern English colonists, the truth is that these settlers along the Atlantic Coast did not engage in exploration on a wide scale. Perhaps the major obstacle was topography. Besides the barrier of the Appalachian Mountains, the neighboring rivers did not compare in length with the St. Lawrence or the Mississippi, and there were no large basins like the Great Lakes. In addition, the colonists already were located in rich fur regions and thus had few incentives to struggle beyond the mountains. Finally, various local enterprises worked to maintain cohesion along the coast. Not until population pressure intensified did widespread interest develop in more land and consequent exploratory expeditions. These English efforts were not as glory-ridden, dramatic, and visionary as those of either the Spanish or the French, but their overall effect was quietly significant.

The period after Boone's expeditions and through the end of the eighteenth century is hazy in detail, for it is difficult to determine exactly who made the most notable discoveries of passageways to the Ohio River and other parts of the continental interior. Indeed, when adventurers from the Atlantic Coast, as well as those who moved east from the Mississippi River, entered the assumed untouched areas between the Appalachians and the Mississippi Valley, they found trees marked by explorers and trails already opened through the wilderness. As historian John B. Brebner has concluded, "It is a matter for regret to us now that their own generations did so little to record and commemorate their achievements."

The Americans The opening of the nineteenth century marked the first major organized campaign by the United States to compete with other nations in exploring the trans-Mississippi sector of the North American continent. In a real sense the area west of the mighty river was largely rediscovered, for discovery resulted primarily from the efforts of early Spanish and French explorers. The American adventurers of the 1800s merely fulfilled or shattered the fondest dreams of those who had come before. Though they did not find the Northwest Passage or the Seven Cities of Cíbola, they were responsible for an image of what the West should be. For several generations, it would be perceived as a haven, a refuge, a safety valve for the discontented, and even a spacious laboratory for experimentation with all kinds of society's ideas.

Lewis and Clark Expedition Exploration of the present American West in this period was mainly a product of the federal government's interest. Despite the timeworn stories of independent frontiersmen braving the hazards of a largely unknown land, the truth is that much of the work resulted from systematic federal support. From the time that Meriwether LEWIS and William CLARK made their way beyond the Missouri River, the government in Washington assumed a vital role. In fact, many explorers with no direct connections with the federal government continually looked to Washington for protection and assistance.

The explorations of Lewis and Clark had worldwide repercussions. Their triumphant return to St. Louis in 1806 signaled the close of a three-century international search for a Northwest Passage to Asia through the heart of the North American continent. Though the two men had not found such a waterway, they had involved the United States in the longtime imperial rivalry over the continent. President Thomas Jefferson's deep interest in the West had spurred the expedition but more than idle curiosity was involved. He had commercial interests, scientific purposes, and cultural goals in mind. By providing information useful to future American settlers, the explorers' work established a pattern for penetration of the West which gave the United States an enormous advantage over competing nations. In short, Lewis and Clark pushed the United States into the international struggle for the North American empire.

Fur trade and Western exploration The fur trade lay at the heart of the contest over the western sector of North America. By the early 1800s Britain's North West Company, founded about 1776, had become the base for Canadian explorations out of Montreal toward the Rocky Mountains and beyond. One of the firm's emissaries had explored the Yellowstone River Valley by 1806, while several of its traders already were wintering with the Mandans and other tribes along the upper Missouri River. David THOMPSON engaged in the most significant exploration, for he scaled the mountains and crossed the entire Columbia River network. His contributions included the establishment of trading posts and the exploration and mapping of adjoining regions. In fact, some historians have noted, Thompson's earlier journeys probably affected the Lewis and Clark Expedition by providing another impetus to President Jefferson's decision to push beyond the Mississippi River.

Thus the focus of British activity in the Northwest centered on the fur trade. When Thompson finally moved toward the Pacific in 1811, Robert Gray from Boston already had sailed into the great mouth of the river named after his ship, the *Columbia,* in 1792, and American fur traders under John Jacob Astor were entrenched at nearby Fort Astoria. Yet the Canadians managed to secure primary control of this vast area largely through the initial weakness of Americans. Consequently, when the War of 1812 began, the British North West Company controlled the Far Northwest to a point below the 49th parallel. Since the only opposition came from a few hostile Sioux Indians, the probability was that the British move southward would continue. East of the mountains, they had great influence along the Missouri River north of the Platte. Their headquarters in Wisconsin and Minnesota enabled them to use the St. Peter's (Minnesota) and Des Moines Rivers to thrive on the Missouri River fur trade as far south as they chose, despite the prohibitory provisions of Jay's Treaty of 1794 and vehement protests from the government in Washington. Yet the preoccupation of the British with the fur trade precluded their support for settlement, thereby leaving potential permanent control of these great regions within the domain of the United States.

American interest in the upper Missouri River fur trade was partially the product of a fortune-seeking, hated, and feared Spaniard from New Orleans, Manuel Lisa. In 1807 he worked with his guide, George Drouillard (Drewyer) of the Lewis and Clark Expedition, to establish trading posts on the upper river as headquarters for entering the fur trade. Encountering unfriendly Indians all along the way, Lisa and his band of forty-two men made their way past the great bend in present North Dakota, along the Yellowstone River, and into new territory surrounding the Bighorn River in central Montana. From Lisa's Fort (Fort Manuel), as he called the ensuing construction, he dispatched several exploratory expeditions into surrounding areas.

One of these was carried out by John Colter (ca. 1774–1813), another Lewis and Clark veteran, who was sent by Lisa in 1807 to establish relations with the Crow Indians. During his remarkable journey, Colter became the first white man to see the Teton Mountains and Jackson Hole and to travel in the Yellowstone Park region. He also saw the hot springs on the Stinkingwater (Shoshone) River, a spot that came to be known as Colter's Hell (though the name has also been applied to the hot springs in Yellowstone Park).

In the Lewis and Clark aftermath, the merchant John Jacob Astor led the march of American explorers into the Rocky Mountains and to the ocean. His Pacific Fur Company (a subsidiary of Astor's American Fur Company established in New York in 1808) was organized in 1810 to exploit the Columbia River area. That same year it dispatched a ship out of New York Harbor to establish a fur-trading post at the mouth of the great river. From Fort Astoria in the spring of the following year, Astor's enterprise supported overland connections back east to St. Louis, most notably those of Wilson Price Hunt and Robert Stuart. Hunt's expedition in 1811–1812, which ascended the Wind River, crossed the mountains by Union Pass and eventually reached the headwaters of the Snake, stimulated American fur interests in the Wind and Snake River areas. Stuart left Astoria on June 29, 1812. After encountering the extreme hardships of the Blue Mountains and the Snake River Valley, his party turned sharply north to cross the Teton Mountains and move into Jackson Hole. At this point near starvation, the men took an Indian trail west of the mountains and in late October came upon the South Pass of the Rockies at the southern tip of the Wind River Range. They then followed the Sweetwater and Platte Rivers and finally arrived in St. Louis on April 30, 1813. Despite the apparent successes, Astor's western enterprise, set up to establish fur-trading connections between the Columbia River and Canton, was no match for Britain's North West Company. The irony is that his work had little effect on the United States move into the Far West but instead encouraged the British to penetrate the Rocky Mountain West and attempt to solidify control over the entire territory west of the mountains above the Great Salt Lake.

Southwestern exploration The Southwest, which included today's Arizona and New Mexico as well as sections of Texas, Oklahoma, Kansas, Colorado, Nevada, Utah, and California, also beckoned to American interests. Some Americans were attracted by the rumor that the resident Spanish sat at the entrance to a land of gold and silver, while others were drawn by the allurement of a strange unknown area. In addition, Santa Fe would be a stepping-stone to the Pacific. As with the famed Northwest Passage, control of this region could determine the fate of the continent.

One of the many great falls of the Yellowstone River. The first American to see the magnificent region that is now Yellowstone National Park was John Colter. [Library of Congress]

One cannot speak accurately of an American "discovery" of the Southwest, for the Spanish had crisscrossed this vast region many times since the great journey of Cabeza de Vaca in the early sixteenth century. Consequently, the trails into the area followed by Jean Baptiste La Lande and James Purcell marked the *rediscovery* of this great area. In 1804 La Lande set out from Kaskaskia, Illinois, toward Santa Fe. Moving up the South Platte River toward the Rockies, he veered south along the mountains and eventually received such a fine welcome by Spanish authorities in Santa Fe that he settled there for the remainder of his life. The following year, Purcell likewise left a group of trappers along the Platte River to retire in Santa Fe. It became obvious that single bands of American explorers could not tear this land from Spain; the federal government in Washington, led by President Jefferson again, would have to take the first steps.

The hazy outlines of the western border of the Louisiana Purchase in 1803 furnished sufficient justification for Jefferson to launch official forays into the Southwest. By late 1804 he planned several scientific expeditions up the Red and Arkansas Rivers. One, directed by Sir William Dunbar, a scientist, and led by Dr. George Hunter, a chemist, reached Natchez by late July before various problems (including Spanish opposition) halted further penetration of the region. But in the winter of 1804–1805 the two men explored the Ouachita River in the present state of Louisiana. In May 1806 Jefferson dispatched Thomas Freeman to explore to the source of the Red River. About 635 miles (1022 kilometers) beyond its mouth, a superior force of Spanish soldiers from Texas ordered his expedition back. By this time the frontier was alive with intrigue and the likelihood of war between the United States and Spain. The master of the spies and counterspies then operating in the Southwest was the notorious Gen. James Wilkinson; not far behind was Aaron Burr.

In this uneasy atmosphere Lieut. Zebulon PIKE, under Wilkinson's orders, began his career of rediscovery. Officially setting out in the summer of 1805 to locate the source of the Mississippi River (which he never found), he undoubtedly had a more important goal of convincing British fur traders that the United States controlled the surrounding areas. In 1806 Wilkinson ordered Pike into the Southwest to settle some business with various Indians and locate the headwaters of the Arkansas and Red Rivers. Evidence suggests, however, that Pike also was under secret orders to investigate Spanish strength in the Santa Fe area. Whatever the truth, the Spanish captured Pike early in 1807, but not before he had explored much of the land from St. Louis to the Rockies and from the mountains south to the Rio Grande. After his release Pike returned to the United States, weighted down with valuable information about Spanish forces in northern Mexico. His report, published in 1810, also confirmed the great commercial possibilities of linking Santa Fe to the ports along the Pacific Ocean. Yet it was not until 1827 that the federal government completed construction of the Santa Fe Trail (opened in 1821 by a Missourian named William Becknell). The source of the Mississippi, which Pike had failed to find, was located in 1832 by geologist and ethnologist Henry Rowe Schoolcraft (1793–1864) at a body of water in Minnesota then known as Lac La Biche (Elk Lake). Schoolcraft is credited with giving the lake its modern name by combining parts of the Latin words for truth (*veritas*) and head (*caput*): Itasca.

Numerous American adventurers followed Pike's initial expeditions into the Southwest, but none won the official support of the federal government until the famed Yellowstone Expedition of 1819–1820. Designed by Secretary of War John C. Calhoun, it aimed to establish a military outpost along the upper Missouri River near the mouth of the Yellowstone which might halt British moves in the region and bring neighboring Indians under Washington's control. The military phase of the expedition, under Col. Henry Atkinson, encountered great difficulties. The steamboats used to transport men and supplies did not perform as expected, and the winter of 1819–1820, spent in a camp near Council Bluffs, Iowa, brought much hardship and suffering to the men, about 100 of whom died of scurvy. The principal accomplishment of the expedition was the resulting explorations of Maj. Stephen H. LONG in the region between the Rockies and the Missouri. Long's description of this area as the Great American Desert further discouraged American settlement there.

British explorers and mountain men Meanwhile, Donald McKenzie tried to revive Britain's still-influential but wavering Rocky Mountain fur trade. After Britain's capture of Fort Astoria during the War of 1812, the North West Company's efforts along the southern frontier of Canada began to suffer from weak leadership and entered a period of decline. The situation changed temporarily with McKenzie's arrival in 1816. Choosing to open the interior fur trade along the Snake River and east to the Green River, he established an outpost at Fort Nez Percé (Fort Walla Walla), located at the confluence of the Walla Walla and Columbia Rivers. By late 1819 his men had trapped the area from the Columbia in the north to Bear Lake in eastern Utah. Penetrating more deeply into the central Rockies than anyone before him, McKenzie for a time instilled new life in the fur trade along the Columbia and Snake Rivers.

No man, however, matched the fur-trade explorations of Peter Skene Ogden (1794–1854), born in Canada of American loyalist parents. Appointed leader of the Snake River brigade by Gov. George Simpson of the Hudson's Bay Company, Ogden extended his proprietor's influence inland from the base at Fort Vancouver along the Columbia River to the heartland of Mexican Utah and California. During the late 1820s he discovered the Humboldt River in Nevada (called by him the "Unknown"), marveled at the Great Salt Lake (though not the first to do so), struggled through the Great Basin, and became the first white man to cross the American West from north to south. In six expeditions between 1824 and 1830, he explored the entire Snake River region, much of Oregon, the areas around the Great Salt Lake and the Bear River, and a large part of California above San Francisco Bay. The irony is that his reports and maps helped Americans drive his fellow British from the Columbia River Valley and the entire Northwest.

Astoria, in Oregon, around the time that it was seized by the British in 1813. It was to become a focal point in the British-American struggle for the Oregon Territory. [Library of Congress]

The forerunners of the final major American assault on the Far West were the MOUNTAIN MEN, rough-hewn, independent fur trappers. Their explorations ranged from the Mississippi River to the Pacific Ocean and from the present American-Canadian border to the Gila River in the Southwest. They opened the Green River fur trade, rediscovered the South Pass through the Rockies, crossed the Great Basin, found and explored the Great Salt Lake, revealed and advertised the wonders of Yellowstone Park, Oregon, and California, and, in so doing, attracted numerous American settlers and fur traders to the West.

Federal interest and the far west The federal government's interest in the Far West increased during the 1830s. Though the trapper-explorers had pointed the way to Oregon and California, they had not marked the trails clearly, and it would be the responsibility of new bands of men, many receiving subsistence from leaders in Washington, to exploit the wilderness. Among these men was Capt. Benjamin Louis Eulalie de Bonneville (1796–1878), made immortal by Washington Irving in *The Adventures of Captain Bonneville* (1837). After securing a leave of absence from the U.S. Army in 1831, he went west as an explorer and fur trader.

Bonneville's instruction from the War Department was more interesting than his stated commercial motives: he was to secure all available information for use of the government. In May 1832 he moved west out of Fort Osage, Missouri, toward the mountains (probably bound for California), leading the first wagon caravan across the continental divide. Bonneville's "unofficial" mission, in short, was to serve the national interest in American expansion west. After he built Fort Bonneville on the Green River, his fellow trapper, Joseph R. Walker (1798–1876), set out for California with forty men in 1833 by way of the Great Salt Lake and the Humboldt River. He and his companions crossed the Sierra Nevada to the Yosemite region, which they were probably the first Americans to see. After a winter in California, Walker recrossed the mountains through Walker Pass, having marked the way for the California Trail, which would become a fact by 1844. Bonneville himself remained in the Rocky Mountains until 1835 but accomplished little, his fame owing largely to Irving's work.

The path to Oregon resulted from a strange set of circumstances. The propagandistic efforts of Hall J. Kelley, a Boston schoolmaster and founder of both the Penitent Female Refuge Society and the Boston Young Men's Education Society, initiated the undertaking. After reading the 1814 edition of *The Lewis and Clark Expedition*, Kelley urged the government in Washington to further the course of America's empire by terminating its long-standing policy with Britain of joint occupation of Oregon. When Congress refused to follow his suggestion, Kelley's efforts seemed wasted. But he had attracted the attention of a Massachusetts ice dealer, Nathaniel J. Wyeth. Interested in the commercial possibilities of the Columbia River, Wyeth left Independence, Missouri, in early May 1832, accompanied by William Sublette and a group of Rocky Mountain fur traders.

Wyeth reached Fort Vancouver (of the Hudson's Bay Company) on the Columbia River the following October. In 1834 he established Fort Hall on the Snake

Fort Laramie, Wyoming, in 1842. An illustration from John C. Frémont's report of the expeditions of 1842 and 1843–1844, which explored the Rocky Mountains and the Oregon Territory. [Library of Congress]

River in present Idaho to serve as a base for his fur-trading activities in the area. The same year Jason Lee, a Methodist missionary, founded a settlement on the Willamette River near present Salem.

The decade of the 1840s thus marked the pivotal point in the exploration of the present United States. Though explorers would open numerous new overland routes west, few of the men involved in these expeditions stand out in the history of exploration. Yet their achievements quietly fulfilled the early efforts of the Mountain Men and at the same time stimulated a new era of national expansion. It would remain for succeeding generations to fill in the broad continental boundaries crudely sketched by the early explorers of the trans-Mississippi West. With the backing of the federal government, men like Lieut. Charles Wilkes of the U.S. Navy and Capt. John C. FRÉMONT of the U.S. Army Topographical Corps would serve as "explorer-diplomats" in solidifying American control of the Far West. If there is no proof that Wilkes's explorations of the Pacific coastal waters, the Columbia River, and the interior waterways directly affected American policy, there can be little doubt that his reports helped to convince American commercialists that the harbor at the Columbia River was useless as a port yet worthwhile as an entrance to the interior of North America (see WILKES EXPEDITION). Frémont's explorations between 1842 and 1845 combined with Wilkes's work to dramatize the immense attraction of Oregon and California. Their enterprise, supported by the federal government, shows that the United States acquired these areas as a result of more than the casual explanation of economic rivalries over the fur trade. As the historian William Goetzmann astutely concluded, America's Western successes were "a continuation and extension of the great clash of empires in North America, at first thought to have ended with the French and Indian War and then finally with Lewis and Clark's discovery of a substitute for the Northwest Passage." By 1850 the United States had emerged victorious in the imperial struggle with Europe over North America from Canada to Mexico. Though there would be scientists, surveyors, artists, and emigrants exploring the West in the future, the American age of exploration had come to a triumphant end.

BIBLIOGRAPHY: Ray A. Billington, *Westward Expansion: A History of the American Frontier*, New York, 1949; Herbert E. Bolton, *Spanish Borderlands*, New Haven, Conn., 1921; Herbert E. Bolton and T. M. Marshall, *Colonization of North America, 1492–1783*, New York, 1920; John B. Brebner, *The Explorers of North America, 1492–1806*, New York, 1933; Edward P. Cheyney, *European Background of American History: 1300–1600*, New York, 1961; H. M. Chittenden, *The American Fur Trade of the Far West*, 2 vols., New York, 1935; William H. Goetzmann, *Exploration and Empire: The Explorer and the Scientist in the Winning of the American West*, New York, 1966; Leroy R. Hafen and Carl C. Rister, *Western America*, Englewood Cliffs, N.J., 1941; Samuel E. Morison, *The European Discovery of America: The Northern Voyages*, New York, 1971; Charles Norman, *Discoverers of America*, New York, 1968; J. H. Parry, *The Age of Reconnaissance*, New York, 1963; David B. Quinn, *North America From Earliest Discoveries to First Settlements: The Norse Voyages to 1612*, New York, 1977; Carl O. Sauer, *Sixteenth Century North America: The Land and the People as Seen by the Europeans*, Berkeley, Calif., 1971; Percy Sykes, *A History of Exploration: From the Earliest Times to the Present Day*, New York, 1934.

Howard Jones

Urdaneta, Andrés de (1508–1568) Spanish navigator and cosmographer. Born near Villafranca de Oria in the province of Guipúzcoa, Urdaneta sailed as a page to fellow Basque Juan Sebastián de Elcano in the expedition to the Moluccas led by Francisco García Jofre de Loaysa, which set sail from La Coruña on July 24, 1525. The expedition, consisting of seven ships and 450 men, was designed as a successor to that of Ferdinand MAGELLAN, but by the time it reached the Moluccas in November 1526 only two vessels remained and more than 300 Spaniards (including Loaysa and Elcano) had died. Moreover, the Portuguese were determined to exclude Spaniards from the islands and the valuable spices they produced. In the ensuing conflict between the Spaniards and the Portuguese and their respective native allies, Urdaneta distinguished himself in both a military and a diplomatic capacity. In 1529, however, King Charles I surrendered his rights in the Moluccas to Portugal in return for 350,000 gold ducats, and the island war came to an end. Urdaneta left the Moluccas on February 15, 1535, and arrived in Lisbon on June 26, 1536. There the Portuguese authorities confiscated his diary of the Loaysa Expedition and his adventures in the Moluccas, but he later wrote another account from memory.

After returning to Spain, Urdaneta agreed to join the Pacific expedition being planned by Pedro de ALVARADO and set sail from Seville on October 16, 1538. His plans were frustrated, however, by the death of Alvarado in 1541 in the Mixtón War in Mexico, in which Urdaneta also took part. He remained in Mexico and served as a royal official before entering the Augustinian order in 1552. He was ordained a priest in 1557.

In 1559 Philip II invited Urdaneta to serve as chief pilot of an expedition to establish Spanish rule in the Philippines. Urdaneta agreed to participate in the expedition but because of his priestly character refused the position offered. As commander he recommended Miguel López de Legazpi (1510–1572), a native of Guipúzcoa long resident in Mexico. The expedition, which consisted of five ships, left the Mexican port of Navidad on November 21, 1564, and reached Samar in the Philippines on February 13, 1565.

Another goal of the expedition was the discovery of a return route from Southeast Asia to the New World, for all previous efforts to cross the Pacific from west to east had been unsuccessful. To this end Urdaneta sailed from the Philippines on the *San Pedro* on June 1, 1565. Following a northerly course, he reached San Miguel Island, off the coast of California, in September 18, 1565, then sailed south to Acapulco. After his return to Mexico, Urdaneta made a detailed chart of his route, which would be followed by the celebrated Manila Galleon for 250 years. Urdaneta's discovery of the trans-Pacific route was anticipated by Alonso de Arellano, another member of the Legazpi Expedition, whose pinnace *San Lucas* was separated from the main body but eventually reached the Philippines, whence he sailed for Mexico, arriving in Navidad on August 8, 1565. However, unlike Urdaneta, Arellano provided no guidance for future sailors.

BIBLIOGRAPHY: Mairin Mitchell, *Friar Andrés de Urdaneta, O.S.A.,* London, 1964; Samuel Eliot Morison, *The European Discovery of America: The Southern Voyages, 1492–1616,* New York, 1974.

Valdivia, Pedro de *(ca. 1502–1553)* Spanish conqueror and explorer. Valdivia was born in the district of La Serena in Extremadura. According to his own account, he served in the Spanish Army in Italy and Flanders and traveled to the New World in 1535, spending a year in Venezuela. He later joined a force sent from Santo Domingo to Peru to assist Francisco PIZARRO in quelling the uprising of the Almagrists. Having been named quartermaster of Pizarro's army, Valdivia distinguished himself at the Battle of Las Salinas and was amply rewarded. He soon astonished Pizarro by applying for a commission to lead an expedition to Chile, which had been in ill repute since the journey of Diego de ALMAGRO in 1535–1537. Pizarro granted Valdivia the commission in 1539, and the latter set out for Chile in January 1540, accompanied by 24 Spaniards, about 1000 Indians, and his mistress, Inés Suárez. After spending 2 months in Copiapó, Valdivia continued southward, his force now augmented to total 150 Spaniards. Overcoming Indian resistance, they reached the site of modern Santiago, which was founded on February 12, 1541. Although Valdivia wanted to explore and occupy the country to the south, the next few years were spent in establishing the new colony and fighting the Indians. An expedition led by Valdivia in 1546 reached the Bío-Bío River before the hostility of the Indians forced him to turn back.

In December 1547 Valdivia returned to Peru, where he played an important role in the suppression of the revolt led by Gonzalo PIZARRO. Valdivia was rewarded with an official appointment as governor of Chile but was then called upon to answer charges of disloyalty and misconduct. Having been exonerated and confirmed in his appointment, Valdivia went back to Chile to resume his plans for southern exploration. He left Santiago in January 1550, initially retracing the steps of his 1546 expedition. As Valdivia moved southward, encountering Indian opposition at every turn, several cities were founded by the Spaniards, among them Concepción (October 5, 1550). Meanwhile, Valdivia sent out several exploratory parties by land and by sea, including an expedition led by Francisco de Ulloa, which entered the Strait of Magellan in 1553. Valdivia himself apparently proceeded as far as the Gulf of Reloncaví, which he mistook for a river. He was killed on December 25, 1553, either during or after a battle with Indians at a fort called Tucapel south of Concepción.

BIBLIOGRAPHY: *Cartas de Pedro de Valdivia*, ed. by José Toribio Medina, Santiago de Chile, 2d ed., 1953; H. R. S. Pocock, *The Conquest of Chile*, New York, 1967.

Vancouver, George *(1757–1798)* English naval officer and explorer. Vancouver was born in King's Lynn, Norfolk, on June 22, 1757, the son of a customs officer. He entered the Royal Navy in 1772 as an able seaman and sailed with James COOK in HMS *Resolution* on Cook's second voyage to the Pacific (1772–

1775). Afterward he was midshipman of the *Discovery* during Cook's last voyage and returned to England in October 1780. On passing his examination, he was promoted lieutenant (October 19, 1780). Appointed to HMS *Martin* and later to the *Fame,* he was engaged in convoy and patrol duty in the North Sea and the Caribbean. He returned to England in 1783 and was appointed to HMS *Europa,* which sailed for Jamaica in 1784 and in 1786 came under the command of Commo. Alan Gardner (later 1st Baron Gardner), who became Vancouver's patron.

In 1789 Vancouver was ordered to sail in HMS *Discovery* on a voyage to plant a small British settlement on the northwest coast of North America to aid British maritime fur traders, then anxious for government support in a new branch of commerce opened by Cook's last voyage. The crisis stemming from the Spanish seizure of several British ships at Nootka Sound forced the British to employ severe measures to stop Spanish pretensions in an area they did not occupy. During the organization of the fleet known as the Spanish Armament, Vancouver was appointed to HMS *Courageux,* commanded by Gardner.

Harbor near Cook Inlet, Alaska, as shown in Voyage de Vancouver. *In 1792 George Vancouver took his* Discovery *around the Cape of Good Hope to the northwestern coast of North America. There he became the first man to chart the coastline accurately and to announce positively that no Northwest Passage existed south of the Arctic Ocean.*

When the government decided to send an officer to Nootka to receive back the land and property seized by the Spanish and to make an accurate survey of the northwest coast north of 30°N, Vancouver was selected. He took command of the *Discovery* on December 15, 1790, and was instructed to sail for Nootka with the tender *Chatham,* Lieut. William R. BROUGHTON commanding. Vancouver sailed via the Cape of Good Hope, surveyed the southwest coast of Australia, examined Dusky Sound, New Zealand, and reached Nootka on August 28, 1792. Before arriving at

Nootka, he charted the Strait of Juan de Fuca, Puget Sound, and the Strait of Georgia, naming many natural features of the area in honor of contemporaries, among them Mount Rainier for Peter Rainier, an officer he had known in the Caribbean, and Puget Sound for Peter Puget, lieutenant of the *Discovery.* Vancouver also circumnavigated the large island which bears his name. Surveying crews under his direction made numerous charts of the coast as far north as the Gulf of Alaska and as far south as San Diego Bay. The first to provide a comprehensive survey of the Pacific coast of North America, Vancouver reported the nonexistence of a Northwest Passage south of the Arctic Sea. He also visited the Hawaiian Islands three times, made the first accurate chart of the group, and accepted on behalf of Great Britain the cession of the island of Hawaii from its king, Kamehameha I.

Vancouver returned to England via Valparaiso, Cape Horn, and St. Helena, arriving at Deal on October 15, 1795. In the meantime, he had been advanced to the rank of captain (August 28, 1794). During the voyage he had proved to be a strict disciplinarian in the Cook tradition, and his punishment of a midshipman, Thomas Pitt, 2d Baron Camelford, for insolent and insubordinate conduct invited censure and some controversy. In retirement he prepared his journals for publication but died, at Petersham, Surrey, on May 12, 1798, a few months before his book *A Voyage of Discovery to the North Pacific* (three volumes with atlas, 1798) appeared in print.

BIBLIOGRAPHY: Bern Anderson, *Surveyor of the Sea: The Life and Voyages of Captain George Vancouver,* Seattle, 1960; George Goodwin, *Vancouver: A Life,* New York, 1931.

Barry M. Gough

Varthema, Lodovico di (fl. 1502–1510)

Varthema, Lodovico di (fl. 1502–1510)   Italian traveler and adventurer. He was born in Bologna between 1465 and 1470. Having a keen interest in foreign lands, he left Venice toward the end of 1502 for Egypt, visiting both Alexandria and Cairo. From Egypt he sailed to the Lebanese coast, disembarking at Beirut and then proceeding inland to Aleppo (Halab), Tripoli (Tarābulus), and Damascus. He later described Damascus as a rich and populous city and a place of great beauty. There he studied Arabic and also enrolled in a Mamlūk garrison. In the period April–June 1503, he joined pilgrims going to Medina (Al Madznah) and Mecca (Makkah), being the first recorded European traveler to visit these holy places of Islam. He next planned a trip to India and embarked from Jidda (Juddah) for that purpose. When the ship stopped at Aden, he was arrested and imprisoned, charged with being a Christian spy in disguise. Through the intercession of one of the local sultan's wives he finally regained his freedom and then spent some time touring southwest Arabia. At Aden he embarked for India, but the ship first touched on the coast of Ethiopia before making the run to the island of Diu. From Diu he backtracked to Julfar, within the Persian Gulf near Cape Musandam, and from there traveled to Muscat, Hormuz (Hormoz), Herat, and Shiraz. At Shiraz he entered into partnership with a wealthy Persian merchant, and the two men sailed together from Hormuz to India. Their voyage took them along the west coast of India, where they stopped at various towns, including the port of Calicut. Varthema made a long stay in Calicut, and a whole book of his travel account is devoted to a description of various aspects of native life which he observed. He next visited Ceylon, the east coast of India, Burma, the islands of Sumatra and Java, and possibly the Moluccas before returning to the west coast of India and Calicut.

Abandoning his Persian companion, he joined the Portuguese garrison at Cannanore and fought for the interests of Portugal against the natives. For his services he was knighted by the Viceroy. In December 1507, Varthema began his return journey to Western Europe, traveling by way of the east coast of Africa, Mozambique, the Cape of Good Hope, and the Azores, finally reaching Lisbon. He was received at a royal palace near Lisbon by Manuel I, who confirmed his honor of knighthood. Varthema then returned to Rome and published an account of his travels in Italian in December 1510. The book was dedicated to a noble lady of literary tastes, Agnesina da Montefeltro, the fourth daughter of Federigo da Montefeltro, Duke of Urbino. This work achieved a remarkable success, and a number of editions were published. As a freelance traveler, Varthema was the first European to reach India by the Red Sea route and to return via the Cape of Good Hope.

BIBLIOGRAPHY: Lodovico di Varthema, *The Travels of Ludovico di Varthema in Egypt, Syria, Arabia Deserta and Arabia Felix, in Persia, India, and Ethiopia, A.D. 1503 to 1508,* tr. by John Winter Jones and ed. by George Percy Badger, Hakluyt Society, 1st ser., no. 32, London, 1863.

Bernerd C. Weber

Vavasour, Mervin

Vavasour, Mervin   See WARRE, HENRY JAMES, AND VAVASOUR, MERVIN.

Verrazzano (Verrazano), Giovanni da (ca. 1485–1528)

Verrazzano (Verrazano), Giovanni da (ca. 1485–1528)   Italian explorer and navigator in the service of France. Although the exact place and date of his birth have not been positively established, he was probably a native of Tuscany, well born and well educated. He entered the service of King Francis I to undertake a voyage to the New World, the first such expedition to North America under the auspices of the French crown. In 1524 in the ship *La Dauphine* and accompanied by a younger brother Girolamo, a map maker, Verrazzano crossed the Atlantic and made landfall at or near Cape Fear, North Carolina. After a short voyage southward he turned toward the north and explored the North American coast probably as far as Newfoundland, anchoring briefly in the Narrows of New York Bay and in Narrangansett Bay. Although this voyage failed in its primary objective of discovering a passage to China, Verrazzano's report of this expedition, written for Francis I immediately after returning to Dieppe, Normandy, does provide the first geographical description of a large section of the North American coast based upon a known exploration. The land discovered in this voyage was named Francesca in honor of the French king. Verrazzano's narrative also contains important data concerning the physical appearance, customs, and way of life of the Indian tribes observed during the voyage. Of the early explorers in North America Verrazzano was the first one to name newly found places in honor of prominent personalities or important spots in France. Few of these place names, however, have survived.

In a subsequent expedition in 1527, sponsored in part by Philippe de Chabot, admiral of France, the Brazilian coast was reached, and a valuable cargo of logwood was brought back to Dieppe. Verrazzano's third voyage got under way in the spring of 1528 and ended in tragedy for the captain. The great navigator attempted on this occasion to find a passage to Asia south of that area which he had explored in the first voyage. Apparently he followed the chain of the Lesser Antilles and stopped at one of the islands, possibly Guadeloupe, where he was seized by hostile Caribs, killed, and then eaten by the natives. The expedition continued on to Brazil and ultimately brought back to France a rich cargo of logwood.

BIBLIOGRAPHY: Samuel Eliot Morison, *The European Discovery of America: The Northern Voyages, A.D. 500–1600,* New York, 1971; Lawrence C. Wroth, *The Voyages of Giovanni da Verrazzano, 1521–1528,* New Haven, Conn., 1970.

Bernerd C. Weber

In 1524 Giovanni da Verrazzano, searching American shores for a passage to China, provided the European world with the first description of the geography of North America based on firsthand exploration. [Library of Congress]

Vespucci, Amerigo *(Americus Vespucius, 1454—1512)*

Italian navigator. Born in Florence, the third son of Stagio Vespucci, a notary, and his wife, Lisabetta Mini, he was educated by his uncle, Father Giorgio Antonio Vespucci, and remained in Italy almost 40 years, mainly in the service of the Medici. In 1492 Vespucci was sent by his employers to Seville, where their manager, Gianetto (Juanoto) Berardi, in addition to merchant banking, outfitted ships. He succeeded Berardi as the Medici agent in Seville in 1496 and made the acquaintance of Christopher COLUMBUS while aiding the admiral in the preparation for his third voyage in 1498.

Profiting perhaps from knowledge gained from his association with Columbus, Vespucci made a voyage of discovery and exploration under Alonso de OJEDA which infringed on the monopoly granted by the Spanish sovereigns to Columbus. The party sailed from Cádiz on May 16, 1499, via the Canary Islands to the Pearl Coast. Vespucci seems to have detached himself from Ojeda, and it is possible that he explored the Brazilian coast on this voyage and sailed to the mouth of the Amazon and beyond to Cabo São (Santo) Agostinho (6°S) before returning to Spain in September 1500. A great furor arose when an account of this voyage (the Soderini Letter) was published in 1504 and the year of the voyage was antedated to 1497, thus giving Vespucci credit for having reached the mainland before Columbus.

Controversy has continued to rage down to the present day about the "Vespucci question." The 1499–1500 voyage is accepted by most scholars. It is also generally acknowledged that Vespucci sailed on a second voyage under the Portuguese flag in the service of King Manuel under the command of Gonçalo Coelho, leaving Lisbon on May 13, 1501. The second voyage, commissioned to investigate the discovery of Brazil by Pedro Álvares CABRAL, took Vespucci from the Cape Verde Islands to Rio de Janeiro, and he may have gone farther south to the Río de la Plata. Claims have been advanced that Vespucci sailed to 50°S on this voyage and discovered South Georgia Island and even the Strait of Magellan, but these claims have been dismissed as farfetched. He returned to Lisbon in the summer of 1502. Most authorities have discounted a voyage in 1497–1498, in which he claimed to have cruised the Caribbean and to have discovered the mainland, and a later one during 1503–1504, in which he claimed to have reached Bahia (Salvador).

Vespucci became a naturalized Castilian and a member of the Casa de Contratación, the clearinghouse for overseas trade, in 1505. He was named the first pilot major of Spain on March 22, 1508. In this position he was responsible for the examination and licensing of mariners and the maintenance of an official up-to-date map of the world. He is also supposed to have developed a lunar method for the determination of longitude; obviously he did not, for even his

The arrival of Amerigo Vespucci in the New World around 1499. Although not truly the discoverer of America, Vespucci deserves credit for recognizing that the vast continent was a new world and not the coast of China. [Library of Congress]

Ioan: Stradanus invent.
Theodor Galle sculp.   Phls Galle excud.

latitudes, easier to determine, are mostly erroneous. His place in history, however, is due chiefly to an egregious error by Martin Waldseemüller, an obscure professor of geography at Saint-Dié in Lorraine who, in his *Cosmographiae introductio* (an essay to accompany an updated version of PTOLEMY published in 1507), applied Vespucci's name rather than that of Columbus to South America, a designation later applied to the northern continent as well.

Vespucci may very well have been little more than an ardent self-promoter. If so, the invention of printing by means of movable type was the greatest boon to his ambitions, for the *Mundus novus*, an account of his voyage of 1501–1502 supposedly written by Vespucci in 1503, went through more than twenty editions in several languages before 1508. Modern scholarship, however, tends to the belief that the *Mundus novus* and the Soderini Letter were forgeries. Nevertheless, Vespucci was the first person to appreciate the immensity of the mainland and to recognize it as a true continent. Furthermore, Vespucci was the first to refer to it as a "new world," although he continued to call it, as Columbus had, Las Indias. He died on February 22, 1512, survived by his wife, the former María Cerezo, who died on December 26, 1524.

BIBLIOGRAPHY: Germán Arciniegas, *Amerigo and the New World*, New York, 1955; Roberto Levillier, *Américo Vespucio*, Madrid, 1966; Samuel Eliot Morison, *The European Discovery of America:*

The Southern Voyages, A.D. 1492–1616, New York, 1974; Frederick J. Pohl, *Americo Vespucci, Pilot Major*, New York, 1944; Vicente D. Sierra, *Amerigo Vespucci: El enigma de la historia de América*, Madrid, 1968.

Martin Torodash

Vinland (*Vinland the Good; Wineland*)

Toponym given by Leifr EIRÍKSSON in 1002 to a region located on the eastern seaboard of North America southwest of Greenland. According to the *Saga of the Greenlanders (Graenlendinga saga)*, Leifr sailed from Greenland with a crew of thirty-five in 1001 in search of the lands which Bjarni Herjólfsson had discovered to the west and southwest of Greenland in 985 or 986. After first visiting and naming Helluland, Markland, and an unnamed island, Leifr landed in Vinland. The exploration party spent the winter of 1001–1002 at Leifrsbuðir (Leifr's Booths), where they erected dwellings.

The earliest-surviving textual reference to Vinland is in Adam of Bremen's *Gesta Hammaburgensis* (1075). Obtaining his information from the Danish king Sweyn Estrithson (Svein Estridsson), Adam briefly writes of an island called Wineland, located in the western ocean. The first mention of Vinland in Icelandic texts dates from the twelfth century. *The Icelandic Annals* record that in 1121 "Eirík, Bishop of Greenland, went in search of Vinland," suggesting that its location had already been forgotten. Whether the bishop ever found Vinland is unknown. Another indirect, laconic reference to Vinland survives in Ari Thorgilsson's *Íslendingabók* (ca. 1122–1132). A number of casual references, some of them of doubtful

value, about Vinland are embedded in twelfth- and thirteenth-century Icelandic historical texts and sagas, including Snorri Sturlusson's *Heimskringla*, *Landnámabók*, and *Eyrbyggja saga*. Surprisingly, the anonymous twelfth- and thirteenth-century manuscripts *Historia Norvegiae* (ca. 1170) and *Konungs skugssjá* (ca. 1280–1300) contain no references at all to the discovery and exploration of Vinland. Neither do the works of the medieval Scandinavian historian Saxo Grammaticus (*Gesta Danorum*, ca. 1185–1223) and the monk Theodoricus (*Historia de antiquitate regum Norvagiensium*, ca. 1170–1180). The primary source for the Vinland voyages and exploration is the *Saga of the Greenlanders (Graenlendinga saga)*, which was first committed to writing in Iceland in about 1200. Another, albeit less reliable source is *Eirík the Red's Saga (Eiríks saga rauda)*, which to some extent is a revision of the older *Saga of the Greenlanders*. *See* NORSE MARITIME DISCOVERIES.

Leifr Eiríksson According to the *Saga of the Greenlanders*, Leifr's landfall in Vinland was near the mouth of a river located to the west of a northward-projecting promontory. After the flood tide refloated the ship, he and his companions conveyed it up the river into a lake where it was anchored at Leifrsbuðir, which served as the base for subsequent exploration of the land. The brief qualitative geographical description of the land they explored and the astronomical observation taken there on or about the winter solstice clearly indicate that Vinland was located considerably south of Greenland. Except for the mention of an island north of a promontory and a river that led to a lake, the geographical description is devoid of topographical information. Indeed, the narrative is highly selective in that it includes references to winter climate, flora, and fish only. Apparently, the land the party explored was uninhabited; at least there is no reference to an indigenous population.

In the following spring, Leifr and his companions sailed for Greenland with a cargo of timber and grapes. How they managed to keep the grapes from spoiling during the winter remains a mystery. Even more troublesome is the meaning of Vinland, for the name has been interpreted from two different perspectives based on the orthography of the element *vin*. Vínland (long vowel) translates "wineland," while Vinland (short vowel) means "meadowland" or "fertile land." The Vínland-Wineland association is vexatious on ecological grounds, for the saga explicitly states that "Leifr named the country after its natural qualities and called it Vinland." Quite obviously wine is a processed liquid and not a "natural quality" of a country. The Vinland-Meadowland interpretation, coupled with the saga narrative about the mild winters and potential for grazing livestock year round, is far more in keeping with the Norse environmental perception and tradition of place naming than is the Vínland-Wineland thesis. The Vinland-Meadowland interpretation has, however, been challenged on phonological grounds and on the ground that Leifr would not have given the country an archaic *vin* name. Yet in the Shetland Islands and the Orkneys the Norse gave composite place names that included the element *vin* (for example, Vinjalok, Vinjari, and Vinbreck) designating pastures and meadows as well as settlement. Even more numerous are the *vin* (pasture, meadow) place names in Norway and Sweden. There are, however, no *vin* place names in Iceland and Greenland, suggesting that the tradition of giving *vin* place names had passed by the time the Norse discovered, explored, and settled these two islands. It may be that the appellation Vinland survived as part of an oral tradition about lands that the Norse had discovered and explored to the west and southwest of Greenland in the eighth or ninth century. Leifr might thus have used the old surviving name in designating the land he explored. Yet others have suggested that the Vínland-Wineland association is simply promotional and has nothing to do with the natural qualities of a country. Clearly, the Vinland-Vínland dilemma has not been satisfactorily resolved. It is of special significance in connection with the question of the location of Vinland: if the country was named Wineland, then it was located to the south of the northern boundary of grapes on the eastern seaboard.

Thorvaldr In 1003 Leifr's brother Thorvaldr with a crew of thirty men left Greenland to explore Vinland further. After spending the first winter at Leifrsbuđir, they reconnoitered the western coast of Vinland, returning in the autumn to Leifrsbuđir. During the second summer exploration proceeded to the east, where again it was limited to shorelands. While reconnoitering along shores in a heavily wooded region, the Norse came upon what at first seemed three bumps or mounds on a sandy beach. On closer inspection they discovered that "these were three skin-boats, with three men under each of them. Thorvaldr and his men divided forces and captured all of them except one, who escaped in his boat. They killed the other eight. . . ." After further surveillance of the area, the Norse observed "a number of humps farther up the fjord and concluded that these were settlements." For some unexplained reason, the cold-blooded killing of the Skraelings (*Skraelingar;* Indians) made Thorvaldr and his men so drowsy that they all fell asleep. They were awakened by what some interpret to have been a "divine voice" warning them of advancing Indians. Considered more realistically, it probably was the war cry of the Indians that awoke the Norse. The Indian who had made his escape apparently had informed others of the fate of his companions. In the ensuing skirmish with the Skraelings, Thorvaldr was mortally wounded. Soon thereafter, Thorvaldr's men returned to Leifr's Booths, and in the spring of 1005 they sailed for Greenland with a cargo of grapes and vines which had been gathered during the previous autumn.

Thorvaldr's voyage of exploration is of importance in that it documents the earliest-known contact between indigenous Americans and intruding Europeans and conveys the incipient European conceptualization of the Indians. It established at least three precedents for subsequent Indian-white relations in that the Norse were the first Europeans to intrude on Indian lands, the first to attack and massacre Indians, and the first to coin and make use of a derogatory epithet (Skraelings) in identifying the Indians. This disparaging noun of Norse origin, meaning "weaklings," "wretches," or "uglies," was especially coined to identify the indigenous populations of America and therefore includes the Eskimos as well.

Thorfinn Karlsefni The next recorded voyage to Vinland was Thorfinn Karlsefni's attempt to settle the country permanently about 1010–1013. According to the *Saga of the Greenlanders*, there were sixty men and five women aboard the ship that left Greenland for Vinland. So far there is no good explanation for the remarkably unbalanced sex ratio of the would-be settlers. *Eirík the Red's Saga*, on the other hand, merely reports that 160 people sailed for Vinland. Livestock, household goods, and other necessities were brought along. According to the *Saga of the Greenlanders*, Karlsefni and his companions reached Leifr's houses in Vinland. There they felled timber, collected grapes, found fish and "game of all kinds," and butchered a stranded whale. During the second summer of their stay in Vinland, in 1011, they met with Skraelings, who emerged from the woods to trade with the Norse. In their packs the Indians brought "furs, sables and all kinds of pelts." Although they wished to trade their goods for weapons of the Norse, Karlsefni prohibited such a barter. Instead, he ordered the women to carry out milk for the purpose of trade. When the Indians observed the milk, they willingly accepted it for their furs and pelts, drinking it immediately. It is most improbable that the Indians, to whom the concept of milking and the consumption of animal milk were entirely foreign, should instantaneously develop a craving for the exotic liquid. Unless the saga narrative represents a deliberate attempt to belittle Indians as traders, it is probable that the so-called milk for which the Indians traded their furs and pelts really was some sort of intoxicating beverage, perhaps the potent Norse mead. The episode might thus describe the first instance of European trade supremacy in America brought about at the expense of planned debauchery. During the subsequent winter the Indians returned to trade their furs and pelts for "milk." When one of the Indians tried to "steal" some weapons, he was immediately killed by one of Karlsefni's men, whereupon the Indians left. Shortly thereafter they returned to battle the Norse. In the hostilities that followed (if we are to believe the saga), "great numbers of the Skraelings were killed," while there is no mention of a single Norse casualty—a highly improbable proposition. During the next spring (1013), Karlsefni and his company sailed for Greenland, having failed to establish a permanent Norse settlement in Vinland.

The less reliable *Eirík the Red's Saga* also narrates Karlsefni's attempted settlement of the western lands. He and his followers settled at a place they called Hope (Hóp). They met and traded with the Skraelings. For their gray pelts the Indians received pieces of red cloth. Hostilities erupted, with casualties on both sides, probably because of unscrupulous trading practices and arrogance on the part of the Norse, not because the Indians were frightened by a bull, as the saga has it. The retreating Norsemen were admonished by Freydis, a Norse amazon: "Why do you flee from these wretches, brave men like you? You should slaughter them like cattle." After the skirmish the Norse abandoned their Hóp settlement and sailed to a place they called Straumfjord. On their way to Straumfjord, they came upon five Skraelings whom they judged to be "outlaws" and therefore killed. Subsequently, after leaving Straumfjord for Greenland, Karlsefni's party met with Skraelings in Markland. They captured two boys and brought them to Greenland. This is the first recorded instance of native Americans being forcibly removed from their lands by Europeans.

With Freydis's voyage and stay at Leifrsbuðir in Vinland in the years 1013–1014, the recorded Norse contact with Vinland came to an end. Overextension of supply lines, racial discrimination on the part of the Skraelings in denying the Norse the privilege of permanent settlement, lack of gunpowder and muskets with which to massacre Indians so as to make room for the Norse settlers, and the "exhaustion of the Norse impetus" are some of the reasons offered by modern scholars to explain the failure of Norse settlements in Vinland and its vicinity.

Location A topic related to the medieval Norse voyages and discoveries in the North Atlantic is the quest for the location of Vinland, a concern that originated in Iceland in post-Columbian times. Since the proposal by the Icelandic historian-clergyman Arngrímur Jónsson (1568–1648) of a Vinland site in Labrador (at about 58°N) and the drawing of the Stefánsson map (ca. 1590) and the Resen map (1605), the first cartographic attempts to locate Vinland, speculation regarding its location has yielded more than 500 definitive Vinland sites, ranging in latitude from Labrador to Florida and in longitude from western Newfoundland to the shores of Lake Superior. So far the search has not produced a Heinrich Schliemann or a Vinland to match his Troy. The very number and geographical diversity of the sites proposed raise embarrassing questions about the credibility of each Vinland location. The seemingly endless speculation has apparently been prompted by a rather remarkable bit of superfluous logic: the surmise that a positive geographical identification of Vinland would somehow verify the Norse pre-Columbian discovery of America.

The incongruous and elastic nature of the saga texts has provided the basis for a variety of interpretations concerning the location of Vinland. For example, qualitative scaleless topographical descriptions of Vinland have been provided with subjective linear and areal scales. Thus, according to one author, the river into which Leifr sailed after his landfall in Vinland is the St. Lawrence River, and the lake where he anchored his ship and along the shore of which he built dwellings is Lake Ontario. Another author, in contrast, holds that the river is the short tidal stream called the Brook, which leads to Leifrsbuðir on Tickle Cove Pond, a basin of a few square miles in southeastern Newfoundland. Similar problems of scale, of the identification of flora and fauna, and of the unraveling of the meaning of the solar observation taken by Leifr face each Vinland locator. Contrary to popular and prevailing opinion, the sagas did not function as itineraries or sailing directions to Vinland. To assume such a function is anachronistic. Nor were the sagas designed as authorities with which to find Vinland. Nor does the famous VINLAND MAP help to locate the Vinland of the *Saga of the Greenlanders*, for it has proved to be a twentieth-century invention. Although the conceptualization of Vinland, including its dimensions, has changed in the last 400 years as a result of conjectures and speculative writing, we are as far from the location of the Vinland of the sagas as was Arngrímur.

Quite contrary to optimistic but premature conclusions, so far archaeology has not corroborated a single event relating to the Norse Vinland voyages lasting from about 1001 to 1014. And that includes the much-publicized L'Anse-aux-Meadows site in Newfoundland, which some contend is Leifr's Vinland. The presence of artifacts in Newfoundland similar in style to artifacts unearthed in the Shetlands, Iceland, Greenland, and other areas of Norse occupation does, on the other hand, document the fact of Norse voyages to the eastern seaboard of America. But which of the voyages were responsible for the artifacts found at the L'Anse-aux-Meadows site, whether the ones recorded in the sagas or others that went unrecorded, is a matter of contention.

BIBLIOGRAPHY: A. W. Brøgger, *Vinlandsferdene*, Oslo, 1937; Johannes Brøndsted, "Problemet om Nordboer i Amerika før Columbus," *Aarbøger for Nordisk Oldkyndighed*, 1950 (1951), pp. 1–152; Anne Stine Ingstad, "The Norse Settlement at L'Anse aux Meadows, Newfoundland," *Acta Archaeologica*, vol. 41, 1971, pp. 111–154; Helge Ingstad, *Vesterveg til Vinland*, Oslo, 1965; *Íslendingabók*. ed. by Finnur Jónsson, Copenhagen, 1930; Gwyn Jones, *The Norse Atlantic Saga, Being the Norse Voyages of Discovery and Settlement of Iceland, Greenland, and Vinland*, London, 1964; Matti Enn Kaups, "Shifting Vinland: Tradition and Myth," *Terrae Incognitae*, vol. II, 1970, pp. 29–60; id., "Shifting Vinland: Tradition and Myth; A Rejoinder," *Terrae Incognitae*, vol. III, 1971, pp. 97–105; id., "Some Observations on Vinland," *Annals of the Association of American Geographers*, vol. LX, no. 3, 1970, pp. 603–608; *Landnámabók*, ed. by Finnur Jónsson, Copenhagen, 1900; Magnus Magnusson and Hermann Pálsson, *The Vinland Sagas*, Harmondsworth, England, 1965; Almar Naess, *Hvor lå Vinland?*, Oslo, 1954; Arthur Middleton Reeves, *The Finding of Wineland the Good: The History of the Icelandic Discovery of America*, London, 1895; V. Tanner, *De gamla Nordbornas Helluland, Markland och Vinland: Ett försök att lokalisera Vinlands-resornas huvudetapper i de isländska sagorna* (Helsingin Yliopiston Maantieteellisen Laitoksen Julkaisuja, no. 5), Åbo, Finland, 1941; Erik Wahlgren, "Fact and Fancy in the Vinland Sagas," in Edgar C. Polomé (ed.), *Old Norse Literature and Mythology*, Austin, Tex., and London, 1969.

Matti Enn Kaups

Vinland Map

Map of the world drawn with pen and ink on parchment and purportedly composed about 1440. It derives its name from the fact that an island labeled VINLAND is located in the northwestern Atlantic west of Greenland. The map is bound with the *Tartar Relation*, a manuscript account of the mission of Friar John of Plano CARPINI to the Mongols in 1245–1247 written by his companion Friar Benedict de Pole, and edited by one Friar C. de Bridia. The map was donated to Yale University in 1965 and brought to the attention of the public on October 11 that year in a volume called *The Vinland Map and the Tartar Relation* by R. A. Skelton, Thomas E. Marston, and George D. Painter.

The map aroused intense interest and controversy from the moment of its appearance because, if authentic, it would be the earliest map to depict any part of the Americas. In 1974, however, Yale University announced that chemical tests had shown that the ink used to draw the map contained anatase, a form of titanium oxide invented in the 1920s. While the university concluded that the map was a forgery, others continued to defend its authenticity.

BIBLIOGRAPHY: *The New York Times*, Jan. 26, 1974, p. 1; Helen Wallis, F. R. Maddison, et al., "The Strange Case of the Vinland Map: A Symposium," *The Geographical Journal*, vol. 140, part 2, June 1974, pp. 183–214.

W

Wallis, Samuel *(1728–1795)* English naval officer and explorer. A native of Cornwall, Wallis received a commission in the British Navy in 1748. During the Seven Years' War he served in North America and in the Channel Fleet. Although he had no experience as an explorer, he was named head of an expedition to search for a southern continent in the Pacific Ocean and sailed from Plymouth on August 21, 1766, on the frigate *Dolphin,* which had recently sailed around the world under the command of John Byron. The *Dolphin's* consort, the *Swallow,* was commanded by Philip CARTERET, a veteran of the Byron Expedition, who resented what he considered the preferential treatment being given to Wallis.

After passing through the Strait of Magellan, the two ships became separated in April 1767. Wallis sailed to the northwest and north, many of his men being afflicted by scurvy. Having turned west, he sighted Pinaki and Nukutavaki and four other islands in the Tuamotu Archipelago, and landings were made to obtain coconuts, scurvy grass, and water. Wallis himself was ill, though not with scurvy, when he sighted his most important discovery, the island of Tahiti, which was named King George the Third's Island, on June 18, 1767. After some early skirmishes between the Englishmen and the natives, friendly relations were established, and the Tahitians supplied the seamen with large quantities of pigs, fowls, and fruit in exchange for nails. What George Robertson, master of the *Dolphin,* called the "old trade" also got

under way, and the seamen were soon stripping the ship of its nails to reward the compliant Tahitian women. Wallis, still ailing after 5 weeks in Tahiti, apparently thought his discovery of sufficient consequence to abandon his search for the southern continent and returned to England, arriving on May 20, 1768. He was later captain of the *Torbay* and of the *Queen,* and from 1782 until his death he was extra commissioner of the Navy.

BIBLIOGRAPHY: Hugh Carrington (ed.), *The Discovery of Tahiti: A Journal of the Second Voyage of H.M.S. "Dolphin" round the World by George Robertson, 1766–1768,* Hakluyt Society, 2d ser., no. 98, London, 1948.

Warre, Henry James *(1819–1898),* **and Vavasour, Mervin** *(ca. 1819–1866)* British soldiers and travelers. In 1845 the Oregon dispute was approaching its climax. The British government, urged by the Hudson's Bay Company to maintain rights established by the Convention of 1818, sent warships to reconnoiter the Pacific Coast and instructed the Governor-General of Canada to send two officers overland to gain accurate knowledge of the country and discover what its "capabilities" might be "in a military point of view." The commander in chief of the British forces in North America selected Lieutenant Warre, his aide-de-camp and nephew, and Lieutenant Vavasour for an ostensible pleasure trip. Warre had already in 1840 visited the "Grand Prairies of the Missouri" on a hunting party. This time sport was to be a cloak for the secret military mission. The officers were to discover whether it would indeed be possible (as Sir George Simpson, governor of the Hudson's Bay Company's territories in North America affirmed) to convey troops to Red River, west of Lake Superior, across the plains, and through the Rocky Mountains to Oregon; whether the company's posts were defensible; and what military positions might be established.

The two men traveled by canoe with Simpson from Lachine, near Montreal, to Fort Garry (modern Winnipeg). There Chief Factor Peter Skene Ogden took charge for the overland journey by horse across the plains and over White Man Pass through the Rockies and by boat down the Columbia from Fort Colvile (Colville) to Fort Vancouver. The 62-day journey (May 5 to August 25) convinced the young officers that it would be quite impossible to move troops with stores and equipment by the route they had taken, while, far from buffalo supplementing rations, not even one was obtained. The "passage of the Rocky Mountains alone would form a sufficient barrier . . . on account of the high, steep and rugged nature of the mountain passes," to say nothing of "the almost impenetrable jungle" on their western side. The trading posts were

"calculated to resist a sudden attack" by Indians but could not "be considered as works of defense against a disciplined force."

The winter passed in visits to the settlements and examination of such strategic positions as Cape Disappointment, as well as Puget Sound and Fort Victoria, Vancouver Island. The return trip, again under company escort, was made by the usual "northern water route," up the Columbia and over the Athabasca Pass, which was still deep in snow, to the Saskatchewan. Going and coming, the officers met the celebrated missionary Father Pierre-Jean de Smet.

Warre published a delightful book of sketches made on the journey. The originals and his journal, now in the Public Archives of Canada, the official reports, and Vavasour's elegant plans of posts and strategic positions are today a useful historical record.

BIBLIOGRAPHY: Joseph Schafer, "Documents Relative to Warre and Vavasour's Military Reconnaissance in Oregon, 1845–6," *The Quarterly of the Oregon Historical Society*, vol. X, March 1909, pp. 1–99; "Secret Mission of Warre and Vavasour," *Washington Historical Quarterly*, vol. III, April 1912, pp. 131–135; Henry J. Warre, *Sketches in North America and the Oregon Territory*, London, 1848.

Irene M. Spry

Oregon City, the American Village, one of many sketches in Henry Warre's record of his "sporting" trip with Mervin Vavasour to northwestern America (1845). The real purpose of the journey was military reconnaissance for the British government. [Library of Congress]

West Indies, Central America, and Mexico

A series of voyages undertaken from Western Europe, and especially Spain, at the end of the fifteenth century and continuing into the sixteenth century brought the Western Hemisphere, the so-called New World, into the political and cultural sphere of Western Europe. These voyages were part of a continuum of interest in parts unknown that had been shown by Western Europeans of many nationalities for several centuries. Exploration and travel had taken place by both land and sea. While the Portuguese had ventured into the Atlantic Ocean before the Spanish became active, the newly unified Spain controlled by Ferdinand of Aragon and Isabella of Castile traditionally has been given credit for the discovery of America.

Christopher Columbus and the Discovery of the New World

The question, probably unanswerable, of who reached the New World first really is not relevant, for there is no doubt that the voyages of Christopher COLUMBUS are what brought the New World into permanent and continuing contact with European civilization. It is perhaps fitting that the Iberian Peninsula, jutting westward from Europe as it does, was the scene of the westward movements by sea that ultimately led to America. For the Iberian peoples, who were formally organized into two meaningful political entities, Portugal and Spain, by the end of the fifteenth century, had had a history more than passingly different from that of the rest of Western Europe. Other Europeans had crusaded abroad, especially in the Middle East, but Iberians had crusaded at home against Muslims whose almost 800-year presence on the Iberian Peninsula was not ended until 1492. A crusading spirit, coupled in Spain with the monarchs' desire for religious purity, underlay an exploring urge, seen first in Portugal and then in Spain, to find places and people unknown.

Portugal's Atlantic Coast and a series of advances in rigging methods and navigational knowledge and instruments made it possible to sail farther with safety and to sail out of sight of land. Portugal's efforts to locate Christians and to find riches led to the discovery and rediscovery of the Atlantic islands—Madeira, the Azores, the Canaries, and the Cape Verde Islands—and to explorations down the west coast of Africa. While Portuguese interests and explorers eventually would work their way around Africa and to the Far East, Spanish activities on the Atlantic took a different tack. The kingdom of Castile claimed the Canary Islands by virtue of a papal grant dating to 1344, but not until the Treaty of Alcaçovas of 1479, which ended a war between Castile and Portugal, was the Castilian title firm, and soon thereafter Castile began the settlement of this island group, fortunately well located for sailing westward across the Atlantic Ocean.

When Christopher Columbus proposed to the Portuguese that they support him in a voyage aimed at reaching Asia by sailing west, they refused. They had invested much in time, effort, funds, and men in the route around Africa and were convinced, quite correctly, that Columbus's estimates of distances were much too low. Columbus eventually turned to Spain, but it would be years before Isabella of Castile could be persuaded to support the project.

First voyage Columbus's first expedition was outfitted at the little port of Palos. Two relatively small vessels, the *Pinta* and the *Niña*, were joined by the larger *Santa María*, which served as the flagship. Columbus recruited about ninety men and boys, mostly local, for the voyage. Among his officers were the Pinzón brothers, veterans of earlier Atlantic voyages. With all preparations made, the party set sail on August 3, 1492, and, after a stop in the Canary Islands, reached land on October 12, 1492, in what is now known as the Bahama Islands. Columbus named the island he landed on first San Salvador; today it is known as Watling Island.

Christopher Columbus and some men went ashore, gave thanks for a safe voyage, claimed the land for Isabella of Castile, and parleyed with the natives. These people, relatively unsophisticated Arawaks, heard about Columbus's Queen and his faith and were asked for directions to the mainland of Asia and the Great Khan. The expedition, with some Arawak Indians serving as guides, sailed southward through the

Christopher Columbus's flagship, the Santa María. Although the facts as to who first came to American shores are still widely disputed, there is no doubt that it was Columbus's voyage that aroused serious interest in the Western Hemisphere.

The Niña, Pinta, *and* Santa María *set sail for the New World. Spain probably owed its exploring fervor to its crusading desire to spread the word of God. [Library of Congress]*

Bahamas and reached the north shore of Cuba late in October. As the Europeans coasted along Cuba, they were welcomed by the Indians and told of a great city inland. But it proved to be just another Indian village. There was some trading: the Indians had some alluvial gold. But friendly natives, open to conversion to Catholicism, nevertheless were not the Asians Columbus had hoped to find.

Martín Alonso Pinzón had taken the *Pinta* and gone off exploring on his own. Columbus had not found what he was looking for while moving westward along the north shore of Cuba; so he reversed his direction, passed the eastern end of Cuba, traversed

French map of the West Indies (1686). [Library of Congress]

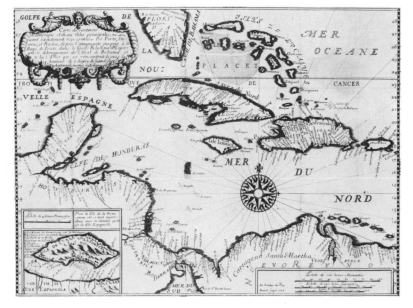

the Windward Passage, and, still sailing to the east, discovered another large island, which he named Española and which now is known as Hispaniola. There, on Christmas Eve, 1492, the *Santa María* ran aground and had to be abandoned. Columbus and his men then set up a little settlement named, appropriately enough, La Navidad.

The local Indians had helped to land the crew of the *Santa María* and to unload its stores. These Arawaks made the Europeans welcome and gave them shelter. They were reported to be loyal and without greed and were described as handsome men and women, but the Arawaks of Hispaniola were the first Indian group known to pay the price for contact with Europeans. They traded away their gold for trinkets, permitted Columbus to take some of them back to Europe with him, and agreed to "look after" those men Columbus had to leave behind. More than forty men from the *Santa María,* who could not be crowded aboard the *Niña,* were to remain at La Navidad. They had orders to search for gold and to explore the land. They were instructed to treat the Indians well and not to abuse the Indian women.

Christopher Columbus promised those of his men left at La Navidad that he would return to them and then set sail again, still going to the east, along the north shore of Hispaniola. Near present Samaná he met Martín Alonso Pinzón and the *Pinta.* The two ships joined in sailing to the north, and then east, and so returned to Europe. Stormy weather delayed Columbus, who finally landed in Portugal, but he successfully brought his expedition back to Europe, even though Pinzón reached Spain first. Differences between the Portuguese and Spanish monarchs over a Line of Demarcation and rights to explore unknown areas were not of primary concern to Columbus. He believed that he had been near the coast of Asia; he had returned to Europe with both gold and natives; and as soon as he could sail again, he would find the Great Khan.

Second voyage The Spanish crown, to secure its claim and to continue the explorations for a route to Asia, quickly made available to Columbus funds for another expedition. The fleet, consisting of seventeen vessels, was ready to leave in less than 6 months. It sailed from Cádiz on September 25, 1493, with about 1500 men aboard, and stopped in the Canary Islands. This time the fleet took a more southerly route and made landfall on November 3, 1493, at an island named Dominica, a high, volcanic island inhabited by Caribs who were anything but the guileless and unwarlike savages that Columbus had reported the Arawaks to be. The fleet sailed north through the Lesser Antilles, sighting islands, landing on some, and naming all. After sailing through the Virgin Islands, along the southern coast of Puerto Rico and through the Mona Passage, Columbus traveled along the north coast of Hispaniola until the expedition reached the site of La Navidad. The local chief was still friendly and reported that the men Columbus had left behind had become greedy (over gold and women) and eventually had exhausted the patience of the Indians, who had killed all the Europeans. Columbus, recognizing that the Europeans no longer really were welcome at La Navidad, moved the entire expedition to the east, where a new site for settlement was selected.

A town, named Isabela after the Queen of Spain, was established on a site that proved to have been poorly chosen. The settlement never thrived, for the shore was unprotected from the open ocean, and the Europeans quickly began to suffer from tropical diseases. Although the expedition had been very well equipped for colonization, the Spanish settlers were unwilling to do the work necessary to make the colony a functional one. What work was done, was done by the local Indians; the Spanish searched for gold on Hispaniola, while Columbus went back to sea to continue his explorations.

Isabela was a proper settlement and was supposed to be a permanent one. It was laid out with streets in a rectangular pattern, and local officials were appointed: *regidores* (town councilors) and *alcaldes* (magistrates). While Christopher Columbus explored (on this trip he discovered Jamaica and sailed along the south shore of Cuba), government for the little town of Isabela was left to his younger brother Diego. By the time Christoper Columbus returned to Isabela in September 1494, he found that the Spanish crown had sent his brother Bartholomew to the New World with three caravels, provisions for the colony, and a title. But newly granted titles of nobility did not make the Columbus brothers successful administrators: they were not very good at the task of governing and were disliked by the colonists because as Italians they were considered foreigners. Columbus early had sent an expeditionary force into the interior of Hispaniola. It was led by Alonso de OJEDA, who forced the Indians to search for gold. The unwillingness of the Spanish colonists to work meant that the Indians were subjected to forced labor. Indian women still were being seized by rapacious Spaniards. The patience and good-

The volcanic island of Dominica, Columbus's landfall on his second voyage. Here he found the native Caribs far less friendly than the Indians he had encountered on his first trip. [Library of Congress]

will of the Indians were rapidly exhausted, and there were Indian revolts. The Spanish crushed these; the remaining Indians fled from the seacoast into the mountainous interior of the island. And European diseases already had begun to take an appalling toll of Indian lives.

Ships and men continued to arrive from Spain; there was regular traffic in both directions across the Atlantic Ocean. But the ships from Spain had to bring provisions, for the colonists still would not work, and foodstuffs remained in short supply on Hispaniola. Christopher Columbus's lack of success (he had not found the mainland of Asia or the Great Khan, nor had he found great riches) helped persuade him to return to Spain in 1496. Also, Spanish malcontents who had gone back to the Old World had registered strong complaints about Columbus with the Spanish government. Before he sailed back to Europe, Colum-

bus left instructions with his brother Bartholomew, who was to be in charge of the colony, to move the settlement from the unprotected and unhealthy site at Isabela across Hispaniola to the south shore. There the colonists found an excellent site and established Santo Domingo, which became the capital of the Spanish Indies for half a century and remains the oldest site of continuous European settlement in the New World.

Third voyage In spite of problems in the New World, complaints by disgruntled colonists who had returned to Spain, and death and disease on Hispaniola for both Indians and Europeans, the Spanish crown retained enough faith in Columbus to authorize a third voyage, which set sail in 1498. Some ships, commanded by subsidiary captains, made for Dominica and nearby Deseada and from there to Hispaniola and Santo Domingo. Columbus himself sailed farther

Santo Domingo, former Spanish colony on the island of Hispaniola. The name is also given to the Dominican Republic, and in early days it applied as well to Haiti. [Library of Congress]

to the south and discovered Trinidad, the mainland of South America, and the mouths of the Orinoco River. The expedition touched the Venezuelan coast, traded with the natives for pearls, then sailed on, sighting and naming Margarita Island, and finally reached the settlement at Santo Domingo.

A royal official, Juan de Aguado, had reached Hispaniola to investigate conditions there before Columbus had returned to Spain in 1496. Upon Columbus's return to Santo Domingo in 1498, he found the colony in rebellion against his brother Bartholomew. The rebels were led by Francisco Roldán and were too strong for Columbus and his supporters. They finally were bought off by a substantial change in the ways the Indians were to be controlled. Earlier Columbus had insisted that the Indians, like other subjects of Isabella of Castile, were to pay a quarterly tribute, preferably in gold, as a tax. The supply of alluvial gold soon was exhausted; the Indians died rapidly when forced to work in mines. Some engineers from Spain had searched for and found likely spots to mine for gold. Columbus then introduced the *repartimiento* system, earlier used in the Canary Islands, whereby Indians were granted to Spanish settlers as laborers on lands distributed by Columbus to Roldán and his followers. The system, based on the Spanish mainland concept of *encomienda*, which could be traced back to the reconquest of Spain from the Muslims, would ultimately come to be used throughout the Spanish New World but would prove to be only a temporary solution to the labor problem on Hispaniola.

Christopher Columbus clearly was not a successful administrator. Ferdinand and Isabella finally realized this and in 1499 appointed Francisco de Bobadilla to supersede Columbus in the government of Hispaniola and to investigate the many complaints against Columbus and his brothers. Bobadilla reached Santo Domingo in August 1500, was met by evidence of still another rebellion against the Columbus brothers, and finally arrested them. They were returned to Spain in irons despite the ship's captain's willingness to remove them from Admiral Columbus. Although, Christopher Columbus would never again be permitted to govern in the Indies, he was allowed to make still another voyage (his fourth) to the New World a few years later. Francisco de Bobadilla was not a particularly successful administrator, but he brought some order to Santo Domingo and gathered much gold. The gold and Bobadilla alike were lost at sea in a hurricane en route to Spain in 1502.

Exploration of Central America

For some years Ferdinand and Isabella had been dissatisfied with their contractual arrangements with Columbus. Particularly galling to the Spanish crown were Columbus's exclusive rights in the lands he had discovered and his right to share in all the profits. As early as 1495, when rumors reached Spain that Columbus was dead, the crown had granted permission to sail west to other would-be explorers, permission that had to be with-

Columbus and his brother Bartholomew are imprisoned. Columbus was a poor administrator, and his governorship of the Indies was characterized by revolts and Indian uprisings. [Library of Congress]

drawn when Columbus protested. Nevertheless, the crown of Castile recognized the success of Columbus's third voyage when the pearls he had gotten by trade with the Indians were presented at court. Licenses soon were granted to seasoned sailors and explorers to go where Columbus had been and to find riches. Although expeditions were authorized as early as 1499, the one led by Rodrigo de Bastidas and Juan de la Cosa was the first to reach Central America. They had been granted a license in 1500 but did not sail until 1501, when their expedition apparently followed Columbus's track toward Trinidad and then coasted west and south along the mainland of South America, called Tierra Firme by the Spanish, and finally reached the coast of Panama in the region of Darién. At various points they traded with the Indians for gold and for brazilwood. They sailed along the coast of Panama and then to Jamaica and Santo Domingo, finally abandoning their ships because of storms. There were difficulties with the Governor in Santo Domingo, and Bastidas and La Cosa returned to Spain. La Cosa was given the right to govern in Urabá on the northwestern coast of South America, where, it was assumed, more gold could be gotten from the Indians.

Columbus's fourth voyage

Columbus left Spain on his fourth voyage in May 1502 and after a rapid crossing reached the island of Martinique. He then sailed for Santo Domingo, where the Governor denied him the right to land and ignored his warnings of a hurricane. Columbus had his own ships avoid the worst of the storm and then sailed westward. The first land sighted was Bonacca (Guanaja), one of the Islas de la Bahía (Bay Islands) off the coast of Honduras. There Columbus and his men found a very large Indian canoe whose occupants had gone to sea to trade. They had come from the nearly mainland and were going to the Yucatán area. Columbus detained its skipper to be his guide and crossed to the mainland, reaching Cabo de Honduras and anchoring off what would become the site of Trujillo. The decision to search for a strait or passage through the land meant a decision to sail to the east. Then it took 28 days of very hard sailing until Cabo Gracias a Dios, where the land turned to the south, was reached. As the party sailed down the coast of Nicaragua, they missed the mouth of the San Juan River, which because it empties from Lake Nicaragua could have brought the Spanish explorers very close to the Pacific Ocean. Finally, late in September 1502, they anchored off what is now Limón, Costa Rica, and traded with the Indians, who offered cloth, an alloy of gold and copper *(guanín)* worked into ornaments, and young girls. An expedition sent inland reported an abundance of game. Early in October the party sailed on, reaching the Chiriquí area of Panama. While the passage to what the Spanish thought was the Indian Ocean was not found, the Indians here willingly traded for their gold disks and other ornaments. Columbus learned that he was on an isthmus, and so sailed on, still searching for the elusive strait. On November 2, 1502, the Spaniards stopped in a natural harbor that they named Puerto Bello (Portobelo), got provisions and cotton from the Indians, and within a week sailed on. Bad weather forced them to put in at the harbor that later was called Nombre de Dios. Although they remained there almost 2 weeks, Columbus again missed learning of the short land passage to the Pacific Ocean.

The expedition sailed on, landing near what now is Escribanos, where Indians who were forced to trade by Columbus's crew later attacked the Spaniards and were shot. Faced with an inhospitable climate and contrary winds, the party returned to the Veraguas area, stopping at a place Columbus named Santa María de Belén, where the expedition was to remain for 3½ months. The region has frequent and heavy rainstorms; the coastal plain is only a few hundred yards wide; behind it is a rugged rain forest. The Europeans soon located a large Indian settlement on the Veragua River which was led by a chief *(cacique)* known as the Quibián. There was an exchange of visits, and the Spaniards quickly began to trade trinkets for gold. But as bad weather continued to prevent Columbus's departure, the Indians soon began to act suspiciously. Columbus finally had the Quibián kidnapped, but he escaped, and the Indians soon attacked the small Spanish trading post, or fort, with bows and arrows and spears. The Indians, though abused, had not attacked until it appeared that the Spaniards planned to remain indefinitely and after their chief had been kidnapped. Columbus finally realized that the Indians had become implacable foes (he remembered the fate of the men he had left at La Navidad) and ordered the evacuation of the garrison and abandoned one of his four ships. The site was abandoned; it has never been settled again.

The three remaining ships set sail for Santo Domingo. Columbus knew that he was west of Santo Domingo and had to sail eastward along the coast until he was south of Hispaniola. The ships were in poor shape; one was abandoned at Puerto Bello. They finally reached Cabo Tiburón, the current boundary between Panama and Colombia, where Columbus's pilots and captains persuaded him to sail north. On May 1, 1503, they began to sail north but were pushed westward by the current and, after passing Little Cayman Island, reached the southern shore of Cuba. Columbus had been there before. While the party again sailed to the east, the condition of the remaining two ships deteriorated so rapidly that Columbus put into St. Ann's Bay, Jamaica, on June 25, 1503. There he and his men were marooned for just over a year. They tried to avoid contacts with the natives and sent men to Hispaniola by small boat. Finally they were taken by ship to Santo Domingo and then went back to Spain. This, Columbus's last voyage, had been most disappointing. He had not followed the Indian canoe to the Yucatán Peninsula, he had not crossed Central America to the Pacific Ocean, and the gold in the Veraguas area could not be exploited by the Spaniards.

Other early expeditions The Spanish crown, having recognized the value of this part of the Indies, soon authorized additional expeditions to it. Juan de la Cosa, with the title of chief constable of Urabá, helped persuade Isabella to authorize the enslavement of Indians there. He reported them to be rebellious and to be cannibals. Isabella now found this reasoning acceptable, and the royal decree *(cédula)* was issued on October 30, 1503. The riches in this region attracted several men who, lacking the ability to work together, finally mounted separate expeditions to go to Urabá and the Pearl Coast near Margarita Island off Venezuela. Cristóbal Guerra sailed in the late spring of 1504, reached the Pearl Coast, bartered with the natives, and then sailed toward Urabá. Indians were persuaded to part with gold, efforts were made to enslave some, and Guerra was killed by Indian opponents.

Juan de la Cosa's expedition sailed late in September 1504, stopped at Gran Canaria, and reached the New World at Margarita. It gathered some pearls and much brazilwood and then sailed westward along the coast. The remnants of the Guerra Expedition, now led by Luis Guerra, were met. Although they jointly attacked Indians and captured some 600, the survivors of Guerra's party were to return to Spain while La Cosa went on to Urabá. Once there, the expedition moved inland looking for gold; the Indians now fled from the Spanish, who found a chest full of drums and masks made of gold. La Cosa and his men crossed to the other side of the Gulf of Urabá, to the region known as Darién, and got more gold. The remnants of the Guerra party, who were taking La Cosa's slaves and brazilwood back to Spain, now appealed for assistance. One of their ships had hit a reef and sunk; the other was not seaworthy, for its hull had been eaten by the *teredos* (shipworms). The rescue was carried out, but La Cosa's ships also were unsafe, so the approximately 200 survivors of both expeditions spent a year on the Urabá beach. More than half of them died of disease. Finally, using the three small boats they still had, they set sail for Caribbean islands, abandoning almost everything except the gold. One boat reached Cuba; the other two landed at Jamaica. After further difficulties, the almost 60 survivors were reunited in Santo Domingo and soon returned to Spain. Juan de la Cosa declared 61 pounds (27.7 kilograms) of gold when he reached Seville; he probably had more. The expedition had been a financial success even though most of the participants died by drowning, disease, or starvation or at the hands of the Indians.

There were other, minor voyages to the area, about which little is known and which seem to have been of no apparent significance. Alonso de Ojeda again sailed to the region during 1505 and returned with some pearls. In 1508 and 1509 Vicente Yáñez PINZÓN and Juan Díaz de SOLÍS sailed to Honduras and Guatemala to try to locate the Line of Demarcation and to find the passage through the Isthmus of Panama. While they failed, the expedition apparently touched the Yucatán Peninsula. These expeditions to the mainland often stopped at Santo Domingo before returning to Spain. There they could unload and sell as slaves the Indians they had captured on the mainland. In Santo Domingo these Indians were used in the mines in place of the island's Indians, most of whom already were dead. In the rush to gain the riches being found on the Central American mainland, the government in Spain did not lose sight of the many islands in the Caribbean Sea discovered by Columbus and others and claimed for Castile. By the time that Columbus had completed his fourth voyage, virtually all the Caribbean islands except Barbados had been discovered. Santo Domingo had become a functioning colony after years of troubles, and it also became the base from which expeditions set out to conquer other islands. Juan de Esquivel first colonized Jamaica for Spain in 1509, moving outward from a site near St. Ann's Bay. The conquest of Cuba began in 1511 and was led by Diego Velásquez. It began on the eastern end of the island, where Santiago de Cuba was founded, but the conquerers killed many Indians, probably unnecessarily, in the process.

Spanish efforts to conquer Puerto Rico had begun as early as 1500, although a serious attempt was not made until 1508, when Juan PONCE DE LEÓN was given rights to the island. While only partially successful in pacifying the island by 1512, Ponce de León nevertheless left Puerto Rico on a voyage of exploration that reached Florida and may have touched the Yucatán Peninsula. Puerto Rico remained less than fully conquered for much of the sixteenth century. The island was at a meeting point of Arawak and Carib Indian cultures; the Caribs, unlike the Arawaks, tended to greet the Spanish with violence. Although Spain later would control Trinidad, off the coast of Venezuela, the Spanish made no serious ef-

forts to conquer or colonize the islands of the Lesser Antilles. Not only were they inhabited by the ferocious Caribs, but they possessed nothing that the Spanish desired. The lure of riches on the mainland in Central America, and later in Mexico, diverted the Spanish from the Lesser Antilles.

In 1508, in spite of the protests of Diego Columbus, the Spanish crown (King Ferdinand) granted two licenses to settle on the mainland. Alonso de Ojeda was granted Nueva Andalucía, which ran eastward from the Gulf of Darién in Panama, while Diego de Nicuesa was authorized to settle Castilla de Oro, which ran from Darién west and north as far as Cabo Gracias a Dios. The expeditions, with more than 1000 men, sailed at the end of 1509. Climate, weather, flora, fauna, and Indians all combined to ravage both expeditions and settlements. Ojeda himself withdrew to Santo Domingo and died about 1515. His partner, Martín Fernández de Enciso, then led a relief expedition that moved the survivors to a site in Darién that actually was part of Nicuesa's Castilla de Oro. The members of the Nicuesa Expedition had settled at Nombre de Dios, then split into factions and fought among themselves. These survivors finally turned up at Darién; Nicuesa had been put to sea in a small boat. Enciso found himself unable to control this combined group, which finally illegally removed him from power and sent him off to Spain.

Balboa and Pedrarias Vasco Núñez de BALBOA, who had sailed to the New World in 1501 as part of the Bastidas Expedition and then settled in Santo Domingo, apparently fled from his creditors by stowing away on the relief expedition to Darién. Balboa took control and brought order to the little colony, using terror and force as well as conciliation and diplomacy to gain ascendancy over the local Indians and to get much food and gold from them. The Spaniards were forced to build homes and plant crops to survive. In September 1513 Balboa discovered the South Sea, later renamed the Pacific Ocean, and was told of pearl islands by the local Indians. He soon returned across the isthmus to Darién, still accompanied by and friendly with the Indians and with gold and pearls they had given him. He notified King Ferdinand of his discovery and sent treasure to Spain.

In Spain exaggerated tales of the wealth of the Darién region circulated widely. The government, through Enciso, had learned of the disastrous failure of both Ojeda and Nicuesa and of Balboa's usurpation in Darién. The Spanish crown was determined to win effective control over this part of the Indies. A major expedition sailed in April 1514. It had nineteen ships and some 2000 men and was commanded by Pedro Arias de ÁVILA, who generally is known as Pedrarias. Among those who sailed with Pedrarias were Diego de ALMAGRO, Sebastián de BENALCÁZAR, Hernando de Luque, and Hernando de SOTO. Francisco PIZARRO already was in Darién. All would have major roles in the Spanish conquest of the New World. Once in Darién, Pedrarias took firm control. There was discord, the efforts to raise food soon broke down, the Indians were alienated, and there was squabbling with Balboa. Finally, Pedrarias accused Balboa of treason and had him tried, convicted, and beheaded in 1519.

Pedrarias continued to govern in Panama. He ignored orders from Spain for humane treatment of the Indians, but he got gold from them and enslaved them. Hot and humid Darién was abandoned in 1524; the capital had been moved to Panama City, which had been set up in 1519 on the Pacific side of the isthmus. From this base in Panama, with outposts on both the Caribbean and Pacific coasts, further expeditions were dispatched west and north into Central America.

With a royal commission, Gil González de Ávila reached Panama in 1519 to continue the explorations begun by Balboa. Disagreements with Pedrarias delayed him until 1522, when he led an expedition of about 100 men along the Pacific Coast from Panama to the Nicaraguan lakes. He was accompanied by a naval expedition commanded by Andrés Niño. The Costa Rican region was a disappointment, but semicivilized Indians lived along the shores of Lake Nicaragua. There was trade, but no settlement was made, and in spite of claims of having baptized some 30,000 Indians, González de Ávila withdrew because of Indian hostility. He returned to Panama with some gold, which aroused further interest in Nicaragua. Rivalry with Pedrarias finally persuaded González de Ávila to withdraw to Santo Domingo with his treasure. Then Pedrarias led an expedition west and north, but was resisted by the Indians in the Chiriquí region of Panama. In 1524 he dispatched an expedition by sea to Nicaragua. Led by Francisco Hernández de Córdoba, it landed at the Gulf of Nicoya and moved inland, founding the towns of Granada, on Lake Nicaragua, and León, on Lake Managua.

Conflicting claims Efforts to settle Central America, encouraged by the Spanish government, were complicated by conflicting claims. González de Ávila returned from Hispaniola and defeated some of Hernández de Córdoba's forces. Hernández de Córdoba then rebelled against Pedrarias, who came north to Nicaragua with an army. After a year of fighting, Hernández de Córdoba surrendered to Pedrarias, who had him executed and remained in León as governor of Nicaragua. But attempts to conquer and settle Central America were not limited to expeditions from Panama. Survivors of a shipwreck off Jamaica had reached the Yucatán Peninsula in 1511. Later expeditions touched the Yucatán area and ultimately opened the way for the conquest of Mexico. Finally, Spaniards from Mexico came to be serious competitors for control in Central America. First, Cristóbal de Olid sailed to the Gulf of Honduras and established the town called El Triunfo de la Cruz. He soon captured González de Ávila and declared his own independence from Hernán CORTÉS in Mexico. Then he captured Francisco de las Casas and the troops sent by Cortés by land from Mexico against him. González de Ávila and

Las Casas turned the tables on their captor and finally had Cristóbal de Olid executed. Hernán Cortés and an army then appeared on the scene after trekking from Mexico to Honduras. González de Ávila was permitted to return to Spain; Las Casas was promoted and established the port of Trujillo. Cortés, having consolidated his control over northern Central America after a journey that really had been unnecessary, returned to Mexico by sea.

Incursions from Mexico into Central America reached even farther south. In December 1523, Cortés's chief lieutenant, Pedro de ALVARADO, had led a land expedition to Guatemala. Smallpox preceded the army, so resistance by the Indians was minimal. But from the Isthmus of Tehuantepec through Chiapas Alvarado and his men had to fight. They reached Guatemala during a war between two major Indian groups, the Cakchiquel and the Quiché. The Spanish became allies of the Cakchiquel, defeated the Quiché in April 1524, and took control of Guatemala. Several new settlements, including a site for a capital, were made in Guatemala, although the Indians in the area already lived in towns and villages. The existing Indian settlements, many of which were remnants of a once-great Mayan civilization, soon were subjected to Hispanicization. Alvarado and his men spent 2 years conquering and pacifying the rest of Guatemala and El Salvador. Soon after they moved on, the Cakchiquel rebelled, but they finally were defeated and reduced to a state of vassalage. Throughout Central America, wherever there were significant Indian populations, the arrival of the Spanish brought the defeat of the local Indian leadership and exploitation of the Indian masses, followed by Indian uprisings that were suppressed by force. After European diseases had thinned the ranks of the Indians, their social, economic, political, religious, and ideological subjugation took place. The Indians then were forced to accept the Spanish Catholic culture—a process that took most of the sixteenth century and still continues.

Indian opposition in Costa Rica kept the area from Spanish control for many years. In 1561 Juan de Cavallón led a successful colonization party into the Gulf of Nicoya area. He was followed by Juan Vásquez de Coronado, who became governor of Nicaragua and Costa Rica and finally firmly established Spanish authority in that region. Thus the Spanish generally gained control of the highlands in Central America, at a great cost in lives. But along the coasts, especially in the Mosquito region, Indians maintained their independence from Spanish rule. Central America had become Spanish, and the instrumentalities and organs of government and administration quickly followed the successes of the conquistadores.

Conquest of Mexico While the Spanish colonized and settled West Indian Islands and searched for wealth there and in Central America, the first contacts with the area that became known as Mexico were the result of shipwreck. A Spanish vessel going from Darién to Hispaniola sank off Jamaica in 1511, and several survivors reached the Yucatán Peninsula. All but two died or were killed by the local Mayan Indians. Gonzalo Guerrero and Gerónimo de Aguilar still were there when Spanish expeditions began to reach Yucatán in force and with regularity. Furthermore, Juan Ponce de León, while returning from Florida in June 1513, may also have landed on the Yucatán Peninsula.

Early expeditions In 1517 the governor of Cuba, Diego Velásquez, dispatched Francisco Fernández de Córdoba on an expedition to capture and enslave Indians. Perhaps blown farther west than he expected to be, perhaps acting on rumors about a rich land to the west, Fernández de Córdoba reached the shores of the Yucatán Peninsula. The architectural efforts of the Mayas were highly visible; the natives were well dressed and well armed. And they fought well, killing about half of the Spanish invaders and wounding the others. The expedition returned to Cuba, where Fernández de Córdoba died of his wounds. The eyewitness reports of wealth in Yucatán and the few gold trinkets brought back excited the Spanish, as did the tales told by two Indians who had been brought to Cuba to be trained as interpreters. Diego Velásquez quickly mounted another expedition to the west, sending some 200 men under the command of his nephew, Juan de Grijalva. They landed first at the island of Cozumel, and then went to the mainland, going around the Yucatán Peninsula and along the coast of Tabasco to the Gulf Coast of Mexico. Grijalva was not authorized to colonize and was quite cautious. When he had collected ample evidence of the wealth in the region, he dispatched a ship to Cuba with the gold and asked for instructions. Certainly he had met Indians who reported the contacts to the Aztec government in Tenochtitlán. Juan de Grijalva returned to Cuba before there was a response to his request for further instructions.

Diego Velásquez wasted no time. The news from Grijalva led to the organization of a major expedition. Velásquez got permission to trade with the mainland from the government in Santo Domingo and wrote to Spain to get authority to colonize the area. The man he placed in charge of the operation was Hernán Cortés, who had moved to Cuba with Velásquez in 1511. Cortés had been in trouble with the authorities, including Velásquez, on several occasions, but in 1518 he was in the Governor's good graces and at Santiago de Cuba actively and rapidly prepared supplies and ships and recruited men. After Grijalva returned and before the expedition was ready to sail, there was another disagreement between Velásquez and Cortés. In November 1518, Cortés ordered the ships to sea before Velásquez could relieve him of the expedition's command. As supplies and men still were needed for this "stolen" expedition, the ships stopped at several small Cuban ports, including Havana, before moving on to Yucatán in February 1519.

Cortés Expedition of 1519 Although the Cortés Expedition was one of the largest assembled in the New World, it was, nevertheless, pitifully small when compared with the size and might that was Aztec Mexico. The eleven ships carried about 700 men, perhaps sixteen horses, some cannon and guns, and the ever-present Spanish war dogs. Cuba, governed by Velásquez, could not be relied upon for additional supplies; nor could the Spanish authorities be expected to approve. The expedition crossed to Cozumel Island and then moved on to the coast of the Yucatán Peninsula. The physical remnants of Mayan civilization were seen, while the resident Maya Indians resisted Spanish attempts to conquer them. But Cortés was lucky. After 8 years among the Indians, Gerónimo de Aguilar rejoined the Spanish world and served as an interpreter as the fleet moved on. (Gonzalo Guerrero remained among the Indians.) In the region of Tabasco the Indians responded to a Spanish request to land for food and water by shooting arrows at the visitors. A Spanish party landed and fought the Indians, but victory was not assured until the cavalry joined the battle. The Indians fled, for they never had seen horses, much less horses with men upon their backs. Cortés soon received a delegation of *caciques* (chiefs) and did his best to impress them with the superiority of the new fair-skinned arrivals. The *caciques* were awed and presented food, gold, and young girls to Cortés and his men. Among these was an Aztec woman of high rank, soon baptized and known as Doña Marina. She knew both Nahuatl, the language of the Aztecs, and Maya, while Aguilar knew both Maya and Spanish. Now Cortés, through his interpreters, could converse with the Aztecs.

Montezuma (Moctezuma) II, in Tenochtitlán, undoubtedly received reports of these strangers on his shores, just as Cortés inquired of all Indians he met, especially *caciques*, about the great inland empire. The expedition finally reached the region near Veracruz and landed in the harbor of San Juan de Ulúa. From here the march into and conquest of central Mexico, the heart of the Aztec empire, would begin. Again Cortés impressed the local Indians with mounted men, firearms, and knowledge of local customs based upon information given him by Marina. Emissaries from Montezuma soon appeared. The Aztec ruler and his advisers did not know whether the foreign invaders at their shores were men or whether the great god Quetzalcoatl had returned and they were his messengers. Marina certainly had informed the Spaniards of the legends concerning the possible return of the god-king Quetzalcoatl, and it was the proper time in the calendar cycle for his return. Although the first envoys were convinced that Cortés and the Spaniards were human, Montezuma was less sure. He dispatched other emissaries to persuade these beings to leave and sent clothing and other rich gifts, including a huge golden disk. Needless to say, neither Cortés nor his men were likely to leave when the evidence clearly showed that there was great wealth inland.

Cortés used the 4 months spent near the current

city of Veracruz to establish a base and to cultivate relationships with the coastal peoples. From a delegation of Totonacs from the nearby town of Cempoala, Cortés learned of the general dissatisfaction of the tribes under Aztec domination. Exactions in the form of taxes and other levies were resented. When the Spanish were able to demonstrate their superiority over Indian methods of fighting, the Totonacs were recruited as allies. In this way Cortés and his followers established a pattern that would serve them well throughout the conquest of Mexico. Indian tribes in vassalage to the Aztecs could be persuaded to join the Spanish and to fight for the Spanish. In this way the Indians would be in the forefront of the battles, would suffer most of the casualties, and would make it possible for a small number of Spaniards to conquer the vast Aztec empire in Mexico.

Before beginning the march inland Cortés took several steps to secure his position. He had no legal authority to conquer Mexico; he had stolen the expedition from Diego Velásquez. Some of Cortés's followers formally organized a municipality, called La

Villa Rica de la Vera Cruz. The men then voted full authority to the city until the Spanish crown gave its approval, and the new city government chose Cortés to lead it. In this way Cortés hoped to legalize his position. A ship was dispatched to Spain recounting all this and the supposed evil actions of Velásquez and was accompanied by almost all the gold and other gifts the Spaniards had received. In spite of orders to the contrary the ship stopped in Cuba, and one sailor got the news to Diego Velásquez. Before Cortés could abandon the coast, moreover, he had to face opposition within the ranks of his own men. Some favored Velásquez, or wished to return to Cuba, or feared the unknown interior of Mexico. So the ships were destroyed—scuttled and dismantled. Cortés's men had no escape, and he correctly assumed that sooner or later ships would arrive from Cuba or from Spain.

A small garrison was left at Veracruz to continue building the town, while Cortés and most of his men headed inland toward Tenochtitlán, the Aztec capital. They were accompanied by their Totonac allies, who had advised Cortés on the best route to Tenochtitlán

Mexico City, formerly Tenochtitlán, in the seventeenth century. The Aztecs sent gifts of gold and young women to the inquisitive Spaniards on their borders, hoping to persuade them to leave this interior city alone. [Library of Congress]

and had provided porters as well as fighting men. They also had told Cortés about Tlaxcala, the one city-state on the plateau that still retained its independence. The usual procedure on the march to Tenochtitlán was a battle with each new Indian group confronted, most often fought by Cortés's Indian allies aided by some of the Spaniards, followed by alliance with the newly defeated Indians, now eager to join the strong Spaniards against their former overlords, the oppressive and hated Aztecs. Although the Tlaxcalans nearly overwhelmed the Spanish in one battle, they finally joined them as allies and remained staunch supporters of Cortés and the Spanish.

Beyond Tlaxcala, the next major town on the route was a traditional holy place, Cholula. Cortés could have avoided Cholula but chose to take the city in order to show the Aztecs his strength. The Cholulans, while ostensibly welcoming Cortés, planned an ambush for the invaders that included pits to trap the cavalry. Warned of the ambush by Marina, the Spanish turned on their hosts, ambushed the ambushers, and captured and massacred the leaders of Cholula. The defeat of the Cholulans really opened the way to Tenochtitlán, for the Aztecs and their remaining allies in the Valley of Mexico seemed to lose their will to fight after the Spanish victory at Cholula. The Spanish, however, had been disgusted by the evidences of the Indians' sacrificial practices in Cholula.

From Cholula the Spanish marched to the rim of the Valley of Mexico, the Anáhuac Basin, and so saw spread before them the center of Aztec civilization. Snow-covered mountains and smoking volcanoes were seen, along with lakes, great areas of cultivated land, and many cities with impressive buildings. All this lay at the Spaniards' feet. Montezuma had concluded that further resistance would be useless. The visitors were to be received as agents of Quetzalcoatl. In November 1519, they were greeted at the shore of Lake Texcoco and escorted along the causeway to Tenochtitlán, where they were met by Montezuma. The Spaniards were quartered in one of the palaces and surrounded by evidence of great wealth and the Aztec religious practices so repellent to Spanish Catholics. Within a few days Cortés and some men visited Montezuma in his palace, questioned him about an attack on the garrison left at Veracruz, and insisted that Montezuma become the "guest" of the Spanish in their quarters. In so simple a way did Cortés get possession of the Aztec ruler, Montezuma, make him into a Spanish puppet, and so gain control over the Aztec empire. For some months this arrangement worked well. The wealth of the Aztec empire now was collected and redirected to the Spanish overlords, many of whom toured Tenochtitlán and other parts of the empire. The Spanish, fearing Aztec discontent and unrest, had gotten *caciques* from outlying areas to come to Tenochtitlán, where they were imprisoned. In spite of Cortés's best efforts, however, the clash between the two civilizations and cultures that differed so drastically was inevitable. From time to

Cortés and Montezuma. Cortés conquered the Aztecs by the simple expedient of inviting Montezuma and other leaders to be his "guests" within the Spanish encampment. [Library of Congress]

time the Spanish interfered with Indian religious practices. Even though most of the principal Aztec officials had acknowledged the sovereignty of the King of Spain, unrest was growing rapidly among the Indians.

Spanish rivalry and Aztec rebellion The first real threat to Cortés's control of Aztec Mexico came from Cuba in May 1520. Once Diego Velásquez had learned where Cortés and the stolen expedition had gone and that there was much treasure there, he rapidly assembled a new expedition to win back what was rightfully his. Aztec runners brought pictorial representations of the new arrivals at Veracruz to Montezuma. Led by Pánfilo de Narváez, they numbered about 900 and had eighty horses and ample munitions and supplies. Cortés met the threat by letting Narváez's men learn of the wealth of the Aztec world and how well Cortés controlled it. Pedro de Alvarado was left in command at Tenochtitlán while Cortés, leading a force of about 250 men, headed for the coast and Narváez's encampment near Cempoala. Even the Tlaxcalans declined to join in the forthcoming battle of Spaniards against Spaniards. But Cortés's psychological warfare had been successful. He attacked at night, after a storm, took the camp by surprise, captured Narváez, and by the next morning had received the allegiance of Narváez and his forces. Cortés now commanded an augmented and unified force of Spaniards.

While Cortés was on the coast, however, the Spaniards still in Tenochtitlán, led by Alvarado, continued to react strongly to the Aztec practices considered reprehensible by the Europeans. Efforts to stop human sacrifices led to an apparent revolt of Aztec nobles, with the result that some 200 were killed by Alvarado and his men. Cortés returned to a Tenochtitlán that soon became a trap. In an effort to mollify the Indians, prisoners were released, including Montezuma's kinsman Cuitláhuac, who soon was chosen by the Aztecs to rule in place of Montezuma. When Cortés had Montezuma appear before his people to try to quell disturbances, Montezuma was stoned and soon died. Now besieged in the city on the lake, Cortés reluctantly decided to abandon Tenochtitlán. The withdrawal, on the night of June 30–July 1, 1520, known as the Noche Triste (Sorrowful Night), was a battle over broken causeways that cost Cortés more than half of his forces, all the horses, and most of the treasure. The survivors regrouped in Tacuba, fought the Aztecs again in the Battle of Otumba, where they suffered further losses, and finally retreated to Tlaxcala. With the Aztec uprising, all Cortés's Indian allies except the Tlaxcalans deserted the Spanish cause.

The remnants of the Spanish forces spent the remainder of 1520 safe in Tlaxcala, while an unbidden invader, smallpox, which had been brought from Cuba with Narváez's expedition, swept through Mexico killing a substantial portion of the population. The experiences of the Spanish on the West Indian islands, where European diseases totally wiped out Indian populations about 20 years after colonization, seemed likely to be repeated in Mexico. Fortunately, they were not, but the devastation brought by the smallpox epidemic undoubtedly helped Cortés, who began to plan the reconquest of the Valley of Mexico and the final defeat of the Aztecs and their allies almost immediately after he reached the safety of Tlaxcala. Once there, the Spaniards were reinforced from garrisons Cortés had established in Veracruz and at several points in the interior of Mexico. More Spaniards arrived from Santo Domingo, Jamaica, and Cuba. Some came in search of treasure, and others came to reinforce Narváez. All were recruited into Cortés's forces with their guns and horses. At the same time a shipwright supervised the building of brigantines. These small sailing ships then were disassembled, transported over the mountains by the Tlaxcalans, and reassembled on the shores of Lake Texcoco.

In May 1521, Cortés again assaulted Tenochtitlán. His brigantines, armed with cannon, easily intercepted Aztec canoes and protected Spaniards along the causeways. Although smallpox raged through Tenochtitlán, the Aztecs resisted fiercely. Now led by Cuauhtémoc (Cuitláhuac had died of smallpox), the Aztecs were defeated only after a campaign that saw a siege, starvation, and much house-to-house fighting. A large part of Tenochtitlán was destroyed. The war and starvation probably killed more than 100,000 Indians. The numbers lost to disease were uncounted.

On August 13, 1521, Cuauhtémoc was captured, and the Aztecs were defeated. Cuauhtémoc was tortured in the hope that he would tell where treasure was hidden, but he remained silent. The lack of treasure made it difficult to appease the soldiers who had taken part in the conquest. Because there was not enough treasure to distribute (much of what there was had been collected by Cortés to be sent to the King in Spain), Cortés began the policy of distributing Indian lands to his followers, making use of traditional Spanish forms—a practice begun by Christopher Columbus on Hispaniola. Cortés also sent out some of his more ambitious captains on expeditions of exploration and conquest beyond the Valley of Mexico.

Expeditions from Mexico City Tenochtitlán, now called Mexico City and being rebuilt to be the Spanish capital, and the Valley of Mexico were secure; so Cortés and his subordinates resumed the search for a passage to the Pacific Ocean that had been the original basis for expeditions to Mexico and to Central America. In October 1522, King Charles I (Emperor Charles V) had named Hernán Cortés governor and captain general of New Spain (the Spanish name for Mexico). This recognition of his rights reached Mexico in 1523, by which time expeditions had been sent into Michoacán and to the Pacific Coast as far north as the Río Grande de Santiago, securing that part of Mexico for Spain. Other expeditions went south into Oaxaca. And in all these areas Indian lands also were distributed to Spaniards.

Cortés sent several expeditions to the south. Late in 1523 Pedro de Alvarado departed for Guatemala, while Cristóbal de Olid was dispatched to Honduras. Their problems in Central America led Cortés to organize a relief expedition that never reported back to him. In 1524 Cortés decided to lead an expedition to Central America by land to deal with Olid's rebellion. The army traveled through appallingly difficult terrain, over mountain ranges and through rain forests, as it marched to Honduras by crossing the base of the Yucatán Peninsula, but it missed the principal sites of the remnants of Mayan civilization. Fearful of a possible Aztec uprising in central Mexico while he was gone, Cortés took Cuauhtémoc and many high-ranking Aztec officials with him. Cuauhtémoc was executed, apparently because Cortés thought that he was rousing the local Indians to ambush the Spanish. The expedition eventually reached Honduras and learned that Olid had been beheaded and that the rebellion was over, whereupon Cortés sailed back to Mexico.

From the established colony of New Spain in central Mexico several expeditions were dispatched during the course of the sixteenth century. Generally they traveled north and west, ultimately reaching much of what later became the southwestern United States. Although the Yucatán Peninsula had been the first part of what is now Mexico to be reached by Spaniards, its real conquest began only in 1527, with a series of expeditions led by Francisco de Montejo and his son. Most of the Mayas were subdued by 1546, at a heavy cost in lives. Pockets of resistance to Spanish authority in Yucatán and elsewhere in Mexico persisted for many years. Much of Mexico and Central America was not thoroughly explored in the early and middle part of the sixteenth century. Many Indian groups found it possible to remain outside the Spanish spheres of influence and power. Exploration, discovery, conquest, and Hispanicization continued throughout the colonial era.

BIBLIOGRAPHY: Charles L. G. Anderson, *Life and Letters of Vasco Núñez de Balboa*, New York, 1941; Robert S. Chamberlain, *The Conquest and Colonization of Honduras, 1502–1550*, Washington, 1953, id., *The Conquest and Colonization of Yucatan, 1517–1550*, Washington, 1948; Hernán Cortés, *Letters to Charles V*, many editions; Bernal Díaz del Castillo, *True History of the Conquest of New Spain*, many editions; J. E. Kelly, *Pedro de Alvarado, Conquistador*, Princeton, N.J., 1932; F. A. Kirkpatrick, *The Spanish Conquistadores*, New York, 1934; Salvador de Madariaga, *Christopher Columbus*, London, 1949; id., *Hernán Cortés, Conqueror of Mexico*, New York, 1941; Samuel E. Morison, *Admiral of the Ocean Sea: A Life of Christopher Columbus*, 2 vols., Boston, 1942; id., *Christopher Columbus, Mariner*, New York, 1958; id., *The European Discovery of America: The Southern Voyages, A.D. 1492–1616*, New York, 1974; R. C. Padden, *The Hummingbird and the Hawk*, New York, 1970; William H. Prescott, *The Conquest of Mexico*, many editions; Kathleen Romoli, *Balboa of Darién: Discoverer of the Pacific*, Garden City, N.Y., 1953; Carl O. Sauer, *The Early Spanish Main*, Berkeley, Calif., 1966; Martin Torodash, "Columbus Historiography since 1939," *Hispanic American Historical Review*, vol. XLVI, November 1966, pp. 409–428; Louis-André Vigneras, *The Discovery of South America and the Andalusian Voyages*, Chicago, 1976; H. R. Wagner, *The Discovery of New Spain in 1518 by Juan de Grijalva*, Berkeley, Calif., 1942; id., *The Rise of Fernando Cortés*, Berkeley, Calif., 1944.

Bruce B. Solnick

Wilkes Expedition

Throughout the early decades of the nineteenth century, exploration in the United States was concerned primarily with learning more about the vast lands which had been acquired west of the Mississippi River. It was not until the late 1820s that consideration began to be given to a program of government-sponsored maritime exploration. Jeremiah Reynolds, a "backwoods scholar" from Ohio, was an early supporter of a national voyage of exploration in the Pacific. American merchants, whalers, and sealers, seeing the commercial opportunities, joined Reynolds in seeking government support. Sincerely interested in science, Reynolds acknowledged the contributions that could be made by American scientists if they had the opportunity to examine the flora, fauna, topography, peoples, and waters of the South Pacific; and he appreciated the prestige which would accrue to the United States if the venture were successful.

On May 14, 1836, President Andrew Jackson signed a bill authorizing the U.S. South Seas Surveying and Exploring Expedition. After a period of conflict, mismanagement, wasteful expenditure of public funds, and confusion over the selection of scientific and naval personnel, a junior officer, Lieut. Charles Wilkes (1798–1877), was selected for command. At last, in mid-August 1838, after many delays, a poorly prepared squadron of six aged and ill-equipped vessels set sail.

Since the primary purpose of the expedition was to obtain scientific knowledge of the waters and regions into which it was sailing, the U.S. Navy reserved for itself the privilege of making the primary geophysical observations. Unfortunately, the naval officers were often unprepared for these tasks. The civilian contingent of nine naturalists was responsible for performing the other scientific investigations.

Most of the first year was spent at sea, and the naturalists had few opportunities to make observations. In January 1839, the squadron rounded Cape Horn, and elements of the squadron made their initial penetration of the Antarctic waters. During that summer, the expedition surveyed among the Pacific islands, charting the islands it encountered. Reaching Sydney, Australia, in November 1839, the naturalists disembarked for investigations in Australia and New Zealand. Wilkes now led part of his squadron south into Antarctic waters again. In ships unsuited for exploration at such high latitudes, Wilkes sailed through the fog-shrouded waters, skillfully avoiding numerous icebergs. Sailing along the great ice barrier which protected the coast, Wilkes claimed that he sighted land. Wilkes sought priority in the discovery of the Antarctic continent, but his claim was contested by Jules DUMONT D'URVILLE and denied by Sir James Clark ROSS.

In 3 years and 10 months, the Wilkes Expedition sailed more than 80,000 miles (128,740 kilometers), explored and charted the waters and islands of the South Pacific, made a successful penetration of Antarctic waters and claimed discovery of the great southern continent, and surveyed along the northwest coast of North America. Its observations and collections included materials on zoology, botany, ethnology, anthropology, geology, meteorology, and hydrography. This was the largest collection of scientific materials to be amassed in nineteenth-century America by a government expedition. A penurious U.S. Congress supported the publication of twenty volumes of scientific reports but allowed only 100 copies of each volume to be printed. The Wilkes Expedition was the first and last major United States government–sponsored voyage of maritime exploration carried out in the age of sail.

Soon after his return to the United States in 1842, Wilkes was court-martialed on several charges stemming from the voyage; he was found guilty of illegally

Charles Wilkes, forty-year-old commander of the U.S. Navy's scientific expedition into southern waters. Wilkes's claim to have discovered Antarctica in the course of this voyage has been widely disputed. [U.S. Navy]

punishing some of the men in the squadron and was publicly reprimanded. In 1861 he became a Northern hero when he seized two Confederate commissioners, James M. Mason and John Slidell, from the British mail steamer *Trent*.

BIBLIOGRAPHY: Daniel C. Haskell, *The United States Exploring Expedition, 1838–1842, and Its Publications*, New York, 1942; Daniel Henderson, *The Hidden Coasts*, New York, 1953; Jessie Poesch, *Titian Ramsay Peale, 1799–1885, and His Journals of the Wilkes Expedition*, Philadelphia, 1961; William Stanton, *The Great United States Exploring Expedition*, Berkeley and Los Angeles, 1975; David B. Tyler, *The Wilkes Expedition*, Philadelphia, 1968; Charles Wilkes, *Narrative of the United States Exploring Expedition*, 5 vols., Philadelphia, 1845.

Phillip Drennon Thomas

Wilkins, George Hubert (1888–1958) Climatologist, naturalist, and polar explorer. Wilkins was born on a sheep station in South Australia. His childhood experience with the destruction caused by drought influenced his life's work. Before leaving Australia in 1908, he was trained as an engineer and a photographer. He covered the Turkish-Bulgarian War in 1912 for the London *Daily Chronicle* and in 1913 was assigned to the Canadian Arctic Expedition of Vilhjalmur STEFANSSON as a correspondent and photographer for *The Times* of London and a cinematographer for the Gaumont Company. He served with Stefansson until 1917, learning well the lessons of successful survival in the polar environment.

Born in Australia in 1888, George Hubert Wilkins was a fine field explorer, whose arduous travels in polar regions uncovered valuable meteorological information, which he hoped to use in establishing a worldwide network of polar weather stations. [National Archives]

Wilkins left the Arctic in 1917 to serve in World War I as a photographer with the Royal Australian Flying Corps in France, where he was awarded the Military Cross with Bar and was wounded nine times. In 1919 he participated in the England-to-Australia air race but crashed in Crete. The following year he went to Antarctica with John Lachlan Cope and later participated in the *Quest* expedition of Ernest SHACKLETON. He made the important scientific collections as a naturalist for the British Museum's biological survey of northern Australia.

Without funding for an Antarctic expedition, he returned to the Arctic in 1926 to explore the area north of Alaska by airplane, and in April 1928 he flew over previously unexplored territory between Alaska and Spitsbergen (Svalbard) with Carl Ben Eielson as pilot. He was knighted the same year in recognition of his accomplishments.

With Eielson he went to Antarctica, and in November 1928 they made the first flight in Antarctica. In two expeditions between 1928 and 1930 Wilkins made important geographical discoveries and observations in the Antarctic Peninsula region.

Wilkins returned to the Arctic in 1931 and attempted to take the submarine *Nautilus* under the pack ice and sail from Spitsbergen westward to the Siberian coast via the North Pole. The expedition had to be abandoned but not before the feasibility of underice submarine use was demonstrated. Wilkins then served as expedition manager for the four Antarctic ventures of Lincoln ELLSWORTH in the 1930s.

During 1937 and 1938 he searched for the Soviet aviator Sigismund Levanevsky, who was lost over the Arctic Ocean near the North Pole during a flight from Moscow to North America. Wilkins's flights during the moonlit winter in the Arctic were pioneering efforts which resulted in important discoveries in meteorology and research in sea-ice movements.

During World War II Wilkins served with the U.S. Office of Strategic Services in the Middle and Far East and as an Arctic expert for the U.S. Army's Quartermaster General Corps. His remaining years were spent working with the U.S. Navy, the Weather Bureau, and the Defense Department's Research and Development Command.

Wilkins died in November 1958. He had frequently asked that his ashes be scattered near the North Pole. This was accomplished in March 1959, when the nuclear submarine *Skate* broke through the ice at 90°N, after sailing under the ice as Wilkins himself had planned.

Wilkins was primarily a field explorer, at home with primitive peoples, whose respect for nature he shared. He was self-sufficient and could adapt his lifestyle to civilized and uncivilized conditions. One of the least-recognized polar explorers of the 1920s and 1930s, he avoided self-promotion and concentrated on the long-term implications of polar exploration. He was convinced that the meteorology of the polar regions had direct implications for weather conditions elsewhere and that a full understanding of polar geography was necessary before his plan for a worldwide meteorological network of polar weather stations could be built.

See also AERIAL EXPLORATION.

BIBLIOGRAPHY: John Grierson, *Sir Hubert Wilkins, Enigma of Exploration*, London, 1960; Hugh Robert Mill, "The Significance of Sir Hubert Wilkins' Antarctic Flights," *The Geographical Review*, July 1929, pp. 377–386; Gordon T. Morris, "Pioneer Arctic Flying: More than a Race to the Pole," *Aerospace Historian*, December 1971, pp. 178–182; Lowell Thomas, *Sir Hubert Wilkins: His World of Adventure*, New York, 1961; Hubert Wilkins, "The Flight from Alaska to Spitzbergen, 1928, and the Preliminary Flights of 1926 and 1927," *The Geographical Review*, October 1928, pp. 527–555; id., "Further Antarctic Explorations," *The Geographical Review*, July 1930, pp. 357–388; id., "The Wilkins-Hearst Antarctic Expedition, 1928–1929," *The Geographical Review*, July 1929, pp. 354–376.

Peter J. Anderson

William of Rubruck *See* RUBRUCK, WILLIAM OF.

Wineland *See* VINLAND.

Wilkins and his plane at the North Pole. He was knighted in 1928 for his aerial accomplishments, among them his flight over unknown territory between Spitsbergen and Alaska. [National Archives]

Women in Travel and Exploration

What has been the contribution of women to knowledge of the world we live in? Compared with that made by men it has been small to date, limited in time to the last 100 years or so and confined to aspects for which women have felt a natural aptitude. They have not been attracted to "the greatness of length of the red-line route of an explorer," as Mary Henrietta Kingsley put it, but rather to what she called "choice spots" in which to botanize and to paint, to study the local people, and to enjoy the local sights. The female traveler in all ages has had one great advantage over the male in enjoying access to the women's quarters, both to the carefully guarded harems of the East and to the simpler conclaves of women in their villages in all parts of the world. Their interest in medicine has enabled them to make the best of such opportunities, and few nineteenth-century "lady travelers" went abroad without taking a course in first aid at least.

Women's contribution has been a personal one and has been restricted by limited resources. Whereas men have been able to call on sponsorship for great projects of exploration, women have had to make do with their savings or with a long-awaited legacy. It follows that women have been tolerated rather than encouraged in the field of travel, and then mostly in the subordinate roles of wife, guide, or servant. Sir Francis Galton, the Victorian scientist and traveler, expressed one idea of the usefulness of women in his *Art of Travel* (1855):

> They are of very great service, and cause no delay; for the body of a caravan must always travel at a foot's pace and a woman will endure a long journey nearly as well as a man, and certainly better than a horse or a bullock. They are invaluable at picking up and retailing information and hearsay gossip, which will give clues to much of importance that, unassisted, you might miss.

What is more, he added, women may be maintained "at a trifling expense; for as they always stand cook, the very licking of their fingers in scarce times, is sufficient for their subsistence." Certainly Halima, the cook of David LIVINGSTONE, was a valuable member of his staff and was awarded a medal for being of the party which carried the explorer's body back to the coast after his death in Central Africa in 1873.

Guides and wives Galton's hint that women make good guides is borne out in several historical instances. Malinche (also known as Doña Marina), who spoke both Nahuatl and Maya, served as an interpreter for Hernán CORTÉS during his conquest of Mexico and became his mistress as well. In 1805 the Shoshoni Indian Sacajawea, with her French Canadian husband and newborn child, joined Meriwether LEWIS and William CLARK on the first American expedition to reach the Pacific Coast. Samuel White BAKER, in his quest for the Nile sources in the 1860s, found one Bacheeta very useful as an interpreter.

The role of guide and interpreter was useful but subordinate; that of explorer's wife, hardly less so. Nevertheless, where the goal of the journey was a new home, the men could hardly have done without such wives as accompanied the covered wagons westward across the Great Plains of the United States in the nineteenth century. The first missionaries in Africa had something of the same experience. A notable example was that of Robert Moffat and Mary Moffat (1795–1871), the Bechuanaland pioneers who, in the 1820s, together created the Christian settlement of Kuruman on the fringes of the Kalahari Desert. No one could pack an ox wagon like Mary Moffat, and she passed her skills on to her daughters. The best known of these was Mary Livingstone (1821–1862), who was lucky in having a doctor for a husband when her babies were born on the trail. Eventually she had to be left behind with the children, rejoining David only to die of fever on the Zambezi River. Annie Hore's lot was happier, and her book *To Lake Tanganyika in a Bath Chair* (1886) is a cheerful record of the long haul from Zanzibar to the lake where her husband, the seaman-turned-missionary Capt. Edward Hore, was stationed.

Bent as they were on the conversion of the heathen to Christianity, clothes, and Western customs, the missionary wives do not tell us much, in fact, about the countryside and the people. Government services and commerce offered wider views, and here Lady Mary Wortley Montagu (1689–1762), who accompanied her husband on an embassy to Turkey in 1716, comes to mind. Lady Mary had the lively curiosity and selective eye of the good reporter. Her interest in the local scene is nowhere more evident than in the inoculation of her son against smallpox after the Turkish fashion, at a time when such a precaution had not been thought of in England. Perhaps she hardly counts as a traveling wife since she spent much of her life on the Continent apart from her husband. Her *Letters Written during her Travels in Europe, Asia and Africa* was published in 1763. Fanny Parks went in 1822 to India, where her husband was employed by the East India Company. Her *Adventures of a Pilgrim in Search of the Picturesque* (1846) is full of information about India in the last years of its administration by the company, when manners and social exchanges were freer than they became later in the century. Mrs. Parks was as much at home in camp as at the grand receptions of Calcutta and could hire and organize a baggage train to take her household up-country when her husband was posted to outlying Oudh.

Florence Baker (1842?–1916) differs from other traveling wives in being the companion not of a missionary or official but of a genuine explorer, Samuel White Baker. Florence's origins are a mystery. Baker met her in the Balkans on one of his earlier journeys, and no one in England knew of her existence until they returned together from Central Africa in 1865. He concluded his first lecture to the ROYAL GEOGRAPHICAL SOCIETY by leading her to the front of the platform and introducing her as "one who though young and tender has the heart of the lion, and without whose courage and devotion I would not be alive to address you tonight."

Lady Franklin (born Jane Griffin, 1792–1875), too, has her place in the picture as the first woman to receive one of the two gold medals awarded annually by the Royal Geographical Society for services to exploration. When Sir John FRANKLIN, who had sailed north in 1845 to look for the NORTHWEST PASSAGE, failed to return, his wife continued to encourage and finance the search for the missing ships after it had been officially abandoned. When her own ship, the *Fox* commanded by Capt. Francis Leopold McCLINTOCK, returned with confirmation of the total loss of the expedition, circumstantial evidence enabled Lady Franklin to claim the discovery of the Northwest Passage for her husband. She received the Patron's Medal in 1860, and McClintock was awarded the Founder's Medal for the same year. *See also* FRANKLIN EXPEDITION AND SEARCH.

Admirable though they were, these traveling wives were no more than marginal to the true business of exploration. Some enjoyed the roving life to which marriage committed them, some did not, but all were concerned primarily with re-creating in the wilderness as near an approximation as possible to the home scene. Many years were to pass before the emergence of the true husband-wife team, typified by Doreen and

Wilfrid Blunt and Lady Anne Blunt in Arab costume. Until well into the twentieth century, women who wished to travel usually had to rely on private means to do so: they were most likely to be found playing the roles of wife-companion, guide-interpreter, or servant.

Harold Ingrams, who in 1940 received jointly the Founder's Medal of the Royal Geographical Society for their explorations in southern Arabia in the 1930s. The ultimate in the independent female companion is surely the Swiss journalist and traveler Ella Maillart (b. 1903), who joined forces with Peter Fleming on a hazardous crossing of Central Asia in 1935, described in *Forbidden Journey* (1937):

> He said coldly, "As a matter of fact, I'm going back to Europe by that route. You can come with me if you like." "I beg your pardon," I had answered. "It's my route, and it's I who'll take you if I can think of some way in which you might be useful to me."

Travelers in Their Own Right Women as travelers in their own right made little impact before the middle years of the nineteenth century. Then they came with a rush, helped along by the movement for female emancipation which was encouraging women to look beyond their homes but which was not yet able to offer entry to the professions. They did not escape easily, however. Some, obliged to earn a living, became governesses overseas, helped by such bodies as the Female Middle Class Emigration Society, founded in 1862 in Britain. Others, following the example of Florence Nightingale, had permissible scope as nurses. The American Kate Field ventured successfully into journalism, and her *Ten Days in Spain* (1875) takes the reader enterprisingly away from the tourist track. Those with no pecuniary necessity to leave home pleaded ill health and their doctor's orders to go abroad for a change of air. Isabella Bird's helpless hypochondria vanished amazingly when she found herself driving cattle on a Colorado ranch or riding unbroken stallion ponies in Korea. Women were helped on their way, too, by an improvement in transport (railways, steamships, better roads) which facilitated greater mobility for men and women alike.

Even so, many obstacles remained in the way of women who wished to see the world and to be recognized as independent travelers. Sir Clements Markham, secretary and later president of the Royal Geographical Society, had "a horror of women of Miss Kingsley's stamp." His contemporary George Nathaniel Curzon (later 1st Marquess Curzon) thought that women's "sex and training render them equally unfit for exploration, and the genus of professional female globe-trotters with which America has lately familiarized us is one of the horrors of the latter end of the nineteenth century." The American traveler May French Sheldon, seeking to penetrate the Masai country of East Africa in the 1890s, found that her project was "a thorough innovation of accepted priorities."

Mrs. Sheldon, author of *Sultan to Sultan* (1892), was one of the twenty-two "well-qualified ladies" elected fellows of the Royal Geographical Society in 1892 and 1893. Their admission was decided by the society's council, whose right to admit women on equal terms with men was instantly challenged by a group of fellows, led by the same McClintock, now

Admiral Sir Leopold, who had shared with Lady Franklin the gold medals in 1860. The opposition was too strong, and election of women ceased, though those who had been admitted might remain. Kate Marsden, however, was refused a ticket to the anniversary dinner in 1894 on the ground that she would be "the only lady among 200 [men], nearly all of them smoking." When the society moved to its present premises in 1913, a new start was made, and women were freely admitted as fellows with full rights, though it was not until 1933 that the first woman was elected to the council. This was Mrs. Patrick Ness, author of *Ten Thousand Miles in Two Continents* (1929) and a pioneer in the use of cinematographic film for travelers.

Historical development The rush of lady travelers, then, begins with our own era, but there were pioneers. Even in medieval times, with no transport but the horse, few roads, and bandits on land and sea, some women managed to see the world. Pilgrimages offered an outlet, as they have done into modern times for the women enclosed in the harems of the East. *The Book of Margery Kempe,* from a manuscript discovered and first published in 1936 (edited by W. Butler-Bowden), contains the experiences of a Norfolk woman who went to Jerusalem and Rome. Mrs. Kempe dictated an account of her travels to a friar in 1436 and so may claim to have been the first woman to write a travel book.

Two centuries later Celia Fiennes (1662–1741) took to the road and kept a journal, first published in 1888 under the title *Through England on a Side-Saddle in the Reign of William and Mary.* A fully annotated edition, with a scholarly introduction, is *The Journeys of Celia Fiennes* (1947), edited by Christopher Morris. Miss Fiennes made "severall journeys into severall parts of England" and strikes a familiar note in claiming that she did so "to regain my health by variety and change of aire and exercise," at the same time collecting information "so that as my bodily health was promoted my mind should not appear totally unoccupied." Meanwhile, on the other side of the world, the painter and naturalist Maria Sibylla Merian (1647–1717) was collecting material for her classic work *Insects of Surinam,* published in Amsterdam in 1705.

Lady Mary Wortley Montagu, already mentioned as a traveling wife, followed a typical pattern of aristocratic travel for men and women alike in the eighteenth century. A more modern note was struck by Mary Wollstonecraft Godwin (1759–1797), author of *Vindication of the Rights of Women* (1792). Her *Letters Written during a Short Residence in Sweden, Norway and Denmark* (1796) also merits inclusion in any survey of travel by women, recording in lively and perceptive style her experiences on a business trip to Scandinavia accompanied by her little girl and the child's nurse. Nothing irritated this early feminist more than the affectation of physical weakness and mental inadequacy by women, and she put precept into practice in the course of her journey, often away from the beaten track, by boat, by coach, and on foot.

To this period belongs an aberration in the pattern of traveling women, the expedient of disguise. The French girl Jeanne Baret saw no other way of escaping into the free world of adventure enjoyed by men than by pretending to be one. She sailed with Louis-Antoine de BOUGAINVILLE on his voyage around the world in 1767–1769 and seems to have been the first women to circumnavigate the globe. It was indeed her ambition to do so which led her to dress as a man and to take service with the botanist Philibert de Commerson, who in *L'Etoile* joined Bougainville in *La Boudeuse* at Rio de Janeiro at the start of the circumnavigation. Jeanne was a plain, strong girl, a hard worker nicknamed his "beast of burden" by the unobservant and highly moral Commerson, whose cabin she shared. It was not until the ships arrived at Tahiti some 3 months after leaving Rio that her secret was discovered by the perceptive islanders of that South Seas paradise. They even tried to kidnap her, and Commerson suffered much raillery from his companions. She saw the voyage through and, to quote Bougainville himself, "her behavior on board was a model of propriety." But what, he mused, would have happened to Jeanne Baret had they been wrecked on a desert island?

Even stranger is the case of Dr. James Miranda Stuart Barry, who qualified as a doctor at Edinburgh University in 1809 and served for 40 years with the British Army. Her career took her to South Africa, Mauritius, Jamaica, St. Helena, Trinidad, Malta, Corfu, and finally Canada, where she was appointed inspector general of hospitals in 1857. Her real sex was not discovered until her death in 1865. Here was a woman mad to be a doctor; a later generation, involved in feminist crusades, would have scorned thus getting into the profession under false pretenses.

The habit of Lady Hester Stanhope (1776–1839) of wearing men's clothes had nothing to do with disguise; she was far too proud of her own identity for that. Rich and aristocratic, she enjoyed immense prestige while she kept house for her uncle William Pitt, Britain's prime minister. At his death she sought wider scope and traveled into the eastern Mediterranean. She claimed to have been "crowned Queen of the Desert" in Palmyra, she made friends with the Bedouin in their tents, she dressed as a man, and she smoked a hookah. Finally, she settled on a mountaintop in Lebanon, whence she cast a spell over the warring tribes which surrounded her and over such chance visitors as the English traveler Alexander William Kinglake and the French poet Alphonse de Lamartine. Similarly autocratic and otherworldly was the Dutch woman Alexine Tinné (1835–1869). Miss Tinné was infected with the then-current obsession with the sources of the Nile and, accompanied by her mother, her aunt, and a large retinue, sailed nearly as far up the river as any individual male explorer had done to date. A later solitary attempt to penetrate the

Lady Hester Stanhope.

Sahara ended in her murder by her Tuareg camel drivers.

These women were isolated eccentrics, but they shared the same inspiration as many who came after, for whom Ida Pfeiffer (1797–1858) of Vienna may speak: "In exactly the same manner as an artist feels an invincible desire to paint, and the poet to give free course to his thoughts, so was I hurried away with an unconquerable wish to see the world." Madame Pfeiffer had saved up for 20 years to enable her to do so. She survived the hardship of traveling with an Arab caravan in the first of her world tours and made sufficient impression on the Austrian government to qualify for a small official grant for the second. English translations of her works include *A Woman's Journey round the World* (1854) and *A Lady's Second Journey round the World* (1856).

Isabella Bird Bishop.

Isabella Bird Bishop (1831–1904) is equally typical of this burst of female energy. She went to the United States in 1854 and explains in *The Englishwoman in America* (1857) that "although bi-weekly steamers ply between England and the States and many mercantile men cross the Atlantic twice annually on business, and think nothing of it, the voyage seems an important event when undertaken for the first time." Forty-two years later, in *The Yangtze Valley and Beyond* (1899), she was describing with equal sangfroid a journey to the navigable limits of the river and her further trek to the borders of Tibet in a carrying chair. Between the two dates, Mrs. Bishop was to visit New Zealand, Hawaii, the Colorado Rockies, Japan, Malaya, India, Persia, and Korea. She was one of the first women to be elected to the Royal Geographical Society.

Mary Kingsley.

Isabella was not alone in her generation. Marianne North (1830–1890) traveled three times round the world painting its tropical flora. Mary Henrietta Kingsley (1862–1900) went to West Africa to study "fish and fetish" and returned with advanced political ideas at a time when Great Britain was taking over large areas of Africa. Kate Marsden (1859–1930), who had trained as a nurse, penetrated Siberia on an errand of mercy, described in her *On Sledge and Horseback to Outcast Siberian Lepers* (1892). Annie Taylor (b. 1855) severed her connection with the China Inland Mission in order to go beyond its prescribed limits in an attempt to reach Lhasa, the capital of Tibet. The American May French Sheldon (1848–1936) came nearest to the male pattern in her daring safari to Mount Kilimanjaro. Her countrywoman Fanny Bullock Workman (1859–1925) not only bicycled, with her husband, the length and breadth of the Indian subcontinent but was also a notable Himalayan mountaineer. Her nearest rival as a climber was also an American, Annie Peck (1850–1935), with whom she disputed heights in the Andes.

These are only a few of the women who traveled as individuals foreshadowing trends observable today in men and women alike. Fanny Bullock Workman, for instance, is an early example of the professional travel-book writer, the author of works with intriguing titles like *Sketches Awheel in Fin-de-Siècle Iberia* (1897), *In the Ice World of the Himálaya* (1900), and *Through Town and Jungle: 14,000 Miles Awheel Among the Temples and Peoples of the Indian Plain* (1904). Edith Harley Tweedie (Mrs. Alec Tweedie; d. 1940), left a widow with two boys and no money, cultivated her talents as a writer, sportswoman, and publicist to amuse a generation of readers with a succession of travelers' tales, among them *Mexico as I Saw It* (1901), *Sunny Sicily* (1904), and *An Adventurous Journey: Russia-Siberia-China* (1929). The trail begins to run out with Rosita Forbes (1890–1967), a daring and flamboyant traveler in Arabia, Africa, India, and South America, whose large literary output includes an autobiography, *Appointment in the Sun* (1939).

Missions The missionary impulse has produced some notable explorers, but among men rather than among women. There are few female counterparts to David Livingstone in Africa and William Carey in India, though the opportunity was there. The China Inland Mission, founded in 1865, almost from the first recruited single women, who were encouraged, as were the men, to carry the Gospel into the far interior. Annie Taylor, who joined the mission in 1884, set off across the China-Tibet border in 1891 with the simple plan of reaching Lhasa, a sacred city forbidden to foreigners, and of claiming Tibet "for the Master." Ill equipped, reduced to one faithful servant, opposed by the united bureaucracy of Tibet and China, she failed inevitably to reach her goal. She fails also in her diary to interest the modern reader, being so preoccupied with her task of saving souls that she tells us no more than that the country is cold, the rivers wide, and the mountains high. The people are benighted: "Poor things, they know no better; no one has ever told them of Jesus." Some years later the Frenchwoman Alexandra David-Neel (1868–1969), an Oriental scholar of distinction, offered a strong contrast in her determination to identify with her hosts rather than expecting them to identify with her. Madame David-Neel made five journeys into Tibet, from 1912 onward, reaching Lhasa in 1924. Accounts of her adventures are to be read in *My Journey to Lhasa* (1927) and *With Mystics and Magicians in Tibet* (1931). Her mastery of the language, her adoption of Tibetan dress and manners, and her total absorption in the mysteries of the country's religion marked Alexandra David-Neel as something out of the ordinary.

The missionary contribution cannot, however, be dismissed in terms of Annie Taylor's lack of observation, contrasted with what one might call the missionary in reverse, Alexandra David-Neel. In the years between World Wars I and II, the China Inland Mission sponsored three remarkable travelers, Mildred Cable (1879–1952) and her colleagues Francesca and Eva French, who crossed and recrossed the Gobi Desert as itinerant missionaries, becoming familiar with the languages and ways of the people. Miss Cable was the author, with Francesca French, of *The Gobi Des-*

ert (1942), one of the great travel books of our time. Though never losing sight of her primary task, Miss Cable assimilated and knew how to impart much information, illustrated with good maps and photographs, on the dwellers of Central Asia. She also conveys the feel of the desert and the hold it gains over certain minds. She describes in few words that synthesis of freedom and discipline which makes traversing great open spaces such an exhilarating experience.

Natural history and anthropology   The scholar Alexandra David-Neel and the missionaries Annie Taylor, Mildred Cable, and the French sisters were all seeking other-than-material delights from their travels. A more homely pattern was followed by those women who beguiled their way with studies of natural history. Here the female lack of education was not such a handicap as might be supposed. These women came from middle-class homes, with books on the shelves which they had the leisure to read. There was talk of the arts in such homes, and the father or even the mother might have a scientific bent and encourage the children to dabble in chemistry. What is more, the men were not very far ahead of women in learning, for scientific education as we know it was almost nonexistent in the schools and universities a century ago, and the great discoveries about our planet were made, as often as not, by men like Charles Darwin and Gregor Mendel for whom science was a hobby. They were hardly better equipped than was Mary Kingsley when she asked Dr. A. C. L. G. Gunther of the British Museum (Natural History) whether she could do anything for him in West Africa. He asked her to collect freshwater fishes, which she did in the Ogowe (Ogooué) River and for good measure brought home beetles, snakes, and lizards. She wrote of her hunting ground, the forest region of equatorial Africa, that "if you fall under its spell, it takes all the colour out of other kinds of living." Marianne North studied natural history in another style, painting her way round the world, in great bold oils which were good enough to be accepted by the Royal Botanical Gardens at Kew, near London. They still hang there in the gallery she had built for them at her own expense. Such studies were, in effect, an extension of the hobbies permissible to the sheltered female child of the time, encouraged to collect wild flowers, to sketch the landscape, to keep rabbits and mice as pets.

Evelyn Cheesman (1881–1969) took the tradition up in the next generation. As a child her delight was in the animals and flowers of the countryside, and in adult life her health actually suffered from not being able to follow her bent. She longed to be a veterinary surgeon, but women were not admitted for training, and she had perforce to take a post as a governess. Eventually she managed to become a canine nurse, but she was 40 before her real opportunity came. A series of chance happenings brought her the offer of a post at the Zoological Gardens of London, as curator of the insect house, an exhibit left derelict at the end

of World War I. So successful was she in restoring and improving the house, so enthusiastic in studying entomology, that she earned a place on a scientific expedition to the Galápagos Islands to collect tropical specimens. She continued through the South Pacific and was away on her quest for some years, returning to study and assess her 500 specimens as a voluntary worker in the Natural History Museum. Miss Cheesman became well known as an entomologist, both for her research and for her travels, which continued into old age. *Things Worth While* (1959) and *Time Well Spent* (1960) are Evelyn Cheesman's autobiographies.

Anthropology was a less acceptable subject 100 years ago than botany or insect collecting, but it is one which has always attracted women, with their interest in people, in social behavior, and in the interrelation of the sexes. Mary Kingsley was originally inspired to take it up by the idea of completing the researches of her father, George Henry Kingsley, into primitive religions and customs, left unfinished at his death. This project seems to have been lost sight of in her increasing absorption in the West African scene, and the results of her researches were embodied in her own *West African Studies* (1899), which followed the more popular *Travels in West Africa* (1897). Even the daring and original Miss Kingsley, however, limited herself by an unexpected diffidence when it came to discussing in mixed company some of her findings. In the following quotation she gave this as one reason for not approving of women's election to the Royal Geographical Society:

> I can go and tell Professor Tylor, or in extreme cases Mrs. T., who can tell him, why they kill twins in West Africa and such things. Women like your own Isabella [Bird Bishop] and myself know lots of things no man can know about the heathen and no doubt men do ditto. This great scientific society ought to know all, but it won't get to know all by just admitting men and women on the same footing.

So she studied the laws, religions, and social customs of West Africa in the raw, traveled and traded with peoples of the virtually unexplored bush, and wrote about them, but never fully shared her knowledge with the male sex. Even so, she was in advance of her time, paving the way for women like Margaret Mead of the United States and Audrey Richards of Britain, who are not afraid to tell "all" in any company.

Scholarly travelers   Miss Kingsley and Miss Cheesman managed pretty well with a minimum of education. So did Marianne North, who claimed to have learned her geography from *Robinson Crusoe* and her history from the novels of Walter Scott. Her sister, Mrs. Addington Symonds, says in her introduction to Marianne's *Recollections of a Happy Life* (1892) that "she painted as a clever child would, everything she thought beautiful in nature and had scarcely any artistic teaching." Nevertheless, the time was coming when both men and women would need to reinforce their natural gifts with the discipline of academic study. Higher education for women began to be avail-

Gertrude Bell.

able during the middle years of the nineteenth century, rather earlier in the United States than in Great Britain. Gertrude Bell (1868–1926) was the first important woman traveler to benefit, entering Lady Margaret Hall, Oxford (founded 1879), when only 16 years old. Women were not admitted to full membership of the university and her first-class degree in modern history was deemed an "equivalent" qualification. A visit to Iran in 1892 aroused her interest in Middle Eastern culture and history, and between 1900 and 1914 she made a number of journeys, to Petra and Palmyra, in Syria and western Anatolia, and within the borders of modern Iraq. In 1913 she traveled deep into the desert country of what is today Saudi Arabia. She learned Persian and Arabic and became an authority on the antiquities of her chosen region. Soon after the outbreak of war in 1914 she was appointed to the Arab Bureau in Cairo and from there seconded to the Mesopotamian Expeditionary Force, first in Basra and then Baghdad. When Iraq became independent under British mandate, she was Oriental secretary in the British High Commission and the first director of antiquities under the new government. She drafted the first Iraqi Antiquities Law and promoted the building of a National Museum in Baghdad. In her will she left money toward the establishment of a British School of Archaeology in Iraq, eventually founded in 1932.

Gertrude Bell's caravan journeys recall the travels of an earlier age. Like Hester Stanope, she was enchanted by Palmyra and was equally adept in the exchange of old-fashioned courtesies with desert worthies. Her career in archaeology, however, foreshadowed the work in our own day of such professional women as the Belgian scholar Jacqueline Pirenne, known for her paleographic studies of south Arabian inscriptions, whose *À la découverte de l'Arabie* was published in 1958. Miss Bell, then, has a foot in both the old and the new camp, as may be said of Dame Freya Stark (b. 1893), who followed her in the Middle East. Both received gold medals from the Royal Geographical Society, in 1918 and 1942 respectively. The likeness between them is more apparent than real.

Gertrude Bell was an enterprising and capable traveler, her goal the achievement of academic excellence and, later, of political power, rather than of the view beyond the hill. Dame Freya is a more joyful companion on the road, her journeyings recorded in book after book of singing prose, sparkling with sharply observed incidents and apt anecdotes. Compared with Gertrude Bell, who had solid home backing and a regular money supply, Dame Freya had to overcome many difficulties. These included the separation of dearly loved parents, constant lack of money, and ill health. By sheer determination Dame Freya made her way into the life she had chosen. She learned Arabic, studied topography, and even endangered her health working long hours on the *Baghdad Times* to pay her living expenses. She traveled first into Iran, later in southern Arabia; her travel books from *Valley of the Assassins* (1934) to *Minaret of Djam* (1970) are too numerous to list. She has also written four volumes of autobiography, of which the first, *Traveller's Prelude* (1950), should be required reading for those interested in what makes people travel. The spontaneity of her style is deceptive, concealing the careful preparation which went into each venture. In old age, Dame Freya explores the mind, seeing death as one more journey into one more delectable land. She brings to a fitting close this all-too-brief survey of women who have found fulfillment in travel.

BIBLIOGRAPHY: Anne Baker, *Morning Star: Florence Baker's Diary of the Expedition to Put Down the Slave Trade on the Nile 1870–1873*, London, 1972; Pat Barr, *A Curious Life for a Lady: The Story of Isabella Bird*, London, 1970; id., *To China with Love: The Lives and Times of Protestant Missionaries in China, 1860–1900*, London, 1972; Elizabeth Burgowyne (ed.), *Gertrude Bell from Her Personal Papers*, 2 vols., London, 1958–1961; Mora Dickson, *Beloved Partner: Mary Moffat of Kuruman*, London, 1974; Barbara Foster, "Memoirs of the Travelling Ladies," *Bulletin*, Geography and Maps Division, Special Libraries Association, New York, nos. 100 and 102, 1975, no. 104, 1976; Penelope Gladstone, *Travels of Alexine: Alexine Tinné, 1835–1869*, London, 1970; Stephen Gwyn, *Life of Mary Kingsley*, 2d ed., London, 1933; Joan Haslip, *Lady Hester Stanhope*, London, 1945; Dorothy Middleton, *Victorian Lady Travellers*, London, 1965; Edna Nixon, *Mary Wollstonecraft: Her Life and Times*, London, 1971; June Rose, *Perfect Gentleman*, London, 1977; Freya Stark, *Beyond Euphrates*, London, 1951; id., *Coast of Incense*, London, 1953; id., *Dust in the Lion's Paw*, London, 1961; id., *Traveller's Prelude*, London, 1950; Ethel Harley Tweedie, *Me and Mine*, London, 1932; id., *Thirteen Years of a Busy Life*, London, 1912.

Dorothy Middleton

Y, Z

Yāqūt al-Rūmī, Shihāb al-Dīn Abū 'Abd-Allāh (1179-1229) Muslim traveler and scholar. Yāqūt al-Rūmī was a Muslim born to non-Arab parents. He was, in fact, apparently of Greek extraction. Captured by Muslim raiders in Asia Minor when he was a youth, he was taken into slavery and purchased by a merchant in Baghad, the capital of the Islamic empire. His master gave him a good Islamic education and sent him to conduct his business affairs in the Persian Gulf region. Yāqūt's commercial voyages awakened in him a particular interest in the study of geography. His master freed him in 1196, and he then began to study and write as well as to undertake further trade journeys for his former master. He settled for a time in Baghdad, but after the death of his former master (some time before 1213), he began to travel once more. He journeyed to various parts of the Islamic world in the years after 1213, studying in various libraries and compiling material for the books which he was in the process of writing. He put the finishing touches to his geographical works in Mosul in 1224 and in Aleppo (Halab) between the first part of 1228 and August 1229, the date of his death.

Yāqūt wrote a number of important books, but it seems that some of these are no longer extant. Two of his most important efforts have survived: the *Mu'jam al Udabā' (Dictionary of Learned Men)* and the *Mu'jam al-Buldān (Dictionary of Countries)*. The former work, as the title shows, is a dictionary of biographies of learned men, incorporating quotations from their prose writings or poetry, or both. The geographical dictionary, a six-volume set, is one of the great works of medieval Islamic travel and geographical literature. It is based upon Yāqūt's own experiences and upon extensive reading in important libraries throughout the Islamic world. This dictionary is a compilation of place names (towns, villages, and so on) that includes relevant physical and sometimes climatic descriptions as well as frequently fascinating historical and literary data. One may find in it, for example, lists of famous individuals from a particular town or region. In its conception and scope, the *Mu'jam al-Buldān* stands as one of the great monuments to the intellectual curiosity and attainment of the Muslim world in the Middle Ages.

BIBLIOGRAPHY: G. Le Strange, *The Lands of the Eastern Caliphate*, 3d ed., London, 1966; Yāqūt al-Hamawī, *The Introductory Chapters of Yāqūt's Mu'jam al-Buldān*, tr. by Wadie Jwaideh, Leiden, 1959.

William Tucker

Yermak (Ermak) Timofeyevich (d. ?1584) Cossack and conqueror of the Siberian khanate. Of uncertain origins, he was first an *ataman* (leader) of one of many cossack bands plundering on the Volga River and robbing Russian merchants, Persian ambassadors, and the Tsar's vessels. Fleeing from government forces, he led about 500 men up the Volga to the Chusovaya River settlements of the Stroganovs, a leading merchant family. There the cossacks helped the Stroganovs defend their property from attacks by natives. In 1581, aided by the Stroganovs, Yermak led his force across the Urals to the khanate of Sibir, where they overthrew the ruler, Kuchum, and established themselves in his capital, Sibir. Envoys sent by the Stroganovs to Tsar Ivan IV with gifts of furs from the newly conquered territory gained his approval for the enterprise, but by the time reinforcements arrived Yermak had perished. The Russians evacuated Sibir but returned 4 years later to establish themselves permanently and to begin the expansion of their power, giving the entire region the name Sibir (Siberia).

BIBLIOGRAPHY: Terence Armstrong (ed.), *Yermak's Campaign in Siberia: A Selection of Documents,* Hakluyt Society, 2d ser., no. 146, London, 1975.

Richard A. Pierce

Zagoskin, Lavrenty Alekseyevich (1807–1890) Russian naval officer and explorer of the interior of Alaska. In 1838 he entered the service of the Russian-American Company and crossed Siberia to Okhotsk, arriving on July 6, 1839. On July 9, he took command of the company brig *Okhotsk* and sailed for Sitka. Between 1840 and 1842 he sailed company ships between Baranof Island and California and from Sitka to Okhotsk and back. In 1842 he headed an expedition to study the Yukon and Kuskokwim Rivers, a project which he himself had proposed as early as 1840. He sailed a company brig from New Archangel to the St. Michael redoubt on the south coast of Norton Sound. From there he went in a *baidarka* (kayak) to the Unalakleet River. During the winter of 1842–1843 he went by dog team to Nulato on the Yukon River and studied its tributary, the lower Koyukuk River. He devoted further study to the Yukon during the summer of 1843, and in 1844 he explored the middle and lower Kuskokwim and the lower Yukon. In 1845 he returned to Okhotsk and left the company's service. Zagoskin's account of his journeys, based on a lengthy report to the Russian-American Company, is one of the most comprehensive works on Alaska during the Russian period.

BIBLIOGRAPHY: Henry N. Michael (ed.), *Lieutenant Zagoskin's Travels in Russian America, 1842–1844: The First Ethnographic and Geographic Investigations in the Yukon and Kuskokwim Valleys of Alaska,* Toronto, 1967.

Richard A. Pierce